TABLE II **Present Value Factors, PVF, Discounted at *r* Percent for *n* Periods:** $PVF_{r,n} = \dfrac{1}{(1+r)^n}$

Discount Rate, *r*

Number of Periods, n	0%	1%	2%	3%	4%	5%	6%	7%	8%	9%	10%	12%	14%	16%	18%	20%	25%	30%	35%	40%	45%	50%
0	1.0000	1.0000	1.0000	1.0000	1.0000	1.0000	1.0000	1.0000	1.0000	1.0000	1.0000	1.0000	1.0000	1.0000	1.0000	1.0000	1.0000	1.0000	1.0000	1.0000	1.0000	1.0000
1	1.0000	0.9901	0.9804	0.9709	0.9615	0.9524	0.9434	0.9346	0.9259	0.9174	0.9091	0.8929	0.8772	0.8621	0.8475	0.8333	0.8000	0.7692	0.7407	0.7143	0.6897	0.6667
2	1.0000	0.9803	0.9612	0.9426	0.9246	0.9070	0.8900	0.8734	0.8573	0.8417	0.8264	0.7972	0.7695	0.7432	0.7182	0.6944	0.6400	0.5917	0.5487	0.5102	0.4756	0.4444
3	1.0000	0.9706	0.9423	0.9151	0.8890	0.8638	0.8396	0.8163	0.7938	0.7722	0.7513	0.7118	0.6750	0.6407	0.6086	0.5787	0.5120	0.4552	0.4064	0.3644	0.3280	0.2963
4	1.0000	0.9610	0.9238	0.8885	0.8548	0.8227	0.7921	0.7629	0.7350	0.7084	0.6830	0.6355	0.5921	0.5523	0.5158	0.4823	0.4096	0.3501	0.3011	0.2603	0.2262	0.1975
5	1.0000	0.9515	0.9057	0.8626	0.8219	0.7835	0.7473	0.7130	0.6806	0.6499	0.6209	0.5674	0.5194	0.4761	0.4371	0.4019	0.3277	0.2693	0.2230	0.1859	0.1560	0.1317
6	1.0000	0.9420	0.8880	0.8375	0.7903	0.7462	0.7050	0.6663	0.6302	0.5963	0.5645	0.5066	0.4556	0.4104	0.3704	0.3349	0.2621	0.2072	0.1652	0.1328	0.1076	0.0878
7	1.0000	0.9327	0.8706	0.8131	0.7599	0.7107	0.6651	0.6227	0.5835	0.5470	0.5132	0.4523	0.3996	0.3538	0.3139	0.2791	0.2097	0.1594	0.1224	0.0949	0.0742	0.0585
8	1.0000	0.9235	0.8535	0.7894	0.7307	0.6768	0.6274	0.5820	0.5403	0.5019	0.4665	0.4039	0.3506	0.3050	0.2660	0.2326	0.1678	0.1226	0.0906	0.0678	0.0512	0.0390
9	1.0000	0.9143	0.8368	0.7664	0.7026	0.6446	0.5919	0.5439	0.5002	0.4604	0.4241	0.3606	0.3075	0.2630	0.2255	0.1938	0.1342	0.0943	0.0671	0.0484	0.0353	0.0260
10	1.0000	0.9053	0.8203	0.7441	0.6756	0.6139	0.5584	0.5083	0.4632	0.4224	0.3855	0.3220	0.2697	0.2267	0.1911	0.1615	0.1074	0.0725	0.0497	0.0346	0.0243	0.0173
11	1.0000	0.8963	0.8043	0.7224	0.6496	0.5847	0.5268	0.4751	0.4289	0.3875	0.3505	0.2875	0.2366	0.1954	0.1619	0.1346	0.0859	0.0558	0.0368	0.0247	0.0168	0.0116
12	1.0000	0.8874	0.7885	0.7014	0.6246	0.5568	0.4970	0.4440	0.3971	0.3555	0.3186	0.2567	0.2076	0.1685	0.1372	0.1122	0.0687	0.0429	0.0273	0.0176	0.0116	0.0077
13	1.0000	0.8787	0.7730	0.6810	0.6006	0.5303	0.4688	0.4150	0.3677	0.3262	0.2897	0.2292	0.1821	0.1452	0.1163	0.0935	0.0550	0.0330	0.0202	0.0126	0.0080	0.0051
14	1.0000	0.8700	0.7579	0.6611	0.5775	0.5051	0.4423	0.3878	0.3405	0.2992	0.2633	0.2046	0.1597	0.1252	0.0985	0.0779	0.0440	0.0254	0.0150	0.0090	0.0055	0.0035
15	1.0000	0.8613	0.7430	0.6419	0.5553	0.4810	0.4173	0.3624	0.3152	0.2745	0.2394	0.1827	0.1401	0.1079	0.0835	0.0649	0.0352	0.0195	0.0111	0.0064	0.0038	0.0023
16			0.7284	0.6232	0.5339	0.4581	0.3936	0.3387	0.2919	0.2519	0.2176	0.1631	0.1229	0.0930	0.0708	0.0541	0.0281	0.0150	0.0082	0.0046	0.0026	0.0015
17			0.7142	0.6050	0.5134	0.4363	0.3714	0.3166	0.2703	0.2311	0.1978	0.1456	0.1078	0.0802	0.0600	0.0451	0.0225	0.0116	0.0061	0.0033	0.0018	0.0010
18			0.7002	0.5874	0.4936	0.4155	0.3503	0.2959	0.2502	0.2120	0.1799	0.1300	0.0946	0.0691	0.0508	0.0376	0.0180	0.0089	0.0045	0.0023	0.0012	0.0007
19			0.6864	0.5703	0.4746	0.3957	0.3305	0.2765	0.2317	0.1945	0.1635	0.1161	0.0829	0.0596	0.0431	0.0313	0.0144	0.0068	0.0033	0.0017	0.0009	0.0005
20			0.6730	0.5537	0.4564	0.3769	0.3118	0.2584	0.2145	0.1784	0.1486	0.1037	0.0728	0.0514	0.0365	0.0261	0.0115	0.0053	0.0025	0.0012	0.0006	0.0003
25			0.6095	0.4776	0.3751	0.2953	0.2330	0.1842	0.1460	0.1160	0.0923	0.0588	0.0378	0.0245	0.0160	0.0105	0.0038	0.0014	0.0006	0.0002	0.0001	0.0000
30			0.5521	0.4120	0.3083	0.2314	0.1741	0.1314	0.0994	0.0754	0.0573	0.0334	0.0196	0.0116	0.0070	0.0042	0.0012	0.0004	0.0001	0.0000	0.0000	0.0000
35			0.5000	0.3554	0.2534	0.1813	0.1301	0.0937	0.0676	0.0490	0.0356	0.0189	0.0102	0.0055	0.0030	0.0017	0.0004	0.0001	0.0000	0.0000	0.0000	0.0000
40			0.4529	0.3066	0.2083	0.1420	0.0972	0.0668	0.0460	0.0318	0.0221	0.0107	0.0053	0.0026	0.0013	0.0007	0.0001	0.0000	0.0000	0.0000	0.0000	0.0000
45	1.0000	0.6391	0.4102	0.2644	0.1712	0.1113	0.0727	0.0476	0.0313	0.0207	0.0137	0.0061	0.0027	0.0013	0.0006	0.0003	0.0001	0.0000	0.0000	0.0000	0.0000	0.0000
50	1.0000	0.6080	0.3715	0.2281	0.1407	0.0872	0.0543	0.0339	0.0213	0.0134	0.0085	0.0035	0.0014	0.0006	0.0003	0.0001	0.0000	0.0000	0.0000	0.0000	0.0000	0.0000

TEXAS INSTRUMENTS

BAII PLUS Rebate Terms and Conditions

This offer is valid only for BAII PLUS purchases between July 1, 1997 and March 31, 1999. All claims must be postmarked by April 30, 1999. Allow 8 to 10 weeks for processing. All purchases must be made in the U.S. or Canada. Rebates will be sent only to addresses in the U.S. and Canada and paid in U.S. dollars. Not redeemable at any store. Send this completed form along with the cash register receipt (original or copy) and the UPC bar code to the address indicated. This original mail-in certificate must accompany your request and may not be duplicated or reproduced. Offer valid only as stated on this form. Offer void where prohibited, taxed, licensed, or restricted. Limit one rebate per household or address. Texas Instruments reserves the right to discontinue this program at any time and without notice.

Yes! I Want $5 Back On My
Purchase of the BAII PLUS.

Principles of FINANCIAL MANAGEMENT

DOUGLAS R. EMERY

The Koffman Fellow
and
Professor of Finance
Binghamton University
(SUNY)

JOHN D. FINNERTY

Partner
Coopers & Lybrand L.L.P.
and
Professor of Finance
Fordham University

JOHN D. STOWE

Professor of Finance
University of Missouri-Columbia
CFA

Prentice Hall, Upper Saddle River, New Jersey 07458

Acquisitions Editor: Paul Donnelly
Development Editor: Michael Buchman
Assistant Editor: Gladys Soto
Editorial Assistant: MaryBeth Sanok
Editorial Director: James Boyd
Director of Development: Steve Deitmer
Marketing Manager: Patrick Lynch
Production Editor: Louise Rothman
Production Coordinator: Carol Samet
Managing Editor: Dee Josephson
Manufacturing Buyer: Kenneth J. Clinton
Manufacturing Supervisor: Arnold Vila
Manufacturing Manager: Vincent Scelta
Senior Designer: Ann France
Design Manager: Patricia Smythe
Interior Design and Cover Design: Maureen Eide
Electronic Art Supervisor: Warren Fischbach
Illustrator (Interior): Steve Frim
Composition: TSI Graphics

Credits and acknowledgments for materials borrowed from other sources and reproduced, with permission, in this textbook, appear on page 785.

 © 1998 by Prentice-Hall, Inc.
A Simon & Schuster Company
Upper Saddle River, New Jersey 07458

Library of Congress Cataloging-in-Publication Data
Emery, Douglas R.
    Principles of financial management / Douglas R. Emery, John D.
Finnerty, John D. Stowe.
        p.   cm.
    Includes bibliographical references and index.
    ISBN 0-13-433541-4
    1. Corporations—Finance.   I. Finnerty, John D.   II. Stowe, John
D.   III. Title.
HG4011.E45   1998
658.15—dc21   97-22392
                                                               CIP

Prentice-Hall International (UK) Limited, London
Prentice-Hall of Australia Pty. Limited, Sydney
Prentice-Hall Canada, Inc., Toronto
Prentice-Hall Hispanoamericana, S.A., Mexico
Prentice-Hall of India Private Limited, New Delhi
Prentice-Hall of Japan, Inc., Tokyo
Simon & Schuster Asia Pte. Ltd., Singapore
Editora Prentice-Hall do Brasil, Ltda., Rio de Janeiro

Printed in the United States of America

10   9   8   7   6   5   4   3   2

To our families with love and appreciation

Cindy, Ryan, Lacey, and Logan   **Louise and William**

Adette, Doug, David, Jason, and Laura

BRIEF CONTENTS

CONTENTS

PART III   CAPITAL BUDGETING: STRATEGIC ASSET ALLOCATION   297

PART IV LONG-TERM FINANCIAL DECISIONS 395

PREFACE

The teaching of finance has evolved over the past 40 years from simple descriptions of observed practice into a sound body of theory that represents our collective understanding of finance. In this book, we have summarized that collective understanding by detailing, for the first time, the principles of finance. Our principles of finance are a set of fundamental tenets designed to help you develop intuition about financial decision making.

Finance continues to evolve at a dizzying pace. Changes in the economic environment and innovations in the practice of finance seem to occur almost daily. How can you prepare for such a fast-paced changing field as finance? The answer lies in the very evolution of finance. You must look past simple descriptions and seek a conceptual understanding. Then, when the inevitable changes occur, you can use that understanding to make good decisions.

TO THE STUDENT: OUR TEACHING PHILOSOPHY

We believe that if you understand the "first principles," every problem and issue can be addressed and solved with these principles. Essentially, if you understand the general theory, you can use it to solve specific problems. This is why we have created the principles of finance, and designed this book around them. Our principles of finance provide an integrated view of the theory of finance so that financial decision making can be treated as an application of our collective understanding. By understanding the principles of finance, rather than simply memorizing a collection of seemingly disparate decision rules, you will be better able to cope with the unforeseen and inevitable changes and problems you will encounter in the future. Our principles of finance provide "ready intuition" for solving problems you have never seen before.

We will show you how to apply this intuition to the world of financial management. Many of our applications come from the "real world," where John Finnerty has spent his entire career of more than 20 years. Most of the applications involve well-known corporations. In other applications, we have changed the name "to protect the innocent." All of the applications are designed to illustrate how financial principles are useful and immediately applicable to the real world.

Of course, as in every field, there is always more to learn. We are honest about the limits of our understanding. We indicate what is known, what is believed, and what is still being debated. The evolution of our understanding is the payoff from the very important process of research. Some professors spend part of their time doing research, and have contributed to the development and testing of financial theory. It's not possible to cite all of them, but many are included in the end-of-chapter bibliographies.

A FEW WORDS FROM A PRACTITIONER ABOUT THE IMPORTANCE OF THEORY

This book focuses on the practice of financial management. It's an applied book. So why should I "waste" your time with talk about theory? Quite simply, because it's important. After all, what is it that *applied* refers to? Theory. Yet some people view theory as an irritation. Almost as though theory gets in the way of good practice. They are wrong.

To be able to apply theory successfully, you must understand it. A "mindless cookbook" approach is fine for routine problems. But what do you do when a problem doesn't fit one of the rules? Understanding the underlying principles—the theoretical concepts—allows you to go beyond simple rules. If you understand the financial theory, you can identify the point of departure for evaluating a newly encountered problem. Then you can ask the questions necessary to get the information you need, process this information, and solve the problem.

Our principles of finance provide the framework for financial theory. The first principle, the Principle of Self-Interested Behavior, is the most basic. Without this principle, we cannot explain financial behavior. However, it also deserves special comment. Regrettably, some people misapply this principle.

I have had the unfortunate experience of encountering individuals who "crossed the line" by pursuing self-interested behavior without regard to the law. They paid a heavy price: in three cases, the price included time in jail and lifelong restriction from the securities industry. In a fourth, the price was still high, even without jail time.

In your career, you are likely to face illegal "opportunities" to make literally millions of dollars by, for example, insider trading. Our Principle of Self-Interested Behavior explicitly excludes such behavior; individuals should obey the rules and regulations to ensure legal—and ethically sound—behavior. There is nothing wrong with pursuing self-interested behavior—provided you play by the rules.

We all marvel at certain people who have had self-interested success in finance without formal training. Some very successful traders and salespeople I've known didn't even have college degrees. What they had developed was an understanding of the principles of finance—and a well-honed ability to apply them. They probably couldn't articulate them, but they surely understood how to apply them in their own self-interest. Whether it's a corporate treasurer deciding what type of security to issue, an investment banker determining the structure of a new security, a bond trader deciding which bonds to buy, or a stock portfolio manager deciding which stocks to sell, in my experience, it is their grasp of financial theory and their ability to apply it in *any* situation that distinguishes the successful people.

So my advice is to take time to understand the basics—the theory—because it's in your own self-interest.

John D. Finnerty

TO THE INSTRUCTOR: OUR GOALS FOR THIS BOOK

Following the Markowitz-Modigliani-Miller-Fama finance revolution, Akerlof (1970), Black and Scholes (1973), and Jensen and Meckling (1976) engendered a follow-on revolution involving asymmetric information, contingent claims, and agency theory. These articles in turn spawned hundreds, perhaps even thousands, of subsequent papers exploring their implications. Our goal in writing this book is to enrich the teaching of finance by weaving these important research advances into the very fabric of the traditional financial management course.

When these research advances are presented, students are fascinated. They are impressed by their immediate application and obvious relevance to the real world. The underlying intuitions are as appealing as a downward-sloping demand curve.

However, over the last 20 years, the textbook treatment of this new material has been almost ornamental. The material's importance may be discussed in the first chapter, and after that, perhaps mentioned in one or two chapter introductions. But if you read the chapters, you will find they really contain only the traditional material.

This book brings the excitement of this profoundly important material directly to the student. These are concepts that students *can*—and should—understand, within the context of finance. This new material is integrated throughout, so you can include it without having to "reinvent the wheel." Many of us have participated in research involving agency theory, contingent claims, or asymmetric information, but have kept it essentially separate from our teaching. We might mention the concepts briefly but, essentially, we only cover the standard material. It's no wonder. The alternative of developing your own unique course material is unreasonably costly, not to mention inefficient.

This book provides the necessary background directly to the students to enrich your topical coverage. Students can read and actually understand much, if not all, of the background material on their own. For example, it takes only a couple of hours to read an enrichment topic such as the one on financial contracting. And our early explanation of contingent claims is given in very intuitive terms, without the usual overwhelming technicalities associated with options. In this way, we have minimized the disruption to the normal in-class topical treatment. In short, the marginal cost can be very low. You don't have to spend a lot of valuable class time on this material. In fact, some of our colleagues assign this material only as outside reading.

TEXTBOOK ORGANIZATION AND DESIGN

The field of finance is a rich and extensive discipline. Quite simply, there is just too much material to jam it all into an introductory course. Further, the objectives of the introductory finance class vary across schools, instructors, and through time. Consequently, we have produced an innovative and flexible design for our text.

The text consists of 18 *chapters* and 6 *enrichment topics*. The chapters are complete and rigorous, and can be covered during lectures. The enrichment topics, by design and by their nature, can be covered in class, but they can also be assigned successfully as outside reading. The instructor can also choose to include or omit some or all of the enrichment topics from the course schedule. The concepts from the enrichment topics are woven into the chapters in such a way that the chapters can be covered without regard to which topics are assigned. The topics can also be covered out of order, if desired.

The organization of chapters and enrichment topics does not prioritize the material regarding its teachability or its importance. We do not advocate covering all of the chapters and then covering enrichment topics to the extent that time permits. The instructor can choose any combination of chapters and enrichment topics that best serves the students. Some instructors will cover most of the chapters and most of the enrichment topics. Some will cover the chapters and only one or two of the enrichment topics. Most, because of time constraints, will have to omit some of the material. Some instructors may omit some of the chapters and emphasize the enrichment topics. Suggested syllabi reflecting differing course designs are included in the instructor's manual.

The enrichment topics can be covered in lectures, assigned as outside reading for all students, assigned as optional reading for selected students, or skipped. Those enrichment topics (and chapters) that were not covered during the course can be good to read after the course is over. Nobody can forecast the academic and professional paths that each student will follow. If we did know these, we could design a separate course of study that would most profit each student. Since we believe in "enlightened self-interest," we challenge each student to study independently any chapters or topics that were skipped during the course or to reread those parts where they wish to attain a higher degree of understanding than was required during the class.

THE CURRICULUM REVOLUTION

This book's design lends itself very comfortably to the new environment in which many of us find ourselves. Business/management programs all over North America are going through, or have already made, dramatic curricular changes. These changes frequently involve integration of material across areas and perhaps team teaching. This new environment is forcing us to rethink, and change, how we teach finance. With change comes opportunity. We believe this new environment provides an excellent opportunity for the finance discipline to provide a leadership role.

The other business/management disciplines have enthusiastically embraced the idea of a corporation as a set of stakeholders. Beyond accounting, areas such as organizational behavior, strategic management, business law, marketing, and production are currently working to incorporate the implications of agency theory, contingent claims, and asymmetric information into their views of the organizational world. This makes the principal-agent framework of financial contracting a natural framework for integrating the areas. Therefore, this book offers the chance for the core finance class to play a central role in the new curricular environment.

OTHER INNOVATIONS OF SPECIAL NOTE

PRINCIPLES OF FINANCE   In Chapter 2, we describe our dozen principles of finance, which provide the foundation for learning finance.

FINANCIAL CONTRACTING   In addition to providing the first formal enumeration of the principles of finance, we further modernize the teaching of finance by including a separate chapter on principal-agent problems in financial contracting. Throughout the book, we recognize the existence of information asymmetries and point out the agency problems it creates. After introducing the problems of financial contracting, we explicitly show how the important insights from this material can be used to solve many practical problems throughout the rest of the book.

OPTIONS   We use the term *option* in its broadest sense: any right without an obligation attached to it. This definition allows us to apply the important insights of option theory to a wide variety of topics. For example, we use option concepts in financial contracting, capital budgeting, and capital structure, among many others. Options analysis is one of the most valuable technologies available in finance.

A PRACTITIONER'S PERSPECTIVE   John Finnerty's more than 20 years of experience in the everyday world of finance brings a unique perspective to this book. Based on his first-hand experience, John brings the real world into the classroom.

INTERNATIONALIZATION   A great deal is heard today about the importance of internationalizing the curriculum. We believe that our country's continued economic well-being demands that we be international in our thinking. It is imperative that today's companies incorporate into their decision-making the specific constraints and additional market imperfections introduced by operating in an international economy. However, the principles of finance don't stop at the border. Therefore, the concepts and principles developed in this book are readily applicable to international transactions. With this in mind, we treat the international aspects of finance throughout the book as both a point of view and a particular market environment in which to operate.

LEARNING AIDS

Several learning aids are embedded in the design of each chapter. Students can profitably use them.

LEARNING OBJECTIVES   The introduction to each chapter includes a set of learning objectives, which highlight the things students should be able to do after mastering the material in the chapter.

PRINCIPLES OF FINANCE BOXES   The chapters have "principles boxes" in their introductions. These boxes highlight how particular finance principles apply to the chapter material. This sets the stage for the material to follow. It also helps students develop and apply financial intuition. In addition, the boxes tie the chapters together and reduce the chance of becoming bogged down in mechanical computations.

EXAMPLES   Numerous examples are included in each chapter. They illustrate the concepts as well as the computational details needed to apply the concepts. Good numerical examples are a fundamental learning device for many business students.

SELF-CHECK QUESTIONS   Following every subsection, there are Self-Check Questions that readers should be able to answer. These questions are very basic, and students should immediately go back and get the answers to any that they don't know.

CHAPTER SUMMARIES   Right before taking a test, students should quickly reread all of the chapter summaries. Students can then selectively refresh their memory by reviewing any material they are uncertain of.

END-OF-CHAPTER SOLVED PROBLEMS   After each chapter summary, we present problems that review some of the important concepts that were covered in the chapter. Solutions follow these review problems.

END-OF-CHAPTER QUESTIONS   These questions are intended to be answered verbally, without calculations. The questions are divided into two groups. The first group of questions should be answerable by direct reference to the chapter. Questions in the second group may require a little more thought because they are more complex, more subtle, or, occasionally, sneaky.

END-OF-CHAPTER PRACTICE PROBLEMS   The end-of-chapter problems are numerous, with an average of more than 35 per chapter. They were written by the authors specifically for this book. The problems are differentiated according to the type of instructional purpose: Problems in problem set A are very straightforward. They review the chapter material and can be answered by direct reference to the text material. Problems in problem set B also relate fairly closely to the material in the chapter but are somewhat more complex. Problems in problem set C are extensions of material presented in the chapter. The C-type problems are designed to challenge the students with complex situations, puzzles, or the examination of more subtle implications of the material in the chapter. Occasionally, problems are drawn from material in earlier chapters to reinforce the retention of important concepts.

NEW TERMS AND JARGON   Terms are defined and redefined in early usage to minimize effort wasted on looking up definitions. Examples given early in the book are deliberately drawn from everyday experience to minimize feelings of being overwhelmed by new jargon. Key terms appear in boldfaced type in their first usage and are emphasized by marginal definitions.

HUMOR   We interrupt the dry dullness from time to time to bring you occasional messages with humor and levity. Our tone is purposefully somewhat informal, so as not to let the words get in the way of the message.

REFERENCES   The body of knowledge in finance is primarily developed and advanced through the academic and professional journals in the field. We have included many references at the end of each chapter, concentrating on the more recent articles in a select set of journals. Our reference list represents only a fraction of the published scholarship, and we humbly apologize for any of your favorite articles that we didn't include. We give these references primarily to invite students to explore those that interest them sometime in the future. We want them to have a feeling for the hundreds of men and women who have made important contributions to the field. We are all indebted to finance researchers for their genius and their hard work.

TARGETED AUDIENCE

This book was written for use in introductory core finance classes. There is an abundance of applications material, so the book can also be used as a text for case classes or retained as a basic reference text for students moving into more advanced finance classes.

We assume throughout the book a familiarity with the standard prerequisites in business/management programs: college-level algebra, financial accounting, microeconomics, and statistics. Although we assume that students have this background, we provide reminders of basic definitions and concepts that were covered in prerequisite courses. Also, while an understanding of mathematics is necessary, we facilitate the learning process by providing simple examples and analogies. By providing both verbal/logical and mathematical descriptions, we hope to enlist each student's "learning strength," as well as have the descriptions reinforce one another.

Finally, this book has been written with the intent that it will become a useful future reference tool for students as they move through their business careers. For example, the abundance of applications material will provide a reference source for material not covered in class; and the chapter summaries provide an easily accessed summary of the important dimensions and concepts connected with particular topics.

SUPPLEMENTARY MATERIALS

STUDY GUIDE   The study guide provides the student with a helpful perspective on how to get the most out of the book. It includes a guide to self-study, and serves as a useful companion to the book. For each chapter, it furnishes an overview, learning objectives, chapter highlights, key terms, worked problems, and a set of exercises with complete solutions.

COMPUTER SOFTWARE   A set of computer software spreadsheets designed to be used on a personal computer is available to adopters at no cost. This software covers specific decision/valuation models such as the Black-Scholes option pricing model, capital budgeting project analysis, and lease-versus-buy analysis, among others. Each topic includes a master model that can be used for calculation, problems that ask the student to complete the logic of partially completed models, and problems that ask the student to use the model for computational purposes.

SOLUTIONS MANUAL   The solutions manual contains solutions to all of the end-of-chapter questions and problems.

INSTRUCTOR'S MANUAL   The instructor's manual provides suggestions on how to use the book as a teaching tool. Each part provides chapter-by-chapter teaching notes that contain a real-world situation to introduce and motivate the material, an outline and summary, including key concepts and definitions, and demonstration problems with transparency masters for class usage. The instructor's manual also includes different class syllabi with suggested problem assignments for alternative course lengths and coverage. A guide for cross-referencing to other texts is also given.

POWERPOINT NOTES   The PowerPoint notes provide a complete set of color slide presentations for lecturing on the material.

TEST BANK   The test bank provides a wide variety of problems like those at the back of the chapters as well as multiple choice and true–false questions, designed to test student comprehension. The test bank is available in both printed form and as a computerized test bank (for Windows).

FINCOACH   *Fincoach*, written by Puneet Handa and published by Prentice Hall, is a wonderful tool that many students enjoy using. *Fincoach* is computer software that provides a large number of problems (like end-of-chapter problems) with randomly generated inputs so that an almost infinite number of problems are available.

PHLIP—PRENTICE HALL'S LEARNING THROUGH THE INTERNET PARTNERSHIP (http://www.prenhall.com/emery)   Developed by Dan Cooper at Marist College, PHLIP provides academic support for faculty adopting this text. From the PHLIP Web site, instructurs can download supplements and lecture aids, including the Instructor's Manuals, PowerPoint presentations, problem and case solutions, and chapter outlines.

PHLIP also helps you bring current events into the classroom. Using our *PHLIPping Through the News* service, you and your students can access the most current news in finance.

To get the necessary username and password to access PHLIP, please call your Prentice Hall sales representative. Or contact Prentice Hall Sales directly at college_sales@pren-hall.com.

ACKNOWLEDGMENTS

As with any book, this book is not simply the work of its authors. Many people have contributed to its creation and development from initial concept to finished product.

We also deeply appreciate the invaluable comments and suggestions we have received from the following people who read all or part of various drafts of the manuscript:

Sankar Acharya, *New York University*

James S. Ang, *Florida State University*

Robert J. Angell, *North Carolina A&T State University*

Mary M. Bange, *Michigan State University*

Shyam B. Bhandari, *Bradley University*

Robert Boldin, *Indiana University of Pennsylvania*

Elizabeth B. Booth, *Louisiana State University*

Ronald C. Braswell, *Florida State University*

Greggory A. Brauer, *Texas Christian University*

Ivan E. Brick, *Rutgers University*

Theodore F. Byrley, *SUC—Buffalo*

Douglas Carman, *Southwest Texas State University*

Richard P. Castanias, *University of California—Davis*

Mary C. Chaffin, *University of Texas—Dallas*

Susan Chaplinsky, *University of Virginia*

K.C. Chen, *California State University—Fresno*

Su-Jane Chen, *University of Wisconsin—Eau Claire*

Elizabeth S. Cooperman, *University of Baltimore*

James J. Cordeiro, *SUNY—Brockport*

Claire Crutchley, *Auburn University*

Larry Y. Dann, *University of Oregon*

Anand S. Desai, *Kansas State University*

Diane K. Denis, *Purdue University*

Upinder S. Dhillon, *Binghamton University*

Eldon L. Ericson, *SUNY—Buffalo*

John R. Ezzell, *Pennsylvania State University*

Richard Fendler, *Georgia State University*

Slim Feriani, *George Washington University*

M. Andrew Fields, *University of Delaware*

Robert L. Finley, *Queens College*

Mona J. Gardner, *Illinois State University*

Chinmoy Gosh, *University of Connecticut*

Atul Gupta, *Bentley College*

Delvin D. Hawley, *University of Mississippi*

Puneet Handa, *University of Iowa*

James D. Harriss, *University of North Carolina at Wilmington*

Kathleen L. Henebry, *University of Nebraska at Omaha*

J. Lawrence Hexter, *Kent State University*

Shalom J. Hochman, *University of Houston*

Keith M. Howe, *DePaul University*

Mai E. Iskandar, *University of Massachusetts*

Robert R. Johnson, *Association for Investment Management and Research*

Steve A. Johnson, *University of Texas— El Paso*

David N. Ketcher, *Drake University*

Daniel P. Klein, *Bowling Green State University*

Ronald J. Kudla, *University of Wisconsin— Eau Claire*

Bruce R. Kuhlman, *University of Toledo*

Raman Kumar, *Virginia Polytechnic Institute and State University*

Robert R. Laatsch, *Bowling Green State University*

Edward C. Lawrence, *University of Missouri—St. Louis*

Ilene F. Levin, *University of Minnesota— Duluth*

Richard D. MacMinn, *University of Texas— Austin*

Judy E. Maese, *New Mexico State University*

J. Robert Malko, *Utah State University*

Gershon N. Mandelker, *University of Pittsburgh*

Terry Maness, *Baylor University*

Surendra K. Mansinghka, *San Francisco State University*

David C. Mauer, *University of Miami*

Ronald W. Melicher, *University of Colorado*

Edward M. Miller, *University of New Orleans*

Mark J. Moran, *Case Western Reserve University*

Ken Motamed, *Columbia College*

Dina Naples, *Baruch College—CUNY*

William Nelson, *Indiana University Northwest*

Dennis T. Officer, *University of Kentucky*

Roger R. Palmer, *University of St. Thomas*

Robert M. Pavlik, *Southwest Texas State University*

Ralph A. Pope, *California State University—Sacramento*

Annette B. Poulson, *University of Georgia*

Gabriel Ramirez, *Binghamton University*

Debra K. Reed, *Texas A&M University*

Jong-Chul Rhim, *University of Southern Indiana*

Ralph W. Sanders, Jr., *University of South Florida*

Barry Schachter, *Office of the Comptroller*

Lemma W. Senbet, *University of Maryland*

Dennis P. Sheehan, *Pennsylvania State University*

David C. Shimko, *University of Southern California*

D. Katherine Spiess, *University of Notre Dame*

Suresh C. Srivastava, *University of Alaska—Anchorage*

Swapan K. Sen, *Michigan Technological University*

Jan R. Squires, *Southwest Missouri State University*

Robert J. Sweeney, *Marquette University*

John Thatcher, *Marquette University*

Ray E. Whitmire, *Texas A&M University*

Daniel T. Winkler, *University of North Carolina—Greensboro*

Emilo Zaruk, *Florida Atlantic University*

We also thank Mark Lerch of Securities Data Company for providing data for several tables, and Stephen B. Land, Esq., of Linklaters & Paines and Robert E. McGrath of Coopers & Lybrand, both of whom reviewed portions of the manuscript dealing with tax issues. As we remind you repeatedly in the book, taxes play an important role in financial decision making, and the tax law changes frequently. It is therefore important to check on the current tax provisions that may affect a financial decision when you undertake a financial analysis.

We are grateful to too many other people for their help and encouragement to mention them all individually. We appreciate the supportive helpful discussions we have had with our many colleagues and friends over the years. We are particularly grateful to several individuals who have helped shape our thinking. These include, but are certainly not limited to, discussions with Victor Marek Borun, Sris Chatterjee, Cynthia L. Cordes, Lawrence A. Darby, III, Uphinder S. Dhillon, Karen K. Dixon, Louis H. Ederington, Adam K. Gehr, Jr., Paul C. Grier, Keith M. Howe, Dennis J. Lasser, Dean Leistikow, Wilbur G. Lewellen, David C. Mauer, Roni Michaely, Philip C. Parr, Gabriel Ramirez, Jong-Chul Rhim, Anthony Saunders, Charles W. Smithson, Michael C. Walker, F. Katherine Warne, and Frank M. Werner.

We thank John Finnerty's partners at Coopers & Lybrand, especially, Rocco J. Maggiotto, Raymond A. Ranelli, Craig M. Jacobsen, Joseph L. D'Amico, and Theodore F. Martens, who provide a stimulating environment within which to apply the principles of finance and a laboratory for testing new analytical techniques based on these principles.

We thank all of the people at Prentice Hall who helped with the project, including Jim Boyd, Teresa Cohan, Dave Cohen, Steve Deitmer, Janet Ferruggia, Leah Jewell, Patrick Lynch, Louise Rothman, Dave Salierno, MaryBeth Sanok, Gladys Soto, and Sandy Steiner. The insights, thoughtfulness, and hard work of our development editor, Mike Buchman, deserve special thanks. He went far beyond the call of duty, and his skills, hard work, and enthusiasm helped us produce a much better book. Finally, Paul Donnelly, our editor at Prentice Hall, brought this project to market. We are grateful for his managerial skills, for his consistent support of the author team, and for his sound judgment on the design and organization of the book itself.

Lifelong appreciation goes to our fathers, E. Ward Emery, John P. Finnerty, and Ronald L. Stowe; to Doug Emery's undergraduate professor, mentor, and friend, William Graziano of Baker University; and to John Finnerty's great uncle, O. K. Taylor, who started his career at what is now Exxon Corporation as an office boy and retired many years later as deputy treasurer. After years of trying they finally got it across to us: "When in doubt, always go back to first principles."

In this book we say a great deal about the 12 principles of finance that are explained in Chapter 2. In writing this book we regularly encountered a 13th principle—the unlucky one that is the bane of all authors. We call it the Underestimation Principle. Its circularity highlights its inevitability: Writing a book always takes longer than you think—even when you take into account the Underestimation Principle! So we sincerely thank our spouses and families for their tremendous forbearance during the long and arduous process that culminated in this book. Yes, it did take considerably longer than we originally estimated, and it even took longer than every subsequent estimation. But we never lied; it's just that the basic principles always assert themselves.

Douglas R. Emery	John D. Finnerty	John D. Stowe
Binghamton, NY	New York, NY	Columbia, MO

ABOUT THE AUTHORS

The authors are long-time friends and collaborators. Currently, Doug Emery and John Finnerty are the editors of *Financial Management*. The journal is one of the oldest finance journals, and has the second largest circulation after the *Financial Analysts Journal*. A major goal of the journal is to bridge the gap between theory and practice. Their most recent book together, *Corporate Financial Management* (Prentice Hall), was published in 1997.

Douglas R. Emery is The Koffman Fellow and Professor of Finance in the School of Management at Binghamton University (SUNY). Doug has also taught at Purdue University, Washington University in St. Louis, the University of Missouri–Columbia, Nanjing University in China, the University of Calgary in Canada, and Kansas University. He currently serves as an Associate Editor of *Decision Sciences* and has been a Director of the Financial Management Association. His research has been published in a wide variety of journals including the *Journal of Finance, Journal of Financial and Quantitative Analysis, Financial Management, Journal of Accounting Research, Journal of Banking and Finance, Decision Sciences, Psychometrika,* and the *Journal of Marketing Research.*

John D. Finnerty is a Partner of Coopers & Lybrand L.L.P. in the Financial Advisory Services practice and is on leave as Professor of Finance in the Graduate School of Business Administration at Fordham University. He has previously worked for Morgan Stanley & Co., Lazard Frères & Co., Houlihan Lokey Howard & Zukin, and was the Chief Financial Officer of the College Savings Bank. He currently serves on the advisory boards of the *Journal of Portfolio Management* and *The Financier,* and is an associate editor of the *Journal of Financial Engineering.* He has served as president of the Fixed Income Analysts Society and been a director of the Financial Management Association. He has authored, co-authored, or co-edited seven other books, including *Corporate Financial Analysis: A Comprehensive Guide to Real-World Approaches for Financial Managers.* His research has been published in a wide variety of journals including the *Journal of Money, Credit and Banking, Journal of Financial and Quantitative Analysis, Financial Management, Journal of Portfolio Management,* and *Management Science.* He co-holds four patents on financial products.

John D. Stowe is Professor of Finance and past chair of the finance department in the College of Business & Public Administration at the University of Missouri-Columbia. He has also taught at the University of Oklahoma, Florida International University, University of California-Irvine, and the University of Houston. He is a CFA charterholder. He currently serves as an associate editor of *Financial Management* and is a past president of the Southwestern Finance Association. He has published his research in several journals, including the *Journal of Finance, Journal of Financial and Quantitative Analysis, Financial Management, Journal of Financial Research, Journal of Risk and Insurance, Journal of Economics and Business, Journal of Business Finance and Accounting, Managerial and Decision Economics,* and *Organizational Behavior and Human Decision Processes.*

Part I

INTRODUCTION TO FINANCIAL MANAGEMENT

P art One introduces financial management. It shows how the business world is a complex web of relationships among a company's various *stakeholders:* its stockholders, bondholders, creditors, employees, customers, and suppliers, among others.

Chapter 1 provides an overview. It shows how financial management fits within the broader area of finance.

Chapter 2 presents the foundation of financial management, the principles of finance, and describes their application within the financial environment.

Chapter 3 reviews basic accounting material, and points out important differences between financial management and accounting. It details some of the limitations and problems connected with using accounting information.

Chapter 4 describes the basics of financial statement analysis. Financial statement analysis provides input and structure for a wide variety of business decisions.

INTRODUCTION AND OVERVIEW

If you're like most people, you have some interest in money. Money, and, therefore, finance, is an integral part of life. Understanding finance can empower you. It can help you use your money more efficiently and, yes, it can even help you make *more* money.

Let's say you have a great idea for a new product or service. It might even be as big an idea as the compact disc, and how it replaced vinyl records for playing music. If you want to make money on your great new idea, how will you go about it? If you don't already have a lot of money, you'll need financing—and critical business know-how. Among other things, you'll need to understand finance. But even if you're not destined to become a business tycoon such as Bill Gates, founder of Microsoft Corporation, you can benefit from finance.

Finance isn't as specialized or complex as you might think. In fact, it's a daily concern of people and organizations, such as businesses and governments. The study of finance can benefit anyone. It can help with your career and your personal financial transactions, such as taking out a loan. It can also help when you're trying to understand world economic events or thinking about investing some money. Learning the ins and outs of finance will enlarge your perspective on important aspects of your present and future life.

This chapter will introduce you to finance, and to the main area of finance on which we focus in this book, financial management.

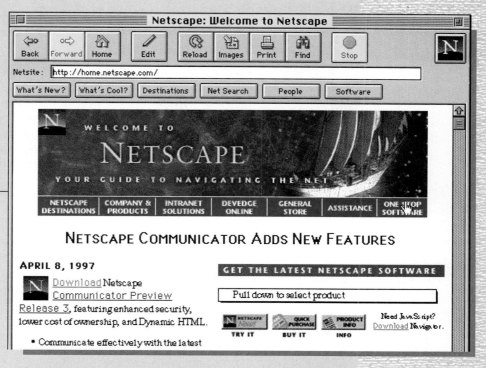

WHAT IS FINANCE?

Finance is primarily concerned with determining value. The question "What is something worth?" is asked again and again. Finance is also concerned with how to make the best decisions. For example, should you make an investment? The decision rule in finance says you should buy an asset if it's worth more than it costs. Though seemingly obvious, this principle can easily be overlooked in a complex situation, as in the heat of a corporate takeover battle, such as when Viacom took over Paramount.

There are three main areas of finance: financial management, investments, and financial markets and intermediaries. These areas often involve the same financial transactions, but each area deals with them from a different viewpoint.

This book focuses on financial management. However, you can apply the principles and theories of finance to your personal financial transactions as well. For example, we'll show you how to calculate which is more valuable when you are buying a car, special financing such as a 1.9% APR loan or a special price such as $1500 cash back.

FINANCE A discipline concerned with determining value and making decisions. The finance function allocates resources, which includes acquiring, investing, and managing the resources.

Financial Management

Financial management focuses on how an organization can create and maintain value. The amounts of money at stake can be huge. For example, Microsoft invested more than $1 billion developing and marketing Windows 95. Financial management decisions are based on fundamental concepts and on the principles of finance, which we describe in this book.

FINANCIAL MANAGEMENT An area of finance that applies financial principles within an organization to create and maintain value through decision making and proper resource management.

3

EXAMPLE

Netscape's Decision to Go Public

In 1994, Jim Clark founded Netscape. Clark put up $4 million. In return, he got 9.4 million shares of the company's stock. This was 30% of the company's ownership. The idea for the company was to produce server software to help other companies set up electronic addresses on the Internet. Netscape also created a software package called Navigator. Navigator helps people browse around ("surf") the Internet. In an effort to build a dominant 75% market share for its server software, Netscape gave away copies of Navigator. It hoped such dominance would help it make money selling its server software, along with the service contracts that go with it.

In 1995, Netscape's growth strategy was working. However, growth was so fast, and continuing to accelerate, that Netscape risked running into a problem keeping up with demand. If it was to meet that demand, it would require substantially more money to finance the company's phenomenal growth. As a result, Netscape was considering *going public*. That is, it was considering selling shares of its common stock to the general public for the first time. But Netscape was a very new company. It was still developing its business. In fact, investment analysts had estimated that Netscape might not become profitable for at least two years. Who would want to invest in a company that was still unprofitable? As it turned out, it seemed like just about everybody.

Netscape went to *underwriters* for advice. Underwriters specialize in selling new shares of stock. The underwriters saw the potential in the new idea. They estimated that Netscape could expect to sell 3.5 million shares for between $12 and $14 per share. That would provide about $40 to $50 million in additional financing. The owners of Netscape found this attractive. They decided to go for it.

The underwriters soon discovered the extent of Wall Street's fascination with the Internet. Anticipated demand for the shares was building far beyond their initial expectations. As the day to issue the new shares approached, the underwriters substantially raised their estimates. They advised Netscape it could sell 5 million new shares at $21 to $24 per share. At $22.50, Netscape would be worth $859 million. Not bad for a company whose gross sales in the first half of 1995 were only $16.6 million! But it didn't stop there.

Demand for the shares continued to build. On August 9, 1995, Netscape went public. It sold the 5 million shares at $28 per share. But when the stock started public trading, it was at a price of $72 per share. It traded as high as $74¾ the first day before closing at $58¼. The first day's volume was nearly 14 million shares—almost 3 times the number of shares available for trading! You might think of this as a sharks' feeding frenzy. Traders described the market for Netscape shares as "frothing."

Based on the first day's closing stock price, Netscape was worth nearly $2 billion. That made Clark's stake worth over $540 million. That's more than 135 times his initial investment just 17 months earlier. Clark's new idea, server software for the Internet, and a free "surfboard" for browsing around the Internet, proved valuable indeed! ■

INVESTMENT DECISIONS ✓
Decisions concerning the asset (left) side of the company's balance sheet, such as the decision to offer a new product.

FINANCING DECISIONS ✓
Decisions concerning the liabilities owed and owners' equity (right) side of the company's balance sheet, such as the decision to issue bonds.

Financial management decisions fall into three major categories. The first two reflect the two sides of a *balance sheet*. **Investment decisions** are primarily concerned with the asset (left) side. They address questions such as should we buy new computers or a warehouse? Should we invest more in inventory, receivables, or marketable securities? These questions are critical because a business is what it owns, whether it is a trucking company, a movie theater, or a clothing store.

Financing decisions are primarily concerned with the liabilities and stockholders' equity (right) side. They determine how the company will obtain the money to make its investments. For example, Netscape obtained additional money for investing by selling new shares of its common stock. Other financing questions are should debt be short- or long-term? Should we borrow in foreign currency, such as the Japanese yen?

Managerial decisions are the third major type of financial management decisions. Such decisions include the company's numerous day-to-day operating and financing decisions. How large should the company be, and how fast should it grow? Should the company grant credit to a customer? Should the company change its advertising program? How should the company compensate its managers and other employees?

MANAGERIAL DECI-
SIONS Decisions concern-
ing the operation of the
company, such as the choice
of the company's size, its
growth, and its employee
wages.

CAREERS IN FINANCIAL MANAGEMENT

Among the three areas of finance, financial management offers the greatest number of job opportunities. It is important to businesses as well as not-for-profit organizations and government agencies.

ENTRY-LEVEL POSITIONS

Financial Analyst

Financial analysts assist in the company's decision-making process. They gather and process
financial information and prepare financial analyses. This work includes capital budgeting
studies, analysis of long-term financing alternatives, capital structure policy studies, dividend
policy studies, and merger analysis, among others. Indeed, a competent analyst should be able
to perform a study involving any of the corporate finance issues discussed in this book.

Credit Analyst

In addition to generalists, there are other more specialized financial analysts. One type is the
credit analyst. They assess the credit strength of the company's customers who apply for credit.
This analysis is useful to the company when it decides whether to grant credit. (Just think, a
former classmate of yours might be the one who processes your next credit card application.)

Cash Manager

Cash managers manage their company's cash investments. This involves comparing the returns on short-term securities, purchasing short-term securities, and monitoring the investments to make sure the company remains fully invested at all times in securities that satisfy its
investment objectives.

MORE SENIOR POSITIONS

Assistant Treasurer

A large company usually has more than one assistant treasurer. They typically divide the responsibility of assisting the treasurer. For example, one may handle international treasury operations, another financial policy, and another working capital management.

Manager of Corporate Financial Analysis

Many companies have found that ensuring high-quality financial analysis is so important that
they've put one individual in overall charge of it. (Titles are flexible, so an assistant treasurer
may be given this role.)

(continued on following page)

(Careers in Financial Management *continued from previous page*)

Corporate Risk Manager

More and more companies are assigning managers responsibility for managing the interest rate risk, foreign exchange risk, and commodity risk the company faces. They are responsible for quantifying these risks and designing and implementing strategies for managing them.

Pension Fund Manager

This individual either manages the company's pension fund investments or else selects and monitors the performance of outside investment managers.

Director of Financial Reporting

Publicly traded companies must meet the financial reporting requirements imposed by the securities laws. The director of financial reporting ensures compliance with these standards.

VERY SENIOR POSITIONS

Chief Financial Officer

The chief financial officer (CFO) is ultimately responsible for all financial aspects of the company's operations, including both day-to-day and long-term decisions. She is one of the most senior executives in the company. Often, the CFO moves on to become the company's chief executive officer (CEO).

Treasurer

The treasurer is usually responsible for the company's day-to-day financial management. The treasurer is concerned with any flow of funds into or out of the company. The treasurer works very closely with, and reports to, the CFO.

Controller

The controller is usually responsible for the auditing, management accounting, and financial reporting functions. In most companies, the treasury and controllership functions complement one another. Like the treasurer, the controller works very closely with, and reports to, the CFO.

Vice President of Corporate Development

This position doesn't have a consistent title. Some companies call it vice president of corporate planning. It involves long-range financial planning, corporate strategy, and mergers and acquisitions.

INVESTMENTS An area of finance that studies financial securities, such as stocks and bonds, from the investor's viewpoint. This area deals with the company's financing decision, but from the other side of the transaction.

FINANCIAL SECURITIES Contracts that provide for the exchange of money at various points in time.

Investments

The area of **investments** studies financial transactions from the viewpoint of investors outside the company. Investors provide funds when they *invest* in (buy) financial securities, such as stocks and bonds. Formally, **financial securities** are contracts that provide for the exchange of money at various times. The positions of the issuing company and investor are mirror images. You can see this clearly with a bond: it's an asset for the investor, but a liability for the company. We can, therefore, view our Netscape example from the "other side" of the transaction: Should you have bought some of the Netscape stock being offered?

CAREERS IN INVESTMENTS

ENTRY-LEVEL POSITIONS

Securities Analyst

Brokerage houses, banks, mutual funds, insurance companies, and other financial institutions employ analysts to evaluate securities as potential investments for the money they manage. College endowments and foundations that manage their own investments also employ securities analysts.

Personal Financial Planner

Personal financial planners help families make financial decisions. This often includes help with managing their investments. Often, this involves helping them save to meet specific needs, such as retirement or college education.

MORE SENIOR POSITIONS

Pension Fund Manager

Pension fund managers manage money on behalf of pension funds. The proportion of financial assets held in public and private pension funds has increased dramatically over the past 25 years. As the assets under management increase, so do the number of job opportunities.

Portfolio Manager

Commercial banks, brokerage houses, investment managers, and other financial institutions that manage funds employ investment portfolio managers. As with pension fund managers, they try to achieve the maximum possible returns consistent with the financial institution's stated investment policies.

VERY SENIOR POSITIONS

Financial institutions involved in the investments area have senior executives who are responsible for the overall day-to-day operations, as well as the long-term strategies, of these companies. These very senior positions are similar to those shown in the "Careers in Financial Management" box.

Capital Markets and Financial Intermediaries

The area of capital markets and intermediaries explores the company's financing decision from yet another viewpoint, that of a third party. This area is that of a go-between who facilitates transactions between investors and corporations.

Capital markets are markets where financial securities, such as stocks and bonds, are bought and sold. Some market participants, like brokers and dealers, facilitate the purchases and sales of securities by other parties. They charge fees or commissions for their services. For example, they helped bring Netscape's stock offering to market. In contrast, financial intermediaries purchase financial securities such as stocks and bonds of other companies but, rather than resell them, hold them as investments. Financial intermediaries finance these investments by issuing claims against themselves (for example, shares of stock in themselves).

CAPITAL MARKETS Markets where financial securities are bought and sold.

FINANCIAL INTERMEDIARIES Companies that purchase financial securities and pay for them by issuing claims against themselves (their own financial securities).

CAREERS IN FINANCIAL MARKETS AND INTERMEDIARIES

ENTRY-LEVEL POSITIONS

Corporate Finance Associate

Corporate finance associates are also known as entry-level *investment bankers*. Investment bankers assist companies in such transactions as issuing securities, merging with other companies, managing outstanding liabilities, and disposing of unwanted assets. Commercial banks and consulting companies have expanded into the investment banking business, so these positions are available at a range of financial institutions. These positions require expertise in all aspects of financial management.[1]

Lending Officer

Lending officers work for banks and other financial institutions that lend money. They help design and negotiate the loan arrangements and monitor the borrower's performance while the loan is outstanding.

Debt-Rating Analyst

The debt-rating agencies employ a flock of credit analysts who participate in the debt-rating process. Usually these analysts specialize in an industry or particular type of security, so these positions offer a good opportunity to learn about particular industries as well as sharpen your credit skills.

Securities Trader

Brokerage houses, banks, money management companies, and many other types of financial institutions employ individuals who actively trade securities. They play an important role in helping the capital markets function.

Stockbroker

Stockbrokers help investors make investments. They usually make investment recommendations as well as place orders to buy or sell securities on behalf of their clients.

Life Insurance Salespersons

Life insurance salespersons help their clients determine how much life insurance is appropriate and which life insurance products are most suitable for them.

Mortgage Broker

These individuals help people and companies arrange mortgage financing for real estate assets they wish to purchase.

MORE SENIOR POSITIONS

Branch Manager

Branch managers are responsible for the day-to-day operations of brokerage house branch offices or insurance sales offices. These are usually persons who have excelled at the respective entry-level positions and earned greater management responsibility.

---

[1]If you're interested in being an investment banker, you should add the C-type problems to your list of things to do in this course.

The Science of Finance

Finance is a science. Like other sciences, it has fundamental concepts, principles, and theories. In chapter 2 we describe the principles of finance, which we will apply throughout the book. A downward-sloping demand curve is an example of an economics principle you already know: If you lower a product's price, you'll sell more of it.

An important tool of science is called modeling. Modeling is a method of describing reality. There are different types of models. Many of our finance models are mathematical models, like a downward-sloping demand curve. The primary benefit of using a mathematical model is its precision in specifying relationships. To the extent we can control the inputs, we can use a model to predict outcomes.

The relationships in a model are established by a variety of methods. One method is empirical estimation. For example, often a company will estimate future sales of a new product using observed past sales during marketing research. Other relationships are contractually specified, such as repaying borrowed money according to a loan agreement. Finally, many come from logical, conceptual, or theoretical ideas, as in the case of expecting a downward-sloping demand curve.

But models have limitations. A famous marketing example cites a case of an *upward*-sloping demand curve. A company sold more after raising its price. The product was the beach sandal, flip-flops.[2] Very few people would buy them at first. Apparently, they thought the sandals couldn't be worth much if they didn't cost very much. When marketers figured out the problem, they raised the price. Sales then increased as people tried the new product. Of course, after flip-flops caught on, competition drove the price back down. Today, flip-flops have a downward-sloping demand curve, as we would expect.[3]

Does this temporary upward-sloping demand curve invalidate the principle of a downward-sloping demand curve? No. The complication in this case was the initial impression that a low price identified a poorly made product. Once this impression was corrected, flip-flops became extraordinarily popular and cheap. They can be cheap because they are inexpensive to make rather than because they are poorly made.

Despite its problems, an imperfect model can provide useful insights and be the best starting point for solving new and challenging problems.

Finance and Accounting

Finance frequently uses accounting information, as we will in the next section when we use an accounting balance sheet to describe a company. Consequently, people often ask, How is finance different from accounting?

The fundamental difference between finance and accounting is the viewpoint. Accounting generally has a historical outlook. Its major purpose is to account for past activities. In marked contrast, finance's emphasis on determining value and making decisions focuses

---

[2]A friend of ours, Phil Parr, calls them "go-aheads." He says, "Did you ever try going backwards in them?"
[3]You might say the demand curve for flip-flops, flip-flopped.

solidly on the future. Picking up from an accounting view, which brings us to the current position, finance concentrates on the implications for the future. Finance asks questions like What do we do now? and Where do we go from here?

Self-Check

1. What is finance, and what are its major concerns?
2. What are the three main areas of finance?
3. Describe the three types of questions financial management addresses.
4. How are finance and accounting fundamentally different?

OWNERSHIP, CONTROL, AND RISK

Businesses are often very large and complex organizations. However, by tracing the development of a company from one person's idea into a major corporation, we can get insights into that complexity. Consider the following fictionalized account of Henry Ford's automobile manufacturing company. Note how each decision in the company's evolution can affect the value and decisions of the company. Each step adds another interested party, called a stakeholder. A **stakeholder** is a constituent who has a legitimate claim of any sort on the company.

STAKEHOLDER Anyone with a legitimate claim of any sort on the company.

Start-up

Henry started with the idea of making a car affordable for a large number of people. Using his own money, he bought raw materials, built one car by himself, and sold it to a satisfied customer, earning a profit. He reinvested the money from the sale, bought more raw materials, and made more cars. Figure 1.1 shows Henry's first *balance sheet*. Note that the **balance sheet identity**

BALANCE SHEET IDENTITY Total Assets = Liabilities + Stockholders' Equity.

$$\left(\text{Total Assets} = \text{Liabilities} + \text{Stockholders' Equity} \right)$$

must always hold. Note also that the financing decision is represented by the right-hand side of the balance sheet.

Henry provided the entire financing himself. (Hence, liabilities and stockholders' equity are made up solely of Henry's equity, HE.) Henry is also the manager of the company. In fact, at this point, besides suppliers and customers, Henry is the only person directly involved in the company.

Henry's primary motivation was to earn money. But what happens if the company is unsuccessful? That is, what happens if Henry can't sell his cars for a profit? Eventually, Henry would run out of money. Under some circumstances, then, Henry can lose the money he invested, but no one else stands to lose anything.

At this initial point, we want to note three things: First, Henry has exclusive *ownership* of the company and its assets. Second, Henry has complete *control* of the company and its assets (within legal limits). Third, Henry is bearing all the *risk* associated with the company's investment.

FIGURE 1.1

Start-up balance sheet for Henry Ford's fictionalized company.

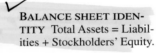

Assets		Liabilities & Owners' Equity	
Cash C			
Raw materials . . . . R			
Tools . . . . T			
Garage . . . . G		Henry's equity . . . . HE	
Total Assets . . . . TA		Liabilities & Stockholders' Equity . . . TA	

Debt

Building one car at a time was OK, but it occurred to Henry that if he could buy more raw materials with each order, he could save money on shipping charges. Henry (and, therefore, the company) did not have enough money to make such large orders. So Henry went to a bank and borrowed some money. He promised to repay the money out of revenues from future car sales. Figure 1.2 shows the revised balance sheet for Henry's company.

Note that the company's financing—its *capital structure*—is now made up of two parts. (We use TA′ to represent the liabilities plus stockholders' equity to emphasize that the accounting identity must always hold.) The two parts of the company's new financing are debt and equity. **Equity** represents ownership, whereas **debt** is a legal obligation for borrowed money. As the only **shareholder** (or **stockholder** or **equityholder**[4]), Henry still has exclusive ownership of the company and its assets. Henry also retains direct control over the company and its assets because he is the manager of the company. However, Henry is now constrained by bank-loan obligations. His company is required to pay interest on the loan and repay the money it borrowed. The bank has become a stakeholder in Henry's company.

As with Henry, the bank's primary motivation for making this loan was to earn money. Because of this, Henry agreed to pay interest in addition to repaying the loan. But now what happens if the company is unsuccessful? That is, what if Henry can't sell his cars for a profit? Under some circumstances, the company might not have enough cash to fully repay the bank. Because of this possibility, the bank is bearing some risk. But how much risk?

On the downside, if it is not fully paid, the bank may still get something, whereas Henry will have lost all of the money he invested. On the upside, if the company does well, the bank will receive only the loan repayment plus promised interest, whereas Henry will get all of the "excess net revenue"—everything above the amount promised to the bank. Therefore, Henry does worse than the bank on the downside and better than the bank on the upside. So Henry is bearing more of the risk than the bank. Also, the bank must trust Henry to act responsibly and not run off to South America without repaying.

You can see that this situation is more complex than in the start-up, where Henry provided all the financing. Determining the values of the claims on the company is more difficult. The company's decisions are more complex because they affect more stakeholders. Let's review the current situation: First, Henry retains exclusive ownership of the company. Second, Henry still controls the company's assets, but he's constrained by bank-loan obligations. Third, the bank now bears some of the risk. Fourth, Henry bears all the *residual* (remaining) risk, which is the majority of the company's risk.

EQUITY An ownership interest in a company.

DEBT A legal obligation to make contractually agreed-upon future payments.

SHAREHOLDER One holding some shares of the company's equity. Also called *stockholder* or *equityholder*.

Employees

After a while, Henry has an even larger number of orders, so large in fact that it would take him longer than the rest of his life to build those cars—and more are coming in every day. To fill the orders, Henry hires some employees. Although the balance sheet doesn't change, Henry's company now has some implicit obligations to its employees. For example, its employees would be upset if the company delayed wage payments. Likewise, the employees

Assets	Liabilities & Owners' Equity
Cash .... C′	
Raw materials .... R′	
Tools ....T′	Bank loan .... B′
Garage .... G′	Henry's equity .... HE′
Total Assets .... TA′	Liabilities & Stockholders' Equity . . . TA′

FIGURE 1.2
Revised balance sheet for Henry's company, right after the bank loan.

---

[4]We follow financial industry practice and use the terms *shareholder, stockholder,* and *equityholder* interchangeably.

have some implicit obligations to the company. For example, an employee shouldn't use an expense account for personal benefit. Therefore, although neither the balance sheet nor the ownership of the company has changed, Henry's control over the company's assets is further constrained.

Multiple Equityholders

Demand for Henry's cars continues to grow. Now, although Henry has employees to build the cars on backorder, he is again short of money to buy raw materials. He goes to the bank, but the bank refuses to loan more money. In short, the bank says it won't take the risk of a bigger loan. The bank will agree to loan more money only if Henry puts up more money. But Henry doesn't have any more money; all his money is already invested in his company. So the bank tells Henry to get other equity financing, and Henry does. Just like Netscape, he sells shares in his company to new equityholders. He also creates a board of directors. Figure 1.3 illustrates the company's new balance sheet.

Where do Henry and his company stand now? First, the company is no longer exclusively Henry's. The company has other equityholders who are part owners. Second, although Henry is still the manager and still has control over the company's assets, he is now even more constrained. In addition to the bank-loan and employee obligations, Henry now has an obligation to act in the best interests of the other equityholders. Third, the bank continues to bear some of the risk of the company. Fourth, Henry no longer bears all of the company's residual risk. He and the new equityholders now share the residual risk of the company in direct proportion to the number of shares each person owns.

Let's also take a moment to point out the new equityholders' motivation for making this investment. As with Henry and the bank, their motivation is to make money. Like Henry, the more money the company makes, the more money each equityholder makes (in proportion to the number of shares each person owns).

Because all of the equityholders, including Henry, have the same motivation, it might appear that all their interests are identical. Not so. Henry is the only equityholder who has *direct* control over the company's assets. Therefore, the other equityholders have to trust Henry to act in their best interests and not, for example, pay himself a huge inappropriate salary.

Separating Ownership from Control

More time has passed, and Henry's company is operating more successfully than ever before. But Henry is now tired of his years of working. He's decided he will retire and live off investment returns. So Henry hires special employees, *managers*, to run the company.

As with other employees, hiring the managers doesn't change the balance sheet. Nevertheless, this change is a *very important* one: Henry no longer has direct control over the company and its assets. The managers now control the company's assets, and Henry has become like the other equityholders. In particular, he must trust the managers to run the company for his benefit, just as the other equityholders trusted him.

Now Henry's company has become a very large and complex corporation. At the start, the right side of the balance sheet was very simple; its total was made up solely of Henry's equity. Now, it has become complex, involving explicit as well as implicit contracts among its

FIGURE 1.3
Revised balance sheet for Henry's company, right after going public.

Assets		Liabilities & Owners' Equity	
Cash . . . . C"			
Raw materials . . . . R"		Bank loan . . . . B"	
Tools . . . . T"		New stockholders' equity . . . . O"	
Garage . . . . G"		Henry's equity . . . . HE"	
Total Assets . . . . TA"		Liabilities & Stockholders' Equity . . . TA"	

many stakeholders. Each change added to the potential for conflicts of interest among the various stakeholders.

For example, consider an equityholder who does not have direct control over the company's assets. This equityholder may be willing to place the company at great risk to have a chance at earning a high return because he has other assets and can "afford" to take the risk. Contrast this equityholder with the company's manager. The manager has direct control over the assets but is affected differently by the company's risk. If the company goes bankrupt, the manager can lose her job. Because of this, the manager may limit the company's risk—even passing up investments that have great potential returns.

Self-Check

1. What are some of the conflicts of interest between Henry and the bank?

2. Describe some of the conflicts of interest between Henry and the other shareholders.

3. What are some of the conflicts of interest between the managers and the other shareholders of Henry's company?

THREE DIFFERENT VIEWS OF A COMPANY

Earlier we talked about modeling. The evolution of Henry's company highlights three different models of the company, the *investment-vehicle*, *accounting*, and *set-of-contracts models*. All three models are important. Each one provides powerful insights into particular problems.

The Investment-Vehicle Model

The investment-vehicle model is the most basic view of the company. It is shown in figure 1.4, along with the three main areas of finance. Investors provide funds (financing) in exchange for financial securities. For example, a bond provides for a specified set of cash payments to its owner (who has previously paid money to purchase the bond).

We have identified the two basic types of financial securities: equity and debt. Equity is the company's ownership. It is typically represented by shares of **common stock.** A person who owns all the shares of common stock owns the company, as Henry did at the start. If more than one person owns shares in the company, each person's ownership portion is simply the number of shares divided by the total number of existing shares. For example, if a shareholder owns 350 of a company's total 1000 shares, that person owns 35% of the company.

COMMON STOCK A proportional ownership interest in the company.

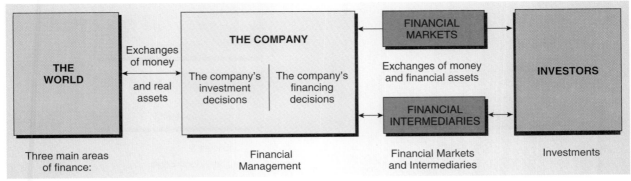

FIGURE 1.4
The investment-vehicle model of the company, and the three main areas of finance.

Debt is a legal obligation to make contractually agreed-upon future payments, identified as interest and repayment of the principal (original debt amount). Debtholders have loaned the company money. They have no claim of ownership as long as the company meets its payment obligations. The company controls the use of the funds.

In the investment-vehicle model, the company's managers are neutral intermediaries who act only in the best interest of the shareholders, the owners of the company. Sometimes, especially in the case of small companies (as when Henry started out), the owner is the manager. In such cases, there is obviously no conflict between the owner and the manager because they are one and the same.

The investment-vehicle model of the company is embodied in an often-stated goal that managers should *maximize shareholder wealth*. In a "perfect" world (one without owner-manager conflicts), maximizing shareholder wealth is the theoretically correct managerial goal. Because of this, the investment-vehicle model is the best starting point for analyzing financial decisions.

The Accounting Model

In a sense, the accounting model is a subset of the investment-vehicle model. In the United States, it's a way to operationalize and approximate the investment-vehicle model. It is embodied in the balance sheet view of the company, an abbreviated version of which is shown in figure 1.5. The company's investment decisions concern the asset side, and the company's financing decisions concern the liabilities and stockholders' equity side. Many day-to-day operating and financial policies (managerial decisions) also can be seen on the balance sheet as well as on the *income statement* and *statement of cash flows*.

One advantage of the accounting model is that it is highly integrated, showing how the company's pieces fit together. Another advantage is that accounting is widely familiar, so the accounting model makes communication easier.

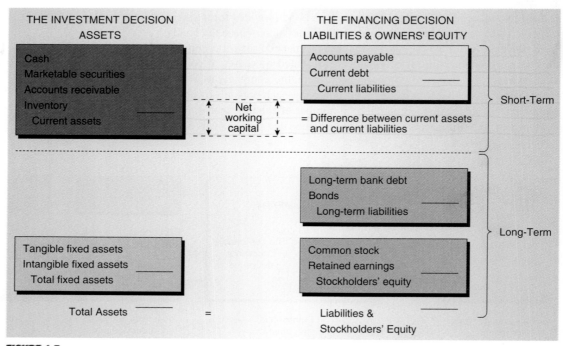

FIGURE 1.5
The accounting model of the company.

There are disadvantages to the accounting model, however. A major one is accounting's primarily historical viewpoint. A lot of the information you use to make decisions is simply not in the accounting system. Although the accounting perspective is important and often helpful, it is frequently inadequate by itself for many corporate decisions.

The Set-of-Contracts Model

The set-of-contracts model is a refinement of the investment-vehicle model. It starts with the investment-vehicle model but recognizes imperfections that can arise in the contracts (relationships) between the company and its stakeholders. Figure 1.6 shows many of the company's major stakeholders.

Contracts in the set-of-contracts model are *implicit* as well as *explicit*. Explicit contracts can be with investors, such as bondholders and creditors, where the company promises to pay them specific amounts of money on specific future dates. They also include such things as outstanding guarantees on previously sold products, severance pay for terminated employees, and pension obligations.

There are implicit contracts to be honest and disclose relevant information. Employees have implicit contracts to give their best effort. Managers have implicit contracts with the shareholders to act in the shareholders' best interests.

Regulatory and legally mandated contracts, such as workplace safety standards and product liability, include both explicit and implicit aspects. A court of law may be needed to determine specific obligations in applying implicit aspects of contracts.

Many contracts depend on the occurrence of particular future outcomes, such as an employee bonus if profits reach a certain level. The bonus is *contingent* on reaching this profit amount. There are many such contingent contracts. Your two-week vacation may be contingent on having worked for the company for the previous 52 weeks. Your participation in the retirement plan may be contingent on having worked for the company for a minimum number of years. This type of contract is called a **contingent claim.** The contract's outcome is contingent on the value of some other asset or a particular occurrence.

CONTINGENT CLAIM A claim that is contingent on the value of some other asset or a particular occurrence.

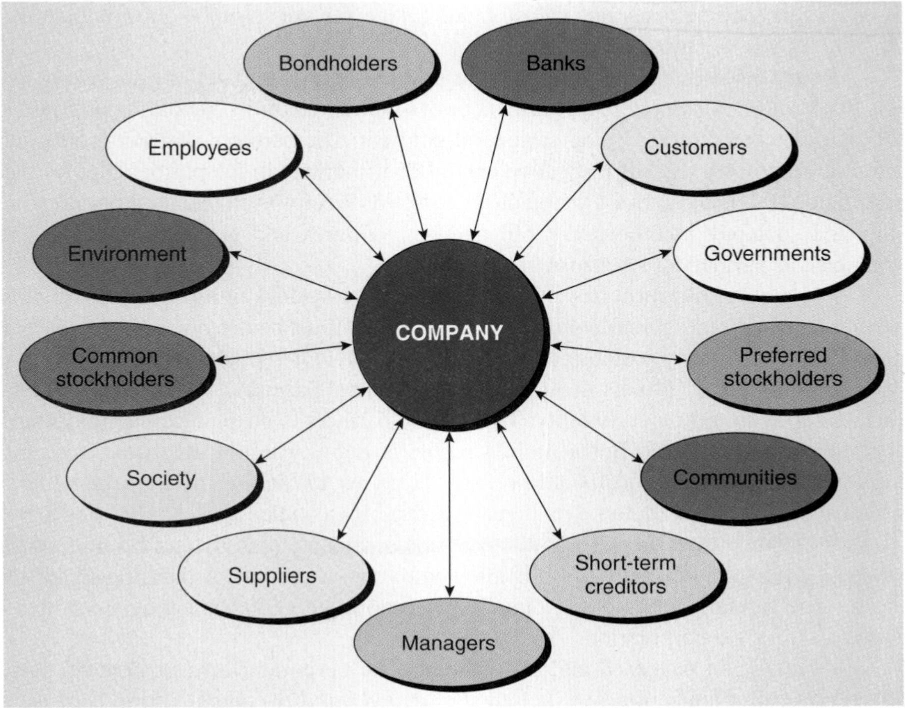

FIGURE 1.6
The set-of-contracts model of the company.

There are many contingent claims in business. A loan can be a contingent claim. If a company doesn't repay, the lender can seize the collateral. However, that claim is contingent on the company's contractual failure. Without such a failure, the lender cannot take the collateral.

Self-Check

1. What is the major difference between debt and equity?

2. How is the accounting model a subset of the investment-vehicle model?

3. How does the set-of-contracts model of the company build on the investment-vehicle model of the company?

4. Which two types of contracts are important according to the set-of-contracts model?

5. What is a contingent claim? Give an example.

THE ROLE OF THE CORPORATION

We focus on the corporate form because it is the predominant form of business organization in the United States. Corporations issue a variety of financial securities, many of which are publicly traded. This section discusses the advantages of the corporate form over the primary alternative forms.

The Corporate Form

SOLE PROPRIETORSHIP A company where a single individual owns all of the company's assets directly and is responsible for all of its liabilities.

There are three basic forms of business organization: sole proprietorship, partnership, and corporation. In a **sole proprietorship,** a single individual owns all the company's assets directly and is directly responsible for all its liabilities. The sole proprietor has *unlimited liability.* That is, the sole proprietor's entire personal wealth is at risk. But a sole proprietorship is not a taxable entity. Instead, the proprietorship's income is added to the owner's other income to determine income taxes due. Most small businesses are set up as proprietorships because they are easy to organize.

PARTNERSHIP A company with two or more individuals who proportionally own the company and who have joint unlimited liability for all the company's actions and liabilities.

A **partnership** is similar to a sole proprietorship except that there are two or more owners. In a *general partnership,* all partners have unlimited liability, including unlimited liability for actions taken entirely by other general partners. The partners share in profits and losses, often in proportion to their respective capital contributions to the partnership. As with a proprietorship, the income from the business is taxed directly to the general partners; a partnership does not pay income taxes. Oil and gas ventures and real estate ventures are often organized as partnerships because of tax laws.

The partnership form has another disadvantage besides unlimited liability. If a general partner leaves the partnership or dies, the partnership must be dissolved. This is very inconvenient if there are many partners. Many states permit *limited partnerships,* in which there are one or more limited partners in addition to the general partners. The general partners run the partnership with unlimited liability. The limited partners contribute capital and share in partnership profits or losses. But a limited partner's liability is limited to the invested capital. Limited partners are typically allowed to withdraw by selling their partnership interests, which avoids the need to dissolve the partnership when someone dies or wishes to withdraw.

CORPORATION A legal "person" that is separate and distinct from its owners. A corporation is allowed to own assets, incur liabilities, and sell securities, among other things.

A **corporation** is legally a "person" that is separate and distinct from its owners, who are its shareholders. A corporation is allowed to own assets, incur liabilities, and sell securities to raise capital, among other things. The corporation's officers are agents who are authorized to act for the corporation.

Table 1.1 on pages 18 and 19 compares the corporate form of organization to three other forms of organization. We include the *limited liability company* form because it has recently emerged as a viable alternative to the corporate form. It offers limited liability, like a corporation, but is taxed like a partnership.

The corporate form of organization has four major advantages over sole proprietorships and partnerships:

- **Limited liability.** Shareholders' liability for corporate obligations is limited to the loss of the shares. If a corporation goes bankrupt or loses a large product-liability suit, the most its shareholders can lose is their respective investments. In a sole proprietorship or a general partnership, the owners can lose considerably more—in the extreme case, virtually everything they own.

- **Permanency.** A corporation's legal existence is not affected when some of its shareholders die or sell their shares. So it's more permanent than a proprietorship or a partnership.

- **Transferability of ownership.** Selling shares in a corporation is normally easier than selling a proprietorship or a general-partnership interest.

- **Better access to external sources of capital.** Because of its permanency and its ability to borrow money or to sell additional shares, a corporation has greater financing flexibility.

The corporate form does have a significant drawback, however. A corporation must pay taxes on its income. Operating income paid to shareholders through cash dividends is taxed twice, first to the corporation and then to the shareholder.

There are many other forms of organization. These include master limited partnerships, limited liability companies, mutual organizations, religious organizations, fraternal organizations, not-for-profit corporations, and many kinds of governmental organizations. Although we focus mostly on profit-making corporations, the principles of finance apply equally well to other forms of organizations.

Ownership Rights

A corporation's shareholders, its owners, can have the following four types of rights:

- **Dividend rights.** Shareholders get an identical per-share amount of any dividends.[5] However, the decision to pay dividends is made by the company's board of directors and is subject to legal and other restrictions.

- **Voting rights.** Shareholders have the right to vote on certain matters, such as the annual election of directors. In most cases, each share of common stock entitles its holder to one vote. A corporation's *articles of incorporation* typically specify either of two voting procedures: majority voting or cumulative voting. Under *majority voting,* with one vote per share, shareholders vote for each director separately, casting one vote per share for each director they support. The candidates receiving the largest numbers of votes are elected to the board. Alternatively, under *cumulative voting,* the directors are voted on jointly, and a shareholder can cast all his votes in favor of a single candidate. Cumulative voting makes it easier for a minority-shareholder group to elect a particular representative to the board.

- **Liquidation rights.** Shareholders have the right to a proportional share of the company's residual value in the event of liquidation. The residual value is what remains after all the corporation's other obligations have been settled.

- **Preemptive rights.** In some corporations, shareholders have the right to subscribe proportionally to any new issue of the corporation's shares. Such offerings are called *rights offerings.*

---

[5]Some corporations have more than one class of common stock. The classes may have different dividend rights. But within each class, the stockholders share equally on a per-share basis in any dividends.

TABLE 1.1

Comparison of Alternative Forms of Organization

	SOLE PROPRIETORSHIP	CORPORATION
Management:	The sole proprietor owns and operates the business.	The corporation owns and operates the business. Employees of the corporation manage the business. The shareholders are represented by the corporation's board of directors.
Liability for Financial Obligations:		
-Nature of liability	The sole proprietor bears full liability.	The shareholders have no direct liability for the corporation's financial obligations.
-Dollar amount of exposure	Liability is unlimited.	Liability is limited to equity invested.
Income Tax Treatment:		
-Taxable entity	Sole proprietor.	Corporation.
-Deductibility, depreciation, and interest expense	All tax consequences of business flow through directly to the sole proprietor. The sole proprietorship is not a taxable entity.	The tax benefits of ownership are claimed by the corporation.
-Limitation on tax deductions	No limitations.	Deductions may not be taken directly by the shareholders.
-Income taxation	Income is taxed at the sole proprietor level only.	Income is taxed at the corporate level. Dividends are taxable to the shareholders as ordinary income.

When a company has two or more classes of common stock with differences in dividend, voting, liquidation, or preemptive rights, the different classes of stock will usually trade at different prices, with the prices reflecting the differential rights.

The Goal of a Business

Many people say a company's goal is to maximize profit. More carefully stated, according to the investment-vehicle model, a company's goal is to *maximize shareholder wealth*. Shareholder wealth maximization is a more specific form of profit maximization.

Why Not Profit Maximization?   There are at least three important reasons why profit maximization is not an operational goal. First, profit maximization is vague. *Profit* has many different definitions. Do we mean accounting profits (based on book values) or economic profits (based on market values, and beyond a fair return)? Are we measuring private profits or social profits, which include any impacts on all parts of society, not just owners? Are we maximizing short-run profits or long-run profits?

Second, profit maximization ignores differences in when we get the money. The longer you have to wait to get the money, the less it's worth. Such timing differences are called the *time value of money*. Profit maximization does not clearly distinguish between getting a dollar today and getting a dollar in the future, such as a year from today. When costs and benefits extend over time, such as a few years, profit measures fail to properly adjust for the effect that timing differences have on value.

PARTNERSHIP	LIMITED LIABILITY COMPANY
The partnership owns and operates the business. One of the general partners is usually designated the manager of partnership operations. The partnership agreement specifies who exercises operating and management authority.	The company owns and operates the business. Employees of the company manage the business.
The general partners are jointly and severally liable for all obligations of the partnership as well as for certain liabilities incurred by any general partner. Limited partners have no liability for partnership obligations except obligations they specifically undertake.	The shareholders have no direct liability for the company's financial obligations.
Liability is unlimited for general partners. Liability is limited to equity invested for limited partners.	Liability is limited to equity invested.
Partners.	Shareholders in the company, which is treated as a partnership for federal income tax purposes.
The tax benefits of ownership usually flow through to partners in the same proportion as ownership percentages.	Tax benefits of ownership usually flow through to shareholders in the same proportion as ownership percentages.
Deductions are usually limited to the tax basis of each partner's investment.	Deductions are usually limited to the tax basis of each shareholder's investment.
Income is taxed at the partner level only.	Income is taxed at the shareholder level only.

Third, profit maximization ignores risk differences between alternative courses of action. When given a choice between two alternatives that have the same return but different risk, most people will take the less risky one. This makes the less risky alternative more valuable. Profit maximization ignores such differences in value.

Shareholder Wealth Maximization

Shareholder wealth maximization focuses the profit motive squarely on the owners. By maximizing shareholder wealth we are directly addressing the problems of profit maximization. First, shareholder wealth is unambiguous. It is based on the future cash flows that are expected to come to the shareholders, rather than an ambiguous notion of profit or other revenues. A cash flow is a transfer of money from one party to another. Second, shareholder wealth depends explicitly on the timing of future cash flows. Finally, our process for measuring shareholder wealth accounts for risk differences.

SHAREHOLDER WEALTH MAXIMIZATION Maximizing the value of the company to its owners. The ownership value of the company is the market value of the shares owned.

Self-Check

1. Discuss the major advantages and disadvantages of the corporate form of organization as compared to sole proprietorships and partnerships.
2. Explain how limited partnerships differ from general partnerships.
3. What four types of rights do corporate stockholders have?
4. State the goal of the company. How is this different from the goal of profit maximization?

The ownership value of a corporation is the market value of the shares owned. Managers should therefore make decisions that increase—or at least maintain—the value of these shares.

THE EVOLUTION OF FINANCE

Finance has flourished only in the broader context of society. It has evolved by addressing the important business, economic, and social problems of its time, thereby contributing to society. For example, finance has long been concerned with the role the company plays in allocating society's resources. Recently, some have begun to question whether the modern corporate form, as we know it, will be eclipsed by a more efficient organizational form. Another form may be better able to function in a global environment and better serve the needs of all its stakeholders.

Historical Development

During the Great Depression in the 1930s, finance was very legalistic and descriptive, dealing with the bankruptcies and reorganizations that were rampant at that time. Following World War II, it remained descriptive but focused on business investment decisions to assist in the postwar economic boom. In the late 1950s, finance took a radical turn. It moved beyond simply describing current practice. It became a science and endeavored to understand the causes and consequences of financial transactions. During the 1960s and 1970s, there were important advances in the pricing of risky assets and in valuing contingent claims. Since then, the field has spent much effort investigating asymmetric information and the problems of financial contracting. The focus has been on efficient contracts that achieve the various participants' objectives.

The scientific quest for understanding has paid off. Several people have been awarded Nobel Prizes for their contributions to understanding finance. Nobel Prize winners to date whose work has contributed to understanding finance are shown in the adjoining box.

NOBEL PRIZE WINNERS WHOSE WORK HAS CONTRIBUTED SIGNIFICANTLY TO FINANCE

James Tobin, 1981
Liquidity and behavior under risk

Franco Modigliani, 1985
Capital structure and dividend policy

Harry M. Markowitz, 1990
Portfolio theory

Merton H. Miller, 1990
Capital structure and dividend policy

William F. Sharpe, 1990
Capital asset pricing

James A. Mirrlees, 1996
Asymmetric information

William S. Vickrey, 1996
Asymmetric information

Other winners whose related work has also been particularly important to finance include Kenneth J. Arrow, 1972; Gerard DeBreu, 1983; Ronald H. Coase, 1992.

Contemporary Trends

Three important trends in finance are globalization, computerization, and corporate reorganization. These trends are rapidly changing the business world.

Globalization   Lower trade barriers, cheaper and more reliable transportation, and instantaneous electronic communication have transformed business into a global marketplace. Large securities companies, such as Salomon Brothers, trade U.S. Treasury securities "around the clock." They transfer the "trading book" from New York to Tokyo to London and back to New York in order to maintain continuous markets. So don't think of globalization as only the importing and exporting of such things as cars and wheat. Globalization is much more.

Almost every product and service has some international content. Financial services are now an important part of the global marketplace. Even corporations themselves are more international. Ownership transcends national boundaries, as do the capital markets. Your working environment is likely to be multinational and diverse in many ways.

Computerization and Telecommunications   Powerful, low-cost computing has become a fact of life. In addition, there has been a simultaneous development of telecommunications media that share databases, information, images, and even conferencing almost anywhere in the world. Individual companies have thrived and disappeared because of their ability, or inability, to use technology effectively. Likewise, individual managers have thrived—or lost their jobs—because they were, or were not, willing and able to use computing and telecommunications technology. If you become a financial analyst, you will have access to vastly more information at the push of a button than would have been possible a decade ago. Today, many financial analysts have on their desks a powerful work station that is capable of doing what required a large mainframe computer not so many years ago!

Corporate Reorganization and Restructuring   We have seen a procession of corporate reorganizations, bankruptcies, mergers, acquisitions, and spinoffs. Within large and small companies, the managerial and professional staffs have, at times, been in turmoil. During a recent period, the Fortune 500 corporations (the 500 largest industrial corporations in the United States) laid off over five million employees. People can no longer expect their first job to be high paying, and secure, in a major corporation. You are not as likely today to spend an entire career with a single company; that dream has been brutally smashed. This reality should provide you with extra motivation for studying finance.

In the past, professionals had one or possibly two distinct careers during their working lives, and only a couple of different employers. Today's generation of managers may have very different career paths. You may go through three, four, or even more distinct careers, and you may work in shorter stretches for more employers before you retire.

Today, a corporation may be less willing to hire, train, and work to retain employees who are not well trained and highly motivated. We sincerely believe that sound training in financial management is critical to your career. Such training provides valuable skills and insights that will enhance your understanding of the nature of business, the marketplace, and your place in it.

Self-Check

1. How have the trends in globalization, computerization and telecommunications, and corporate reorganization affected the business world?

2. Is a recent graduate more or less likely than in the past to spend her entire career with a single company?

3. How can sound training in financial management affect your career?

A FEW WORDS OF ADVICE

There are some things we encourage you to keep in mind as you study. These are things we have found to be helpful to our students.

Financial Principles

This book was written with an overriding belief that if you understand the "first principles," you can solve every problem and issue using these principles. Essentially, we believe that if you understand the general, you can always apply that understanding to a specific situation. Once you understand the principles and the structure of the financial world, using those principles can be interesting and even fun.

Financial Jargon

When you first encounter a subject, you must learn new terms. Finance is no exception. It has its own language, or jargon. When you learn a new language, it's better to add vocabulary in sequence, rather than try to learn all of it at once. A rich language has many terms for essentially the same thing, but each term has subtle differences that make it the "best" term to use in a particular situation. This richness provides more precise communication and is welcome in technical situations. However, it can be overwhelming at first.

Toward this end, we will help you avoid getting bogged down in terminology. For now, we'll keep it simple, concentrating on helping you understand the basic concepts rather than forcing you to memorize new terms. While the new terminology is essential, we will endeavor to familiarize you with the terminology of finance in a way that promotes your understanding of the basics. In the longer term, however, it's very important that you learn the language of finance. Unless you do, it can be very difficult to comprehend fully the more subtle concepts.

Business Calculators

We recommend you purchase a good business calculator. You may have a calculator that will add, subtract, multiply, and divide, or a "scientific" calculator with complex math functions. These calculators are good for balancing your checkbook or for courses in statistics, engineering, chemistry, and the like. However, this is a finance course, and we have written this book with a business calculator in mind.

Business calculators are necessary equipment in the business world. For convenience, we'll simply say "calculator" when we mean a business calculator. Such a calculator will also serve you well in other classes, in your professional life, and in your personal investing and borrowing.

Finance Isn't Just for Finance Majors

Regardless of your major, we believe this will be an important and worthwhile course for you. The principles can be immediately used in your personal financial transactions, such as borrowing money or using a credit card. This course will also provide important preparation for additional study. Even if you are majoring in another subject, this course will provide you with the ability to apply financial principles in that field. If you are undecided about a major, this course will help you to decide. We are admittedly biased, but we encourage you to consider finance.

We appreciate the opportunity to teach you about finance. We believe finance can enhance your professional and personal lives in many ways. We hope your finance studies pay you generous dividends.

SUMMARY

The purpose of chapter 1 is to introduce you to the field of finance and the objective of financial management. These are some of the key concepts covered in the chapter:

- Finance is the field concerned with acquiring, investing, and managing capital.
- The fundamental questions that finance addresses are: (1) What assets should the company acquire? (2) How should the company be financed? (3) What operating and financial decisions are consistent with the goal of the company to maximize shareholder wealth?
- The three basic areas of finance are corporate finance, investments, and financial markets and intermediaries.
- Three basic models of the company are (1) the investment-vehicle model, which views the company from the viewpoint of stockholders, (2) the accounting model, which represents the company as a set of financial statements, and (3) the set-of-contracts model, which views the company as a set of contracts among its various stakeholders.
- The corporate form of organization benefits from limited liability, permanency, transferability of ownership, and better access to capital markets. A big disadvantage can be double taxation of income.
- The rights of stockholders include dividend rights, voting rights, liquidation rights, and (sometimes) preemptive rights.
- Profit maximization suffers from vagueness, does not account for the time value of money, and does not account for risk.
- Shareholder wealth maximization is the goal of the company in the investment-vehicle view of the company. Shareholder wealth maximization means maximizing the value of the company to its owners.
- The field of finance has evolved in response to the major societal and economic needs of the times.
- Current significant trends in finance involve globalization, computerization and telecommunications, and restructuring of the business environment and the workplace.

CHAPTER REVIEW ACTIVITIES

QUESTIONS

1. What is finance? What is financial management? What are the three major questions that financial managers deal with?
2. What are the two basic types of financial securities that companies issue? What are the differences between them?
3. What are three problems associated with using profit maximization as the goal of the company? What is shareholder wealth maximization? How does shareholder wealth maximization deal with these three problems?
4. What are the advantages of the corporate form of organization over the sole proprietorship and partnership forms? What is the primary disadvantage of the corporate form?
5. Distinguish between investing decisions and financing decisions within the area of financial management. Give one example of each.
6. Give examples of a company's stakeholders in the set-of-contracts view of the company. Distinguish between an explicit contract and an implicit contract and give an example of each.
7. What is a contingent claim? Give an example of a contingent claim.
8. Explain the four types of rights common stockholders can have.

CHALLENGING QUESTIONS

9. Classify each of the following jobs into one of the three areas of finance: (1) financial management, (2) investments, or (3) financial markets and intermediaries.

a. A credit analyst for a manufacturing company who decides which customers receive credit.

b. A financial planner who advises individuals on how to invest to achieve their long-term financial needs.

c. An individual who is looking at several stocks as potential additions to her investment portfolio.

d. A manager who is evaluating long-term equipment purchases for her employer.

e. A stockbroker who helps his clients buy and sell securities.

f. A bank loan officer who attempts to identify good customers to whom his bank should lend money.

g. A manager who is deciding how an expansion of her business should be financed.

10. Consider the fictionalized account of Henry's car company.

a. Describe some of the conflicts of interest between Henry and the bank.

b. Describe some of the conflicts of interest between Henry and the other shareholders.

c. Describe some of the conflicts of interest between the managers and the other shareholders of Henry's company.

BIBLIOGRAPHY

Balachandran, Bala V., Nandu J. Nagarajan, and Alfred Rappaport. "Threshold Margins for Creating Economic Value," *Financial Management,* 1986, 15(1):68–77.

Bessembinder, Hendrik, Kalok Chan, and Paul J. Seguin. "An Empirical Examination of Information, Differences of Opinion, and Trading Activity," *Journal of Financial Economics,* 1996, 40(1):105–134.

Brennan, Michael J. "Corporate Finance Over the Past 25 Years," *Financial Management,* 1995, 24(2):9–22.

Choi, Frederick D. S. "International Data Sources for Empirical Research in Financial Management," *Financial Management,* 1988, 17(2):80–98.

Cooper, Dan, and Glenn Petry. "Corporate Performance and Adherence to Shareholder Wealth-Maximizing Principles," *Financial Management,* 1994, 23(1):71–78.

Cornell, Bradford, and Alan C. Shapiro. "Corporate Stakeholders and Corporate Finance," *Financial Management,* 1987, 16(1):5–14.

Donaldson, Gordon. *Managing Corporate Wealth: The Operations of a Comprehensive Financial Goals System.* New York: Praeger, 1984.

Fama, Eugene F., and Kenneth R. French. "The Cross-Section of Expected Stock Returns," *Journal of Finance,* 1992, 47(2):427–466.

Froot, Kenneth A., David S. Scharfstein, and Jeremy C. Stein. "Herd on the Street: Informational Inefficiencies in a Market with Short-Term Speculation," *Journal of Finance,* 1992, 47(4):1461–1484.

Glosten, Lawrence R. "Is the Electronic Open Limit Order Book Inevitable?" *Journal of Finance,* 1994, 49(4):1127–1161.

Gordon, Lilli A., and John Pound. "Information, Ownership Structure, and Shareholder Voting: Evidence from Shareholder-Sponsored Corporate Governance Proposals," *Journal of Finance,* 1993, 48(2):697–718.

Gordon, M. J. "Corporate Finance Under the MM Theorems," *Financial Management,* 1989, 18(2):19–28.

Jensen, Michael C. "Presidential Address: The Modern Industrial Revolution, Exit, and the Failure of Internal Control Systems," *Journal of Finance,* 1993, 48(3):831–880.

Jensen, Michael C., and William H. Meckling. "Theory of the Firm: Managerial Behavior, Agency Costs, and Ownership Structure," *Journal of Financial Economics,* 1976, 3(4):305–360.

Moyer, R. Charles, Ramesh Rao, and Phillip M. Sisneros. "Substitutes for Voting Rights: Evidence from Dual Class Recapitalizations," *Financial Management,* 1992, 21(3):35–48.

Ramirez, Gabriel G., David A. Waldman, and Dennis J. Lasser. "Research Needs in Corporate Finance: Perspectives from Financial Managers," *Financial Management,* 1991, 20(2):17–29.

Roll, Richard. "What Every CFO Should Know About Scientific Progress in Financial Economics: What Is Known and What Remains to Be Resolved," *Financial Management,* 1994, 23(2):69–75.

Scholes, Myron S. "Presidential Address: Stock and Compensation," *Journal of Finance,* 1991, 46(3):803–824.

Seitz, Neil. "Shareholder Goals, Firm Goals and Firm Financing Decisions," *Financial Management,* 1982, 11(3):20–26.

Seward, James K. "Corporate Financial Policy and the Theory of Financial Intermediation," *Journal of Finance,* 1990, 45(2):351–378.

Shefrin, Hersh, and Meir Statman. "Behavioral Aspects of the Design of Financial Products," *Financial Management,* 1993, 22(2):123–134.

Thakor, Anjan V. "Corporate Investments and Finance," *Financial Management,* 1993, 22(2):135–144.

Treynor, Jack L. "The Financial Objective in the Widely Held Corporation," *Financial Analysts Journal,* 1981, 37(2):68–71.

Weston, J. Fred. "What MM Have Wrought," *Financial Management,* 1989, 18(2):29–38.

THE FINANCIAL ENVIRONMENT: CONCEPTS AND PRINCIPLES

OBJECTIVES

1. Explain each of the principles of finance.

2. Interpret real situations using these principles.

3. Distinguish clearly among expected rates of return, realized rates of return, and required rates of return.

4. Describe the characteristics of the major securities in the capital markets.

5. Distinguish among the roles of investment bankers, brokers and dealers, and financial intermediaries.

6. Explain the *term structure of interest rates*.

7. Discuss the role of business ethics in corporate finance.

Every field of endeavor has fundamental laws, principles, or tenets that help guide you in understanding that field. Finance is no exception. There are important, basic principles that can help you understand mundane practices in finance as well as new and complex situations.

If you wanted to sell your car, would you want to get the highest possible price? Sure. Do you think a person who wanted to buy it would want to pay the lowest possible price? Undoubtedly. Suppose you wanted to invest some money. Would you like to triple your money in the next year? That would be nice. But do you want to risk losing all your money? Not really. Do you think you might have to take some risk to get a superior return? Probably. If someone guaranteed to double your money in six months with absolutely no risk, would you doubt them? We hope so. If we owed you $100, would you rather have it today or in three years? Today, of course.

The answers to these questions are obvious in such straightforward situations. They come from intuition you have developed, based on an understanding of the world. In more complex situations, answers are not always so easy. So you need principles to help you.

In this chapter we describe the principles of finance. They are the foundation on which financial management is built. We will help you understand their application to the practice of finance.

We also take a quick look at the capital markets. Recall that a financial security, which we'll call simply a *security,* is issued by a company to finance itself. A security, such as a stock or bond, is essentially a claim on future cash flows, such as dividend and interest payments. Capital market transactions (buying and selling securities) are important, both as a part of financial management and as a place to observe and apply the principles of finance.

PRINCIPLES OF FINANCE: THE COMPETITIVE ECONOMIC ENVIRONMENT

The principles of finance, described in this section and the two that follow, are based on logical deduction and on empirical observation. Even if every principle is not absolutely correct in every case, most practitioners accept the principles as a valid way to describe their world.

Our first group of principles deals with competition in an economic environment.

The Principle of Self-Interested Behavior: People Act in Their Own Financial Self-Interest

To make good business decisions you need to understand human behavior. Although there may be individual exceptions, we assume that people act in an economically rational way. That is, people act in their own financial self-interest.

It may be hard to swallow the Principle of Self-Interested Behavior at first. One reason is that most of us realize money isn't everything. The Principle of Self-Interested Behavior does not deny this truth. Nor does it deny the importance of "human" considerations. Also, it is not saying money is *the most important thing* in life.

This principle says that when all else is equal, all parties to a financial transaction will choose the course of action most financially advantageous to themselves. It explains actual behavior very well. This is because most business interactions are "arm's-length" transactions. In such impersonal transactions, getting the most good out of available resources is the primary consideration.

You also might think that giving money to a charity, having children, and being honest on your tax return are violations of the Principle of Self-Interested Behavior. These decisions involve more than money. But even if certain actions do violate the Principle of Self-Interested Behavior, the principle is still useful for our purposes. This is because it is right on average. So it's a very good approximation of human behavior.

There is an important corollary to the Principle of Self-Interested Behavior. Frequently, competing desirable actions can be taken. When someone takes an action, that action eliminates other possible actions. The difference between the value of one action and the value of the best alternative is called an **opportunity cost.**

OPPORTUNITY COST The difference between the value of one action and the value of the best alternative action.

An opportunity cost provides an indication of the relative importance of a decision. When the opportunity cost is small, the cost of an incorrect choice is small. Similarly, when the opportunity cost is large, the cost of not making the best choice is large.

EXAMPLE

The Opportunity Cost of Selling a Used Car

Suppose you sell a car for $3200 without much forethought. You find out the next day that the car could have been sold for $3300. You have incurred an opportunity cost of at least $100. You might not consider that very significant. But suppose you discovered the next day that the car could have been sold for $4500. You probably would consider the opportunity cost of $1300 on an asset worth $4500 significant. ■

AGENCY THEORY The analysis of participant behavior in a *principal-agent relationship.*

PRINCIPAL-AGENT RELATIONSHIP A situation in which one participant, the *agent,* makes decisions that affect another participant, the *principal.*

AGENT One of the participants in a *principal-agent relationship.*

PRINCIPAL One of the participants in a *principal-agent relationship.*

Don't let the simplicity of our used-car example lull you into thinking such costs are obvious and easy to calculate. In some cases, opportunity costs are very subtle and difficult even to define, let alone calculate. However, the importance of opportunity costs cannot be overstated.

An important application of the Principle of Self-Interested Behavior is called **agency theory.** Agency theory analyzes conflicts of interest and behavior in a principal-agent relationship. A **principal-agent relationship** is a relationship in which one participant, an **agent,** makes decisions that affect another participant, a **principal.**

The set-of-contracts model we discussed in chapter 1 views contracts as principal-agent relationships. Examples include those between the company (as the principal) and its employees (agents), such as its managers, salespeople, and others. The company also has a principal-agent relationship with pension fund managers, with lawyers, and with real estate, travel, and insurance agents. An important principal-agent relationship is that between the company's stockholders (principals) and managers (agents).

EXAMPLE

Death of Occidental Petroleum's Founder

The longtime chairman of Occidental Petroleum Corporation, Armand Hammer, died in December 1990. Hammer's name had come to be synonymous with Occidental. He had built it into a major corporation. Now he was gone. What happened to Occidental's stock price when his death was announced? It jumped up 9%. Trading volume exceeded 8 million shares, many times the stock's average trading volume, making it the most active stock on the New York Stock Exchange that day. Why?

Many oil industry analysts felt that Hammer had begun to operate the company as his personal fiefdom. They accused him of using the company's resources to support his own pet projects (such as an art museum to house his collection), even when investing in them was not in the best interests of stockholders. Stockholders believed his successor, Ray Irani, would make better business decisions. Indeed, most would agree that the company fared much better under Irani. ■

The problem of **moral hazard** is a critical consideration in principal-agent relationships. Moral hazard refers to situations wherein the agent can take unseen actions for personal benefit even though such actions are costly to the principal. By carefully analyzing individual behavior, agency theory helps us develop more effective provisions for contracts between a principal and an agent. A typical goal of such contract provisions is to reduce conflicts of interest, thereby reducing moral hazard problems.

MORAL HAZARD A situation in which an agent can take unseen actions for personal benefit even though such actions are costly to the principal.

The Principle of Two-Sided Transactions: Each Financial Transaction Has at Least Two Sides

The Principle of Two-Sided Transactions may seem very straightforward, yet it is sometimes forgotten when things become complex. Understanding financial transactions requires that we not become self-centered. Don't forget that while we're following self-interested behavior, others are also acting in *their own* financial self-interest. That includes those with whom we are transacting business. Consider the sale of an asset—or should we say the purchase? That's just the point. For every sale, there is a purchase. For each buyer, there is a seller. When we analyze our side of a transaction, we must keep in mind that there is someone else analyzing the other side.

So Who Was Buying?

EXAMPLE

An example of the confusion regarding the Principle of Two-Sided Transactions involves reporting stock market transactions. Media commentators sometimes refer to "profit takers *selling off* their holdings" and causing a decline in the price of a particular common stock. The implication is that there was more selling than buying. You may even read in the newspaper that changes in market prices are the result of an "imbalance" between the amount of buying and the amount of selling that is taking place. We know this, of course, is not true.

When stocks are traded, there is a buyer and a seller for each share that changes hands. If you will recall the Principle of Self-Interested Behavior, you know the buyers didn't deliberately buy a stock that was going to decline in value. They thought the stock would maintain or increase its value. It just happened that the buyers turned out to be wrong! Quite simply, it is these differences in expectations that lead to many of the securities trades in the first place. ■

We can describe this sort of situation as one where more people believe the stock is overvalued than believe the stock is undervalued. This difference in beliefs may lead to more *sell orders* than *buy orders*. However, in spite of the disequilibrium in orders (those *willing* to buy or sell), there is *exactly* one share purchased for each share sold. In such situations, people buy or sell until the market price reaches what they think is the correct value of each share.

Most financial transactions are zero-sum games. A **zero-sum game** is a situation in which one player can gain *only* at the expense of another player. In these situations, my gain is your loss, and vice versa. This is exactly the case with most buyer-seller relations. A higher price costs the buyer and benefits the seller, and vice versa. Nevertheless, some transactions may not appear to be zero-sum games. Consider the case of municipal bonds (*munis*; pronounced "mu-nees").

ZERO-SUM GAME A situation in which one player can gain only at the expense of another player.

Tax-Free Municipal Bonds

EXAMPLE

Municipal bonds are issued by state and local governments. For constitutional reasons, the interest payments on such bonds are exempt from federal taxes. This allows state and local governments to issue munis at a lower interest rate than they would have to pay if the interest were taxable. Purchasers of munis will get a higher after-tax return than they would if they had

(continued on following page)

(Tax-Free Municipal Bonds *continued from previous page*)

bought otherwise similar but fully taxable bonds. It appears, then, that this is not a zero-sum game. Both sides are better off. However, this is not so clear when you consider some other parties to the transaction. How about other taxpayers? Reducing one group of tax-payers' tax payments may cause others to bear a larger portion of the cost of running the government. ■

Many transactions that are not zero-sum games result from provisions in the tax code. Because this is a finance textbook, we won't debate whether these provisions are good or bad. Suffice it to say that, with few exceptions, people and corporations seek out ways to pay less in taxes. This is consistent with the Principle of Self-Interested Behavior. People will seek out tax-created exceptions to the usual zero-sum-game condition and exploit them whenever possible.

Sometimes, people overlook the Principle of Two-Sided Transactions. Egotistical people can suffer from *hubris,* an arrogance due to excessive pride and an insolence toward others. They believe, mistakenly, that they are superior to those with whom they are doing business. Such hubris has led to many unfortunate decisions. For example, companies have often paid what seems to be an excessive amount to buy another company. The managers might justify the price by saying that the current market price is too low. Such managers are implicitly saying that the marketplace is stupid. Unfortunately, an accurate assessment is possible only after the fact in most cases. Empirical evidence shows that, on average, a company's value doesn't increase by acquiring another company.

EXAMPLE   *Sun's Offer to Take Over Apple Computer*

The management of Sun Microsystems Inc. had met with executives of Apple Computer Inc. to discuss a possible business combination. In mid-January 1996, the *Wall Street Journal* reported that Sun might bid $25 per share for Apple. What do you think happened to Sun's stock price? It fell that day from $48.56 per share to $44.13. Investors apparently felt that Sun would be making a bad investment and paying too much for Apple. They registered their opinion "loudly" by reducing the price they were willing to pay for Sun stock. ■

There are at least two sides to every transaction, and the parties on the other side can be just as bright, hard working, and creative as you are. Underestimating your competitors can lead to disaster.

The Signaling Principle: Actions Convey Information

The Signaling Principle is another extension of the Principle of Self-Interested Behavior. Assuming self-interested behavior, we can guess at the information or opinions behind the decisions that we observe. For example, a decision to buy or sell an asset can imply information about the condition of the asset or about a decision maker's expectations or plans for the future. Likewise, a company's decision to enter a new line of business may reveal something about the company's position and its belief in the venture's potential. Similarly, when a company announces a dividend, stock split, or new securities issue, people frequently interpret these actions in terms of the company's future earnings. In fact, when actions are at odds with announcements, the actions are usually louder than words.

Actions versus Words

Janus Chemtech's chief executive officer announces at a securities analysts' meeting that he is very encouraged by his company's prospects for future earnings growth. At the same time, he reports to the Securities and Exchange Commission that the company's executives—including the chief executive officer—are selling large numbers of their own shares of the company's stock. The analyst community is understandably suspicious. ■

Of course, decisions can be misinterpreted. For example, recall the temporarily upward-sloping demand curve for flip-flops, discussed in chapter 1. Many consumers incorrectly thought the incredibly low price signaled that the product was worthless.

The flip-flop example illustrates what is known as adverse selection. The problem of **adverse selection** is operating when offering something for sale seems to indicate something negative about the item being offered for sale. Adverse selection discourages people from offering to sell good-quality products. This problem is common in used-equipment markets, because the equipment offered for sale can be broken or even worthless as opposed to no longer needed.

ADVERSE SELECTION
When offering something for sale seems to indicate something negative about the item being offered for sale.

The Behavioral Principle: When All Else Fails, Look at What Others Are Doing for Guidance

The Behavioral Principle is a direct application of the Signaling Principle. The Signaling Principle says that actions convey information. The Behavioral Principle says, in essence, "Let's try to use such information."

To help you understand the Behavioral Principle, we want you to imagine that you've already earned your degree and have been working for a medium-size corporation for about a year and a half in three different positions. Recently, your hard work and the long hours you have been putting in have been noticed by your boss, Mr. Womack, the financial vice president. In recognition of your accomplishments, Mr. Womack has invited you and your spouse to his home for dinner, along with several other members of the department and their spouses.

You and your spouse are just congratulating each other for having successfully navigated the very formal cocktail hour when you arrive at the dining room. It's larger than your whole apartment. As you seat yourselves in your assigned seats, you and your spouse simultaneously nudge each other, motioning toward the silverware. There's more silverware at your place setting alone than you have in your entire kitchen. You haven't got a clue about which piece should be used for which food. What do you do?

There is only one reasonable way to proceed. Discreetly look down the table as each course is served and use the same piece of silverware that Mr. Womack is using. But suppose this isn't possible—you can't see Mr. Womack very well from where you sit. What should you do? You can simply check out the people immediately around you. Most of us will go with the majority if there isn't someone we especially trust.

Now change the scenario from dinner to finance. Suppose you're a financial manager. You are facing a major decision that seems to have no single, clearly correct course of action. For example, suppose the board of directors has asked you to assess how the company is currently being financed and perhaps recommend changes. As it turns out, there is no prescribed single optimal capital structure for a company; managers must make an informed judgment. What should you do?

One reasonable approach is to look for guidance in what other companies similar to your company are currently doing and have done in the recent past. Either you can imitate the companies that you feel are most likely to be the best guides, or you can imitate the majority. In particular, the policy choices made by other companies in the same industry can provide useful guidance. This form of behavior is sometimes referred to as the "industry effect." This is what we mean by the Behavioral Principle of Finance: When all else fails, look at what others are doing for guidance.

In practice, the Behavioral Principle is typically applied in two types of situations. In some cases, such as the choice of a capital structure, theory doesn't provide a clear solution to the problem. In other cases, theory provides a clear solution, but the cost of gathering the necessary information outweighs the potential benefit. Valuing certain assets is an example of the latter case. The value of some assets, such as stock or a piece of real estate, can often be estimated at relatively low cost from the observed recent purchase prices of similar assets. In cases such as these, managers use the Behavioral Principle to arrive at an inexpensive approximation of the correct answer.

We have just cited two appropriate applications of the Behavioral Principle: (1) the case where there is a limit to our understanding and (2) the case where its use is more cost-effective than the most accurate method. One application that sometimes occurs in practice is *not* appropriate: "blind imitation" to minimize personal cost and risk. We want to leave you with an important warning to avoid this misapplication.

The Behavioral Principle can be tricky to apply. You have to decide when there's no single, clearly correct, best course of action. Furthermore, having decided this, you must decide whether there is a "best" other or group of others to look to for guidance. Finally, you must determine from their actions what your best course of action would be. The Behavioral Principle is, admittedly, a second-best principle. It leads to approximate solutions in the best of situations and, in the worst, to imitating the errors of others. Still, it is useful in certain situations, despite its potential shortcomings.

FREE RIDER A follower who avoids the cost of finding the best course of action by simply imitating the leader's behavior.

This principle also has an important corollary. Its application can lead to what is called the **free-rider** problem. In such situations, a "leader" expends resources to determine a best course of action, and a "follower" receives the benefit of the expenditure by simply imitating. So the leader is subsidizing the follower. For example, McDonald's does extensive research and analysis concerning the placement of its restaurants. Other fast-food chains have at times chosen their new restaurant locations by simply building near a McDonald's restaurant. Patent and copyright laws are designed to protect innovators, at least to some extent, from the free-rider problem and to reward the introduction of valuable new ideas that improve society.

Self-Check

1. Explain in your own words the Principle of Self-Interested Behavior.

2. What is a principal-agent relationship? Give some examples.

3. Why is it important to remember the Principle of Two-Sided Transactions?

4. Give an example of the Signaling Principle, where actions convey information.

5. What are two good reasons to employ the Behavioral Principle? Explain why the Behavioral Principle does *not* suggest blind imitation.

6. Define the following concepts: *opportunity cost, zero-sum game, adverse selection,* and *free rider.*

PRINCIPLES OF FINANCE: VALUE AND ECONOMIC EFFICIENCY

Our second group of principles deals with ways of creating value and economic efficiency.

The Principle of Valuable Ideas: Extraordinary Returns Are Achievable with New Ideas

The Principle of Valuable Ideas says you might find a way to get rich! New products or services can create value, so if you have a new idea, you might then transform it into *extraordinary positive value* for yourself.

Most valuable new ideas occur in the physical-asset markets. Physical assets are more likely than financial assets to be unique. For example, the founders of Apple Computer became wealthy by inventing and successfully introducing the personal computer.

Physical assets can be unique in a number of ways. Consider patents. Thomas Edison became a very wealthy man from having invented a large number of unique products, such as the light bulb, the phonograph, the motion picture, and many others. If patent protection had not been available, it is unlikely that he would have become so wealthy. The ability to hold the exclusive rights to produce a unique product enhances the value of a physical asset. Even without patent protection, some companies have been successful at building brand loyalty. They convince consumers that they are the only companies that can produce particular types of products, and this conviction generates more repeat purchases and purchases of related products.

New ideas may also take the form of improved business practices or marketing. For example, a man named Ray Kroc bought a small chain of hamburger stands. By applying his ideas about how to operate the business, he made himself and a large number of other people very wealthy. You might have heard of Ray's little chain—it is called McDonald's. The list of such products and services is almost endless, and the potential for new products and services *is* endless.

The Principle of Comparative Advantage: Expertise Can Create Value

The Principle of Comparative Advantage may be familiar. In a broad sense, it's the very idea underlying our economic system. If everyone does what they do best, we will have the most qualified people doing each type of work. This creates economic efficiency: We pay others to do what they can do better than we can, and they pay us to do what we can do better than they can.

The Principle of Comparative Advantage is the basis for foreign trade. Each country produces the goods and services that it can make most efficiently. Then, when countries trade, each can be better off.

Michael Jordan Plays Better Basketball

EXAMPLE

Michael Jordan is arguably the best basketball player ever, but for personal reasons, he left basketball and tried out for a baseball team. He then played only one season of minor league baseball before "throwing in the towel." He left baseball to others who did that better than he did, and he went back to playing basketball, which he does better than anyone else. ■

The Options Principle: Options Are Valuable

An **option** is a right, without an obligation, to do something. In other words, the owner (the buyer of the option) can require the writer (the seller of the option) to make the transaction specified in the option contract (for example, sell a parcel of land), but the writer cannot require the owner to do anything. Often, in finance, an explicit option contract refers to the right to buy or sell an asset for a prespecified price.

The right to buy is a **call option,** and the right to sell is a **put option.** Call options are frequently used by real estate developers. A call option allows the developer to gain the consent of all necessary parties *before* investing a large amount of money—money that could be lost if any of the parties later refused to sell their land.

Insurance is a kind of put option. Suppose you have insurance on your car, and, while it is parked, the car is destroyed by a cement truck. The insurance settlement can be viewed as selling the destroyed car to the insurance company. Now you may or may not decide to buy another car, but that's your choice.

The Options Principle also has a corollary: An option can't have a negative value to the owner. This is because the owner can always decide to do nothing. Of course, the option can

OPTION The right, without an obligation, to do something.

CALL OPTION The right to *buy* something at a given price during the life of the option.

PUT OPTION The right to *sell* something at a given price during the life of the option.

be worthless. However, even the smallest chance of a positive payoff at *any* time in the future gives the option some positive value, however tiny that value might be.

The word *options* makes some people think of explicit financial contracts such as call options and put options. However, we use the term in its broadest sense: a right with no obligation attached. With such a broad definition, you can see that options are widespread. In fact, they exist in many situations without being noticed. The importance of options extends well beyond their easily identified existence, because many assets contain "hidden" options.

One important hidden option is created by what is called limited liability. **Limited liability is a legal concept within bankruptcy that limits an investor's possible loss to what has already been invested**. For example, suppose a corporation fails to repay a debt. The debtholder can't sue the stockholders for the money. So the most the stockholders can lose is the money they have already invested.

Limited liability creates the option to default, the *option* to not fully repay a debt. Of course, this isn't an option you think of right away as being valuable, but it is nevertheless a valuable option.

LIMITED LIABILITY A legal concept within bankruptcy that limits an investor's possible loss to what has already been invested.

EXAMPLE

TWA Uses Its Option to Default

A few years ago, Transworld Airlines (TWA) was unable to meet its financial obligations. It filed for protection and reorganization under what is called *Chapter 11 of the Bankruptcy Code*. The result was that some of TWA's creditors did not—and never will—get all the money they were owed. Of course, such situations are complex, and they have many other negative consequences and related problems. However, the fact of the matter is that TWA failed to make legally required payments, it *defaulted,* and yet it continued to operate its business. ■

Hidden options dramatically complicate the process of measuring value. In some cases, such options actually provide an alternative way to value an asset, as we will see when we consider valuing shares of common stock. We'll discuss options in greater detail at several points in this text. For now, we hope you can see that an asset plus an option is more valuable than the asset alone.

The Principle of Incremental Benefits: Financial Decisions Are Based on Incremental Benefits

The Principle of Incremental Benefits states that the value derived from choosing a particular alternative is determined by the net extra—that is, incremental—benefit the decision provides compared to its alternative. The term *incremental* is very important. The incremental costs and benefits are those that would occur *with* a particular course of action but would not occur *without* taking that course of action.

For example, if General Motors spends nothing this year on advertising its products, some people will nevertheless buy GM products. So the value to GM of advertising its products is based on the difference between whatever future sales they would make *with* the advertising expenditure and whatever future sales they would make *without* the advertising expenditure. GM's decision, whether and how much to advertise, is based on the profit from the incremental sales that results from the advertising compared to the cost of the advertising. In other words, the advertising decision is based on the *net* (incremental) change in profit.

The incremental benefits are cash flows in many situations. The incremental cash flow is the cash flow that would occur as a result of the decision minus the cash flow that would occur without the decision.

As with other principles, the Principle of Incremental Benefits can get lost when things become complex. But this principle is easily overlooked even in some relatively simple situations. There is one situation in which it may be difficult to accept and apply this principle. It involves the concept of a sunk cost. A **sunk cost** is a cost that has already been incurred; subsequent decisions cannot change it.

SUNK COST A cost that has already been incurred and cannot be altered by subsequent decisions.

Creating the Lockheed Tri-Star

When Lockheed Corporation developed its L-1011 tri-star jet, critical decisions were made about whether or not to continue the project. When the wide-body jet was first proposed, there was enthusiasm in the corporation about its potential. But after considerable work on the project, it became clear that the tri-star project would not be nearly as valuable as expected. Some decision makers at Lockheed proposed abandoning the tri-star. Others argued against such a strategy, because so much had already been spent on its development. The decision to continue with the project proved to be a disaster for Lockheed. Bankruptcy was only narrowly avoided, and the tri-star project was eventually scrapped.[1]

If Lockheed decision makers had applied the Principle of Incremental Benefits, they might have saved a lot of money. At some point, the potential benefits from finishing the project were insufficient to justify the remaining development costs. Concentrating on previous expenditures can obscure the fact that in such cases, the company should proceed with a project only if the necessary *remaining* costs are less than the projected final benefits from the project. Whatever expenditures have already been incurred—sunk costs—are not relevant to the decision to continue the project, because they cannot be changed. ■

Another example of a sunk cost you've probably seen, or even confronted yourself, involves changing majors. Suppose an economics major is considering changing majors, to marketing. Some people have difficulty making such a decision because of what they have already "invested" in economics. In fact, this past history is a sunk cost. Given today's situation, the decision to continue in economics or change to marketing should be based on the future costs and benefits of each choice. Of course, an important cost is that of completing either degree, and the past investment in economics reduces the incremental future cost of completing that major. Nevertheless, the decision to change should be based on whatever the incremental benefits and costs are *now*. That requires ignoring sunk costs.

In spite of the Principle of Incremental Benefits, some individuals seem to have an emotional attachment to sunk costs. These people continue to own an asset even though they know they could sell the asset and reinvest their money more profitably elsewhere. Clearly, these individuals are not applying the Principle of Incremental Benefits. They are continuing to incur an opportunity cost. Unfortunately, identifying such situations can be very difficult. Still, remember that an asset isn't like a family member. Most of us are emotional about people, but we recommend you not be emotional about your investments.

Self-Check

1. Explain in your own words the Principle of Comparative Advantage.

2. What is the main difference between a call option and a put option?

3. Give an example of a successful business that illustrates the Principle of Valuable Ideas.

4. Which principle does the following situation violate? A company has invested $50 million in a new computer chip. Its chief scientist wants to abandon the effort, but the vice president for research and development tells securities analysts that the company "can't afford to abandon the project now."

5. Define the following terms: *incremental costs and benefits, sunk costs, option, call option,* and *put option.*

---

[1] It was said by someone other than us: "Sunk costs nearly sunk Lockheed."

PRINCIPLES OF FINANCE: FINANCIAL TRANSACTIONS

Our last group of principles emerges from observing financial transactions.

The Principle of Risk-Return Trade-Off: There Is a Trade-Off Between Risk and Return

The Principle of Risk-Return Trade-Off is another way of saying that if you want to have a chance at some really great outcomes, you have to take a chance on having a really bad outcome. Even without providing a formal definition of *risk,* we can agree on some of the effects of risk. One important dimension of risk is that higher risk brings with it either a greater chance of a bad outcome or worse possible outcomes. You simply cannot expect to get high returns without simultaneously exposing yourself to the chance of low returns.

When we discussed the Principle of Self-Interested Behavior, we didn't talk about how to operationalize it. We'll do that now. In a financial transaction, we assume that *when all else is equal, people prefer higher return and lower risk.* To appreciate the justification for this assumption, simply ask yourself this question: If you are faced with two alternatives that are identical (including their riskiness), except that alternative A provides a higher return than B, which alternative will you choose? We predict you'll choose A.

Similarly, if you are offered two alternatives that are identical (including their return), except that A is riskier than B, which alternative will you choose? If you're like most people, you'll choose B. This behavior is called **risk aversion:** avoiding risk when all else is equal. In other words, investors are not indifferent to risk but require compensation for bearing it.

✓ **RISK AVERSION** Avoiding risk when all else is equal.

People generally behave as though they are averse to risk. Almost any decision or choice you make involves risk. For example, decisions to make an investment, take a job, or lend money involve varying degrees of risk. Personal decisions also involve risk, and your personal choices will generally reflect your attitude toward risk.

If people prefer higher return and lower risk and they act in their own financial self-interest, competition then creates the Principle of Risk-Return Trade-Off. Competition forces people to make a trade-off between the return and the risk of their investment. You just can't get high returns and low risk simultaneously because that's what *everyone* wants. Therefore, to get a higher expected return, you'll have to take more risk.

A corollary to the Principle of Risk-Return Trade-Off is that most people are willing to take less return in exchange for less risk. When an asset is purchased, its expected future return can be adjusted by altering its purchase price. A lower (higher) purchase price increases (decreases) the buyer's expected future return. Capital markets, such as the stock market, offer such opportunities, and each participant makes his risk-return trade-off.

The Principle of Diversification: Diversification Is Beneficial

✓ **DIVERSIFICATION** Spreading your investments across several alternatives instead of concentrating them in a single investment.

✓ **PORTFOLIO** A group of investments, as opposed to a single investment.

The Principle of Diversification is really quite straightforward and requires little explanation. A prudent investor won't invest her entire wealth in a single company. That would expose her entire wealth to the risk that the company might fail. But if the investment is divided among many companies, the entire investment won't be lost unless all of those companies fail. This is much less likely than that one of them will fail. Spreading investments around, instead of concentrating them, is called **diversification.** We will explain in chapter 7 how investors can lower their risk by investing in a group of securities, called a **portfolio,** rather than by investing exclusively in one security.

EXAMPLE   *Examples of Diversification*

Mutual funds, commercial banks, and other financial intermediaries all have very diversified portfolios. No single investment makes up a very large part of their overall portfolios. Individual investors are advised to diversify their portfolios broadly. Operating businesses diversify themselves in many ways. They operate in different business segments. They try to diversify their customer base; that is, they try not to depend too heavily on only a few customers. They diversify their sources of supply. Your college curriculum is diversified, because you cannot concentrate too heavily in one area of study to the exclusion of others. Even a healthy diet should be diversified.

Why is diversification so widespread? Quite simply, because it reduces risk. ■

The Principle of Capital Market Efficiency: The Capital Markets Reflect All Information Quickly

Buying and selling securities is referred to as **trading.** Probably the best-known capital markets are in New York, London, and Tokyo. The New York and American Stock Exchanges and, especially because of recent television advertising, the NASDAQ (National Association of Securities Dealers Automated Quotation) stock markets are the most widely known in the United States. Together with other stock exchanges around the world and smaller ones around the country, they are collectively referred to as the *stock market.* There are many other capital markets as well.

Formally, the Principle of Capital Market Efficiency says: *Market prices of financial assets that are traded regularly in the capital markets reflect all available information and adjust fully and quickly to "new" information.*

How do share prices react to new information? We'll use the stock market for illustrative purposes at this point, because it is probably familiar to you.

TRADING Buying and selling securities. ✓

Capital Markets React to New Information

EXAMPLE

Suppose an oil company were to announce the discovery in the United States of a massive new oil field comparable to the North Slope of Alaska. What stock market trading prices would change? Clearly, the share price of the discovering company would rise. But what about other oil company stocks? Because of the increase in the supply of oil, the price of oil would decline, bringing down the value of the oil reserves owned by other companies. Therefore, we would expect that the share prices of the other oil companies would tend to fall (unless they were participating in the new discovery). Other share prices might change as well.

For example, cheaper oil should lead to cheaper plastic and increased business for a plastics manufacturer. That would suggest higher share prices for plastics manufacturers. However, the share prices of banks that have loaned Mexico a lot of money might decrease. The lower price of oil would reduce Mexico's oil revenue and increase the likelihood that those banks would not be fully repaid.

Alert traders who recognize these effects would act upon the information. Among other things, they might (1) buy the shares of the oil company that made the discovery, (2) sell the shares of oil companies not involved in the discovery, (3) buy the shares of companies such as plastics manufacturers that would benefit from the lower price of oil, and (4) sell the shares of lenders to Mexico that would be hurt by a lower price of oil.

This active trading is the mechanism by which new information becomes reflected in share prices. As you may have gathered by now, an event like a major oil discovery would provide opportunities to make a great deal of money quickly in many different capital markets. This opportunity to profit from new information provides the incentive to act (recall the Principle of Self-Interested Behavior) that causes share prices to respond to new information. ■

Capital market efficiency depends on how quickly new information is reflected in share prices. For a machine, perfect efficiency means there's no wasted energy—no loss to friction. This is certainly one aspect of capital market efficiency. The capital markets are well organized. The cost of making a transaction (buying or selling) is very low, especially when compared to transaction costs in the real-asset markets (such as machines, real estate, and raw materials). It's generally much easier, cheaper, and faster to buy and sell financial assets than to buy and sell real assets.

For example, companies such as Merrill Lynch charge a sales commission of about 1% of the sales value to execute an order to trade 1000 shares of stock selling for $60 per share, a $60,000 transaction. There are somewhat lower (higher) rates to handle larger (smaller) transactions. In contrast, companies such as Century 21 charge about 6% of the sale value to sell a $60,000 house. We'll have more to say about why this difference exists, but for now let's just note the difference.

In addition to offering convenience, low cost, and high speed, the capital markets are unimaginably large. The New York Stock Exchange alone averages more than $10 billion worth of stock traded each day. There are numerous participants, and competition is intense. When new information arrives, there are plenty of people paying close attention because there is a lot of money at stake. Those people can buy or sell their financial assets in minutes or even seconds. This explains why transaction costs and operational efficiencies play an important role in the speed and accuracy with which prices fully reflect new information. The lower the transaction costs and the easier it is to trade, the easier it is to act on new information, and the more quickly share prices adjust to reflect the new information.

In an efficient market that had no impediments to trading, the price of each asset would be the same everywhere in the market, except for temporary differences during periods of disequilibrium. In such a market environment, if price differentials existed, traders would take immediate actions to benefit from those differences through arbitrage. **Arbitrage is the act of buying and selling an asset simultaneously, where the sale price is greater than the purchase price, so that the difference provides a riskless profit.** As long as selling prices exceed buying prices, traders can earn a riskless arbitrage profit, and they can continue to do so until the price differential no longer exists.

Arbitrage opportunities enforce the economic principle called the *law of one price.* This law states that equivalent securities must trade at the same price. The law of one price may not hold strictly when there are transaction costs or other impediments to trading, but it is a good approximation of reality. Arbitrage activity ensures that whatever price differentials exist are smaller than the cost of arbitraging them away. For example, you might see small differences in price between the New York and London prices of gold, despite intense competition. This is due to the cost of shipping gold from one place to another. In the capital markets, with the same kind of intense competition but with essentially zero "shipping costs,"[2] differences in the prices of any particular security tend to be virtually zero.

It's easy to accept the Principle of Capital Market Efficiency. Yet it is probably the hardest to "internalize" of all of the principles of finance. We all know there are people who win the lottery and people who occasionally amass vast fortunes trading in the stock market. How can we become winners? How can we start with a small sum and amass a great fortune trading in stocks? (The answer to both questions is the same: only with luck or illegal activity!) If there were a reliable way to amass such a fortune, everyone would do it, of course, and then, instead of one great fortune, there would be a multitude of smaller "fortunes." Yet hope springs eternal!

ARBITRAGE The act of buying and selling an asset simultaneously, where the sale price is greater than the purchase price, so that the difference provides a riskless profit.

---

[2]The cost to "ship" a security is essentially zero because there is nothing physical to move. It's only information exchanged electronically. Although there were fixed costs to set up the system, the incremental cost (what economists call the variable, or marginal, cost) is simply the electricity cost, which is virtually zero for a single transaction.

Hot Tips and Easy Money

The logic of the Principle of Capital Market Efficiency is impeccable, and a lot of empirical research supports it. Nevertheless, investors gobble up hot tips and continue to search for "bargains" in the stock market. Just about every major brokerage house regularly publishes a list of "undervalued stocks." If a stock appears on such a list, investors will evaluate the security and bid up the stock's price if they agree with the brokerage analysts' conclusion. In an efficient market, a stock does not remain undervalued for very long. So how can brokerage houses regularly identify and publish extensive lists of them? What special powers do their analysts possess that enable them to identify such undervalued companies?

If you're skeptical of the value of such lists, you are not alone. Empirical research has not shown them to provide extra value. People who seem to have the gift of "second sight" are more likely to trade for their own account (take the profits for themselves) than to publish a list so that other people can help themselves to the money. Why? You guessed it—the Principle of Self-Interested Behavior. ∎

Competition, size, and the similarity of assets combine to make the capital markets extremely efficient. Frequently, we assume that the capital markets are *perfect* (100% efficient—no losses due to friction) in order to build a decision model. In fact, a perfect market is the best approximation we have of the capital markets. The assumption of perfect capital markets is like the assumption of risk aversion. Though not always correct, it is widely accepted and useful.

Reconciling Capital Market Efficiency with Valuable New Ideas

You may find it difficult to reconcile the Principle of Valuable Ideas with the Principle of Capital Market Efficiency. Together, they state that the capital markets are efficient, but that even in the capital markets, with all the competition that exists, a *new* market, product, or service can be created that provides an extraordinary return.

Here is the critical difference between the two principles. The Principle of Valuable Ideas applies to the return associated with being part of the creation of the opportunity. The Principle of Capital Market Efficiency involves the return associated with simply purchasing part of an opportunity that has become known to everyone. The founders of Apple Computer earned a tremendous rate of return on their investment as a result of their innovations. But what happened as other people became aware of the unique advantages that Apple's computer offered? Those advantages became fully reflected in Apple Computer's share price. So once the stock became actively traded, a purchaser of Apple Computer common stock could expect, because of capital market efficiency, to earn only a rate of return commensurate with the risk of the investment. Because of the very nature of risk, the outcome could be quite different from what was expected.

The Time-Value-of-Money Principle: Money Has a Time Value

If you own some money, you can "rent" it to someone else. The borrower must pay you interest for the use of your money (or you won't make the loan). Simply stated, the time value of money is how much it costs to rent money.

You can think of the time value of money as the opportunity to earn interest on a bank savings account. A sizable amount of money kept in cash at home creates an opportunity cost, the cost of missing the opportunity to earn interest on the money. For this reason, we think of the interest rate as a measure of the opportunity cost. In fact, because of capital market efficiency, we can use our capital market alternatives as benchmarks against which to measure other investment opportunities: Don't make the investment unless it is at least as good as comparable capital market investments.

Suppose you deposit $1000 today in a bank savings account that is paying 7% per year. One year from today, the account will have $1070. Let's call the starting amount PV (for present value) and next year's account balance FV (for future value). Let r be the interest rate. The interest earned over a time period is the interest rate times the amount deposited initially, $r(\text{PV})$. Then FV is the sum of the starting amount, PV, plus the interest, or

$$FV = PV + r(PV) = PV(1 + r) \tag{2.1}$$

For PV = $1000 and $r = 0.07$, in one year FV is $1070 (= (1000)1.07). In words, equation (2.1) says the future value equals the present value times 1 plus the interest rate.

Equation (2.1) is based on *per-year* interest. But suppose you save the money for two years? At the end of the first year, the account contains $1070. By reapplying equation (2.1), at the end of two years, you will have

$$FV = \$1070(1.07) = \$1144.90$$

Note that the account will earn $70 interest the first year and an additional $74.90 interest the second year. This is because the interest paid at the end of the first year itself earns interest the second year, amounting to $4.90 (7% of $70). Paying interest on interest already earned is called paying **compound interest.** The process of compounding interest can be handled by extending equation (2.1). Let n be the number of time periods the money remains in the account. Then

$$FV = PV(1 + r)^n \tag{2.2}$$

Now let's reverse the logic of equation (2.2). This time, let's rewrite the equation so that we can solve for PV (instead of FV).

$$PV = \frac{FV}{(1 + r)^n} \tag{2.3}$$

This is the form in which the equation is most often used. In words, equation (2.3) says a dollar today is worth more than a dollar in the future. This is because today's dollar can be invested to earn interest until tomorrow. To determine the present value of an amount of money that will be received in the future, divide the future value by the quantity $(1 + r)^n$. This adjustment reflects the cost to rent money at an interest rate of r per period for n periods. That is, it represents the cost from now until you expect to receive the payment.

To compute a present value, you must estimate the amounts to be received in the future. The future amounts are referred to as *expected future cash flows*. Next, you must estimate the appropriate "rental" rate for each of the expected future cash flows from now until you expect to receive each of them. This rental rate has many different names, but the generic term for it is the **discount rate**.

Equation (2.3) is often referred to as the basic **discounted cash flow (DCF) framework** for valuation. It is simple in the form given, but it can become complex as we combine multiple expected future cash flows and allow the discount rate to change over time. Equation (2.3) can be used to value any asset, provided we can estimate the expected future cash flows and determine an appropriate discount rate for each cash flow. The discount rate must accurately reflect each cash flow's riskiness. Selecting the appropriate discount rate often represents a difficult challenge, even for an expert in finance. Estimating expected future cash flows also requires skill.

The Time-Value-of-Money Principle is probably the most useful concept you can learn in this class. The importance of this principle (and for that matter, of all the principles) rests on its ability to keep our thinking clear and logical. Chapter 5 is devoted to the time value of money, and applications of the principle appear throughout the book. You will encounter the time value of money repeatedly for the rest of your life.

COMPOUND INTEREST Earning additional interest on interest previously earned.

DISCOUNT RATE The generic term for a rate of return that measures the time value of money.

DISCOUNTED CASH FLOW (DCF) FRAMEWORK Valuing an asset by discounting its expected future cash flows at some discount rate.

Self-Check

1. What does it mean to say an investor is risk averse?

2. Why do investors diversify their investment portfolios? (Answer in three words or less.)

3. Explain the Principle of Capital Market Efficiency in your own words.

4. Why is a dollar today worth more than a dollar to be received a year from today?

5. Compute the present value of $100 due in one year if the discount rate is 10%.

6. Define the following terms: *risk aversion, portfolio, diversification, arbitrage, compound interest,* and *discount rate.*

RATES OF RETURN AND NET PRESENT VALUE

Most investors want to know about an investment's rate of return. An investment's *return* for a period equals its income during the period, which is its cash flows plus its increase (or decrease) in value, divided by its starting value:

$$Return = \text{Rate of return} = \frac{\text{Cash flow} + (\text{Ending value} - \text{Beginning value})}{\text{Beginning value}} \quad (2.4)$$

For example, suppose you bought a share of stock for $20, it paid you a $0.50 dividend during the next year, and was worth $24.50 at the end of one year. Your rate of return for the year would be

$$Return = \frac{0.50 + (24.50 - 20.00)}{20.00} = \frac{5.00}{20.00} = 25\%$$

Your total income consists of $0.50 of dividends and $4.50 in increased value, for a total of $5.00. With $5.00 of income, and an original investment of $20.00, your return was 25%.

Realized, Expected, and Required Returns

The example we just gave is of a realized (or actual) return. There are, however, other concepts of return. We describe and discuss here three different returns. Distinguishing among these three concepts is critical.

Realized Return The **realized return** is the rate of return actually earned on an investment during a given time period. The realized return depends on what the future cash flows turn out to be after the investment is made. In the return example above, with the same $0.50 dividend, but an unchanged stock price, the realized return would have been 2.5% ($0.50 divided by $20). Or, if the stock price declined to $16.00, the realized return would have been *minus* 17.5% (= [0.50 + (16.00 − 20.00)]/20.00).

It's critical to understand that a realized return is an outcome, the result of having made the decision to invest. You cannot go back and change the realized return. You can only make new decisions in reaction to it.

> **REALIZED RETURN** The return actually earned on an investment during a given time period. The realized return can be known only after the fact.

Expected Return The **expected return** is the rate of return you expect to earn if you make the investment. If you expected to make 15% in our example investment, including an expected $0.50 dividend, you would be expecting the value of the stock next year to be $22.50 (15% = [0.50 + (22.50 − 20.00)]/20.00).

> **EXPECTED RETURN** The return you expect to earn if you make an investment.

REQUIRED RETURN The return that exactly reflects the riskiness of an investment.

Required Return   The **required return** is the rate of return that exactly reflects the riskiness of the expected future cash flows. This is the return the market would require of an investment of identical risk. The market evaluates all of the available information about an investment and prices it in comparison with all other investments. This pricing process establishes an investment's required return, the fair return for an investment.

Net Present Value

NET PRESENT VALUE (NPV) The present value of a set of expected future cash flows minus their cost.

Using the required return to calculate the present value of an asset's expected future cash flows—equation (2.3)—is one way to value the asset. Another way is to find out what it would cost to *buy* such an asset. The difference between what an asset is worth (the present value of its expected future cash flows) and its cost is the asset's **net present value (NPV).**

$$\text{NPV} = \text{Net present value} = \text{Present value of expected future cash flows} - \text{Cost} \qquad (2.5)$$

A positive NPV increases wealth because the asset is worth more than it costs. A negative NPV decreases wealth, because the asset costs more than it is worth.

The net-present-value concept is important because it provides a framework for decision making. NPV appears in connection with virtually every topic in this book, and most financial decisions can be viewed in terms of net present value. NPV measures the value created or lost by a financial decision. However, NPV is measured from a benchmark of the "normal" market return. Therefore, a zero-NPV decision earns the required return and is "fair." A decision that earns less than the required return is undesirable and has a negative NPV. Positive-NPV decisions earn more than the appropriate return. Companies that pursue the goal of maximizing shareholder wealth seek to make positive-NPV decisions.

FAIR PRICE A price that does not favor either the buyer's or seller's side of the transaction.

Another way to state the Principle of Capital Market Efficiency is to say that financial securities are priced fairly. A **fair price** is a price that does not favor either the buyer's or seller's side of the transaction. A fair price makes the NPV from investing equal zero. Sometimes, people ask, "If the NPV is zero, why would anyone purchase a financial security?" The answer is to earn a profit. Remember, a zero NPV implies that the investor will earn the required return for the investment risk, *not* a zero return.

The Principle of Risk-Return Trade-Off implies that investors who take more risk will earn a larger profit, on average. The decision to invest in (purchase) a financial security with NPV = 0 often involves risk. But in exchange for that risk, you get a chance at a higher return.

Confusion between the expected and required returns arises because, if capital markets were *perfect,* an investment's expected return would *always* equal its required return and the investment's NPV would be zero. In fact, financial analysis often starts off assuming a perfect capital market environment, where everyone can expect to earn the required return for the risk they bear. While this is a good starting place for analysis, and the capital markets are efficient, we must add that they are not, if fact, perfect.

Confusion between the expected and realized returns is created by risk. Because of risk, the outcome rarely equals the expected amount. In fact, one way to think about risk is to consider how different the outcome can be from the expected amount. The risk is high when the difference can be great. The risk is low when there cannot be much difference.

Let's review and summarize the relationships among these concepts by using an investment you might make. First, on the basis of other possible market investments of the same risk, you determine a minimum return you would have to earn to be willing to invest. (Otherwise, you would simply invest your money in one of these alternatives.) This is the *required* return. Next, you estimate the return if you were to make the investment. This is the *expected* return. Then you decide whether to make the investment. If the expected return is more than the required return, the investment is worth more than its cost, and the NPV is positive. A positive NPV creates value, whereas a negative NPV loses value. Let's say the NPV is positive, and you make the investment.

Finally, later on, the investment pays off. The payoff is the *realized* return. If the realized return is bad (low, negative, or perhaps even zero—you get nothing back), you are not happy, but that is the fundamental nature of risk! After the return is realized, you can't turn back the clock and decide not to make the investment after all. (Of course, if the realized return is good—equal to or greater than the expected return—you're glad you made the investment.) Therefore, the realized return is disconnected—by risk—from the required and expected returns, despite its vital importance and our desire for it to be large.

Self-Check

1. Distinguish among the concepts of expected, realized, and required returns.

2. Assume you buy a share of General Motors stock for $48.00. During the next year, you receive $2.25 in cash dividends and sell the stock for $55.00 per share at the end of the year. What is your realized return?

3. If the required return is 12% and projects A, B, and C have expected returns of 15%, 9%, and 13%, respectively, in which if any projects should you invest?

4. Why would anyone ever make a *zero*-NPV investment?

5. If the expected return is above the required return, does this mean that the realized return also will be above the required return?

CAPITAL MARKETS

The capital markets are important and are watched very carefully by financial managers for several reasons. One reason is simply that companies have many direct transactions with financial markets, such as issuing their own securities, redeeming or repurchasing their own securities, and investing in other companies' securities. A second reason is that many of the concepts and principles that apply to financial markets are concepts and principles that managers also apply to the management of the company's real assets. Finally, capital markets provide information and signals that help managers make decisions.

This section describes many of these types of securities and the capital markets in which they are traded. The section also describes the roles of the professionals in the capital markets. These include a true smorgasbord of investment bankers, brokers, dealers, banks, mutual funds, and other financial intermediaries.

Money Market Securities

Money market securities are short-term claims with an original life that is generally one year or less. The largest markets for money market securities are for Treasury bills, commercial paper, certificates of deposit, and bankers' acceptances. Money market securities tend to be high-grade securities with little risk of default. Because of the short time involved, the amount of interest earned simply does not allow much margin for default or for expensive credit investigations. Similarly, the securities rarely offer **collateral**, assets that can be claimed if the borrower defaults. The risk and amount of interest income are too small to justify the added expense involved with collateral.

COLLATERAL Assets that can be claimed if the borrower defaults.

Treasury Bills   A Treasury bill (T-bill) is a short-term security issued by the U.S. government. The government regularly issues T-bills with original lives of 13 weeks, 26 weeks, and 52 weeks. Most T-bills are sold in $10,000 denominations. T-bills do not have explicitly stated interest. Instead, they are sold on what is called a discount basis. For example, suppose a 52-week T-bill that will pay $10,000 at the end of its life is sold for $9400. The $600 discount is the implicit interest the investor would earn.

Commercial Paper   Commercial paper is a promissory note sold by very large, creditworthy corporations. The minimum size is typically $100,000. Lives range from 1 day to 270 days. Longer lives require registration with the Securities and Exchange Commission, which is a fairly expensive process, so corporations simply don't issue commercial paper with lives longer than 270 days. Corporations that issue commercial paper typically have a standby line of credit from a major bank. That way, if the company finds itself short of the cash it needs to redeem the commercial paper, it can quickly and easily borrow the necessary funds to fulfill its obligation.

Certificates of Deposit   Certificates of deposit (CDs) are promises to pay, written by a commercial bank or a savings bank, with lives typically ranging between six months and five years. CDs are sold at face value and pay a fixed interest rate. The principal and the last period's interest are paid to the lender at the end of the CD's life. Negotiable CDs have denominations of $100,000 or more and can be traded in the capital markets.

Bankers' Acceptances   Bankers' acceptances are short-term loans made to importers and exporters. They help facilitate international trade. The acceptance occurs when the bank "accepts" a customer's promise to pay. The bankers' acceptance is a guarantee that promises to pay the face amount of the security to whoever presents it for payment. The bank customer uses the bankers' acceptance to finance a transaction by giving the security to a supplier in exchange for goods or services. The supplier can either hold the acceptance until the end of its life and collect from the bank or sell it at a discount. Bankers' acceptances usually have short lives (180 days or less). The security is a two-party obligation, a direct customer liability and a contingent liability for the bank. Therefore, the risk of default is very low.

Bonds and Stocks

Bonds and stocks are long-term securities issued by corporations or governments.

Long-Term Debt   Bonds are long-term debt securities. Recall that debt is a legal obligation for borrowed money. A debt security is a promise to pay interest, and to repay the borrowed money, the *principal,* on prespecified terms. Failure to make the promised payments is default. It can lead to bankruptcy. *Bonds* have lives of ten or more years. *Notes* have lives between one and ten years. Bonds and notes are often referred to as fixed-income securities, because they promise to pay specific (fixed) amounts to their owners.

Stocks   A share of stock is equity in a corporation. Recall that equity represents ownership. *Common stock* is the residual interest in the company. It is residual because it is a claim on the earnings and assets of the company *after* all of the company's other, more senior, obligations have been met. The common shareholders have the dividend rights, voting rights, liquidation rights, and preemptive rights we described in chapter 1. Common stock does not have a fixed life.

   Preferred stock also represents an equity claim. There are some important differences between common stock and preferred stock. Preferred stockholders are promised a specific periodic dividend, whereas common stockholders receive whatever dividends are decided on (perhaps none) by the board of directors of the corporation each quarter. Preferred stockholders have a higher priority with respect to the payment of dividends and the distribution of liquidation proceeds. This means that preferred stockholders must be paid their dividends before common stockholders can be paid any dividends. However, if the company is unable to pay its preferred dividends, it cannot be forced into bankruptcy. Preferred stockholders usually do not have a residual claim on the assets of the company, as do the common shareholders. Nor do preferred stockholders normally have a right to vote on general corporate matters.

Derivative Securities

A **derivative** is a security that derives its value from the value of another security. Options, forward contracts, and futures are among the most common derivatives.

Options   Call options and put options, which we described above with the Options Principle, are very visible examples of derivatives. For example, suppose you own a call option on a share of stock giving you the right to buy the stock at a fixed price of $20 any time during the next three months. The value of your call option depends on the value of the underlying stock. The current stock price is $15. If stock goes up to $35 per share, you can use your call option and your gain will be $15 (the $35 value of the stock minus the $20 you pay to use your call option). By contrast, if the stock stays at $15, you won't use your option to buy the stock for $20 because you can buy it for less in the market.

There are many securities with option-like features in addition to puts and calls. A warrant is a long-term call option issued by a corporation, giving its holder the right to buy the stock at a fixed price directly from the corporation. A convertible security gives holders the right to exchange the security for common shares.

Futures   A **futures contract** is a standardized **forward contract** that is traded in a futures market. Standardized means that only contracts with certain features are created, such as in certain amounts and for certain time periods. A forward contract is an agreement to buy or sell something for a particular price at a future point in time. Note that a forward contract is not an option—the owner has the obligation to make the transaction. Futures are traded on commodities such as corn, oil, and gold. Futures are also traded on financial assets such as bonds, stocks, and foreign currencies. It may seem odd at first to contract to buy something in the future. Why not simply buy it now or wait and buy it when you need it?

The answer lies in the need to plan. Suppose you don't have a way to store what you are going to need. Suppose what you are going to need hasn't been produced yet, as in the case of next fall's crop of corn. Market prices change according to supply and demand, so future prices may be different from what we expect. By making the contract now, we can lock in our future needs at an agreed-upon price.

For example, a food packer such as Kraft Foods can plan for its needs for corn meal, and farmers can sell their corn before it is harvested. This enables both parties to benefit from the Principle of Comparative Advantage. By arranging the sale-purchase ahead of time, each side of the transaction can concentrate its efforts on what it does best. It need not worry constantly about what it will pay or earn for corn.

Forward contracts are also traded in private transactions. Though useful and common, such nonstandard contracts do not have the liquidity that the futures market provides.

A **spot market** is a market in which assets are bought and sold for immediate delivery. Some of the same assets traded in spot markets are also traded in the futures markets.

Primary and Secondary Markets

A **primary market** transaction involves the sale by a company of newly created securities to get additional financing. The issuing company receives the proceeds from the sale of the securities. A **secondary market** is a market where previously issued securities are bought and sold. The vast majority of trading in the capital markets is secondary. This is because a primary transaction takes place only once, when issued. However, those securities can be traded later many times.

Brokers, Dealers, and Investment Bankers

Brokers, dealers, and investment bankers facilitate securities trading. Brokers and dealers assist investors in trading securities in the secondary market. A broker *helps* investors sell or buy securities, charging a sales commission but without taking ownership of the shares. In

DERIVATIVE A security that derives its value from the value of another security.

FUTURES CONTRACT A standardized *forward contract* that is traded in a futures market.

FORWARD CONTRACT A contract to exchange an asset for cash at a specific future date.

SPOT MARKET A market in which assets are bought and sold for immediate delivery.

PRIMARY MARKET A market in which companies sell newly created securities to raise capital.

SECONDARY MARKET A market in which previously created securities are traded.

contrast, a dealer actually takes ownership. She buys securities for, and sells them from, her own account. Suppose you buy 100 shares of Sears stock through a broker. The broker arranges the purchase from someone else, typically through a stock exchange. If instead you buy the shares from a dealer, you are buying the shares from that person.

Although some companies get additional financing by selling securities directly to investors, many others raise capital with the assistance of investment bankers. Investment bankers specialize in marketing new securities in the primary market. The people who buy the securities can be individuals or financial institutions, such as pension funds, mutual funds, and insurance companies. In some cases, the investment banker acts as a broker, without taking ownership of the securities. In other cases, the investment banker acts as an **underwriter,** who guarantees a minimum price, thereby acting, in effect, as a dealer. The first time a company issues shares to the public, it is called an **initial public offering (IPO).** If the company later issues additional shares to the public, such an offering is called a **seasoned offering.**

UNDERWRITER A party that guarantees the proceeds to the company from a security sale, thereby taking effective (but usually very brief) ownership of the securities.

INITIAL PUBLIC OFFERING (IPO) The first time a company issues shares to sell to the public.

SEASONED OFFERING An offering of additional new shares to the public, subsequent to the company's *IPO*.

Financial Intermediaries

Financial intermediaries are *institutions* that assist in the financing of companies. Financial intermediaries include commercial banks and pension funds. They invest in securities but are themselves financed by other financial claims.

Commercial banks invest primarily in business and personal loans and in marketable securities. They finance their assets by selling various kinds of deposits, such as checking accounts, money market accounts, savings accounts, and certificates of deposit. Pension funds invest primarily in stocks, bonds, and mortgages. They finance their portfolios with the cash contributions made on behalf of pension beneficiaries and keep the funds invested until it is time to pay them out as benefits. With financial intermediaries, savers are investing in securities but are doing so indirectly. Their savings are used to buy securities. Table 2.1 lists examples of the assets and obligations of various financial intermediaries.

Self-Check

1. What are the primary kinds of money market securities?

2. How is preferred stock different from common stock?

3. What is a derivative? Define option contract and forward contract. What is a spot market, a forward market, and a futures market?

4. Distinguish between primary and secondary markets.

5. What are investment bankers, brokers, dealers, and financial intermediaries?

TABLE 2.1

Examples of Financial Intermediaries

TYPE OF FINANCIAL INTERMEDIARY	PRIMARY KINDS OF INVESTMENTS	TYPES OF OBLIGATIONS
Commercial banks	Short-term loans and securities	Deposit liabilities
Pension funds	Stocks, bonds, mortgages	Obligations to pension beneficiaries
Savings and loans	Mortgages	Deposit liabilities
Mutual savings banks	Mortgages	Share deposits
Credit unions	Personal loans, car loans	Share deposits
Mutual funds	Stocks, bonds, or money market securities	Mutual fund shares
Insurance companies	Bonds, mortgages, stocks	Policy obligations

THE TERM STRUCTURE OF INTEREST RATES

One way to describe the great variety of debt securities is to graph the relationship between interest rate and security life for a particular class of debt securities, such as U.S. Treasury securities. This shows how the interest rate depends on the amount of time the money will be invested. This relationship is called a *yield curve*. One form of yield curve has a special name. The yield curve for zero-coupon U.S. Treasury securities is called the *term structure of interest rates*. (Zero-coupon means there are no payments until the end of the security's life, so that such securities always trade on a discount basis.) Informally, the phrase **term structure** is sometimes used to refer to the relationship between the life of a debt security and interest rates generally. We will use this phrase as well.

Available lives vary widely. At one extreme, investors borrow for less than a day. For example, banks borrow overnight in the federal funds market. At the other extreme, governments and companies regularly issue bonds with lives of up to 30 years, and sometimes even as long as 100 years. A virtual continuum of lives exists between these extremes.

More often than not, interest rates increase with remaining life. Figure 2.1 shows an example of the common upward-sloping term structure of interest rates. There are much less frequent periods when the reverse is true; the term structure is downward sloping. Figure 2.2 illustrates this unusual structure. Note that in both cases the curve flattens out as remaining life increases, because differences in interest rates typically become less and less significant with longer life.

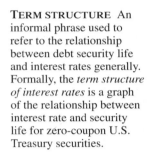

TERM STRUCTURE An informal phrase used to refer to the relationship between debt security life and interest rates generally. Formally, the *term structure of interest rates* is a graph of the relationship between interest rate and security life for zero-coupon U.S. Treasury securities.

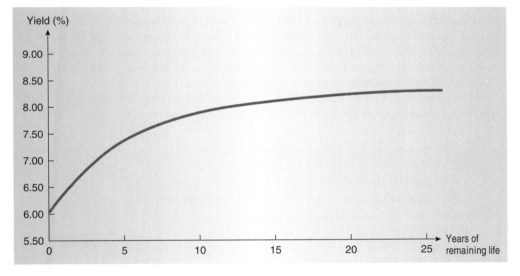

FIGURE 2.1
An example of the common upward-sloping term structure of interest rates.

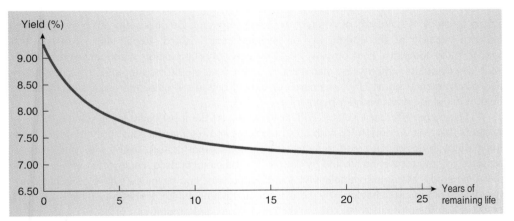

FIGURE 2.2
An example of the uncommon downward-sloping term structure of interest rates.

Interest rates are affected by the risk of default and the taxability of the returns. Investors require higher returns to offset tax liabilities and the possibility of default. For this reason, the securities used to compile a yield curve must all have the same default risk and tax status, such as the zero-coupon U.S. Treasury securities used to create the term structure of interest rates. In addition to tax considerations, several other factors affect the term structure of interest rates.

At the most basic level, investors sometimes have a particular desired security life because they plan to use the money for specific needs, such as retirement or a down payment on a house. So investors may seek to invest in securities with lives that match their needs. Beyond specific needs, shorter lives provide more liquidity and greater financial flexibility, a form of option that the Options Principle tells us is valuable.

As we explain in chapter 6, if all else is equal, longer-lived securities are riskier. Much of this risk depends on inflation expectations, which are an important determinant of interest rates. Therefore, if all else is equal, the Principle of Risk-Return Trade-Off implies that investors will require a higher interest rate (return) to bear the extra risk. This is the basis for the idea that the term structure *should* usually be upward sloping.

Finally, investors also take into consideration what they expect interest rates to be in the future. That is, if investors believe that long-term interest rates are going to be higher next year, they will want to wait to make a long-term investment. But investors don't hold the cash in a cookie jar while they wait. They put the money in short-term investments, such as money market securities. This kind of "waiting" increases the supply of short-term funds and at the same time decreases the supply of long-term funds. The shift in these supplies lowers the short-term rate and increases the long-term rate, which increases the upward slope of the curve. The reverse happens when investors believe interest rates are going to decrease. This can bring about a downward-sloping term structure. Unusual expectations can even lead to oddly shaped curves that are not consistently upward or downward sloping.

The Principle of Capital Market Efficiency tells us that the term structure reflects all the available information about the collective impact of all these factors at any point in time.

Self-Check

1. What is a yield curve?

2. What class of securities are used to compile the term structure of interest rates?

3. Why is the term structure usually upward sloping?

BUSINESS ETHICS

Ethics consists of standards of conduct or moral judgment. Business ethics is a topic of great concern because of the complexity of business relationships. Recall the set-of-contracts model of the company. The company is at the center of relationships with many stakeholders, such as customers, employees, managers, shareholders, creditors, suppliers, the community, and governmental units. High standards of ethical conduct require that each stakeholder be dealt with in an honest and fair manner.

There are different levels of ethical behavior. At the most basic level, ethical behavior requires that you comply fully with all of the rules and regulations that apply to your behavior. Failure to do so can result in substantial penalties that include time in jail and fines assessed by regulatory agencies and by courts. The financial consequences often go far beyond these penalties. Many individuals have lost their careers, and businesses have gone bankrupt, because of unethical behavior. The gains from unethical behavior sometimes have been small compared to the ultimate losses due to the loss of trust and reputation.

But behaving ethically means much more than simply following rules and regulations—it requires making personal judgments about right and wrong. Some people believe business is inherently corrupt, immoral, and unethical. However, many others assert that high ethical standards are essential to the profitability and survival of the company and that ethics in business may be higher than in other segments of society. Why do so many feel that ethical behavior is essential to profitability? There are some clear answers.

1. Ethical behavior avoids fines and legal expenses.
2. It builds customer loyalty and sales.
3. It helps attract and keep high-quality employees and managers.
4. It builds public confidence and adds to the economic development of the communities in which the company operates.
5. A good reputation enhances relations with the company's investors.

Ethical behavior can be a necessity for companies to operate profitably and to survive.

Many companies have formal codes of ethics that are a prominent part of their corporate cultures. Managers are often very careful to explore the ethical dimensions of their decisions. Furthermore, if you join a profession—such as accounting, financial analysis, personnel management, or real estate brokerage—there will be professional societies with codes of ethics you must know and follow. In addition, professionals in many fields are regulated by government agencies and are thus subject to special licensing procedures and rules of conduct.

CODE OF ETHICS FOR CHARTERED FINANCIAL ANALYSTS

The Association for Investment Management and Research requires that Chartered Financial Analysts (CFAs) adhere to a detailed set of Standards of Professional Conduct that cover the relationships of CFAs with the public, clients, customers, employers, employees, and fellow analysts. The topics covered in the Standards of Professional Conduct are:

I. Fundamental responsibilities
II. Relationships with and responsibilities to the profession
   A. Use of professional designation
   B. Professional misconduct
   C. Prohibition against plagiarism
III. Relationships with and responsibilities to the employer
   A. Obligation to inform employer of code and standards
   B. Duty to employer
   C. Disclosure of conflicts to employer
   D. Disclosure of additional compensation arrangements
   E. Responsibilities of supervisors

(continued on following page)

(Code of Ethics for Chartered Financial Analysts *continued from previous page*)

IV. Relationships with and responsibilities to clients and prospects
   A. Investment process
      1. Reasonable basis and representations
      2. Research reports
      3. Independence and objectivity
   B. Interactions with clients and prospects
      1. Fiduciary duties
      2. Portfolio investment recommendations and actions
      3. Fair dealing
      4. Priority of transactions
      5. Preservation of confidentiality
      6. Prohibition against misrepresentation
      7. Disclosure of conflicts to clients and prospects
      8. Disclosure of referral fees
V. Relationships with and responsibilities to the investing public
   A. Prohibition against use of material nonpublic information
   B. Performance presentation

Source: Standards of Practice Handbook, 7th edition, Charlottesville, Va.: Association for Investment Management and Research, 1996.

Self-Check

1. Why should a financial manager be concerned with business ethics?

2. Why is ethical behavior essential to profitability?

SUMMARY

Financial markets, financial principles, and business ethics are all a foundation for the financial decisions that managers routinely make.

- The principles of finance describe typical behavior in financial transactions and provide guidance for decision making.
  - Financial self-interest guides rational decision making.
  - Many financial decisions must consider the time value of money.
  - All transactions are two-sided, with each party considering his or her self-interest.
  - Incremental costs and benefits are the basis for choices among alternatives.
  - Investors are risk-averse.
  - The marketplace rewards risk because rational investors require a reward to bear it.
  - Diversification can reduce risk.
  - Options are valuable because they contain rights but not obligations.
  - Market prices in an efficient market reflect all available information.
  - Actions can be valuable signals.
  - Look to what others are doing for guidance.
  - Extraordinary returns are possible with new ideas.
- Expected return is what you expect to earn, required return is the return the marketplace assigns to securities of similar characteristics, and actual or realized return is what you actually get.
- Money markets are short-term markets where Treasury bills, commercial paper, certificates of deposit, and bankers' acceptances are traded.

- Capital markets are long-term markets where stocks and bonds are traded.
- Derivative markets trade derivative securities such as options and futures.
- Primary markets are the markets where corporations raise capital, while secondary markets are where previously issued and outstanding securities are traded.
- Investment bankers, brokers, and dealers primarily facilitate the trading of securities. Financial intermediaries buy and hold the securities of others while issuing claims against themselves.
- The term structure of interest rates represents the relationship between interest rates and security life. The main factors that affect the term structure include expected future changes in interest rates, taxes, and default risk.
- Business ethics, standards of conduct, and moral judgment are central to the operations and profitability of many businesses.

EQUATION SUMMARY

(2.1) $$FV = PV + r(PV) = PV(1 + r)$$

(2.2) $$FV = PV(1 + r)^n$$

(2.3) $$PV = \frac{FV}{(1 + r)^n}$$

(2.4) $$Return = \text{Rate of Return} = \frac{\text{Cash flow} + (\text{Ending value} - \text{Beginning value})}{\text{Beginning value}}$$

(2.5) $$NPV = \text{Net present value} = \text{Present value of expected future cash flows} - \text{Cost}$$

CHAPTER REVIEW ACTIVITIES

2 a. $1000 (1+.1)^1 = 1000 (1.1) = \$100.00$

b. $1000 (1.1)^2 = \$1210.00$

SELF-TEST PROBLEMS

1. (Expected, required, and realized returns) An investment of $20 in Stock A is expected to pay no dividend and have a value of $24 in 1 year. An investment of $70 in Stock B is expected to generate a $2.50 dividend next year and the price of the stock is expected to be $78.

a. What are the expected returns for Stock A and Stock B?

b. If the required return is 10%, which stocks should be profitable investments?

c. One year from now, Stock A has paid no dividend and is selling for $19. Stock B has paid a $3.00 dividend and is selling for $81. What are the realized returns for the two stocks?

2. (Present and future values)

a. What is the future value of $1000 invested today if it earns 10% interest for 1 year? for 2 years?

b. What is the present value of $1000 discounted at 10% if it is received in 1 year? in 2 years?

2)b. $PV = \dfrac{1000}{(1.1)^1}$

$= 909.09$

$PV = \dfrac{1000}{(1.1)^2}$

$= 826.45$

SOLUTIONS TO SELF-TEST PROBLEMS

1. Using equation (2.4):

a. Expected return for A = [0 + (24 − 20)]/20 = 4/20 = 20%
   Expected return for B = [2.50 + (78 − 70)]/70 = 10.5/70 = 15%

b. Invest in both stocks, since their expected returns are greater than the required return.

c. Realized return for A = [0 + (19 − 20)]/20 = −1/20 = −5%
   Realized return for B = [3.00 + (81 − 70)]/70 = 14.00/70 = 20%

2. Using equation (2.2):

a. FV = 1000(1 + 0.10)^1 = 1000(1.10) = 1100
   FV = 1000(1 + 0.10)^2 = 1000(1.21) = 1210

b. Using equation (2.3):
   PV = 1000[1/(1 + 0.10)^1] = 1000[1/1.10] = 909.09
   PV = 1000[1/(1 + 0.10)^2] = 1000[1/1.21] = 826.45

QUESTIONS

1. Define these terms: *opportunity cost, principal-agent relationship, moral hazard, zero-sum game, sunk cost, hubris, adverse selection.*
2. Define the terms *option, call option,* and *put option.*
3. What is a portfolio? Why is diversification beneficial?
4. Distinguish between each of the following:
   a. Spot market and futures market
   b. Call option and put option
   c. Option contract and futures contract
   d. Broker and dealer
   e. Investment banker and financial intermediary
   f. Primary market and secondary market
   g. Initial public offering and seasoned equity offering
   h. Forward contract and futures contract
   i. Stock and bond
5. Define the term *limited liability.* How does limited liability create an option for a borrower?
6. Describe in your own words what is meant by the term *efficient capital market.* What is arbitrage?
7. Explain in your own words the idea of compound interest.
8. What are the factors that cause the term structure to be upward sloping or downward sloping?
9. What is ethics? If you follow all applicable rules and regulations, are you an ethical person?
10. Why do many business managers feel that ethical behavior is essential to the profitability and survival of their company?

CHALLENGING QUESTIONS

11. Cite an example that involves information signaling.
12. Describe a situation in which the problem of adverse selection can arise.
13. Explain why the Principle of Two-Sided Transactions is important to financial decision making.
14. *USA Today* once reported that executives of Teradyne had told Wall Street analysts that "business was jumping," but the next day the company's chairman sold 24,800 shares of his stock in the company for $32 each, or $793,600. The chairman's secretary said the shares belonged to his daughter. Interpret these events in light of the Signaling Principle.
15. Explain how the Behavioral Principle is derived directly from the Signaling Principle.
16. Cite two appropriate applications and one inappropriate application of the Behavioral Principle.
17. Explain how the Signaling Principle is derived directly from the Principle of Self-Interested Behavior.
18. Describe a situation where you might want to guard against the free-rider problem.
19. How do the Principles of Self-Interested Behavior and Two-Sided Transactions relate to the Principle of Capital Market Efficiency?
20. Imagine yourself as a manager in a nonfinancial business, a business that provides real goods and services (that is, you are not in a financial business such as a bank or brokerage company). How are financial markets relevant to the effective performance of your job?

PROBLEM SET A

A1. (Present and future values)
   a. What is the future value of $1000 invested today if it earns 25% interest for 1 year? for 2 years?
   b. What is the present value of $1000 discounted at 25% if it is received in 1 year? in 2 years?

A2. (Future value) An investor deposits $1000 into a bank account that pays interest at the rate of 6% per year (payable at the end of each year). She leaves the money and all accrued interest in the account for 5 years.
   a. How much money does she have after 1 year?
   b. How much money does she have at the end of year 5?

PROBLEM SET B

B1. (Expected, required, and realized returns) If you buy shares of Rivas Resorts, it will cost you $45 per share and you expect to receive $1.00 in dividends and sell the stock for $56 in one year. If you invest in Carreras Holdings, the investment would be $125 per share with an expected dividend of $5.00 and stock price of $132 in one year.

a. What are the expected returns for Rivas and Carreras?

b. If the required return is 15%, which stocks should be profitable investments?

c. One year from now, Rivas has paid a $1.00 dividend and is selling for $52. Carreras has paid a $5.00 dividend and is selling for $155. What were the realized returns for the two stocks?

B2. (Future value) An investor deposits $1000 into a bank account that pays interest at the rate of 10% per year (payable at the end of each year). She leaves the money and all accrued interest in the account for 5 years.

a. How much money does she have after 1 year?

b. How much money does she have at the end of year 5?

c. Compared to the bank account in problem A2 above (that paid only 6% interest), how much additional money does she have after 1 year and after year 5?

B3. (Present value) What is the present value of $10,000 to be received 7 years from today when the annual discount rate is 12%?

B4. (Future value) What is the future value in 7 years of $10,000 invested today when the annual interest rate is 12%?

B5. (Present and future values) Assume that you are starting with an investment of $10,000.

a. What is the future value of the investment after 1 year if it earns 10% per year? What is the present value of this future value discounted at 10%?

b. What is the future value of the investment after 1 year if it earns 20% per year? What is the present value of this future value discounted at 10%?

c. What is the future value of the investment after 1 year if it earns 10% per year? What is the present value of this future value discounted at 20%?

B6. (Options) Assume you pay $1000 for a call option that gives you the right to buy a piece of property for $20,000 anytime within the next year.

a. Assume the property appreciates and you can sell it for $30,000 at the end of the year. If you use the option, what is your gain (the difference between the property value and the price using the option)? Will you use your call option? What is your profit in dollars after you subtract the cost of the option? What is your realized return?

b. Assume the property can be sold for $15,000 at the end of the year. If you use the option, what is your gain? Will you use your call option?

B7. (Opportunity cost) You own a small duplex near campus. You bought it several years ago for $120,000. You can sell the duplex today for $160,000, or you can add on to the duplex and sell it for $220,000. The addition would cost $80,000. Should you sell the duplex "as is," or should you invest in the addition and then sell? At what selling price would you change your mind?

PROBLEM SET C

C1. (Options) Assume you buy a call option for $2.00 that gives you the right to buy a share of stock for $20 at any time during the next year. You can buy a put option for $1.00 to sell the same stock for $20 at any time during the next year. The stock does not pay a dividend.

a. At the end of the year, the stock is selling for $24. What is the realized return on the stock, the call option, and the put option?

b. At the end of the year, the stock is selling for $17. What is the realized return on the stock, the call option, and the put option?

BIBLIOGRAPHY

Ackert, Lucy F., and Brian F. Smith. "Stock Price Volatility, Ordinary Dividends, and Other Cash Flows to Shareholders," *Journal of Finance,* 1993, 48(4):1147–1160.

Akerlof, George A. "The Market for 'Lemons': Quality Uncertainty and the Market Mechanism," *Quarterly Journal of Economics,* 1970, 84(August):488–500.

Ambrose, Brent W., and Drew B. Winters. "Does an Industry Effect Exist for Leveraged Buyouts?" *Financial Management,* 1992, 21(1):89–101.

Asquith, Paul, and David W. Mullins, Jr. "Signalling with Dividends, Stock Repurchases, and Equity Issues," *Financial Management,* 1986, 15(3):27–44.

Baker, George P., Michael C. Jensen, and Kevin J. Murphy. "Compensation and Incentives: Practice vs. Theory," *Journal of Finance,* 1988, 43(3):593–616.

Balvers, Ronald J., Thomas F. Cosimano, and Bill McDonald. "Predicting Stock Returns in an Efficient Market," *Journal of Finance,* 1990, 45(4):1109–1128.

Berry, Thomas D., and Keith M. Howe. "Public Information Arrival," *Journal of Finance,* 1994, 49(4):1331–1346.

Black, Fischer, and Myron Scholes. "The Pricing of Options and Corporate Liabilities," *Journal of Political Economy,* 1973, 81(May/June):637–654.

Brous, Peter Alan. "Common Stock Offerings and Earnings Expectations: A Test of the Release of Unfavorable Information," *Journal of Finance,* 1992, 47(4):1517–1536.

Christie, William G., Jeffrey H. Harris, and Paul H. Schultz. "Why Did NASDAQ Market Makers Stop Avoiding Odd-Eighth Quotes?" *Journal of Finance,* 1994, 49(5):1841–1860.

Christie, William G., and Paul H. Schultz. "Why Do NASDAQ Market Makers Avoid Odd-Eighth Quotes?" *Journal of Finance,* 1994, 49(5):1813–1840.

Conrad, Jennifer, and Gautam Kaul. "Long-Term Market Overreaction or Biases in Computed Returns?" *Journal of Finance,* 1993, 48(1):39–64.

Crutchley, Claire E., and Robert S. Hansen. "A Test of the Agency Theory of Managerial Ownership, Corporate Leverage, and Corporate Dividends," *Financial Management,* 1989, 18(4):36–46.

Ederington, Louis H., and Jae Ha Lee. "How Markets Process Information: News Releases and Volatility," *Journal of Finance,* 1993, 48(4):1161–1192.

Fama, Eugene. "Efficient Capital Markets: A Review of Theory and Empirical Work," *Journal of Finance,* 1970, 25(2):383–417.

Fama, Eugene F. "Efficient Capital Markets: II," *Journal of Finance,* 1991, 46(5):1575–1618.

Fisher, Irving. *The Theory of Interest.* New York: Augustus M. Kelley, 1965 (reprinted from the original edition published in 1930).

Froot, Kenneth A., David S. Scharfstein, and Jeremy C. Stein. "Herd on the Street: Informational Inefficiencies in a Market with Short-Term Speculation," *Journal of Finance,* 1992, 47(4): 1461–1484.

Hasbrouck, Joel, and George Sofianos. "The Trades of Market Makers: An Empirical Analysis of NYSE Specialists," *Journal of Finance,* 1993, 48(5):1565–1593.

Hirshleifer, David, Avanidhar Subrahmanyam, and Sheridan Titman. "Security Analysis and Trading Patterns When Some Investors Receive Information Before Others," *Journal of Finance,* 1994, 49(5):1665–1698.

Jegadeesh, Narasimhan, and Sheridan Titman. "Returns to Buying Winners and Selling Losers: Implications for Stock Market Efficiency," *Journal of Finance,* 1993, 48(1):65–92.

Jensen, Michael C., and William H. Meckling. "Theory of the Firm: Managerial Behavior, Agency Costs, and Ownership Structure," *Journal of Financial Economics,* 1976, 3(4):305–360.

Jordan, James V. "Tax Effects in Term Structure Estimation," *Journal of Finance,* 1984, 39(2):393–406.

Jose, Manuel L., Len M. Nichols, and Jerry L. Stevens. "Contributions of Diversification, Promotion, and R&D to the Value of Multiproduct Firms: A Tobin's q Approach," *Financial Management,* 1986, 15(4):33–42.

Krueger, Thomas M., and William F. Kennedy. "An Examination of the Super Bowl Stock Market Predictor," *Journal of Finance,* 1990, 45(2):691–698.

Lee, Winson B., and Elizabeth S. Cooperman. "Conglomerates in the 1980s: A Performance Appraisal," *Financial Management,* 1989, 18(1):45–54.

Leland, Hayne E., and David H. Pyle. "Informational Asymmetries, Financial Structure, and Financial Intermediation," *Journal of Finance,* 1977, 32(2):371–387.

Liu, Pu, Stanley D. Smith, and Azmat A. Syed. "Stock Price Reactions to the *Wall Street Journal*'s Securities Recommendations," *Journal of Financial and Quantitative Analysis,* 1990, 25(3):399–410.

Longstaff, Francis A., and Eduardo S. Schwartz. "Interest Rate Volatility and the Term Structure: A Two-Factor General Equilibrium Model," *Journal of Finance,* 1992, 47(4):1259–1282.

Markowitz, Harry M. "Portfolio Selection," *Journal of Finance,* 1952, 7(1):77–91.

McCulloch, J. Huston. "A Reexamination of Traditional Hypotheses About the Term Structure: A Comment," *Journal of Finance,* 1993, 48(2):779–789.

McInish, Thomas H., and Robert A. Wood. "An Analysis of Intraday Patterns in Bid/Ask for NYSE Stocks," *Journal of Finance,* 1992, 47(2):753–764.

Merton, Robert C. "A Functional Perspective of Financial Intermediation," *Financial Management,* 1995, 24(2):23–41.

Michel, Allen, and Israel Shaked. "Does Business Diversification Affect Performance?" *Financial Management,* 1984, 13(4): 18–25.

Miller, Merton H., and Franco Modigliani. "Dividend Policy, Growth, and the Valuation of Shares," *Journal of Business,* 1961, 34(October):411–433.

Mitchell, Mark L., and J. Harold Mulherin. "The Impact of Public Information on the Stock Market," *Journal of Finance,* 1994, 49(3):923–950.

Modigliani, Franco, and Merton H. Miller. "The Cost of Capital, Corporation Finance, and the Theory of Investment," *American Economic Review,* 1958, 48(June):261–297.

Myers, Stewart C., and Nicholas S. Majluf. "Corporate Financing and Investment Decisions When Firms Have Information That Investors Do Not Have," *Journal of Financial Economics,* 1984, 13(2):187–221.

Netter, Jeffry, and Annette Poulsen. "State Corporation Laws and Shareholders: The Recent Experience," *Financial Management*, 1989, 18(3):29–40.

Pearson, Neil D., and Tong-Sheng Sun. "Exploiting the Conditional Density in Estimating the Term Structure: An Application of the Cox, Ingersoll, and Ross Model," *Journal of Finance*, 1994, 49(4):1279–1304.

Ravid, S. Abraham, and Oded H. Sarig. "Financial Signalling by Committing to Cash Outflows," *Journal of Financial and Quantitative Analysis*, 1991, 26(2):165–180.

Roll, Richard. "What Every CFO Should Know About Scientific Progress in Financial Economics: What Is Known and What Remains to Be Resolved," *Financial Management*, 1994, 23(2):69–75.

Sharpe, William F. "Capital Asset Prices: A Theory of Market Equilibrium Under Conditions of Risk," *Journal of Finance*, 1964, 19(3):425–442.

Shefrin, Hersh, and Meir Statman. "Behavioral Aspects of the Design of Financial Products," *Financial Management*, 1993, 22(2):123–134.

Singh, Ajai K., Mir A. Zaman, and Chandrasekhar Krishnamurti. "Liquidity Changes Associated with Open Market Repurchases," *Financial Management*, 1994, 23(1):47–55.

Slovin, Myron B., and Marie E. Sushka. "Ownership Concentration, Corporate Control Activity, and Firm Value: Evidence from the Death of Inside Blockholders," *Journal of Finance*, 1993, 48(4):1293–1321.

Spence, Michael. "Competitive and Optimal Responses to Signals: Analysis of Efficiency and Distribution," *Journal of Economic Theory*, 1974, 7:296–332.

Tobin, J. "Liquidity Preference as Behavior Towards Risk," *Review of Economic Studies*, 1958, 26(February):65–86.

Winton, Andrew. "Limitation of Liability and the Ownership Structure of the Firm," *Journal of Finance*, 1993, 48(2):487–512.

ACCOUNTING, CASH FLOWS, AND TAXES

OBJECTIVES

1. Describe the structure of a company's balance sheet, income statement, and statement of cash flows.

2. Construct and complete financial statements in standard format.

3. Discuss the inherent limitations of historical accounting information.

4. Explain the differences between net income and cash flow.

5. Calculate and explain the differences between book values and market values.

6. Explain and apply the key features of corporate and personal income taxation that will have significant implications for financial management.

7. Calculate a company's economic income and explain how it differs from its accounting income.

Chapters 1 and 2 introduced you to the business world as a complex web of relationships among the company's various stakeholders: its stockholders, bondholders, creditors, employees, customers, and suppliers, among others. Beyond complexity, the sheer size of many corporations makes it difficult to comprehend all their activities. The accounting system is a framework for keeping track of it all. It has evolved to serve two basic purposes: reporting the financial activities of the company to outside stakeholders and providing information to assist decision makers within the company.

The accounting material covered in this chapter is a review of material from basic accounting classes. We outline the basics of the accounting statements, without going into the details of how they are prepared. We describe important differences between accounting and economic information. Our focus in financial management is on how to use and interpret this information, rather than on operating an accounting system and creating financial reports.

Financial managers need to understand accounting statements for several very good reasons. Accounting statements are used to communicate with stakeholders outside the company, such as stockholders, bondholders, and other creditors. They are used within the company to help plan and organize its activities. Accounting statements are used to monitor employees in connection with such things as performance or even theft. Furthermore, they are used by the Internal Revenue Service to determine the company's taxes.

Finally, we review the federal income tax system. In finance, we make decisions on an *after-tax* basis, so understanding tax effects is very important. Because taxes affect value, they affect many of a company's financial management decisions. Even at the most basic level, taxes are a significant cost of doing business. Throughout the book we will point out

situations where taxes might make a difference. We aren't going to make you a tax expert. Rather, we feel it is important that you realize how tax factors can affect decisions. Thus, when you encounter them in practice, you will know when to seek expert tax advice.

ACCOUNTING, TAXES, AND THE PRINCIPLES OF FINANCE

◆ *Two-Sided Transactions:* Recognize that the accounting system always records two sides to every transaction, and there are real people or real companies on each side of the transaction.

◆ *Incremental Benefits:* Use financial statements and the accounting system to help identify and estimate the incremental expected cash flows that will be used to make a financial decision.

◆ *Risk-Return Trade-Off:* Keep in mind that managerial decisions are based on future risks and returns. Accounting tends to measure historical or past returns. Consequently, many decisions require information and perspectives that are unavailable from the accounting system.

◆ *Behavioral Principle:* Use the wealth of financial information available on thousands of companies to apply this principle.

◆ *Signaling:* Recognize that financial information provides many observable signals about customers, competitors, and suppliers.

THE LAYOUT OF ACCOUNTING STATEMENTS

GENERALLY ACCEPTED ACCOUNTING PRINCIPLES (GAAP) A technical accounting term that encompasses the conventions, rules, and procedures necessary to define accepted accounting practice at a particular time.

Accounting statements in the United States are prepared according to what are called **generally accepted accounting principles (GAAP).** GAAP include the conventions, rules, and procedures that define how companies should maintain records and prepare financial reports.[1] In the United States, these rules and procedures are based on guidelines issued by the *Financial Accounting Standards Board (FASB).* The FASB is the U.S. accounting profession's rule-making organization.

Internationally, the set of generally accepted accounting principles varies from one country to another. In some cases U.S. GAAP are different from another country's GAAP. British GAAP, for example, differ substantially from U.S. GAAP. As a result, a company's financial statements can look quite different depending on which country's GAAP are used to prepare them. In any case, you cannot compare the information contained in the financial statements of two companies when the statements were prepared under different systems of GAAP until you first adjust for the differences.

Even under U.S. GAAP, it is possible for accounting numbers to distort economic reality. One of the tasks facing a good manager is to use accounting information effectively. Managers must know what accounting information can—and cannot—be used for. This is a balancing act. They have to combine their knowledge of accounting with other sources of information to make sound business decisions.

The accounting material covered in this chapter is a review of material covered in basic accounting courses. Our focus in financial management is on how to use and interpret this information, rather than on operating an accounting system and generating reports.

Financial Statements

ANNUAL REPORT A report issued annually by a company. It includes, at a minimum, an income statement, a balance sheet, a statement of cash flows, and accompanying notes.

A company's published **annual report** includes, at a minimum, an income statement, a balance sheet, a statement of cash flows, and accompanying notes.[2] We review these statements below, using a basic set of statements for OutBack SportWear, Inc. as an example.[3] They are the "raw material" for a variety of techniques and procedures that managers and analysts use in financial statement analysis. But first, let's introduce some basic terms we will need.

MATURITY The end of an asset's life.

The **maturity** of an asset is the end of its life. When a financial asset is created (issued), the length of its life is called its **original maturity.** The amount of time remaining until maturity is called the **remaining maturity.**

ORIGINAL MATURITY The length of an asset's life when it is created.

The **liquidity** of an asset expresses how quickly and easily it can be sold without loss of value. Cash is the most liquid asset.

REMAINING MATURITY The length of time remaining until an asset's maturity.

Market value is the price for which something could be bought or sold in a "reasonable" length of time. A reasonable length of time is defined in terms of the asset's liquidity. It

LIQUIDITY The extent to which something can be sold for cash quickly and easily without loss of value.

MARKET VALUE The price for which something could be bought or sold in a reasonable length of time, where "reasonable length of time" is defined in terms of the item's liquidity.

---

[1]According to the American Institute of Certified Public Accountants (AICPA), the "phrase 'generally accepted accounting principles' is a technical accounting term that encompasses the conventions, rules, and procedures necessary to define accepted accounting practice at a particular time. It includes not only broad guidelines of general application, but also detailed practices and procedures. . . . Those conventions, rules, and procedures provide a standard by which to measure financial presentations."

[2]A company's annual report includes income statements and statements of cash flows for the latest three years and balance sheets for the latest two years. It also includes a separate statement of stockholders' equity. This shows how the company's total stockholders' equity changed from one balance sheet to the next during the past three years.

[3]Publicly traded companies also publish quarterly reports and make public announcements of important information. They also file, with the Securities and Exchange Commission (SEC), disclosures that investors use. Such disclosures include 10-K annual reports (the information in the annual report plus more disclosures), 10-Q reports (the information in quarterly reports plus more), 8-K statements (describing significant events of interest to investors as the events occur), and registration statements (large documents containing financial and business information that must be filed before new securities can be publicly issued).

might be several months or even a year for buildings and land, but only a few days for publicly traded stocks and bonds. **Book value (net book value)** is a net amount shown in the accounting statements.

Balance Sheet

The **balance sheet** reports the financial position of a company at a particular point in time. The balance sheet shows the **assets** of the company, which are the productive resources used in its operations. The balance sheet also shows the **liabilities and stockholders' equity** of the company, which are the total claims of creditors and owners against the assets.

A typical balance sheet, that of OutBack SportWear, is shown in table 3.1. Note that the *balance sheet identity* is satisfied:

$$\text{Assets} = \text{Liabilities} + \text{Stockholders' equity} \tag{3.1}$$

Assets and liabilities are both broken down into short-term and long-term parts. In accounting statements, **current (short-term)** refers to a period of up to one year. **Long-term** refers to more than one year. Current assets are expected to become cash within one year. Current liabilities mature or are expected to be paid off with cash within one year. A long-term asset and a long-term liability have remaining maturities of more than one year. Current assets and liabilities are usually arranged in approximate order of remaining maturity, from shortest to longest. This arrangement reflects the fact that, generally, the book values of the short-remaining-maturity assets and liabilities tend to be closer to their current market values than those that have long maturities. For example, the book value of receivables may be fairly close to their market value. In contrast, the current market value of net fixed assets can be very different from their book value.

The liabilities and stockholders' equity (right-hand) side of the balance sheet shows the company's choice of its **capital structure:** the proportions of debt versus equity financing and the mixture of debt maturities, short-term versus long-term.

The difference between current assets and current liabilities is the company's net working capital, often simply called **working capital:**

$$\text{Working capital} = \text{Current assets} - \text{Current liabilities} \tag{3.2}$$

Working capital provides a measure of the business's liquidity, or its ability to meet its short-term obligations as they come due.

BOOK VALUE (NET BOOK VALUE) The net amount (net book value) for something shown in accounting statements.

BALANCE SHEET A statement of a company's financial position at one point in time, including its assets and the claims on those assets by creditors (liabilities) and owners (stockholders' equity).

ASSETS A company's productive resources.

LIABILITIES AND STOCKHOLDERS' EQUITY The total claims of creditors and owners against the company's assets.

CURRENT (SHORT-TERM) Typically refers to a period of up to one year.

LONG-TERM In accounting information, more than one year.

CAPITAL STRUCTURE The makeup of the liabilities and stockholders' equity side of the balance sheet, especially the proportion of debt versus equity and mixture of short- versus long-term debt maturities.

WORKING CAPITAL Current assets minus current liabilities.

TABLE 3.1
OutBack SportWear, Inc. Annual Balance Sheet ($ millions) December 31

	1997	1996		1997	1996
ASSETS			**LIABILITIES & STOCKHOLDERS' EQUITY**		
Cash and equivalents	$ 9.5	$ 12.0	Accounts payable	$ 18.8	$ 14.7
Accounts receivable	233.2	203.3	Notes payable	66.2	33.2
Inventories	133.9	118.8	Accrued expenses	77.7	62.0
Total current assets	$376.6	$334.1	Total current liabilities	$162.7	$109.9
Net plant and equipment	203.8	167.0	Long-term bonds	74.4	70.2
Total assets	$580.4	$501.1	Other long-term liabilities	19.6	17.7
			Total liabilities	$256.7	$197.8
			Preferred stock	10.0	10.0
			Common stock	45.4	45.4
			Retained earnings	268.3	247.9
			Total common equity	$323.7	$303.3
			Liabilities and stockholders' equity	$580.4	$501.1

INCOME STATEMENT A financial statement that reports the revenues, expenses, and profit (or loss) for a company over a specific interval of time, usually a year or a quarter of a year.

Income Statement   *Read All*

The **income statement** reports the revenues, expenses, and profit (or loss) for a company over a specific interval of time, typically a year or a quarter of a year. Net income, sometimes referred to as profit, is the difference between total revenue and total cost for the period. Table 3.2 shows the income statement for OutBack SportWear. In this income statement, the gross profit is the net sales minus the cost of goods sold. The cost of goods sold is the direct cost for the materials, labor, and other expenses directly associated with the production of the goods or services sold by the company.

EARNINGS BEFORE INTEREST AND TAXES (EBIT) Operating profit plus nonoperating profit, such as investment income, calculated before the deduction of interest and income taxes.

To compute the operating profit, subtract from gross profit (1) the indirect costs associated with selling, general, and administrative expenses and (2) depreciation and amortization (which are noncash items). **Earnings before interest and taxes (EBIT)** equals operating profit plus nonoperating profit (such as investment income). Subtracting interest expense from EBIT gives pretax income of $44.0 million in 1997. Finally, subtracting income taxes yields net income: $25.9 million in 1997, up from $18.0 million in 1996.

If the company has preferred stock outstanding, preferred dividends paid are subtracted from net income to get net income available for common stock. After subtracting whatever common stock dividends the company paid, the remaining earnings are the current period's addition to retained earnings on the balance sheet.

Dividends per share and earnings per share (EPS) are given in the bottom part of the income statement. The company's common stockholders have a residual claim on the company's assets after all debts and preferred stock have been paid. The stockholders' welfare, then, depends on the current and future profitability and dividends of the company. The per-share figures indicate how large the net income is relative to the number of common shares.[4] With 9 million shares outstanding, OutBack shows $2.77 in EPS in 1997.

Corporations occasionally declare an extraordinary gain or loss in addition to income or loss from their normal operations. OutBack SportWear did not report any extraordinary income. If a corporation had an extraordinary gain or loss, the income statement would show net income before and after (that is, without and with) the extraordinary gain or loss. In addition, EPS would be reported before and after the extraordinary income. For valuation purposes, EPS before extraordinary items (without taking them into account) is a more meaningful measure of the company's sustainable profit.

PAYOUT RATIO Generally, the proportion of earnings paid out to common stockholders as cash dividends. More specifically, the company's cash dividend divided by the company's earnings in the same period.

Finally, dividends per share divided by EPS gives the company's **payout ratio.** The payout ratio is the proportion of earnings that the company paid out to common shareholders as cash dividends. OutBack's 1997 payout ratio is about 18% (= 0.50/2.77).

STATEMENT OF CASH FLOWS A financial statement that shows cash receipts and payments, and how the company's cash position has changed, over a specific period of time, such as a year.

Statement of Cash Flows   *Read All*

The **statement of cash flows** indicates how the cash position of the company has changed during the period covered by the income statement. Thus, it complements the income statement and the balance sheet. Changes in a company's cash position can be the result of any of the company's many transactions.

The statement of cash flows breaks down the sources and uses of cash into three components. These are cash flows from (1) operating, (2) investing, and (3) financing activities. The flows of funds between a company and its investors, creditors, workers, customers, and other stakeholders serve as a fundamental starting point for the analysis of the company, its

---

[4]The earnings-per-share calculation can be fairly complicated. Simple earnings per share is net income divided by the weighted average number of common shares outstanding during the period. Other definitions, such as primary earnings per share and fully diluted earnings per share, take into account what are called the *dilutive effects* of option-like instruments (warrants, convertibles, executive stock options). The rules for computing earnings per share are given in Accounting Principles Board, "Earnings Per Share," APB Opinion No. 15 (New York: AICPA, 1969).

TABLE 3.2

OutBack SportWear, Inc. Annual Income Statement ($ millions, except per share data) Years Ended December 31

	1997	1996
Sales	$546.9	$485.8
Cost of goods sold	286.3	247.3
Gross profit	$260.6	$238.5
Selling, general & administrative exp.	186.2	180.5
Depreciation & amortization	22.7	20.1
Earnings before interest and taxes (EBIT)	$ 51.7	$ 37.9
Interest expense	7.7	8.0
Earnings before tax	$ 44.0	$ 29.9
Total income tax	18.1	11.9
Net income	$ 25.9	$ 18.0
Preferred dividends	1.0	1.0
Net income available for common	$ 24.9	$ 17.0
Dividends on common stock	4.5	3.6
Addition to retained earnings	$ 20.4	$ 13.4
Per Share Data:		
Earnings per share	$ 2.77	$ 1.89
Dividends per share	$ 0.50	$ 0.40
Shares outstanding (millions)	9.000	9.000

capital investment projects, and corporate acquisitions, as well as the analysis underlying many other decisions.

Table 3.3 on page 62 shows a typical statement of cash flows, that of OutBack SportWear. The sources and amounts of cash flows from operating activities, investing activities, and financing activities are itemized.[5]

Let's look more closely at the cash flow from operating activities. The net income is taken from OutBack's income statement (table 3.2). To arrive at net income, various items are deducted from sales, including some that are noncash expenses. Depreciation is usually the largest of these items. Because these items are not cash flows, they must be added back to determine cash flow. Dividends are *not* subtracted from operating activities. Instead, they are a discretionary part of financing activities. The other items represent changes in several working capital accounts, which are part of operating activities. Decreases (increases) in asset (liability) accounts are positive cash flows (*inflows*). The opposites are negative cash flows (*outflows*). One short-term liability, notes payable, is considered a financing activity and is not included in operating activities.

Investing activities cash flows include those connected with buying or selling long-term assets, acquiring other companies, and selling subsidiaries. OutBack used $59.5 million to purchase plant and equipment, which is an outflow (negative cash flow).

---

[5]The format of the statement of cash flows shown in table 3.3 is a presentation called the *indirect method.* Another method, called the *direct method,* sums the cash inflows and outflows associated with operating the company. The first part of the statement of cash flows (cash flows from operating activities) looks different depending on whether the direct or the indirect method is used; the other two parts are the same. Although their formats differ, the methods give the same numerical result. We use the indirect method here because it is used most widely in published financial statements.

TABLE 3.3

OutBack SportWear, Inc. Statement of Cash Flows ($ millions) Year Ended
December 31

	1997
CASH FLOWS FROM OPERATING ACTIVITIES	
Net income	$ 25.9
Depreciation and amortization	22.7
Accounts receivables decrease (increase)	(29.9)
Inventories decrease (increase)	(15.1)
Accounts payable increase (decrease)	4.1
Accrued expenses increase (decrease)	15.7
Net cash provided by (used in) operating activities	$ 23.4
CASH FLOWS FROM INVESTING ACTIVITIES	
Purchase of plant and equipment	$(59.5)
Net cash provided by (used in) investing activities	$(59.5)
CASH FLOWS FROM FINANCING ACTIVITIES	
Notes payable increase (decrease)	$ 33.0
Issuance of long-term debt, net	4.2
Increase in other long-term liabilities	1.9
Cash dividends (preferred and common)	(5.5)
Net cash provided by (used in) financing activities	$ 33.6
Net increase (decrease) in cash and equivalents	$ (2.5)
Cash and equivalents at beginning of year	12.0
Cash and equivalents at end of year	$ 9.5

Financing activities cash flows include those connected with selling or repurchasing common and preferred stock, issuing or retiring long-term debt, issuing and repaying short-term notes, and paying dividends on common stock or preferred stock. For example, OutBack borrowed $33.0 million in notes payable, which was an inflow.

Net increase (decrease) in cash and equivalents is the sum of the cash flows from the three sections: $23.4 - 59.5 + 33.6 = \$(2.5)$ million. This change is then added to the beginning cash balance of $12.0 million, leaving the ending cash balance of $9.5 million.

In many financial decisions, such as long-term investments, we separate the investing, financing, and operating cash flows. It is important to understand that such separations in the statement of cash flows are somewhat arbitrary, particularly in the case of the first part of the statement, which shows the cash flows from operating activities. For example, dividends are included with financing cash flows, whereas interest expense is treated as an operating cash flow.

NOTES TO THE FINAN-CIAL STATEMENTS A detailed set of notes immediately following the financial statements that explain and expand on the information in the financial statements.

Notes to the Financial Statements

The **notes to the financial statements** are an integral part of the statements. The notes disclose the significant accounting policies used to prepare the financial statements. They also provide additional detail concerning several of the items in the accounting statements. Table 3.4 lists subjects usually included in such notes.

TABLE 3.4

Subjects Typically Covered as Notes to Financial Statements in Annual Reports

- more detailed breakdowns of other income, interest and other financial charges, and provision for income taxes
- a description of the earnings-per-share calculation
- details concerning extraordinary items, if any, and foreign exchange gains or losses
- breakdown of inventories, investments (including nonconsolidated subsidiaries), property, plant, and equipment, and other assets
- costs and amounts of short-term borrowings
- schedules of long-term debt, preferred stock, and capitalized and operating lease obligations
- schedule of capital stock issued or reserved for issuance and statement of changes in shareholders' equity (which is often included as a separate financial statement)
- details concerning significant acquisitions or disposals of assets
- information concerning employee pension and stock option plans
- commitments and contingent liabilities
- events subsequent to the balance sheet date, but prior to the release of the financial statements to the public, which might significantly affect their interpretation
- quarterly operating results
- business segment information (by line of business and by geographic region)
- a five-year summary comparison of financial performance and financial position

Published annual reports also include **management's discussion** of recent operating results. Management's discussion is included along with the financial statements. Usually there is also a letter to the stockholders, which appears at the front of the annual report. This letter and the management's discussion can help you interpret the accounting statements. They can also provide insights into management's philosophy and strategy that simply don't appear in the numerical sections of the annual report.

The notes to the financial statements and management's discussion contain a wealth of useful information. You cannot fully appreciate the information contained in a company's accounting statements unless you read the notes to the financial statements and the management's discussion.[6]

MANAGEMENT'S DISCUSSION A report from management to the stockholders that accompanies the company's financial statements in the annual report. This report explains the period's financial results and enables management to discuss other ideas that may not be apparent in the financial statements in the annual report.

Self-Check

1. Suppose a company issues $10 million of new bonds and repurchases $10 million of its common stock. What happens to Total Assets, Net Working Capital, and Common Stockholders' Equity?

2. Suppose a company issues $10 million of new bonds. It then pays off $2 million of accounts payable, purchases $6 million of capital equipment, and purchases $2 million of additional inventory. What happens to Total Assets, Net Working Capital, and Common Stockholders' Equity?

3. Sales increase by $100. The cost of goods sold goes up by $60, and depreciation and interest expenses are unchanged. The tax rate is 40% and the company does not change its dividend. What happens to Net Income and the Addition to Retained Earnings as a result of the increased sales?

4. Indicate whether each of the following transactions is classed as a cash flow in the company's operating activities, investing activities, or financing activities and whether it increases or decreases the company's cash balance.

(continued on following page)

---

[6]This is why accounting and securities regulations required companies to furnish this information!

(Self-Check *continued from previous page*)

a. The company increases its inventory.

b. The company decreases its accounts receivable.

c. The company increases its accounts payable.

d. The company sells some of its long-term plant and equipment.

e. The company reduces the balance on its long-term mortgage.

BOOK VALUES VERSUS MARKET VALUES

Accounting statements are invaluable aids to analysts and managers. But the statements do not provide certain critical information, and as a result they have inherent limitations. Accounting statements are historical. They don't provide any information about cash flows that might be expected in the future. They also don't provide critically important information about the *current* market values of assets and liabilities. Thus accounting statements not only fail to look ahead, they do not even report the current situation. Such missing information limits the usefulness of accounting information.

There are several reasons why accounting statements are historical, but we will not contribute here to the debate over how accounting statements might better be prepared. We will simply review the information accounting statements provide, based on today's practice, and note important implications of the procedures.

Market versus Book Value of Assets

The current market value of an asset can be *very* different from its book value. Therefore, an asset probably can't be sold for its book value. If an asset can't be sold for its book value, it can't be bought for that value, either. So the cost to replace an asset that breaks down is probably different from its current book value as well. At the same time, four factors make a disparity between market and book values more or less likely: the time since the asset was acquired, inflation, the asset's liquidity, and whether the asset is tangible or intangible.

Time Since Acquisition As a rule, the more time that has passed since an asset was acquired, the greater the chance that the asset's current market value will differ from its book value. When an asset is acquired, it is recorded in the accounting statements at its cost. That cost is a market value, at least in some sense. Therefore, the initial book value is quite likely to be similar to the market value of the asset *at the time it is acquired.* Over time, however, the market value can diverge significantly from the book value. This is because changes in the book value (depreciation each period) are specified by GAAP rather than by economic considerations.

EXAMPLE   *Differences in Car Usage*

Suppose two companies buy identical cars. In one case, a sales representative is going to drive the car about 10,000 miles per month. In the second case, a manager is going to drive the car about 1000 miles per month. GAAP specify identical depreciation rules for these cars. The rule is based on the type of asset (an automobile), not on how it will be used. Thus after any significant time, say a year, the book values of the cars will be identical, but the more heavily used car will have a much lower market value. The more time that passes, the larger the difference is likely to be. ■

The Sampson Company Waterfront Warehouse

The Sampson Company purchased a warehouse 15 years ago. Since then, the area surrounding the building has changed dramatically from an industrial area of factories and shipping warehouses into an exclusive high-rise condominium area overlooking the waterfront. Sampson's building and land currently have a combined book value of $231,000 (after accounting for depreciation on the building; depreciation cannot be claimed on land). Today the building could be sold for $15 million. Such a difference fundamentally changes the value of the company. It also has profound implications for the best use of the company's assets at this point in time. Sampson should consider moving its operations elsewhere and selling the current location. Of course, in other cases the market value may be well *below* the book value, which could have very different policy implications! ■

Inflation Inflation during the time since the asset was acquired is a second important factor that can cause a significant difference between market value and book value. When prices change because of inflation, the market values of existing assets also change to reflect the difference in purchasing power. Such changes can be dramatic. For example, from 1970 until 1995, inflation caused the purchasing power of a dollar to change by a factor of 5. This means that what could be purchased for $1.00 in 1970 cost about $5.00 in 1995.

SunTrust's Shares of Coca-Cola Stock

In the early part of this century, when the Coca-Cola Company first issued shares of its common stock to the public, some of the shares went to a predecessor of SunTrust Banks in Atlanta. At the time, the value of the stock was recorded at its current market value of $100,000. Until very recently, the stock was shown on SunTrust's balance sheet as an asset with a book value of $100,000. However, the stock had since gone up in value. Currently, those shares are worth about $1.5 billion, an increase of about 15,000 times over their original value. We know that the stock value has increased well in excess of inflation over the intervening 80 or so years. However, inflation during the same time period was substantial, perhaps changing purchasing power by a factor of 50 or more. Therefore, even if the value of the shares had increased only in step with inflation, the shares would be worth in excess of $5 million. In that case, then, only the remaining 300-times increase (= 15,000/50) is due to the success of the Coca-Cola Company! ■

Liquidity An asset's liquidity is a third factor that affects the likelihood that the asset's current market value will differ from its book value. Less liquid assets have higher transaction costs when they are sold, so there's greater uncertainty about the *net* proceeds from a sale. As a consequence, if all else is equal, the current market values of less liquid assets can differ more from their book values.

For example, compare a two-year-old pickup truck to a unique patented process for producing plastic bags. The pickup truck is a more liquid asset, because it is commonly available and there are many alternatives to that particular truck. In fact, there are established used-truck markets for selling such assets with low transaction costs. Contrast this with the plastic-bag-production process. Such a production process may be worth much more than its book value if it is the leading production technology. It may be essentially worthless if another technology has made it obsolete. But in either case, it could be very costly and time consuming to find the buyer who will pay the most for the process, because there isn't an established market for used plastic-bag-production processes.

Read ──→ **Tangible versus Intangible**   A fourth factor that affects the likelihood of there being a significant difference between market and book values is whether the asset is tangible or intangible. The values of intangible assets are much more variable. As with our example of the plastic-bag-production process, intangible assets can be extremely valuable or essentially worthless. Valuation differences can also be caused by extreme differences in liquidity. Even long-term assets such as plant and equipment are more likely to have established markets (real estate and used equipment) than are intangible assets such as patents or the design for a new product. Intangible assets tend to be unique. There aren't active markets for selling them. Consequently, intangible assets tend to be extremely illiquid. Therefore, the current market value of an intangible asset is especially likely to differ from its book value.

EXAMPLE

Developing a New Product at Murray Corporation

Suppose the Murray Corporation has spent $14 million developing a new product. Now, it can more accurately estimate that the product will provide only about $5 million in profit to offset the development cost. At this point, Murray would like to sell the rights to its product to another company and let that company manufacture and market the new product. Would you pay $14 million for something that is worth only $5 million? Despite the $14 million historical cost on Murray's balance sheet, a potential buyer will assess the value of the new product on the basis of its *future* potential.[7] ∎

We noted earlier that placement on the balance sheet reflects the general remaining maturity of the assets. We should now point out that balance sheet placement also reflects the general likelihood that there will be a difference between the asset's book value and its market value. As you move down the list of assets, they are less liquid and have generally been held longer. Intangible assets are shown last.

Consider two types of assets that represent opposite extremes in liquidity: cash and a manufacturing plant. Cash is extremely liquid (actually, it is the very *definition* of liquidity), whereas it would probably require considerable effort to find a buyer for the plant.[8] However, despite the fact that the market values of other current assets are generally less likely to differ from their book values, care is always in order when valuing a company. Accounts receivable can include bad debts. Inventory can be obsolete or can be shown at very low values because of a "last-in–first-out" policy of accounting for inventory. Thus even the book values of current assets other than cash and equivalents can be poor approximations of market value. Therefore, it is wise to look especially carefully at assets other than cash and equivalents when trying to value them.

Market versus Book Value of Liabilities

As with assets, the current market value of a liability can differ from its book value. Generally, however, the potential divergence is smaller, and the relationship between the market and book values is less complex.

Remaining Maturity   The time until a liability must be paid off—its remaining maturity—is the main factor that affects the difference between the market and book values of a healthy company's liabilities. Liabilities have explicit contractual amounts that must be paid at specific

---

[7]This problem is a major reason why GAAP call for expensing (depreciating) research and development costs over a relatively short time period. The other side to this is that when a company does make a great and valuable discovery, its book value grossly *under*states its market value.

[8]If the company really wanted to sell the plant quickly, it could probably find a buyer almost instantly for a low enough price, say $2.39. (But even this price might be too high if the plant sat on top of a chemical waste dump that would cost the new owner $100 million to clean up.)

points in time. Failure to meet these contractual obligations creates the possibility of bankruptcy. Therefore, when a liability becomes due, the market value of the liability is essentially equal to its book value. In contrast, the market value of liabilities that do not have to be repaid for a long time reflects current economic conditions, as well as expectations about the future.

Consider a loan for $10 million that is due to be paid off in four months. Because the remaining maturity is short, the cost of interest is relatively insignificant compared to the amount borrowed. Now consider a long-term loan for $10 million at 6% interest per year that doesn't have to be repaid for another 25 years, except for yearly interest. If the borrowing rate today is 10%, the market value of this liability is smaller than its book value because its remaining maturity of 25 years provides the company with 25 more years over which to enjoy the low 6% interest cost on the existing loan.

Financial Distress   In our discussion of the impact of remaining maturity, we referred to a *healthy* company's liabilities. A second factor that affects the difference between the market and book values of liabilities is the company's financial health. The market values of a financially distressed company's liabilities are likely to be below their book values. This state of affairs reflects the fact that the distressed company may not be able to meet its obligations. Recall that corporate stockholders have limited liability. This increases the likelihood that the liability holders will not get paid. A distressed company's long-term liabilities are especially likely to have a market value that is below book value because of the uncertainty about the company's long-term viability. Thus financial distress can intensify the effect of remaining maturity on the market value of a company's liabilities.

Total Value

The total value of a company is simply the sum of the market values of all its assets. Because the market values of the individual assets can be very different from their book values, the balance sheet amount *Total Assets* should *never* be taken as a reliable estimate of the current value of the company.

Equity Value

The current book value of the company's equity is probably the least informative item on a balance sheet. Every factor that affects the difference between the market and book values of each individual item on the balance sheet affects the difference between the market and book values of the company's equity. This is because the difference between the market and book values of equity is the sum of the differences between the market and book values of all the other items on the balance sheet.

Look back at equation (3.1), the balance sheet identity. We can rewrite that equation as

$$Stockholders' \ equity = Assets - Liabilities$$

This form makes it is easy to see the residual nature of the equity value, which we discussed in chapter 1. We have just said that the Assets amount is not the market value of the company's assets and that the Liabilities amount is not the market value of the company's liabilities. Therefore, it should be clear that the difference between the two isn't miraculously going to become an accurate measure of market value, either!

If, instead of being book (historical) values, the Assets and Liabilities amounts were current market values, this equation would provide the true residual value of the stockholders' equity. In a GAAP balance sheet, however, the value of Stockholders' Equity is simply the result of applying the required rules to the historical cost of the assets and liabilities—in essence, an amount that forces the balance sheet identity to hold. In a sense, then, the book value of stockholders' equity is a "plug" figure that enforces the balance sheet identity.

As we will explain in detail later, stock prices observed in public market trading are a much more accurate basis for estimating the current market value of a company.

Self-Check

1. Why might the market value of an asset differ from its book value?

2. Why is the difference between market value and book value likely to be greater for intangible assets than tangible assets?

3. How does the maturity of a liability affect the difference between its book and market value?

4. Your friend believes that the book value of Microsoft Corporation's stockholders' equity is a good measure of what Microsoft's equity is really worth. Do you agree? Explain.

5. The book value of the company's assets is $100 and the market value of the assets is $200. The book value of the company's liabilities is $40 and the market value is $44. What is the book value of stockholder's equity and the market value of equity?

ACCOUNTING NET INCOME VERSUS CASH FLOW

The income statement contains noncash expenses and accruals. Because of this, net income is not an accurate measure of cash inflow. In fact, this is part of the reason for requiring a Statement of Cash Flows.

Noncash Items

Certain items in the income statement are called noncash items. These are items for which the cash flow connected with the expense occurs at a point in time outside of the reporting period. GAAP require the allocation of all or part of the expense to a time period other than the one in which the cash flow occurs. Depreciation is the most significant such item. When a company purchases certain assets, such as plant and equipment, the use of the asset is over a prolonged period that spans many income statement periods. On this basis, GAAP require that the total expense for the asset be spread over some extended number of income periods, such as 5, 10, or even 30 years.

The only thing at issue here is *timing*. The claim of expense for accounting purposes is separated in time from when the cash flow actually occurs. The cash flow for the item occurs at the time of purchase. The expense charged against income occurs in stages over several income statement periods. Therefore, noncash items make the company's net income figure very different from its cash inflow. Deferred and accrued taxes are two other examples of noncash items.

Accruals

The revenues and expenses on the income statement include items for which no cash has yet been received. For example, a sale of merchandise that has been agreed to and perhaps even delivered, but that the customer has not yet paid for, can be included. Also, a sale for which some cash has already been received may not be included, because it has not met certain GAAP requirements. Despite this, the revenues shown over a long time represent a good estimate of the actual revenue that will *ultimately* be collected. However, within a limited time period of, say, one or two years, because of accruals the revenue shown on the income statement can be significantly different from the cash revenue that actually came into the company.

Estimating Cash Flow

Cash flow is often estimated by adding back noncash items to the net income, as in the first two lines of the operating activities part of the statement of cash flows (table 3.3). This is because the distortion from accruals is typically relatively small. We will use such an estimate in connection with long-term investment decisions, called *capital budgeting decisions,* which are covered in Part III of this book.

Accounting Income versus Economic Income

Economic income is the total return on an investment, made up of the cash inflow plus the change in the market value of the assets and liabilities. As we have just discussed, however, net income is not cash flow, and GAAP changes in the company's assets and liabilities do not reflect changes in market values. Thus the Net Income figure shown on the income statement can be quite different from the company's actual economic income. As with the balance sheet, however, some items on the income statement are more or less likely than others to be good estimates of economic reality.

Operating Income   Operating income can be a good estimate of the true economic operating income, provided that (1) the company has made no changes in its accounting procedures, such as switching inventory accounting from a "last-in–first-out" (LIFO) to a "first-in–first-out" (FIFO) basis, and (2) the accounting period is sufficiently long. With respect to changes in accounting procedures, certain changes make the amounts reported in that period larger or smaller and can therefore distort the amounts reported. With respect to the length of the accounting period, several years is preferable. Good or poor performance may not be revealed in income statements of one or two years. However, over time, significant changes in performance are likely to be revealed in any extended series of income statements.

Extraordinary Income   Interpreting the economic meaning of extraordinary income requires that we understand its nature and origin. Without such an understanding, it can be impossible to determine the implications of extraordinary income for the company's future.

For example, consider an extraordinary item that is the sale of some land that was worth much more than its current book value. Suppose this difference between book and market values was widely known. In such a case, the extraordinary income that is recognized by the land sale is probably only a matter of bookkeeping. Managers and stockholders will have already taken the higher value into account.

In general, extraordinary items occur only once. They do not reflect the company's *sustainable net income.* We therefore recommend that you use *net income before extraordinary items* when doing calculations that involve net income.

Self-Check
1. What are the main differences between net income and cash flows?
2. Why might the economic income of the company differ significantly from its net income?
3. Why should you use net income *before extraordinary items* when doing calculations that involve net income?
4. How would it be possible for a company to report positive accounting income and yet have negative economic income?

CORPORATE AND PERSONAL INCOME TAXES

Taxes make the federal government, and any state and local government that levies income taxes, a partner with every company. With so much money at stake, taxes can have a significant impact on financial decisions. Both corporate and personal taxes are relevant to financial management. We focus here on income taxes for illustrative purposes and because they are currently the most significant form of taxes.

MARGINAL TAX RATE
The tax rate applied to the marginal (incremental, or last) dollar of income.

AVERAGE TAX RATE
Taxes as a fraction of income: total taxes divided by total taxable income.

Corporate Income Taxes

The corporate income tax system is complicated. As table 3.5 shows, the federal tax rate generally increases with the level of income. The tax rate applied to the last dollar of income is called the **marginal tax rate.** The **average tax rate** is the total taxes paid divided by taxable income. A **progressive tax system** has an average tax rate that increases for some increases in the level of income but never decreases with such increases. The marginal tax rate is greater than the average tax rate in a progressive tax system.

E X A M P L E

Corporate Income Taxes for Sidewell, Inc.

Suppose Sidewell, Inc. has taxable corporate income of $200,000. What will be the corporation's federal corporate income tax liability on this amount?

From the tax rates in table 3.5, the tax liability will be

$$\text{Tax} = 22{,}250 + 0.39(200{,}000 - 100{,}000) = 22{,}250 + 39{,}000 = \$61{,}250$$

The marginal tax rate is 39%, but the average tax rate on this level of income is

$$\text{Average tax rate} = 61{,}250/200{,}000 = 30.625\%$$

At this income level, the marginal tax rate exceeds the average tax rate. ■

PROGRESSIVE TAX SYSTEM A tax system wherein the average tax rate increases for some increases in income but never decreases with an increase in income.

As income is taxed at the higher marginal tax rate in a progressive tax system, the average tax rate continues to increase toward the marginal tax rate. Figure 3.1 shows the relationship between the marginal and average tax rates at various levels of taxable corporate income for the tax structure shown in table 3.5. In the first range, indicated by an A (where taxable income is between zero and $50,000), the average and marginal rates are both 15%. In range B, the marginal tax rate is 25%, and the average tax rate increases over the range to 18.3%. In range C, the marginal rate is 34%, and the average rate increases over the range to 22.3%. Because of the lower rate on the "earlier" income, the average tax rate will never become equal to the marginal rate.

To equalize the two rates, Congress set the marginal rate at 39% on income over $100,000 until the average rate increases to 34%. At a taxable income of $335,000, the average and marginal rates are both equal to 34%. For taxable incomes between $335,000 and $10 million, the marginal rate is set back to 34%. For taxable incomes between $10 and $15 million, the marginal tax rate is increased again, to 35%. Once again to raise the average tax rate to this higher marginal rate, the marginal rate is 38% for taxable incomes between $15 and $18.33 million. Above $18.33 million, all incomes are taxed at both a marginal and an average rate of 35%.

There are two more important complications. First, tax structures are often modified. Thus the average and marginal tax rates that apply to a corporation can and do change from

TABLE 3.5
Corporate Income Tax Rates

CORPORATE TAXABLE INCOME ($)	PAY THIS AMOUNT ON THE BASE OF THE RANGE ($)	PLUS THIS RATE TIMES THE EXCESS OVER THE BASE[a]
0 – 50,000	0	15%
50,000 – 75,000	7,500	25%
75,000 – 100,000	13,750	34%
100,000 – 335,000	22,250	39%
335,000 – 10,000,000	113,900	34%
10,000,000 – 15,000,000	3,400,000	35%
15,000,000 – 18,333,333	5,150,000	38%
over 18,333,333	6,416,667	35%

[a]These tax rates apply to 1997 taxable income.

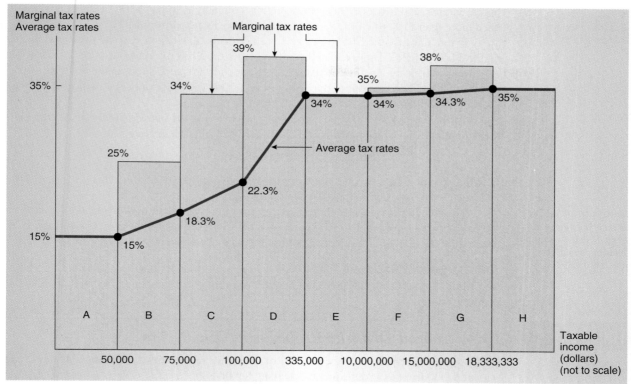

FIGURE 3.1
Marginal and average corporate income tax rates.

time to time, sometimes dramatically. Second, state and local governments often impose additional income (and other) taxes on corporations, so the total tax is the sum of the federal, state, and local tax levies. The result is that no single tax rate will endure through time, and no single tax rate will apply across all geographical locations.

Throughout this book, we'll simply specify an income tax rate, such as 40%. We intend whatever rate we specify to reflect all taxes from all levels. The single rate is a simplified approximation of taxes. We use different tax rates to emphasize that actual tax rates vary over time and from one location to another.

Corporate Capital Gains   A long-term capital gain or loss, referred to simply as a **capital gain,** occurs *for tax purposes* when an asset that has been owned for a sufficiently long time (currently, at least one year) is sold for more or less than its tax basis (that is, its net book value for tax purposes). Although an actual gain or loss occurs every time the market value of the asset changes, the gain or loss is not recognized for tax purposes until the asset is sold. This means that the tax on the gain is postponed—indefinitely—until the asset is sold. Of course, this also means no tax-reducing losses can be claimed until the asset is sold. This is an important complicating feature of the tax system. It creates what is called a **tax-timing option.** We will describe and discuss tax-timing options in more detail later.

Corporate capital gains are currently taxed at the same rates as regular income. Before 1987 corporate capital gains were taxed at a lower rate. A lower tax rate on capital gains provides extra incentive to invest in capital assets. Short-term capital gains (or losses) that result from holding assets for less than the required year are taxed as regular income.

Tax Treatment of Interest Expense and Dividends Paid   Interest paid on debt obligations is a tax-deductible expense. Dividends paid to common and preferred stockholders are not. If a company is to pay $100 of interest, the company needs $100 of earnings

CAPITAL GAIN The difference between what an asset is sold for and its book value, typically referring to an asset that has been owned for a sufficiently long time, such as a year or more.

TAX-TIMING OPTION The option to sell an asset and claim a loss for tax purposes or not to sell the asset and defer a capital gain tax.

before interest and taxes (EBIT). However, if a company is to pay $100 of dividends, it will need more than $100 of EBIT, because taxes will be deducted from EBIT.

In the first case the $100 of interest is a tax-deductible expense, so no taxes will be due on the $100 of EBIT. However, in the second case, the $100 of dividends is not a deductible expense, so taxes are due on the $100 before dividends are paid. Suppose the tax rate is 40%. Taxes of $40 will be paid out of the $100 of EBIT. This will leave only $60 to pay the planned $100 of dividends.

To find the amount of EBIT necessary to cover the dividends, simply divide the dividend amount by 1 minus the marginal tax rate. If the marginal tax rate is 40%,

$$\text{EBIT needed} = 100/(1 - 0.40) = 100/0.6 = \$166.67$$

If EBIT is $166.67, taxes due on this will be $66.67 (= [0.40]166.67). This will leave $100 (= 166.67 − 66.67) after taxes to pay the dividend.

This unequal, or **asymmetric,** treatment of interest expense and dividend payments effectively lowers the tax bills of corporations that use more debt financing. Conversely, it increases the tax bills of corporations that use more equity financing.

ASYMMETRIC A lack of equivalence between two things, such as the unequal tax treatment of interest expense and dividend payments.

Intercorporate Dividend Exclusion   At least 70% of dividends *received* by a corporation from another corporation are not taxed.[9] The remaining dividends received are taxed at ordinary rates.

EXAMPLE

Intercorporate Dividend Exclusion at Epic Records

Suppose Epic Records receives $10,000 of dividend income from Columbia Music. It can deduct $7000 from its taxable income, leaving $3000 to be taxed.[10] If Epic's marginal tax rate is 35%, it will owe $1050 (= [0.35]3000) in taxes on the $10,000 of dividends. This means that the *effective* tax rate on an intercorporate dividend payment is 30% of the marginal tax rate. In this example, it is 10.5% (= 1050/10,000 = 0.30 × 35%) for Epic Records. ■

The reason for an intercorporate dividend exclusion involves the concept of multiple taxation. In the U.S. tax system, income is taxed once at the corporate level when the company earns the income, and it is taxed a second time at the personal level when dividends are paid to individual shareholders. This results in what is called double taxation. Fully taxing intercorporate dividends would amount to triple taxation. To reduce the impact of this, a substantial part of intercorporate dividends, currently 70%, is effectively excluded from taxation.

Incidentally, *interest received* by one corporation from another is fully taxable. There are situations wherein a corporation might prefer to purchase preferred stock (over a debt instrument) because an intercorporate dividend exclusion results in lower taxes and a higher *after-tax* return on the investment.

Improper Accumulations of Income to Avoid Payment of Taxes   If a corporation does not pay a dividend, its shareholders do not receive the dividend income and do not incur a personal tax liability. The U.S. tax code imposes a substantial penalty on a corporation if it accumulates earnings for the purpose of enabling its shareholders to avoid the payment of personal income taxes. A corporation is allowed to accumulate $250,000 of retained earnings without being subject to this tax. Accumulations above $250,000 are subject to the penalty tax if they are considered unnecessary for the reasonable needs of the business. However, if these funds are reinvested in the company to buy more assets, to pay off debt obligations, or to provide a reasonable amount of liquidity, the improper-accumulations tax is not imposed. Al-

---

[9]The proportion not taxed ranges from 70% to 100%, depending on the percentage of ownership.
[10]The effect of the intercorporate dividend exclusion is to exclude the amount from income. It is as though the deducted amount is simply not counted as part of Epic's income.

though this penalty tax is very rarely imposed, the threat of the penalty is real. It encourages corporations either to use the funds in the company or to distribute them as dividends.

Tax Loss Carry-backs and Carry-forwards If a corporation shows a loss (has a negative net income), this loss can be "carried back" as much as three years or "carried forward" for as much as 15 years to offset taxable income in those years. For example, suppose a corporation has negative net income this year but had positive net income and paid taxes within the last three years. This year's loss can be used to offset previous profits (carried back), and the government will refund some previously paid taxes. If the corporation's current loss exceeds its previous income, the company can use the loss to offset future profits (carry the loss forward) and reduce its future taxes.

S Corporations The so-called Subchapter S regulation permits small businesses that meet certain requirements to choose to be taxed as partnerships or proprietorships instead of as corporations. This allows the corporation to receive some of the benefits of the corporate form of organization and yet avoid the double taxation of income. Subchapter S corporate income is reported as personal income by its owners. The individual owners then pay personal income taxes on the part of the income that is allocated to each of them.

Personal Income Taxes

Personal income taxes are the federal government's largest source of income. In a recent year, they made up 36% of its total income. Here we'll look at some of the features of the personal income tax system that have implications for financial management.

Personal Income Tax Rates Like corporate income tax rates, personal income tax rates increase with income, going from zero to a maximum of 39.6%. The marginal tax rates for the two most common filing status categories ("single" and "married, filing jointly") are shown in table 3.6. There are other schedules for people classified as "married, filing separately" or as "head of household." Personal tax rates are further complicated by the elimination of certain exemptions and deductions for higher incomes. The elimination of an exemption or deduction raises the effective tax rate. In addition, individuals pay social security and Medicare taxes and income taxes to state and local governments, so the effective tax rates for individuals can be much higher than the rates in table 3.6.

TABLE 3.6
1995 Personal Income Tax Rates

PERSONAL TAXABLE INCOME ($)	PAY THIS AMOUNT ON THE BASE OF THE RANGE ($)	PLUS THIS RATE TIMES THE EXCESS OVER THE BASE[a]
Single taxpayer		
0 – 23,350	0	15%
23,350 – 56,550	3,502.50	28%
56,550 – 117,950	12,798.50	31%
117,950 – 256,500	31,832.50	36%
over 256,500	81,710.50	39.6%
Married taxpayers, filing jointly		
0 – 39,000	0	15%
39,000 – 94,250	5,850	28%
94,250 – 143,600	21,320	31%
143,600 – 256,500	36,618.50	36%
over 256,500	77,262.50	39.6%

[a]The marginal tax rates are the same in 1997 but the income brackets are slightly higher.

Exemptions and Deductions

Taxable income is equal to gross income minus allowable exemptions and deductions. For each dependent there is an exemption, which was $2650 in 1997 and increases each year with inflation. In addition, you can choose either to itemize your deductions or to take a standard deduction that is based on your filing status. Itemized deductions include such things as home mortgage interest, gifts to charity, state and local income taxes paid, real estate taxes paid, and some medical and job-related expenses. As mentioned above, some exemptions and deductions are eliminated for incomes above certain levels.

Dividend and Interest Income

Dividend income received from common stock and preferred stock is fully taxable. Income from interest paid by corporations, financial institutions, and individuals is also fully taxable. However, recall from our discussion of the Principle of Two-Sided Transactions that interest on munis (municipals), certain state and local government bonds, is not taxable by the federal government. Consequently, munis can be attractive investments. However, their relative attractiveness depends on one's marginal income tax rate. With a zero income tax rate, the after-income-tax yield on the muni is its before-income-tax yield. The after-income-tax yield on the taxable bond is

$$After\text{-}income\text{-}tax\ yield = Before\text{-}income\text{-}tax\ yield\ (1 - Marginal\ income\ tax\ rate)$$

EXAMPLE

Yields on Munis versus Taxable Securities

Suppose Phil and Marcia can invest in a taxable bond yielding 8.0% or a muni yielding 6.5%. Phil's marginal income tax rate is 15%, whereas Marcia's is 31%. Which bond should each one invest in?

The after-income-tax muni yield is 6.5% for both of them. If Marcia invests in the taxable bond, she will have an after-income-tax yield of 5.52%:

$$After\text{-}income\text{-}tax\ yield = 8.0(1 - 0.31) = 8.0(0.69) = 5.52\%$$

Therefore, the muni is more attractive for Marcia.

However, if Phil invests in the taxable bond, he will have an after-income-tax yield of 6.80%:

$$After\text{-}income\text{-}tax\ yield = 8.0(1 - 0.15) = 8.0(0.85) = 6.80\%$$

So Phil is better off investing in the taxable bond, despite the taxation on its interest. ■

Dividend income received from common stock and preferred stock is fully taxable. This is the double taxation noted above in the discussion of corporate income taxes.

Personal Capital Gains Taxes

Like corporate income, the personal income tax system has special provisions for long-term capital gains that result from owning assets for more than one year. They also lead to tax-timing options.

As with corporate income, short-term capital gains (or losses) that result from holding assets for less than the required one year are taxed as regular income. However, personal (long-term) capital gains may be taxed at a lower rate because the maximum capital gains rate is currently 28%. Thus if your marginal ordinary rate is above 28% (such as 31%, 36%, or 39.6%), your capital gains are taxed at the lower rate of 28%. The lower capital gains tax rate provides extra incentive to invest in assets such as stocks, real estate, and, more generally, business.

A Capital Gain Tax-Timing Option on Goodyear Stock

EXAMPLE

Suppose you bought 100 shares of Goodyear for $3000 a little more than a year ago and the shares are worth $4500 today. If you sell the shares for $4500, you will be taxed on a $1500 capital gain. But for as long as you continue to own the shares, you will not have to pay a capital gains tax. Now suppose instead that your shares have gone down in value to $2200. If you sell the shares for $2200, you will be able to claim a capital loss of $800, which could reduce your taxes this year. ■

Self-Check

1. What is a progressive tax system? How do the marginal and average tax rates usually compare in such a system?

2. Explain an important difference in corporate income taxes between interest expense and dividends paid.

3. How does the intercorporate dividend exclusion work?

4. Explain how capital gains are taxed differently from ordinary income.

5. What is a tax-timing option?

SUMMARY

The purpose of chapter 3 is to review the major financial statements, emphasize the difference between accounting and economic concepts of value and income, and detail the major corporate and personal tax features that affect a company's financial policy.

- The primary financial statements are the balance sheet, income statement, and statement of cash flows. The footnotes and management's discussion are also important parts of the company's annual report.

- The balance sheet shows the assets, liabilities, and stockholders' equity of the company. The balance sheet shows the company's financial position at a point in time.

- The income statement reports the company's revenues, costs, and net income for a period of time, such as one year or one quarter.

- The statement of cash flows shows the cash flows that result in a period's change in cash balances. The cash flows are broken into three parts, cash flows from operating activities, investing activities, and financing activities.

- Market values are based on expected future cash flows. Book values are based on historical costs. The market values and book values of assets, liabilities, and stockholders' equity can be substantially different.

- Economic income (cash flow plus capital gain) differs from accounting income.

- Corporate and personal income taxes are levied by the federal government as well as by most states and many local governments.

- Marginal and average tax rates for both corporations and individuals are fairly high and taxes are a major expense of doing business.

- Currently, capital gains tax rates are similar to ordinary income rates. When they exist, lower capital gains rates are an incentive to invest in capital assets.

- For corporations, interest paid is a tax-deductible expense, but dividends paid are not tax deductible. This encourages the use of debt financing.

- Double taxation is the system of taxing income twice, once at the corporate level and a second time when dividends are paid to stockholders. Seventy percent (and in some cases, more) of intercorporate dividends are excluded from taxable income to avoid triple taxation.

- S corporations are certain small businesses that can avoid double taxation (if they qualify) by allocating their income to their owners, who pay personal taxes on the corporation's income.

- Personal tax rates and corporate tax rates are progressive, where low-income individuals and corporations have lower marginal and average tax rates.
- Interest income on qualifying municipal bonds is not taxable by the federal government.

EQUATION SUMMARY

(3.1)	Assets = Liabilities + Stockholders' equity.
(3.2)	Working capital = Current assets − Current liabilities

CHAPTER REVIEW ACTIVITIES

SELF-TEST PROBLEMS

1. (Personal income taxes)
   a. For 1995, Bob and Carol each have a total income of $20,000. They got married in December 1995 and had a tax status of "married, filing jointly." They get two personal exemptions at $2500 each and take the standard deduction of $6550. What is their federal income tax liability? Use the personal tax rate schedule shown in table 3.6.
   b. For 1995, Ted and Alice each have a total income of $20,000. They do not get married in 1995 and each files a return as a "single" taxpayer. They get personal exemptions of $2500 and itemized deductions of $3900. How much federal income tax does Ted owe? Alice? Ted and Alice combined?
   c. Suppose that Bob and Carol receive an additional $500 of interest on a municipal bond. What is the impact of this on their tax obligation?
   d. Suppose that Bob and Carol receive an additional $1000 of long-term capital gains. What is the impact of the capital gain on their tax obligation?

2. (Corporate income taxes) Linn Oil Field Service Company has sales of $5,000,000, cost of goods sold of $2,000,000, selling and administrative costs of $500,000, and depreciation expense of $500,000. Linn also paid $25,000 of interest expense and received $400,000 of dividends from other corporations. Linn had a long-term capital loss of $200,000 and paid dividends of $250,000 to shareholders.
   a. What is Linn Oil Field Service Company's federal tax liability?
   b. What are the marginal and average tax rates for Linn?

SOLUTIONS TO SELF-TEST PROBLEMS

1. a. 1995 U.S. Individual Income Tax Return for Bob and Carol:

Total income	$40,000
minus: two	
exemptions	
2($2500)	−5,000
standard	
deduction	−6,550
Taxable income	$28,450

Tax = 0.15(28,450) = $4267.50

b. 1995 U.S. Individual Tax Return for Ted:

Total income	$20,000
minus: one	
exemption	−2,500
standard	
deduction	−3,900
Taxable income	$13,600

Tax = 0.15(13,600) = $2040.00

Alice's tax return is identical to Ted's. Ted and Alice's combined income tax is 2(2040) = $4080. Notice that Ted and Alice pay $187.50 less total income tax than Bob and Carol. This extra tax that Bob and Carol pay is often called the marriage penalty tax.

   c. Interest on a qualifying municipal security is not taxable by the federal government, so no additional tax is due.
   d. Long-term capital gains are usually taxed at the ordinary rate. In this case, the additional tax would be 0.15(1000) = $150. If Bob and Carol had been in a high-income bracket with a marginal rate above 28%, the capital gain would be taxed at the lower rate of 28%.

2. **a.** Linn's tax liability is:

Sales	$5,000,000
Less:	
Cost of goods sold	2,000,000
Selling and administrative costs	500,000
Depreciation	500,000
Interest expense	25,000
Taxable ordinary income	$1,975,000
Plus 30% of intercorporate dividends	
0.30(400,000)	120,000
Minus long-term capital loss	−200,000
Total taxable income	$1,895,000

(handwritten: ?)

The tax is computed on this taxable income using the tax rate schedule in table 3.5 on page 70.

Tax = 113,900 + 0.34(1,895,000 − 335,000)

Tax = 113,900 + 0.34(1,560,000)

Tax = 113,900 + 530,400 = $644,300

b. The marginal tax rate is 34%. The average tax rate is 644,300/1,895,000 = 34.00%. Linn is in an income range where the marginal and average rates are equal. Dividends paid by a corporation are not a tax-deductible expense.

QUESTIONS

1. Explain the purpose of each of the following financial statements: income statement, balance sheet, and statement of cash flows.
2. In a corporation's annual report, what do you think would be the order of presentation of the following items? Balance sheet, income statement, statement of cash flows, management's discussion, notes to the financial statements.
3. What is the balance sheet identity?
4. Assume that interest rates have increased substantially. Would this tend to increase or decrease the market value of a company's liabilities (relative to the book value of liabilities)?
5. Assume that inflation rates have been fairly high. Would this tend to increase or decrease the market value of a company's assets (relative to their book values)?
6. Describe the difference between economic income and accounting net income.

CHALLENGING QUESTIONS

7. What important feature of the corporate tax system tends to favor the use of debt financing over equity financing?
8. Why do you think each of the following features is part of the tax code applied to corporations?
   a. Progressive tax rates (low rates for low levels of corporate income).
   b. Intercorporate dividend exclusion.
   c. A tax on improper accumulations of income to avoid payment of personal taxes on dividends.
9. "For high-income individuals, capital gains are taxed at a lower rate than ordinary income. Additionally, the payment of a capital gains tax can be deferred by postponing the sale of an asset that has gone up in value." Do you agree with this opinion?
10. "Because interest on municipal bonds is not taxable, individuals should always buy municipal bonds instead of taxable corporate bonds." Is this advice sound? Do munis always have a higher after-tax yield? When do munis have a higher after-tax yield?

PROBLEM SET A

A1. (Balance sheet and income statement) Rimbey Sporting Goods has a weird accountant who reported the balance sheet and income statement items in alphabetical order. Please put these items in the correct format for a balance sheet and income statement for Rimbey Sporting Goods for the year ending January 31. All of the data are in thousands of dollars.

Accounts payable	$500	Cost of goods sold	3700
Accounts receivable	600	Depreciation	300
Addition to retained earnings	250	Dividends on common shares	150
Cash and equivalents	200	Earnings before interest and taxes	800
Common stock	100	Earnings before taxes	700

Gross profit	$2300	Sales	6000
Interest expense	100	Selling, general and	
Inventories	700	administrative expenses	1200
Long-term debt	1100	Taxes	300
Net income	400	Total assets	4000
Net plant and equipment	2500	Total current assets	1500
Notes payable	300	Total current liabilities	1300
Other current liabilities	500	Total liabilities and equity	4000
Retained earnings	1500	Total liabilities	2400

A2. (Statement of cash flows) Rimbey's accountant also presented all of the items in the statement of cash flows in alphabetical order. Please put these items in the correct format for a statement of cash flows for Rimbey Sporting Goods for the year ending January 31. All data are in thousands of dollars.

Accounts payable increase	$50	Net cash provided by (used in)	
Accounts receivable increase	(100)	financing activities	100
Cash dividends (common stock)	(100)	Net cash provided by (used in)	
Cash and equivalents at beginning		investing activities	(500)
of year	100	Net cash provided by (used in)	
Cash and equivalents at end of year	200	operating activities ·	500
Depreciation and amortization	300	Net income	400
Increase in other long-term liabilities	(50)	Net increase in cash and equivalents	100
Inventories increase	(150)	Notes payable increase	50
Issuance of long-term debt, net	200	Purchase of plant and equipment	(500)

A3. (Financial statements) For the year ended December 31, 1997, Dominion Resources, Inc. recorded the items listed below. Prepare an income statement for the year ended December 31, 1997 for Dominion Resources, Inc. Please use an appropriate format, such as the one in table 3.2.

Cost of goods sold	$485	Administrative expenses	125
Interest expense	20	Depreciation expense	100
Preferred dividends paid	5	Sales revenues	700
Common dividends paid	10	Taxes = 40% of taxable income	
Selling expenses	30		

A4. (Financial statements) Construct a balance sheet for Solomon Mines from the following data. Use a format similar to the balance sheet in table 3.1. What is stockholders' equity?

Cash	$100	Accounts payable	100
Inventory	200	Accrued expenses	50
Accounts receivable	200	Long-term debt	300
Fixed assets	400		

A5. (Financial statements) For 1998, Utah Ski Tours has a cash flow from operating activities of $700,000, a cash flow from investing activities of −$450,000, and a cash flow from financing activities of −$100,000. If Utah Ski Tours has a beginning cash balance for 1998 of $300,000, what is the company's ending cash balance?

A6. (Financial statements) Ivan Brick Company earned net income after taxes of $850,000 during 1998. Retained earnings on its balance sheet equaled $1,740,000 on December 31, 1997 and $2,040,000 on December 31, 1998. What cash dividends did Ivan Brick Company pay during 1998?

A7. (Corporate taxes) The Boston Publishing Company has taxable income of $250,000.

a. What is its federal corporate tax liability?

b. What are its average and marginal tax rates?

c. If Boston had an additional $10,000 from interest income, what additional taxes would it owe?

d. If Boston had an additional $10,000 of dividend income (from other corporations), what additional taxes would it owe? Assume a 70% dividend exclusion rate.

A8. (Corporate taxes) Newbould Industries, Inc. has earnings before interest and taxes of $1,500,000. Newbould has interest expense of $300,000 and paid cash dividends of $200,000 to its common stockholders. Newbould received no dividends from other corporations. Its income tax rate is 35%.

a. What is Newbould's income tax liability?   b. What is Newbould's after-tax income?

A9. (Corporate taxes) The Welch Trading Corporation is in the 35% marginal tax bracket. What would be its after-tax yield from investing in each of the following securities?
  a. A Treasury bond paying 8.0% interest.
  b. A municipal bond paying 5.2% interest.
  c. Preferred stock paying a 5.81% dividend
yield. Don't forget the 70% intercorpo-rate dividend exclusion.

A10. (Personal taxes) Two of your friends are trying to decide between buying taxable bonds yielding 8.0% and municipal bonds yielding 6.0%. Gary is in the 20% marginal tax bracket, which includes the combined effect of federal and state personal income taxes. Anna is in the 40% marginal tax bracket.
  a. What are the after-tax yields of the two kinds of bonds for Gary?
  b. What are the after-tax yields of the two kinds of bonds for Anna?
  c. What marginal tax rate would cause both bonds to have the same after-tax yield?

(handwritten: 6%/8% subtract by 1)

PROBLEM SET B

B1. (Financial statements) Consider the financial information for Spartan Video given below.
  a. What is stockholders' equity in 1997 and 1998?
  b. Assume a tax rate of 40%. What are income taxes paid and net income after taxes for 1998?
  c. The company did not issue or repurchase any stock during 1998. What dividend was paid?
  d. Given the change in net fixed assets and depreciation expense, what is the amount
  of fixed assets purchased during 1998?
  e. What is net working capital in 1997 and 1998?
  f. What is cash provided (used) by operations during 1998 (the increase in working capital is a use of cash)? What is cash provided (used) by investing activities? What is cash provided (used) by financing activities?

Balance Sheet, December 31
(Figures in millions of dollars)

ASSETS	1998	1997	LIABILITIES & STOCKHOLDERS' EQUITY	1998	1997
Current assets	$200	$150	Current liabilities	$100	$ 80
Net fixed assets	500	400	Long-term debt	300	300

Partial Income Statement, year ending December 31, 1998
(Figures in millions of dollars)

Sales	$1000
Cost of goods sold	300
Selling and administrative expenses	100
Depreciation	60
Interest expense	40

B2. (Book and market values) Bill's Lanes, a Louisiana corporation that owns several bowling alleys, has the balance sheet given below. Assume that the market value of the current assets is equal to the book value and that the market value of the net fixed assets is three times the book value. The market value of current liabilities is equal to the book value and the market value of long-term debt is 90% of its book value.
  a. What is the market value of Bill's Lanes's assets?
  b. What is the market value of Bill's Lanes's liabilities?
  c. If the market value of equity is equal to the market value of assets minus the market value of liabilities, what is the market value of the equity in Bill's Lanes?

Bill's Lanes Corporation
Balance Sheet, December 31, 1997
(Figures in thousands of dollars)

ASSETS		LIABILITIES & STOCKHOLDERS' EQUITY	
Current assets	$1200	Current liabilities	$ 800
Net fixed assets	3000	Long-term debt	1000
Total	$4200	Stockholders' equity	2400
		Total	$4200

B3. (Book and market values) Consider the information given below about the Peachtree Construction Company. All data are in millions of dollars.

a. What is the book value of stockholders' equity at the end of 1997 and 1998?

b. What is the market value of stockholders' equity at the end of 1997 and 1998?

c. For the year ending December 31, 1998, net income was $150 million. If Peachtree paid its stockholders cash dividends of $75 million, what is the total economic income of the stockholders during this year?

	Book Value	Market Value
Assets, December 31, 1997	800	1400
Assets, December 31, 1998	900	1650
Liabilities, December 31, 1997	400	425
Liabilities, December 31, 1998	425	475

B4. (Corporate income taxes) Santiago's Chile Company has sales of $15,000,000, cost of goods sold of $6,000,000, selling and administrative costs of $2,500,000, and depreciation expense of $500,000. Santiago's also paid $200,000 of interest expense and received $150,000 of dividends from other corporations. Santiago's Chile had a long-term capital gain of $400,000 and paid dividends of $250,000 to shareholders. Use the federal income tax rates for 1997 that are given in table 3.5.

a. What is the federal income tax liability for Santiago's Chile Company?

b. What are the marginal and average tax rates for Santiago's?

B5. (Personal income taxes) Assume that you are a single taxpayer and have one personal exemption for $2500 and itemized deductions of $7500. Calculate your federal income tax liability for the three cases given below. What is your marginal income tax rate and your average income tax rate for each case? Use the personal tax rate schedule in table 3.6.

a. Your taxable income is $25,000.

b. Your taxable income is $75,000.

c. Your taxable income is $125,000.

PROBLEM SET C

C1. (Accounting versus economic income) During 1997, McGowan Construction earned net income of $250,000. The company neither bought nor sold any capital assets, and the book value of its assets declined by the year's depreciation charge, which was $200,000. The company's operating cash flow for the year was $450,000, and the market value of its assets increased by $300,000. What was McGowan Construction's economic income for the year? Why is this figure different from its accounting net income?

C2. (Personal taxes and realized return) Ed Lawrence invests $100,000, buying 2000 shares of Yolo Freight for $50 per share. After one year, he receives a cash dividend of $1.50 per share and sells the stock for $62.00 per share.

a. Assume no taxes. What is the ending value of Ed's investment (including the value of the stock and the cash dividend)? What is the realized return on his investment?

b. Assume that Ed pays taxes of 39.6% on dividends and 28% on capital gains. After taxes, what is the ending value of his portfolio? What is the after-tax realized return on his investment?

C3. (Personal income taxes) Reconsider Self-Test Problem 1. Assume that Bob and Carol and Ted and Alice now earn $40,000 each.

a. For 1995, Bob and Carol each have total income of $40,000. They got married in December 1995 and had a tax status of "married, filing jointly." They get two personal exemptions at $2500 each and take the standard deduction of $6550. What is their federal income tax liabil-

ity? Use the personal tax rate schedule shown in table 3.6.

b. For 1995, Ted and Alice each have a total income of $40,000. They do not get married in 1995 and each files a return as a "single" taxpayer. They get personal exemptions of $2500 and itemized deductions of $3900. How much federal income tax does Ted owe? Alice? Ted and Alice combined?

c. Based on your answer to parts a. and b., what is the marriage penalty for Bob and Carol?

d. Get a copy of the latest federal income tax forms. There will be new personal exemptions, standard deductions, and a revised tax rate schedule. Recalculate the tax liabilities for Bob and Carol and Ted and Alice. Does the marriage penalty still exist?

BIBLIOGRAPHY

AICPA. "The Meaning of Presenting Fairly in Conformity with Generally Accepted Accounting Principles in the Independent Auditor's Report," *Statement on Auditing Standards.* New York: AICPA, 1992.

Amihud, Yakov, and Haim Mendelson. "Liquidity and Asset Prices: Financial Management Implications," *Financial Management,* 1988, 17(1):5–15.

Badrinath, S. G., and Wilbur G. Lewellen. "Evidence on Tax-Motivated Securities Trading Behavior," *Journal of Finance,* 1991, 46(1):369–382.

Ben-Horim, Moshe, Shalom Hochman, and Oded Palmon. "The Impact of the 1986 Tax Reform Act on Corporate Financial Policy," *Financial Management,* 1987, 16(3):29–35.

Brick, Ivan E., and William K. H. Fung. "The Effect of Taxes on the Trade Credit Decision," *Financial Management,* 1984, 13(2):24–30.

Brick, Ivan E., William Fung, and Marti Subrahmanyam. "Leasing and Financial Intermediation: Comparative Tax Advantages," *Financial Management,* 1987, 16(1):55–59.

Dammon, Robert M., and Lemma W. Senbet. "The Effect of Taxes and Depreciation on Corporate Investment and Financial Leverage," *Journal of Finance,* 1988, 43(2):357–373.

Davis, Alfred H. R. "Effective Tax Rates as Determinants of Canadian Capital Structure," *Financial Management,* 1987, 16(3):22–28.

Ferri, Michael G., Steven J. Goldstein, and It-Keong Chew. "Interest Rates and the Announcement of Inflation," *Financial Management,* 1983, 12(3):52–61.

Gombola, Michael J., Mark E. Haskins, J. Edward Ketz, and David D. Williams. "Cash Flow in Bankruptcy Prediction," *Financial Management,* 1987, 16(4):55–65.

Gordon, Roger H. "Can Capital Income Taxes Survive in Open Economies?," *Journal of Finance,* 1992, 47(3):1159–1180.

Green, Richard C., and Eli Talmor. "The Structure and Incentive Effects of Corporate Tax Liabilities," *Journal of Finance,* 1985, 40(4):1095–1114.

Griffiths, Mark D., and Robert W. White. "Tax-Induced Trading and the Turn-of-the-Year Anomaly: An Intraday Study," *Journal of Finance,* 1993, 48(2):575–598.

Haugen, Robert A., and Lemma W. Senbet. "Corporate Finance and Taxes: A Review," *Financial Management,* 1986, 15(3):5–21.

Hochman, Shalom J., Oded Palmon, and Alex P. Tang. "Tax-Induced Intra-Year Patterns in Bonds Yields," *Journal of Finance,* 1993, 48(1):331–344.

Jaffe, Jeffrey F. "Taxes and the Capital Structure of Partnerships, REIT's, and Related Entities," *Journal of Finance,* 1991, 46(1):401–408.

Kroll, Yoram. "On the Differences Between Accrual Accounting Figures and Cash Flows: The Case of Working Capital," *Financial Management,* 1985, 14(1):75–82.

Lewis, Craig M. "A Multiperiod Theory of Corporate Financial Policy Under Taxation," *Journal of Financial and Quantitative Analysis,* 1990, 25(1):25–44.

MacKie-Mason, Jeffrey K. "Do Taxes Affect Corporate Financing Decisions?" *Journal of Finance,* 1990, 45(5):1471–1494.

Maloney, Kevin J., and Thomas I. Selling. "Simplifying Tax Simplification: An Analysis of Its Impact on the Profitability of Capital Investment," *Financial Management,* 1985, 14(2):33–42.

Manzon, Gil B., Jr., David J. Sharp, and Nickolaos G. Travlos. "An Empirical Study of the Consequences of U.S. Tax Rules for International Acquisitions by U.S. Firms," *Journal of Finance,* 1994, 49(5):1893–1904.

Mauer, David C., and Wilbur G. Lewellen. "Securityholder Taxes and Corporate Restructurings," *Journal of Financial and Quantitative Analysis,* 1990, 25(3):341–360.

Newbould, Gerald D., Robert E. Chatfield, and Ronald F. Anderson. "Leveraged Buyouts and Tax Incentives," *Financial Management,* 1992, 21(1):50–57.

Papaioannou, George J., and Craig M. Savarese. "Corporate Dividend Policy Response to the Tax Reform Act of 1986," *Financial Management,* 1994, 23(1):56–63.

Pilotte, Eugene. "The Economic Recovery Tax Act of 1981 and Corporate Capital Structure," *Financial Management,* 1990, 19(4):98–107.

Robin, Ashok J. "The Impact of the 1986 Tax Reform Act on Ex-Dividend Day Returns," *Financial Management,* 1991, 20(1):60–70.

Servaes, Henri, and Marc Zenner. "Taxes and the Returns to Foreign Acquisitions in the United States," *Financial Management,* 1994, 23(4):42–56.

Talmor, Eli, and Sheridan Titman. "Taxes and Dividend Policy," *Financial Management,* 1990, 19(2):32–35.

FINANCIAL STATEMENT ANALYSIS

OBJECTIVES

1. Calculate and explain a variety of financial ratios—liquidity, asset turnover, leverage, coverage, profitability, and market value ratios.

2. Calculate and explain common-size and common-base-year financial statements.

3. Use the DuPont equation to show how operating efficiency, profit margins, and financial leverage determine a company's return on equity.

4. Interpret financial information carefully by knowing the strengths and weaknesses of financial statement analysis.

In chapter 3, we detailed certain limitations and problems in connection with accounting information. In spite of these limitations, a company's published financial statements can reveal a great deal about the business to a trained financial analyst.   Such information can guide managers, investors, and other stakeholders as they assess a company's prospects and plans.

In this chapter we present the basic tools of financial statement analysis. Financial analysts and managers find it helpful to calculate *financial ratios* when interpreting a company's accounting statements. A financial ratio is simply one quantity divided by another. Financial ratios compare key financial elements in order to judge such characteristics as liquidity, asset activity, leverage, and profitability. *Common-size statements* are used to compare performance between companies, or to track a company as it changes in size. *DuPont Analysis* helps us examine the components of the investor's return on equity.

Financial statement analysis can be useful in at least two ways. First, it can help structure your thinking about business decisions. Second, it can provide some information that is helpful in making those decisions.

We'll illustrate the techniques of financial statement analysis using Anheuser-Busch Companies, Inc. as an example throughout this chapter. As you apply these techniques, you can better draw inferences about companies from readily available reports.

FINANCIAL STATEMENT ANALYSIS AND THE PRINCIPLES OF FINANCE

◆ *Two-Sided Transactions:* Keep in mind that each transaction has at least two sides, and the company is the result of thousands or millions of transactions. Financial statements are an attempt to grasp the totality of these transactions.

◆ *Risk-Return Trade-Off:* Use financial statement analysis to help measure the risks in the loans, investments, and other business decisions.

◆ *Capital Market Efficiency:* Recognize that publicly available information, such as that in a company's financial statements, is reflected in the price of a company's common stock.

◆ *The Behavioral Principle:* Develop your knowledge and understanding of financial statements to help you better use this principle.

◆ *Signaling:* Recognize that financial statements provide information for all of the company's stakeholders, not just investors.

THE USE OF FINANCIAL STATEMENT ANALYSIS

Let's begin by having you use your interpretive abilities on the five proportional balance sheets shown in table 4.1 on page 84. They give the percentage breakdown of accounts on the balance sheets of Merck & Co. (an ethical drug company headquartered in New Jersey), FPL

Group (the parent for Florida Power and Light, an electric utility headquartered in Miami), BankAmerica Corporation (commercial bank based in San Francisco), J. C. Penney Company (retail department store chain based in Dallas), and Dow Chemical Company (a chemical company based in Michigan). As you can see, the table doesn't indicate which corporation goes with each set of financial statement information. That's your assignment: determine which balance sheet, A through E, goes with which company.

Incidentally, since bank financial statements are different from those of nonfinancial businesses, we altered BankAmerica's statement slightly. We classified the bank's loans as accounts receivable and we classified its deposit liabilities as accounts payable.

How did you do?

Company A is BankAmerica. This company has a large investment in bank loans (accounts receivable) and owes a lot of accounts payable (deposit liabilities). Compared to the other companies, BankAmerica has a large investment in cash and marketable securities and very little invested in inventories or in fixed assets. This bank, like other banks, has very little stockholders' equity compared to nonfinancial businesses. Banks rely very heavily on debt financing.

Company B is FPL Group, the electric company. This is apparent because of the large investment in long-term assets, the generating and transmission facilities that electric companies must have. FPL Group has very low receivables and inventory, too. Because they provide an essential service and have a degree of monopoly power in their service areas, public utilities have been fairly low-risk companies. This has allowed them to use debt financing very heavily. You can see that FPL Group has fairly high long-term debt and modestly low shareholders' equity.

Company C is J. C. Penney. The giveaway is that, as a retailer, J. C. Penney should have much more invested in receivables and in inventory than the other companies.

This leaves Companies D and E, and Merck and Dow. If you don't know which is which, here's a clue. Merck is in a riskier business than Dow. Drug companies risk a

TABLE 4.1

Selected Balance Sheet Information for Five Companies

	COMPANY				
	A	**B**	**C**	**D**	**E**
ASSETS					
Cash and marketable securities	32.0%	3.2%	2.3%	10.1%	5.1%
Receivables	65.7	3.9	31.6	10.5	15.0
Inventories	0.3	2.5	24.0	8.2	9.9
Fixed assets	2.0	90.4	42.1	71.2	70.0
Total assets	100.0%	100.0%	100.0%	100.0%	100.0%
LIABILITIES & STOCKHOLDERS' EQUITY					
Accounts payable	75.8%	2.5%	7.0%	11.9%	5.8%
Other short-term debt	7.4	11.6	19.3	17.7	16.4
Long-term debt	7.6	51.1	37.4	20.1	46.3
Stockholders' equity	9.2	34.8	36.3	50.3	31.5
Total liabilities and stockholders' equity	100.0%	100.0%	100.0%	100.0%	100.0%

Which balance sheet belongs to each of the following companies?
BankAmerica Corporation (commercial bank)
J. C. Penney Company (retail department store)
FPL Group (electric utility)
Merck & Co. (ethical drug supplier)
Dow Chemical Company (chemical company)

tremendous amount on the success of new drugs they develop and introduce. If its new drugs are unsuccessful or are delayed, a drug company can be in serious jeopardy. Consequently, drug companies employ two important risk management strategies that are apparent in table 4.1. First, drug companies maintain relatively large cash balances. Such a balance would allow them to operate for a long time in the face of revenue shortfalls. Second, drug companies try to minimize the fixed-interest obligations associated with debt financing. As you can see, Company D holds much more cash and equivalents than Company E. Company D also uses much less long-term debt financing and has a much greater stockholders' equity than Company E. In fact, Company D is Merck and Company E is Dow.

As the Behavioral Principle predicts, obvious differences among companies in different industries can emerge from a careful reading of their financial statements. More detailed financial statement analysis, however, can be a costly exercise. Therefore, you should not undertake this work unless you expect its benefits to outweigh its costs. This leads to the questions of *who* uses financial statement analysis, *why* do they use it, and *how* do they use it? Some answers include:

1. *Equity investors.* Investors use financial statement analysis to help them decide whether to buy, sell, or hold particular common stocks.

2. *Creditors.* Long-term lenders use financial statement analysis to decide which bonds to invest in. Short-term lenders use this information when deciding to make short-term loans or to purchase money market instruments.

3. *Management.* Managers use financial analysis to help make decisions about resource allocation or about mergers and acquisitions. Financial statement analysis is also used to evaluate and reward the performance of various managers. As a manager, your raises, your promotions, and even your termination can depend on meeting certain financial targets.

4. *Other professionals.* Auditors use financial statement analysis to supplement some of their audit procedures. The Internal Revenue Service reviews the structure of financial statements to help determine the reasonableness of tax reports. Government and regulatory agencies use it to monitor and regulate companies in many industries. Labor unions carefully review the financial health of employers when they engage in collective bargaining. Marketing managers use this information to enhance the marketing of their companies' goods and services. Customers are very concerned about the financial health of their suppliers whenever they have concerns about product quality or whenever they need a long-term dependable supplier.

5. *Students.* Job seekers use financial information both to learn as much as possible about prospective employers and to help them display their knowledge and talents to recruiters. Students often conduct financial statement analysis to help them avoid an economic phenomenon commonly known as unemployment!

COMMON-SIZE FINANCIAL STATEMENTS

A company's financial statements, such as the income statement and balance sheet for Anheuser-Busch contained in tables 4.2 and 4.3 on pages 86 and 87, can be difficult to interpret at first glance. Fortunately, such statements can be manipulated to make them more "user friendly" and more amenable to careful analysis. A common analytical procedure is the creation of **common-size statements.** These modified statements are simply standardized versions of the company's balance sheets and income statements. The items are expressed as percentages instead of in dollars. Common-size statements can be extremely helpful to highlight changes over time in the financial performance and financial condition of the company.

COMMON-SIZE STATEMENTS Financial statements that show components as percentages instead of dollars. Balance sheet components are expressed as percentages of assets, and income statement components are expressed as percentages of sales.

TABLE 4.2

Anheuser-Busch Companies, Inc. Annual Income Statement ($ millions, except per share amounts) Year Ended December 31

	1993	1992	1991
Sales	$ 11,505	$ 11,394	$ 10,996
Cost of goods sold	6,811	6,742	6,614
Gross profit	4,694	4,652	4,382
Selling, general, & administrative expenses	2,309	2,309	2,126
Depreciation, depletion, & amortization	608	567	534
Operating profit	1,777	1,776	1,722
Interest expense	(208)	(200)	(239)
Capitalized interest	37	48	47
Nonoperating profit (loss)	(556)	(9)	(9)
Earnings before tax	1,050	1,615	1,521
Total income tax	456	621	581
Net income	594	994	940
Preferred dividends	0	0	0
Available for common	$ 594	$ 994	$ 940
Earnings per share	$2.17	$3.48	$3.26
Dividends per share	$1.36	$1.20	$1.06
Shares outstanding (000)	273,963	285,690	288,282

Common-Size Income Statements and Balance Sheets

Common-size statements provide a percentage breakdown of the income statement and balance sheet. In the common-size income statement, each item is expressed as a percentage of sales. In the common-size balance sheet, each asset, liability, or equity item is expressed as a percentage of total assets. Standardizing the income statement and balance sheet by making them sum to 100% can make it much simpler to spot changes or trends in the statements.

Table 4.4 contains the common-size balance sheets for Anheuser-Busch for 1991, 1992, and 1993. Table 4.5 on page 88 contains the common-size balance sheets for Anheuser-Busch for the years ending December 31, 1991, 1992, and 1993. As you can see, the format of the common-size financial statements is the same as the income statement and balance sheet in tables 4.2 and 4.3. Expressing items as a percentage of sales or of assets gives the reader a feel for the relative sizes of the various items. This feel is harder to achieve when looking at the dollar amounts in the original statements.

Common-size statements are especially helpful when looking at the financial statements of several companies. The balance sheets for the five companies in table 4.1 are common-sized, which makes comparisons easier. Because the sizes of the companies will differ, common-size statements allow you to focus on the relative structures of the financial statements. You can spot structural differences between companies very easily with common-size statements.

Common-size statements are also used to track changes in a given company's financial statements over time. You can see very quickly which items have increased or decreased as a percentage of sales or assets. Because common-size statements are easy to create and because they are easy to interpret, these statements are popular.

TABLE 4.3

Anheuser-Busch Companies, Inc. Annual Balance Sheet ($ millions) December 31

	1993	1992	1991
ASSETS			
Cash and equivalents	$ 127.4	$ 215.0	$ 97.3
Accounts receivable	751.1	649.8	654.8
Inventories	626.7	660.7	635.6
Other current assets	290.0	290.3	240.0
Total current assets	$ 1,795.2	$ 1,815.8	$ 1,627.7
Gross fixed assets	11,727.1	11,385.1	10,589.6
Accumulated depreciation	(4,230.0)	(3,861.4)	(3,393.1)
Net fixed assets	7,497.1	7,523.7	7,196.5
Other assets	1,588.0	1,198.4	1,162.3
Total assets	$10,880.3	$10,537.9	$ 9,986.5
LIABILITIES & STOCKHOLDERS' EQUITY			
Accounts payable	$ 812.5	$ 737.4	$ 709.8
Taxes payable	91.0	38.8	45.2
Accrued expenses	609.7	426.7	392.7
Other current liabilities	302.4	256.9	255.1
Total current liabilities	$ 1,815.6	$ 1,459.8	$ 1,402.8
Long-term debt	3,031.7	2,642.5	2,644.9
Deferred taxes	1,170.4	1,276.9	1,500.7
Other liabilities	607.1	538.3	0.0
Total liabilities	$ 6,624.8	$ 5,917.5	$ 5,548.4
Preferred stock	$ 0.0	$ 0.0	$ 0.0
Common stock	342.5	341.3	338.5
Capital surplus	402.2	328.5	193.3
Retained earnings	5,990.4	5,793.5	5,230.5
Less: Treasury stock	(2,479.6)	(1,842.9)	(1,324.2)
Total common equity	$ 4,255.5	$ 4,620.4	$ 4,438.1
Total liabilities & stockholders' equity	$10,880.3	$10,537.9	$ 9,986.5

TABLE 4.4

Anheuser-Busch Companies, Inc. Common-Size Income Statement (Percentage) Year Ended December 31

	1993	1992	1991
Sales	100.00%	100.00%	100.00%
Cost of goods sold	59.20	59.17	60.15
Gross profit	40.80	40.83	39.85
Selling, general, & administrative expenses	20.07	20.27	19.33
Depreciation, depletion, & amortization	5.28	4.98	4.86
Operating profit	15.45	15.59	15.66
Interest expense	(1.81)	(1.76)	(2.17)
Capitalized interest	0.32	0.42	0.43
Nonoperating profit (loss)	(4.83)	(0.08)	(0.09)
Earnings before tax	9.13	14.17	13.83
Total income tax	3.96	5.45	5.28
Net income	5.16	8.72	8.55
Preferred dividends	0.00	0.00	0.00
Available for common	5.16%	8.72%	8.55%

The common-size income statement is created by dividing each item on the company's income statement by total sales.

TABLE 4.5

Anheuser-Busch Companies, Inc. Common-Size Balance Sheet (Percentage) December 31

	1993	1992	1991
ASSETS			
Cash and equivalents	1.17%	2.04%	0.97%
Accounts receivable	6.90	6.17	6.57
Inventories	5.76	6.27	6.36
Other current assets	2.67	2.75	2.40
Total current assets	16.50%	17.23%	16.30%
Gross fixed assets	107.78	108.04	106.04
Accumulated depreciation	38.88	36.64	33.98
Net fixed assets	68.90	71.40	72.06
Other assets	14.60	11.37	11.64
Total assets	100.00%	100.00%	100.00%
LIABILITIES & STOCKHOLDERS' EQUITY			
Accounts payable	7.47%	7.00%	7.12%
Taxes payable	0.84	0.37	0.45
Accrued expenses	5.60	4.04	3.93
Other current liabilities	2.78	2.44	2.55
Total current liabilities	16.69%	13.85%	14.05%
Long-term debt	27.86	25.07	26.48
Deferred taxes	10.76	12.12	15.03
Other liabilities	5.58	5.11	0.00
Total liabilities	60.89%	56.15%	55.56%
Preferred stock	0.00%	0.00%	0.00%
Common stock	3.15	3.24	3.39
Capital surplus	3.70	3.12	1.94
Retained earnings	55.06	54.98	52.38
Less: Treasury stock	(22.79)	(17.49)	(13.26)
Total common equity	39.11%	43.85%	44.44%
Total liabilities & stockholders' equity	100.00%	100.00%	100.00%

A common-size balance sheet is created by dividing each item on the company's balance sheet by its total assets.

Read Common-Base-Year Financial Statements

Another device that analysts use to track changes in a company's financial structure is common-base-year statements. In these statements, a common base year is selected, such as five years ago. Then for each year after the base year, every income statement and balance sheet item is expressed as a percentage of its base-year value. For example, if any item, such as cash, increases from its base-year level, that item is expressed as a number exceeding 100%, and if the item decreases, it is expressed as some number less than 100%. It is easy to see which items are growing faster or slower than others in these common-base-year statements.

Self-Check

1. Why do analysts create common-size statements?

2. Explain the differences in common-size statements and common-base-year statements.

FINANCIAL RATIOS

Financial analysts and managers find it helpful to calculate financial ratios when interpreting a company's financial statements. A **financial ratio** is simply one quantity divided by another. You'll find almost any decision that uses accounting information relies on financial ratios that focus on specific aspects of the company. The number of financial ratios that might be created is virtually limitless, but there are certain basic ratios that are frequently used. These ratios can be placed into six classes: *liquidity ratios, asset turnover ratios, leverage ratios, coverage ratios, profitability ratios,* and *market value ratios.* We illustrate and discuss the calculation and interpretation of these six classes of ratios below. All our illustrations are based on tables 4.2 and 4.3, and other information about Anheuser-Busch. Calculations are for 1992, if not otherwise noted.

FINANCIAL RATIO The result of dividing one financial statement item by another. Ratios help analysts interpret financial statements by focusing on specific relationships.

Liquidity Ratios

Recall that *liquidity* refers to how quickly and efficiently (in the sense of low transaction costs) an asset can be exchanged for cash. **Liquidity ratios** provide a measure of the company's liquidity, that is, its ability to meet its financial obligations on time. Four widely used liquidity ratios are the current ratio, quick ratio, working capital ratio, and the cash ratio.

LIQUIDITY RATIOS Ratios that measure a company's ability to meet its short-term financial obligations on time.

The most commonly used measure of overall liquidity is the **current ratio:**

$$\text{Current ratio} = \frac{\text{Current assets}}{\text{Current liabilities}} = \frac{1816}{1460} = 1.24x \qquad (4.1)$$

CURRENT RATIO A liquidity ratio that measures the number of times a company's current assets cover its current liabilities.

The current ratio measures the number of times the company's current assets cover its current liabilities. The higher the current ratio, the greater the company's ability to meet its short-term obligations as they come due. A widely held but conservative rule of thumb holds that a current ratio of 2.0 is an appropriate target for most companies. In fact, the average current ratio for companies included in the S&P 500 is about 1.5.

Inventories are considered current assets, so they are included in the current ratio calculation. Inventories, however, are less liquid than marketable securities and accounts receivable. This is because it is normally more difficult to turn inventory into cash on short notice. Thus analysts often exclude inventories from the numerator in the current ratio and calculate the **quick ratio** (also called the **acid test ratio**).

$$\text{Quick (Acid test) ratio} = \frac{\text{Current assets} - \text{Inventories}}{\text{Current liabilities}} = \frac{1816 - 661}{1460} = 0.79x \qquad (4.2)$$

QUICK (ACID TEST) RATIO A liquidity ratio that measures the number of times a company can cover its current liabilities using its current assets (but not including its inventories, which are less liquid).

Another widely held but rough rule of thumb holds that a quick ratio of at least 1.0 is desirable. The average S&P 500 company has a quick ratio of about 0.9.

Net working capital (or, simply, *working capital*) is the difference between current assets and current liabilities. The **working capital ratio** is simply net working capital expressed as a proportion of sales:

$$\text{Working capital ratio} = \frac{\text{Current assets} - \text{Current liabilities}}{\text{Sales}} = \frac{1816 - 1460}{11,394} = 3.1\% \qquad (4.3)$$

WORKING CAPITAL RATIO Net working capital expressed as a proportion of sales.

Net working capital is often considered a measure of liquidity. This ratio shows the amount of liquidity relative to sales.

The **cash ratio** is calculated by dividing cash and equivalents by total assets:

$$\text{Cash ratio} = \frac{\text{Cash and equivalents}}{\text{Total assets}} = \frac{215}{10,538} = 2.0\% \qquad (4.4)$$

CASH RATIO The proportion of a company's assets held as cash.

Cash and equivalents (which include marketable securities) is the most liquid asset. The cash ratio simply shows the proportion of its assets that the company is holding in the most liquid possible form.

Comparing Liquidity Ratios

Ratios for other companies in the same industry and time period are often compared to judge a company's relative strengths and weaknesses. For example, we can compare Anheuser-Busch's ratios to average ratios for the other large companies in the alcoholic beverages industry.[1]

	Anheuser-Busch	Other Alcoholic Beverage Companies
Current ratio	1.24x	2.12x
Quick ratio	0.79x	0.90x
Working capital ratio	3.1%	24.0%
Cash ratio	2.0%	3.0%

Anheuser-Busch has lower liquidity ratios than the other alcoholic beverage companies. Nevertheless, Anheuser-Busch is a healthy company; nobody expects it to have trouble meeting its obligations as they come due. Its health allows it to carry much greater current liabilities, and it simply doesn't need as much liquidity as the rules of thumb prescribe, a current ratio of 2.0 and a quick ratio of 1.0. Note that the other alcoholic beverage companies have current and quick ratios that are very close to 2.0 and 1.0, respectively. ■

Asset Turnover Ratios

Asset turnover ratios are designed to measure how effectively a company manages its assets. A business faces fundamental decisions about how much to invest in assets such as receivables, inventories, and fixed assets, and then it has the responsibility of using these assets effectively. Several ratios have evolved that focus on the management of specific assets as well as total assets.

The **receivables turnover ratio** is:

$$\text{Receivables turnover} = \frac{\text{Annual credit sales}}{\text{Accounts receivable}} = \frac{11,394}{650} = 17.53x \qquad (4.5)$$

It measures the number of times the accounts receivable balance "turns over" during the year. Note that annual credit sales, which give rise to receivables, are used in the numerator. If a figure for annual credit sales is not available, the company's net sales figure is used instead. Making that substitution is like assuming all sales were credit sales.

A closely related figure is the **days' sales outstanding (DSO).** It is the number of days in a year divided by the receivables turnover ratio.[2]

$$\text{Days' sales outstanding} = \frac{365}{\text{Receivables turnover}} = \frac{\text{Accounts receivable}}{\text{Annual credit sales}/365} = \frac{365}{17.53} = 20.8 \text{ days} \quad (4.6)$$

The days' sales outstanding shows approximately how many days on average it takes to collect the company's accounts receivable. The days' sales outstanding is also called the **average collection period.**

A more detailed picture of the company's accounts receivable can be obtained by preparing an **aging schedule** for accounts receivable. An aging schedule shows the amounts of receivables that have been outstanding for different periods, such as 0 to 30

RECEIVABLES TURNOVER RATIO The number of times receivables turn over in a year, measured as the total annual credit sales divided by the current accounts receivable balance.

DAYS' SALES OUTSTANDING (DSO) Also called **average collection period,** the approximate number of days required to collect a company's accounts receivable.

AGING SCHEDULE A table of accounts receivable broken down into age categories (such as 0–30 days, 30–60 days, and 60–90 days) to see if customer payments are keeping close to schedule.

---

[1]Brown-Forman Corporation, Canandaigua Wine Co., Adolph Coors Company, The Molson Companies Ltd., and Seagram Co. are the others followed by *The Value Line Investment Survey.* The enormous difference between the working capital ratios for Anheuser-Busch and the other alcoholic beverage companies may look odd. You will find in a moment that Anheuser-Busch also has relatively high receivables and inventory turnover ratios.

[2]Before calculators and computers were widely used, analysts often used a 360-day year for simplicity. Although much of the financial press has continued this practice so far, it is becoming less popular. We will always use a 365-day year.

days, 30 to 60 days, 60 to 90 days, and more than 90 days. An example of an accounts receivable aging schedule is given in table 4.6. An external analyst typically lacks the detailed information in an aging schedule unless the company has chosen to provide it. Of course, managers within the company want this information to help monitor the quality of their accounts receivable.

A measure of the effectiveness of inventory management is the **inventory turnover ratio,** which is calculated as follows:

$$\text{Inventory turnover} = \frac{\text{Cost of goods sold}}{\text{Inventory}} = \frac{6742}{661} = 10.20x \qquad (4.7)$$

INVENTORY TURNOVER RATIO An asset turnover ratio that shows how many times inventory turns over in a year.

Inventory turnover is a good estimate of how many times per year the inventory is physically turning over. In the past, some analysts calculated the inventory turnover by dividing net sales by inventory. However, this calculation overstates the turnover rate of physical inventory.[3]

Another way to measure inventory turnover is the **days' sales in inventory ratio.** This is the time for "one turnover." For example, if inventory turnover were 12.0x, one turnover would be 1/12 of a year, which in days is 30.42 (= 365/12). For Anheuser-Busch, it is

$$\text{Days' sales in inventory} = \frac{365}{\text{Inventory turnover}} = \frac{\text{Inventory}}{\text{Cost of goods sold}/365} = \frac{365}{10.20} = 35.8 \text{ days} \qquad (4.8)$$

DAYS' SALES IN INVENTORY RATIO The average number of days' worth of sales that is held in inventory.

The day's sales in inventory ratio estimates the average time inventory stays with the company before it's sold.

Finally, two more ratios show how productively the company is using its assets. They are the **fixed asset turnover ratio** and the **total asset turnover ratio.**

$$\text{Fixed asset turnover} = \frac{\text{Sales}}{\text{Net fixed assets}} = \frac{11,394}{7524} = 1.51x \qquad (4.9)$$

FIXED ASSET TURNOVER RATIO The ratio of sales to fixed assets.

$$\text{Total asset turnover} = \frac{\text{Sales}}{\text{Total assets}} = \frac{11,394}{10,538} = 1.08x \qquad (4.10)$$

TOTAL ASSET TURNOVER RATIO The ratio of sales to total assets.

These two ratios show the sales volume generated per book-value dollar of fixed assets and total assets, respectively. Because total assets is never smaller than fixed assets, the total asset turnover is virtually always smaller than the fixed asset turnover.

TABLE 4.6

Accounts Receivable Aging Schedule

AGE IN DAYS	ACCOUNTS RECEIVABLE ($)	ACCOUNTS RECEIVABLE (%)
0–30	$1500	50.0%
30–60	900	30.0
60–90	450	15.0
90+	150	5.0
Total	$3000	100.0%

[3]An example illustrates the problem: 60 units of the company's product were sold last year; sales were $600; cost of goods sold on these units was $360; and inventory was $120 with 20 units in it. Dividing *sales* by inventory, 600/120 = 5.0x. Dividing *cost of goods sold* by inventory, 360/120 = 3.0x. From knowing the number of units, we can see that the physical turnover rate is in fact 60/20 = 3.0x. The turnover rate of 5.0x is larger than the physical turnover rate, because sales are on a different basis; sales include profit. Cost of goods sold does not include profit. Cost of goods sold is on the same cost basis as inventory.

EXAMPLE

Comparing Asset Turnover Ratios

We can again compare Anheuser-Busch's ratios to those of the other alcoholic beverage companies.

	Anheuser-Busch	Other Alcoholic Beverage Companies
Receivables turnover	17.53x	8.11x
Days' sales outstanding	20.8 days	50.9 days
Inventory turnover	10.20x	2.89x
Days' sales in inventory	35.8 days	189.2 days
Fixed asset turnover	1.51x	3.84x
Total asset turnover	1.08x	1.01x

Anheuser-Busch turns over its receivables and inventory more rapidly than the other companies.[4] Anheuser-Busch's fixed assets turn over more slowly. This implies that Anheuser-Busch requires a larger investment in fixed assets (relative to sales) than these other companies. ■

Leverage Ratios

Financial leverage is the extent to which a company is financed with debt. The amount of debt a company uses has both positive and negative effects. The more debt, the more likely it is that the company will have trouble meeting its obligations. Thus the more debt, the higher the probability of financial distress and even bankruptcy. Furthermore, the chance of financial distress, and debt obligations generally, may create conflicts of interest among the stakeholders.

Despite this, debt is a major source of financing. It provides a significant tax advantage, because interest is tax-deductible, as we noted in this chapter. Debt also has lower transaction costs and is generally easier to obtain. Finally, debt affects how the company's stakeholders bear the risk of the company. One particular effect is that debt makes the stock riskier because of the increased chance of financial distress. These factors are discussed at length later in the book. At this point, suffice it to say that leverage is very important, and **leverage ratios** measure the amount of (financial) leverage.

Three common leverage ratios are the debt ratio, the debt/equity ratio, and the equity multiplier. The **debt ratio** is the proportion of debt financing.

$$\text{Debt ratio} = \frac{\text{Total debt}}{\text{Total assets}} = \frac{10{,}538 - 4620}{10{,}538} = \frac{5918}{10{,}538} = 0.56x \qquad (4.11)$$

The debt/equity ratio is a simple rearrangement of the debt ratio and expresses the same information on a different scale. Whereas the debt ratio can be as small as zero but, assuming positive equity, is always less than 1.0, the debt/equity ratio ranges from zero to infinity. The **debt/equity ratio** is

$$\text{Debt/equity ratio} = \frac{\text{Total debt}}{\text{Stockholders' equity}} = \frac{5918}{4620} = 1.28x \qquad (4.12)$$

The equity multiplier is yet another representation of the same information. It shows how much total assets the company has for each dollar of equity. The **equity multiplier** is

$$\text{Equity multiplier} = \frac{\text{Total assets}}{\text{Stockholders' equity}} = \frac{10{,}538}{4620} = 2.28x \qquad (4.13)$$

All three of these leverage ratios are widely used. As we have said, they are simply different representations of the same information. If you know any one of them, you can derive the other two. For example, suppose a company has a debt ratio of 0.40x, so it's 40% debt-financed. From this we know that the company is 60% equity-financed. Therefore, the company's debt/equity ratio is 40/60 = 0.67x. Because total assets are equal to 100% of the financing (the balance sheet identity, A = L + SE), the equity multiplier is 100/60 = 1.67. Generalizing, we have

FINANCIAL LEVERAGE The proportion of a company's assets that is financed by debt (as opposed to equity).

LEVERAGE RATIO A measure of a company's amount of financial leverage.

DEBT RATIO Total debt/Total assets, which is the fraction of the assets of the company that is financed by debt.

DEBT/EQUITY RATIO Total debt/Total common stockholders's equity, which is the amount of debt per dollar of equity.

EQUITY MULTIPLIER Total assets/Total common stockholders' equity, which is the amount of total assets per dollar of equity.

[4]We suggest you draw your own conclusions concerning the reasons for this rapid turnover in inventory.

$$\text{Debt/equity ratio} = \frac{\text{Debt ratio}}{1.0 - \text{Debt ratio}}$$

$$\text{Equity multiplier} = \text{Debt/equity ratio} + 1.0 = \frac{1.0}{1.0 - \text{Debt ratio}}$$

Because it doesn't make any difference which of the three measures is used, we use the debt ratio throughout this book for simplicity and consistency.

Comparing Leverage Ratios

EXAMPLE

Here we again compare Anheuser-Busch to the other alcoholic beverage companies.

	Anheuser-Busch	Other Alcoholic Beverage Companies
Debt ratio	0.56x	0.24x
Debt/equity ratio	1.28x	0.51x
Equity multiplier	2.28x	1.51x

The debt ratio shows that Anheuser-Busch is 56% debt-financed. The debt/equity ratio shows that the company has $1.28 in debt for each $1.00 of equity. The equity multiplier shows that the company has about $2.28 in total assets for each $1.00 of equity. The comparison shows that Anheuser-Busch has more leverage than the other companies. ∎

Coverage Ratios

Coverage ratios show the number of times a company can "cover" or meet a particular financial obligation. The **times-interest-earned ratio,** which is also called the **interest coverage ratio,** measures the number of times the income available to pay interest charges covers the company's interest expense. It is Earnings Before Interest and Income Taxes (EBIT) divided by the company's interest expense. For Anheuser-Busch, EBIT is 1767 (= operating profit (1776) plus nonoperating profit (−9)). So the times-interest-earned ratio is

$$\text{Times-interest-earned ratio} = \frac{\text{EBIT}}{\text{Interest expense}} = \frac{1767}{200} = 8.84x \qquad \textbf{(4.14)}$$

COVERAGE RATIOS Ratios that show the amount of funds available to cover a particular financial obligation compared to the size of that obligation.

TIMES-INTEREST-EARNED RATIO The ratio of EBIT to interest expense, also called the **interest coverage ratio.**

Many companies lease or rent assets that require contractual payments. Long-term leases are reported on the balance sheet, and the periodic lease payments are included in the company's interest expense. Rental agreements are different. They are not on the balance sheet. Renting an asset is an alternative to owning it. (Rental payments are therefore an alternative to the interest payments the company would make if it borrowed the money to buy the same assets). Rental expense is reported in the notes to the financial statements. For these companies, the **fixed-charge coverage ratio** is useful, where fixed charges consist of interest expense plus rental payments:[5]

$$\frac{\text{Fixed-charge}}{\text{coverage ratio}} = \frac{\text{EBIT} + \text{Rental payments}}{\text{Interest charges} + \text{Rental payments}} = \frac{1767 + 5}{200 + 5} = 8.64x \qquad \textbf{(4.15)}$$

FIXED-CHARGE COVERAGE RATIO The number of times that interest charges and rental payments are covered by earnings before interest, taxes, and rental payments.

The **cash flow coverage ratio** is the company's operating cash flows divided by its payment obligations for interest, principal, preferred stock dividends, and rent.[6]

$$\frac{\text{Cash flow}}{\text{coverage ratio}} = \frac{\text{EBIT} + \text{Rental payments} + \text{Depreciation}}{\text{Rental payments} + \text{Interest charges} + \dfrac{\text{Preferred stock dividends}}{1 - T} + \dfrac{\text{Debt repayment}}{1 - T}} \qquad \textbf{(4.16)}$$

$$\frac{\text{Cash flow}}{\text{coverage ratio}} = \frac{1767 + 5 + 567}{5 + 200 + \dfrac{0}{1 - 0.4} + \dfrac{344}{1 - 0.4}} = 3.01x$$

CASH FLOW COVERAGE RATIO The number of times that financial obligations (for interest, principal payments, preferred stock dividends, and rental payments) are covered by earnings before interest, taxes, rental payments, and depreciation.

---

[5]Rental expense in 1992 is $5 million.
[6]Debt repayment in 1992 is $344 million. The marginal tax rate is 40%.

Note that two of the financial obligations in the denominator of the cash flow coverage ratio are divided by $(1 - T)$, where T is the marginal income tax rate. Rental payments and interest charges are tax-deductible expenses. Only one dollar of before-tax cash flow is required to meet one dollar of these obligations. In contrast, preferred stock dividends and principal repayments must be made out of after-tax cash flows. As a consequence, they are divided by $(1 - T)$ to calculate the equivalent before-tax operating cash flow necessary to meet them. For example, with a marginal tax rate of 40% and a $100 non-tax-deductible obligation, the company needs $166.67 (= 100/(1 - 0.4)) of before-tax dollars to meet this obligation. Note that the $166.67 before-tax cash flow provides $100 after paying taxes of $66.67 (= [0.40]166.67).

EXAMPLE

Comparing Coverage Ratios

Anheuser-Busch's coverage ratios compared to the other alcoholic beverage companies are:

	Anheuser-Busch	Other Alcoholic Beverage Companies
Times-interest-earned ratio	8.84x	6.28x
Fixed-charge coverage ratio	8.64x	6.17x
Cash flow coverage ratio	3.01x	8.26x

Anheuser-Busch has comparatively better coverage of its interest and fixed-charge obligations. Its cash flow coverage is lower because it had greater long-term debt repayment obligations. ■

Profitability Ratios

PROFITABILITY RATIOS
Ratios that focus on the profitability of the company. *Profit margins* measure performance in relation to sales, and *return ratios* measure performance relative to some measure of the size of the investment.

GROSS PROFIT MARGIN
Gross profit divided by sales. It is the amount of each sales dollar left after paying the cost of goods sold.

NET PROFIT MARGIN
Net income divided by sales. It is the amount of each sales dollar left after paying all expenses.

Profitability ratios focus on the company's effectiveness at generating profit. They reflect the operating performance, its riskiness, and the effect of leverage. We'll look at two kinds of profitability ratios: *profit margins,* which measure performance in relation to sales, and *return ratios,* which measure performance relative to some measure of the size of the investment.

Gross profit is the difference between sales and the cost of goods sold. Gross profit is critical because it represents the amount of money remaining to pay operating costs, financing costs, and taxes, and to provide for profit. The **gross profit margin** is the amount of each sales dollar left over after paying the cost of goods sold.

$$\text{Gross profit margin} = \frac{\text{Gross profit}}{\text{Sales}} = \frac{\text{Sales} - \text{Cost of goods sold}}{\text{Sales}} = \frac{4652}{11{,}394} = 40.8\% \quad (4.17)$$

The **net profit margin** measures the profit that is available from each dollar of sales after *all* expenses have been paid, including cost of goods sold; selling, general, and administrative expenses; depreciation; interest; and taxes.

$$\text{Net profit margin} = \frac{\text{Net income before extraordinary items}}{\text{Sales}} = \frac{994}{11{,}394} = 8.7\% \quad (4.18)$$

Note that the gross profit margin and net profit margin are identical to the percentages of sales for gross profit and net profit on the common-size income statement.

EXAMPLE

Comparing Profit Margins

Here's how Anheuser-Busch stacks up against the other alcoholic beverage companies:

	Anheuser-Busch	Other Alcoholic Beverage Companies
Gross profit margin	40.8%	40.5%
Net profit margin	8.7%	7.2%

Anheuser–Busch has done well. Its gross profit margin is about the same, but its net profit margin is higher than the other companies' average. ■

Unlike profit margins, *return ratios* express profitability in relation to various measures of the investment in the company. Their potential usefulness is inherently limited, however, because they are based on book values. Three ratios are commonly used: return on assets, earning power, and the return on equity.

Return on assets (ROA) corresponds to the net profit margin, except that net income is expressed as a proportion of total assets.

RETURN ON ASSETS (ROA) Net income divided by total assets.

$$\text{ROA} = \text{Return on assets} = \frac{\text{Net income}}{\text{Total assets}} = \frac{994}{10{,}538} = 9.4\% \qquad (4.19)$$

Earning power is EBIT divided by total assets.

EARNING POWER Earnings before interest and taxes (EBIT) divided by total assets.

$$\text{Earning power} = \frac{\text{EBIT}}{\text{Total assets}} = \frac{1767}{10{,}538} = 16.8\% \qquad (4.20)$$

The difference between ROA and earning power is due to debt financing. Net income is EBIT minus interest and taxes, so ROA will always be less than earning power. Earning power represents the "raw" operating results, whereas ROA represents the combined results of operating and financing.

Return on equity (ROE) is the return on common stockholders' equity:

RETURN ON EQUITY (ROE) Net income available to common stockholders divided by common stockholders' equity.

$$\text{ROE} = \frac{\text{Return on common}}{\text{stockholders' equity}} = \frac{\begin{array}{c}\text{Earnings available for common stock}\\ \text{before extraordinary items}\end{array}}{\text{Common stockholders' equity}} = \frac{994}{4620} = 21.5\% \quad (4.21)$$

where common stockholders' equity includes common stock (at par value), capital surplus, and retained earnings. ROE shows the company's residual profits as a proportion of the book value of common stockholders' equity. The amount of financial leverage affects both the numerator and denominator of the ROE. Typically, ROE is greater than ROA for healthy companies. In bad years, however, ROE can be below ROA. This is because financial leverage increases the risk of the stock, as we noted earlier.

Comparing Return Ratios

EXAMPLE

Comparing Anheuser-Busch to the other alcoholic beverage companies, we have

	Anheuser-Busch	Other Alcoholic Beverage Companies
Return on assets (ROA)	9.4%	5.8%
Earning power	16.8%	10.6%
Return on stockholders' equity (ROE)	21.5%	11.4%

Anheuser-Busch has higher profitability than the other companies. Note once again, however, that these ratios collectively reflect not only the operating performance but also its riskiness and the company's financial leverage. ∎

Market Value Ratios

At the time the 1992 statements were prepared, the market price of Anheuser-Busch common stock was $58.50 per share. Analysts look at several ratios that use the market value of the company's common stock.

The **price/earnings ratio (P/E)** is the market price per share of common stock divided by the earnings per share (EPS).

PRICE/EARNINGS (P/E) RATIO The market price per share divided by the earnings per share.

$$\text{P/E} = \text{Price/earnings ratio} = \frac{\text{Market price per share}}{\text{Earnings per share}} = \frac{58.50}{3.48} = 16.8x \qquad (4.22)$$

Negative earnings make EPS negative, which in turn make the P/E negative. Also, when EPS gets close to zero, the P/E becomes extremely large, because of dividing by the EPS. In such cases, the P/E is not considered economically meaningful. As a result, the P/E is not generally reported when EPS is negative or excessively small.

EARNINGS YIELD The earnings per share divided by the market price per share, equaling the reciprocal of the P/E.

The **earnings yield** is another form of the same information. It is the reciprocal:

$$\text{Earnings yield} = \frac{\text{Earnings per share}}{\text{Market price per share}} = \frac{3.48}{58.50} = 5.95\% \qquad \textbf{(4.23)}$$

EPS is in the numerator of the earnings yield and so avoids the division-by-zero problem. So, unlike the P/E, the earnings yield doesn't "break down" when EPS is negative or excessively small. A very small EPS simply leads to a very small earnings yield. A negative EPS simply represents such losses as a negative return, a rate of losing value.

DIVIDEND YIELD The dividend per share divided by the share price.

The ratio of dividends per share to market price per share is called the **dividend yield.**

$$\text{Dividend yield} = \frac{\text{Dividend per share}}{\text{Market price per share}} = \frac{1.20}{58.50} = 2.05\% \qquad \textbf{(4.24)}$$

Many companies are not currently paying a cash dividend. Such companies will have a dividend yield of zero. The decision to pay cash dividends is essentially a choice between paying out earnings to the owners or reinvesting the money in the company.

MARKET-TO-BOOK RATIO The ratio of the market price per share to the book value per share.

Finally, the **market-to-book ratio** is the market price per share divided by the book value per share. The book value per share is total common equity divided by the number of common shares outstanding. At year-end 1992, Anheuser-Busch's book value per share was $16.17 (= 4620/285.69).

$$\text{Market-to-book ratio} = \frac{\text{Market price per share}}{\text{Book value per share}} = \frac{58.50}{16.17} = 3.62x \qquad \textbf{(4.25)}$$

The market-to-book ratio is a very rough index of a company's historical performance. The higher the ratio, the greater is market value relative to book value. A high ratio says the company has created more in market value than the GAAP rules have recorded in book value. The implied message is that the company has done well. Of course, as we noted earlier, there are many possible explanations for a difference between market and book values. Although the implied message of a high market-to-book ratio is likely to be correct in most cases, additional information is generally needed to reach a confident conclusion.

EXAMPLE

Comparing Market Value Ratios

Here's how Anheuser-Busch stacks up against the other alcoholic beverage companies:

	Anheuser-Busch	Other Alcoholic Beverage Companies
Price/earnings ratio	16.8x	15.4x
Earnings yield	5.95%	6.40%
Dividend yield	2.05%	2.00%
Market-to-book ratio	3.62x	1.93x

Apparently, Anheuser-Busch has enjoyed past increases in the market value of its stock that have significantly exceeded increases in the book value per share. This has put its market-to-book ratio and P/E above the average of the other companies. Its earnings yield and dividend yield are about the same. ■

All of the ratios in this section are summarized in the Equation Summary Box at the end of the chapter.

Self-Check

1. What are the six general categories of financial ratios? Give examples of ratios in each category.

2. What is the purpose in creating financial ratios?

3. Consider each of the following transactions. Decide whether the transaction increases, decreases, or does not affect the ratios below.

Transaction 1: The company issues new long-term bonds and uses the proceeds to pay off some short-term debts.

Transaction 2: The company pays a cash dividend to common stockholders.

Transaction 3: The company sells some inventory. (The selling price is above the book value of the inventory. The sale is for credit, so the sale is recorded in accounts receivable.)

Transaction 4: The company buys new plant and equipment, paying cash.

Financial ratios: Current ratio, Quick ratio, Cash ratio, Debt/equity ratio, Return on assets, Earning power.

DUPONT ANALYSIS

Managers and investors are concerned with the return on common stockholders' equity (ROE). An important linkage between ROE and three other ratios has been called DuPont Analysis, named for the large chemical company that popularized its use. ROE can be expressed as the product of three other ratios; the net profit margin, the total asset turnover, and the equity multiplier.

$$\text{Return on equity} = \left(\text{Net profit margin}\right)\left(\text{Total asset turnover}\right)\left(\text{Equity multiplier}\right) \tag{4.26}$$

This relationship can be seen by noting that the components of the middle ratio cancel out the denominator and numerator, respectively, of the first and third ratios. That leaves the left side of the equation.

$$\frac{\text{Net income}}{\text{Stockholders' equity}} = \left(\frac{\text{Net income}}{\text{Sales}}\right)\left(\frac{\text{Sales}}{\text{Total assets}}\right)\left(\frac{\text{Total assets}}{\text{Stockholders' equity}}\right)$$

Changes in ROE can be traced to changes in the net profit margin, total asset turnover, or equity multiplier. This relationship helps diagnose problems and assists managers in deciding where improvements must occur to improve the company's ROE.

DuPont Analysis for Anheuser-Busch

EXAMPLE

For Anheuser-Busch, the ROE calculated by substituting the values for the net profit margin, total asset turnover, and the equity multiplier into the DuPont equation is:

$$\text{Return on equity} = (8.7\%)(1.08)(2.28) = 21.5\% \quad \blacksquare$$

Figure 4.1 on page 98 shows the variables that make up the DuPont Analysis system in diagrammatic form. You can move up or down the diagram and see how the pieces fit together. The financial statement values for Anheuser-Busch have been included in the figure to show how the various costs, revenues, assets, and liabilities make up the system. If the company has a problem, the system helps diagnose the location of the problem.

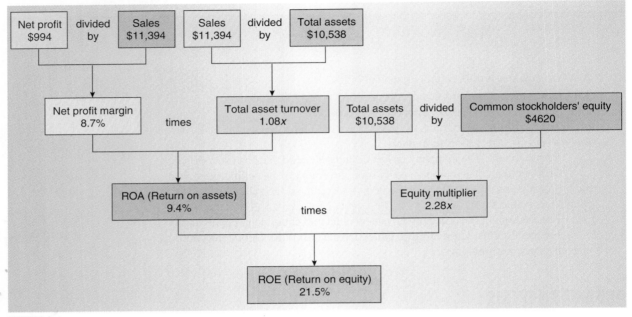

FIGURE 4.1
DuPont chart for Anheuser-Busch.

Of course, a company would like to have a high net profit margin, a high total asset turnover, and a high equity multiplier, which would result in an extremely high ROE. Unfortunately, there is usually a trade-off between the various parts of the DuPont System. For example, companies with high turnovers usually have low profit margins, and vice versa. In addition, companies with a low return on assets (which is the net profit margin times the total asset turnover) sometimes have a high equity multiplier, which gives them a more normal (competitive) ROE.

Table 4.7 illustrates this trade-off among industries. The total asset turnover is largely determined by the production and marketing processes in each particular industry. For example, it's not possible to generate electricity without a large investment in plant and equipment. Similarly, banks must invest heavily in loans, and jewelers must maintain very expensive inventories. Total asset turnover rates for electric companies, jewelry stores, and commercial banks, then, are relatively low compared to restaurants.

You can see in table 4.7 that net profit margin and total asset turnover tend to be inversely related. Similarly, companies with a low ROA sometimes have a high equity multiplier. Such trade-offs are in part because profit margins are competitively determined in the marketplace for the goods and services the companies are supplying. Restaurants, for example, operate on lower profit margins than electric companies, jewelers, or banks. Finally, even the amount of leverage a company chooses is influenced by the industry's risk and its ROA, which tends to further enforce these patterns.

Self-Check
1. Explain the logic underlying the DuPont equation.
2. Why is there often a trade-off between the values for the three components of the DuPont equation?

TABLE 4.7

Comparing the Components of the ROE in Different Businesses

COMPANY	NET PROFIT MARGIN	TOTAL ASSET TURNOVER	EQUITY MULTIPLIER	RETURN ON EQUITY
Food wholesaler	2%	10	1.2	24.0%
Jewelry store	30%	0.5	1.5	22.5%
Commercial bank	10%	0.15	16.0	24.0%
Electric company	20%	0.5	2.3	23.0%
Restaurant	5%	3.0	1.5	22.5%
Department store	5%	1.5	3.0	22.5%

USING AND INTERPRETING FINANCIAL STATEMENT INFORMATION

Financial ratios are used by analysts, investors, lenders, and managers to judge a company's financial performance and condition. Still, financial analysis is more of an art than a science. The set of ratios that proves most useful in any particular application depends on the company being analyzed, the purpose of the analysis, and the analyst's judgments. Lenders typically are most concerned with the company's liquidity, coverage, and leverage ratios. They may believe that the greater the liquidity and the lower the leverage, the greater the likelihood that interest and principal payments will be made on time. Managers are also likely to be concerned with the profitability of the enterprise. They must be concerned with turnover ratios and profitability measures too, because these ratios show how effectively the company is using its assets. Shareholders are most concerned with investment returns. As a result, common stockholders tend to emphasize profitability ratios, return on common stockholders' equity, and market value ratios.

Financial information can be obtained from the company itself as well as from financial service companies, government agencies, trade associations, and many other sources. Information is increasingly available in electronic form instead of in a printed medium. Table 4.8 on page 100 provides examples of several important providers of financial information.

Analysts, investors, and managers face a number of challenging and interesting situations whenever they undertake financial statement analysis. Several important tools you can use and several problems you may encounter are described and discussed below.

Choosing Financial Ratios

Earlier in the chapter, we presented a set of basic financial ratios. As we noted then, however, many other ratios are used to meet the needs of specialized analysts representing particular clienteles or focusing on specific industries. Fortunately, each specialty tends to use a limited set of ratios. Unfortunately, the names of financial ratios are not standardized. A particular ratio might have several names (as does the acid test ratio and the quick ratio). Even more disturbing is the fact that many ratios called by the same name have different definitions.

For example, when calculating an inventory turnover ratio, some analysts use the end-of-year inventory in the denominator, as we did. But others use an average of the inventory over the year. Also, some analysts use sales in the numerator of the inventory turnover ratio instead of cost of goods sold.

Similarly, the P/E may be calculated in different ways. It's most often calculated (and reported in the financial press) by dividing the current market price by the last year's EPS (that is, total EPS for the last four quarters). Alternative P/Es are constructed by dividing the current market price by the *forecasted* earnings per share for the next year.

As you can see, unlike a rose, a ratio by any other name (or even by the same name) may not smell as sweet. Therefore, whenever ratios are supplied by others, you must know their exact definition if they are to be of any use.

TABLE 4.8
Major Sources of Financial Information

Information from Company: Annual reports, Quarterly reports
General Financial Press:

Wall Street Journal	*Forbes*
Barron's	*Institutional Investor*
Business Week	*Inc.*
Fortune	*The Economist*

Financial Vendors:
    Dun & Bradstreet, Inc.—Business Norms and Key Business Ratios
    Moody's Investors Service—Moody's Manuals
    Robert Morris Associates—Annual Statement Studies
    Standard & Poor's Corporation—Industry Surveys and Corporation Records
    Leo Troy—Almanac of Business and Industrial Financial Ratios
    Value Line Publishing, Inc.—Value Line Investment Survey
Federal Agencies:
    Small Business Administration
    Department of Commerce
    Department of the Treasury
    Federal Trade Commission
    Securities and Exchange Commission
    Internal Revenue Service
Computerized Databases:
    ABI/Inform—on-line, CD-ROM
    Corporate Information Research Reports (CIRR)—microfiche, on-line, and CD-ROM
    Compact Disclosure—CD-ROM
    Compustat—computer tapes and CD-ROM
    Lotus OneSource—CD-ROM
    There are also numerous sources of information on the Internet or the World Wide Web. Corporations usually have their own Web sites, financial vendors are on the Web, and government agencies have sites (such as EDGAR, maintained by the Securities and Exchange Commission).

Discriminant Analysis and Credit Scoring

DISCRIMINANT ANALYSIS A statistical method of grouping companies according to selected characteristics.

One tool used to assess the financial health of a company is called **discriminant analysis.** This statistical procedure combines several variables (such as a company's financial ratios) into a single score in an attempt to classify the company into one of various groupings. Such analysis can be used to predict significant events, such as bankruptcy or a bond rating change.

In the case of bond ratings, the rating predicted by discriminant analysis is compared with the actual rating. For example, a discriminant analysis might reveal that a company whose bonds are currently rated BBB has financial characteristics more similar to those companies whose bonds are rated A. This would suggest that the bonds have lower default risk than the BBB rating would indicate. The analysis would predict an improvement in the rating.

CREDIT SCORING MODELS Models used to evaluate loan applications based on multivariate discriminant analysis.

Discriminant analysis models are also used for evaluating commercial loans, consumer loans, and credit card applications. Such models are often called **credit scoring models.** As with bankruptcy analysis for a company, the basic idea for a credit scoring model is to predict the likelihood of default.

Cross-Sectional Analysis

Cross-sectional analysis evaluates a company's financial ratios against industry averages or averages for a selected set of comparable companies. As you would expect from the Behavioral Principle, more meaningful comparisons are often possible using specific companies. Table 4.9 shows selected financial ratios from the Annual Statement Survey published by

TABLE 4.9

Selected Ratios for SIC# 5942, Retailers-Books

COMPANY SIZE (SALES IN 1000S): PERCENTILE:	$0 TO 500 25th, 50th, 75th	$500 TO 2000 25th, 50th, 75th	$2000 TO 10,000 25th, 50th, 75th
Current ratio	0.9, 1.5, 2.5	1.1, 1.5, 2.7	1.1, 1.5, 2.6
Quick ratio	0.1, 0.1, 0.5	0.1, 0.2, 0.6	0.1, 0.2, 0.6
Inventory turnover	2.6, 3.2, 5.6	1.4, 2.2, 3.2	2.6, 3.3, 4.7
%Profit before taxes/Total assets	2.4, 12.3, 25.9	0.6, 4.1, 11.7	1.6, 6.8, 12.3
Total asset turnover	2.8, 3.8, 5.1	1.6, 2.2, 2.9	2.1, 2.6, 3.3

Source: Robert Morris Associates Ratios from Annual Statement Studies.

Robert Morris Associates. The information in the table illustrates the distribution of a financial ratio within an industry.

Suppose you're interested in book retailers. Table 4.9 divides the firms into three size classes, and shows the 25th percentile, 50th percentile, and 75th percentile of five ratios for this industry. The industry averages are broken down further by company size, as measured by most recent total annual sales. For example, for the smallest companies, the 25th percentile current ratio (25% are below this amount) is 0.9. The 50th percentile (median) current ratio is 1.5, and the 75th percentile current ratio is 2.5. Using this kind of information, a company can compare itself to other companies of similar size in the same industry.

Beyond simple industry/size comparisons, many companies engage in benchmarking. **Benchmarking** is a comparison to a more specific set of *benchmark companies*. For example, suppose the Olin Corporation wants to compare itself to Dow Chemical, DuPont, Monsanto, and Union Carbide. Table 4.10 provides the ratios for all five companies. As you can see, Olin is most like Union Carbide. Olin's inventory turnover, receivables turnover, and total asset turnover are higher than those of Dow, DuPont, and Monsanto, but similar to those of Union Carbide. Days' sales outstanding and the days' sales in inventory are below the benchmark companies, except for Union Carbide.

BENCHMARKING A comparison of a company's financial results with those of a set of companies chosen as benchmark companies.

Time-Series Analysis

Trends in financial ratios and of common-size statement items are studied very carefully by managers and analysts. Changes in a company's liquidity, financial leverage, asset turnover, or profitability ratios over time can be very meaningful.

TABLE 4.10

Asset Turnover Ratios for Benchmark Company Group

	Olin Corporation	BENCHMARK COMPANIES			
		Dow	DuPont	Monsanto	Union Carbide
Inventory turnover	5.70x	4.16x	5.32x	3.50x	8.54x
Receivables turnover	6.88x	4.78x	6.49x	5.55x	6.46x
Total asset turnover	1.22x	0.71x	0.86x	0.89x	0.96x
Days' sales outstanding	52	75	55	65	56
Days' sales in inventory	63	87	68	103	42

In this table, Olin Corporation's asset turnover ratios are being compared to those of four benchmark companies.

General economic conditions, industry conditions, specific managerial decisions, or simply good or bad luck might explain what is happening. Table 4.11 shows an eight-year series of profitability ratios for three companies. Notice how the net profit margin, return on assets, and return on equity declined significantly from 1988 until 1993 for Chrysler. In 1994 and 1995, Chrysler recovered dramatically. Compare Chrysler's ratios to those of McDonald's and PepsiCo, the soft drink and food conglomerate. The profitability ratios for McDonald's and PepsiCo were fairly stable. The patterns in these ratios imply that Chrysler is a riskier company than McDonald's and PepsiCo.

Financial Planning Models and Strategic Planning Models

The structure of financial statements underlies many models that companies build for internal as well as external use. For example, a company applying for a bank loan might be required to submit historical financial statements as well as projected (what are called *pro forma*) financial statements for the next several years. Banks use such projected statements to help judge the likelihood the company will be able to repay the loan. Other models are used internally by management to plan the company's future investments and financing.

Inflation and Book Values

Financial decisions should be based on current and expected future conditions. However, as we emphasized in the previous chapter, accounting statements are historical in the United States and many other countries. In particular, we showed how several factors, such as inflation, can distort the balance sheet.

Inflation can also distort a company's reported income. When a company gets an inflated price from selling its finished goods from inventory, it appears to have had higher income. However, it must then in turn pay an inflated price for the cost of goods to replenish its inventory for the next sale. If the company uses the so called LIFO (last in, first out) convention to overcome this problem, that will distort its balance sheet by understating the inventory value.

Fixed assets also will have to be replaced at inflated prices in the future. However, U.S. tax laws compute depreciation on a historical cost basis. This too inflates the company's income. Taxes are paid on this overstated income, which further impinges on cash flow.

In fact, inflation is the major reason for using common-size and common-base-year financial statements. Many, but not all, of the distortions caused by inflation are reduced by scaling the information by a common base.

Some countries with high inflation rates, such as Mexico, actually *require* that accounting statements be adjusted for inflation. Without such adjustments, meaningful interperiod

TABLE 4.11

Time-Series Profitability Ratios for Chrysler, McDonald's, and PepsiCo (All ratios are in percent)

	1995	1994	1993	1992	1991	1990	1989	1988
Chrysler								
Net profit margin	4.0	7.3	−6.0	2.0	−2.8	0.2	1.0	3.0
Return on assets	3.9	8.0	−6.0	1.7	−1.7	0.1	0.7	3.1
Return on equity	18.7	42.4	−35.5	10.6	−12.3	1.0	4.8	14.9
McDonald's								
Net profit margin	14.6	14.7	14.6	13.4	12.8	12.1	12.0	11.7
Return on assets	9.9	9.5	9.1	8.3	7.8	8.1	8.4	8.5
Return on equity	20.2	19.9	19.1	18.6	19.1	20.8	20.8	20.4
PepsiCo								
Net profit margin	5.3	6.2	6.3	1.7	5.5	6.0	5.9	5.9
Return on assets	6.4	7.2	7.1	1.9	6.0	6.7	6.9	7.6
Return on equity	22.7	26.6	27.2	6.9	20.7	24.5	25.6	26.9

comparisons or comparisons among companies can be almost impossible. As Mexico becomes a larger trading partner with the United States, in part because of the North American Free Trade Agreement (NAFTA), accounting for differences in inflation will remain important to all stakeholders in Mexican companies.

International Accounting

In the previous chapter, we noted how accounting standards can differ substantially across countries. This is an additional significant impediment to using and interpreting financial information. In addition, there are the problems of language translation and foreign currency conversion. There are other differences as well. Auditing standards vary. *Disclosure* ranges from fairly open to almost completely secret. Legal systems, business practices, educational levels, and management sophistication all vary widely. In fact, even seemingly similar countries, such as the United States and Great Britain, have differences that can surprise you.[7] Just as it takes considerable effort to learn to read and interpret U.S. financial statements, it takes additional effort to learn how to understand those from other countries.

Judgment, Experience, and Hard Work

There is no unique set of theoretically correct financial ratios. A manager's decisions, such as those about a company's liquidity or leverage, are not simple decisions. A business is a complex and dynamic organization. Most decisions involve some sorts of trade-offs, frequently including the Principle of Risk-Return Trade-Off. For example, a company can lower its risk by maintaining greater liquidity, but that's likely to reduce profitability. A company can lower its risk by using less debt, but that too will reduce the stockholders' expected return.[8] Such decisions require judgment and analysis.

Likewise, an outside analyst must exercise judgment and draw on experience to understand a company's financial position. People outside the company must be aware of the possibility that managers are manipulating the company's financial information through careful decision making involving such things as choices of accounting treatments, timing of decisions, and public relations. Alternative accounting treatments can alter the picture of the company's financial statements.[9] A certain amount of manipulation of financial information, which is called *window dressing,* is legally permissible and fairly routine. As an outside user of financial information, you should be carefully skeptical. If you are providing financial information about your company, you should recall our admonition about ethics. Avoid unethical manipulations. They can be fraudulent and land you in prison!

Corporate practice must deal with ever-increasing complexity, and that's part of what managers are paid for. If you're not an accounting major, you still must understand a critical mass of accounting to be an intelligent user of accounting information.

Why We Use Financial Statement Analysis

Financial statement analysis is useful in at least two ways. First, it provides a structure for understanding the dynamics of a company. For example, how would some event affect a company? Is it good or bad; is it significant or insignificant; how does it affect specific parts of the company? A financial framework allows you to more quickly understand the importance of new information.

---

[7]Winston Churchill, prime minister of England during the Second World War, once commented that the United Kingdom and the United States were two countries "separated by a common language." Despite the efforts of the accounting profession to reconcile the different accounting systems, Churchill's statement could well be applied to the problems financial statement users face in trying to reconcile financial statements prepared under different accounting systems.

[8]Choosing higher risk to obtain a higher expected return can, of course, backfire. Recall that risk disconnects the stockholders' *realized* return from their expected return.

[9]Have you heard about the accountants applying for a job who were asked the question, "What is one plus one?" The accountant who got the job answered, "What would you like it to be?"

Second, financial statements provide information. But there is a good-news/bad-news story here. The good news is that accounting information is readily available and can be very helpful. The bad news is that this information is rarely sufficient to make sound business decisions. Don't overestimate the value of financial statement information. Much of it is not news; it's already been anticipated from other outside information. When a financial statement does contain a surprise, markets will react accordingly. Still, we would caution you against an overreliance on financial statement information and recommend you maintain a heathy skepticism about it.

Self-Check

1. What is the difference between cross-sectional analysis and time-series analysis?

2. What is benchmarking?

3. Describe some of the problems inflation can create when you analyze financial statements.

4. "The primary problem in international financial statement analysis is to translate the foreign languages into English." Do you agree? Why or why not?

5. Why is financial statement analysis important? Cite some of the potential pitfalls.

SUMMARY

Analysts and managers use financial reports to compare businesses and to study them over time. Financial ratios often make comparisons and trends clearer.

- Common-size financial statements show percentage breakdowns of the income statement and balance sheet that allow easier comparisons across companies.
- Financial ratio analysis focuses on specific relationships in the financial statements.
- Liquidity ratios show the ability of the company to meet its maturing short-term obligations. These ratios include the current ratio, the quick (acid test) ratio, the working capital ratio, and the cash ratio.
- Asset turnover ratios show how effectively the company is using its assets. These ratios include the receivables turnover, days' sales outstanding, inventory turnover, days' sales in inventory, fixed asset turnover, and total asset turnover ratios.
- Leverage ratios show the relative contribution of creditors and owners to the financing of the company. These include ratios such as the debt ratio, debt-to-equity ratio, and the equity multiplier.
- Coverage ratios show the amount of funds available to cover a particular financial obligation compared to the size of that obligation. These include times-interest-earned, fixed-charge coverage, and cash flow coverage ratios.
- Profitability ratios include profit margins and return ratios. The profit margin ratios are the gross profit margin and the net profit margin. The return ratios include the return on assets, earning power ratio, and return on equity.
- Market value ratios are based on the market price of the company's common stock. These ratios include the price/earnings ratio, the earnings yield, the dividend yield, and the market-to-book ratio.
- DuPont analysis shows how the net profit margin, the total asset turnover, and the equity multiplier are linked to determine the return on equity.
- Discriminant analysis computes an overall measure of the likelihood of an event, such as bankruptcy or default on a loan.
- Cross-sectional analysis lets you compare your financial ratios to industry averages and industry norms, or compare your financial ratios to those for a set of benchmark companies.
- In time-series analysis, trends in financial ratios are followed over a period of time.
- Financial statement concepts are used to help build financial planning and strategic planning models.
- Inflation can distort financial statements in many ways. Inflation can cause reported profits to be unrealistic, cause income taxes to be higher than they should be, and understate the value of some assets and liabilities.

- Accounting principles and procedures differ greatly across countries. Thus, the challenges of international financial statement analysis are much more complicated than simply translating from one language to another.
- Financial statement analysis can be useful in two fundamental ways. First, it can help structure your thinking about business decisions. Second, it can provide some information that is helpful in making those decisions.

EQUATION SUMMARY

Liquidity ratios

(4.1)
$$\text{Current ratio} = \frac{\text{Current assets}}{\text{Current liabilities}}$$

(4.2)
$$\text{Quick (Acid test) ratio} = \frac{\text{Current assets} - \text{Inventories}}{\text{Current liabilities}}$$

(4.3)
$$\text{Working capital ratio} = \frac{\text{Current assets} - \text{Current liabilities}}{\text{Sales}}$$

(4.4)
$$\text{Cash ratio} = \frac{\text{Cash and equivalents}}{\text{Total assets}}$$

Asset turnover ratios

(4.5)
$$\text{Receivables turnover} = \frac{\text{Annual credit sales}}{\text{Accounts receivable}}$$

(4.6)
$$\text{Days' sales outstanding} = \frac{365}{\text{Receivables turnover}} = \frac{\text{Accounts receivable}}{\text{Annual credit sales}/365}$$

(4.7)
$$\text{Inventory turnover} = \frac{\text{Cost of goods sold}}{\text{Inventory}}$$

(4.8)
$$\text{Days' sales in inventory} = \frac{365}{\text{Inventory turnover}} = \frac{\text{Inventory}}{\text{Cost of goods sold}/365}$$

(4.9)
$$\text{Fixed asset turnover} = \frac{\text{Sales}}{\text{Net fixed assets}}$$

(4.10)
$$\text{Total asset turnover} = \frac{\text{Sales}}{\text{Total assets}}$$

Leverage ratios

(4.11)
$$\text{Debt ratio} = \frac{\text{Total debt}}{\text{Total assets}}$$

(4.12)
$$\text{Debt/equity ratio} = \frac{\text{Total debt}}{\text{Stockholders' equity}} = \frac{\text{Debt ratio}}{1.0 - \text{Debt ratio}}$$

(4.13)
$$\text{Equity multiplier} = \frac{\text{Total assets}}{\text{Stockholders' equity}} = \frac{1.0}{1.0 - \text{Debt ratio}}$$

Coverage ratios

(4.14)
$$\text{Times-interest-earned ratio} = \frac{\text{EBIT}}{\text{Interest expense}}$$

(4.15)
$$\frac{\text{Fixed-charge}}{\text{coverage ratio}} = \frac{\text{EBIT} + \text{Rental payments}}{\text{Interest charges} + \text{Rental payments}}$$

(continued on following page)

(Equation Summary *continued from previous page*)

$$(4.16) \quad \text{Cash flow coverage ratio} = \frac{\text{EBIT} + \text{Rental payments} + \text{Depreciation}}{\text{Rental payments} + \text{Interest charges} + \frac{\text{Preferred stock dividends}}{1 - T} + \frac{\text{Debt repayment}}{1 - T}}$$

Profitability ratios

$$(4.17) \quad \text{Gross profit margin} = \frac{\text{Gross profit}}{\text{Sales}} = \frac{\text{Sales} - \text{Cost of goods sold}}{\text{Sales}}$$

$$(4.18) \quad \text{Net profit margin} = \frac{\text{Net income before extraordinary items}}{\text{Sales}}$$

$$(4.19) \quad \text{ROA} = \text{Return on assets} = \frac{\text{Net income}}{\text{Total assets}}$$

$$(4.20) \quad \text{Earning power} = \frac{\text{EBIT}}{\text{Total assets}}$$

$$(4.21) \quad \text{ROE} = \frac{\text{Return on common stockholders' equity}}{} = \frac{\text{Earnings available for common stock before extraordinary items}}{\text{Common stockholders' equity}}$$

Market value ratios

$$(4.22) \quad \text{P/E} = \text{Price/earnings ratio} = \frac{\text{Market price per share}}{\text{Earnings per share}}$$

$$(4.23) \quad \text{Earnings yield} = \frac{\text{Earnings per share}}{\text{Market price per share}}$$

$$(4.24) \quad \text{Dividend yield} = \frac{\text{Dividend per share}}{\text{Market price per share}}$$

$$(4.25) \quad \text{Market-to-book ratio} = \frac{\text{Market price per share}}{\text{Book value per share}}$$

DuPont equation

$$(4.26) \quad \frac{\text{Return on equity}}{} = \left(\frac{\text{Net profit margin}}{}\right)\left(\frac{\text{Total asset turnover}}{}\right)\left(\frac{\text{Equity multiplier}}{}\right)$$

CHAPTER REVIEW ACTIVITIES

SELF-TEST PROBLEMS

Use the financial information for the Zumwalt Corporation to answer the self-test problems.

Zumwalt Corporation
Balance Sheet as of December 31, 1997
(Millions of dollars)

Current assets		Current liabilities	
Cash	$ 80	Accounts payable	$ 95
Accounts receivable	140	Notes payable	110
Inventory	155	Total	$205
Total	$375	Long-term debt	120
Fixed assets		Common stock	40
Net fixed assets	265	Retained earnings	275
Total assets	$640	Total liabilities and stockholders' equity	$640

Zumwalt Corporation
Income Statement for Year Ended December 31, 1997
(Millions of dollars)

Sales	$910
Cost of goods sold	470
General, selling, and admin. expenses	210
Depreciation	60
Earnings before interest and taxes	$170
Interest expense	40
Earnings before taxes	$130
Taxes (40%)	52
Net income	$ 78
Per share data:	
Outstanding shares (millions)	40
Earnings per share	$1.95
Dividends per share	$0.50
Market price per share	$18.00
Book value per share	$7.88

1. (Common-size statements) Prepare a common-size balance sheet and income statement for Zumwalt Corporation. What are the largest two expense categories for the company? What percentage of the company is financed by short-term sources of funds and how much is financed by long-term sources?
2. (Financial ratios) Based on its 1997 financial statements, calculate the following ratios for Zumwalt: Current ratio, quick ratio, working capital ratio, cash ratio, receivables turnover, days' sales outstanding, inventory turnover, days' sales in inventory, fixed asset turnover, total asset turnover, debt ratio, debt/equity ratio, equity multiplier, times-interest-earned ratio, gross profit margin, net profit margin, return on assets, earning power, return on equity, price/earnings ratio, earnings yield, dividend yield, market-to-book ratio.
3. (DuPont analysis) What is Zumwalt's ROE? Break the ROE into its component parts using the DuPont equation.

SOLUTIONS TO SELF-TEST PROBLEMS

1. The common-size statements are a percentage breakdown of the balance sheet and income statement. Each balance sheet item is expressed as a percentage of total assets and each income statement item is expressed as a percentage of sales.

Zumwalt Corporation
Common-Size Balance Sheet as of December 31, 1997

Current assets		Current liabilities	
Cash	12.5%	Accounts payable	14.8%
Accounts receivable	21.9	Notes payable	17.2
Inventory	24.2	Total	32.0%
Total	58.6%	Long-term debt	18.8
Fixed assets		Common stock	6.2
Net fixed assets	41.4%	Retained earnings	43.0
Total assets	100.0%	Total liabilities	
		and stockholders' equity	100.0%

Zumwalt Corporation
Common-Size Income Statement for Year Ended December 31, 1997

Sales	100.0%
Cost of goods sold	51.6
General, selling, and admin. expenses	23.1
Depreciation	6.6
Earnings before interest and taxes	18.7%
Interest expense	4.4
Earnings before taxes	14.3%
Taxes (40%)	5.7
Net income	8.6%

Zumwalt's largest two expense categories are Cost of goods sold, which is 51.6% of sales, and General, selling, and administrative expenses, which is 23.1% of sales. The right-hand side of the common-size balance sheet shows that short-term financing is 32.0% of total assets. Long-term financing, which would include long-term debt, common stock, and retained earnings, is 68.0% of financing.

2. These are the calculations of the ratios for Zumwalt. If you do not understand how the numbers for the calculation were obtained for any particular ratio, refer to the definition of that ratio in the chapter.

Ratio	Inputs	Result
Current ratio	375/205	1.83x
Quick ratio	220/205	1.07x
Working capital ratio	170/910	18.7%
Cash ratio	80/640	12.5%
Receivables turnover	910/140	6.50x
Days' sales outstanding	140/(910/365)	56.2 days
Inventory turnover	470/155	3.03x
Days' sales in inventory	155/(470/365)	120.4 days
Fixed asset turnover	910/265	3.43x
Total asset turnover	910/640	1.42x
Debt ratio	325/640	50.8%
Debt/equity ratio	325/315	1.03x
Equity multiplier	640/315	2.03x
Times-interest-earned ratio	170/40	4.25x
Gross profit margin	440/910	48.4%
Net profit margin	78/910	8.6%
Return on assets	78/640	12.2%
Earning power	170/640	26.6%
Return on equity	78/315	24.8%
Price/earnings ratio	18.00/1.95	9.2x
Earnings yield	1.95/18.00	10.8%
Dividend yield	0.50/18.00	2.8%
Market-to-book ratio	18.00/7.88	2.28x

3. Zumwalt's ROE is $78/315 = 24.8\%$, which was one of the ratios we calculated in self-test question 2. The ROE can be decomposed into three parts:

$$\text{ROE} = (\text{Net profit margin})(\text{Total asset turnover})(\text{Equity multiplier})$$
$$\text{ROE} = (78/910)(910/640)(640/315) = (8.6\%)(1.42)(2.03) = 24.8\%$$

The product of the first two components (Net profit margin × Total asset turnover) is equal to the Return on assets (ROA). Hence,

$$\text{ROE} = (\text{Return on assets})(\text{Equity multiplier}) = (78/640)(640/315) = (12.2\%)(2.03) = 24.8\%$$

QUESTIONS

1. Give four examples of persons who use financial statement analysis and what they might use it for.
2. Give as many examples as you can of financial ratios that are classed as the following:
   a. liquidity ratios
   b. asset turnover ratios
   c. leverage ratios
   d. coverage ratios
   e. profitability ratios
   f. market value ratios
3. Ratios can also be classed as *balance sheet* ratios, *income statement* ratios, and *mixed* ratios. A balance sheet ratio uses only information from the balance sheet, an income statement ratio uses only information from the income statement, and a mixed ratio uses information from both the balance sheet and the income statement. For the ratios presented in this chapter, classify each of them as a balance sheet, income statement, or mixed ratio. (Ignore the market value ratios.)
4. Assume that the company has a current ratio of 2.0 and a debt ratio of 60%. Indicate whether each of the following transactions would increase or decrease the current ratio and the debt ratio.
   a. A long-term debt obligation is paid off with cash.
   b. An account receivable is collected (in cash).

c. An account payable is paid off (with cash).

d. Long-term equipment is purchased with cash.

e. Long-term equipment is purchased and financed with long-term debt.

f. Inventory is purchased with cash.

g. Inventory is purchased and financed with accounts payable.

5. The return on equity (ROE) of Wal-Mart Stores has declined in recent years. Please look at the components of the DuPont equation given below.

Year	ROE (Net income/Equity)	Net profit margin (Net income/Sales)	Total asset turnover (Sales/Assets)	Equity multiplier (Assets/Equity)
1993	24.1%	3.5%	2.86	2.41
1992	25.4	3.6	3.08	2.29
1991	26.3	3.7	3.27	2.17
1990	28.0	4.0	3.33	2.10
1989	31.2	4.2	3.55	2.09
1988	32.1	4.1	3.59	2.18

Why did the ROE decline?

6. Describe the difference between doing a cross-sectional analysis and a time-series analysis. What is benchmarking?

7. What are some of the limitations on the use of ratio analysis and financial statement analysis?

CHALLENGING QUESTIONS

8. Quantrock Mining has a return on assets of 10%, which is above average for its industry, and a return on equity of 15%, which is below average for its industry. Why isn't Quantrock's ROE also above the industry average?

9. Under what company circumstances would an analyst have a strong preference for using the quick ratio instead of the current ratio? What company circumstance would cause an analyst to have a strong preference for using the fixed-charge coverage ratio instead of the times-interest-earned ratio?

10. Dross Development Company has reported some exaggerated, or perhaps even fraudulent, annual results. The income statement includes $5 million of nonexistent sales, which are also included as accounts receivable on the balance sheet. When these misrepresentations are removed from the financial statements, what should happen to Dross Development's current ratio, quick ratio, net profit margin, return on equity, and debt/equity ratio?

11. In the United States, financial accounting is intended to disseminate as much information as quickly as possible to investors. Securities regulations and accounting practices are oriented to serving a very large number of common stock investors. In Germany, large banks and wealthy families own a much larger fraction of the country's companies. As a result, would you expect German financial statements to be disseminated more (or less) rapidly than in the United States? Would you expect the amount of disclosure (amount of information) to be more (or less) than in the United States? Would you expect the accounting principles in Germany to be more conservative (favoring creditors) or less conservative (favoring equity investors)?

PROBLEM SET A

A1. (Liquidity ratios) A company has current liabilities of $100, net working capital of $80, and inventory of $60. What are the company's current ratio and quick ratio?

A2. (Asset turnover ratios) Record Distributors had sales of $1,225,000 and a cost of goods sold of $775,000. Record had an inventory of $275,000 and accounts receivable of $225,000. Calculate Record Distributors' gross profit margin, inventory turnover, days' sales in inventory, receivables turnover, and days' sales outstanding.

A3. (Liquidity ratios) The Buchanan Group, Inc. has $4,000,000 in cash, $8,000,000 in receivables, $10,000,000 in inventory, $6,000,000 in accounts payable, and $2,000,000 in other short-term debt.

a. What is Buchanan's net working capital? What are the current ratio and quick ratio?

b. Buchanan pays $2,000,000 cash to reduce accounts payable. Recalculate Buchanan's working capital ratio, current ratio, and quick ratio.

A4. (Ratio analysis) Kentucky Archery Suppliers expects sales of $800,000. With a gross profit margin of 40%, an inventory turnover of 4.0 and a receivables turnover of 5.0, what assets should Kentucky have invested in receivables and inventory?

A5. (Leverage ratios) The equity multiplier is 3.0. What is the debt/equity ratio? What is the debt ratio?

A6. (Asset turnover ratios) Sales are $750,000, cost of goods sold is $500,000, accounts receivable is $125,000, inventory is $100,000, net fixed assets are $300,000, and total assets are $900,000. Calculate the following ratios:
a. receivables turnover
b. days' sales outstanding
c. inventory turnover
d. days' sales in inventory
e. fixed asset turnover
f. total asset turnover

A7. (Leverage ratios) Fill in the missing ratio values.

	Debt ratio	Debt/equity ratio	Equity multiplier
a.	50%	_____	_____
b.	_____	0.50x	_____
c.	_____	_____	4.0x

A8. (Times-interest-earned ratio) Phoenix Sports Corporation has total sales of $11,000,000. Phoenix also has cost of goods sold of $4,000,000, selling, general and administrative expenses of $2,500,000, depreciation expenses of $1,000,000, interest expenses of $800,000, income taxes of $1,000,000, and net income of $1,700,000. Calculate the times-interest-earned ratio.

A9. (Coverage ratios) Conway Trucking has net income of $25,000,000, taxes of $15,000,000, interest expenses of $10,000,000, rental expenses of $15,000,000, depreciation charges of $12,000,000, no preferred stock dividends, and a debt principal repayment of $10,000,000. Conway's marginal tax rate is 37.5%. Calculate each of the following coverage ratios:
a. times-interest-earned ratio;
b. fixed-charge coverage ratio;
c. cash flow coverage ratio.

A10. (Market value ratios) Datta Data has a total book value of stockholders' equity of $72,000,000, net income of $16,000,000, and 4,000,000 outstanding shares. Datta paid cash dividends of $3,600,000 during the year. The market price per share is $42.00. Calculate each of the following for Datta Data:
a. price/earnings ratio;
b. earnings yield;
c. dividend yield;
d. market-to-book ratio.

A11. (Asset turnover ratios) The receivables turnover is 7.2 and the inventory turnover is 12.5. What is the days' sales outstanding and the days' sales in inventory?

A12. (Market value ratios) Dominion Resources has projected earnings per share of $3.60 for next year. Analysts also expect Dominion to pay cash dividends that are 75% of earnings.
a. If the price/earnings ratio is 11.0x, what should be Dominion's stock price?
b. Given this stock price, what is the dividend yield?

A13. (Ratio analysis) You are given the following information for Pelaez Products Company: Sales = $1,000,000; net profit margin = 10%; return on equity = 20%; debt/equity ratio = 0.50x. Estimate each of the following for Pelaez: net income, stockholders' equity, total debt, and total assets.

A14. (Ratio analysis) You have the following information for Pelaez Products Company: Sales = $1,000,000; gross profit margin = 40%; receivables turnover = 6.0x; inventory turnover = 5.0x. How much does Pelaez have invested in accounts receivable and in inventory?

A15. (DuPont analysis) Gehr Hair, Inc. has a net profit margin of 12%, a total asset turnover of 0.7, and an equity multiplier of 2.0. What is Gehr Hair's ROE?

A16. (DuPont analysis) The equity multiplier is 1.50 and the total asset turnover is 2.5. What net profit margin is required to achieve a return on equity of 30%?

A17. (DuPont analysis) Fill in the missing ratio values.

	Return on equity	Return on assets	Equity multiplier
a.	_____	4%	4.0x
b.	25%	_____	2.0x
c.	18%	12%	_____

A18. (DuPont analysis) Fill in the missing ratio values.

	Return on equity	Net profit margin	Total asset turnover	Equity multiplier
a.	15%	2%	5.00x	1.50x
b.	21%	7%	1.50x	2.00x
c.	28%	7%		2.00x
d.	36%	12%	0.80x	2.75x

A19. (Differing ratio definitions) For the recent fiscal year, Becker Partners had sales of $4,400,000 and cost of goods sold of $2,200,000. Inventory balances were $300,000 at the beginning of the year and $500,000 at the end of the year. Calculate inventory turnover using each of the following definitions:

a. Cost of goods sold divided by ending inventory.

b. Cost of goods sold divided by the average of beginning and ending inventory.

c. Sales divided by ending inventory.

d. Sales divided by the average of beginning and ending inventory.

e. One of your friends says it is not important to know how a ratio is calculated. Do you agree?

A20. (Differing ratio definitions) GM earned $8.20 per share in the just-concluded fiscal year. Security analysts are projecting earnings per share of $9.75 in the next fiscal year. The current stock price is $57.00 per share. The earnings per share in the denominator of the price/earnings ratio can be either last year's actual earnings or next year's projected earnings. The "trailing P/E" ratio uses last year's earnings, while the "leading P/E" uses next year's earnings.

a. What is GM's trailing price/earnings ratio?

b. What is GM's leading price/earnings ratio?

PROBLEM SET B

B1. (Ratio analysis) Fill out the balance sheet and other information in the table below for the Morales Well Supply Company. These ratios are sufficient for you to derive the missing information: Current ratio = 2.0x; debt ratio = 50%; total asset turnover = 1.60x; gross profit margin = 40%; net profit margin = 10%; inventory turnover = 5x; receivables turnover = 10x.

Balance Sheet

Cash	_____	Accounts payable	_____
Accounts receivable	_____	Long-term debt	100,000
Inventory	_____	Common stock	20,000
Fixed assets	_____	Retained earnings	_____
Total assets	500,000	Total liabilities and equity	_____
Sales	_____	Cost of goods sold _____	Net income _____

B2. (Ratio analysis) Fill out the balance sheet and other missing information below for the Champion Sales Company. These ratios will help you: Current ratio = 2.0x; cash ratio = 0; debt/equity ratio = 70%; gross profit margin = 20%; net profit margin = 6%; inventory turnover = 8x; receivables turnover = 10x.

Balance Sheet

Cash	_____	Current liabilities	_____
Accounts receivable	_____	Long-term debt	1,000,000
Inventory	_____	Stockholders' equity	_____
Current assets	_____		
Fixed assets	_____		
Total assets	_____	Total liabilities and equity	_____
Sales	$10,000,000	Quick ratio	_____
Cost of goods sold	_____	Total asset turnover	_____
Net income	_____	Working capital ratio	_____

B3. (Ratio analysis) The Osborn Company has $4,500,000 in current assets and $3,000,000 in current liabilities. Osborn has a loan agreement in which it promises to maintain a current ratio of 2.0 or more.

a. Is Osborn in violation of the terms of the loan agreement?

b. If the owners of the company decide to contribute additional equity capital that will be invested in marketable securities, how much must they contribute to achieve a current ratio of 2.0?

c. If the owners decide to contribute additional equity capital that will be used to pay down current liabilities, how much must they contribute to achieve a current ratio of 2.0?

d. Osborn can sell some of its accounts receivable for 100% of their face value and use the proceeds to reduce current liabilities. How much must the company sell to achieve a 2.0 current ratio?

e. Osborn can sell some of its accounts receivable for 90% of their face value. If the proceeds are used to reduce current liabilities, how much must the company sell to achieve a current ratio of 2.0?

B4. (Ratio analysis) Waller Distributing has the following financial results: Sales = $500,000; cost of goods sold = $350,000; net income = $30,000; total debt = $150,000; common stock = $50,000; retained earnings = $100,000; receivables turnover = 8.0x; inventory turnover = 7.0x.

a. Calculate the net profit margin, total asset turnover, return on assets, and return on equity.

b. Suppose that a new computer system would allow Waller to increase its receivables turnover to 10.0 and the inventory turnover to 10.0. Calculate the reductions in receivables and inventory that would be achieved.

c. Assume the new system would not change sales or the cost of goods sold.

d. Assume that the costs of running the computer system are such that net income is also left unchanged. Assume that the funds freed up by reducing receivables and inventories are distributed to stockholders as a cash dividend. (Both total assets and retained earnings will go down by this amount.) Recalculate the net profit margin, total asset turnover, return on assets, and return on equity.

B5. (Common-size statements) Based on the financial statements below, construct a common-size balance sheet and income statement for Dallas Storage Devices.

Dallas Storage Devices
Balance Sheet as of December 31, 1997
(Thousands of dollars)

Current assets		Current liabilities	
Cash	$ 2,006	Accounts payable	$ 2,325
Accounts receivable	4,782	Other current debt	3,009
Inventory	3,401	Total	$ 5,334
Total	$10,189	Long-term debt	1,977
Fixed assets		Common stock	5,215
Net fixed assets	4,346	Retained earnings	2,009
Total assets	$14,535	Total liabilities	
		and stockholders' equity	$14,535

Dallas Storage Devices
Income Statement for year ended December 31, 1997
(Thousands of dollars)

Sales	$20,909
Cost of goods sold	14,407
General, selling, and admin. expenses	3,801
Depreciation	1,225
Earnings before interest and taxes	$ 1,476
Interest expense	639
Earnings before taxes	$ 837
Taxes (40%)	335
Net income	$ 502
Per share data:	
Outstanding shares (thousands)	1,205

Earnings per share	$ 0.42
Dividends per share	$ 0.00
Market price per share	$19.25
Book value per share	$ 5.99

B6. (Ratio analysis and DuPont analysis) For Dallas Storage Devices, whose balance sheet and income statement are given in problem B5, calculate all the financial ratios in the Equation Summary Box. The company made no rental payments and no debt repayments in the latest year.

PROBLEM SET C

C1. (International accounting) Suppose that Dallas Storage Devices is located in a country that has different accounting practices than those used in preparing the financial statements presented in problem B5. In this country, short-term financial assets and obligations are simply netted off against each other, and only a net figure is given on the balance sheet. (If short-term financial assets minus short-term debt is positive, a net figure is included as a short-term asset. If this figure is negative, it is reported as a short-term liability. Inventory is considered a real asset, the rest of the short-term and long-term accounts are considered to be financial.) In addition, fixed assets are depreciated more rapidly, resulting in net fixed assets being $1,000 lower than the figure given. (Since depreciation has been more rapid, this results in a comparable reduction in retained earnings, too.) Recast the balance sheet to reflect these financial practices.

Dallas Storage Devices
Balance Sheet as of December 31, 1997
(Thousands of dollars)

Net short-term			
financial assets	$_____	Long-term debt	$1,977
Inventory	3,401	Common stock	5,215
Net current assets	$_____	Retained earnings	_____
Net fixed assets	_____	Total liabilities	
Total assets	$_____	and stockholders' equity	$_____

BIBLIOGRAPHY

Altman, Edward I. "Financial Ratios, Discriminant Analysis and the Prediction of Corporate Bankruptcy," *Journal of Finance,* 1968, 23(4):589–609.

Bernstein, Leopold A. *Financial Statement Analysis: Theory, Application, and Interpretation,* 5th ed. Homewood, Ill.: Richard D. Irwin, 1993.

Dun & Bradstreet. *Industry Norms and Key Business Ratios.* Parsippany, N.J.: Dun & Bradstreet Information Services, 1996.

Foster, George. *Financial Statement Analysis,* 2nd ed. Englewood Cliffs, N.J.: Prentice-Hall, 1986.

Gombola, Michael J., and J. Edward Ketz. "Financial Ratio Patterns in Retail and Manufacturing Organizations," *Financial Management,* 1983, 12(2):45–56.

John, Teresa A. "Accounting Measures of Corporate Liquidity, Leverage, and Costs of Financial Distress," *Financial Management,* 1993, 22(3):91–100.

Johnson, W. Bruce. "The Cross-Sectional Stability of Financial Ratio Patterns," *Journal of Financial and Quantitative Analysis,* 1979, 14(5):1035–1048.

Mueller, Gerhard G., Helen Gernon, and Gary Meek. *Accounting: An International Perspective.* Homewood, Ill.: Richard D. Irwin, 1994.

O'Connor, Melvin C. "On the Usefulness of Financial Ratios to Investors in Common Stock," *Accounting Review,* 1963, 48(2):339–352.

RMA Annual Statement Studies. Philadelphia, Pa.: Robert Morris Associates, 1995.

Troy, Leo. *Almanac of Business and Industrial Financial Ratios.* Englewood Cliffs, N.J.: Prentice-Hall, 1996.

Part II

BASIC VALUATION

Part Two builds on the foundation established in Part One and provides the valuation framework used throughout the rest of the book. Valuation is critical to almost everything in finance.

Chapter 5 is devoted to the Time-Value-of-Money Principle. In it we develop the tools for measuring the time value of money. We demonstrate how to calculate *present value* and how to determine the value, at *any* point in time, of cash flows that actually occur at other points in time. The time-value-of-money tools are used in Chapter 6 to value *bonds* and *stocks*, which are the most common and basic types of financial securities.

The value of a security is the present value of its expected future cash flows. The present value reflects both the time value and the risk of the expected cash flows. Chapter 7 explains how to measure risk. We show that an asset's risk, and therefore its *required return*, depends on how the asset's expected future cash flows *covary* with all other assets. This result leads to a very useful model, the *capital-asset-pricing model*, for calculating an asset's required return.

THE TIME VALUE OF MONEY

Have you ever paid for something with monthly payments? Suppose you wanted to buy a $10,000 car and were told the payments would be $273.11 per month for 48 months. How would you know whether you were being offered a great deal, a fair deal, or a bad deal?

Now suppose you have $10,000 to invest for a long time, and someone tells you about an investment that will double your money, without any risk: Invest your $10,000 now, and you'll get back $20,000 in 15 years. How does this compare with other no-risk investments?

This chapter will teach you how to answer such questions; it's devoted entirely to the Time-Value-of-Money Principle. You'll learn how to determine the present value of future cash flows and, more generally, how to value at one point in time cash flows that actually occur at other points in time. We develop the logic underlying these calculations and show you procedures for solving problems using a financial calculator. We urge you, however, not to use these calculator procedures like cookbook recipes. Understanding the logic will prepare you to apply the Time-Value-of-Money Principle in the business world to new types of problems, ones that don't fit neatly into classroom examples.

Like you, companies also have to choose among investments and borrowing alternatives. In fact, their success *depends* on those choices. Financial decisions are measured by their net present value (NPV). Recall that NPV is the present value of the expected future cash flows minus the cost. The NPV is the value created or lost by a decision. Therefore, to be successful, companies must find positive-NPV opportunities and avoid negative-NPV choices.

◆ *Time-Value-of-Money:* Note that the value of a cash flow depends on when it will occur.

◆ *Two-Sided Transactions:* Be specific about the timing of cash flows to be fair to both sides of a transaction.

◆ *Risk-Return Trade-Off:* Recognize that a higher-risk investment has a higher required return. Therefore, the time value of money is especially important to the profitability of long-term investments.

◆ *Capital Market Efficiency:* Use efficient capital markets to estimate an investment's expected and required returns.

SINGLE CASH FLOWS

We introduced the concept of present values and future values in our brief discussion of the Time-Value-of-Money Principle in chapter 2. We also defined three different rates of return: expected, required, and realized. The expected return is the return you expect to earn if you make the investment. The required return is the minimum return you must expect to get to be willing to make the investment. The realized return is the return you actually earned on an investment during a given time period. We showed you that finding the present value or the

117

future value of a single cash flow is a simple calculation. After a brief recap, we'll extend its logic to deal with multiple cash flows.

DEFINITIONS, ASSUMPTIONS, AND SOME ADVICE

We need to give you several additional definitions and underlying assumptions. Please read through the complete list of notations and assumptions now, even though we won't explain some of the terms until later.

Cash Flows Occur at the End of the Time Period Unless otherwise stated, cash flows occur at the end of the time period.

Cash Outflows Are Negative Values Positive cash flows are inflows and negative cash flows are outflows from the decision maker's viewpoint. The decision maker can be a company or an individual. In other words, the algebraic sign indicates whether the amount is an inflow (+) or an outflow (−) to the decision maker.

The Decision Point Is $t = 0$ Unless otherwise stated, "now" is the instant before $t = 0$. That is, at $t = 0$, cash flows (in or out) are just about to occur. In other words, you can still make a decision that affects them, such as choosing to make an investment.

Compounding Frequency Is the Same as Payment Frequency Unless otherwise stated, financial transactions assume the compounding frequency is identical to the payment frequency. For example, if payments are monthly, compounding is also monthly.

Notation

t	A time period. For example, $t = 3$ is time period 3.
CF_t	The net cash flow at time t. For example, CF_3 is the net cash flow at the end of time period 3.
PMT	The net cash flow each period for an annuity.
r	The discount rate per period. For example, $r = 0.02$ is 2% per time period.
m	The number of compounding periods per year.
APR	The annual percentage rate (nominal annual rate). The APR equals r times m.
APY	The annual percentage yield (effective annual rate). The APY is the amount you would actually earn if you invested for exactly one year and if the investment paid interest at r per period for m periods.
n	A number of time periods. For example, n might be 36 months.
FV_n	A future value at time n. For example, FV_5 is a future value at the end of time period 5.
FVA_n	The future value of an n-period annuity (at $t = n$).
PV	A present-value amount.
PVA_n	The present value of an n-period annuity.
$PVF_{r,n}$	The present-value factor for n periods at r per period.
$FVF_{r,n}$	The future-value factor for n periods at r per period.
$PVAF_{r,n}$	The present-value-annuity factor for an n-period annuity at r per period.
$FVAF_{r,n}$	The future-value-annuity factor for an n-period annuity at r per period.
NPV	The net present value.

Advice Always use a time line. Valuation problems are easier to understand and the error rate is lower with the visual aid of a time line. Also, you should make the calculations in the chapter yourself. Doing so is critical to help develop your abilities. Similarly, you should follow through the conceptual development carefully, because this will help you understand the concepts.

Finding the Future Value of an Investment

The future value (FV) is the value an investment will grow to after a given time period. Let's say you invest $1000 today. Table 5.1 shows the amount of money you'll have accumulated at the end of each of the next six years if the bank is paying 10% interest. After one year:

$$FV_1 = \$1000 + \$100 = \$1100$$

In the second year, you'll earn $110 more—10% interest on your accumulated investment $(= [0.10]1100)$, for a total of

$$FV_2 = \$1100 + \$110 = \$1210$$

The extra $10 of interest earned in the second year is called compound interest. **Compound interest** is a way of computing interest earned where interest is earned on both the original investment *and* on the reinvested interest. As you can see in table 5.1, the interest earned each year grows because of compound interest.

Table 5.1 also shows how fast your $1000 investment grows if invested funds earn simple interest instead of compound interest. **Simple interest** is a way of computing interest earned where interest is earned on *only* the original investment. Note that in year 1 with simple interest, the interest earned is $100, the same as with compound interest. However, after that, the story changes. In year 2 with simple interest, the interest earned is again $100. No interest is earned on the first year's $100 interest. All other years also earn only $100, 10% of the original investment.

Would you rather earn compound interest or simple interest? Obviously, if the interest rates are the same, you'll have more money with compound interest than with simple interest. Because of today's technology, the use of simple interest has largely disappeared.

One way to find a future value is to calculate interest each year, adding it to the previous year's balance, and accumulating the result for the desired number of years. In table 5.1, we stopped at six years. Suppose you were investing for 20 years. It's repetitive, and such a large number of hand calculations can cause errors. Consequently, we use shortcut methods whenever we can. One shortcut method of finding future values is to use the **future-value formula:**

The Future-Value Formula

$$FV_n = PV(1 + r)^n = PV(FVF_{r,n}) \tag{5.1}$$

The amount $(1 + r)^n$ above is called the future-value factor. The **future-value factor,** $FVF_{r,n}$, is the value $1.00 will grow to if it's invested at r per period for n periods. Figure 5.1 on page 120 is a graph of $FVF_{r,n}$ as a function of n and r. As you can see there, future value is directly related to both time and the discount rate. The larger the discount rate, the larger the future value. For positive discount rates, the more time, the larger the future value.

COMPOUND INTEREST A way of computing interest earned where interest is earned on both the original investment and on interest reinvested from previous periods.

SIMPLE INTEREST A way of computing interest earned where interest is earned on only the original investment and not on interest reinvested from previous periods.

FUTURE-VALUE FORMULA A formula showing the future value, the amount that PV dollars will become, if invested at r per period for n periods.

FUTURE-VALUE FACTOR The amount $1.00 will become if it is invested at r per period for n periods.

TABLE 5.1
Future Value of an Investment of $1000

	COMPOUND INTEREST, $r = 10\%$			SIMPLE INTEREST, $r = 10\%$		
Year	Beginning Balance	Interest Earned	Ending Balance	Beginning Balance	Interest Earned	Ending Balance
1	$1000	$100	$1100	$1000	$100	$1100
2	1100	110	1210	1100	100	1200
3	1210	121	1331	1200	100	1300
4	1331	133.10	1464.10	1300	100	1400
5	1464.10	146.41	1610.51	1400	100	1500
6	1610.51	161.05	1771.56	1500	100	1600

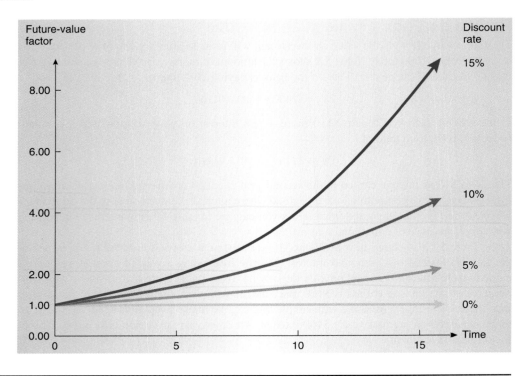

FIGURE 5.1
The future-value factor, $FVF_{r,n}$, as a function of time and various discount rates.

E X A M P L E

Finding the Future Value of an Investment

Let's redo one of the calculations in table 5.1. What is the future value of $1000 invested at 10% per year for 6 years?

Using the future-value formula with these values:

$$FV_n = PV(FVF_{r,n}) = PV(1 + r)^n = 1000(1.10)^6 = 1000(1.771561) = \$1771.56$$

To do this on a calculator, you can first raise 1.10 (= 1 + the discount rate) to the power six, using the y^x key where y = 1.10 and x = 6. Then multiply the answer by 1000, to get 1771.56. [Put in 1.1 and press $[y^x]$, put in 6 and press [=] (the display will show 1.1771561), multiply by 1000 (the display will show 1771.56).] ■

FINANCIAL CALCULATORS

There are five basic input variables to a financial (also called business) calculator:

PV	Present value
FV	Future value
n	The number of time periods
$i, k,$ or r	The discount rate per period (We use r throughout this book)
PMT	The cash flow (payment) for an annuity

The basic calculator formula encompasses each of the four basic time-value-of-money formulas we explain in this chapter. For this reason, at the start, you may need to put in a zero for some variables we haven't yet explained. Even though you may not fully appreciate the basic calculator formula right away, we state it now so you can refer back to it. Then, you can see how each of the basic time-value-of-money formulas is part of it, as we explain that formula.

The Basic Calculator Formula

$$PV = PMT\left[\frac{(1+r)^n - 1}{r(1+r)^n}\right] + FV\left[\frac{1}{(1+r)^n}\right]$$

The calculator solves this equation for each time-value-of-money calculation. It computes the variable you want on the basis of the values you put in for all the other variables. Amounts can be positive or negative. However, to use your calculator, you must understand how it handles positive and negative amounts.

Confusion about positives and negatives can occur because some calculators use a slightly modified version of the basic calculator formula: They put all the cash flows on one side and require the amount to sum to zero. You can think of this in terms of the decision maker's cash flows we described earlier: You are paying out (−) one amount to get in (+) another. For example, let's say you borrow $10,000 (PV), and the money comes to you, which is a positive. But then you pay back $248.85 per month for 48 months, and those payments go from you, which are negatives. For this modified basic calculator formula, then, after you enter the PV as a positive amount, the calculator will display the computed payment as a negative amount. Appendix A at the end of the book shows the key strokes for standard calculations on a calculator of this type, the BAII PLUS.

Whichever type you have, if you put in a negative value that should be entered as a positive in a simple calculation, the calculator will give you an error message and not compute an answer. You can adapt quickly to either type. We use positive amounts in our calculations for convenience.

Another common problem that can arise is when a calculator retains one or more values from previous calculations. If you don't put in a value for a variable, your calculator may use a value from a previous calculation and give you an incorrect answer. You can avoid this problem in two ways. One way is to push the "clear-all" button to zero out all entries. (Be sure to use the "clear-all" rather than the "clear-the-latest-entry" button. The calculator's "how-to" book will describe both procedures.) Another way to avoid the problem is to enter a zero for any variables not otherwise used. We'll use this approach for our calculator computations.

An easier way to make our future-value calculation is to use a financial calculator: Put in PV = 1000, n = 6, r = 10%, and PMT = 0, then compute FV = $1771.56. Note that, for most financial calculators, you enter the discount rate as a whole percent, 10, *not* as a decimal number, 0.10. Throughout the rest of the book, we'll show you such calculator calculations in a standardized format. The amount the calculator solves for is in bold type. The other amounts are inputs.

| N = 6 | r = 10 | PV = 1000 | PMT = 0 | **FV = 1771.56** |

Let's practice on another example.

Grandma's Savings Bond

EXAMPLE

Suppose your grandma bought you a savings bond for $100 when you were born. If the bond earns 6% interest, what will the bond be worth on your 21st birthday?

(continued on following page)

(Grandma's Savings Bond *continued from previous page*)

Using the future-value formula, the bond will be worth:

$$FV_n = PV(FVF_{r,n}) = PV(1 + r)^n$$
$$FV_{21} = 100(1.06)^{21} = 100(3.39956) = \$339.96$$

| | N = 21 | r = 6 | PV = 100 | PMT = 0 | **FV = 339.96** |

What would your bond be worth if it earned 10% instead of 6%? Do this one on your calculator. The answer is $740.02.

| | N = 21 | r = 10 | PV = 100 | PMT = 0 | **FV = 740.02** |

Present Value of a Future Cash Flow

Now, let's find the *present* value of an expected *future* cash flow. The present value (PV) is the amount that if invested today at *r* per period would provide a given future value at time *n*. We can compute a PV using the **present-value formula:**

PRESENT-VALUE FOR-MULA A formula showing the present value, the amount that must be invested today at *r* per period for *n* periods to grow to a particular future value.

The Present-Value Formula

$$PV = FV_n\left[\frac{1}{(1 + r)^n}\right] = FV_n(PVF_{r,n}) \tag{5.2}$$

The present-value formula is simply a rearrangement of the future-value formula. We're solving for PV instead of FV. In the present-value formula, the amount $[1/(1 + r)^n]$ is called the present-value factor. The **present-value factor,** $PVF_{r,n}$, is the amount that, if invested today at *r* per period will grow to exactly $1.00 *n* years from today.

PRESENT-VALUE FACTOR The amount that must be invested today at *r* per period for *n* periods to result in a future value of $1.00.

Figure 5.2 is a graph of $PVF_{r,n}$ as a function of time and various discount rates. It shows that present value is inversely related to both time and the discount rate. That is, the larger the discount rate, the smaller the present value. For positive discount rates, the more time until you get the cash flow, the smaller the present value will be. Like two kids on a seesaw, when one goes up the other goes down.

EXAMPLE

Present Value of a Future Cash Flow

What is the present value of $2000 to be received 2 years from today if the required return is 8% per year?

Using the present-value formula,

$$PV = FV_n(PVF_{r,n}) = FV_n\left[\frac{1}{(1 + r)^n}\right] = 2000\left[\frac{1}{(1.08)^2}\right] = 2000(0.857339) = \$1714.68$$

$PVF_{8\%,2}$ is 0.857339, and the present value of the future $2000 is $1714.68.

| | N = 2 | r = 8 | **PV = 1714.68** | PMT = 0 | FV = 2000 |

Solving for a Return

If you look back at the basic calculator formula, you can see how the present-value formula is part of it. You can also see that if you know any four of the five input variables, the formula can be solved for the fifth.

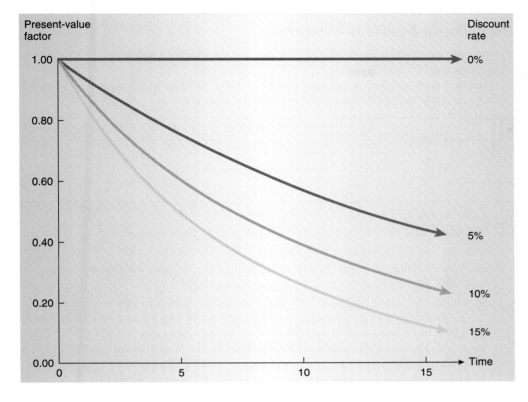

Present-value factor

Discount rate

FIGURE 5.2
The present-value factor, $PVF_{r,n}$, as a function of time and various discount rates.

For example, to find a PV, we put in FV (the expected future cash flow), n (the time the cash flow will occur), r (the required return), and PMT = 0. However, suppose you already know PV from a market price, but you don't know the discount rate. You can rearrange the formula to solve for the expected return. Solving for r, with PMT = 0, we get

$$r = \left(\frac{FV}{PV}\right)^{1/n} - 1$$

The Expected Return for a Bank One Certificate of Deposit

EXAMPLE

Suppose Bank One offers a certificate of deposit that pays $10,000 in 3 years in exchange for $7938.32 today. What interest rate is Bank One offering? In other words, what is the expected return from investing in this certificate of deposit?

Using our rearranged formula, with $n = 3$, FV = 10,000, and PV = 7938.32, we find that the expected return is

$$r = \left(\frac{10,000}{7938.32}\right)^{0.3333} - 1 = 1.08 - 1 = 8.00\%$$

N = 3	**r = 8**	PV = 7938.32	PMT = 0 FV = 10,000

Solving for the Number of Time Periods

We could also rearrange the basic calculator formula to solve for n, using natural logarithms. However, it's much easier to let the calculator do the work.

EXAMPLE

How Long to Double Your Salary?

Are you earning a salary currently? If you are, and your salary grew at 6% per year, how many years would it take to double?

Even though we don't know how much you make, so long as it's more than zero, we can tell you it will take 11.9 years to double if it's growing at 6% per year. Try it.

$N = 11.9$ $r = 6$ $PV = 1$ $PMT = 0$ $FV = 2$

Self-Check

1. What is the future-value formula? What is the present-value formula?

2. Is the present-value factor the reciprocal of the future-value factor?

3. What is the future value of $100 invested for 1 year at 0%? What is the present value of $100 received in 1 year discounted back at 100%?

4. *Choose the correct word in each set of parentheses:* **a.** The future-value factor is (positively/negatively) related to the discount rate. **b.** The present-value factor is (positively/negatively) related to the discount rate. **c.** The future-value factor is (positively/negatively) related to the number of time periods. **d.** The present-value factor is (positively/negatively) related to the number of time periods.

5. Explain why present value and the discount rate are inversely related.

VALUING ANNUITIES

ANNUITY A series of regular periodic payments of equal size.

Annuity payments are a very common financial arrangement. An **annuity** is a series of equal periodic payments. The payments occur regularly, such as every month or every year.

Annuities occur in many different financial transactions. Monthly payments on a car loan, a student loan, or a mortgage are annuities. Monthly rent is an annuity. A paycheck, with a fixed salary, is an annuity. Lease, interest, and dividend payments are annuities. Any series of equal, periodic payments is an annuity.

The majority of annuities have end-of-period payments. For example, car loans usually require end-of-month payments. If it's a 48-month loan, the first payment is made at the end of the first month and the 48th (and last) is made at the end of month 48. This kind of annuity, where payments occur at the end of each period, is called an **ordinary annuity.**

ORDINARY ANNUITY An annuity with payments at the end of each period.

Other annuities, such as for a rental, require beginning-of-period payments. For a 12-month apartment lease, the first rent payment is due at the beginning of the first month, and the 12th (and last) is due at the beginning of the 12th month. This kind of annuity, where payments occur at the beginning of each period, is called an **annuity due.**

ANNUITY DUE An annuity with payments at the beginning of each period.

We know the timing of payments affects value. Therefore, it's critical to know whether you are dealing with an ordinary annuity or an annuity due. We'll start by analyzing the future and present values of an ordinary annuity. Later, we'll show you how to handle an annuity due.

The Future Value of an Annuity

We started our discussion of the time value of money in chapter 2 with an example of depositing money in a savings account. Now consider a savings plan for depositing the same amount every period for n periods. How much will you have at the end of the n periods?

Let the periodic cash flow, PMT, be the amount deposited at the end of each time period (that is, $CF_1 = CF_2 = \ldots = CF_n = PMT$). Figure 5.3 illustrates the future value of an n-period annuity.

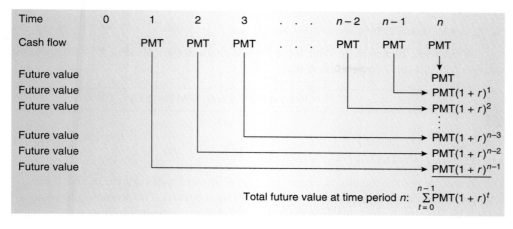

Total future value at time period n: $\sum_{t=0}^{n-1} PMT(1+r)^t$

FIGURE 5.3
The future value of an
n-period annuity.

The future value of an annuity is the total value that will have accumulated at the end of the annuity if the annuity payments are all invested at r per period. The future value of an annuity can be computed using the future value formula to value each payment and then adding up the individual values to get the total. If we start with the last payment at time $t = n$ and proceed backward to the first payment at time $t = 1$, the future value of the annuity at time n, FVA_n, is

$$FVA_n = PMT(1+r)^0 + PMT(1+r)^1 + \ldots + PMT(1+r)^{n-1}$$

Figure 5.3 illustrates this calculation. Note that the first payment (at $t = 1$) earns interest for $(n - 1)$ periods, *not* n periods. Each subsequent payment earns interest for one less period than the previous one. Note that the last payment occurs exactly at the end of the annuity, so it doesn't earn any interest; $(1+r)^0 = 1$.

The equation for FVA_n has a PMT in every term on the right-hand side. If the PMT is factored out, the equation can be rewritten as

$$FVA_n = PMT[(1+r)^0 + (1+r)^1 + \ldots + (1+r)^{n-1}] = PMT\sum_{t=0}^{n-1}(1+r)^t$$

where Σ is a summation. This equation can be simplified to

$$\times \quad FVA_n = PMT\left[\frac{(1+r)^n - 1}{r}\right] = PMT(FVAF_{r,n}) \quad \times \qquad (5.3)$$

The quantity in large brackets in equation (5.3) is called the future-value-annuity factor. The **future-value-annuity factor,** $FVAF_{r,n}$, is the total future value of $1.00 per period for n periods invested at r per period. The particular values for PMT, n, and r along with equation (5.3) are all that's needed to determine the future value of the annuity, regardless of the number of payments.

FUTURE-VALUE-ANNUITY FACTOR The total future value of an annuity of $1.00 per period for n periods invested at rate r per period.

Saving for Retirement at Citibank

EXAMPLE

Suppose you save $2000 per year at the end of each year for 30 years at Citibank, and the money earns 5% interest per year. How much will you have at the end of the 30 years?

The cash flows are like those in figure 5.3 with $n = 30$. Therefore, using equation (5.3),

$$FVA_{30} = PMT(FVAF_{5\%,30}) = 2000\left[\frac{(1.05)^{30} - 1}{0.05}\right] = 2000(66.43885) = \$132{,}877.70$$

$FVAF_{5\%,30}$ is 66.43885, and the future value of the annuity is $132,877.70.

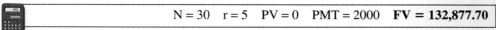

$$N = 30 \quad r = 5 \quad PV = 0 \quad PMT = 2000 \quad \textbf{FV = 132,877.70}$$

(continued on following page)

(Saving for Retirement at Citibank *continued from previous page*)

What would be the future value if the interest rate was 6% instead of 5%? Compute the answer of $158,116.37 on your calculator.

| $N = 30$ | $r = 6$ | $PV = 0$ | $PMT = 2000$ | **$FV = 158{,}116.37$** |

The Present Value of an Annuity

The present value of an annuity is the amount that, if invested today at r per period, could exactly provide equal payments of PMT every period for n periods. The present value of an annuity, PVA_n, is simply the sum of the present values of the n individual payments:

$$PVA_n = PMT\frac{1}{(1+r)^1} + PMT\frac{1}{(1+r)^2} + \ldots + PMT\frac{1}{(1+r)^n}$$

The present value of an n-period annuity is illustrated in figure 5.4. Because the cash flows or payments are all identical, we can rewrite this as

$$PVA_n = PMT\left[\frac{1}{(1+r)^1} + \frac{1}{(1+r)^2} + \ldots + \frac{1}{(1+r)^n}\right] = PMT\sum_{t=1}^{n}\frac{1}{(1+r)^t}$$

This equation for PVA_n can also be simplified; it becomes

$$PVA_n = PMT\left[\frac{(1+r)^n - 1}{r(1+r)^n}\right] = PMT(PVAF_{r,n}) \tag{5.4}$$

FIGURE 5.4
The present value of an n-period annuity.

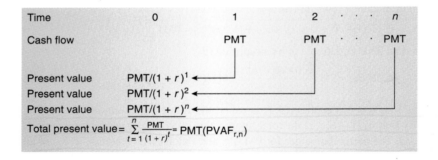

PRESENT-VALUE-ANNUITY FACTOR The total present value of an annuity of $1.00 per period for n periods discounted back at r per period.

The quantity in large brackets in equation (5.4) is called the present-value-annuity factor.[1] The **present-value-annuity factor**, $PVAF_{r,n}$, is the total present value of an annuity of $1.00 per period for n periods discounted at r per period. The particular values for PMT, n, and r are all that is needed to determine the present value of the annuity.

Calculating Annuity Payments

We've shown how to compute the present and future values of an annuity, given a set of payments and a discount rate. When you borrow money, the amount is the present value, and the annuity is the loan payments. We can solve for the payments by rearranging equation (5.4):

$$PMT = PVA_n\left[\frac{r(1+r)^n}{(1+r)^n - 1}\right] = \frac{PVA_n}{PVAF_{r,n}} \tag{5.5}$$

---

[1]The present value of an annuity can also be expressed as the PV of FVA_n. To see this, show that $PVAF_{r,n} = FVAF_{r,n}$ times $PVF_{r,n}$.

Computing the Present Value of a Car Loan from GMAC

Suppose General Motors Acceptance Corporation (GMAC) expects to receive future car-loan payments of $200 per month for the next 36 months from one of its customers. The first payment is due 1 month from today. The interest rate on the loan is 1% per month. How much money is being borrowed? In other words, what is the present value of the loan?

Using equation (5.4) with PMT = $200, $n = 36$, and $r = 1\%$:

$$PVA_{36} = PMT(PVAF_{1\%,36}) = 200\left[\frac{(1.01)^{36} - 1}{0.01(1.01)^{36}}\right] = 200(30.1075) = \$6021.50$$

$PVAF_{1\%,36}$ is 30.1075, and the present value is $6021.50.

N = 36	r = 1	**PV = 6021.50**	PMT = 200	FV = 0

Computing Annual Loan Payments

Consider a $10,000 loan requiring equal payments at the end of each of the next five years. If the interest rate is 9% per year, what are the payments?

Using equation (5.5) we get:

$$PMT = PVA_5\left[\frac{(0.09)(1.09)^5}{(1.09)^5 - 1}\right] = \frac{10,000}{PVAF_{9\%,5}} = \frac{10,000}{3.88965} = \$2570.92$$

$PVAF_{9\%,5}$ is 3.88965, and the payments are $2570.92.

N = 5	r = 9	PV = 10,000	**PMT = 2570.92**	FV = 0

Now suppose you're getting ahead of the game and saving money regularly rather than paying off a loan. The accumulated amount is a future value. We can solve for the amount that must be saved regularly to accumulate a given future value, this time by rearranging equation (5.3):

$$\times \quad PMT = FVA_n\left[\frac{r}{(1 + r)^n - 1}\right] = \frac{FVA_n}{FVAF_{r,n}} \quad \times \qquad (5.6)$$

Saving at the IBM Credit Union for a Down Payment on a House

Dina Naples is saving money at the IBM Credit Union for a down payment on a house. How much does she have to save at the end of every month to accumulate a total of $12,000 at the end of 5 years if the money is invested at 0.5% per month?

Using equation (5.6) we get:

$$PMT = FVA_{60}\left[\frac{0.005}{(1.005)^{60} - 1}\right] = \frac{12,000}{FVAF_{0.5\%,60}} = \frac{12,000}{69.77} = \$171.99$$

$FVAF_{0.5\%,60}$ is 69.77, and the payments are $171.99.

N = 60	r = 0.5	PV = 0	**PMT = 171.99**	FV = 12,000

Amortizing a Loan

LOAN AMORTIZATION SCHEDULE A table showing, for each loan payment, the size of the payment, the amount of interest paid, the reduction in the loan balance, and the remaining loan balance.

A **loan amortization schedule** shows how the loan is paid off over time. That is, it shows how the principal (the original amount borrowed) and interest are paid. Because an installment loan is an annuity, an amortization schedule for such a loan shows the relationships among the payments, principal, and interest rate.

To create an amortization schedule, start with the amount borrowed. To this amount add the first period's interest, and then subtract the first period's payment. The result is the remaining balance, which is the starting amount for the second period. Repeat this procedure each period until the remainder becomes zero at the end of the last period.

E X A M P L E

Amortizing a Loan

Suppose a $1000 loan with an interest rate of 10% requires equal payments at the end of each of the next 3 years. The annual loan payments will be $402.11.

| N = 3 | r = 10 | PV = 1000 | **PMT = 402.11** | FV = 0 |

What is this loan's amortization schedule?

This loan's amortization schedule is given in table 5.2. Each period's interest increases the remaining balance by the interest rate times the previous period's remaining balance. The loan payment then reduces the remaining balance. Since the loan payment exceeds the first year's interest charge, the remaining balance is sequentially reduced to zero after *n* periods.

The loan in table 5.2 is not amortized precisely to zero because the loan payment was rounded off to the nearest penny. Note how the breakdown of the loan payment into interest paid and principal reduction changes during the life of the loan. Early in the loan's life, the interest portion is high and the principal reduction is low. Later on, as principal has been paid off, the interest portion is low, and the principal reduction is high. ∎

Calculating the Discount Rate and Number of Annuity Payments

In addition to solving for the payments, future value, or present value of an annuity, we can solve for the discount rate or the number of annuity payments. However, unlike the payments, we cannot always rearrange our equation to solve for these variables. Instead, the equation must be solved using trial and error. So the calculator is especially convenient for calculating these variables because it performs the tedious trial-and-error calculations automatically.

TABLE 5.2
A Loan Amortization Schedule

	PERIOD		
	1	**2**	**3**
a. Principal at start of period	$1000.00	$697.89	$365.57
b. Interest for the period	100.00	69.79	36.56
(10% of starting principal)			
c. Balance	1100.00	767.68	402.13
(a + b)			
d. Payment	402.11	402.11	402.11
e. Principal at start of next period	697.89	365.57	.02*
(c − d)			

*Not zero because of rounding error.

Computing the Interest Rate on a Mortgage from Chase Home Mortgage

EXAMPLE

Suppose Chase Home Mortgage offers a mortgage loan of $97,218.33 to buy a house. It requires payments of $1000 a month for 30 years (360 payments). What interest rate is Chase charging?

Using equation (5.4):

$$97,218.33 = 1000(\text{PVAF}_{r,360}) = 1000\left[\frac{(1+r)^{360} - 1}{r(1+r)^{360}}\right]$$

An r of 1% solves this equation, so Chase is charging 1% per month.

$$N = 360 \quad \mathbf{r = 1} \quad PV = 97,218.33 \quad PMT = 1000 \quad FV = 0$$

Calculating the Remaining Life of a Car Loan

EXAMPLE

Let's say you borrowed $15,000 to buy a car. The loan was originally a 48-month loan charging 0.75% per month on the unpaid balance. Your monthly payment is $373.28.

$$N = 48 \quad r = 0.75 \quad PV = 15,000 \quad \mathbf{PMT = 373.28} \quad FV = 0$$

Now you don't remember how many payments are remaining, but your statement says that your remaining balance is now $9092.81. How many more monthly payments are left?

Again, using equation (5.4):

$$9092.81 = 373.28(\text{PVAF}_{0.75\%,n}) = 373.28\left[\frac{(1 + 0.0075)^n - 1}{0.0075(1 + 0.0075)^n}\right]$$

An n of 27 solves this equation, so you have to make 27 more monthly payments.

$$\mathbf{N = 27} \quad r = 0.75 \quad PV = 9092.81 \quad PMT = 373.28 \quad FV = 0$$

Valuing Annuities Not Starting Today

Sometimes, annuities start at a time other than right away (where the first payment is at $t = 1$). The present value of such an annuity can be computed from the difference between the present values of two other annuities. The first annuity goes from now until the end of the one in question. The second annuity goes from now until the start of the one in question. The difference between the two values is the value of the annuity in question.

EXAMPLE

Computing the Present Value of an Annuity Starting in the Future

What is the present value of $5000 to be received at the end of each of the years 4 through 7 if the required return is 12% per year?

This kind of "postponed" annuity, one not starting until sometime in the future, is equivalent to the difference between two other annuities. In this case, the *difference* is between a 7-year annuity and a 3-year annuity. That is, the net cash flow in each period in the postponed annuity equals the cash flow for that period in a 7-year annuity minus the cash flow for that period in a 3-year annuity. The cash flows cancel each other out in the first three periods. This is illustrated in figure 5.5.

Therefore, the present value of the postponed annuity equals the present value of a 7-year annuity minus the present value of a 3-year annuity, $22,818.78 - 12,009.16 = \$10,809.62$.

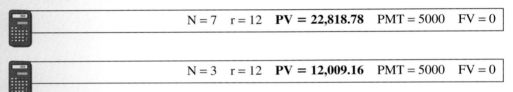

| N = 7 | r = 12 | **PV = 22,818.78** | PMT = 5000 | FV = 0 |

| N = 3 | r = 12 | **PV = 12,009.16** | PMT = 5000 | FV = 0 |

Perpetuities

PERPETUITY An annuity that has an infinite life.

An annuity that goes on forever is called a **perpetuity.** Although perpetuities actually exist in some situations, the most important reason for studying them is that they can be used as a simple and fairly accurate approximation of a long-term annuity.

As we showed in figure 5.2, the present-value factor becomes smaller as n becomes larger. Therefore, later payments in a long annuity add little to the present value of the annu-

FIGURE 5.5
Duplicating the annuity cash flows for a "postponed" annuity.

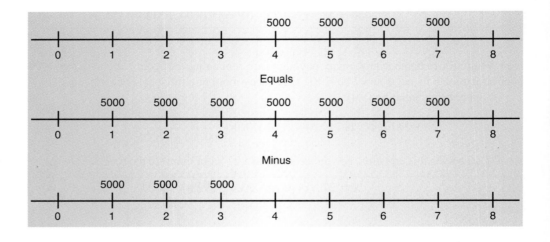

ity. For example, at a required return of 10% per year, the present value of getting $100 in 30 years is only $5.73. It is a mere 85 cents if payment is going to take 50 years. As it turns out, the present value of an annuity has a maximum value, no matter how many payments are expected. That maximum value is the value of a perpetuity.

To examine the present value of a perpetuity, we can start with the present value of an annuity and see what happens when the life of the annuity, n, becomes very large. Let's start by rewriting equation (5.4), the present-value-of-an-annuity formula:

$$PVA_n = PMT\left[\frac{(1+r)^n - 1}{r(1+r)^n}\right] = PMT\left[\frac{(1+r)^n}{r(1+r)^n}\right] - PMT\left[\frac{1}{r(1+r)^n}\right]$$

$$PVA_n = \left[\frac{PMT}{r}\right] - \left[\frac{PMT}{r(1+r)^n}\right]$$

Written this way, you can see what happens when n becomes large. The first term on the right-hand side of the bottom expression is not affected by n. But the second term gets smaller because $(1+r)^n$ gets larger when n increases. As n gets really big, the second term goes to zero. Therefore, the present value of a perpetuity is

$$\times \quad PVA_{perpetuity} = \frac{PMT}{r} \quad \times \tag{5.7}$$

Present Value of a Perpetuity

What is the present value of $1000 per year, forever, if the required return is 8% per year?
Using equation (5.7):

$$PVA_{perpetuity} = \frac{PMT}{r} = \frac{1000}{0.08} = \$12,500.00$$

Now let's say the $1000 per year lasted for only 50 years. What would be the present value, and how well does the present value of the perpetuity approximate this present value?
The actual present value for the 50-year annuity is

$$PVA_{50} = PMT(PVAF_{8\%,50}) = 1000\left[\frac{(1.08)^{50} - 1}{0.08(1.08)^{50}}\right] = 1000(12.23348) = \$12,233.48$$

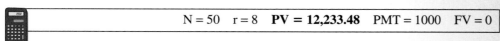

N = 50   r = 8   **PV = 12,233.48**   PMT = 1000   FV = 0

In this case, the perpetuity is worth only about 2% more than a 50-year annuity. This is because the present value of the very distant (the 51st and subsequent) payments is very small. ■

Valuing an Annuity Due

The payments for an annuity due occur at the beginning of each period instead of at the end. Because each payment occurs one period earlier, an annuity due has a higher present value than a comparable ordinary annuity. Likewise, an annuity due has a higher future value than a comparable ordinary annuity because each payment has an additional period to compound. In fact, a simple way to value an annuity due is to multiply the value of a comparable ordinary annuity by $(1+r)$.

EXAMPLE

Computing the Future Value and Present Value of an Annuity Due

What are the future and present values of an annuity due of $100 per year for 3 years, if the required return is 10% per year?

If this were an ordinary annuity, the future and present values would be:

$$FVA_n = PMT(FVAF_{10\%,3}) = 100\left[\frac{(1.10)^3 - 1}{0.10}\right] = \$331.00$$

N = 3	r = 10	PV = 0	PMT = 100	**FV = 331.00**

$$PVA_n = PMT(PVAF_{10\%,3}) = 100\left[\frac{(1.10)^3 - 1}{0.10(1.10)^3}\right] = \$248.69$$

N = 3	r = 10	**PV = 248.69**	PMT = 100	FV = 0

Then, for the annuity due:

Future value of annuity due = $FVA_n (1 + r)$ = 331 (1.10) = $364.10

Present value of annuity due = $PVA_n (1 + r)$ = 248.69 (1.10) = $273.56

You can also use a financial calculator to compute the FV and PV of the ordinary annuity due directly. To do so, put your calculator into the BEGIN mode and make the FV and PV calculations in the ordinary way. ■

Self-Check

1. Describe the layout of a loan amortization schedule.

2. Why is the value of a perpetuity a good estimate of an otherwise comparable long-term annuity?

3. Indicate whether each of the following is typically an ordinary annuity or an annuity due: **a.** Monthly installment on a car loan **b.** Monthly rent payment on an apartment **c.** Monthly paycheck for someone on a fixed monthly salary **d.** The monthly payment on your cable television hookup

MULTIPLE EXPECTED FUTURE CASH FLOWS

Unlike an annuity, in some cases future cash flows vary in size. In this section, we demonstrate a few common-sense methods for computing the value of a set of unequal future cash flows. We'll describe three of these methods through the use of the following example.

EXAMPLE

Computing the Present Value of a Set of Unequal Future Cash Flows

Suppose you expect to receive the following cash flows at the times indicated:

Time	0	1	2	3
Cash flow	$3000	$2000	$8000	$5000

If the required return is 10%, what is the total present value of these cash flows?

The total present value of these cash flows can be calculated by calculating the present value of each cash flow and then adding them together:

$$PV = \frac{3000}{(1.1)^0} + \frac{2000}{(1.1)^1} + \frac{8000}{(1.1)^2} + \frac{5000}{(1.1)^3}$$

$$PV = 3000 + 1818.182 + 6611.570 + 3756.574 = \$15,186.326$$

This calculation is illustrated in figure 5.6.

An alternative method for calculating the total present value of our set of unequal future cash flows is called the "rollback" method: Start with the most distant cash flow ($5000 at time 3) and discount it back one period (at 10%). Its value at $t = 2$ is $4545.45 (= 5000/1.10). Add this amount to the time 2 cash flow of $8000 to get $12,545.45. Discount this amount back one period. Its value at $t = 1$ is $11,404.96 (= 12,545.45/1.10). Add the time 1 cash flow to this amount to get $13,404.96. Discount this amount back one period. Its value is $12,186.33 (= 13,404.96/1.10). Finally, this amount plus the $3000 time 0 cash flow equals the total present value of $15,186.33. Figure 5.7 illustrates the rollback method of calculating a present value.

Finally, many financial calculators provide a third method for valuing this unequal set of future cash flows. Because calculators are not identical, you'll have to use your own calculator's manual to learn how to use this method. There is an important advantage to using this calculator feature: If you already know the present value, but don't know the discount rate, the calculator can automatically compute the expected return for the set of unequal cash flows. This can eliminate the hassle of very tedious trial-and-error calculations. ■

Valuing Cash Flows at Other Points Along the Time Line

Thus far, we've calculated a present value ($t = 0$) or a future value at $t = n$. But suppose we want to know the total value of a set of cash flows at some other point in time. Calculating such a value directly may require extra care, but it uses the same formulas. If you already know the present or future value, calculating such values is quite straightforward. Our next example illustrates this process by building on our last example.

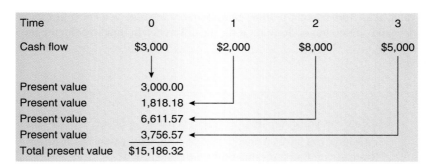

FIGURE 5.6
Computing the present value of a set of unequal future cash flows.

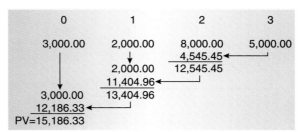

FIGURE 5.7
The rollback method for calculating a present value.

EXAMPLE

Computing Total Value at Other Points in Time

Let's reconsider the value of our set of unequal cash flows. What is their total value at $t = 2$? Cash flows before $t = 2$ must be compounded forward. Cash flows on or after $t = 2$ must be discounted back. The sum of these compounded and discounted cash flows plus the $t = 2$ cash flow equals FV_2, the total value at $t = 2$:

$$FV_2 = 3000(1.10)^2 + 2000(1.10)^1 + 8000(1.10)^0 + 5000\frac{1}{(1.10)^1}$$

$$= 3630 + 2200 + 8000 + 4545.45 = \$18,375.45$$

This calculation is illustrated in figure 5.8.

In this case, there's a shortcut for computing FV_2. In our previous example, we computed the present value of this set of cash flows. This value can be used directly to find FV_2. Simply compound the total present value forward two periods, just as though it's a single cash flow at $t = 0$:

$$FV_n = PV(FVF_{r,n}) = PV(1 + r)^n$$
$$FV_2 = 15,186.326(1.10)^2 = \$18,375.45$$

| $N = 2$ | $r = 10$ | $PV = 15,186.326$ | $PMT = 0$ | **FV = 18,375.45** |

In a parallel way, FV_2 can also be used directly to find FV_3. Simply compound 18,375.45 forward one period, just as though it's a single cash flow at $t = 2$:

$$FV_3 = FV_2(FVF_{10\%,1}) = 18,375.45(1.10) = \$20,213.00$$

| $N = 1$ | $r = 10$ | $PV = 18,375.45$ | $PMT = 0$ | **FV = 20,213.00** |

The example illustrates a very important point we want to emphasize. Once you have the total value of a set of cash flows at *any* point in time, you can easily compute the total value at any *other* point in time. Simply *treat the value you know as though it's a single cash flow* and compound or discount it for the difference in time to compute the value you're looking for.

Self-Check

1. How can you compute the present value of an unequal set of future cash flows?

2. Assume you have an unequal set of cash flows extending from $t = 1$ through $t = 10$. How can you find the value of this stream at $t = 4$?

FIGURE 5.8
Computing the future value at time period 2 of an unequal set of future cash flows.

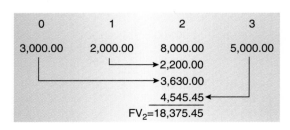

COMPOUNDING FREQUENCY

Thus far, we've been careful to use a discount rate that is consistent with the frequency of the cash flows—for example, 1% per *month* with *monthly* payments or 10% per *year* with *annual* payments. In practice, interest rates are typically stated in one of two ways, as an annual percentage rate (APR) or as an annual percentage yield (APY), even though interest may be calculated and paid more often than annually.

Annual Percentage Rate (APR)

The **annual percentage rate (APR)** is the periodic rate times the number of periods in a year. The APR is a nominal rate, a rate "in name only." The true (effective) annual rate may be different from the APR because of the compounding frequency.

The **compounding frequency** is how often interest is compounded. For example, the compounding frequency might be monthly (12 times per year), quarterly (4 times), or annually (once). The periodic rate is an effective rate, but recall that two periods of interest is more than double one. The second period's interest includes interest on the first period's interest.

With *m* compounding periods per year and a periodic rate of *r*, the APR is:

$$\text{APR} = (m)(r) \tag{5.8}$$

ANNUAL PERCENTAGE RATE (APR) The nominal annual rate that ignores the effect of compound interest within the year. The APR is the periodic rate (*r*) times the number of compounding periods per year (*m*).

COMPOUNDING FREQUENCY The number of times interest is compounded in a year.

Computing an APR at Bankers Trust

EXAMPLE

Suppose Bankers Trust offers a loan, charging 1% per month. What is the APR?
Using equation (5.8), the APR is 12%:

$$\text{APR} = 12(0.01) = 0.12 = 12.00\%$$

Note: The compounding frequency is the same as the payment frequency, unless it is otherwise specified.

Annual Percentage Yield (APY)

The **annual percentage yield (APY)** is the effective (true) annual rate of return. It is the rate you actually earn or pay in one year, taking into account the effect of compounding. The APY is computed by compounding the periodic rate for the compounding frequency:

$$\text{APY} = \left(1 + \frac{\text{APR}}{m}\right)^m - 1 \tag{5.9}$$

ANNUAL PERCENTAGE YIELD (APY) The effective (true) annual rate, which takes into account the effect of compound interest.

If interest is compounded once per year, *m* = 1, the APY and the APR have the same value. Whenever compounding occurs more than once, the APY, the true rate, is more than the APR.

Computing the APY from Bankers Trust's APR

EXAMPLE

What is the APY on Bankers Trust's 12% APR loan, with monthly compounding?
Using equation (5.9), the APY is 12.68%:

$$\text{APY} = (1 + r)^m - 1 = (1.01)^{12} - 1 = 0.1268 = 12.68\%$$

We can also compute the APY from the future value (= 1.1268): APY = FV − 1 = 0.1268 = 12.68%.

| N = 12 | r = 1 | PV = 1.00 | PMT = 0 | **FV = 1.1268** |

EXAMPLE *Computing the APY for a Credit Card*

Suppose a credit card charges 1.50% per month on unpaid balances. The periodic rate $r =$ 1.5% and $m = 12$. The APR $= 0.015(12) = 0.18 = 18.00\%$. What is the APY? That is, what is the true, or effective annual return?

Using equation (5.9):

$$APY = (1 + r)^m - 1 = (1.015)^{12} - 1 = 0.1956 = 19.56\%$$

This means that APY $=$ FV $- 1 = 0.1956 = 19.56\%$.

$N = 12 \quad r = 1.5 \quad PV = 1.00 \quad PMT = 0 \quad \textbf{FV = 1.1956}$

The Effect of Compounding Frequency on Future Value

How does compounding frequency affect future value? To answer this question, let's compare yearly, semiannually, quarterly, monthly, and weekly compounding for saving $10,000 for a year at a 12% APR.

The future value of $10,000 in one year is shown in table 5.3 for all of these compounding frequencies. The APY equals the 12% APR for yearly compounding. But the table shows how the future value and APY increase as the compounding frequency increases.

Another way to understand an APY is to say that it's the total interest earned in a year (annual interest) divided by the principal. That is,

$$APY = \frac{\text{annual interest}}{\text{principal}}$$

For example, the annual interest for monthly compounding is $1268.25, which, divided by $10,000, gives the same 12.68% we got using equation (5.9) and a calculator.

TABLE 5.3
Future Values and APYs for Various Compounding Frequencies

COMPOUNDING FREQUENCY	m	PV	FV_{YEAR}	ANNUAL INTEREST	APY
Yearly	1	$10,000	$11,200.00	$1,200.00	12.0000%
Semiannually	2	10,000	11,236.00	1,236.00	12.3600
Quarterly	4	10,000	11,255.09	1,255.09	12.5509
Monthly	12	10,000	11,268.25	1,268.25	12.6825
Weekly	52	10,000	11,273.41	1,273.41	12.7341
Daily	365	10,000	11,274.75	1,274.75	12.7475
Continuous	∞	10,000	11,274.97	1,274.97	12.7497

The APR is 12%.
m = number of times interest is compounded per year
When $t = 1$, FV $= PV(1 + APR/m)^m = 10,000(1 + 0.12/m)^m$
Interest $=$ FV $-$ PV
APY $= (1 + APR/m)^m - 1 =$ Interest/PV
For continuous compounding, FV $= PV\,e^{APR} = 10,000e^{0.12}$
For continuous compounding, APY $= e^{APR} - 1 = e^{0.12} - 1 =$ Interest/PV

Continuous Compounding

If more frequent compounding increases the future value, what if we compound daily, hourly, or even every minute? These are all examples of *discrete compounding,* where interest is compounded a finite number of times per year. If interest is compounded an infinite number of times per year, we have *continuous compounding.*

The APR and APY with Continuous Compounding

When m, the compounding frequency, becomes large enough, compounding becomes essentially continuous. Without giving the proof, it turns out that with continuous compounding:

$$\times \quad \text{APY} = e^{\text{APR}} - 1 \quad \times \tag{5.10}$$

where e is approximately 2.718.[2] The function e^x is called an exponential function. It is usually found on a calculator with either an "e^x" or "exp" on the key.

Computing an APY with Continuous Compounding

What is the APY for a 12% APR continuously compounded?
  Using equation (5.10), we have

$$\text{APY} = e^{\text{APR}} - 1 = e^{0.12} - 1 = 0.1274969 = 12.74969\%$$

An alternative to this calculation is to approximate APY using a very large value for m. For example, $m = 6656$ (compounding about 18 times per day) yields APY = 12.74956%.

| $N = 6656$ | $r = 12/6656$ | $PV = 1.00$ | $PMT = 0$ | **FV = 1.1274956** |

This is very close to the APY. So you can see that a large value for m in equation (5.9) is a good approximation for the APY with continuous compounding, equation (5.10). ■

Figure 5.9 on page 138 shows how compounding frequency affects future value by graphing future value as a function of annual, semiannual, and continuous compounding for 20% APR. Note how the "stair steps" are smaller and more frequent for semiannual compounding and how they become a smooth curve with continuous compounding. Note also that the amount increases faster with more frequent compounding.

Self-Check

1. What is the APR (annual percentage rate)? Does it reflect the frequency of compounding?

2. What is the APY (annual percentage yield)? How does it take into account the effect of compounding?

3. Explain in your own words the meaning of continuous compounding.

4. Suppose a bank offers you a 10% APR certificate of deposit. You can specify annual, semiannual, quarterly, monthly, or daily compounding. Which would you choose?

5. Suppose you're going to borrow from a bank at 10% APR. You can specify annual, semiannual, quarterly, monthly, or daily compounding. Which would you choose?

---

[2]This number occurs frequently in the mathematical and natural sciences. It is the base for what are called *natural logarithms,* usually denoted *ln; ln* is the inverse function of e. That is, *ln(e^x)* = x.

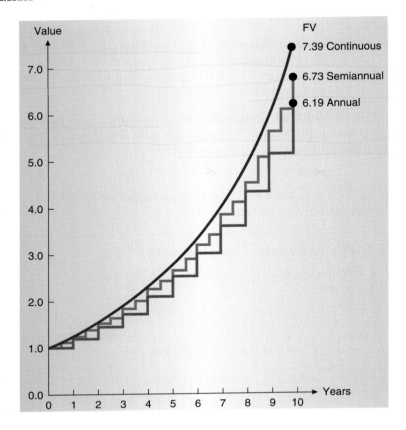

FIGURE 5.9
Future value as a function
of annual, semiannual, and
continuous compounding
for 20% APR.

PARTIAL TIME PERIODS

Earlier, we used a fractional exponent (0.333) to solve for the 8% expected return from a
Bank One certificate of deposit. Using the time-value-of-money formulas with partial time
periods requires care and an understanding of the assumptions underlying the formulas.
Drawing a time line can be helpful when solving problems involving partial time periods.

Single Cash Flows

Computing present and/or future values of single cash flows between partial time periods is
straightforward, because a fractional exponent can be used directly.

EXAMPLE   *Computing the Present Value of a Single Future Cash Flow*

What is the present value of $1000 to be received 46 months from today if the required return
is 12% APY?

Using the present value formula with $n = 3.8333$ (= 46/12):

$$PV = 1000\left[\frac{1}{(1.12)^{3.8333}}\right] = \$647.64$$

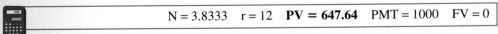

$$N = 3.8333 \quad r = 12 \quad \mathbf{PV = 647.64} \quad PMT = 1000 \quad FV = 0$$

Annuities with Partial Time Periods

Unfortunately, calculators treat annuities with partial time periods inconsistently. Some "round down" and treat the partial time period and payment as though they aren't there. Others "round up" and treat the partial time period and payment as a full period and payment. Still others account for the partial time period but assume no payment. Our advice is to either (1) carefully study how your calculator works and use it successfully or (2) "take matters into your own hands" and account for annuities with partial time periods in other ways. Here are two examples of how to compute a future value using a two-step process, without relying on whatever assumptions are programmed into your calculator.

Computing the Future Value of an Annuity After It Has Ended

EXAMPLE

What is the value 3.75 years from now of a 3-year annuity, with the first $1000 payment being made 1 year from today, if the expected return is 10% APY?

The value in 3 years is: $1000(\text{FVAF}_{10\%,3}) = \$3310$.

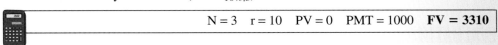

$$N = 3 \quad r = 10 \quad PV = 0 \quad PMT = 1000 \quad \mathbf{FV = 3310}$$

The future value in 3.75 years can then be computed by simply treating the $3310 as though it's a single cash flow at $t = 3$ and compounding that amount for 0.75 time periods to get: $3310(\text{FVF}_{10\%,0.75}) = 3310[1.1]^{0.75} = \$3555.27$.

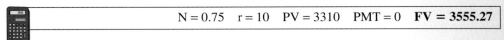

$$N = 0.75 \quad r = 10 \quad PV = 3310 \quad PMT = 0 \quad \mathbf{FV = 3555.27}$$

Figure 5.10 illustrates the solution to this example using a time line. ■

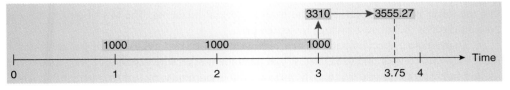

FIGURE 5.10
Solution using a time line.

Computing the Present Value of an Annuity with Early Cash Flows

EXAMPLE

What is the present value of a 4-year annuity, with the first $5000 payment being made 9 months from today, if the required return is 8% APY?

Three months ago, this annuity would be a "normal" 4-year annuity. So its value as of 3 months ago (at $t = -0.25$) is $5000(\text{PVAF}_{8\%,4}) = \$16,560.63$.

$$N = 4 \quad r = 8 \quad \mathbf{PV = 16,560.63} \quad PMT = 5000 \quad FV = 0$$

The present value can then be computed by simply treating $16,560.63 as though it's a single cash flow and compounding it forward to the present for 0.25 time periods, to get $16,560.63(\text{FVF}_{8\%,0.25}) = 16,560.63[1.08]^{0.25}) = \$16,882.35$.

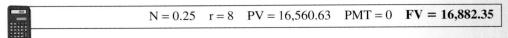

$$N = 0.25 \quad r = 8 \quad PV = 16,560.63 \quad PMT = 0 \quad \mathbf{FV = 16,882.35}$$

Figure 5.11 on page 140 illustrates the solution using a time line. ■

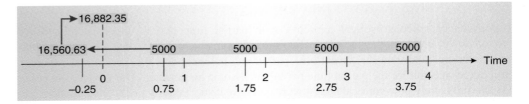

FIGURE 5.11
Solution using a time line.

Self-Check
1. How can you compute the present or future value of a single cash flow when there is a partial time period involved?
2. Why must you be especially careful when using a calculator to compute the present or future value of an annuity when there is a partial time period involved?

EVALUATING SPECIAL-FINANCING OFFERS

"Special-financing" offers are often used as part of a sales promotion for consumer goods, such as cars, furniture, and even condominiums. In short, special financing has become part of the package in many types of consumer purchases. But how can you tell whether the financing is really special in anything but name only? In this section, we provide an example and some guidelines for dealing with special financing.

Often the interest rate creates the most confusion with special financing. This is because the special rate offered, such as 3.9% APR, is not the opportunity cost for borrowing money. You can't really borrow money at that rate. The special financing is simply a promotional gimmick. In essence, the company is lowering the effective price to encourage sales. It's just that the lower price is expressed in the form of special financing. The key question, then, is how much does the interest savings lower the price?

To evaluate a special financing deal, you need the interest rate at which you can borrow money for *any* comparable use. That is, you need the market interest rate for such loans. The market interest rate provides a way to measure the opportunity cost of the special financing. You use the market rate to compute the "real" price for the product. The real price is the present value of the payments you would have to make using the special-financing offer. If the present value is smaller than the cash price, the special financing is a better deal; the real price with special financing is lower than the cash price.

EXAMPLE

Cash Back or 3.9% APR from Chevy

Let's say Chevy is offering a choice of either "special financing" or "cash back" to buy a car you have already decided to buy. The stated price is $20,000. Either you can have $1500 cash back, for a cash price of $18,500, or you can borrow the "$20,000" at 3.9% APR, 0.325% per month (= 3.9/12). Monthly payments would be $589.59 for the next 36 months.

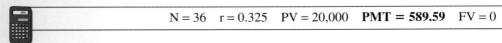

N = 36   r = 0.325   PV = 20,000   **PMT = 589.59**   FV = 0

You could also borrow $18,500 from Citibank (or any of several other banks) at 8% APR and pay cash for the car. Should you take the special-financing offer or take the cash-back offer and borrow from a bank?

The best choice has the lowest present-value cost. The difference between the two costs is the NPV of the choice. On the basis of 8% APR (0.6667% per month), the present value of the special-financing loan payments is $18,814.77.

N = 36	r = 0.6667	**PV = 18,814.77**	PMT = 589.59	FV = 0

This is more than the $18,500 cash-back-offer price, so taking the cash-back offer and borrowing from the bank is the better deal. The NPV is $314.77 (= $18,814.77 − $18,500.00).

There's another way to see the difference between the two alternatives: Compute what the payments would be on the Citibank loan if Citibank required the same 36 monthly payments.[3] The payments for such a Citibank loan would be $579.73.

N = 36	r = 0.6667	PV = 18,500	**PMT = 579.73**	FV = 0

The bank loan would be about $10 a month cheaper. The monthly savings have a present value of $314.65, which is the NPV for the bank loan, except for rounding error.

N = 36	r = 0.6667	**PV = 314.65**	PMT = 9.86 (= 589.59 − 579.73)	FV = 0

In the prior example, you had already decided to purchase that particular car. But what if you're still shopping? In the next example, we'll show how to evaluate competing product offers.

Computing the Value of a Special-Financing Offer from Chrysler   EXAMPLE

Suppose that just before you "sign on the dotted line" for the Chevy, you hear about another offer from Chrysler. It's a nicer model that you actually like better—except for its higher price of $25,000. Now Chrysler is offering 1% APR for 48 months on this "$25,000" model. Therefore, you could buy the nicer model for $531.53 per month for the next 48 months.

N = 48	r = 0.0833 (= 1/12)	PV = 25,000	**PMT = 531.53**	FV = 0

However, because the loan on the more expensive model is over a different period, the lower monthly payment is not necessarily the best deal.[4]

Is Chrysler's price on the better model less than the $18,500 cash price on Chevy's more basic model? It is a lower monthly payment at a "lower" interest rate, but it is for 12 more months. What is the real price for the Chrysler? There's no cash-back offer on this nicer model to give a guideline for the price discount.

(continued on following page)

---

[3]To make a fair comparison possible, the repayment process for the bank loan *must* be identical to that for the special-financing offer: 36 equal monthly payments. If the size of the period is different (say, weekly), if the length of the loan is different (say, 48 months), or if the payments are not identical each period, a comparison of payments can lead to the wrong choice.
[4]We also want to caution that you must *never* multiply the payment amount times the number of payments. Remember, even identical cash flows, if they occur at different times, do not have the same value—because of the time value of money.

(Computing the Value of a Special-Financing Offer from Chrysler *continued from previous page*)

Again, the real price with the special financing is the present value of the loan payments at the opportunity cost (market) interest rate. On the basis of the bank's 8% APR interest rate, the real price is $21,772.32.

$N = 48$ $r = 0.6667$ **PV = 21,772.32** $PMT = 531.53$ $FV = 0$	

Therefore, even with the 1% APR special-financing offer, Chrysler's nicer model still costs $3272.32 more (= 21,772.32 − 18,500) than the best deal (cash back) on Chevy's more basic model. ■

Self-Check

1. Why is special financing just like reduction in the real price of the car?

2. Why is it so important to calculate the value of special-financing offers correctly when deciding which brand to buy?

SUMMARY

This chapter explored the Time-Value-of-Money Principle and established the following concepts:

- The present value and future value formulas can be used to compute the value of cash flows at times other than when they will be paid or received. These formulas can be used to find the PV (present value), FV (future value), PMT (annuity cash flow), n (number of periods), or r (the periodic rate of return).

- An annuity is a set of equal periodic payments for a given number of periods. Annuities are common in financial contracts. Annuity formulas allow complex problems to be solved in a routine manner.

- Time-value-of-money formulas can also be used to find a loan's payments or true interest cost—its APY.

- A loan's APY—its true annual cost—can differ from its APR, which is a nominal rate.

- Present value and the discount rate are inversely related: Present value goes down when r goes up, and vice versa—like two kids on a seesaw.

- NPV (net present value) is the present value minus the cost. NPV measures the value created by a financial decision. A positive (negative) NPV creates (destroys) value.

EQUATION SUMMARY

The Basic Calculator Formula

$$PV = PMT \left[\frac{(1 + r)^n - 1}{r(1 + r)^n} \right] + FV \left[\frac{1}{(1 + r)^n} \right]$$

(5.1)
$$FV_n = PV(1 + r)^n = PV(FVF_{r,n})$$

(5.2)
$$PV = FV_n \left[\frac{1}{(1+r)^n} \right] = FV_n(PVF_{r,n})$$

(5.3)
$$FVA_n = PMT \left[\frac{(1+r)^n - 1}{r} \right] = PMT(FVAF_{r,n})$$

(5.4)
$$PVA_n = PMT \left[\frac{(1+r)^n - 1}{r(1+r)^n} \right] = PMT(PVAF_{r,n})$$

(5.5)
$$PMT = PVA_n \left[\frac{r(1+r)^n}{(1+r)^n - 1} \right] = \frac{PVA_n}{PVAF_{r,n}}$$

(5.6)
$$PMT = FVA_n \left[\frac{r}{(1+r)^n - 1} \right] = \frac{FVA_n}{FVAF_{r,n}}$$

(5.7)
$$PVA_{perpetuity} = \frac{PMT}{r}$$

(5.8)
$$APR = (m)(r)$$

(5.9)
$$APY = \left(1 + \frac{APR}{m} \right)^m - 1$$

(5.10)
$$APY = e^{APR} - 1$$

CHAPTER REVIEW ACTIVITIES

SELF-TEST PROBLEMS

1. (Calculating FVs) If you invest $1000 in a savings account paying 12% APY, what will be your account balance at the end of the following periods?
   a. 1 year
   b. 5 years
   c. 1.75 years

2. (Calculating PVs) What is the present value of $20,000 discounted back at 6% if the money is received at the end of the following periods?
   a. 1 year
   b. 5 years
   c. 1.75 years

3. (Calculating the PV) A scam artist collected $20,000,000 from gullible investors for an oil well drilling scheme. The scam artist promised that he would pay off the investors in full within 8 years if the oil wells, for some reason, were not drilled. He purchased zero-coupon bonds that paid off the $20,000,000 in a single payment at the end of 8 years. He then mailed the bonds to his investors, pocketing the difference between the price of the bonds and the $20,000,000, and skipped the country. The rate of return on the bonds was 9%.
   a. What is the present value of $20,000,000 in 8 years discounted at 9%?
   b. How much did the scam artist pocket?

4. (Calculating the PV and FV of an annuity) Assume an ordinary annuity of $500 at the end of each of the next 3 years.
   a. What is the future value at the end of year 3 if cash flows can be invested at 10%?
   b. What is the present value discounted at 10%?

5. (PV of a delayed annuity) What is the present value of $1000 to be received at the end of each of years 6 through 15 with 10% APY?

6. (Finding interest rates) Find the APY for the following:
   a. The APR is 8% compounded semi-annually.
   b. The APR is 21.6% compounded monthly.
   c. The APR is 6% compounded continuously.

7. (Special-financing offer) Reduced financing costs are often used as part of a sales promotion for consumer goods, such as cars, furniture, or even condominiums. In short, special financing has become part of the package in many types of consumer purchases. Ford is offering you a choice of either special financing or cash back to buy a car you have already decided to buy. Which offer is better?

You have negotiated a price of $20,000 for the car. Ford will either give you $1,500 cash back, for a real price of $18,500, or a loan of the "$20,000" at 3.9% APR. Monthly payments would be $589.59 for the next 36 months.

$$N = 36 \quad r = 0.325 \quad PV = 20{,}000 \quad \textbf{PMT = 589.59} \quad FV = 0$$

The loan is at a bargain rate. You could also borrow $18,500 from Citibank (or any of several other banks) at a 10% APR, and pay cash for the car. Should you take the special-financing offer, or take the cash-back offer and borrow from a bank?

a. What is the present value of the special-financing loan payments discounted at the going market rate of 10% APR (0.8333% per month)? How does this present value compare to the cash price of $18,500?

b. Take the $18,500 cash price and finance this amount with Citibank at a 10% APR (0.8333% per month) for 36 months. How does the monthly payment on this loan compare to the monthly payments on the 3.9% special-financing loan?

c. What should you do?

SOLUTIONS TO SELF-TEST PROBLEMS

1. a. $FV = PV(1 + r)^n = 1000(1.12)^1 = 1000(1.12)^1 = \$1120$

$$N = 1 \quad r = 12 \quad PV = 1000 \quad PMT = 0 \quad \textbf{FV = 1120}$$

b. $FV = 1000(1.12)^5 = \$1762.34$

$$N = 5 \quad r = 12 \quad PV = 1000 \quad PMT = 0 \quad \textbf{FV = 1762.34}$$

c. $FV = 1000(1.12)^{1.75} = \$1219.36$

$$N = 1.75 \quad r = 12 \quad PV = 1000 \quad PMT = 0 \quad \textbf{FV = 1219.36}$$

2. a. $PV = FV/(1 + r)^n = 20{,}000/(1.06)^1 = \$18{,}867.92$

$$N = 1 \quad r = 6 \quad \textbf{PV = 18,867.92} \quad PMT = 0 \quad FV = 20{,}000$$

b. $PV = 20{,}000/(1.06)^5 = \$14{,}945.16$

$$N = 5 \quad r = 6 \quad \textbf{PV = 14,945.16} \quad PMT = 0 \quad FV = 20{,}000$$

c. $PV = 20{,}000/(1.06)^{1.75} = \$18{,}061.12$

$$N = 1.75 \quad r = 6 \quad \textbf{PV = 18,061.12} \quad PMT = 0 \quad FV = 20{,}000$$

3. a. The cost of the bonds is
$$PV = FV/(1 + r)^n = 20{,}000{,}000/(1.09)^8 = \$10{,}037{,}326$$

$$N = 8 \quad r = 9 \quad \mathbf{PV = 10{,}037{,}326} \quad PMT = 0 \quad FV = 20{,}000{,}000$$

b. The scam artist pocketed the difference between \$20,000,000 and the PV, which was
\$20,000,000 − \$10,037,326 = \$9,962,674.

4. a. $FV = 500(1.10)^2 + 500(1.10)^1 + 500(1.10)^0 = 605 + 550 + 500 = \$1655$

$$N = 3 \quad r = 10 \quad PV = 0 \quad PMT = 500 \quad \mathbf{FV = 1655.00}$$

b. $PV = 500/(1.10)^1 + 500/(1.10)^2 + 500/(1.10)^3 = 454.55 + 413.22 + 375.66 = \$1243.43$

$$N = 3 \quad r = 10 \quad \mathbf{PV = 1243.43} \quad PMT = 500 \quad FV = 0$$

5. The present value of the delayed annuity is the difference between the present values of a 15-year annuity and a 6-year annuity. $PV = 7606.08 - 4355.26 = \$3250.82$.

$$N = 15 \quad r = 10 \quad \mathbf{PV = 7606.08} \quad PMT = 1000 \quad FV = 0$$

$$N = 6 \quad r = 10 \quad \mathbf{PV = 4355.26} \quad PMT = 1000 \quad FV = 0$$

6. a. For semiannual compounding, $m = 2$ and $r = 8/2 = 4\%$ every 6 months.
$$APY = (1 + APR/m)^m - 1 = (1.04)^2 - 1 = 1.0816 - 1 = .0816 = 8.16\%$$

$$N = 2 \quad r = 4 \quad PV = 1 \quad PMT = 0 \quad \mathbf{FV = 1.0816}$$

b. For monthly compounding, $m = 12$ and $r = 21.6/12 = 1.80\%$ per month.
$$APY = (1 + APR/m)^m - 1 = (1.018)^{12} - 1 = 1.2387 - 1 = .2387 = 23.87\%$$

$$N = 12 \quad r = 1.8 \quad PV = 1 \quad PMT = 0 \quad \mathbf{FV = 1.2387}$$

c. For continuous compounding,
$$APY = e^{APR} - 1 = e^{.06} - 1 = 1.0618 - 1 = .0618 = 6.18\%$$

7. a. The present value of the special-financing loan payments discounted at a 10% APR is \$18,272.23.

$$N = 36 \quad r = 0.8333 \quad \mathbf{PV = 18{,}272.23} \quad PMT = 589.59 \quad FV = 0$$

This is less than the \$18,500 cash-back offer price, so taking the special-financing offer is \$227.77 cheaper (\$18,500.00 − \$18,272.23 = \$227.77).

b. The monthly payment of financing the \$18,500 for 36 months at a 10% APR is \$596.94. The bank loan would be about \$7.35 a month more expensive (\$596.94 − \$589.59 = \$7.35).

$$N = 36 \quad r = 0.8333 \quad PV = 18{,}500 \quad \mathbf{PMT = 596.94} \quad FV = 0$$

c. The special-financing offer is better. Its present value ($18,272.23) is less than the present value of the cash price ($18,500). If you want to finance the cash price, a regular 10% APR loan will have a monthly payment about $7.35 more than the special-financing loan.

QUESTIONS

1. Assume that the rate of return r is equal to zero.
   a. What is the future value of $1.00 in 5 years?
   b. What is the present value of $1.00 received 5 years in the future?
   c. What is the future value of an ordinary annuity of $1.00 per year for 5 years?
   d. What is the present value of an ordinary annuity of $1.00 per year for 5 years?
2. Why is the present value of a future cash flow inversely related to the discount rate?
3. What is an ordinary annuity? What is an annuity due? Why is the present value of an annuity due greater than the present value of an ordinary annuity?
4. Give a formula for each of the following:
   a. Future-value formula
   b. Present-value formula
   c. Future-value-of-an-annuity formula
   d. Present-value-of-an-annuity formula
5. Indicate which item in each of the following pairs is larger. Answer without computing the results.
   a. The FV of $100 invested at 10% compounded annually for 3 years or the FV of $100 invested at 10% compounded monthly for 3 years.
   b. The PV of $100 received in 3 years discounted back at 10% compounded annually or the PV of $100 received in 3 years discounted back at 10% compounded monthly.
   c. The FV of an ordinary annuity or the FV of an annuity due.
   d. The PV of an ordinary annuity or the PV of an annuity due.
6. Dewey No computed the value of a 10-year annuity of $100 per year. The value was $700. Now he can't remember whether it was a *present* value or a *future* value. Which is it? Why?
7. Why should a business undertake an investment that has a positive net present value?

CHALLENGING QUESTIONS

8. Explain the format or layout of a loan amortization table.
9. What is the present value of $100 received in one year at each of the following rates?
   a. 0%
   b. 100%
   c. −50%
10. Assume that you extend the life of an annuity by one year. For example, assume that you increase the life from 10 years to 11 years. How much does this increase the present value of the annuity?

PROBLEM SET A

A1. (PV and FV of single payments) Fill in the missing information below:

	PV	FV	r	n
a.	___	20	10%	10
b.	10	___	10%	10
c.	10	20	___	10
d.	10	20	10%	___

A2. (PV and FV of single payments) Fill in the missing information:

	PV	FV	r	n
a.	___	22,000	5.6%	3.0
b.	1,000	___	12.1%	5.5
c.	400	400	___	4.0
d.	25,000	50,000	7.75%	___

A3. (Return) Adrian Trennepohl bought shares of a small company stock 3 years ago for $12.00 per share. What would be Adrian's annual return if she sells the stock today for each of the following prices?
   a. $72.00
   b. $13.50
   c. $15.00
   d. $6.00

A4. (Return) After graduation, Florence moved across the country to Greenville and bought a small house for $108,000. Clarence moved to Columbia and bought a house for $145,000. Four years later, they both sold their houses. Florence netted $135,000 when she sold her house and Clarence netted $115,000 on his.

a. What annual return did Florence realize on the price of her house?

b. What annual return did Clarence realize on the price of his house?

A5. (PV of lump sum) George Jetson invests $100 for 1 year at 10%. He expects to have $110 in 1 year.

a. What is the present value of this future amount discounted at 10%?

b. What is the present value discounted at 8%?

c. What is the present value discounted at 12%?

A6. (PV of an annuity) What is the present value of $500 per year for 8 years if the required return is 8.5% per year?

A7. (FV of an annuity) What is the future value at the end of year 6 of a 6-year annuity of $1000 per year if the expected return is 10%?

A8. (FV of an annuity) What is the future value, at the end of year 5, of $1200 per year for each of the next 5 years if the expected return is 7% per year?

A9. (FV of an annuity) What is the future value 7 years from now of an annuity of $350 per year for each of the next 7 years if the expected return is 10% per year?

A10. (PV of an annuity) What is the present value of a 6-year annuity of $1000 per year if the required return is 10% per year?

A11. (Annuity payments) What are the monthly payments on a 3-year $5000 loan if the interest rate is 1% per month?

A12. (Amortizing a loan) What are the annual payments for a 4-year $4000 loan if the interest rate is 9% per year? Make up a loan amortization schedule for this loan.

A13. (Amortizing a loan) Create a loan amortization schedule for borrowing $7500 at an interest rate of 20% per year, to be paid off in four equal annual payments.

A14. (Ordinary annuity and annuity due) Assume an annuity payment of $125, an annuity life of 10 years, and a discount rate of 10%.

a. If the annuity is an ordinary annuity, what is the future value of the annuity?

b. If the annuity is an ordinary annuity, what is its present value?

c. If the annuity is an annuity due, what is its future value?

d. If the annuity is an annuity due, what is its present value?

A15. (PV of a perpetuity) What is the present value of a perpetuity of $800 per year if the required return is 11% per year?

A16. (Annuity payments) What are the monthly payments on a $15,000 4-year loan if the required return is 9% APR?

A17. (PV of an annuity) What is the present value of $100 per week for 5 years if the required return is 10% APR?

A18. (FV of an annuity) What is the future value after 10 years of $200 per month if the expected return is 6% APR?

A19. (Annuity payments) What are the monthly payments on a $150,000 25-year mortgage if the required return is 7.5% APR?

A20. (PV and FV of multiple cash flows) You expect to receive the following future cash flows at the end of the years indicated: $500 in year 2, $1200 in year 4, $800 in year 5, and $1500 in year 6. If the discount rate is 7% per year:

a. What is the present value of all four expected future cash flows?

b. What is the value of the four flows at year 5?

c. What is the value of the four flows at year 10?

A21. (PV and FV of multiple cash flows) The following future cash flows will be received at the end of the years indicated: $1000 in year 1, $1400 in year 2, $900 in year 4, and $600 in year 5. If the discount rate is 8% per year:

a. What is the present value of all four expected future cash flows?

b. What is the value of the four flows at year 5?

c. What is the value of the four flows at year 3?

A22. (PV of single payment) What is the present value of $10,000 to be received 7.8 years from today, if the required return is 8.2% APY?

PROBLEM SET B

B1. (Finding the APY) You expect to receive $2000 3 years from today. If the present value of this amount is $1423.56, what is the APY?

B2. (PV of an annuity) If the required return is 8% per year, what is the present value of $1000 per year for:

a. 10 years?

b. 20 years?

c. 50 years?

d. 100 years?

e. forever?

B3. (Finding a monthly return) A bank offers to pay you $200 per month for 5 years if you will give them $10,345.11 today. What return would you earn per month if you accept the bank's offer?

B4. (APR and APY) Corey Christian has a $4000 balance on a credit card. The APR on the card is 18%, compounded monthly.

a. What is the APY?

b. If he makes no payments and no further charges, what will be the credit card balance in 1 year?

c. What will be the balance in 4 years?

B5. (Finding APR and APY of a loan) Suppose a bank offers to lend you $18,000 if you will pay back $439.43 per month for 48 months.

a. What monthly interest rate is the bank charging?

b. What APR interest rate is the bank charging on this loan?

c. What APY interest rate is the bank charging on this loan?

B6. (Finding the APY) What is the APY for a 15% APR with monthly compounding?

B7. (Finding the APY) What is the APY for a 15% APR with continuous compounding?

B8. (Finding the APR and APY for a mortgage) Suppose a bank offers a $130,000 20-year mortgage if you will pay back $1007.89 per month.

a. What monthly interest rate is the bank charging?

b. What APR interest rate is the bank charging on this mortgage?

c. What APY interest rate is the bank charging on this loan?

B9. (PV of single payment with continuous compounding) What is the present value of $3400 to be received 3 years from today if the required return is 11% APR compounded continuously?

B10. (PV of a single payment) What is the present value of $4500 to be received 31 months from today if the required return is 10% APY?

B11. (FV of discrete payments with continuous compounding) What is the future value of $20,000 received as a lump sum at the end of each year for 5 years if the expected return is 10% per year compounded continuously?

B12. (PV of an annuity) What is the present value of a 5-year annuity, with the first $3000 payment being made 3 months from today, if the required return is 7% APY?

B13. (FV of an annuity) What is the value 4.35 years from now of a 4-year annuity, with the first $1200 payment being made 1 year from today, if the expected return is APY = 10%?

B14. (PV of an annuity) What is the present value of a 6-year annuity, with the first $2500 payment being made 7 months from today if the required return is APY = 12%?

B15. (PV of an annuity) What is the present value of a stream of $1500 payments received at the end of each of years 3 through 9 if the required return is 10% per year?

B16. (Finding the time period) You expect to receive $1000 sometime in the future. If the present value of this amount is $592.03 and the discount rate is 10% APY, when is the cash flow expected to occur?

B17. (Time to double your money) How long does it take a present-value amount to double if the expected return is
   a. 4%?   c. 15%?
   b. 9%?

B18. (Finding the APY) If an annuity of $5000 per year for 8 years has a present value of $27,469.57, what is the expected APY?

B19. (Valuing annuities not starting today) What is the present value of a 15-year annuity with payments of $1800 per year, where the first payment is expected to occur 4 years from today and the required return is 7.3% APY?

B20. (Finding the PV of an annuity with missing payments) Suppose you expect to receive $1000 per year for each of the next 15 years, except that you will not receive any payments in years 3 and 5. What is the present value of this annuity if the required return is 12% APR?

B21. (Mortgage loan interest rates) Bob's Bank has offered you a $40,000 mortgage on a house. Payments are to be $374.90 per month for 30 years.
   a. What monthly interest rate is Bob charg-   b. What is the APR on this loan?
      ing?   c. What is the APY on this loan?

B22. (Special-financing arrangement) Let's say Chrysler is offering 42-month 2.2% APR financing or $2000 cash back on a car you have decided to buy. The stated price for the car is $23,000.
   a. What are the monthly payments required   from several different banks at 8.3%
      for Chrysler's special-financing deal?   APR, would you be better off taking the
   b. If you can borrow the cash to buy the car   cash-back offer?

B23. (Special-financing arrangement) Performance Auto is offering you a choice of either special financing or a price discount on their new sports car, the QT-123. The stated price for the car is $31,000, but you can pay $25,500 cash and "drive it home today." Alternatively, you can borrow the $31,000 from Performance Auto and make monthly payments for 3 years with a 1% APR. Suppose the best financing currently available is to borrow money from Bob's Bank for 3 years at 12% APR with monthly installment payments and you have decided to buy a QT-123 from Performance Auto. Should you take the special financing or borrow the money from Bob's Bank and pay the cash price?

B24. (Monthly annuity payments) What are the monthly payments on a 3-year $10,000 loan (36 equal payments) if the interest rate is 10% APY?

B25. (FV and PV of an annuity) Suppose you would like to be paid $20,000 per year during your retirement, which starts in 20 years. Assume the $20,000 is an annual perpetuity and that the expected return is 4% APY. How much should you save per year for the next 20 years so that you can achieve your retirement goal?

B26. (Special-financing offer) Let's say Toyota is offering 36-month 1.9% APR financing or $1400 cash back on a car you have decided to buy. The stated price for the car is $18,000. You can borrow the cash to buy the car from several different banks at 8.1% APR. Which alternative has the lower "real" price, the special-financing deal or the cash-back offer?

B27. (PV of an annuity due) Congratulations! You have just won a $10,000,000 lottery prize. The prize is paid out to you in 20 equal installments at the beginning of each of the next 20 years.
   a. What is the present value of your lottery   ule like yours, the present value of lottery
      winnings if the discount rate is 7%?   prizes is less than 50% of tickets sold.
   b. The lottery commission claims that lot-   The PV of lottery prizes is what percent-
      tery prizes are 50% of lottery tickets sold.   age of lottery revenue?
      If all prizes have a 20-year payout sched-

PROBLEM SET C

C1. (Annuity due)

a. What is the present value of an 8-year *annuity due* of $750 per year if the required return is 8.2% APY?

b. What is the future value at the end of 6 years of a 6-year *annuity due* of $400 per year if the expected return is 10.4% APY?

C2. (Annuity payments) Harry's Home Finance is offering to lend you $10,000 for a home improvement. The loan is to be repaid in monthly installments over 9 years. If the interest rate on this loan is 15% APR, compounded continuously, what would your monthly payments be if you accepted Harry's offer?

C3. (PV of an annuity) Billy Bob won a lottery that will pay him $10,000 per year for 10 years. He got the first payment 9 months ago, so the second payment will occur 3 months from today. Billy Bob has decided to sell the rest of the payments. He is offering them to you for $61,825.00. Assume the appropriate required return on this stream of expected future cash flows is 10% APY.

a. What is the present value of this set of cash flows?

b. What is the net present value of buying this set of expected future cash flows from Billy Bob for $61,825.00?

C4. (FV of a single payment over a partial time period) What is the future value, 1.75 years from now, if the present value is $900 and the expected return is 12% APR, compounded semi-annually?

C5. (PV of an annuity) What is the present value of $5000 per year received at the end of each year for 20 years if the required return is 8% APR, compounded continuously?

C6. (PV of an annuity) What is the present value of $10,000 per year received at the end of each year in perpetuity with a required return of 7.4% APR?

C7. (FV and PV of an annuity) Suppose your parents have decided that after you graduate at the end of this year, they will start saving money to help pay for your younger sister to attend college. They plan to save money for 5 years before she starts college. The instant after they make the last payment, they will withdraw the first payment for her. The payments to her will be $8000 per year at the start of each of her 4 college years. They will save an equal amount at the end of every month for 5 years. The monthly interest rate they will earn on their savings is 0.45%. How much must they save each month in order to be able to make the four payments with no money left over?

C8. (Annuity payments) Suppose your parents have decided that after you graduate at the end of this year, they will start saving money to help pay for your younger brother to attend college. They plan to save money for 5 years before he starts college and to continue to save during his college years. They plan to contribute $8000 per year at the start of each of his 4 college years. Your parents will thus make monthly payments for 8 years, 5 prior to and 3 during your brother's college education. The monthly interest rate earned on their savings is 0.45%. How much must the monthly savings be under these conditions?

C9. (PV of an annuity) What is the present value of $1000 every 2 years forever, with the first payment 2 years from today, if the required return is 12% APY?

C10. (PV of an annuity) What is the present value of $500 every 4 years forever, with the first payment 2 years from today, if the required return is 12% APY?

C11. (Finding an APY) A company advertising early-retirement programs promises to repay you forever whatever amount you pay them per year for 12 years. What interest rate are they promising?

C12. (Annuity payment) Suppose you would like to be paid $30,000 per year during your retirement, which starts in 25 years. Assume the $30,000 is an annual perpetuity and that the expected return is 6% APY. What should you save *per month* for the next 25 years so that you can achieve your retirement goal?

C13. (Finding loan interest rates) Suppose you are paying $31.73 per week for 10 years to repay a $10,000 loan.

    a. What is the weekly interest rate on this loan?

    b. What is the APR?

    c. What is the APY?

C14. (Annuity payments) What are the monthly payments on a $50,000 25-year loan if the interest rate is 13% APR with continuous compounding?

BIBLIOGRAPHY

Black, Fischer. "A Simple Discounting Rule," *Financial Management,* 1988, 17(2):7–11.

Fisher, Irving. *The Theory of Interest.* New York: Augustus M. Kelley, 1965 (reprinted from the original edition published in 1930).

Hirshleifer, J. *Investment, Interest and Capital.* Englewood Cliffs, N.J.: Prentice-Hall, 1970.

Ross, Stephen A. "Uses, Abuses, and Alternatives to the Net-Present-Value Rule," *Financial Management,* 1995, 24(3):96–102.

VALUING BONDS AND STOCKS

Stocks and bonds are the most common and basic types of financial securities. Financial securities provide much of the financing (liabilities and stockholders' equity) for companies. When a company decides to expand and lacks the necessary cash, it can obtain the money it needs by selling new securities.

In this chapter, we cover the basics of how bonds and stocks are valued. Recall that stocks and bonds have a fundamental difference. Stock is equity, a form of ownership. A bond is debt, a type of loan. In later chapters, we'll examine many important details about the numerous alternatives companies have for financing and explore theories about how companies should be financed.

We know from previous chapters that the value of something can be expressed as the present value of its expected future cash flows. This is especially convenient for financial securities because they are nothing but a claim on future cash flows. We can make immediate use of the time-value-of-money tools from the previous chapter to value bonds and stocks.

For a bond, the periodic expected future cash flows are the contractually promised interest and principal payments. For a stock, the periodic expected future cash flows are cash dividends. Both have one additional expected future cash flow, the cash received if the bond is paid off or sold or if the stock is sold. The basic valuation procedure for any asset is the following:

1. Estimate the expected future cash flows.
2. Determine the required return, which depends on the riskiness of the expected future cash flows.
3. Compute the present value, which is what the asset is worth.

◆ *Incremental Benefits:* Note that the incremental benefits from owning a financial security are its expected future cash flows.

◆ *Time-Value-of-Money:* Determine the value of a financial security by computing the present value of its expected future cash flows.

◆ *Risk-Return Trade-Off:* Recognize that a financial security's value and required return reflect its risk.

◆ *Two-Sided Transactions:* Use the fair price of a financial security to compute its expected return, because the fair price does not favor either side of the transaction.

◆ *Efficient Capital Markets:* Estimate the required return for a financial security with its expected return.

BONDS

A **bond** is a long-term obligation for borrowed money. It's a promise to pay interest and repay the borrowed money on terms specified in a contract called a **bond indenture.** The indenture is the legal contract between the issuing corporation and the bondholders.

In addition to U.S. corporations, many other entities sell bonds to borrow money. The U.S. government, federal agencies, state governments, municipalities, non–U.S. companies,

BOND A long-term obligation for borrowed money. ✓

BOND INDENTURE The explicit legal contract between the issuing corporation and the bondholders. ✓

153

foreign governments, and international agencies account for most other bond issues. We'll use U.S. corporate bonds for illustrative purposes. These same bond valuation techniques apply to virtually any bond.

Let's start with an example. A bond contract for a six-year $100 million loan specifies an interest rate of 7% per year payable semiannually (7% APR[1]). It also requires principal repayment in equal installments three, four, five, and six years from the date the bond was issued. The borrower would then be obligated to pay the lender 3.5% (one-half of 7%) of the unpaid bond loan balance every six months. Table 6.1 specifies the bond's future cash flows promised by the borrower.

Typical Bond Features

There are many different types of bonds. They can be described by their pattern of promised future payments. A typical bond indenture includes at a minimum the following provisions:

1. The **par value,** which is also called the **face value,** specifies the amount of money that must be repaid at the end of the bond's life. Most U.S. corporate bonds have a par value of $1000. A bond issue of $100,000,000 would involve the sale of 100,000 such bonds, each with a par value of $1000.

2. A promise to make **coupon payments** periodically over the life of the bond. Coupon payments are the finance term for what are called interest payments in everyday language. The large majority of U.S. corporate bonds make semiannual coupon payments. Coupon payments are determined by the **coupon rate.** In the example given above, the coupon rate is 7% and, assuming a $1000 par value and semiannual interest payments, calls for coupon payments of $35 (one-half the coupon rate times the par value) every six months.

3. A promise to repay the **principal** of the bond issue in one or more installments over the life of the bond issue. The principal is the total amount of money being borrowed. Typically, it's simply the total of the par values of all the bonds that make up the bond issue.

4. The **maturity** of a bond is the end of its life, which occurs at the **maturity date,** when it is fully repaid. When a bond is issued (created), the length of its life is its **original**

PAR VALUE The amount of money to be repaid for a bond at the end of its life. The par value is also called the **face value.**

COUPON PAYMENTS A bond's interest payments.

COUPON RATE A bond's annual coupon divided by the face value.

PRINCIPAL The total amount of money being borrowed in exchange for all of the bonds.

MATURITY The end of a bond's life.

MATURITY DATE The date a bond is fully repaid.

ORIGINAL MATURITY The length of a bond's life when it is issued.

TABLE 6.1
Schedule of Semiannual Bond Payments

PERIOD	INITIAL LOAN BALANCE	INTEREST PAYMENT	PRINCIPAL REPAYMENT	ENDING LOAN BALANCE	TOTAL DEBT SERVICE PAYMENT
0.5	$100,000,000	$3,500,000	—	$100,000,000	$ 3,500,000
1.0	100,000,000	3,500,000	—	100,000,000	3,500,000
1.5	100,000,000	3,500,000	—	100,000,000	3,500,000
2.0	100,000,000	3,500,000	—	100,000,000	3,500,000
2.5	100,000,000	3,500,000	—	100,000,000	3,500,000
3.0	100,000,000	3,500,000	$25,000,000	75,000,000	28,500,000
3.5	75,000,000	2,625,000	—	75,000,000	2,625,000
4.0	75,000,000	2,625,000	25,000,000	50,000,000	27,625,000
4.5	50,000,000	1,750,000	—	50,000,000	1,750,000
5.0	50,000,000	1,750,000	25,000,000	25,000,000	26,750,000
5.5	25,000,000	875,000	—	25,000,000	875,000
6.0	25,000,000	875,000	25,000,000	—	25,875,000

[1]Recall that the APR, annual percentage rate, is the rate per compounding period times the number of compounding periods in a year.

maturity. The amount of time remaining until maturity is called the **remaining maturity.** Virtually any original maturity is possible, but most U.S. corporate bonds issued in recent years have had original maturities between 5 and 30 years.

5. A **call provision** gives the issuer (the company) the right (option) to pay off the bonds prior to their maturity. When you first think about it, it may seem odd to need the right to pay back the money you owe. After all, if you don't need the borrowed money anymore, just return it. But like other options, this one is valuable. Let's step to the other side of the transaction to see how.

If you buy a bond that pays 8% interest and then market interest rates go down, you would be pretty happy to continue to earn 8%. That would be more than you could get in other comparable market investments. But the company would want to repay you and reborrow the money from others at the new lower interest rate. Because of this difference in view from the two sides of the transaction, the contract must carefully specify the rights of each side. Call provisions typically have a "grace period" of several years after issuance during which the company cannot repay the bonds. A bond's call price usually starts at a premium above the bond's par value and then declines over time, reaching par value at or near maturity.

A bond issue that requires the repayment of the entire face value at maturity is said to have a **bullet maturity.** When a bond issue is repaid in multiple installments, the method of repayment is called a **sinking fund.** Typically, bond issues that have a sinking fund require annual payments that begin after some specified grace period. Sinking fund payments are a fixed obligation from the company's viewpoint, but not from the bondholder's. The bonds to be repaid in a given year are chosen by lottery. So any particular bondholder doesn't know her bond will be repaid until just before it happens.[2] Sometimes companies repurchase the bonds in the capital markets from owners wanting to sell them, rather than by lottery selection. This is especially likely when a bond is selling for less than its par value.[3]

The final repayment of principal is typically larger than the others. When it is, it's called the **balloon payment** (or balloon, for short).

Obtaining Bond Information

Suppose you wanted to find out information about a publicly traded bond. One source is a current *Wall Street Journal*. It has bond quotes similar to the one shown in figure 6.1.

From the highlighted Coca-Cola bond quote, you know the

1. *Coupon rate.* Coca-Cola pays a coupon rate of 6% on these bonds, or $30.00 (one-half of 6.00% of $1000) every six months.

2. *Maturity year.* Assuming the bonds don't have a sinking fund, Coca-Cola will pay owners $1000 per bond at the bond's maturity in 2003 (indicated by the 03).

REMAINING MATURITY The length of time remaining until a bond's maturity.

CALL PROVISION A provision that gives the company the right to repay the bonds before the maturity date.

BULLET MATURITY A bond issue that requires the repayment of the entire principal amount at maturity.

SINKING FUND A bond provision requiring principal repayments prior to the maturity date.

BALLOON PAYMENT A final principal repayment that's larger than other repayments.

Bonds	Cur Yld	Vol	Close	Net Chg.
Caterpinc 9³/₈ 01	8.3	30	112¹/₂	−1¹/₂
Chryslr 10.95s17	9.8	37	111¹/₂	...
Citicp 6¹/₂ 04	6.5	2	99¹/₂	+ ¹/₈
ClevEl 8³/₄ 05	8.7	10	101¹/₈	− ⁵/₈
Coca-Cola 6 03	7.7	49	78¹/₄	+ ¹/₂
CrayRs 6¹/₈ 11	cv	31	79¹/₂	− ³/₄

FIGURE 6.1
Hypothetical bond quotes with a Coca-Cola bond highlighted.

---

[2]This is frequently the opposite of the typical lottery: In this case, you win by *not* being picked!
[3]A sinking fund effectively changes the maturity of the total bond issue. This is because some of the bonds are repaid before the stated maturity date. A calculation that takes this difference into account is called *duration*. Duration provides a measure of the "effective" length of a bond issue's life.

3. *Current yield.* The bond's current yield is 7.7%. As discussed below, this is a measure of return based on the current price.

4. *Trading volume.* Yesterday, 49 of these bonds were traded.

5. *Closing price.* Yesterday's **closing price** for this bond was 78¼. The closing price is simply the price of a financial security in the last trade before the market closed. Bond prices are quoted as a percentage of the par value. The Coca-Cola bond was selling for 78¼% of its face value. The quote indicates a dollar price of $782.50 (78.25% of $1000).

6. *Net change in price.* The closing price is $5 higher than the previous day's closing price (½% of $1000).

A variety of additional symbols and notation can provide further information in the quote. For example, the Cray bond has *cv* for its current yield. This means the bond is a convertible bond. It can be exchanged at the bondholder's option for a given number of shares of Cray common stock.

A **bond guide,** such as those published by *Moody's* or *Standard & Poor's,* provides more information about this and other bonds. For example, you can determine the exact date a bond pays interest, its maturity date, and its sinking fund provisions (that is, how the principal is to be repaid). Figure 6.2 illustrates hypothetical information from a bond guide. Check the highlighted bond.

From this quote, you know that

1. Coca-Cola pays interest on January 15 and July 15 of each year.

2. Coca-Cola's 6 03 bonds mature on July 15, 2003.

3. Coca-Cola has $150 million worth of these bonds outstanding.

4. This bond issue does not include a sinking-fund provision.

CLOSING PRICE The price of a financial security in the last trade before the market closed.

BOND GUIDE A publication that provides particular information about specific bonds.

FIGURE 6.2
Hypothetical excerpt from a bond guide with a Coca-Cola bond highlighted.

CUSIP	ISSUE	RATING	AMT. OUTST. MIL. $	INTEREST DATES
126117AC	CNA Financial Corp. nts 6.25 2003.	A3	250	M&N 15
126117AE	deb. 7.25 2023	A3	250	M&N 15
12613BAA	CNC Holding Corp. sr.sub.nts. 13.00 1997	B3 r	188.6	M&S 1
190348AC	Coast Fed. Bank FSB cap.nts. 13.00 2002.	Ba2	50.0	MJS&D31
19039MAA	Coast Savings Fin., Inc. sr.nts. 10.00 2000	Ba2	58.0	M&S 1
19041PAA	Coastal Bancorp, Inc. TX sr.nts. 10.00 2002	B1 r	50.0	MJS&D30
190441AN	Coastal Corp. sr.nts. 8.75 1999.	Baa3r	150	M&N 15
190441AJ	• sr.nts. 10.375 2000	Baa3	250	A&O 1
190441AL	sr.nts. 10.00 2001	Baa3	300	F&A 1
190441AQ	• nts. 8.125 2002	Baa3	250	M&S 15
190441AM	• deb. 9.75 2003	Baa3r	300	F&A 1
190441AH	sr.deb. 10.25 2004.	Baa3r	200	A&O 15
190441AF	• sr.deb. 11.75 2006	Baa3r	400	J&D 15
190441AK	sr.deb. 10.75 201.	Baa3	150	A&O 1
190441AP	sr.deb. 9.625 2012.	Baa3r	150	M&N 15
190441AR	• deb. 7.75 2035	Baa3	150	A&O 15
191098AB	Coca-Cola Bottling Consol nts. 6.85 2007	Baa3r	100	M&N 1
191175AB	Coca-Cola Bottling Group sr.sub.nts.9.00 2003	B2 r	140	M&N 15
191216AB	Coca-Cola nts. 7.75 1996.	Aa3r	250	F&A 15
191216AC	nts. 7.875 1998	Aa3r	250	M&S 15
191216AD	nts. 6.625 2002	Aa3	150	A&O 1
191216AE	nts. 6.00 2003	Aa3r	150	J&J 15
191216AF	deb. 7.375 2093	Aa3	117	J&J 29
191219AR	Coca-Cola Enterprises nts. 6.50 1997	A3 r	300	M&N 15
191219AT	nts. 7.00 1999	A3 r	200	M&N 15
191219AM	nts. 7.875 2002	A3	500	F&A 1
191219AN	nts. 8.50 2012	A3	250	F&A 1
191219AB	deb 5.75 2005	A3 r	153.3	F&A 2
191219AV	zero cpn.nts. 2020.	A3		N.P.
191219AP	deb. 8.50 2022	A3	750	F&A 1

Current Yield The **current yield** equals the annual coupon payment divided by the closing dollar price. It is a measure of the rate of income from the coupon payments. However, it ignores the gain or loss that will result from the difference between the purchase price and the principal repayment. The yield to maturity, which is discussed below, is a better measure of the return, because it measures the *total* return from owning a bond, including changes in market value. Given that current computer and information technology could easily provide the yield to maturity, there is little need for the bond quote to include the current yield. It appears that the current yield is still in the bond quote simply because of tradition. Traditions are often hard to break!

CURRENT YIELD The annual coupon payment divided by the current market price.

Self-Check

1. Define the following terms: *bond indenture, par* or *face value, coupon, principal, maturity, call provision,* and *sinking fund.*

2. What is the par value of most U.S. corporate bonds?

3. How often do U.S. corporate bonds usually pay interest?

4. A corporate bond is quoted at a price of 95 in a newspaper. What is its dollar price?

BOND VALUATION

The value of a bond, its fair price, is the present value of its promised future coupon and principal repayments. This present value is determined by the bond's required return. Recall that the required return is the minimum return you must expect to be willing to make the investment (buy the bond).

CURRENT PRICE		YIELD TO MAT.	1995		CURRENT CALL PRICE	CALL DATE	SINK FUND PROV.	ISSUED	PRICE	YLD.
			HIGH	LOW						
99⅛	bid	6.38	99⅛	83⅛	N.C.			11-9-93	99.82	6.28
99⅛	bid	7.31	99⅛	78⅜	N.C.			11-9-93	99.68	7.28
—		—	—	—	104.87 to	9-1-97	Yes	N.A.	0.00	
113¾	bid	10.20	113¾	108½	105.57 fr	12-31-97		12-18-92	100.00	13.00
—		—	—	—		—		4-1-93	100.00	10.00
—		—	—	—	100.00 fr	6-30-00	No	6-23-95	100.00	10.00
104	bid	7.38	104	101⅛	N.C.	—		5-13-92	100.00	8.75
112⅝	bid	7.18	111½	109¼	N.C.	—	No	9-25-90	99.88	10.40
111¾	bid	7.20	111¾	111¾	N.C.	—	No	1-29-91	99.50	10.08
109	bid	6.45	108½	95¼	N.C.	—	No	9-11-92	99.62	8.18
113⅛	bid	7.45	112⅞	103⅛	N.C.	—	No	7-30-91	99.44	9.83
118⅛	bid	7.40	117½	108	N.C.	—	No	10-3-89	99.85	10.27
105¾	sale	10.81	109⅛	104⅛	103.92 fr	6-15-96	Yes	6-24-86	100.00	11.75
118⅛	bid	8.56	120	107	N.C.	—	No	9-25-90	99.59	10.80
108	bid	8.69	108⅞	106	N.C.	—	No	5-13-92	99.34	9.70
106⅜	bid	7.25	—	—	N.C.	—	No	10-16-95	99.96	7.75
103½	bid	6.42	103½	99⅛	N.C.	—	No	11-1-95	100.00	6.85
100¾	bid	8.86	100¾	87½	104.50 fr	11-15-98		11-8-93	100.00	9.00
100¼	bid	5.50	101⅛	100⅛	N.C.	—	No	2-12-91	100.00	7.75
105⅞	bid	5.45	105⅞	98⅞	N.C.	—	No	9-9-91	99.69	7.93
104¼	bid	5.84	104¼	90⅞	N.C.	—	No	9-30-92	99.32	6.71
100⅜	bid	5.93	100⅜	86½	N.C.	—	No	7-15-93	99.81	6.03
110⅝	bid	6.66	110⅝	86⅜	N.C.	—	No	7-22-93	98.93	7.46
101⅞	bid	5.42	101⅞	95½	N.C.	—		11-12-92	99.63	
104½	bid	5.68	104½	94⅞	N.C.	—		11-12-92	99.31	
109¾	bid	5.92	109¾	97⅛	N.C.	—	No	1-29-92	100.00	7.87
118¼	bid	6.63	118¼	99⅝	N.C.	—	No	1-29-92	100.00	8.50
100¾	bid	5.89	103	98⅝	§104.89 to	3-31-96	Yes	1-29-76	98.83	7.98
—	—	—	—	—		—		5-9-95	12.93	
122⅛	bid	6.69	122⅛	98½	N.C.	—	Yes	Ref. fr. 4-1-97 @ 104.08		

When a bond is issued, its terms are set by the issuing company to achieve a particular fair price for the bond. Most often, companies set the terms so that, when the bond is issued, the fair price will be very close to the bond's par value. However, after the bonds have been issued, their fair price will reflect current market conditions for that contract.

In other words, bond values change over time. This is because the contract terms, especially the schedule of payments, are usually fixed. But the required return always reflects *current* market conditions. As a result, whenever the interest rate (required return) changes, the bond price (the present value of its future payments) changes.

Bond Value When the Required Return Equals the Coupon Rate

Let's consider a two-year bond with a 6% coupon rate. The bond pays $30 every six months for the next two years plus a $1000 principal repayment at maturity, the time of the last coupon payment. Currently, the bond's required return equals the coupon rate, 3% per six-month period. So the fair price of the bond, B_0, is:

$$B_0 = \frac{30}{(1.03)} + \frac{30}{(1.03)^2} + \frac{30}{(1.03)^3} + \frac{30}{(1.03)^4} + \frac{1000}{(1.03)^4} = \$1000.00$$

 Figure 6.3 illustrates this present-value computation. For all bonds of this type it is always the case that *when the required return equals the coupon rate, the fair price equals the par value.*

Valuing Interest and Principal Separately

Another way to make this same computation is to view the expected future cash flows as two parts: (1) a four-period annuity of $30 every six months and (2) a single $1000 payment two years from today. The bond's value is the present value of the two parts:

$$B_0 = PV(\text{coupon payments}) + PV(\text{par value}) = 30 PVAF_{3\%,4} + 1000 PVF_{3\%,4}$$

$$B_0 = 30 \left[\frac{(1.03)^4 - 1}{(0.03)(1.03)^4} \right] + \frac{1000}{(1.03)^4} = 111.51 + 888.49 = \$1000.00$$

| N = 4   r = 3   **PV = 1000.00**   PMT = 30   FV = 1000 |

Note that in this case we're not putting in zero for one of the calculator inputs. This case further illustrates the power of a financial calculator and demonstrates the logic of the Basic Calculator Formula, given in chapter 5. The calculator computes the sum of these two present values in one calculation.

FIGURE 6.3
The present value of a bond's expected future cash flows when the required return equals the bond's coupon rate.

	Now	6 months	1 year	18 months	2 years
Time	0	1	2	3	4
Cash flow		30.00	30.00	30.00	1030.00
Present value	29.13				
Present value	28.28				
Present value	27.45				
Present value	915.14				
Total present value:	$1000.00				
Required return:	6% APR				

Bond Value When the Required Return Differs from the Coupon Rate

Now let's look at the value of this bond if its required return is 12% APR, which is higher than the coupon rate. The only difference in our computation will be the discount rate, which is now 6% per six-month period. Under these conditions, the bond is worth

$$B_0 = \text{PV(coupon payments)} + \text{PV(par value)} = 30\text{PVAF}_{6\%,4} + 1000\text{PVF}_{6\%,4}$$

$$B_0 = 30\left[\frac{(1.06)^4 - 1}{(0.06)(1.06)^4}\right] + \frac{1000}{(1.06)^4} = 103.953 + 792.094 = \$896.05$$

N = 4 r = 6 **PV = 896.05** PMT = 30 FV = 1000	

We know the discount rate and present value are inversely related. So, as expected, the higher discount rate produces a lower bond value.

Bond Valuation Formula for a Bond with Semiannual Coupon Payments   Let's generalize our valuation method to value any bond of this type:

$$B_0 = \text{PV(coupon payments)} + \text{PV(par value)}$$

$$B_0 = \left(\frac{\text{CPN}}{2}\right)\text{PVAF}_{(r/2)\%,2N} + 1000\text{PVF}_{(r/2)\%,2N}$$

$$B_0 = \left[\frac{\text{CPN}}{2}\right]\left[\frac{(1 + r/2)^{2N} - 1}{(r/2)(1 + r/2)^{2N}}\right] + \frac{1000}{(1 + r/2)^{2N}} \tag{6.1}$$

where   CPN = the coupon rate times the par value
          N = the number of remaining years until maturity
          r = the bond's current required return

   In practice, bond returns are normally quoted as an APR with semiannual compounding. For example, in equation (6.1), if the bond's required return is quoted as 10%, that means 5% per six-month period. That's why we use r/2 in the formula. Of course, when compounding is more frequent than once a year, the APY (the true, or effective, return) exceeds the APR. A 10% APR with semiannual compounding provides an APY of 10.25% (= $[1.05]^2 - 1 = 0.1025 = 10.25\%$).

N = 2 r = 5 PV = 1.0 PMT = 0 **FV = 1.1025**	

Computing the Fair Price of a Ford Credit Bond   E X A M P L E

Suppose a Ford Credit bond has a coupon rate of 8.5% and a remaining maturity of exactly 12 years. If the required return on this bond is 10% APR, what is the bond's current fair price?

   The semiannual coupon payments in this case will be $42.50 (= one-half of 8.5% of $1000 = 85/2$), and the semiannual required return is 5%. Using equation (6.1), the fair price of the bond—the present value of its expected future cash flows—is

$$B_0 = 42.50\text{PVAF}_{5\%,24} + 1000\text{PVF}_{5\%,24} = (42.50)\left[\frac{(1.05)^{24} - 1}{(0.05)(1.05)^{24}}\right] + \frac{1000}{(1.05)^{24}}$$

$$B_0 = 586.44 + 310.07 = \$896.51$$

N = 24 r = 5 **PV = 896.51** PMT = 42.50 FV = 1000	

(continued on following page)

(Computing the Fair Price of a Ford Credit Bond *continued from previous page*)

Buying this bond for less than $896.51 would be a positive-NPV investment. That's because it would be worth more than it cost. Paying more than $896.51 would be a negative-NPV investment. At its fair price of exactly $896.51, buying it would be a zero-NPV investment. ■

Estimating a Bond's Expected Return: The Yield to Maturity

The expected return is the return you expect to earn if you make the investment (buy the bond). A bond's expected return can be estimated by its yield to maturity. The **yield to maturity (YTM)** is the return that will be earned if all the payments are made exactly as promised. Therefore, the YTM is the APR that makes the bond's market price equal the present value of its promised future cash flows.[4]

This relationship is again given by equation (6.1). But instead of putting in the required return and solving for B_0, we put in the current market price and solve for the r, which is the YTM.

YIELD TO MATURITY (YTM) The APR that makes a bond's market price equal the present value of its promised future cash flows.

EXAMPLE

Computing the YTM of a Coca-Cola Bond

What is the YTM of a Coca-Cola bond that is currently selling for $782.50, has a 6% coupon rate, and matures in exactly 6 years?

The inputs are $B_0 = 782.50$, CPN/2 = 30.00 (one-half of 6.0% of $1000), and $2N = 12$. Putting these into equation (6.1), we have:

$$782.50 = 30.00\left[\frac{(1 + r/2)^{12} - 1}{(r/2)(1 + r/2)^{12}}\right] + \frac{1000}{(1 + r/2)^{12}}$$

The $r/2$ that solves this equation is 5.528%; r is the YTM.

N = 12	**r = 5.528**	PV = 782.50	PMT = 30.00	FV = 1000

So the YTM for this bond is two times $r/2$ or 11.056%. Practitioners would say the bond's YTM is about 11.1%.[5]

This example is another case where a financial calculator really pays off. After you key in the inputs, the calculator will automatically perform the trial-and-error process needed to solve for the expected return.[6] ■

ZERO-COUPON BOND A bond that makes no payments until maturity. A zero-coupon bond is also called a **pure-discount bond**.

Zero-Coupon Bonds   A **zero-coupon bond** (also called a **pure-discount bond**) is a bond that makes no payments until its maturity. Its par value, which is paid at maturity, is the combined repayment of principal and all the interest over the bond's life. Despite the seeming difference, equation (6.1) can be used to value a zero-coupon bond or to determine its YTM.

---

[4]The YTM is only an estimate of the expected return because it ignores risk. We discuss bond risk in the next section.
[5]As we noted earlier, bond returns are quoted as an APR. This bond's YTM produces an APY of 11.36% (= [1 + 0.05528]^2 − 1 = 0.1136).

N = 2	r = 5.528	PV = 1.0	PMT = 0	**FV = 1.1136**

[6]The trial-and-error process without a financial calculator is as follows: Pick a discount rate and calculate the present value. If the present value is above the price, choose a higher discount rate and try again. If the present value is below the price, choose a lower discount rate and try again. Continue trying discount rates until one provides a price that is "close enough" to the target price.

Computing the YTM on a J.C. Penney Zero-Coupon Bond

Suppose J.C. Penney has a zero-coupon bond that will pay $1000 at maturity on April 9, 2018, and today is April 9, 1998. The bond is selling for $178.43. What is its YTM?

Using equation (6.1) with semiannual compounding[7] and $CPN/2 = 0$

$$\frac{1000}{(1 + r/2)^{40}} = \$178.43$$

The $r/2$ that solves this is 4.40, so the YTM is 8.8% (= 2[4.4]).

$$N = 40 \quad \mathbf{r = 4.403} \quad PV = 178.43 \quad PMT = 0 \quad FV = 1000$$

Self-Check

1. A recent bond quote provides a good estimate of a bond's value. How else can you estimate the value of a bond?

2. What is the fair price of a Texaco bond that has an 8% coupon rate, a required return of 10%, and matures in exactly 4 years?

3. What is a yield to maturity (YTM)? How do you compute it?

BOND RISKINESS

The YTM is the bond's *promised* return, which is its expected return—if the payments are certain. But what if the bond issuer may not make all the payments exactly as promised?

If the company fails to make a payment, or even if it's just late making a payment, the investor's realized return will be less than the promised return. But the company is not going to pay more than the contract requires, so the realized return (to maturity) will never be more than the promised return. Therefore, when there is any chance the payments will not be made exactly as promised—any payment risk—the expected return is less than the YTM.

Nevertheless, the YTM is a good estimate of the expected return on high-grade bonds because the payment risk is low. The YTM is not always a good estimate of the expected return on so-called junk bonds, named precisely for their higher payment risk.

Interest-Rate Risk

Bonds rarely sell for exactly face (par) value, even if that was their original selling price. Whenever a bond's required return changes, the bond's fair price also changes. A bond selling below its par value is called a **discount bond**. A bond selling above its par value is called a **premium bond**.

A bond's price changes because its present value depends on its required return. With contractually fixed cash flows (interest and principal payments), a drop in the required return raises the present value, and vice versa. Figure 6.4 on page 162 illustrates how the value of a bond that has a fixed-coupon rate varies with its required return.

In chapter 2, we described the *term structure of interest rates*. The term structure shows how interest rates depend on maturity. We described several factors that affect the term structure.

DISCOUNT BOND A bond that's selling for less than its par value.

PREMIUM BOND A bond that's selling for more than its par value.

---

[7]We chose semiannual compounding for comparability with other bonds. You could use annual compounding, in which case the calculation would provide the bond's APY.

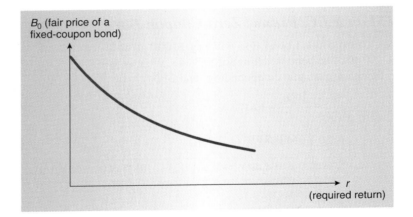

FIGURE 6.4
Relationship between a bond's fair price and its required return.

INTEREST-RATE RISK
The risk of a change in the value of a bond because of a change in the interest rate.

A very important factor is the risk of interest rate changes. As we said, changes in required return most often result from changes in the expected rate of inflation.

Because a change in the required return causes a change in a bond's fair price, owning a bond is risky. This risk, that market prices will fluctuate, exists even if the company is healthy and makes all of the required payments. This risk is called **interest-rate risk.** Because of interest-rate risk, even bonds that are guaranteed against default have some risk.

A bond can be riskless (or as close as possible to being riskless) *only* in the sense that the future cash flows will occur as promised. If you sell the bond before its maturity, you'll probably sell it for a price that differs from your purchase price. In fact, a decline in market value can easily exceed the income received from the interest payments while you own the bond!

How much interest-rate risk is there? It depends primarily on the bond's remaining maturity. When all else is equal, interest-rate risk is greater with a longer remaining maturity.

Remaining Maturity and Interest-Rate Risk

The present value of a payment due in the distant future changes more with a change in the required return than does a payment due in the near future. To see this, compare a one-year bond and a ten-year bond, both with an 8% coupon rate. Table 6.2 compares the values of these bonds at required returns between 4% and 15%.

At 4% per year, the one-year bond is worth $1038.83 and the ten-year bond is worth $1327.03. At 15% per year, the one-year bond is worth $937.16 and the ten-year bond is worth $643.19. Therefore, an increase in the required return on these bonds from 4% to 15% causes less than a 10% drop in the value of the one-year bond. In contrast, that same rate change causes more than a 50% drop in the value of the ten-year bond.

Figure 6.5 graphs the values of these same bonds as a function of required return. The slope of the curve for the value of the ten-year bond is much steeper. As a result, any change in the required return will cause a larger change in its value than in the value of the one-year bond.

Bond Values, Maturity, and Default

Although a bond's value may vary over time, it is constrained by its *terminal value.* In most cases, a bond's terminal value is simply its par value to be paid at maturity. As a result, the bond's price will tend to converge to its par value as the bond matures. Therefore, although a bond's value may fluctuate (due to changes in interest rates), the typical path of a bond's value is somewhat constrained, ending at its par value. This concept is illustrated in figure 6.6 on page 164 by hypothetical price paths for both a discount bond (selling below par) and a premium bond (selling above par).

TABLE 6.2

A Comparison of Bond Value Sensitivity to Changes in the Required Return

REQUIRED RETURN	FAIR PRICE FOR AN 8% COUPON BOND WITH A ONE-YEAR REMAINING MATURITY	FAIR PRICE FOR AN 8% COUPON BOND WITH A TEN-YEAR REMAINING MATURITY
4%	$1038.83	$1327.03
5%	1028.92	1233.84
6%	1019.14	1148.77
7%	1009.51	1071.06
8%	1000.00	1000.00
9%	990.64	934.96
10%	981.41	875.38
11%	972.31	820.74
12%	963.33	770.60
13%	954.48	724.54
14%	945.76	682.18
15%	937.16	643.19
Interest rate *increases* from 4% to 15%:		
Decrease in value:	$101.67	$683.84
Percentage decrease:	9.8%	51.5%
Interest rate *increases* from 8% to 12%:		
Decrease in value:	$36.67	$229.40
Percentage decrease:	3.7%	22.9%
Interest rate *decreases* from 8% to 4%:		
Increase in value:	$38.83	$327.03
Percentage increase:	3.9%	32.7%

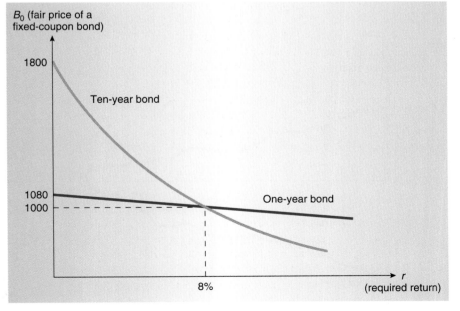

FIGURE 6.5

A comparison of bond value sensitivity to changes in the required return.

The price paths shown in figure 6.6 ignore two alternative outcomes: *default* and *early repayment.* We'll consider the possibility of default now and discuss the issue of early repayment in the next section.

Suppose there is a significant chance that the company won't be able to pay off its bonds at maturity. If you were going to purchase one of these bonds, how would you take this potential problem into account? You would offer a lower price. If the company did pay off the bonds on time, you would earn a higher return (having paid less for the bond). But this possibility is your reward for taking the higher risk that you may not get the full promised payments on time. This is another illustration of the Principle of Risk-Return Trade-Off. Because others will have the same reaction, the bond will be worth less than it would be if full repayment were not in doubt.

If repayment continues to be in doubt as the bond approaches maturity, the bond's price will converge to a lower value. The bond's price at maturity will be the discounted value of the payment the bondholders expect to receive eventually (when the company makes a settlement after defaulting).

Bond Values and Call Provisions

The call provision (the company's option to pay off the bonds early) can also change the bond's terminal value and its maturity. This is because the company can repay the bonds early by paying the call price to the bondholders. If the bonds might be called at any time, you won't pay much more than the call price for one of them, because the company could call the bonds right after you buy one.

For example, suppose you could buy a bond for $1230, but it could be called for $1080 anytime after you buy it. If you pay $1230 for the bond today, tomorrow you could be forced to sell it back to the company for only $1080, producing a one-day loss of $150, or −12.2%. So it's clear you don't want to pay much more than the call price for a bond.

✓ **YIELD TO CALL (YTC)**
The APR of a bond, assuming it will be paid off at the first possible call date.

However, what if the bond can't be called now but could be called five years from today? In such cases, practitioners compute what is called the bond's **yield to call (YTC)** on bonds selling above their call price. The YTC is a bond's promised return, assuming the company will pay off the bonds (pay the bondholders the call price) on a specified call date.

FIGURE 6.6
Hypothetical price paths for a discount bond and a premium bond.

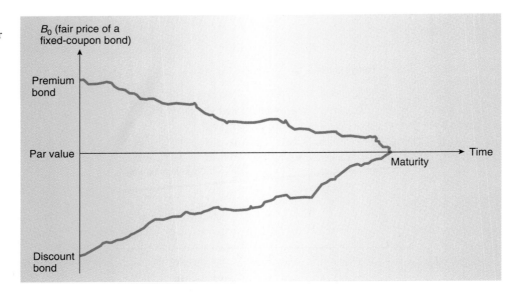

Computing the YTC on an IBM Bond

Suppose IBM has a bond that can't be called today but can be called in 3 years at a call price of $1090. The bond has a remaining maturity of 18 years and a coupon rate of 12%. It currently sells for $1175.97. What is the bond's YTC? In other words, what return will be earned from buying this bond today for $1175.97, if the company makes all promised payments and redeems the bonds in 3 years by paying $1090?

Once again we apply equation (6.1), but with the call price in place of the par value. The inputs are $B_0 = 1175.97$, CPN/2 is 60.00 (one-half of 12% of $1000), future value is 1090, and $2N = 6$ (3 years until the call):

$$\$1175.97 = 60.00\left[\frac{(1 + r/2)^6 - 1}{(r/2)(1 + r/2)^6}\right] + \frac{1090}{(1 + r/2)^6}$$

The $r/2$ that solves the equation is 4.0%. Therefore, this bond's YTC is 8.0%.

$$N = 6 \quad r = 4.00 \quad PV = 1175.97 \quad PMT = 60.00 \quad FV = 1090$$

If IBM doesn't call the bond 3 years from now, but continues to make all the required payments throughout the life of the bond, the realized return will be the YTM, which is higher than the YTC. Of course, that's a "big if" you might not want to count on!

You can verify that the bond's YTM is currently 9.89%.

$$N = 36 \quad r = 4.944 \quad PV = 1175.97 \quad PMT = 60.00 \quad FV = 1000$$

The key point in the IBM bond example is that if the company calls the bond at its earliest chance, you'll earn only an 8% yield, not the 9.89% YTM. This is an important risk to take into account. This risk of calling is why the YTC is, and the YTM is not, the appropriate measure of return when a bond is selling above its call price.

The YTC computation alerts the potential bond buyer to the possibility that the company will repay the bonds at the first opportunity the contract allows. We cannot know for certain what will happen. As with every option, the outcome is contingent on the decision of the optionholder—in this case, the company. And that decision in turn depends on other contingencies—in this case, future market interest rates.

Other Bond Risks

Bondholders are taking several other risks, including inflation risk, currency risk, and marketability risk.

Inflation Risk   Bond principal payments are stated in nominal dollars. That is, they ignore inflation—and the decreasing purchasing power it causes. Current inflationary expectations are built into the required return. If inflation turns out to be less than expected, the future cash flows will have more purchasing power than had been expected, which would be a gain. On the other hand, if inflation turns out to be more than expected, the future cash flows will have less purchasing power, a loss. Fixed-income securities can have considerable inflation risk.

Currency Risk   Many people invest in foreign securities. Payments from foreign securities are usually made in a foreign currency. If the value of that currency changes, relative to the value of a dollar, the dollar-denominated value of your investment will change. For example, suppose you buy a Japanese bond that makes payments in yen. If the yen appreciates relative to the dollar, the bond's payments will be worth more when you convert them into dollars. On the other hand, if the yen depreciates relative to the dollar, the payments will be worth less when you convert them into dollars.

Marketability Risk   The volume of trading in corporate bonds is lower than the volume in common stocks. Bonds are less liquid and have larger trading costs. This reduces the bond's return. If a bond's liquidity changes significantly, the bond's required return will change to reflect the change in trading costs. The possibility of significant changes in liquidity creates marketability risk, which affects bond values.

Self-Check

1. Define *interest-rate risk, default risk, call risk, inflation risk, currency risk,* and *marketability risk.*

2. Suppose you buy a bond that has some default risk. If the bond doesn't default, is the realized return above or below the expected return?

3. What is a YTC, yield to call? How is it different from a YTM?

STOCK VALUATION

Stocks are of two basic types, common stock and preferred stock. *Common stock* represents the residual ownership interest in a company. Collectively, the common stockholders are the owners of the company. They elect the company's directors. In the event the company is liquidated, they share proportionately in what is left after the bondholders and other claimants of higher legal priority are legally satisfied (for example, the government gets any taxes owed).

The common stockholders receive dividends, which the company pays out of cash, presumably out of profits it earns. Profits are calculated after making interest payments. But dividends are not a contractual obligation of the company. If the company doesn't earn any profit, it may even be legally barred from paying dividends in certain cases. As a result, the common stockholders bear more risk than the bondholders. There is greater uncertainty about the payments they will receive. In fact, common stock has no explicitly promised future payments. But we expect the company to pay cash dividends to its common stockholders, at least at some point in the future.

Preferred Stock

Preferred stock has a claim higher in priority than the company's common stock but lower in priority than the company's debt. There's a stated cash dividend rate, which is like the stated interest rate on debt. But if the company fails to pay the dividends, the preferred stockholders cannot force the company into bankruptcy. Compared to common stockholders, preferred stockholders typically have only very limited rights to vote on corporate matters.

Preferred stock is therefore a hybrid; it falls between bonds and common stock in the legal-priority hierarchy of financial securities. The risk of preferred stock also falls between that of the company's common stock and that of its bonds. However, a company that wants to keep a good financial reputation will make every effort to pay its preferred stock obligations.

Preferred stock payment obligations are typically viewed like debt obligations, and they look like debt payment obligations. As a result, the bond valuation model can also be used to value preferred stock—under the assumption that the company will meet its preferred stock payment obligations. However, an adjustment is required. Preferred stock pays dividends quarterly, whereas bonds pay interest semiannually.

Valuing New York Edison Preferred Stock

Let's say New York Edison has preferred stock outstanding that pays a $2.00 per quarter dividend. New York Edison must repay the $100 par value 20 years from today. The market price of the stock is $97.50. What is the stock's YTM?

The formula is like equation (6.1), but with quarterly payments and compounding:

$$\text{Preferred stock value} = (\text{Coupon payment})\text{PVAF}_{(r/4)\%,4N} + (\text{Par value})\text{PVF}_{(r/4)\%,4N}$$

$$\$97.50 = 2.00\left[\frac{(1 + r/4)^{4N} - 1}{(r/4)(1 + r/4)^{4N}}\right] + \frac{100}{(1 + r/4)^{4N}}$$

The YTM on this preferred stock equals four times the quarterly rate, or 8.256%.

| N = 80 | **r = 2.064** | PV = 97.50 | PMT = 2.00 | FV = 100 |

Some preferred stocks never mature. Such a *perpetual preferred stock* therefore has no final principal payment and is expected to pay dividends every period into the future. In such situations, the valuation formula collapses to the simpler perpetuity formula (equation 5.7), and stock value equals dividend/required return.

Valuing United Airlines Perpetual Preferred Stock

Suppose United Airlines has perpetual preferred stock outstanding that pays a $0.40 quarterly dividend. It has a required return of 12% APR (3% per quarter). What is the stock worth?

Using equation (5.7), with PMT = 0.40 and r = 0.03, the stock's value is

$$\text{Stock value} = \text{PVA}_{\text{perpetuity}} = \frac{\text{PMT}}{r} = \frac{0.40}{0.03} = \$13.33$$

Valuing Common Stock

There are two important differences between the factors for valuing common stock and those for valuing bonds. First, the horizon, or life, of the investment can be *infinite* rather than finite. For a bond the horizon is called the maturity. Because corporations have potentially infinite life, common stocks have infinite lives; corporations never have to redeem them. When an investor sells a stock, its value depends on future expected cash flows, which theoretically continue forever.

Second, as we previously mentioned, the future cash flows are not explicitly promised. The future cash flows must be estimated on the basis of expectations about the company's future earnings and dividend policy.

From a financial point of view, the value of a share of common stock depends *entirely* on the cash flows the company will distribute to its owners and the required return on such cash flows. This is a strong statement, but it is the fundamental way in which stocks are valued.

The Fair Price of a Share of Common Stock

When you own a stock, you know that its future sale price can largely determine your profit or loss. During your investment holding period, you expect to receive cash dividends plus the sale price at the end of the holding period.

Let the value of a share of common stock today be P_0. The expected future cash dividends are $D_1, D_2, \ldots, D_n$, for time periods $1, 2, \ldots, n$. The cash dividend just paid by the company is D_0. P_0 is the present value of the expected future cash dividends plus the present value of P_n, the expected future cash sale price of the share of stock at time n, or

$$P_0 = \frac{D_1}{(1+r)^1} + \frac{D_2}{(1+r)^2} + \ldots + \frac{D_n}{(1+r)^n} + \frac{P_n}{(1+r)^n} \qquad (6.2)$$

where r is the stock's required return.[8]

If equation (6.2) looks suspiciously like the bond valuation model, that's because it involves the same valuation concept: The price of a financial security equals the present value of its expected future cash flows. For a share of common stock, these are its periodic dividends plus a terminal amount. As we've said, valuing a share of common stock is more difficult than valuing a bond because its expected future cash flows are so uncertain.

A stock's value has two components. Its dividends are often called the income component. Cash dividends are similar to other income sources. The second component is the change in value, which is often called the capital-gain component. Capital gain represents the growth (or loss) in stock value from the time of purchase until the time of sale.

For an investor who has a one-year horizon, $n = 1$ and the value of the stock is:

$$P_0 = \frac{D_1}{(1+r)^1} + \frac{P_1}{(1+r)^1}$$

For an investor with a two-year horizon, $n = 2$ and the value of the stock is:

$$P_0 = \frac{D_1}{(1+r)^1} + \frac{D_2}{(1+r)^2} + \frac{P_2}{(1+r)^2}$$

and so forth.

EXAMPLE

Investing in Pepperidge Farm Common Stock

Steve Wyatt is considering an investment in Pepperidge Farm common stock. He expects Pepperidge Farm to pay a $1.48 dividend in 1 year and $1.80 in 2 years. He believes Pepperidge Farm will sell for $26.00 in 2 years. What's the stock worth if its required return is 12%?

The present value of Steve's investment is:

$$P_0 = \frac{1.48}{(1.12)^1} + \frac{1.80}{(1.12)^2} + \frac{26.00}{(1.12)^2} = 1.32 + 1.43 + 20.73 = \$23.48$$

So the stock is worth $23.48 to Steve. ∎

You might wonder how Steve estimated that the stock would sell for $26 in two years. That is, what determines the stock price at time n? The answer is that the value at time n is once again the present value (as of time n) of the expected future (after time n) dividends and eventual selling price.

Therefore, P_0 depends *directly* on the dividends the investor receives for n periods and *indirectly* on dividends after time n. That is, the dividends after time n determine the stock price at n. This concept holds regardless of how many times the stock might be sold in the future. For example, Joe can buy the stock now. Joe can sell it to Mary in the future. Mary can

---

[8]For now, we're ignoring tax considerations and treating cash dividends as though payments occur annually rather than quarterly as they typically do, and thus compounding yearly. These simplifications might significantly affect valuation in practice, but they are useful simplifications that allow us to concentrate on the important concepts.

later sell it to Gordo. Gordo can sell it to you. You can sell it to someone else, and so forth. At any point in time, the stock's value depends on the dividends and future sale price the investor expects to receive. But the expected future sale price in turn depends on subsequent dividends and another selling price. Conceptually, then, the expected future sale price drops out.

As a result, a stock's fair price can be expressed as the present value of *all* its expected future dividends, of an *infinite* stream of expected future cash dividend payments, or

$$P_0 = \frac{D_1}{(1+r)} + \frac{D_2}{(1+r)^2} + \dots = \sum_{t=1}^{\infty} \frac{D_t}{(1+r)^t} \qquad (6.3)$$

Equation (6.3) is a very general expression for the value of a share of stock. It doesn't assume any specific pattern of future cash dividends. Also, it makes no specific assumption about when the share of stock will be sold; the share might be sold any number of future times—or never.

But What Determines Future Dividends?

If the value of a share of common stock is based on expected future cash dividends, a logical next question is: What determines future dividends? There are two factors that determine cash dividends: (1) the company's earnings and (2) its dividend policy. A company's future profitability ultimately determines how much income the company has available to distribute as dividends.

The decision to distribute cash dividends to stockholders is made by the board of directors. The board must choose between either reinvesting or paying out the earnings as dividends. A company's **dividend policy** guides its payment of cash dividends.

A simple but convenient way to describe a dividend policy is to compute the payout ratio. The **payout ratio** expresses the company's cash dividend as a proportion of its earnings:

$$Payout\ ratio = \frac{Dividends}{Earnings}$$

Although a payout ratio is an oversimplification of a company's dividend policy, we can use this measure to analyze stock valuation. Chapter 13 examines dividend policy in more depth.

DIVIDEND POLICY An established guide for the company to determine the amount of money it will pay out as dividends.

PAYOUT RATIO The company's cash dividend divided by the company's earnings in the same period.

Self-Check

1. Why is preferred stock often called a hybrid security?

2. Why is the bond valuation model useful for valuing preferred stock?

3. What are the two components of a stock's value?

4. How can a share of common stock be valued without regard to a future sale price?

5. Why might a payout ratio be a kind of indicator of a company's emphasis on growth?

APPLYING THE DIVIDEND VALUATION MODEL

Investors look at a company (and its stock) as a source of growing wealth. Therefore, they are interested in the underlying rate of growth of a company and the implications of that growth rate for the stock's value. We're going to assume cash dividends will change at some average rate *g* from one period to the next, forever into the future. This characterization of cash dividends is very useful. It's general enough to apply to many situations (for example, the rate of change can be positive or negative). It's also a good *approximation* of actual patterns of dividends.

Although an infinite horizon may seem to be unbelievable (after all, corporations don't really live forever, or at least none has yet), it's also a good approximation. This is because most of a stock's value is determined by the value of its nearest dividends. As with any cash flow, the further in the future a dividend will occur, the smaller is its present value. As figure 6.7 shows, very distant future dividends contribute little to the present value of the stock. For example, the present value at 10% of a $2 dividend, expected 60 years from now, is less than a penny (= $2.00/1.10^{60} = 0.007$).

The Constant Growth Model

Assume cash dividend payments change at the rate of g from one period to the next forever into the future. For example, suppose the latest year's dividends totaled $1.00 and dividends are growing 10% per year. Future dividends would then total $1.10 next year, $1.21 the year after, $1.331 in the third year, and so on. Then the dividend payment for period t, D_t, can be expressed as the previous dividend, D_{t-1}, times (1 plus g). Thus, D_t can be expressed as a function of any dividend between now and time t, or

$$D_t = (1 + g)D_{t-1} = (1 + g)^2 D_{t-2} = \ldots = (1 + g)^{(t-1)}D_1 = D_0(1 + g)^t$$

If each future dividend in equation (6.3) is represented in this way, P_0, the current price, can be rewritten as the sum of the growing dividends, discounted at the required return, r:

$$P_0 = \frac{D_0(1 + g)}{(1 + r)} + \frac{D_0(1 + g)^2}{(1 + r)^2} + \frac{D_0(1 + g)^3}{(1 + r)^3} + \ldots = D_0 \sum_{t=1}^{\infty} \frac{(1 + g)^t}{(1 + r)^t}$$

This is an infinite geometric series, like the perpetuity we described in chapter 5 (equation 5.7). This one simplifies to

$$P_0 = \frac{D_1}{(r - g)}$$

In this situation, D_t is a *growing* perpetuity. A positive growth ($g > 0$) makes the denominator less than r. This in turn makes the present value, P_0, larger than it would be if the perpetual cash flow were not growing. The positive growth increases the value of the stock. Logically, the larger the growth rate, the larger the stock's value.

We can use this same notion to determine a stock's fair price at any point in time. That price, P_t, can be expressed in two different ways. The first is in terms of the next period's dividend

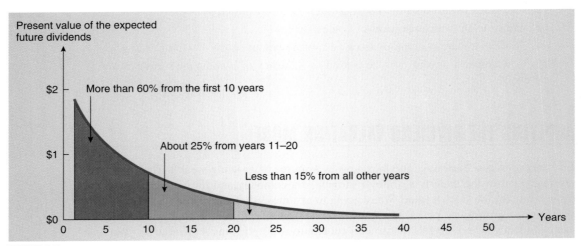

FIGURE 6.7
Relative contribution to stock price of near and distant future dividends.

(D_{t+1}), the growth rate (g), and the required return (r), whenever dividends from D_{t+1} on are expected to grow by g every period forever into the future. So whenever g is expected to be constant from time $t + 1$ on, P_t can be written as

$$P_t = \frac{D_{t+1}}{(r - g)} \qquad (6.4)$$

The second way to express P_t is in terms of the previous period's price, P_{t-1}. By substituting $(1 + g)D_t$ for D_{t+1} and P_{t-1} for $D_t/(r - g)$ into the above equation, we get:

$$P_t = (1 + g)P_{t-1}$$

Therefore, just like dividends, P_t also grows by g each period.

Valuing a Constant-Growth Stock: Procter & Gamble

EXAMPLE

Suppose Procter & Gamble is expected to pay a dividend of $3.00 next year on its common stock, the required return is 12%, and dividend payments are expected to grow at 4% per year forever. What is the fair price for a share of Procter & Gamble common stock?

Using equation (6.4) with $t = 0$, $D_1 = \$3.00$, $r = 0.12$, and $g = 0.04$, we have

$$P_0 = \frac{3.00}{(0.12 - 0.04)} = \$37.50 \quad \blacksquare$$

Valuing a Zero-Growth Stock: Sargasso

EXAMPLE

Suppose Sargasso is expected to pay a dividend of $3.00 per year on its common stock forever into the future but has no growth prospects whatsoever. If the required return on Sargasso's common stock is 12%, what is a share worth?

In this case, we simply put in a growth rate of zero. So, using equation (6.4) with $t = 0$, $D_1 = \$2.50$, $r = 0.10$, and $g = 0$, we have

$$P_0 = \frac{3.00}{(0.12 - 0)} = \$25.00 \quad \blacksquare$$

An Important Comment on the Relationship Between g and r   One of the first questions about equation (6.4) is what happens if g equals r, or if g is greater than r. The question arises because if we blindly apply equation (6.4), it implies that the stock's value is infinite if g equals r and that it is negative if g is greater than r. Neither situation makes economic sense. A faster-growing company is riskier and will have a higher required return, so the larger g is, the larger r will be.

Quite simply, g can never be greater than or equal to r. Although we won't prove this, consider the following argument: g is the rate at which cash dividends are expected to grow *every period, forever.* In the long run, dividends are paid from a company's earnings. Therefore, for cash dividends to grow at g, the company's earnings must grow at a rate that equals or exceeds g (at least, on average over a long time) to have sufficient income to pay the dividends.

It's easy to imagine very high earnings growth. However, any situation you can imagine will involve a *limited* time period. No company can grow faster than the economy forever. If a company grew fast enough for long enough, its total revenue would equal the economy's total output. In the limit, the company would become the entire economy. After that, it couldn't grow faster than itself!

One other comment concerning g might be helpful. Even though g acts like a discount rate in that it compounds amounts, it is a *growth* rate. Be careful to distinguish between the two; it's easy to mix up the rates when you are working problems.

Estimating a Stock's Required Return Using the Constant Growth Model

For a publicly traded stock, the most recent price paid is the best available estimate of its value. This price can be used in the constant growth model, equation (6.4), to estimate the required return for a stock. A stock's required return is often called its **capitalization rate.**

✓ **CAPITALIZATION RATE**
A stock's required return.

Rearranging equation (6.4) provides a model for computing a stock's expected return. Based on the Principle of Capital Market Efficiency, a stock's expected return is in turn a good estimate of its required return, or capitalization rate:

$$r = \frac{D_1}{P_0} + g \tag{6.5}$$

✓ **DIVIDEND YIELD** The dividend income portion of a stock's return.

✓ **CAPITAL-GAIN YIELD** The price change portion of a stock's return.

Earlier, we referred to the two components of a stock's value, income and capital gains. You see these in equation (6.5). The income component is also called the **dividend yield,** which is the dividend divided by the price. The capital-gain component, or **capital-gain yield,** is g. The total return is simply the sum of the two.

E X A M P L E

Estimating International Paper's Capitalization Rate

Suppose you look in today's *Wall Street Journal* and see that International Paper's stock price is $51.00 and its last year's dividend was $1.52. If International Paper's dividend growth rate is expected to be 5.25% per year forever, what is the capitalization rate on its common stock?

First, note that next year's dividend, D_1, is expected to be $1.60 (= 1.52[1.0525]). Then, with a price of 51 for P_0, and $g = 0.0525$ in equation (6.5), the expected return is

$$r = \frac{D_1}{P_0} + g = \frac{1.60}{51.00} + 0.0525 = 0.0315 + 0.0525 = 0.084$$

So the implied capitalization rate, our estimate of International Paper's required return, is 8.4%. This rate consists of a 3.15% dividend yield plus a 5.25% capital-gain yield. ∎

Valuing a Supernormal Growth Stock

Consider a company that is currently experiencing high dividend growth, which is expected to continue for some finite time. After this period of supernormal growth, dividend growth will be at a normal rate forever into the future. We can compute the value of this company's stock by using equation (6.2) and breaking the dividends into two parts: a normal-growth part, which goes on forever into the future, and a supernormal-growth part, which is finite. The normal-growth part makes up the sale price, P_n, which can be computed using equation (6.4). The supernormal-growth part is D_1 through D_{n-1}. Applying equation (6.2), then, P_0 equals the present value of the two parts.

E X A M P L E

Valuing a Supernormal Growth Stock: Netscape

Let's say Netscape is operating in a new industry that has recently caught on with the public. Sales are growing 80% per year. This high sales growth rate is expected to translate into a 25% growth rate in cash dividends for each of the next 4 years. After that, the dividend growth rate is expected to be 5% per year forever. The latest annual dividend, paid yesterday, is $0.75. The stock's required return is 22%. What is a share of Netscape common stock worth?

First, compute the expected future cash dividends.

Time	0	1	2	3	4	5	6	...
Dividend	0.75	0.938	1.172	1.465	1.831	1.923	2.019	...
Growth		25%	25%	25%	25%	5%	5%	5% ...

Second, compute the stock's fair price at a future point in time, using equation (6.4). To be able to use equation (6.4), you must pick a point after the dividend growth rate has become constant forever. Using time 5, the hypothetical sale value of the stock, P_5, is

$$P_5 = \frac{D_6}{r - g} = \frac{2.019}{0.22 - 0.05} = \$11.876$$

Finally, compute the present value of the expected future sale price and add that to the present value of all the expected cash dividends between now and then. Using equation (6.2), with $n = 5$, we have

$$P_0 = \frac{0.938}{(1.22)} + \frac{1.172}{(1.22)^2} + \frac{1.465}{(1.22)^3} + \frac{1.831}{(1.22)^4} + \frac{1.923}{(1.22)^5} + \frac{11.876}{(1.22)^5}$$

$$= 0.768 + 0.787 + 0.807 + 0.827 + 0.711 + 4.394 = \$8.295$$

Note that the choice of time period 5 for the hypothetical sale is somewhat arbitrary. We could have used period 6 or period 7. In fact, any fair price from period 3 onward can be used. (Period 3 is not a misprint; dividends will grow at the 5% rate from period 4 on. Therefore D_4 can be used to compute P_3, which is $10.77. Again, the present value of the dividends and the sale price equals $8.295. Try it!) ∎

Valuing an Erratic-Growth Stock

Now consider a company that is expected to have erratic dividend growth for some finite time, followed by a normal rate forever into the future. We can again break the dividend stream into two parts and use equation (6.2). In fact, we can generalize our procedure further.

Suppose expected dividend growth varies for n periods but is constant at g forever after that. At time n, the next dividend is $D_{n+1} = (1 + g)D_n$. Using equation (6.4), the stock's value at n is

$$P_n = \frac{(1 + g)D_n}{r - g}$$

We can now use this expression in place of P_n in equation (6.2), which gives

$$P_0 = \frac{D_1}{(1 + r)} + \frac{D_2}{(1 + r)^2} + \ldots + \frac{D_n}{(1 + r)^n} + \frac{(1 + g)D_n}{(1 + r)^n(r - g)} \tag{6.6}$$

Equation (6.6) is a general formula for valuing common stocks with *any* variable dividend growth rates over a finite time period that is followed by a constant growth rate forever. It simply combines equations (6.4) and (6.2) into a single formula.

EXAMPLE

Valuing an Erratic-Growth Stock: Novell

Let's say Novell is currently in a building stage. It's not expected to change its annual cash dividend while new projects are being developed over the next 3 years. Its dividend was $1 last year and is to be $1 for each of the next 3 years. After the projects have been developed, earnings are expected to grow at a high rate for 2 years as the sales resulting from the new projects are realized. The higher earnings are expected to result in a 40% increase in dividends for 2 years. After these two extraordinary increases in dividends, the dividend growth rate is expected to be 3% per year forever. If Novell's common stock required return is 12%, what is a share worth today?

As with our Netscape example, first compute the expected future dividends.

Time	0	1	2	3	4	5	6	7	...
Dividend	1.00	1.00	1.00	1.00	1.40	1.96	2.019	2.079	...
Growth	0%	0%	0%	40%	40%	3%	3%	3%	...

Second, note that D_5 is where the growth rate in the dividends is expected to become constant forever. This is the earliest point that satisfies the constant-growth assumption. Using equation (6.6) with $D_5 = \$1.96$, $g = 3\%$, and $r = 12\%$, we have

$$P_0 = \frac{1.00}{(1.12)} + \frac{1.00}{(1.12)^2} + \frac{1.00}{(1.12)^3} + \frac{1.40}{(1.12)^4} + \frac{1.96}{(1.12)^5} + \frac{(1+0.03)1.96}{(1.12)^5(0.12-0.03)} = \$17.13 \quad \blacksquare$$

Self-Check

1. With constant dividend growth, equation (6.4), what's the relationship between one dividend and the next, such as between D_t and D_{t+1}? What's the relationship between one price and the previous price?

2. Why is it that g can never equal or exceed r when dividend growth is constant forever after?

3. What is a stock's capitalization rate?

4. Explain in your own words how equation (6.6) combines equations (6.4) and (6.2).

OBTAINING COMMON STOCK INFORMATION

Suppose you wanted to get information about a particular common stock, say PepsiCo, makers of Pepsi-Cola. You could look in a newspaper, such as the *Wall Street Journal* or the *New York Times,* and find New York Stock Exchange quotes like those in figure 6.8.

From the PepsiCo quote you know PepsiCo's

1. *Latest 12 months' price range.* The highest and lowest prices paid in the last 52 weeks for a share of PepsiCo common stock were $52.75 and $31.875, respectively.

2. *Exchange symbol.* PepsiCo's stock symbol on the NYSE is PEP.

3. *Estimated dividend.* PepsiCo's estimated current annual dividend rate (based on the latest quarter's dividend) is $0.80.

52 Weeks		Stock	Sym	Div	Yld %	P/E	Sales 100s	High	Low	Last	Chg
HI	LO										
$9^1/8$	$4^3/4$	PaylessC	PCS	...	...	8	486	$5^1/4$	$5^1/8$	$5^1/8$	...
$50^1/4$	$35^3/8$	Pennzoil	PZL	1.00	2.4	11	1348	$40^1/2$	$39^7/8$	$40^1/8$	$-^1/8$
$52^3/4$	$31^7/8$	PepsiCo	PEP	.80	1.6	24	14546	$49^1/8$	$48^5/8$	$48^7/8$	$+^1/4$
$38^5/8$	$26^1/4$	PerkElmer	PKN	.68	1.8	28	1890	38	$37^1/8$	$37^3/4$	+1
$66^7/8$	$36^1/8$	Pfizer	PFE	1.04	1.6	26	13254	$64^1/8$	$62^1/4$	$62^3/8$	$-1^1/4$
$69^1/2$	$51^5/8$	PhilLongD	PHI	1.80	2.8	7	412	$64^5/8$	$61^1/8$	$63^3/8$	$+2^1/4$
$62^5/8$	47	PhilLongD pf		4.12	7.9	...	260	$52^3/8$	$51^1/2$	$52^3/8$	$+^3/4$
18	$9^1/8$	PhillpsVanH	PVH	.15	1.6	41	2511	$9^5/8$	$9^1/4$	$9^1/2$	$-^1/8$

FIGURE 6.8
Hypothetical stock quote with PepsiCo highlighted.

4. *Dividend yield.* PepsiCo's dividend yield is 1.6%; it is the dividend rate divided by the closing price (= 0.80/48.875).

5. *Price-earnings ratio.* PepsiCo's P/E is 24; it is the closing price divided by the latest 12 months' earnings per share.

6. *Trading volume.* 1,454,600 shares (= [14,546]100) changed ownership yesterday.

7. *Latest day's high, low, and closing prices.* Yesterday's high, low, and closing prices for PepsiCo common stock were $49.125, $48.625, and $48.875, respectively.

8. *Change in closing price.* Yesterday's closing price was $0.25 (= [1/4]1) higher than the previous day's closing price.

A variety of additional symbols and notations can provide further information in the quote. For example, the second PhilLongD stock has a *pf* after it and no symbol. This indicates that the stock is a preferred rather than a common stock. Other notations indicate such things as a new 52-week high or low price, or that a dividend has been declared.

You can find out more about these and other items by looking in a **stock guide,** such as *Standard & Poor's Stock Guide.* Additional information published in a stock guide includes the number of shares outstanding and the stated dividend rate for preferred stock. Figure 6.9 on pages 176 and 177 illustrates hypothetical information from a stock guide.

STOCK GUIDE A publication that provides particular information about specific stocks.

From this stock guide quote, we know that

1. PepsiCo has 797,315,000 shares of common stock outstanding and no publicly traded preferred stock.

2. PepsiCo has paid $0.58 per share in dividends for the year so far.

3. PepsiCo has $7.675 billion in long-term debt.

4. PepsiCo had $1.405 billion in cash and equivalents on September 4.

Self-Check

1. Define the following terms: *exchange symbol, dividend yield, trading volume, closing price.*

2. Assume you have a copy of the *Wall Street Journal* and *Standard & Poor's Stock Guide.* Which one would you look in to find each of the following pieces of information? **a.** Yesterday's closing stock price; **b.** The number of outstanding shares; **c.** Yesterday's trading volume in a stock; **d.** A corporation's total long-term debt; **e.** The stock's exchange symbol.

3. A share of stock is quoted at 24¼ in the newspaper. What is its dollar price?

FIGURE 6.9

Hypothetical excerpt from a stock guide with PepsiCo highlighted.

◆ S&P 500 # MidCap ·Options Index	Ticker Symbol	NAME OF ISSUE (Call Price of pfd. Stocks)	Market	PRINCIPAL BUSINESS	Com. Rank & Pfd. Rating	Par Val.	Inst. Hold Cos.	Inst. Hold Shs. (000)
1	PTEL	√Peoples Telephone Co	NMS	Oper private pay tel system	NR	1¢	70	7483
2	PSFT	√PeopleSoft Inc	NMS	Mfr human resource mgmt softwr	NR	1¢	90	6645
◆3[a]	PBY	√Pep Boys-Man,Mo,Ja	NY,B,Ch,P,Ph	Retail chain: auto parts, etc.	A+	1	273	39582
◆4[b]	PEP	√PepsiCo Inc	NY,B,C,Ch,P,Ph	Soft drink: snack fd/food svc	A+	1¢	1022	463605
5	PRCP	√Perceptron Inc	NMS	Laser-based sensor/image sys	NR	1¢	11	300
6	PFGC	√Performance Food Group	NMS	Market, dstr food products	NR	1¢	24	1021
7	PCR	√Perini Corp	AS,B,Ch	Construction: R.E. develop	C	1	27	1363
8	Pr	$2.12551Dep Cv52Ex Pfd (5326.275).	AS		NR	No	6	198
◆9[c]	PFR	√Perkin-Elmer	NY,B,Ch,P,Ph	Analytical instruments, optics	B–	1	263	34497
10	PKN	√Perkins Family Rest L.P.	NY,Ch,Ph	Family style restaurant svc	B+	No	24	267
11	PBT	√Permian Basin Try Tr55..........................	NY,B,Ch,P,Ph	Royalty oil interests, Texas	NR	No	24	1098
#12	PRGO	√Perrigo Co	NMS	Mfr store brand pharmac'l prd	NR	No	186	29307
13	PDS	√Perry Drug Stores.......	NY,B,Ch,Ph	Drug chain in Michigan	#C	5¢	41	3914
14	PCPI	√Personal Computer Prod..........................	NSC	Dvlp. mkt laser printers/prod	*B-	.005¢	4	414
◆15	PT	Pet Inc	NY,B,Ch,P,Ph	Specialty food & confections prd	NR	1¢	259	59474

◆ S&P 500 # MidCap ·Options Index	Ticker Symbol	PRICE RANGE 1971–91 High	1971–91 Low	1992 High	1992 Low	1993 High	1993 Low	Dec. Sales in 100s	December, 1993 Last Sale or Bid High	Low	Last	% Div. Yield	P-E Ratio
1	PTEL	7	2	8⅝	5½	13¾	7⅜	24570	11½	9¾	9¾	...	28
2	PSFT	...	...	32	17	40½	23½	40064	33½	27⅜	31¼	...	51
◆3[a]	PBY	19½	⅓	27⅜	15⅛	27⅜	19⅞	25809	27⅜	25½	26¼	0.6	25
◆4[b]	PEP	35⅝	1⅓	43⅜	30½	43⅜	34½	227685	42⅛	39⅝	40⅞	1.6	20
5	PRCP	...	...	8¼	5⅜	13¼	5¼	9248	13¼	10¾	13¼	...	38
6	PFGC	...	...	...	...	24¾	14	3683	24¾	18¾	24½	...	31
7	PCR	44	3	18¾	10	18⅝	9⅞	1279	11⅞	10⅛	11⅝	...	d
8	Pr	28⅛	11½	24⅜	16½	25⅞	21	117	23¼	22½	22⅝	9.4	...
◆9[c]	PFR	41⅛	7¼	36	27¼	39¾	28½	31149	39	33¾	38½	1.8	...
10	PKN	18⅞	7⅜	21½	15⅞	23⅝	17¼	1086	22¼	21¼	21⅜	6.1	14
11	PBT	25	3¾	5⅛	3⅞	5	3½	5998	4⅞	4½	4¾	8.4	11
#12	PRGO	15⅜	8	22⅝	12	34⅞	19⅛	49075	34⅞	30	34¼	...	54
13	PDS	20⅞	½	11⅝	7⅝	9⅝	5⅜	10269	6¾	5⅞	6⅛	...	d
14	PCPI	6⅛	¼	1⅛	⅜	1⅞	⅛	22634	1⅜	⅞	1⅛	...	24
◆15	PT	23¾	15	23¾	14⅜	18⅜	14⅝	54540	17¾	16½	17½	1.8	25

CAPITALIZATION			FINANCIAL POSITION				DIVIDENDS					
	Shs. 000		Mil—$				Latest Payment			Total $		
Lg. Trm. Debt Mil—$	Pfd.	Com.	Cash & Equiv.	Curr. Assets	Curr. Liab.	Balance Sheet Date	Period $	Date	Ex Div.	So Far 1993	Ind. Rate	Paid 1992
40.2	...	14374	3.84	23.1	20.0	9-30-93	None Since Public			...	Nil	...
0.97	...	11610	56.3	87.1	27.0	9-30-93	None Since Public			...	Nil	...
265	...	60986	12.8	355	200	10-31-93	Q0.038	1-24-94	1-4	0.14¾	0.15	0.135
7675	...	797315	1405	4759	5141	9-04-93	Q0.16	1-1-94	12-6	0.58	0.64	0.5
0.08	...	3580	0.91	9.01	1.85	9-30-93	None Since Public			...	Nil	...
6.01	...	6032	4.47	52.8	33.9	10-02-93	None Since Public			...	Nil	...
85.8	100	4331	30.4	266	238	9-30-93	1-0-00	12-18-90	11-20	...	Nil	...
...	1000	...	Cv into 0.662 com, $37.75				Q0.53⅛	12-15-93	11-18	2.12½	2.125	
6.97	...	43944	29.0	496	400	9-30-93	Q0.17	1-3-94	11-24	2.12½		
35.6	...	10390	2.46	12.9	23.9	9-30-93	Q0.32½	2-15-94	12-27	0.68	0.68	0.68
										1.3	1.3	1.3
...	...	46609	Southland Royalty (prop)				0.031	1-14-94	12-27			
										0.40¾	0.4	0.456
77.0	...	75266	0.35	236	111	9-30-93	None Since Public			...	Nil	...
94.4	...	12027	3.80	157	78.0	7-31-93	0.05½	9-14-87	8-24	...	Nil	...
1.20	3	12121	0.54	6.05	2.82	9-30-93	None Since Public			...	Nil	...
										...	Nil	...
★720	...	104125	21.3	368	316	9-30-93	Q0.08	1-1-94	12-13			

EARNINGS $ PER SHARE							INTERIM EARNINGS			
	Years							$ Per Share		
End	1989	1990	1991	1992	1993	Last 12 Mos.	Period	1992	1993	Index
Dc	△0.19	0.14	0.25	0.28	...	0.35	9 Mo Sep	0.21	0.28	1
Dc	d0.07	0.07	0.2	0.48	...	0.61	9 Mo Sep	0.29	0.42	2
Ja	0.63	0.67	0.69	0.9	E1.05	1.01	9 Mo Oct	0.7	0.81	3
Dc	1.13	1.35	1.35	□1.61	E2.00	1.73	36 Wk Sep	□1.29	1.41	4
Dc	d8.87	0.38	d0.57	0.57	...	0.35	9 Mo Sep		0.2	5
Dc	0.41	0.28	0.16	□0.54	...	0.79	9 Mo Sep	□0.38	0.63	6
Dc	3.11	d1.20	0.27	d4.69	...	d5.38	9 Mo Sep	0.88	0.19	7
Dc	b1.94	b0.31	b0.91	bd0.94	...	...				8
Je	d0.56	1.1	d0.47	p540.81	□0.54	0.26	3 Mo Sep	□0.30	0.02	9
Dc	1.14	1.31	1.47	1.48	...	1.55	9 Mo Sep	1.23	1.3	10
Dc	0.46	0.53	0.51	0.45	...	0.45	9 Mo Sep	0.31	0.31	11
Je	...	...	p0.26	p.41	0.57	0.63	3 Mo Sep	0.13	0.19	12
Oc	0.7	0.06	0.3	0.75	Pd1.54	d1.54				13
Je	d0.33	d0.30	d1.14	0.01	0.05	0.05	3 Mo Sep	Nil	Nil	14
Je	...	p560.39	p570.39	p0.96	□0.68	0.69	9 Mo Sep	□0.19	0.2	15

HISTORICAL SECURITY RETURNS IN THE UNITED STATES

In this section, we take a quick look at past returns for investing in U.S. bonds and stocks. This provides a perspective on actual investments in stocks and bonds.

Suppose someone earned 10% on one security and 20% on another. Which was the better investment? The answer seems obvious. But what if the 10% was earned over the last six months and the 20% was over the last six years? Clearly, the amount of time the money was invested affects our opinion of the investment. This amount of time is called the **holding period.**

HOLDING PERIOD An amount of time money is invested.

A realized return—the return actually earned on an investment—has little meaning without knowing the holding period. To standardize comparisons of realized returns, investors often calculate an annual equivalent return, a realized APY. In chapter 5 we showed how to compute an APY for periods less than a year in equation (5.9). But how do you compute an APY when the holding period is more than a year?

Suppose someone tells you that a particular investment produced a return r_1 the first year, r_2 the second year, . . . , and r_N in year N when it was finally sold. The N-year realized return, r, is simply the result of compounding the N annual returns:

$$r = (1 + r_1)(1 + r_2) \ldots (1 + r_N) - 1$$

But what's the realized APY in this case?

Normally, we think of compounding from the smaller period to the larger. So for an N-year holding period, we can compound the APY for N years to compute the holding period realized return:

$$1 + r = (1 + \text{realized APY})^N \tag{6.7}$$

EXAMPLE

Calculating a Realized APY for the Hasbeen Corporation

Suppose a friend told you he bought $12,000 worth of Hasbeen Corporation common stock 45 months (3.75 years) ago. Hasbeen has paid no dividends since he bought the stock. Your friend's stock is currently worth $13,680. What is his realized APY?

First, the realized return for the 3.75-year holding period is 14% (= [13,680/12,000] − 1). Using equation (6.7), we have a realized APY of 3.56%:

$$1.14 = (1 + 0.0356)^{3.75}$$

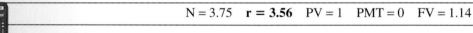

| N = 3.75 | r = 3.56 | PV = 1 | PMT = 0 | FV = 1.14 |

A Historical View

Figure 6.10 compares the cumulative returns since year-end 1925 from investing $1 in each of six classes of securities: large-company common stocks, small-company common stocks, long-term corporate bonds, long-term U.S. government bonds, intermediate-term U.S. government bonds, and U.S. Treasury bills. The vertical (y) axis shows the realized returns for all holding periods starting from the end of 1925.

For example, if one dollar had been invested in large-company common stocks at year-end 1925, with all dividends reinvested in additional shares of common stock, the investment would have grown to $1370.95 by year-end 1996. This is a 71-year holding period with a realized return of 136,995% (= [1370.95 − 1.00]/1.00) and a realized APY of 10.71%.

| N = 71 | r = 10.71 | PV = 1.00 | PMT = 0 | FV = 1370.95 |

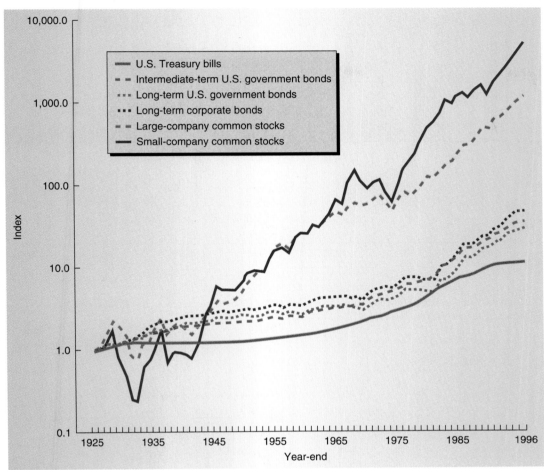

FIGURE 6.10
Cumulative returns from investing in different classes of securities, 1926–1996.   Source: *Stocks, Bonds, Bills, and Inflation 1997 Yearbook* (Chicago, Ill.: Ibbotson Associates, 1997), pp. 232–249.

Small-company common stocks produced the greatest cumulative return, and Treasury bills produced the smallest. But the small-company stock returns also have the most variability.

Table 6.3 shows the average annual total percentage returns. It also shows the average standard deviations of these returns. Standard deviation is a measure of variability. We explain standard deviation, and how it serves as a measure of risk, in the next chapter.

TABLE 6.3
Average Annual Realized Returns for Different Classes of Securities, 1926–1996

CLASS OF SECURITY	ARITHMETIC MEAN	GEOMETRIC MEAN	STANDARD DEVIATION
Large-firm common stocks	12.7%	10.7%	20.3%
Small-firm common stocks	17.7	12.6	34.1
Long-term corporate bonds	6.0	5.6	8.7
Long-term U.S. government bonds	5.4	5.1	9.2
Intermediate-term U.S. government bonds	5.4	5.2	5.8
U.S. Treasury bills	3.8	3.7	3.3

Source: *Stocks, Bonds, Bills, and Inflation 1997 Yearbook* (Chicago, Ill.: Ibbotson Associates, 1997), p. 118.

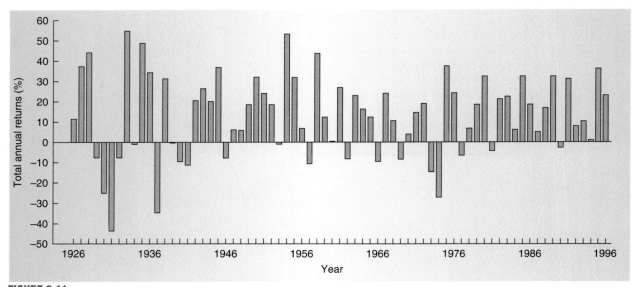

FIGURE 6.11
Yearly realized APYs from investing in large-company common stocks, 1926–1996.   Source: *Stocks, Bonds, Bills, and Inflation 1997 Yearbook* (Chicago, Ill.: Ibbotson Associates, 1997), pp. 180–181.

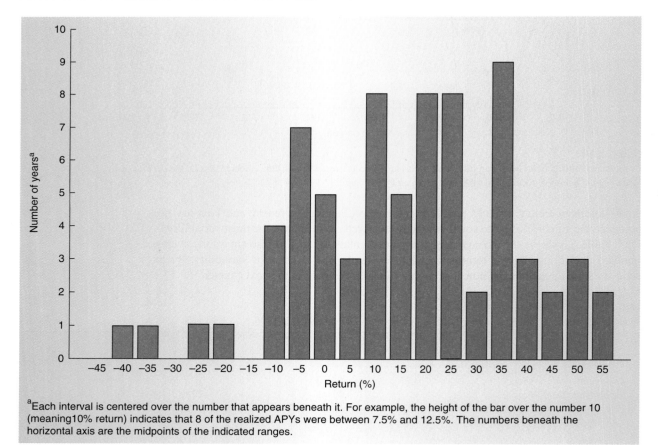

[a]Each interval is centered over the number that appears beneath it. For example, the height of the bar over the number 10 (meaning10% return) indicates that 8 of the realized APYs were between 7.5% and 12.5%. The numbers beneath the horizontal axis are the midpoints of the indicated ranges.

FIGURE 6.12
The frequency of the APYs shown in figure 6.11.   Source: *Stocks, Bonds, Bills, and Inflation 1997 Yearbook* (Chicago, Ill.: Ibbotson Associates, 1997), pp. 180–181.

Common Stock Realized APYs

Figure 6.11 shows average yearly realized APYs for common stocks in each year from 1926 to 1996. The highest (53.99%) occurred in 1933 and the lowest (−43.34%) in 1931. Figure 6.12 shows the frequency of these APYs. You can see that realized returns from investing in securities are spread out over a wide range.

Self-Check

1. What are the realized return and realized APY from an investment that cost $10,000 and returned $13,000 27 months later?

2. In how many years did the average realized APY for large-firm common stocks exceed 40 percent? In how many was it below 30 percent?

3. For common stocks, what was the longest period without a negative annual return? What was the longest period of consecutive losing years?

SUMMARY

This chapter described the typical features of bonds and stocks, and presented valuation models for both securities. Fundamental points in the chapter include:

- Information about stocks and bonds is readily available from a variety of sources.
- A security's fair price is the present value of its expected future cash flows.
- Conversely, we can compute a security's expected return from its market price. The expected return is called the yield to maturity, YTM, for a bond and the capitalization rate for a stock.
- A bond's expected future cash flows are its future coupon payments and terminal value.
- Interest-rate risk is the sensitivity of a bond's value to interest-rate changes. Interest-rate risk depends primarily on a bond's remaining maturity.
- If an investor's bond is likely to be called, its yield to call, YTC, may be more relevant than its YTM.
- Bonds are subject to inflation risk, currency risk, and marketability risk.
- A stock's expected future cash flows are more uncertain and are more difficult to estimate than a bond's. A stock's expected future cash flows are its cash dividends and selling price.
- The chapter provided a brief historical perspective on realized returns from investing in securities.

EQUATION SUMMARY

$$B_0 = \left(\frac{CPN}{2}\right)PVAF_{(r/2)\%,2N} + 1000PVF_{(r/2)\%,2N}$$

(6.1)
$$B_0 = \left[\frac{CPN}{2}\right]\left[\frac{(1 + r/2)^{2N} - 1}{(r/2)(1 + r/2)^{2N}}\right] + \frac{1000}{(1 + r/2)^{2N}}$$

(6.2)
$$P_0 = \frac{D_1}{(1 + r)^1} + \frac{D_2}{(1 + r)^2} + \ldots + \frac{D_n}{(1 + r)^n} + \frac{P_n}{(1 + r)^n}$$

(6.3)
$$P_0 = \frac{D_1}{(1 + r)} + \frac{D_2}{(1 + r)^2} + \ldots = \sum_{t=1}^{\infty} \frac{D_t}{(1 + r)^t}$$

(continued on following page)

(Equation Summary *continued from previous page*)

(6.4)
$$P_t = \frac{D_{t+1}}{(r-g)}$$

(6.5)
$$r = \frac{D_1}{P_0} + g$$

(6.6)
$$P_0 = \frac{D_1}{(1+r)} + \frac{D_2}{(1+r)^2} + \ldots + \frac{D_n}{(1+r)^n} + \frac{(1+g)D_n}{(1+r)^n(r-g)}$$

(6.7)
$$1 + r = (1 + \text{realized APY})^N$$

CHAPTER REVIEW ACTIVITIES

SELF-TEST PROBLEMS

1. (Bond value) A bond has a remaining maturity of 10 years and a required return of 9%. The bond's coupon rate is 7.4%. What is the fair value of this bond?

2. (Yield to maturity) Marstel Industries has a 9.2% bond maturing in 15 years. What is the yield to maturity if the current market price of the bond is:
   a. $1120?   c. $785?
   b. $1000?

3. (Constant growth model)
   a. The current dividend for Birmingham Electric is $2.40 and is growing at 5% annually. If the required return is 13%, what is the value of one share of stock?

   b. Montgomery Audio is expected to pay a $1.30 dividend next year. The dividend is expected to grow at 6% annually. If the current stock price is $21.25, what is Montgomery's required return?

4. (Supernormal growth model) Crockett Paintball Company has a current dividend of $1.00. The dividend is expected to grow at 40% annually for 3 years and to grow thereafter at 5% per year. If the required return is 14%, what is the value per share?

SOLUTIONS TO SELF-TEST PROBLEMS

1. The semiannual coupon is $0.074(1000)/2 = \$37.00$. The semiannual required return is $9\%/2 = 4.5\%$. There are $N = 20$ semiannual periods in the bond's remaining life.

$$B_0 = 37(\text{PVAF}_{4.5\%,20}) + 1000(\text{PVF}_{4.5\%,20}) = 37\left[\frac{(1.045)^{20} - 1}{(0.045)(1.045)^{20}}\right] + \frac{1000}{(1.045)^{20}}$$

$$B_0 = 481.294 + 414.643 = \$895.94$$

| $N = 20$ | $r = 4.5$ | **PV = 895.94** | PMT $= 37.00$ | FV $= 1000$ |

2. The semiannual coupon is $0.092(1000)/2 = \$46.00$. There are $N = 30$ semiannual periods in the bond's remaining life.
   a.

| $N = 30$ | **r = 3.913** | PV $= 1120.00$ | PMT $= 46.00$ | FV $= 1000$ |
| | | | | APR $= 2(3.913) = 7.83\%$ |

b.

$N = 30$	$r = \mathbf{4.60}$	$PV = 1000.00$	$PMT = 46.00$	$FV = 1000$
				$APR = 2(4.60) = 9.20\%$

c.

$N = 30$	$r = \mathbf{6.195}$	$PV = 785.00$	$PMT = 46.00$	$FV = 1000$
				$APR = 2(6.195) = 12.39\%$

3. a. Next year's dividend is 5% greater than the current dividend: $D_1 = 2.40(1.05) = \$2.52$. You can use equation (6.4) to get the current stock price:

$$P_0 = \frac{D_1}{(r-g)} = \frac{2.52}{0.13 - 0.05} = \frac{2.52}{0.08} = \$31.50 \text{ per share}$$

b. Use equation (6.5) to find the expected return. Then from the Principle of Capital Market Efficiency, this equals the required return.

$$r = \frac{D_1}{P_0} + g = \frac{1.30}{21.25} + 0.06 = 0.0612 + 0.06 = 12.12\%$$

4. First the expected future dividends are: $D_1 = 1.00(1.4) = \$1.40$; $D_2 = 1.00(1.4)^2 = \$1.96$; $D_3 = 1.00(1.4)^3 = \$2.744$. Then, using equation (6.6):

$$P_0 = \frac{D_1}{(1+r)} + \frac{D_2}{(1+r)^2} + \frac{D_3}{(1+r)^3} + \frac{(1+g)D_3}{(1+r)^3(r-g)}$$

$$= \frac{1.40}{(1.14)} + \frac{1.96}{(1.14)^2} + \frac{2.744}{(1.14)^3} + \frac{(1.05)2.744}{(1.14)^3(0.14-0.05)}$$

$$= 1.228 + 1.508 + 1.852 + 21.608 = \$26.20$$

QUESTIONS

1. What is the basic approach that is used to value any asset, including bonds and common stocks?
2. What information is needed to calculate the yield to maturity for a bond? Once you have this information, how do you calculate the yield to maturity?
3. Assume that a long-term bond is selling at a discount. If you calculate the current yield, coupon rate, and yield to maturity, which will have the highest value? Which will have the lowest value?
4. What is a yield to call? When is a yield to call a more reasonable estimate of your expected return than the yield to maturity?
5. What are the assumptions behind the dividend growth model? What is the value of a share of stock using the dividend growth model? What is the required return for a stock using the dividend growth model?

CHALLENGING QUESTIONS

6. What is interest-rate risk? How is interest-rate risk related to the maturity of a bond and to the coupon rate for a bond?
7. Assume that the Federal Reserve unexpectedly raises interest rates. As a result, bond prices and stock prices both fall. What explanation can you give for this?
8. Cite and explain three reasons why a P/E ratio may not be a reliable indicator of a stock's expected future performance.
9. Cite and discuss two important factors that limit the usefulness of the stock valuation model.
10. Explain, in your own words, why the growth rate in the dividend growth model, g, cannot be larger than the required return, r.

PROBLEM SET A

A1. (Bond valuation) Find the missing information for each of the following bonds. The coupons are paid in semiannual installments, so the number of payments is equal to twice the bond's life in years. The annual percentage yield is compounded semiannually.

Bond	N (years)	Yield to maturity	Present value	Coupon rate	Face value
1	10	7.8%	_____	7.8%	$1000
2	5	10.5%	_____	9.5%	$1000
3	25	8.2%	_____	5.5%	$1000
4	15	_____	$1050	7.4%	$1000
5	_____	9.0%	$977.20	8.5%	$1000
6	8	7.0%	$1120.94	_____	$1000

A2. (Bond valuation) RCA made a coupon payment yesterday on its "6.25s06" bonds that mature on October 9, 2006. If the required return on these bonds is 9.2% nominal annual and today is April 10, 1997, what should be the market price of these bonds?

A3. (Bond valuation) Dow made a coupon payment yesterday on its "7.75s07" bonds that mature on April 9, 2007. If the required return on these bonds is 8.4% nominal annual and today is April 10, 1997, what should be the market price of these bonds?

A4. (Yield to maturity) Long Island Lighting has a 8.9% coupon bond maturing in 20 years. The current market price of the bond is $915. What is the bond's yield to maturity?

A5. (Yield to maturity) Pacific Bell's 6.25% coupon bond that matures in 10 years is selling for $937.50.
   a. What is the yield to maturity?   b. What is the current yield?

A6. (One-period dividend discount model) Mead is expected to pay a $1.40 dividend in the next year and to sell for $68.00 in 1 year. Discounted at a required return of 12%, what is the value of one share of Mead today?

A7. (Two-period dividend discount model) New England Electric has projected dividends of $2.72 in one year and $3.10 in two years. If the stock is projected to sell for $48.00 in two years, what is the value of the stock today if the required return is 10%?

A8. (Dividend discount model) Assume that IBM is expected to pay a total cash dividend of $5.60 next year and that dividends are expected to grow at a rate of 6% per year forever. Assuming annual dividend payments, what is the current market value of a share of IBM stock if the required return on IBM common stock is 10%?

A9. (Required return) Northern States Power has a projected dividend of $3.60 next year. The current stock price is $50.50 per share. If the dividend is projected to grow at 3.5% annually, what is the expected return on Northern States stock?

A10. (Required return for a preferred stock) James River $3.38 preferred is selling for $45.25. The preferred dividend is nongrowing. What is the required return on James River preferred stock?

PROBLEM SET B

B1. (Yield to maturity) DuPont's "8.45s12" bonds closed yesterday at 103. If these bonds mature on October 9, 2012, and today is April 10, 1997, what is the yield to maturity of these bonds? What is their APY?

B2. (Yield to maturity) GMAC's "8-3/4s08" bonds closed yesterday at 95¼. If these bonds mature on April 9, 2008, and today is April 10, 1997, what is the yield to maturity of these bonds? What is their APY?

B3. (Remaining maturity) IBM's "9-3/8s" bonds closed yesterday at 95⅛. If a coupon payment was made yesterday, April 9, 1997, and the yield to maturity on these bonds is 10%, when do these bonds mature?

B4. (Remaining maturity) ATT's "7-1/8s11" bonds closed yesterday at 92¾. If a coupon payment was made yesterday, April 9, 1997, and the yield to maturity on these bonds is 8%, when do these bonds mature?

B5. (Yield to call) Bowen Mills has a 10.5% coupon bond that has a remaining maturity of 14 years. The bond is callable in four years at a price of $1080. Its current market price is $1090.

a. If the required return for this bond is 8.0% (assuming that it is not callable), what would be the value of the bond?

b. What is the yield to maturity (based on its current market price)?

c. What is the yield to call?

B6. (Required return) What required return is implied by the Constant Growth Model for a stock that is selling for $25.00 per share, and is expected to pay a single cash dividend next year of $1.80, and whose growth in dividend payments is expected to be 2% per year forever?

B7. (Expected dividend growth rate) Suppose that GM is expected to pay $4.00 in cash dividends next year and that the required return on GM stock is 14%. If GM is currently selling for $37.50 per share, what is the expected growth rate in dividends for GM based on the Constant Growth Model?

B8. (Interest-rate risk) A quick look in the NYSE bond-quote section will tell you that GMAC has many different issues of bonds outstanding. Suppose that four of them have identical coupon rates of 7¼% but mature on four different dates. One matures in 2 years, one in 5 years, one in 10 years, and the last in 20 years. Assume that they all made coupon payments yesterday.

a. If the yield curve was flat and all four bonds had the same yield to maturity of 9%, what is the fair price of each bond today?

b. Suppose that during the first hour of operation of the capital markets today, the term structure shifts and the yield to maturity of all these bonds changes to 10%. What is the fair price of each bond now?

c. Suppose that in the second hour of trading, the yield to maturity of all these

bonds changes once more to 8%. Now what is the fair price of each bond?

d. Based on the price changes in response to the changes in yield to maturity, how is interest-rate risk a function of the bond's maturity? That is, is interest-rate risk the same for all four bonds, or does it depend on the bond's maturity?

B9. (Interest-rate risk) Philadelphia Electric has many bonds trading on the New York Stock Exchange. Suppose PhilEl's bonds have identical coupon rates of 9⅜% but that one issue matures in 1 year, one in 7 years, and the third in 15 years. Assume that a coupon payment was made yesterday.

a. If the yield to maturity for all three bonds is 8%, what is the fair price of each bond?

b. Suppose that the yield to maturity for all of these bonds changed instantaneously to 7%. What is the fair price of each bond now?

c. Suppose that the yield to maturity for all of these bonds changed instantaneously

again, this time to 9%. Now what is the fair price of each bond?

d. Based on the fair prices at the various yields to maturity, is interest-rate risk the same, higher, or lower, for longer- versus shorter- maturity bonds?

B10. (Default risk) You buy a very risky bond that promises an 8.8% coupon and return of the $1000 principal in 10 years. You pay only $500 for the bond.

a. You receive the coupon payments for two years and the bond defaults. After liquidating the company, the bondholders receive a distribution of $150 per bond at the end of 2.5 years. What is the realized return on your investment?

b. The company does far better than expected and bondholders receive all of the promised interest and principal payments. What is the realized return on your investment?

B11. (Dividend valuation) Medtrans is a profitable company that is not paying a dividend on its common stock. James Weber, an analyst for A. G. Edwards, believes that Medtrans will begin paying a $1.00 per share dividend in 2 years and that the dividend will increase 6% annually thereafter. Bret Kimes, one of James's colleagues at the same company, is less optimistic. Bret thinks that Medtrans will begin paying a dividend in 4 years, that the dividend will be $1.00, and that it will grow at 4% annually. James and Bret agree that the required return for Medtrans is 13%.

a. What value would James estimate for this company?

b. What value would Bret assign to the Medtrans stock?

B12. (Dividend valuation) Wichita Realty Trust is expected to pay a modest dividend of $1.00 per share for 2 years and then $2.00 per share for years 3–5. Then in year 6, Wichita Realty Trust is planning to pay a $40.00 per share liquidating dividend and go out of business. What is the value of a share of this company if the required return is 10%?

B13. (Supernormal growth model) Gebhardt Corporation has recently undertaken a major expansion project that is expected to provide growth in earnings per share of 400% within the coming year and 75% growth in each of the subsequent 3 years. After that time, normal growth of 3% per year forever is expected. The cash dividend was $0.10 per share this last year and is expected to be that amount for each of the next 5 years. In year 6, it is expected that the payout ratio will be 80% of the earnings per share, and the payout ratio is expected to remain at that level forever. If the required return on Gebhardt common stock is 32% per year and the latest earnings per share was $0.25, at what price should Gebhardt common stock be selling in the market?

B14. (Supernormal growth model) Losh Key Corporation common stock is selling for $25.00 per share with an expected cash dividend next year of $1.00. Short-term prospects are excellent for Losh Key: A 25% annual growth rate in dividend payments is expected for the 3 years following next year's dividend. After that, a normal growth rate of 4% per year forever is expected. What required return is implied by the current $25.00 price?

B15. (Valuing a perpetual bond) Suppose a bond pays $90 per year forever. If the bond's required return is 10.3%, what is the bond selling for in the capital markets?

PROBLEM SET C

C1. (Bond valuation between coupon payments) Gehr's Gears, Inc. has bonds outstanding that mature in 14 years and 3 months from today. The bonds have an annual coupon rate of 15% and pay interest every 6 months. The bonds are currently selling for $1100.

a. Assuming a coupon payment was made yesterday and there are 29 more coupon payments remaining to be paid in the life of the bond, what is the YTM on this bond? What is the APY for this bond under these assumptions?

b. Assuming a coupon payment was made yesterday and there are 28 more coupon payments remaining to be paid in the life of the bond, what is the YTM on this bond? What is the APY for this bond under these assumptions?

c. Assuming a coupon payment was made, as it actually was, 3 months ago and there are 29 more coupon payments remaining to be paid in the life of the bond, what is the YTM on this bond? What is the APY for this bond under these assumptions?

C2. (Bond valuation between coupon payments) Kay Patteris owns a bond that matures in 6 years and 4 months from today. The bond has an annual coupon rate of 6% and pays interest every 6 months. Currently, the bond is selling for $825.

a. Assuming a coupon payment was made yesterday and there are 13 more coupon payments remaining to be paid in the life of the bond, what is the YTM on this bond? What is the APY for this bond under these assumptions?

b. Assuming a coupon payment was made yesterday and there are 12 more coupon payments remaining to be paid in the life of the bond, what is the YTM on this bond? What is the APY for this bond under these assumptions?

c. Assuming a coupon payment was made, as it actually was, 2 months ago and there are 13 more coupon payments remaining to be paid in the life of the bond, what is the YTM on this bond? What is the APY for this bond under these assumptions?

C3. (Supernormal growth model) Managers of the Biden-Time Company, makers of Mickey Moose watches, are currently considering suspending the company's cash dividends for the next 3 years to invest the money in a project they call Court Jesters. Biden-Time's *current* operations are expected to earn $0.85 per share next year and with a constant payout ratio of 75% are expected to grow at 5% per year forever. Under the *proposed* Court Jesters plan, earnings are expected to grow at 17% per year for the investment years. After the investment, the company expects to have a payout ratio of 70% and a growth rate in earnings of 6.5% forever. If the required return on Biden-Time's stock is 20% per year, what is the NPV per share of the Court Jesters plan?

C4. (Dividend valuation) The copy service Quick Quality in Quantity (Q3) has a payout ratio of 80%, and a required return of 10%, and is expected to pay a dividend next year of $2.00. If Q3 is selling for $25 per share, what is its expected return? What is the expected market value of a share of Q3 4 years from now?

C5. (Dividend valuation) Philip Quick, owner of a chain of self-service gas stations, has several investments. One of them is 2,000 shares of Getty Oil. Getty is expected to pay a dividend next year of $2.38 and has expected growth of 6% per year forever. If Getty is selling for $19.45 per share, what is Phil's expected return on Getty Oil? Another of Phil's investments is 1200 shares of ConEdison, which has an expected growth rate in dividends of 4% per year forever, sells for $41⅞, and is expected to pay a dividend of $3.35 per share next year. What is Phil's expected return on ConEdison? Now the real question: How can Phil's expected returns be different for these two investments? Why doesn't Phil sell the one with the lower expected return and buy more of the one with the higher expected return?

BIBLIOGRAPHY

Fuller, Russell J., and Chi-Cheng Hsia. "A Simplified Common Stock Valuation Model," *Financial Analysts Journal,* 1984, 40(September-October):49–56.

Gordon, M. J., and L. I. Gould. "Comparison of the DCF and HPR Measures of the Yield on Common Shares," *Financial Management,* 1984, 13(4):40–47.

Siegel, Jeremy J. "The Application of the DCF Methodology for Determining the Cost of Equity Capital," *Financial Management,* 1985, 14(1):46–53.

Woods, John C., and Maury R. Randall. "The Net Present Value of Future Investment Opportunities: Its Impact on Shareholder Wealth and Implications for Capital Budgeting Theory," *Financial Management,* 1989, 18(2):85–92.

RISK AND RETURN

1. Estimate a portfolio's expected return from the expected returns of the securities that make up the portfolio.

2. Calculate a portfolio's standard deviation from the standard deviations of the securities that make up the portfolio and the correlation coefficients for the securities' returns.

3. Explain why diversification can be beneficial when assets have returns that are less-than-perfectly positively correlated.

4. Explain why investors should invest on the capital market line (CML) by investing part of their money in the market portfolio and lending or borrowing at the riskless return.

5. Describe the basic makeup of the capital-asset-pricing model (CAPM) and use it to calculate an asset's required return.

6. Recognize that international investing may provide potentially beneficial added diversification.

Everyone knows about risk. Some people won't skydive because they think it's too risky. Others won't even fly in an airplane because of risk. Most of us would say there's more risk in jumping out of a flying airplane (even with a parachute) than simply being up in the plane, but *how much* more risk? We don't know how to measure this risk difference. We can't even measure the amount of risk connected with getting in the plane in the first place. But you don't need to measure the risk precisely to decide whether you'll fly in an airplane—and, once you are flying, whether you will jump out.

Now think about investing. It too can be risky. But, as in skydiving, you could invest without measuring the risk precisely. Most of us, however, would want to know about the risk and would consider an investment in terms of its opportunity costs. That is, we would ask, "Compared to what?" To do that, we must measure the risk.

In this chapter, we tackle the problem of measuring risk, using realized returns on stocks. We start by examining the variability of realized stock returns. We then develop a model for calculating an asset's required return. This model is more general than solving for a stock's capitalization rate, as we did in the previous chapter.

Surprisingly, the variability of an individual security's returns is not always the best way to measure risk. Investors typically hold groups of assets called *diversified portfolios*. An investor is therefore concerned with each security's incremental contribution to the risk of the entire portfolio.

Let's say the returns from a particular security are highly variable. Does such a security then have high risk? Suppose the security's returns tend to be high when the returns on the rest of the portfolio are low. Adding that security to the portfolio could actually reduce the risk of the

portfolio because of the Principle of Diversification. We would say such a security has high *specific risk* when the security is considered in isolation but that it has low *market risk* when placed in the portfolio. We will show you how to measure market risk based on the correlation between a security's returns and the returns on the rest of the portfolio.

Our model of required return is intuitively appealing. In it, a required return is simply a "base," riskless return *plus* an added return to compensate for the asset's risk. The added return is for the asset's *market* risk.

RISK AND RETURN AND THE PRINCIPLES OF FINANCE

◆ *Diversification:* Invest in a group of assets, a *portfolio,* to reduce the total risk of your entire investment.

◆ *Risk-Return Trade-Off:* Invest in the amounts of the risky *market portfolio* and the *riskless asset* that provide the investment risk level you choose.

◆ *Efficient Capital Markets:* Estimate a security's risk and required return from its past realized returns.

◆ *Incremental Benefits:* Measure the incremental benefits from owning a security, which are its expected future cash flows.

(continued on following page)

189

(Risk and Return and the Principles of Finance *continued from previous page*)

◆ *Time-Value-of-Money:* Determine the value of a security by computing the present value of its expected future cash flows.

◆ *Two-Sided Transactions:* Use a security's fair price to compute its expected return, because the fair price does not favor either side of the transaction.

◆ *Self-Interested Behavior:* Recognize that prices will be set by the highest bidder, because owners will sell to the highest bidder.

◆ *Valuable Ideas:* Look for innovative management or information services that might provide a positive NPV by creating value for capital market participants.

PROBABILITY AND STATISTICS

Intuitively, the risk of an asset is the likelihood its realized return will vary substantially from its expected return. That is, an important dimension of risk is the probability (chance) a really bad outcome will occur. In this section we briefly develop some basic concepts from probability and statistics, which are important to risk and return.

Random Variables

A *random variable* is not perfectly predictable. For example, the amount of Exxon Corporation's earnings for next year is a random variable. We might have in mind some possible outcomes for this random variable, but we can't know the value for sure until the year ends and Exxon reports its earnings.

Probabilities

Because the value of a random variable is uncertain, we need a way to measure the relative likelihood of each possible outcome. We do this by assigning a *probability* to each possible outcome. Probabilities must satisfy two conditions: (1) A probability can't be negative and (2) the probabilities of all possible outcomes must sum to 1.0.

The first condition says we're interested only in possible (positive probability) outcomes. The second ensures that the specified set includes all possible values.

EXAMPLE

Exxon's EPS for Next Year

The Great Jones Securities Service gathers earnings forecasts and analyzes them for its subscribers. Ten analysts forecast Exxon's earnings. Three predict earnings per share (EPS) next year of $5.75, two forecast $5.90, one predicts $6.25, and four forecast $6.30. What are the probabilities associated with these forecasts?

There are four different predictions: $5.75, $5.90, $6.25, and $6.30. For simplicity, assume these are the only possible outcomes and the analysts are equally likely to be correct. Then the probability of an outcome is its frequency divided by the total number of predictions. So Exxon's EPS for next year will be $5.75 with probability 0.3(= 3/10), $5.90 with probability 0.2(= 2/10), $6.25 with probability 0.1(= 1/10), and $6.30 with probability 0.4(= 4/10). ■

MEAN The probability-weighted average of all possible outcomes for a random variable.

The Mean

Thus far, we've talked about expected cash flows without really defining the term *expected*. An expected amount is the mean of the random variable. The **mean** of a random variable is its long-run average. It's the average value we would get if we repeated the random experiment a very large number of times.[1] The mean is usually shown by writing a lower-case letter with a bar over it. For example $\bar{x}$ is the mean of X.

Suppose a random variable X can take on N possible values x_n, $n = 1, 2, \ldots, N$. The probability associated with x_n is p_n. Then

$$\bar{x} = \sum_{n=1}^{N} p_n x_n \qquad\qquad (7.1)$$

In words, equation (7.1) says multiply each possible outcome x_n by its probability of occurrence p_n, and sum the products. The mean is the weighted average of the possible outcomes, where the weights are the probabilities.

Calculating the Mean of Exxon's EPS   E X A M P L E

Let's continue our previous example. The mean of Exxon's EPS for next year is

$$\bar{x} = (0.3)(5.75) + (0.2)(5.90) + 0.1(6.25) + 0.4(6.30) = \$6.05$$

Figure 7.1 shows how the mean locates the "weighted center" of the probability distribution. The mean is like a fulcrum that balances the probability weighted value on either side of it.

We've said the mean is the average outcome when an experiment is repeated many times (actually, an infinite number of times). However, suppose we have only one outcome, such as Exxon's actual realized EPS next year. The mean doesn't provide a complete picture of what might happen when there will be only one outcome. Any single outcome might vary tremendously from its mean. (If the possible outcomes are 0 and 1, the mean is 0.5, which is not even a possible outcome.) In spite of this and other limitations, the mean is very useful as a *summary statistical measure*.

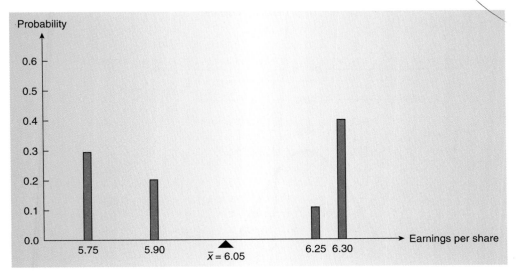

FIGURE 7.1
Mean value of Exxon's earnings per share.

---

[1]In your statistics class, you might have flipped coins or rolled dice. What is the mean value for rolling a pair of dice? It's 7.0. If you roll a pair of dice many, many times, the average of all the rolls will get closer and closer to 7.0 as you continue rolling.

Variance and Standard Deviation

VARIANCE A probability-weighted measure of the dispersion of all possible outcomes around the mean.

The **variance** is a measure of the dispersion of all possible outcomes around the mean. Variance is typically shown using a Greek letter, as σ^2, sometimes with an identifying subscript. The formula for variance is

$$\sigma_x^2 = \sum_{n=1}^{N} p_n(x_n - \bar{x})^2 \tag{7.2}$$

STANDARD DEVIATION The square root of the variance.

The **standard deviation** is the square root of the variance, sometimes with an identifying subscript. For example, σ_x is the standard deviation of X.

Figure 7.2 shows the bell-shaped probability density function for what is known as the *normal random variable* (normal pdf). The normal pdf is frequently encountered in finance. In such situations, we know that there is a 68% probability that any single outcome will fall within one standard deviation (plus or minus) of the mean, a 95% probability that it will fall within two standard deviations of the mean, and a 99.7% probability that it will fall within three standard deviations of the mean.

Suppose we know the variance (or standard deviation), but nothing else. Like a mean, variance provides limited insight without other information. For example, suppose we told you the variance of X is 100. That doesn't mean much by itself. Suppose the variance of television prices for all current models is 100, or the variance of prices for all fast food hamburgers is 100. In the first case, the variance would be small. In the second case, it would be large.

Because of this problem, the mean and variance are used *together*. Look at figure 7.2. Knowing $\bar{x}$ and σ_x would enable you to draw the normal pdf *exactly*.

EXAMPLE   *Computing the Variance and Standard Deviation of Exxon's EPS*

Continuing our Exxon example, the variance of possible earnings per share next year is

$$\sigma^2 = (0.3)(5.75 - 6.05)^2 + (0.2)(5.90 - 6.05)^2 + (0.1)(6.25 - 6.05)^2 + (0.4)(6.30 - 6.05)^2 = 0.0605$$

The standard deviation is

$$\sigma = \sqrt{0.0605} = 0.2460$$

FIGURE 7.2
Dispersion of possible outcomes for a normal random variable (normal pdf).

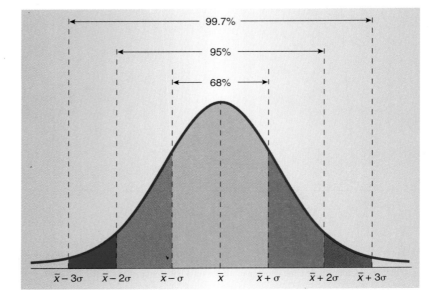

Covariance and Correlation Coefficient

Covariance is a measure of how two random variables vary together, or "covary." Covariance can be positive, negative, or zero. A positive covariance indicates that when one random variable has an outcome above its mean, the other also tends to be above its mean. A negative covariance indicates the reverse—a higher outcome for one tends to be associated with a lower outcome for the other. A covariance of zero indicates that a simple pairing of outcomes does not reveal any regular pattern.

The covariance of two random variables, say X and Y, is usually shown as $\text{Cov}(X,Y)$, or sometimes σ_{XY}. The formula for the covariance is

$$\text{Covariance} = \text{Cov}(X,Y) = \sum_{n=1}^{N} p_n \, (x_n - \bar{x})(y_n - \bar{y}) \tag{7.3}$$

The covariance is sensitive to the particular units of measurement. The **correlation coefficient** removes this sensitivity. Although covariance can take on any value, the correlation coefficient can be only between minus 1 and plus 1. The correlation coefficient is usually shown as $\text{Corr}(X,Y)$. The formula for the correlation coefficient is

$$\text{Corr}(X,Y) = \frac{\text{Cov}(X,Y)}{\sigma_X \sigma_Y} \tag{7.4}$$

Dividing by the standard deviations cancels out the units of measurement, leaving $\text{Corr}(X,Y)$ unit-free.

COVARIANCE A measure of how two random variables vary together, or "covary."

CORRELATION COEFFICIENT The covariance divided by the standard deviations of the two random variables.

Self-Check

1. Explain the meaning of the terms *mean* and *standard deviation.*

2. What does a positive correlation coefficient between two random variables signify? What does a negative correlation coefficient between them signify?

EXPECTED RETURN AND SPECIFIC RISK

In the previous chapter, we showed how to compute a realized APY. However, in selecting investments, we are concerned with the *future* returns, which are uncertain. Therefore, in making an investment, we're interested in the expected return.

Measuring the Expected Future Return

One measure of the expected return is the mean of future possible returns. Remember, however, the drawback to using the mean. It represents the average outcome when the experiment is repeated many times. But suppose you can get only *one* of those outcomes?

Recall our discussion in chapter 2 about how risk disconnects the expected and realized returns. If you own an asset for the next year, it will provide you with *one* realized return. That return may turn out to be positive, zero, or negative. More important, it can turn out to be very different from its mean. Once next year's outcome is realized, the experiment is not repeated. (The second year might be considered a repeat. However, conditions may have changed so much that the possible outcomes are quite different from those of the first year.) After the fact, when you have the outcome, it doesn't really matter what the mean was.

Despite this drawback, investment decisions must be made before the outcome is known. You may remember the *law of large numbers* from your statistics class. Applied to finance, it says that if you have a large enough group of investments, the good and bad outcomes tend to cancel each other out. In that way, the average of the outcomes will approximate the mean of the group more and more closely as the number of investments increases.[2] In this sense, the mean is a good measure of the expected return when you have a large number of investments.

A Definition of Expected Return

Now, after six and a half chapters, we can finally give you a precise definition of expected return: An asset's **expected return** is the mean of its future possible returns.

✓ **EXPECTED RETURN** The mean of an asset's future possible returns.

EXAMPLE

Calculating IBM's Expected Return

During work one day, suppose a friend recommends investing in IBM common stock. She has researched it for her finance class. She thinks it has a 0.35 probability of producing a 15% return, a 0.25 probability of a 25% return, and a 0.10 probability of a 40% return. However, she says a bad outcome of −10% is also possible, with probability 0.30. What is the expected return?

Using equation (7.1), we get

$$\text{Expected return} = (0.30)(-10) + (0.35)(15) + (0.25)(25) + (0.10)(40) = 12.5\%$$

Measuring Specific Risk

The other aspect of the risk-return trade-off is risk. First, we'll consider the risk of an investment by itself, its *specific risk*. Later, we'll consider the risk of an asset that belongs to a group, called a *portfolio*, of assets.

People usually come up with two notions when they think about why an investment is risky: (1) uncertainty about the future return and (2) the possibility of a large negative return—that is, a bad outcome. By bad outcome we mean an outcome that is truly undesirable. Failing to win a lottery may not be a good outcome, but it's not a really negative outcome. So most people don't think of buying a lottery ticket as a risky investment. On the other hand, losing an entire investment—say your life savings of $80,000—because the company went bankrupt would be a bad outcome!

A good definition of risk, then, should include a measure of variability and a measure of the possibility of negative outcomes. Standard deviation reflects variability both above and below the mean return. Strictly speaking, the standard deviation captures only one dimension of risk. An asset with a return that has a very large standard deviation, such as a lottery ticket, may be interpreted as having a great deal of risk when it's not really very risky. However, suppose an asset has a return distribution that is approximately symmetrical around the mean (like the normal pdf in figure 7.2). In such cases, the larger the standard deviation, the riskier the investment. When the return distribution is symmetrical, standard deviation captures both dimensions of risk.

Despite its apparent shortcomings, the standard deviation of the return (just "standard deviation," for short) is actually a pretty good measure of risk. First, return distributions tend to be approximately symmetrical. Second, evidence indicates that, as a practical matter, other conceptually superior measures don't perform any better.

A Definition of Risk

An investment's **specific risk** is its standard deviation.

✓ **SPECIFIC RISK** The standard deviation of an investment's return.

---

[2]Literally, the law of large numbers states that the average of the outcomes approaches the mean in the limit (that is, as the number of trials increases without limit).

Self-Check

1. Explain the drawbacks to using the historical mean return when evaluating the returns you might realize next year from holding 100 shares of AT&T common stock.

2. Explain why the mean is a good measure of expected return when you have a large number of different investments.

3. According to your broker, a share of Microsoft common stock might produce three possible returns next year, 15%, 25%, or 50%. The respective probabilities, again according to your broker, are 0.20, 0.45, and 0.35. What is the expected return?

4. What are the two dimensions of risk? Explain the practical meaning of each.

5. What are the drawbacks to using standard deviation to measure risk when the return distribution isn't symmetrical? Why is standard deviation a relatively good measure of risk as long as the return distribution is approximately symmetrical?

INVESTMENT PORTFOLIOS

An investment made up of a group of assets is called a **portfolio.** Combining securities into portfolios reduces risk. This follows from the Principle of Diversification. Stocks with "good" returns tend to cancel out those with "bad" returns. Rational investors hold a portfolio of stocks rather than put all their eggs in one basket.

PORTFOLIO A group of assets or securities.

Efficient Portfolios   An **efficient portfolio** is one that provides the highest expected return for a given amount of risk. Equivalently, an efficient portfolio provides the lowest risk for a given expected return. According to the Principle of Risk-Return Trade-Off, investors want high return and low risk. Therefore, investors will want to invest only in efficient portfolios.

EFFICIENT PORTFOLIO A portfolio that provides the highest expected return for a given level of risk or, equivalently, provides the lowest risk for a given expected return.

Risk and Return in Two-Asset Portfolios

Now let's see how the risks and expected returns of individual assets combine to create a portfolio's risk and expected return.

Let the return to asset 1 be R_1 with expected return $\bar{r}_1$ and specific risk σ_1. The return to asset 2 is R_2 with expected return $\bar{r}_2$ and specific σ_2. Suppose a proportion w_1 of portfolio value is invested in asset 1, and the remainder $(1 - w_1)$ is invested in asset 2. The *portfolio's expected return, $\bar{r}_p$,* is

$$\bar{r}_p = w_1\bar{r}_1 + (1 - w_1)\bar{r}_2 \qquad (7.5)$$

Equation (7.5) says the portfolio's expected return is simply the weighted average of the individual assets' expected returns. The weights are the proportions of money invested in each asset. Therefore, $\bar{r}_p$ is a linear function of $\bar{r}_1$ and $\bar{r}_2$.

The portfolio's risk is related to the individual assets' risks in a more complex way. The portfolio's standard deviation, σ_p, is

$$\sigma_p = [w_1^2\sigma_1^2 + (1 - w_1)^2\sigma_2^2 + 2w_1(1 - w_1)\mathrm{Corr}(R_1,R_2)\sigma_1\sigma_2]^{\frac{1}{2}} \qquad (7.6)$$

where $\mathrm{Corr}(R_1,R_2)$ stands for the correlation coefficient between the returns on the two assets. As you can see, σ_p is not a simple weighted average of σ_1 and σ_2. (There is a single exception to this statement, which we'll explore later.)

| EXAMPLE | *Calculating a Portfolio's Risk and Expected Return* |

Table 7.1 provides the possible returns and their probability for two assets, "mature stock" and "growth stock," in each of four scenarios. Equation (7.1) is used to calculate the expected return. Equation (7.2) is used to calculate the variance, the square root of which is the standard deviation, σ. Suppose equal amounts are invested in the two stocks. What will be the portfolio's expected return and risk?

First, because the stocks are equally weighted, $w_1 = 0.5$. Therefore, using equation (7.5), we find that the portfolio's expected return is

$$\bar{r}_p = 0.5(5.4) + 0.5(9.4) = 7.4\%$$

Next, we calculate the correlation coefficient using equations (7.3) and (7.4).

$$Cov(R_1,R_2) = 0.1(-8.4)(-7.4) + 0.3(-2.4)(-5.4) + 0.4(1.6)(0.6) + 0.2(4.6)(10.6) = 20.24$$

$$Corr(R_1,R_2) = \frac{20.24}{(3.7)(6.1)} = 0.90$$

Finally, using equation (7.6), the portfolio's standard deviation is

$$\sigma_p = [(0.5)^2(3.7)^2 + (0.5)^2(6.1)^2 + 2(0.5)(0.5)(0.90)(3.7)(6.1)]^{\frac{1}{2}} = 4.8\%$$

Portfolio-Asset Risk-Return Interactions

Our portfolio example looked at an equally weighted two-asset portfolio. But what about other, unequal combinations? Figure 7.3 graphs the expected return and risk for each asset. Expected return is measured along the vertical (y) axis, and risk (standard deviation) along the horizontal (x) axis. Suppose all the money is invested in either asset 1 or asset 2. Then the risk-return combinations are at A_1 and at A_2, respectively. But we're more interested in "true" portfolios involving both assets. These are cases where money is invested in each asset.

Equation (7.5) shows the portfolio's expected return in terms of the assets' expected returns. Equation (7.6) shows σ_p in terms of σ_1 and σ_2. Let's explore the combined effect of equations (7.5) and (7.6) by substituting a value for the correlation coefficient, $Corr(R_1,R_2)$, and looking at all possible values for w_1 between 0 and 1.

Perfect Negative Correlation   Figure 7.4 graphs the portfolio risk-return combinations given by equations (7.5) and (7.6) for $0 \leq w_1 \leq 1.0$ when $Corr(R_1,R_2) = -1.0$. Note in figure 7.4 that it is possible to combine investments in the two risky assets so that the portfolio risk is zero. This result is a direct consequence of the perfect negative correlation. When asset 1's realized return is high, asset 2's realized return is low, and vice versa. When asset 1 has a

TABLE 7.1
Return Estimates for Two Stocks

STATE OF THE ECONOMY	PROBABILITY OF OCCURRENCE	MATURE STOCK	GROWTH STOCK
Recession	0.10	−3.0%	2.0%
Stable	0.30	3.0	4.0
Moderate growth	0.40	7.0	10.0
Boom	0.20	10.0	20.0
	1.00		
Expected return, $\bar{r}$		5.4%	9.4%
Standard deviation, σ		3.7%	6.1%
Correlation coefficient, Corr		0.90	

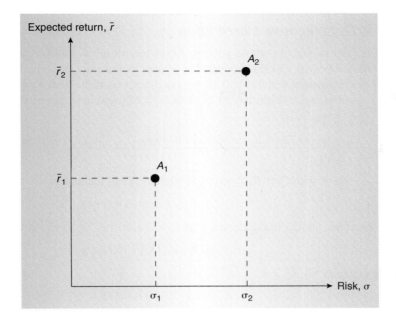

FIGURE 7.3
Expected return and risk of
asset 1 and asset 2.

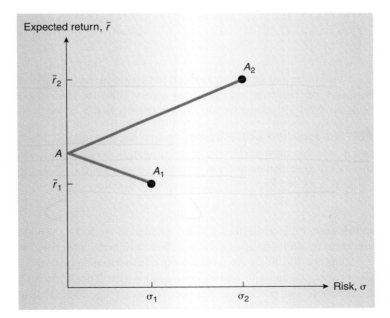

FIGURE 7.4
Perfect negative correlation
$(\text{Corr}(R_1, R_2) = -1.0)$.

medium return, so does asset 2. Therefore, when the two assets are combined in the proportions represented by portfolio A in figure 7.4, high and low returns always cancel each other out *exactly*. The portfolio earns the same return every period.

The idea that you might be able to invest in two assets, both of which are risky, and yet have your total investment be riskless is not at all intuitive. Harry Markowitz pointed out this phenomenon in 1952 and started a revolution in the way people think about investing.

Figure 7.4 illustrates the special case in which the minimum value of portfolio risk is $\sigma_p = 0$. When Corr $= -1.0$, we can determine analytically the exact proportions to invest in the two risky assets, w_1 and $(1 - w_1)$, so that the portfolio is riskless. These proportions can be derived by setting equation (7.6) equal to zero and solving for w_1.

EXAMPLE

Perfect Negative Correlation

Consider two stocks whose possible future returns are as indicated in Table 7.2. The five scenarios are equally likely to occur. The returns to these stocks are perfect negatively correlated. What investment weights will create a two-asset portfolio with $\sigma_p = 0$?

First, we'll show that the correlation coefficient is in fact -1.0:

$$\text{Corr}(R_1, R_2) =$$

$$\frac{0.2(11.0)(-13.2) + 0.2(-19.0)(22.8) + 0.2(6.0)(-7.2) + 0.2(-14.0)(16.8) + 0.2(16.0)(-19.2)}{(13.9)(16.7)} = -1.00$$

Next, with $\text{Corr}(R_1, R_2) = -1.0$, equation (7.6) reduces to

$$\sigma_p = w_1(\sigma_1 + \sigma_2) - \sigma_2$$

Therefore, putting in the known values, we have

$$0 = w_1(13.9 + 16.7) - 16.7$$

Solving for w_1, we get

$$w_1 = 0.54575$$

Verifying our answer, with this value for w_1:

$$\sigma_p = [(0.54575)^2(13.9)^2 + (0.45425)^2(16.7)^2 - 2(0.54575)(0.45425)(13.9)(16.7)]^{1/2} = 0.0$$

Are there two securities to invest in that are perfectly negatively correlated? No, not that we know of. However, this provides a very powerful starting point, which we're going to build on. Now let's consider some other, more realistic, cases.

Perfect Positive Correlation

Unlike our first case, it's both realistic and easy to find two assets that have perfect positive correlation between their returns. A simple example is two identical securities, such as two shares of common stock in the same company.

When $\text{Corr}(R_1, R_2) = +1.0$, equation (7.6) reduces to

$$\sigma_p = w_1\sigma_1 + (1 - w_1)\sigma_2$$

In this case, σ_p is a simple weighted average of σ_1 and σ_2. This is the single exception to a nonlinear relationship among the standard deviations, which we mentioned earlier.

Figure 7.5 shows the possible expected returns to portfolio combinations for values of w_1 between 0.0 and 1.0, when $\text{Corr}(R_1, R_2) = +1.0$. They form a straight line between A_1 and A_2, and there's no portfolio interaction. Although this case is realistic, it's not very interesting. The next case we look at is both realistic *and* interesting. In fact, it's the usual case.

TABLE 7.2

Future Returns for Two Stocks that Have $\text{Corr}(R_1, R_2) = -1.0$

SCENARIO	1	2	3	4	5	AVERAGE	STANDARD DEVIATION
Stock A return	20%	−10%	15%	−5%	25%	9.0%	13.9%
Stock B return	15	51	21	45	9	28.2	16.7

Positive Correlation   Figure 7.6 shows the curve linking all possible combinations of portfolio risk and return for assets 1 and 2 when $Corr(R_1,R_2) = 0.4$. It's not a straight line. Compare portfolios with $w_1 = 1.0$ (all the money invested in asset 1) and $w_1 = 0.5$. A portfolio with $w_1 = 0.5$ has an expected return exactly halfway between the expected returns of assets 1 and 2. However, its standard deviation is only about one-fifth of the way toward asset 2 from asset 1. Think about that.

In this case, the trade-off between how much expected return you get and how much risk you take on is more favorable where w_1 is greater than 0.5 than it is where w_1 is less than 0.5. In mathematical terms, the slope is greater when w_1 is close to 1.0 and smaller when it's near zero.

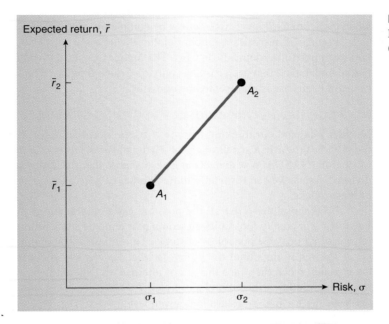

FIGURE 7.5
Perfect positive correlation $(Corr(R_1,R_2) = +1.0)$.

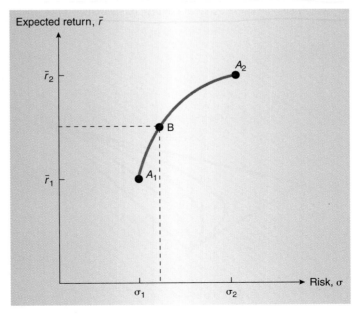

FIGURE 7.6
Positive correlation $(Corr(R_1,R_2) = 0.4)$.

We can also look at the investment possibilities by starting with $w_1 = 0.0$ (all the money invested in asset 2): By investing half the money in asset 1, risk can be decreased 80% of the way toward σ_1, but expected return decreases only half the way toward $\bar{r}_1$.

Some people might be so risk averse they would not invest anything in asset 2. Others might have such little risk aversion that they would invest all their money in asset 2. But we believe most people will find it attractive to diversify. This leads us to an interesting generalization:

> When asset returns are not perfectly positively correlated, diversification can increase the ratio of the portfolio's expected return to its risk.

In other words, when asset returns are not perfectly positively correlated, diversification can change the risk-return trade-off among our set of possible investments as we move along the curve in figure 7.6. Note that although risk is reduced by combining stocks into portfolios when $0 < \text{Corr}(R_1, R_2) < 1$, risk *cannot* be completely eliminated.

Figure 7.7 provides a graphic picture of how the set of all possible combinations for two-asset portfolios depends on Corr. The higher Corr is, the straighter the curve. It's important to understand that each case has only one value for Corr. The set of all possible combinations for each case is represented by one line.

An Expanded Framework: Portfolios with More than Two Assets

Now let's expand our thinking from two assets. Consider all of the stocks that are traded on the NYSE, the AMEX, or through the National Association of Securities Dealers Automated Quotation (NASDAQ) system. That gives us more than 10,000 stocks. In addition to these individual assets, we can form an infinite number of portfolios containing different proportions of these stocks.

It's impossible to list all the possible asset combinations. Nevertheless, we can show you what it generally looks like, based on past realized stock returns. Figure 7.8 illustrates the returns of all possible portfolios of stocks. (It reminds us of an umbrella without a handle.)

The really important thing here is what we can say about how investors should invest their money when they face this set of alternatives. Should they invest in portfolio G, which lies in the middle of the umbrella in figure 7.8? No, because G isn't an *efficient portfolio*, one that provides the highest return for a given level of risk. They can instead invest in portfolio E_2. It has the same risk, but a higher expected return. They can also invest in the efficient portfolio E_1, which has the same expected return, but the lowest possible risk for that expected return.

FIGURE 7.7

How the set of all possible combinations for two-asset portfolios depends on Corr.

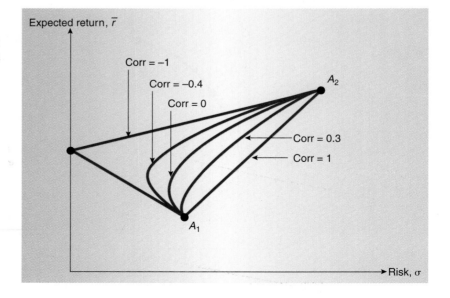

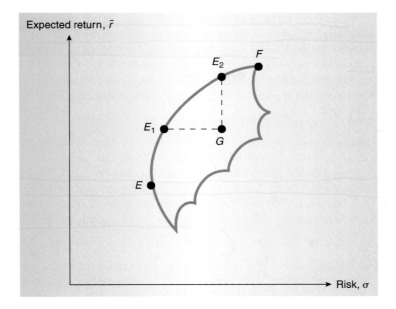

Expected return, $\bar{r}$

Risk, σ

FIGURE 7.8
The expected returns to all possible combinations of risky assets.

As we noted, investors will want to invest only in efficient portfolios, those with the highest possible expected return for a given risk level. The set of efficient portfolios—those on the curve between *E* and *F*—is called the **efficient frontier.** This leads to an important recommendation:

EFFICIENT FRONTIER
The set of efficient portfolios.

> You shouldn't invest in a portfolio that lies below the efficient frontier—regardless of how much or how little risk you are willing to take.

Self-Check

1. Define the term *portfolio.* Can a portfolio contain just one asset?

2. If the returns from two assets are perfectly negatively correlated, how can it be possible to find a combination of investments in these two assets that has zero portfolio risk?

3. When the returns from two assets are less-than-perfectly positively correlated, how can diversification be beneficial?

4. What is an efficient portfolio? What is the efficient frontier?

5. Explain why a rational investor would never knowingly invest money in a portfolio that is below the efficient frontier.

A PRESCRIPTION FOR INVESTING

Another element of investing is a *riskless asset.* Surprisingly, the "riskless" asset's return critically affects how everyone should invest money in *risky* assets. The existence of a riskless asset also allows us to establish the market-determined trade-off between risk and expected return. This risk-return trade-off provides the key to pricing individual risky assets.

A Riskless Asset

By *riskless asset* we mean an asset with a zero standard deviation; that is, one with no uncertainty about its future return. Its realized return will always equal its expected return.

Can there be such an asset? Literally, no. There's always some chance, no matter how small, that the debtor (even the U.S. government) will fail to make timely payment.[3] But for practical purposes, some investments have a small enough standard deviation to be considered riskless. Most experts think of U.S. government 90-day Treasury bills as riskless investments. The risk of default by the U.S. Treasury is negligible. Although such investments are not *literally* riskless, we'll go along with the majority and assume them to be essentially riskless.

Investing in the Riskless Asset

Combining one investment in a risky portfolio of assets with a second investment in a riskless asset is the two-asset portfolio problem we looked at earlier. Let's build on what we learned. Let asset 1 be the riskless asset and asset 2 a risky portfolio. The (total) portfolio is a combination of asset 1 (the riskless asset) and asset 2 (the risky portfolio).

Equations (7.5) and (7.6) express the portfolio's expected return and standard deviation. But we can simplify things a little. With $\sigma_1 = 0.0$, equation (7.6) reduces to

$$\sigma_p = [(1 - w_1)^2 \sigma_2^2]^{1/2} = (1 - w_1)\sigma_2$$

This equation shows that the (total) portfolio's risk (that of the combined investments in the riskless asset and the risky portfolio), σ_p, is a simple linear function of σ_2. Therefore, the set of all possible combinations of asset 1 and asset 2 forms a straight line between the riskless asset and the chosen risky portfolio (asset 2). Figure 7.9 shows this relationship for an arbitrarily chosen risky portfolio, G, from among our "umbrella set" of all possible portfolios.

Note that some of the line from the riskless return, r_f,[4] to G's return dominates part of the efficient frontier. The problem is further complicated because the amount it dominates depends on the choice of G. This brings up a logical question: Is there a "best" risky portfolio? Yes. Now let's see why, and what that portfolio is.

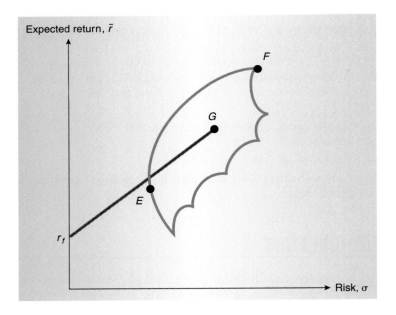

FIGURE 7.9

Combinations of a risky portfolio and the riskless asset.

---

[3]You never know—the eastern United States might be destroyed by a huge meteorite during the next period. Perhaps, as nearly happened in 1995, the federal government might default because the U.S. Congress refuses to raise the debt ceiling and the U.S. Treasury runs out of cash.
[4]The f in r_f is to indicate that the return is *free* of risk.

Choosing the Best Risky Portfolio

Figure 7.9 suggests the following decision rule: Choose the risky portfolio that dominates the largest portion of the efficient frontier. If we follow this rule, the *best* risky portfolio is the one that produces a line of combinations tangent to the efficient frontier. This best risky portfolio is identified as *M* in figure 7.10.

Lending and Borrowing

Investing in the riskless asset is really simply lending the money. The opposite, borrowing, is like having a *negative* investment in the riskless asset (asset 1). That is, borrowing money to invest makes the proportion invested in the riskless asset, w_1, negative. In effect, what we owe you is negative to us—but positive to you. (The Principle of Two-Sided Transactions strikes again!) So borrowed money is simply a negative investment.

One problem with using negative values for w_1 to represent a borrowed amount is that the implied borrowing rate of interest is the same as the lending rate of interest. At first, this may seem very troublesome. We know that banks we go to charge a higher rate for borrowing than they pay for lending (the rate paid on deposits).

Different borrowing and lending rates are certainly a fact of life for most of us. However, consider large corporations. Many invest and borrow in the commercial paper market. One day a company is a lender, but the next day that same company may be a borrower. The commercial paper rate is generally quoted as a single rate.

The main difference between the bank's borrowing and lending rates in practice is the charge for transacting in small amounts. In other words, the bank is simply charging (a transaction cost) for separating large amounts into small ones or putting small amounts together to make large ones. Therefore, using a single rate for borrowing and lending is essentially equivalent to assuming costless transactions. On the basis of the Principle of Capital Market Efficiency, costless transactions are a good starting point for forming estimations.

The Capital Market Line

Letting w_1 be negative doesn't change equations (7.5) and (7.6). With the possibility of borrowing (negative investment in asset 1), the line of investment possibilities simply continues past *M* with the same slope. Figure 7.11 on page 204 shows the line that links possible investment combinations when you can borrow at the riskless return. It's called the **capital market line**

CAPITAL MARKET LINE (CML) The risk-return combinations of the risky portfolio *M* and lending or borrowing at the riskless return.

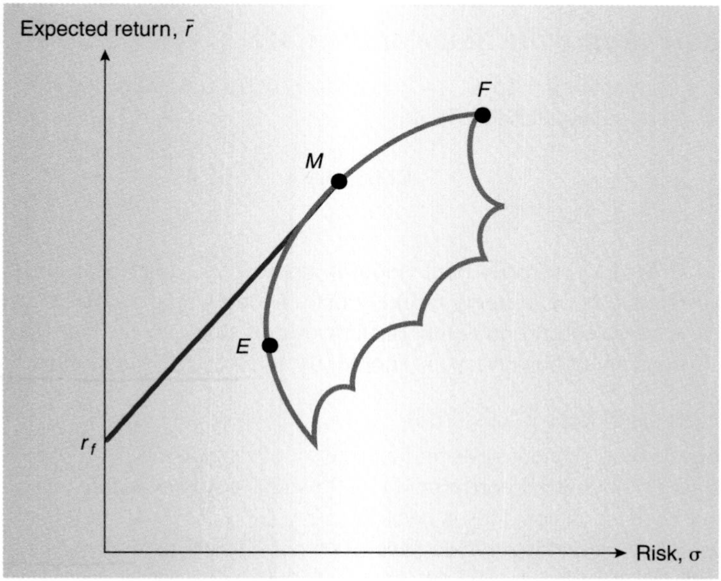

FIGURE 7.10
Combinations of *M* and the riskless asset.

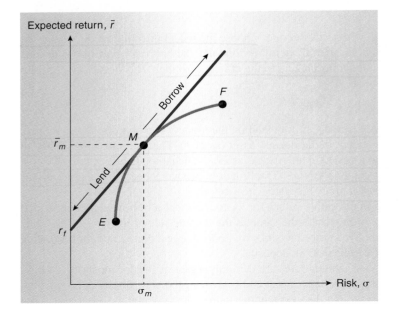

FIGURE 7.11
The capital market line
(CML): Combinations of
the risky portfolio M and
lending and borrowing at
the riskless return.

(CML). The CML touches the efficient frontier at M and dominates the efficient frontier everywhere else. Figure 7.11 provides another important recommendation:

> You should invest your money in the risky portfolio M, and set your portfolio's return and risk levels by lending or borrowing.

The Slope of the CML A slope is the "rise" over the "run." For the CML, the rise is $\bar{r}_M - r_f$, and the run is $\sigma_M - \sigma_f$. But with $\sigma_f = 0$, the run becomes simply σ_M. Therefore,

$$\text{CML slope} = \frac{\bar{r}_M - r_f}{\sigma_M} \qquad (7.7)$$

MARKET RISK PREMIUM
The difference between the
expected return on the market portfolio and the riskless return.

The slope of the CML is the amount of expected return per unit of risk. The numerator of the slope, $\bar{r}_M - r_f$, is called the **market risk premium.**

EXAMPLE

Calculating the Slope of the CML

Let's say that $\bar{r}_M = 15\%$, $r_f = 7\%$, and $\sigma_M = 16\%$. What is the slope of the CML?
Using equation (7.7), it is

$$\text{CML slope} = \frac{\bar{r}_M - r_f}{\sigma_M} = \frac{15 - 7}{16} = 0.50$$

When you really think about it, figure 7.11 suggests a startling approach to picking investments. It's extremely unlikely that anyone would arrive at such an approach intuitively. However, a careful modeling of the world of stock investments has produced surprising conclusions about how everyone should invest. Everyone should invest in M. But what is M?

The Market Portfolio

MARKET PORTFOLIO A
portfolio that includes every
asset that is available in the
market.

Because everyone invests in the same set of risky assets, everyone will own a portion of every asset in this special portfolio M (for "market"). Any available market asset that's not in M cannot have an owner. This is because everyone owns a part of the same set of assets. But every available market asset must have an owner. Therefore, every asset must be included in M. Because M includes every available market asset, it's called the **market portfolio.**

In this view, all investors diversify their ownership of risky assets by owning some of everything. But what proportion of their money should they invest in each asset? This question is more easily analyzed by examining a simplified example of a market, rather than the stock market with its more than 10,000 stocks.

The Market Portfolio's Composition

EXAMPLE

Consider a market with three risky assets: 1, 2, and 3. They are worth $100, $200, and $300, respectively, for a total market value of $600. Suppose there are two investors, A and B. Investor A owns $450 worth of the market portfolio, *M*, and B owns $150 worth of *M*. They invest the rest of their money in the riskless asset. Because Investor A owns 75% of *M*, A will own 75% of each asset. Similarly, B owns 25% of *M* and 25% of each asset. The investors own identical mixes of risky assets. But what proportion of each investor's portfolio is invested in asset 1?

The answer is one-sixth, because asset 1 is one-sixth (= 100/600) of the total market value. If an investor C decides to invest in this market, she should invest one-sixth of her money in asset 1, one-third (= 200/600) in asset 2, and one-half (= 300/600) in asset 3. In this way, C would be investing in the market portfolio. ∎

If we translate our three-asset example into a large market of risky assets such as the stock market, the principle for determining the market portfolio is the same. However, identifying the value of each asset can be tricky. An asset's value is not the market value *per share*. Instead, it's the total market value of all the company's stock.

That is, the asset value to use in determining the proper investment proportions is the market value per share multiplied by the number of shares the corporation has outstanding. For example, if IBM is selling for $150 per share and there are 200 million shares of IBM, the stock market value of IBM is $30 billion.

We determine the proportion of money to invest in each stock in the following manner. First, sum the stock market values of all the corporations in the market. Then divide the corporation's stock market value by the sum of all the values. The resulting fraction is the proportion of the portfolio to invest in the stock. Continuing our hypothetical example of IBM, suppose the sum of the values for all stocks is $3.5 trillion. Then *M* would contain 0.86% (= 30 billion/3.5 trillion) invested in IBM stock.

If finding the proportions to invest in each stock sounds tedious, that's because it would be! Fortunately, when such information is valuable to one set of people, other people apply the Principle of Valuable Ideas. They recognize the potential to make a positive NPV by producing the information for a profit, or by creating investment funds that approximate the market portfolio.

Currently, information about the market portfolio's makeup can be purchased from a variety of information services. Also, many so-called stock index funds have been created. The fund's portfolio of common stocks matches the composition of an index, such as the Standard & Poor's 500 Index, which is a diversified set of common stocks that is generally accepted as a good estimate for the (common stock) market. For example, the oldest and largest of the S&P 500 mutual funds, the Vanguard Index Trust-500 Portfolio, had approximately $39.1 billion under management at May 31, 1997. The 73 S&P 500 mutual funds tracked by Lipper Analytical Services, Inc. had $84.9 billion under management at May 31, 1997.

Self-Check

1. What is a riskless asset?

2. In what sense is a 90-day Treasury bill a riskless asset? In what sense is a 30-year Treasury bond *not* a riskless asset?

(*continued on following page*)

(Self-Check *continued from previous page*)

3. Explain how the existence of a riskless asset alters an investor's set of investment opportunities.

4. What is the CML?

5. Which assets are in the market portfolio, *M?*

THE CAPITAL-ASSET-PRICING MODEL (CAPM)

Our investment prescription is to be on the CML by investing in some mix of the market portfolio and the riskless asset. We arrived at this prescription without really saying much about the risk and return of the individual stocks in the market portfolio. Now, we can do that by building on what we've learned. We can, in a sense, reverse our thought process; we can invert the CML. That is, we can ask, "What must a particular security's risk and expected return be, given the CML?"

Diversifiable and Nondiversifiable Risk

Earlier in the chapter, we showed that a portfolio's standard deviation is not a simple linear combination of its assets' standard deviations. The Principle of Diversification asserts itself. Some of the risk can be diversified away. So a security's specific risk is the sum of two parts:

$$\text{Specific risk} = \text{Diversifiable risk} + \text{Nondiversifiable risk} \tag{7.8}$$

DIVERSIFIABLE RISK
Risk that can be eliminated by diversification. Also called **unsystematic risk.**

Diversifiable risk (or *unsystematic risk*) is risk that can be eliminated by diversification. **Nondiversifiable risk** (or *systematic risk*) is risk that can't be eliminated by diversification.

    Nondiversifiable risk is really *market risk.* Therefore, a security's nondiversifiable risk is the part of its standard deviation that correlates with the market portfolio. So the nondiversifiable risk of particular security *j* is its correlation with the market times its standard deviation.

NONDIVERSIFIABLE RISK Risk that cannot be eliminated by diversification. Also called **market risk** or **systematic risk.**

$$\text{Nondiversifiable risk of security } j = [\text{Corr}(j,M)]\sigma_j$$

    Security *j*'s nondiversifiable risk is the amount of risk it contributes to the market portfolio. So the nondiversifiable risk sets its expected return. But how much does the market "pay" in expected return for taking on risk? The price for market risk is the slope of the CML, equation (7.7). It's the amount of expected return per unit of risk. Therefore, security *j*'s risk premium, the amount above the riskless return, is its nondiversifiable risk times the slope of the CML:

$$\text{Security } j\text{'s risk premium} = (\text{Nondiversifiable risk})(\text{CML slope}) = [\text{Corr}(j,M)]\sigma_j\left(\frac{\bar{r}_M - r_f}{\sigma_M}\right)$$

    This relationship is typically rearranged and expressed in terms of a variable, β_j (the Greek letter beta—pronounced "bay–tah"—subscripted to identify the asset).

BETA The covariance of an asset's return with the market portfolio's return divided by the variance of the market portfolio's return. Beta is a measure of nondiversifiable or market risk.

$$\text{Security } j\text{'s risk premium} = [\text{Corr}(j,M)]\sigma_j\left(\frac{\bar{r}_M - r_f}{\sigma_M}\right)$$
$$= \left(\frac{[\text{Corr}(j,M)]\sigma_j}{\sigma_M}\right)(\bar{r}_M - r_f) = \beta_j(\bar{r}_M - r_f)$$

A stock's **beta** is a measure of its market—that is, nondiversifiable—risk. Beta can be expressed either in terms of Corr(*j,M*) or in terms of Cov(*j,M*):

$$\beta_j = \frac{\text{Corr}(j,M)\sigma_j}{\sigma_M} = \frac{\text{Corr}(j,M)\sigma_j\sigma_M}{\sigma_M\sigma_M} = \frac{\text{Cov}(j,M)}{\sigma_M{}^2} \tag{7.9}$$

The Security Market Line

Security j's total expected return is the sum of the riskless return and its risk premium:

$$r_j = r_f + \beta_j(\bar{r}_M - r_f) \tag{7.10}$$

When the capital market is in equilibrium, equation (7.10) is called the **security market line (SML)**. Based on the Principle of Capital Market Efficiency, at such an equilibrium, the required return equals the expected return. Therefore, the SML also identifies the required return for security j that is implied by the CML. Let's compute an expected/required return.

SECURITY MARKET LINE (SML) The line showing the relationship between an asset's expected return and its beta.

Computing an Expected Return

EXAMPLE

Suppose $r_f = 7\%$, $\text{Cov}(j,M) = 250$, $\sigma_M^2 = 225$, and $\bar{r}_M = 15\%$. What is security j's required return?

First, using equation (7.9), β_j is 1.11:

$$\beta_j = \frac{\text{Cov}(j,M)}{\sigma_M^2} = \frac{250}{225} = 1.11$$

Second, using equation (7.10), security j's required return equals 15.89%:

$$r_j = r_f + \beta_j(\bar{r}_M - r_f) = 7\% + 1.11(15\% - 7\%) = 15.89\%$$

The SML, equation (7.10), expresses a security's return as the sum of the riskless return and a risk premium. The risk premium is the product of two factors. The first is β_j (beta). The second is the market risk premium ($\bar{r}_M - r_f$), which is also the slope of the SML.[5] The slope of the SML is the amount of return per unit of *nondiversifiable* (market) risk, just as the CML slope is the amount of return per unit of specific (total) risk. The greater the degree of collective risk aversion, the higher the market risk premium, and the steeper the slope of the SML.

Figure 7.12 shows the SML as a function of β_j on May 31, 1995. The riskless return—the yield on 3-month Treasury bills is used as the estimate—was 5.8%. The riskless return has a beta of zero, where the SML crosses the expected return (y) axis. The market risk premium

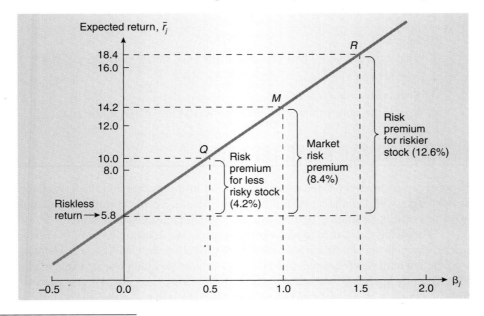

FIGURE 7.12
The security market line at May 31, 1995.   Sources: Bloomberg, L.P., and *Stocks, Bonds, Bills, and Inflation 1995 Yearbook* (Chicago, Ill.: Ibbotson Associates, 1995), p. 157.

---

[5]It's especially important to understand that beta is *not* the slope of the SML. Beta is the variable plotted along the horizontal axis in figure 7.12.

(slope) was 8.4%. The beta of the market portfolio, which is the value-weighted average of all common stock betas, equals 1.0, and the expected return on the market portfolio was (which corresponds to the point M) 14.2%:

$$\bar{r}_M = 5.8\% + (1.0)8.4\% = 14.2\%$$

EXAMPLE

The Stock Market Risk-Return Trade-Off

What risk-return trade-off is reflected in figure 7.12?

Riskier (higher beta) stocks have higher required returns. Consider point R, where $\beta_j = 1.50$. Using equation (7.10), we find that

$$r_R = 5.8 + 1.5(8.4) = 18.4\%$$

Next consider point Q. Less risky (lower beta) stocks have lower required returns. Point Q has a beta of 0.50, and a required return of

$$r_Q = 5.8 + 0.5(8.4) = 10.0\%$$

In more general terms, a stock is a *capital asset*. The SML (in conjunction with the Principle of Capital Market Efficiency) prices stocks by specifying a required (equal to the expected) return. Can we generalize and use it to specify a required return to *any* capital asset? Yes, if the model is appropriate to the situation.

CAPITAL-ASSET-PRICING MODEL (CAPM) An asset-pricing model that expresses the required return as the sum of the riskless return and a risk premium that depends on the price of market risk and how the asset's returns covary with those of the market portfolio.

When we use the more general concept that *j* is a capital asset, rather than specifically a stock, equation (7.10) becomes one form of what is called the **capital-asset-pricing model (CAPM).** Just as the name implies, it's a model for pricing capital assets. In it, an asset's required return is simply the sum of the riskless return and an asset-specific risk premium.

The CAPM is so appealing that it might make you wonder why we have gone to such great lengths to derive this model. The reason is that it shows that the appropriate risk adjustment is not immediately obvious. The risk adjustment is based on how an asset's return *covaries* with the market portfolio's return. It shows what an individual asset contributes to the risk of an investor's total portfolio.

Self-Check

1. What's the difference between diversifiable and nondiversifiable risk?

2. Does beta measure specific risk or market risk?

3. What is the SML?

4. What is the slope of the SML, and how is it a kind of "price" for risk?

ESTIMATING AND USING THE CAPM

Suppose we knew every asset return distribution in the market and the covariance of each asset's return with the market portfolio's return. Then we could specify a required return for every asset using equation (7.10). In practice, we don't have this information.

In applying the CAPM to real-world situations, we're taking it out of the perfect capital market environment in which it was derived. Nevertheless, the CAPM is still useful in estimating required returns. We can measure how stock returns vary with respect to the market portfolio's return by applying a statistical method called *linear regression.* We can express stock *j*'s realized return, r_j, as a linear function of the realized market risk premium $(r_M - r_f)$, so that

$$r_j = r_f + \tilde{\beta}_j (r_M - r_f) \tag{7.11}$$

We use the tilde ($\sim$) to indicate that $\tilde{\beta}_j$ is a random variable.

To estimate β_j from historical data, collect a sample of simultaneous observations of r_j, r_M, and r_f. Then use equation (7.11) to estimate the regression coefficient β_j.

Equation (7.11) is why the coefficient β_j came to be called the common stock's *beta*. Beta plays a critical role in asset pricing. It's a *linear measure* of how much an individual asset contributes to the market portfolio's standard deviation (specific risk). So an asset's beta is a simple, well-behaved measure of the asset's market risk.

Computing a Beta

EXAMPLE

Table 7.3 provides the monthly returns for Merck common stock (symbol MRK) and the market (with the Standard & Poor's 500 Index as the market portfolio estimate). MRK's beta is calculated by using linear regression to estimate equation (7.11):

$$r_{MRK,t} - r_{f,t} = \beta(r_{M,t} - r_{f,t}) + \epsilon$$

where $r_{MRK,t}$ is the realized return (including dividends) on Merck common stock during month t, $r_{f,t}$ is the realized return on Treasury bills during month t, $r_{M,t}$ is the realized return on the S&P 500 Index during month t, β is the regression coefficient, and ϵ is a linear regression error term. In this example, the y intercept is constrained to equal zero.

We applied ordinary least squares regression analysis (using the data regression function in a spreadsheet package). The estimated β coefficient for Merck common stock, based on monthly 1994 data, is 1.05.

Figure 7.13 on page 210 plots the regression equation. This plot is called the stock's **characteristic line.** A security's beta is thus the slope of the stock's characteristic line.

Most experts prefer to use a larger number of observations to reduce the likelihood that transitory factors might affect the beta estimate. It's customary to use at least three years' but not more than seven years' data. We used 12 months of data to simplify the example. ∎

CHARACTERISTIC LINE A linear regression of the historical relationship between a stock's return and the market portfolio's return.

Table 7.4 on page 210 shows the beta coefficients for 20 companies, many of which are familiar to you. (Having lunch at McDonald's anytime this week? Had a Pepsi lately?)

Beta indicates how sensitive a security's returns are to changes in the returns on the market portfolio. If a security's beta is 1.0, its returns tend to track the market portfolio. If the market portfolio increases or decreases by 10%, the stock also tends to move up or down by 10%.

If a stock has a beta less than 1.0, it will tend to rise or fall less than the market. For example, suppose a stock has a beta of 0.5. If the market portfolio increases or decreases by 10%, the stock will tend to move up or down only 5%.

A stock with a beta greater than 1.0 will rise or fall more than the market. For example, a stock with a beta of 1.5 will tend to rise or fall by 15% when the market portfolio increases or decreases 10%. Values of beta for most common stocks fall within the range from 0.75 to 1.50.

TABLE 7.3
Monthly Returns on Merck Common Stock, the S&P 500 Index, and Treasury Bills During 1994

MONTH	MRK	MARKET (S&P 500)	RISKLESS SECURITY	MONTH	MRK	MARKET (S&P 500)	RISKLESS SECURITY
JAN	6.18%	3.25%	0.25%	JUL	−1.35%	3.15%	0.28%
FEB	−11.30	−3.00	0.21	AUG	15.19	3.76	0.37
MAR	−7.24	−4.58	0.27	SEP	5.27	−2.69	0.37
APR	−1.35	1.16	0.27	OCT	−0.84	2.08	0.38
MAY	2.95	1.24	0.32	NOV	4.56	−3.95	0.37
JUN	−1.54	−2.68	0.31	DEC	3.15	1.23	0.44

Sources: Bloomberg, L. P., and *Stocks, Bonds, Bills, and Inflation 1995 Yearbook* (Chicago, Ill.: Ibbotson Associates, 1995), p. 203.

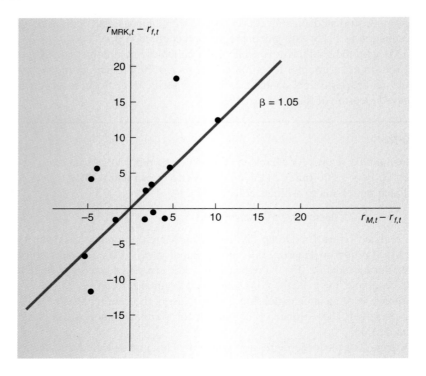

FIGURE 7.13
A stock's characteristic line.

Take note that beta can be negative. Accordingly, an asset with a negative beta can have a required return that is *less* than the riskless return. At first glance, this seems counterintuitive: How can any asset have an expected return that's less than the riskless return?[6]

Remember, these are assets held in a fully diversified portfolio, the market portfolio. Therefore, the measure of risk for the individual asset depends on how the standard deviation of the portfolio return changes when that asset is added to the portfolio. When a negative-beta asset is added to the market portfolio, it actually lowers the market portfolio's standard deviation. So although the notion of negative risk is counterintuitive, it makes sense in this context.

TABLE 7.4
Beta Coefficients for Selected Companies

COMMON STOCK	BETA	COMMON STOCK	BETA
Alex. Brown	1.95	Boeing	0.95
Magma Copper "B"	1.30	Minnesota Mining & Mfg.	0.95
ITT Corp.	1.20	PepsiCo, Inc.	0.90
Microsoft Corp.	1.15	Berkshire Hathaway	0.90
General Electric	1.15	Quaker Oats	0.80
J. P. Morgan & Co.	1.10	Idaho Power	0.70
NIKE, Inc. "B"	1.05	Boston Edison	0.70
McDonald's Corp.	1.00	AT&T Corp.	0.65
Gibson Greetings	1.00	Florida Progress Corp.	0.65
Neiman Marcus	0.95	Exxon Corp.	0.65

Source: *The Value Line Investment Survey* (March 28, 1997).

---

[6]Admittedly, such assets are rare. The common stocks of some gold mining companies have negative betas.

Arbitrage and the SML

As the name *security market line* suggests, the [beta/expected return] combinations of all securities in the market portfolio must lie along the SML. Consider a security *l* whose [beta/expected return] combination lies below the SML, as represented by the point *l* in figure 7.14. Would anyone want to invest in asset *l*? No.

There's an asset whose [beta/expected return] combination, located at *l'* on the SML, is superior. Asset *l'* has the same β as asset *l*. Thus, both contribute identically to portfolio risk. However, asset *l'* has a higher expected return. In a perfect capital market, an asset such as *l* would give rise to an *arbitrage opportunity*. Investors could earn an *arbitrage profit*, without changing their portfolio's risk, by selling *l* short and buying asset *l'*.

Selling short involves borrowing a security and selling it with the expectation of buying it back later at a lower price (to make a profit). The expected profit is $r_{l'} - r_l$.

How long would such an arbitrage opportunity continue to exist? Until the price of asset *l* had been driven down to such an extent that the [beta/expected return] combination for asset *l* shifted to the SML. That is, until the [beta/expected return] combinations for assets *l* and *l'* are equal.

Can a security whose [beta/expected return] combination lies above the SML, such as security *k* depicted in figure 7.14, exist for long? Again, not in a perfect capital market. Investors would purchase asset *k* and sell asset *k'* short, thereby earning an arbitrage profit without changing their portfolio's risk. The expected profit is $r_k - r_{k'}$. Arbitrage activity would continue until the market value of asset *k* had been driven up to such an extent that the [beta/expected return] combination for asset *k* shifted down to the SML.

In a perfect capital market environment, one with no impediments to arbitrage activity (no restrictions on short selling, for example), the [beta/expected return] combinations for all securities *and* for all portfolios of securities must lie along the SML.

Approximating the Market Portfolio

In our discussion of an asset's expected return, we cited the law of large numbers as a justification for using the mean of the distribution to represent a portfolio's expected return. The concept of large numbers, and more specifically random samples, can also be used here. The law of large numbers can help determine an accurate approximation of the market portfolio.

When we want to estimate the unknown mean of a probability distribution, we compute the sample mean for a reasonably large random sample. The definition of large doesn't necessarily depend on the size of the underlying population. A large sample in statistics may contain only 25 to 30 observations.

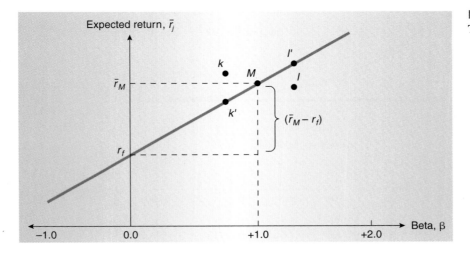

FIGURE 7.14
The SML and arbitrage.

Therefore, we can predict that the realized return to a portfolio of approximately equal investments in 25–30 *randomly* chosen stocks will be consistently close to the market portfolio's realized return. In fact, this result has been shown empirically countless times. The accuracy of this approximation depends on the size of the random sample. Figure 7.15 graphs portfolio standard deviation as a function of the number of randomly selected securities in the portfolio.

Prices Are Set by Diversified Investors

Figure 7.15 is another way of showing how diversification reduces portfolio risk. Recall that every asset has both diversifiable and nondiversifiable risk. Adding securities reduces diversifiable risk. Look back at equation (7.11). The market compensates investors only for taking on nondiversifiable risk. It won't pay them for taking on diversifiable risk. Why is this?

Nondiversified investors will be taking more risk than diversified investors. For nondiversified investors, the added (diversifiable) risk lowers the value of, and price they should pay for, the security. Diversified investors will be taking less risk and can afford to pay more for the security. People wanting to sell the security will follow the Principle of Self-Interested Behavior and sell to the highest bidders—diversified investors. Therefore, the market price will reflect the security's higher value to diversified investors.

This point can be seen in another way. With a large number of assets, such as in the U.S. stock market, it's both easy and relatively inexpensive to diversify. So U.S. investors are not able to require payment for something that's negative to them, when they can easily (and close to costlessly) eliminate it. In other words, investors can choose whether to take on diversifiable risk. Consequently, they can't require payment for taking it on.

A Word of Warning

The CAPM appears to work reasonably well in most situations. However, there are two situations we must warn you about. The CAPM tends to *understate* the required return for common stocks of companies that are *small* or are *highly leveraged* (a company with a comparatively large proportion of debt financing). Using the CAPM in such situations requires adjustments for these effects. The end-of-chapter bibliography contains sources for learning more about these issues and how to make such adjustments.

FIGURE 7.15

Portfolio standard deviation as a function of portfolio size.

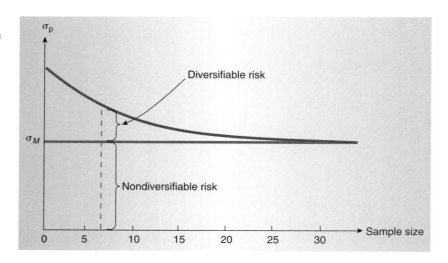

Self-Check

1. Is all the information we need for using the CAPM readily available?

2. Do returns on a stock with a beta greater than 1.0 tend to vary more or less than the market return?

3. If you can't duplicate the market portfolio exactly, how can you approximate it?

INTERNATIONAL CONSIDERATIONS

There are many multinational companies. These companies make investments in more than one country. Should the required return on such foreign investments be greater than the required return on an otherwise identical domestic investment? Many believe a risk premium should be added when evaluating foreign investments, because of higher economic and political risks. You may be surprised to learn that an international investment's required return may actually be *less* than that for an otherwise identical domestic investment.

International Diversification

Just as companies invest internationally, investors purchase both domestic and foreign securities. We know that the relevant risk for pricing an asset is its nondiversifiable risk.

Suppose there's a single world capital market. In such a market, most of the economic and political risk is specific to the investment and can be eliminated by diversification. Consequently, investors face the same nondiversifiable risk on a foreign investment as on an otherwise identical domestic project. Therefore, the required return for the two projects would be the same. We could still use the CAPM, but *M* would be a **world market portfolio.** It would include all the capital assets in the world. Beta would be based on the world market portfolio return.

WORLD MARKET PORTFOLIO A portfolio that contains all the capital assets in the world.

Now let's consider the opposite of a single world market. Suppose the various national capital markets are essentially separated. Investors purchase domestic stocks. Suppose you get a chance to make either a domestic or foreign investment. The investments are otherwise identical. Because the Principle of Diversification doesn't depend on national boundaries, you may be better off making the international investment.

To see this, consider adding a negative-beta stock to the market portfolio. The reduction in portfolio risk overcomes the fact that the stock's return is actually below the riskless return.

In a similar way, the international investment has two benefits: (1) the "basic" return like that from an otherwise identical domestic investment, and (2) the potential risk-reducing benefits from international diversification. With separated capital markets, investors may not get this specific diversification in other ways. In such a case, therefore, the foreign investment may be more valuable than the otherwise identical domestic investment.

International Opportunities

In reality, the world capital markets are not fully integrated. Certain countries have restrictions. In practice, U.S. investors have not invested very much internationally. We don't know why. Possible factors include problems obtaining foreign financial information,[7] foreign tax considerations, costs of converting currencies, higher transaction costs, and expropriation risk, as well as legal and other forms of political risk. But things seem to be changing.

In recent years, U.S. financial institutions have increased their foreign investing. In addition, many foreign companies have listed their shares on the NYSE. Mutual funds have

---

[7] Foreign countries generally impose less exacting disclosure requirements than exist in the United States.

been created that invest in companies located in a specific region (for example, there are several Latin American funds) or in a particular country (there are dozens of country funds, including funds investing in Argentina, India, Korea, Mexico, and Spain). These changes have made it easier and less expensive for Americans to make foreign investments.

Unfortunately, the bottom line is that we don't have an exact formula for a foreign investment's required return. However, we can say that it is *not* the required return for an otherwise identical domestic investment plus a "tacked-on" risk premium.

Self-Check

1. Describe what is meant by the term *world market portfolio.*

2. Should a foreign investment have an extra risk premium added to its required return compared to a domestic investment?

SUMMARY

An asset's expected return and risk are based on its future possible returns. The risk-return trade-off is fundamental to many business and personal decisions.

- The analysis of risk and return uses several basic statistical concepts, including the mean, variance, standard deviation, covariance, and correlation.
- An investment's expected return is its mean or weighted value of its possible future returns. The weights are the probabilities of each possible future return.
- Risk has two dimensions: (1) uncertainty about the future outcome and (2) the possibility of a negative outcome. The standard deviation of a distribution of future returns that is approximately symmetrical around the mean captures both dimensions. Thus, in most cases, we can use an asset's standard deviation of return to measure its specific risk.
- Combining stocks into portfolios reduces risk because of the Principle of Diversification. Stocks that perform better than expected tend to offset to some degree the returns from stocks that perform worse than expected.
- A portfolio's expected return is the weighted average of the individual security expected returns. The proportions of portfolio value invested in each security are the weights.
- The portfolio's standard deviation of return depends on the standard deviations of the individual securities in the portfolio and correlation coefficients between the returns of the securities that compose the portfolio. It is *not* simply a weighted average of the standard deviations of the individual securities.
- The amount of risk reduction in a two-asset portfolio depends on the correlation between the two assets' returns. In a portfolio consisting of two assets whose returns are perfectly negatively correlated, it's possible to find a set of investment proportions for which the portfolio is riskless. If the two assets are perfectly positively correlated, the risk-return trade-off is a straight line with no risk reduction from diversification. With correlations between −1 and +1, the risk-return trade-off is usually a curved, nonlinear function.
- An efficient portfolio is one that provides the greatest possible expected return for a given risk level or, equivalently, provides the smallest risk level for a given expected return. The set of efficient portfolios makes up the efficient frontier.
- By combining the efficient frontier with the possibility of lending or borrowing at the riskless return, the best investment strategy is to invest part of the money in the market portfolio and the rest in the riskless asset.
- The capital market line (CML), which goes through the riskless return and is tangent to the efficient frontier at *M,* traces out the available risk-return possibilities. Investors should invest in the risky portfolio *M* and set their return and risk levels by lending or borrowing to achieve their most desired position on the CML. As a result, investors' choices of which risky portfolio to invest in are not based on their attitude toward risk. Everyone should invest in *M.*

- For diversified investors, the proper measure of a stock's risk is its nondiversifiable risk, not its specific risk. Nondiversifiable risk is also called market risk or systematic risk. A stock's required return is based on its nondiversifiable risk.

- The capital-asset-pricing model (CAPM) expresses the required return as the riskless return plus a risk premium. The risk premium is a function of two variables, the investment's beta and the market price of risk. Beta is a measure of market risk. Beta is the covariance between the security's return and the market return divided by the variance of the market portfolio's return. The market price of risk is the difference between the expected market return and the riskless return.

- The CAPM expresses an asset's required return as the riskless return plus a risk premium

$$r_j = r_f + \beta_j(\bar{r}_M - r_f)$$

where r_j is the expected return on security j, r_f is the riskless return, β_j is the security's beta, and $\bar{r}_M$ is the expected return on the market portfolio.

- The CAPM prices only nondiversifiable risk. U.S. investors can easily eliminate diversifiable risk at low cost. Therefore, stock prices reflect the stock's value to diversified investors.

- Beta can be estimated using linear regression. Many analytical services provide beta estimates for actively traded common stocks.

- The market portfolio includes all assets. In practice, a stock market index, such as the S&P 500, is used as a proxy for the market portfolio.

- The CAPM appears to work reasonably well in most situations. However, there is evidence that it tends to *understate* the required return for the common shares of companies that are *small* or are *highly leveraged* (a company with a comparatively large proportion of debt financing). Using the CAPM in such situations requires adjustments for these effects.

- International investing may provide benefits from diversification. A foreign investment's required return is not found by "tacking on" an additional risk premium to the required return for an otherwise identical domestic investment.

EQUATION SUMMARY

(7.1)
$$\bar{x} = \sum_{n=1}^{N} p_n x_n$$

(7.2)
$$\sigma_x^2 = \sum_{n=1}^{N} p_n(x_n - \bar{x})^2$$

(7.3)
$$\text{Covariance} = \text{Cov}(X,Y) = \sum_{n=1}^{N} p_n(x_n - \bar{x})(y_n - \bar{y})$$

(7.4)
$$\text{Corr}(X,Y) = \frac{\text{Cov}(X,Y)}{\sigma_X \sigma_Y}$$

(7.5)
$$\bar{r}_p = w_1 \bar{r}_1 + (1 - w_1)\bar{r}_2$$

(7.6)
$$\sigma_p = [w_1^2 \sigma_1^2 + (1 - w_1)^2 \sigma_2^2 + 2w_1(1 - w_1)\text{Corr}(R_1,R_2)\sigma_1\sigma_2]^{\frac{1}{2}}$$

(7.7)
$$\text{CML slope} = \frac{\bar{r}_M - r_f}{\sigma_M}$$

(7.8)
$$\text{Specific risk} = \text{Diversifiable risk} + \text{Nondiversifiable risk}$$

(7.9)
$$\beta_j = \frac{\text{Corr}(j,M)\sigma_j}{\sigma_M} = \frac{\text{Corr}(j,M)\sigma_j\sigma_M}{\sigma_M\sigma_M} = \frac{\text{Cov}(j,M)}{\sigma_M^2}$$

(7.10)
$$r_j = r_f + \beta_j(\bar{r}_M - r_f)$$

(7.11)
$$r_j = r_f + \tilde{\beta}_j(r_M - r_f)$$

CHAPTER REVIEW ACTIVITIES

SELF-TEST PROBLEMS

1. (Expected return and standard deviation) An investment has four possible returns, each with its own probability given below.
  a. What is the expected return?   b. What are the variance and the standard deviation of returns?

Return:	−7.5%	0%	10%	20%
Probability	0.20	0.25	0.35	0.20

2. (Portfolio return and standard deviation) Two stocks have the expected returns and standard deviations given below. The correlation between the returns of the two stocks is 0.50. As the portfolio weights show, 40% of the total portfolio is invested in stock 1 and 60% is in stock 2.
  a. What is the expected portfolio return?   b. What is the portfolio standard deviation?

Stock	Expected return	Standard deviation	Portfolio weights
1	12%	10%	0.40
2	16%	20%	0.60

3. (Beta and required return) The riskless return is 6% and the expected market return is 14%. The market standard deviation is 20% and the standard deviation for Uplift stock is 36%. The correlation between market and Uplift returns is 0.80.
  a. What is the beta for shares of Uplift stock?   b. Using the CAPM, what is the required return on Uplift?

SOLUTIONS TO SELF-TEST PROBLEMS

1. a. The expected return is: $\bar{r} = 0.20(-7.5) + 0.25(0) + 0.35(10) + 0.20(20) = 6.0\%$
  b. The variance and standard deviation of returns are:
  $\sigma^2 = 0.20(-7.5 - 6)^2 + 0.25(0 - 6)^2 + 0.35(10 - 6)^2 + 0.20(20 - 6)^2 = 78.8875;$
  $\sigma = (78.8875)^{1/2} = 8.88\%$
2. a. The expected portfolio return is: $\bar{r}_p = w_1\bar{r}_1 + (1 - w_1)\bar{r}_2 = 0.40(12) + 0.60(16) = 14.4\%$
  b. The portfolio variance is: $\sigma_p^2 = w_1^2\sigma_1^2 + (1 - w_1)^2\sigma_2^2 + 2w_1(1 - w_1)\text{Corr}(R_1,R_2)\sigma_1\sigma_2$
  $\sigma_p^2 = (0.40)^2(10)^2 + (0.60)^2(20)^2 + 2(0.40)(0.60)(0.50)(10)(20) = 208$
  The standard deviation is: $\sigma_p = (208)^{1/2} = 14.42\%$
3. a.

$$\beta_{\text{Uplift}} = \frac{\text{Corr}(j,M)\sigma_j}{\sigma_M} = \frac{0.80(36)}{20} = 1.44$$

  b. $r = r_f + \beta_{\text{Uplift}}(\bar{r}_M - r_f) = 6\% + 1.44(14\% - 6\%) = 6\% + 11.52\% = 17.52\%$

QUESTIONS

1. What is meant by the term *expected return?*
2. Define the term *mean.*
3. What are the two dimensions of risk?
4. How is *risk* defined in this chapter?
5. Define the term *efficient frontier.* Why is it desirable to invest in a portfolio that lies on the efficient frontier?
6. a. Suppose you own $1,000,000 worth of 30-year Treasury bonds. Is this asset riskless?
  b. Let's say you own $1,000,000 worth of 90-day Treasury bills. You "roll over" this investment every 90 days by reinvesting the proceeds in another issue of 90-day Treasury bills. Is this investment riskless?
  c. Can you think of an asset that is truly riskless?
7. Explain what is meant by the term *market price of risk.*
8. Common stock A has an expected return of 10%, a standard deviation of future returns of 25%, and a beta of 1.25. Common stock B has an expected return of 12%, a standard deviation of future returns of 15%, and a beta of 1.50. Which stock is riskier? Explain.

9. a. Define the term *capital market line, CML.*

   b. Define the term *security market line, SML.*

   c. What's the difference between the CML and the SML?

10. What is the difference between diversifiable risk and nondiversifiable risk?

11. Why is it that the market will pay an investor for taking on nondiversifiable risk, but will not pay an investor for taking on diversifiable risk?

CHALLENGING QUESTIONS

12. Explain the fallacy in the following statement: "I bought the stock for $30 per share. It's now selling for $20 per share. But I haven't lost anything because I haven't sold it yet."

13. Explain how it is possible to invest in two risky assets that are perfectly negatively correlated (that is, $\text{Corr}(R_1, R_2) = -1.0$) and earn a riskless return.

14. Respond to the following statement: First you say σ measures the risk of investing. Then you say β measures the risk of investing. Which is right?

15. Suppose an investor's degree of risk aversion increases. How will the investor's required return on a particular stock be affected? Does it matter whether the stock's beta is high or low?

16. Explain why a foreign investment project might have a lower required return than an otherwise identical domestic project.

17. According to the CAPM, an asset with a beta of zero has a required return equal to the riskless return, r_f. Does this mean that the asset is riskless? Can an asset with a positive standard deviation of return, σ, have a beta of zero?

18. Figure 7.8 shows what the group of all possible portfolio combinations for stocks in the stock market looks like. Is it possible that any two of these portfolios have a correlation coefficient between them that is equal to *negative* 1.0? If it is possible, give an example. If it is not possible, explain why.

19. Suppose r_f is 5% and $\bar{r}_M$ is 10%. According to the SML and the CAPM, an asset with a beta −2.0 has a required return of *negative* 5% (= 5 − 2[10 − 5]). Can this be possible? Does this mean that the asset has negative risk? Why would anyone ever invest in an asset that has an expected and required return that is negative? Explain.

PROBLEM SET A

A1. (Calculating portfolio weights) Consider a market with four risky assets, 1, 2, 3, and 4, worth $1000, $2500, $1500, and $5000, respectively. If an investor wants to replicate the market portfolio, what proportion of each investor's portfolio should be invested in each risky asset?

A2. (Expected portfolio return) Musumeci Capital Management has invested its portfolio as shown below. What is Musumeci's expected portfolio return?

Asset	Portfolio Weight	Expected Return
Money market securities	10%	4%
Corporate bonds	20	8
Equities	70	12

A3. (Calculating beta) What's the beta of a stock whose covariance with the market portfolio return is 0.0045 if the variance of the return on the market portfolio is 0.002?

A4. (Calculating beta) Malhotra Computers has a standard deviation of monthly returns of 9% and has a 0.70 correlation with market returns. The standard deviation of market monthly returns is 6%. What is Malhotra's beta?

A5. (Plotting the SML and a company's required return) General Electric's beta in May 1995 was approximately 1.10, according to the *Value Line Investment Survey.* The riskless return at the time was 5.75%. The historical risk premium on the market portfolio is 8.4%. Graph the SML for May 1995 and plot General Electric's required return.

A6. (Required return) According to the CAPM, what would be the required return on an asset that has a beta of 1.35 when the expected return on the market portfolio is 12% and the riskless return is 7%?

A7. (Market price of risk) The market portfolio has an expected return of 12.4% and a standard deviation of 20%. The riskless return is 4.4%.
a. What is the market price of risk ($\bar{r}_M - r_f$)?
b. What is the slope of the capital market line (which is the price of market risk divided by the standard deviation of the market return)?

PROBLEM SET B

B1. (Expected return and standard deviation) What is the expected return and standard deviation of the return for the next year on a stock that is selling for $30 now and has probabilities of 0.2, 0.6, and 0.2 of selling 1 year from now at $24, $33, and $39, respectively? Assume that no dividends will be paid on the stock during the next year and ignore taxes.

B2. (Expected return and risk) General Eclectic Corporation is considering three possible capital investment projects. The projected returns depend on the future state of the economy as shown below.

State of the Economy	Probability of Occurrence	Projected Return		
		1	2	3
Recession	0.20	10%	8%	12%
Stable	0.60	15	13	10
Boom	0.20	21	25	8

a. Calculate each project's expected return, variance, and standard deviation.
b. Rank the projects on the basis of (1) expected return and (2) risk. Which project would you choose?

B3. (Beta) What is the beta of an asset whose correlation coefficient with the market portfolio's returns is 0.62 and variance is 0.1 if the variance of the market portfolio's return is 0.0025?

B4. (CAPM) The required return on an asset with a beta of 1.4 is 17% and the riskless return is 7%. What is the expected return on the market portfolio?

B5. (CAPM) Suppose the expected return and variance of the market portfolio are 0.11 and 0.0016, respectively. If the riskless return is 0.06 (6%), what will be the required return on a stock whose return variance is 0.12 and correlation with the market portfolio's returns is 0.46?

B6. (CAPM) What's the beta of a stock when its expected return is 15%, its standard deviation of return is 25%, its correlation coefficient with the market is 0.2, and the return to the market portfolio is 14% with a standard deviation of 4%? Assuming the market for this stock is in equilibrium, what is the riskless return that is implied by the information given?

B7. (CAPM) Stock A has a beta of 2.0 and a required return of 15%. The market return is 10%. What will be the required return on stock B, which has a beta of 1.4?

B8. (CAPM) Not-so-Swift Meat Processors is considering building a new meat processing facility in Omaha, Nebraska. Not-so-Swift has 75,000,000 common shares outstanding. The share price is $25. Assume $r_f = 6.5\%$, $\beta = 0.95$, and $\bar{r}_M - r_f = 8.4\%$. Estimate Not-so-Swift's required return on its equity investment in the new facility.

B9. (Calculating means, standard deviations, covariance, and correlation) Given the probability distribution for returns for stock X and stock Y, compute the following:

	Returns	
Probability	Stock X	Stock Y
0.1	−10%	4%
0.3	0	8
0.3	6	0
0.2	10	−5
0.1	20	15

a. The expected return for each stock, $\bar{x}$ and $\bar{y}$.
b. The variance of the return for each stock.
c. The covariance between the returns for stock X and stock Y.
d. The correlation coefficient between the returns for stock X and stock Y.

PROBLEM SET C

C1. (Capital market line) Plot the ten investment portfolio risks and returns shown below.

Portfolio	1	2	3	4	5	6	7	8	9	10
Expected return	10.0	12.0	7.5	8.3	6.1	13.2	14.1	7.9	9.2	13.1
Risk	15.5	18.7	14.3	17.2	22.3	23.0	25.2	17.1	16.7	23.4

a. Identify the efficient portfolios and plot the efficient frontier.

b. Suppose the riskless return is 10%. Which is the best portfolio?

c. Suppose you are prepared to experience a standard deviation of 10%. What is your best investment strategy? What is your expected return?

d. Suppose you are prepared to experience a standard deviation of 30%. What is your best investment strategy? What is your expected return?

C2. (Calculating expected returns, standard deviations, covariance, and correlation) The following table provides the monthly returns for Microsoft Corp. (symbol MSFT) common stock and the S&P 500 Index during 1994. Compute the following:

Month	Market (S&P 500)	MSFT	Month	Market (S&P 500)	MSFT
JAN	3.25	5.58	JUL	3.15	−0.24
FEB	−3.00	−3.08	AUG	3.76	12.86
MAR	−4.58	2.73	SEP	−2.69	−3.44
APR	1.16	9.14	OCT	2.08	12.25
MAY	1.24	16.22	NOV	−3.95	−0.20
JUN	−2.68	−3.95	DEC	1.23	−2.78

a. The average monthly return for the market and for MSFT over these 12 months.

b. The variance of the monthly return for each over these 12 months.

c. The covariance between the returns for the market and MSFT over these 12 months.

d. The correlation coefficient between the returns for the market and MSFT for these 12 months.

C3. (Beta and required return) Will Eatem, a portfolio manager for the Conservative Retirement Equity Fund (CREF), is considering investing in the common stock of Big Caesar's Pizza (stock symbol PIES). His analysts have compiled the return data given below.

Year:	1	2	3	4	5	6	7	8	9	10
S&P 500:	−10.2	5.8	12.2	−7.3	−1.5	10.5	8.3	15.7	−2.1	8.6
PIES:	−5.3	13.2	6.1	2.1	−8.8	15.7	3.9	12.6	−7.3	10.2

a. Calculate the beta coefficient for PIES.

b. The riskless return is 6% and the market risk premium is 8.4%. Plot the SML.

c. You have recently met with the management of PIES. You are favorably im-

pressed, and you estimate that the stock will earn a return of 19% over the next 12 months. Should you invest in PIES?

C4. (Portfolio returns and risk) There are four securities and five possible economic scenarios. The probability of occurrence and security returns are given below.

State of the Economy	Probability of Occurrence	U.S. T-bills	Government Bonds	Corporate Bonds	Common Stock
High growth	0.10	6.0%	8.0%	10.0%	25.0%
Moderate growth	0.25	6.0	7.5	9.0	15.5
Slow growth	0.35	6.0	7.0	8.5	11.5
Stagnation	0.15	6.0	6.0	6.0	−1.0
Recession	0.15	6.0	4.0	−2.0	−11.5
	1.00				

a. Calculate the expected return and standard deviation of returns for each security.

b. Calculate the correlation coefficient for each pair of securities.

c. Assuming the four securities are weighted equally, calculate the expected return to the portfolio and the standard deviation of the return to the portfolio.

d. Assuming 20% of the portfolio is invested in each of U.S. T-bills and govern- ment bonds and 30% is invested in each of corporate bonds and common stock, calculate the expected return to the port- folio and the standard deviation of the re- turn to the portfolio.

C5. (Calculating beta from historical returns) Many analysts subtract the riskless return from the market and security returns, and use these excess returns to calculate betas. Use this convention for this problem. The following table provides the monthly returns for Exxon common stock (symbol XON) and the market as estimated by the S&P 500 Index, both during 1994. Compute the following:

Month	Market (S&P 500)	XON	Riskless Security	Month	Market (S&P 500)	XON	Riskless Security
JAN	3.25%	5.35%	0.25%	JUL	3.15%	4.85%	0.28%
FEB	−3.00	−1.36	0.21	AUG	3.76	1.21	0.37
MAR	−4.58	−4.15	0.27	SEP	−2.69	−4.52	0.37
APR	1.16	0.00	0.27	OCT	2.08	9.35	0.38
MAY	1.24	−1.64	0.32	NOV	−3.95	−2.78	0.37
JUN	−2.68	−8.24	0.31	DEC	1.23	−0.61	0.44

a. The average monthly returns for the mar- ket and for XON over these 12 months.

b. The variance of the monthly returns for each over these 12 months.

c. The covariance between the returns for the market and XON over these 12 months.

d. The correlation coefficient between the returns for the market and XON for these 12 months.

e. The beta for XON, using linear regres- sion for these 12 months.

C6. (Beta and required return) The riskless return is currently 6%, and Chicago Gear has estimated the contingent returns given below.

State of the Market	Probability that State Occurs	Realized Return	
		Stock Market	Chicago Gear
Stagnant	0.20	(10%)	(15%)
Slow Growth	0.35	10	15
Average Growth	0.30	15	25
Rapid Growth	0.15	25	35

a. Calculate the expected returns on the stock market and on the project.

b. What is Chicago Gear's beta?

c. What is Chicago Gear's required return according to the CAPM?

BIBLIOGRAPHY

Affleck-Graves, John, and Bill McDonald. "Nonnormalities and Tests of Asset Pricing Theories," *Journal of Finance,* 1989, 44(4):889–908.

Amihud, Yakov, and Haim Mendelson. "Liquidity and Asset Prices: Financial Management Implications," *Financial Manage- ment,* 1988, 17(1):5–15.

Ball, Ray. "Anomalies in Relationships Between Securities' Yields and Yield-Surrogates," *Journal of Financial Economics,* 1978, 6(2/3):103–126.

Banz, Rolf W. "The Relationship Between Return and Market Value of Common Stocks," *Journal of Financial Economics,* 1981, 9(1):3–18.

Basu, Sanjoy. "The Relationship Between Earnings' Yield, Mar- ket Value and Return for NYSE Common Stocks: Further Evi- dence," *Journal of Financial Economics,* 1983, 12(1):129–156.

Bhandari, Laxmi Chand. "Debt/Equity Ratio and Expected Com- mon Stock Returns: Empirical Evidence," *Journal of Finance,* 1988, 43(2):507–528.

Black, Fischer. "Estimating Expected Return," *Financial Ana- lysts Journal,* 1993, 49(5):36–38. Reprinted in *Financial Ana- lysts Journal,* 1995, 51(1):168–171.

Black, Fischer. "Return and Beta," *Journal of Portfolio Manage- ment,* 1993, 20(1):8–18.

Boquist, John A., and William T. Moore. "Estimating the Systematic Risk of an Industry Segment: A Mathematical Programming Approach," *Financial Management*, 1983, 12(4):11–18.

Breeden, Douglas T., Michael R. Gibbons, and Robert H. Litzenberger. "Empirical Tests of the Consumption-Oriented CAPM," *Journal of Finance*, 1989, 44(2):231–262.

Bremer, Marc, and Richard J. Sweeney. "The Reversal of Large Stock-Price Decreases," *Journal of Finance*, 1991, 46(2):747–754.

Brennan, Michael J. "The Optimal Number of Securities in a Risky Asset Portfolio When There Are Fixed Costs of Transaction: Theory and Some Empirical Evidence," *Journal of Financial and Quantitative Analysis*, 1975, 10(3):483–496.

Brigham, Eugene F., Dilip K. Shome, and Steve R. Vinson. "The Risk Premium Approach to Measuring a Utility's Cost of Equity," *Financial Management*, 1985, 14(1):33–45.

Brown, Stephen J. "The Number of Factors in Security Returns," *Journal of Finance*, 1989, 44(5):1247–1262.

Burmeister, Edwin, and Marjorie B. McElroy. "Joint Estimation of Factor Sensitivities and Risk Premia for the Arbitrage Pricing Theory," *Journal of Finance*, 1988, 43(3):721–733.

Chan, K. C., and Nai-Fu Chen. "An Unconditional Asset-Pricing Test and the Role of Firm Size as an Instrumental Variable for Risk," *Journal of Finance*, 1988, 43(2):309–325.

Chan, K. C., and Nai-Fu Chen. "Structural and Return Characteristics of Small and Large Firms," *Journal of Finance*, 1991, 46(4):1467–1484.

Chan, Kalok. "Imperfect Information and Cross-Autocorrelation among Stock Returns," *Journal of Finance*, 1993, 48(4):1211–1230.

Chan, Louis K. C., Yasushi Hamao, and Josef Lakonishok. "Fundamentals and Stock Returns in Japan," *Journal of Finance*, 1991, 46(5):1739–1764.

Chang, Eric C., and J. Michael Pinegar. "A Fundamental Study of the Seasonal Risk-Return Relationship: A Note," *Journal of Finance*, 1988, 43(4):1035–1039.

Cho, D. Chinhyung, Cheol S. Eun, and Lemma W. Senbet. "International Arbitrage Pricing Theory: An Empirical Investigation," *Journal of Finance*, 1986, 41(2):313–330.

Conine, Thomas E., Jr., and Maurry Tamarkin. "Implications of Skewness in Returns for Utilities' Cost of Equity Capital," *Financial Management*, 1985, 14(4):66–71.

Connor, Gregory, and Robert A. Korajczyk. "A Test for the Number of Factors in an Approximate Factor Model," *Journal of Finance*, 1993, 48(4):1263–1291.

Conrad, Jennifer S., Allaudeen Hameed, and Cathy Niden. "Volume and Autocovariances in Short-Horizon Individual Security Returns," *Journal of Finance*, 1994, 49(4):1305–1330.

Cooper, Ian A., and Evi Kaplanis. "Cost to Crossborder Investment and International Equity Market Equilibrium." In J. Edwards, Julian Franks, C. Mayer, and Stephen Schaefer, eds. *Recent Developments in Corporate Finance*. Cambridge, England: Cambridge University Press, 1986, 209–240.

Crum, Roy L., and Keqian Bi. "An Observation of Estimating the Systematic Risk of an Industry Segment," *Financial Management*, 1988, 17(1):60–62.

Davis, James L. "The Cross-Section of Realized Stock Returns: The Pre-COMPUSTAT Evidence," *Journal of Finance*, 1994, 49(5):1579–1593.

Donaldson, R. Glen, and Harald Uhlig. "The Impact of Large Portfolio Insurers on Asset Prices," *Journal of Finance*, 1993, 48(5):1943–1955.

Dubofsky, David A. "Volatility Increases Subsequent to NYSE and AMEX Stock Splits," *Journal of Finance*, 1991, 46(1):421–432.

Easley, David, and Maureen O'Hara. "Order from and Information in Securities Markets," *Journal of Finance*, 1991, 46(3):905–928.

Ehrhardt, Michael C., and Yatin N. Bhagwat. "A Full-Information Approach for Estimating Divisional Betas," *Financial Management*, 1991, 20(2):60–69.

Fama, Eugene F. "Stock Returns, Expected Returns, and Real Activity," *Journal of Finance*, 1990, 45(4):1089–1108.

Fama, Eugene F., and Kenneth R. French. "The Cross-Section of Expected Stock Returns," *Journal of Finance*, 1992, 47(2):427–466.

Fama, Eugene F., and Kenneth R. French. "Multifactor Explanations of Asset Pricing Anomalies," *Journal of Finance*, 1996, 51(1):55–84.

Fama, Eugene F., and Kenneth R. French. "Size and Book-to-Market Factors in Earnings and Returns," *Journal of Finance*, 1995, 50(1):131–155.

Fama, Eugene F., and James D. MacBeth. "Risk, Return and Equilibrium: Empirical Tests," *Journal of Political Economy*, 1973, 81(May):607–636.

Ferson, Wayne E., and Campbell R. Harvey. "Seasonality and Consumption-Based Asset Pricing," *Journal of Finance*, 1992, 47(2):511–552.

Gehr, Adam K., Jr. "Some Tests of the Arbitrage Pricing Theory," *Journal of the Midwest Finance Association*, 1978, 7:91–105.

Glosten, Lawrence R., Ravi Jagannathan, and David E. Runkle. "On the Relation Between the Expected Value and the Volatility of the Nominal Excess Return on Stocks," *Journal of Finance*, 1993, 48(5):1779–1801.

Gombola, Michael J., and Douglas R. Kahl. "Time-Series Processes of Utility Betas: Implications for Forecasting Systematic Risk," *Financial Management*, 1990, 19(3):84–93.

Gultekin, Mustafa N., and N. Bulent Gultekin. "Stock Return Anomalies and the Tests of the APT," *Journal of Finance*, 1987, 42(5):1213–1224.

Handa, Puneet, S. P. Kothari, and Charles Wasley. "Sensitivity of Multivariate Tests of the Capital Asset-Pricing Model to the Return Measurement Interval," *Journal of Finance*, 1993, 48(4):1543–1551.

Harris, Robert S., and Felicia C. Marston. "Estimating Shareholder Risk Premia Using Analysts' Growth Forecasts," *Financial Management,* 1992, 21(2):63–70.

Haugen, Robert A., Eli Talmor, and Walter N. Torous. "The Effect of Volatility Changes on the Level of Stock Prices and Subsequent Expected Returns," *Journal of Finance,* 1991, 46(3):985–1008.

Ibbotson Associates. *Stocks, Bonds, Bills, and Inflation 1997 Yearbook.* Chicago, Ill.: Ibbotson Associates, 1997.

Jagannathan, Ravi, and Zhenyu Wang. "The Conditional CAPM and the Cross-Section of Expected Returns," *Journal of Finance,* 1996, 51(1): 3–53.

Jegadeesh, Narasimhan. "Seasonality in Stock Price Mean Reversion: Evidence from the U.S. and the U.K.," *Journal of Finance,* 1991, 46(4):1427–1444.

Jones, Steven L., Winson Lee, and Rudolf Apenbrink. "New Evidence on the January Effect Before Personal Income Taxes," *Journal of Finance,* 1991, 46(5):1909–1924.

Kothari, S. P., Jay Shanken, and Richard G. Sloan. "Another Look at the Cross-section of Expected Stock Returns," *Journal of Finance,* 1995, 50(1):185–224.

Lintner, John. "The Valuation of Risk Assets and the Selection of Risky Investments in Stock Portfolios and Capital Budgets," *The Review of Economics and Statistics,* 1965, 47(1):13–37.

Loderer, Claudio, John W. Cooney, and Leonard D. Van Drunen. "The Price Elasticity of Demand for Common Stock," *Journal of Finance,* 1991, 46(2):621–652.

Longstaff, Francis A. "How Much Can Marketability Affect Security Values?" *Journal of Finance,* 1995, 50(5):1767–1774.

MacKinlay, A. Craig. "Multifactor Models Do Not Explain Deviations from the CAPM," *Journal of Financial Economics,* 1995, 38(1):3–28.

Maddox, Farris M., Donna T. Pippert, and Rodney N. Sullivan. "An Empirical Study of Ex Ante Risk Premiums for the Electric Utility Industry," *Financial Management,* 1995, 24(3):89–95.

Markowitz, Harry M. "Foundations of Portfolio Theory," *Journal of Finance,* 1991, 46(2):469–478.

Markowitz, Harry M. "Portfolio Selection," *Journal of Finance,* 1952, 7(1):77–91.

Markowitz, Harry M. *Portfolio Selection: Efficient Diversification of Investments.* New York: Wiley, 1959.

McQueen, Grant, and Steven Thorley. "Are Stock Returns Predictable? A Test Using Markov Chains," *Journal of Finance,* 1991, 46(1):239–264.

Mossin, Jan. "Equilibrium in a Capital Asset Market," *Econometrica,* 1966, October:768–783.

Pettengill, Glenn N., Sridhar Sundaram, and Ike Mathur. "The Conditional Relation Between Beta and Returns," *Journal of Financial and Quantitative Analysis,* 1995, 30(1):101–116.

Roll, Richard. "A Critique of the Asset Pricing Theory's Tests; Part I: On Past and Potential Testability of Theory," *Journal of Financial Economics,* 1977, 4(2):129–176.

Roll, Richard. "Industrial Structure and the Comparative Behavior of International Stock Market Indexes," *Journal of Finance,* 1992, 47(1):3–42.

Roll, Richard, and Stephen A. Ross. "On the Cross-Sectional Relation Between Expected Returns and Betas," *Journal of Finance,* 1994, 49(1):101–121.

Rosenberg, Barr, Kenneth Reid, and Ronald Lanstein. "Persuasive Evidence of Market Inefficiency," *Journal of Portfolio Management,* 1985, 11(3):9–17.

Ross, Stephen A. "The Arbitrage Theory of Capital Asset Pricing," *Journal of Economic Theory,* 1976, 13(December):341–360.

Sarig, Oded, and Arthur Warga. "Some Empirical Estimates of the Risk Structure of Interest Rates," *Journal of Finance,* 1989, 44(5):1351–1360.

Seyhun, H. Nejat. "Overreaction or Fundamentals: Some Lessons from Insiders' Response to the Market Crash of 1987," *Journal of Finance,* 1990, 45(5):1363–1388.

Shanken, Jay. "The Current State of the Arbitrage Pricing Theory," *Journal of Finance,* 1992, 47(4):1569–1574.

Shanken, Jay, and Clifford W. Smith, Jr. "Implications of Capital Market Research for Corporate Finance," *Financial Management,* 1996, 25(1):98–104.

Sharpe, William F. "Capital Asset Prices: A Theory of Market Equilibrium Under Conditions of Risk," *Journal of Finance,* 1964, 19(3):425–442.

Sharpe, William F. "Capital Asset Prices with and without Negative Holdings," *Journal of Finance,* 1991, 46(2):489–510.

Shukla, Ravi, and Charles Trzcinka. "Sequential Tests of the Arbitrage Pricing Theory: A Comparison of Principal Components and Maximum Likelihood Factors," *Journal of Finance,* 1990, 45(5):1541–1564.

Stattman, Dennis. "Book Values and Stock Returns," *The Chicago MBA: A Journal of Selected Papers,* 1980, 4, 25–45.

Stulz, Rene M., and Walter Wasserfallen. "Foreign Equity Investment Restrictions, Capital Flight, and Shareholder Wealth Maximization: Theory and Evidence," *Review of Financial Studies,* 8(4):1019–1057.

Trzcinka, Charles. "On the Number of Factors in the Arbitrage Pricing Model," *Journal of Finance,* 1986, 41(2):347–368.

Wei, K. C. John. "An Asset-Pricing Theory Unifying the CAPM and APT," *Journal of Finance,* 1988, 43(4):881–892.

VALUATION

Topic A: Capital Market Efficiency
Topic B: Options and Contingent Outcomes
Topic C: Financial Contracting

This section provides additional background material designed to enrich your understanding of the valuation process. Topic A focuses on the Principle of Capital Market Efficiency. We explain why it makes sense that capital markets should be efficient. You'll see that competition to profit from new information lies at the heart of capital market efficiency. We also explain how three persistent capital market imperfections, *asymmetric information, asymmetric taxes,* and *transaction costs,* interfere with capital market efficiency.

Topic B explores contingent claims, ownership rights that become valuable under certain circumstances. Such claims can also be called options, and they can occur naturally in the course of business dealings. They are not always easy to spot, however, and we point out several "hidden options" that can affect value and decision making.

Topic C is devoted to financial contracting, which is an important source of potential conflict among some of the company's many stakeholders, such as its stockholders, managers, debtholders, and consumers. We illustrate how these conflicts give rise to *agency costs* that affect the value of the company, and we explain how proper financial contracting can minimize these costs.

TOPIC A

Capital Market Efficiency

The prices of securities traded in *efficient* capital markets reflect all available information. Such prices adjust fully and quickly to new information. We first described the concept of capital market efficiency in chapter 2. Here, we explain why it makes sense that capital markets *should be* efficient. You'll see how the Principle of Capital Market Efficiency is a by-product of many people applying other principles of finance to the capital market environment. We'll also explain the limitations of capital market efficiency and how three persistent *capital market imperfections* interfere with capital market efficiency.

The capital markets have evolved to perform several important functions. To explain capital market efficiency, we must first examine these functions and see how capital markets should operate. We can then understand how (1) new information becomes reflected in securities prices, (2) transaction costs can inhibit this process, and (3) information about differences in value can create opportunities for profit. The first person to recognize and take advantage of such an opportunity can indeed profit but will, at the same time, eliminate the difference (*and* the opportunity). The competition to find and take advantage of such opportunities lies at the heart of capital market efficiency.

CAPITAL MARKET EFFICIENCY AND THE PRINCIPLES OF FINANCE

◆ *Self-Interested Behavior:* Self-interested capital market transactions force market prices toward being fair prices.

◆ *Two-Sided Transactions*: Intense capital market competition to get and use information to take advantage of arbitrage opportunities eliminates such opportunities.

◆ *Signaling:* Information in the transactions of others can be valuable, such as providing an accurate measure of current market value, or information about expected future value.

◆ *Risk-Return Trade-Off:* Differences between financial assets are measured primarily in terms of risk and return. Investors choose the highest return for a given risk level.

◆ *Capital Market Efficiency:* The fact that people apply the Principles of Self-Interested Behavior, Two-Sided Transactions, and Signaling to an environment characterized by similar financial assets, low transaction costs, and intense competition leads to capital market efficiency.

◆ *Valuable Ideas:* New ideas can provide value when first introduced, even in an efficient capital market.

◆ *Comparative Advantage:* Capital market efficiency allows a company to concentrate its primary efforts on its comparative advantage rather than on its day-to-day financing.

EFFICIENCY

Thinking of capital markets as being *perfect* can be hard to accept at first. But it's the right place to start out. It provides several important insights. The first is that investors cannot consistently earn abnormally high risk-adjusted returns, other than through extraordinarily good luck. This rather surprising implication has led to a great deal of criticism of the idea of perfect capital markets and to much doubt about the theory even though extensive evidence suggests that capital markets are efficient. We hope the following analogy will help you see the logic of capital market efficiency.

Efficiency refers to the amount of wasted energy. Efficient machines don't waste much energy. Friction—the "stickiness" between things—is the main reason for the waste of energy in a machine. Lubricants, such as oil, are used to increase the efficiency of machines by reducing friction that wastes energy. The more efficient a machine is, the better it is. So too for capital markets.

A capital market is like a machine. In a capital market, **frictions** are the "stickiness" in making transactions. They are the total "hassle," including the time, effort, money, and associated tax effects of gathering information and making a transaction such as buying stock or borrowing money. As with machines, efficiency is critical. Perfect efficiency represents an ideal, because unavoidable frictions keep a system (machine or market) from being perfectly efficient.

Conserving Energy

The physical law of energy conservation states that energy is neither created nor destroyed. Instead, energy is transformed from one form into another within a system. This law implies that no machine can be more than 100% efficient. So the energy output from a machine can never exceed the energy input to the machine. Simply stated, you can't get something for nothing! In the financial world, schemes that seem to provide more output than input are known as scams. They are illegal, yet they persist. We will talk more about them later.

Our story uses refrigeration to illustrate the limits of efficiency. Suppose it's a hot summer day and you're a poor student who can't afford the electric bills for running an air conditioner, let alone its initial cost. But on this particular day it is so hot you can't stand it. You go into the kitchen and open the refrigerator door to feel a blast of cool, refreshing air across your face. Thinking you have solved the problem, you decide to stay in the kitchen with the refrigerator door open. What will happen?

Refrigerators work like air conditioners, so why shouldn't it be able to cool the kitchen? A refrigerator takes heat from inside itself and puts that heat outside itself. But outside itself is still *inside* the kitchen, so the kitchen will not be cooled at all. In fact, because a refrigerator is substantially less than 100% efficient, energy escapes in the form of heat with each transfer. Thus the kitchen will actually heat up if you leave the refrigerator door open!

A machine's efficiency can't exceed 100% because of the law of energy conservation. In fact, machines don't ever have 100% efficiency because energy is lost to friction. If the refrigerator were 100% efficient, we could say that the transaction (leaving the door open) was costless (made no difference) in terms of increased temperature. But as we've said, transactions aren't costless.

Frictions in the Capital Markets: Transaction Costs

The analogy with the capital markets is that the transfer of assets from one party to another is like a transfer of heat from one area to another within the kitchen. The total wealth of the parties is like the temperature in the kitchen, with lower temperature corresponding to greater wealth. It makes no more sense to say that the total wealth of a group of people can be increased by the simple transfer of assets among them than it does to say that opening the refrigerator door can cool the kitchen! The only thing involved is a transfer from one to another.

You can make one individual better off at the expense of another individual, just as you can decrease the temperature inside the refrigerator by increasing the temperature outside it. So it's possible to make unbalanced transfers between people. (For example, we won't protest if you pay us $1000 for an asset that's worth only $800.) But the wealth of the two individuals, taken together, cannot be increased by a transfer between them, any more than the kitchen can be cooled by a transfer of heat within its boundaries.

Pressing the analogy a little further, just as the kitchen will heat up as a result of wasted energy from many heat transfers, the total wealth of two parties will be wasted by many transfers of assets between them. The waste occurs because of factors that we classify as *transaction costs, asymmetric taxes,* or *asymmetric information.* **Transaction costs** are the time, effort, and money necessary to make a transaction, including such things as commission fees and the cost of physically moving an asset from seller to buyer. We'll say a lot more about the other two later. These three factors are very much like friction: They slow down the process and waste resources (energy).

LIQUIDITY AND VALUE

The concept of **capital market efficiency** is linked to the concept of wasted wealth. An efficient capital market allows the transfer of assets with little loss of wealth. Capital market efficiency results from market prices reflecting all available information so that prices are *fair.* But what does it mean to reflect all available information?

There are three forms of capital market efficiency. The **strong form of capital market efficiency** requires that prices reflect *all* information that exists about the asset's value. This includes every bit of information known to anyone in the world that has any relevance whatsoever to the asset's value. The **semi-strong form of capital market efficiency** requires only that prices fully reflect *publicly available* information. Publicly available information is a subset of all the information that exists about an asset's value. The **weak form of capital market efficiency** requires only that prices fully reflect the information *contained in past asset market prices,* the prices at which assets have been exchanged. Past asset prices are a small subset of the publicly available information about an asset's value.

The relationships among various sets of information pertaining to the strong, semi-strong, and weak forms of capital market efficiency can be seen in figure A.1. It shows how the information sets are nested, or contained, within one another.

The Principle of Capital Market Efficiency refers to the semi-strong form of capital market efficiency. So when we use the phrase *all available information,* we mean all publicly available information. Infamous *insider-trading* scandals clearly demonstrate that the capital markets are not efficient in the strong form.

The Reason for Capital Markets: Liquidity

Society has evolved by developing new ideas and proce-dures that facilitate life, retaining the best and discarding the rest. In ancient times, each person met all his or her own needs. Over time, cooperative societies developed, and in-dividuals specialized in certain tasks. This change embod-ied the initial recognition and application of the Principle of Comparative Advantage. Still later, a barter society devel-oped, in which individuals exchanged goods and services to meet their needs. Finally, money was used to *represent* the goods and services—to collect and store resources—be-cause it's so easily exchanged. Money has proved so useful that today its logic is rarely questioned.

Money allows for the easy transfer of resources, just as liquids can flow through a tube better than solids. The rate at which a liquid flows through a tube depends on how thick the liquid is. This analogy leads to the idea of asset *liquidity.* Liquidity reflects how easily assets are trans-ferred without loss of value. Cash is the most liquid asset, because it is most easily transferred from one entity to an-other without loss of value. Real property, such as a build-ing, is a less liquid type of asset. Considerable time, effort, and money can be spent in finding a buyer willing to pay a fair price for a building. Alternatively, a substantially re-

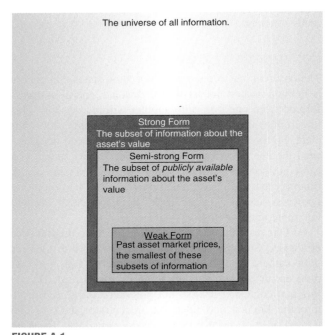

FIGURE A.1

Information, and the nested subsets of information about an asset's value pertaining to the strong, semi-strong, and weak forms of capital market efficiency.

duced price may attract a buyer quickly. Either way, it can be costly.

Liquidity is the primary reason for using money. Money enables us to exchange our efforts for another person's efforts without having to trade our services directly. Money also makes it possible to exchange one asset for another readily.

Exchanging Shares of IBM for Xerox Stock

EXAMPLE

Suppose you own 100 shares of IBM, but you'd rather have your money invested in Xerox stock (maybe you think Xerox is about to announce some great new computer technology). Although you might be open to the possibility of trading the IBM shares for Xerox shares directly, it's generally much easier to sell the IBM shares and then buy the Xerox shares. This saves your having to find a trading partner who wants exactly what you are offering (100 IBM shares) and who offers exactly what you want (Xerox shares of corresponding value). ■

Stocks are more liquid because of the stock market. Without it, you'd have to incur higher transaction costs—extra time, effort, and money. The stock market reduces the total transaction cost. In many markets, such as the New York Stock Exchange (NYSE), there is a *market maker* who increases liquidity by handling transactions in a particular asset. For example, when your orders to sell 100 IBM shares and buy Xerox stock are carried out on the NYSE, a *specialist* (market maker) handling each stock, rather than another individual investor like yourself, may be on the other side of the transaction.

In fact, markets are generally set up specifically to increase liquidity by reducing the transaction costs of asset transfer. Think about what you would do if there were no stock market and you wanted to sell your IBM shares. One possibility is to consider the Principle of Valuable Ideas: Set up a stock market yourself, provide a service to other people, and earn money. If you were the first, you might earn a positive NPV. Setting up a new market to provide liquidity for particular assets may be a valuable idea. Creating a viable new market provides a service that might earn a positive NPV. Creating a viable market can also make the Principle of Capital Market Efficiency come true.

This is exactly why capital markets exist. There are real benefits to the participants, which can be exploited for profit by those clever enough to do so.

An Unexpected Benefit: A Measure of Value

Even though markets are created in response to the need for liquidity, there's an additional benefit when market transactions are made public. Such transaction prices provide a measure of value that is visible to everyone.

Pricing GM Stock

EXAMPLE

Imagine you're going to invest in General Motors common stock. What price will you have to pay for the stock? There are a couple of ways to establish a fair price. You could call a broker and ask for the latest trading price. You could look in the finance or business section of a newspaper, such as the *Wall Street Journal,* to find yesterday's closing price. Which price would be likely to be more accurate? The latest price is the more accurate one, because it reflects any new information that has come to light since yesterday's close. But, yesterday's closing price is generally a very good approximation of the security's current fair price. ■

Most capital market transactions are reported publicly, and the information is conveniently available shortly after the transactions take place. This means that fair market prices for many securities are freely observable at any time.

So if you want to know what a share of GM is worth, find out the most recent actual transaction price, and you will have an accurate estimate of a share's value. After all, two parties actually transferred a share at that price. They didn't just talk about it or *offer* to buy or sell it. Moreover, the price isn't an average of many transactions from the last few weeks or months. The parties actually transferred shares within the last few minutes, and either one of them would have been willing for *you* to have been the other party in the transaction. (In most cases, they would not have known the difference if you had been!)

Therefore, even though liquidity is the main reason to create a market, a "spin-off" benefit of a public market is that it provides an inexpensive, fast, and accurate method of estimating fair prices: current market values.

Self-Check

1. What are the strong form, semi-strong form, and weak form of capital market efficiency? Which of these does the Principle of Capital Market Efficiency refer to?

2. What is publicly available information? What is its importance to the three forms of capital market efficiency?

3. What relevance do the infamous insider-trading scandals have to the three forms of capital market efficiency?

4. What benefits do markets provide?

5. Suppose you wanted to know the most current value of Colgate-Palmolive common stock. What price would contain that information?

ARBITRAGE: STRIVING FOR EFFICIENCY

Now that we know why capital markets were created, let's turn to their operation. In this and the next section we will present two concepts very important to the operation of the capital markets: *arbitrage* and *signaling*.

Getting Rich Quick?

Suppose the current price of a security in one market differs from the current price of that same security in a different market. Assume too that this information is available to one or more market participants. Someone who possesses this information can exploit it for profit by engaging in what is called arbitrage. **Arbitrage** refers to buying an asset in one market for the purpose of immediately re-selling it, at a higher price, in another market.[1] Arbitrage is an important factor in the efficient operation of any market, but especially a capital market.

When people first learn about arbitrage, their usual reaction is to say that it sounds wonderful but that they are skeptical about the existence of such opportunities. In spite of their (very healthy) skepticism, market prices do in fact differ between two markets for short periods. For example, consider an asset that is traded in two markets, such as shares of Exxon common stock. If Exxon shares were trading at a higher price on the Pacific Stock Exchange than on the NYSE, it would be possible to buy Exxon shares on the NYSE and resell them on the Pacific Stock Exchange for more than you paid for them.

Arbitrage is possible, whenever there is a price differential, by simply buying at the lower price and selling at the higher. The transactions, taken together, "lock in" a profit equal to the price differential multiplied by the number of shares simultaneously purchased and sold. This profit is riskless, because the shares purchased and sold offset one another exactly. There are people who earn a living exploiting arbitrage opportunities that they observe while watching different capital markets that trade the same asset.

One Definition of a Perfect Market   Later on, we'll list seven conditions that create a **perfect capital market.** But without getting into detail now, a convenient way to define a perfect capital market is simply to say that it's a market in which there are never any arbitrage opportunities.

Competition: If It's That Easy . . .

Now that you know what arbitrage is and that opportunities for earning a riskless arbitrage profit do exist, if you're like many of us, you may be considering applying the Principle of Self-Interested Behavior to participate in such a delightful process. You're not alone. Consequently, how often do you think trading price differences exist for the same asset between two markets? When they do exist, how large do you think the price differences are?

That's right—not very often, and not very large. Further, the larger the difference you're looking for, the less likely it is to occur. Rather than think this one through, we could have used a shortcut, the Principle of Capital Market Efficiency. Perhaps you were already applying it with your skepticism when we first told you about arbitrage.

There is an important implication of investor arbitrage. Suppose one investor discovers an arbitrage opportunity and trades securities to take advantage of it. When other investors become aware of this opportunity, the competition will eventually eliminate it. Consider the following example.

---

[1]We start by using the dictionary definition of arbitrage, or what may be termed "riskless arbitrage." The term *arbitrage* is also used in the sense of "risk arbitrage" to describe the purchase of stock in companies that are expected to increase in value in the future for reasons such as becoming a takeover target. Such purchases involve a large element of speculation. We'll discuss arbitrage versus speculation later.

Eliminating Arbitrage Opportunities

A few years ago, Edward O. Thorp, a "onetime university professor and mathematical whiz" who had developed arbitrage strategies for exploiting price discrepancies between a company's common stock and securities that were convertible into its common stock, closed his money management business after more than 20 years in the business and returned $200 million of his clients' money. Mr. Thorp had published some of his ideas in a book entitled *Beat the Market* and had set up a successful investment partnership that traded securities using his strategies. Mr. Thorp said he was withdrawing from the money management business because his ideas had become so widespread that only those investors with the lowest transaction costs could still use his arbitrage strategies profitably. His own success had helped to eliminate his arbitrage opportunities. ■

Competition among people engaged in arbitrage is actually an important contributing factor to capital market efficiency. The very existence of people, **arbitrageurs,** who are constantly looking for arbitrage opportunities, ensures that prices for a particular asset will not differ very much among the various markets where the asset is traded. If it is easy to access both markets, then there isn't much need for arbitrageurs. People making a transaction would buy or sell their assets for the best price provided by the two markets. When two markets are not easily accessed simultaneously, then it is worthwhile for arbitrageurs to incur the cost of accessing them, and in so doing to make transactions that push the two markets toward identical prices for a given asset. In time, competition among arbitrageurs will drive their NPV to zero. (Careful now—that doesn't mean the arbitrageur has a zero profit.)

When the NPV is zero, participants are getting exactly a fair return for the effort they are expending and an appropriate positive return for the risk they are taking on, and capital market efficiency is enforced.

Another important factor that contributes to the competitive environment of the capital markets is the similarity of financial assets. Financial assets are very similar. For example, consider a simple financial asset, a $10 bill. Would you exchange one $10 bill for another? Of course. Would you exchange a $10 bill for two $5 bills? Certainly. For the most part, people are indifferent to such exchanges. Forms of money are essentially equivalent. Almost any positive incentive (such as additional money or a polite request for change) will get people to exchange one form of money for another.

Similarity applies to securities as well as money. Let's say there are two securities that are exactly alike except for their expected return. The Principle of Risk-Return Trade-Off says that investors will choose the alternative with the higher expected return. Investors are fairly indifferent to owning shares in one company versus another, except for differences in return and risk. For example, most people do not have strong feelings, beyond the financial considerations of return and risk, about owning shares of stock in Ford versus Chrysler. Corporate bonds are also similar to government bonds, except that corporate bonds are riskier. For that matter, bonds are relatively similar to stocks, except that stocks are riskier.

When you think about it, compared to physical assets, financial assets are very similar to one another. Physical assets tend to be unique. There are many paintings, but there is only one Mona Lisa. Even two cars that are identical when they're made, can be very different after being used—one in excellent condition, the other a mess.

Because financial assets are so similar, investors can concentrate on the risk and return of an asset. When investors find two identical or even very similar investment opportunities, they will make transactions to increase the return on their investments, just as arbitrageurs do. Therefore, even though not all investors are primarily pursuing arbitrage opportunities, arbitrageurs must compete with the investing population as well as with each other.

Limits to Arbitrage: Transaction Costs

But how can arbitrage opportunities occur in efficient capital markets? How far apart do prices have to be for arbitrage opportunities to exist?

In theory, any price difference is an opportunity. In practice, however, transaction costs are not zero, and therefore if the difference between the prices is too small, arbitrageurs will not make a transaction because it won't be profitable. As you've probably already guessed, an arbitrage transaction is worth making only if the benefit exceeds the cost of the transaction.

Arbitrageurs have fixed and variable transaction costs. Variable transaction costs are specific to a particular arbitrage opportunity. For example, suppose a stock sells for 31⅛ in London and 31⅜ in New York, and that it will cost you ¹⁄₁₆ to buy in London, ¹⁄₁₆ to sell in New York, and ¹⁄₁₆ for transfer and communications costs. Consequently, it will cost you ³⁄₁₆ to make ¼ point. If you can buy and sell 1000 shares, you make $62.50.

This sounds good. You will have more than covered your variable costs, and earned a riskless arbitrage profit. But what about the cost of setting up your office and communication lines, educating yourself, and paying your support staff? These are fixed transaction costs, and they must be considered, too.

When two or more markets for the same asset exist, the differential between trading prices for the asset will exceed the variable cost of making a transaction only for a brief period. This period will be only as long as it takes arbitrageurs to buy and sell enough assets to reduce the price differential to less than the variable costs of making another transaction.

Because of arbitrage, *the price differential between markets is generally smaller than the variable transaction costs* for an asset traded in two markets.

How do variable transaction costs compare among different assets? How do the transaction costs of buying a used car in Los Angeles, taking it to Chicago, and selling it there compare with the costs of buying, transporting, and selling a share (or 1000 shares) of stock? Unless you have someone who wants to drive across the United States from Los Angeles to Chicago, getting a car between those points can be costly in time (yours or someone you pay) as well as in gas and vehicle wear. In contrast, the stock ownership can be transferred quickly and easily via telecommunications, and all at a fairly low cost.

Transaction costs for buying and selling financial assets are low compared with transaction costs for physical assets, for several reasons. The most important reason is simply the physical difference. A few sheets of paper, or instructions typed at a computer keyboard, are much easier to transport than 3000 pounds of automobile. A second important reason is market size. An enormous number of financial assets change hands every day. When many transactions take place, the fixed transaction costs are less on a per-transaction basis, because they can be spread over more transactions.

Since transaction costs for financial assets are so low (in both relative and absolute terms), price differentials for financial assets in different markets are tiny compared with price differentials for physical assets in different markets. Even on a percentage basis, price differentials for financial assets are relatively small because of low transaction costs and high competition among arbitrageurs. The low price differentials among markets reflect capital market efficiency.

Arbitrage versus Speculation

Let's return to our car example. Could we risklessly arbitrage used cars between areas of the country that have different market values for the same type of car?[2] Probably not, because the cars might need to be at both the purchase and sale points for careful inspection. This would eliminate the possibility of simultaneous purchase and sale. Literally speaking, a transaction that involves holding an asset for any length of time is not arbitrage.

We can't be specific about the time that determines where riskless arbitrage leaves off and speculation begins. But we can say that when the asset is held for any positive time, risk is introduced into the transaction. The longer the time between purchase and sale, the greater the risk. People who buy and sell a particular asset are not arbitrageurs but traders. **Traders** are people who engage in short-term speculation.

The continuum from arbitrage to speculation is important because in many cases, traders anticipate price changes using less than perfect information. Traders are involved in "small gambles." But they are investments, because they average a positive return. After all, if the average return were not positive, the trader could not continue to do business while sustaining losses.

"Slightly" speculative transactions, which anticipate price changes, smooth the transition from one price level to another. New information does not generally occur in a complete and correct form. The first inkling of new information may come as a rumor. A trader's talent for determining more quickly than other traders which rumors are true and which are false is valuable, because facts can translate directly into price changes that can be turned into profit.

Some talents can't be taught, and interpreting information may be one of them. But we can point out that some actions carry with them subtle implications about a company's current condition or its prospects for the future. This brings us to the topic of the next section.

---

[2]This is not a hypothetical example. Auto brokers are extensively involved in this process.

Self-Check

1. What is arbitrage? How does it contribute to capital market efficiency?

2. How long do arbitrage opportunities exist in an efficient capital market?

3. What is a perfect capital market? How long do arbitrage opportunities exist in such a market?

4. For an asset traded in two markets, what is the relationship between the price differential and the variable transaction costs?

5. Which type of assets has smaller price differentials between markets, common stocks or used motor homes?

6. What is the difference between arbitrage and speculation?

SIGNALING AND INFORMATION GATHERING

There is a very important concept underlying the Principle of Capital Market Efficiency: Market participants react quickly to events that convey useful information. This quick reaction is due in part to the Signaling Principle, which states that actions convey information.

Recall that *signaling* refers to using actual behavior to infer things you can't observe directly or find out in other ways. Signaling involves inferences concerning asymmetric information. **Asymmetric information** is information that is known to some people but not to others. Actions convey the asymmetric information, and in so doing eliminate it. Asymmetric information is a second imperfection, another one of the significant frictions in the capital markets.

We discuss the signaling aspects of dividend announcements in chapter 13. In an efficient market, participants react to the information signals contained in such announcements by making buy and sell decisions. Executing the trades will cause securities prices to change. This is the mechanism by which the information content of the signals becomes reflected in securities prices.

What Is Signaling?

In our discussion of the Signaling Principle in chapter 2, we introduced the concept of *adverse selection*. Adverse selection is a process of inferring negative information about a product or service. Adverse selection can discourage offering "good-quality" products or services, because doing so may give a seemingly negative signal. Consider the following example.

Selling a Used Car

EXAMPLE

Suppose you decide to sell your car. The question for a buyer is *why* do you want to sell the car? One possible reason for selling it is that it doesn't run well, and then buyers would be foolish to buy it. If the car is in fact a good car, one that buyers would like to buy, why would you be selling it?

This line of reasoning leads to the problem of adverse selection. Simply offering the car for sale can be a negative signal. How negative the signal is depends on how often sellers voluntarily sell good cars. Used-car prices will reflect this frequency.

If the only reason for selling a car is that it isn't worth fixing, all used cars would be worthless. In fact, there are used cars that turn out to be exceptionally good as well as exceptionally bad. Because there are reasons for selling a car other than its not being worth the trouble to repair, and because people have different levels of tolerance for car trouble, all used cars are not worthless. There is a chance that buying a used car will turn out well, and a chance it will turn out poorly. Many people who are not skilled at determining the quality of used cars always buy new cars to protect themselves from this problem. Others, skilled in evaluating the quality of a used car, put that skill to use and pay less for their dependable transportation. The savings represent the difficulty and cost—in time, effort, and money—of obtaining and using this valuable skill. ■

There have been many applications of the concept of signaling to financial transactions. Most applications are too technical to be detailed here, but it should be obvious that many daily events can be thought of as information signals. Companies make decisions nearly every day that provide an almost continuous flow of information about their current operations and intended future direction. For example, decisions about new equipment and raw materials, such as how much to buy and who to buy from, occur regularly. Other less frequent but telling information signals concern financing, such as decisions to issue new stock or bonds, or to change the dividend rate. Still other signals are decisions made not by the company itself but by people outside the company, such as decisions to buy the company's products.

Conditional Signals: Watching Management

It's important to note that some information signals are sent intentionally and others inadvertently. Suppose you're listening to a chief executive officer (CEO) of a corporation speak about the company's prospects for the future. The CEO paints a rosy picture, outlining plans for expanded production facilities to handle the projected increase in sales that will result in "big profits" for the next several years. The CEO is dynamic, enthusiastic, and persuasive.

But a week later, you find out the CEO sold 10,000 of the 15,000 shares she owned just 3 days after you heard the better-things-are-coming speech. How would it make you feel to learn that the CEO sold that stock? After you hear about the stock sale, what do you think the CEO really believed about the company's prospects for the next several years?

It's possible that the CEO merely sold the 10,000 shares to pay for a new yacht, and that the sale didn't negatively reflect on the company's prospects. However, most of us would consider it a negative signal if a person sells an asset while telling everyone else to buy it because of its investment value. Insider stock sales are often perceived as an indication of an upcoming change in a company's profitability.

Although this negative signal was fairly easy to read, many other signals can be positive or negative, depending on additional facts or decisions. For example, when a company announces that it plans to borrow money, you would want to know why. Without any further information, that announcement couldn't be considered positive or negative. Borrowing can be a positive signal of new investment opportunities, a negative signal of low sales or poor management, or a neutral signal of replacing worn-out equipment.

Interpreting Signals: A Very Valuable Talent

Most information is easily and costlessly available if you just wait long enough. IBM's sales data for last year are easily obtained from the library. But knowing what IBM's sales were for last year is not going to help you determine whether IBM's stock price will be higher or lower in the future. Some information, like the number of shares owned by management and how much money a company has borrowed, is published on a regular basis (every quarter or year), as required by the Securities and Exchange Commission (SEC). However, just like the sales figure from the library, it is unlikely that the information can be profitably used *after* it's published.

Traders, as well as speculators, who own stock for longer periods, are constantly searching for new information that will tell them if a stock price is going to increase or decrease in the future, so they'll know whether to buy or sell the shares now. Competition is intense to obtain information before prices reflect that information. The more often a trader or speculator obtains valuable new information *first,* the more money she makes. (Such competition has led some people to breach ethical and legal standards, creating insider-trading scandals.)

Of course, the more current that information is, the more difficult and costly it is to obtain. For example, a trader dealing in Wal-Mart's stock might pay someone to check local stores for the number of customers at various times and make statistical estimates of current sales, so that when Wal-Mart announces the latest sales figures, the trader has anticipated any stock price change that is due to higher- or lower-than-expected sales. Profits that a trader earns are the result of the cost—in time, effort, and money—of gathering information and using it to make informed trades.

When considering information like recent sales figures or amounts of borrowing, we are dealing with "hard facts." However, just as there is a continuum from arbitrage to speculation, there is a continuum for the quality of information. That continuum might be described, from one end to the other, as starting with hard information and moving to interpretive information, speculation, intuition, and finally to blind guess.

We interpret information using inductive reasoning. Most of us are familiar with **deductive reasoning,** where a *general* fact provides accurate information about a *specific* situation. For example, if a friend tells you he just got a new cat, you can predict with a high probability of being correct that the animal has four legs and a tail.

In contrast, **inductive reasoning** attempts the reverse, to use a *specific* situation to make *general* conclusions. Therefore, accuracy depends on having sufficient information. For example, suppose a friend tells you he has just brought home an animal that has four legs and a tail. Without more information, making an accurate prediction of what kind of animal your friend got is virtually impossible. The pieces of information that are uncovered for use with inductive reasoning may be obvious—such as knowing that your friend had planned to visit a person whose cat recently had kittens. However, the missing pieces of information are often quite subtle, such as spotting a few cat hairs on your friend's knee.

Some information can be drawn from truly obscure facts and interpreted in many different ways. Therefore, a person's talent for dealing with new or uncertain information is like any other talent a person might have, say in music, sports, or art. To some extent it's possible to teach people how to go about interpreting new or uncertain information. But as with other activities, there are differences in abilities among people despite identical training. Exceptional talent for dealing with new or uncertain information and interpreting information signals correctly has great value. For those of us who do not possess that unusual talent, it is still important to understand the process.

Self-Check

1. What is *signaling*? How is the information signaling conveys reflected in securities prices?

2. What is asymmetric information? How is signaling useful in eliminating asymmetric information?

3. Explain the concept of adverse selection.

4. Why is new information about a company whose shares are actively traded unlikely to create profitable opportunities after it is published?

THE COLLECTIVE WISDOM

With many different ways to interpret new and uncertain information, and with so many people competing for information, could one person be consistently right? The answer is no. Yet, surprisingly, stock prices are good predictors of the future. How can this be? The information about the future is contained in the collective wisdom. The **collective wisdom** is the combination of all of the individual opinions about a stock's value. It is the *net* opinion that results from intense competition, and it is more accurate than any single assessment.

Information in Stock Price Movement

As you know, prices in efficient markets reflect all available information. A logical implication of this statement is that any transaction you make in an efficient market has a zero NPV (that is, the cost equals the value). So why bother to invest? The answer is that a zero NPV includes a profit that is appropriate for the risk of the investment. So the reason to invest, then, is to earn a profit (and perhaps a large profit, if you're willing to take on considerable risk).

This is another very important implication of market prices reflecting all available information: *Price movements are random in an efficient market.* If you think about it, this *must* be the case. If price movements could be predicted before new information arrived, the information would already be here! Instead, price movements take place only after someone can better assess an asset's value based on new information. Thus, because price movements depend on information arrival and information arrives randomly, price movements must reflect that randomness.

It's important to distinguish between *anticipated* and *unanticipated* new information. Some information, such as earnings and dividend announcements, is available at regular intervals, such as quarterly. It is therefore anticipated by market participants, who will use whatever other information is available to formulate expectations and may then enter into securities transactions in anticipation of the release of the new information.

If traders were skilled enough to anticipate the new information perfectly, market prices would actually reflect fully the new information even *before* the official announcement. When the new information is not perfectly anticipated—as when market participants expect an earnings increase, but instead there is a decrease—there can be price adjustments both before and after the announcement.

Other information cannot be anticipated. An example would be a fire that destroys a company's production facilities, or the discovery of a revolutionary product. The occurrence of such events is essentially random in nature. In such cases, the market can react only after the event occurs and is disclosed.

Information can arrive over time, which causes the likelihood of a particular outcome to increase from unlikely to likely, and then from likely to actual occurrence. Securities analysts generate earnings forecasts and keep revising them up to the time of the actual earnings announcement. Although each securities analyst may have perfectly valid reasons for each earnings forecast revision, the series of earnings forecasts and revisions taken collectively looks like a random process. With each tiny change in the likelihood of an outcome, the value of that stock changes. Because new information arrives almost continuously, and its interpretation goes on continuously, there will be many price changes, and they will be random. In fact, stock prices change almost constantly for precisely this reason.

The virtually constant movement of stock prices may appear, at first glance, to reflect uncertainty about what a stock is worth. At this point, however, we hope you can see that the movement in stock prices is the result of constantly *reassessing* what a stock is worth. Price changes are the result of competition in the ongoing interpretation of all available information, so random stock price movement can result from *rational* behavior.

The amount of time it normally takes for a market price to adjust to new information is a measure of capital market efficiency. As we've said, in an efficient market, prices adjust quickly and fully (within minutes) to new information. The process can be shown visually.

Three alternative price reactions to new information about a stock's value are shown in figure A.2: The perfect-market reaction, in which the price adjusts instantaneously; an overreaction, where the price drops too much and then increases during the adjustment period to the correct level; and an underreaction, where the price does not react immediately but declines during the adjustment pe-

riod to the correct level. The smaller the adjustment period, the more efficient the market.

The Stock Market as an Important Leading Economic Indicator

Random stock price movement implies that no single person can consistently predict future stock prices correctly. Traders use information that lies somewhere along the continuum ranging from hard facts to blind guesses. Still, most of their decisions are educated guesses.

A trader who has extraordinary talent in interpreting information and predicting future stock prices with great accuracy can amass a fortune very quickly. People observing this talent will value that trader's opinion more highly than the opinions of others. These people, then, by watching, would be interpreting the information available to them. They would have another signal to watch: the expert trader.

Thus far, no single trader, analyst, or company has yet been consistently accurate enough to convince the rest of the world that he is *the* expert. Of course, some are more highly respected than others. As a group, however, their work and competition create prices that reflect the chances of future events more accurately than any single trader, analyst, or company. In fact, stock prices are so accurate at assessing the probabilities of future events that stock market indexes such as the Standard & Poor's 500 Index of common stock prices are among the most accurate leading economic indicators known.

Traders, or their representatives (who provide a valuable service for which traders are willing to pay), expend a lot of resources doing things like counting customers at Wal-Mart stores so they can translate those statistics into sales estimates, the sales into profit estimates, the profit into dividend estimates, the dividend estimates into predicted stock value, and finally, the predicted stock value into decisions to buy or sell.

The collective wisdom, as contained in a competitive price, generally provides a much more accurate assessment of value than any single assessment. It's always possible to find an assessment that at a particular point in time turns out to be more accurate than the market's assessment. However, we can establish this only after the fact. What has not yet been observed is an individual's assessment that is consistently, over a long period, more accurate than the market's competitive price.

There have been many temporary successes, with people who appear better than the market for a while. But even random guesses achieve some successes. For example, if you always pick heads when a coin is flipped, you'll choose correctly 50% of the time. Think about the next example.

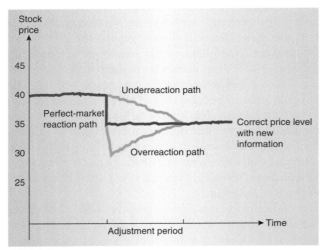

FIGURE A.2

Alternative price reactions to new information indicating a stock is worth less than previously thought.

Stock Market Prediction Experts

Suppose there are 4096 market forecasters, and their predictions are evaluated quarterly. Every quarter each forecaster is just as likely to pick the stock market's direction correctly as incorrectly. With a 0.5 probability of being correct each time, we can use the binomial probability distribution to show that during an average year, 256 will be correct in every quarter $(= [0.5]^4 = 6.25\%$; 6.25% of 4096 = 256).

Over a typical 2-year period, 16 will have correctly predicted the stock market's movement each quarter. Even over a 3-year period, on average, one of the forecasters will be exactly right *every* quarter. In spite of the equal likelihood of being right or wrong in any one quarter, 1 out of 4096 prognosticators on average will make 12 correct predictions in a row $(2^{12} = 4096)$.

From this you can see that a market forecaster can have a good run of luck, even if he doesn't possess any extraordinary predictive powers. Perhaps that's why an individual's time as a market "guru" is short lived! In fact, some forecasters have been strikingly accurate—but only for a limited time. (Note that 4096 is a very small number of forecasters compared to the actual number.) In any case, the competitive market price reflects the collective wisdom about the probabilities of all the possible outcomes, taking into account the cost of being wrong as well as the benefit of being right. ■

Self-Check

1. Why bother to invest when any transaction you make in an efficient market has a zero NPV?

2. How do prices behave in an efficient market? Why must this be so?

3. Explain how random stock price movement results from rational investor behavior. When stock prices behave this way, can any single trader expect to be able to consistently predict future stock prices correctly?

4. Explain the stock market's role as an important leading economic indicator.

5. Why is a string of correct forecasts not necessarily proof that a particular forecaster is smarter than the collective wisdom?

VALUE CONSERVATION

Perfect markets—meaning entirely frictionless—are perfectly efficient. Another important, and startling, implication of perfect markets is the concept of value additivity. **Value additivity** means that the value of the whole (a group of assets) exactly equals the sum of the values of the parts (the individual assets). Value additivity holds in a perfect capital market. If this weren't the case, there would be a profitable arbitrage opportunity. As we discussed earlier, people would exploit this opportunity until further profits were no longer possible; at that point value additivity would have been restored.

The Law of Value Conservation

The law of value conservation in finance is like the law of energy conservation in physics. If value is conserved across transactions, as it is in a perfect market, value additivity will exist among assets. In the case of two assets, value additivity can be stated in this way: The value of two assets combined equals the sum of their two individual values. Algebraically, if V(A) stands for the value of A, V(B) stands for the value of B, and V(A + B) stands for the combined assets, value additivity can be represented as

$$V(A + B) = V(A) + V(B) \qquad \text{(A.1)}$$

Note that this equation describes the process of separating assets as well as combining them. Also note that the equation can easily be generalized to more than two assets.

The two people most responsible for introducing the concept of value conservation into finance are Franco Modigliani and Merton Miller, commonly referred to as MM (pronounced "M 'n' M"). Both are Nobel Prize winners for their work because they changed the way people think about finance.

Recall that a zero-sum game is a situation where one person's gain (loss) is always another person's loss (gain). In the absence of any new information, an efficient market represents a *zero-sum-game* environment at a specific point in time. Value additivity results from competition within such an environment. It is an implication of the combined effect of capital market efficiency and two-sided transactions.

A word of caution is in order. As we said in chapter 2, the one significant factor that can cause capital markets to deviate from being a zero-sum-game environment is taxes. (We also pointed out, however, that even in the presence of taxes, the capital markets still represent a zero-sum-game environment when we include the government in the game.) Taxes are another imperfection, the last of our set of three significant frictions in the capital markets.

It sounds so simple to say that value is neither created nor destroyed when assets are exchanged, and yet extraordinary time and effort has gone into debating this issue. The fundamental question is whether an asset can be worth different amounts, depending upon whether it's attached to another asset. The Principle of Valuable Ideas says, in effect, that it may be possible to combine assets in value-increasing ways. But the Principle of Capital Market Efficiency says it isn't possible if people are already aware of the value-increasing possibility. How do we resolve this apparent contradiction?

Reconciling Valuable New Ideas with Capital Market Efficiency   A financial asset is really only a set of expected cash flows. If we combine cash flows from various sources, can they be worth more in total after they're combined than before? *Only if we are the first ones to think of making this valuable combination.* If the owners of the separate cash flow streams know that the cash flows are worth more when combined, they will either make the combination themselves or charge us the equivalent combined value for the assets because they *could* combine the cash flows themselves.

We could also ask the opposite question: Can cash flows be worth more if they're split up? Again, only if we're the first ones to think of a value-increasing breakup.

To appreciate the concept underlying the law of value additivity, recall our example of that simple financial asset, a $10 bill. Would you exchange a $10 bill for nine $1 bills? Of course not. But how about exchanging it for 11 of them? More interested? Value additivity says that breaking a $10 bill into several smaller assets does not change the total value—you'll still have $10 worth of assets.

Similarly, suppose you have two $5 bills. Can combining the two bills by exchanging them for one $10 bill make the total worth more than the sum of the two taken separately? No. Consider the following example.

EXAMPLE   *Dismembering a $10 Bill*

What if a $10 bill has been torn into four equal pieces, with each piece given to a different person. Individually, the pieces are all worthless—or are they? Suppose you know the four people who each hold a piece. You point out to each individual that the piece is worthless, but that you will be happy to take it off their hands at no cost to them. If everyone gives you their pieces, you'll have an asset worth $10. Assuming each person knows that the other three pieces are obtainable, however, the holders are not likely to *give* their pieces to you. The holders would be willing to *sell* their pieces to you for $2.50 each, but then there would be no reason for you to bother with the transaction, because it would cost you $10 for an asset worth $10. If the four individuals didn't want to bother spending the time, effort, and money to get together and make the deal themselves, however, you might get them to sell their pieces for less than $2.50 each. If they sold you the pieces for $2 each, you would make a "commission" of $2 on the transaction, and they would be paying a transaction cost of 50 cents each.[3] ∎

---

[3]Note that an interesting sunk-cost problem could arise. If you bought three of the pieces for $2.50 each and the holder of the fourth piece discovers that information, he could bargain for a higher price. How much higher? The $7.50 you have already paid is a sunk cost. If your three pieces are not worth anything without the fourth piece, the fourth person can demand up to $9.99, and you would be better off making the transaction, in spite of the $7.50 you already spent! (Of course, you might take nothing rather than let the fourth person "fleece" you. Acting out of frustration would be due to emotional rather than financial considerations.) To avoid this problem, you could bargain with each person separately and purchase options from them before making any transactions. Although the options would complicate the valuation problem by creating more "pieces," the whole would still be worth exactly $10.

The capital markets are just a more sophisticated application of this $10-bill example. Value additivity holds exactly when all the parts are included. That is, when the loss due to frictions is included, there is perfect conservation of value. More importantly, however, value additivity is the best approximation of a situation with relatively low transaction costs, as is the case with the capital markets.

A Chance for a Bigger Pie to Split: Lowering Your Taxes

Taxes can create a situation in which the environment is no longer a zero-sum game. This can happen when two parties pay taxes at different rates. When one records a dollar of revenue and the other records a dollar of expense in a single transaction, an asymmetry in taxes occurs if the two parties pay taxes at different rates. This is true because the revenue increases taxes collected, and the expense decreases taxes collected. But because the increase and decrease are taxed at different rates, the tax amounts are not equal. So the government may collect more or less taxes on the revenue than it gives up on the expense. This means there can be an advantage if the transaction reduces their combined tax bill. Such a situation is called a **tax asymmetry.**

Because people understand the phenomenon, the government generally collects fewer tax dollars when such tax asymmetries occur. Of course, in many of these cases people are doing exactly what the government is encouraging them to do.

For example, the government uses the tax code to encourage saving for retirement. It creates special advantages for Individual Retirement Accounts. The goal is to reduce the future burden on social programs. As a second example, the government has sometimes encouraged investment in new capital equipment to spur the economy by providing an investment tax credit.

The Tax Treatment of Zero-Coupon Bonds

EXAMPLE

A tax asymmetry Congress may not have intended involves zero-coupon bonds. A zero-coupon bond (sometimes called a pure-discount bond) is like a Treasury bill, except that it has a much longer life. A zero-coupon bond sells on a discount basis because it makes no interest payments between the time it's issued and the time it matures.

For example, a zero-coupon bond might be sold for $100 when issued and pay $1000 20 years later. The interest compounds over the life of the bond. That is, the discount ($900 in the example) is the total amount of interest over the bond's entire life.

The Internal Revenue Code, at one time, permitted the issuer and the holders to allocate equal amounts of the discount to each year of the bond's existence, rather than allocate the discount on the basis of how interest would truly compound. By using the straight-line allocation of interest expense, the company lowers its present value cost of taxes because it claims the interest sooner, even though the total amount claimed over the life of the security is the same.

Continuing our example, interest would be allocated as $45 for each of the 20 years (= 900/20). This amount was both claimed by the company as an expense and recorded as income by each bondholder. As we know, the dollar amount of interest actually compounds slowly at first but increases over time. That is, the interest earned on past interest grows from one year to the next. The actual interest accrued is $12.20 in the first year and $108.75 in the last year. Thus, the company is overstating its interest expense for tax purposes in the early years ($45 vs. $12.20 in the first year), and understating its interest expense in the later years.

This "incorrect" allocation of the interest expense causes a shift in the company's tax payments: Lower taxes are paid in the early years, and higher taxes are paid in the later years, than would be paid under the "correct" allocation. Although the total underpayment in the early years exactly equals the total overpayment in the later years, this shift is valuable to the company because of the time value of money. The company can invest the tax underpayments in the early years so that it will have more than enough money to cover the added cost of the tax overpayments in the later years.

(continued on following page)

(The Tax Treatment of Zero-Coupon Bonds *continued from previous page*)

The shift in tax payments is good for the company, but the Principle of Two-Sided Transactions reminds us to look at the other side of the transaction—the bondholders' position in the scheme of things. Sure enough, the shift in tax payments is bad for the bondholders. However, in spite of the apparently bad position for the bondholders, several billion dollars worth of zero-coupon bonds were issued in the years 1979 through 1982. The buyers were primarily tax-exempt investors, such as pension funds. Such investors pay no taxes, so that the shift in interest payments for tax purposes is irrelevant to them. The decrease in taxes collected from the issuing corporations was not being offset by an increase in taxes collected from the bondholders.

As more companies learned about this opportunity, the number of new zero-coupon bonds being issued each month began to dramatically increase. When the IRS realized that this tax asymmetry was occurring on a large scale and significantly affecting the taxes being collected, it asked Congress to change the tax law. Congress agreed, and the rule for allocating interest expense/income for a zero-coupon bond was changed to how it actually compounds, to accurately reflect each year's interest cost. ■

Zero-coupon bonds are only one example of many tax asymmetries that have occurred or that still exist. A lot of attention has been given to tax asymmetries connected with leasing. For example, a significant reduction in the tax deductibility of personal interest at one point substantially increased the attractiveness of leasing to many individuals, and dramatically increased the car leasing market. Although most tax asymmetries exist by congressional design, many people spend considerable effort looking for others to exploit for profit.

Apparent Exceptions to Value Additivity

People are often reluctant to believe that value conservation is the best approximation of the valuation of assets traded in capital markets. To some extent, this skepticism may rest on the hope for an easy way to riches, or on what people perceive as exceptions to the conservation of value.

There are some apparent exceptions worth mentioning. The first concerns a privately owned company that issues its stock publicly for the first time. Frequently, the value of the shares is larger after going public. This situation looks like a clear violation of the law of value conservation and therefore a violation of value additivity as well. However, it isn't necessarily a violation of value additivity, because going public increases the liquidity of the shares.

EXAMPLE   *Going Public*

Consider the owners of a privately held company who've decided they want to sell shares of stock in their company. The first step in the process is to find potential buyers for the stock. It can take substantial time, anxiety, and money to locate buyers. In many markets there are specialists paid to *search* for potential buyers. After locating one or more potential buyers, each of the parties (the company and each buyer) must assess the value of the company. This is a second task that takes time, effort, and money. After valuing the company, they must negotiate to reach agreement for any sale.

When a potential buyer is thinking about buying stock, she must consider resale, especially due to unforeseen future events. Purchasers in a private transaction face significant restrictions on their ability to resell their shares of stock unless they register them under the U.S. securities laws.

Assume for the moment that the stock in question is unregistered. What would happen if it becomes necessary to resell shares? Who would buy them? Realistically, "sophisticated purchasers" (high-net-worth individuals and financial institutions) would be the only potential buyers for the unregistered shares, unless the holder could convince the company to go to the time, trouble, and expense of registering the stock before the resale.

What would these *other* investors be willing to pay for the shares? They would have an awareness of the resources used to get this far in the negotiations for *this* sale. These contingencies increase the buyer's risk. Because of the higher risk, the Principle of Risk-Return Trade-Off tells us that buyers will lower the price they're willing to pay in order to raise their expected return to compensate for the higher risk.

Now consider the same scenario but with the resources that the current owners put into finding potential buyers instead going into registration for public sale. In this second case, when potential buyers consider the purchase of shares, one aspect of risk and transaction costs has been removed. With the stock registered for public sale, there is a much higher likelihood that a resale could be transacted quickly and at low cost. Shareholders can sell in the public market. They are not restricted to selling to sophisticated investors, as they are in the case of a private transaction. (Registration does nothing to guarantee the resale price.)

The process of going public appears to add value to the company. However, we hope you can see that value has not actually been *created*. Rather, transaction costs have been reduced: There is a broader market, so the time and cost of locating buyers have been reduced. Investment risk has also been reduced, because of increased liquidity and the greater valuation accuracy that comes from public prices and more people valuing the company. Finally, the costs of transferring ownership have been reduced. In short, the increased liquidity of the shares, due to their public registration and their being traded in the stock market, is valuable. ∎

Let's look at one other apparent exception to value additivity.

Pyramid Schemes

EXAMPLE

The **pyramid scheme** is a scam in which a con artist tells victims that they can earn an extraordinary return on their money, such as 10% per quarter, with no risk. The con artist takes the money, then returns the investment with the promised interest one quarter later, and inquires about reinvesting. The soon-to-be victim is pleased because he has gotten the money back with tremendous interest, as promised. Usually people reinvest their money and can be called upon to cajole some friends into investing, too.

The con artist takes in the invested money, using the new money coming in to pay off any investors who want to quit. Most people naturally want to keep their money invested in such a great investment, so the outflow for "quitters" is small for quite a while. In the meantime, a lot of money comes in.

From the start, the amount of promised money exceeds the amount of money actually held by the con artist, and over time, the difference between promised returns and funds available grows and eventually becomes enormous. At some point, the con artist disappears, along with whatever money actually remains.

This may seem to be an unlikely scenario because of the difficulty of pulling it off. The scheme is illegal, and there are many checks in the system to prevent its occurrence. However, in each of the last three decades there have been one or more pyramid schemes that have been at least partially successful for the con artist.

The pyramid scheme is not an exception to value additivity, because the cash to pay interest to those who wish to withdraw is obtained from others who have been sucked in. Value is not created; it is simply transferred from one group of participants to another, while the promoter takes a sizable "commission." ∎

PERFECT CAPITAL MARKETS

Earlier, we noted that certain market imperfections such as transaction costs can limit market efficiency, chiefly by interfering with the arbitrage process. We also defined a perfect capital market simply as a market in which there are never any arbitrage opportunities. More formally, a perfect capital market is one in which the following are true:

1. There are no barriers to entry that would keep any potential suppliers or users of funds out of the market.

2. There is perfect competition—that is, each participant is sufficiently small that its actions cannot affect prices.

3. Financial assets are infinitely divisible.

4. There are no transaction costs, including no bankruptcy costs.

5. All existing information is fully available to every capital market participant without charge.

6. There are no tax asymmetries.

7. There are no government or other restrictions on trading.

Do these perfect market conditions describe existing capital markets? The answer is yes, very well, but not *perfectly* (contradiction—and pun—intended). How far a market deviates from these seven conditions determines how "imperfect" the market is. For example, if there are few participants in the market for a stock, and the flow of information to investors is very poor because there are no securities analysts who monitor the stock and prepare research reports on it, the market for the stock may not always behave efficiently.

Despite their lack of perfection, the idea of a perfect market is an excellent starting point for analysis. The Principle of Capital Market Efficiency states that the capital markets are efficient—but how far is "efficient" from perfect? We don't have a precise way of separating the two concepts, but our seven conditions provide us with guidance in looking for important exceptions to a perfect capital market. If you think about it, you might see that we've already told you how the capital markets are imperfect. We have identified three significant frictions in the capital markets, three persistent capital market imperfections. Let's summarize.

Asymmetric Taxes

Asymmetric taxes are one significant type of market imperfection. Because tax laws change quite frequently, we generally refrain from getting into too much detail about them in this book. At various points, we describe some tax asymmetries that have existed for quite a while and are relevant to major corporate decisions. However, even those tax asymmetries might be changed by Congress. It's important to remember to check for tax asymmetries as a potential explanation for transactions that otherwise would appear to be a zero-sum game.

Asymmetric Information

A second type of significant market imperfection concerns the availability of information. In our discussion on speculation we pointed out the importance and cost of obtaining information. New information relevant to pricing a security is not costless and available to everyone. However, because competition puts new information into prices so quickly and information is published almost as quickly, it is a good approximation of the environment to say that information is freely available to everyone. Signaling is an important component of the flow and interpretation of information. As with tax asymmetries, information flow—sending signals—is a potential explanation for transactions that otherwise would appear to be a zero-sum game.

Transaction Costs

Transaction costs are a third imperfection we discussed. Unbelievable as this may sound, transaction costs may be less important than asymmetric taxes and asymmetric information. Transaction costs affect transactions in a way that is fundamentally different from the effects of asymmetric taxes and asymmetric information. Transaction costs are usually symmetrical. Although they may inhibit arbitrageurs, traders, and speculators from making transactions, transaction costs do not *bias* prices upward or downward, nor do they provide an incentive for making a transaction. That is, they do not create profit in and of themselves, except for the financial intermediary collecting a commission or finding a way to structure a transaction that reduces transaction costs.

The significant effect that transaction costs can have is to favor one *type* of transaction over another. For example, the existence of fixed transaction costs favors less frequent larger transactions over more frequent smaller ones. Note that price discounts because of a lack of liquidity are transaction costs.

Despite the existence of these three imperfections, perfect is a very good approximation for most segments of the capital markets. Value conservation—value is neither created nor destroyed through splitting or combining cash flows—is the best *starting* point for financial analysis. This is why we so often use this "starting-with-a-clean-slate" approach in our analyses.

Self-Check

1. Cite the seven characteristics of a perfect capital market.

2. Describe three significant capital market imperfections.

3. Are transaction costs likely to be more, or less, important than asymmetric taxes and asymmetric information in inhibiting capital market efficiency?

4. Why does a perfect capital market serve as the best starting point from which to analyze capital market transactions?

SUMMARY

The Principles of Self-Interested Behavior, Two-Sided Transactions, Signaling, and Risk-Return Trade-Off combine with the similarity of financial assets, low transaction costs, and large size in a very competitive market environment and lead us to the Principle of Capital Market Efficiency.

- Transaction costs are the time, effort, and money necessary to make a transaction.

- Capital market efficiency states that, at any point in time, capital market prices reflect all available information and adjust fully and quickly to new information. Although disparities in valuation can occur, these will prove temporary when transaction costs are low, because arbitrage activity will tend to eliminate them quickly and restore efficient pricing.

- The strong form of capital market efficiency requires that market prices reflect *all* information that exists about the asset's value. The semi-strong form of capital market efficiency requires that market prices reflect all *publicly available* information. The weak form of capital market efficiency requires that prices fully reflect the information *contained in past asset market prices.*

- Price movements in an efficient market are random because market participants will react to each new piece of information, and the events that generate this new information occur randomly.

- Market prices at any point in time will reflect the up-to-date collective wisdom of the market participants about the "correct" value of each asset.

- Arbitrage is the act of buying and selling an asset simultaneously, where the sale price is more than the purchase price, providing a riskless profit.

- Market participants will interpret each new event and respond with buy and sell decisions. This involves the interpretation of many events, such as dividend or new product announcements, as *signals* regarding possible changes in the company's financial condition or prospects.

- A perfect market is a market where there are never any arbitrage opportunities. A perfect market is one in which:
  - There are no barriers to entry
  - There is perfect competition
  - Financial assets are infinitely divisible
  - There are no transaction costs
  - All information is fully available to everyone without cost
  - There are no tax asymmetries
  - There are no restrictions on trading

- Conservation of value across transactions leads to value additivity. In the special case of a perfect capital market, where there are no frictions such as asymmetric taxation or transaction costs and information is fully and costlessly available to everyone, the value of combined assets exactly equals the sum of their individual values. As a result, the law of value conservation holds: Value is neither created nor destroyed when assets are combined or separated. Transaction costs appear to cause only minor departures from value additivity because they are not biased. That is, in most cases, both parties to a transaction must pay approximately equivalent transaction costs.

- Asymmetric taxes can cause the capital markets to deviate from being a zero-sum-game environment. So tax-related factors might be responsible for transactions that would otherwise seem to be zero-sum games. In practice, tax-related factors are often the driving force behind a transaction.

- Asymmetric information is an important capital market imperfection and a frequent reason for making transactions. Such transactions can be the method by which the asymmetric information is eliminated and put into security prices.

- Transaction costs don't generally cause a bias in prices. However, as we show later, transaction costs can have important effects on decisions.

- In spite of capital market imperfections, the assumption of a perfect capital market usually serves as the best starting point from which to analyze capital market transactions.

TOPIC REVIEW ACTIVITIES

SELF-TEST PROBLEMS

1. (Arbitrage opportunities) Which of the following transactions would allow you to make arbitrage profits?
   a. You may buy 1,000 shares of Benet Bancorporation for 61¼ per share in Toronto and sell them for 61½ in Seattle. Transactions costs will be ½ per share.
   b. You may buy a used diesel engine in Phoenix for $4500 and ship it to St. Louis and sell it for $5700. Transaction and shipping costs total $700.
   c. You may buy a Richmond Utility bond for $700 from a small Georgia bank and sell it for $730 to a Baltimore bond dealer. Commissions will be $40.

2. (Transaction costs) Jackie Dunn sold her condo for $150,000. She paid a sales commission of 6% ($9000) to the real estate brokers, had legal fees of $750, and had additional selling costs of $1250.
   a. What are Jackie's total transaction costs?
   b. What are her transaction costs as a percentage of the gross selling price?
   c. What are her transaction costs as a percentage of her net proceeds?

SOLUTIONS TO SELF-TEST PROBLEMS

1. a. Transaction costs of $0.50 per share are greater than the price spread of $0.25 per share, so no profit is possible.
   b. The price spread of $1200 exceeds the transaction and shipping costs of $700 by $500, so this is a profitable transaction.
   c. The $40 commission exceeds the $30 price difference, so do not transact.

2. a. Total transaction costs = $9000 + $750 + $1250 = $11,000.
   b. Transaction costs/gross selling price = 11,000/150,000 = 7.33%

   c. Net proceeds = Gross selling price − Transaction costs = $150,000 − $11,000 = $139,000.
      Transaction costs/Net proceeds = 11,000/139,000 = 7.91%

QUESTIONS

1. Explain how public securities prices provide a measure of value.
2. Define the term *riskless arbitrage.*
3. How can arbitrage be used to define a perfect market?
4. What are the conditions that must exist for a perfect market to exist?
5. Respond to the following: "Why should I invest in the capital markets when I don't earn any money—that is, when I get a zero NPV?"
6. What do we mean when we say that financial assets are very similar?
7. What does the term *collective wisdom* mean?
8. Why is it important to distinguish between anticipated and unanticipated new information?
9. What is value additivity?
10. Describe what we mean by the term *asymmetric taxes.*
11. What is asymmetric information?
12. Cite and briefly discuss three types of capital market imperfections that may affect corporate decision making.
13. Originally, the capital markets were created to bring users and suppliers of capital together. In addition to this important purpose, we now find that there are important side benefits. Cite and discuss three benefits that capital markets provide for society.
14. Explain the importance of arbitrage to the efficiency of the capital markets.
15. Is the following statement true or false? Because arbitrageurs sell assets for more than they paid for them, arbitrageurs must make a lot of money. Justify your answer.
16. Explain how an increase in the liquidity of a financial security can appear to be a violation of value additivity.
17. Explain how the similarity of assets contributes to the efficiency of the capital markets.
18. Describe the problem of adverse selection in your own words.
19. Describe the law of value conservation in your own words.

CHALLENGING QUESTIONS

20. Applying the Signaling Principle involves inductive reasoning. Cite an important aspect of inductive reasoning that can make some applications of this principle extremely difficult.
21. Evaluate the following statement. As the evidence seems to suggest, price movements are random; this clearly implies that the capital markets are not functioning well.
22. Rank the following assets from the most liquid to the least:
    a. Cash
    b. 400 shares of McDonald's Corporation
    c. A two-year-old Ford Taurus
    d. One of Chagall's lesser-known paintings

23. In each of the following situations, indicate whether the strategy is a violation of the weak form of market efficiency, the semi-strong form of market efficiency, or the strong form of market efficiency. Each person expects to earn an abnormally high return from his or her decision.

a. Michael buys 100 shares of ABBA Corporation because it had an extraordinary total return exceeding 100% last year.

b. Sheila buys stock in Utah Gaming because it has a high ratio of the market value of the stock to book value.

c. Edward has been selling cocaine to Charles, an employee of a financial printer. Edward has decided to invest in Memphis Multimedia because Charles has confided in him that the company is about to report quarterly earnings that are substantially above analysts' expectations.

d. Susan is buying a pharmaceutical stock because the Food and Drug Administration announced approval of an important new drug that the company will market in the United States.

24. Two companies both announce 20% earnings increases. One company's stock increases substantially and the other company's stock is basically unchanged. Why did the market react differently to these announcements?

25. Explain how the effect of transaction costs on market prices is fundamentally different from the effects of asymmetric taxes and asymmetric information.

26. Comment on the following statement: "If *all* markets were perfect, it would be both a blessing and a curse."

PROBLEMS

B1. (Arbitrage) You can purchase gold bullion in Zurich for $450.50 per ounce and sell it in London for $452.75 per ounce.

a. If transaction costs are $3.50 per ounce, can you earn an arbitrage profit on trading gold?

b. What is the largest transaction cost you could absorb with these gold prices and still make a profit?

B2. (Arbitrage) A large investor wants your company to help him sell a large block of 50,000 shares of a stock. The current market price of the stock is $36.00 per share. When this block of stock hits the market, it may depress prices from their current level. Consequently, this investor is willing to sell to your company at a price of $34.00 per share.

a. If transaction costs are $0.40 per share and the market price does not move, what profit would your company make with this deal?

b. If the market price drops to $33.00 per share, what profit would your company make?

c. What is the largest price drop that would still enable your company to make a profit?

B3. (Arbitrage opportunities) Which of the following transactions would allow you to make arbitrage profits?

a. You may buy 15,000 shares of Denver Crude Drilling Company for 2⅛ per share in New York and sell them for 2⅝ in Atlanta. Transactions costs will be ¼ per share.

b. You may buy a used single-engine plane in Phoenix for $135,000 and fly it to Vancouver and sell it for $148,000. Transaction, licensing, and shipping costs total $18,000.

c. You may buy a Tuscarora general obligation bond for $1050 from an acquaintance and sell it to a municipal bond dealer. Commissions will be $20.

B4. (Transaction costs) Steve Bolten sold his sailboat for $225,000. He paid a sales commission of 10% ($22,500) to the boat brokers, had legal fees of $500, and had additional selling costs of $1000.

a. What are Steve's total transaction costs?

b. What are his transaction costs as a percentage of the gross selling price?

c. What are his transaction costs as a percentage of his net proceeds?

BIBLIOGRAPHY

Ackert, Lucy F., and Brian F. Smith. "Stock Price Volatility, Ordinary Dividends, and Other Cash Flows to Shareholders," *Journal of Finance,* 1993, 48(4):1147–1160.

Affleck-Graves, John, Shantaram P. Hegde, and Robert E. Miller. "Trading Mechanisms and the Components of Bid-Ask Spreads," *Journal of Finance,* 1994, 49(4):1471–1488.

Affleck-Graves, John, and Richard R. Mendenhall. "The Relation Between the Value Line Enigma and Post-Earnings-Announcement Drift," *Journal of Financial Economics,* 1992, 31(1):75–96.

Akerlof, George A. "The Market for 'Lemons': Quality Uncertainty and the Market Mechanism," *Quarterly Journal of Economics,* 1970, 84(August):488–500.

Ariel, Robert. "High Cost Returns Before Holidays: Existence and Evidence on Possible Causes," *Journal of Finance,* 1990, 45(5):1611–1626.

Baker, H. Kent, and Richard B. Edelman. "AMEX-to-NYSE Transfers, Market Microstructure, and Shareholder Wealth," *Financial Management,* 1992, 21(4):60–72.

Balvers, Ronald J., Thomas F. Cosimano, and Bill McDonald. "Predicting Stock Returns in an Efficient Market," *Journal of Finance,* 1990, 45(4):1109–1128.

Bathala, Chenchuramaiah T., Kenneth P. Moon, and Ramesh P. Rao. "Managerial Ownership, Debt Policy, and the Impact of Institutional Holdings: An Agency Perspective," *Financial Management,* 1994, 23(3):38–50.

Benveniste, Lawrence M., Alan J. Marcus, and William J. Wilhelm. "What's Special About the Specialist?" *Journal of Financial Economics,* 1992, 32(1):61–86.

Berry, Thomas D., and Keith M. Howe. "Public Information Arrival," *Journal of Finance,* 1994, 49(4):1331–1346.

Best, Ronald, and Hang Zhang. "Alternative Information Sources and the Information Content of Bank Loans," *Journal of Finance,* 1993, 48(4):1507–1522.

Bhardwaj, Ravinder K., and LeRoy D. Brooks. "The January Anomaly: Effects of Low Share Price, Transaction Costs, and Bid-Ask Bias," *Journal of Finance,* 1992, 47(2):553–576.

Bhide, Amar. "The Hidden Costs of Stock Market Liquidity," *Journal of Financial Economics,* 1993, 34(1):31–51.

Black, Fischer. "Presidential Address: Noise," *Journal of Finance,* 1986, 41(3):529–544.

Blume, Lawrence, David Easley, and Maureen O'Hara. "Market Statistics and Technical Analysis: The Role of Volume," *Journal of Finance,* 1994, 49(1):153–181.

Brennan, Michael J., and Patricia J. Hughes. "Stock Prices and the Supply of Information," *Journal of Finance,* 1991, 46(5):1665–1692.

Brous, Peter A., and Omesh Kini. "The Valuation Effects of Equity Issues and the Level of Institutional Ownership: Evidence from Analysts' Earnings Forecasts," *Financial Management,* 1994, 23(1):33–46.

Campbell, Cynthia J., Louis Ederington, and Prashant Vankrudre. "Tax Shields, Sample-Selection Bias, and the Information Content of Conversion-Forcing Bond Calls," *Journal of Finance,* 1991, 46(4):1291–1324.

Chan, Kalok, Y. Peter Chung, and Herb Johnson. "Why Option Prices Lag Stock Prices: A Trading-Based Explanation," *Journal of Finance,* 1993, 48(5):1957–1967.

Chatterjea, Arkadev, Joseph A. Cherian, and Robert A. Jarrow. "Market Manipulation and Corporate Finance: A New Perspective," *Financial Management,* 1993, 22(2):200–209.

Christie, William G., Jeffrey H. Harris, and Paul H. Schultz. "Why Did NASDAQ Market Makers Stop Avoiding Odd-Eighth Quotes?" *Journal of Finance,* 1994, 49(5):1841–1860.

Christie, William G., and Paul H. Schultz. "Why Do NASDAQ Market Makers Avoid Odd-Eighth Quotes?" *Journal of Finance,* 1994, 49(5):1813–1840.

Conrad, Jennifer, and Gautam Kaul. "Long-Term Market Overreaction or Biases in Computed Returns?" *Journal of Finance,* 1993, 48(1):39–64.

Conroy, Robert M., Robert S. Harris, and Bruce A. Benet. "The Effects of Stock Splits on Bid-Ask Spreads," *Journal of Finance,* 1990, 45(4):1285–1295.

Copeland, Thomas E., and Won Heum Lee. "Exchange Offers and Stock Swaps—New Evidence," *Financial Management,* 1991, 20(3):34–48.

Cornell, Bradford, and Erik R. Sirri. "The Reaction of Investors and Stock Prices to Insider Trading," *Journal of Finance,* 1992, 47(3):1031–1060.

Cox, Don R., and David R. Peterson. "Stock Returns Following Large One-Day Declines: Evidence on Short-Term Reversals and Longer-Term Performance," *Journal of Finance,* 1994, 49(1):255–268.

Daves, Phillip R., and Michael C. Ehrhardt. "Liquidity, Reconstruction, and the Value of U.S. Treasury Strips," *Journal of Finance,* 1993, 48(1):315–330.

DeBondt, Werner F. M., and Richard H. Thaler. "Further Evidence on Investor Overreaction and Stock Market Seasonality," *Journal of Finance,* 1987, 42(3):557–581.

Dezhbakhsh, Hashem, and Asli Demirguc-Kunt. "On the Presence of Speculative Bubbles in Stock Prices," *Journal of Financial and Quantitative Analysis,* 1990, 25(1):101–112.

Dubofsky, David A. "A Market Microstructure Explanation of Ex-Day Abnormal Returns," *Financial Management,* 1992, 21(4): 32–43.

Easley, David, and Maureen O'Hara. "Time and the Process of Security Price Adjustment," *Journal of Finance,* 1992, 47(2):577–606.

Ederington, Louis H., and Jae Ha Lee. "How Markets Process Information: News Releases and Volatility," *Journal of Finance,* 1993, 48(4):1161–1192.

Fama, Eugene F. "Efficient Capital Markets: II," *Journal of Finance,* 1991, 46(5):1575–1618.

Froot, Kenneth A., David S. Scharfstein, and Jeremy C. Stein. "Herd on the Street: Informational Inefficiencies in a Market with Short-Term Speculation," *Journal of Finance,* 1992, 47(4):1461–1484.

Furbush, Dean. "Program Trading and Price Movement: Evidence from the October 1987 Market Crash," *Financial Management,* 1989, 18(3):68–83.

Glosten, Lawrence R. "Is the Electronic Open Limit Order Book Inevitable?" *Journal of Finance,* 1994, 49(4):1127–1161.

Golec, Joseph, and Maurry Tamarkin. "The Degree of Inefficiency in the Football Betting Market," *Journal of Financial Economics,* 1991, 30(2):311–324.

Gombola, Michael J., and George P. Tsetsekos. "The Information Content of Plant Closing Announcements: Evidence from Financial Profiles and the Stock Price Reaction," *Financial Management,* 1992, 21(2):31–40.

Gosnell, Thomas, Arthur J. Keown, and John M. Pinkerton. "Bankruptcy and Insider Trading: Differences Between Exchange-Listed and OTC Firms," *Journal of Finance,* 1992, 47(1):349–362.

Griffiths, Mark D., and Robert W. White. "Tax-Induced Trading and the Turn-of-the-Year Anomaly: An Intraday Study," *Journal of Finance,* 1993, 48(2):575–598.

Harlow, W. V., and John S. Howe. "Leveraged Buyouts and Insider Nontrading," *Financial Management,* 1993, 22(1):109–118.

Harris, Milton, and Artur Raviv. "Capital Structure and the Informational Role of Debt," *Journal of Finance,* 1990, 45(2):321–350.

Hasbrouck, Joel, and George Sofianos. "The Trade of Market Makers: An Empirical Analysis of NYSE Specialists," *Journal of Finance,* 1993, 48(5):1565–1593.

Haugen, Robert A. "Finance from a New Perspective," *Financial Management,* 1996, 25(1):86–97.

Haugen, Robert A. *The New Finance: The Case Against Efficient Markets.* Englewood Cliffs, N.J.: Prentice-Hall, 1995.

Hertzel, Michael G. "The Effects of Stock Repurchases on Rival Firms," *Journal of Finance,* 1991, 46(2):707–716.

Hirshleifer, David, Avanidhar Subrahmanyam, and Sheridan Titman. "Security Analysis and Trading Patterns When Some Investors Receive Information Before Others," *Journal of Finance,* 1994, 49(5):1665–1698.

Hochman, Shalom J., Oded Palmon, and Alex P. Tang. "Tax-Induced Intra-Year Patterns in Bonds Yields," *Journal of Finance,* 1993, 48(1):331–344.

Holden, Craig W., and Avanidhar Subrahmanyam. "Long-Lived Private Information and Imperfect Competition," *Journal of Finance,* 1992, 47(1):247–270.

Holthausen, Robert W., Richard W. Leftwich, and David Mayers. "Large-Block Transactions, the Speed of Response, and Temporary and Permanent Stock-Price Effects," *Journal of Financial Economics,* 1990, 26(1):71–96.

Jarrow, Robert A., and Maureen O'Hara. "Primes and Scores: An Essay on Market Imperfections," *Journal of Finance,* 1989, 44(5):1263–1288.

Jegadeesh, Narasimhan, and Sheridan Titman. "Returns to Buying Winners and Selling Losers: Implications for Stock Market Efficiency," *Journal of Finance,* 1993, 48(1):65–92.

Jones, Charles M., Gautam Kaul, and Marc L. Lipson. "Information, Trading, and Volatility," *Journal of Financial Economics,* 1994, 36(1):127–154.

Kadlec, Gregory B., and John J. McConnell. "The Effect of Market Segmentation and Illiquidity on Asset Prices: Evidence from Exchange Listings," *Journal of Finance,* 1994, 49(2):611–636.

Krueger, Thomas M., and William F. Kennedy. "An Examination of the Super Bowl Stock Market Predictor," *Journal of Finance,* 1990, 45(2):691–698.

Kryzanowski, Lawrence, and Hao Zhang. "The Contrarian Investment Strategy Does Not Work in Canadian Markets," *Journal of Financial and Quantitative Analysis,* 1992, 27(3):383–396.

Kumar, Raman, Atulya Sarin, and Kuldeep Shastri. "The Behavior of Option Price Around Large Block Transactions in the Underlying Security," *Journal of Finance,* 1992, 47(3):879–890.

Lakonishok, Josef, Andrei Shleifer, and Robert W. Vishny. "Contrarian Investment, Extrapolation, and Risk," *Journal of Finance,* 1994, 49(5):1541–1578.

Lee, Chun I., Stuart Rosenstein, Nanda Rangan, and Wallace N. Davidson, III. "Board Composition and Shareholder Wealth: The Case of Management Buyouts," *Financial Management,* 1992, 21(1):58–72.

Lee, D. Scott. "Management Buyout Proposals and Inside Information," *Journal of Finance,* 1992, 47(3):1061–1080.

Lee, Winson B., and Elizabeth S. Cooperman. "Conglomerates in the 1980s: A Performance Appraisal," *Financial Management,* 1989, 18(1):45–54.

Lin, Ji-Chai, and John S. Howe. "Insider Trading in the OTC Market," *Journal of Finance,* 1990, 45(4):1273–1284.

Liu, Pu, Stanley D. Smith, and Azmat A. Syed. "Stock Price Reactions to the *Wall Street Journal's* Securities Recommendations," *Journal of Financial and Quantitative Analysis,* 1990, 25(3):399–410.

Lockwood, Larry J., and Scott C. Linn. "An Examination of Stock Market Return Volatility During Overnight and Intraday Periods, 1964–1989," *Journal of Finance,* 1990, 45(2):591–602.

Long, Michael S. "The Incentives Behind the Adoption of Executive Stock Option Plans in U.S. Corporations," *Financial Management,* 1992, 21(3):12–21.

Loughran, Tim. "NYSE vs. NASDAQ Returns: Market Microstructure or the Poor Performance of Initial Public Offerings," *Journal of Financial Economics,* 1993, 33(2):241–260.

Maloney, Michael T., and J. Harold Mulherin. "The Effects of Splitting on the Ex: A Microstructure Reconciliation," *Financial Management,* 1992, 21(4):44–59.

McInish, Thomas H., and Robert A. Wood. "An Analysis of Intraday Patterns in Bid/Ask for NYSE Stocks," *Journal of Finance,* 1992, 47(2):753–764.

McQueen, Grant, and Steven Thorley. "Are Stock Returns Predictable? A Test Using Markov Chains," *Journal of Finance,* 1991, 46(1):239–264.

Merton, Robert C. "Presidential Address: A Simple Model of Capital Market Equilibrium with Incomplete Information," *Journal of Finance,* 1987, 42(3):483–510.

Michaely, Roni. "Ex-Dividend Day Stock Price Behavior: The Case of the 1986 Tax Reform Act," *Journal of Finance,* 1991, 46(3):845–860.

Miller, Merton, and Franco Modigliani. "Dividend Policy, Growth, and the Valuation of Shares," *Journal of Business,* 1961, 34(October):411–433.

Miller, Merton H., Jayaram Muthuswamy, and Robert E. Whaley. "Mean Reversion of Standard & Poor's 500 Index Basis Changes: Arbitrage-Induced or Statistical Illusion?" *Journal of Finance,* 1994, 49(2):479–513.

Mitchell, Mark L., and J. Harold Mulherin. "The Impact of Public Information on the Stock Market," *Journal of Finance,* 1994, 49(3):923–950.

Modigliani, Franco, and Merton Miller. "The Cost of Capital, Corporation Finance, and the Theory of Investments," *American Economic Review,* 1958, 48(June):261–297.

Moyer, R. Charles, Ramesh Rao, and Phillip M. Sisneros. "Substitutes for Voting Rights: Evidence from Dual Class Recapitalizations," *Financial Management,* 1992, 21(3):35–48.

Netter, Jeffry M., and Mark L. Mitchell. "Stock-Repurchase Announcements and Insider Transactions after the October 1987 Stock Market Crash," *Financial Management,* 1989, 18(3):84–96.

Pearce, Douglas K., and V. Vance Roley. "Firm Characteristics, Unanticipated Inflation, and Stock Returns," *Journal of Finance,* 1988, 43(4):965–981.

Persons, John C. "Signaling and Takeover Deterrence with Stock Repurchases: Dutch Auctions versus Fixed Price Tender Offers," *Journal of Finance,* 1994, 49(4):1373–1402.

Pound, John. "Proxy Voting and the SEC: Investor Protection versus Market Efficiency," *Journal of Financial Economics,* 1991, 29(2):241–286.

Pruitt, Stephen W., and K. C. John Wei. "Institutional Ownership and Changes in the S&P 500," *Journal of Finance,* 1989, 44(2):509–514.

Rosen, Corey. "The Record of Employee Ownership," *Financial Management,* 1990, 19(1):39–47.

Schall, Lawrence D. "Asset Valuation, Firm Investment, and Firm Diversification," *Journal of Business,* 1972, 45(January):11–28.

Schwert, G. William. "Stock Returns and Real Activity: A Century of Evidence," *Journal of Finance,* 1990, 45(4):1237–1257.

Seguin, Paul J., and Gregg A. Jarrell. "The Irrelevance of Margin: Evidence from the Crash of '87," *Journal of Finance,* 1993, 48(4):1457–1473.

Shanken, Jay, and Clifford W. Smith. "Implications of Capital Markets Research for Corporate Finance," *Financial Management,* 1996, 25(1):98–104.

Shefrin, Hersh, and Meir Statman. "The Disposition to Sell Winners Too Early and Ride Losers Too Long: Theory and Evidence," *Journal of Finance,* 1985, 40(3):777–782.

Sivakumar, Kumar, and Gregory Waymire. "Insider Trading Following Material New Events: Evidence from Earnings," *Financial Management,* 1994, 23(1):23–32.

Young, Philip J., James A. Millar, and G. William Glezen. "Trading Volume, Management Solicitation, and Shareholder Voting," *Journal of Financial Economics,* 1993, 33(1):57–72.

TOPIC B

Options and Contingent Outcomes

Options are everywhere. People often use the term *option* to refer to a choice or alternative. For example, someone might say he has a lot of options, or no options. We all know the first situation is good, and the second is bad. That's because we understand the Options Principle: Options are valuable.

People like options because options provide a measure of control over uncertain events. Insurance is an option that you purchase to provide protection against bad events such as death or fire. At the heart of an option is a contingency—something that may happen but isn't certain to. An option is a contingent claim to particular outcomes; it comes into play only when certain conditions occur, such as having an accident or winning the lottery.

Of course, most options don't come with a "tag" attached that says *option*. Many of the options we focus on here are subtle or even difficult to recognize. They are implicit options inherent in a situation, such as the examples of hidden options we cited in our discussion of the Options Principle.

Having told you that options are valuable, we must also say that options can be extremely complex. In some situations, measuring the exact value of an option can be very difficult. This can be the case even with obvious and explicit options, such as those traded in the capital markets.

This topic explores what an option means in terms of participants' rights to a situation's possible outcomes. We identify and discuss both explicit and hidden options. We examine the factors that determine an option's value and how changes in those factors alter an option's value.

The purpose of this topic is not to make you an expert at valuing options. Rather, we want to help you understand some important and very useful generalizations about options. These generalizations are powerful weapons in the valuation arsenal.

OPTIONS AND THE PRINCIPLES OF FINANCE

◆ *Options:* Look for options that can significantly affect value.

◆ *Two-Sided Transactions:* Always consider both sides. The option buyer has the right, but the option seller has the obligation.

◆ *Incremental Benefits:* Measure the impact of options on an incremental basis.

◆ *Time-Value-of-Money:* Include its impact on the value of an option.

◆ *Risk-Return Trade-Off:* An option splits the returns from an investment into pieces, altering risk and return for the buyers and sellers of the option.

◆ *Self-Interested Behavior:* People will exercise an option when it benefits them. Options can be used to provide incentives to influence behavior.

OPTIONS

An **option** is the right to do something, without the obligation to do it. We use the term in its broadest sense: An option is *any* right that has no obligation attached to it. However, there are also specific types of options. A **call option** is the right to buy an asset. A **put option** is the right to sell an asset. In both cases the asset on which the option is written is known as the **underlying asset.** The **strike price** is the price at which the option-holder may buy or sell the underlying asset when the option is exercised. When you **exercise** an option, you make the exchange specified in the option contract.

When exercising an option would provide an advantage over buying or selling the underlying asset in the open market, the option is **in-the-money.** For example, an option to sell (put) an asset for $100 when you can sell it for only $80 in the market is in-the-money. The option would allow the optionholder to sell the asset for $20 more than it is currently worth.

When exercising an option would *not* provide an advantage over buying or selling the underlying asset currently in the market, the option is **out-of-the-money.** For example, an option to buy (call) an asset at a strike price of $100, when you could buy it for $80 in the market, is out-of-the-money. Exercising the option contract, the option-holder would pay $20 more for the asset than it is currently worth. Out-of-the money options are not exercised because it would be a disadvantage, but they are frequently sold to others who believe the option might become in-the-money in the future.

The **exercise value** (also called *intrinsic value*) is the amount of advantage an in-the-money option provides over buying or selling the underlying asset currently in the market. For example, the $20 just noted in the in-the-money example is its exercise value. An out-of-the-money option has a zero exercise value. After all, optionholders have the right without the obligation, so they will "walk away from the option" rather than exercise an out-of-the-money option.

Like most things, options don't live forever. An option's **expiration** is the point in time the option contract ceases to exist, the point at which the option expires or dies. Also, options are of two types. An **American option** is an option that can be exercised at any time prior to its expiration. In contrast, a **European option** can be exercised only at the end of the contract, not before.

The complexity of an option stems from its very nature. It is a contingency that creates a discontinuity in the possible outcomes. Because the outcome is contingent, it may not matter at all or it may matter a lot. Sometimes a seemingly small difference in conditions can make a *big* difference in the outcome. Alternatively, a seemingly big difference in conditions may make little or no difference in the outcome. The set of possible outcomes is cut off, or truncated. Let's start by viewing an everyday item through "option glasses." Consider an example of something you might not think of as an option, a lottery ticket.

EXAMPLE   *An Option View of a Lottery Ticket*

Suppose you bought a lottery ticket for $2.00. The first prize is $5000 a week for life. There are five second prizes of $1000 a week for life, and 20 third prizes of $250 a week for life. You, of course, would like to win the first prize. But you also understand that isn't too likely; 17.5 million tickets will have been sold. Upon reflection, the condition that it be *first* prize isn't critical. You would rather win than not win—if you could choose. This is because the difference between winning one prize or another is relatively small compared with the difference between not winning and winning any of the prizes.

Your ticket is marked 1X4U2C. Watching the big drawing on TV, you see the 26 winning numbers. Your heart jumps; one of the second prizes is 1X4U2B. (None of the others is close.) Sooooo close! If only the last letter had been the next one in the alphabet. A small difference in the one drawn—a *C* rather than a *B* in that last place—would have made a *big* difference in your outcome. At the same time, a big difference in the one drawn—an outcome of 9A8B7C—would not have changed your outcome at all. You would still not have been a winner. This is what we mean by a discontinuity in the outcomes. The outcomes for your lottery ticket are shown in figure B.1.

Your lottery ticket is a contingent claim. A **contingent claim** can be made only if particular conditions occur. You can claim a prize only if your ticket is drawn a winner. In most cases (17,499,974 of the 17.5 million possible outcomes to be precise), your ticket is worthless and you get nothing. But if one of the 26 tickets that gets drawn happens to be yours, you can claim a prize in exchange for your lottery ticket. A contingent claim is an option in its broadest sense: the right without an obligation to do something.

Your lottery ticket is a European call option on a prize, which is the *underlying asset.* It is a *call option* because it gives you the right to "buy" the underlying asset for a *strike price* of zero. You would *exercise* your option by turning in your ticket if it has a winning number. It is a *European option* because you can do this only at its *expiration,* the end of the option's life just after the big drawing. The $2.00 price you paid for the ticket is the value of the option when you purchased it. Your option had an *exercise value* of zero during its life because it gave zero advantage to claiming the prize before the drawing, so it was *out-of-the-money.* As it turned out, after the drawing, your option was still out-of-the-money when it *expired.* ∎

A Call Option on an Asset

The lottery ticket example shows how something you don't think of as an option can be implicitly an option. Now let's look at an explicit call option on an asset.

Suppose Alice buys some land for $100,000 and immediately sells Carl a *European call option* on the same piece of land with a *strike price* of $110,000 and *expiration* one year from today. Both of their outcomes with respect to this land (the *underlying asset*) now include a contingency. While the call option exists, the most Alice can sell the land for is $110,000; she might get less. The most Carl will have to pay for the land is $110,000; he might be able to buy it for less. We can express this contingency for Alice as

$$\text{Alice's value} = \min\,[\text{market value}; 110,000]$$

The **min function** expresses the contingency in the situation mathematically. Its value is whichever is smaller, the market value *or* $110,000.

Basic Option Value: The Exercise Value

The Principle of Two-Sided Transactions reminds us to consider the other side of the transaction. Carl's situation is the mirror image, or opposite, of Alice's because he's on the other side of the transaction. We can show the basic value of Carl's call option, its *exercise value,* using a mir-

ror image of the min function, the **max function,** which takes the largest of a set:

Exercise value of Carl's call option
$$= \max\,[(\text{market value} - 110,000);\ 0]$$

We know Carl's option is never worth less than zero because an option cannot have a negative value. That is represented by the zero inside the max function. If the option is *out-of-the-money,* the exercise value is zero, and the option provides no advantage over an open market purchase. If the option is *in-the-money,* it would provide an advantage of (market value − 110,000) over an open market purchase.

Note that the strike price is a break point in the outcomes for both sides of the transaction. If the market value is below the strike price on a call option at expiration, it doesn't matter how much below. Being just a little less is the same as being a great deal less. Whether the land's market value is $109,000 or only $1, the option is out-of-the-money and won't be *exercised.* But if the market value is above the strike price on a call option at expiration, the option is in-the-money and will be exercised. The farther the market value is above the strike price, the larger the exercise value is.

The exercise value changes dollar-for-dollar with the market value whenever the market price is above the call option's strike price. This is shown in figure B.2, which

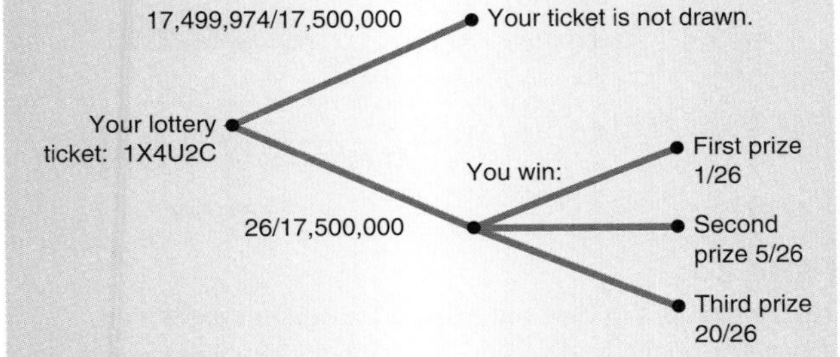

FIGURE B.1
Lottery ticket outcomes.

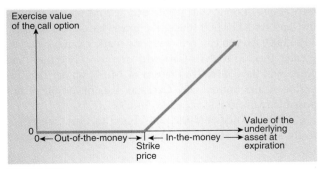

FIGURE B.2
How the exercise value of a call option depends on the value of the underlying asset.

graphs the exercise value of a call option against the market value of the underlying asset. The line going up from the strike price at a 45° angle shows the dollar-for-dollar relationship as the asset's market value increases and the option becomes deeper in-the-money. The flat line shows how the exercise value is zero everywhere in the out-of-the-money area.

There is an important point to keep in mind when you look at a figure such as figure B.2. *There will be only one outcome.* At expiration, the underlying asset will have a sin-gle value, represented as one point on the horizontal axis. But before expiration, we don't know which point it will be. That is the nature of a risky—that is, uncertain—outcome. This is just like the distinction between a realized return and, say, an expected return. If we knew ahead of time what that outcome was going to be, we would know which side of the transaction was going to "win." If we knew that, we wouldn't need a complex analysis of option value. We would already know the exact value of the option!

Self-Check

1. What is an option?

2. What is the difference between an American option and a European option?

3. What is the difference between a call option and a put option?

4. What does it mean to say that an option is in-the-money?

BUYING AND SELLING PARTS OF AN ASSET'S RETURN DISTRIBUTION

We can think of an asset as a probability distribution of possible realized returns. Let's continue our example of Alice's land purchase. If she sells the land a year later for $126,000, she will have a realized return of 26% (= (126 − 100)/100). Now consider the impact of Carl's option on Alice's realized return.

A Call Option

Suppose Alice sold Carl the call option for $4000. Figure B.3 shows the net gain or loss to Alice and Carl a year later at the option's expiration, as a function of the market value of the land. Note once again that neither Alice nor Carl can choose the outcome. There will be only one value for the land a year later and they don't know what it will be.

Having sold the call option, a next-year market value outcome of $126,000 would give Alice a realized return of only about 14.6%.[1] Carl would exercise his option and buy the land for $110,000 (the strike price) because it is worth $126,000. As you can see, with any market value outcome greater than $110,000, Carl will exercise his option and Alice will have a realized return of 14.6% on her land investment and option sale. Carl has a claim on all of her possible realized returns above 14.6%.

When Alice sold the call option to Carl, she effectively sold him all her outcomes above a 14.6% realized return. So an option can be described as a claim to some of the possible realized returns on the underlying asset. Figure B.4 presents the probability distribution of Alice's realized returns in terms of the sale value of the land.

We can divide the outcome distribution into two parts: one part above and the other part below $110,000. Alice would prefer the higher possible outcomes (those to the right of $110,000) over the lower possible outcomes (those to the left of $110,000). Of course, knowing that people prefer higher to lower return (Principle of Risk Aversion), this same statement can be made if we partition

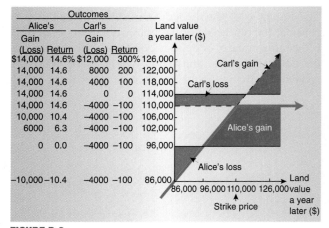

FIGURE B.3
The gain or loss to Carl and Alice at the option's expiration, depending on the land's value. Remember, there will be only one outcome for the land value (one point on the *x* axis), which creates all of the *y* axis outcomes. Alice's net investment is $96,000.

---

[1] Alice spent $100,000 for the land and sold the option for $4000, so her net investment is $96,000. Her net gain of $14,000 provides a return of 14.6% (= 14/96).

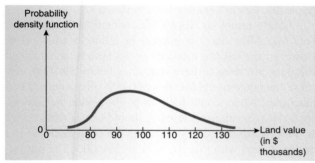

FIGURE B.4

The probability distribution of the future value of Alice's land.

the distribution into two parts at *any* point. On this basis, we can view outcomes to the right of *any* split point as good outcomes and those to the left as bad outcomes, because all asset owners like Alice want the good outcomes but don't want the bad. As a result, asset owners must be

paid to give up their claim to the good possible outcomes. This is why Carl had to pay Alice for his call option.

The split point between the good and bad outcomes is the strike price for the option. When an asset owner is paid for giving up good outcomes, the owner has sold a call option on the asset.

Figure B.5 illustrates the claim portion of the return distribution for Carl's call option. A call option gives the optionholder the right to claim all of the good outcomes (the highlighted portion above the strike price) by exercising the option. Carl can avoid bad outcomes (those below the strike price) by simply not exercising his option. But if the outcome is more than $110,000, say $116,000, Carl can claim the return by buying the land from Alice for $110,000 and reselling it to someone else for $116,000, thereby gaining the $6000 exercise value. You can see in figure B.3 that his net gain would then be $2000 ($6000 minus the $4000 he paid for the call option).

Computing Outcomes for a Call Option

Barb Wyre purchased a building in downtown San Francisco for $2.3 million. Right after this, she sold a one-year European call option on the building, with a strike price of $2.5 million, for $150,000 to Bob N. Weave. So Barb's net investment is $2.15 million. What are Barb's and Bob's outcomes, in terms of the land's possible value when the option expires?

They will be (in $ millions):

LAND VALUE	BARB'S GAIN (LOSS)	BARB'S RETURN	BOB'S GAIN (LOSS)	BOB'S RETURN
$3.00	$0.35	16.28%	$0.35	233.33%
2.75	0.35	16.28	0.10	66.67
2.50	0.35	16.28	−0.15	−100.00
2.25	0.10	4.65	−0.15	−100.00
2.00	−0.15	−6.98	−0.15	−100.00
1.75	−0.40	−18.60	−0.15	−100.00

A Put Option

Now consider the bad outcomes. Naturally, an asset owner like Alice would have to *pay* someone to get rid of the bad outcomes. When an asset owner pays someone else to take the bad outcomes, the asset owner has purchased a *put option* on the asset. The split point is again the (put) option's strike price. Figure B.6 on page 252 shows how the exercise value of a put option (the savings from not having to keep the bad outcomes) depends on the value of the underlying asset.

If you look back at figure B.2, you can see how the exercise value of a put option is simply a mirror image of that for a call option. The 45° line, going up and to the left from the strike price in figure B.6, shows the one-for-one relationship between exercise value and asset value as the asset's

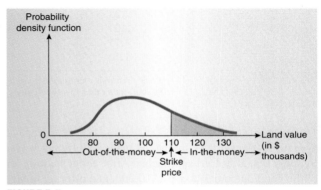

FIGURE B.5

Carl's call option claim.

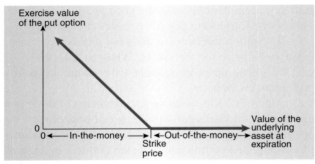

FIGURE B.6
How the exercise value of a put option depends on the value of
the underlying asset.

market value decreases and the option becomes deeper in-
the-money. The flat line shows how the exercise value is
zero everywhere in the out-of-the-money area.

Buying a put option is like purchasing insurance on
an asset. For example, automobile collision insurance is
like a put option on a car, exercisable only in the event of an
accident. In the event of an accident, the insurance company covers your loss (in an agreed-upon way, such as all
but $100 if you have "$100 deductible" insurance). In effect, you had a bad outcome (an accident), so you "sell" the
destroyed car to the insurance company for the strike price

(typically, the car's market value before it was destroyed).

Let's return to Alice's land situation. Suppose for
now that Alice has lost interest in selling a call option.
However, she has just heard about put options and decided
she does not want to have outcomes below $90,000. Be-
cause the outcomes below this $90,000 split point are bad
outcomes, Alice would have to pay a person to take responsibility for those outcomes, should one of them occur.
In other words, Alice buys a put option from Paul (the put
option writer) with a strike price of $90,000. The put op-
tion gives Alice the right to sell the land to Paul for
$90,000.

Figure B.7 illustrates Paul's put option obligation.
The put option gives Alice the right to avoid all of the bad
outcomes (the highlighted portion below the strike price)
by exercising her option should one of them occur. Alice
can claim the good outcomes simply by failing to exercise
her put option. Therefore, if the land is worth more than
$90,000, Alice will accept the outcome and let the put op-
tion expire without exercising it. With a land value less
than $90,000, Alice will sell the land to Paul for $90,000,
thereby gaining the exercise value of the put option—the
difference between $90,000 and the market value of the
land. Her net gain would then be the exercise value minus
whatever she paid Paul for the option.

EXAMPLE   *Computing Outcomes for a Put Option*

Barb Wyre purchased a building in downtown San Francisco for $2.3 million. Right after this,
she bought a one-year European put option on the building, with a strike price of $2.1 million,
for $150,000 from Peter N. Da'Wolfe. So Barb's net investment is $2.45 million. What are
Barb's and Peter's outcomes, in terms of the land's possible value when the option expires?
They will be (in $ millions):

LAND VALUE	BARB'S GAIN (LOSS)	BARB'S RETURN	PETER'S GAIN (LOSS)	PETER'S RETURN[2]
$3.00	$0.55	22.45%	$0.15	100.00%
2.75	0.30	12.24	0.15	100.00
2.50	0.05	2.04	0.15	100.00
2.25	−0.20	−8.16	0.15	100.00
2.00	−0.35	−14.29	0.05	33.33
1.75	−0.35	−14.29	−0.20	−133.33
1.50	−0.35	−14.29	−0.45	−300.00

[2]Peter's return is expressed here as a percentage of the initial option value. Peter is taking risk, but he gets money at
the start, rather than investing money. So this return is not "normal" in an economic sense.

Equivalent Claims, or Put-Call Parity

Sometimes the same claim can be made in different ways.
Suppose that after Carl approached Alice about wanting all
of the good outcomes above $110,000, and offering to buy
a call option, Alice reconsidered her situation. She decided
Carl's idea of claiming only the good outcomes above

$110,000 sounded better than all the other possibilities we
have talked about. So she purchased a put option from Paul
with a strike price of $110,000. What does her claim look
like? Think about it. She has claim to all the good outcomes above $110,000, but the put option allows her to
avoid all the bad ones below $110,000. If you think this

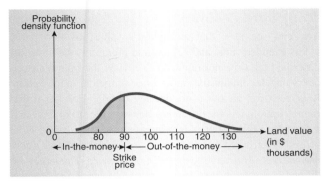

FIGURE B.7
Paul's put option obligation (Alice's put option claim).

sounds familiar, you're right. Alice's claim portion will be the same as Carl's would have been with the call option, the one shown in figure B.5.

The equivalence between this new claim of Alice's and Carl's claim is called put-call parity. **Put-call parity** expresses the relationship between the values of put and call options. Put-call parity is interesting, but it can also be confusing: *Every situation that can be described in terms of a call option has a parallel description using a put option.* In this book, we try to use the description that seems easiest to see in a situation. However, because a situation can always be described in terms of *either* a call or a put option, we sometimes simply talk about the "optionality" in the situation.

Self-Check

1. How does buying a call option let you benefit from the really good outcomes?

2. Why is buying a put option like purchasing insurance?

3. Suppose you don't want to sell a particular stock you own right now, because of tax reasons. But you're concerned its value might decline before you do sell it. Should you buy a call option or a put option?

4. What sort of relationship does put-call parity express?

VALUING AN OPTION

Thus far, we haven't said much about the prices paid for options, except that Carl would have paid $4000 for his call option. But where did that price come from? We referred to the exercise value of an option as the *basic* (or intrinsic) value of an option. Would Alice sell the call option to Carl for its exercise value? No. In fact, the exercise value of Carl's call option is zero when he was to buy it—the option was out-of-the-money. The land is worth $100,000 (Alice just bought it for that price) and the strike price is $110,000. Alice would require more than the exercise value because she is taking on an obligation. Carl would have the right to buy the land for $110,000, because he would own the option (the right without the obligation). However, if Alice sold the option, she would have the obligation to sell the land for $110,000 if Carl decided to use his right. So there is more to an option's value than its exercise value.

Additional Option Value: The Time Premium

The **time premium of an option** (time premium for short) is the value of its "optionality." That is, the time premium is the extra value (above the exercise value) provided by having control. Control is the right without the obligation. It allows the optionholder to claim good outcomes and avoid bad ones. We call this part the time premium because it decreases as the option approaches expiration and be-

comes zero when the option is just about to expire. The time premium is determined by three factors: *time until expiration, risk of the underlying asset,* and market *riskless return.*

Time Until Expiration
It's easy to see why time is a determinant of option value. If you have a choice between two options, where the only difference between them is their time until expiration, which option would you prefer to own? You can never be worse off with the option that has the longer time until expiration. Another way to think about this is to say that more time allows more chance for the option to be more in-the-money.[3]

Risk of the Underlying Asset
Less obvious is how the *risk* (potential variation of the realized return) of the underlying asset affects the time premium. Figure B.8 on page 254 demonstrates the effect of risk on a call option. It illustrates the claim portions for identical call options on assets with identical market values and strike prices but different risk levels. Asset A has an outcome distribution with a relatively small variation, whereas asset B has an outcome distribution with a relatively large variation. As you can see, asset B's claim portion is much larger. It has a much greater probability (the area under the curve) of

---

[3]Some cynics might point out that it also allows more chance to be more out-of-the-money. But remember, the optionholder can avoid bad outcomes—at least those beyond the strike price in the out-of-the-money direction.

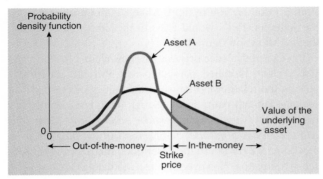

FIGURE B.8
The effect of risk on the value of a call option.

having a good outcome than asset A. Therefore, the call option for asset B is worth more than the call option for asset A. Although we illustrated this with a call option, the same concept holds for a put option. That is, greater asset risk also enlarges the value of a put option.

Here are two other ways to see the impact of asset risk on option value. First, the greater the risk, the more the underlying asset value can change in a given amount of time. Because the optionholder has control (to claim the good outcomes but leave the bad), if everything else is the same, the greater the possible change is, the more the option is worth.

Finally, note that an increase in risk (a flatter probability distribution) increases the number of outcomes at the extremes of the distribution. That means there are more extremely good outcomes to be claimed and also more extremely bad outcomes to be avoided. Again, with optionholder control, the more outcomes that are covered, the more valuable is the option.

Riskless Return
The final determinant of the value of an option is the riskless return. It has opposite effects on call and put option values. We can think of the riskless return as the pure, or base, market required return. It is the basic, or benchmark, opportunity cost of money. The effect of the riskless return depends primarily on who has to pay the strike price if the option is exercised. The higher the riskless return is, the lower will be the present value of this payment, because the payment will not take place until the future, when the option is exercised. A complexity of the riskless return is that its effect is reversed for call and put options. This is because the owner of a call option *pays* the strike price to obtain the underlying asset, whereas the owner of a put option *receives* the strike price to give the asset up.

As a result, an increase in the riskless return increases the value of a call option but decreases the value of a put option.

Total Option Value
You can see now that an option's value has two parts: (1) its exercise value and (2) its time premium. We have just described the time premium. Let's review the option's exercise value. It contains the cutoff, or contingency, in the option. It is zero for an out-of-the-money option. For an in-the-money option, it is the difference between the strike price and the market value of the underlying asset. So the exercise value is itself determined by two factors: the *underlying asset's current market value* and the option's *strike price*. The larger the difference for an in-the-money option, the larger the exercise value and the more the option is worth. In other words, the deeper in-the-money an option is, the more it's worth.

Maximum Option Value Although Alice may require Carl to pay more than the exercise value for the call option, there is a limit to what Carl will be willing to pay. In the extreme, that limit is the value of the land. After all, if he paid any more he would be better off simply buying the land now. So the extreme upper limit on the value of a call option is the value of the underlying asset. In fact, except in the most extraordinary of situations, a call option's value would never even approach this limit.

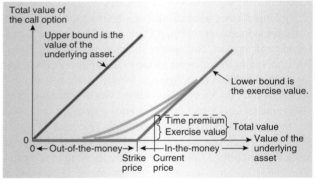

FIGURE B.9
Total call option value as a function of underlying asset value.

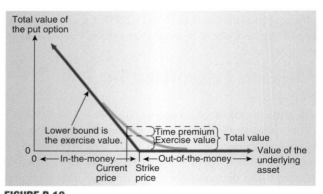

FIGURE B.10
Total put option value as a function of underlying asset value.

We can now show you the boundaries of an option's value and what the total value of a typical call option looks like as a function of the value of the underlying asset. Figure B.9 illustrates the value of two call options. As you can see, the options are worth more than their exercise values. The additional amount is the time premium. You can also see that one option is worth more than the other. Such a higher value can be due to a longer time until expiration, greater risk in the underlying asset, or an increase in the riskless return.

Figure B.10 illustrates the value of a put option as a function of underlying asset value. As with exercise value, you can see that the total value of a put option is a mirror image of a call option's total value.

Self-Check

1. Why is there more to an option's value than its exercise value?

2. What is an option's time premium?

3. What three factors determine an option's time premium?

4. Why does greater asset risk increase the value of call options *and* put options?

5. What two factors determine an option's exercise value?

SOME IMPORTANT GENERALIZATIONS ABOUT OPTIONS

Using the determinants of an option's value, we can establish some generalizations about option valuation. These generalizations provide easy intuitions about the options, their values, and how the determinants affect value in a given situation. The generalizations we discuss here are extremely important, because we will use them to provide quick insights into many situations in the rest of the book.

We start by looking at the determinants of option value. Table B.1 summarizes these factors and indicates how an increase in each will affect the value of an option.

The Largest Time Premium for an Option Occurs When the Underlying Asset's Value Equals the Strike Price
You can see this for the options illustrated in figure B.9. The time premium is at its maximum here because it could go either way. That is, at the split point, when the underlying asset value exactly equals the strike price, the uncertainty is greatest about whether the option will expire in- or out-of-the-money.

An Option's Time Premium Decreases as the Option Becomes More In- or Out-of-the-Money
This phenomenon is also illustrated in figure B.9, and we note it in table B.1 as well. It occurs because there is less uncertainty about whether the option will expire in- or out-of-the-money when the underlying asset is *already* worth more or less than the strike price. Quite simply, an option that is already in- or out-of-the-money is more likely to stay that way than it is to change. (That is not to say it *can't* change, but the likelihood is smaller. We are dealing with probabilities.)

An American Option Is Never Worth Less Than a Comparable European Option
This is easy to understand. Essentially, there is more optionality in an American option. Consider two options that are comparable except that one is American and the other is European. The

---

TABLE B.1
The Determinants of Option Value

AN INCREASE IN THIS FACTOR	HAS THIS EFFECT ON THE OPTION'S VALUE
The option's exercise value	
depth in-the-money	increases it
depth out-of-the-money	has no effect on it
The option's time premium	
time until expiration	increases it
risk of the underlying asset	increases it
increase in riskless return	increases the value of a call option
increase in riskless return	decreases the value of a put option
depth in-the-money	decreases it
depth out-of-the-money	decreases it

American option has everything the European option has, but in addition provides the added option of allowing exercise prior to expiration. Like any option, this added option cannot have a negative value. Therefore the American option is never worth less than the comparable European option. The added optionality has positive value in some situations, so in those cases the American option would be worth more than the comparable European option.

An Option's Time Premium Is Generally Positive

This always holds for an out-of-the-money option because an option cannot have a negative value. (This is our corollary to the Options Principle.) For an in-the-money American option, if the time premium were negative, a person could buy and immediately exercise the option for an arbitrage profit. So market competition naturally enforces a positive time premium. This generalization does not hold strictly because in-the-money European options cannot be exercised during their life. It is therefore possible (although not frequent) to have a case where we know the asset's value is going down in the future, and the time premium becomes somewhat negative.

For example, consider a high-coupon bond that is currently selling above par value because of low interest rates. In the future, at maturity, the bond will be worth only its par value. Therefore, in such a case, we know the bond's value is going down in the future.

It Is Generally Better to Sell Rather Than Exercise an Option Prior to Its Expiration

Although this follows directly from the previous generalization, it is a very important insight. Quite simply, if you exercise an option, you give up its time premium. If you exercise the option you get only its exercise value. If you sell the option, you get the exercise value *plus* the time premium. (This generalization also breaks down in the unlikely case of a negative time premium.)

The Further an Option Is Out-of-the-Money, the Less It Is Worth

This generalization follows directly from two previous observations. First, an out-of-the-money option is worth only its time premium because its exercise value is zero. Second, the time premium decreases as the option gets further out-of-the-money.

But remember our lottery ticket example earlier. Even a very unlikely event *can* happen. Whenever one does, it can dramatically change things. When an option is far out-of-the-money, it's not worth very much and its existence seems insignificant. But if an unlikely event occurs and that option becomes in-the-money, the option's claim and value suddenly become very important. Topic C shows you how such things can happen with contingent stakeholder claims when a company falls into financial distress.

Self-Check

1. What underlying asset value leads to the largest time premium?

2. What happens to an option's time premium as the option becomes more in-the-money? What about when it becomes more out-of-the-money?

3. Can an American option ever be worth less than a comparable European option? Explain.

4. Is it generally better to sell or exercise an option prior to its expiration?

PLACES TO LOOK FOR OPTIONS

We said that options exist in *many* forms. The following sections show a number of places to look for options, to help you develop insight into their pervasive existence.

Insurance

As we noted earlier, in its simplest form, insurance is a put option. For complex insurance contracts, a put option is also the best starting point for understanding and valuing the insurance.

Real Estate Options

Options have been used for many years in real estate. For example, consider a person trying to develop a new shopping mall. The development depends on many things, such as buying several pieces of real estate, obtaining financing, and gaining commitments from retailers to lease shops. The development can proceed only if *all* the parts come together. Rather than invest in each piece of land sequentially, the developer can purchase call options from the landowners with agreed upon strike prices. Then, *if* everything comes together, the developer has claim to the land for a particular price. Without the call option, the later landowners could hold out for extraordinary prices. Actually, the last landowner could require a price of almost the total positive NPV of the project.

To see this point, suppose the NPV of the project is $5 million at the start of the development, based on estimates for purchasing all the pieces. Also assume that everything has happened exactly according to plan—so far. Only one last piece of land, which was expected to cost

$100,000, remains to be purchased. Assuming the investment project *must* have this parcel of land to be completed, the owner of the land can refuse to sell for the expected $100,000 price. How much will the developer be willing to pay?

The developer will be better off as long as the price for the land is less than the $5 million in positive NPV. That, of course, is considerably more than what the land was worth before the project was this far along. Now, however, if the landowner sets a price of $4 million for the land, the developer will be $1 million ahead, even after paying the "inflated" price. A call option can keep the developer from being caught in the position of having to give up a substantial portion of the positive NPV of the project to a holdout.

Convertibles   Convertible bonds and convertible preferred stock can be converted into shares of common stock at the securityholder's option. Such securities can be viewed as combinations of other securities. For example, a convertible bond can be seen as a "straight" corporate bond *plus* a call option on shares of the company's common stock.

Warrants   A **warrant** is a long-term call option on a stock. Warrants generally have very long lives when they are issued, such as ten years or longer. They are issued by a company on its own stock. Warrants differ from many other call options in that if they are exercised, the company typically issues new shares of stock so that it actually creates new equity. Often, new warrants are issued together with new "straight" bonds. In effect, the package is like a convertible bond, except that the two parts are independent and can be bought and sold separately. Sometimes warrants are referred to as "sweeteners" that are added to the bond to make it more attractive to buy.[4]

Call Provisions   Many corporate bonds include a call provision that allows the *company* to redeem the bond for a preset amount prior to maturity. A call provision is a call option. As with any option, it increases the company's financial flexibility. More specifically, if interest rates decline, it allows the company to save money: The company can replace its high-interest-rate loan with a new lower-interest-rate loan. So, in simple terms, this call option is a formal contract provision that says the company can pay off the money it owes sooner than was originally expected. Therefore, even the typical corporate bond is not a simple security. It is a combination of even more basic securities. The bondholder owns the asset (a "straight" bond) but also has written a call option on that asset. The company is on the "other side of the transaction." It has sold the bond but also purchased a call option.

The Option in Gibson Greetings's Treasury-Linked Swap   **EXAMPLE**

In April 1994, Gibson Greetings, Inc. announced that it had lost approximately $20 million on a series of "swap" transactions with a major bank.[5] One of them was a "Treasury-linked swap."

At the end of eight months, Gibson was to pay the bank $30 million in principal plus interest on that amount. Interest was to be charged at a well-known and regularly published variable market rate called LIBOR.[6] The "swap" (exchange) called for the bank to pay Gibson interest on $30 million at LIBOR *plus* 2%. (For example, if LIBOR turned out to be 8%, the bank would pay 10%). In addition, the bank was to pay a principal amount of the smaller of either (1) $30.6 million or (2) a contingent amount P determined by a complex formula. P depended on future yields on two-year Treasury notes and 30-year Treasury bonds. The higher the yields, the lower P would be.[7]

Figure B.11 shows the bank's savings on the principal amount (payoff) on the swap in terms of Treasury yields. The Treasury-linked swap contained an option. Compare figures B.6

(continued on following page)

---

[4]It seems to us that the "sweetener" concept must have to do with a psychological marketing notion, like a rebate for buying a car. The rebate is simply a cut in the purchase price. Likewise, rather than adding the warrants, the company could have offered the bonds for a lower price—the value of the warrants!

[5]The swaps are described in Overdahl and Schachter (1995).

[6]London Interbank Offer Rate.

[7]However, in the formula for P, the input variable representing the 30-year yield was the market *price* of the 30-year Treasury bond. This increased the complexity of the formula and apparently caused Gibson to misunderstand the deal.

(The Option in Gibson Greetings's Treasury-Linked Swap *continued from previous page*)

and B.11. In effect, Gibson had sold the bank a put option in exchange for the extra 2% interest. (The bank was paying Gibson 2% above LIBOR, whereas Gibson was paying the bank LIBOR.)

Unfortunately for Gibson, Treasury yields rose during the spring and summer of 1994. As they did, the contingent amount P fell farther and farther below the $30.6 million. This resulted in a large loss for Gibson. The bank, being on the other side of the transaction, did quite well, thank you, with an equally large gain. ∎

Publicly Traded Options   In addition to the Chicago Board Options Exchange, standardized puts and calls are also traded on the American and Philadelphia Stock Exchanges, among others. Warrants are also sometimes traded on the stock exchanges. Other publicly traded options, such as stock index options, interest rate options, commodity options, and currency options are listed in the Money & Investing section (section C) of the *Wall Street Journal*.

"Hidden" Options

As we have noted before, the importance of options extends well beyond those cases where they can be easily identified. Many assets contain implicit, or "hidden," options. Whenever a claim is contingent upon particular outcomes, there is probably a hidden option involved. For example, being able to claim a tax loss on an asset requires that you sell the asset for a loss. So the option to claim the tax loss is contingent on having incurred the loss. Hidden options dramatically complicate the valuation process. This may seem an obvious statement, because the option is hidden. However, even in cases that are known to contain an option, identifying it can pose a significant analytical

puzzle. The difficulties are dramatically illustrated in the following examples.

Common Stock as an Option

In our overview of the Options Principle, we pointed out that *limited liability* creates the option to default and not fully repay a debt. When a debt contract is created, it is as though the debtholders have written the stockholders a sequence of European call options on the company. Each required debt payment represents a strike price. Whenever *any* payment is due, interest or principal, the shareholders have in effect a decision whether they should "exercise" their call option.[8] If the company is worth more than the payment that is due, the shareholders will exercise their option and "buy back" the company from the debtholders by making the required payment. If the company is ever worth less than the strike price (the required payment), the stockholders will simply refuse to exercise their call option, and the debtholders "keep" the company. Therefore, when a company has one or more debts, it is as though the shareholders have a call option on the company.

We said earlier in our discussion of the concept of put-call parity that we would try to use the description that is easiest to see in a situation. Here is such a case where it might be easier to see this idea from the alternative viewpoint. So let's look at the optionality in this situation by trying on our "put option glasses."

The stockholders' option can also be viewed as a put option with a strike price of $0. If the stockholders do not want to make the required debt payment, they can "sell" the company's assets to the debtholders for $0—and the debtholders have no choice but to accept the "sale." You might say the stockholders are "putting" it to the debtholders!

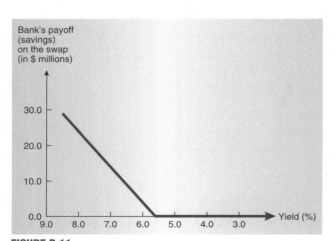

FIGURE B.11
The bank's payoff on the Treasury-linked swap.

---

[8]Naturally, the smaller the required payment, the less likely it is that the assets will not be worth the strike price. So default is much more likely when a large payment is due, such as when a $200 million loan comes due.

Although common stock can be described *exactly* as an option only under certain restrictive conditions, it is a very good approximation. More importantly, it can provide very important insights into a situation. For example, topic C shows you how the stock-as-an-option view provides insights into stakeholder relationships and the practical management of a company.

It is interesting to note that the hidden default option adds yet again to the complexity of the typical corporate bond. We pointed out that many corporate bonds include a call provision. Now you can see that they also include a hidden default option. So not only is the typical corporate bond not a simple security, but determining the makeup of its exact value is much more complex than it appeared to be in chapter 6.

Other "Hidden" Options

There are many other situations that contain hidden or implicit options that are not obvious. Here are a few.

Stakeholder Relationships in Financial Contracting
Topic C uses our generalizations about option valuation to study the contingent claims that the company's various stakeholders—such as the employees, stockholders, bondholders, and customers—have on the company's assets and on each other.

Refunding a Home Mortgage
When a mortgage on a home permits prepayment of the loan (mortgage), if interest rates go down the borrower can refinance the home loan at a lower interest rate. In effect, the right to refinance the loan involves a hidden call option; the homeowner can take out a new (lower-interest) loan and use the proceeds to prepay the original high-interest loan. The option to prepay the home mortgage loan is analogous to the call provision we noted on a corporate bond. Some banks charge the customer extra for prepaying a home mortgage. This additional charge can be viewed as a strike price for the hidden call option of prepayment. Naturally, the larger such a charge is, the larger the interest savings would have to be to make refinancing attractive.

Tax-Timing Options
Tax laws include many contingencies. Some of them create valuable options. For example, one of them involves capital gains. Suppose a taxpayer purchased two stocks last year. Since then, one has increased and the other has decreased in value. So our taxpayer has earned "income" on one and lost "income" on the other. If this were regular income, the taxpayer would pay taxes on the gain and save taxes on the loss. But because this is subject to the capital gains tax rules, the taxes apply only when the taxpayer sells the stock, which is his "option." The taxpayer can use this option to his advantage: Keep the first stock, thereby continuing to postpone the tax liability; sell the second stock, thereby claiming the tax savings on the loss right away.

Options Connected with Capital Investments
In capital budgeting, we discuss options the company has in connection with its capital investment projects. Such options include product price setting, as well as postponing, expanding, and abandoning an investment project.

Variable Cost Reduction
In chapter 11, we talk about operating leverage, which is how much a company spends on fixed cost versus how much it spends on variable costs. Companies sometimes have choices about these proportions. For example, companies have increased their use of robotic equipment in manufacturing as technology has advanced. Overall, companies determined that the robotic equipment would produce the product more cheaply. However, compared to human labor, robotic equipment has higher fixed cost (it is more costly to buy) and lower variable cost (it is cheaper to use). Consider what happens if production is temporarily suspended. Variable costs are no longer incurred then, but fixed costs must still be paid. So if production is temporarily suspended, the company would have the option of reducing its costs more if it had not invested in robotic equipment. Thus, a production process with relatively more variable cost and less fixed cost provides a hidden option to reduce total cost should production ever have to be temporarily suspended.

Self-Check

1. What is the relationship between a convertible bond and a straight bond?

2. What is a warrant? How are warrants used as "sweeteners" in bond financing?

3. Why is a bond's call provision valuable to the company that issued the bonds?

4. How can the common stock of a company be described as an option on the company's assets?

5. What type of option does the right to prepay a home mortgage involve?

A SIMPLE MODEL OF OPTION VALUATION

Determining the exact value of an option can be difficult. There are companies that sell complex mathematical models for valuing options. It's high-tech. So, unfortunately, we are not going to be able to make you a whiz at valuing options in the space available here, but we will illustrate the basic relationships using a simplified valuation method. This model determines the value of an option by computing the present value of the option's expected outcomes. The model has four steps:

1. Compute the probabilities of possible price changes on the basis of what an investor can earn on the riskless asset.

2. Calculate the possible exercise values at expiration.

3. Determine the expected outcome as the probability-weighted average of the outcomes.

4. Compute the present value of the expected outcome by discounting at the riskless return.

EXAMPLE

The Value of Carl's Call Option

Let's take a final look at Carl's call option on Alice's land. Suppose that Alice's land can have only one of two possible values next year, $120,000 or $94,138. In other words, the land can go up 20% or down 5.862% in value from its current $100,000 price. Nothing else. Also assume that the riskless return is 5% per year. What is Carl's call option worth?

Our first step is to compute the probabilities of the two possible outcomes if the return on the land must equal the riskless return of 5%. Recall that the probabilities of all possible outcomes have to sum to 1.0. Since there are only two possible outcomes, the probability of a decrease is one minus the probability of an increase. Thus,

$$5\% = (\text{probability of an increase})(+20\%) + (1 - \text{probability of an increase})(-5.862\%)$$

Solving for the probability of an increase, we get 0.42, or 42%. The probability of a decrease is 1 minus this, so it is 0.58, or 58%.

We now move on to the second step, which is to compute the call option's possible exercise values at expiration. Recall that

$$\text{Exercise value of Carl's call option} = \max[(\text{market value} - 110{,}000); 0]$$

Because the land has only two possible values, Carl's call option can have only two possible exercise values as well. These are 0 or $10,000. (With the decrease, the out-of-the-money option has an exercise value of 0. With the increase, the exercise value is 120,000 − 110,000.)

Armed with the probabilities and exercise values, we can compute the expected value of Carl's outcome. It is simply the outcomes times their probabilities, or

$$(0.42)(10{,}000) + (0.58)(0) = \$4200$$

Finally, the value of Carl's call option is the present value of the expected value of his outcome, or

$$(4200)/(1.05) = \$4000$$

So under these conditions, Carl's call option is worth $4000. ■

Self-Check

1. Why is it difficult to determine the exact value of an option?

2. What are the four steps in the simple option valuation model described in this section?

COMBINING OPTION VALUES

An important problem is how option values combine. For traded options, this is straightforward: The value of owning multiple options is simply the sum of the values of the individual options. But it is not always this simple. In some cases, exercising one option can affect the value of another option. This is more likely when the options exist on the same asset. Such complex situations arise most often in connection with hidden options. This is because hidden options often do not require an incremental payment to create them. They occur naturally. Frequently, outside forces create them. In the case of the default option, it is part of our laws.

Overlapping Hidden Options

Here is another useful generalization: *The value of two or more hidden options may be less than the sum of their indi-* *vidual option values.* This often occurs when the options provide "coverage" for some of the same outcomes.

Think about buying car insurance. Suppose you buy car insurance and then have an accident. Your put option (insurance) contract will require the insurance company to reimburse you for most, but not all, of your loss. Now consider buying car insurance from two different companies on the same car at the same time. If you did this and then had an accident, you could be reimbursed for all of your loss. However, you would not get more than your total loss. The companies would split the repair bill. Although you might get reimbursed more with two insurance policies than you would with one, the incremental cost for the second policy doesn't add enough value to be worth it. In short, if you are covered by one policy, the second policy doesn't add very much.

The Price-Setting and Production Quantity Options

EXAMPLE

Consider two hidden options a company has in connection with the manufacture and sale of a product, the option to set the selling price and the option to choose the quantity produced. These options exist without action on the company's part. They cannot be separated from the ownership of the underlying asset, the manufacturing process. Figure B.12 (a one-stop convenience figure) is a Venn diagram of outcomes for price and production quantity choices. The circle marked A contains the "in-the-money outcomes" for the price-setting option. That is, the circle includes the price choices where the company would make more money than it does now. (This can be a higher price if demand has been exceeding production, or a lower price with more sold if inventory has been accumulating.) The price-setting option is out-of-the-money for all other price choices, and its value is $12,000. The choices in the circle marked A, and option value, are based on the quantity the company is currently producing.

However, the company can choose a different production quantity. The circle marked B in figure B.12 contains the "in-the-money outcomes" for the production quantity option. That is, circle B includes the production quantity choices where the company would make more money than it does now. (This can be a larger quantity if demand has been exceeding

(continued on following page)

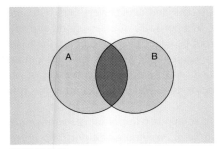

FIGURE B.12
A Venn diagram of outcomes for choices of price and production quantity.

(The Price-Setting and Production Quantity Options *continued from previous page*)

production, or a smaller quantity if inventory has been accumulating.) The production quantity option is out-of-the-money for all other quantity choices, and its value is $10,000. Once again, these choices and values are based on current conditions, in this case including the price the company is now charging.

Now look again at figure B.12. What additional value does the production quantity option offer, because the company already has the price-setting option? The price-setting option "covers" the company for all of the outcomes in circle A, and the production quantity option covers it for all of the outcomes in circle B. Because the company owns the price-setting option, however, the production quantity option adds coverage *only* for those outcomes that are not also in circle A. In other words, the intersection of circles A and B is redundant, as long as the company has either one of the options. If the company isn't selling all that it is producing, it can *either* lower its price *or* reduce the quantity it is producing. Even if it can't do one of these, the other can take care of the problem.

Suppose the value of the overlap of the option coverage of outcomes is $6000. In this case, the combined value of the price-setting and production quantity options, V(A + B), is the sum of the values of the individual options, V(A) + V(B) = $22,000 (= 12,000 + 10,000), *minus* the value of the intersection, V(A ∩ B) = $6000, or

$$V(A + B) = V(A) + V(B) - V(A \cap B) = 22,000 - 6000 = \$16,000$$

So the value of having these two options is not equal to the sum of the separate values of the individual options. This lack of simple additivity is typically the case with overlapping hidden options. ∎

A similar situation can occur when exercising one option affects the value of another option. The simplest case is where exercising one option eliminates another. Suppose a company has an investment opportunity to build a new plant with a positive NPV. Just prior to starting, an alternative place to build becomes available. Building the plant on the newly discovered alternative spot is also a positive-NPV investment opportunity. In effect, the company now has two options. But if the company exercises one of the options, the other will become worthless. You may recognize this situation as an option view of an *opportunity cost:* Taking one action eliminates the possibility of taking other desirable actions. Although they can be difficult to determine accurately, such costs can be very significant. Therefore, it is important to include the lost value of options that are eliminated by exercising another option.

A Portfolio of Options

Consider two ways of holding options on a set of assets. You could buy an option on each asset individually, or you could buy a single option on the whole set of assets. In the first case, you would have a portfolio of options. In the second case, you would have a single option on a portfolio of assets. Would one way of holding options always be more valuable than the other? We just showed that sometimes an option doesn't add its entire stand-alone value. Still, we've told you options are valuable, and an additional option never decreases your wealth.

The effects of diversification can help us understand the relative values of the two alternatives. An option is a claim on the good outcomes without the obligation to take the bad. So an option on each asset allows you to claim every good outcome and avoid every bad outcome among all the assets. In a portfolio of assets, good and bad outcomes are netted out by each. This is, after all, the basis for saying that diversification is beneficial. A single option on the portfolio allows you to claim only the *net* of all the outcomes if the net is good and avoid claiming it if it is bad.

We therefore have another important generalization about options: *The value of an option on a portfolio of assets is always less than or equal to the value of a portfolio of comparable options on the individual assets.*

A Portfolio of Options

Suppose you can invest in two different assets using call options. Each asset can have a future value of $200, $400, $600, or $800. You can have either a single call option on a portfolio of the two assets with a strike price of $1000, or you can have two separate call options, one on each asset, each with a strike price of $500. Which is worth more?

Table B.2 shows the values of the assets, options, and combinations for each of the possible outcomes. As you can see, the portfolio of options has a higher value in four of the nine possible outcomes, and it has the same value as the single option on the portfolio of assets for all the other outcomes.

So the portfolio of options is worth more than the single option on the portfolio of assets. ■

Self-Check

1. Can the value of two options ever be less than the sum of their separate option values?

2. Why is it that a company's price-setting option may not add its entire stand-alone value when considered in addition to the company's production quantity option?

3. What's the relationship between the value of an option on a portfolio of assets and the value of a portfolio of comparable options on the individual assets?

SUMMARY

We described various types of options and showed how option contracts are a part of many business relationships. The factors that determine an option's value and how changes in those factors alter an option's value were examined. We explained several powerful and practical generalizations regarding options.

- An option is the right without the obligation to do something. A call option is the right to buy an asset at the strike price while a put option is an option to sell an asset at the strike price. An option is often referred to as a contingent claim because its use depends on some event.

- An option takes an asset's distribution of returns and divides it in some way between the buyer of the option and the seller of the option. An option can be viewed as a claim on a portion of an asset's return distribution.

- An option's value is the sum of its exercise value and its time premium.

- An option's exercise value is the difference between the underlying asset's market value and the strike price for in-the-money options. It is zero for out-of-the-money options.

- An option's time premium (1) increases with the option's time until expiration, (2) increases with the risk of the underlying asset, and (3) decreases with the option's depth in- or out-of-the-money (how far the underlying asset's value is from the strike price). A call (put) option's time premium (4) increases (decreases) with the market riskless return.

TABLE B.2

The Value of a Portfolio of Options (O_1 and O_2) versus the Value of a Single Option on a Portfolio of Assets (O_p)

ASSET$_1$	O_1	ASSET$_2$	O_2	PORTFOLIO	O_P	$O_1 + O_2$	$(O_1 + O_2) - O_P$
400	0	400	0	800	0	0	0
400	0	600	100	1000	0	100	100
400	0	800	300	1200	200	300	100
600	100	400	0	1000	0	100	100
600	100	600	100	1200	200	200	0
600	100	800	300	1400	400	400	0
800	300	400	0	1200	200	300	100
800	300	600	100	1400	400	400	0
800	300	800	300	1600	600	600	0

- It is generally better to sell, rather than exercise, an option prior to expiration, because an option's value includes both the exercise value and a time premium. Exercising an option terminates its time premium.

- Options are found in many places. Options are inherent in insurance contracts, real estate contracts, bonds (callable bonds and convertible bonds), warrants, executive stock options, and publicly traded options.

- Many "hidden" options can also significantly affect the value of an asset. Tax-timing options, options in capital investments, and refunded mortgages are examples. The most important hidden option is that the company's common stock can be considered a call option on the company's assets.

- The chapter gives a simple option pricing model. More sophisticated models exist and should be used to value options.

- The "optionality" in a situation can always be described in terms of either a put or a call option. This relationship is referred to as put-call parity.

- The value of two or more "hidden" options may be less than the sum of the values of the individual options.

- The value of a portfolio of options is greater than or equal to the value of a comparable single option on a portfolio of the assets.

TOPIC REVIEW ACTIVITIES

SELF-TEST PROBLEMS

1. (Exercise value of a call option) Marilyn Wiley owns a call option on 100 shares of Chrysler with an exercise price of $70 per share. What is the exercise value of her call option for each of the following market values of Chrysler common stock: $60, $65, $70, $75, $80?

2. (Exercise value of a portfolio of common stock minus a call option) Charles DeGaulle owns 100 shares of Chrysler common stock. Charles has sold a call option on the 100 shares with an exercise price of $70. What is the value of his portfolio (the stock owned and the option sold) for each of the following market values of Chrysler common stock: $60, $65, $70, $75, $80?

3. (Common stock as a call option) Waste King Enterprises has total debts of $15 million that are maturing at the end of the year. If the assets of the company are worth $22 million at the end of the year, do you expect Waste King to pay its debt obligations? If the assets are worth $9 million, will Waste King pay its debt?

4. (Exercise value and time premium) Motorola is currently selling for 65½. A call option expiring in 50 days with an exercise price of 65 is selling for 3¼. A put option with the same exercise price and expiration is selling for 2⅜.
   a. What is the exercise value and the time premium of the call option?
   b. What is the exercise value and the time premium of the put option?

5. (Simple option valuation model) You own a call option on shares of Advanced Business Systems. Your option expires in 1 year and the exercise price is $55 per share. The current stock price is $50. By the end of the year, the stock will increase 25% (to $62.50) or drop 10% (to $45). The riskless return is 8%. Using the simple option valuation model, determine the value of this call option.

SOLUTIONS TO SELF-TEST PROBLEMS

1. The exercise values of Marilyn Wiley's call option will be:

Price of Chrysler:	$60	65	70	75	80
Exercise value per share:	$0	0	0	5	10
Exercise value for 100 shares:	$0	0	0	500	1000

2. The values of Charles DeGaulle's portfolio will be:

Price of Chrysler	Exercise value per share for call	Value of 100 shares	Exercise value for 100 shares	Value of Portfolio
$60	$0	$6000	$0	$6000
65	0	6500	0	6500
70	0	7000	0	7000
75	− 5	7500	−500	7000
80	−10	8000	−1000	7000

3. The Waste King Enterprises stockholders have a call option on the company's assets. The exercise price is equal to the $15 million they owe to the creditors. If the assets are worth $22 million, the exercise value of the call option is $7 million, so the company will pay the creditors what is owed. If the assets are worth $9 million, the company will not exercise its call option. Stockholders will not pay $15 million for assets worth only $9 million, so they will default, turning over ownership of the assets to the creditors.

4. a. For the call option, the exercise value is max [(stock price − exercise price); 0], which is the greater of 65.50 − 65 = $0.50 or zero. The exercise value is $0.50. The time premium is the price of the option minus its exercise value, which is 3.25 − 0.50 = $2.75.
   b. For the put option, the exercise value is max [(exercise price − stock price); 0], which is the greater of 65 − 65.50 = −$0.50 or zero. The exercise value is zero. The time premium is the price of the option minus its exercise value, which is $2.375 − 0 = $2.375.

5. Let's use the four-step simple option valuation model:

Step 1: Find the probabilities of the price changes based on what an investor can earn on a riskless investment:

$$8\% = (\text{probability of increase})(25\%) + (1 - \text{probability of increase})(-10\%)$$

$$8\% = p(25\%) + (1 - p)(-10\%)$$

Solving this for p, we get the probability of an increase = 0.5143.

Step 2: Calculate the exercise values at expiration:

For increase, exercise value = max [(62.5 − 55); 0] = $7.50

For decrease, exercise value = max [(45 − 55); 0] = $0

Step 3: Find the expected outcome as the probability-weighted average of the outcomes:

Expected outcome = 0.5143(7.50) + (1 − 0.5143)(0) = $3.85725

Step 4: Find the present value of the expected outcome by discounting at the riskless return:

$$\text{Present value} = 3.85725/(1.08) = \$3.57$$

The value of your call option is $3.57.

QUESTIONS

1. Define the terms *option, call option,* and *put option.*
2. Define the terms *strike price, in-the-money, out-of-the-money, exercise value,* and *time premium.*
3. Cite three situations involving hidden options.
4. In your own words, explain how limited liability makes shares of common stock like an option.
5. Explain how auto insurance can be viewed as a put option.
6. Why would an American call option traded in an efficient capital market never be worth less than its exercise value?
7. The value of an option includes its (a) exercise value and (b) time premium. Name the parameters that determine each of these two parts and explain how each parameter affects the option's value.
8. Why is the time premium for an American option never negative?
9. Explain how shares of stock can be viewed as a put option on the company's assets.
10. Why is it generally better to sell rather than exercise an American option?
11. What is the relationship between the value of an American option and the value of a comparable European option? For example, is it always greater or less, or does the relationship depend on some parameter? Explain why the relationship is that way.
12. Explain why an option on a portfolio of assets is never worth more than a portfolio of comparable options on the individual assets.

CHALLENGING QUESTIONS

13. Explain how shares of stock can be viewed as a series of European call options on the company's assets.
14. Consider the following statement: "A call option is a great way to make money. If the asset goes up in value, you get the increase, but if the asset goes down in value, you do not exercise the option and don't lose any money. Therefore, everyone should invest in call options." Is this statement true, false, or partly true and partly false? Explain why.
15. Why does the maximum time premium for an option occur when the underlying asset's value equals the strike price? Why does the time premium decrease as the option becomes more in- or out-of-the-money?
16. Most stock options are not dividend-protected. This means that if dividends are paid, the option terms are not adjusted to reflect the cash paid out and the accompanying reduction in the value of the stock. Assume that a large cash dividend reduces the stock price from $100 to $95 on October 18. A call option with an exercise price of $80 expires on October 20. What could the holder of an American call op-

tion do to protect the value of her option? What could the holder of a European call option do to protect the value of her option?

17. Why is an American put option worth more than a comparable European put option when the options are certain to be in the money during their entire remaining time until maturity?

PROBLEM SET A

A1. (Computing exercise values) What is the exercise value of the following options?

Type of option	Stock price	Exercise price	Exercise value
call	$20	$25	_____
call	25	20	_____
put	20	25	_____
put	25	20	_____

A2. (Recognizing puts and calls) Indicate whether the stock price, exercise price, and exercise value given below are for a call option or a put option.

Stock price	Exercise price	Exercise value	Type of option: Put or call?
$44	$40	$0	_____
25⅜	20	5⅜	_____
5	50	45	_____
34	40	0	_____

A3. (Computing exercise values) You have a weird aunt who will give you your choice of one of the following options. They expire today, and all are an option on 100 shares. Which one is the most valuable?
   a. A put option on Gannett. The exercise price is $70 and the stock price is $65.
   b. A call option on Apple. The exercise price is $30 and the stock price is $25⅛.
   c. A call option on Xerox. The exercise price is $150 and the stock price is $162½.
   d. A put option on Hilton. The exercise price is $100 and the stock price is $114½.

A4. (Insurance as a put option) You own a $100,000 house and pay $500 for fire insurance.
   a. What is the exercise value of the fire insurance put option if the house does not burn (and you have no claim)? What is the realized return on your investment in fire insurance?
   b. What is the exercise value of the fire insurance put option if the house burns and you have $80,000 of damage? What is the realized return on your investment in fire insurance?

A5. (Exercise value of executive stock options) Your employer announces a new compensation plan that includes stock options for the company's managers. You are granted stock options on 10,000 shares with an exercise price equal to the current stock price of $70. In five years, when the options expire, what is the exercise value of your options if the stock price has risen to $135? What is the exercise value of your options if the stock price is $50?

A6. (Early exercise versus selling a call option) Joan Junkus owns IBM options expiring in 6 weeks. The exercise price for her options is $100. The current stock price is $104⅞ and the current market price for her options is $5¾. Would she be better off selling her options or exercising her options? Why?

A7. (Exercise value and time premium) Find the missing option values below:

Type of option	Stock price	Exercise price	Exercise value	Time premium of option	Market value of option
call	$30	$20	_____	$1.00	_____
call	66	70	_____	_____	$2.50
put	42	40	_____	1.50	_____
put	24	30	_____	_____	8.00

A8. (Exercise value and time premium) General Motors common stock is currently selling for 56⅞. A call option expiring in 90 days with an exercise price of 55 is selling for 4¼. A put option with the same exercise price and expiration is selling for 2.
   a. What are the exercise value and the time premium of the call option?
   b. What are the exercise value and the time premium of the put option?

A9. (Exercise value and time premium) Microsoft common stock is currently selling for 120⅞. A call option expiring in 50 days with an exercise price of 125 is selling for 3⅝. A put option with the same exercise price and expiration is selling for 6½.
   a. What are the exercise value and the time premium of the call option?
   b. What are the exercise value and the time premium of the put option?

A10. (Graphing exercise values) Assume an exercise price of $50.
   a. Show the exercise value of a call option as a function of the underlying stock price. Put the stock price on the horizontal axis and let it range from $0 to $100. Put the option value on the vertical axis.
   b. On a similar graph, show the exercise value of a put option.
   c. Increase the exercise price to $60 and redraw the value of a call option.
   d. Increase the exercise price to $60 and redraw the value of a put option.

PROBLEM SET B

B1. (Exercise value of a convertible bond) John Houston owns several convertible BIT Company bonds. Given their coupon, maturity, and riskiness, the bonds would have a straight bond value of $850 each if they were nonconvertible. Each bond can be exchanged for 24 shares of BIT stock. The stock is currently selling for $45 per share.
   a. If John converts his bond, what is the conversion value of the 24 shares?

   b. Consider the straight bond value to be the exercise price. What is the exercise value of converting the bond to common stock?
   c. Assume the stock is selling for $20 per share. What would be the exercise value at this price? Should John convert?

B2. (Option values for both buyer and seller) Tom Smith purchased a building in uptown Indianapolis for $50,000. Right after this, he sold a 1-year European call option on the building, with a strike price of $54,000, for $2200 to Sarah Smyth. What are Tom's and Sarah's outcomes, in terms of the land's possible value when the option expires?

B3. (Option values for both buyer and seller) Jenny Johnson purchased a building on New York's lower east side for $1,500,000. Right after this, she bought a 1-year European put option on the building, with a strike price of $1,600,000, for $350,000 from Jimmy Johnsen. What are Jenny's and Jimmy's outcomes, in terms of the land's possible value when the option expires?

B4. (Value of a call option) Suppose you can buy a call option on a business that is currently worth $10,000,000 but will be worth either 25% more or 15% less 1 year from today. The option's strike price is $11,000,000, and the riskless return is 6% per year. What is this call option worth today? Use the simple model of option valuation.

B5. (Value of a call option) Suppose you can buy a call option on a parcel of land that is currently worth $200,000 but will be worth either 15% more or 8% less than this 1 year from today. The option's strike price is $215,000, and the riskless return is 7% per year. What is this call option worth today? Use the simple model of option valuation.

B6. (Value of a portfolio of options versus value of an option on a portfolio) Cheryl Jones has a call option on one share of Cytrans with an exercise price of $20 and a call option on one share of Mallmax with an exercise price of $30. Susan Parker has a call option on a portfolio that has one share of Cytrans and one share of Mallmax. The exercise price on Susan's call option is $50. These options are all expiring today.
   a. If Cytrans is selling for $40 and Mallmax for $25, what is the value of Cheryl's options? What is the value of Susan's option?
   b. If Cytrans is selling for $15 and Mallmax for $35, what is the value of Cheryl's options? What is the value of Susan's option?
   c. If Cytrans is selling for $40 and Mallmax for $35, what is the value of Cheryl's options? What is the value of Susan's option?

PROBLEM SET C

C1. (Put-call parity) The current stock value of Absteel Products is $19. At the end of the year, the price will be either $24 or $16. The riskless return is 5%.
   a. What is the value of a 1-year call option with an exercise price of $20?

b. What is the value of a 1-year put option with an exercise price of $20?

c. Calculate the value of the call (calculated in **a**) plus the present value of the exercise price ($20 discounted at 5% for 1 year) minus the current stock price.

d. Compare your answers to **a** and **b**.

C2. (Put-call parity) Rick Dark purchased some stock from Roger Muns. As part of the transaction, Rick gave Roger a 1-year call option with an exercise price of $100 and received a 1-year put option with an exercise price of $100.

a. In 1 year, if the stock is worth more than $100, what cash should Rick receive?

b. In 1 year, if the stock is worth less than $100, what cash should Rick receive?

c. Assume that Rick's net investment (price of the stock - price of the call option + price of the put option) was $80. What return should Rick earn on his investment?

C3. (Describing an option) A particular type of bond that has actually been issued from time to time allows for the bond to be redeemed, at the option of the bondholder, at either of two future points in time. Suppose such a bond can be redeemed for its face value after either 10 or 20 years. That is, at the 10-year point, the bondholder makes a one-time decision to redeem or not. Clearly there is an option in this contract. Describe this complex bond in terms of one or more (a) option contracts and (b) bonds that are otherwise identical but do not have the two-points-of-redemption option.

C4. (Early exercise of an American put option) Assume that you hold an American put option on Netplus Communications. The option has an exercise price of $50 and expires in 1 year. Netplus has utterly failed and its stock price has dropped to zero. It has no hope of recovering. The riskless return is 10%.

a. If you exercise your put option in 1 year, what will be the payoff? What is the present value of this payoff?

b. If you exercise your put option now, what will be your payoff? What is the present value of this payoff?

c. Consider your answers to **a** and **b**. Should you exercise now or wait? It is generally considered unattractive to exercise an option prior to maturity. Is this an exception to this rule? Can you devise a rule for when it is favorable to exercise an American put option early?

d. Why is an American put option worth more than a comparable European put option?

C5. (Value of a call option) An investor is considering investing $5 million to acquire a thrift institution that currently has $1 billion of assets and zero net worth on its balance sheet. The thrift's liabilities consist principally of federally insured deposits. Its assets include principally real estate loans, which were recently written down to their supposed "fair market value" by the thrift's regulators to enhance the thrift's salability. What does option theory tell you about how the investor should view the prospective $5 million investment?

C6. (Designing option contracts) Suppose you live in a state that has a usury law prohibiting interest charges above 9%. Current market interest rates are 18% for a project. You are a wealthy individual who wants to offer a 1-year construction loan of $100,000 to Storage Partners to build a miniwarehouse.

a. If you lend the money at 9%, what will be your loan payoff in one year?

b. You want to receive a fair market return of 18%. Design a portfolio of contracts that will promise you a $118,000 payoff in 1 year.

BIBLIOGRAPHY

Adams, Paul D., Steve B. Wyatt, and Yong H. Kim. "A Contingent Claims Analysis of Trade Credit," *Financial Management,* 1992, 21(3):95–103.

Biger, Nahum, and John Hull. "The Valuation of Currency Options," *Financial Management,* 1983, 12(1):24–28.

Black, Fischer. "Fact and Fantasy in the Use of Options and Corporate Liabilities," *Financial Analysts Journal,* 1975, 31(July-August):36–41:61–72.

Black, Fischer, and Myron Scholes. "The Pricing of Options and Corporate Liabilities," *Journal of Political Economy,* 1973, 81(May/June):637–654.

Block, Stanley B., and Timothy J. Gallagher. "The Use of Interest Rate Futures and Options by Corporate Financial Managers," *Financial Management,* 1986, 15(3):73–78.

Bodnar, Gordon, Greg Hayt, Richard Marston, and Charles Smithson. "Wharton Survey of Derivatives Usage by U.S. Non-Financial Firms," *Financial Management,* 1995, 24(2):104–114.

Brown, Keith C., and Scott L. Lummer. "A Reexamination of the Covered Call Option Strategy for Corporate Cash Management," *Financial Management,* 1986, 15(2):13–17.

Carr, Peter. "The Valuation of Sequential Exchange Opportunities," *Journal of Finance,* 1988, 43(5):1235–1256.

Carter, Richard B, and Frederick H. Dark. "The Use of the Over-Allotment Option in Initial Public Offerings of Equity: Risks and Underwriter Prestige," *Financial Management,* 1990, 19(3):55–64.

Chatfield, Robert E., and R. Charles Moyer. "'Putting' Away Bond Risk: An Empirical Examination of the Value of the Put Option on Bonds," *Financial Management,* 1986, 15(2):26–33.

Chung, Kee H., and Charlie Charoenwong. "Investment Options, Assets in Place, and the Risk of Stocks," *Financial Management,* 1991, 20(3):21–33.

Cook, Douglas O., and John C. Easterwood. "Poison Put Bonds: An Analysis of Their Economic Role," *Journal of Finance,* 1994, 49(5):1905–1920,

De, Sankar, and Jayant R. Kale. "Contingent Payments and Debt Contracts," *Financial Management,* 1993, 22(2):106–122.

Dufey, Gunter, and S. L. Srinivasulu. "The Case for Corporate Management of Foreign Exchange Risk," *Financial Management*, 1983, 12(4):54–62.

Eckbo, B. Espen, and Ronald W. Masulis. "Adverse Selection and the Rights Offer Paradox," *Journal of Financial Economics*, 1992, 32(3):293–332.

Emery, Douglas R., and Adam K. Gehr, Jr. "Tax Options, Capital Structure, and Miller Equilibrium: A Numerical Illustration," *Financial Management*, 1988, 17(2):30–40.

Fleming, Jeff, and Robert E. Whaley. "The Value of Wildcard Options," *Journal of Finance*, 1994, 49(1):215–236.

Flood, Eugene, Jr., and Donald R. Lessard. "On the Measurement of Operating Exposure to Exchange Rates: A Conceptual Approach," *Financial Management*, 1986, 15(1):25–36.

Galai, Dan, and Ronald W. Masulis. "The Option Pricing Model and the Risk Factor of Stock," *Journal of Financial Economics*, 1976, 3(1/2):53–81.

Grenadier, Steven R. "Valuing Lease Contracts: A Real-Options Approach," *Journal of Financial Economics*, 1995, 38(3):297–332.

Grundy, Bruce D. "Option Prices and the Underlying Asset's Return Distribution," *Journal of Finance*, 1991, 46(3): 1045–1070.

Hansen, Robert S., Beverly R. Fuller, and Vahan Janjigian. "The Over-Allotment Option and Equity Financing Flotation Costs: An Empirical Investigation," *Financial Management*, 1987, 16(2):24–32.

Jacob, David P., Graham Lord, and James A. Tilley. "A Generalized Framework for Pricing Contingent Cash Flows," *Financial Management*, 1987, 16(3):5–14.

Jameson, Mel, and William Wilhelm. "Market Making in the Options Markets and the Costs of Discrete Hedge Rebalancing," *Journal of Finance*, 1992, 47(2):765–780.

Kalotay, Andrew, and Bruce Tuckman. "Sinking Fund Prepurchases and the Designation Option," *Financial Management*, 1992, 21(4):110–118.

Kemna, Angelien G. Z. "Case Studies on Real Options," *Financial Management*, 1993, 22(3):259–270.

Kim, In Joon, Krishna Ramaswamy, and Suresh Sundaresan. "Does Default Risk in Coupons Affect the Valuation of Corporate Bonds? A Contingent Claims Model," *Financial Management*, 1993, 22(3):117–131.

Kulatilaka, Nalin. "The Value of Flexibility: The Case of a Dual-Fuel Industrial Steam Boiler," *Financial Management*, 1993, 22(3):271–280.

Laber, Gene. "Bond Covenants and Managerial Flexibility: Two Cases of Special Redemption Provisions," *Financial Management*, 1990, 19(1):82–89.

Laughton, David G., and Henry D. Jacoby. "Reversion, Timing Options, and Long-Term Decision-Making," *Financial Management*, 1993, 22(3):225–240.

Longstaff, Francis A. "Pricing Options with Extendible Maturities: Analysis and Applications," *Journal of Finance*, 1990, 45(3):935–958.

Mason, Scott P., and Robert C. Merton. "The Role of Contingent Claims Analysis in Corporate Finance." In *Recent Advances in Corporate Finance*, ed. Edward I. Altman and Marti G. Subrahmanyam. Homewood, Ill.: Irwin, 1985.

McLaughlin, Robyn, and Robert A. Taggart, Jr. "The Opportunity Cost of Using Excess Capacity," *Financial Management*, 1992, 21(2):12–23.

Merton, Robert C. "Theory of Rational Option Pricing," *Bell Journal of Economics and Management Science*, 1973, 4(Spring):141–183.

Mozes, Haim A. "An Upper Bound for the Firm's Cost of Employee Stock Options," *Financial Management*, 1995, 24(4):66–77.

Overdahl, James, and Barry Schachter. "Derivatives Regulation and Financial Management: Lessons from Gibson Greetings," *Financial Management*, 1995, 24(1):68–78.

Phillips, Aaron L. "1995 Derivatives Practices and Instruments Survey," *Financial Management*, 1995, 24(2):115–125.

Rendleman, Richard J., Jr., and Brit J. Bartter. "Two-State Option Pricing," *Journal of Finance*, 1979, 34(5):1093–1110.

Ritchken, Peter, L. Sandarasubramanian, and Anand M. Vijh. "Averaging Options for Capping Total Costs," *Financial Management*, 1990, 19(3):35–41.

Smit, Han T. J., and L. A. Ankum. "A Real Options and Game-Theoretic Approach to Corporate Investment Strategy Under Competition," *Financial Management*, 1993, 22(3):241–250.

Sprenkle, Case. "Warrant Prices as Indications of Expectations," *Yale Economic Essays*, 1961, 1:179–232.

Sterk, William Edward. "Option Pricing: Dividends and the In- and Out-of-the-Money Bias," *Financial Management*, 1983, 12(4):47–53.

Triantis, Alexander J., and James E. Hodder. "Valuing Flexibility as a Complex Option," *Journal of Finance*, 1990, 45(2):549–566.

Trigeorgis, Lenos. "Real Options and Interactions with Financial Flexibility," *Financial Management*, 1993, 22(3):202–224.

Winton, Andrew. "Limitation of Liability and the Ownership Structure of the Firm," *Journal of Finance*, 1993, 48(2):487–512.

Woods, John C., and Maury R. Randall. "The Net Present Value of Future Investment Opportunities: Its Impact on Shareholder Wealth and Implications for Capital Budgeting Theory," *Financial Management*, 1989, 18(2):85–92.

Yermack, David. "Do Corporations Award CEO Stock Options Effectively?" *Journal of Financial Economics*, 1995, 39(2&3):237–270.

Zivney, Terry L., and Michael J. Alderson. "Hedged Dividend Capture with Stock Index Options," *Financial Management*, 1986, 15(2):5–12.

Financial Contracting

The modern corporation is exceedingly complex. Chapter 1 touched on a little of that complexity in our fictionalized account of Henry Ford's car company. A lot of the complexity occurs because there are so many implicit contractual relationships in addition to all the explicit ones.

Financial contracting describes the business world in terms of *both* types of contracts, implicit and explicit. The purpose is to identify important practical considerations, such as the implicit aspects of the "stake," or contingent claim each stakeholder has in the company.

The main issue in financial contracting is how to minimize the costs of having someone else make decisions that affect you. This really refers to the cost of managing a situation in which you have a stake *through* other people. The answer lies in (1) creating incentives, constraints, and punishments; (2) having reasonable monitoring procedures; and (3) identifying and using contracts that minimize the *possibility* of conflicts of interest at the outset.

Costs associated with financial contracting occur throughout the business decision-making process and can be very significant. Therefore, these costs play an important role in many of the topics covered in this book.

FINANCIAL CONTRACTING AND THE PRINCIPLES OF FINANCE

◆ *Self-Interested Behavior:* Look for the incentives that influence an agent's decision making.

◆ *Incremental Benefits:* Measure the incentives on an incremental basis.

◆ *Signaling:* Interpret the information contained in the actions of others. Recognize the incentive value of building and maintaining a good reputation.

◆ *Options:* Include all of the contingencies and their impact on incentives and value.

◆ *Two-Sided Transactions:* Consider every situation from both the principal's and the agent's points of view.

◆ *Valuable Idea:* Beware of free riders who might illegally copy your valuable ideas.

◆ *Diversification:* Recognize that human capital is extremely difficult to diversify.

◆ *Risk-Return Trade-Off:* Require a higher return from unique assets.

PRINCIPAL-AGENT RELATIONSHIPS

As Chapter 1 discusses, the **set-of-contracts model** views a company as a set of obligations among its stakeholders. This model highlights the complexity of the modern corporation. The model was developed using **agency theory,** which is the analysis of **principal-agent relationships.** Stakeholder relationships can be described as principal-agent relationships, where an **agent** is making decisions that affect a **principal.**

Some of the more visible examples of *explicit* principal-agent relationships include money managers, lawyers, and agents of real estate, travel, and insurance. Many other situations can be described in the principal-agent framework *as though* the two parties were principal and agent—even though one party is not literally an agent for the other. For example, even though most employees are not explicitly classified as agents for their employer, most act as agents at some point.

EXAMPLE

A Principal-Agent Conflict

Seldon C. Fish is the CEO of a large financial company. While looking over the company's financial reports, he found that the latest quarter was great. A large change in interest rates provided a windfall for the company. Although the extra income was not caused by anything the company did, Sel was of course delighted. However, he knew competition would not allow his company to have the same big margins next year, so the extra income was only a one-time bit of luck.

Now the company must decide what to do with the extra income. Sel will be making a recommendation on this matter to the company's board of directors. He has narrowed it down to two possibilities: (1) extra-large employee bonuses as a reward for having such a successful year, or (2) a one-time "extra" cash dividend to the stockholders for getting lucky.

Suppose you are a stockholder (part owner) of this company—but you're not also an employee. As a principal in this example, which alternative would you want Sel to recommend?

Now suppose you are an employee who gets part of the employee bonuses—but you're not also a stockholder. As an agent in this example, which alternative would you like Sel to recommend?

Finally, consider the CEO, Mr. Fish. He is both a stockholder (principal) and a bonus-earning employee (agent). How would he fare under each alternative? In other words, what are his incentives? To develop an opinion of which alternative you think he might like, here are some additional facts. The CEO will himself get 4% of this year's employee bonus money. If paid, the extra dividend would be split equally among the 9 million shares of the company's stock. Sel owns 27,000 of these shares, so he would get 0.3% of the extra dividend. If you consider only these one-time financial incentives, what do you think Sel Fish is likely to recommend?

You can see that the CEO's incentives in this example favor the extra-large employee bonuses. Regardless of how much the extra is, Sel Fish would get more of this one-time extra if it is paid out in employee bonuses (4% versus 0.3%). Note that for other bonus-earning employees who are stockholders, the employee bonus is also likely to be larger than their share of the dividend. Although they would get a smaller portion of the bonus, most own much less stock and would get less in dividends as well. Compared to other stockholders and employees, the CEO has a large stake. You might say he's a "big fish." ∎

A potential conflict of interests between the agent and the principal creates an **agency problem.** Such conflicts can be as simple as the agent not putting forth "full effort." From the Principle of Self-Interested Behavior, we know that agents may be tempted to put their own self-interest ahead of those of the principal. As a result, an agent's decision making becomes suspect when the interests of the agent and principal diverge.

For example, is it ok for an employee (an agent) who is traveling on behalf of the company to take a side-trip vacation along the way? Answering this question can be difficult or even impossible. On the one hand, if travel is necessary for the employee to do the job, what's wrong with the employee getting personal benefit from the trip? That is, if the employee benefits at no cost to the company, why not allow the employee to take the side trip? The prob-

lem lies in making sure it's truly costless to the company. It may be impossible to make sure the employee's travel decision was not influenced by a personal side benefit.

Agency problems occur because of asymmetric information. If the principal knows everything an agent does, the agent would never be able to take actions that were not in the best interest of the principal. Thus, if it were possible and not unreasonably costly for the principal to **monitor** the agent's actions perfectly, there would be no agency problems. Obviously, perfect monitoring, even if it were truly possible, is exorbitantly expensive. Most people would quickly conclude that "it's easier to do it myself." Therefore, contracts rarely have perfect monitoring, and the problem of **moral hazard** can arise. Moral hazard occurs whenever agents can take unobserved actions in their own interest, to the detriment of the principal.

The amount of monitoring is important with respect to efficient resource allocation. The more monitoring there is, the harder it is for an agent to misbehave—but the extra monitoring costs money. Not all agents will take self-interested actions to the detriment of the principal; therefore, spending too much on monitoring agent behavior is wasteful. For any specific situation, there is a trade-off between the resources spent on monitoring and the possibility of agent misbehavior.

Alternatives to monitoring include constraints, incentives, and punishments that encourage an agent to act in the principal's best interest. An example of constraints are the legal regulations on insider trading. Managerial stock options, performance share plans, and sales commissions are examples of incentives. Getting fired would be a punishment.

If it were possible to create a contract that paid agents in perfect accord with the best interests of the principal, the need for monitoring would be eliminated. This is because when the agents act in their own best financial interest they would also be acting in the principals' best interest. But our world is not characterized by perfect accord or perfect information. Consequently, we need to search for better contracts, ones that minimize the *possibility* of conflicts of interest.

Self-Check

1. What is a principal-agent relationship?

2. Why do principal-agent relationships give rise to agency problems?

3. How can monitoring reduce agency problems? Is there a cost involved?

4. What are some alternatives to monitoring an agent's behavior?

AGENCY COSTS

Monitoring, constraints, incentives, and punishments are designed to push agents to act in the principals' best interests, but they are costly. The costs of doing these things are called **agency costs.** Agency costs are the extra costs of having an agent act for a principal, those in excess of what it would cost the principals to "do it themselves." These costs are like friction in a machine—the more there is, the less efficient the machine, and the more energy that will be wasted.

Agency costs are defined in terms of the Principle of Incremental Benefits: The agency cost is the *incremental* cost of working *through* others, who serve as agents. In a perfect world, the agent would be paid exactly the fair amount without any waste. In our imperfect world, agency costs are a waste that is lost to the system.

Agency costs consist of three types:

1. Direct contracting costs, which include the following:

   a. The transaction costs of setting up the contract, such as the selling commissions and legal fees of issuing bonds.

   b. The opportunity costs imposed by constraints that preclude otherwise optimal decisions (for example, an inability to undertake a positive-NPV investment because of a restrictive bond covenant).

   c. The incentive fees paid to the agent to encourage behavior consistent with the principal's goals, such as employee bonuses.

2. The costs to the principal of monitoring the agent (for example, auditing costs).

3. The loss of wealth the principal suffers as a result of misbehavior in spite of monitoring, such as unidentified excessive employee expense accounts or employees wasting time.

A major goal is to find the optimal contract. The **optimal contract** minimizes the relationship's total agency costs. It transfers the decision-making authority in the most efficient way. It provides the smallest waste. Note that in some cases, the cost of periodic misbehavior is less than the cost of monitoring. In most cases, the optimal contract entails some attention to each of the three component costs.

In our search for better contracts, it's important to identify those situations where conflicts of interest arise naturally. In the following sections, we examine several important relationships and conditions that are prone to such conflicts. But no set of contracts can cover all possible contingencies. Therefore, it is impossible to eliminate all potential for conflict. This is an especially good reason to keep the Principles of Self-Interested Behavior and Two-Sided Transactions in your mind as you interact in the business world.

Self-Check

1. What are agency costs and how do they arise?

2. What are the three types of agency costs? Give an example of each.

3. How can financial contracting deal with agency costs?

A FEW WORDS ABOUT ETHICS

The goal of stockholder wealth maximization should be pursued subject to a fundamental restriction: Corporate managers should take only steps that are legal and ethically sound.

You may encounter situations in your career that tempt you to "play it close to the edge" or even cross over the line that separates ethical from unethical behavior in order to enhance a company's—and your own—position. But modest transgressions tend to lead to more serious transgressions and eventually to serious legal difficulties.

History offers many examples of price fixing, insider trading, market manipulation, and similar activities that people undertook after convincing themselves that it was somehow in their companies' best interests to do so. We explicitly exclude such behavior when we talk about maximizing stockholder wealth.

We have also said that managers may act in their own self-interest to the detriment of the stockholders. In some cases, these actions may not be illegal, or even explicitly prohibited, but they are not good for the corporation. Managers who abuse their positions set a bad example for everyone else. Still, as a practical matter, we must acknowledge that such behavior does exist.

For example, empirical evidence shows a difference in administrative costs (including management benefits) based on a difference in monitoring. The most important benefit from this acknowledgment is probably an increase in awareness. Such an awareness can help protect you from unethical behavior.

STOCKHOLDER-MANAGER CONFLICTS

The stockholder-manager relationship is created by separating ownership and control. In simple companies, the owners are the managers. In more complex companies, many stockholders have nothing to do with the daily operation of the company. Still, in theory, the managers work for all the stockholders. If managers don't do a good job, the stockholders can fire them and hire new managers. But such a process is cumbersome and difficult to accomplish in practice.

Strictly speaking, the common stockholders of a publicly held corporation don't even own the company; they own shares of common stock that entitle them to voting rights and certain other rights. Such corporations are operated by professional managers who may or may not own shares themselves. The company's board of directors hires the managers. Although the directors serve as the shareholders' elected representatives and have a legal responsibility to the shareholders, they are typically nominated for election by top management. You can see the problem right away. It seems almost circular if you ignore the obligation to the shareholders.

Managers, therefore, are the primary decision makers. They have considerable control over the company and its assets. In some cases, managers have even been accused of using the company's assets against the owners. So two important questions arise: Are the managers' interests different from the nonmanagement shareholders' interests? If they are, whose interests are the managers really promoting?

How Stockholders' and Managers' Goals May Diverge

Based on the Principle of Self-Interested Behavior, the theory of finance holds that the goal of the stockholders is to maximize the present value of their investment.

Also on the basis of the Principle of Self-Interested Behavior, the theory of finance allows that managers' goals can differ from the stockholders' goal of maximizing stockholder wealth. Managers are alleged to favor growth and large size for a variety of reasons. Managers appear to value salary, power, and status, all of which are positively correlated with the size of the company. Larger size, it is argued, provides management with (1) greater job security and (2) larger compensation. Faster growth creates more opportunities for the internal promotion of lower- and middle-level managers. Growth also creates opportunities to distinguish oneself as a productive member of the organization, one who is worthy of promotion. Other potential managerial objectives include greater prestige and discretionary expense accounts.

Differences in the goals of stockholders and managers lead to several specific points of possible goal divergence, which we will now discuss. Note that, in this relationship, the stockholders are the principals who are trying to get the managers (agents) to act in their best interest.

Employee Perquisites

One of the most obvious examples of moral hazard (the possibility of agent misbehavior) involves employee decisions that affect personal benefits, or **perquisites.** These include direct benefits, such as the use of a company car or expense account for personal business, and also indirect benefits such as an up-to-date office decor. When excessive money is spent on such things, it is money lost to the stockholders.

Employee Effort

Some employees would like to get paid without having to put forth any effort. It's been said that 20% of the people do 80% of the work.[1] The problem of an agent being neglectful or putting forth less than "full effort" is referred to as **shirking.**

The Nondiversifiability of Human Capital

The unique capabilities and expertise of individuals are referred to as **human capital.** Typically, human capital is tied to employment, and employees devote most of their efforts to a single company. Therefore, employees cannot easily diversify their human capital. They become specialists in the company they serve and in the role they play. This creates a problem called the **nondiversifiability of human capital.**

We know about the benefits of diversification from the Principle of Diversification. Still, even if a person wants to, it's extremely difficult to diversify human capital. Professionals, such as corporate managers, engineers, physicians, accountants, and lawyers, simply don't have the time to become proficient in several areas—and certainly not a sufficient number to provide reasonable diversification. The nondiversifiability of human capital leads to yet other goal divergences between managers and stockholders.

Capital Investment Choices   The stockholders of large publicly traded corporations typically hold many different stocks in their financial investment portfolios. Therefore, they are not overly concerned with random fluctuations in the value of one particular company. This is because the random fluctuations in the many different stock values tend to cancel each other out. In marked contrast, managers can be "wiped out" by a random fluctuation in the value of their company. As a result, the stockholder and manager incentives for making investments can be quite different. But it is the managers who routinely make the company's investment decisions.

To see this divergence of incentives, consider the impact of bankruptcy on a well-diversified stockholder versus its impact on an employee. Let's take the extreme bankruptcy case where the company becomes worthless. Despite the lost stock value, the bankruptcy has no effect on the value of the stockholder's other investments, nor does it affect his job. Employees, however, lose their jobs—even though their financial investments are unaffected. The important question is one of differential impact: Is the loss of a job worse than the loss of, say, 5% of one's financial investments? In the overwhelming majority of cases, job income is much larger than one's income from financial investments. Therefore, the impact of bankruptcy is much greater on the employee than it is on the stockholder.

This divergence of incentives results in an investment decision-making bias. Because employees have more to lose from a really bad outcome, they will have a bias against the company's making high-risk investments. Because the bias is based on risk (rather than return), it can still exist even if the investment has a large positive NPV.

Asset Uniqueness   Another impact of the nondiversifiability of human capital on agency costs involves the company's products and services. If the products and/or services are unique (as opposed to generic), the employee's human capital will have even less than normal diversification. Highly specialized employees may be able to sell their services *only* to this company, because no one else is in this exact business. In such cases, the stockholders will have to pay the employees extra to compensate them for the lack of other job alternatives. After all, employees doing more generic work have options to work for other companies (and we know options are valuable!).

The problems of capital investment choices and asset uniqueness impose their costs at different times. The agency cost with capital investment choices is the possibility of passing up positive-NPV investments. This effect is on the choice of *new* investments. The agency cost of unique assets is the higher wages paid to employees to induce them to work for the company. This effect is on *existing* investments.

---

[1]Shareholders would naturally like to have only "20%-type" employees, in which case—conceptually—the shareholders would need only one-quarter as many employees: $X/100\% = 20\%/80\%$ implies that $X = 25\%$.

Self-Check

1. How can stockholders' and managers' goals diverge?

2. What is shirking? Why is it an agency problem?

3. How does the nondiversifiability of human capital give rise to a stockholder-manager conflict?

4. How does asset uniqueness intensify the problem of the nondiversifiability of human capital?

DEBTHOLDER-STOCKHOLDER CONFLICTS

In a general sense, the stockholders can be viewed as having an option against the debtholders (bondholders): The stockholders have *limited liability,* the option to default. Consequently, there is always some possibility (even if extremely small) that the contractually required payments to corporate debtholders will not be the full amount promised on or before the specified due dates. For this reason, the debt is called **risky debt.**

Incentive conflicts occur between the debtholders and the stockholders because the debt is risky. These conflicts lead to several specific problems we discuss in this section. First, let's get the roles straight. In the previous section, the stockholders are principals with respect to their corporate managers (agents). In this section, the stockholders reverse their role. Here, we are examining them in their role as agents in their relationship with debtholders (principals). The debtholders want to protect themselves against actions taken by the agent stockholders who in turn make their decisions through the company managers.

The Asset Substitution Problem

Companies routinely make decisions that result in the substitution of assets. In the simplest and most common instance, cash is used to buy equipment or materials. In fact, for every investment, some assets are substituted for others. Prudent managers weigh the risks and returns of these investments. But with risky debt, stockholders may be motivated to substitute riskier assets for the company's existing assets. The **asset substitution** problem occurs when riskier assets are substituted for the company's existing assets, thereby expropriating value from the company's debtholders.

Here is how the asset substitution problem happens. The total value of a company is the market value of all its assets. The debtholders have a claim that is secured by this total value. The stockholders have the residual claim to the remaining company value. But the debtholders' claim is a fixed promised amount. What can change is the likelihood that they will actually get the amount they have been promised. With the promised payment fixed, an increase in the risk of the assets decreases the value of the debtholders' claim. After all, with higher risk there is more chance the debtholders will not be repaid the promised amount. This lowers the expected value of the payment.

The asset substitution problem arises because of the stockholders' valuable default option. So we can view the problem in terms of options (contingent claims). The value of an option increases and decreases with the risk of the underlying asset. In this case the "underlying asset" is all of the company's assets. Therefore, if the company (that is, the stockholders) increases the risk of its assets through substitution, the value of this option goes up. This lowers the expected value of the debt payment, as we just noted. Expropriating this value from the debtholders distorts the stockholders' incentives. In fact, it can even cause a negative-NPV investment to actually *increase* stockholder wealth.

Consider the case where the asset substitution does not change the total value of the company's assets. This is illustrated in figure C.1. With the same total value—the same-sized "pie"—and only the debtholders and stockholders as claimants, a decrease in the value of the debtholders' claim must cause an exactly offsetting increase in the value of the stockholders' claim. It is a zero-sum game between the debtholders and the stockholders. After making the risky asset substitution, the stockholders could sell their shares for more than before. If the

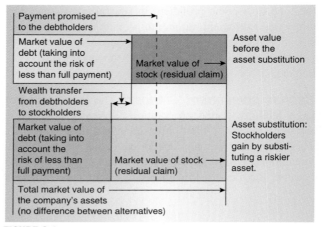

FIGURE C.1

The asset substitution problem. Stockholders gain at the expense of the debtholders.

debtholders sold their bonds, however, they would get equivalently less, because the marketplace would factor in the increased risk of default.

Figure C.1 is a useful way of illustrating the debtholder-stockholder conflict. We use the same framework in figures C.2 through C.6 on pages 276 and 277 to illustrate other aspects of this conflict. So it's "worth your while" to spend enough time with figure C.1 to understand and become comfortable with it.

The idea behind the asset substitution problem might seem puzzling at first. It *is* tricky. But examining its potentially dramatic implications in the following detailed example may help your intuition. Because it's so amazing, we want to stress that we didn't make it up. It actually happened!

The Green Canyon Project

EXAMPLE

The Hunt brothers' Green Canyon oil and gas drilling project illustrates the asset substitution problem. Placid Oil Co. defaulted on its bank loan agreement in March 1986 after oil prices plummeted. The company was owned by trusts of the three Hunt brothers of Dallas, sons of the legendary H. L. Hunt. Placid filed for bankruptcy protection from its creditors in September 1986. Placid wanted to stretch out its loan payments in order to fund its Green Canyon project. Understandably, the banks wanted Placid to pay them off before undertaking new investments—especially highly risky ones.

The Hunt brothers had embarked on the highly risky $340 million Green Canyon project in the hope that a massive oil and gas discovery would save their business. (At one time the Hunts contended that they might find a 70-million-barrel oil reserve worth upwards of $1 billion.) At that time they apparently had debts they were unable to repay. These debts included Placid's debt, debts of Placid's sister company Penrod Drilling Co., and personal debts that grew out of their unsuccessful, very expensive attempt to corner the world silver market in 1979 to 1980.

The Green Canyon project entailed drilling for oil and gas in very deep water in the Gulf of Mexico. One well, drilled through 2243 feet of water, set a world water-depth record for drilling. This is a very hostile operating environment. Hurricane gusts can reach 150 miles per hour. Also, they used an untested technology, a one-of-a-kind floating drilling and production system. The Hunts were "betting the ranch" on one of the world's riskiest ventures. Many industry experts questioned the project's economic viability. Understandably, the banks went to extraordinary lengths in their efforts to stop the project, arguing that if the project failed there would be little left of Placid for them to collect toward their loans.

Consider the situation in terms of the hidden option that common stock can be viewed as being a call option on the company's assets. When the company's assets are worth less than its debt obligations, the stock is like an out-of-the-money call option. As such, the stock isn't worth a whole lot. To risk such a relatively small equity value on an unlikely chance of the company earning a lot of money is something like buying a lottery ticket: The stockholders have a lot to gain—but not much to lose. This is the essence of the asset substitution problem in a financially distressed company. Increasing the risk of the underlying asset (the company's total assets), by using cash to invest in highly risky assets, increases the value of the call option (the company's common stock). The gamble may not be very likely to pay off, but hey, you never know!

Afterword: Eventually, all three Hunt brothers' trusts and two of the Hunt brothers and their wives wound up in bankruptcy as their financial woes mounted. The Green Canyon project did not pay off and Placid finally abandoned it. The banks didn't do so badly after all. They got back their principal, but only some of the interest they were owed.

The effect of the Green Canyon project on Placid Oil Co. is illustrated in figure C.2 on page 276. It's important to note that even though "everyone lost," it could have turned out differently. Winning this big gamble would have provided enough for everyone. The problem, of course, was that the debtholders put up all the money for the gamble—even though they didn't want to. The stockholders chose the gamble, without putting up any additional money. Perhaps more of us would play the lottery if we could get other people to purchase the tickets for us! ■

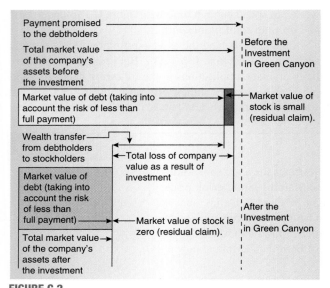

FIGURE C.2
The effect of the Green Canyon project on Placid Oil Co. The debtholders bore the risk of the investment made by the stockholders.

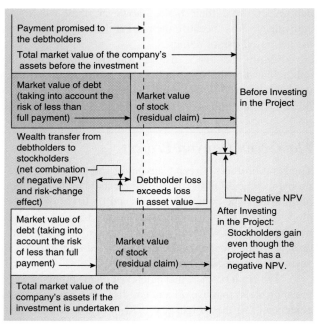

FIGURE C.3
The problem of asset substitution with a negative-NPV investment. The stockholders gain more in wealth transfer from the debtholders than they lose in negative NPV.

Now let's consider a more general asset substitution situation where the increase in risk changes the total value of the company. The change in assets may have either a positive or a negative NPV. Let's look at the good investments first. Because the debt claim is fixed, the stockholders get the positive NPV (increase in "pie" size). If the value of the debtholders' claim is also reduced by the simultaneous increase in risk, the stockholders get that value as well. This is because it's a zero-sum game.

What happens with bad investments? Even with a smaller-sized "pie" (a smaller company value due to the negative NPV), if the decrease in the debtholders' claim value is *more* than the loss in the size of the pie, the value of the stockholders' claim *increases*. That is, if the wealth transfer dominates the negative NPV, the stockholders still gain. The debtholders suffer the entire negative NPV and then some.[2] The asset substitution problem is illustrated with a negative-NPV investment in figure C.3.

Let's summarize. The asset substitution problem occurs when the stockholders substitute riskier assets for the company's existing assets and expropriate value from the debtholders. This can be accomplished in the process of new investment (growth) or by selling some existing assets and purchasing new ones. Although the total value of the company may stay the same, increase, or decrease, the value of the debtholders' claim goes down because of the greater chance of default. The decrease in debtholder value

causes an exactly offsetting increase in stockholder value because of the zero-sum-game condition between the two claimants.

The Underinvestment Problem

Underinvestment is essentially the mirror image, or reverse, of the asset substitution problem. With risky debt outstanding, the stockholders may *lose* value if the company makes a low-risk investment. This can happen even if the investment has a positive NPV. As we saw in the asset substitution problem, with a neutral (zero-NPV) investment, the stockholders gain with an increase in risk. Logically, under the same conditions, the stockholders will lose with a decrease in risk. With asset substitution, stockholders may undertake a bad (negative-NPV), but high-risk, investment to expropriate wealth from the debtholders.

With underinvestment, stockholders refuse to undertake a good (positive-NPV), but low-risk, investment so as not to shift wealth away from themselves to the debtholders. Despite the loss from such a risk change, of course, stockholders can gain from an investment—if it has a sufficiently large positive NPV. However, if the decrease in stockholder value from lowering the asset risk outweighs the positive NPV of an investment, stockholders will refuse to undertake the investment. Figure C.4 illustrates the underinvestment problem.

---

[2]You can see right away why the debtholders don't like this game!

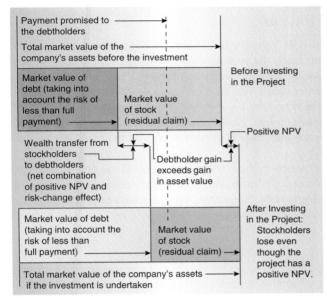

FIGURE C.4
The underinvestment problem. The stockholders would lose more in wealth to the debtholders than they would gain in positive NPV.

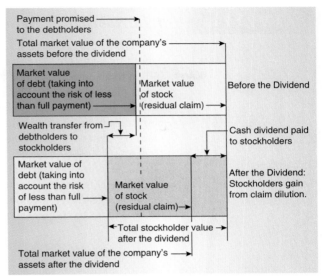

FIGURE C.5
The problem of claim dilution via dividend policy. Since cash is a riskless asset, paying it out to stockholders as a dividend increases the risk of the remaining assets. The value of the stock declines, because of the drop in assets, but by less than the value of the dividend.

Claim Dilution via Dividend Policy

Paying out a large cash dividend may dilute the existing debtholders' claim. The dividend simultaneously reduces the company's cash and its owners' equity. The equity reduction enlarges the company's proportion of debt financing, thereby increasing the risk of the debt and reducing the value of its claim.

This is simply a different form of asset substitution. The substituted assets are the same except for having a smaller amount of cash. Because cash is a riskless asset, removing some of it (paying it out to the stockholders) raises the average risk of the remaining assets. As you now know, the increase in risk will decrease the value of the company's outstanding debt. Figure C.5 illustrates the problem of claim dilution via dividend policy.

Claim dilution via dividend policy is why many bond issues (and virtually all "junk," or high-yield, issues) have some form of dividend restriction. Such a restriction typically limits cash dividends to a fraction of earnings or cash flow. For companies with a large portion of debt financing, it may prohibit the payment of cash dividends altogether until long-term debt is repaid to some specified level.

Claim Dilution via New Debt

A substantial increase in debt may also dilute the existing debtholders' claim on the company's assets. Claim dilution occurs if the new debt increases the chance that the existing debtholders will not be repaid the promised amount. As with

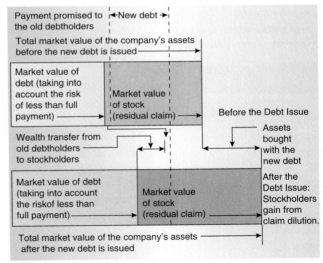

FIGURE C.6
The problem of claim dilution via new debt. The stockholders gain from a wealth transfer from the old debtholders.

asset substitution, the increased risk decreases the value of the company's outstanding debt. Once again, because of the nature of the zero-sum game and the contingent claim, the stockholders get the benefit of the debtholders' loss in value. Figure C.6 illustrates the problem.

We have just explained how a company may engage in claim dilution by paying a large dividend, or by deliber-

| **E X A M P L E** | ***RJR Nabisco's Leveraged Buyout*** |

The real-world leveraged buyout of RJR Nabisco, Inc. illustrates how claim dilution can be caused by new debt. The buyout increased the company's outstanding debt from about $5.7 billion to about $23.2 billion. Following the announcement of the bid, existing RJR Nabisco bonds plunged roughly 20% in market value. The pre-existing debt did not have a legal restriction preventing a large amount of new debt. Existing bondholders had expected the company to continue to use similar amounts of debt. But the bondholders were rudely confronted: Once the debt was issued, the company constrained its actions *only* by the explicit legal debt contract.

Following the RJR Nabisco experience, there was near turmoil in the market for high-grade bonds issued by consumer products companies. After things settled down, many investors had learned a lesson from this incident. Since then, investors have required additional restrictions to try to prevent other companies from doing the same thing that RJR Nabisco did. ■

ately changing its *capital structure* (its mix of liabilities and stockholders' equity) by taking on a significant amount of new debt. A significant economic downturn can also cause claim dilution. This is because poor economic conditions increase the probability of default. In such cases the claim dilution certainly may not have been the company's choice!

Asset Uniqueness

In general, when a company's assets are unique, as opposed to generic, there is more risk associated with the dis-

posal of those assets, should that become necessary. So the collateral provided by the assets to the debtholders is of lower value. Although the assets might be highly sought after because of their uniqueness, they also might become worthless (or perhaps even costly to dispose of). This is the essence of a risk-return trade-off. Therefore, if everything else is equal, a company with unique assets would have to pay a higher interest cost to compensate the debtholders for the increased risk.

| **E X A M P L E** | ***The Effect of Asset Uniqueness on Making a Loan*** |

Suppose you're a banker considering two different loan applications. Each loan would enable its respective company to build a business facility that would be almost entirely controlled by robotics equipment. The new facility would be the collateral for the loan. One is a storage facility that can be used for virtually anything that does not need specialized treatment such as refrigeration. The other is a facility for manufacturing a new kind of home entertainment product, such as a video laser disc player. The cost of building the facilities would be identical. What would be the comparative risk of loaning money to these two companies?

The storage facility would be built by one company for a specific use, but it could easily be used for something different at little extra cost. The manufacturing facility would also be built for a specific use, but using it for something else would require considerable additional cost. Therefore, if the second company defaulted, it is likely that the facility would be worthless for its intended purpose. That is, if the product was unsuccessful, the robotics facility would require extensive and costly modifications to make it useful for another purpose. But if the first company defaulted, the bank would stand a better chance of reselling the collateral to another business without having to spend much money to modify it.

As the banker, would you be willing to loan the same amount of money to the two companies? We wouldn't. Even if the likelihood of default were identical, the bank's risk would be greater with the manufacturing facility because the value of the facility would be considerably less if it had to be used for something else. Therefore, for the manufacturing company, we would either not loan as much money, or we would charge a higher interest rate on a loan of the same amount as the loan for the storage facility. ■

Just as the manager of a company in a unique business would charge more for her labor, so a lender would charge the company more. If the unique business defaults, the manager would need to become reeducated to recover the value of her human capital. The lender would have to reinvest to make the collateral assets equal their original value. When a company heads for uncharted waters, the increased risk has its costs.

Self-Check

1. Why is corporate debt risky?

2. What is the asset substitution problem, and how are debtholders hurt by it?

3. What is the underinvestment problem, and how are the debtholders hurt by it?

4. What does claim dilution mean? How does paying a cash dividend give rise to claim dilution? How does a new debt issue lead to claim dilution?

5. How does an asset's uniqueness affect its value as collateral for a loan?

CONSUMER-COMPANY CONFLICTS

Even some consumer-company interactions can be viewed as principal-agent relationships. However, it's important to keep in mind who the players are. In the first situation we discuss, the company is the agent and the consumer is the principal. In the second situation, the company is the principal and the consumer is the agent.

Guarantees and Service After the Sale

In its agent role, the company promises future service, should it become necessary. The fundamental question is whether the consumer can "trust" the company to fulfill its future obligations. If the consumer (principal) is confident the company will live up to its promise, the company can get full value for its products and services. The level of confidence is the essence of the company's reputation. A good reputation is the assurance that promises will be fulfilled to the consumer's satisfaction. Needless to say, a company in financial distress—even one with a great reputation—may not be able to provide adequate assurance of future service. When it comes time for service, the company may be long gone!

Consumer-Company Conflicts and Chrysler's Financial Distress   **EXAMPLE**

Several years ago Chrysler Corporation experienced financial distress. This led the federal government to provide more than $1.5 billion of loan guarantees. It stands as one of the few times the federal government has stepped in to "bail out" a private company.

Warranties were a critical factor that compounded Chrysler's trouble. As Chrysler's financial woes mounted, consumers grew more concerned that Chrysler might not be around to honor its warranties and sell replacement parts. Sales plummeted, which led to greater losses. Even the cars that were sold brought much lower prices compared with comparable competitor models. The federal government loan guarantees came just before Chrysler would have had to file for bankruptcy. ∎

The Free-Rider Problem

What a customer does with a company's product can in some cases significantly affect the company. For example, a company may be hurt by a customer who duplicates and sells the company's products and/or services without proper agreement. (The "option" to do this is yet another hidden option.) As such, this relationship also can be viewed in a principal-agent framework. Recall the concept of a free rider, one who receives the benefit of someone else's expenditure (money, effort, or creativity) simply by imitation. The potential for consumers (the agents in this case) to duplicate and sell the company's (the principal's) products and/or services without proper agreement is another example of the free-rider problem.

Consider the copying (or plagiarism) of books, computer software, videotapes, audiotapes, and so on. Copyright laws make such misuse illegal. Similarly, patent laws make certain kinds of copying of a valuable idea illegal. The purpose of such laws is to provide incentives for people to be creative. In other words, our society has recognized the Principle of Valuable Ideas and encourages people to create value in this manner. In many cases these laws work very well. However, new products and technologies sometimes require the modification of existing laws. Such a modification was deemed necessary with respect to video-movie rentals. During the 1980s, royalties for movie rentals became mandated by law.

Another free-rider problem area involves international law. Making and enforcing copyright, patent, and royalty laws are important to international trade and relations. As markets become truly international, countries that do not recognize and enforce such laws become places where pirated material can be easily created. Alleged blatant violations are a major issue of contention in international talks, as they were recently in U.S.-China trade negotiations. Such pirated material can cause a significant loss to the creators.

How can the company protect itself from unscrupulous consumers who exercise the hidden option to free-ride? It is rumored that the Coca-Cola Company has employed people to order "Coke" in establishments that do not sell their product. If they failed to clarify that the drink served was not actually Coke, Coca-Cola is said to have sued the establishment for violation of its trademark. Although this may sound like a harsh measure, it may be one of the few methods available to protect a valuable trademark.[3]

Self-Check

1. Describe two consumer-company conflicts.

2. How does financial distress affect the consumer-company conflict relating to promises of future service?

3. What is the free-rider problem, and how does it involve a hidden option?

WORKING IN CONTRACTUAL RELATIONSHIPS

There are a number of other practical considerations in ongoing explicit and implicit contractual relationships.

Financial Distress

Financial distress can intensify the problem of goal divergence. As an example, consider again the debtholder-stockholder relationship. After a debt contract has been made, stockholders make company decisions (through the managers) within the constraints of the contract. But the incentives to "push the edge of the contract" and engage in asset substitution and underinvestment increase dramatically if a company becomes financially distressed. We saw this in practice in the Green Canyon project example.

In figure C.7, we illustrate two companies that are facing the same two alternative investments: a positive-NPV low-risk investment, and a negative-NPV high-risk investment. Company A is financially healthy, but company B is financially distressed. As you can see, the incentives differ for the two companies' stockholders. The stockholders of the financially distressed company are better off engaging in asset substitution and underinvestment, taking the negative-NPV investment and leaving the positive-NPV investment. In contrast, the financially healthy company has the incentives to take the positive-NPV investment and leave the negative-NPV one.

Claimant Coalitions Financial distress can distort other situations as well. It can create incentives for the company's various claimants (stakeholders) to form coalitions and "gang up" on one another. For example, suppose a company is in financial distress, and liquidation would produce the largest total value. Despite this, the managers might contract with a bank for a loan to continue operations.

Each claimant will favor or oppose liquidation on the basis of its own outcome, not on the basis of maximizing total company value. The loan provides the managers with another chance to save their jobs (an option!), even though continuing hurts the stockholders. But the stockholders might support the loan, even though it hurts the debtholders. This can happen if the stockholders will get little from liquidation but might get a lot if the company recovers. If you have ever played the board game Monopoly with several players until only one player was left, you probably saw, or even engaged in, a claimant coalition game. Of course, the play is considerably more intense when there is real money at stake!

The dramatic shift in incentives brought on by financial distress in each case happens because the contingent claim—the option—inherent in the situation falls to or out-of-the-money. At that point, the optionholder has little more to lose—perhaps only the time premium. The downside risk is limited, since an option cannot have a negative value. At the same time, the option is worthless if it expires out-of-the-money, so the possibility of it coming back into the money can make it worth fighting to keep the option alive. You can't lose much but you might win. This combination can create powerful incentives to take risks and engage in protracted legal battles.

---

[3]Perhaps Coca-Cola has reason to worry. Many years ago Bayer lost its trademark name *aspirin* after the term became commonly used to refer to the drug, regardless of the manufacturer.

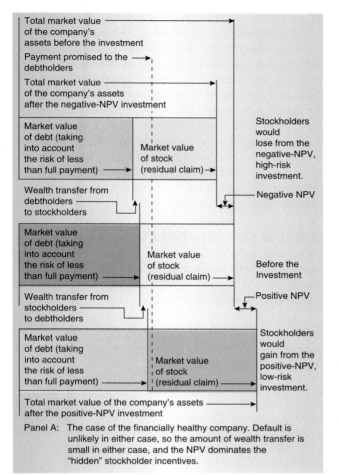

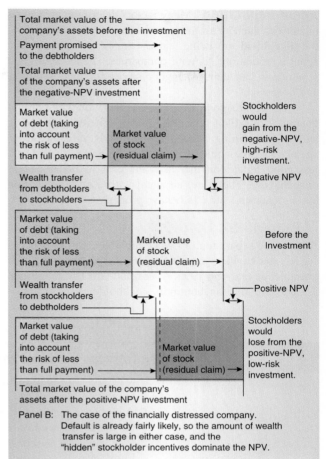

FIGURE C.7
The potential effect of financial distress on investment choice.

Information

A financial contract is complex because it involves imperfect information. In a perfect capital market, complete information is available to all participants at no cost. In a real capital market, you can apply the Signaling Principle to interpret actions. Although it would be nice if the meaning of all actions were absolutely clear, this is not the case. Interpretation can be complex and difficult. For example, when is a "sale" really a sale? Some retailers have essentially continuous sales. When is this or any other advertising claim credible?[4] This represents a significant and ongoing asymmetric information problem.

Even when the meaning of an action is clear, other problems can arise. For example, to avoid being taken advantage of, one might choose to camouflage some actions.

Suppose a company always reduced its price on a model that was about to be discontinued. If you knew this, you wouldn't think the sale was such a good deal. After all, the item might not be worth much after a new model comes out. So the company faces the problem of adverse selection: Offering the reduced price is a negative signal indicating imminent model discontinuation. How can the company reduce this problem?

One approach to this problem is to deliberately add uncertainty. Thus, the company could occasionally (randomly) offer a lower price on items not being discontinued—a "real" sale. In that way, a reduced price can be a good deal rather than an obvious signal of a model discontinuation.

Incentives also play an important role. Ideally, an agent would have incentives to send accurate signals. But consider managers whose earnings depend on the company's performance. Such managers might be tempted to mislead, or even falsely report better company performance, unless they face penalties for being found out later. Properly structured, penalties lead to more credible signals by making it unattractive to mimic the activities of a "better" agent.

---

[4]You've probably wondered about particular advertising claims. Our own risk aversion toward lawsuits keeps us from citing specific examples.

Agent Reputation   Many factors determine an agent's incentives, such as rewards, punishments, ethical attitudes, the likelihood of being caught misbehaving, and the agent's reputation. As with companies, agents with good reputations can demand higher prices for their products and/or services.

An agent's good reputation carries with it an implicit guarantee of satisfactory performance. Therefore, building and/or maintaining a good reputation is valuable. Conversely, its loss would be costly. The opportunity cost of a lost good reputation increases the cost of being caught misbehaving. Therefore, an agent with a good reputation has a greater incentive to behave properly.

Management Contracts

Beyond the separation of ownership and control we noted earlier, stockholders can be a widely dispersed group. For example, at year-end 1995, AT&T and GM had more than 2.2 and 1.3 million common stockholders, respectively.

This tremendous diffusion of ownership appears to intensify stockholder-manager conflicts. There are some who cite large executive salaries as evidence that the managers are winning the conflict, at least in the instances cited. However, empirical studies have reached conflicting conclusions about whether manager-controlled companies differ significantly from stockholder-controlled companies.

Even with widely diffused share ownership—and managerial control—stockholders possess several devices that help align managerial goals with their own. These devices include designing incentive compensation plans for managers, the right to sell their own shares, the right to replace managers, and the right to elect directors.

Incentive Compensation Plans   Management contracts often include stock options, performance shares, and bonuses. Because accounting measures can sometimes be manipulated, it is generally preferable to base bonuses on appreciation in the company's share price.

EXAMPLE	*Lee Iacocca's First-Year Compensation Package*

When Chrysler Corporation hired Lee Iacocca, he insisted on taking only one dollar in salary the first year. In place of the typical salary, he chose an incentive package that included options to purchase approximately 350,000 shares of Chrysler common stock. These options were far out-of-the-money. He argued that if he was successful in turning the company around, he would be well paid; if he wasn't successful, he would appropriately get nothing.

Eight years later, Iacocca cashed in his options for a gain of roughly $20 million. Unfortunately, it was incorrectly reported that the $20 million was his pay for the single year in which he cashed in his options. Understandably, others have since cited this payment as evidence that corporate executives are being paid too much.

We won't take a position on the issue of whether executive compensation is fair. However, we believe the starting place for such a debate must be accurate facts and a complete understanding of the contract. ■

The Stockholders' Right to Sell Their Shares
Except in special cases, stockholders can sell the shares they own. This can create the threat of a takeover. If many stockholders offer to sell their shares, and the market price per share falls, others may buy up the shares and take over the company if the price is low enough.

The right to tender shares to a prospective acquirer, or sell them in the market, is potentially the most effective (although last-resort) measure open to shareholders. However, many recently introduced anti-takeover measures may have reduced the threat of takeover. So-called poison pills are an example of an anti-takeover measure.

Poison pills typically take the form of an option to purchase shares in the target company at a bargain price. The option becomes exercisable in the hands of the target company's stockholders once an "unfriendly" suitor (one not approved by the company's board of directors) acquires some specified percentage of the outstanding shares, often just 20%. The poison pill provision gets its name from the pill of cyanide a spy is given to swallow when capture becomes imminent. While such a poison pill sure does prevent talking after being captured, it also has some other profound side effects!

Chrysler's Poison Pill

In November 1994, Chrysler Corporation's largest stockholder, billionaire Kirk Kerkorian, demanded action from Chrysler. He owned about 9% of Chrysler's stock and felt it was undervalued. He wanted the company to raise its dividend and buy back some of its shares.

At the time, Chrysler had a poison pill that prevented a shareholder from controlling 10% or more of Chrysler's shares without board approval. Kerkorian wanted to increase his ownership proportion to 15%. He asked Chrysler's board to modify the poison pill. Several large investors went even farther. They urged Chrysler to eliminate the poison pill.

Within a few weeks, Chrysler took action. The dividend was boosted 60%. A $1 billion stock buy-back program was announced. Finally, Chrysler modified its "shareholder-rights plan" to permit a shareholder to own up to 15% of the stock. Chrysler's board diluted the poison pill but didn't discard it. ∎

Replacing Managers   Managers, like all agents, have significant incentives to build and/or maintain a good reputation. On average, executives who lose their jobs in connection with a financially distressed company do not subsequently find comparable or better-paying jobs. In contrast, when a person is recruited away from an existing job into a higher-paying job, their past success is almost always cited as the basis for hiring them.[5]

How Much Will Michael Ovitz Make at Disney?

In August 1995, the Walt Disney Company hired Michael Ovitz as president and a director of Disney. Ovitz had co-founded Creative Artists Agency and was very highly regarded in Hollywood. It was rumored that MCA Inc. had tried to hire him just a few months before. To get Ovitz to leave Creative Artists, Disney offered 10-year options on 5 million of its shares. Compensation experts valued the option package at between $107 million and $140 million. ∎

The Stockholders' Election of Directors   Unhappy stockholders can elect new directors or even mount a *proxy fight*.[6] However, this is difficult. Further, the recent practice of staggering directorships (such as electing one-third each year) makes winning a proxy fight even harder.

Sallie Mae's Proxy Fight

The Student Loan Marketing Association (nicknamed Sallie Mae) buys and services student loans under federally sponsored student loan programs. In 1995, a group of shareholders, led by former Sallie Mae chief operating officer Albert Lord, started a proxy fight. They said Sallie Mae was poorly managed and blamed current management for not paying enough attention to the company's profit margin and stock price.[7] Earnings had slumped in 1994 for the first time in the company's 21-year history.

The proxy fight succeeded. At the 1995 annual meeting, the dissidents elected 8 new directors to the 21-member board. (Of the other 13, 6 were management candidates, and the other 7 were appointed by President Clinton.) Management started a legal battle to keep the new directors from serving but gave up after a month. Meanwhile, Sallie Mae announced that it was considering changes in the way it runs its business. ∎

---

[5]Sadly, we must point out that many people who are quite successful never get hired away for "big bucks!"

[6]Sometimes one or more shareholders lead a takeover attempt by asking other shareholders to precommit to vote with them. This precommitment is called a *proxy*.

[7]Apparently, the market agreed. The company's stock jumped 30% in value when the proxy fight was announced.

Available empirical evidence indicates that, on average, there is not a sharp divergence between managers' and stockholders' interests. Still, we recommend the continued use of monitoring, because that may be a critical ingredient to this general consistency!

Debt Contracts

How will debtholders react to the risks of asset substitution, underinvestment, and claim dilution? They will try to restrict the company's ability to engage in these behaviors. For example, debt contracts may include specific limits on the company's activities, such as restricting the company from issuing new bonds without first paying off, or otherwise protecting, existing bonds. As we noted earlier, restrictions of this sort became much more widely used after the RJR Nabisco leveraged buyout. The debtholders may also attempt legal action with respect to an existing contract, as in the case of Placid Oil's Green Canyon project.

Despite all attempts at restriction, some possibility remains that stockholders will be able to expropriate wealth from the debtholders. The essential question is how large is the possibility. The larger it is, the higher the rate of interest the debtholders will require to compensate them for that risk. Such a higher rate is part of the agency costs borne by the stockholders. Also, contractual limitations may restrict more than just the targeted activities. Therefore, another part of the agency cost is reduced decision-making flexibility that might unintentionally prevent the company from making a positive-NPV investment.

The legal contract for a publicly traded bond is called the *bond indenture.* The structure of this explicit contract affects the incentives by detailing responsibilities, constraints, punishments, and required monitoring. For example, such contracts specify the timing and amounts of all interest and principal payments. They also appoint a particular agent, called the *trustee,* who has a legal responsibility to look after the bondholders' interests.

Certain contractual provisions within a bond indenture are called **bond covenants.** These are designed to protect the interests of the bondholders. They are of two types. A **negative covenant** *prohibits* or *limits* certain actions, such as incurring more debt or paying dividends. A **positive covenant** *requires* certain actions, such as regularly making tax payments and providing periodic financial statements.

Bond covenants are a form of monitoring. They provide a warning system that is triggered when a company fails to comply with a covenant. The warning system is activated only with a failure to comply. This can save resources because more complete monitoring—such as a monthly review of the company's actions—is more costly and time consuming. Further, even when a covenant is violated, corrective action can often be taken before the problem becomes more severe and the company falls into financial distress. As such, a bond covenant can be an *early* warning device.

Bond covenants provide value by lowering the risk of the bonds. The bondholder gets increased protection against certain events and therefore agrees to a lower interest rate. This benefits the company. However, the value of a specific covenant depends on the particular situation. This is quite like the overlapping options problem discussed in topic B.

With hidden options, the addition of an option may not add much value if the contingency it "covers" is already covered by other options. If the bondholder is protected in other ways, a covenant may not add much value. Generally, covenants are more valuable to bondholders in a higher-risk company because the likelihood of running into a problem is greater.

However, bond covenants are also costly. They restrict the company's operating flexibility and can eliminate positive-NPV investment opportunities. In short, they can eliminate valuable options for the company. It's possible to solicit consent from the bondholders to relax a restrictive covenant. But such a process is cumbersome, time consuming, and often expensive. Bondholders normally demand some form of payment, either an immediate cash payment or an increase in the coupon rate—in exchange for their consent. Even when the company does go to the trouble and cost of eliminating a covenant that is constraining it, the lost time it takes to do it adds to the opportunity cost of that covenant. As with so many other things, there's a trade-off between the benefits and costs of bond covenants.

EXAMPLE

Removing a Restrictive Covenant

A few years ago, the owners of the Seven-Up Company offered a group of its bondholders incentives in return for changes in the bond indenture: (1) an immediate one-time payment of $25 per $1000 bond, (2) an increase in the coupon rate from 12⅛% to 12⅜% for the next 2½ years, and (3) a further increase in the coupon rate to 12⅝% for the remaining 5 years of the bonds' life. At the same time, the Dr. Pepper Company offered a similar financial incentive to a group of its bondholders. The offers were in exchange for a consent to allow a leveraged buyout of each company to form a single merged company. The cost of the cash payment if all bondholders consented (a majority was required in each case) was $9.3 million. The increase in coupon rate, which would benefit every bondholder as long as a majority consented, amounted to $934,000 per year for the first increase and a further $934,000 per year for the second.

This is a particularly interesting example of managing *implicit* stakeholder claims. Both solicitation statements pointed out that the bondholder consents were not *legally* required for the planned leveraged buyout. Did this mean that the company was paying something and getting nothing? No. The company offered a financial incentive in exchange for *explicit* consent to preempt potential legal action from the bondholders. This was important because even if all protesting bondholders lost their legal complaints, they could have caused a costly, or even disastrous, delay in the company's plans.[8] ■

---

[8]This can be viewed as one more hidden option—the option to "make trouble" by suing, even though you don't expect to win!

One alternative to an extensive array of restrictive bond covenants is the use of a conversion option to create a **convertible bond.** A convertible bond can be exchanged for a pre-set number of shares of the company's common stock at the bondholder's option. The option in a convertible bond allows the securityholder to share in the upside if the investments the company makes are especially successful. Smaller, younger companies often issue convertible bonds, rather than bonds without the conversion option, for precisely this reason.

Optimal Contracts

An optimal contract balances the three types of agency costs (contracting, monitoring, and misbehavior) against one another to minimize the total cost. In some cases, the optimal contract involves a fixed wage and some degree of monitoring, as is typically the case for employees. In other cases, the cost of monitoring is not worth it. When its cost exceeds the expected cost of agent misbehavior, the optimal contract is a simple bonus based on the outcome. An example of such is a salesperson who earns only a commission, which is a percentage of sales.

Some of the decisions connected with the choice of a financial contract are similar to trade-offs an agent might make in an effort to earn a good reputation: Agents may forgo profiting from misbehaving in the short run to earn more in the long run. Demonstrating good behavior can increase the value of their services. Similarly, agents may agree to "severe" monitoring to earn more for their services. The principal agrees to the higher price because the severe monitoring reduces the chance of agent misbehavior. Again, it is a cost trade-off.

Choosing the Best Contract   EXAMPLE

Let's say the Nintendo Corporation can choose one of four managerial contracts. The estimated annual total and component contracting costs (in millions of dollars) of these alternatives are given below. Which managerial contract should Nintendo choose?

	DIRECT	MONITORING	MISBEHAVIOR	TOTAL
Contract #1	1.4	0.0	5.1	6.5
Contract #2	1.1	2.4	0.1	3.6
Contract #3	2.2	0.4	0.4	3.0
Contract #4	2.6	0.1	0.7	3.4

Contract #3 is the best choice because it provides the lowest *total* costs among the alternatives. Based on the company's estimates, it's the best game in town. ■

Unfortunately, a financial contract cannot cover every possible contingency; beforehand, you can't conceive of everything that might go wrong. In any case, dealing with every possible situation would involve tremendous time and expense. Each party must take reasonable precautions but must ultimately rely on the other parties to behave ethically and responsibly in those situations not explicitly covered by the agreement. If either party behaves unethically, the contractual provisions may not prove very effective anyway.

Self-Check

1. Why does financial distress intensify the problem of goal divergence?

2. What devices do stockholders have for aligning managerial goals with their own?

3. What is a poison pill, and how does it help current management keep their jobs in the face of a takeover threat?

4. What is the purpose of bond covenants?

5. Describe an optimal contract in your own words.

MONITORING

A financial contract is complex because it involves imperfect information. Despite this complexity, there are a number of potentially cost-effective monitoring devices.

New External Financing

Whenever a company seeks new external financing, it is exposed to special scrutiny, which is a form of monitoring. The company must reveal new information. If the information is public, existing investors can look more closely at the company. Even if the new information is not made public, the new investors provide a form of monitoring. They provide reassurance to existing investors by their willingness to invest their own money.

This reassurance concept is quite broad. Suppose a company has a valuable new idea that would be damaged if it were made public, because of the free-rider problem. That is, others would copy the idea. In such cases, the company may be able to issue new securities through investment bankers who underwrite the issue.

Here's how it works. The company explains the idea to the investment bankers now but doesn't make the idea public until it is marketed. With an underwritten issue, the investment bankers actually purchase the securities before reselling them to the public. Taking ownership, even for a short time, is much riskier than simply marketing the securities for a commission. Presumably, investment bankers would not take on this risk if they thought it was large. The investment bankers' purchase signals the market about the value of the new idea. As reputable middlemen, they can profit from their role as third-party monitor.

Other Monitoring Devices

Many elements of the financial environment serve as monitoring devices. People openly offer and seek information in the normal course of business. They also signal information through their actions. Information is revealed through government enforcement of laws and regulations. Even a company's reputation and structure convey information. Common monitoring devices include the following:

◆ **Financial statements** Audited accounting statements are a monitoring device for stockholder-manager, debtholder-stockholder, and consumer-company relationships. They provide an early warning system.

◆ **Cash dividends** Cash dividends can be a monitoring device in two ways. First, the failure to declare a cash dividend in the expected amount provides a warning. Although it may or may not be negative information, it prompts investors to look further. They must determine the meaning of the deviation. Second, paying cash dividends may force the company to seek new external financing more frequently, the benefits of which we just noted.

◆ **Bond ratings** Bond ratings by agencies such as Moody's or Standard & Poor's provide monitoring at issuance and, to a lesser extent, over the bonds' life.

◆ **Bond covenants** Bond covenants provide a kind of warning system.

◆ **Government regulation** Governments continue to evolve their monitoring devices in the public interest. For example, numerous federal agencies, such as the IRS, SEC, and FDA, monitor companies for various legal violations.

◆ **The entire legal system** Theft, fraud, and many other forms of agent misbehavior are illegal. The legal system provides various forms of monitoring for everyone.

◆ **Reputation** Reputation, and the general information it contains, is a form of monitoring. As we noted earlier, building and/or maintaining a good reputation is valuable. This creates incentives for providing accurate information, which also facilitates monitoring.

◆ **Multilevel organizations** A company that uses many levels of authority to review and evaluate decisions also provides a structural form of monitoring. Misbehavior is more difficult when you need a large number of people to do it. To get approval in such a company, a plan must be widely discussed. Large groups are more likely to include honest people, braggarts, and blabbermouths. Not everyone can keep a secret.

Throughout the book we examine information from these and other sources to better understand the motivations contained in implicit and explicit financial contracts.

The Barings Bankruptcy

EXAMPLE

Barings PLC was a venerable 233-year-old British investment bank. It had helped Britain reopen trade with the United States after the Revolutionary War. In 1803, it helped the United States double in size by financing the purchase of the Louisiana Territory from France. Despite a long and distinguished history, early in 1995 it took a single 28-year-old trader just a month of undetected trading to create a $1 billion loss, which caused the company's demise.

Nicholas Leeson had been an arbitrage trader at Barings Securities. He was trading futures contracts in Singapore and Japan. He simultaneously bought in one market and sold the same contract in the other to exploit price differences. Profits were small but so were the risks.

One day in late January 1995, Leeson decided that "plain vanilla" arbitrage was too tame. So he changed tactics. He stopped matching buy and sell orders. He became a buyer who thought he knew which way Japanese stock prices and interest rates were headed. Without authorization, he bet big.

By the time Leeson's betting was finally discovered, he had bought stock futures contracts representing $7 billion worth of Japanese shares, and interest rate futures contracts representing $22 billion worth of Japanese government bonds. (That's right, we said *billion.*) Unfortunately, Leeson didn't know as much as he thought he did. He racked up about a $1 billion loss.

The regulators found there had been a "failure of control." Apparently, the company didn't really understand what Leeson was doing. It was reported that someone at a Barings risk committee meeting asked whether the high level of trading by Leeson was "safe." Barings's head of derivatives assured them it was. This is particularly surprising in light of press reports that Leeson's trading was large enough to generate comment throughout the Asian markets about his aggressive strategy.[9] As it turned out, the derivatives head's belief was based on reports filed by Leeson! Leeson's superiors thought he was trading on behalf of clients, rather than for the company's own account.

Barings's lack of controls surprised Wall Street risk managers. Unlike most salesmen, Leeson was allowed to go to the trading floor to trade. Barings didn't limit the size of Leeson's trading positions. In contrast to industry practice, he was both head derivatives trader and head of the back-office settlement department. He was therefore monitoring himself. This enabled him to withhold information from the head office and send in falsified reports. That crippled the monitoring process.

It seems that Barings's monitoring problem ought to be unique, but it's not! Kidder Peabody & Co. said its head government bond trader racked up $350 million in fake profits by entering false trades into its computer system. Daiwa Bank Ltd. suffered $1.1 billion of losses over an 11-year period due to questionable trading by a lone trader. Like Leeson, he headed a back-office department responsible for monitoring trading (including his own).

As these examples vividly illustrate, monitoring isn't very effective when the individual being monitored is the one doing the monitoring! ■

---

[9]At one point, his trades accounted for *half* the outstanding positions on the Nikkei-225 futures contract.

Self-Check

1. Describe three external monitoring devices. How cost-effective is each?

2. How do investment bankers function as monitors when they underwrite a new issue of securities?

3. How do audited financial statements assist in monitoring?

SUMMARY

We described many of the problems that are revealed by a principal-agent framework in the set-of-contracts model of the company. Figure C.8 shows the contractual relationships we examined, each in a separate principal-agent framework.

Agency issues are everywhere. Agency theory has been used to an increasing extent to explain financial contracting phenomena that were not previously well understood. Several important concepts include:

- The modern corporation involves a large number of both explicit and implicit contracts.
- Both implicit and explicit contracts frequently involve contingent claims.
- The interests of principals and agents often diverge. For example, managers operate the company but may own only a tiny fraction of it. Therefore, the company's various stakeholders (such as managers, employees, stockholders, debtholders, and customers) may not have identical interests.
- Incentives, constraints, punishments, and monitoring are necessary to ensure that an agent acts in the principal's best interest. Such things impose agency costs. Agency problems and costs arise in many of the relationships that compose the set of contracts making up the modern corporation.

- An agency cost is the incremental cost of working through agents. The agency cost is the amount above whatever cost would be incurred in a perfect market environment.
- Financial distress complicates and intensifies many agency problems and costs.
- The existence of agency problems adds agency costs to the cost of financial contracting.
- An optimal financial contract minimizes the total agency cost, which is made up of financial contracting costs (transaction costs, opportunity costs, and incentive fees), monitoring costs, and misbehavior costs.
- Conflicts of interest can arise naturally between stockholders and managers because of employee perquisites, employee effort, and the nondiversifiability of an employee's human capital, among other things.
- Ultimately, if stockholders are dissatisfied, they can sell their shares. If the market value of a poorly run company falls sufficiently, another company or investor can purchase sufficient shares to gain control and fire inept managers.
- Conflicts of interest can arise naturally between debtholders and stockholders because of the possibility of asset substitution, underinvestment, and claim dilution, among other things.
- Debt contracts typically include provisions designed to control agency costs.
- The contingent-claim view of the company's various stakeholders provides important insights into how the incentives can dramatically shift if the contingent claim (option) comes to be at or out-of-the-money. Because the option cannot have a negative value, the downside risk is limited. As such, it is somewhat like a lottery ticket. The agent has little to lose, but the upside potential can be tremendous.
- Conflicts of interest can arise naturally between consumers and the company because of guarantees and product imitation, among other things.
- The value of building and maintaining a good reputation provides important long-term incentives that help reduce some agency problems.
- Agency cost considerations are important in many decisions, including the capital budgeting process, the choice of capital structure, the choice of dividend policy, many of the company's day-to-day decisions, the design of new securities issues, the choice between leasing and buying an asset, and merger and acquisition decisions.

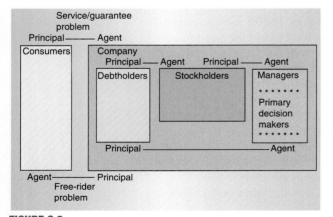

FIGURE C.8

Important implicit principal-agent relationships connected with a company.

TOPIC REVIEW ACTIVITIES

SELF-TEST PROBLEMS

1. (Asset substitution problem) Michigan Mining and Manufacturing has a debt obligation of $100 million and assets with a value of $90 million. This debt must be paid off very shortly. When this happens, the value of the debt will be $90 million and the value of equity will be $0.

Prior to paying off the debt, MMM has an opportunity to make a high-risk investment. MMM is considering an investment of $20 million that will pay off $40 million or zero. The investment would have an NPV of either $20 million or −$20 million (NPV = the value of the payoff minus the investment). The investment would be paid for with the company's liquid cash holdings.

a. If the $40 million payoff (NPV = $20 million) occurs, what is the value of equity? What is the value of debt?

b. If the zero payoff (NPV = −$20 million) occurs, what is the value of equity? What is the value of debt?

c. Assume the probability of the high payoff is 0.25 and the probability of the low payoff is 0.75. What is the expected NPV of the investment?

d. What is the expected value of equity? What is the expected value of debt?

e. How can stockholders benefit from a negative-NPV project?

2. (Underinvestment problem) Assume that the value of the company's assets is $100 and that the company has debts of $80. If a catastrophe occurs, the assets are completely destroyed and have a value of $0. The probability of a catastrophe is 1%.

a. What is the value of debt and equity with no catastrophe? What is the value of debt and equity with a catastrophe? What is the expected value of debt and equity?

b. Assume that an insurance policy can be purchased for $1. It pays off $100 in the event of a catastrophe. Recompute the value of debt and equity with no catastrophe. Recompute the value of debt and equity with a catastrophe. (Remember to deduct the cost of the $1 insurance premium.)

c. This insurance policy was a zero-NPV investment because its cost of $1 exactly equaled the expected payoff of $1 (1% of $100). What was the impact of the investment in the insurance policy on the value of debt and equity? Who benefited from the insurance policy, stockholders or debtholders?

3. (Contracting costs and the cost of borrowing) Fuqua Computers is arranging a $20 million, 3-year loan. Fuqua will repay the loan with three interest payments of $2 million at the end of each year and will repay the principal at the end of year 3.

a. Assuming no contracting costs, what is the effective cost of this loan to Fuqua?

b. Assume now that Fuqua incurs one-time setup costs of $400,000 at time 0 for legal and other contracting costs. In addition, Fuqua incurs an additional $100,000 of contracting costs at the end of each of the next 3 years. What is the effective annual cost of this loan including these contracting costs?

SOLUTIONS TO SELF-TEST PROBLEMS

1. a. If the high payoff occurs, the value of the assets is $110 million, the original $90 million value minus the investment of $20 million plus the payoff of $40 million. The debt will be paid in full and will be worth $100 million, and the stockholders receive the residual value of $10 million.

b. If the low payoff occurs, the value of the assets is $70 million, the original $90 million value minus the investment of $20 million plus the payoff of zero. The debt will not be paid in full and will be worth $70 million. The stockholders have limited liability, which means that they do not have to pay off the losses of the debtholders. The stock is worth zero.

c. The expected NPV is the sum of the two NPVs weighted by their probabilities:

Expected NPV
= $20 million (0.25) + (−$20 million)(0.75) = −$10 million.

d. The expected value of equity is the sum of the two equity values weighted by their probabilities:

Expected value of equity
= $10 million (0.25) + (zero)(0.75) = $2.5 million

The expected value of debt is the sum of the two debt values weighted by their probabilities:

Expected value of debt
= $100 million (0.25) + $70 million (0.75) = $77.5 million.

Notice that the value of debt and equity combined is now $80 million ($2.5 million + $77.5 million).

The value of equity has increased from zero to $2.5 million.

The value of debt has declined from $90 million to $77.5 million.

The value of the company declined from $90 million to $80 million, which is the original total value of the company plus the NPV of −$10 million.

e. Even though the NPV is negative, the value of the debt payoffs declined by more than the loss on the investment. This is a shift in wealth from bondholders to stockholders.

For this investment, stockholders keep any excess of the value of assets over the $100 million debt, even though the probability is low. If the company loses more money, the stockholders aren't liable and don't lose any more, because their equity was worthless anyway. The payoffs to stockholders are not symmetrical; they can keep some of the gains, but they don't share in the losses.

2. a. With no catastrophe:
Value of debt = $80
Value of equity = $20
With a catastrophe:
Value of debt = $0
Value of equity = $0

The expected value of debt and equity is the sum of the possible debt and equity values, respectively, weighted by their probabilities:

Expected value of debt = $80 (0.99) + $0 (0.01) = $79.2

Expected value of equity = $20 (0.99) + $0 (0.01) = $19.8.

b. The company now has purchased insurance against the catastrophic loss. With no catastrophe, the value of the company is the original $100 minus the $1 insurance premium, or $99. The values of debt and equity are:

> Value of debt = $80
> Value of equity = $19

With a catastrophe, the value of the company is $0 plus the insurance settlement of $100 minus the $1 insurance premium, or $99. This causes the value of debt and equity to be:

> Value of debt = $80
> Value of equity = $19

The expected values of debt and equity are now:

Expected value of debt = $80 (0.99) + $80 (0.01) = $80

Expected value of equity = $19 (0.99) + $19 (0.99) = $19.

c. The insurance increased the expected value of debt from $79.20 to $80, an increase of $0.80. The insurance decreased the value of equity from $19.20 to $19, a decrease of $0.20. The bondholders benefited from the insurance while the stockholders lost. This is because most of the benefit of the insurance payoff goes to the bondholders, but the stockholders, in essence, are paying all of the insurance premium. This example shows why debt contracts almost always require the borrower to insure the assets against loss. The borrowers (the equity holders) would underinvest in insurance if it were left up to them.

3. a. The cost with no contracting costs is 10% per year.

N = 3	r = 10	PV = 20,000,000
PMT = 2,000,000		FV = 20,000,000

b. Contracting costs reduce your loan proceeds to $19,600,000 (= $20,000,000 − $400,000). Contracting costs increase your annual costs to $2,100,000 ($2,000,000 + $100,000).

N = 3	r = 11.32	PV = 19,600,000
PMT = 2,100,000		FV = 20,000,000

Contracting costs increase the effective cost of the loan from 10% to 11.32%.

QUESTIONS

1. In your own words, describe a principal-agent relationship. Cite two examples of explicit principal-agent relationships and two others that are not explicit but can be viewed as such.
2. Describe and discuss the asset substitution problem.
3. Describe and discuss the underinvestment problem.
4. Define the term *moral hazard.*
5. Define the term *free rider* and explain why it causes problems. Cite an example of the free-rider problem and a contract form that is typically used to reduce or eliminate the problem.
6. Define the concept of agency problems and cite three examples of such problems.
7. Cite three goals managers might have that are not necessarily consistent with the goal of maximizing shareholder wealth.
8. What is an agency cost? What are its three components? Cite an example of each one.
9. Cite and describe two ways that the uniqueness of assets creates agency costs for shareholders.
10. How can employee perquisites create a conflict between the shareholders and the employees?
11. How can product and service guarantees create an agency problem between the company and its consumers?
12. Cite and briefly discuss four devices that naturally monitor agent behavior for the principal.
13. Define and explain in your own words the concept of an optimal contract.
14. Explain how covenants in a bond indenture help to reduce a company's agency costs, thereby reducing the company's cost of financing.
15. Explain why debtholders typically require covenants in the bond indenture that restrict the company's ability to take on additional debt. Cite two such covenants that are common and relate them to your explanation.
16. Using the stock-as-an-option view, explain why stockholders might choose to undertake a high-risk investment, even if the NPV of the investment is negative. What group is on the other side of this transaction?
17. Using the stock-as-an-option view, explain why stockholders might choose not to undertake a low-risk investment, even if the expected NPV of the investment is positive. What group is on the other side of this transaction?
18. Describe the problem of claim dilution, using the stock-as-an-option view.
19. How does having a manager who is also a stockholder reduce potential conflicts of interest?
20. Explain the problem of the nondiversifiability of human capital.
21. How does the nondiversifiability of human capital cause a conflict of interest between the managers and the stockholders regarding the company's choice of investments?
22. Explain how an agent's desire to maintain the ongoing value of a good reputation can facilitate shareholder monitoring of the agent.
23. Using a contingent claim view, describe in your own words how financial distress can intensify conflicts of interest among the company's claimants. Cite three specific examples of situations in which this can occur.
24. Explain why the stock price of a company that is undergoing bankruptcy proceedings is virtually always positive and never negative.

CHALLENGING QUESTIONS

25. What methods do shareholders have at their disposal for aligning managers' goals with their goals?
26. Perfect monitoring in a perfect market environment always provides an optimal contract. Explain why monitoring is not always the best choice, even in a well-functioning market environment with low transaction costs.

27. Respond to the following statement: "Since a company can lower its interest cost by including more restrictive covenants in its bond indentures, a company should use the most restrictive set of covenants it can in order to achieve the lowest interest cost." (Obviously, there is the trade-off between lower interest cost and reduced decision-making flexibility. The subtle point here is the possibility of overlapping restrictions that don't add much protection for the debtholders but can be quite costly for the company. As such they are truly wasted costs.)

28. Is it possible to have an agency problem if there is no asymmetric information? If so, cite an example; if not, explain why not.

29. In some bankruptcy settlements, the debtholders accept less than full payment on the claim and at the same time they agree to having the stockholders get a payment as well. Because the stockholders are only the *residual* claimants (after the debtholders get what they have been promised), why do the debtholders agree to let the stockholders get something? (*Hint:* Consider our example of the "unnecessary" payment the Seven-Up Company and Dr. Pepper Company made to their debtholders in exchange for their consent to the leveraged buyout—the hidden option to sue.)

30. Suppose you were a company's debtholder. Would you be concerned about the company's dividend policy? Explain why or why not.

31. How can employee perquisites create an agency problem between managers and the *debtholders?*

32. Explain in your own words how a complex multilevel organization provides a natural form of agent monitoring.

33. How does convertible debt help to reduce the agency problem between the shareholders and the debtholders?

34. We said that in cases of financial distress, various claimant coalitions can form. Is it possible to predict what those coalitions will be when the company is healthy? If so, explain how. If not, explain why.

PROBLEM SET A

A1. (Value of a managerial contract) John Hall is considering a new managerial contract for his company. The contract will increase direct contracting costs (mostly cash incentive awards) by $1,000,000. John estimates that the contract should save $400,000 in monitoring costs such as accounting and oversight costs. It should also reduce misbehavior costs by $950,000 by reducing excessive perk consumption and managerial shirking. If his estimates are correct, what is the net cost or net benefit of Hall's proposed managerial contract?

A2. (Optimal managerial contract) Estimates of the direct, monitoring, and misbehavior costs for three different managerial contracts are given below. Which of the contracts is optimal?

Contract	Direct Costs	Monitoring Costs	Misbehavior Costs
A	$4.5	$3.5	$7.0
B	6.0	2.5	4.5
C	8.0	2.0	3.5

A3. (Optimal managerial contract) Because of excessive perk consumption, high salaries and compensation of executives, and a pattern of negligent and mediocre decision making, Michael Alderson has recommended that the company restructure its managerial contracts. Michael expects that heightened monitoring will add $750,000 of costs annually.
  a. What decrease in direct costs and misbehavior costs is required to offset the additional monitoring costs?
  b. If direct costs are reduced by $250,000, what is the minimum reduction in misbehavior costs required to justify Michael's recommendation?

A4. (Effect of contracting costs on a lender) Frank Laatsch is considering a loan of $500,000 to Regency Partners. Frank estimates that he will incur $15,000 of costs per year to monitor this loan.
  a. Regency is promising to pay 12% annually on the loan. After paying monitoring costs, what return is Frank receiving?
  b. If a fair return on this loan is 10%, what is the minimum interest rate that Frank would require on this loan?

A5. (Claim dilution via dividend policy) Bosco Company purchased the common stock of Redux Insurance Company for $10 million (1,000,000 shares at $10 each). At the time of its acquisition, Redux had assets valued at $90 million and liabilities of $80 million.
  a. What was the surplus of assets over obligations at the time of the purchase?
  b. Immediately after the purchase, the board of directors of Redux, which Bosco now controlled, paid an $18 per share dividend to Bosco. After this transaction, what is the surplus of assets over obligations for Redux Insurance Company?

A6. (Cost of a restrictive covenant) Peachtree Construction has a restrictive covenant in a loan contract that essentially prohibits the expansion of the company into a new line of business that it is considering. The cost of this restriction is estimated to be $20 million. The debt can be called and paid off early by paying a $5 million penalty. What should Peachtree do?

PROBLEM SET B

B1. (Misbehavior costs) This has been a poor year for the company. A little checking has revealed several questionable transactions that benefit the company's president. (1) The company purchased a condominium for $800,000 and gave the president an option to purchase it for $500,000. She exercised this option immediately. (2) She put her spouse on the payroll for a total cost of $150,000 annually. The husband's contributions were considered to have a zero value. (Luckily, they were not negative.) (3) She redecorated her office at a cost of $150,000. The office had been redecorated only 2 years previous. (4) She has four club memberships costing $100,000 per year and has total travel and entertainment expenses of $120,000. A good guess is that one-half of these are not justifiable.

(5) She set up consulting contracts with her brother that cost $40,000 total. No tangible benefit from the contracts exists. (6) She made several decisions that violate labor, environmental, and securities laws that will expose the company to future penalties. (7) Her behavior causes many other executives and employees to engage in similar misbehavior. Several employees have resigned the company because of their concerns about legal, ethical, and poor business practices. Ignoring items (6) and (7), which are not yet quantified, what do the other misbehavior costs sum to?

B2. (Management incentives) The board of directors for Ettinger Manufacturing is considering a $.75 per share dividend on its 4,000,000 shares. The board is also considering a $2,000,000 bonus payment to be shared by its top managers.
  a. Sharon Conn, the company controller, will receive 8% of the bonus pool and also owns 20,000 shares. How much will Sharon receive in dividends and bonus?
  b. Marilyn Ettinger, the president and chief executive officer, will receive 15% of the bonus pool and owns 800,000 shares. What distributions will Marilyn receive?
  c. One of the directors is advocating a shift of funds from the bonus pool to cash dividends. This plan would reduce the bonus pool to $1,000,000 and increase the dividend to $1.00 per share. Recalculate the distributions for Sharon and for Marilyn.
  d. Which plan do you think Sharon and Marilyn would favor?

B3. (Asset substitution problem) Your loan to Kansas City Construction Company (KCCC) is due at the end of the year. At that time, KCCC must pay you $500,000.
  a. If the collateral for the loan is expected to be worth either $600,000 or $700,000, what payment would you expect from KCCC?
  b. Assume that KCCC sells some of the collateral and replaces it with riskier assets. The value of the collateral at the end of the year is now expected to be either $350,000 or $950,000. What loan payments might you now expect from KCCC?

B4. (Claim dilution via new debt) Your loan to Penguin Development is now due. Penguin has assets of $200 and your loan, the company's only debt, has a $100 balance.
  a. What loan payment do you expect from Penguin?
  b. Penguin has taken on an additional $150 of debt, which has the same claim on assets as your debt. The company still has $200 of assets. What loan payment do you now expect from Penguin?

B5. (Claim dilution) J & B Piano Company owes you $200,000. J & B sells all of the company's assets for $100,000 cash. Then J & B pays a $40,000 cash dividend to its stockholders. Finally, J & B pays a $60,000 bonus to its managers. What is the value of your loan?

B6. (After-tax cost of compensation) Singh Financial Services has a handful of professionals, all of whom own stock in the company. Singh is considering a year-end distribution to its professional staff. The marginal tax rate is 40%.
  a. If Singh Financial Services pays $1,000,000 in cash dividends, what is the effect on taxable income, taxes due, and net income? What is the cash outlay on an after-tax basis?
  b. If Singh pays $1,000,000 of salary and bonuses, what is the effect on taxable income, taxes due, and net income? What is the cash outlay on an after-tax basis?

PROBLEM SET C

C1. (Claim dilution via new debt) Assume that you work for Bank of North America and that you have made a large loan to Kinkus Publishing. At the end of the year, Kinkus must pay off the $20 million loan. Kinkus has undertaken a major expansion, and the value of its assets when the loan is due is expected to be either $25 million or $50 million. Let's call these two outcomes the "good" and "bad" scenarios.
  a. Under these two scenarios, what loan repayment do you expect from Kinkus at the end of the year?
  b. Assume now that Kinkus has issued some new debt to another party. Kinkus must pay $20 million to this other lender at the end of the year. Kinkus distributed the loan proceeds to its stockholders, so the assets of the company are unaffected and the value of the company's assets is still expected to be $25 or $50 million. If Kinkus is unable to pay its debts, your loan has the same priority as the new loan. If Kinkus cannot pay 100% of its debt, you will get the same percentage payoff as the other lender. What loan repayment do you now expect from Kinkus under the "good" and "bad" scenarios?

C2. (Asset substitution problem) Integrity Plastics has a debt obligation of $25 and assets with a value of $20. This debt must be paid off soon. When this happens, the value of the debt will be $20 and the value of equity will be $0. Prior to paying off the debt, Integrity has an opportunity to swap all of its assets for a high-risk investment that will pay off $40 or zero. The investment would have an NPV of either $20 or −$20 (NPV = the value of the payoff minus the investment).
  a. If the $40 payoff (NPV = $20) occurs, what is the value of equity? What is the value of debt?
  b. If the zero payoff (NPV = −$20) occurs, what is the value of equity? What is the value of debt?
  c. Assume the probability of the high payoff is 0.40 and the probability of the low payoff is 0.60. What is the expected NPV of the investment? What is the expected value of the company?
  d. What is the expected value of equity? What is the expected value of debt?
  e. How can Integrity stockholders benefit from a negative-NPV project?

C3. (Asset substitution problem) Reconsider the self-test problem for Michigan Mining and Manufacturing. Assume that the company now has assets worth slightly more than its debts. MMM has a debt obligation of $100 million and assets with a value of $102 million. This debt must be paid off soon. When this happens, the value of the debt will be $100 million and the value of equity will be $2 million. Prior to paying off the debt, MMM has an opportunity to make a high-risk investment. MMM is considering an investment of $20 million that will pay off $40 million or zero. The investment would have an NPV of either $20 million or –$20 million (NPV = the value of the payoff minus the investment). The investment would be paid for with the company's liquid cash holdings.

a. If the $40 million payoff (NPV = $20 million) occurs, what is the value of equity? What is the value of debt?

b. If the zero payoff (NPV = –$20 million) occurs, what is the value of equity? What is the value of debt?

c. Assume the probability of the high payoff is 0.25 and the probability of the low payoff is 0.75. What is the expected NPV of the investment? What is the expected value of the company?

d. What is the expected value of equity? What is the expected value of debt?

e. Do the stockholders benefit from the negative-NPV project?

C4. (Underinvestment problem) The value of a company's assets is $1000 and it has debts of $750. If a catastrophe occurs, the assets are completely destroyed and have a value of $0. The probability of a catastrophe is 5%.

a. What is the value of debt and equity with no catastrophe? What is the value of debt and equity with a catastrophe? What is the expected value of debt and equity?

b. Assume an insurance policy can be purchased for $60. It pays $1000 in the event of a catastrophe. Recompute the value of debt and equity with no catastrophe. Recompute the value of debt and equity with a catastrophe. (Remember to deduct the cost of the $60 insurance premium.)

c. What would be the impact of the investment in the insurance policy on the value of debt and equity? Who would benefit from this insurance policy, stockholders or debtholders?

C5. (Contracting costs and the cost of borrowing) Uff Brothers Shipping is setting up a $200,000 loan. Uff Brothers makes interest payments of $22,000 at the end of each year for 4 years and will repay the principal at the end of year 4.

a. Assuming no contracting costs, what is the effective cost of this loan to Uff Brothers?

b. Assume now that Uff Brothers incurs one-time setup costs of $10,000 at time 0 for legal and other contracting costs. In addition, Uff Brothers incurs an additional $1000 of contracting costs at the end of each of the next 4 years. What is the effective annual cost of this loan including the contracting costs?

BIBLIOGRAPHY

Admati, Anat R., and Paul Pfleiderer. "Robust Financial Contracts and the Role of Venture Capitalists," *Journal of Finance,* 1994, 49(2):371–402.

Agrawal, Anup, and Nandu J. Nagarajan. "Corporate Capital Structure, Agency Costs, and Ownership Control: The Case of All-Equity Firms," *Journal of Finance,* 1990, 45(4):1325–1331.

Agrawal, Anup, and Ralph A. Walkling. "Executive Careers and Compensation Surrounding Takeover Bids," *Journal of Finance,* 1994, 49(3):985–1014.

Bagnani, Elizabeth Strock, Nickolaos T. Milonas, Anthony Saunders, and Nickolaos G. Travlos. "Managers, Owners, and the Pricing of Risky Debt: An Empirical Analysis," *Journal of Finance,* 1994, 49(2): 453–477.

Baker, George P., Michael C. Jensen, and Kevin J. Murphy. "Compensation and Incentives: Practice vs. Theory," *Journal of Finance,* 1988, 43(3):593–616.

Barnea, Amir, Robert A. Haugen, and Lemma W. Senbet. *Agency Problems and Financial Contracting.* Englewood Cliffs, N.J.: Prentice-Hall, 1985.

Barry, Christopher B., Chris J. Muscarella, and Michael R. Vetsuypens. "Underwriter Warrants, Underwriter Compensation, and the Costs of Going Public," *Journal of Financial Economics,* 1991, 29(1):113–136.

Barton, Sidney L., Ned C. Hill, and Srinivasan Sundaram. "An Empirical Test of Stakeholder Theory Predictions of Capital Structure," *Financial Management,* 1989, 18(1):36–44.

Bergman, Yaacov Z., and Jeffrey L. Callen. "Opportunistic Underinvestment in Debt Renegotiation and Capital Structure," *Journal of Financial Economics,* 1991, 29(1):137–172.

Berkovitch, Elazar, and Stuart I. Greenbaum. "The Loan Commitment as an Optimal Financing Contract," *Journal of Financial and Quantitative Analysis,* 1991, 26(1):83–96.

Berkovitch, Elazar, and E. Han Kim. "Financial Contracting and Leverage Induced Over- and Under-Investment Incentives," *Journal of Finance,* 1990, 45(3):765–794.

Berlin, Mitchell, and Jan Loeys. "Bond Covenants and Delegated Monitoring," *Journal of Finance,* 1988, 43(2):397–412.

Bessembinder, Hendrik. "Forward Contracts and Firm Value: Investment Incentive and Contracting Effects," *Journal of Financial and Quantitative Analysis,* 1991, 26(4):519–532.

Boot, Arnoud W. A., and Anjan V. Thakor. "Security Design," *Journal of Finance,* 1993, 48(4): 1349–1378.

Booth, James R., and Daniel N. Deli. "Factors Affecting the Number of Outside Directorships Held by CEOs," *Journal of Financial Economics,* 1996, 40(1):81–104.

Born, Jeffrey A. "Insider Ownership and Signals—Evidence from Dividend Initiation Announcement Effects," *Financial Management,* 1988, 17(1):38–45.

Born, Jeffrey A., and Victoria B. McWilliams. "Shareholder Responses to Equity-for-Debt Exchange Offers: A Free-Cash-Flow Interpretation," *Financial Management,* 1993, 22(4): 19–20.

Borstadt, Lisa F., and Thomas J. Zwirlein. "The Efficient Monitoring Role of Proxy Contests: An Empirical Analysis of Post-Contest Control Changes and Firm Performance," *Financial Management,* 1992, 21(3):22–34.

Brickley, James A., Frederick H. Dark, and Michael S. Weisbach. "An Agency Perspective on Franchising," *Financial Management,* 1991, 20(1):27–35.

Brickley, James A., and Kathleen T. Hevert. "Direct Employees Stock Ownership: An Empirical Investigation," *Financial Management,* 1991, 20(2):70–84.

Brook, Yaron, and Ramesh K. S. Rao. "Shareholder Wealth Effects of Directors' Liability Limitation Provisions," *Journal of Financial and Quantitative Analysis,* 1994, 29(3):481–497.

Bulow, Jeremy I., and John B. Shoven. "Bankruptcy Decision," *Bell Journal of Economics,* 1978, 9(Autumn):437–456.

Byrd, John W., and Kent A. Hickman. "Do Outside Directors Monitor Managers? Evidence from Tender Offer Bids," *Journal of Financial Economics,* 1992, 32(2):195–222.

Campbell, Tim S., and William A. Kracaw. "Corporate Risk Management and the Incentive Effects of Debt," *Journal of Finance,* 1990, 45(5):1673–1686.

Cannella, Albert A., Jr., Donald R. Fraser, and D. Scott Lee. "Firm Failure and Managerial Labor Markets: Evidence from Texas Banking," *Journal of Financial Economics,* 1995, 38(2):185–210.

Carter, Richard B., and Roger D. Stover. "Management Ownership and Firm Compensation Policy: Evidence from Converting Savings and Loan Associations," *Financial Management,* 1991, 20(4):80–90.

Chan, Yuk-Shee, Stuart I. Greenbaum, and Anjan V. Thakor. "Is Fairly Priced Deposit Insurance Possible?" *Journal of Finance,* 1992, 47(1): 227–246.

Chang, Chun. "Capital Structure as an Optimal Contract Between Employees and Investors," *Journal of Finance,* 1992, 47(3):1141–1158.

Chang, Saeyoung. "Employee Stock Ownership Plans and Shareholder Wealth: An Empirical Investigation," *Financial Management,* 1990, 19(1):48–58.

Choi, Yoon K. "The Choice of Organizational Form: The Case of Post-Merger Managerial Incentive Structure," *Financial Management,* 1993, 22(4):69–81.

Clayton, Ronnie J., and William Beranek. "Disassociations and Legal Combinations," *Financial Management,* 1985, 14(2):24–28.

Conte, Michael A., and Douglas Kruse. "ESOPs and Profit-Sharing Plans: Do They Link Employee Pay to Company Performance?" *Financial Management,* 1991, 20(4):91–100.

Cook, Douglas O., John C. Easterwood, and John D. Martin. "Bondholder Wealth Effects of Management Buyouts," *Financial Management,* 1992, 21(1):102–112.

Cornell, Bradford, and Alan C. Shapiro. "Corporate Stakeholders and Corporate Finance," *Financial Management,* 1987, 16(1):5–14.

Cornett, Marcia Millon, and Nickolaos G. Travlos. "Information Effects Associated with Debt-for-Equity and Equity-for-Debt Exchange Offers," *Journal of Finance,* 1989, 44(2): 451–468.

Cotter, James F., and Marc Zenner. "How Managerial Wealth Affects the Tender Offer Process," *Journal of Financial Economics,* 1994, 35(1):63–97.

Crabbe, Leland. "Event Risk: An Analysis of Losses to Bondholders and 'Super Poison Put' Bond Covenants," *Journal of Finance,* 1991, 46(2):689–706.

Crutchley, Claire E., and Robert S. Hansen. "A Test of the Agency Theory of Managerial Ownership, Corporate Leverage, and Corporate Dividends," *Financial Management,* 1989, 18(4):36–46.

DeFusco, Richard A., Thomas S. Zorn, and Robert R. Johnson. "The Association Between Executive Stock Option Plan Changes and Managerial Decision Making," *Financial Management,* 1991, 20(1):36–43.

Denis, David J. "Organizational Form and the Consequences of Highly Leveraged Transactions: Kroger's Recapitalization and Safeway's LBO," *Journal of Financial Economics,* 1994, 36(2):193–224.

Denis, David J., and Diane K. Denis. "Performance Changes Following Top Management Dismissals," *Journal of Finance,* 1995, 50(4):1029–1057.

Denning, Karen C., and Kuldeep Shastri. "Changes in Organizational Structure and Shareholder Wealth: The Case of Limited Partnerships," *Journal of Financial and Quantitative Analysis,* 1993, 28(4):553–564.

Diamond, Douglas W. "Optimal Release of Information by Firms," *Journal of Finance,* 1985, 40(4):1071–1094.

Diamond, Douglas W. "Reputation Acquisition in Debt Markets," *Journal of Political Economy,* 1989, 97(August):828–862.

Donaldson, Gordon. *Managing Corporate Wealth: The Operations of a Comprehensive Financial Goals System.* New York: Praeger, 1984.

Fields, L. Paige, and Eric L. Mais. "Managerial Voting Rights and Seasoned Public Equity Issues," *Journal of Financial and Quantitative Analysis,* 1994, 29(3):445–457.

Finnerty, John D. "Stock-for-Debt Swaps and Shareholder Returns," *Financial Management,* 1985, 14(3): 5–17.

Fischer, Paul E. "Optimal Contracting and Insider Trading Restrictions," *Journal of Finance,* 1992, 47(2):673–694.

Fridson, Martin S. "Do High-Yield Bonds Have an Equity Component?" *Financial Management,* 1994, 23(2): 82–84.

Furtado, Eugene P. H., and Vijay Karan. "Causes, Consequences, and Shareholder Wealth Effects of Management Turnover: A Review of the Empirical Evidence," *Financial Management,* 1990, 19(2):60–75.

Giammarino, Ronald M., Tracy R. Lewis, and David E. M. Sappington. "An Incentive Approach to Banking Regulation," *Journal of Finance,* 1993, 48(4):1523–1542.

Gilson, Stuart C. "Bankruptcy, Boards, Banks, and Blockholders: Evidence on Changes in Corporate Ownership and Control When Firms Default," *Journal of Financial Economics,* 1990, 27(2):355–388.

Gilson, Stuart C., and Michael R. Vetsuypens. "CEO Compensation in Financially Distressed Firms: An Empirical Analysis," *Journal of Finance,* 1993, 48(2):425–458.

Gombola, Michael J., and George P. Tsetsekos. "The Information Content of Plant Closing Announcements: Evidence from Financial Profiles and the Stock Price Reaction," *Financial Management,* 1992, 21(2):31–40.

Gupta, Atul, and Leonard Rosenthal. "Ownership Structure, Leverage, and Firm Value: The Case of Leveraged Recapitalizations," *Financial Management,* 1991, 20(3):69–83.

Handa, Puneet, and A. R. Radhakrishnan. "An Empirical Investigation of Leveraged Recapitalizations with Cash Payout as Takeover Defense," *Financial Management,* 1991, 20(3):58–68.

Harris, Milton, and Artur Raviv. "Capital Structure and the Informational Role of Debt," *Journal of Finance,* 1990, 45(2):321–350.

Hasbrouck, Joel. "Measuring the Information Content of Stock Trades," *Journal of Finance,* 1991, 46(1):179–208.

Hermalin, Benjamin E., and Michael S. Weisbach. "The Effects of Board Composition and Direct Incentives on Firm Performance," *Financial Management,* 1991, 20(4):101–112.

Hertzel, Michael, and Richard L. Smith. "Market Discounts and Shareholder Gains for Placing Equity Privately," *Journal of Finance,* 1993, 48(2):459–485.

Hirshleifer, David. "Managerial Reputation and Corporate Investment Decisions," *Financial Management,* 1993, 22(2):145–160.

Jensen, Michael C., and William H. Meckling. "Theory of the Firm: Managerial Behavior, Agency Costs and Ownership Structure," *Journal of Financial Economics,* 1976, 3(4): 305–360.

Jordan, James V., and George Emir Morgan. "Default Risk in Futures Markets: The Customer-Broker Relationship," *Journal of Finance,* 1990, 45(3):909–934.

Kaplan, Steven N., and David Reishus. "Outside Directorships and Corporate Performance," *Journal of Financial Economics,* 1990, 27(2):389–410.

Kumar, Raman, and Parvez R. Sopariwala. "The Effect of Adoption of Long-Term Performance Plans on Stock Prices and Accounting Numbers," *Journal of Financial and Quantitative Analysis,* 1992, 27(4):561–574.

Laber, Gene. "Bond Covenants and Forgone Opportunities: The Case of Burlington Northern Railroad Company," *Financial Management,* 1992, 21(2):71–77.

Lippert, Robert L., and William T. Moore. "Monitoring versus Bonding: Shareholder Rights and Management Compensation," *Financial Management,* 1995, 24(3):54–62.

Loderer, Claudio P., and Dennis P. Sheehan. "Corporate Bankruptcy and Managers' Self-Serving Behavior," *Journal of Finance,* 1989, 44(4):1059–1076.

Logue, Dennis E., James K. Seward, and James P. Walsh. "Rearranging Residual Claims: A Case for Targeted Stock," *Financial Management,* 1996, 25(1):43–61.

Long, Michael S. "The Incentives Behind the Adoption of Executive Stock Option Plans in U.S. Corporations," *Financial Management,* 1992, 21(3):12–21.

Mahajan, Arvind. "Pricing Expropriation Risk," *Financial Management,* 1990, 19(4):77–86.

Maksimovic, Vojislav. "Product Market Imperfections and Loan Commitments," *Journal of Finance,* 1990, 45(5):1641–1654.

Maksimovic, Vojislav, and Josef Zechner. "Debt, Agency Costs, and Industry Equilibrium," *Journal of Finance,* 1991, 46(5):1619–1644.

Malitz, Ileen. "On Financial Contracting: The Determinants of Bond Covenants," *Financial Management,* 1986, 15(2):18–25.

McLaughlin, Robyn M. "Does the Form of Compensation Matter? Investment Banker Fee Contracts in Tender Offers," *Journal of Financial Economics,* 1992, 32(2):223–260.

Mehran, Hamid. "Executive Compensation Structure, Ownership, and Firm Performance," *Journal of Financial Economics,* 1995, 38(2):163–184.

Merton, Robert C., and Zvi Bodie. "On the Management of Financial Guarantees," *Financial Management,* 1992, 21(4):87–109.

Michel, Allen, and Israel Shaked. "Airline Performance Under Deregulation: The Shareholders' Perspective," *Financial Management,* 1984, 13(2):5–14.

Murphy, J. Austin. "Analyzing Sub-Classes of General Motors Common Stock," *Financial Management,* 1989, 18(1):64–71.

Netter, Jeffry, and Annette Poulsen. "State Corporation Laws and Shareholders: The Recent Experience," *Financial Management,* 1989, 18(3):29–40.

Park, Sangsoo, and Moon H. Song. "Employee Stock Ownership Plans, Firm Performance, and Monitoring by Outside Blockholders," *Financial Management,* 1995, 24(4):52–65.

Perotti, Enrico C., and Serhat E. Guney. "The Structure of Privatization Plans," *Financial Management,* 1993, 22(1):84–98.

Persons, John C. "Signaling and Takeover Deterrence with Stock Repurchases: Dutch Auctions versus Fixed Price Tender Offers," *Journal of Finance,* 1994, 49(4):1373–1402.

Petersen, Mitchell A., and Raghuram G. Rajan. "The Benefits of Lending Relationships: Evidence from Small Business Data," *Journal of Finance,* 1994, 49(1):3–37.

Rosen, Corey. "The Record of Employee Ownership," *Financial Management,* 1990, 19(1):39–47.

Rosenstein, Stuart, and Jeffrey G. Wyatt. "Outside Directors, Board Independence, and Shareholder Wealth," *Journal of Financial Economics,* 1990, 26(2):175–192.

Roy, Asim. "Partial Acquisition Strategies for Business Combinations," *Financial Management,* 1985, 14(2):16–23.

Sanders, Ralph W., Jr., and John S. Zdanowicz. "Target Firm Abnormal Returns and Trading Volume Around the Initiation of Change in Control Transactions," *Journal of Financial and Quantitative Analysis,* 1992, 27(1):109–130.

Schwartz, Eduardo S., and Salvador Zurita. "Sovereign Debt: Optimal Contract, Underinvestment, and Forgiveness," *Journal of Finance,* 1992, 47(3):981–1004.

Slovin, Myron B., and Marie E. Sushka. "Ownership Concentration, Corporate Control Activity, and Firm Value: Evidence from the Death of Inside Blockholders," *Journal of Finance,* 1993, 48(4):1293–1321.

Slovin, Myron B., Marie E. Sushka, and John A. Polonchek. "The Value of Bank Durability: Borrowers as Bank Stakeholders," *Journal of Finance,* 1993, 48(1):247–266.

Smith, Clifford W., Jr., and Ross L. Watts. "The Investment Opportunity Set and Corporate Financing, Dividend, and Compensation Policies," *Journal of Financial Economics,* 1992, 32(3):263–292.

Spatt, Chester S., and Frederic P. Sterbenz. "Incentive Conflicts, Bundling Claims, and the Interaction Among Financial Claimants," *Journal of Finance,* 1993, 48(2):513–528.

Szewczyk, Samuel H., and George T. Tsetsekos. "State Intervention in the Market for Corporate Control: The Case of Pennsylvania Senate Bill 1310," *Journal of Financial Economics,* 1992, 31(1):3–22.

Thakor, Anjan V. "Game Theory in Finance," *Financial Management,* 1991, 20(1):71–94.

Thakor, Anjan V. "Strategic Issues in Financial Contracting: An Overview," *Financial Management,* 1989, 18(2):39–58.

Williamson, Oliver E. "Corporate Finance and Corporate Governance," *Journal of Finance,* 1988, 43(3):567–591.

Part III

CAPITAL BUDGETING: STRATEGIC ASSET ALLOCATION

Capital budgeting is the process of choosing the company's long-term capital investments. This includes investments in such things as land, plant, and equipment. Capital budgeting is fundamental because a company is essentially defined by its assets and the products and services those assets produce. For example, Chrysler is a car maker, regardless of how it is financed. A company's choices of which products to produce and which services to offer, then, are capital budgeting decisions—and those choices are intertwined with all the other decisions facing the company.

A company has an almost limitless number of possible investments, but past and current choices constrain its future choices. This is why we have added the phrase, "strategic asset allocation," to the title of part III. The strategic nature of these choices can be seen in the time horizons of capital assets, which may span years or even decades. In some cases, such as forest product management, capital assets may not produce returns for generations.

Regardless of their time horizons, capital budgeting projects are judged on the value they create. When you buy a stock or bond that's worth more than it costs—one with a positive NPV—your wealth will increase by the amount of the difference. When a company undertakes a capital budgeting project with a positive NPV, the value of the company's stock will increase by that amount. However, a negative-NPV project will decrease its stock value.

So you can see why we say capital budgeting decisions are the most important decisions facing a company. Capital budgeting has a direct link to shareholder wealth. The more successful a company's capital budgeting decisions, the higher the value of the company's stock.

BUSINESS INVESTMENT CRITERIA

When making capital budgeting decisions, a company evaluates the expected future cash flows in relation to the required initial investment. The objective is to find investment projects that will add value to the company. These are projects that are worth more to the company than they cost—projects that have a positive NPV.

The pivotal role of capital budgeting, and the risks associated with capital investments, are dramatically demonstrated by comparing the initial cash outflow, which can be huge, to that of the relatively much smaller expected periodic future cash inflows. The risk is especially obvious if you consider the tremendous uncertainty associated with the timing and size of the future cash flows. A company might invest $200 million now, *hoping* to net $30 million per year *after* several years of development!

A company's evaluation of a long-term investment project is like an individual's investment decision. The steps are the same:

1. Estimate the expected future cash flows from the project. This is like estimating the coupon payments for a bond or the dividend stream for a stock and a maturity value or terminal sale price.
2. Assess the risk and determine a required return for discounting the expected future cash flows.
3. Compute the present value of the expected future cash flows.
4. Determine the cost of the project and compare it to what the project is worth. If the project is worth more than it costs—if it has a positive NPV—it will create value.

In this chapter we'll present the process of capital budgeting as it is practiced in most corporations. We'll show you ways to measure the attractiveness of projects. As you'll see, some badly flawed methods remain

in practice and can lead to bad decisions. We'll also show how sound methods of evaluating business investments can be applied to both proposed projects and to current operations. When combined with reasonable estimates of future outcomes, these methods support good decisions.

Throughout this first chapter on capital budgeting, we'll ignore taxes and certain other complications to focus on basic investment criteria and the process of capital budgeting.

BUSINESS INVESTMENT CRITERIA AND THE PRINCIPLES OF FINANCE

◆ *Valuable Ideas:* Look for new ideas to use as a basis for capital budgeting projects that will create value.

◆ *Comparative Advantage:* Look for capital budgeting projects that will use the company's comparative advantage to create value.

◆ *Incremental Benefits:* Identify and estimate the expected future cash flows for a capital budgeting project on an incremental basis.

◆ *Risk-Return Trade-Off:* Incorporate the risk of a capital budgeting project into its *cost of capital:* the project's required return.

(continued on following page)

(Business Investment Criteria and the Principles of Finance continued from previous page)

◆ *Time Value of Money:* Measure the current value a capital budgeting project will create: its NPV.

◆ *Options:* Recognize the value of options, such as the options to expand, postpone, or abandon a capital budgeting project.

◆ *Two-Sided Transactions:* Consider why the other party to a transaction is willing to participate.

◆ *Signaling:* Consider the products and actions of competitors.

THE CAPITAL BUDGETING PROCESS

CAPITAL BUDGETING
The process of choosing the company's long-term capital investments.

CAPITAL BUDGET A company's set of planned capital expenditures.

Let's start by looking at how **capital budgeting** works in practice. The overall process can be broken down into five steps as a project moves from idea to reality:

1. Generating ideas for capital budgeting projects
2. Preparing proposals
3. Reviewing existing projects and facilities
4. Evaluating proposed projects and creating the **capital budget,** the company's set of planned capital expenditures
5. Preparing appropriation requests

Idea Generation

The first—and most important—part of the capital budgeting process is generating new ideas. Its critical importance is obvious from the Principle of Valuable Ideas. Unfortunately, we can't teach people how to come up with valuable new ideas. If we could, we would already be wealthy from having followed the procedure ourselves! However, although we don't have a process that ensures the creation of new ideas, it's important to stress their value. Such an emphasis makes it more likely that those ideas that do occur to us and to others will be given serious consideration.

Where do new ideas come from? Ideas for capital budgeting projects come from all levels within an organization. Figure 8.1 shows the typical flow of capital investment ideas within a company. Often plant managers are responsible for identifying potential projects that will enable their plants to operate on a different scale or on a more efficient basis. For instance, a plant manager might suggest adding 10,000 square feet of production space to a plant or replacing a piece of equipment with a newer, more efficient machine. After screening out the less advantageous or less attractive ideas, the manager would send the ones that appear to be attractive to the divisional level, with supporting documentation.

Division management not only reviews such proposals but also adds ideas of its own. For example, division management may propose the introduction of a new product line or combination of two plants and elimination of the less efficient one. Such ideas are less likely to come from the plant managers!

This bottom-up process results in ideas percolating upward through the organization. At each level, ideas submitted by lower-level managers are screened, and some are forwarded to the next level. In addition, the managers at successively higher levels, who are in a position to take a broader view of the company's business, add ideas that may not be visible to lower-level managers.

At the same time, there is also a top-down process at work in most companies. Strategic planners will generate ideas regarding new businesses the company should enter, other com-

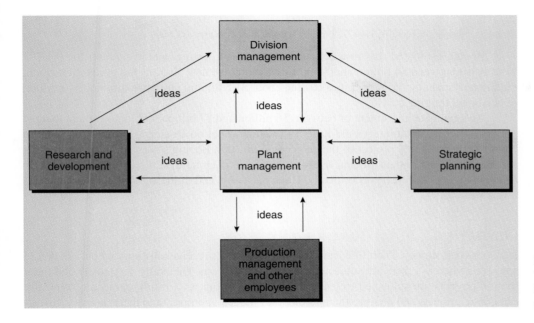

FIGURE 8.1
The typical flow of capital investment ideas within a company.

panies it might acquire, and ways to modify its existing businesses to achieve greater profitability. Strategic planning is a critical element in the capital budgeting process. The processes complement one another; the top-down process generates ideas of a broader, more strategic nature, whereas the bottom-up process generates ideas of a more project-specific nature.

In addition, some companies have a research-and-development group, either within a production division or as a separate department. A research-and-development group often provides new ideas for products that can be sent on to a marketing research department. Table 8.1 lists the typical stages for the development and approval of a capital investment proposal.

Each stage in table 8.1 involves a capital budgeting decision at one or more levels of the company. Therefore, at each stage, the company re-estimates the NPV of going ahead. With this kind of sequential appropriation of funds, an automatic progress review is enforced, enabling early cancellation of unsuccessful projects. So each stage includes options, for example, to abandon, postpone, change, or continue.

TABLE 8.1
Development and Approval Stages for a Proposed Capital Budgeting Project

1. Approve funds for research that may result in a product *idea*.
2. Approve funds for market research that may result in a product *proposal*.
3. Approve funds for product development that may result in a usable *product*.
4. Approve funds for plant and/or equipment for the *production* and sale of the new product.

Boeing's Strategic Decision: Will the 777 Project Fly?

EXAMPLE

The Boeing Company is the world's leading maker of commercial aircraft. Just a few years ago, the company faced a critical capital budgeting decision: whether to develop a new generation of passenger aircraft, the 777. Developing new aircraft is very expensive, as Boeing well knows.

(*continued on following page*)

(Boeing's Strategic Decision: Will the 777 Project Fly? *continued from previous page*)

Boeing estimated that research and development, testing, and evaluation for the 777 would cost between $4 billion and $5 billion. Placing the new aircraft into production would require new manufacturing facilities costing about $1.5 billion, plus an additional $0.5 billion in personnel training costs.

An aggregate investment of between $6 billion and $7 billion was large enough that the project's success or failure would have a profound effect on Boeing's fortunes for years to come. An unprofitable project of that size could threaten Boeing's very survival, whereas its success would strengthen Boeing's leadership in commercial aviation. Therefore, correctly analyzing the 777 project was critical to Boeing's future and to the value of its shareholders' investment. ■

Classifying Capital Budgeting Projects

Analysis costs money. Therefore, certain types of projects receive only cursory checks before approval, whereas others are subjected to extensive analysis. Generally, less costly and more routine projects are subjected to less extensive evaluation. As a result, companies typically categorize projects and analyze them to the level judged appropriate to their category. Investments in each category may have a lot in common and can be analyzed similarly. A useful set of investment classifications is:

Maintenance projects

Cost-saving/Revenue-enhancement projects

Capacity expansions in current businesses

New products and new businesses

Projects required by government regulation or company policy

Maintenance Expenditures At a most basic level, a company must make certain investments to continue to be a healthy, profitable business. Replacing worn-out or damaged equipment is a necessity to continue business. Therefore, the major questions concerning such investments are "Should we continue in this business?" and if so, "Should we continue to use the same production process?" Since the answers to these questions are so frequently "yes," an elaborate decision-making process is not a good use of resources, and typically such decisions are approved with only routine review.

Cost Savings/Revenue Enhancement Projects in this class include improvements in production technology to realize cost savings and marketing campaigns to achieve revenue enhancement. The central issue is increasing the difference between revenue and cost; the result must be sufficient to justify the investment. Cost-reducing investments involve not only the requirement that the purchase and installation of the equipment must be profitable, but also that current action is better than waiting until a later time—there may be a valuable option to postpone.

Capacity Expansion in Current Businesses Deciding to expand the current business is inherently more difficult than approving maintenance or cost-savings proposals. Firms have to consider the economics of expanding or adding new facilities. They also must prepare demand forecasts, and the Principle of Two-Sided Transactions reminds us to consider competitors' likely strategies. Marketing consultants may help, but the cash flow projections for this type of project have naturally greater uncertainty than do maintenance or replacement projects.

New Products and New Businesses Projects in this category, which include research-and-development activities, are among the most difficult to evaluate. Their newness and long lead times make it very difficult to forecast product demand accurately. In many cases, the project may be of special interest because it would give the company an option to break into a new market. For example, a company that possesses a proprietary technology might spend additional research-and-development funds trying to develop new products based on this technology. If successful, these new products could pave the way for future profitable investment opportunities. Access to such follow-on opportunities represents options for the company, which you know are valuable.

Meeting Regulatory and Policy Requirements Government regulations and/or company policies concerning such things as pollution control and health or safety factors are viewed as costs. Often, the critical issue in such projects is meeting the standards in the most efficient manner—at the minimum present-value cost—rather than realizing the value added by the project. Engineering analyses of alternative technologies often provide critical information in such cases. The company must also consider the possibility that the option to abandon the business is worth more than making the required investments and continuing.

Capital Budgeting Proposals

Small expenditures may be handled informally, but in general, the originator presents a proposal in writing. Sometimes proposals are not formally written in smaller privately owned companies, which tend to have relatively informal organizational structures. Most companies use standard forms, and these are typically supplemented by written memoranda for larger, more complex projects. Also, there may be consulting or other studies prepared by outside experts; for example, economic forecasts from economic consultants.

For a healthy company, a maintenance project might require only limited supporting information. In contrast, a new product would require extensive information gathering and analysis. At the same time, within a category, managers at each level typically have upper limits on their authority regarding both expenditures on individual assets and the total expenditure for a budgeting period. In this way, larger projects require the approval of higher authority.

For example, at the lowest level, a department head may have the authority to approve $25,000 in total equipment purchases for the year. However, that same person might have to obtain specific approval from higher authority to spend more than $5000 for any single piece of equipment. A plant manager might have authorization limits of $250,000 per year and $50,000 per piece of equipment, and so forth.

A system of authorization such as this requires more extensive review and a greater number of inputs to approve larger expenditures. The hierarchical review structure reflects the obvious fact that misjudging a larger project is potentially more costly than misjudging a smaller one. Hence, the need for a greater number of reviews before deciding to proceed.

Capital Budgeting and the Required Return

Recall that the required return is the minimum return that you need to earn to be willing to make an investment. It's the return that exactly reflects the riskiness of the expected future cash flows. In capital budgeting, the required return has several different names. The most widely used term is the **cost of capital.** Other names are the *hurdle rate* and the *appropriate discount rate,* or simply the *discount rate.* While these terms may be used interchangeably, it is important to remember that the cost of capital reflects the riskiness of the capital budgeting project's cash flows, not the interest rate on its bonds, nor the riskiness of the company's *existing* assets.

COST OF CAPITAL The required return for a capital budgeting project. Also called the *hurdle rate, appropriate discount rate,* or simply the *discount rate.*

NET PRESENT VALUE (NPV)

Net present value (NPV) is the difference between what a capital budgeting project costs and what it is worth (its market value).

Can something really be worth more than it costs? Yes, it happens. But being the skeptical and insightful person you are, you know that we are not going to give you a list of such opportunities; we would rather keep it for ourselves. In fact, the major difficulty of finding positive-NPV projects rests on the need to see situations differently from other people in the market. That translates into an assumption of risk based on special knowledge or valuable ideas. At best we can estimate a project's NPV in advance. We will not know its true market value, or what it is *really* worth, until the project is completed and the returns are collected.

EXAMPLE

Discovering a Positive-NPV Opportunity

Suppose you have noticed a run-down office building in downtown Chicago that you think has possibilities. You decide to buy it for $420,000, and invest $300,000 more in renovations over the next 6 months. After this, you offer the building for sale and sell it to the highest bidder for $910,000. Because the building turned out to be worth more than you paid for it, that is, its market value of $910,000 exceeded its cost of $720,000 (= $420,000 + 300,000), your management will have created about $190,000 (= $910,000 − 720,000) in value.

Although it's delightful to contemplate the money you made in our example, think about how you could have known enough to undertake this capital budgeting project in the first place. To estimate the market value after renovation, you might have looked at other buildings in good repair to see what they were worth, and then adjusted for differences between these buildings and the run-down one you were thinking of buying. You would also estimate the cost of the needed renovations and add that to the cost of buying the building to determine the total cost. Finally, you would compare your market value estimate to your total cost estimate.

If the estimates tell you the project creates value, and your estimates are correct, then you get the value that is created. You can see right away how important accurate estimates are! ■

Let's generalize from our building renovation example. You could find the building's market value by offering it for sale—the highest offer you get is its market value. However, that's possible only after doing the renovations. Although you might be able to offer the building for sale before doing the renovations by describing your plans, at best this would be awkward, time consuming, and expensive. Furthermore, keep in mind the Principle of Two-Sided

Transactions: Once you pointed out the potential value of renovating the building to other people, some of them might decide to bid on the building now for more than the $420,000 you hoped to pay for it.

As an alternative, the example mentioned a method of estimating market value without offering it for sale: Find the market value of a similar asset and adjust for whatever differences there are between the two.

Yet another way to determine value is to use **discounted cash flow (DCF) analysis** and compute the present value of all the cash flows connected with ownership. This is like discounting the interest payments on a bond or dividends on a stock.

The NPV of a capital budgeting project is the present value of *all* of the cash flows connected with the project, all its costs and revenues, now and in the future:

DISCOUNTED CASH FLOW (DCF) ANALYSIS The process of valuing capital budgeting projects by discounting their expected future cash flows.

$$\left(\begin{array}{c} \text{NPV} = \text{CF}_0 + \dfrac{\text{CF}_1}{(1+r)} + \dfrac{\text{CF}_2}{(1+r)^2} + \ldots + \dfrac{\text{CF}_n}{(1+r)^n} \\[2ex] = \displaystyle\sum_{t=0}^{n} \dfrac{\text{CF}_t}{(1+r)^t} \end{array} \right) \qquad (8.1)$$

DECISION RULE for net present value: Undertake the capital budgeting project if the NPV is positive.

EXAMPLE

Computing an NPV

Let's suppose that instead of expecting to sell the building after you renovate it, you expect to lease it out for 20 years, after which time you estimate you can sell the building for $250,000. You expect the lease to pay you $110,000 per year. Finally, the cost of capital in this case is 12%. What is the NPV of this renovation project?

Using equation (8.1), the NPV is $127,555.49:

$$\text{NPV} = -(420,000 + 300,000) + 110,000 \sum_{t=1}^{20} \frac{1}{(1.12)^t} + 250,000 \frac{1}{(1.12)^{20}}$$

$$= -720,000 + 821,639.80 + 25,916.69 = \$127,556.49$$

The NPV is the present value of the future cash flows, which is $847,556.49

| N = 20 | r = 12 | **PV = 847,556.49** | PMT = 110,000 | FV = 250,000 |

minus the initial cost of $720,000. ■

It's important to note that the uncertainty connected with the assumptions about revenues, costs, and selling price are included in the cost of capital (required return). That is to say, computing the NPV does *not* reduce the risk. If the assumptions work out, however, you'll be richer for undertaking the project.

Adding Value per Share

How much value would this renovation project add to a share of a company's stock if the company undertook the building renovation project? Each share of stock has a claim on the company. Typically, this would be 1/n, where n is the number of outstanding shares, and the claim would extend to the NPV of the new project. Assuming such a claim, then, if the company had 100,000 shares of common stock outstanding, and our estimates are correct, the project would simply add a fractional share of its NPV to the stock's price. The company's stock price would therefore increase by $1.28 per share (= 127,556.49/100,000).

Self-Check
1. What is the NPV of a capital budgeting project?
2. State the decision rule for net present value.
3. What is discounted cash flow analysis?

INTERNAL RATE OF RETURN (IRR)

INTERNAL RATE OF RETURN (IRR) The expected return for a capital budgeting project. The IRR is the discount rate that makes the total present value of all of the expected cash flows from a project sum to zero.

Another method of evaluating a capital budgeting project is called the internal-rate-of-return method. The **internal rate of return (IRR)** is the project's expected return. If the cost of capital (required return) equals the IRR (expected return), the NPV equals zero. So one way of viewing the IRR is to say that it's the discount rate that makes the total present value of all of a project's cash flows sum to zero. Because of risk, the project's realized return will almost surely be different from its IRR. Recall from chapter 6 how to compute a bond's yield to maturity (YTM). We use the same sort of procedure to compute an IRR:

$$CF_0 + \frac{CF_1}{(1 + IRR)} + \frac{CF_2}{(1 + IRR)^2} + \ldots + \frac{CF_n}{(1 + IRR)^n} = 0$$

$$\sum_{t=0}^{n} \frac{CF_t}{(1 + IRR)^t} = 0 \qquad (8.2)$$

DECISION RULE for internal rate of return: Undertake the capital budgeting project if the IRR exceeds r, the project's cost of capital.

In its simplest form, the IRR rule is intuitively appealing. In essence, it asks whether the capital budgeting project's expected return exceeds its required return. In other words, will it create value?

At first glance, this seems to be saying the same thing the NPV rule says. As we'll see, this is generally true—but not always. The intuitive appeal of the IRR rule, however, probably accounts for its widespread use (some analysts even prefer it).

Like other expected returns, the IRR must be calculated by trial and error. Although some calculators and spreadsheets can solve for the IRR, they also are using trial and error.[1] Let's work through a detailed trial-and-error calculation to help you understand the problem.

EXAMPLE

Computing an IRR for Reebok

Suppose Reebok can invest in a capital budgeting project that has a 12% cost of capital. The project's expected future net cash flows are shown in figure 8.2. What is the IRR of Reebok's capital budgeting project?

FIGURE 8.2
Expected future net cash flows for Reebok's capital budgeting project.

Year	0	1	2	3	4
Cash flows	− 800	300	300	300	150

---

[1]When it seems as if the calculator is taking time to "think," it is going through a trial-and-error calculation. Its answer is actually an estimate that is accurate to within some prespecified degree, such as 9 decimal places.

When in doubt, start by trying 10%. At a discount rate of 10%, the NPV of this project would be

$$\text{NPV}_{10\%} = -800 + \frac{300}{(1.10)^1} + \frac{300}{(1.10)^2} + \frac{300}{(1.10)^3} + \frac{150}{(1.10)^4} = +48.51$$

Because $\text{NPV}_{10\%}$ is positive, we must try a larger discount rate. Let's try 12%. It's the cost of capital anyway.

$$\text{NPV}_{12\%} = -800 + \frac{300}{(1.12)^1} + \frac{300}{(1.12)^2} + \frac{300}{(1.12)^3} + \frac{150}{(1.12)^4} = +15.88$$

This is still too low. Let's try 14%:

$$\text{NPV}_{14\%} = -800 + \frac{300}{(1.14)^1} + \frac{300}{(1.14)^2} + \frac{300}{(1.14)^3} + \frac{150}{(1.14)^4} = -14.70$$

Because 14% would make the NPV negative, it must be too high. Let's try 13%:

$$\text{NPV}_{13\%} = -800 + \frac{300}{(1.13)^1} + \frac{300}{(1.13)^2} + \frac{300}{(1.13)^3} + \frac{150}{(1.13)^4} = +0.34$$

That's pretty close, but you could keep going with this process and find that, to 4-decimal accuracy, the IRR is 13.0225%. With a cost of capital of 12%, then, the IRR decision rule would tell us to undertake this project, which is the same advice the NPV decision rule offers. ■

Self-Check

1. What is a capital budgeting project's IRR?

2. State the decision rule for internal rate of return. What does it mean in practical terms?

3. Does the IRR rule usually lead to the same investment decisions as the NPV rule?

USING THE NPV AND IRR CRITERIA

In many applications, the NPV and IRR are both valuable guides to making capital budgeting decisions. Frequently, the NPV and IRR agree and can be trusted to provide a valid assessment. There are some instances, however, where the NPV and IRR disagree on the relative merits of projects, and there are other instances where the IRR is very difficult to interpret. In this section, we discuss when both methods can be trusted. We also show cases where they disagree. When in doubt, as we show, use the NPV rule.

When the IRR and NPV Methods Agree: Independent, Conventional Projects

In the example just given, the IRR and NPV methods agree. This will happen whenever the projects are both independent and conventional. An **independent project** is one that can be chosen independently of other projects. That is, undertaking it neither requires nor precludes any other investment. A project that requires other investments is simply part of a larger capital budgeting project, which must be evaluated together with all of its parts. When undertaking one project prevents investing in another project, and vice versa, the projects are said to be **mutually exclusive projects.**

INDEPENDENT PROJECT A project that can be chosen without requiring or precluding any other investment.

MUTUALLY EXCLUSIVE PROJECTS Two capital budgeting projects that cannot both be undertaken; choosing one precludes choosing the other.

CONVENTIONAL PRO-
JECT A project with a negative initial cash flow (an
*out*flow), which is expected
to be followed by one or
more future positive cash
flows (cash *in*flows).

A **conventional project** is a project with an initial cash outflow that is followed by one or more expected future cash inflows. That is, after making the investment, the total cash flow in each future year is expected to be positive. Purchasing a stock or bond is a simple example of a conventional capital budgeting project: You buy the security (a negative cash flow), and the terminal sale price and any dividends or interest payments while you own it will be positive cash flows—or at the worst zero. They cannot be negative because you have limited liability.

NPV Profile

NPV PROFILE A graph of
the NPV as a function of
the discount rate.

Another way to look at this problem is to graph NPV as a function of the discount rate. This graph is called an **NPV profile.** The NPV profile is one of the most useful tools of discounted cash flow analysis.

The NPV profile includes both NPV and IRR. It also shows the value of the project at different possible costs of capital. Therefore, if you are unsure about the project's cost of capital, you can use the NPV profile to identify costs of capital at which the project would not create value.

An NPV profile for our IRR computation example is presented in figure 8.3. To construct this NPV profile, we used the calculations in the example and a couple more. One of the additional calculations assumes a cost of capital of 0%, in which case the NPV would be +250. This calculation is straightforward because it's simply the undiscounted sum of all the cash flows. We also calculated what the NPV would be at discount rates of 5% and 20%, to fill in the graph.

The NPV profile in figure 8.3 shows the general relationship between IRR and NPV for independent, conventional projects. If the IRR exceeds the cost of capital, the NPV is positive. If the IRR is less than the cost of capital, the NPV is negative. The vertical distance from the *x* axis to the NPV line is the project's NPV at each required return, *r.*

When IRR and NPV Can Differ: Mutually Exclusive Capital Budgeting Projects

Thus far, we've looked at the question of whether or not to undertake an independent project. But often we must choose from a set of mutually exclusive projects. If we undertake one, we can't undertake any of the others.

For example, a company that plans to build a new assembly plant might have three possible locations and four possible plant configurations. But the company needs only *one* plant.

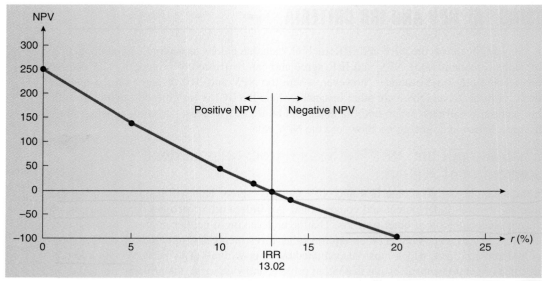

FIGURE 8.3
An NPV profile.

Therefore, it must choose one configuration in one location, and the alternatives are effectively mutually exclusive. In such cases, we can get conflicting recommendations from the IRR and NPV methods.

Conflicting recommendations can occur because there is a difference in (1) the *size* of the projects, or (2) the *cash flow timing.* An example of the latter occurs when cash flows from one project come in mostly early and cash flows from the other project come in later. We'll look at each of these types of differences in turn.

Size Differences When one project is larger than another, the smaller project can have a larger IRR but a smaller NPV. For example, suppose project A has an IRR of 30% and an NPV of $100, and project B has an IRR of 20% and an NPV of $200. The choice between these two projects—and therefore the resolution of such conflicts—is fairly straightforward: You need only decide whether you would you rather have more wealth or a larger IRR. Like you, we'll take the wealth, thank you. Therefore, the NPV decision rule is the better rule to follow when mutually exclusive projects differ in size.

Cash Flow Timing Differences The problem of cash flow timing can arise because of the **reinvestment rate assumption.** The question is "What will the cash inflows from the investment earn when they are subsequently reinvested in other projects?" The IRR method assumes the future cash inflows will earn the project's IRR. The NPV method assumes they will earn the cost of capital.

The following example illustrates the reinvestment rate assumption conflict that results from a difference in cash flow timing. As you'll see, the NPV profiles diverge at a crossover point, a cost of capital at which the two projects have equal NPV.

REINVESTMENT RATE ASSUMPTION The rate of return that the cash flows from a capital budgeting project are expected (assumed) to earn when they are reinvested.

Comparing IRR with NPV at Guess, Inc.

EXAMPLE

Suppose Guess, Inc. can invest in only one of two projects, S (for short term) and L (for long term). The cost of capital is 10%, and the projects have the expected future cash flows shown in figure 8.4. Which is the better project?

Project S has an IRR of 22.08%, and project L has an IRR of 20.01%. But project S has an NPV of $76.29, and project L has an NPV of $94.08. Thus, the IRR method tells us to choose S, but the NPV method says choose L.

Take a look at figure 8.5 on page 310. It compares NPV and IRR. You can see there that project S will have a higher NPV than project L whenever the cost of capital is higher than 15.40%, the **crossover rate.**[2] Both projects would have an NPV of $37.86 if the cost of capital were 15.40%. You can also see that project L has a steeper NPV profile than project S. This is because the present values of cash flows farther in the future are more sensitive to the discount rate. We saw this in the case of bonds, where the market value of a long-term bond changes more than that of a short-term bond in response to a given interest rate change. ■

CROSSOVER RATE The rate of return at which two alternative projects have the same NPV.

FIGURE 8.4
Alternative short- and long-term capital budgeting projects for Guess.

YEAR	0	1	2	3	4	5	6	IRR	NPV
Project S	−250	100	100	75	75	50	25	22.08%	76.29
Project L	−250	50	50	75	100	100	125	20.01%	94.08

---

[2]You can compute the crossover rate by finding the rate that makes the present value of the cash flow differences equal zero. Thus, for this example, the yearly differences are:

Year	0	1	2	3	4	5	6
Cash flow difference	0	50	50	0	−25	−50	−100

You can verify that 15.3985% will make the present value of this cash flow stream equal zero.

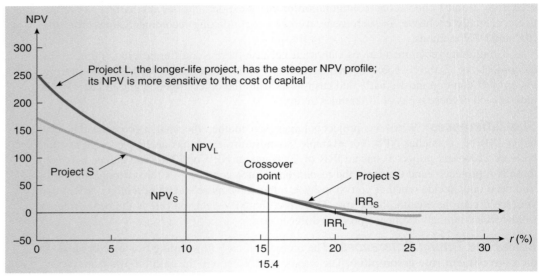

FIGURE 8.5
A comparison of NPV and IRR.

Which method makes the better assumption about what the reinvested cash flows will earn? If the cost of capital is computed correctly, it's the project's required return. In equilibrium, the required return equals the expected return, and over time, competitive forces drive investment returns to equilibrium.

Although new ideas can be very valuable, after a while most people will be using them, and they will no longer command a positive NPV. So the NPV from future projects based on the same sort of idea will tend toward zero. In the long run, then, reinvested cash flows can earn the cost of capital, but not the higher IRR. So the NPV method's assumption that the reinvestment rate will equal the cost of capital is the better assumption. Again, the NPV decision rule is superior to the IRR decision rule.

Another Case Where IRR and NPV Can Differ: Nonconventional Projects

NONCONVENTIONAL PROJECT A project with a pattern of investments and returns different from conventional projects.

We defined a conventional capital budgeting project earlier in the chapter. A **nonconventional project** has a cash flow pattern that is different in some way from conventional projects. Nonconventional projects can create a conflict between the NPV and IRR decision rules.

In some cases, a nonconventional project is simply the reverse of a conventional project, one in which the initial cash flow is positive and the subsequent flows are all negative. A lifetime annuity, which insurance companies sell to retired persons, is an example. From the insurance company's viewpoint, it receives a lump-sum amount at the start of the investment. It then makes monthly payments to the annuity's owner for the rest of that person's life.

Analyzing such cases using IRR is straightforward: Simply reverse the IRR decision rule. That is, for a reverse conventional project, undertake the project if the IRR is *less than* the cost of capital. If you forget to reverse the IRR rule in such cases, you'll make exactly the wrong decision.

Unfortunately, complications can arise. When some future cash flows are expected to be positive and others negative, there can be multiple IRRs. Such cases can occur, for example, when an environmental cleanup is necessary at the end of the project. The company makes an initial investment, receives positive cash flows while the project is operating, and then must make a cash outlay to clean up when the project is terminated. Another example is a project that requires one or more major renovations during its life. Let's take a look at the kinds of conflicts that can arise in these more complex situations.

Multiple IRRs for Triborg, Inc.

Suppose Triborg, Inc. can invest in a project that has an initial cost of −$15,625, with expected future cash flows of $36,875 after 1 year and −$21,750 after 2 years. So the net expected cash flows are negative, positive, and negative. Is this a problem? It can be.

   The best way to see the problem we are illustrating here is to look at the NPV profile for this project, which is shown in figure 8.6. You can see the problem right away. With possible discount rates from 0 to 30%, the NPV goes from negative to positive, and back to negative again. The project has two IRRs, 16% and 20%. That is, there are two points where the NPV would be zero if that were the cost of capital.[3]

   In this case, the IRR decision rule breaks down completely. If we applied the IRR decision rule blindly to this choice, we could make a serious mistake.

   For example, if the cost of capital were 10%, we would undertake the project because both IRRs exceed this. However, at a 10% cost of capital, the project has a negative NPV. Reversing the rule as we did with reverse conventional projects doesn't help either. If the cost of capital exceeded 20%, the rule would again lead to an incorrect decision. Moreover, to the extent that we don't know the project's cost of capital, 16% to 20% is a small "window" to hit. Finally, even in the range where the NPV is positive, it's not very large, and the project wouldn't create much wealth, anyway. ■

   Unfortunately, calculators and currently available PC software generally are not fully equipped to handle the problem of multiple IRRs. They often report only the IRR their trial-and-error process happens to find first. However, they can be used to create an NPV profile. In any case, that provides a much more complete view of the project's potential value.

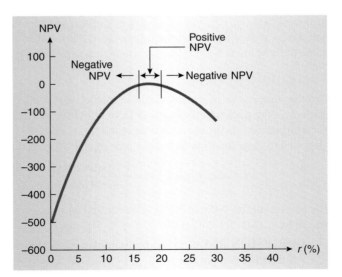

FIGURE 8.6
A capital budgeting project with multiple IRRs.

---

[3]The number of IRRs is never more than the number of sign reversals in the stream of cash flows. So conventional projects and reverse conventional projects have only one IRR because they have only one sign reversal—a negative followed by all positives, or a positive followed by all negatives. In this example, there can be at most two IRRs because there are two reversals; the flows go from negative to positive, and back to negative.

Internal Rate of Return, on Balance

At this point, you may ask "Why use the IRR rule, when you may have to make several NPV calculations in the course of computing the IRR?" Our answer is that you shouldn't use the IRR rule. Use NPV instead.

In practice, however, the IRR rule is more widely used than the NPV rule. Many people prefer the intuitive feel of the IRR rule: After all, if the expected return is big enough, it will surely exceed the required return, and the project is a good investment. Such straightforward simplicity is appealing. For example, in cases where the cost of capital is especially uncertain, as in the case of an entirely new product, using the IRR rule gets around having to compute the cost of capital carefully.

Also, if the IRR for a conventional project is large enough, say 88%, it's probably not worth the trouble to estimate the cost of capital accurately. Because the cost of capital would virtually never be that high, we can simply undertake the project without wasting additional resources on analysis. Those resources can be spent instead on making the project successful!

Self-Check

1. What's the difference between mutually exclusive projects and independent projects?
2. Distinguish between a conventional project and a nonconventional project.
3. When do the NPV and IRR methods agree? Under what circumstances can they differ?
4. When the NPV and IRR methods disagree, which is more likely to provide the best advice?
5. Describe an NPV profile in your own words. Why is it so useful?

OTHER WIDELY USED CAPITAL BUDGETING CRITERIA

Several capital budgeting criteria besides the NPV and IRR are widely used. These include the *profitability index, payback, discounted payback, average rate of return, return on investment,* and *urgency.* We'll describe them here as background in case you encounter them. Because some of these are not economically sound, it is critical to know their strengths and weaknesses.

Profitability Index

PROFITABILITY INDEX (PI) The present value of the future cash flows divided by the initial investment. Also called the **benefit-cost ratio.**

Another time-value-of-money-adjusted method that can be used to evaluate capital budgeting projects is the **profitability index (PI),** or **benefit-cost ratio,** as it is sometimes called. The PI for a project equals the present value of the future cash flows divided by the initial investment. One way to view the PI is that it is 1 plus the NPV divided by the initial investment:

$$\text{Profitability Index} = PI = \frac{\text{PV(future cash flows)}}{\text{initial investment}} = 1 + \frac{\text{NPV}}{\text{initial investment}} \tag{8.3}$$

If a project had an NPV of $240, and required an initial cash flow of −$1000, the project's PI would be 1.24 (= 1 + 240/1000).

DECISION RULE for the profitability index: Undertake the capital budgeting project if the PI is greater than 1.0.

You probably wonder why we bother introducing this method, because it's obvious the NPV decision rule will give you the identical recommendation.[4] The idea underlying the PI is

---

[4]In fact, some people define the PI as simply the NPV divided by the initial investment. Such a definition changes the scale to center on zero, rather than 1.0. There's no substantive difference because such a definition simply changes the cutoff for the PI rule to zero from 1.0.

to measure the capital budgeting project's "bang for the buck." By scaling (dividing) the present value of the future cash flows by the initial outlay, you can see how much return is obtained *per dollar* invested. For example, with a PI of 1.24, you get $1.24 of present value back for each $1 invested, or an NPV of $0.24 for each $1 invested.

Although the PI works fine for independent projects, the scale problem of mutually exclusive projects we saw with IRR also occurs with PI. For example, suppose project A has a PI of 1.6 and an NPV of $100. Project B has a PI of 1.3 and an NPV of $200. The choice between these two projects is again straightforward: Would you rather have more wealth or a larger PI? (Again, like you, we'll take the wealth.) Therefore, the NPV decision rule is the better rule to follow when mutually exclusive projects differ in size.

Profitability Index, on Balance
Although PI offers a perspective on "bang for the buck," it is best used in conjunction with NPV, rather than in place of NPV. PI gets some use in practice, but less than IRR. Its most beneficial use is in situations where the company is restricting the amount of investment it makes, rather than investing in all worthwhile projects. Such a situation is called *capital rationing,* which we discuss in chapter 10.

Payback

An appealing investment concept is that of "getting your money back." Risk may intervene, but investors often want an estimate of the time it will take to recover the initial cash outflow. When this amount of time is calculated without regard to the time value of money, it's called a project's payback. **Payback** is computed by simply summing all the expected cash flows (without discounting them) in sequential order until the sum equals the initial outflow.

> **PAYBACK** The length of time it takes to recover the initial cost of a capital budgeting project, without regard to the time value of money.

> **DECISION RULE** for payback: Undertake the capital budgeting project if the payback is less than a preset number of years.

Computing a Payback

EXAMPLE

Let's turn again to the building renovation example we used earlier in the chapter to illustrate the NPV method. We expected to purchase the building for $420,000 and spend $300,000 on renovations. After renovation, we expected to be able to lease the building out for $110,000 per year. Ignoring taxes, this would give the cash flows in figure 8.7. What is this project's payback?

The payback is 6.55 years, because $110,000 per year for 6.55 years equals $720,000, the initial investment. ■

The idea underlying the payback method is simple: The shorter the payback the better. But there are serious deficiencies in the payback method. You're probably already saying "But, but, but—it ignores the time value of money!" This is true. It also ignores risk differences. In fact, the cutoff is entirely arbitrary, and all cash flows beyond the cutoff are effectively ignored. Let's compare the payback method with the NPV method.

FIGURE 8.7
Payback for the building renovation project.

YEAR	0	1	2	3	4	5	6	7	8
Cash flows	−720	110	110	110	110	′110	110	110	110
Cumulative	−720	−610	−500	−390	−280	−170	−60	+50	+160
Payback:								↑6.55 years	

EXAMPLE

Payback and NPV at Neiman Marcus

Let's say Neiman Marcus requires a 2-year payback. The cost of capital is 15% for two projects it's considering, S (for short term) and L (for long term). These projects have the expected future cash flows given in figure 8.8. What does the payback rule advise in this case?

Project S has a 2-year payback, and project L has a 3-year payback. Therefore, the payback rule would tell us to invest in project S, but not in project L. But is this good advice? Frankly, no. First, consider the project NPVs:

$$\text{NPV}_S = -1000 + \frac{500}{(1.15)^1} + \frac{500}{(1.15)^2} + \frac{150}{(1.15)^3} + \frac{100}{(1.15)^4} = -31.34$$

$$\text{NPV}_L = -1000 + \frac{300}{(1.15)^1} + \frac{300}{(1.15)^2} + \frac{400}{(1.15)^3} + \frac{500}{(1.15)^4} + \frac{500}{(1.15)^5} = +285$$

Is this a problem? Clearly it is. Project S will actually decrease shareholder wealth, even though it has the shorter payback; and the opposite holds for L. Although we would urge the company to undertake L and "pass" on S, in practice, most companies require that projects meet multiple tests. In this case, a company that used both NPV and a 2-year payback rule might decide not to invest in either project. ∎

As we've seen, payback ignores the time value of money. In effect, it assumes the cost of capital is 0%. This underestimates the time required to recover the real (present) value of the initial investment. It can even recommend projects that actually decrease wealth. In addition, managers who use payback set an arbitrary cutoff for project profitability. If the payback exceeds the maximum time, the project is rejected—period. Furthermore, it's impossible to estimate the project's value using payback alone, because all cash flows beyond the payback cutoff are ignored. Obviously, this method has major deficiencies: It can rule out attractive long-term opportunities.

Practical Value of the Payback   Despite the drawbacks of the payback method, the gut reaction of wanting to "at least get your money back" is a powerful feeling to overcome. Moreover, payback provides a control on liquidity, offers a different type of risk control, is easy to compute, and is simple to understand.

Payback controls liquidity because it rejects excessively long-term projects. This may be important for a smaller, less liquid company, because it favors investments that will return cash sooner. That cash can be reinvested in other profitable projects.

Cash flows further in the future are arguably more risky. As a risk control device, payback addresses this harshly by simply ignoring those beyond the payback period, which is an arbitrary cutoff.

Finally, we would add two other practical considerations: First, most investments with a short payback, and additional benefits beyond that, will also have a positive NPV. Second, for relatively small investments, the cost of extensive analysis can exceed the potential loss from a mistake. This can make the simplicity of payback attractive.

Payback, on Balance   Probably because of the practical considerations just noted, the payback rule is still widely used in practice despite its serious deficiencies. However, very few companies use payback by itself. Most companies also require investments to be accept-

FIGURE 8.8

Short- and long-term investment alternatives for Neiman Marcus.

Year	0	1	2	3	4	5
Project S	−1000	500	500	150	100	0
Project L	−1000	300	300	400	500	500

able on the basis of other rules, such as NPV. Because of its weaknesses, payback should be viewed as a supplement to the discounted-cash-flow techniques, at best.

Discounted Payback

If a company wants to use the payback method, a better measure is a variation of payback called **discounted payback.** The discounted payback is the amount of time it takes for the project's *discounted* cash flows to equal the project's initial cost. The idea underlying the discounted payback period is to incorporate the time value of money into the basic notion of getting your money back.

> **DISCOUNTED PAYBACK**
> The length of time it takes for an investment's *discounted* future cash flows to equal the investment's initial cost.

> **DECISION RULE** for discounted payback: Undertake the capital budgeting project if the discounted payback is less than a preset cutoff.

Discounted Payback at Neiman Marcus

EXAMPLE

Let's look again Neiman Marcus's two alternative projects we used to compare payback and NPV, with a discounted payback cutoff of 4 years. What are the discounted paybacks for these investments? What investment decisions would the discounted payback rule imply?

Discounted payback computations for the projects are shown in figure 8.9. Project S has an infinite discounted payback, whereas project L has a 3.87-year discounted payback. The prorated portion of the fourth year is determined by the amount of the year-4 benefit needed to sum to the initial cost. In this case, it is 0.87 (= (286 − 37)/286). Therefore, the discounted payback rule would tell us to invest in project L, but not in project S. ∎

Is this good advice? We know from the past calculations that NPV_S is negative and NPV_L is positive, so this advice matches that of the NPV rule. In fact, you can probably see that for conventional projects, which are the most common type, a project that meets a discounted payback cutoff will always have a positive NPV. This is because the present value of the future cash flows during the discounted payback period alone cover the initial cost.

The project's NPV, then, is the present value of the remaining cash flows—those ignored by the discounted payback period computation. You can see this by noting that the cumulative sum for all the project cash flows equals the NPV of the project, $285. Figure 8.10 on page 316 illustrates the cumulative present values of the cash flows for project L.

The discounted payback is superior to the payback method because it includes the effects of the time value of money. However, it too is arbitrary, and it too suffers from the weakness of ignoring all cash flows beyond the cutoff. This can be a significant problem when there are negative expected future cash flows. The rule can break down in such cases.

			PROJECT S			
YEAR	**0**	**1**	**2**	**3**	**4**	**5**
Cash flows	−1000	500	500	150	100	0
PV	−1000	435	378	99	57	0
Cumulative	−1000	−565	−187	−88	−31	−31
Discounted payback: infinite because the initial investment is not returned						

			PROJECT L			
YEAR	**0**	**1**	**2**	**3**	**4**	**5**
Cash flows	−1000	300	300	400	500	500
PV	−1000	261	227	263	286	248
Cumulative	−1000	−739	−512	−249	+ 37	+285
Discounted payback:					↑3.87 years	

FIGURE 8.9
Discounted payback for Neiman Marcus's alternative short- and long-term capital budgeting projects.

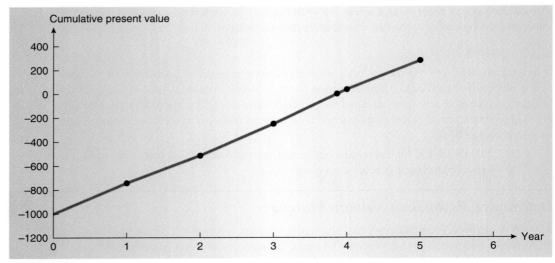

FIGURE 8.10
Cumulative present values of the cash flows for Neiman Marcus's project L.

For example, let's say project L had a year-6 cash flow of −$700, such as might be connected with the cost of cleaning up an environmental hazard after the project was done. If that were the case, the project would have an NPV of −$18, but the discounted payback rule would still favor undertaking the project because the discounted payback period would still be 3.87 years, less than the 4-year cutoff. So the discounted payback rule can break down with nonconventional projects.

Discounted Payback, on Balance   Although it is better than payback, the discounted payback method is still not an adequate indicator by itself. It too should be viewed as, at best, a supplement to the NPV method. Discounted payback is neither as conceptually correct as NPV nor as simple as payback. If you can understand the notion of discounted payback, you can understand and use net present value. So why bother with discounted payback? This is probably why discounted payback is not very widely used in practice.

Average Rate of Return

The **average rate of return (ARR)** is the ratio of the average cash inflow to the average amount invested:

$$\text{Average Rate of Return} = \text{ARR} = \frac{\text{Average cash inflow}}{\text{Average amount invested}}$$

For example, consider a capital budgeting project requiring an initial cost of $2 million and providing a cash inflow of $250,000 per year for five years. The average cash inflow is then simply $250,000. The average investment is the average over the life of the investment. For the typical case of a constant rate of decline over its life, this is simply the average of the initial and final values (the sum of the two divided by 2). If the project is worthless at the end of the five years, the average investment is $1,000,000 (= (2,000,000 + 0)/2). Therefore, ARR in this example is 25% (= 250,000/1,000,000).

The ARR method contains a fatal flaw that makes it completely unacceptable as a decision method. It averages cash flows across time periods, actually *distorting* the representation of the cash flows. After all, a project may offer an attractive cash flow for a year or two and then end without repaying the initial investment. The ARR considers only the average cash flow per period, not the total over the project's life. Note that in the example we just gave, the payback period is infinite. That is, the investment is not even expected to return the initial investment, without regard to the time value of money. So you can see that the 25% is indeed an odd measure of rate of return. In fact, it has no economic meaning whatsoever.

Average Rate of Return, on Balance   ARR has no redeeming features. Don't use it.

Return on Investment (ROI)

Another investment criterion is called **return on investment (ROI).** This term is used by many companies to refer to their own measure of a project's profitability. Unfortunately, different companies define ROI in different ways. Some define ROI to be much like an IRR. Others define ROI to be much like ARR. Still others have unique definitions. Some companies make the mistake of using accounting income rather than cash flow for investment returns to compute ROI. We discuss the problems associated with this mistake in the next chapter.

> **RETURN ON INVEST-MENT (ROI)** A term many firms use to refer to a measure of a project's profitability. Since the ROI is defined very differently by some users, be sure you know how the ROI is being defined and calculated.

Return on Investment, on Balance   You must carefully examine the definition of ROI whenever you encounter it. Only after determining its precise definition can you assess its usefulness as an evaluation method. Whenever the definition differs from IRR, it may be an inappropriate method that should not be used.

Urgency

The final method we look at can be described by inverting Ben Franklin's advice and asking, "Why do today what you can put off until tomorrow?" The corollary to this perverse statement as applied to capital budgeting is "Let's not replace it until we _absolutely_ have to." No need for replacement studies. Wait until the machine breaks down, then air-freight in a new one. At that point, the specter of costly downtime will be sufficient to convince management to skip the analysis and simply order the replacement equipment.

Such a policy has obvious disadvantages, yet stories of plants that have critical equipment held together by "chewing gum and baling wire" loom large in industrial folklore. Capital budgeting projects and key pieces of equipment should be reviewed at regular intervals. A company should develop a program of preventive maintenance and should estimate a probable replacement date each time it acquires a significant piece of equipment. This will help to ensure that the assets are used with maximum efficiency and that equipment is replaced when it is most advantageous to do so—rather than when the baling wire finally snaps and the equipment stops working!

Urgency, on Balance   Urgency is a frequently used but extremely poor basis for decision making, and it should be avoided. Companies should instead plan ahead. Drawing on Ben Franklin again, with accuracy this time, "An ounce of prevention is worth a pound of cure."

Self-Check

1. What is the profitability index? How is it calculated? What is its decision rule?

2. Explain how the profitability index rule breaks down when there's a size difference between mutually exclusive projects.

3. What is the payback rule? Why is it inferior to NPV? Does it have any practical value? Does the discounted payback method avoid the shortcomings of the simple payback method?

4. What is the major problem with using the return on investment (ROI) rule?

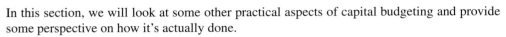

BUSINESS INVESTMENT IN PRACTICE

In this section, we will look at some other practical aspects of capital budgeting and provide some perspective on how it's actually done.

Methods of Evaluation

Just about all companies use the evaluation methods we have discussed, in one form or another. *The single most useful tool is the NPV profile.* This is because it provides the most complete view of the project. It incorporates both NPV and IRR, and also sheds light on the problem of an uncertain required return.

Understandably, however, most companies use more than one evaluation technique. Over the last 30 years, the use of techniques based on the time value of money, especially the NPV method, has increased substantially. We hope that means that when you finish school and apply the things you've learned here, you'll be able to convince your employer to use the better discounted-cash-flow techniques that are available for capital budgeting if they're not already being used.

Appropriations

A decision to include an investment in the capital budget seldom means automatic approval of the required expenditures. Most companies require that plant managers or division heads submit detailed appropriation requests before funds can be released for a project.

Companies often create manuals that specify how the appropriations request should be prepared. This helps maintain managerial control over investments and their associated costs.

Conducting a review of budgeted capital expenditures just prior to releasing funds provides one last check before making the expenditure. This can be valuable in cases where new information has come to light that might make one or more changes advantageous.

Review and Performance Measurement

As we've said, capital budgeting has a critical role in the company's strategic plan. Therefore, companies must systematically review the status of all projects. Such a process is sometimes called a **post-audit.** Managers should examine projects not yet completely under way to determine whether or not development should continue.

POST-AUDIT A review of capital budgeting projects that have been undertaken.

They also must assess the performance of the company's existing assets. Consideration should be given to whether projects should, for example, be expanded, contracted, liquidated, sold off, reconfigured, or simply continued. The basic capital budgeting techniques discussed in this chapter can be applied to the review and performance-measurement process.

The major goal of the post-audit is improvement. Improvements can come primarily in two areas: (1) forecasting and (2) operations. When people know that records of estimates, either forecasts or operational goals, will be maintained and later compared to the actual outcomes, they tend to be more careful making their estimates in the first place. The fact that they are being monitored and will be evaluated and held accountable for their work tends to motivate people to seek better methods and work to eliminate both conscious and unconscious biases. This kind of process is sometimes referred to as *continuous improvement,* and it is part of the concept of *total quality management (TQM).*

Although very difficult in some situations, post-audits are extremely important because of their potential impact on value. Chapter 10 discusses post-audits further.

Self-Check

1. What is the single most useful capital budgeting evaluation tool?

2. Why are appropriation requests useful in the capital budgeting process?

3. What is a post-audit? Why are post-audits useful in the capital budgeting process?

SUMMARY

This chapter described the capital budgeting process and several investment criteria. Capital budgeting decisions are critical because companies are effectively defined by the products and services that flow from their capital assets.

- **Idea generation** is the first and most important part of the capital budgeting process. Sources of potentially valuable ideas include production employees, managers at all levels, sales and marketing staff, research and development groups, and the strategic planning process.

- The **net present value** (NPV) method discounts all cash flows at the project's required return— its *cost of capital*. The NPV measures the value the project will create, which is the difference between what the project is worth and what it will cost to undertake the project. The NPV method recommends that all independent projects with a positive NPV be undertaken. The NPV method is widely used in practice.

- The **internal rate of return** (IRR) is the project's expected return. It's the return that would make the NPV zero if it were the project's cost of capital. The IRR method recommends that every independent conventional capital budgeting project with an IRR greater than its cost of capital be undertaken. Caution is needed, because the IRR decision rule can break down when projects are mutually exclusive or nonconventional. IRR is widely used in practice, probably because of its "intuitive feel."

- The **profitability index** (PI) method calculates one plus the project's NPV divided by its initial cost. The idea is to measure the project's "bang for the buck." The PI rule can break down when projects are mutually exclusive.

- The **payback** method finds the length of time it takes to recover the initial investment, without regard to the time value of money. It recommends acceptance of projects that "return the investment" quickly. The payback method has several serious deficiencies that can cause it to make bad recommendations, but it may have some practical value. In particular, it can provide a liquidity screen, which might be desirable in some situations. Although widely used in conjunction with other methods, payback is rarely used alone.

- The **discounted payback** method is like payback but incorporates the effect of the time value of money. The discounted payback is the time it takes the project to earn a present value equal to its initial cost. Although this method is superior to the payback method, it's still inferior to NPV because it ignores the value of cash flows after the payback point. Discounted payback is not widely used in practice, probably because it is neither as conceptually correct as NPV nor as simple as payback.

- The **average rate of return** (ARR) method is fatally flawed and should not be used to evaluate a capital budgeting project. Fortunately, its use has substantially declined over the last 30 years.

- The **return on investment** (ROI) method does not have a consistent definition. You must find out what definition is being used to determine the potential usefulness of the ROI method.

- **Urgency** is a dangerous but widely used method of allocating resources. Its use is always short-sighted. Many potential crises can be avoided through good planning.

- In practice, most companies use multiple evaluation methods for investments of any significance. However, the **NPV profile** is the single most useful tool. It provides the project's NPV, IRR, and sensitivity to the discount rate at a glance.

- The **post-audit** is a critical and ongoing part of capital budgeting. It provides a significant opportunity to create value through *continuous improvement* in forecasting outcomes and in choosing and operating projects.

EQUATION SUMMARY

(8.1)

$$NPV = CF_0 + \frac{CF_1}{(1 + r)} + \frac{CF_2}{(1 + r)^2} + \ldots + \frac{CF_n}{(1 + r)^n}$$

$$= \sum_{t=0}^{n} \frac{CF_t}{(1 + r)^t}$$

(continued on following page)

(Equation Summary *continued from previous page*)

(8.2)
$$CF_0 + \frac{CF_1}{(1+IRR)} + \frac{CF_2}{(1+IRR)^2} + \ldots + \frac{CF_n}{(1+IRR)^n} = 0$$

$$\sum_{t=0}^{n} \frac{CF_t}{(1+IRR)^t} = 0$$

(8.3) $$\text{Profitability Index} = PI = \frac{PV(\text{future cash flows})}{\text{initial investment}} = 1 + \frac{NPV}{\text{initial investment}}$$

CHAPTER REVIEW ACTIVITIES

SELF-TEST PROBLEMS

1. (Investment criteria) Compute the NPV, IRR, and payback period for the following investment. The cost of capital is 10%.

Year	0	1	2	3
Cash flow	−200	100	100	150

2. (Choosing among mutually exclusive projects) The cash flows for two mutually exclusive investments are given below.

Year	0	1	2	3	4
Project A	−500	200	200	200	200
Project B	−500	0	0	0	1000

a. Compute the total present value of each project's cash flows discounted at 0%, 5%, 10%, 15%, 20%, and 25%.
b. What is the NPV of each project assuming a 10% cost of capital?
c. What is the IRR for each project?

d. What is the crossover rate (the discount rate that gives the same NPV for both projects)? What is the NPV discounted at the crossover rate?
e. Which project should be chosen?

3. (Investment criteria) Consider an investment that has the cash flows given below. The cost of capital is 10%. Compute the following:

Year	0	1	2	3	4
Cash flow	−1000	300	400	500	500

a. Payback;
b. Discounted payback;
c. Net present value;

d. Profitability index;
e. Internal rate of return.

SOLUTIONS TO SELF-TEST PROBLEMS

1. The NPV is:

Year	Cash flow	PV@10%
0	−$200	−$200.00
1	100	90.91
2	100	82.64
3	150	112.70
		NPV = $86.25

The IRR can be found by trial and error. Since the NPV @10% = 86.25, we can try higher rates until we converge on an NPV of zero. NPV @ 20% = 39.58. NPV @ 30% = 4.37. NPV @ 40% = −22.89. NPV @ 31% = 1.33. NPV @ 32% = −1.63. The IRR is 31.45%.

The payback is 2 years. It takes exactly 2 years for the cumulative future cash flows to equal the $200 outlay at time 0.

2. a. Project A is a 4-year annuity of $200 and Project B is a single future payment of $1,000 in 4 years. The NPVs of the future cash flows minus the $500 outlays for the given discount rates are:

Discount rate	NPV(A)	NPV(B)
0%	$300.00	$500.00
5	209.19	322.70
10	133.97	183.01
15	71.00	71.75
20	17.75	−17.75
25	−27.68	−90.40

b. The NPVs using a 10% cost of capital are already calculated above. NPV(A) = $133.97 and NPV(B) = $183.01.

c. The IRR for A is between 20% and 25%. Solving for it using a financial calculator gives the IRR(A) = 21.86%. The IRR for B is between 15% and 20%. Solving for it using a financial calculator gives the IRR(B) = 18.92%.

d. Looking at the NPVs for part A shows us that the crossover rate is close to 15%. The actual crossover rate is 15.091%. Discounted at 15.091%, NPV(A) = NPV(B) = $69.94.

e. The cost of capital is 10%. Even though project A has the higher IRR, project B, which has the higher NPV, should be chosen.

3. a. To find the payback, we need to find how long it takes for the cumulative future cash flows to equal the $1000 investment:

Year	Cash flow	Cumulative CF
1	$300	$ 300
2	400	700
3	500	1200
4	500	1700

The payback occurs between 2 and 3 years. After 2 years, the recovery is $700, so $300 out of the $500 cash flow for year 3 is needed to reach payback. The payback then is 2 years + 300/500 years = 2.60 years.

b. For the discounted payback, we need to know how long it takes the accumulated present values of the future cash flows to reach the $1000 investment. The future cash flows are discounted at the 10% cost of capital:

Year	Cash flow	PV of CF	Cumulative PV of CF
1	$300	$272.73	$ 272.73
2	400	330.58	603.31
3	500	375.66	978.97
4	500	341.51	1320.48

It takes a little over 3 years to reach the discounted payback. You need $21.03 (= 1000 − 978.97) of the fourth year's discounted cash flow of $341.41. So the discounted payback is 3 years + 21.03/341.51 years = 3.06 years

c. Using the PV of the future cash flows (= 1320.48) from **b,** the NPV = 1320.48 − 1000 = $320.48.

d. PI = 1320.48/1000 = 1.32.

e. You can compute the IRR using trial and error, or a calculator. The IRR is 22.77%.

QUESTIONS

1. Briefly describe the five steps in the capital budgeting process.
2. Why is the Principle of Valuable Ideas of critical importance to the capital budgeting process?
3. Define the term *independent project.*
4. Define the terms *conventional project* and *nonconventional project.*
5. Define the term *mutually exclusive projects.*
6. Define the term *profitability index* and describe the concept.
7. Define the term *payback* and describe the concept.
8. What is an internal rate of return (IRR)?

9. Briefly explain why capital budgeting projects are frequently classified into groups such as maintenance projects, cost savings/revenue enhancement projects, capacity expansion projects, new product/new business projects, and projects mandated by regulation or company policy.

10. Why can the NPV and IRR methods disagree on the rankings for mutually exclusive projects?

11. What are the strengths and weaknesses of the payback and the discounted payback?

12. Which of the capital budgeting criteria are the most sound? Which are the least sound?

13. Suppose you were restricted to using only one method of analysis to evaluate a capital budgeting project. Briefly explain why the NPV profile is the best method to use.

14. Why do firms perform post-audits, reviewing and measuring the performance of their previous capital investments?

PROBLEM SET A

A1. (NPV and IRR) An investment of $100 at time 0 generates a cash flow of $150 at time 1. If the cost of capital is 10%, what is the NPV? What is the IRR?

A2. (Mutually exclusive projects) Consider the cash flows given below for the mutually exclusive projects S and L.

Year	0	1	2
Project S	−100	160	0
Project L	−100	0	200

a. If the cost of capital is 10%, what is the NPV of each investment?

b. What is the IRR of each investment?
c. Which investment should you accept?

A3. (NPV and PI) Vu Trading Company is evaluating a project that has the estimated cash flows given below. The cost of capital is 14%.

Year	0	1	2	3	4
Cash flow	−100,000	30,000	30,000	60,000	60,000

a. What is the project's NPV?

b. What is the profitability index?

A4. (Investment criteria) An investment of $100 returns exactly $100 in 1 year. The cost of capital is 10%.

a. What are the payback, NPV, and IRR for this investment?

b. Is this a profitable investment?

A5. (Payback and discounted payback) Find the payback and the discounted payback for a project with the cash flows given below. The cost of capital is 12%.

Year	0	1	2	3	4
Cash flow	−10	3	3	4	6

A6. (NPV and IRR) A project is expected to generate cash flows of $50,000 annually for 5 years plus an additional $100,000 in year 6. The cost of capital is 10%.

a. What is the most that you can invest in this project at time 0 and still have a positive NPV?

b. What is the most that you can invest in this project at time 0 if you want to have a 15% IRR?

A7. (Investment criteria) Compute the NPV, IRR, and payback period for the project given below. The cost of capital is 10%.

Year	0	1	2	3
Cash flow	−250,000	100,000	200,000	100,000

A8. (Investment criteria) An investment of $100,000 generates cash flows of $30,000 annually for the next 3 years. Using a 10% cost of capital, find the NPV, the internal rate of return, and the payback period.

A9. (NPV) An investment of $10 will generate an annual cash flow of $1 forever. If the cost of capital is 8%, what is the NPV of this investment?

A10. (Payback and NPV) Three projects have the cash flows given below. The cost of capital is 10%.

Year	0	1	2	3	4	5
Project 1	−10	4	3	2	1	5
Project 2	−10	1	2	3	4	5
Project 3	−10	4	3	2	1	10

a. Calculate the paybacks for all three projects. Rank the projects from best to
worst based on their paybacks.

b. Calculate the NPVs for all three projects.
Rank the projects from best to worst
based on their NPVs.

c. Why are these two sets of rankings different?

PROBLEM SET B

B1. (Reverse conventional project) You have an opportunity to undertake a project that has a positive
cash flow of $100 at time 0 and a negative cash flow of $100 at time 1. The cost of capital is 10%.

a. What is the IRR?

b. What is the NPV?

c. Should you accept this project?

B2. (Reverse conventional project) You can undertake a project with the cash flows given below. The
cost of capital is 10%. The internal rate of return is 15.8%. Should you accept this project? Why
or why not?

CF_0	CF_1	CF_2
+5000	+5000	−12,500

B3. (NPV) Truman State University is evaluating an investment in new air handling systems for some
of its major buildings. The expected outlays and the expected savings, in millions of dollars, are
given below. What is the net present value of this investment if the required return is 8%?

Time	0	1	2	3	4 through 10
Outlays	2.0	3.0	4.0	0	0
Savings	0	0.5	1.0	1.5	2.0

B4. (NPV and shareholder wealth) Stockholders are surprised to learn that the company has invested
$43 million in a project that has an expected payoff of $8 million per year for 6 years. The project's cost of capital is 12%.

a. What is the project's NPV?

b. There are 3 million outstanding shares.
What should be the direct impact of this

investment on the per-share value of the
common stock?

B5. (Average rate of return and IRR) Breckinridge Products has two investments that its analysts are
evaluating. One of the projects has a 4-year life and the other an 8-year life. The cash flows for
the two projects, in thousands of dollars, are given below. Josee Dumas, the analyst, is providing
two ROI figures for each project. The first is an average rate of return, defined as the average
cash flow during the project's life divided by the average investment. The average investment, in
this case, will be one-half of the original investment. The other ROI figure will be the internal
rate of return. Josee considers 12% to be an appropriate hurdle rate for these investments.

Time	0	1	2	3	4	5	6	7	8
Pneumatic Blower	−100	30	30	30	30				
Microwave Blower	−100	28	28	28	28	28	28	28	28

a. What is the average rate of return for
each investment?

b. What is the IRR for each investment?

c. Which investment should be accepted?

B6. (Investment criteria) Pierre Bouvier is evaluating four projects. The cash flows for the four projects are given below.

Time	0	1	2	3	4
Project K	−100	40	40	40	40
Project L	−100	40	80	0	40
Project M	− 90	40	80	0	30
Project N	− 90	40	80	0	40

a. Pierre thinks you can rank these projects
from best to worst by simply inspecting
the cash flows (and not calculating anything). Try to do so.

b. Pierre next found the NPV of each project, discounting future cash flows at
10%. What is the NPV for each project?

c. Do your rankings in parts **a** and **b** agree?

B7. (Investment criteria) Consider the cash flows for the two capital budgeting projects given below. The cost of capital is 10%.

Year	0	1	2	3	4
Project A	−10,000	4000	4000	4000	4000
Project B	−5,000	2000	2000	2000	2000

a. Calculate the NPV for both projects.
b. Calculate the IRR for both.
c. Calculate the PI for both.

d. Calculate the payback for both.
e. Which is the better project? Why?

B8. (NPV profile) Consider the projects shown below.

Project	CF_0	CF_1	CF_2	NPV@10%	IRR
R1	−100	70	70	$21.49	25.7%
R2	−150	100	100	$23.55	21.5%

a. Which is the better project?
b. Is this an example of size differences or cash flow timing differences?
c. What is the crossover rate, the discount rate that would have the same NPV for

both projects? (*Hint:* Find the differential cash flows between the two projects. Then find the IRR for the differential cash flows.)

B9. (Investment criteria) Consider a project that has the cash flows shown below. The required return on the investment is 10%. Compute the following:

Year	0	1	2	3	4
Cash flow	−175,000	30,000	80,000	65,000	95,000

a. Payback;
b. Discounted payback;
c. Average rate of return;

d. NPV;
e. Profitability index;
f. IRR.

B10. (NPV) Bill Scott estimates that a project will involve an outlay of $125,000 and will return $40,000 per year for 6 years. The required return is 12%.
a. What is the NPV using Bill's estimates?
b. David Scott is less optimistic about the project. David thinks the outlay will be 10% higher, the annual cash flows will be

5% lower, and the project will have a 5-year life. David does agree with Bill's required return. What is the NPV using David's estimates?

B11. (NPV profile) Helix Inc. is considering two mutually exclusive one-time projects. Both require an initial investment of $80,000. Project A will last for 6 years and has expected net future cash flows of $40,222 per year. Project B will last for 5 years and has expected net future cash flows of $44,967 per year. The cost of capital for both projects is 12%.
a. Calculate the NPV for each project.
b. Calculate the IRR for each project.
c. Graph the NPV of the projects as a function of the discount rate, including solv-

ing for the crossover rate by trial and error.
d. Which project should Helix take?

B12. (Investment criteria) Suppose Reebok has a possible capital budgeting project with a cost of capital of 10% and the expected cash flows shown below.

Year	0	1	2	3	4	5
Cash flow	−100	25	50	50	25	10

a. Calculate the project's NPV. Should Reebok accept the project?
b. Calculate the project's IRR. Should Reebok accept the project according to the IRR rule?

c. Calculate the project's payback. What does payback tell you about the project's acceptability?

B13. (Investment criteria) Texaco has a capital budgeting project with a cost of capital of 12% and the following expected cash flow pattern.

Year	0	1	2	3
Cash flow	50	100	−20	−50

a. Calculate NPV. Should the company accept the project?

b. Calculate IRR. Should the company accept the project?

c. Calculate payback period.

d. Calculate the project's average rate of return (ARR).

e. What do payback period and ARR tell you about the project's acceptability?

f. How would your answers to parts **a** or **b** change if you were told that the project is one of two mutually exclusive projects the company has under consideration?

B14. (Mutually exclusive projects) Sperry is considering two mutually exclusive capital budgeting projects with a cost of capital of 14% and the expected cash flows shown below. Which, if either, project should Sperry undertake? Justify your answer.

Year	0	1	2	3	4	5
Project A	−100	30	40	50	40	30
Project B	−150	45	60	75	60	60

PROBLEM SET C

C1. (Investment criteria) Nassau Manufacturing Company is considering two capital budgeting projects with a cost of capital of 15%, and the expected cash flows shown below.

Year	0	1	2	3	4	5
Project A	−100	25	30	40	30	25
Project B	−50	10	15	25	15	15

a. Calculate the NPV and IRR for each project. Which project(s) should Nassau accept, assuming they are:

b. Independent?

c. Dependent (both or neither are required)?

d. Mutually exclusive?

C2. (Discounted payback and NPV) A staff analyst has just brought you an incomplete capital budgeting analysis that shows you only that the discounted payback of this conventional project is 5.24 years. A moment later, before you can fully collect your thoughts and ask the analyst any questions, the marketing vice president calls you and asks if the project analysis shows a positive NPV. You answer yes. Explain how you know this.

BIBLIOGRAPHY

Brick, Ivan E., and Daniel G. Weaver. "A Comparison of Capital Budgeting Techniques in Identifying Profitable Investments," *Financial Management,* 1984, 13(4):29–39.

Brigham, Eugene F., and T. Craig Tapley. "Financial Leverage and Use of the Net Present Value Investment Criterion: A Reexamination," *Financial Management,* 1985, 14(2):48–52.

Flannery, Mark J., Joel F. Houston, and Subramanyam Venkataraman. "Financing Multiple Investment Projects," *Financial Management,* 1993, 22(2):161–172.

Golbe, Devra L., and Barry Schachter. "The Net Present Value Rule and an Algorithm for Maintaining a Constant Debt-Equity Ratio," *Financial Management,* 1985, 14(2):53–58.

Greenfield, Robert L., Maury R. Randall, and John C. Woods. "Financial Leverage and Use of the Net Present Value Investment Criterion," *Financial Management,* 1983, 12(3):40–44.

Howe, Keith M. "A Note on Flotation Costs and Capital Budgeting," *Financial Management,* 1982, 11(4):30–33.

Howe, Keith M. "Perpetuity Rate of Return Analysis," *Engineering Economist,* 1991, 36(3):248–257.

Kasanen, Eero. "Creating Value by Spawning Investment Opportunities," *Financial Management,* 1993, 22(3):251–258.

Ross, Stephen A. "Uses, Abuses, and Alternatives to the Net-Present-Value Rule," *Financial Management,* 1995, 24(3):96–102.

Viswanath, P. V. "Adjusting Capital Budgeting Rules for Information Asymmetry," *Financial Management,* 1993, 22(4):22–23.

CAPITAL BUDGETING CASH FLOWS

This chapter continues our investigation of capital budgeting. In the previous chapter we described the capital budgeting process and examined several investment criteria. Most investment criteria, such as NPV and IRR, depend on a project's expected future cash flows.

In this chapter we'll show you how to estimate a capital budgeting project's expected future cash flows—its incremental after-tax cash flows. Such estimates critically affect the accuracy of the various capital budgeting investment criteria. As you read the chapter, you should remember five very important things about cash flow estimation. The phrase *incremental after-tax cash flows* actually includes three of them.

First, it is indeed cash flow that's relevant. Chapter 3 showed that cash flow is distinctly different from a company's accounting net income. Second, these cash flows are measured on an after-tax basis. The relevant cash flow is the amount left after all taxes have been paid. Third, the Principle of Incremental Benefits reminds us that it is the incremental cash flow that's relevant. Fourth, the Time-Value-of-Money Principle reminds us that the value of a cash flow depends on its timing. Money is worth more, the sooner you get it. Fifth, the standard cash flow estimation does not explicitly identify the financing costs. The incremental financing costs are implicitly included in the project's cost of capital—its required return.

We'll also look at inflation and optimal replacement cycles. These things can complicate capital budgeting. However, as we'll see, the key to proper treatment of these considerations in a capital budgeting analysis is carefully applying the Time-Value-of-Money Principle.

CAPITAL BUDGETING CASH FLOWS AND THE PRINCIPLES OF FINANCE

◆ *Incremental Benefits:* Identify and estimate the incremental expected *after-tax* future cash flows for a capital budgeting project. Special care is necessary to deal with projects that will erode or enhance the company's current operations.

◆ *Time Value of Money:* Measure the value the capital budgeting project will create—its NPV.

◆ *Risk-Return Trade-Off:* Incorporate the risk of a capital budgeting project into its cost of capital, its required return.

◆ *Valuable Ideas:* Look for new ideas to use as a basis for capital budgeting projects that will create value.

◆ *Comparative Advantage:* Look for capital budgeting projects that use the company's comparative advantage to add value.

◆ *Options:* Recognize the value of options, such as the options to expand, postpone, or abandon a capital budgeting project.

◆ *Two-Sided Transactions:* Consider why the other party to a transaction is willing to participate.

◆ *Signaling:* Consider the actions and products of competitors.

AN OVERVIEW OF ESTIMATING CASH FLOWS

As a prelude to the more detailed analysis of estimating cash flows given in this chapter, we would first like to cover some of the basic concepts used in estimating these cash flows and then give a simple numerical example. After this quick preview, we will go into more detail.

Basic Concepts Behind Capital Budgeting Cash Flows

There are five basic concepts to keep in mind when calculating a project's cash flows.

First, as with any investment, a capital budgeting project's costs and benefits are measured in terms of cash flow rather than income. This distinction is critical. Income calculations also reflect noncash items. But ultimately, only cash flow provides the cash needed to pay shareholders dividends, either immediately or later after getting the returns from reinvestment. Also, including indirect noncash benefits leads to ambiguity and subjective (nonfinancial) choices that might hide any principal-agent problems between the managers and shareholders.[1]

Second, cash flow timing is critical because timing affects value, even beyond simple time-value-of-money considerations. Companies often depend on expected cash inflows to meet their financial obligations. Insufficient cash inflow can cause failure to meet these obligations, which in turn can lead to penalty fees and even bankruptcy.

The third important concept is embodied in the Principle of Incremental Benefits: Cash flows must be measured on an incremental, or marginal, basis. They are the difference between the company's cash flows with and without the project. For example, consider a sequential set of capital budgeting decisions concerning the research and development of a new product. Initial funds are spent for research; subsequent funds may or may not be approved for product development, test marketing, and production. At each stage, previous expenditures are sunk costs. Therefore, at each stage of the decision-making process, only *future* expenditures and revenues are relevant to the decision of whether to proceed with product development.

Fourth, the Principle of Incremental Benefits further requires that expected future cash flows are measured on an after-tax basis. A company is concerned with after-tax cash flows in the same way that you as an individual are interested in take-home pay: Ultimately, that's what you can spend. Shareholders are interested in the *net* gain in wealth, and taxes take away from the wealth gain.

Finally, we want to alert you to a subtle aspect of the standard capital budgeting analysis: Financing costs are not explicitly identified. However, please don't think they have been left out. The incremental financing costs are implicitly included in the project's cost of capital—its required return. In other words, when we compute a project's NPV or IRR, the discount rate includes in it the opportunity cost for obtaining financing for the project.

An Example Comparing Project Cash Flows and Income

Let's look at a simplified example first, to give you the "big picture" before delving into the details.

Let's say a company has the following capital budgeting project:

1. The initial outlay is $5000.
2. The investment is depreciated straight-line to a salvage value of $1000 in four years, so depreciation is $1000 per year (= [5000 − 1000]/4).

---

[1]Nonquantified items can be valid and a very important part of a capital budgeting project. However, such items should be introduced into the analysis only *after* the direct cash flows have been identified and incorporated. This is so that the nonquantified items are not double counted but do get proper consideration. This also minimizes potential principal-agent conflicts by explicitly identifying these items.

3. At the end of the four years, the investment will be sold for exactly its then net book value of $1000.

4. Each year for four years, the investment will generate incremental sales of $4000 and cash operating expenses of $1500.

5. The company pays income taxes at the rate of 40% of taxable income.

6. The project's cost of capital is 10%.

What are the project's cash flows? What are the project's NPV and IRR?

There are three different types of cash flows: an initial outlay (the "cost" of the investment), annual after-tax operating cash flows, and a salvage value. The initial outlay (at time 0) is $5000 and the salvage value (at time 4) is $1000. That leaves the operating cash flows.

As part of the company's operations, we can think of the project's contribution to the company's income statement as though it were its own "mini" income statement, shown in table 9.1. The project's net income is its revenue minus all its expenses (cash operating expenses, depreciation, and income taxes). Project net income is $900.

Now let's examine the income statement for those transactions that are cash flows. You can see that sales are a cash *inflow* of $4000, cash operating expenses an *outflow* of $1500, and taxes an *outflow* of $600. So the net cash flow is +$1900.

Note that we did not include any financing or interest expenses in the project's hypothetical mini income statement. This income statement shows operating revenues and costs only. Notice also that the $1900 net cash flow is equal to net income + depreciation (= 900 + 1000). Depreciation is a noncash charge, so we add it back to net income to get the cash flow.

Over the project's four-year life, the cash flows for our investment are as follows:

Time	0	1	2	3	4
(1) Investment	−5000				
(2) Annual operating cash flows		+1900	+1900	+1900	+1900
(3) Salvage value					+1000
Totals	−5000	+1900	+1900	+1900	+2900

For these cash flows, the NPV (using the 10% cost of capital) is $1705.76. The IRR is 23.91%. Because the NPV is positive, this is a profitable investment.

Self-Check

1. What are the five basic concepts to keep in mind when calculating a project's cash flows?

2. Why don't we explicitly include financing costs when estimating a project's cash flows?

3. In addition to the initial outlay, what are two other categories of project cash flows?

TABLE 9.1
"Mini" Income Statement for the Project

	INCOME STATEMENT	CASH FLOWS
Sales	$4000	+$4000
Cash operating costs	1500	− 1500
Depreciation	1000	
Taxable income	$1500	
Taxes at 40%	600	− 600
Net income	$900	
		+$1900 = Net cash flow

CALCULATING A PROJECT'S INCREMENTAL CASH FLOWS

A capital budgeting project's cash flows fall into four basic categories: **1.** Net initial investment outlay, **2.** Expected future net operating cash flows, **3.** Non-operating cash flows to support the project, such as those for an overhaul, **4.** Net salvage value, which is the after-tax total amount of cash received and/or spent when the project ends. In this section, we'll look at each of these cash flow types in turn.

Net Initial Outlay

The net initial outlay can be broken down into cash expenditures for the new capital assets, changes in net working capital, cash flow from the sale of old equipment, and the tax impact of the sale of old equipment:

(1) Cash paid for new capital assets $\qquad\qquad -I$

(2) Increase in net working capital $\qquad\qquad -\Delta W$

(3) Cash received on sale of old equipment $\qquad\quad S$

(4) Tax paid (saved) on sale of old equipment $\qquad -T(S-B)$

$$\text{Net cash flow for initial investment} = -I - \Delta W + S - T(S-B) \qquad\qquad (9.1)$$

Negative (positive) signs indicate cash outflows (inflows). The first item includes the purchase price, freight or shipping costs, and setup costs. An increase in net working capital is also part of the project's initial outlay. Additional production and sales usually require additional inventory and accounts receivable, which must be financed. If a project would reduce the company's net working capital, those funds would be freed up to be invested elsewhere.

The third item in the initial outlay is the net cash flow from the sale of old equipment.

Finally, the fourth item is any tax effect on the sale of old equipment. A tax effect occurs whenever an asset is sold for a net sale price other than the asset's net book value. The taxes due are the tax rate times the excess of the sale price over the book value, which is $T(S-B)$.

For example, suppose an asset was purchased five years ago for $2000 and there has been $300 of depreciation expense claimed for tax purposes for each of the five years. The net book value of that asset is currently $500 $(= 2000 - (5)300)$. If the asset is sold today for more than $500, then "too much" depreciation was claimed. In such a case, the government will "recapture" the excess depreciation by taxing the amount above the net book value. In the same way, if the asset is sold today for less than $500, "too little" depreciation was claimed, and the company now claims the amount below the net book value as an expense.[2]

A potential fifth item, an investment tax credit, is not currently in effect. We describe the investment tax credit a little later.

The Investment in Net Working Capital

The investment in net working capital can be easily overlooked. In order to operate a new project, additional investments in short-term assets such as cash, receivables, and inventory may be required. Some spontaneous short-term financing, such as from accounts payable, may also occur with the new project. The increase in net working capital is the additional short-term assets required minus the additional short-term liabilities generated.

---

[2]The gain is taxed at ordinary income tax rates until all prior depreciation deductions have been fully "recaptured." If, for example, as a result of inflation, the asset is sold for more than was initially paid for it, all prior depreciation deductions are recaptured, and the excess above the original purchase price is taxed as a capital gain.

Recall that net working capital is current assets minus current liabilities. But exactly what is working capital? To get a better understanding, consider the following simple (even silly) example about an entrepreneurial child named Terry.

It is a hot summer afternoon, and after watching people walk uncomfortably through the neighborhood because of the heat, Terry decides there is money to be made selling lemonade. Terry makes some lemonade and a sign, *Lemonade: 25 cents.*[3] After Terry has made several trips to the curb in front of the house—taking the sign, a table, a chair, some cups, and the lemonade—a customer walks by and asks Terry for a glass of lemonade. Terry pours the glass and says, "That will be twenty-five cents, please." The customer hands over a $1 bill, to which Terry responds, "Would you like to buy four glasses?" The customer is not that thirsty and asks for change. Terry puts the customer on hold, runs into the house, and borrows $3 worth of change from Mom. After returning and making change for the customer, Terry settles into selling lemonade all afternoon.

That evening at the dinner table, Dad asks about everyone's day. Terry proudly reports making $11 selling lemonade. This prompts Mom to ask about the $3 in change. Terry hands $3 to Mom and revises the profit estimate down to $8. Mom, however, points out that money has a time value and that Terry had the use of her money all afternoon. Terry agrees and pays Mom the loan-shark rate of five cents interest on the $3 loan.

Terry's working capital was the $3 in change. It was put in at the start, and when operations were shut down, it was there in the bottom of the cash register at the end. The only cost of having the working capital was the time value of money. However, Terry could not operate the lemonade stand without the working capital. Although the time value of money is trivial for $3 for an afternoon, it *can* be a substantial cost, as in the case of a ten-year project that requires $5 million in working capital.

When we analyze a capital budgeting project, the cost of the investment in working capital due to the time value of money is accounted for by the incremental cash flows. Increases in working capital are outflows. Decreases in, and releases of, working capital are inflows. The difference in the present values of these cash flows is the time-value-of-money cost of using the working capital during the project's life.

Tax Considerations

Two important tax considerations for a capital budgeting project are whether the assets will be expensed or capitalized and the tax consequences of selling old assets. Other tax regulations may also be relevant to the investment cash flows.

Expensing or Capitalizing the New Investment   When a company makes a cash outlay for a capital asset, the cost of this asset usually is not recognized immediately and the company depreciates the asset in the future. **Capitalizing** an asset involves recording the outlay as an asset and allocating (depreciating) the cost over future time periods. Capitalizing leads to depreciation expense. It allocates the cost of the asset to two or more time periods. The entire cost is not an immediately recognized expense. Instead, the expenditure is recognized as a prespecified series of expenses at various times in the future.

CAPITALIZE Record an outlay as an asset and allocate (depreciate) the cost over future time periods.

In contrast, cash expenditures that are not required to be capitalized can be expensed immediately. Cash expenditures that are **expensed** are recognized for tax purposes entirely at the time of expenditure. Therefore, expensed items do not have any *subsequent* tax consequences, because they do not involve the process of depreciation. Generally, the earlier an expense is recognized, the earlier the tax savings will occur. The importance of this is seen in the next example.

EXPENSE Recognize an outlay as an expense for tax purposes at the time it was incurred.

---

[3]Terry considered charging $25 per glass. That way, selling only one glass would make a successful day. Then Terry remembered about downward-sloping demand curves: such a high price would eliminate the demand for lemonade.

EXAMPLE

Capitalizing versus Expensing at Boeing

Suppose The Boeing Company is going to purchase an asset that costs $1 million. Let's say that Boeing's marginal tax rate is 40%. How does the pattern of expenses recognized for tax purposes differ between (1) capitalizing the asset on a straight-line basis over 4 years and (2) expensing the $1 million right now? What are the tax savings generated by these expenses? What is the present value of the tax savings discounted at 8%?

The answers to these questions are shown in table 9.2. If the investment is capitalized and depreciated, the total expense of $1,000,000 is allocated over the next 4 years, or $250,000 per year. The tax savings are equal to 40% of the depreciation charge, which is $100,000 per year. The present value of the tax savings equals $331,213. If Boeing can expense this item, the full cost is recognized immediately, resulting in a tax savings and a present value of the tax savings of $400,000. Expensing the item increases the present value of the tax savings by $68,787, from $331,213 to $400,000. Clearly, Boeing would be better off expensing rather than capitalizing its asset. ∎

The present value of taxes saved is greater the sooner the expense is allowed as a tax deductible expense. To the extent a company can expense instead of capitalize an outlay it will effectively reduce its taxes.

For example, assume that you are investing $100,000, and that you are able to expense $20,000 and are capitalizing the balance of $80,000. This additional expense reduces your current outlay by the tax rate times the $20,000. With a 40% tax rate, your outlay is reduced by $8000, making your outlay $92,000 instead of $100,000. Expensing part of the investment results in a smaller capitalized investment and smaller depreciation charges in the future.

As the Boeing example demonstrates, companies will not generally choose to capitalize rather than expense an asset. However, the tax code *requires* that certain assets be capitalized.[4]

Tax on Sale of Existing Assets   If a project involves replacing or disposing of existing assets, there can be tax consequences. If an asset has been fully depreciated and has a book value of zero, taxes will be due on 100% of the selling price. If the asset has a positive book value, the taxes due will equal the excess of the selling price over the book value, $T(S - B)$, or there will be a tax saving equal to $T(S - B)$ when the selling price is less than the book value.

TABLE 9.2

Capitalizing versus Expensing an Investment at Boeing

Capitalizing and depreciating a $1,000,000 investment:					
Time	0	1	2	3	4	Total
Expense	0	250,000	250,000	250,000	250,000	1,000,000
Tax savings	0	100,000	100,000	100,000	100,000	400,000
PV of tax savings	0	92,593	85,734	79,383	73,503	331,213

Expensing a $1,000,000 investment:					
Time	0	1	2	3	4	Total
Expense	1,000,000	0	0	0	0	1,000,000
Tax savings	400,000	0	0	0	0	400,000
PV of tax savings	400,000	0	0	0	0	400,000

---

[4]We are assuming the company has sufficient income to use the tax credit or that loss carryforwards work properly. Exceptions to this assumption (and therefore this generalization) occur infrequently. However, when they do, it is often a unique situation that requires careful analysis.

For example, suppose that the remaining book value $B = \$200$ and that the tax rate is 40%. The tax consequence for various selling prices between 0 and $400 is as follows:

Selling price: (S)	Excess over book value: (S − B)	Taxes due: T(S − B)	Net cash flow: S − T(S − B)
$400	$200	$80	$320
300	100	40	260
200	0	0	200
100	−100	−40	140
0	−200	−80	80

Selling existing assets for more than their net book value generates a tax liability that increases the initial outlay. Conversely, selling existing assets for less than their net book value generates a tax saving that reduces the initial outlay.

Other Taxes   There are other tax considerations that can also affect business investments. One of these, not currently in effect, is the **investment tax credit,** which is a credit against taxes due based on new capital investment. For example, with a 10% investment tax credit, businesses receive a tax credit equal to 10% of new capital outlays. This tax credit is applied to a company's tax bill, reducing it by the amount of the credit. The effect of such a credit is to reduce the cost of purchasing the assets. For example, a 10% investment tax credit would reduce the cost by 10%. The stated government purpose of having an investment tax credit is to stimulate business investment.

INVESTMENT TAX CREDIT A credit against taxes due that is based on the amount of new capital outlays.

Other taxes that can affect a company include sales taxes, property taxes, payroll taxes, and many others. These are typically included as a cost of doing business. Businesses also receive subsidies from the federal, state, and local governments that can reduce the cost of doing business.

Self-Check

1. What is the net cash flow for the initial investment, and how is it calculated?

2. What is the difference between capitalizing an expenditure and expensing it for tax purposes? Which is more advantageous to the company?

3. How can taxes affect the initial investment?

4. What is the net investment in working capital?

Net Operating Cash Flows

After the initial investment, a project generates future cash inflows and outflows. Let ΔR be the change in periodic revenue and ΔE be the change in periodic cash operating expense connected with undertaking the project in each period. The **net operating cash flow, CFAT (cash flow after tax),** can then be expressed as $\Delta R - \Delta E$ minus the tax liability on this amount:

NET OPERATING CASH FLOW, CFAT (CASH FLOW AFTER TAX) The change in cash receipts minus the change in cash operating expense minus the taxes paid.

$$\text{Net operating cash flow} = \text{CFAT} = \Delta R - \Delta E - \text{tax liability}$$

The tax liability depends on the change in depreciation as well as ΔR and ΔE. Let ΔD be the depreciation change; then the tax liability will be $T(\Delta R - \Delta E - \Delta D)$, and the net operating cash flow will be

$$\text{CFAT} = \Delta R - \Delta E - T(\Delta R - \Delta E - \Delta D)$$

This equation is typically rearranged into two other forms. The first is:

$$\text{CFAT} = (\Delta R - \Delta E)(1 - T) + T\Delta D \qquad (9.2)$$

In this form, CFAT is after-tax cash revenues and cash expenses plus the "tax shield" from the depreciation expense. Equation (9.2) can be considered the incremental *operating cash flows after taxes plus the depreciation tax shield.*

The other form in which CFAT is commonly expressed is:

$$CFAT = (\Delta R - \Delta E - \Delta D)(1 - T) + \Delta D \qquad (9.3)$$

In this form, CFAT can be thought of as incremental *net income plus depreciation.* This is because $(\Delta R - \Delta E - \Delta D)(1 - T)$ would be the net income from the project if the company were all-equity financed (and therefore had no interest expenses). Depreciation is added back to net income because it is a noncash charge. The following example shows that the two methods of finding CFAT produce the same results.

E X A M P L E

Equivalence of Two Methods of Computing CFAT

In order to illustrate the equivalence of the two methods of computing CFAT, let's assume that $\Delta R = \$4000$, $\Delta E = \$1500$, $\Delta D = \$1000$, and $T = 40\%$. You may recognize these values from the numerical example earlier in this chapter.

The first method, equation (9.2), finds the cash flow as *operating cash flows after taxes plus the depreciation tax shield:*

$$CFAT = (\Delta R - \Delta E)(1 - T) + T\Delta D$$
$$CFAT = (4000 - 1500)(1 - 0.40) + 0.40(1000)$$
$$CFAT = 2500(0.60) + 0.40(1000) = 1500 + 400 = \$1900$$

Operating cash flows before tax are $2500, and after paying the 40% tax, operating cash flows after tax are $1500. The depreciation is $1000, which, at the 40% tax rate, provides a $400 tax shield. The cash flow is $1500 plus $400, or $1900.

The second method, equation (9.3), finds the cash flow as *net income plus depreciation:*

$$CFAT = (\Delta R - \Delta E - \Delta D)(1 - T) + \Delta D$$
$$CFAT = (4000 - 1500 - 1000)(1 - 0.40) + 1000$$
$$CFAT = 1500(0.60) + 1000 = 900 + 1000 = \$1900$$

Income before taxes is $1500. Income after taxes is $900. Adding the net income and the depreciation gives the net cash flow of $1900.

Obviously, CFAT calculated as operating cash flows after taxes plus the depreciation tax shield is identical to CFAT calculated as net income plus depreciation. ∎

Non-Operating Cash Flows

NON-OPERATING CASH FLOWS Future cash flows that are not associated with current operations. These are usually additions or subtractions from the investment in capital assets or working capital.

Non-operating cash flows, cash flows that are not associated with operations, can occur at various points during the life of a capital project. There are many possible examples of these non-operating cash flows. Required maintenance or upgrades can occur periodically, and they can be treated the same as the cash expenditures for the initial investment outlay. Equipment such as boats, trucks, or airplanes can require engine overhauls every few years, while the rest of the boat, truck, or airplane needs major repairs on a less frequent basis. These non-operating cash flows can be either capitalized or expensed immediately. Expensed non-operating cash flows are multiplied by $(1 - T)$ to adjust for taxes. Capitalized non-operating cash flows have a non-adjusted net cash outflow when they occur and depreciation expenses that follow.

Future changes in net working capital are another common non-operating cash flow. A future increase in net working capital is a cash outflow and a future decrease in net working capital is a cash inflow. These future non-operating cash flows, just like future operating cash flows, are discounted back to find a project's NPV.

Net Salvage Value

The **net salvage value** is the after-tax net cash flow for terminating the project. It can be broken into four parts: sale of assets, taxes owed or saved on the sale, cleanup and removal expenses, and release of net working capital.

NET SALVAGE VALUE
The after-tax net cash flow for terminating the project.

The taxes due on the sale of assets are computed exactly as described earlier in our discussion of the net initial outlay. The taxes due are $T(S - B)$, the tax rate times the difference between the sale price and the book value. Cleanup and removal expenses are generally expensed immediately. Therefore, they are multiplied by $(1 - T)$ to adjust for taxes. The release of net working capital is unaffected by taxes. Tax law treats it as an internal transfer of funds. Therefore, the release of net working capital is simply an added cash flow. With cleanup and removal expenses represented as REX, net salvage value can be broken into four parts:

(1) Cash received on sale of old equipment S

(2) Tax paid (saved) on sale of old equipment $-T(S - B)$

(3) After-tax cleanup and removal expenses $-(1 - T)\text{REX}$

(4) Release of investment in working capital $\underline{\Delta W}$

$$\text{Net salvage value} = S - T(S - B) - (1 - T)\text{REX} + \Delta W \qquad (9.4)$$

SALVAGE VALUE The before-tax difference between the sale price of the assets and the cleanup and removal expenses.

The term **salvage value** typically refers to the before-tax difference between the sale price (S) and the clean up and removal expense (REX). That is, salvage value $= S - \text{REX}$.

Self-Check

1. There are two equivalent equations for calculating the net operating cash flow after tax (CFAT). Give the equation for *operating cash flows after taxes plus the depreciation tax shield*. Give the equation for *net income plus depreciation*.

2. If the tax rate increases, will CFAT increase or decrease? Why?

3. What are the two types of non-operating cash flows?

4. What is net salvage value? Give the equation for net salvage value and explain each of its four parts. Under what circumstances would taxes not affect the net salvage value?

AN EXAMPLE OF INCREMENTAL CASH FLOW ANALYSIS

Rocky Mountain Chemical Corporation (RMC) is thinking of replacing the packaging machines in its Texas plant. Each packaging machine currently in use has a net book value of $1 million and will continue to be depreciated on a straight-line basis to a net book value of zero over the next five years. The plant engineer estimates that the old machines could be used for as many as ten more years. The purchase price for the new machines is $5 million apiece, which would be depreciated over a ten-year period on a straight-line basis to a net book value of $500,000 each. Each new machine is expected to produce a pretax operating savings of $1.5 million per year over the machine it would replace.

RMC estimates that it could sell the old packaging machines for $250,000 each. Installation of each new machine would be expected to cost $600,000 in addition to the purchase price. Of this amount, $500,000 would be capitalized in the same way as the purchase price, and the remaining $100,000 would be expensed immediately. Because the new machines are so much faster than the ones they would replace, the company's average raw materials inventory account would need to be increased by $30,000 for each new machine. Simultaneously, because of trade credit, accounts payable would increase by $10,000. Finally, management believes that even though the new machines would have a net book value of $500,000 at the end of ten years, it would be possible to sell them for only $300,000, with removal and cleanup cost of $40,000.

If RMC has a marginal tax rate of 40%, what would be the after-tax incremental expected future cash flows associated with each new machine?

The Net Cash Flow for the Initial Investment

The net cash flow for the initial investment includes the $5 million purchase price, the $500,000 capitalized installation cost, and the $100,000 expensed installation cost, which sums to $5.6 million. Of this amount, $5.5 million will be depreciated over the life of the investment. The $100,000 expensed installation cost creates an immediate tax saving of $40,000, that is, the tax rate times the expense, 0.40(100,000). Thus, the initial cash investment for the new equipment is $5.56 million (5,600,000 − 40,000). The increases in inventory and accounts payable cause a required increase in net working capital of $\Delta W = \$20,000$. The sale of the machine currently in use would have two effects on future cash flows. First, we receive a cash inflow of the sale price of $250,000, along with the taxes due or saved on the sale. In this case, we have a tax *loss* on the sale of $750,000 ($S − B = 250,000 − 1,000,000$). With a marginal tax rate of 40%, this creates a tax saving of $300,000 (= (0.40)750,000). This tax saving is a positive cash flow of this amount. The second tax effect occurs in the depreciation expenses that would *not* be claimed for the old machine in each of the next five years. This effect would be accounted for in the expected future annual cash flows. We can compute the net initial outlay using equation (9.1):

$$\text{Net cash flow for initial outlay} = -I - \Delta W + S - T(S - B)$$
$$= -5,560,000 - 20,000 + 250,000 - 0.40(250,000 - 1,000,000)$$
$$= -5,560,000 - 20,000 + 250,000 + 300,000 = -\$5,030,000$$

So the net cash outlay on the investment is $5.03 million.

Note that the original purchase price of the old machine does not enter into this calculation. The original cost is a *sunk cost*. It was incurred in the past and therefore cannot be affected by the decision to replace the old machine. Similarly, care must be taken to correctly treat sunk costs that have been incurred more recently. Dollars that have already been spent—for example, on feasibility studies, prior research and development, and site preparation—are irrelevant for purposes of capital budgeting analysis. They are also sunk costs. Whether or not the company proceeds with the project, the timing and amounts of prior capital expenditures can't change, because these expenditures have already been made.

The Annual Operating Cash Flows (CFAT)

The net operating cash flows resulting from purchasing the new machine can be calculated using either equation (9.2) or (9.3). The change in revenue, ΔR, is zero. The change in expenses, ΔE, is −$1.5 million. Depreciation would increase $500,000 per year (= [5,500,000 − 500,000]/10) for the next ten years because of the new machine. It would decrease $200,000 per year (1,000,000/5) for the next five years because of the sale of the old machine. Therefore, ΔD is $300,000 (= 500,000 − 200,000) for years 1 through 5 and then ΔD is $500,000 for years 6 through 10.

Now let's use equation (9.2), the *operating cash flows after taxes plus the depreciation tax shield*. For years 1 through 5,

$$\text{CFAT} = (\Delta R - \Delta E)(1 - T) + T\Delta D$$
$$\text{CFAT(1 through 5)} = [0 - (-1,500,000)](1 - 0.4) + (0.4)(300,000) = \$1,020,000$$

For years 6 through 10, $\Delta D = \$500,000$, and

$$\text{CFAT(6 through 10)} = [0 - (-1,500,000)](1 - 0.4) + (0.4)(500,000) = \$1,100,000$$

If you prefer, you can also use equation (9.3), the *net income plus depreciation* method. For years 1 through 5:

$$CFAT = (\Delta R - \Delta E - \Delta D)(1 - T) + \Delta D$$

$$CFAT(1 \text{ through } 5) = [0 - (-1,500,000) - 300,000](1 - 0.4) + (300,000) = \$1,020,000$$

For years 6 through 10:

$$CFAT(6 \text{ through } 10) = [0 - (-1,500,000) - 500,000](1 - 0.4) + (500,000) = \$1,100,000$$

No non-operating cash flows are expected over the life of this project, and so no non-operating cash flows need be included in the project's cash flow stream.

Salvage Value

Even though these machines will be depreciated to a book value of $500,000 over ten years, they are expected to have a market value of $300,000 at the end of the project's life. A removal and cleanup expenditure of $40,000 is expected, which is tax deductible. In addition, the $20,000 investment in net working capital is recovered. From equation (9.4), the net salvage value is

$$\text{Net salvage value} = S - T(S - B) - (1 - T)\text{REX} + \Delta W$$
$$= 300,000 - 0.4(300,000 - 500,000) - 0.6(40,000) + 20,000$$
$$= 300,000 - (-80,000) - 24,000 + 20,000 = \$376,000$$

Over the next ten years, the incremental cash flows for this project are then (in $ millions):

Year	0	1	2	3	4	5	6	7	8	9	10
CF	−5.03	1.02	1.02	1.02	1.02	1.02	1.1	1.1	1.1	1.1	1.476

The final step, calculating the net present value from the expected cash flows, is shown in the following example.

Computing the NPV of Rocky Mountain's Packaging Machine   **E X A M P L E**

Let's continue our earlier example of RMC's packaging-machine replacement. If the project's required return is 12%, what is the NPV?

Computing the NPV of the project's annual incremental cash flows, we have

$$NPV = \sum_{t=0}^{n} \frac{CF_t}{(1 + r)^t} = -5.03 + \sum_{t=1}^{5} \frac{1.02}{(1.12)^t} + \sum_{t=6}^{9} \frac{1.10}{(1.12)^t} + \frac{1.476}{(1.12)^{10}} = \$1,017,925$$

So the project should be accepted because the NPV is positive. ∎

A More Convenient Computation Procedure

Our computation of the NPV for the packaging machine is partitioned by years. That is, $CFAT_t$ for each year is computed, and then the NPV is given by the sum of the present values of $CFAT_t$.

An alternative to this procedure is to compute the CFAT for each item (for example, the initial cost, the change in working capital, and so on), in which case the NPV is given by the sum of the present values of the CFATs for the items. Most people make fewer mistakes grouping by item because we think in terms of items rather than annual cash flows.

Naturally, the total discounted cash flows will be the same, regardless of whether we group them by year or by item. In the previous example, we totaled the cash flows in each year, discounted their values, and summed them. The column totals in table 9.3 on page 338 show these cash flows by year before discounting. The row totals in table 9.3 show them undiscounted by item. Table 9.4 then shows the NPV calculation for the example, using item cash flow groupings. In table 9.4, CFBT refers to the item's before-tax cash flow, and the formulas for each item's CFBT and CFAT are shown below the amount.

TABLE 9.3
Alternative Groupings of the Cash Flows for RMC's Packaging-Machine Replacement, by Years and by Items (in $ millions)

ITEM	0	1	2	3	4	5	6	7	8	9	10	TOTAL BY ITEM	
Capitalized installation and equipment cost	−5.50											−5.50	$t = 0$
Expensed installation cost	−0.06											−0.06	$t = 0$
Change in net working capital	−0.02											−0.02	$t = 0$
Sale of old equipment	0.55											0.55	$t = 0$
Investment tax credit	0.00											0.00	$t = 0$
Lost depreciation from sale of old equipment		−0.08	−0.08	−0.08	−0.08	−0.08						−0.08/yr	$t = 1 - 5$
Depreciation		0.20	0.20	0.20	0.20	0.20	0.20	0.20	0.20	0.20	0.20	0.20/yr	$t = 1 - 10$
Change in revenues minus expenses		0.90	0.90	0.90	0.90	0.90	0.90	0.90	0.90	0.90	0.90	0.90/yr	$t = 1 - 10$
Sale of equipment											0.38	0.38	$t = 10$
Removal expense											−0.024	−0.024	$t = 10$
Return of net working capital											0.02	0.02	$t = 10$
Total by year	−5.03	1.02	1.02	1.02	1.02	1.02	1.10	1.10	1.10	1.10	1.476		

TABLE 9.4
Alternative NPV Calculation for RMC's Packaging-Machine Replacement, with the Cash Flows Grouped by Item (in $ millions)

TIME	ITEM	CFBT[a]	CFAT	PV AT 12%
0	Capitalized installation and equipment cost	−5,500,000 / $-I$	−5,500,000 / $-I$	−5,500,000
0	Expensed installation cost	−100,000	−60,000	−60,000
0	Change in net working capital	−20,000 / $-\Delta W$	−20,000 / $-\Delta W$	−20,000
0	Sale of old equipment	250,000 / S	550,000 / $S - T(S - B)$	550,000
0	Investment tax credit	0	0	0
1–5	Lost depreciation from sale of old equipment[b]	0	−80,000/yr / $-TD_{old}$	−288,382
1–10	Depreciation[c]	0	200,000/yr / TD_{new}	6,215,245
1–10	Change in revenues minus expenses	1,500,000/yr / $\Delta R - \Delta E$	900,000/yr / $(1 - T)(\Delta R - \Delta E)$	
10	Sale of equipment	300,000 / S	380,000 / $S - T(S - B)$	121,062
10	Removal expense	−40,000 / $-REX$	−24,000 / $-(1 - T)REX$	
10	Return of net working capital	20,000 / ΔW	20,000 / ΔW	
				NPV = $1,017,925

[a]Note that noncash items have zero before-tax cash flow.
[b]D_{old} = annual depreciation expense on the old item.
[c]D_{new} = annual depreciation expense on the new (replacement) item.

Erosion and Enhancement

RMC's decision to replace its packaging machines involves many aspects of the company's operations, yet all the incremental cash flows were identified, and the decision could be made separately from other decisions. Some capital budgeting decisions cannot be made so independently. For example, a new product can interact with the company's existing products and services.

Suppose a company has discovered how to make a product that would be better than one of its existing products. For example, suppose Procter & Gamble creates a new soap. Such a new product can cause what is called **erosion** of one or more existing products. Sales of the new product will erode (reduce) sales of the existing products.

Perhaps less obvious is the decline in the market value of the production facilities for existing products caused by the innovation. Because of reduced or eliminated sales opportunities, the value of plant and equipment used by *other companies,* as well as that of the company introducing the innovation, declines. Therefore, as perverse as it might seem, a company may be best served by delaying introduction of an innovation until it can be incorporated into the company's natural replacement of equipment. A company might also introduce the innovation sooner than it might have otherwise done, as a defensive move against competitors.

Just as one interaction among products may cause a decrease in value, another interaction may cause an increase in value. Such an increase is called **enhancement.** Enhancement occurs when the production and/or sales of one product increases the value of another. For example, an innovation that causes a reduction in the cost of making or installing a home swimming pool may cause an increase in the sales of swimming pool maintenance equipment.

EROSION An innovation that has a negative impact on one or more of a company's existing products.

ENHANCEMENT An innovation that has a positive impact on one or more of a company's existing products.

New Computer Game Systems at Nintendo

E X A M P L E

What if Nintendo discovered a computer graphics innovation that would require a new type of machine, such as when Sega introduced its Genesis system? The company would face the problems of erosion and enhancement. Sales of existing products, and the value of existing production facilities, for Nintendo and its competitors, would probably be eroded by a superior system. At the same time, a new system might provide Nintendo with an enhancement of some existing and potential future products. The company could develop the new system to facilitate such enhancement. ■

It's vital to include dependencies that cause significant erosion or enhancement in order to correctly measure a project's NPV. Without their inclusion, you won't have measured the NPV, even though you think you have! The next chapter examines several project interdependencies.

Self-Check

1. In an equipment replacement decision, explain how the incremental cash flows are measured for the initial outlay, annual net operating cash flows, and net salvage value.
2. Describe two alternative ways of grouping a project's incremental after-tax cash flows. Why are they equivalent?
3. Explain the concepts of erosion and enhancement.
4. Why is it so important to include any significant effects of erosion and enhancement in capital budgeting cash flows?

INFLATION

Expectations about inflation affect required returns. So a project's required return—its cost of capital—depends on inflation expectations. Expectations about inflation also affect the project's expected future cash flows. Therefore, it seems obvious that inflation expectations can affect a project's value. However, surprisingly, the changes may actually cancel each other out.

It's very important to keep in mind the relationship among the required return, expected cash flows, and present value. Present value depends on both the required return *and* the expected cash flows. When any one of these three things changes, at least one of the others must also change.

For example, if the required return increases, present value will decrease if the expected cash flows don't also change. This is the case for bonds. With constant coupon payments, the market value of a bond changes whenever market interest rates change. As a result, even U.S. government bonds are not truly riskless because of inflation uncertainty, as chapter 6 shows.[5] Similarly, an increase in the expected cash flows will increase present value *if* the required return (and therefore risk) has not changed.

The possibility most easily forgotten with respect to the relationships among present value, required return, and expected future cash flows is that *present values can remain constant even if there are changes in both the expected cash flows and the required return.* The changes can actually offset each other, exactly. Present value might be constant, even though the required return and expected cash flows change.

Capital Budgeting and Inflation

The effect of inflation can be complex because asset value is a function of both the required return and the expected future cash flows. As we noted, inflation affects the project's expected future cash flows as well as its required return. Yet, as we also noted, the changes can cancel each other out, leaving the project's NPV unchanged.

To analyze a capital budgeting decision, either include inflation in all the estimates of expected future cash flows and the required return, or exclude inflation everywhere. When an estimate includes inflation, it is said to be stated in *nominal* terms. When an estimate excludes inflation, it is said to be stated in *real* terms.[6] For proper measurement, then, all of the parts must be stated either entirely in real terms or entirely in nominal terms.

To explore the effects of inflation, let's look first at its effect on the required return. Let the required return in real terms be r_r, the required return in nominal terms be r_n, and the inflation rate be i. The nominal rate can be obtained by simply compounding the real rate and the inflation rate, or

$$(1 + r_n) = (1 + r_r)(1 + i)$$

Multiplying the right-hand side and rearranging, the nominal rate can be expressed as a function of the real and inflation rates:

$$r_n = r_r + i + ir_r \qquad\qquad (9.5)$$

This relationship may surprise you. You may have seen the nominal rate expressed simply as the sum of the real and inflation rates, without including the cross-term, ir_r. Because the cross-term is relatively small compared to the other terms, the sum is a good approximation and is often used in practice. However, equation (9.5) is the correct expression.

---

[5]It is very important to note that the relevant measure is that of the *expected* future inflation rate. This can be quite different from the inflation rate actually realized, although recent realized inflation rates are often highly correlated with expected future inflation rates.

[6]As we said in chapter 5, the term *nominal* means that the value is a value "in name only." Cash flows that are expressed in nominal dollar terms are not comparable in purchasing power to today's dollars, which is the reason the phrase "constant purchasing power dollars" is often used in place of the term *real.*

A major problem that occurs with inflation is that while revenues and expenses inflate, the depreciation tax credits do not inflate. This is because depreciation expense is based on the historical cost of the equipment. Thus, either the depreciation tax credits must be converted into real terms, or the expected revenue and expense cash flows must be converted into nominal terms. You can see this problem in the following example, in which the NPV of the project is computed in both real and nominal terms.

Monogramming at Christian Dior

EXAMPLE

Suppose Christian Dior is thinking of buying a monogramming machine. The machine has a 4-year useful life and would require an initial outlay of $100,000. The machine would be depreciated to a zero book value over 4 years on a straight-line basis, so depreciation would be $25,000 per year. The machine would generate an incremental increase in operating income of $50,000 per year before taxes, and the relevant tax rate is 40%. Inflation is expected to be 8% per year, and the project's required return in real terms would be $r_r = 10\%$. What is the NPV of purchasing this machine?

First, let's compute the NPV of Christian Dior's project in real terms. The real cash flow $(\Delta R - \Delta E)$ before taxes is $50,000, and it is $30,000 after taxes. Depreciation is fixed in nominal terms, so the depreciation charge and the depreciation tax shield must be converted into real terms. The nominal tax credit for the first year would be $T\Delta D = 0.4(25,000) = 10,000$. With 8% inflation, this would be worth $9259 (= 10,000/1.08) in real terms, or dollars of constant purchasing power. The tax credit for the second year would be worth $8573 (= 10,000/[1.08]^2)$. The other tax credits would be determined in a similar manner, by discounting them for the appropriate number of years at the inflation rate. The real cash flow after taxes is the sum of $30,000 plus the real depreciation charge, which is shown in table 9.5. These real cash flows are discounted at the real cost of capital of 10%. This gives a final NPV of $21,583.

The alternative method to compute the NPV is to find the present values of *nominal* after-tax cash flows with a *nominal* cost of capital. The nominal discount rate is found with equation (9.5):

$$r_n = r_r + i + ir_r = 0.10 + 0.08 + (0.08)(0.10) = 18.8\%$$

In nominal dollars, the first year's $\Delta R - \Delta E$ would be $54,000 (= 50,000[1.08])$. After taxes, this nets $32,400. The depreciation is $25,000, which gives a depreciation tax shield of $10,000 (= 0.4(25,000))$, so the nominal cash flow the first year is $42,400. The second year's $\Delta R - \Delta E$ would be $58,320 (= 50,000[1.08]^2)$, with the subsequent flows computed in a similar manner, by compounding them forward at the inflation rate. The future nominal depreciation charges, however, are fixed and don't increase. Table 9.6 on page 342 gives the calculations for the nominal cash flows after tax each year for the investment project. These nominal cash flows are then discounted at the nominal discount rate of 18.8%, producing an NPV of $21,583.

As you can see, the two calculations produce exactly the same NPV. ■

TABLE 9.5

NPV Calculation in Real Terms for Christian Dior's Monogramming Machine

TIME	ITEM	CFBT	CFAT (REAL)	PV AT 10%
0	I	−100,000	−100,000	−100,000
1–4	$\Delta R - \Delta E$	50,000/yr	30,000/yr	95,096
1	Depreciation	0	9,259	8,418
2	Depreciation	0	8,573	7,085
3	Depreciation	0	7,938	5,964
4	Depreciation	0	7,350	5,020
				NPV = $21,583

TABLE 9.6
NPV Calculation in Nominal Terms for Christian Dior's Monogramming Machine

TIME	ITEM	CFBT	CFAT (NOMINAL)	PV AT 18.8%
0	I	−100,000	−100,000	−100,000
1	$\Delta R - \Delta E$	54,000	32,400/yr	27,273
2	$\Delta R - \Delta E$	58,320	34,992	24,793
3	$\Delta R - \Delta E$	62,986	37,791	22,539
4	$\Delta R - \Delta E$	68,024	40,815	20,491
1–4	Depreciation	0	10,000/yr	26,487
				NPV = $21,583

If inflation affects various component cash flows differently—for example, if revenues are expected to increase 6% per year, but expenses are expected to increase 9%—those differences must be incorporated into the analysis. Differences in inflation rates among cash flows can cause complexity, as can differences in the effect of inflation on the required return and the expected cash flows. Still, this merely complicates the problem. Such complexity does not change the way we incorporate the effects of inflation. Whatever the case, the analysis should be cast in a consistent manner, *entirely in real terms or entirely in nominal terms.*

Self-Check

1. Explain why it is important when analyzing a capital budgeting decision either to include inflation in all the estimates of expected future cash flows and the cost of capital, or else to exclude it everywhere.

2. Why is the nominal cost of capital not simply the sum of the real cost of capital and the expected inflation rate?

3. True or false? A capital budgeting analysis must be cast entirely in real terms.

A FEW MORE WORDS ABOUT THE TAX ENVIRONMENT

Early in this century, Congress instituted a procedure for collecting taxes, now familiar to most Americans, called the income tax. Since that time, income tax has come to provide the primary source of tax revenue for the federal government. Income tax provisions and rates have changed frequently. Table 9.7 shows the statutory federal tax rates on corporate income from 1909 through 1997.

Another way tax laws have changed over the years is in the provisions for capitalizing equipment expense—depreciation—and for claiming investment tax credit. In the last three decades there have been no fewer than five major changes in the depreciation rules in addition to numerous minor changes. MACRS (pronounced "makers"), which stands for *Modified* ACRS (accelerated cost recovery system, pronounced "acres") is the latest provision. ACRS was originally introduced to replace the asset depreciation range (ADR) method. ADR had been an attempt to specify carefully (once and for all!) the rules for using the three allowable depreciation methods, which were, at that time, *double-declining-balance, sum-of-the-years'-digits,* and *straight-line.* The designation of these three depreciation methods as the allowable methods for federal income tax purposes had occurred many years earlier, but the rules governing their use had changed often during the intervening years.

TABLE 9.7
Statutory Corporate Income Tax Rates from 1909 through 1997

YEAR	RATE BRACKETS OR EXEMPTIONS	RATE[a] (PERCENT)
1909–1913	$5000 exemption	1
1913–1915	No exemption after March 1, 1913	1
1916	None	2
1917	None	6
1918	$2000 exemption	12
1919–1921	$2000 exemption	10
1922–1924	$2000 exemption	12.5
1925	$2000 exemption	13
1926–1927	$2000 exemption	13.5
1928	$3000 exemption	12
1929	$3000 exemption	11
1930–1931	$3000 exemption	12
1932–1935	None	13.75
1936–1937	Graduated normal tax	
	First $2000	8
	Over $40,000	15
	Graduated surtax on undistributed profits	7–27
1938–1939	First $25,000	12.5–16
	Over $25,000	19[b]
1940	First $25,000	14.85–18.7
	$25,000 to $31,964.30	38.3
	$31,964,30 to $38,565.89	36.9
	Over $38,565.89	24
1941	First $25,000	21–25
	$25,000 to $38,461.54	44
	Over $38,461.54	31
1942–1945	First $25,000	25–29
	$25,000 to $50,000	53
	Over $50,000	40
1946–1949	First $25,000	21–25
	$25,000 to $50,000	53
	Over $50,000	38
1950	First $25,000	23
	Over $25,000	42
1951	First $25,000	28.75
	Over $25,000	50.75
1952–1963	First $25,000	30
	Over $25,000	52
1964	First $25,000	22
	Over $25,000	50
1965–1967	First $25,000	22
	Over $25,000	48
1968–1969	First $25,000	24.2[c]
	Over $25,000	52.8[c]
1970	First $25,000	22.55[c]
	Over $25,000	49.2[c]
1971–1974	First $25,000	22
	Over $25,000	48

(continued on following page)

(Statutory Corporate Income Tax Rates from 1909 through 1997 *continued from previous page*)

YEAR	RATE BRACKETS OR EXEMPTIONS	RATE[a] (PERCENT)
1975–1978	First $25,000	20
	Next $25,000	22
	Over $50,000	48
1979–1981	First $25,000	17
	$25,000 to $50,000	20
	$50,000 to $75,000	30
	$75,000 to $100,000	40
	Over $100,000	46
1982	First $25,000	16
	$25,000 to $50,000	19
	$50,000 to $75,000	30
	$75,000 to $100,000	40
	Over $100,000	46
1983–1986	First $25,000	15
	$25,000 to $50,000	18
	$50,000 to $75,000	30
	$75,000 to $100,000	40
	Over $100,000	46
1987–1990[d]	First $50,000	15
	$50,000 to $75,000	25
	Over $75,000[e]	34
1991–1992	First $50,000	15
	$50,000 to $75,000	25
	$75,000 to $100,000	34
	$100,000 to $335,000	39
	Over $335,000	34
1993–1997	First $50,000	15
	$50,000 to $75,000	25
	$75,000 to $100,000	34
	$100,000 to $335,000	39
	$335,000 to $10,000,000	34
	$10,000,000 to $15,000,000	35
	$15,000,000 to $18,333,333	38
	Over $18,333,333	35

[a]In addition to the rates shown, certain types of "excess profits" taxes were in effect in 1917–1921, 1933–1945, and 1950–1953.
[b]Less adjustments: 14.025% of dividends received and 2.5% of dividends paid.
[c]Includes surcharge of 10% in 1968 and 1969 and 2.5% in 1970.
[d]Rates shown effective for tax years beginning on or after July 1, 1987. Income in taxable years that include July 1, 1987 (other than as the first date of such year) is subject to a blended rate.
[e]An additional 5% tax is imposed on a corporation's taxable income in excess of $100,000. Maximum additional tax is $11,750; this provision phases out the benefit of graduated rates for corporations with taxable income between $100,000 and $335,000; corporations with income above $335,000, in effect, pay a flat tax at a 34% rate.
Source: Treasury Department, Office of Tax Analysis.

Looking at this history of change, we see little reason to assume that the modified ACRS procedure is permanent.

Because tax law changes occur often, it's critical to *use the current tax laws to determine after-tax cash flows* for a capital budgeting decision (or for that matter, for any financial decision). However, because of the frequency of changes, there isn't much point in memorizing all of the tax provisions. When you make a financial decision, determine exactly what the treatment for each item will be under current tax law by consulting current tax guides (federal, state, or private) or tax experts within or outside your organization.

Even though the federal corporate income taxes are the largest part of a business's total tax bill, there are other tax provisions. Most states have an income tax. Consequently, the marginal tax rate usually isn't the federal income tax rate but a higher rate that reflects the combined effect of federal, state, and local taxes. A business may also face other taxes that aren't directly related to its income. These include federal and state excise taxes, payroll taxes, property taxes, and state and local sales taxes. The effect of these taxes is included by reducing revenues or increasing cash expenses (ΔR and ΔE) by the amount of the tax.

Because of the complexity of the tax laws, we don't attempt to specify taxes perfectly. In our presentations, we follow the convention of using a single marginal tax rate that people often think of as the federal income tax rate. To remind us that normally the rate is larger than the federal rate, we generally use a tax rate in our examples that's different from the most common corporate tax rate (before surtax) of 34%.

Depreciation

In many of the examples and problems in this book, we use straight-line depreciation, even though companies actually use the MACRS system, an accelerated depreciation method, for tax purposes or capital budgeting analysis. (Most companies *do* use straight-line depreciation for financial reporting purposes.) Straight-line depreciation isn't used for tax purposes because of the time value of money. As long as a company has enough income that it can fully use all of its tax credits and deductions, the sooner it claims the depreciation, the sooner it can put the money from the tax shield to work earning more money. Over the life of an investment, the total amount of depreciation tax deductions will be the same, regardless of the depreciation schedule that's used.

Under current tax laws, an investment is assigned to a property class, and each class of property has a separate depreciation schedule. Property is put into a class based on a rough estimate of its useful life. Some of the asset classes are shown in table 9.8. Each MACRS property class has a separate depreciation schedule, which is shown in table 9.9 on page 346. MACRS is an accelerated depreciation method, which results in higher depreciation charges in the early years of a project's life. This reduces taxable income, taxes, and net income during the early years. But it also results in a higher after-tax cash flow because of these lower taxes.

Which depreciation method is best? The answer comes from determining which provides the largest present value of the tax credits (the product of depreciation deduction times the marginal tax rate). The answer is not necessarily the same from year to year, because the allowable methods and procedures change with disturbing regularity. Therefore, there's little point in memorizing the fact that a particular method is optimal now, because it probably won't be by the time you get around to using it.

TABLE 9.8
MACRS Asset Classes

MACRS ASSET CLASSES	TYPES OF PROPERTY
3-year	Tractor units, racehorses over 2 years old, special tools
5-year	Cars, light and heavy trucks, computer and office equipment
7-year	Office furniture and fixtures, railroad property, and any property that does not have a designated class life
10-year	Fruit trees, water transportation (boats)
15-year	Depreciable land improvements, wastewater plants, pipelines
20-year	Farm buildings, municipal sewers
27.5-year	Residential property
39-year	Nonresidential real property

TABLE 9.9
Depreciation Rates under MACRS (Modified Accelerated Cost Recovery System)

YEARS	RECOVERY PERIOD CLASS					
	3-YEAR	5-YEAR	7-YEAR	10-YEAR	15-YEAR	20-YEAR
1	33.33%	20.00%	14.29%	10.00%	5.00%	3.75%
2	44.45	32.00	24.49	18.00	9.50	7.22
3	14.81	19.20	17.49	14.40	8.55	6.68
4	7.41	11.52	12.49	11.52	7.70	6.18
5		11.52	8.93	9.22	6.93	5.71
6		5.76	8.93	7.37	6.23	5.28
7			8.93	6.55	5.90	4.89
8			4.45	6.55	5.90	4.52
9				6.55	5.90	4.46
10				6.55	5.90	4.46
11				3.29	5.90	4.46
12					5.90	4.46
13					5.90	4.46
14					5.90	4.46
15					5.90	4.46
16					2.99	4.46
17						4.46
18						4.46
19						4.46
20						4.46
21						2.25

Notes:
1. Depreciation is lower in year 1 because assets are assumed to be in service for only six months.
2. Rates for four asset classes (3-year, 5-year, 7-year, and 10-year) are 200% declining balance with a half-year convention and a switch to straight-line when optimal. Only half the formula amount is claimed the first year.
3. Rates for 10-year and 15-year property are 150% declining balance with a half-year convention and a switch to straight-line when optimal.
4. Residential real property is depreciated straight-line over 27.5 years. Nonresidential real property is depreciated straight-line over 39 years.

There is considerable value, however, in describing a general method for identifying the optimal depreciation schedule from whatever schedules are allowable at the time you have to choose one. Despite all the changes, the way to determine the best method hasn't changed since the income tax laws first began requiring companies to capitalize equipment costs. *A company should use the depreciation method that provides the largest present value of depreciation tax credits.*

EXAMPLE

Alternative Depreciation Methods at General Electric

Let's say that General Electric invests in a capital asset that costs $100,000. GE can depreciate this asset as 5-year property using the MACRS schedule. Assume GE's marginal tax rate is 40% and the asset's required return is 10%. What are the asset's annual depreciation charges, its annual tax shields, and the present value of the tax shields?

They are shown in table 9.10. As you can see, the total depreciation charge using the MACRS schedule is $100,000 and the tax shield, undiscounted, totals $40,000. The present value of the tax shield is $30,931. But what if GE used straight-line depreciation instead?

Table 9.10 also shows the comparable calculations using straight-line depreciation. Although the *total* depreciation and undiscounted tax shields are the same, the present value of the tax shields, $30,326, is less. MACRS is more beneficial because it provides a greater depreciation in the early years of the project's life. Getting the depreciation earlier increases the present value. ■

TABLE 9.10
GE Depreciation

YEAR	MACRS PERCENTAGE	MACRS DEPRECIATION	TAX SHIELD	PV @10%	STRAIGHT-LINE DEPRECIATION	TAX SHIELD	PV @10%
1	20.00	$20,000	8,000	$ 7,273	$20,000	$8,000	$7,273
2	32.00	32,000	12,800	10,579	20,000	8,000	6,611
3	19.20	19,200	7,680	5,770	20,000	8,000	6,011
4	11.52	11,520	4,608	3,147	20,000	8,000	5,464
5	11.52	11,520	4,608	2,861	20,000	8,000	4,967
6	5.76	5,760	2,304	1,301			
Totals	100.00%	$100,000	$40,000	$30,931	$100,000	$40,000	$30,326

Based on the general superiority of expensing over capitalizing (which we illustrated earlier in the Boeing example), we could have predicted the superiority of the MACRS method in the GE example. The comparison in the General Electric example was between straight-line and an "accelerated" method. Although not as quick as expensing, an accelerated method allows depreciation to be claimed more quickly than straight-line. As long as a company can use the tax credits, accelerated depreciation provides the more advantageous treatment.

Self-Check
1. When is the effective income tax rate higher than the federal rate?
2. Explain how to calculate MACRS depreciation.

EVALUATING REPLACEMENT CYCLES

RMC's packaging-machine replacement involved replacing specialized equipment that is subject to periodic technological design improvements. In such cases, the replacement decision is basically a one-time decision. Later, when the chosen machine becomes worn out or technologically outmoded, its replacement is essentially an entirely new project. Such a replacement decision is, in effect, a decision of whether to continue producing a product or even to remain in that line of business.

But many replacement decisions are not like the packaging machine. Instead, they are routine decisions, involving machinery and equipment that does not change very much over time. The asset is replaced or overhauled because of worn-out parts rather than technological improvement. Essentially, the new asset is identical to the one it replaces. In such cases, there is a routine pattern, or **replacement cycle.** The asset is purchased, maintained, and replaced on a regular basis. An example would be a delivery vehicle for Federal Express.

A problem arises when investment alternatives have differing useful lives. When alternatives in a routine replacement decision do not have identical life cycles, the asset with the largest single-cycle NPV isn't necessarily the best choice. Instead, the choice must be made on a comparable basis. For example, if a company is choosing between two assets, one with a five-year life and the other with a ten-year life, two sequential five-year assets would be needed to do the job of one ten-year asset.

One way to choose among alternatives in a replacement cycle decision, then, is to find a common horizon where some number of sequential replacements of one asset equals that for the alternative.[7] This approach can be cumbersome, however.

REPLACEMENT CYCLE
The elapsed time during which an asset is purchased, operated, and then replaced with an essentially equivalent asset.

---

[7]This is called the "least common multiple of lives" or the "common horizon" approach.

For example, comparing a six-year type A asset with a seven-year type B asset would involve a horizon of 42 years—seven sequential purchases of A types versus six of B types. If there was a C-type alternative with an eight-year life, the process would become even more tedious. A more convenient method of choosing among alternatives in such situations is on the basis of equivalent annual cost.

Equivalent Annual Cost

EQUIVALENT ANNUAL COST (EAC) The *equivalent* cost per year of owning an asset over its entire life. The EAC is calculated as an ordinary annuity payment that has the same present value as the asset's costs.

Equivalent annual cost (EAC) is the *equivalent* cost per year of owning an asset over its entire life. The method is a simple two-step application of time-value-of-money mathematics. The first step is to compute the present value of all costs associated with owning the asset over its entire life. These costs include the purchase price, maintenance costs, and operating costs over the period of expected ownership. Let the net initial outlay be C_0 and the yearly CFAT costs be $C_1, C_2, \ldots, C_n$, where n is the length of the asset's life. The cost of capital is r. The total present value of costs over the life of the asset, TC, is

$$TC = C_0 + \sum_{t=1}^{n} \frac{C_t}{(1+r)^t}$$

The second step is to determine the cash flow that, if it was paid out each year, would have the same present value, TC. In other words, what annuity payment has a present value of TC? This cash flow is the equivalent annual cost (EAC). It is given by the formula for determining the payments of an ordinary annuity, equation (5.5). In EAC notation, it is:

$$EAC = \frac{TC}{PVAF_{r,n}} = TC\left[\frac{r(1+r)^n}{(1+r)^n - 1}\right] \tag{9.6}$$

EXAMPLE

Changing Inventory Equipment at Hoover

Let's say the Hoover Corporation is considering the replacement of a machine used for its inventory storage. Hoover can buy two alternative machines, A or B. Which machine should Hoover buy?

Hoover should choose the machine with the lower equivalent annual cost, so we must calculate each machine's EAC. Machine A costs $49,000 to purchase and install, has a 5-year life, and will be depreciated over 5 years on a straight-line basis to a book value of $4000, so depreciation will be $9000 per year for 5 years (= [49,000 − 4000]/5). At the end of the 5 years, Hoover expects to be able to sell machine A for $10,000. For the expected production level, it will cost $25,000 per year to operate machine A. The relevant tax rate is 40%, and the project's cost of capital is 12%.

The present value of all of machine A's costs is −$85,783, as given in table 9.11. The EAC can then be calculated using equation (9.6):

$$EAC = TC\left[\frac{r(1+r)^n}{(1+r)^n - 1}\right] = 85,783\left[\frac{0.12(1.12)^5}{(1.12)^5 - 1}\right] = \$23,797$$

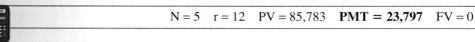

| N = 5 | r = 12 | PV = 85,783 | **PMT = 23,797** | FV = 0 |

For convenience, we drop the minus sign on total cost (TC) when we apply equation (9.6).

Machine B has a 10-year life but costs $72,000 to purchase and install. It will be depreciated over 8 years on a straight-line basis to a book value of zero, so depreciation will be $9000 per year for the first 8 years (= 72,000/8) and zero for the last 2 years of use. Machine

B is expected to require an overhaul at the end of year 6 that will cost $18,000 and will be expensed, rather than capitalized. At the end of the 10 years, Hoover expects to be able to sell machine B for a scrap value that will equal the cost of removal and cleanup. Machine B is slightly less expensive to run than machine A, costing $24,000 per year to operate.

The present value of all the costs for machine B is −$140,952, as given in table 9.12. The EAC can then be calculated using equation (9.6) as $24,946.

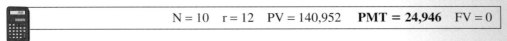

$$N = 10 \quad r = 12 \quad PV = 140{,}952 \quad \textbf{PMT = 24{,}946} \quad FV = 0$$

Based on the EACs, then, Hoover should buy machine A with its lower EAC. Note that we disregarded the revenues, because both alternatives have the same revenues and risk. ■

Figure 9.1 compares the costs over ten years of using the two machines. The comparison shows both the EACs and the present values of total cost outlays over a common ten-year horizon. Figure 9.1 illustrates how comparing EACs is equivalent to comparing costs over a common horizon, which happens in all cases. However, as we noted earlier, the EAC method is more convenient, especially with more than two alternatives.

TABLE 9.11
Present Value of the Total Cost for Hoover's Machine A

TIME	ITEM	CFBT	CFAT	PV AT 12%
0	I	−49,000	−49,000	−49,000
1–5	−ΔE	−25,000/yr	−15,000/yr	−54,072
1–5	Depreciation	0/yr	3,600/yr	12,977
5	Salvage value	10,000	7,600	4,312
		(B = 4,000)	S − T(S − B)	
				TC = −$85,783

TABLE 9.12
Present Value of the Total Cost for Hoover's Machine B

TIME	ITEM	CFBT	CFAT	PV AT 12%
0	I	−72,000	−72,000	−72,000
1–10	−ΔE	−24,000/yr	−14,400/yr	−81,363
1–8	Depreciation	0/yr	3,600/yr	17,883
6	Overhaul	−18,000	−10,800	−5,472
				TC = −$140,952

FIGURE 9.1
Comparison of the equivalent annual cost and common horizon methods.

EAC_A =	23,797	23,797	23,797	23,797	23,797	23,797	23,797	23,797	23,797	23,797
EAC_B =	24,946	24,946	24,946	24,946	24,946	24,946	24,946	24,946	24,946	24,946
	0	1	2	3	4	5	6	7	8	9	10

85,783   85,783

48,675 ◄

134,458 = Present value of total costs for machine A over a 10-year horizon
140,952 = Present value of total costs for machine B over a 10-year horizon

Replacement Frequency

The preferred shorter replacement cycle in the Hoover example has an additional option associated with it. Because of the shorter life cycle, there is less chance that a mechanically sound machine will be made useless by a technological advance. In essence, the company has the option to change production technologies more often when it purchases the machine with the shorter life cycle. Therefore, if the two machines had identical EACs (including removal costs), the machine with the shorter life cycle would be preferred. Although we do not have an option pricing model for conveniently determining an estimate for the value of more frequent replacement, it is nevertheless a valuable option. Other capital budgeting options are discussed in the next chapter.

The Hoover example compared two alternative machines. It is also useful to consider alternative replacement cycles for a given machine. The optimal replacement cycle is the one that minimizes the EAC. Salvage values and maintenance costs vary with the type and usage of a machine. (Salvage value is also a function of the potential future uses of the equipment.) One life cycle is not necessarily optimal for *all* situations. Let's investigate replacement cycle frequency by extending the Hoover example to consider various life cycles for machine A. Note that the depreciation schedule doesn't change, despite the change in usage.

EXAMPLE

Replacement Cycle Frequency at Hoover

Let's say that instead of after 5 years, machine A could be replaced early, at the end of 4 years. It could also be used an extra year and replaced after 6 years. With less use, the machine would have an expected $16,000 resale value at the end of 4 years. With more use, the machine would require maintenance costing $1000 at the end of year 5 and is expected to have a zero salvage value at the end of year 6. Which replacement cycle is best?

The total cost over one 4-year life cycle is −$74,220, as given in table 9.13. From equation (9.6), the EAC for a 4-year cycle is $24,436.

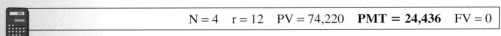

$$N = 4 \quad r = 12 \quad PV = 74{,}220 \quad \textbf{PMT} = \textbf{24{,}436} \quad FV = 0$$

The total cost over one 6-year life cycle is −$97,223, as given in table 9.14. From equation (9.6), the EAC for a 6-year cycle is $23,647.

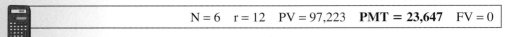

$$N = 6 \quad r = 12 \quad PV = 97{,}223 \quad \textbf{PMT} = \textbf{23{,}647} \quad FV = 0$$

So the 6-year replacement cycle is best. ■

TABLE 9.13

Present Value of the Total Cost of Machine A if It's Replaced after 4 Years

TIME	ITEM	CFBT	CFAT	PV AT 12%
0	I	−49,000	−49,000	−49,000
1–4	−ΔE	−25,000/yr	−15,000/yr	−45,560
1–4	Depreciation	0/yr	3,600/yr	10,934
4	Salvage	16,000	14,800	9,406
		(B = 13,000)	S − T(S − B)	
				TC = −$74,220

TABLE 9.14

Present Value of the Total Cost of Machine A if It's Replaced after 6 Years

TIME	ITEM	CFBT	CFAT	PV AT 12%
0	I	−49,000	−49,000	−49,000
1–6	−ΔE	−25,000/yr	−15,000/yr	−61,671
1–5	Depreciation	0/yr	3,600/yr	12,977
5	Maintenance	−1,000	−600	−340
6	Salvage	0	1,600	811
		$(B = 4,000)$	$S − T(S − B)$	
				TC = −$97,223

As we pointed out earlier, the choice of machine A (over B), with its shorter replacement cycle, provides more flexibility with respect to technological innovations. Similarly, flexibility in a machine's replacement cycle is also valuable because even if one cycle is projected at one point in time, the company has the option to change when replacement will occur, depending upon conditions that develop.

In the replacement cycle frequency example, the alternative EACs are very similar. Therefore, the company can purchase machine A, run it for four years, and reevaluate the replacement decision then. The reevaluation would include technological considerations, the condition of the machine, replacement cost, salvage values, maintenance experience over the four years, and more accurate maintenance cost projections for its continued use, among other things.

Equivalent Annual Annuities

The EAC calculation annualizes the total cost of a project over its life. The same type of calculation can be used to annualize *any* amount, such as a project's NPV, its total revenue, and so on. In such cases, the amount is called an *equivalent annual benefit*. The general term for an annualized amount is **equivalent annual annuity (EAA).** The EAA is a useful measure whenever the project horizon is indefinitely long, so that the assumption of an infinite, or permanent, stream is a good characterization of the situation.

EQUIVALENT ANNUAL ANNUITY (EAA) An annualized annuity payment with a present value equal to the present value of a project. The EAA is the ordinary annuity payment with a present value equal to the project's NPV.

Computing an Equivalent Annual Annuity (EAA)

EXAMPLE

Suppose one 5-year cycle of a machine has an NPV of $2800. Assuming a required return of 11%, what is the project's EAA?

Using equation (9.6) with EAA in place of EAC and NPV in place of TC, the EAA for this project's NPV would be $757.60.

| N = 5 | r = 11 | PV = 2800 | **PMT = 757.60** | FV = 0 |

With an infinite horizon of sequential replacement, the NPV from the sequence would be the present value of a perpetuity of EAA inflows, or $6887.27 (= 757.60/0.11). ■

Other Replacement Scenarios

Chapter 8 looks at one-time replacement decisions. Such decisions should be made using the one-time NPV decision criterion: *Choose the asset with the largest NPV.* In this section on replacement cycles, we assume that a project would be replaced periodically, with an infinitely long horizon. The choice of replacement cycle for the *routine* like-for-like replacement of assets is made on the basis of equivalent annual cost: *Choose the asset with the lowest EAC or the highest EAA.*

When future significant technological advances are likely, the replacement cycle decision becomes more complex. Among other things, the decision must include the option connected with a shorter replacement cycle to make technological change sooner. In practice, technological advances can be difficult to predict. Nevertheless, their possible occurrence can materially affect a company's choice of asset.

Self-Check

1. How do periodic replacement decisions differ from one-time replacement decisions? What is the best way to handle assets with replacement cycles in capital budgeting analysis?

2. What is the equivalent annual cost of owning an asset? How is it related to an ordinary annuity?

3. How is the EAC (equivalent annual cost) approach used to decide which of two machines to purchase?

4. What is an equivalent annual annuity (EAA)? How can it be used in capital budgeting analysis?

SUMMARY

In this chapter, we described the critical problem of estimating a capital budgeting project's incremental cash flows. We want to leave you with one final observation. *The accuracy of the estimates used in capital budgeting is critically important.* Bad estimates will not lead to good decisions, regardless of the evaluation methods you choose or how well you apply them. Having said that, however, we must sadly note that no one ever has completely accurate estimates of investment outcomes.

The basic points in chapter 9 are:

- A project's net initial outlay includes cash expenditures, changes in net working capital, after-tax cash flows from selling old equipment, and any investment tax credits. The net cash flow for initial investment $= -I - \Delta W + S - T(S - B)$.

- A project's periodic net operating cash flow, its CFAT, can be described as incremental *operating cash flows after taxes plus the depreciation tax shield:* $\text{CFAT} = (\Delta R - \Delta E)(1 - T) + T\Delta D$.

- Net operating cash flow can also be described as incremental *net income plus depreciation:* $\text{CFAT} = (\Delta R - \Delta E - \Delta D)(1 - T) + \Delta D$.

- A project's non-operating cash flows, nonregular cash flows during its life, must be included.

- A project's net salvage value includes the after-tax cash flow from the sale of assets, all cleanup and removal expenses, and any release of net working capital. Net salvage value $= S - T(S - B) - (1 - T)\text{REX} + \Delta W$.

- Be sure to include the effects of all economic dependencies that cause erosion or enhancement in the value of existing or other potential projects.

- Be sure to use the *current* tax laws to determine after-tax cash flows.

- For tax and capital budgeting purposes, a company should use the depreciation method that provides the largest present value of depreciation tax credits.

- The modified accelerated cost recovery system, MACRS, is required under current tax laws. Corporations usually use straight-line depreciation for financial reporting. In the text, we frequently use straight-line depreciation to simplify the calculations.

- Include the effect of inflation by representing all cash flows and discount rates for a decision on a consistent basis—in either real *or* nominal terms.

- The nominal discount rate depends on the real rate and the expected inflation rate: $r_n = r_r + i + ir_r$.

- Because present value is a function of both cash flow and required return, in many cases inflation doesn't have a significant effect on the decision, although it can increase the complexity of calculations.
- When an investment is part of a replacement cycle, the correct method for evaluating alternative investments is the Equivalent Annual Cost (EAC) or the Equivalent Annual Annuity (EAA).

EQUATION SUMMARY

(9.1) $\qquad$ Net cash flow for initial investment $= -I - \Delta W + S - T(S - B)$

(9.2) $\qquad$ $\text{CFAT} = (\Delta R - \Delta E)(1 - T) + T\Delta D$

(9.3) $\qquad$ $\text{CFAT} = (\Delta R - \Delta E - \Delta D)(1 - T) + \Delta D$

(9.4) $\qquad$ Net salvage value $= S - T(S - B) - (1 - T)\text{REX} + \Delta W$

(9.5) $\qquad$ $r_n = r_r + i + ir_r$

(9.6) $\qquad$ $\text{EAC} = \dfrac{\text{TC}}{\text{PVAF}_{r,n}} = \text{TC}\left[\dfrac{r(1 + r)^n}{(1 + r)^n - 1}\right]$

CHAPTER REVIEW ACTIVITIES

SELF-TEST PROBLEMS

1. (Cash flows and NPV for a new project) Syracuse Roadbuilding Company is considering the purchase of a new tandem box dump truck. The truck costs $95,000, and an additional $5000 is needed to paint it with the company logo and install radio equipment. Assume the truck falls into the MACRS 3-year class. The truck will generate no additional revenues, but it will reduce cash operating expenses by $35,000 per year. The truck will be sold for $40,000 after its 5-year life. An inventory investment of $4000 is required during the life of the investment. Syracuse Roadbuilding is in the 45% income tax bracket.

   a. What is the net investment?

   b. What is the after-tax operating net cash flow for each of the 5 years?

   c. What is the after-tax salvage value?

   d. Assuming a 10% cost of capital, what is the net present value of this investment?

2. (Cash flows and NPV for a replacement decision) Andrew Thompson Interests (ATI) is using a mechanical switching system that it bought 5 years ago for $400,000. This mechanical system is being depreciated straight-line to an estimated salvage value of zero over a 10-year life. Thus, the annual depreciation charge is $40,000 and current book value is $200,000. At the end of its life, the actual salvage value is expected to be $25,000. If ATI sold this equipment today, it would fetch $100,000.

   ATI is evaluating a new digital switching system that will cost $500,000. The digital system is depreciated straight-line to a zero salvage value over a 5-year life. At the end of the 5 years, ATI expects to sell the system for $150,000. The new digital system should have a favorable impact on operating cash flows, increasing revenues by $100,000 annually and decreasing cash operating expenses by $50,000 annually. The new equipment has no effect on the investment in working capital.

   Andrew Thompson Interests is in the 40% tax bracket and has a 12% cost of capital. Consider each of the following questions, assuming that ATI sells the old mechanical switching system and replaces it with the new digital system.

   a. What is the net investment?

   b. What is the after-tax operating net cash flow for each of the 5 years?

   c. What is the after-tax salvage value?

   d. What is the net present value of this investment?

3. (Replacement cycle) Barry Marks is looking for the optimal replacement cycle for his company's towmotors. New towmotors cost $70,000 each. Their resale value, like that of new cars, drops rapidly at first and then declines more slowly. However, annual operating costs increase with age.

Barry has carefully assessed these factors and boiled down the cash flows from various replacement cycles to those given below. The data are in $thousands. The operating costs are after taxes and after the effect of the depreciation tax shield. The salvage value is also after taxes. The cost of capital is 10%. What is the equivalent annual cost (EAC) for replacing the towmotors after every 1, 2, 3, or 4 years?

Year	1	2	3	4
Operating costs each year after purchase	20	30	40	50
Salvage value if held for this time period	45	30	25	20

SOLUTIONS TO SELF-TEST PROBLEMS

1. a. The net investment is the cash paid for the new truck, plus setup costs, plus the investment in working capital: Net investment = 95,000 + 5000 + 4000 = $104,000. Of the total net investment, $100,000 will be depreciated, and the $4000 investment in working capital will be reversed at the end of the project.

   b. The annual net cash flow is found with this equation: $CFAT = (\Delta R - \Delta E - \Delta D)(1 - T) + \Delta D$. The increase in revenues each year is zero, the increase in cash operating expenses is –$35,000 each year, and the depreciation each year is the MACRS depreciation percentage for 3-year property times the $100,000 depreciable basis of the investment. The depreciation percentages are in table 9.9.

	Year 1	Year 2	Year 3	Year 4	Year 5
ΔR	$ 0	$ 0	$ 0	$ 0	$ 0
ΔE	−35,000	−35,000	−35,000	−35,000	−35,000
ΔD	33,330	44,450	14,810	7,410	0
$(\Delta R - \Delta E - \Delta D)$	1,670	− 9,450	20,190	27,590	35,000
$(1 - T)$	0.60	0.60	0.60	0.60	0.60
$(\Delta R - \Delta E - \Delta D)(1 - T)$	1,002	− 5,670	12,114	16,554	21,000
$(\Delta R - \Delta E - \Delta D)(1 - T) + \Delta D$	34,332	38,780	26,924	23,964	21,000

   c. When the truck is sold for $40,000, its book value is zero, so this entire amount is taxable. Thus, the after-tax salvage value for the truck is $40,000(1 − 0.4) = $24,000. In addition, the investment in inventory will be liquidated for an additional $4000, or a total after-tax salvage value of $28,000.

   d. The net present value is found by discounting and then summing the present values of the project's after-tax net cash flows:

Year	Cash flow type	Cash flow	Present value @ 10%
0	Net investment	−$104,000	−$104,000.00
1	CFAT	34,332	31,210.91
2	CFAT	38,780	32,049.59
3	CFAT	26,924	20,228.40
4	CFAT	23,964	16,367.73
5	CFAT	21,000	13,039.35
5	After-tax salvage	28,000	17,385.80
	Net Present Value		$ 26,281.78

The future cash flows have a total present value of $130,281.77. When this is reduced by the $104,000 investment, the NPV is $26,281.77.

2. a. Net cash flow for initial investment = $-I - \Delta W + S - T(S - B)$ = −$360,000
   (1) Cash paid for new capital assets = $-I$ = −500,000
   (2) Increase in net working capital = $-\Delta W$ = 0
   (3) Cash received on sale of old equipment = S = 100,000
   (4) Tax paid (saved) on sale of old equipment = $-T(S - B)$ = 40,000
                                          −$360,000

   Except for the tax paid (saved), most of these are straightforward. The company incurs a tax loss of $100,000 when it sells the old equipment (the selling price S = $100,000 minus the current book value B = $200,000). This tax saving is the tax rate times the tax loss, 0.40(100,000) = $40,000.

b. The annual operating cash flows are found by taking the cash flows *with* the new investment minus the cash flows *without* the new investment: $\Delta R = +100{,}000$; $\Delta E = -50{,}000$; $\Delta D = 100{,}000 - 40{,}000 = 60{,}000$. The cash flow after taxes is found with either equation (9.2) or (9.3): $\text{CFAT} = (\Delta R - \Delta E)(1 - T) + T\Delta D = [100{,}000 - (-50{,}000)](1 - 0.40) + 0.40(60{,}000) = 90{,}000 + 24{,}000 = 114{,}000$. The operating revenues and cash expenses, after taxes, are \$90,000. Add back the depreciation tax shield of \$24,000, and the CFAT is \$114,000 per year. The CFAT is the same for all 5 years.

The other form in which CFAT is commonly expressed is: $\text{CFAT} = \text{Net income} + \text{depreciation} = (\Delta R - \Delta E - \Delta D)(1 - T) + \Delta D = [100{,}000 - (-50{,}000) - 60{,}000](1 - 0.40) + 60{,}000 = 54{,}000 + 60{,}000 = \$114{,}000$.

c. The net salvage value is the salvage value of the digital system minus the salvage value for the mechanical system (the new minus the original): Net salvage value $= S - T(S - B) - (1 - T)\text{REX} + \Delta W = \$75{,}000$:

(1) Cash received on sale of old equipment $= S = 150{,}000 - 25{,}000$ $= \$125{,}000$
(2) Tax paid (saved) on sale of old equipment $= -T(S - B) = -0.40(150{,}000 - 25{,}000) = -50{,}000$
(3) After-tax cleanup and removal expenses $= -(1 - T)\text{REX} = -(1 - 0.40)0$ $= 0$
(4) Release of investment in working capital $= \Delta W$ $= \underline{\quad 0\quad}$
     $\$75{,}000$

The differential salvage before taxes is \$125,000. After paying net additional taxes of \$50,000 on the taxable gain of salvage over book value, the net salvage value is a positive cash flow of \$75,000.

d. The cash flows are an outlay of \$360,000, an annuity of \$114,000 annually for 5 years, and a salvage value of \$75,000 in 5 years. The present value of these cash flows discounted at 12% is:

Time	Cash flow type	Cash flow	PV @ 12%
0	Initial investment	−360,000	−\$360,000.00
1–5	CFAT	114,000	410,944.49
5	Net salvage value	75,000	42,557.01
	Net present value =		\$ 93,501.50

Since the NPV > 0, it is profitable to replace the old system with the new one.

3. For annual replacement, a 1-year cycle, the present value of future costs is

$$TC = 70{,}000 + \frac{20{,}000 - 45{,}000}{(1.10)^1} = \$47{,}273$$

and the EAC is \$52,000.30.

$$N = 1 \quad r = 10 \quad PV = 47{,}273 \quad \textbf{PMT} = \textbf{52,000.30} \quad FV = 0$$

For a 2-year replacement cycle, the present value of future costs is

$$TC = 70{,}000 + \frac{20{,}000}{(1.10)^1} + \frac{30{,}000 - 30{,}000}{(1.10)^2} = \$88{,}181.81$$

and the EAC is \$50,809.52.

$$N = 2 \quad r = 10 \quad PV = 88{,}181.81 \quad \textbf{PMT} = \textbf{50,809.52} \quad FV = 0$$

For a 3-year replacement cycle the present value of future costs is

$$TC = 70{,}000 + \frac{20{,}000}{(1.10)^1} + \frac{30{,}000}{(1.10)^2} + \frac{40{,}000 - 25{,}000}{(1.10)^3} = \$124{,}245$$

and the EAC is \$49,960.70.

$$N = 3 \quad r = 10 \quad PV = 124{,}245 \quad \textbf{PMT} = \textbf{49,960.70} \quad FV = 0$$

Finally, for replacement every 4 years, the present value of future costs is

$$TC = 70,000 + \frac{20,000}{(1.10)^1} + \frac{30,000}{(1.10)^2} + \frac{40,000}{(1.10)^3} + \frac{50,000 - 20,000}{(1.10)^4} = \$163,518$$

and the EAC is $51,585.15.

N = 4 r = 10 PV = 163,518 **PMT = 51,585.15** FV = 0		

The 3-year replacement cycle is the most economical.

QUESTIONS

1. Choose one of each of the bracketed terms that correctly states a concept used in assembling project cash flows.

    The costs and benefits should be measured in terms of [cash flow/net income].

    Cash flows are measured on an [incremental/total] basis.

    Future cash flows are measured on a [before-tax/after-tax] basis.

    Financing costs are [ignored/included].

2. Explain the basic cash flows that are included in the net cash flow for the initial investment.

3. Why is it important to recognize and exclude sunk costs from a capital budgeting analysis?

4. Describe the calculation of the net operating cash flow as operating cash flows after tax plus the depreciation tax shield. Describe the calculation of the net operating cash flow as net income plus depreciation.

5. What are two types of non-operating cash flows that can occur during a project's life?

6. Explain the calculation of a project's net salvage value.

7. How are financing charges normally accounted for in a capital budgeting analysis?

8. Why is a change in net working capital an important and necessary part of the incremental cost of a capital budgeting project?

9. What is the relationship between the nominal return, the real return, and the rate of inflation?

10. Why are *current* tax laws very important to the proper evaluation of a capital budgeting project?

11. Explain the concept of an equivalent annual cost in your own words.

12. Suppose that you invested $10,000 in an asset that is depreciated as 5-year property under the modified accelerated cost recovery system. Explain how you would calculate the investment's depreciation charges.

13. Define the terms *erosion* and *enhancement* as they relate to the company's capital investment decisions.

CHALLENGING QUESTIONS

14. Phyllis believes that the company should use straight-line depreciation for a capital project because it results in higher net income during the early years of the project's life. Joanna believes that the company should use the modified accelerated cost recovery system depreciation because it reduces the tax liability during the early years of the project's life. Assuming you had a choice between depreciation methods, whose advice should you follow? Why?

15. From one point of view, inflation does not create a problem in the evaluation of a capital budgeting project. From another point of view, inflation creates tremendous problems in the evaluation of a capital budgeting project. What are these two points of view?

PROBLEM SET A

A1. (Net income and net cash flows) Julie Stansfield has a bicycle rental shop with annual revenues of $200,000. Cash operating expenses for rent, labor, and utilities are $70,000. Depreciation is $40,000. Julie's tax rate is 40%.

    a. What should be Julie's net income?   b. What is her net cash flow?

A2. (Net income and net cash flows) Annual revenues are $100, cash operating expenses are $40, depreciation is $10, and the tax rate is 40%.

a. What is net income?   b. What is the net cash flow?

A3. (MACRS depreciation) Modigliani Jet Ski Company has purchased several company cars for a total of $150,000. They are classed as 5-year property.

a. What is the annual depreciation charge for these assets?

b. If Modigliani's marginal tax rate is 40%, what is the annual depreciation tax shield?

c. Discounted at 8%, what is the present value of the depreciation tax shield?

A4. (MACRS depreciation) Modigliani Jet Ski Company also purchased some special tools for a total of $150,000. The tools are classed as 3-year property.

a. What is the annual depreciation charge for these assets?

b. If Modigliani's marginal tax rate is 40%, what is the annual depreciation tax shield?

c. Discounted at 8%, what is the present value of the depreciation tax shield?

A5. (Capitalizing versus expensing) Suppose the Caltron Corporation is going to purchase an asset that costs $500,000. Caltron's marginal tax rate is 35%. How does the pattern of expenses recognized for tax purposes differ between (1) capitalizing the asset on a straight-line basis over 5 years and (2) expensing the $500,000 right now?

A6. (Net investment outlay) You purchase a new machine for $100. You pay an additional $30 for freight and setup costs. The old machine that is being replaced has a book value of $10 and can be sold for $20. An investment of $40 in working capital is also required. The marginal tax rate is 30%. What is the net investment outlay?

A7. (Net investment outlay) The cost of a new machine is $70,000 plus an additional $8000 for freight and setup costs. The old machine that is being replaced has a book value of $15,000 and can be sold for $7000. An investment of $15,000 in working capital is also required. The marginal tax rate is 30%. What is the net investment outlay?

A8. (Cash flows after tax) Assume that revenues increase by $400,000, cash operating expenses increase by $180,000, and depreciation increases by $45,000. The tax rate is 34%.

a. Calculate the cash flow after tax using the formula that the CFAT is operating cash flows after taxes plus the depreciation tax shield.

b. Calculate the cash flow after tax using the formula that the CFAT is net income plus depreciation.

c. Should the answers to **a** and **b** be the same?

A9. (Cash flows after tax) Revenues increase by $16,000, cash operating expenses increase by $6000, and depreciation increases by $2000. The tax rate is 45%.

a. Calculate the cash flow after tax using the formula that the CFAT is operating cash flows after taxes plus the depreciation tax shield.

b. Calculate the cash flow after tax using the formula that the CFAT is net income plus depreciation.

c. Should the answers to **a** and **b** be the same?

A10. (Salvage value) Zydeco Shrimping is selling off one of its boats. The boat has been depreciated to a $100,000 book value and can be sold for $150,000. Net working capital of $20,000 can be liquidated. Zydeco will have before-tax cleanup and removal expenses at their dock of $5000. If Zydeco is in the 40% tax bracket, what is the net salvage value?

A11. (Salvage value) Booth Broadcasting is decommissioning one of its Southwestern radio stations at the end of its economic life. The equipment and building have been depreciated to zero and the land has a $400,000 book value. Working capital of $200,000 can be liquidated. Booth has before-tax cleanup and removal expenses of $100,000. Booth is selling the property to an Australian investor for $1,500,000. If Booth Broadcasting is in the 45% tax bracket, what is the net salvage value?

A12. (Investment in working capital) Nelson Store's expansion plans are expected to increase its inventories by $30 million. Nelson will also increase its accounts receivable by $15 million and its accounts payable by $8 million. What investment in net working capital is required?

A13. (Nominal and real discount rates) The real required return is 8% and the inflation rate is 5%.

a. What is the nominal required return if you add the two rates and ignore the cross-term?

b. What is the nominal required return including the cross-term?

A14. (Nominal and real discount rates) The nominal and real discount rates are 18% and 8%.
    a. What is the expected inflation rate (ignoring the cross-term)?
    b. What is the expected inflation rate (including the effect of the cross-term)?

A15. (EAC) The total present value of all costs associated with an asset over a 7-year life is $73,285. If the asset has a cost of capital of 11%, what is the EAC of using this asset?

A16. (EAC) A machine that costs $10,000 new can be replaced after being used from 4 to 7 years. Annual maintenance costs are identical for all possible replacement cycles. The machine has a cost of capital of 12%. The alternative net salvage values at the end of 4 to 7 years of use are, respectively, $3800, $2800, $1000, −$1000. Ignoring taxes and inflation, what is the optimal replacement cycle?

PROBLEM SET B

B1. (Capitalizing versus expensing) Bey Travel Agency is a small company owned by David Bey that has just purchased $20,000 worth of computer upgrades. Under current tax laws, Bey has a choice of expensing or depreciating a small investment such as this. Bey's marginal tax rate is 40%.
    a. What is the present value of the depreciation tax shield if the computers are depreciated straight-line over the next 5 years? The cost of capital is 10%.
    b. What is the present value of the tax saving if the computers are expensed immediately?
    c. Would you recommend that Bey expense or capitalize this investment?

B2. (Incremental cash flows and NPV) The Canton Sundae Corporation is considering the replacement of an existing machine. The new machine, called an X-tender, would provide better sundaes, but it costs $120,000. The X-tender requires $20,000 in setup costs that are expensed immediately and $20,000 in additional working capital. The X-tender's useful life is 10 years, after which it can be sold for a salvage value of $40,000. Canton uses straight-line depreciation, and the machine will be depreciated to a book value of zero on a 6-year basis. Canton has a tax rate of 45% and a 16% cost of capital on projects like this one. The X-tender is expected to increase revenues minus expenses by $35,000 per year. What is the NPV of buying the X-tender?

B3. (Replacement frequency) In the section on replacement frequency in this chapter, the example considered Hoover's inventory equipment. Suppose that machine A could be used for a seventh year if $18,000 is spent for maintenance at the end of year 6. This is in addition to $1000 necessary at the end of year 5 to use the machine a sixth year. The net salvage value will be zero. What is the EAC for a 7-year replacement cycle?

B4. (Incremental cash flows and NPV) Let's say Johnson & Johnson currently has a machine that has 5 years of useful life remaining. Its current net book value is $50,000, and it is being straight-line depreciated to its expected zero salvage value in 5 years. It generates $60,000 per year in sales revenue, requiring $30,000 in operating expenses, excluding depreciation. If the firm sells the machine now, it could get $30,000 for it. The firm is considering buying a new machine to replace this one. The new machine will have a useful life of 5 years and a salvage value of $5000. It costs $65,000. It is expected to generate $70,000 in sales revenue and require $25,000 in operating expenses annually, excluding depreciation. The project's cost of capital is 10%, the firm uses straight-line depreciation, and the relevant tax rate is 40%. Compute the NPV from replacing the old machine.

B5. (Capitalizing versus expensing) Suppose Hydrex can either expense or capitalize an asset it has just purchased for $9000. If it capitalizes the asset, it will depreciate the asset to a book value of zero on a straight-line basis over 3 years. Hydrex has a marginal tax rate of 38%, and the cost of capital for this asset is 12%. What is the present-value difference to Hydrex between expensing and capitalizing the asset? Assume Hydrex will have sufficient income over the next 3 years to use all possible tax credits.

B6. (Inflation) A project's initial investment is $40,000, and it has a 5-year life. At the end of the fifth year, the equipment is expected to be sold for $12,000, at which time its net book value will be

$5000. The CFATs (including inflation and net salvage value) for the next 5 years are expected to be $20,000, $25,000, $10,000, $10,000, and $10,000. In real terms, the project's cost of capital is 10%, and the riskless return is 7%. The tax rate is 46%, and the inflation rate is 3%. What is the project's NPV?

B7. (Incremental cash flows and NPV) A new product called AW-SUM is being considered by Egg Streams, Unlimited. An outlay of $16 million is required for equipment to produce the new product, and additional net working capital in the amount of $3.2 million is also required. The project is expected to have an 8-year life and the equipment will be depreciated on a straight-line basis to a zero book value over 8 years. Although the equipment will be depreciated to a zero book value, it is expected to have a salvage value of $2 million. Revenues minus expenses for the project are expected to be $5 million per year. The project's cost of capital is 16%, and the relevant tax rate is 35%. Compute the NPV of the AW-SUM project.

B8. (Taxes and NPV) Depreciation provides a sort of shield against taxes. If there were no taxes, there would be no depreciation tax shields.

a. Does this mean that the NPV of the AW-SUM project in problem B7 would be less if there were no taxes?

b. Compute the NPV of the AW-SUM project in problem B7, assuming a tax rate of 0% and cost of capital of 16%.

B9. (Taxes) The investment is $1,000,000, which is depreciated straight-line to a zero salvage value over a 10-year life. The asset will be worthless in 10 years. The project will generate, annually, revenues of $800,000, cash operating expenses of $500,000, and depreciation of $100,000. The tax rate is 30% and the cost of capital is 10%.

a. What is the annual cash flow and NPV?

b. What would be the annual cash flow and NPV if the tax rate were 0%?

c. What tax rate would result in a zero NPV?

B10. (Investment in net working capital) You are reviewing the project analysis submitted by one of your staff analysts. You find the analysis to be correct except that the analyst ignored the effects of changes in net working capital. You expect an increase in net working capital of $400,000 at time 0, another increase of $400,000 in 1 year, a decrease of $200,000 in 5 years, and a liquidation of remaining working capital at the end of 10 years. If the analyst had calculated an NPV of $360,000, what should be the project's NPV including the effect of changes in net working capital? The cost of capital is 10%.

B11. (Analysis of cash flows) Corpus Christi Partners has evaluated a major expansion that had a positive NPV of $4,500,000. Joe Whitman believes that if the Partners invest an additional $500,000 in net working capital, the annual revenues would be increased by $140,000 per year and the annual cash operating expenses would be increased by $40,000 per year. These changes would persist over the 10-year life of the project. The investment in net working capital would not affect depreciation schedules and would be reversed at the end of 10 years. Corpus Christi Partners is in the 30% tax bracket and has a 10% cost of capital.

a. Assuming that Joe's estimates are correct, what is the outlay, annual net cash flow, and after-tax salvage value?

b. What is the net present value of the additional investment in net working capital?

c. What is the total NPV of the project including the additional investment in working capital?

B12. (NPV and product pricing) You are bidding on a contract to supply 10,000 Lat Blasters per year for 5 years. The cash expenses are $200 per Lat Blaster, or $2,000,000 per year. This contract would require an investment of $5,000,000, which would be depreciated straight-line over the 5-year life of the project. The salvage value will be zero. Your marginal tax rate is 40% and cost of capital is 10%. Your annual revenue is the price per Lat Blaster times 10,000 units per year. What minimum annual revenue and what price per Lat Blaster is required to produce a zero net present value?

B13. (Solving for an unknown salvage value) Wendy Guo is investing $800,000 in a property that will generate fairly low profits for 2 years, at which time she plans to sell the project. The profitability of her investment hinges on the selling price. For the 2 years while she owns the project, annual revenues of $80,000, cash expenses of $30,000, and depreciation of $30,000 are expected. Wendy's tax rate is 40% and her cost of capital is 12%. What minimum selling price for the property is needed for Wendy to make a profit (have a zero NPV)? Do not forget the taxes that Wendy must pay if she sells the property for more than book value.

B14. (EAC) Y. B. Blue Corporation is considering two alternative machines. Machine A will cost $50,000, have expenses (excluding depreciation) of $34,000 per year, and have a useful life of 6 years. Machine B will cost $70,000, have expenses (excluding depreciation) of $26,000 per year, and have a useful life of 5 years. Y. B. uses straight-line depreciation and pays taxes at the rate of 35%. The project's cost of capital is 13%. Net salvage value is zero for each machine at the end of its useful life. Assuming the project for which the machine will be used is profitable, which machine should be purchased?

B15. (EAC) Billy Bob's Big Eat'n Place has decided to purchase a new cornhusker. Billy Bob will buy one of two machines. Both machines cost $1500. Machine A has a 4-year life, a salvage value of $1000, and expenses of $475 per year. Machine B has a 5-year life, a salvage value of $500, and expenses of $460 per year. Whichever machine is used, revenues for this project are $1200 per year, and machines will be replaced at the end of their lives. Using straight-line depreciation to the salvage value, a tax rate of 35%, and a cost of capital of 20%, which machine should Billy Bob buy, and why?

PROBLEM SET C

C1. (Inflation) Letter-Fly, Unlimited, a conglomerate corporation with investments in overnight mail service and skeet-shooting franchises, is contemplating a 5-year investment project that requires an initial investment of $200,000 for equipment (depreciated over 5 years on a straight-line basis to a zero salvage value). The project also requires $25,000 in additional net working capital and is expected to have a salvage value of zero. The revenues from the project are expected to be $100,000 in the first year and to grow with inflation at 3.5% per year over the life of the project. Expenses are expected to be $25,000 in the first year and to grow at a different inflation rate of 6% per year. The general level of inflation for the economy is expected to be 5% per year. If the required return on this project in real terms is 8% and taxes are paid at the rate of 32%, should Letter-Fly undertake the investment project?

C2. (Replacement cycles) Suppose Federal Express is considering which of two delivery trucks to purchase. The German model will cost $75,000, will have expenses (excluding depreciation) of $250,000 per year, and will have a useful life of 3 years. The Japanese model will cost $100,000, will have expenses (excluding depreciation) of $240,000 per year, and will have a useful life of 4 years. Suppose Federal Express uses straight-line depreciation to a zero book value and pays taxes at a 40% rate. The cost of capital for the project is 12%. The salvage values are $15,000 for the German model and $12,000 for the Japanese model. Which model of delivery truck should Federal Express purchase?

C3. (Replacement cycles) Suppose Federal Express in Problem C2 could refit either model of delivery truck at the end of its estimated useful life. An expenditure of $5000 would extend either truck's useful life by 1 year. Operating expenses would be $10,000 higher in the extra year for either truck. Alternatively, spending $10,000 would extend either truck's original estimated useful life by 2 years. Operating expenses would be $20,000 per year higher in the extra years under this alternative. The depreciation schedules would remain as given in C2. Estimated salvage values for the 1- and 2-year extensions are, respectively, $12,000 and $10,000 for the German truck, and $10,000 and $8000 for the Japanese truck.

a. What is the optimal replacement cycle for each truck?

b. Which one should Federal Express purchase?

BIBLIOGRAPHY

Angell, Robert J. "Depreciable Basis/ITC Decisions When the ITC Is Deferred," *Financial Management,* 1985, 14(2):43–47.

Bathala, Chenchuramaiah T., and Steven J. Carlson. "Repeal of the Investment Tax Credit and Firms' Investment Spending," *Financial Management,* 1994, 23(1):13.

Cason, Roger L. "Leasing, Asset Lives and Uncertainty: A Practitioner's Comments," *Financial Management,* 1987, 16(2):13–16.

Flannery, Mark J., Joel F. Houston, and Subramanyam Venkataraman. "Financing Multiple Investment Projects," *Financial Management,* 1993, 22(2):161–172.

Gaumnitz, Jack E., and Douglas R. Emery. "Asset Growth, Abandonment Value and the Replacement of Like-for-Like Capital Assets," *Journal of Financial and Quantitative Analysis,* 1980, 15(2):407–419.

Howe, Keith M. "Does Inflationary Change Affect Capital Asset Life?" *Financial Management,* 1987, 16(2):63–67.

Howe, Keith M., and George M. McCabe. "On Optimal Asset Abandonment and Replacement," *Journal of Financial and Quantitative Analysis,* 1983, 18(3):295–305.

Hubbard, Carl M. "Flotation Costs in Capital Budgeting: A Note on the Tax Effect," *Financial Management,* 1984, 13(2):38–40.

Kwan, Clarence C. Y., and Yufei Yuan. "Optimal Sequential Selection in Capital Budgeting: A Shortcut," *Financial Management,* 1988, 17(1):54–59.

Marcus, Alan J. "Depreciation Rules and Rate Shock in Rate of Return Regulation," *Financial Management,* 1986, 15(4):61–68.

McCarty, Daniel E., and William R. McDaniel. "A Note on Expensing versus Depreciating Under the Accelerated Cost Recovery System: Comment," *Financial Management,* 1983, 12(2):37–39.

Mehta, Dileep R., Michael D. Curley, and Hung-Gay Fung. "Inflation, Cost of Capital, and Capital Budgeting Procedures," *Financial Management,* 1984, 13(4):48–54.

Pohlman, Randolph A., Emmanuel S. Santiago, and F. Lynn Markel. "Cash Flow Estimation Practices of Large Firms," *Financial Management,* 1988, 17(2):71–79.

Prezas, Alexandros P. "Effects of Depreciation and Corporate Taxes on Asset Life under Debt-Equity Financing," *Financial Management,* 1992, 21(2):24–30.

Pruitt, Stephen W., and Lawrence J. Gitman. "Capital Budgeting Forecast Biases: Evidence from the Fortune 500," *Financial Management,* 1987, 16(1):46–51.

Rappaport, A., and R. A. Taggart, Jr. "Evaluation of Capital Expenditure Proposals under Inflation," *Financial Management,* 1982, 11(1):5–13.

Sick, Gordon A. "A Certainty-Equivalent Approach to Capital Budgeting," *Financial Management,* 1986, 15(4):23–32.

Statman, Meir, and Tyzoon T. Tyebjee. "Optimistic Capital Budgeting Forecasts: An Experiment," *Financial Management,* 1985, 14(3):27–33.

Vogt, Stephen C. "The Cash Flow/Investment Relationship: Evidence from U.S. Manufacturing Firms," *Financial Management,* 1994, 23(2):3–20.

CAPITAL BUDGETING IN PRACTICE

OBJECTIVES

1. Describe the critical role of capital budgeting options, and the opportunity costs they can create, in properly valuing capital budgeting projects. Such options include price-setting options, future investment options, abandonment options, and postponement options.

2. Explain the pitfalls of "hard" capital rationing, and cite the benefits of "soft" capital rationing as a tool for planning and controlling a company's capital budget.

3. Describe the practice of capital budgeting, including important practical considerations that are difficult to quantify, such as the role of managerial responsibility and incentives.

4. Explain why a set of simple mechanical rules cannot consistently win out in complex and competitive business situations.

5. Recognize project interactions and capital budgeting options and apply the principles of finance to capital budgeting decisions.

The capital budgeting principles and techniques we've learned so far provide an excellent framework. However, we don't want you to think that capital budgeting decisions are mechanical and straightforward. Practical realities introduce complexities that can make capital budgeting decision making intellectually challenging.

For example, the principle that options are valuable is straightforward, but applying it in valuing a capital budgeting project can be challenging. Similarly, opportunity costs play a very important role in determining the value of a project, but first we have to identify them. This chapter suggests places to look for options and opportunity costs caused by interaction among existing operations and new projects.

Another kind of interaction among projects comes from *capital rationing*. Capital rationing places limits on what a company spends, such as placing a cap on the amount available to spend on projects this year. On the one hand, such limits can seem bad, because they might eliminate positive-NPV projects. On the other hand, there are good reasons for such limits, and what is called *"soft" capital rationing* can be a practical tool for planning and coordinating a company's capital budget. Controlling managerial responsibility and incentives are two other useful tools for managing a company's capital budgeting decisions.

The chapter ends with a discussion of additional practical considerations in the capital budgeting process. We examine several factors that can be subtle and difficult to deal with in practice. Finally, we provide an overview, with practical reminders of the importance of the principles of finance.

CAPITAL BUDGETING AND THE PRINCIPLES OF FINANCE

◆ *Options:* Recognize the value of options, such as the options to expand, postpone, or abandon a capital budgeting project.

◆ *Two-Sided Transactions:* Consider why the other party to a transaction is willing to participate.

◆ *Signaling:* Consider the actions and products of competitors.

◆ *Valuable Ideas:* Look for new ideas to use as a basis for capital budgeting projects that will create value.

◆ *Comparative Advantage:* Look for capital budgeting projects that use the company's comparative advantage to add value.

◆ *Incremental Benefits:* Identify and estimate a project's incremental expected future cash flows.

◆ *Risk-Return Trade-Off:* Consider the risk of the capital budgeting project when determining the project's cost of capital, its required return.

◆ *Time Value of Money:* Measure the value the capital budgeting project will create—its NPV.

A PROPOSAL FOR CAPACITY EXPANSION: THE PRICE-SETTING OPTION

Remember Rocky Mountain Chemical Corporation's packaging-machine proposal, which we analyzed in chapter 9? Well, let's assume that besides the new packaging-machine proposal, RMC has several other projects under consideration. If undertaken, these projects will be financed with funds from a new bond issue RMC made earlier this month.

One project is an expansion of RMC's production capacity for a consumer product produced at its Colorado plant, a specialty facial soap called Smooooth. This year's sales are running substantially ahead of last year's and are currently just about at the plant capacity of 10 million bars per year. Next year's sales might top 11 million bars if RMC had the capacity to produce that much soap. Furthermore, management estimates that if RMC spent an additional $500,000 per year on advertising in each of the next three years, sales would rise to 12 million bars next year, 13 million the year after, and 14.5 million per year following that for the foreseeable future.

The proposal under consideration is to increase RMC's production capacity for Smooooth soap by 65%. Before-tax initial outlays for the project are expected to total $1.85 million. Of this amount, $50,000 would be an increase in working capital. Capitalized space and equipment costs would be $1.45 million, installation costs that would have to be capitalized would be $250,000, and costs associated with the installation that could be expensed immediately would be $100,000.

This last amount could be expensed immediately because it would stem from the temporary reassignment of current employees.[1] The capitalized expenses would be depreciated to a zero book value on a straight-line basis over eight years. However, the additional facility is expected to be able to produce for ten years if a substantial overhaul of the equipment were done at the end of the sixth year. The overhaul would be expected to cost $200,000 and would be expensed (rather than capitalized) when it is done. Depreciation, therefore, would be $212,500 per year ($= [1.45 + 0.25]/8$) for the first eight years and zero for the last two years of the project. The salvage value of the new equipment (scrap value minus the cost of removal and cleanup) would be zero at the end of the ten years.

The wholesale price for Smooooth is $0.612 per bar, and the variable cost of production is $0.387 per bar. So RMC earns a contribution margin of $0.225 per bar on Smooooth. The additional 4.5 million bars sold in years 3 through 10 would therefore generate an increase of $1,012,500 ($= [0.225]4.5$ million) in revenue minus expenses each year. The increase for years 1 and 2 would be $450,000 and $675,000, respectively. RMC's marginal tax rate is 40%, and the project's required return is 16%. What's the project's NPV?

Table 10.1 shows the NPV calculation for the proposed expansion. Note once again that financing charges don't appear explicitly anywhere in the analysis, even though we know the incremental funds for the project will come from RMC's recent bond issue. The financing opportunity costs are part of the project's required return. The NPV is $342,266. By trial and error, the IRR is found to be about 19.7%, which exceeds the 16% required return. Finally, because the NPV is positive, the profitability index is also positive and equals 1.189 ($= 1 + 342,266/[1,700,000 + 60,000 + 50,000]$).

At this point, it would be easy to say "Let's do it!" However, although the project looks good so far, we've left an important option out of the analysis.

---

[1] Although these employees will be paid anyway, their wages become an opportunity cost if the project is undertaken. This is because the company will lose the work normally done by these employees while they help with the installation process. This phenomenon can also occur with respect to managerial time.

TABLE 10.1

NPV Calculation for Smooooth Production Capacity Expansion

TIME	ITEM	CFBT	CFAT	PV AT 16%
0	Capitalized installation and equipment cost	−1,700,000 $-I$	−1,700,000 $-I$	−1,700,000
0	Expensed installation cost	−100,000	−60,000 Included in I	−60,000
0	Change in net working capital	−50,000 $-\Delta W$	−50,000 $-\Delta W$	−50,000
1–3	Additional advertising expense	−500,000/yr $-\Delta E$	−300,000/yr $-(1-T)\Delta E$	−673,767
1–8	Depreciation	0	85,000/yr TD	369,205
1	Change in revenues minus expenses	450,000/yr $\Delta R - \Delta E$	270,000/yr $(1-T)(\Delta R - \Delta E)$	232,759
2	Change in revenues minus expenses	675,000/yr $\Delta R - \Delta E$	405,000/yr $(1-T)(\Delta R - \Delta E)$	300,981
3–10	Change in revenues minus expenses	1,012,500/yr $\Delta R - \Delta E$	607,500/yr $(1-T)(\Delta R - \Delta E)$	1,961,007
6	Overhaul expense	−200,000 $-\Delta E$	−120,000 $-(1-T)\Delta E$	−49,253
10	Return of net working capital	50,000 ΔW	50,000 ΔW	11,334
				NPV = $342,266

The Price-Setting Option

What we didn't consider in our NPV calculation is the option to raise Smooooth's wholesale price. That option creates a significant opportunity cost.

What if we raised the price less than 2 cents, from $0.612 to $0.629 per bar? If this price increase decreased next year's demand to 10.2 million bars, the current plant's entire capacity of 10 million bars could be sold at the higher price. This would be possible without *any* additional cash outflows!

Based on the sales projections, demand at a wholesale price of $0.629 is expected to exceed 10 million bars per year for the next ten years. With an increase of $0.017 over the current price, RMC would have additional before-tax revenues of $170,000 (= 0.017[10 million]) per year. This translates into an increase in after-tax revenues of $102,000 (= [1 − 0.4]170,000) per year.

As an alternative to the expansion plan, then, RMC could increase its wholesale price and obtain an increase of $102,000 in its annual CFAT—*with no other changes whatsoever in its after-tax cash flows.* You can verify that the present value of $102,000 per year for ten years at 16% is $492,989, which exceeds the $342,266 from the expansion plan. Therefore, although the expansion plan is better than the status quo, the alternative of increasing the price is even better than expansion.

Let's say that, based on extensive marketing research, RMC determines that the demand curve for Smooooth soap is 2.538 million/price^3. RMC can optimize its price setting based on its *current* production capacity. Set the demand equal to the maximum production (10 million bars) and solve for the price, which is $0.633. This is the highest possible price that will produce the desired 10 million in demand.

Of course, estimating a demand curve isn't easy. Many dimensions must be taken into account, such as consumers substituting other products, and the likelihood that a competing product will become available. But in spite of the cost and difficulty of obtaining it, an estimate of the demand curve for a product may be very valuable. In any case, the analysis for a proposed expansion should always include consideration of the price-setting option, and the opportunity costs associated with it.

Another thing to consider is the cost of capital. The required return for RMC's proposed wholesale price change would probably be less than the required return for the capacity expansion proposal. That's because it's a less risky alternative. The company will have committed more fixed costs for plant and equipment if it undertook the expansion. If demand were to decline in the future, the price could be reduced under either alternative to stimulate demand. However, the company's fixed costs would be higher under the expansion alternative. Using a cost of capital that's less than 16% would raise the NPV of the price increase alternative. We discuss the cost of capital in the next chapter.

Flexibility in product pricing is another illustration of the importance of hidden options and demonstrates once again the value of options. Price flexibility is a very valuable tool. Automobile manufacturers have exercised this option, popularizing cash rebates as a form of price reduction to stimulate demand. Similarly, companies should consider price *increases* among their alternative actions. Of course, in some cases, keeping a constant price can have benefits as well.

Self-Check

1. Define the price-setting option and explain why it can be so valuable.

2. Explain why expanding production facilities would involve greater business risk than raising the price of the product.

3. Why might the cost of capital for a proposed price change be less than the cost of capital for a proposed capacity expansion?

CAPITAL BUDGETING OPTIONS

Numerous options can be connected with any investment a company might make. In the expansion example just given, we saw the value of the price-setting option. In chapter 9, we analyzed the replacement decision and noted the options a company has in connection with equipment replacement. If an option is ignored, the company may be incurring an opportunity cost. We must consider the value of all options connected with a capital budgeting project in order to correctly measure the project's NPV.

What are capital budgeting options worth? An option is the right to do something without any obligation to do it. When the option is costless, it simply adds to the project's value. Not all options are costless. Therefore, a project's NPV can be expressed as its "basic" NPV from discounted cash flows (DCF-NPV) *plus* the value of all options associated with the project *minus* any costs connected with getting or maintaining those options:

$$\text{NPV} = \text{DCF-NPV} + \text{Value of options} - \text{Cost of options} \qquad (10.1)$$

Unfortunately, we do not have an option-pricing model for many options, so we cannot readily get the "value of options" to use in equation (10.1). However, it is important to understand that the lack of a convenient option-pricing model does not diminish the importance of an option.

Managerial options have been shown to have substantial value. For example, consider mineral mining operations. A mining company has the option to suspend mining operations during times when the price of the mineral is too low to make extraction profitable. The company can then restart operations whenever mineral prices rise and extraction becomes profitable again. This option substantially increases the value of the mine.

Options are valuable, but there are certain problems associated with combining option values. When a capital budgeting option is exercised, other options are often precluded. In effect, when one option is exercised, other options are eliminated, and simultaneously many costs become sunk costs. Thus, the decision to exercise an option must include the value of all alternative actions in the analysis. Otherwise, a company may incur an opportunity cost by choosing an alternative that wasn't the best.

We will now discuss three other capital budgeting options: (1) future investment opportunities, (2) the abandonment option, and (3) the postponement option.

Future Investment Opportunities

Future investment opportunities are options to identify additional, more valuable investment possibilities in the future that result from a current investment. For example, manufacturing and distributing a product now puts a distribution and marketing network in place. This creates an option to sell additional products, should they be developed from valuable new ideas or a comparative advantage.

FUTURE INVESTMENT OPPORTUNITIES The options to identify additional valuable investment opportunities in the future that result from a current investment.

Money is spent on research and development in the hope of discovering a new idea first. Being first secures the option of developing it into a product, production technique, or service.

Chapter 6 presented a dividend growth method of valuing stock. We found that the most important factor in determining a stock's value is the capital gain component created by reinvesting the company's earnings. In fact, managers often say that the largest part of a project's value comes from its future investment opportunities. Unfortunately, we must emphasize that accurately measuring such future investment opportunities can be a difficult, if not impossible, task.

Future Investment Option for Strickland Accounting

EXAMPLE

Tom Strickland is considering the expansion of his accounting business by opening an office in a nearby small town. Tom has carefully considered the revenues and costs this accounting office might generate and finds that it's unprofitable; the DCF-NPV is −$50,000. However, by investing today, Tom thinks he might have a future option to expand into providing financial services such as personal financial planning and investment advice. It would cost Tom an additional $100,000 in personnel, licensing, and facilities costs to have this option for future growth. Does the growth option make investment now a positive NPV?

If this future opportunity occurs, Tom estimates the present value of this option to be $500,000. There's a 60% chance of this occurring, and a 40% chance that this investment will not be worthwhile. So the expected value of the future investment option is $300,000 (= 0.6[500,000]).

Using equation (10.1), then, the NPV is actually $150,000:

NPV = DCF-NPV + Value of option − Cost of option = −50,000 + 300,000 − 100,000 = $150,000

So the future investment option makes the new accounting office an attractive investment. ■

The Abandonment Option

Another option to consider in capital budgeting is the possibility of stopping a project earlier than originally planned. This is the **abandonment option.** The abandonment value of a project is simply the NPV from terminating the project by selling or scrapping its assets. The decision rule on abandonment is simple. *Abandon only if the abandonment value is greater than the present value of the future cash flows without abandonment.*

ABANDONMENT OPTION The option of terminating an investment earlier than originally planned.

A project's or asset's abandonment value depends on a number of things, but it's higher when there's an active used-equipment market. Generic and widely used brands of tangible assets are more likely to have such markets, as in the case of cars and trucks.

Intangible assets—such as special production processes, patents, and copyrights—are less likely to have organized markets. Therefore, intangible assets usually have higher transaction costs to find buyers and are more difficult to sell than generic, tangible assets. Of course, there are rarely any cleanup or removal costs associated with disposing of an intangible asset. Consequently, highly specialized tangible assets subject to technological obsolescence tend to have even higher transaction costs than intangible assets.[2]

We considered the importance of deciding whether to *continue to develop* an investment project in chapter 8's discussion of the capital budgeting process. This is simply the abandonment option during the development stage of a project. In addition to its importance during development, the abandonment option should be considered periodically after a project is actually under way. It is possible that abandonment of part, or even all, of its operations could have a positive NPV (bearing in mind that sunk costs should be ignored).

EXAMPLE

To Sell or Not to Sell Joe's Diner

Joe's Diner has been operating for about as long as anyone can remember. Pete has run it for the last 18 years since he took it over from his father, Jack. Last month, Pete was approached by a developer about selling the place. Diane, the developer, wouldn't say exactly what she had in mind, except that Pete could move the diner if he wanted to. She was interested only in the land. At the end of their conversation, Diane offered Pete $350,000 for the land.

Pete was confident that this was a fair price—indeed, the most he could hope to get for the place at this time. Pete thought about moving the diner, but he found out that it wasn't feasible to move the physical structure. Also, there was no place he could move into that was close enough to keep the clientele and good name of Joe's Diner. If he sold, he would have no choice but to abandon the business.

Pete gathered the following information to analyze his decision whether to sell the diner: The sale price of $350,000 would provide an after-tax amount of $280,000. The equipment could be sold at auction for about $30,000, on which he would have to pay $5,000 in taxes. The building needed renovation about every 10 years. The before-tax equivalent annual cost (EAC) of this periodic maintenance was $24,000, and the after-tax EAC, including the effect of depreciation, was $18,000. The annual revenues minus expenses from running the diner were $100,000 per year, and Pete paid taxes at the rate of 25% on this amount. Pete determined that his required return is 12%. The one thing Pete almost forgot to include in the analysis was the opportunity cost for his time.

A friend recently offered Pete $35,000 per year, including retirement and other benefits, to come and work for him. Pete figured that it would not be exactly a 40-hour work week, but it would average less than his 55-hour work week in the diner. With the change in income sources, Pete's tax specialist estimated that the $35,000 per year would be taxed at a rate of 20%. Finally, Pete had been planning for quite a while to sell the diner and retire 12 years from now. He estimated that the land would sell for the same price then as now, after adjusting for the effect of inflation.

From this information, and help from a friend who had taken a finance class, Pete created the NPV calculation for abandoning his investment in the diner (table 10.2). Note that the

---

[2]Mainframe computers in the 1970s are an example of such highly specialized equipment subject to technological obsolescence. Many universities were offered mainframe computers as gifts if the university would pay the cost of removal and reinstallation. Several universities made the mistake of accepting such gifts, only to discover that they could have gotten greater computing capability for less money by purchasing a new machine! Corporations were sorry when universities began refusing such gifts, because not only did the corporation then have to pay the removal cost, but in some cases it also lost a significant tax benefit that would accrue from having made a gift to a nonprofit organization.

positive and negative signs are reversed from what they would normally be, because Pete is selling, rather than undertaking, the project.

So the "basic" NPV—the DCF-NPV—of abandonment was positive, $53,494. But in spite of this, Pete turned Diane down. He decided he enjoyed what he was doing more than he would enjoy increasing his wealth by $53,494.

We want to emphasize that this was *not* necessarily an irrational choice on Pete's part. For him, the nonmonetary values he received from owning the diner exceeded $53,494. Pete said he was just relieved that his opportunity cost of staying in the diner wasn't larger, because at some amount, he would have had to sell the diner, because the nonmonetary values wouldn't have been large enough to overcome the opportunity cost.

Postscript: Diane came back 2 years later and offered Pete $600,000 for the diner. He took it! ◼

It is important to understand in the example that Pete needed to have an accurate estimate of the monetary opportunity cost of continuing to own the diner, in order to make a rational decision about whether the nonmonetary values exceeded that cost. The nonmonetary values are not irrelevant, but it is simply more accurate to include them after all other costs that are more easily quantified have been included.

The Postponement Option

We illustrated the price-setting option earlier in the chapter. Another logical option to consider is the **postponement option,** which is the option to postpone, rather than cancel, an expansion alternative. A price increase now, followed by an expansion in production capacity, additional advertising, and perhaps even a price *decrease* later, might be superior to a simple price increase now. Of course, the analysis can become very complex when such additional alternatives are included, because of interactions among the various alternatives.

POSTPONEMENT OPTION The option of postponing a project without eliminating the possibility of undertaking it.

There are many postponement decisions in your personal life. Should you study for an exam now or postpone your studying? Should you try to enter an MBA program now or delay for a period of time? In business, the timing of investments is critical. A profitable investment is sometimes more profitable if it's delayed. Timing decisions are not easy, as the next example reminds us. The example is about a college basketball player considering entering the pro draft before his college eligibility has been completed.

TABLE 10.2
NPV Calculation for Abandoning Joe's Diner

TIME	ITEM	CFBT	CFAT	PV AT 12%
0	Land sale	350,000	280,000	280,000
0	Equipment sale	30,000	25,000	25,000
1–12	EAC-building (saved)	24,000/yr	18,000/yr	
1–12	$\Delta R - \Delta E$ (forgone)	−100,000/yr	−75,000/yr	−179,637
1–12	Wages	35,000/yr	28,000/yr	
12	Land sale (forgone)	−350,000	−280,000	−71,869
				NPV = $53,494

EXAMPLE

Entering the NBA Draft Early

After three years of college ball, Arnell Johnson owns most of his college's offensive records. Arnell is considering declaring himself eligible for the NBA draft and skipping his senior year. If he goes pro now, agents tell him that his likely contract and the rest of his basketball earnings will have a present value of around $10 million. What should Arnell do?

Arnell needs to compare the benefits of going pro now versus the benefits of postponing for a year. If he waits, he might actually get a smaller contract next year. He might be injured. On the other hand, a year of weight lifting and additional basketball experience might result in a substantially better contract.

Many professional prospects weigh the costs and benefits and find that acting now is preferred to postponement. Others choose to postpone. ∎

A Warning About Capital Budgeting Options

In chapter 8, we discussed different decision rules used in making capital budgeting decisions. Often, people in practice talk about the "gut feel," or special expertise, that allows them to say a project should be undertaken even though it doesn't appear to have a positive NPV. Options are frequently at the heart of the matter. It is difficult to quantify their value, so the gut feel approach is often simply to "guesstimate" that the project is profitable and then to go ahead with it. Although the gut feel approach is not entirely wrong, it should be applied very sparingly. Otherwise, the value of one or more vague options can be used to justify undertaking *any* project, no matter how unprofitable it might appear or actually be.

It is best to quantify the additional value for the options that would be necessary to justify the project. Then you can see if that additional value is at all reasonable.

EXAMPLE

Follow-on Markets at Hess, Inc.

Suppose Hess, Inc. has a project with a DCF-NPV of −$1 million, before adding the value of a significant option to the NPV calculation. Therefore, if that option is worth more than $1 million, the project would actually have a positive NPV and should be undertaken.

The option that exists for Hess consists of a 25% chance of having an entry into a new market 5 years from now. The project's required return is 20%. What must be the future value of the follow-on market entry, in order to make the current project's NPV positive?

For the present value of the option to exceed $1 million, the expected future value (5 years from now) must be greater than about $2.5 million (= $[1.2]^5 1,000,000 = 2,488,320$). With a 25% chance of achieving market entry, the future project within the option must then be expected to produce almost $10 million (= $0.25[10] + 0.75[0] = 2.5$ million) in additional NPV (5 years from now) for the current project to have a positive total NPV. This might be possible—but that's a lot of NPV! ∎

Self-Check

1. Why is it important to consider all options connected with a proposed capital budgeting project?

2. What is the relationship between the "basic" NPV of a project, its DCF-NPV, and the value and cost of project-related options?

3. List three capital budgeting options. Describe each one.

4. What is the major pitfall that can result from hidden options?

CAPITAL RATIONING

As the name implies, **capital rationing** limits (rations) the company's capital expenditures. A company can impose such limits in a number of different ways, but two are widely used.

One method is to use a cost of capital that exceeds the project's required return by, for example, 3%. Although this is a form of rationing, the use of a "higher" rate can be subtle, because in many cases it is not explicitly acknowledged. Often, management argues on the basis of conservatism, and a "few points" are added, or the number is "rounded up" when a required return is established. Obviously, the effect of increasing the discount rate is to reduce the calculated NPVs of capital projects. Many projects that had positive NPVs will have negative NPVs at the higher rate and thereby be rationed out of the company's planned capital expenditures.

CAPITAL RATIONING
Placing one or more limits on the amount of new investment undertaken by a company, either by using a higher required return or by setting a maximum on the capital budget.

Rationing Capital with Artificially High Discount Rates

EXAMPLE

Chula Vista Entertainment has five capital budgeting projects that have positive NPVs using a cost of capital that equals the required return. Management wants to raise the cost of capital by three percentage points and invest only in those projects that still have a positive NPV at the higher cost of capital. The projects and their NPVs are shown table 10.3.

Without rationing capital by using a higher cost of capital, all five projects have a positive NPV and the total outlay for the five projects is $4,200,000. When the cost of capital is raised 3%, projects 3 and 5 have negative NPVs and would be rejected. Rejecting these projects reduces the total capital outlay by $1,450,000, to $2,750,000. ■

A second method of capital rationing is to set a maximum on parts of, or the total, capital budget. For example, a company decides that it will invest a maximum of $1.2 million in new projects this year. This second method of capital rationing is the more visible method, because rationing is explicitly acknowledged. However, because of this explicit acknowledgment, it appears to be the more widely used of the two methods.

Capital Rationing with a Budget Constraint

EXAMPLE

Bayless Enterprises has the six projects listed in table 10.4 on page 372. The six projects require a total outlay of $1,550,000 if they are all accepted. Bayless has chosen to invest only $1,000,000, and would like the set of projects from this list that would have the highest total NPV without exceeding this budget.

One way to find the optimal set of projects is to enumerate all possible sets of projects and take the one with the highest total NPV. This can be tedious. As a guide, you can use the

(continued on following page)

TABLE 10.3
Chula Vista's Capital Budgeting Projects

PROJECT	INITIAL OUTLAY	NPV AT COST OF CAPITAL	NPV AT COST OF CAPITAL + 3%
1	$1,000,000	$440,000	$310,000
2	500,000	105,000	50,000
3	750,000	122,000	−40,000
4	1,250,000	210,000	110,000
5	700,000	66,000	−90,000

(Capital Rationing with a Budget Constraint *continued from previous page*)

PI (Profitability Index) to try to find the best projects. Recall that the PI is the project's total present value divided by the initial outlay, or one plus the NPV divided by the initial outlay. The PI s are also shown in table 10.4, along with their PI rank, from best (1) to worst (6).

In lucky cases, the projects with the highest-ranking PIs make up the best set. In this case, however, the optimal set of projects isn't so easy. Projects A, B, C, and E have a total outlay of $900,000 and total NPV of $271,000. Projects C, D, and E have a total outlay of $1,000,000 and total NPV of $291,000. Projects A, D, and E have a total outlay of $950,000 and NPV of $246,000. So the optimal set of projects is C, D, and E. ■

Pitfalls of Capital Rationing

One obvious consequence of using a higher discount rate is that for conventional projects (an outflow followed by one or more inflows), the project's NPV will be understated. Some financial managers are not bothered by this fact, because they like the idea that value is being "conservatively" measured. Likewise, limiting the total amount of money spent on new capital budgeting projects can also be viewed as conservative. This conservatism, however, can create opportunity costs if the company passes up positive-NPV projects.

Unfortunately, management may be eager to incur this opportunity cost because of an agency cost. Enrichment topic C describes the nondiversifiability of human capital. This is the difficulty people have in diversifying their unique capabilities and expertise (human capital). This difficulty causes a divergence of incentives between shareholders and managers over the choice of capital budgeting projects.

Shareholders hold diversified investment portfolios and are concerned only about nondiversifiable risk. But because managers' human capital is not well diversified, managers can be "wiped out" if the company goes bankrupt, so managers are concerned about the company's total risk (diversifiable plus nondiversifiable).

As a result, managers may want to choose projects conservatively so that only projects with a greater margin of safety will be chosen. In this way, managers reduce the likelihood of bankruptcy, the company's total risk, and the likelihood they will lose their jobs. When managers choose projects conservatively to reduce their personal risk, such choices create opportunity costs, which add to the company's agency costs.

Capital Rationing and Capital Market Efficiency

Capital rationing has been widely criticized because of the efficiency of the capital markets, which should make rationing unnecessary. In a perfect capital market, a company could *always* obtain funds needed to undertake a positive-NPV project, because the project would be better than other capital market opportunities. Therefore, given that existing capital markets

TABLE 10.4

Bayless Enterprises's Six Capital Budgeting Projects

PROJECT	OUTLAY	NPV	PV	PI	PI RANK
A	$250,000	$ 75,000	$325,000	1.30	2
B	150,000	30,000	180,000	1.20	5
C	300,000	120,000	420,000	1.40	1
D	500,000	125,000	625,000	1.25	3
E	200,000	46,000	246,000	1.23	4
F	150,000	15,000	165,000	1.10	6

are very efficient, companies should simply obtain whatever additional funds are needed to undertake all positive-NPV projects.

In practice, however, companies regularly ration their capital expenditures. As it turns out, there can be some practical benefits from capital rationing.

Benefits of Capital Rationing

Enrichment topic A identifies three persistent capital market imperfections: tax asymmetries, information asymmetries, and transaction costs. We show here how two of these imperfections, information asymmetries and transaction costs, can make capital rationing beneficial for a company.

To obtain funds from the capital market, a company must convince investors that they can expect to earn at least their required return. However, recall the problem of *adverse selection* from our discussion of the Signaling Principle, where offering something for sale appears to be a negative signal. Adverse selection leads investors to ask, "If this investment is so good, why is the company willing to let me in on it? Why doesn't the company want to keep all of the positive NPV for itself?"

Only the managers know the answer. This creates what is called **asymmetric information** between investors and the company. Asymmetric information is a situation where information is known to some participants but not others. Investors will raise their required return to protect themselves from the risk of being "taken." The higher required return lowers the amount of funds obtained from selling new securities to the outside investors. As a result, the company must have special circumstances to make the sale of new securities attractive.

Two such special circumstances include a "really great" new investment opportunity and a "really bad" set of current operations. The benefits from really great new investment opportunities are obvious, but let's examine the second case. Additional funds can help a troubled company in the following way.

When people learn that a company's current operations are worth less than was previously believed, the market value of the company declines, and investors incur a loss in value. By bringing in new investors prior to such a decline in market value, the new investors will help the existing investors by sharing in the value loss, so the existing investors' loss is smaller than it would have been.

Without going on to explain this idea fully, this brief discussion should help you to appreciate the importance of problems of asymmetric information. Capital rationing can be beneficial because it is a way a company can manage the problems and costs of asymmetric information connected with getting additional financing for new projects.

The direct transaction costs of obtaining additional financing, such as the issuance costs of new bonds, provide another way in which capital rationing can benefit a company. As with asymmetric information considerations in the capital markets, we will look at the impact of transaction costs in depth in later chapters, but we provide some insight into the problem here because it relates to the use of capital rationing.

Simply stated, the cost of obtaining additional financing is a declining function of the amount of new financing. That is, the cost, as a percentage of the amount of new financing, is lower when more funds are obtained. For example, the total flotation costs for $200 million worth of bonds might be only 1% of the value of the new bonds. In contrast, $10 million worth of bonds might have total flotation costs of 6% or more of the value of the bonds.

Let's say a company has a project with a basic NPV that is positive, but insufficient funds to undertake it. If the transaction costs of obtaining the needed funds exceed the project's NPV, the project's true NPV would be negative, and the project is undesirable after all. A capital rationing process can help avoid such situations.[3]

ASYMMETRIC INFORMATION Information that is known to some participants but not others.

---

[3]It might be argued that in such cases, the company wouldn't really be rationing capital. It would simply be measuring the project's NPV more accurately by including all the costs, including those of obtaining the needed financing. As a practical matter, however, the process used would look like capital rationing.

Another market imperfection that can make capital rationing beneficial takes place in the labor, as opposed to the capital, markets. When a company invests, it must have a manager for the project. Existing managers can often manage additional small projects without too much difficulty. However, a large new project may require managerial expertise beyond what the company's existing employees can provide.[4] Although a company may be confident of the high quality of its current employees, it cannot be so confident of being able to hire similar employees off the street.

Many current employees have been extensively trained and have grown into their current positions over time. Others were not promoted because they were less qualified. Again, as between investors and the company's managers, there is an information asymmetry between the company and potential new employees who could be hired so the company could undertake a positive-NPV project. That information asymmetry causes an increase in the transaction costs associated with undertaking the proposed project and decreases the NPV. As with capital market transaction costs, a capital rationing process provides a way to include otherwise ignored costs and measure the project's NPV more accurately.

Capital Rationing, on Balance

Agency costs create pitfalls for the use of capital rationing. But other market imperfections can make capital rationing beneficial. We suspect that both factors contribute to the fact that almost all companies engage in some sort of capital rationing process.

We'll build on this later in the chapter and show how capital rationing can also be beneficial in planning and managing capital expenditures.

Self-Check

1. What is capital rationing?

2. What are two methods companies use to impose capital rationing? Which method is more widely used?

3. Explain how the profitability index can serve as a useful tool for identifying the best projects under capital rationing.

4. What are some of the pitfalls of capital rationing?

5. Explain why capital rationing would be unnecessary in a perfect capital market environment.

6. Are there any practical benefits to capital rationing? Explain.

MANAGING THE COMPANY'S CAPITAL BUDGET

Earlier, we discussed the abandonment option. We noted that replacement decisions often provide natural opportunities for considering abandonment. However, the abandonment option probably should be considered with respect to a company's ongoing operations more frequently and systematically than simply whenever a replacement decision is being considered.

We also said earlier that capital rationing can create opportunity costs if it causes the company to pass up positive-NPV projects. This can be even more significant if forgone projects are more valuable than the company's current operations. This opportunity cost can be controlled by the effective use of the abandonment option. The company can abandon less

---

[4]Of course, new employees may be assigned to current operations to allow existing employees to manage the new operations. Whatever the distribution of assignments, however, the company must hire additional qualified managers.

profitable current operations and use the freed-up funds to increase its (rationed) capital budget and undertake more new positive-NPV projects.

As you can see, there is an important interaction between capital rationing and abandonment. In fact, there are many interactions between capital rationing and the various options of price flexibility and replacing, postponing, accelerating, or abandoning projects. These interactions lead to the idea of a planning horizon, whereby capital rationing can be used as a tool for managing interactions between a company's investment and financing decisions. For example, capital rationing this year can ensure the availability of funds for a project planned to be undertaken next year.

Plans can change for any number of reasons. For example, a competitor can make a project unattractive by changing a price or introducing a new product. Although planning can't guarantee a great outcome, it can improve the expected value of the outcome. Therefore, planning is critical to good financial management.

Capital Rationing as a Planning Tool

Capital rationing can be of two types. **"Hard" capital rationing** refers to how the maximum total expenditure is viewed, implying that under no circumstances can that maximum be exceeded. When a set of projects is particularly attractive, management may decide to exceed its self-imposed capital expenditure limit. In fact, companies often establish a condition called **"soft" capital rationing:** The company sets a target for its total amount of capital expenditures, but depending upon project desirability and the company's condition at the time decisions are actually made, the company may over- or underspend relative to that target.

A company can get a good picture of the trade-offs among alternative projects using *sensitivity analysis,* which entails varying the maximum expenditure limit. For example, a company may find that a small increase in the total expenditure would allow it to undertake the next most desirable project, which management may consider a worthwhile trade-off. Computer software is particularly useful for soft capital rationing and sensitivity analysis. Once the problem has been formulated, the computer can be conveniently used to obtain alternative solutions simply by changing the constraint values.

"HARD" CAPITAL RATIONING Strict capital rationing that allows no circumstances where the constraints can be violated.

"SOFT" CAPITAL RATIONING Capital rationing that allows certain circumstances where the constraints can be violated or even viewed as targets rather than absolute constraints.

Managerial Authority and Responsibility

Good decision making requires cooperation. This holds for capital budgeting as well. Interpersonal relationships can play a key role. Feuds between people and/or divisions hurt the company. People within the same functional area, such as marketing research, obviously must be able to work together successfully. In addition, cooperation among the various decision-making *levels* plays a critical role.

Good capital budgeting decisions also require members of different functional areas to work together successfully. For example, marketing research and finance must exchange information to estimate project cash flows. Procedures that provide authority by area and amount, with a hierarchy of amounts, are designed to minimize problems among individuals, levels, and areas. Unfortunately, although such procedures generally provide a net gain by reducing or eliminating certain kinds of problems, they may create others.

Chapter 8 described a typical budgetary authority system where a manager could approve capital expenditures—but only within certain limits. However, a manager can break up expenditures that exceed the limit into smaller ones that do not require additional approval, spread them out over time, or both. In this way, a manager can undertake a project without having to obtain prior approval from a higher decision-making level.

It may sound extreme, yet cases have been cited where a division of a corporation actually built and equipped a whole new plant using plant expense orders. In one such case, corporate headquarters discovered the new plant only after its managers submitted an expenditure request for a chimney. They had to. They couldn't figure out how to break a key component of the chimney expense into smaller amounts!

The problem illustrated by this example is that the division thought the company needed the new plant but felt that corporate headquarters would turn down the project. In essence, the division thought it knew better than headquarters. The division managers probably felt that corporate-level managers lacked the hands-on viewpoint. They might have been right, but they might just as easily have been wrong. The responsibility for that decision was not theirs. The viewpoint from the division level does not encompass the breadth of the higher level of decision-making authority.

This example illustrates a tremendous breakdown of the system of authority and responsibility. The division's responsibility was to communicate its viewpoint to higher levels. Headquarters had the responsibility of trying to understand that viewpoint, weighing it along with other information, and deciding on the best course of action.

At the other extreme, having top management review all decisions could lead to the absurd case where the CEO has to approve a salesperson's purchase of a new pencil. In essence, budgetary authority is designed to reduce transaction costs. Lowering the level of decision-making authority within a company may reduce the net cost of making decisions, including the opportunity cost of delay when time is critical.

The problems just cited point out the need to balance decision-making authority against transaction costs. In spite of these and other problems that can arise, recall from chapter 8 that multiple layers of decision-making authority provide a monitoring function that can reduce agency costs. The multiple layers and divisions of authority make collusion among employees more difficult, and it is less likely that employees will take self-interested actions at the expense of the shareholders. Therefore, the multiple layers may provide a form of agency cost reduction that also enters into the choice of decision-making authority for each level of the company.

In practice, the procedures outlined in chapters 8 and 9, along with intelligent and honest employees best using their abilities, provide methods of coping with the complexities encountered in practice and generally produce sensible capital budgeting decisions.

Managerial Incentives and Performance Evaluation

Capital rationing can provide additional opportunities for managers to take self-interested behavior, thus increasing the company's agency costs. This points out once again the value of managerial incentives that reduce agency costs.

A typical example of poor incentives is the case where managers are evaluated on the basis of the company's or the division's return on the book value of assets. This rate is often called a return on investment (ROI). Recall that ROI has several different definitions. Thus, the definition for ROI does not have a consistent relationship with NPV. Therefore, it does not measure managerial success in choosing projects that create value.

When managers are evaluated and rewarded for a measure of performance, self-interested behavior leads them to actions that will increase it. Consequently, it is important to choose performance measures that are consistent with the company's goals. Otherwise, you might get exactly what you asked for—even though it was not at all what you wanted!

Post-audits

As we discussed in chapter 8, *post-audit* is a set of procedures for evaluating a capital budgeting decision after the fact. Post-audits are valuable. However, some words of caution are in order, because post-audits can pose practical challenges and must be done carefully. Sometimes the opportunity costs of forgone alternatives and options are simply impossible to measure. Also, as the cliché "hindsight is better than foresight" points out, using hindsight to evaluate foresight is not reasonable. Outcomes can occur that were not even thought possible, let alone predicted. In some cases, as in the following example, identifying and measuring the incremental cash flows that actually resulted from a decision can be impossible.

Kroger's Optical Scanners

Suppose Kroger installed optical scanners in its grocery checkout counters six years ago. The scanners were installed for a variety of reasons. It was argued that they would dramatically improve the store's inventory management by reducing the chance of over- and understocking, reducing the time to take inventory, and reducing the cost of ordering. In addition, the scanners were expected to improve customer service by reducing the time for customers to check out. If Kroger is now interested in determining whether installing the scanners was a good decision, what can be determined from a post-audit?

The current costs of ordering and taking inventory can be compared to such costs before the scanners were installed to measure any savings. Also, it might be possible to establish a cost savings for any reduction in overstocking. However, estimating the incremental revenues associated with a reduction in the number of lost sales, because of being out of stock, would be very difficult at best.

An observed increase in sales could have been caused by many things, such as improved economy-wide conditions. Similarly, connecting the sales level to an improvement in the customer service level is not possible. Although Kroger could survey its customers to measure improvement in customer service, suppose total sales have not increased. We cannot establish what the sales level would have been if the scanners had not been installed. After all, competitors may also have put in scanners, so the store might have experienced a substantial drop in sales had the scanners *not* been installed.

In this case, it's just not possible to measure exactly the incremental cash inflows that were generated by installing the optical scanners. At this point, only the financial condition of the entire store can be meaningfully established. ∎

In spite of the problems of evaluating a decision after the fact, post-audits made up of sensible evaluation procedures can be useful and are often undertaken in practice. One valuable and typical procedure is to evaluate some or all of the expected future cash flow estimates. This process is often aimed more at improving the analysts' ability to forecast expected future cash flows on current and future projects than simply evaluating the analyst's performance. Some analysts have relatively consistent biases in their estimates (either optimistically above or pessimistically below). It might be possible to correct such a bias over time through the review and evaluation of the analyst's work.

A second form of post-audit is to determine the value of abandonment, versus continued operation, of an entire project. Often, as in the optical-scanner example, determining the value of the entire operation is the only reasonable method of evaluating a project. However, although this may determine the project's current value, it does not indicate whether a particular decision was good or bad. The current value provides a measure of the outcome from the entire set of past decisions, but that outcome could be more the result of good or bad luck than good or bad decision making.

The Capital Budgeting Framework

The capital budgeting/NPV framework is a useful decision-making tool. It's based on sound principles and techniques. However, practical realities can significantly complicate its use. In practice, there can be a great deal of "squish" in the decision-making process. But it's important to have a rationally based system for making decisions as a guide. Otherwise, managers could justify self-interested choices with enough "subjective add-ons." Recall our warning about this problem in our discussion of the value that options add to a project's DCF-NPV.

Don't be swayed by the following kind of argument: Because estimating and planning are complex, difficult, and uncertain, in the final analysis, decisions are subjective. Therefore, forget all the complex analysis—"Just take your best shot." Although the first statement is true, the conclusion does not follow. A decision is certainly easier to make if it is simply the result of a coin flip or a "gut-feel best guess," but it can lead to disaster.

If a decision is worth considering, and can benefit from additional information, gather the most cost-efficient information set and make the decision based on that information. Sometimes the most cost-efficient information is what you already have. In such cases, choose the optimal alternative based on that information. But often, gathering extra information is a cost-effective method of making a better decision, even if the information isn't perfect.

Remember, if capital budgeting decisions were trivial, there would not be much reason to study the process. Framing the analysis and decision properly improves understanding and subjective judgments and puts them in proper context. Of course, using the NPV framework will not save you from the effects of inaccurate forecasts of incremental cash flows, or from the effects of using the wrong cost of capital.

Self-Check

1. What is hard capital rationing? How is soft capital rationing different?

2. Are different analytical techniques required to apply the two types of capital rationing?

3. Why is soft capital rationing a useful managerial tool for planning?

4. What is the purpose of having multiple layers of decision-making authority within a company?

5. What is a post-audit? How is it useful in capital budgeting?

OTHER FACTORS THAT ARE DIFFICULT TO QUANTIFY

We've already mentioned several factors that are difficult to quantify in a capital budgeting analysis, such as options, incorporating the effects of erosion and enhancement, predicting the likelihood of technological advances, and hiring qualified managers.

Overlooking such factors that create opportunity costs can lead to bad decision making. However, we've emphasized the importance of care in performing incremental analysis to reflect such factors (when they are important) while avoiding double counting and/or overestimating the impact of these factors, particularly with respect to options.

Here's a list of some other factors that can also increase or decrease project value. For the most part, these factors have a much smaller impact on project value than those already mentioned.

1. *Working relationships with suppliers*—either good or bad. The importance of interpersonal relationships within a company that we noted earlier extends to relationships with individuals and departments in other companies. An individual working for a supplier can cause a costly delay because of a personal vendetta.

2. *Particular expertise* concerning a project, or the lack of it, among current employees. In our discussion of capital rationing, we pointed out the problems of information asymmetry in the labor markets and noted the difficulty of identifying high-quality employees. When transaction costs must be incurred to identify and hire additional employees, those costs decrease the project's NPV. Similarly, when existing employees have expertise that can be used for a project, transaction costs associated with undertaking the project, such as training, will be lower, which in turn increases the project's NPV.

3. *Experience* with the quality of machines and/or service from particular manufacturers. As with relationships with suppliers, good or bad service or parts availability from a manufacturer can decrease or increase the company's expenses. Likewise, when a ma-

chine is known to have a better or worse "cost/quality" relationship, it will increase or decrease the project's NPV. Also, improved knowledge of the expenses connected with using a machine may increase the accuracy of the forecast cash flows. Such improved knowledge is more likely when dealing with machines that use existing technology than machines using innovative technology.

The same warning we gave about options applies to the above and similar factors: As long as a person does not provide specific values that can be carefully examined, a proponent of a project can always find a long enough list of vague add-ons with which to "shout down" an opponent of the project. Don't be fooled. *A long list is not a substitute for a large NPV!*

Self-Check

1. Name three factors that can have an important effect on the NPV of a capital budgeting project but are difficult to quantify.

2. Explain why it's important to describe thoroughly the benefits that you expect to result from a factor that cannot be readily quantified. What problem do vague add-ons present?

SOME PRACTICAL ADVICE

Decision making in a complex world is difficult because no single approach *always* works best. As with earning extraordinary returns in the stock market, if it were that easy, everyone would already be doing it. At one extreme, the analyst-manager should gather all the relevant information to make the optimal choice. But of course there is more information that could be gathered in just about every situation, and so with that strategy, the decision maker would never make a decision.

At the other extreme, gathering information costs money and takes time. Therefore, in order to minimize cost, one could conclude that the analyst-manager should never gather more information.

Either approach may in fact be best in a particular situation, but both are too extreme to be applied to every situation. Extreme solutions involving "always" or "never"—such as always wait (or never wait), always purchase more information (or never purchase more information)—are too simplistic to be consistently successful in complex situations. Our advice is to be wary of simplistic decision-making procedures that are like cure-all medicines, claimed to be appropriate for all situations.

Despite the need to be wary, the capital budgeting/NPV framework for decision making described in chapters 8 and 9 is *always* correct! The problem is that following the framework is sometimes extremely difficult because of a variety of complicating factors, such as opportunity costs, options, erosion, and enhancement. The tools we've described provide methods of coping in an environment where it is not only impossible to predict future outcomes but often impossible even to describe the possible outcomes. In other words, in some cases, we cannot even imagine some of the outcomes.

When your investment depends on unknown future events, you simply do the best you can. We can talk about the possibility of a technological advance, but often we cannot say anything more about it than to make some general statements about rendering an existing product obsolete. Also, some possible outcomes are so unlikely that they have no significant effect on the analysis, yet if one occurs, its effect will be catastrophic. We discussed this phenomenon in chapter 7, in connection with contingent claims.

As we said in chapter 8, we know of no way to teach a person how to generate new ideas. Our ability to teach a person to assimilate information is also limited.

Applying the Principles of Finance

Despite all the difficulties, several principles of finance are especially important to remember with respect to capital budgeting decisions.

Valuable New Ideas   Bad financing decisions can destroy a company. On the other hand, although good financing decisions can contribute to a company's profitability, the possibility of extraordinary success rests primarily on investment decisions. Because of capital market efficiency, great financial management rarely makes a company extraordinarily profitable. The Principle of Valuable Ideas is alive and well. *Pursuing valuable ideas is the best way to achieve extraordinary returns.*

Valuable new ideas are not necessarily limited to new products. A valuable new idea can be related to many dimensions of the business. An improved management technique can be valuable. Ray Kroc employed valuable new management procedures in helping to make McDonald's a profitable corporation. He had many new ideas in addition to his idea of serving hamburgers quickly. For example, McDonald's introduced fast food in a family restaurant, a substantive change from the take-out hamburger joint.

At the same time, a company must adjust for erosion or enhancement. Introducing new ideas in the form of products, services, management, and/or technology can erode (reduce) the value of current ideas or even render current ideas worthless. For example, what are typewriters worth today, compared with what they were worth when new?

Comparative Advantage   Beyond new ideas, a company should look for ways to make good use of its comparative advantages or current expertise. Promising places to look for opportunities include the use of patents and marketing or distribution networks.

Market Efficiency   In chapter 6 we showed how bond and stock values can be easily found by looking at their latest trading price. Yet we've noted that the physical asset markets are not as efficient as the capital markets. In spite of lower efficiency, there is useful information contained in a physical asset's market-traded price.

If you're not going to trust a market price, you should have a very good reason. This is true in the physical asset markets as well as the capital markets. Beware of an analysis that places a value on an asset that is very different from prices observed in a competitive market. Even if the market is less efficient than the capital markets, you need to have one or more good reasons why it should be different, such as a new idea or comparative advantage.

When there is a market for an asset, *you should think long and hard before you conclude that a market price is "wrong."* Ask yourself what value you are bringing to the asset. That is, how will your use of the asset be different, so that the asset is worth more to you than it is to other people? If an asset will be used more profitably by others because, for example, they hold a patent, it's probably not good to compete with them for the use of that asset.

Two-Sided Transactions   Why is the other party to the transaction willing to sell the asset to you or purchase it from you? For example, why is the other party willing to sell you the asset for less than you think it's worth? Remember, those on the other side of the transaction are acting in their self-interest. Establishing reasons for the difference will help you understand the project you are analyzing.

Signaling   Watch the competition. Try to understand their actions. Often, but not always, their actions contain information. The question is what information do the actions contain? The actions could simply be an application of the Behavioral Principle, which can lead to a "herd" mentality. If you're the first to recognize such behavior, you can profit from it by doing something different.

Finally, *plan ahead.* Undertaking a major project is not as simple as discounting cash flows. It requires management. The capital budgeting/NPV framework is useful for making decisions. It is always correct. The difficulty is in correctly estimating future values. But just because it is difficult or the process becomes complex, don't just blow it off and flip a coin. Use the information you have in the best way you can to decide whether to go ahead, quit, or seek additional information.

> **Self-Check**
> **1.** Which capital budgeting decision criterion is always correct?
> **2.** What's the most promising way to achieve extraordinary returns?
> **3.** True or false? You should *always* think long and hard before concluding that the market price of an asset is wrong.

SUMMARY

When businesses are actually making capital budgeting decisions, factors such as project interactions and investment options can greatly complicate the process. However, the decision-making process based on maximizing NPV provides a *framework* for making the best possible capital budgeting decisions.

- Options and the opportunity costs they create play a very important role in capital budgeting decisions. The following capital budgeting options were identified: Expansion option, price-setting option, abandonment option, postponement option, replacement option, and future investment opportunities.
- When capital budgeting options exist, the NPV of a project is its DCF-NPV plus the expected value of the options minus the cost of the options.
- "Soft" capital rationing is a useful framework for the planning process and can be conveniently accomplished using specialized software packages.
- Pursuing valuable new ideas and using the company's comparative advantages are the best ways to achieve extraordinary returns.
- Factors such as the level of expertise among employees, working relationships with other companies, and past experience with machines and/or service can play valuable, but lesser roles, in capital budgeting decisions.
- Watch how other people and companies act—the competition and those on the other side of your transactions.
- Have good reasons for being able to get a positive NPV from a project, especially if there is no innovative idea or comparative advantage involved.
- The framework presented in this chapter for making capital budgeting decisions helps structure the decision and can enhance one's understanding of complex situations, even though its application is not as simple as hastily calculating an NPV.

EQUATION SUMMARY

(10.1)	$NPV = DCF\text{-}NPV + \text{Value of options} - \text{Cost of options}$

CHAPTER REVIEW ACTIVITIES

SELF-TEST PROBLEM

1. The current level of production for Adam's Gears, Inc. (the original gear) is limited by its production facilities, so Adam is considering an expansion of production capacity. Because the product has become essentially generic, raising the price is not an option for Adam. There are two types of processes that can be installed for the expansion. One process is riskier than the other, but the total production capacity is the same for the two processes, as is the expected value of the additional gear sales ($1,300,000 per year). Process A costs $1,560,000 to install and has variable

costs of $740,000 per year. Process B costs $390,000 to install and has variable costs of $935,000 per year. Both investments would be depreciated on a straight-line basis to a zero book value over 8 years, but both have a 10-year useful life and expected salvage values of zero at the end of 10 years. The cost of capital for process A is 15%. Because of lower risk, the cost of capital for process B is 12%. Adam's Gears has a marginal tax rate of 30%. Which, if either, project should Adam undertake?

SOLUTION TO SELF-TEST PROBLEM

1.

Process A

Time	Item	CFBT	CFAT	PV @ 15%
0	I	−1,560,000	−1,560,000	−1,560,000
1–8	Depreciation	0	58,500	262,508
1–10	$\Delta R - \Delta E$	560,000	392,000	1,967,357
				NPV = $669,865

Process B

Time	Item	CFBT	CFAT	PV @ 12%
0	I	−390,000	−390,000	−390,000
1–8	Depreciation	0	14,625	72,652
1–10	$\Delta R - \Delta E$	365,000	255,500	1,443,632
				NPV = $1,126,284

So Adam should undertake the expansion using process B because it has the higher NPV.

QUESTIONS

1. Cite and briefly discuss six areas in which to look for options that might be connected with a company's capital budgeting opportunities.
2. Define *capital rationing*.
3. Contrast the concepts of "soft" and "hard" capital rationing.
4. How can capital rationing be used as a tool for managerial planning?
5. Why might it be important to review and assess (post-audit) a company's decisions? What are some of the pitfalls associated with such a task?
6. Briefly explain how the pricing of a product can interact with a company's decision whether to expand production capacity.
7. Why might the consideration of abandonment value be more important for a company engaging in capital rationing than for companies that simply take on all positive-NPV projects?
8. Cite and briefly discuss six factors that can be especially difficult to quantify for inclusion in a capital budgeting NPV calculation.
9. Respond to the following comment: "First you tell us the value of a project is its NPV. Now you say that the project's value is its NPV plus the value of its options minus the cost of those options. Which is right?"
10. Cite and briefly discuss potential pitfalls encountered in estimating the value of future investment opportunities, in the context of our warning about capital budgeting options.
11. Explain why no single approach will always work in a complex and competitive business world.

CHALLENGING QUESTIONS

12. Based on the Principle of Two-Sided Transactions, what would you tell a company that has "discovered" a large positive-NPV project that requires the company to purchase the assets (which are necessary to undertake the project) from another corporation?
13. Cite an example of a situation in which "hard" capital rationing would be appropriate for at least a limited time.
14. Suppose you're a manager considering a capital budgeting project. You have examined the proposed project, and, according to every relevant piece of information you can find, you feel the project should be undertaken. After submitting your analysis, the division head informs you that the project has not been approved for funding. Briefly discuss the possible causes of the difference between your opinion of the project and that of upper management.

15. We've said that abandonment should always be considered with respect to a company's current operations. Suppose a company has the opportunity to sell one of its subsidiaries that is doing poorly. As a general rule, why would it *not* be likely that a company can "limit its losses" by selling off such subsidiaries?

16. Cite and discuss four broad factors that can cause the NPV of a capital budgeting project to be incorrectly measured.

17. Capital rationing would not be a shareholder wealth-maximizing strategy in a perfect capital market. How might the capital market imperfections such as information asymmetries and transaction costs render capital rationing a rational tool?

18. Discuss the importance of erosion and enhancement to a company such as IBM when it considers introducing a new product.

19. How might the agency costs associated with the separation of ownership and control contribute to a tendency for companies to expand rather than raise the prices of their products?

PROBLEM SET A

A1. (Future investment option) You are evaluating an investment in a very nice Indian restaurant in Wichita Falls. The NPV of the investment is −$1,500,000. For an additional outlay of $200,000, you will have the option to add additional restaurants in the region. If circumstances are favorable, which has a probability of 0.5, the expansion option has an NPV of $6 million. If circumstances are unfavorable, a probability of 0.5, the expansion option has an NPV of 0. What is the total NPV of the investment, including the cost and expected value of the expansion option?

A2. (Capital rationing) Consider the capital projects shown below.

Project	Outlay	NPV	PV	Profitability Index	Rank (1 = highest PI)
A	$150	$ 60	$210	1.40	1
B	300	105	405	1.35	2
C	200	60	260	1.30	3

a. With no limit on capital outlays, which projects should be accepted? What is the total outlay and the total NPV?

b. Assume the capital budget is limited to $450. Which projects should be accepted? What is the total outlay and the total NPV?

c. Assume the capital budget is limited to $400. Which projects should be accepted? What is the total outlay and the total NPV?

A3. (Postponement option) A real estate developer can build a golf course now or wait one year. The cash flows for investing now or postponing one year are given below. If the cost of capital is 10%, should the developer invest now or postpone and invest in one year?

Time	0	1	2	3	4	5	6
Invest now	−50	10	20	20	20	20	20
Invest in one year		−55	24	24	24	24	24

A4. (Abandonment) Five years ago, your company installed a quick-lube store on Connolly Avenue. Southwest Cellular would like your store to convert to one of its own outlets. They have made you an offer that nets you $600,000 after taxes. Your required return is 12%.

a. You expect a $75,000 cash flow after tax for each of the next 10 years. Should you abandon?

b. Assume your annual cash flow is $120,000. What is the minimum offer you would accept?

A5. (Capital rationing) Consider the projects shown below (amounts in $ thousands).

Project	A	B	C	D	E	F	G
Initial cost	10	20	20	15	30	40	20
NPV	1.1	3.6	0.8	1.6	4.0	3.0	1.4

a. Compute the profitability index for each project.

b. If you were rationed to $115,000 for the initial investment, which projects should you choose?

c. If you were rationed to $95,000 for the initial investment, which projects should you choose?

A6. (Salvage value) Suppose GAF Corporation is contemplating a capital budgeting project with capital assets that will be depreciated to a book value of $10,000 but that GAF expects to have a salvage value of $18,000. GAF's marginal tax rate is 34%. Cleanup and removal expenses are expected to be $1000, and there will be no return of working capital. What is the net salvage value?

A7. (Basic capital budgeting problem) The investment is $1,000,000, which is depreciated straight-line for 10 years down to a zero salvage value. For its 10-year life, the investment will generate annual sales of $800,000 and annual cash operating expenses of $250,000. Although the investment is depreciated to a zero book value, you expect to sell it for $200,000 in 10 years. The marginal income tax rate is 30% and the cost of capital is 10%.

a. What is the after-tax net cash flow expected each year?

b. What is the net present value of the investment?

A8. (Basic capital budgeting problem) An investment of $60,000 will be depreciated straight-line for 10 years down to a zero salvage value. For its 10-year life, the investment will generate annual sales of $30,000 and annual cash operating expenses of $12,000. Although the investment is depreciated to a zero book value, it should sell for $10,000 in 10 years. The marginal income tax rate is 40% and the cost of capital is 10%.

a. What is the after-tax net cash flow expected each year?

b. What is the net present value of the investment?

PROBLEM SET B

B1. (Future investment option) Virginia Matteson is considering a major investment in new technology for her executive recruiting business. Virginia has carefully considered the revenues and costs that this investment will generate, and finds that it is unprofitable. Her discounted cash flow analysis reveals an expected NPV of −$100,000. However, Virginia believes that this new technology could enable her to expand her business into a new area, that of renting professional staff such as accountants, lawyers, and computer specialists to her clients. The additional cost of preparing for the temporary professional business would have a present value of $100,000. Virginia believes that this new business, if future conditions justified it, would be worth a present value of $1,000,000. The probability of the temporary professional business becoming a reality, she estimates, is about 40%. What is the NPV of the investment in new technology if you include the cost and expected value of the future investment option?

B2. (Abandonment) You can invest $1,000,000 in a new business. There is a 50% probability that the business will be worth $1,600,000 and a 50% probability that it will be worth $600,000.

a. What is your expected NPV?

b. After you invest in the business, you can abandon it for $900,000. If you use the abandonment option rationally, what is your expected NPV?

B3. (Abandonment) Your dance/karate studio generates a cash flow after taxes of $220,000 per year. A national chain wants to purchase your studio for $1,500,000. You believe the fair value of your business is the capitalized cash flow for 10 years, discounted at 14%. Should you keep the business or sell out?

B4. (Incremental cash flows and NPV) The Howe Fix-It Corporation is considering buying a new machine called a TX2 that costs $60,000. The TX2 requires $10,000 in setup costs that are expensed immediately and $10,000 in additional working capital. The TX2's useful life is 10 years, after which it can be sold for a salvage value of $20,000. The TX2 requires a maintenance overhaul costing $30,000 at the end of year 7. The overhaul is fully expensed when it is done. Howe uses straight-line depreciation, and the machine will be depreciated to a book value of zero on a 6-year basis. Howe has a tax rate of 40% and the project's cost of capital is 15%. The TX2 is expected to increase revenues minus expenses by $17,500 per year. What is the NPV of buying the TX2?

B5. (Incremental cash flows and NPV) The Miller Corporation is considering a new product. An outlay of $6,000,000 is required for equipment to produce the new product, and additional net working capital of $500,000 is required to support production and marketing. The equipment will be depreciated on a straight-line basis to a zero book value over 8 years. Although the depreciable life is 8 years, the project is expected to have a production life of only 6 years, and it will have a salvage value of zero at that time (removal cost − scrap value). Revenues minus expenses for the first 2 years of the project will be $5,000,000 per year, but, because of competition, revenues minus expenses in years 3 through 6 will be only $3,000,000. The cost of capital for this project is 16%, and the relevant tax rate is 35%. Compute the NPV of Miller's new product.

B6. (NPV and abandonment) The owners of Egg Sauce, Ltd. are tired of their business. In fact, they are so *exhausted* that they are considering abandoning the business. The building and land could be sold for $700,000 and would provide an after-tax amount of $640,000. The equipment could be sold at auction for about $55,000, and at that price, they could claim a tax credit of $5,000 in addition. The building needed renovation about every 10 years, the before-tax EAC of this periodic maintenance is $40,000, and the after-tax EAC, including the effect of depreciation, is $30,000. The annual revenues minus expenses (including all employee costs) from running Egg Sauce are $200,000 per year, and the company pays taxes at the rate of 35% on this amount. The investment's cost of capital is 15%. What is the NPV from abandoning Egg Sauce?

B7. (Future investment option) Suppose Upjohn's research team would like to spend $50 million on final development and testing of a new kidney drug. The DCF-NPV is −$10 million. Production cannot begin until testing has been completed, which will take several years, and success is not assured. There is a 40% chance that the research might also give Upjohn the option to produce a related drug that could stimulate hair growth and eliminate baldness.

a. Suppose the hair growth stimulant could be marketable within 3 years and yield CFATs of $5 million per year forever. If the cost of capital for the research project is 15%, should Upjohn proceed with it?

b. What's the minimum option value necessary to justify the research project?

c. What's the minimum level of perpetual annual CFATs needed to justify the research project?

B8. (Replacement cycles) Suppose Chrysler Corporation is considering which of two emission testing devices to buy. Machine A costs $100,000, has a 5-year useful life, and has operating expenses of $40,000 per year. Machine B costs $36,000, has a 6-year useful life, and has operating expenses of $62,000 per year. Both machines will have zero salvage value and revenues of $85,000 per year, and both will be replaced at the end of their lives. Chrysler's tax rate is 35%.

a. Assume a 12% cost of capital for each machine. Which one should Chrysler buy?

b. Suppose instead that machine A requires a higher cost of capital, 15%, because it's a riskier process. Machine B's cost of capital is still 12%. Which machine should Chrysler buy?

B9. (Inflation) Suppose Starter, makers of athletic wear, is considering purchasing a new knitting machine that will cost $250,000. It will have an 8-year useful life. It can be depreciated to a $10,000 book value on a straight-line basis. Incremental operating income will be $100,000 per year before taxes. Starter's marginal tax rate is 40%. Inflation is expected to average 5% per year, and the project's cost of capital in real terms is 8%. The salvage value will be $10,000.

a. Calculate the NPV in real terms.

b. Calculate the NPV in nominal terms.

B10. (Inflation and NPV) Suppose Starter in problem B9 believes the inflation rate will be 10%, rather than 5%. How does that affect the NPV?

B11. (Incremental cash flows and NPV) A Wendy's franchisee is considering replacing his kitchen equipment. The equipment currently has a net book value of $60,000 and will continue to be depreciated on a straight-line basis to a net book value of zero over the next 3 years. The franchisee estimates that the current equipment could be used for up to an additional 6 years. The purchase price for the new equipment is $300,000, and it would be depreciated over a 6-year period on a straight-line basis to a net book value of $50,000. The new equipment would produce pretax operating savings of $80,000 per year as compared to the replaced equipment. The old equipment can be sold for $25,000. Installation would cost $30,000 in addition to the purchase price and would be expensed immediately. The franchisee believes the new equipment would have a net salvage value of $40,000 at the end of 6 years.

a. If the franchisee has a marginal tax rate of 30%, what would be the after-tax incremental expected future cash flows associated with the new equipment by year and by item?

b. Approximately what is the IRR for the project?

c. If the cost of capital for the project is 12%, what is the NPV?

d. Compute the NPV assuming costs of capital of 0%, 4%, 8%, 12%, and 16%. Prepare an NPV profile for the project.

PROBLEM SET C

C1. (Abandonment) An investment of $200 will generate one of two outcomes: $144 in 1 year and $172.8 in 2 years *or* $120 in 1 year and $120 in 2 years. Each outcome has a 50% probability. The cost of capital is 20%.

a. What is the expected NPV?

b. Assume you have the option to abandon in 1 year for $120. If you abandon, you keep the year 1 cash flow and give up the year 2 cash flow. Is abandonment rational for either outcome? What is the NPV of the investment, assuming rational abandonment?

C2. (Incremental cash flows and NPV) Ivan's Onion-Brick Restaurant has been very successful for 10 years. However, the growth potential in Ivan's area has declined, and therefore Ivan is contemplating investment in a new business line: consulting. Ivan can enter this new field by purchasing and renovating a small building in downtown Newark at a cost of $100,000, all of which will be depreciated on a straight-line basis to a zero book value over 10 years. Although it will be depreciated to a zero book value, the entire project is expected to be sold off for a salvage value of $65,000 at the end of 8 years. It is estimated that the revenues from the project will be $100,000 per year during the next 2 years and $150,000 in years 3 through 8. Variable costs (including all labor and material) will be 65% of revenues. At the expected revenue levels, Ivan expects to average about $30,000 in receivables, and accounts payable are expected to average $5000. Ivan has determined that the project's cost of capital is 17.31%, and the tax rate is 35%. What is the NPV of this project?

APPENDIX: ADDITIONAL METHODS OF PROJECT ANALYSIS

Chapter 11 describes more explicitly the most widely used method of incorporating the risk of a project into the analysis. In that method, risk, as measured by what is called the *nondiversifiable business risk* of the project, is embedded in the project's cost of capital, its required return. When the cash flows are discounted at the risk-adjusted cost of capital, the effect of risk is thereby included in the calculation of the project's NPV.

The purpose of this appendix is to look at some other methods that are sometimes used to incorporate risk into capital budgeting decisions. In particular, we examine NPV breakeven analysis, sensitivity analysis, scenario analysis, and Monte Carlo simulation.

Before proceeding, we need to alert you to a problem with using the methods we'll describe: These methods can make it difficult to separate diversifiable and nondiversifiable risk, and the distinction between them can be overlooked in the analysis. In other words, special care is necessary to ensure that the risk measured is that of nondiversifiable risk. As we discussed in chapter 7, diversifiable risk is not relevant to shareholders. However, it can be very relevant to managers personally because of the difficulty of diversifying the managers' human capital, which enrichment topic C describes.

The use of the methods discussed in this appendix, then, presents a particular problem because managers have an incentive to use them improperly. By focusing on total risk (and deliberately including diversifiable risk), managers may be able to use risk as a basis for rejecting projects that have a large amount of diversifiable risk. Thus, these methods may inadvertently provide managers with a justification for rejecting projects that are undesirable from their viewpoint—even though the projects may be desirable from the shareholders' viewpoint. This aspect of capital budgeting analysis represents another example in which divergent interests can cause a conflict between shareholders and managers.

Despite this problem, the methods presented here can be useful when it isn't possible to determine a market-based estimate of a project's cost of capital. Generally, using these techniques takes more expertise than is provided here. However, it's important to know of their existence and their potential benefits and problems. Additional expertise can be obtained from additional study or from support staff who are well versed in such quantitative methods. You may have encountered (or will encounter) some or all of these methods in other course work.

Break-Even

The **break-even point** is where the total contribution margin exactly equals the total fixed cost of producing a product or service. Recall that the contribution margin is the difference between revenue and variable cost. For example, if revenue is $15 per unit for a product, and the variable cost of producing a unit of the product is $10, the contribution margin is $5 per unit. With a total fixed cost of $500,000, break-even is 100,000 units (= 500,000/5).

Break-even is the point at which the accounting income is zero. But accounting income ignores the opportunity cost associated with the time value of money (among other problems), so break-even is *not* the point at which the NPV equals zero. In spite of this, break-even is commonly used as a point of analysis, so it is important to understand the pitfalls of using break-even as part of the decision criteria.

It's easy for people to believe that as long as sales stay above the break-even point, the company is "making money." But this is true only in the sense that accounting income will be positive. If sales were to continue essentially at the break-even point forever, it is most likely that the company would be better off if it exercised its abandonment option on the project.

Consider the break-even example just given. Suppose the company could sell the entire project and everything connected with it for an after-tax net salvage value of $1.2 million. Then selling the project would be a positive-NPV decision if sales would fall exactly at the break-even point forever into the future. With sales forever at the break-even point, the company's net cash flow from the project each year would equal the tax credit from the depreciation. The company could sell the project and create value by investing the money elsewhere.

The actual point of indifference is the level of sales at which the NPV from selling or abandoning the project is zero. We need more information to determine that point.

BREAK-EVEN POINT An accounting term defined as the point at which the total contribution margin equals the total fixed cost of producing a product or service. At this point, total revenue equals total cost and profit equals zero.

Determining the Zero-NPV Sales Level

EXAMPLE

Suppose our project has 6 more years of useful life, after which it will have a net salvage value of zero. Also assume that depreciation would be $150,000 per year for the next 4 years and zero for the last 2 years, that the relevant tax rate is 40%, and that the project's required return is 12%. The level of sales for which the NPV of selling the project equals zero can be determined by first setting the NPV from selling equal to zero. Next, work backward to the present value of the CFAT it would require, which must result from a particular value of $\Delta R - \Delta E$. Finally, you can solve for the zero-NPV sales level using the necessary $\Delta R - \Delta E$ and the contribution margin per unit.

The NPV calculation with these unknowns is given in table 10.5 on page 388. To have a zero NPV, the project must produce a present value of $1,017,759 (= 1,200,000 − 182,241). Solving for the corresponding annuity payment implies that the CFAT is $247,545 per year. Therefore the CFBT equals $412,575 per year (= 247,545/[1 − 0.4]). The CFBT per year for $\Delta R - \Delta E$ is the total contribution margin minus the fixed cost. Showing the number of units sold as Q, the contribution margin per unit as c, and the fixed cost per year as F, CFBT is given as

$$\text{CFBT} = cQ - F \qquad (10.2)$$

(continued on following page)

(Determining the Zero-NPV Sales Level *continued from previous page*)

Solving for Q, we have

$$Q = \frac{\text{CFBT} + F}{c} = \frac{412{,}575 + 500{,}000}{5} = 182{,}515$$

Therefore, the point at which the company is actually indifferent to having the project—which we might call the "true" break-even point—is a sales level of 182,515 units per year for the next 6 years. This sales level is almost twice the 100,000 units at which accounting income is zero. Although the relationship between this indifference point and the break-even point is specific to the situation, in most cases it's much larger. ∎

Determining a project's indifference point—the unit sales level per period at which the project's NPV is zero—provides a feel for the project by putting the NPV in terms of the minimum number of units that must be sold per year to have a positive-NPV investment. This applies to prospective new, as well as ongoing, projects. You can get still more of a feel for a project by determining how sensitive the project's NPV is to variations in sales. This is called sensitivity analysis, which we turn to next.

Sensitivity Analysis

SENSITIVITY ANALYSIS
Varying key values in a process to determine the sensitivity of outcomes to the variation.

Sensitivity analysis varies key parameters in a process to determine the sensitivity of outcomes to the variation in each item. The question sensitivity analysis addresses is "What occurs if things don't go as predicted?"

NPV sensitivity to variations in sales is characterized by the relative steepness of the slope that expresses the relationship between profit and sales in a graph. This slope is largely determined by the contribution margin. A large contribution margin makes a steep slope, in which case profits are very sensitive to changes in sales. A small contribution margin makes a flatter slope, and profits are less sensitive to changes in sales. Increasing the contribution margin, then, magnifies the sensitivity of profit to changes in sales.

EXAMPLE   *Sensitivity Analysis*

A common way to get a feel for a project's profit sensitivity is to estimate optimistic, expected, and pessimistic levels for future annual sales. Extending our break-even example, suppose optimistic, expected, and pessimistic estimates for future sales levels are 250,000, 200,000, and 150,000, respectively. At the expected sales level, yearly CFBT for $\Delta R - \Delta E$ is given by equation (10.2):

$$\text{CFBT} = cQ - F = 5(200{,}000) - 500{,}000 = \$500{,}000$$

The NPV calculation for keeping the project, given the expected sales level, is shown in table 10.6. Similar calculations for $Q = 250{,}000$ and $Q = 150{,}000$ show that the NPVs range from −\$401,048 to \$832,374. ∎

TABLE 10.5

NPV Calculation for the Production Amount That Will Yield a Zero NPV

TIME	ITEM	CFBT	CFAT	PV AT 12%
0	Salvage value	1,200,000	1,200,000	1,200,000
1–6	$\Delta R - \Delta E$	?	?	?
1–4	Depreciation (lost)	0	−60,000/yr	−182,241
				NPV = 0

If the optimistic and pessimistic sales estimates had been 75,000 and 400,000 instead of 150,000 and 250,000, respectively, the variation in the NPVs would have been much larger, ranging from −$1,326,115 to +$3,195,930. Comparisons such as these may provide further insight into the nature of a project. ■

Obviously, you can perform sensitivity analysis with respect to any parameter in the NPV computation. However, as we said earlier, great care is necessary to identify the nondiversifiable risk in the analysis. This is especially difficult when combining optimistic and pessimistic estimates for multiple parameters.

Scenario Analysis

Sensitivity analysis measures the sensitivity of NPV by varying one variable at a time. In contrast, **scenario analysis** constructs scenarios where *several* variables change in each scenario. A project is evaluated by looking at its NPVs in all of the constructed scenarios.

Although it's possible to create a large number of alternative scenarios, it's very common to use only three or four. The scenarios are constructed to span the good and bad outcomes that the project might encounter.

SCENARIO ANALYSIS Finding the profitability of a project for alternative "scenarios" where the values for the key variables are different for each scenario.

Scenario Analysis at Kingdom Catheter

EXAMPLE

Kingdom Catheter Company is considering an investment in a new product where future cash flows are hard to predict. The team leader has constructed three possible scenarios for future sales, which are shown in table 10.7. These sales and costs are projected to be the same each year over the project's 10-year life. The project requires a $2,000,000 investment, which is depreciated straight-line to zero over 10 years (depreciation is $200,000 per year). Salvage value will be zero. The required return is 12% and the marginal tax rate is 30%. What is the NPV for each scenario?

(continued on following page)

TABLE 10.6
NPV Calculation for Keeping the Project, at the Expected Sales Level

TIME	ITEM	CFBT	CFAT	PV AT 12%
0	Salvage value (forgone)	−1,200,000	−1,200,000	−1,200,000
1–6	ΔR − ΔE	500,000/yr	300,000/yr	1,233,422
1–4	Depreciation	0	60,000/yr	182,241
				NPV = $215,663

TABLE 10.7
Kingdom Catheter's Three Possible Investment Scenarios

SCENARIO	WORST-CASE	MOST-LIKELY	BEST-CASE
Unit sales	10,000	14,000	18,000
Unit price	$150	$170	$190
Sales revenue	$1,500,000	$2,380,000	$3,420,000
Variable cost per unit	$105	$100	$95
Variable cash expenses	$1,050,000	$1,400,000	$1,710,000
Fixed cash expenses	$70,000	$80,000	$90,000

(Scenario Analysis at Kingdom Catheter *continued from previous page*)

For the worst-case scenario, the annual CFAT is:

$$\text{CFAT} = (\Delta R - \Delta E - \Delta D)(1 - T) + \Delta D$$
$$\text{CFAT} = (1,500,000 - 1,050,000 - 70,000 - 200,000)(1 - 0.3) + 200,000 = \$326,000$$

The present value of a 10-year annuity of $326,000 at 12% is $1,841,973,

| N = 10 | r = 12 | **PV = 1,841,973** | PMT = 326,000 | FV = 0 |

and the NPV is −$158,027 (= 1,841,973 − 2,000,000).

For the most-likely scenario, the annual CFAT is:

$$\text{CFAT} = (2,380,000 - 1,400,000 - 80,000 - 200,000)(1 - 0.3) + 200,000 = \$690,000$$

The present value of this cash flow stream is $3,898,654,

| N = 10 | r = 12 | **PV = 3,898,654** | PMT = 690,000 | FV = 0 |

and the NPV is $1,898,654 (= 3,898,654 − 2,000,000).

Finally, for the best-case scenario, the annual CFAT is $1,190,000. The present value of this cash flow stream is $6,723,765,

| N = 10 | r = 12 | **PV = 6,723,765** | PMT = 1,190,000 | FV = 0 |

and the NPV is $4,723,765 (= 6,723,765 − 2,000,000).

So this project has a somewhat negative NPV for the worst-case scenario. But it has very large positive NPVs in the most-likely and best-case scenarios. ■

Monte Carlo Simulation

Airline pilots get some of their training on flight simulators. A flight simulator is a physical model that simulates or imitates (as realistically as possible) what it is like to fly an airplane in a variety of circumstances. Physically, the pilot sits in the model, which is an exact replica of the cockpit of the plane being simulated. Video equipment provides a visual scene that appears for the pilot through the cockpit windows. The model is mounted on a complex construction of hydraulic equipment that creates motion like that of flying. Although expensive, flight simulators help train pilots in a variety of situations. Inexpensive computer programs are also available that can make a PC seem like a flight simulator, minus the physical movement.

SIMULATION Using a mathematical model to imitate a situation many times to estimate the likelihood of possible outcomes.

Monte Carlo simulation, or more simply, **simulation,** is a technique that uses a mathematical model to represent a financial decision or other phenomenon. Simulation imitates a risky situation many times to build a distribution of the possible outcomes. As with a flight simulator, the intention is to make good decisions without having to risk life and limb actually flying the airplane (or in this case, making the financial decision).

A simulation model is similar to sensitivity analysis, in that it can be used to attempt to answer "what-if" questions. The model relies on random sampling from probability distributions of outcomes. Using a computer, a simulation model can assess the likelihood of particular outcomes by trying out a large number of outcomes.

Often, in statistics courses, a coin is flipped a number of times to illustrate that the number of resulting heads actually does turn out to be very close to the 50% that is theoretically estimated using probability theory. This is a simple simulation experiment. Flipping two coins and observing that both are heads about 25% of the time is a slightly more complex simulation experiment. With two coins, of course, the probability of two heads can be calculated by multiplying the probabilities of the individual outcomes together—0.5 for the occurrence of heads on the first coin times 0.5 for heads on the second coin equals 0.25 for the combined event. Although we can use probability theory to determine the probabilities of combined outcomes in simple cases like these coin examples, it isn't hard to imagine situations too complex to mathematically derive the probabilities of all possible outcomes. By making assumptions about the joint probability distributions of the random variables, outcome probabilities can be determined for complex situations using a simulation model.

The major drawback to simulation is that it may be simply impossible to identify the nondiversifiable risk in the analysis.

SUMMARY

- Be sure to distinguish between the break-even point and the zero-NPV sales level.
- Sensitivity analysis can provide insight into a project's profitability by examining "what-if" questions, such as "How does the NPV respond to specific changes in a variable?"
- Scenario analysis provides an overview of a project's profitability under different possible scenarios.

APPENDIX REVIEW ACTIVITIES

SELF-TEST PROBLEM

1. (Break-even) Patty's Stores is evaluating a $4,000,000 outlay in a new store. The investment will be depreciated straight-line over 10 years to a zero salvage value. Annual cash operating expenses will be $200,000 plus 60% of sales. Patty's marginal tax rate is 40% and the required return is 10%.

a. What annual sales volume is required for accounting break-even (zero profits)?

b. What annual sales volume is required for a zero NPV?

SOLUTION TO SELF-TEST PROBLEM

1. a. Accounting fixed costs are $200,000 for cash operating expenses and $400,000 for depreciation. Each dollar of sales has $0.60 of cash expenses and contributes $0.40 to cover fixed costs. The accounting break-even point is: Break-even point = 600,000/0.40 = $1,500,000.

b. If we let X = the dollar sales volume, the annual CFAT is: $CFAT = (\Delta R - \Delta E - \Delta D)(1 - T) + \Delta D$

$$CFAT = [X - 0.6X - 200,000 - 400,000](1 - 0.40) + 400,000$$
$$CFAT = 0.24X + 40,000$$

Setting the NPV equal to zero, we have

$$NPV = -4,000,000 + CFAT \sum_{t=1}^{10} \frac{1}{(1.10)^t} = 0$$

$$NPV = -4,000,000 + (0.24X + 40,000)(6.1445671) = 0$$
$$24X = 4,000,000/6.1445671 - 40,000 = 610,981.58$$
$$X = 610,981.58/.24 = \$2,545,757$$

Annual sales must be $2,545,757 to have a zero NPV. The NPV break-even sales volume is much higher than the accounting break-even of $1,500,000.

APPENDIX QUESTIONS

1. What is a break-even point? How is it different from the zero-NPV sales level?
2. What is sensitivity analysis?

3. What is scenario analysis?

4. What is Monte Carlo simulation? How is simulation similar to scenario analysis?

APPENDIX PROBLEM SET

B1. (Sensitivity analysis) The baseline case has expected sales of 1000 units per year, price of $500 per unit, cash operating expenses of $200 per unit, straight-line depreciation to zero over a 10-year life, cost of capital of 10%, investment of $100,000, and tax rate of 40%.

a. What is the NPV of the baseline case?

b. Calculate the effect on NPV of each of the following changes: Sales are 1100 units; cost of capital is 11%; initial outlay is $110,000; tax rate is 45%. In each case, all values have their baseline values except for the one that is changed.

B2. (Sensitivity analysis) Expected sales are 100,000 units per year, the price is $60 per unit, cash operating expenses are $25 per unit, straight-line depreciation to zero over a 10-year life will be used, the required return is 10%, the investment is $9,000,000, and the tax rate is 40%.

a. What is the NPV of the baseline case?

b. Calculate the effect on NPV of each of the following changes: Unit sales are 10% higher than expected; the price is 10% higher than expected; the unit costs are 10% higher than expected; the required return is 11%; the initial outlay is $10,000,000; the tax rate is 45%. In each case, all values have their baseline values except for the one that is changed.

B3. (Scenario analysis) An analyst at Centenary Cement Company is evaluating a new plant. The plant will cost $2,000,000 and be depreciated straight-line to zero over the plant's 10-year life. The analyst developed the three scenarios given below, based on the outlook in highway and commercial construction. Calculate the NPV and IRR for each scenario.

	Worst-case scenario	Most-likely scenario	Best-case scenario
Unit sales volume	500	600	700
Unit price	$2000	$2200	$2500
Variable cash expenses per unit	$1000	$1000	$900
Fixed cash expenses	$400,000	$500,000	$600,000
Tax rate	40%	40%	40%
Cost of capital	12%	12%	12%

C1. (Break-even) Pledge Macrobiotics is a new company investing $800,000 in itself. The investment will be depreciated straight-line to zero over the expected 10-year life of the business. Fixed cash operating expenses will be $170,000 annually. Variable cash expenses should be equal to 75% of sales. Pledge is in the 40% tax bracket and has a 14% required return.

a. What is the accounting break-even sales volume?

b. What is the NPV break-even sales volume?

C2. (Break-even) Florida Avocado Products is investing $4,000,000 in a new project. The investment will be depreciated straight-line to zero over the expected 10-year life. Fixed cash operating expenses will be $500,000 annually. Variable cash expenses should be equal to 40% of sales. Florida Avocado is in the 40% tax bracket and has a 12% cost of capital.

a. What is the accounting break-even sales volume?

b. What is the NPV break-even sales volume?

BIBLIOGRAPHY

Bebchuk, Lucian Arye, and Chaim Fershtman. "Insider Trading and the Management Choice Among Risky Projects," *Journal of Financial and Quantitative Analysis,* 1994, 29(1):1–14.

Berkovitch, Elazar, and E. Han Kim. "Financial Contracting and Leverage Induced Over- and Under-Investment Incentives," *Journal of Finance,* 1990, 45(3):765–794.

Bjerksund, Petter, and Steinar Ekern. "Managing Investment Opportunities Under Price Uncertainty: From 'Last Chance' to 'Wait and See' Strategies," *Financial Management,* 1990, 19(3):65–83.

Blackwell, David W., M. Wayne Marr, and Michael F. Spivey. "Plant-Closing Decisions and the Market Value of the Firm," *Journal of Financial Economics,* 1990, 26(2):277–288.

Brennan, Michael J. "Presidential Address: Latent Assets," *Journal of Finance,* 1990, 45(3):709–730.

Brennan, Michael J., and Eduardo S. Schwartz. "A New Approach to Evaluating Natural Resource Investments," *Midland Corporate Finance Journal,* 1985, 3(Spring):37–47.

Butler, J. S., and Barry Schachter. "The Investment Decision: Estimation Risk and Risk Adjusted Discount Rates," *Financial Management,* 1989, 18(4):13–22.

Campbell, Tim S., and William A. Kracaw. "Corporate Risk Management and the Incentive Effects of Debt," *Journal of Finance,* 1990, 45(5):1673–1686.

Chan, Su Han, John D. Martin, and John W. Kensinger. "Corporate Research and Development Expenditures and Share Value," *Journal of Financial Economics,* 1990, 26(2):255–276.

Chauvin, Keith W., and Mark Hirschey. "Advertising, R&D Expenditures, and the Market Value of the Firm," *Financial Management,* 1993, 22(4):128–140.

Chung, Kee H., and Charlie Charoenwong. "Investment Options, Assets in Place, and the Risk of Stocks," *Financial Management,* 1991, 20(3):21–33.

Cooper, Kerry, and R. Malcolm Richards. "Investing the Alaskan Project Cash Flows: The Sohio Experience," *Financial Management,* 1988, 17(2):58–70.

Copeland, Thomas. "Improving Capital Efficiency," *Financial Management,* 1993, 22(4):25–26.

Denis, David J. "Corporate Investment Decisions and Corporate Control: Evidence from Going-Private Transactions," *Financial Management,* 1992, 21(3):80–94.

Flannery, Mark J., Joel F. Houston, and Subramanyam Venkataraman. "Financing Multiple Investment Projects," *Financial Management,* 1993, 22(2):161–172.

Harris, Milton, and Artur Raviv. "The Capital Budgeting Process, Incentives and Information," *Journal of Finance,* 1996, 51(4):1139–1174.

Hearth, Douglas, and Janis K. Zaima. "Voluntary Corporate Divestitures and Value," *Financial Management,* 1984, 13(1):10–16.

Heinkel, Robert, and Josef Zechner. "The Role of Debt and Preferred Stock as a Solution to Adverse Investment Incentives," *Journal of Financial and Quantitative Analysis,* 1990, 25(1):1–24.

Hirshleifer, David. "Managerial Reputation and Corporate Investment Decisions," *Financial Management,* 1993, 22(2):145–160.

John, Kose, and BaniKanta Mishra. "Information Content of Insider Trading Around Corporate Announcements: The Case of Capital Expenditures," *Journal of Finance,* 1990, 45(3):835–856.

Kasanen, Eero. "Creating Value by Spawning Investment Opportunities," *Financial Management,* 1993, 22(3):251–258.

Kemna, Angelien G. Z. "Case Studies on Real Options," *Financial Management,* 1993, 22(3):259–270.

Kulatilaka, Nalin. "The Value of Flexibility: The Case of a Dual-Fuel Industrial Steam Boiler," *Financial Management,* 1993, 22(3):271–280.

Laber, Gene. "Bond Covenants and Managerial Flexibility: Two Cases of Special Redemption Provisions," *Financial Management,* 1990, 19(1):82–89.

Laughton, David G., and Henry D. Jacoby. "Reversion, Timing Options, and Long-Term Decision-Making," *Financial Management,* 1993, 22(3):225–240.

Long, Michael S., Ileen B. Malitz, and S. Abraham Ravid. "Trade Credit, Quality Guarantees, and Product Marketability," *Financial Management,* 1993, 22(4):117–127.

Maksimovic, Vojislav. "Product Market Imperfections and Loan Commitments," *Journal of Finance,* 1990, 45(5):1641–1654.

McLaughlin, Robyn, and Robert A. Taggart, Jr. "The Opportunity Cost of Using Excess Capacity," *Financial Management,* 1992, 21(2):12–23.

Merton, Robert C., and Zvi Bodie. "On the Management of Financial Guarantees," *Financial Management,* 1992, 21(4):87–109.

Opler, Tim C., and Sheridan Titman. "Financial Distress and Corporate Performance," *Journal of Finance,* 1994, 49(3):1015–1040.

Sicherman, Neil W., and Richard H. Pettway. "Wealth Effects for Buyers and Sellers of the Same Divested Assets," *Financial Management,* 1992, 21(4):119–128.

Smit, Han T. J., and L. A. Ankum. "A Real Options and Game-Theoretic Approach to Corporate Investment Strategy Under Competition," *Financial Management,* 1993, 22(3):241–250.

Smith, Clifford W., Jr., and Ross L. Watts. "The Investment Opportunity Set and Corporate Financing, Dividend, and Compensation Policies," *Journal of Financial Economics,* 1992, 32(3):263–292.

Statman, Meir, and James F. Sepe. "Project Termination Announcements and the Market Value of the Firm," *Financial Management,* 1989, 18(4):74–81.

Thakor, Anjan V. "Corporate Investments and Finance," *Financial Management,* 1993, 22(2):135–144.

Triantis, Alexander J., and James E. Hodder. "Valuing Flexibility as a Complex Option," *Journal of Finance,* 1990, 45(2):549–566.

Trigeorgis, Lenos. "The Nature of Option Interactions and the Valuation of Investments with Multiple Real Options," *Journal of Financial and Quantitative Analysis,* 1993, 28(1):1–20.

Trigeorgis, Lenos. "Real Options and Interactions with Financial Flexibility," *Financial Management,* 1993, 22(3):202–224.

Trigeorgis, Lenos, and Scott P. Mason. "Valuing Managerial Flexibility," *Midland Corporate Finance Journal,* 1987, 5(Spring):14–21.

Viswanath, P. V. "Adjusting Capital Budgeting Rules for Information Asymmetry," *Financial Management,* 1993, 22(4):22–23.

Vogt, Stephen C. "The Cash Flow/Investment Relationship: Evidence from U.S. Manufacturing Firms," *Financial Management,* 1994, 23(2):3–20.

Williams, Joseph. "Efficient Signalling with Dividends, Investment, and Stock Repurchases," *Journal of Finance,* 1988, 43(3):737–747.

Woods, John C., and Maury R. Randall. "The Net Present Value of Future Investment Opportunities: Its Impact on Shareholder Wealth and Implications for Capital Budgeting Theory," *Financial Management,* 1989, 18(2),85–92.

Part IV

LONG-TERM FINANCIAL DECISIONS

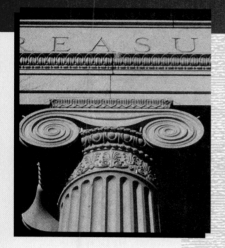

Chapter 11 shows that a capital budgeting project's cost of capital (its required return) depends on the project's risk. However, whether other things, such as the company's choices of *capital structure* (its mix of debt and equity) and dividend policy can affect the cost of capital—and if so, how—is controversial. Practitioners certainly behave as though these decisions are important, but exactly how they matter is still being debated. What we do know is that their relevance depends primarily on three groups of persistent capital market imperfections: asymmetric taxes, asymmetric information, and transaction costs.

Chapters 12 and 13 explore how companies choose their capital structure and dividend policies in an efficient capital market. Practical methods of managing each policy are presented.

Chapter 14 examines alternative external sources of financing a company's capital assets, including common stock, preferred stock, debt, leases, debt-related options, and more.

Successful companies today have a global perspective. Although the principles of finance don't stop at the border, international considerations do introduce significant complications into business decisions. Chapter 15 describes the major international considerations that can be incorporated into financial decisions.

COST OF CAPITAL

OBJECTIVES

1. Explain why the cost of capital is based on the concept of an opportunity cost, not on the historical cost of funds.

2. Distinguish among the cost of capital, the required return to equity, and the required return to debt, and identify the major determinants of each.

3. Distinguish between business risk and financial risk, and identify the important differences between operating leverage and financial leverage.

4. Estimate the cost of capital for a capital budgeting project.

In chapter 1, we described the investment-vehicle model. In that model, the company's managers are neutral intermediaries who act only in the best interest of the shareholders. In such a world, the company is simply a conduit for shareholders to invest in the company's assets. Figure 1.4 in chapter 1 shows this "investment-pass-through" effect.

In a perfect capital market environment, then, the cost of capital—a capital budgeting project's required return—would be the investors' required return for investing in the company's assets, because it's perfectly "passed through" from investors to the company's choice of assets—its capital budgeting decisions. In other words, the cost of capital would be the investors' required return for the project. Because of this, and the Principle of Capital Market Efficiency, we will start our analysis of the cost of capital assuming a perfect capital market environment. Chapters 12 through 14 examine how capital market imperfections affect the cost of capital.

Another way to view the cost of capital is to say it's an opportunity cost. If a company undertakes a project, it creates an opportunity cost: It gives up the chance to make other investments—including investments in publicly traded financial securities. So the cost of capital is the required return on comparable publicly traded securities.[1] In this chapter, we use the idea of comparable publicly traded securities to determine the cost of capital. We'll use what we learned about required returns in chapters 6 and 7 to estimate a capital budgeting project's required return.

---

[1]Such comparability is admittedly difficult to define in some cases. However, recall that nondiversifiable risk is the primary dimension. As a practical matter, then, investments are considered to be comparable when they have identical nondiversifiable risk.

COST OF CAPITAL AND THE PRINCIPLES OF FINANCE

◆ *Risk-Return Trade-Off:* Consider the risk of the capital budgeting project when determining the project's cost of capital.

◆ *Time Value of Money:* The value a capital budgeting project will create—its NPV—depends on its *cost of capital,* its required return.

◆ *Valuable Ideas:* Look for new ideas to use as a basis for capital budgeting projects that will create value.

◆ *Comparative Advantage:* Look for capital budgeting projects that use the company's comparative advantage to add value.

◆ *Incremental Benefits:* Identify and estimate the incremental expected future cash flows for a capital budgeting project.

◆ *Options:* Recognize the value of options, such as the options to expand, postpone, or abandon a capital budgeting project.

◆ *Two-Sided Transactions:* Consider why others are willing to participate in a transaction.

◆ *Signaling:* Consider the actions and products of competitors.

397

HISTORICAL VERSUS INCREMENTAL COST OF CAPITAL

COST OF CAPITAL The required return for a capital budgeting project.

Unfortunately, the term **cost of capital** can be very misleading. It is *not* the company's historical cost of funds, such as coupon payments on existing bonds, that determines the cost of capital. The relevant cost of funds is an *opportunity cost*. It is the rate at which investors would provide financing for the capital budgeting project under consideration *today*. If the company's historical cost of capital is used to evaluate capital budgeting projects, the analysis will be wrong if market rates have changed.

Observing capital markets for just a short time will convince you that market rates are not constant. However, at any one time, there is only *one* expected/required return for a given risk level in an efficient capital market. Any differential in returns for comparable investments, or between a single investment's expected and required returns, will be eliminated quickly by arbitrage activity.

A second problem with the historical perspective involves risk differences. The cost of capital also is *not* the required return on the company's existing (historical) operations. This is because the company's current cost of capital reflects the average risk of *all* the company's existing assets, but the new project's risk (the incremental project) may be very different from this average.

The cost of capital is the required return for a capital budgeting project. Any investment's required return is the minimum return investors must expect to earn in order to be willing to finance the investment today. When management acts in the shareholders' best interest, the cost of capital is the project's required return—that is, the return investors could earn today on comparable capital market investments, capital market securities that have the same risk.

Self-Check

1. What is the cost of capital? Why is it *not* the company's historical cost of funds?

2. Why is an investment's required return the minimum return investors must expect to earn in order to be willing to finance it today?

CORPORATE VALUATION

In a perfect capital market environment, a company cannot affect its market value by changing the way it is financed. The company's value depends only on the size of its expected future cash flows and the required return on those expected future cash flows. Company value does not depend on how those cash flows must be divided between the debtholders and the shareholders. Therefore, a company's capital structure—how the company is financed—is irrelevant to the company's value in a perfect capital market environment.

The Financing Decision

If the financing decision doesn't affect a company's value, you might wonder why we're interested in it. There are at least three reasons. First, even if the financing decision does not affect the company's value, it can provide us with important insight into how to estimate the cost of capital. Second, as a practical matter, even in an efficient capital market, mistakes can be made. It's important to understand the financing decision, if only to avoid making stupid mistakes in operating the company. Finally, examining the financing decision in a perfect capital market environment provides a good foundation for understanding, later on, why and how certain capital market imperfections cause the financing decision to, in fact, affect company value after all.

The value of a company can be expressed as the value of the claims on its assets. That is, company value equals the total market value of its liabilities plus the total market value of its stockholders' equity:

$$\text{Company value} = \text{Equity} + \text{Debt}$$

Although this may look suspiciously like the balance sheet equation, it's important to emphasize that it is given in *market values* rather than book values. Equity is the current value of all of the company's outstanding shares of stock. This value is often estimated by multiplying the current market value per share times the number of outstanding shares.

For example, suppose CBS's stock is currently selling for $48.25, and there are 20 million shares outstanding. CBS's equity would be estimated to be $965 million (= [20]48.25). Similarly, debt is the market value of all of the company's outstanding liabilities.

The Investment Decision

We can also express a company's value in terms of its assets. That is, company value is also the sum of the market values of its assets, shown as $A_1, A_2, \ldots$:

$$\text{Company value} = A_1 + A_2 + A_3 + \ldots$$

This representation is also a market value expression, but in this case it is for the asset (left-hand) side of the balance sheet. Here, the company's value is represented as the value of a portfolio of its real assets.[2] The company's investment decision consists of choosing which assets to add or remove from its portfolio. That choice is based on earning at least the required return on each asset.

This view of company value as the value of a portfolio of assets is important, because it shows how each asset must "rest on its own bottom." That is, each asset (or group of interrelated assets) has its own unique value, required return, and expected return. Recall that a capital budgeting project's expected return is called its *internal rate of return (IRR)*. An asset must be expected to earn at least its cost of capital (required return) to justify its inclusion in the company's asset portfolio. In simple terms, then, the IRR must equal or exceed the cost of capital. But as chapter 9 shows, this rule can break down in some situations. Still, the simple notion that the expected return must equal or exceed the required return provides us with important intuition about the concept of a cost of capital.

The Market Line for Capital Budgeting Projects

Our derivation of the capital-asset-pricing model (CAPM) in chapter 7 was based on shares of common stock. However, the concept can be extended to include all real assets as well. We can build on the idea of the security market line (SML) and create what might be called the capital budgeting project market line (PML). The cost of capital for capital budgeting project j, r_j, can then be expressed as a function of the nondiversifiable risk of the project, its beta:

$$r_j = r_f + \beta_j(r_M - r_f)$$

where r_f is the riskless return, β_j is the beta for project j, and r_M is the required return on the market portfolio. Capital budgeting projects are then evaluated on the basis of the PML in the same way securities are evaluated using the SML.

---

[2]Note that by equating these two expressions for company value, we can see the "investment-pass-through" effect of the investment-vehicle model shown in figure 1.4.

EXAMPLE   *Capital Budgeting for Kmart*

Suppose Kmart Corporation is considering five capital budgeting projects. Undertaking any single project does not preclude, or require, undertaking any of the others. Each project costs an identical $1,000,000 but has a unique beta (and therefore its own cost of capital), and promises a unique perpetual annual cash flow amount. The required return on the market portfolio is 15%, and the riskless return is 7%.

Table 11.1 shows the beta, cost of capital, annual cash flow, IRR, and NPV of each project. For example, the beta for project A is 1.30, and so its cost of capital is 17.4% (= 7 + 1.30[15 − 7]). Project A's annual cash flow is $200,000, making its IRR 20% (= 200,000/1,000,000). Finally, the NPV for project A is $149,430, which is the present value of the expected future cash flows, $1,149,430 (= 200,000/0.174), minus its initial cost of $1,000,000.

Figure 11.1 graphs the costs of capital and IRRs for the projects Kmart is considering, along with the PML. The costs of capital fall on the PML, because they were determined by the PML equation. As with the SML, investments that are above the line have a positive NPV. So projects A, B, and E have positive NPVs, whereas projects C and D have negative NPVs. ■

TABLE 11.1

Kmart's Capital Budgeting Projects

PROJECT	BETA	REQUIRED RETURN	ANNUAL CASH FLOW	EXPECTED RETURN	NPV
A	1.30	17.4%	$200,000	20%	$149,430
B	1.75	21.0	220,000	22	47,620
C	0.95	14.6	140,000	14	−41,100
D	1.50	19.0	170,000	17	−105,260
E	0.60	11.8	140,000	14	186,440

FIGURE 11.1

Kmart's alternative capital budgeting projects and the PML (NPV in $ thousands).

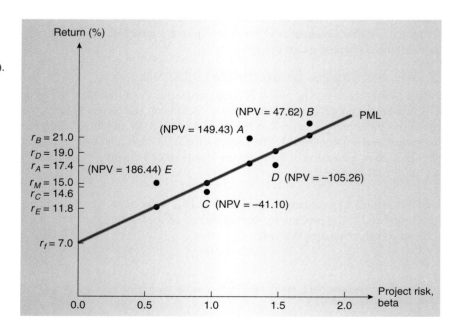

Self-Check

1. True or false? A company's capital structure does not affect its value in a perfect capital market environment.

2. Why should we be interested in how a company finances itself?

3. Describe two ways to interpret this equation: Company Value = Equity + Debt.

4. What is the capital budgeting project market line (PML)? How is it like the security market line (SML)?

VALUE AND THE RISK-RETURN TRADE-OFF

It's very important to keep in mind the relationship among the cost of capital, expected cash flows, and present value. Present value depends on both the cost of capital *and* the expected cash flows. When any one of these three things changes, at least one of the others must also change.

For example, if the cost of capital increases, present value will decrease if the expected cash flows don't also change. We have seen this in the case of a bond. With constant coupon payments, the market value of a bond changes whenever market interest rates change.

Similarly, an increase in the expected cash flows will increase present value *if* the cost of capital (and therefore risk) has not changed. The relationship most easily forgotten with respect to this concept is that *present value can remain constant even if there are changes in both the expected cash flows and the cost of capital (required return)*. The changes can exactly offset each other. This is precisely what the Principle of Risk-Return Trade-Off means. Present value is constant, even though the required return and expected cash flows change. Consider the following simple example.

A Pure Risk-Return Trade-Off

EXAMPLE

Assume you have an asset that has an expected cash payment of $100 per year forever. Some years the yearly cash payment may be more, and other years less. The risk of this asset makes its required return 10%. So the asset's value is $1000 (= 100/0.1). Now suppose you can exchange this asset for some other asset that has an expected cash payment of $200 per year forever, but because of higher risk, its required return is 20%. The alternative asset's cash flow can be much smaller or larger than the expected $200 per year. Should you make the exchange?

The value of the alternative asset is also $1000 (= 200/0.2). Therefore, your choice depends *only* on your attitude toward risk. In other words, your choice represents a pure risk-return trade-off. Even though the other asset's expected cash flows are larger, *there is no difference in value.* Such is the case when an investor moves along the SML or a company moves along the PML. Value is enhanced only when the increase (decrease) in expected cash flows exceeds (is less than) the increase (decrease) in risk. ■

Self-Check

1. What happens to present value when the expected cash flows all increase and the cost of capital doesn't change?

2. What happens to present value when the cost of capital decreases and the expected cash flows don't change?

3. How can the present value remain constant if the expected cash flows and the cost of capital are changing?

LEVERAGE

According to the CAPM, the required return depends only on the nondiversifiable risk of an investment. However, nondiversifiable risk borne by the shareholders can be further split into two parts. It's very important to distinguish between these two types of risk, because they affect required returns in different ways.

The main part of nondiversifiable risk is often called **business risk** or **operating risk.** Business risk is the inherent or fundamental risk of a business without regard to how it is financed. Business risk comes from operating the business; it's based on the company's assets, the left-hand side of its balance sheet.

The secondary part of nondiversifiable risk is called **financial risk.** Financial risk comes from how the company is financed; it's based on the company's capital structure (its proportions of debt and equity), which is the company's liabilities and owners' equity or right-hand side of its balance sheet.

In many cases, a company cannot control its business risk. It is simply the inherent risk of an investment. By contrast, a company's financial risk is determined by the amount of debt it has, its financial leverage or simply **leverage.** More leverage increases financial risk.

The term *leverage* is derived from the mechanical lever that allows you to lift more weight than you can by yourself. Financial leverage allows shareholders to control (lift, so to speak) more assets than is possible using only their own money. In addition to (financial) leverage there is a second type of leverage, called operating leverage. We now turn to this.

BUSINESS OR OPERATING RISK The inherent or fundamental risk of a business, without regard to *financial risk.* The risk that is created by *operating leverage.*

FINANCIAL RISK Risk that is created by financial leverage, which is the financial makeup, or *capital structure.*

LEVERAGE The use of debt financing.

Operating Leverage

OPERATING LEVERAGE The relative mix of fixed and variable costs used to produce a product or service.

Operating leverage is the relative mix of fixed and variable costs used to produce a product or service. Multiple methods of producing a product or service may exist, whereby a company spends more on fixed costs and less on variable costs, or vice versa. A decrease in the variable cost per unit creates an increase in the contribution margin (the selling price minus the variable cost). With a larger contribution margin, the company's profit is more sensitive to changes in sales. That is, a small change in sales makes a large change in profit because the fixed costs are spent in either case.

By contrast, an increase in the variable cost per unit causes a decrease in the contribution margin. With a smaller contribution margin, the change in profit caused by a change in the sales level will not be as large. Therefore, lowering the variable cost per unit (by increasing fixed costs) increases the sensitivity of the company's profit to changes in the level of sales. Such an increase in fixed cost is referred to as an increase in operating leverage.

EXAMPLE

Eastern Mountain Apparel Ski Cap Production

Eastern Mountain Apparel will purchase one of two alternative production methods for manufacturing ski caps. Method A costs $30,000 to install and $6 to make one cap. Method B costs $54,000 to install and $4 to make one cap. Eastern sells caps for $11 apiece. Which production method should Eastern purchase?

The answer, of course, depends on how many ski caps will be sold. For simplicity, let's ignore taxes and the time value of money. Profit will be the contribution margin times the number of caps sold, N, minus the fixed cost. The profit will be $5N – $30,000 for method A, and $7N – $54,000 for method B. Figure 11.2 illustrates Eastern's profit as a function of the number of ski caps sold for both methods.

As you might predict from our discussion above, method B with its higher operating leverage (larger fixed and smaller variable costs) will make Eastern's profit more sensitive to the number of units sold. The slope of the profit line for method B is steeper. If the number sold turns out to be more than 12,000 (the point where the profit functions are equal, $5N - 30,000 = 7N - 54,000$), then method B will have been the better choice. On the other hand, if sales turn out to be less than 12,000 units, then method A will have been the better choice. Of course, the best choice may not be obvious if the sales amount is highly variable or expected to be about 12,000. ■

Operating leverage is important because of its impact on the risk of the investment. However, a company's choice of operating leverage is limited by the number of possible different methods of producing a product and/or service. In some cases, a company has no choice because there is a single (or significantly most efficient) method of production.

There are two important things to remember about operating leverage. First, operating leverage is generally unique for each investment rather than identical for all the company's investments. Second, operating leverage affects the total risk of the capital budgeting project, both diversifiable and nondiversifiable risk. Because operating leverage affects nondiversifiable risk, it also affects both the beta and the project's cost of capital.

Financial Leverage

Operating risk depends principally on the nature of the investment, and to a lesser extent on the company's choice of operating leverage. In contrast, financial risk depends mostly on financial leverage. When a company has some debt financing, that portion of its financing costs are fixed rather than variable. Although we would expect a larger return to shareholders than to debtholders, shareholder return can vary from one period to the next without affecting the operation of the company. However, failure to make required debt payments can result in bankruptcy. We could say, then, that financial leverage substitutes fixed payments to debtholders for variable payments to shareholders.

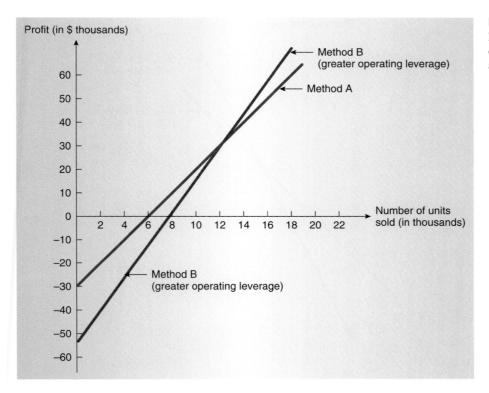

FIGURE 11.2
Eastern Mountain Apparel's operating leverage alternatives.

Graphically, financial leverage looks similar to operating leverage. The realized return to the shareholders (owners) in an all-equity-financed company is the same as the realized return to the company. The realized return to the shareholders in a leveraged company is the realized return *after* the fixed payment to the debtholders has been taken out. The shareholders are the *residual* owners.

Figure 11.3 illustrates the shareholders' realized return as a function of the company's realized return with and without leverage. The leverage alternative assumes 50% debt financing. Figure 11.3 ignores taxes and assumes that the company pays a 10% interest rate on its debt.

We've come across the concept of financial leverage before. Recall that investors in a perfect capital market should all invest in the same risky portfolio—the market portfolio. Investors set their risk and return levels by lending or borrowing. This kind of lending and borrowing is simply personal financial leverage.

There is a very important fact we learned about personal leverage: The choice of lending or borrowing (personal financial leverage) does not alter the *total* value of an investment. It is just like our example of a pure risk-return trade-off. Any change in the expected cash flows is exactly offset by a change in risk and required return.

So the choice of personal leverage is yet another pure risk-return trade-off. It is the investor's choice of personal capital structure that puts the investor at a particular point on the capital market line (CML). We will see that this same conclusion holds for a company's choice of capital structure in a perfect capital market environment. Financial leverage is not a matter of value. It is a question of risk-return preference, subject to a market-determined risk-return trade-off.

As with operating leverage, financial leverage also has two important corresponding (and almost opposite) things to remember about it. First, a company's choice of leverage is for the most part made for the entire company rather than separately for each of the company's investments. Second, leverage affects the risk borne by each class of investor (debt, equity, and so on), but does not affect the cost of capital for the investment in a perfect capital market environment.

FIGURE 11.3

An illustration of the effect of (financial) leverage on shareholder return.

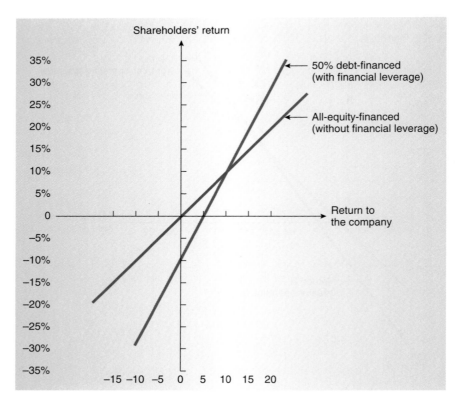

Self-Check

1. What are the two parts of nondiversifiable risk?

2. What is operating leverage? How does it differ from financial leverage? How is it similar?

3. How does a company's choice of financial leverage affect its cost of capital in a perfect capital market environment?

LEVERAGE AND RISK BEARING

In a perfect capital market environment, leverage does not affect a company's value or the cost of capital. However, even in a perfect capital market environment, leverage does affect the required returns for the debtholders and shareholders. This is because leverage affects how the risk of the company is borne by each group. To see this, consider the following simple example.

Leveraging Per-Pet, Inc.

EXAMPLE

Per-Pet, Inc. is financed only with equity. It has a perpetual expected cash inflow each year of $150, which can be larger or smaller, but is never less than $50 per year. Per-Pet's cost of capital is 15%, so Per-Pet is worth $1000 (= 150/0.15). Recently, the shareholders heard the old adage that "the way to get rich is to use someone else's money."

The manager agrees, and has pointed out that the company could borrow $500 at 10% per year and give the $500 to the shareholders. Then the shareholders' expected return on their remaining $500 investment would increase to 20% per year. If $500 of financing is converted into debt, the company would be taking on leverage and have a capital structure that is half debt and half equity.

First of all, why would the debtholders accept a return of only 10% when the company's cost of capital is 15%? The answer, of course, is the risk-return trade-off: The debtholders will get their 10% return *every* period without fail—their return is riskless. But the shareholders are the *residual* claim holders. They get what is left after the debtholders have been paid. Their risk will increase with leverage.

When the company is all-equity-financed, the shareholders bear all the company's risk, spread out over an investment of $1000. With the proposed 50% debt capital structure, the shareholders also bear all the company's risk, but the risk is spread out over an investment of only $500. Thus, the risk *per dollar invested* for the shareholders will be twice as large with the leverage as it is currently. So the shareholders "pay" for their increased expected return with an increase in risk. ∎

What conclusions can we draw from the Per-Pet example? First, you can see once again that the expected operating income of $150 coming into Per-Pet each year is not affected by how it must be paid out to those financing the company. In other words, the return distribution for a capital budgeting project is not altered by a change in leverage in a perfect capital market environment.

Second, the shareholders' expected return increases with an increase in leverage, but so does their required return. The shareholders' increased risk from leverage exactly offsets their increase in expected return, so there is no change in the shareholders' collective wealth. Without leverage, shareholders have $1000 invested. Under the proposed leveraging, shareholders will have $500 in cash to invest as they wish and $500 of invested value (= 100/0.2) in Per-Pet stock, for an unchanged *total* value of $1000.

Finally, with the proposed leverage, debtholders provide $500 in cash for promised future payments worth *exactly* $500 (= 50/0.1).

This example also demonstrates that because of financial risk, all investors do not bear the same amount of risk. The shareholders bear more risk per dollar invested than do the debtholders, because they are the residual claim holders. At the same time, leverage does not affect the company's cost of capital (required return). The cost of capital, when it is all-equity-financed, is 15%. The weighted average of debt and equity required returns with the proposed leverage is also 15% (= 0.5[0.2] + 0.5[0.1]). This is not an accident. This must hold in all cases in a perfect capital market environment.

Self-Check

1. As a company's leverage increases, how will each of the following be affected in a perfect capital market environment: required return for debtholders, required return for shareholders, and cost of capital?

2. How does an increase in a company's leverage affect its shareholders' collective wealth in a perfect capital market environment?

THE WEIGHTED AVERAGE COST OF CAPITAL

WEIGHTED AVERAGE COST OF CAPITAL (WACC) The weighted average of financing costs for a financing package that would allow a project to be undertaken.

We always come back to opportunity cost. The **weighted average cost of capital (WACC)** can be described in terms of financing rates. Therefore, it can *always* be represented as the weighted average cost of the components of *any* financing package that will allow the project to be undertaken. For example, such a financing package could be 20% debt plus 80% equity, 55% debt plus 45% equity, and so on. Or it could be 30% 30-year debt, 10% 180-day debt, 10% preferred stock, 15% 20-year convertible debt, and 35% common stock.

The cost of capital is the return required by a group of investors to take on the risk of the project. But the investors can share the burden of that risk in any way they agree on. In a perfect capital market environment, each investor will require the fair return for the amount of risk borne. However, the *average* will always be the same—regardless of the components.

Certain capital market imperfections, such as asymmetric taxes, asymmetric information, and transaction costs, might cause the package to have an impact on the average cost, but we leave that part of the story for later. For now, it's most important to understand that the required return for each participant depends on the proportion of risk being borne by that participant.

Before proceeding, we need to say exactly what we mean by the components of a financing package. For simplicity, we'll just use the proportions of financing provided by debt and equity. Let $L = D/(D + E)$ be the ratio of debt financing to total investment value. D is the market value of debt, E is the market value of equity, and $(D + E)$ is the company's total market value.

For example, suppose a project has a total present value of $10,000 and $4000 of debt will be used to finance the project. Then $L = D/(D + E) = 0.4$. It's very important to note that L does not depend on the initial cost of the project; it depends on the total value of the project.

Suppose our example project has an initial cost of $8000 and an NPV of $2000, making up its present value of $10,000. Then the shareholders of this project will be putting up $4000 and getting $6000 because they get the NPV. So the shareholders own 60% of the value, even though they will be putting up only 50% of the initial cost ($4000 of the $8000). The project is referred to as 40% debt-financed and 60% equity-financed because those proportions reflect the distribution of the *market* value of the project among the claimants. Proportions of the initial cost are not relevant because that would disregard the project's NPV.

The Per-Pet example illustrates that the shareholders' required return depends on leverage. The same phenomenon occurs with respect to the debtholders' required return. It also depends on leverage. This might not be obvious because, as long as there is no chance of default, the debtholders' required return is the riskless return. However, when default is possible, the debtholders' required return must increase to reflect the risk that debtholders will not receive full payment.[3]

A Cost of Capital Formula

The WACC (weighted average cost of capital) can be expressed as the weighted average of the required return for equity, r_e, and the required return for debt, r_d, as we illustrated in the Per-Pet example. The weights are based on the market values of the company's debt and equity.

$$\text{WACC} = \frac{E}{(D+E)}r_e + \frac{D}{(D+E)}(1-T)r_d = (1-L)r_e + L(1-T)r_d \qquad (11.1)$$

where L is the market value proportion of debt financing, and T represents the marginal corporate tax rate on income from the project.

Note that the WACC is expressed as the after-corporate-tax return. Because the returns to equity investors are paid after corporate taxes, r_e, is also an after-corporate-tax return (to equity). The return to debt, r_d, is a pretax return and must be multiplied by $(1-T)$ to convert it to an after-tax basis.[4]

General Patent's Cost of Capital

E X A M P L E

General Patent, Inc. makes innovative military equipment and has only long-term debt and common equity financing. Both securities are traded regularly on a securities exchange. What is the WACC for General Patent?

To begin, we gather the following information:

Current market value of General Patent's common stock	
(5 million shares outstanding)	$33.25/share
Total market value of equity (= [5]33.25)	$166.25 million
Next year's expected cash dividend	$2.83/share
Expected constant annual dividend growth	10%
Current market value of General Patent's bonds	
(70,000 bonds outstanding, 7.5% coupon rate, maturing in 17 years)	$800.00/bond
Yield to maturity on General Patent's bonds	10%
Total market value of debt (= [70,000]800)	$56.00 million
Current total market value of General Patent (= 166.25 + 56.0)	$222.25 million
General Patent's marginal corporate tax rate	34%

Based on this information, we can use the dividend growth model from chapter 6 to estimate r_e. From equation (6.5):

$$r_e = \frac{D_1}{P_0} + g = \frac{2.83}{33.25} + 0.10 = 0.185$$

The yield to maturity (YTM) on the long-term bonds, 10%, provides an approximation of r_d.[5] The proportion of debt financing, $L = D/(D+E)$, is 0.252 (=56/222.25). From equation (11.1), then, our estimate of General Patent's WACC is 15.5%:

$$\text{WACC} = (1-L)r_e + L(1-T)r_d = (0.748)(0.185) + (0.252)(0.66)(0.10) = 0.155$$

---

[3]Note that full payment includes the time value of money. That is, late payments reduce the value debtholders receive.
[4]We first discussed using this kind of adjustment in chapter 3 in connection with ratios and the difference in tax treatment between interest expense and dividends.
[5]The yield to maturity is only an approximation because of tax considerations.

The estimated 15.5% WACC in the General Patent example can be used as a cost of capital for capital budgeting projects that essentially duplicate (with respect to operating risk level and financing mix) the company's current operations. But how can we estimate a cost of capital for projects that are significantly different from the company's current operations?

The company's own securities are not appropriate because they reflect only the riskiness of the company's existing asset mix. Conceptually, a company could offer a financing package in the capital market to determine a project's cost of capital. However, this would be cumbersome, to say the least. The transaction costs would almost certainly outweigh the benefits of this method.

In practice, a company looks at existing market-traded securities of comparable risk to estimate a cost of capital. The estimate is derived from such market rates. We'll get back to this later in the chapter.

Self-Check

1. What is the WACC? How is it calculated?

2. How is the ratio L calculated? Is it based on market or book values?

3. Suppose a project costs $10,000. Its NPV is $5000. Shareholders put up $5000 and debtholders lend $5000. What is L in this case?

4. In the WACC formula, why do we multiply only r_d by $1 - T$?

5. Suppose a company wanted to estimate the cost of capital for a project that differs from its current operations. Should the company use its current WACC as the project's cost of capital? Explain.

A POTENTIAL MISUSE OF THE WEIGHTED AVERAGE COST OF CAPITAL

We've said that a project's cost of capital must reflect its own risk, not the risk of a company's existing operations. But what happens if a company incorrectly uses its weighted average cost of capital (WACC) for existing operations to evaluate all capital budgeting projects, regardless of risk? Figure 11.4 graphs the risk (beta) versus the IRR for some capital budgeting projects.

FIGURE 11.4

Misapplication of the WACC concept to capital budgeting project selection.

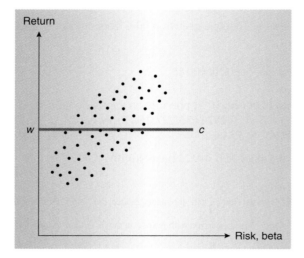

Assume the company's existing operations have a risk equal to the average risk of the set of capital budgeting projects, and the rate w correctly reflects the WACC of the company's current operations. The horizontal line wc in figure 11.4 represents the use of the company's WACC to evaluate the projects, where all projects with an IRR above w are accepted and all those below w are rejected.

If this decision rule is followed, the new projects undertaken will tend to be riskier than the company's existing operations. This is because, taken as a group, the projects that would be accepted using this decision rule are riskier than the remaining set that would not be undertaken. (You can see this by visually estimating the center point of the groups, above and below wc, and comparing the two points.) Therefore, following such a decision rule will cause the risk of the company to increase over time as new projects are undertaken. As a result, the company's WACC will also increase to reflect the greater investor risk.

Taken to the extreme, misusing a company's WACC to evaluate new projects could lead a company with low operating risk, such as a utility, to take on high-risk projects, such as drilling exploratory oil wells. The incorrect low rate could make the project appear to be very desirable by incorrectly computing the project's NPV. Other companies that regularly undertake such projects would find the project to have a (correctly computed) negative NPV! Note also that in addition to undertaking bad projects, the company would be incurring opportunity costs by passing up good projects.

Alternatively, consider what happens if a company applies the PML concept and uses risk-adjusted costs of capital, such as those on the line connecting r_f and j in figure 11-5. As with the single cost of capital decision rule, projects above the line will be accepted, whereas projects falling below the line are rejected. In this case, the average risk of those above the line is approximately the same as those that are rejected. So the application of project-specific risk-adjusted costs of capital does not, as a matter of course, cause the risk of a company to increase over time. In other cases, the total risk could also change. However, a change in total risk will not matter as long as the company earns the returns sufficient to compensate for the risk.

Enrichment topic C on Financial Contracting discusses the implications associated with increased company risk in connection with the *asset substitution problem*. Asset substitution is a technique that shareholders can use to expropriate wealth from the debtholders. The company deliberately undertakes riskier investments to reduce the value of the company's outstanding debt. The value of the debt is reduced because of the increased risk of default. The present situation differs from the asset substitution problem in one major respect. In cases of asset substitution, shareholders are knowingly taking self-interested action. The present case is simply the result of a misapplication of the concept of a cost of capital.

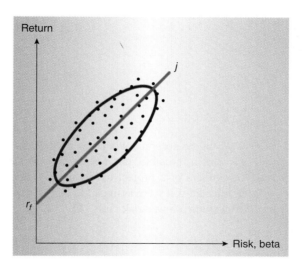

FIGURE 11.5
Proper capital budgeting project selection.

EXAMPLE	*Capital Budgeting at American Airlines*

Suppose American Airlines has a beta of 1.3. It is considering issuing stock to raise money for a project that has a beta of 1.0. The project has an IRR (internal rate of return) of 18%. The riskless return is 5%, and the expected return on the market is 10%. Should American go ahead with the project?

The project's cost of capital from the PML (project market line) is 10% (= 5 + 1.0[10 − 5]). Because the project's expected return, its IRR, of 18% is greater than its required return, its cost of capital, of 10%, American should go ahead with the project. Note that American's current beta of 1.3 is not relevant to the investment decision. Note also that how American will finance the project does not change the answer. ■

RISK CLASS A group of projects that have approximately the same amount of risk.

In practice, companies considering projects with differing risk levels often use a *set* of costs of capital to capture risk differences among capital budgeting projects. Each cost of capital corresponds to a particular **risk class.** For example, a company might have a unique cost of capital for each of its divisions, or it might have a cost of capital for each of various types of projects, such as maintenance, expansion, and new products.

Five risk classes will eliminate virtually all of the problem of shifting risk created by the misuse of a single cost of capital. Therefore, using more than five risk classes is probably unnecessary and a waste of resources. However, using at least three different risk classes appears to be valuable.

EXAMPLE	*Using Risk Classes at Cornett Company*

Cornett Company assigns capital budgeting proposals to three risk classes. Risk Class A, which typically includes modernization and equipment replacement proposals, is for the lowest-risk projects, and these projects are assigned a 12% required return. Risk Class B projects, frequently expansions of existing lines of business, are riskier and have a 14% required return. Finally, Risk Class C projects, new products and new businesses, are given a 16% hurdle rate.

Seven capital budgeting proposals are briefly described in the table below:

PROJECT NUMBER	PROJECT IRR	RISK CLASS	COST OF CAPITAL	DECISION
1412	15%	A	12%	Accept
1416	11	A	12	Reject
1429	13	B	14	Reject
1430	16	B	14	Accept
1431	19	B	14	Accept
1435	15	C	16	Reject
1436	26	C	16	Accept

A project should be accepted whenever its IRR exceeds the required return for its risk class. As you can see in the table, this results in four projects being accepted and three being rejected. Assignment of a project to the appropriate risk class is crucial. Project 1412 would have been rejected if it were assigned to Risk Class C and project 1435 would have been accepted if it were in a lower-risk class. ■

Self-Check

1. What happens to the company if it uses its (overall) WACC for existing operations to evaluate all capital budgeting projects?

2. Why does using the company's WACC to evaluate all capital budgeting projects lead to incorrect investment decisions? Might the use cause the company to accept some negative-NPV projects? Might it cause the company to reject some positive-NPV projects?

3. Explain why applying the PML concept should lead to correct capital budgeting decisions.

4. How can a company use risk classes to evaluate its capital budgeting projects? How many risk classes are usually sufficient?

FINANCIAL RISK

A company's operating risk is determined by the characteristics of the individual assets in the company's portfolio of assets. Therefore, as a portfolio, the betas of the individual assets combine to determine the operating risk of the entire company.

In contrast to operating risk, financial risk depends on company rather than individual asset characteristics. In some sense, an asset or new project undertaken by an ongoing company has no financial risk; only the company itself has financial risk. This is because financial risk is created by financial obligation.

If a company is *all*-equity-financed (no money owed at any time, no matter what), then the company has no financial risk. Such a company would not have even one creditor. All the risk of this hypothetical company would be its operating risk, because the company never owes anyone anything. In such a case there is no possibility of, or option to, default. In effect, the shareholders' limited liability has no effect on value.

Such a company could still go bust. But although the shareholders could lose everything they invested in the company, no wealth can be transferred because no loss can ever be inflicted on anyone other than the shareholders. So although such shareholders still cannot lose more than they have invested in the company, they also cannot benefit from limited liability and the default option.

Because financial risk depends on financial leverage, adjusting for the impact of financial risk must be done on the basis of whatever unit has responsibility for that financial obligation. Except in very special cases, the shareholders' obligation is not limited by the results of one capital budgeting project. Rather, financial obligation extends to the entire company.

When one project does poorly, the company is still obligated to pay its debts from the proceeds of all its other projects. (Only when the company's total performance from all its operations is inadequate to meet its promised obligations can the shareholders be relieved of their obligation—that is, exercise their option to default.)

Therefore, in marked contrast to considerations of operating risk, financing considerations cannot generally be accounted for on a project-by-project basis. Instead, because financial obligations are at the level of the company, the impact of leverage on required returns is determined by the capital structure of the whole company.

Another difference between financial risk and operating risk is the extent to which a company can control each type of risk. A company can control its financial risk to a reasonable extent (and typically at reasonable cost) by its choice of capital structure and the maturities of its financial obligations. As previously noted, in theory a company could have zero financial risk if it was financed entirely with equity. By contrast, the company's operating risk is not as easily controlled.

Although a company's choice of assets affects its operating risk via operating leverage (commitments to fixed as opposed to variable costs), the choice of assets is often constrained in some way. Technological considerations may force a company to use certain processes that have a large component of either fixed or variable expense. For example, some products can be produced by one method only. Thus, we point out again: operating risk is not easily manipulated, whereas financial risk is controlled by the company's financial policy.

Subsidiaries

Whenever a company splits itself into separate units, with each unit having limited liability with respect to its financing, the capital structure of each unit becomes the relevant consideration for a cost of capital. Therefore, if a company is considering a capital budgeting project where the financing will be obtained by creating a subsidiary for which the company has limited liability, the cost of capital for financing that project must reflect the capital structure of the subsidiary.

How Leverage Affects the Cost of Capital

In a perfect capital market environment, capital structure (the choice of leverage) is a pure risk-return trade-off and doesn't affect value. We saw this in the Per-Pet example earlier in the chapter. This fact allows us to draw some important conclusions about the various required returns in equation (11.1).

Most importantly, if capital structure is irrelevant, the value of a capital budgeting project is unaffected by how the project is financed. This means that WACC *does not* vary with L; WACC is constant for *all* values of L because changes in L don't affect the total value of the project or its expected cash flows. If the present value and the expected cash flows are constant, the third parameter in the present value equation, WACC, must also be constant. However, as we saw in the Per-Pet example, changes in leverage alter how the risk of the project is borne by the debtholders and shareholders. Therefore, leverage *does* affect r_e and r_d, even in a perfect capital market environment.

Based on the fact that WACC is constant across all possible values of $L = D/(D + E)$, we can determine the values of r_e and r_d when L takes on either of its extreme possible values. When the company is all-equity-financed, $L = 0.0$, the second term in equation (11.1) drops out, so that WACC $= r_e$. At the other extreme, when the company is all-debt-financed, the first term drops out because $(1 - L) = 0.0$, and WACC $= (1 - T)r_d$.[6]

The result that WACC $= r_e$ (with $L = 0.0$) and that WACC $= (1 - T)r_d$ (with $L = 1.0$) makes intuitive sense. The debtholders of a company that is financed totally with debt would bear all of the company's business risk. As such, the debtholders' risk would be the same as the risk borne by the shareholders if the company were all-equity-financed. Therefore, these two returns must be equal because the risks are equal. The only difference between the all-debt and all-equity alternatives would be in taxes—assuming an otherwise perfect capital market: An all-debt-financed company that is just earning its required return would not pay any income taxes because interest would exactly offset its taxable income; the all-equity-financed company would pay corporate income taxes because it would have no interest expense, and all its income would therefore be taxable.

A second implication to be drawn from a perfect capital market analysis involves the return that debtholders will require for financing only an infinitesimal fraction of the investment—r_d when L is tiny. We established above that a company that is truly

---

[6]We know of no company that is literally all-debt-financed ($L = 1.0$). Strictly speaking, L is always less than 1.0. For convenience, rather than continue to indicate that L is as close to 1.0 as possible, we will simply refer to $L = 1.0$.

100%-equity-financed has no chance of default. Such a hypothetical company can borrow a *very small* amount of money in our assumed environment at the riskless return. For example, the amount of money such a company could borrow at the riskless return may be only 1 cent for 1 minute. Still, conceptually, the required return on the first fraction of debt in a perfect capital market environment *must be* the required return for the riskless asset, r_f.

Based on these two implications from a perfect market analysis (and hypothetical functions for r_e and r_d), figure 11.6 illustrates the relationships that can be established in a perfect capital market environment.

Toshiba's Leveraged Investment   EXAMPLE

Let's say Toshiba plans to invest $1 million in a one-year capital budgeting project. The company will borrow $500,000 from a bank and put up $500,000 in cash. The bank is charging 9% interest. Assume Toshiba pays no taxes and operates in a perfect capital market environment. With this arrangement, Toshiba expects a return of 16% on its equity investment. What would Toshiba's return be without the leverage?

Toshiba expects a dollar return (above its return of capital) of $80,000 (= [0.16]500,000) after paying interest (above its repayment of capital) of $45,000 (= [0.09]500,000). So the project is expected to have a total dollar return of $125,000 (= 80,000 + 45,000). Without leverage, therefore, the project has an expected return of 12.5% (= 125,000/1,000,000).

Another way to answer the question is to calculate the weighted average of the returns. The project's 12.5% expected return = (0.5)16% + (0.5)9%. ■

How Leverage Affects Beta

We now know that leverage entails a pure risk-return trade-off. But how does leverage affect beta?

An investor's risky portfolio, the market portfolio, is made up of individual stocks. Each has its own beta. Each stock then contributes to the beta of the market portfolio. The investor then makes a choice about personal leverage (lending or borrowing). That leverage choice puts the investor's total investment at a specific point on the CML and determines the investor's risk-return trade-off.

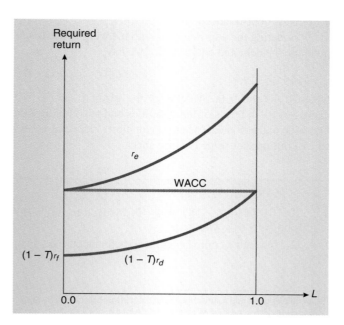

FIGURE 11.6
WACC (weighted average cost of capital), r_e (required return for equity), and r_d (required return for debt) as hypothetical functions of L (leverage ratio) in a perfect capital market environment.

The process is similar for the company's leverage but actually occurs *before* the investor makes the personal leverage choice. So the stock's beta already has embedded in it the effect of the company's leverage choice.

As we noted earlier, the company can be viewed as a portfolio of assets. Therefore, the asset beta for the company, β_A, is simply the weighted average of its asset betas, or

$$\beta_A = \sum_{j=1}^{J} w_j\beta_j \tag{11.2}$$

where J is the company's total number of assets and w_j is the proportion of company value invested in asset $j(j = 1, 2, \ldots, J)$. The company's WACC can then be expressed in terms of β_A as

$$\text{WACC} = r_f + \beta_A(r_M - r_f) \tag{11.3}$$

This expression is based on the asset (left-hand) side of our market value balance sheet view of the company. In contrast, equation (11.1) is based on the liabilities and stockholders' equity (right-hand) side of our market value balance sheet. Comparing the two expressions points out once again that the required return for equity, r_e, is not necessarily the WACC to use for measuring the NPV of a capital budgeting project, even if the risk of the project is identical to the risk of the company as a whole. The difference is the company's leverage. As shown in figure 11.6, WACC and r_e are equal only if the company has no leverage ($L = 0.0$).

Now we can draw the parallel between the company's leverage and the shareholder's personal leverage. After choosing its assets, and therefore β_A, the company then chooses its leverage, which determines the stock's beta, β.

What must be the relationship between the asset beta for the company, β_A (which is a weighted average of asset betas), and the shareholders' beta? β_A can be thought of as the shareholders' beta if the company were all-equity-financed. But now we need to add the effect of debt. Just as there are equity betas and asset betas, there are debt betas.

A portfolio's beta is simply the weighted average of its components. Although the idea for a company is the same, the equity and debt components are taxed in different ways. Corporate interest payments are tax deductible. Therefore, we must adjust the asset beta for this taxation difference, just as we did in other cases. The adjustment requires multiplying the asset beta by an adjustment factor that includes L and the corporate tax rate, T. The factor TL is simply adjusting for the tax deductibility of the interest on the proportion L of the project cost that is debt-financed.

Equating the adjusted beta with the weighted average of the betas of the financing components, the debt and equity betas, we have:

$$(1 - TL)\beta_A = L\beta_d + (1 - L)\beta \tag{11.4}$$

where β_d is the beta of debt for the given L, and β is the equity beta.[7] Equation (11.4) expresses β_A in terms of the liabilities and stockholders' equity (right-hand) side of our market value balance sheet, whereas equation (11.2) expresses β_A in terms of the asset (left-hand) side of our market value balance sheet.

Self-Check

1. True or false? Operating risk exists project by project. Financial risk exists for the company as a whole.

2. How can a company control its financial risk? Is operating risk easier to control?

---

[7]Sometimes people add a subscript e to make it clear that it is the equity beta. In order to emphasize that it is the same β we used to derive the CAPM in chapter 7, we have not added the subscript e.

3. Suppose a company will finance a project through a subsidiary for which it will have only limited liability. Which capital structure should it use to calculate the WACC for the project?

4. True or false? A company's asset beta, β_A, is simply the weighted average of its separate asset betas.

5. How is a company's WACC related to its asset beta in a perfect capital market environment?

A PRACTICAL PRESCRIPTION FOR ESTIMATING A COST OF CAPITAL

When a company takes on financial leverage, the risk borne by the debtholders is generally quite low.[8] If the debtholders bear no risk, β_d is zero. In such a case the debtholders will earn the riskless return, r_f. Even when the debtholders bear some of the company's risk, the amount is typically small compared with other investment opportunities. As a practical matter, if we approximate β_d as zero and solve for β_A, we can rewrite equation (11.4) as

$$\beta_A = \frac{(1-L)\beta}{(1-TL)} \tag{11.5}$$

We can use this expression to approximate β_A.

Calculating Officemate's β_A

Suppose Officemate International Corporation is contemplating an expansion of its current operations. To evaluate the proposed expansion, the financial vice president has asked you to estimate the cost of capital for the project. How do you proceed?

First, you look in an investor's guide and find that the beta for shares of common stock in Officemate is estimated to be 1.30. Second, you note that the current market value of a share of Officemate is $8.25 and that there are 2 million shares outstanding, so the market value of Officemate's equity is $16.5 million (=[8.25]2 million). From Officemate's balance sheet you determine that the total book value of all of Officemate's liabilities is $8.5 million.[9] For convenience, assume that the market value of debt is close to the book value. Based on these figures, L is approximately 0.34 (= 8.5/[8.5 + 16.5]). From Officemate's income statement, you estimate a marginal corporate tax rate of $T = 0.37$. Then, using equation (11.5), β_A is about 0.981:

$$\beta_A = \frac{(1-L)\beta}{(1-TL)} = \frac{(1-0.34)1.30}{[1-(0.37)(0.34)]} = 0.981$$

Finally, you estimate that r_f and r_M are 5% and 13%, respectively. Therefore, based on equation (11.3), Officemate should use a cost of capital for its expansion of about 12.8%:

$$\text{WACC} = r_f + \beta_A(r_M - r_f) = 0.05 + 0.981(0.13 - 0.05) = 0.128, \text{ or } 12.8\% \blacksquare$$

---

[8]An exception to this is a so-called junk (or high-risk) bond.
[9]Theoretically, the market value of the liabilities should be used rather than the book value. In practice, the book value is often used. This conceptual violation is not significant when the difference between the two measures is not large, for example less than 15%, which is often the case.

Estimating the Cost of Capital for a Capital Budgeting Project

In the Officemate example, the capital budgeting project was of the same risk class as the company's overall current operations. Now let's consider how to estimate the cost of capital for a project that is significantly different, such as one either in an area where the company has no experience or that has significantly different risk from the company's average.

In the next example, we'll show you how to use a group of companies as surrogates for estimating the risk of a project. The surrogate companies stand in place, or substitute, for the project for estimation purposes. Because the leverage and tax rates of the surrogate companies vary from our company and from each other, we cannot use these companies' stock betas directly. Instead, we must use equation (11.5) to compute each company's asset beta. The asset betas then provide a good estimate of our project's nondiversifiable operating risk.

EXAMPLE

Expanding Compact-Disk Player Production at Poly-brands

Poly-brands, Inc. is a multinational conglomerate with worldwide operations involving products and services that range from a ski resort in Vail, Colorado, to a high-tech ball-bearings manufacturing plant located in Bonn, Germany. The audio division of Poly is considering an expansion of its compact-disk player manufacturing facilities located just outside of Tokyo. Poly needs to estimate the project's cost of capital.

Poly's stock and bonds are publicly traded on major exchanges and we can estimate Poly's WACC. However, in this case, Poly's WACC is not a good estimate of the project's cost of capital, because the manufacture of compact-disk players has greater operating risk than the average risk of all of Poly's assets.

The steps for estimating the beta for this project are

1. Obtain estimates of stock betas for a sample of surrogate companies whose primary business is the manufacture of audio products, especially compact-disk players.

2. Estimate β_A for each of the companies in the manner illustrated in the Officemate example.

3. The average of all the company betas is the estimate of beta for Poly's project.

4. Estimate the expected market return, r_M, and riskless return, r_f, as 5% and 13%, respectively.

Table 11.2 summarizes the beta estimation procedure. The estimate for the asset beta is 1.31. The cost of capital for Poly's project is then calculated using equation (11.3):

$$\text{WACC} = 0.05 + 1.31(0.13 - 0.05) = 0.155, \text{ or } 15.5\% \;\blacksquare$$

TABLE 11.2

Estimating the Beta of Poly-brands, Inc.'s Capital Budgeting Project

SAMPLE COMPANY	β	L	T	$\dfrac{(1 - L)\beta}{(1 - TL)}$
A	1.70	0.29	0.42	1.37
B	1.85	0.45	0.31	1.18
C	1.95	0.37	0.34	1.41
D	1.90	0.43	0.28	1.23
E	2.00	0.42	0.34	1.35
F	1.60	0.35	0.38	1.20
G	1.65	0.26	0.42	1.37
H	1.80	0.34	0.37	1.36
				Average asset beta = 1.31

How Operating Leverage Affects Beta and the Cost of Capital

We said earlier that operating risk is the primary determinant of a project's cost of capital. We also noted that often a company has little control over a project's operating leverage because of technological, efficiency, or other production considerations. However, for those projects where a company has a choice of operating leverage, how does operating leverage affect the project's beta and cost of capital?

Unlike financial leverage, operating leverage affects β_A, and therefore affects the WACC. Its effect is similar to the effect of leverage on r_e—an increase in operating leverage increases β_A and the WACC. Changes in the WACC then in turn affect both r_e and r_d.

The Cost of Capital with a Choice of Operating Leverage

Because operating risk affects the beta of a capital budgeting project, the estimation method outlined above must have one more condition added to it when there is a choice of operating leverage. If there are significant differences in operating risk among potential production methods, the sample of representative companies must be restricted to those companies that are using a set of assets and production methods that are approximately equivalent to those in the proposed project.

Estimating the Cost of Capital with a Choice of Operating Leverage   **EXAMPLE**

Let's reexamine Poly-brands, Inc.'s capital budgeting project. A technological advance in the production process for manufacturing CD players has recently occurred. Poly's project will use this new process. Assume that companies B, D, and F in table 11.2 are using the new process. The other companies are more established and have not yet upgraded their production process. What cost of capital should Poly use?

In this case, the subsample of only companies B, D, and F are used to estimate beta. They have an average implied company beta of about 1.20. So the estimated project beta would be 1.20, rather than the 1.31 average for all eight companies. This produces a slightly lower WACC of 14.6% $(= 0.05 + 1.20[0.13 - 0.05])$. ■

Self-Check

1. Describe a three-step procedure for estimating the beta for a project whose risk differs from that of the company considering it.

2. How does operating leverage affect a project's beta and its cost of capital?

3. How do differences in operating risk affect the choice of companies to use in estimating the beta for a project?

SUMMARY

The cost of capital—a capital budgeting project's required return—is based on the concept of an opportunity cost. It is estimated from the expected return on comparable publicly traded securities. The relevant question is "What else can be done with the money?" Chapter 11 makes several fundamental points about estimating the cost of capital. Chapter 12 examines the effect of capital market imperfections such as asymmetric taxes, asymmetric information, and transaction costs on a company's financing decision.

- The cost of capital is not the historical cost of funds. Market rates change regularly because of changes in expected inflation and in the supply and demand for money. Investment decisions must be based on the alternatives that are *currently* available.

- The cost of capital depends on a project's operating risk. Theoretically, each project has its own cost of capital. In practice, however, projects are typically categorized by risk classes, each of which has a different cost of capital.
- A project's cost of capital is the same as the cost of capital for the company's current operations *only* if the nondiversifiable risk of the project is identical to the nondiversifiable risk of the existing company taken as a whole.
- Present value is a function of both expected cash flows and the required return. With a pure risk-return trade-off, present value is constant, and changes in the other two parameters offset one another.
- Except for capital market imperfections, changes in financial leverage involve a pure risk-return trade-off. Therefore, a capital budgeting project's cost of capital does not vary as the degree of financial leverage changes—in a perfect capital market environment.
- A project's cost of capital does not equal either the required return on debt or the required return on leveraged equity. The cost of capital is the *weighted average* of the current required returns on debt and equity, where the weights are the market-value proportions of debt and equity in the company's capital structure. In a perfect capital market environment, this weighted average is constant across alternative financing packages and is equal to the required return for an all-equity-financed company.
- The leverage ratio, L, depends on the market values of the company's debt and equity, not on the initial cost of the investment. The cost and the market value differ by the NPV of the investment.
- Potential differences in the value of a project between one company and another undertaking the project are reflected in the expected cash flows rather than the cost of capital.
- With riskless (or very low risk) debt, the relationship between the asset beta and the equity beta depends on the leverage ratio and marginal tax rate as given in equation (11.5). If debt is risky, the relationship between the asset beta and the equity beta is given by equation (11.4).
- When a project's risk differs from the average risk of the company's existing assets, its cost of capital can be estimated using the risk and cost of capital for other businesses (surrogate companies) with lines of business that resemble the project.

EQUATION SUMMARY

(11.1) $$\text{WACC} = \frac{E}{(D+E)}r_e + \frac{D}{(D+E)}(1-T)r_d = (1-L)r_e + L(1-T)r_d$$

(11.2) $$\beta_A = \sum_{j=1}^{J} w_j\beta_j$$

(11.3) $$\text{WACC} = r_f + \beta_A(r_M - r_f)$$

(11.4) $$(1-TL)\beta_A = L\beta_d + (1-L)\beta$$

(11.5) $$\beta_A = \frac{(1-L)\beta}{(1-TL)}$$

CHAPTER REVIEW ACTIVITIES

SELF-TEST PROBLEMS

1. (Calculating the WACC) Sopranzetti Sports has 50,000 bonds and 1,000,000 shares outstanding. The bonds have a $1000 face value, $950 market value, and 10% yield to maturity. The stock has a market price of $62.50 per share and an estimated required return of 16%. Sopranzetti's tax rate is 34%.

   a. What is the after-tax cost of debt financing?

   b. What is the after-tax cost of equity financing?

   c. What is the weighted average cost of capital?

2. (Estimating the WACC using a surrogate company) Dyl Pickle is a new company in the condiment business. Dyl has $25 million in debt and its equity is worth an estimated $50 million. Since Dyl is not publicly traded, it is unsure of its cost of capital and cost of equity. Dyl considers Mercado Products to be very similar to itself and will use Mercado as a surrogate company to estimate its own WACC. Mercado's equity beta is 1.40, its leverage ratio is 40%, and its marginal tax rate is 34%. Dyl's tax rate is also 34%.
   a. Estimate Mercado's and Dyl's asset beta.
   b. Estimate Dyl's equity beta.
   c. Assuming a riskless return of 6% and an expected return on the market of 14%,

   what should be Dyl Pickle's cost of capital and cost of equity?

SOLUTIONS TO SELF-TEST PROBLEMS

1. a. The after-tax cost of debt financing is $(1 - T)r_d = 0.66(10\%) = 6.6\%$.
   b. The after-tax cost of equity financing is $r_e = 16\%$.
   c.

Component	Number	Price	Total Value	Weight	Cost	Weighted Cost
Bonds	50,000	950	47,500,000	0.4318	6.6%	2.85%
Stock	1,000,000	62.5	62,500,000	0.5682	16	9.09
			110,000,000	1.0000	WACC =	11.94%

The weights are the proportions of the $110,000,000 total market value represented by bonds and stock. The weighted average cost of capital is 11.94%.

2. a. Using Mercado's tax rate and leverage ratio, Mercado's asset beta is:
$$\beta_A = \frac{(1-L)\beta}{(1-TL)} = \frac{(1-0.40)(1.40)}{(1-(0.34)0.40)} = 0.972$$

This is also the estimate for Dyl's asset beta.
   b. Dyl's leverage ratio is $L = \$25$ million / ($25 million + $50 million) = 1/3. Using the same equation as in part a, we now solve for the equity beta (β) instead of the asset beta (β_A):
$$0.972 = \frac{(1-1/3)\beta}{[1-0.34(1/3)]}$$

Solving this for the equity beta gives us $\beta = 1.293$.
   c. Dyl's cost of capital is:
$$\text{WACC} = r_f + \beta_A(r_M - r_f) = 6\% + 0.972(14\% - 6\%) = 13.776\%$$

The cost of equity is:
$$r_e = r_f + \beta(r_M - r_f) = 6\% + 1.293(14\% - 6\%) = 16.344\%$$

QUESTIONS

1. Define what we mean by the company's financing decision and the company's investment decision. What entities are on the "other side" of these decisions?
2. What is the NPV of a project that has an IRR exactly equal to its cost of capital?
3. What are the two factors on which present value depends?
4. Distinguish between operating leverage and financial leverage.
5. Give an example of a case where the expected future cash flows are increased but the present value of the cash flows remains unchanged.
6. A company uses a single discount rate to compute the NPV of all its potential capital budgeting projects, even though the projects have a wide range of nondiversifiable risk. The company then undertakes all those projects with positive NPVs. Briefly explain why such a company would tend to become riskier over time.
7. The treasurer of a large company is considering investing $50 million in 10-year Treasury notes that yield 8.5%. The company's WACC is 15%. Is this a negative-NPV project? Explain.
8. Yukon Etiquette, Inc. has a beta of 1.85 and is deciding whether to issue stock to raise money for a capital budgeting project that has the same risk as the market and an IRR of 20%. If the riskless return is 10% and the expected return on the market is 15%, under what conditions should the company go ahead with the investment?

9. What are the important differences in the way operating risk (versus financial risk) enters into the consideration of a capital budgeting project?

CHALLENGING QUESTIONS

10. Describe how you would go about estimating a required return for computing the NPV of a project.

11. Assume that the value of a company is not identical when it is computed using the left-hand versus right-hand sides of our market value balance sheet. In particular, suppose that the value of the assets $(A_1 + A_2 + \dots)$ is $10 million, whereas the value of the liabilities and stockholders' equity (Equity + Debt) is $8.5 million, both on the basis of market values in their respective markets. Assuming both values are correct, what transactions could you make to profit from this situation? Can you think of a second set of transactions you could use as an alternative way to profit from the situation?

12. A company calculates its cost of debt and finds it to be 9.75%. It then calculates its cost of equity capital and finds it to be 16.25%. The company's chairman tells the chief financial officer that the company should issue debt because it is cheaper than equity. How should the chief financial officer respond to the chairman? (You may assume that the chief financial officer's job is secure!)

PROBLEM SET A

A1. (Calculating the WACC) The required return on debt is 8%, the required return on equity is 14%, and the marginal tax rate is 40%. If the company is financed 70% equity and 30% debt, what is the weighted average cost of capital?

A2. (Calculating the WACC) The following values apply to the Drop Corporation: $r_d = 7.5\%$, $r_e = 13\%$, $T = 38\%$, $D = \$100$, and $E = \$200$. What is the weighted average cost of capital?

A3. (Market versus book value weights) Prakesh Productions has 10,000 outstanding bonds that have a book value of $1000 per bond and a market value of $1050 per bond. Prakesh has 40,000 outstanding shares with a per-share book value of $20 and market value of $45. When estimating the weighted average cost of capital, what proportions of debt and equity capital should be used?

A4. (Estimating the WACC with three sources of capital) Eschevarria Research has the capital structure given below. If Eschevarria's tax rate is 30%, what is its weighted average cost of capital?

	Book value	Market value	Before-tax cost
Bonds	$1000	$1000	8%
Preferred stock	400	300	9%
Common stock	600	1700	14%

A5. (Calculating the WACC) Exxon's required return for equity, r_e, is 14%. Its required return for debt, r_d, is 8%, its debt-to-total-value ratio, L, is 35%, and its marginal tax rate, T, is 40%. Calculate Exxon's WACC.

A6. (Finding NPVs with differing project risks) Assume that the expected return on the market portfolio is 15% and the riskless return is 9%. Also assume that all of the projects listed below are perpetuities with annual cash flows (in $) and betas as indicated. None of the projects requires or precludes any of the other projects and each project costs $2000.

Project	A	B	C	D	E	F
Annual cash flow	310	500	435	270	385	450
Beta	1.00	2.25	2.22	0.65	1.37	2.36

a. What is the NPV of each project?   b. Which projects should the company undertake?

A7. (Asset and equity betas) Goh Travel, Inc. is a diversified conglomerate with six different business lines. The investments, their betas, and the proportion of the company's value invested in each are given below. Goh has a 30% tax rate.

Project	A	B	C	D	E	F
Proportion of company value	20%	10%	12%	10%	34%	14%
Beta	1.00	2.25	2.22	0.65	1.37	2.36

a. What is β_A for Goh Travel?

b. If Goh is 20% debt-financed, what is Goh's equity beta, β?

A8. (Asset and equity betas) If Goodyear has a debt-to-total-value ratio, L, of 43%, a tax rate of 34%, and its common stock has a beta of 1.32, what is the approximate value of Goodyear's company beta, β_A?

PROBLEM SET B

B1. (Cost of equity) The cost of capital is 10%, the after-tax cost of debt is 5%, and the company is 50% debt-financed. What is the cost of equity?

B2. (Cost of equity) The cost of capital is 11%, the before-tax cost of debt is 8%, and the marginal income tax rate is 40%. The market value of debt is $40 million and the market value of equity is $80 million. What is the cost of equity?

B3. (Capital structure weights) The cost of capital is 14%, the after-tax cost of debt is 6%, and the cost of equity is 16%. What proportions of the company are financed with debt and equity?

B4. (Capital structure weights) The required return on debt (before taxes) is 7.5%, the required return on equity is 15%, and the cost of capital is 10%. If the marginal income tax rate is 40%, what are the proportions of debt and equity financing?

B5. (Evaluating investments with differing risks) You are considering three stocks for investment purposes. The required return on the market portfolio is 14%, and the riskless return is 9%. Based on the information given below, in which (if any) of these stocks should you invest?

Stock	Beta	Current Price	Last Dividend	Growth Rate
A	1.3	$15	$1.20	5%
B	0.9	28	1.30	10
C	1.1	31	2.40	8

B6. (Finding the WACC) The information given below has been gathered about O'ryan Swim-Where, Ltd. Based on this information, estimate O'ryan's WACC.

Current market value of common shares (10 million outstanding)	$23.63/share
Next year's expected cash dividend	$1.92/share
Expected constant annual dividend growth rate	8%
Current market value of bonds	
(100,000 bonds outstanding, 8.5% coupon, maturing in 21 years)	$835.00/bond
Corporate tax rate	34%

B7. (Graphing the cost of capital) The D. B. Spiess Finance Corporation is financed with 80% debt and 20% common equity. Its required return on equity is $r_e = 25\%$ and its pretax cost of debt is 10%. Its marginal ordinary income tax rate is 40%. The riskless return is 8% (pretax). Graph WACC, r_e, and $(1 - T)r_d$ for values of L between 0 and 1. What have you assumed in drawing these curves?

B8. (All-equity and leveraged returns) You plan to invest $10,000 in a security, borrowing $6000 of the cost from a friend, thus putting up $4000 of your own money. The cost of debt is 12%, and there are no taxes. With this arrangement, you expect a return of 20% on your equity investment. What would your return be without the leverage? That is, what would your return be if the entire $10,000 was your own money?

B9. (Estimating the WACC) Seitz Nails has 2000 bonds outstanding with a $1000 face value per bond, 7% annual coupon, 15-year maturity, and $950 market value. Seitz has 50,000 shares out with a market value of $60 per share, expected dividend next year of $3.00, and a perpetual dividend growth rate of 6%. The marginal tax rate is 40%.

a. What is the after-tax cost of debt financing?

c. What is the weighted average cost of capital?

b. What is the after-tax cost of equity financing?

B10. (Estimating the WACC) Latin Pollo has 10,000 bonds and 400,000 shares outstanding. The bonds have a 10% annual coupon, $1000 face value, $1050 market value, and 10-year maturity.

The beta on the stock is 1.30 and its price per share is $40. The riskless return is 6%, the expected market return is 14%, and Latin Pollo's tax rate is 40%.

a. What is the after-tax cost of debt financing?

b. What is the after-tax cost of equity financing?

c. What is the weighted average cost of capital?

B11. (Estimating the WACC from the asset structure) McCabe Interests has three major investments, which are given below. What should be McCabe's weighted average cost of capital?

Investment	Market value	Required return
Storage sheds	$35 million	12%
Ice rinks	15 million	17%
Office furniture sales	50 million	15%

B12. (Project market line) Parr's Poultry Place, Inc. is considering two mutually exclusive 1-year capital budgeting projects, A and B. A costs $100,000, and its expected payoff 1 year later is $114,000. The variance of its return is 25%. B costs $50,000, and its expected payoff 1 year later is $56,000. The variance of its return is also 25%. The expected return and variance of return on the market portfolio are 14% and 16%, respectively. The going rate on government bonds is 9%, and Parr has bonds outstanding with a current yield of 10.5%. The correlation coefficient, Corr, between the returns for A and the market is 0.8, whereas the correlation coefficient between the returns for B and the market is 0.32. Ignoring taxes and depreciation, determine what investment decision Parr should make concerning these projects. (*Hint:* you may want to refer to equation (7.9).)

PROBLEM SET C

C1. (Finding the WACC using surrogate companies) Eastern Chemical has an oil and gas subsidiary that is considering the purchase of $100 million worth of proven oil and gas properties. Eastern's financial staff has compiled the following list of companies in the same business as the project under consideration, which is given below. All eight companies as well as Eastern pay income tax at a 34% marginal rate. Eastern's target debt ratio is 0.40, and its oil and gas subsidiary's target debt ratio is 0.50.

Company	Equity Beta	Debt Ratio, L
N.J. Chemical	1.35	0.35
Great Lakes Chemical	1.25	0.25
Johnson Chemical	1.50	0.45
Clark Chemical	1.40	0.40
Franklin Oil	1.40	0.50
Oscar Oil	1.45	0.50
VMB Oil & Gas	1.30	0.45
Peters Oil & Gas	1.55	0.60

a. Calculate an estimate of the unleveraged beta, β_A, for the proven oil and gas project. Eastern's subsidiary has bonds outstanding with a yield to maturity of 15.15%.

b. Assuming a 10% riskless return and a 16% expected return on the market port-

folio, calculate the required return on unleveraged equity, r_e, for the project.

c. Calculate the weighted average cost of capital, WACC.

C2. (Finding the WACC using surrogate companies) A company considering a capital budgeting project identifies five comparable companies and collects the information given below. The project should be one-third debt-financed, and the company's marginal tax rate is 34%.

Company	Beta	Debt Ratio, L
A	1.10	0.25
B	1.20	0.30
C	1.15	0.20
D	1.30	0.50
E	1.25	0.25

a. Calculate the leveraged beta for the project.

b. The riskless return is 9%, and the expected return on the market portfolio is 15%. Calculate the required return on project equity.

c. The cost of debt for the project (before taxes) is 11%. Calculate the cost of capital for the project.

C3. (Asset beta if debt is risky) Calimari Fisheries, Ltd. is financed with $L = 0.72$ proportion of debt, which is large enough that the beta of the company's debt, β_d, is 0.32—too large to ignore. If the beta of Calimari's common stock is 3.1 and the tax rate is 34%, what is the beta for the company's assets, β_A? (*Hint:* Because equation (11.5) assumes that the debt beta is zero, use equation (11.4), which allows risky debt.)

BIBLIOGRAPHY

Booth, Laurence. "The Influence of Production Technology on Risk and the Cost of Capital," *Journal of Financial and Quantitative Analysis,* 1991, 26(1):109–128.

Brigham, Eugene F., Dilip K. Shome, and Steve R. Vinson. "The Risk Premium Approach to Measuring a Utility's Cost of Equity," *Financial Management,* 1985, 14(1):33–45.

Brown, Keith C., W. V. Harlow, and Seha M. Tinic. "The Risk and Required Return of Common Stock Following Major Price Innovations," *Journal of Financial and Quantitative Analysis,* 1993, 28(1):101–116.

Butler, J. S., and Barry Schachter. "The Investment Decision: Estimation Risk and Risk-Adjusted Discount Rates," *Financial Management,* 1989, 18(4):13–22.

Chambers, Donald R., Robert S. Harris, and John J. Pringle. "Treatment of Financing Mix in Analyzing Investment Opportunities," *Financial Management,* 1982, 11(2):24–41.

Conine, Thomas E., Jr., and Maurry Tamarkin. "Divisional Cost of Capital Estimation: Adjusting for Leverage," *Financial Management,* 1985, 14(1):54–58.

Diamond, Douglas W., and Robert E. Verrecchia. "Disclosure, Liquidity, and the Cost of Capital," *Journal of Finance,* 1991, 46(4):1325–1360.

Durand, David. "Afterthoughts on a Controversy with MM, Plus Thoughts on Growth and the Cost of Capital," *Financial Management,* 1989, 18(2):12–18.

Ehrhardt, Michael C., and Yatin N. Bhagwat. "A Full-Information Approach for Estimating Divisional Betas," *Financial Management,* 1991, 20(2):60–69.

Fama, Eugene F. "Risk-Adjusted Discount Rates and Capital Budgeting Under Uncertainty," *Journal of Financial Economics,* 1977, 5(1):3–24.

Harris, Robert S. "Using Analysts' Growth Forecasts to Estimate Shareholder Required Rates of Return," *Financial Management,* 1986, 15(1):58–67.

Harris, Robert S., Thomas J. O'Brien, and Doug Wakeman. "Divisional Cost-of-Capital Estimation for Multi-Industry Firms," *Financial Management,* 1989, 18(2):74–84.

Kale, Jayant R., Thomas H. Noe, and Gabriel G. Ramirez. "The Effect of Business Risk on Corporate Capital Structure: Theory and Evidence," *Journal of Finance,* 1991, 46(5):1693–1716.

Krueger, Mark K., and Charles M. Linke. "A Spanning Approach for Estimating Divisional Cost of Capital," *Financial Management,* 1994, 23(1):64–70.

Linke, Charles M., and J. Kenton Zumwalt. "Estimation Biases in Discounted Cash Flow Analyses of Equity Capital Cost in Rate Regulation," *Financial Management,* 1984, 13(3):15–21.

Linke, Charles M., and J. Kenton Zumwalt. "The Irrelevance of Compounding Frequency in Determining a Utility's Cost of Equity," *Financial Management,* 1987, 16(3):65–69.

Mehta, Dileep R., Michael D. Curley, and Hung-Gay Fung. "Inflation, Cost of Capital, and Capital Budgeting Procedures," *Financial Management,* 1984, 13(4):48–54.

Modigliani, Franco, and Merton H. Miller. "The Cost of Capital, Corporation Finance, and the Theory of Investment," *American Economic Review,* 1958, 48(June):261–297.

Myers, Stewart C. "Determinants of Corporate Borrowing," *Journal of Financial Economics,* 1977, 5(2):147–175.

O'Brien, Thomas J., and Paul A. Vanderheiden. "Empirical Measurement of Operating Leverage for Growing Firms," *Financial Management,* 1987, 16(2):45–53.

Prezas, Alexandros P. "Effects of Debt on the Degrees of Operating and Financial Leverage," *Financial Management,* 1987, 16(2):39–44.

Ravid, S. Abraham. "On Interactions of Production and Financial Decisions," *Financial Management,* 1988, 17(3):87–99.

Siegel, Jeremy J. "The Application of the DCF Methodology for Determining the Cost of Equity Capital," *Financial Management,* 1985, 14(1):46–53.

Sundem, Gary L. "Evaluating Capital Budgeting Models in Simulated Environments," *Journal of Finance,* 1975, 30(4):977–991.

Taggart, Robert A., Jr. "Consistent Valuation and Cost of Capital Expressions with Corporate and Personal Taxes," *Financial Management,* 1991, 20(3):8–20.

Yagil, Joseph. "Divisional Beta Estimation Under the Old and New Tax Laws," *Financial Management,* 1987, 16(4):16–21.

CAPITAL STRUCTURE POLICY

OBJECTIVES

1. Describe six different views of capital structure: perfect market, corporate tax, personal tax, agency cost, bankruptcy cost, and pecking order.

2. Describe how these views depend on the three capital market imperfections—asymmetric taxes, asymmetric information, and transaction costs—and combine to create an environment in which a company's capital structure can affect its total value.

3. Explain how this combination of factors, which we call the capital market imperfections view of capital structure, leads to a preference order among financing alternatives in which retained earnings are the preferred source, debt is next, and new external equity is the least preferred source of new financing.

4. Explain why adjusting a company's WACC (weighted average cost of capital) for the impact of capital structure on company value is equivalent to adjusting the expected cash flows and required returns on equity and debt.

5. Adjust the cost of capital for the effect of capital structure on total company value.

424

A company's mix of financing methods is called its **capital structure.** In simple terms, capital structure refers to the company's proportion of debt financing, its leverage ratio. The leverage ratio was represented by L in equation (11.1). In practice, leverage ratios tend to be similar within an industry. For example, real estate investors such as Donald Trump and Merv Griffin use extensive debt financing.

In chapter 11, we said that capital structure does not affect company value—*in a perfect capital market environment*. Capital structure choice is a pure risk-return trade-off. We then showed that this is equivalent to saying that leverage does not affect the cost of capital—in a perfect capital market environment.

The question of whether capital structure affects company value in real capital markets has been called the *capital structure puzzle*. Puzzle is a particularly appropriate term because our understanding has evolved in much the same way that a puzzle is pieced together. Currently, pieces are still being added, and we still don't have the complete picture.

Capital structure matters in practice if for no other reason than that companies actually behave as though it does. The empirical evidence shows consistent patterns of leverage ratios, as though there are definite reasons for following certain policies. Some argue that companies are simply following the Behavioral Principle of Finance—just copying each other—and that these patterns continue from habit and imitation even though they don't affect company value. We believe this is too simplistic.

We've found that companies manage their capital structures carefully. The factors involved with choosing a capital structure are complex, and the impact of each factor on the value of the company is not clear-cut. However, we can describe such factors and classify them into three possible groups of persistent capital market imperfections: asymmetric taxes, asymmetric information, and transaction costs. (These three imperfec-

tions are described and discussed in more detail in enrichment topic A, Capital Market Efficiency.)

In principle, a company should balance the incremental advantage of more financial leverage against the incremental costs. Unfortunately, we don't have methods to precisely measure all the factors that are important.

A number of methods exist for analyzing the impact of alternative capital structures, but in the end, the choice of capital structure requires expert judgment. The analytical models give us a range of reasonable capital structures, rather than pinpoint the absolute best. In this chapter, we'll show you how a company can take into account the various relevant factors to select an appropriate capital structure. In the appendix to the chapter, we describe a practical method a company can use to manage its capital structure.

CAPITAL STRUCTURE
The makeup of the liabilities and stockholders' equity side of the balance sheet, especially the ratio of debt to equity.

CAPITAL STRUCTURE AND THE PRINCIPLES OF FINANCE

◆ *Incremental Benefits:* Consider the possible ways to minimize the value lost to capital market imperfections, such as asymmetric taxes, asymmetric information, and transaction costs. At the same time, be sure to include all of the transaction costs of making potentially beneficial financing transactions, because they reduce the *net* benefit from such transactions.

(continued on following page)

(Capital Structure and the Principles of Finance continued from previous page)

◆ *Capital Market Efficiency:* Recognize that the potential to increase company value through capital structure is smaller than the potential to increase company value through the introduction of *valuable new ideas* and wise use of the company's *comparative advantages.*

◆ *Signaling:* Consider any possible change in capital structure carefully, because financing transactions and capital structure changes convey information to outsiders and can be misunderstood.

◆ *Time Value of Money:* Include any time-value-of-money tax benefits from capital structure choices.

◆ *Valuable Ideas:* Look for opportunities to create value by issuing securities that are in short supply, perhaps resulting from changes in tax law.

◆ *Behavioral:* Look to the information contained in the capital structure decisions and financing transactions of other companies for guidance in choosing a capital structure.

◆ *Risk-Return Trade-Off:* Recognize that capital structure changes made at fair market security prices, which also change equity-debt risk bearing, are simply a risk-return trade-off. Such transactions don't affect company value (except for possible signaling effects).

DOES CAPITAL STRUCTURE MATTER?

PERFECT MARKET VIEW OF CAPITAL STRUCTURE
The analysis showing that a company's capital structure does not affect its value in a perfect capital market environment.

In chapter 11, we asserted that a company's capital structure does not affect its value in a perfect capital market environment. We demonstrated in the Per-Pet example that leverage is a pure risk-return trade-off in such an environment. This result is called the **perfect market view of capital structure.** The value of a company depends only on the size of its expected future operating cash flows and the cost of capital, not on how those cash flows are divided between the debtholders and the shareholders. Enrichment topic A, Capital Market Efficiency, discusses the concept of value conservation, which is the fundamental concept underlying the perfect market view.

Let's review our Per-Pet example. With or without leverage, the total value of the company is $1000. With leverage, the shareholders get $500 in exchange for half their claim on the company. Figure 12.1 illustrates these cases in terms of "pies." The total size of the pie is the same whether the company is leveraged or all-equity-financed. The only difference is in the claims on that pie. Figure 12.1 expresses the perfect market view in terms of total company value, the present value of the expected future cash flows.

Figure 12.2 is a reproduction of figure 11.6. Figure 12.2 also illustrates the perfect market view, but it does so in terms of the cost of capital, WACC, and the required returns on the expected future cash flows.

Recall that present value depends on both the cost of capital and the expected cash flows. If the cash flows don't change and one of the other parameters doesn't change, then the third must also remain constant. However, also recall that even though the leverage ratio L (the market-value proportion of debt financing—$D/[D + E]$) doesn't affect the WACC, it does affect how the risk of the company is borne by the shareholders and debtholders. Therefore, the required returns on equity and debt (r_e and r_d, respectively) depend on L.

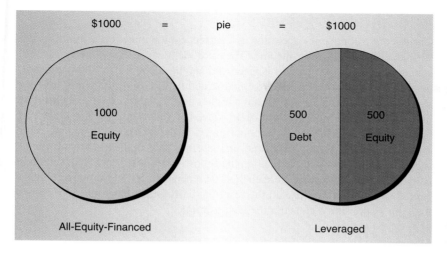

FIGURE 12.1
A "pie" representation of the perfect market view of capital structure.

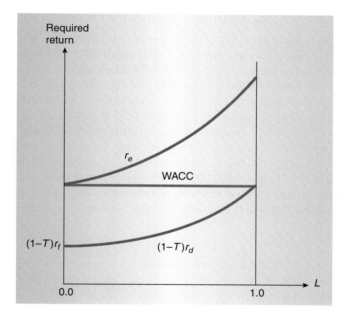

FIGURE 12.2
WACC (weighted average cost of capital), r_e (required return for equity), and r_d (required return for debt) as hypothetical functions of L (the leverage ratio) under the perfect market view of capital structure.

Finally, recall that the WACC can always be expressed as the weighted average cost of any financing package. With only equity and debt, the WACC is the weighted average of r_e and r_d adjusted for taxes,[1] or

$$\text{WACC} = (1 - L)r_e + L(1 - T)r_d \qquad (12.1)$$

Note how the weight is shifted from the higher return r_e to the lower return r_d as L increases and $(1 - L)$ decreases, leaving the WACC unchanged.

Another way of illustrating capital structure irrelevance is with an arbitrage argument. We show below that if two companies have identical operating profitability but different capital structures, arbitrage among investors will ensure that the two companies have equal market values.

---

[1]As we discussed in chapter 3 and again in chapter 11, the tax adjustment is necessary because interest payments are paid out *before* corporate taxes are levied on the company's income, but dividends are not paid out until after. See figure 12.6 for a visual representation of this process that includes personal taxes.

An Arbitrage Argument

Consider two companies operating in a perfect capital market environment. Each will generate $10,000,000 of operating income. They are identical in every other respect except for their capital structures. Company L is leveraged and has debt in its capital structure. Company U is unleveraged; it has an all-equity capital structure. The two companies have the market values shown in table 12.1. Company L has a higher market value, supposedly because of its leverage.

According to the perfect market view, the situation shown in table 12.1 cannot persist because of a profitable arbitrage opportunity. Shareholders of company L can realize a greater return on their investment, with no increase in either their investment risk or the amount of funds they have invested, by making the following transactions. First, sell their shares of company L. Second, borrow and create their own personal 50% leverage to duplicate company L's capital structure. Third, use all the resulting cash to purchase shares of company U. To illustrate this opportunity, consider the next example.

EXAMPLE

Arbitraging Leverage Valuation Differences

An investor owns 1% of the shares of company L. The first step in the arbitrage process is to sell these shares at their market value of $300,000 (1% of $30,000,000). The second step is to borrow an identical amount, $300,000, at an interest rate of 12% per year. This creates a personal capital structure that is 50% debt and 50% equity, exactly company L's capital structure. The final step is to use the total funds to purchase $600,000 (= 300,000 + 300,000) of company U shares, which happens to be 1.2% (= 600,000/50,000,000) of company U.

Now let's compare the return before and after. Before the three-step transaction, the investor's return per year is 1% of company L's expected net income, $64,000. After, the return per year is $120,000 (1.2% of company U's expected net income) minus an interest charge of $36,000 (12% of $300,000), or $84,000. Thus, without adding any funds, our investor has an investment with an identical amount of leverage (and therefore identical risk) that earns $20,000 (= 84,000 − 64,000) per year more after completing the arbitrage transaction. ∎

With self-interested arbitrage activity, investors will continue to sell company L and buy company U until the total market values of the two companies (debt and equity) are equal. Only when the total company values are equal will there be no further profitable arbitrage opportunity.

TABLE 12.1
An Illustration of Capital Structure Arbitrage

	COMPANY L	COMPANY U
Leverage ratio [= debt/(debt + equity)]	50%	0
Operating income	$10,000,000	$10,000,000
−Interest expense[a]	3,600,000	0
Net income	$ 6,400,000	$10,000,000
Market value of equity	$30,000,000	$50,000,000
Market value of debt	30,000,000	0
Total market value	$60,000,000	$50,000,000

[a]At a 12% interest rate.

Capital Market Imperfections

In our chapter introduction we mentioned three persistent capital market imperfections: tax asymmetries, information asymmetries, and transaction costs. So an important place to look for value-changing market imperfections is in the tax code. Whenever tax rates differ for the two sides of a transaction, there is a tax asymmetry that might be used to enhance company value.

Self-Check

1. What is the perfect market view of capital structure?

2. What is the formula for the WACC? Explain each variable and how it contributes to the WACC.

3. What is the shape of the WACC curve according to the perfect market view?

THE ROLE OF INCOME TAXES

We've pointed out numerous times that interest payments are tax deductible to the company, whereas dividend payments are not. This tax asymmetry gives rise to the **corporate tax view of capital structure.** In this view, corporate taxes cause debt to be cheaper than equity. The corporate tax view concludes that the maximum company value results from being essentially all-*debt*-financed.

CORPORATE TAX VIEW OF CAPITAL STRUCTURE The argument that double (corporate and individual) taxation of equity returns makes debt a cheaper financing method.

Corporate Income Taxes

We'll illustrate the corporate tax view by extending our Per-Pet example.

Corporate Taxes at Per-Pet, Inc.

EXAMPLE

As in our chapter 11 example, we'll start with an all-equity company and examine the effect of leverage on company value. We assume that Per-Pet must pay corporate taxes on its net income at the rate of 37.5% but operates in an otherwise perfect capital market environment. What is Per-Pet worth if it is all-equity-financed, and what is it worth with leverage?

Per-Pet has a perpetual expected cash inflow each year of $150, which can be larger or smaller, but is never less than $50 per year. Therefore, its expected after-tax net income is $93.75 per year (= [1 − 0.375]150). Per-Pet's cost of capital is 15%, so Per-Pet is worth $625 (= 93.75/0.15), compared with a $1000 value without corporate taxes (= 150/0.15).

Now suppose the company borrows $500 at 10% per year and gives the $500 to the shareholders. This debt will require $50 per year in interest payments. Because the interest payments are made *before* corporate taxes are assessed, they cost only $31.25 (= [1 − 0.375]50) in after-tax cash flow. After the capital structure change, then, the residual expected future cash flow to be paid out to shareholders each year is $62.50 (= 93.75 − 31.25).[2] Once again, the leverage would increase the shareholders' required return to 20%. Therefore, under the proposed leveraging, shareholders would get $500 from the debtholders in cash to invest as they wish and have a remaining investment worth $312.50 (= 62.50/0.20), for a total value of $812.50. Thus, in this environment, the proposed leveraging increases shareholder value by $187.50 (= 812.50 − 625.00).

Simultaneously, the total value of Per-Pet would also increase by the same $187.50. With no leverage, the company is worth $625.00 (= 93.75/0.15). Under the proposed leveraging, total company value is the value of the debt (500) plus the value of the equity (312.50), for a total value of $812.50. ∎

---

[2]This amount can also be computed starting with the company's expected income of $150 per year: Subtract the $50 interest payment and apply the corporate tax rate so that (1 − 0.375)(150 − 50) = $62.50.

The extra value for the Per-Pet shareholders can be traced directly to the tax asymmetry. The expected after-tax cash flows to investors increase because the government collects fewer tax dollars from the leveraged company. Specifically, with the all-equity capital structure, the company pays an average of $56.25 (= [0.375]150) in taxes per year. It pays an average of only $37.50 (= [0.375][150 − 50]) per year with the leveraged capital structure.

Figure 12.3 illustrates the corporate tax view of capital structure, showing the Per-Pet alternatives in terms of "pies." Once again, the total size of the pie is the same whether the company is leveraged or all-equity-financed, $1000. The only difference is in the claims on the pie. However, this time, under the corporate tax view, there are three claimants: shareholders, debtholders, and the government. When part of the cash flow is sold to the debtholders, the government collects less in taxes. This shrinks the government claim and leaves more for investors. Leverage increases the total after-tax company value from $625 to $812.50.

The Cost of Capital with Corporate Income Taxes

Although leverage actually changes the after-tax cash flows, the effect can be equivalently accounted for by adjusting the cost of capital. Let $\bar{I}$ represent the expected perpetual cash inflow per year. Then the unleveraged company pays taxes of $T\bar{I}$ each year, and the shareholders get the rest, an expected yearly after-tax cash flow of $\bar{I}(1 − T)$. The value of the unleveraged company, V_U, is then

$$V_U = \frac{\bar{I}(1 − T)}{r} \tag{12.2}$$

where r is the unleveraged cost of capital (15% in the Per-Pet example).

In the Per-Pet example, we adjusted the after-tax cash flows and the required returns for equity (20%) and debt (10%) to find the value of the leveraged company. Alternatively, we can represent the value of the leveraged company, V_L, in terms of the "basic" after-tax cash flow to the company and an appropriately adjusted cost of capital. The "basic" cash flow is the cash flow to the shareholders if the company were unleveraged, $\bar{I}(1 − T)$. This flow is what we called CFAT in capital budgeting (see chapter 9). Then

$$V_L = \frac{\bar{I}(1 − T)}{\text{WACC}} \tag{12.3}$$

FIGURE 12.3
A "pie" representation of the corporate tax view of capital structure.

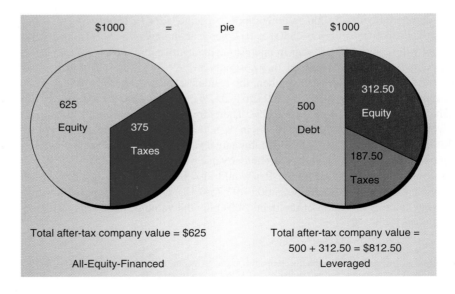

where WACC is the weighted average cost of capital, which has been adjusted for the effect of corporate taxes. Now we need to determine just what that adjustment is.

The company uses an amount of debt, $D = LV_L$, with interest payments of $r_d D$, the interest rate times the amount of debt. The debtholders earn a *risky* (rather than riskless) amount each period, which has an expected payment of $r_d D$.

The company pays taxes on all its income that is not paid out as interest. So the company's annual taxes are expected to be

$$T(\bar{I} - r_d D)$$

The combined after-tax cash flow expected to be paid out to debtholders and shareholders is a yearly perpetuity of

$$\bar{I} - T(\bar{I} - r_d D) = \bar{I}(1 - T) + T r_d D$$

The cash flows in this equation don't all have the same risk. The tax savings due to interest ($T r_d D$) have exactly the same riskiness as the debt (because they are strictly proportional to debt), and so the tax savings are discounted at r_d. However, the "basic" after-tax cash flows to equity ($\bar{I}[1 - T]$) are discounted at r, because they have the same risk as the company's assets, which is riskier than the debt payments. The value of the leveraged company is then the present value of these two cash flow streams:

$$V_L = \frac{\bar{I}(1 - T)}{r} + \frac{T r_d D}{r_d} = \frac{\bar{I}(1 - T)}{r} + TD \tag{12.4}$$

Because $\bar{I}(1 - T)/r$ is equal to the value of the unleveraged company, equation (12.2),

$$V_L = V_U + TD \tag{12.5}$$

This is the most common way of mathematically expressing the corporate tax view. The value of the leveraged company is equal to the value of the unleveraged company plus the tax rate times the amount of debt.

We can build on this result. A value for the WACC can be derived by setting equations (12.3) and (12.4) equal to each other and solving for the WACC. We'll spare you the details, and just give you the result:

$$\text{WACC} = r(1 - TL) \tag{12.6}$$

Figure 12.4 on page 432 illustrates the corporate tax view of capital structure in terms of the WACC and hypothetical functions for the required returns on equity and debt. Note that the function for the WACC is a straight line. The WACC decreases as leverage increases. The lowest value for the WACC, $r(1 - T)$, occurs when the company is financed entirely with debt, that is, when $L = D/(D + E) = 1.0$. Under the corporate tax view, then, the optimal capital structure—the one that creates the most valuable company—is the one that contains as much debt as possible.

The Cost of Capital at Per–Pet, Inc.

EXAMPLE

Now we can check our work by applying the adjusted cost of capital given in equation (12.6) to our Per-Pet example with corporate taxes. Under the proposed leveraging, the company borrows $500 and leveraged company value is $812.50. This means that Per-Pet's leveraged capital structure would be $L = D/(D + E) = 0.61538$ (= 500/812.50). (Remember, the leverage ratio is based on market values.) What is Per-Pet's cost of capital under the proposed leveraging?

From equation (12.6), we have

$$\text{WACC} = r(1 - TL) = (0.15)[1 - (0.375)(0.61538)] = 0.115385 = 11.5385\%$$

(continued on following page)

(The Cost of Capital at Per-Pet, Inc. *continued from previous page*)

Alternatively, we can also find the WACC using equation (12.1):

$$\text{WACC} = (1 - L)r_e + L(1 - T)r_d$$
$$= (0.38462)(0.20) + (0.61538)(1 - 0.375)(0.10) = 0.115385 = 11.5385\%$$

We can also verify that our adjustment produces the correct value for V_L using this WACC and Per-Pet's CFAT of $93.75 in equation (12.3):

$$V_L = \frac{\overline{I}(1 - T)}{\text{WACC}} = \frac{93.75}{0.115385} = \$812.50$$

Before moving on, we want to emphasize the equivalence between (1) adjusting the WACC and (2) adjusting the after-tax cash flows and required returns on equity and debt. Adjusting the WACC has become more commonly used, probably because of convenience. It involves only a single adjustment.

Also, it's important to reemphasize that *the leverage ratio is based on market values.*

Self-Check

1. What is the corporate tax view of capital structure?

2. Why does the U.S. corporate tax system seem to favor debt financing over equity financing?

3. According to the corporate tax view, what is the relationship between the leveraged value of the company V_L and its unleveraged value V_U?

4. What is the shape of the WACC curve according to the corporate tax view?

FIGURE 12.4

WACC (weighted average cost of capital), r_e (required return for equity), and r_d (required return for debt) as hypothetical functions of L (the leverage ratio) under the corporate tax view of capital structure.

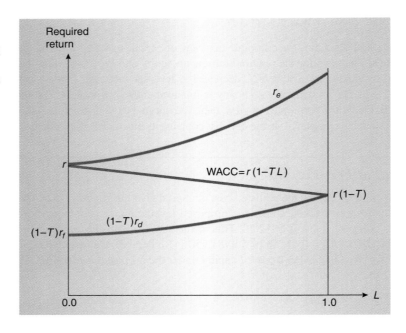

Personal Income Taxes

From an income tax perspective, our Per-Pet corporate tax example is incomplete. There are other significant taxes besides corporate income taxes. The company pays taxes on its income, but investors then pay personal income taxes on their income from the company. The rates investors pay are not all the same. The rates depend on the form of the investment, in particular whether it is equity or debt.

Interest and dividends are taxed when they are received, but capital gains are not taxed until the asset is sold. Therefore, a shareholder can postpone the tax on a gain by not selling the shares. At the same time, there is a mirror image treatment of losses. The shareholder can claim the tax shield resulting from a loss right away by selling the asset. This creates the valuable tax-timing option we first described in chapter 3. The capital gain tax-timing option lowers the effective tax rate on shareholder income. In turn, this lower effective rate leads to the **personal tax view of capital structure.** According to this view, the company is still operating in a perfect capital market environment, except for corporate *and* personal income taxes.

The personal tax view concludes that the differential between tax rates on personal income from equity and from debt cancels out the corporate tax asymmetry. The outcome is that leverage has no effect on company value in this environment and, once again, capital structure is irrelevant.

To illustrate the personal tax view of capital structure, let's extend our Per-Pet example one more time.

PERSONAL TAX VIEW OF CAPITAL STRUCTURE The argument that the difference in personal tax rates between income from debt and income from equity eliminates the disadvantage from the double (corporate and individual) taxation of income from equity.

Personal Taxes at Per-Pet, Inc.

EXAMPLE

Once again, we'll start with an all-equity company and examine the effect of leverage on company value. Suppose Per-Pet's debtholders' tax rate is 50%, whereas the shareholders' rate is 20%. Per-Pet's corporate tax rate is the same 37.5%, and it operates in an otherwise perfect capital market environment. What is Per-Pet worth if it is all-equity-financed, and what is it worth with leverage?

After paying 20% in personal taxes, the shareholders get to keep 80% (= 1.0 − 0.20) of their cash flow from the company, which after corporate taxes is expected to be $93.75 (= [1 − 0.375]150). With an all-equity capital structure, then, the shareholders' expected cash flow after corporate *and* personal taxes is $75.00 (= [0.8]93.75). On the basis of Per-Pet's 15% unleveraged cost of capital, Per-Pet is worth $500 (= 75.00/0.15).

Now suppose the company borrows $250 at an after-personal-taxes required return of 10%. The debtholders must receive 10% of $250, or $25 after taxes. Therefore, the interest payment from the company must be $50 (= 25/[1 − 0.5]) per year. This interest payment and corporate taxes leave an expected amount for the shareholders of $62.50 (= [1 − 0.375] [150 − 50]), on which they must pay personal taxes. Therefore, under the proposed leveraging, the shareholders have an expected annual cash flow after corporate and personal taxes of $50 (= [1 − 0.2]62.50). Again, the leverage would increase the shareholders' required return to 20%. Under the proposed leveraging, then, shareholders would get $250 from the debtholders in cash to invest as they wish and have a remaining investment in Per-Pet worth $250 (= 50/0.20). Thus, shareholders will have the same total value of $500 whether or not the company is leveraged.

The total value of Per-Pet is not changed, and capital structure is irrelevant in this environment. In both cases, the company is worth $500—either $500 worth of equity, or $250 worth of equity plus $250 worth of debt. ∎

Figure 12.5 illustrates the personal tax view of capital structure, showing the alternatives in our personal taxes Per-Pet example in terms of "pies." In this case, the total size of the pie is the same and the total taxes paid are the same. The only difference is the amounts paid for each type of tax. With all-equity financing, more in corporate taxes and less in personal taxes are paid than under the proposed leveraging. So in this case the total after-tax value is $500 either way.

If it occurs to you that the results illustrated in figure 12.5 depend on the personal tax rates we use, you're right. The critical issue is the amount that reaches the investor after corporate and personal taxes. Let T_d, T_e, and T represent the tax rates for debtholders, equityholders, and the corporation, respectively. The difference in equity and debt personal taxes exactly cancels out the corporate tax asymmetry *only* when

$$(1 - T_d) = (1 - T_e)(1 - T) \tag{12.7}$$

When this condition holds, the after-corporate-and-personal-taxes portion of the company's cash flow that "reaches" an investor is the same, whether the investor has an equity or debt claim. That is, a before-tax dollar singly taxed at T_d provides the same net amount to an investor as a before-tax dollar taxed at T and then taxed again at T_e.

E X A M P L E

Neutral Tax Rates

If the $T_e = 10\%$, $T = 30\%$, and $T_d = 37\%$, then equation (12.7) is satisfied:

$$(1 - 0.37) = (1 - 0.1)(1 - 0.3) = 0.63$$

Figure 12.6 illustrates the tax process using these tax rates. Note once again how the cash flows to the shareholders are taxed twice, whereas those going to the debtholders are taxed only once, but at a higher rate. ◼

It's important to understand that the personal tax view that capital structure is irrelevant depends on having tax rates that satisfy equation (12.7).

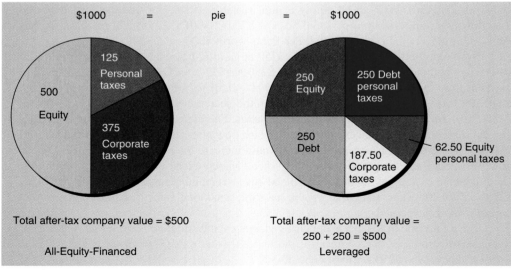

FIGURE 12.5
A "pie" representation of the personal tax view of capital structure.

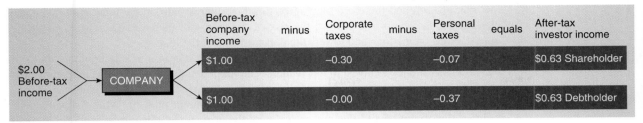

		Before-tax company income	minus	Corporate taxes	minus	Personal taxes	equals	After-tax investor income
$2.00 Before-tax income	COMPANY	$1.00		−0.30		−0.07		$0.63 Shareholder
		$1.00		−0.00		−0.37		$0.63 Debtholder

FIGURE 12.6
An example of corporate and personal taxation of cash flows going to shareholders and debtholders.

Combined Effect of Corporate and Personal Income Taxes

Suppose tax rates are such that (1) personal taxes do not *exactly* cancel out the corporate tax asymmetry and (2) the single tax rate on debt income is smaller than the combined tax rate on corporate income and equity returns. Then the conclusion of the corporate tax view of capital structure still holds—more leverage increases company value by reducing the net loss to taxes. But the benefit to leverage is significantly less than if we ignore personal taxes. Therefore, even if personal taxes don't eliminate the corporate tax asymmetry, they significantly reduce it, along with the net benefit to leverage.

We believe—and we think we have the support of most of our colleagues in the finance profession—that there is a net tax benefit to leverage. If so, why don't companies employ 100% leverage? Let's see why.

Self-Check

1. What is the personal tax view of capital structure?

2. If $T = 0.3$ and $T_d = 0.35$, what tax rate on equity income T_e leads equation (12.7) to hold?

3. How can the personal tax view reach the same conclusion as the perfect market view concerning the irrelevance of capital structure?

4. How do personal taxes modify the conclusion of the corporate tax view of capital structure?

5. Explain how capital gains tax law creates a tax-timing option.

THE ROLE OF AGENCY COSTS AND FINANCIAL DISTRESS COSTS

Certain conflicts of interest among the debtholders, shareholders, and managers that are caused by the problem of asymmetric information create agency costs. These conflicts give rise to the **agency cost view of capital structure.** In this view, capital market imperfections resulting from agency cost considerations create a complex environment in which capital structure affects a company's value. This view also concludes that a company's value is maximized by some mixture of debt and equity.

We'll discuss a few of these conflicts of interest here to illustrate the potential role of agency costs. A more complete discussion of these and other agency cost considerations is contained in enrichment topic C, Financial Contracting.

AGENCY COST VIEW OF CAPITAL STRUCTURE
The argument that some level of debt financing (more than zero but less than 100%) minimizes total agency costs.

Agency Costs of Debt

A major conflict that arises from the use of debt financing is the possibility that shareholders will expropriate wealth from the debtholders. Recall the problem of *asset substitution.* Suppose debtholders loan money to the company assuming that the company will invest in a low-risk project, and therefore they agree to a low interest rate on the loan. If the company then invests in a high-risk project, the risk of the loan will increase. This increases the required return on the loan and lowers the present value of the loan.

As a second example, recall the problem of *claim dilution.* Let's assume that the company borrows money to invest in its business, and immediately thereafter the company's managers do a leveraged buyout. That is, they take over ownership of the company with a very small amount of equity financing and a tremendous amount of debt. What happens to the value of the original debt? The present value of the original debt decreases, and the decrease is lost to those debtholders, but gained by the shareholders.[3]

Agency conflicts among the company's various claimants must be resolved in some way. When possible, contracts that eliminate these conflicts are created. For example, restrictive covenants, such as a restriction on leverage, are used to limit potential conflicts. The agency costs of debt tend to increase with leverage. These costs limit how much leverage is beneficial to shareholders.

The trade-off among the agency costs of all the company's various claimants (stakeholders) leads to the agency cost view. This view holds that the optimal capital structure is a mix of multiple types of securities, rather than all debt or all equity. This mix minimizes the company's *total* agency costs.

Self-Check

1. What is the agency cost view of capital structure?

2. How does increased leverage provide incentives for asset substitution?

3. How does increased leverage lead to claim dilution?

Financial Distress and Bankruptcy Costs

BANKRUPTCY COST VIEW OF CAPITAL STRUCTURE The argument that the expected indirect and direct costs of financial distress and bankruptcy reduce the benefits to additional debt financing.

With debt in its capital structure, a company has an expected cost of bankruptcy. This gives rise to the **bankruptcy cost view of capital structure.** In this view, capital market imperfections associated with financial distress and bankruptcy offset the other benefits from leverage from such things as taxes and agency costs.

It's an Expected Cost Financial distress or bankruptcy costs occur only if financial distress or bankruptcy actually occurs. Therefore, it is important to note that with an ongoing company that is not in financial distress, the cost is a mathematical expectation. This expected value is considerably less than the actual cost when there is only a small chance of bankruptcy.

The expected cost of financial distress and bankruptcy includes *indirect costs* and *direct costs* such as notification costs, court costs, and legal fees. Somewhat surprisingly, the direct costs are relatively small when compared to the company's value or the indirect costs of bankruptcy.

The indirect costs of financial distress and bankruptcy can involve virtually every aspect of the company. It can be very costly to have management's attention diverted from the day-to-day operation of the business in order to deal with the financial distress and bankruptcy process. After filing for bankruptcy, every major decision a company makes may require approval by the bankruptcy court. When financial distress occurs, suppliers may refuse to ship goods other than on a COD basis, or even refuse to ship altogether. For example, at one point, Macy's Department Stores experienced financial difficulties that led many suppliers to halt shipments of goods.

---

[3]Other debtholder-stockholder conflicts that are relevant to a company's capital structure include the underinvestment problem and the effect of asset uniqueness.

A company may lose tax shields during periods of financial distress. This is another tax asymmetry that can affect a company's value.[4] Loss carryforwards and loss carrybacks are sometimes limited. As a result, some of the corporate tax shields due to leverage may be lost during a period of financial distress. Further, even if all current losses can be fully carried forward and eventually deducted from future income, the company still loses the time value of money on the tax shields. So the possibility of lost tax shield value limits the net tax benefits of leverage and makes "too much" leverage undesirable.

The most significant potential cost of financial distress and bankruptcy is an indirect cost that can be difficult to measure but should not be underestimated. It arises because of the possibility that the company will not continue as a going concern. This likelihood is important, because it can dramatically affect the value of the company's products. Consider the case where consumers believe the company may not be able to honor warranties, provide service, or even supply replacement parts in the future.[5] Such a belief can dramatically hurt sales, as it would with a car manufacturer in financial distress.[6]

When potential customers fear product discontinuation, they will force the company to sell its product for a lower price than what it would otherwise be worth. The lower price reduces and can easily eliminate the manufacturer's profit margin on the product. This forgone profit can be very substantial. In fact, even though it is an opportunity cost that's difficult to measure, *this loss is the largest of the financial distress and bankruptcy costs by a wide margin.*

Effect of Leverage   The expected costs of financial distress and bankruptcy depend in part on the uniqueness, or degree of specialization, of the company's assets. The higher the degree of specialization, the lower the degree of liquidity and the greater the sales transaction costs. In the extreme case, a specially designed piece of equipment that is unique to just one company's production process might be worth only its scrap value if the company goes bankrupt.

An argument similar to the argument concerning specialized assets is based on a company's type of assets: A company with primarily tangible assets can borrow more than an otherwise comparable company with primarily intangible assets (such as patents and trademarks). Intangible assets are less liquid and have higher sales transaction costs than tangible assets, and their value may be more company-specific. The values of patents and trademarks depend on how they are used and past conditions. Another company may not be able to realize as much value from some of them. For example, the good-service reputation of a trademark product may be damaged or even destroyed by bad service resulting from otherwise unrelated financial distress problems. As a consequence, companies with more intangible assets have larger expected bankruptcy costs.

Possible financial distress and bankruptcy costs have the following effect on capital structure: Suppose all other factors combined—such as personal and corporate taxes, agency costs, and other transaction costs—create a net value benefit to leverage, thereby making leverage desirable. But it will be desirable only up to a certain point because, as the company increases its leverage, expected bankruptcy costs also increase and offset that benefit. So bankruptcy costs reduce the net value benefit of leverage and make "too much" leverage undesirable. (But if there were no net benefit to leverage from all the other factors combined, expected bankruptcy costs would make it so that even the first dollar of leverage would reduce a company's value and therefore be undesirable.)

---

[4]This loss includes lost tax deductions and lost tax credits. Tax credits are the more valuable of the two. Tax credits offset taxes owed dollar-for-dollar. Tax deductions reduce taxable income; their value equals the tax rate times the reduction in the amount of taxable income.

[5]Additional coverage of consumer-company conflicts is contained in enrichment topic C, Financial Contracting.

[6]This possibility helped convince the U.S. Congress to provide loan guarantees for the Chrysler Corporation when it was in financial distress. The loan guarantees made Chrysler's warranties and promises of future service and parts availability believable.

The bankruptcy effect produces an "optimal" capital structure that balances the expected bankruptcy cost off against the other benefits. This is similar to the net effect of the various agency costs. Also like agency costs, a solution is hard to quantify. The bankruptcy view, however, is more satisfying than the corporate tax view, because it does not call for the extreme of 100% debt financing.

Self-Check

1. What is the bankruptcy cost view of capital structure?

2. Describe the difference between the direct and indirect costs of financial distress and bankruptcy. Which is more significant?

3. Explain why "too much" leverage is undesirable if the company may lose tax shields.

4. Why do tangible assets support higher leverage than intangible assets?

EXTERNAL FINANCING TRANSACTION COSTS

PECKING ORDER VIEW OF CAPITAL STRUCTURE
The argument that external financing transaction costs create a preference, or pecking order, of preferred sources of financing.

The transaction costs associated with obtaining new external financing can play an important role in a company's capital structure decisions. As in the case of bankruptcy, there are both direct and indirect costs. These costs lead to the **pecking order view of capital structure.** In the pecking order view, companies use internally generated funds as much as possible for financing new projects. New debt is less preferred than internal funds, but more preferable than other sources. Debt-equity combinations, such as convertible debt, are third in the pecking order, with securities that have smaller proportions of equity being preferred to those with larger proportions of equity. Last in the pecking order comes new external equity.

The cost of obtaining new financing affects the company's management of its capital structure in ways similar to other factors we've discussed, but also in a way that is different. These costs affect the company's capital structure decisions over time, in a dynamic way. We touched on this dynamic dimension in chapter 10, when we said that the transaction costs connected with additional financing are a legitimate reason for capital rationing.

The transaction costs associated with obtaining new external financing make it much more costly for a company to sell a series of small issues compared to issuing a single large amount when it needs to obtain additional external funds. So the company should sell larger issues, less often, to reduce the net transaction costs of new external financing.

The idea of issuing a relatively larger amount of a security when the company does obtain new external financing does not imply a preference for any particular method of financing. However, it does imply that the dynamic management of the company's capital structure is important to the value of the company. A company can waste resources on issuance expenses if it does not manage its capital structure carefully.

Concerning particular methods, the total cost of new debt (negotiating private debt, or the combination of underwriting spread and direct issuance expenses connected with public debt) is typically lower than the total cost of obtaining other new external financing. Therefore, whether or not other factors create a net value benefit to leverage, debt is generally attractive *relative* to equity when a company has already decided that it is going to obtain additional outside financing.

Signaling and the Choice of Financing Method

A company's decision as to how to finance a project reflects its choice of capital structure. It may also convey information about the project and about how the company's managers view its current market value.

Consider two examples. The first illustrates how the choice between internal (equity) and external financing can convey information about project value. The second illustrates how the debt-equity choice can convey information about any perceived under- or overvaluation of the company's shares.

Internal Financing versus Issuing Securities

EXAMPLE

Two companies, G and N, are identical except for new projects they are about to undertake. G has a good project that has a large positive NPV, whereas B has a neutral project that has a zero NPV. The owners of G are eager to provide the financing for the new project themselves, using personal funds so that they alone will earn the large expected NPV. In contrast, the owners of N are indifferent to allowing outside investors to invest in the new project because it has a zero NPV. Generalizing the argument, then, the percentage of owner financing may provide a signal about the owners' opinion of investment opportunities. ∎

Debt versus Equity Financing

EXAMPLE

Suppose the shareholders know the company is currently overvalued. They would like to have partners to share in the decline in market value that will take place in the future when others realize the company is overvalued. Suppose instead they know the company is currently undervalued. Then they would not want to have new partners who will get a share of the increase in market value that will take place in the future when others realize the company is undervalued. Shareholders of properly valued companies would be indifferent to having new partners.

This leads to the idea that if additional financing is to be obtained, the company will choose debt or equity depending on whether or not they want new partners. That is, undervalued companies will issue new debt, whereas overvalued companies will issue new equity. Of course, in this simple world we have just described, shareholders of overvalued companies may not want to be identified as such. Therefore, they may try to imitate undervalued companies by issuing debt instead of equity. Situations such as this will require other information to allow investors to interpret the company's actions. ∎

Sometimes companies with existing publicly traded stock issue additional new shares. Apparently, therefore, there are cases where managers believe a new project is sufficiently good to justify the potential loss connected with issuing new equity.

One way in which companies may try to overcome the negative impression of issuing additional new shares is to use underwriters, rather than sell securities themselves. This can be especially useful if there is a need to protect trade secrets. The underwriter may be able to "certify" the value of the company and its new projects by standing ready to purchase all the new shares without revealing (and therefore destroying the value of) certain types of private information.

Changes in Capital Structure

Evidence indicates that the stock market reacts favorably to increases in leverage and negatively to decreases in leverage. Investors apparently interpret an increase in leverage as a signal that the company's prospects have improved. Its future cash flow will support greater leverage. A decrease in leverage signals the opposite. Weaker prospects reduce the company's ability to service debt.

Self-Check

1. Why do transaction costs make it more costly to sell a series of small issues as compared with a single large issue?

2. Based on the transaction costs of obtaining funds, what is the pecking order among internally generated funds, external debt financing, external debt-equity financing (such as convertible debt), and external equity?

3. Why is internal financing often a more positive signal about the company than external financing?

4. Why is debt financing often a more positive signal about the company than equity financing?

5. Explain how using underwriters might help a company to reduce the negative impression connected with issuing additional new shares.

FINANCIAL LEVERAGE CLIENTELES

Both personal tax and corporate tax considerations affect the desirability of a particular capital structure. Investors will take their own tax situations into account in deciding whether to invest in a particular company. The idea that investors "sort" themselves into groups, where each group prefers the companies it invests in to follow a certain type of policy, is called the **clientele effect.**

CLIENTELE EFFECT The grouping of investors who have a preference that the company follow a particular financing policy, such as the amount of leverage it uses.

How the Clientele Effect Works

When applied to financial leverage, the clientele effect refers to those investors who prefer a particular type of security or capital structure. A similar concept in marketing is called *market segmentation.* A market segment is an identifiable group of consumers who purchase a product with particular attributes distinct from the attributes of alternative products. An example would be a market segment that buys luxury cars versus one that buys economy cars.

The existence of various leverage clienteles mitigates some, but not all, of the arguments in favor of capital structure relevance. With respect to taxes, some securities may be a more or less attractive investment for certain investors. For example, investors with a high marginal income tax rate may find debt securities less attractive, whereas tax-exempt investors may find debt securities relatively more attractive. Similarly, investors with a low marginal income tax rate may prefer company leverage to personal leverage because of the higher corporate tax rate. Investors preferring a company with a particular capital structure strictly because of their own risk preferences are able to avoid the transaction costs of personal leverage by simply investing in a company that already has their preferred amount of leverage.

Taxes and transaction costs reduce the return to shareholders. Therefore, investors should, and do, invest in securities that minimize their aggregate taxes and transaction costs for any particular combination of risk and return. The result of taking taxes and transaction costs into account is that a particular clientele group may pay a premium for a certain type of security. (Note that the premium is measured relative to the prices of securities that are equivalent.) Such a premium gives companies an incentive to follow particular policies that appeal to various clientele groups. Of course, this is simply another application of the Principle of Valuable Ideas: Being the first to have the idea has the potential to create value.

The result is that it may be possible to earn a premium for supplying a security or capital structure policy that is in short supply. (Note that this gain must be weighed against the transaction costs of investors' rearranging their security holdings.) Whenever a change in law affects the taxes and transaction costs for a particular financial leverage clientele, opportunities may be created for a company to earn a positive NPV by changing its capital structure.

Practical Limitations

Opportunities to profit from capital structure changes have natural limitations. First, direct transaction costs to the company reduce the potential benefit from a change in capital structure. Second, shareholder transaction costs make it expensive for investors to buy and sell shares, which can affect the market price of the company's stock.

These factors make sudden or frequent shifts in a company's capital structure generally undesirable. Too sudden a shift may be disruptive to the company's stock price in the near term, and frequent major shifts may be disruptive over the longer term.

In practice, most companies maintain a stable capital structure. It appears, then, that companies depart from a stable capital structure only when the managers believe there are valid reasons to do so. Such reasons include significant changes in the company's investment opportunities, its earnings, or its own or shareholders' tax position.

Self-Check

1. Explain what is meant by the clientele effect.

2. According to the clientele effect, investors with low marginal income tax rates should prefer to invest in companies with high leverage. Do you agree? Explain.

3. How might a company profit when a change in tax law causes a particular financial leverage clientele to change its investment preferences?

THE CAPITAL MARKET IMPERFECTIONS VIEW OF CAPITAL STRUCTURE

Taken in total, the view that emerges from the various factors we've discussed can be characterized as a dynamic process that involves various trade-offs and results in a general preference order among a company's financing alternatives. We call this the **capital market imperfections view of capital structure.** In this view, debt is generally valuable. With relatively low leverage, where there is little chance of incurring the costs associated with financial distress, the *expected* value of the costs of financial distress will be low. Therefore, for small amounts of leverage, the value-enhancing considerations of leverage resulting from taxes dominate the expected costs of financial distress. At some point, the expected costs of financial distress and agency costs become large enough to overcome the other value-enhancing considerations.

CAPITAL MARKET IMPERFECTIONS VIEW OF CAPITAL STRUCTURE The view that debt financing is generally valuable, but a company's optimal choice of capital structure is a dynamic process in a complex environment that involves a mixture of financing methods. The exact mix at any particular point results from considerations of asymmetric taxes, asymmetric information, and transaction costs.

Total Market Value and Market Imperfections

The optimal capital structure is the one that maximizes the company's value. Figure 12.7 on page 442 is a conceptual picture of the effect on company value of all the various factors we've discussed. Note that the picture is only a "snapshot"; it cannot include the dynamic considerations that transaction costs connected with external financing introduce into the picture. These managerial considerations mean that the optimal capital structure may not be a simple fixed proportion of debt financing.

The Cost of Capital and Market Imperfections

Figure 12.7 illustrates the capital market imperfections view in terms of a company's total value. Once again, the view can be represented in a corresponding way in terms of the company's WACC, its weighted average cost of capital. The optimal capital structure is the point where company value reaches its maximum by minimizing the company's WACC.

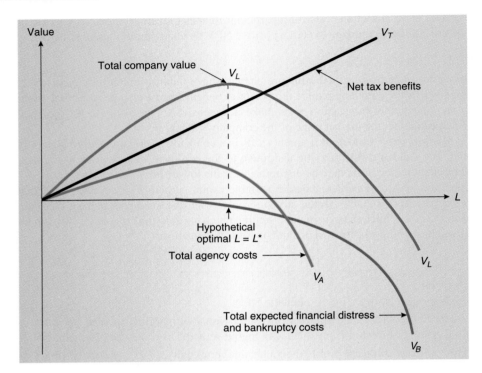

FIGURE 12.7
The capital market imperfections view of capital structure.

Figure 12.8 illustrates the capital market imperfections view of capital structure that takes into account all of the factors we have discussed. In figure 12.8, the WACC is expressed in terms of hypothetical functions of r_d and r_e.

Figure 12.8 is a snapshot like figure 12.7. So the company's optimal capital structure is in truth more complex than these figures indicate. Although figure 12.8 provides a visual aid to understanding the impact of capital structure on the WACC and company value, we need an equation for the WACC in order to determine more precise values.

FIGURE 12.8
WACC (weighted average cost of capital), r_e (required return for equity), and r_d (required return for debt) as hypothetical functions of L (the leverage ratio) under the capital market imperfections view of capital structure.

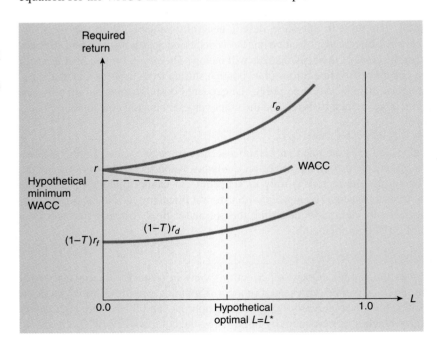

The Net Benefit to Leverage

To capture the impact of *all* the relevant dimensions connected with debt financing, define T^* as the **net-benefit-to-leverage factor.** T^* is assumed to be derived from a linear approximation to the actual net-benefit-to-leverage relationship over some relevant range of values for the leverage ratio L. T^* allows us to operationalize the total impact of leverage on company value in the capital market imperfections view. We can use the same sort of mathematics we used with the corporate tax view to adjust the WACC for all of the relevant factors. In this more general case, we can express the value of the leveraged company as

$$V_L = V_U + T^*D = \frac{\bar{I}(1-T)}{r} + \frac{T^*r_dD}{r_d} \tag{12.8}$$

NET-BENEFIT-TO-LEVERAGE FACTOR A linear approximation of a factor, T^*, that allows us to operationalize the total impact of leverage on company value in the capital market imperfections view of capital structure.

which is a generalization of equation (12.5).

Once again, V_L can be viewed as being made up of two components. The first component is the basic value of the company if it is unleveraged, V_U. The second component is the net benefit from leverage. Each component represents the present value of a stream of expected future cash flows. The first stream is $\bar{I}(1-T)$, the company's after-tax income each period, its CFAT. The second stream is the net benefit from maintaining an amount D of debt. This net benefit can be expressed as T^* times the interest payment each period, or T^*r_dD.

For the perpetuity case, the present value is simply these cash flow streams divided by their required returns. The required return for the company's (unleveraged) after-tax income stream, its CFAT, is r. Because of lower risk, the required return for the net-benefit-to-leverage stream is r_d, which is lower than r.

Finally, the parallel is completed by expressing the impact on company value in terms of the company's WACC (its required return). As before, we won't prove it, but the result is

$$\text{WACC} = r(1 - T^*L) \tag{12.9}$$

The usefulness of equation (12.9) is based on how easily it fits into our framework for making capital budgeting decisions. It is simply an adjustment made to the project's cost of capital, which accounts for the effect of leverage on project value. The adjusted rate is then used to compute the present value of the project's CFATs, its NPV.

Total Company Value and Capital Market Imperfections

There's one final point we want to make. All of the views of capital structure, beyond that of a perfect capital market, are based on minimizing the value lost to one or more imperfections. Therefore, even though we talk about using leverage to increase company value, in fact we're actually describing ways to use leverage to *reduce the loss* connected with various imperfections. What this means is that the total value of the company is never more than what it would be in a perfect capital market. We illustrate this point in figure 12.9 on page 444 by using three "pie" views of a $1000 company.

In figure 12.9 the far-left "pie" shows the perfect market view. In it, there is no loss in value from imperfections. A company's value does not depend on its capital structure. The other two pies reflect the capital market imperfections view of capital structure. In them, a dynamic optimal capital structure minimizes the total loss from all the various imperfections. In the middle pie, the company is all-equity-financed. In the far-right pie, the company has multiple types and amounts of financing that might typically be found in the practice of financial management.

The net benefit to leverage can be seen in figure 12.9. It is the difference between the value of the company on the far right (the combined values of common equity, preferred equity, and debt) and the value of the company in the middle (equity). However, despite this positive net benefit to leverage, the total value of the company on the far right is substantially less than the company value would be in a perfect capital market. This is because of losses to capital market imperfections.

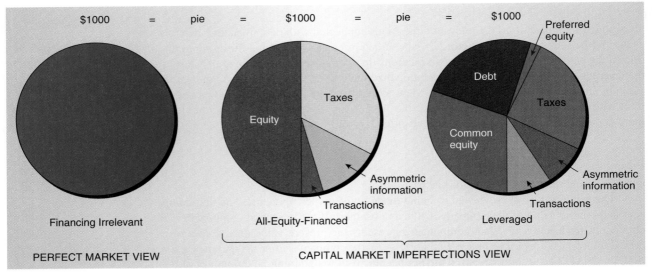

FIGURE 12.9
These three "pie" views of capital structure illustrate the loss of company value from all the various capital market imperfections and the minimization of that loss through the choice of capital structure.

Self-Check

1. What is the capital market imperfections view of capital structure?

2. What is the shape of the WACC curve according to the capital market imperfections view?

3. What is the net-benefit-to-leverage factor?

4. Suppose the net-benefit-to-leverage factor is $T^* = 0.20$. How would you interpret this value?

SUMMARY

The critical issue concerning capital structure is whether it affects the value of the company.

- In a perfect capital market, a company's capital structure has no effect on its value. A company's value is based entirely on the profitability of its assets and the expected NPVs of its future projects. Even if leverage enhanced investment value, shareholders could borrow to create personal leverage. Therefore, in a perfect capital market, companies cannot capture any value due to leverage, because shareholders can do it themselves just as cheaply as the company.

- Our financial system contains some important persistent imperfections. Information is not costless and freely available to everyone, so the Signaling Principle (actions contain information) is a very important consideration. Capital structure and capital structure changes may provide information about the company to the public. Thus, a company should be careful to choose the best method of financing, taking all costs into account—including the information investors will infer from the company's financing transactions.

- There are other market imperfections. The system of corporate income taxation imposes a bias in favor of debt over equity, as do issuance costs.

- However, the system of individual income taxation, as well as direct and indirect financial distress/bankruptcy costs, have an opposite bias.
- Aggregate agency costs and tax-timing options both favor a mix of debt and equity rather than using one or the other exclusively. Taken together, these market imperfections lead to a view that there is some dynamic optimal capital structure that maximizes the value of a company.
- The clientele effect, where personal investments are made in companies that have adopted capital structures that are best for the individual investors, may mitigate some of these considerations. Changes in laws, particularly the tax code, sometimes create a demand for new types of securities or alter the demand for existing ones. Such changes in demand may in turn create profitable opportunities for a company to supply a particular type of security to satisfy this new demand.
- Companies manage their capital structures carefully. Choosing an appropriate capital structure involves balancing the net tax advantage against the agency costs, the larger expected cost of financial distress, and the cost of reduced financial flexibility from additional leverage. Simultaneously, transaction costs and information effects must also be considered. Unfortunately, these costs cannot be measured precisely. As a result, the "best" capital structure cannot be pinpointed.

EQUATION SUMMARY

(12.1) $$\text{WACC} = (1 - L)r_e + L(1 - T)r_d$$

(12.2) $$V_U = \frac{\bar{I}(1 - T)}{r}$$

(12.3) $$V_L = \frac{\bar{I}(1 - T)}{\text{WACC}}$$

(12.4) $$V_L = \frac{\bar{I}(1 - T)}{r} + \frac{Tr_d D}{r_d} = \frac{\bar{I}(1 - T)}{r} + TD$$

(12.5) $$V_L = V_U + TD$$

(12.6) $$\text{WACC} = r(1 - TL)$$

(12.7) $$(1 - T_d) = (1 - T_e)(1 - T)$$

(12.8) $$V_L = V_U + T^*D = \frac{\bar{I}(1 - T)}{r} + \frac{T^* r_d D}{r_d}$$

(12.9) $$\text{WACC} = r(1 - T^*L)$$

CHAPTER REVIEW ACTIVITIES

SELF-TEST PROBLEMS

1. (Corporate taxes and leverage) An unleveraged company has an operating cash flow of a perpetuity of $100, a marginal tax rate of 40%, and an unleveraged cost of capital of 10%. An otherwise identical company is leveraged with $400 of perpetual debt paying 8% interest.
   a. What is the after-tax cash flow to stockholders of the unleveraged company? What is the value of the unleveraged company?
   b. What is the after-tax cash flow to stockholders and bondholders of the leveraged company? What is the value of the leveraged company? What is the leveraged company's cost of capital?
   c. What accounts for the difference in the value of the two companies?

2. (Corporate and personal taxes) Trussler Corporation has a corporate tax rate of 40%, its bond-holders have a personal tax rate of 30%, and the effective tax rate that its stockholders pay is 20%.

a. Trussler has $100 of before-tax cash flows which it pays as interest to its bondholders. What is the total corporate and personal tax on this cash flow? What is after-tax bondholder income?

b. Trussler has $100 of before-tax cash flows. After corporate taxes, it is distrib-

uting the balance to stockholders. What is the total corporate and personal tax on this cash flow? What is after-tax stock-holder income?

c. Are these tax rates neutral? Which form of financing is favored, debt or equity fi-nancing?

SOLUTIONS TO SELF-TEST PROBLEMS

1. a. The after-tax cash flow to stockholders is $\bar{I}(1 - T) = 100(1 - 0.40) = \$60$. The value of the un-leveraged company is $\bar{I}(1 - T)/r = 60/0.10 = \$600$.

   b. The cash flow to stockholders of the leveraged company is $\bar{I} - r_dD - T(\bar{I} - r_dD) = 100 - 32 - 0.40(100 - 32) = 100 - 32 - 27.20 = \$40.80$. The bondholders are paid $32. Stockholders and bondholders combined are paid $40.80 + 32 = \$72.80$.

   The value of the leveraged company is

   $$V_L = \bar{I}(1 - T)/r + TD = 60/0.10 + 0.40(400) = 600 + 160 = \$760$$

   The WACC for the leveraged company is

   $$\text{WACC} = r(1 - TL) = 0.10(1 - 0.40(400/760)) = 0.078947 = 7.8947\%$$

   The leverage ratio (L) is the value of debt (400) divided by the total value of the company (760). Notice that the tax deductibility of interest expense increases the value of the leveraged company by $760 - 600 = \$160$ compared to the unleveraged company. The tax deductibility of interest expense also reduces the WACC from 10% to 7.89%.

   c. The tax savings due to the tax deductibility of interest expense causes the leveraged company to be more valuable. The annual tax savings are $Tr_dD = 0.40(0.08)(400) = 0.40(32) = \$12.80$. This reduction in taxes precisely equals the increase in cash flows received by stockholders and bond-holders combined in the leveraged company ($12.80 = 72.80 - 60$).

   The present value of these tax savings is found by capitalizing it by an appropriate discount rate, the rate on the debt. $\text{PV} = Tr_dD/r_d = 12.80/.08 = \$160$. This PV of the tax savings equals the excess in the value of the leveraged company over the unleveraged company ($160 = 760 - 600$).

2. a. The corporate taxes are zero because the interest expense offsets the $100 of before-tax cash flows. The bondholders pay personal taxes of $0.30(100) = \$30$, so the combined corporate and personal tax bill is $0 + 30 = 30$.

   The after-tax bondholder income is $100 - 30 = \$70$.

   b. Corporate taxes are $0.40(100) = \$40$. This leaves $100 - 40 = \$60$ to be distributed to stockhold-ers. Stockholders pay personal taxes of $0.20(60) = \$12$. The combined corporate and personal tax bill is $40 + 12 = \$52$.

   The after-tax stockholder income is $100 - 40 - 12 = \$48$.

   c. These tax rates are not neutral. Stockholder income is taxed more heavily when both corporate and personal income taxes are considered. This favors debt financing. Equation (12.7) indicates that personal taxes on debt and equity cancel out the corporate tax asymmetry and that the tax system is neutral if

   $$(1 - T_d) = (1 - T_e)(1 - T)$$

   In this example, the personal tax rate for bondholders is $T_d = 0.30$, the personal tax rate for stock-holders is $T_e = .20$, and the corporate tax rate is $T = 0.40$. For a $1 distribution to bondholders, bondholders receive

   $$1(1 - T_d) = 1(1 - 0.30) = \$.70.$$

   For a $1 corporate cash flow, the ultimate distribution to stockholders is

   $$1(1 - T_e)(1 - T) = 1(1 - 0.20)(1 - 0.40) = \$0.48$$

QUESTIONS

1. Briefly explain the corporate tax view of capital structure.
2. Give an example of a tax-timing option and explain why it is valuable.
3. Cite an example of how transaction costs might affect a company's choice of financing.
4. Define the term *financial leverage clientele.*
5. Briefly explain in your own words why taxes would not be asymmetric if equation (12.7) holds.
6. What is the shape of the WACC curve according to the perfect market view?
7. What is the shape of the WACC curve according to the capital market imperfections view?
8. Briefly explain how the personal tax view of capital structure mitigates the corporate tax view.
9. True or false? The *direct* transaction costs connected with financial distress and bankruptcy are large as a proportion of the value of the company.
10. True or false? The *direct* transaction costs connected with financial distress and bankruptcy are much larger than the indirect, implicit opportunity costs such as lost sales, depressed product price, and lost tax credits.
11. Why might potential new equity investors in a company be leery of buying newly issued stock in a company?
12. Why should a company's ability to use tax credits affect its capital structure?
13. Describe the capital market imperfections view of capital structure.

CHALLENGING QUESTIONS

14. Show how financial distress can affect the value of the company through its tax credits, even when a company is able to use completely all tax credits via loss carryforwards.
15. Suppose a company is operating with corporate and personal taxes in an otherwise perfect capital market and equation (12.7) currently holds. In such a world, a company would never take on any risky debt. Why not? (*Hint:* Consider what would happen in financial distress.)
16. Leverage increases the risk (and therefore the required return) of the equityholders. Above some point, an increase in leverage also increases the risk (and required return) of the debtholders. How is it possible, then, that in a perfect capital market environment the weighted average of the two is constant, because both required returns are increasing?
17. How can restrictive debt covenants reduce agency costs?
18. Respond to the following statement: "Because a company can lower its interest cost by including more restrictive covenants in its bonds, a company should use the most restrictive set of covenants it can in order to achieve the lowest interest cost."
19. Why might a company that manufactures a unique product using specialized employee expertise tend to finance with less debt than an otherwise identical company that manufactures a generic product?
20. What is the basis for the view that a company's total market value is invariant to its choice of capital structure? Cite three broad types of capital market imperfections that can cause the capital structure of a company to have an effect on the value of that company. Give three examples (one for each type) where such an imperfection would cause a company's capital structure to have an effect on the value of that company. Explain *how* each of the three examples you gave would cause a company's capital structure to have an effect on the value of that company.
21. The good fairy has decided to smile on you and has offered you a choice between two "great" outcomes. The alternatives concern an investment that has the same risk as the market portfolio and requires an initial investment of $10 million. The alternatives are (1) the cost of financing for the investment will be three standard deviations less than the current average market required return for financing such investments, but the investment will have an otherwise zero NPV or (2) the expected future cash inflows from the investment will be three standard deviations larger than those that would make the investment have a zero NPV, but the cost of financing for the investment will be at the current average market required return for financing such investments. Therefore, either alternative will provide you with a positive-NPV investment. Alternative 1 does so by virtue of "great" financing, whereas alternative 2 does so by virtue of "great" investing. Which alternative should you choose, and why?

PROBLEM SET A

A1. (Calculating a leverage ratio) William Bates is contemplating starting a new company that will provide background music for elevators, dentists' offices, and the like. He estimates a positive NPV of $270,000 for the investment. Mr. Bates plans to call the company Tarry-Tune, Unlimited. He estimates that the initial investment needed to start Tarry-Tune is $325,000. He plans to borrow $200,000 of the initial investment. What is the expected leverage ratio, L, for Tarry-Tune?

A2. (Taxes, leverage, and WACC) Suppose a company is unleveraged and has an unleveraged required return of $r = 15\%$. The company borrows 30% of the value of the company at $r_d = 8\%$. Because of the financial leverage, r_e becomes 18%. What is the company's WACC:

  a. Assuming the company is operating in a perfect capital market (including no taxes)?

  b. Assuming there are only corporate taxes at a rate of 35% in an otherwise perfect capital market?

A3. (Value of company and WACC) Suppose a company currently has an unleveraged required return of 10% and perpetual unleveraged after-tax income of $140,301 per year. The company has come up with an investment opportunity that would alter the company's asset makeup so that it would increase its perpetual unleveraged after-tax income to $170,650 per year. Because the new asset mix is riskier, the company's unleveraged required return would also increase to 12.165%. Should the company undertake this investment opportunity?

A4. (Corporate taxes and company value) Jahera Mines issues $50,000,000 of perpetual new debt paying 9% interest. Jahera is in the 40% marginal income tax bracket. Assume no market imperfections beyond corporate taxes.

  a. What are the annual tax savings that result from the debt financing?

  b. What is the increase in the value of

  Jahera Mines that results from this debt issue?

A5. (Corporate taxes and leverage) Caples Communications is evaluating how to finance the company. Caples expects to have an operating cash flow of a perpetuity of $1,000 and a marginal tax rate of 40%. As an unleveraged company, Caples will have a cost of capital of 12%. As a leveraged company, Caples will issue $3,000 of perpetual debt paying 8% interest.

  a. Assume that Caples chooses to be an all-equity (unleveraged) company. What is the after-tax cash flow to stockholders? What is the value of Caples as an unleveraged company?

  b. Assume that Caples chooses the leveraged capital structure. What is the after-

  tax cash flow to stockholders and bondholders of the leveraged company? What is the value of the unleveraged company? What is the leveraged company's cost of capital?

  c. What accounts for the difference in the value of the two companies?

A6. (Corporate and personal taxes) Sarin Software Corporation has a corporate tax rate of 30%, its bondholders have a personal tax rate of 30%, and the effective tax rate that its stockholders pay is 20%.

  a. Sarin has $100 of before-tax cash flows, which it pays as interest to its bondholders. What is the total corporate and personal tax on this cash flow? What is after-tax bondholder income?

  b. Sarin has $100 of before-tax cash flows. After corporate taxes, it is distributing

  the balance to stockholders. What is the total corporate and personal tax on this cash flow? What is after-tax stockholder income?

  c. Are these tax rates neutral? Which form of financing is favored, debt or equity financing?

A7. (Corporate and personal taxes) LaPlante Company has a corporate tax rate of 30%, its bondholders have a personal tax rate of 44%, and the effective tax rate that its stockholders pay is 20%.

  a. LaPlante has $100 of before-tax cash flows, which it pays as interest to its bondholders. What is the total corporate

  and personal tax on this cash flow? What is after-tax bondholder income?

b. LaPlante has $100 of before-tax cash flows. After corporate taxes, it is distributing the balance to stockholders. What is the total corporate and personal tax on this cash flow? What is after-tax stockholder income?

c. Are these tax rates neutral? Which form of financing is favored, debt or equity financing?

PROBLEM SET B

B1. (Leveraged and unleveraged returns) You invest $12,000 in Joe's Garage, Inc., borrowing $5000 of the money at 10%. If you expect to earn 24% on your investment under this arrangement, what would you expect to earn if you put up the entire $12,000 from your own money? Ignore taxes.

B2. (Capital structure arbitrage) Consider two companies operating in a perfect capital market environment. Each will generate $10 million of operating income, and they are identical in every other respect, except that company A has debt in its capital structure and company B has an all-equity capital structure. Suppose that investors currently value A as indicated in table 12.1, but the market value of the equity in B is $65 million. According to the perfect market view, this situation cannot persist. Suppose an investor owns 1% of the shares of B. Show how this owner can profit from arbitrage.

B3. (Capital structure arbitrage) Miles's Manor, an unassuming resort in mid-state Pennsylvania, currently has an all-equity capital structure. Miles's Manor has an expected income of $10,000 per year forever and a required return to equity of 16%. There are no personal taxes, but Miles's pays corporate taxes at the rate of 35%, and all transactions take place in an otherwise perfect capital market.

a. What is Miles's Manor worth?

b. How much will the value of the company increase if Miles's Manor leverages the company by borrowing half the value of the unleveraged company at an interest rate of 10% and the leverage causes the required return on equity to increase to 18.89%?

B4. (Corporate and personal taxes) Dick's Pet-Way Corporation (DPC) is a chain of pet stores that has an expected cash inflow of $1000 each year forever. DPC's required return is 20% per year. Assume all of DPC's income is paid out to the company's investors.

a. If DPC is all-equity-financed and there are no taxes, what would DPC be worth in a perfect capital market?

Now suppose DPC's corporate tax rate is 30%.

b. If DPC is all-equity-financed and there are no personal taxes, what would DPC be worth in an otherwise perfect capital market?

In addition to corporate taxes, suppose DPC borrows $1400 at a required return on the debt of 10%. (*Note:* Because of risk, the required return on equity increases to 23.89%.)

c. If there are no personal taxes, what would DPC be worth in an otherwise perfect capital market? What would be DPC's leverage ratio, L?

d. If there are personal taxes on debt income at a rate of 37%, and personal taxes on equity income at a rate of 10%, what would DPC be worth in an otherwise perfect capital market?

e. If there are personal taxes on debt income at a rate of 25%, and personal taxes on equity income at a rate of 10%, what would DPC be worth in an otherwise perfect capital market?

f. Finally, compute the value of DPC as a 35.7% leveraged company, with a 10% interest rate on the debt when there are no taxes at all in a perfect capital market.

B5. (Cost of capital) The Query Company has identified two alternative capital structures. If the company borrows 15% of the value of the company, it can borrow the money at $r_d = 10\%$, and the shareholders will have a required return of $r_e = 18\%$. If the company borrows 45% of the value of the company, it can borrow the money at $r_d = 12\%$, and the shareholders will have a required return of $r_e = 23.21\%$. Query pays corporate taxes at the rate of 35%. Which capital structure should Query adopt? If Query is operating in an essentially perfect capital market except for taxes, are the taxes approximately symmetric, or are they asymmetric?

B6. (Leverage, taxes, and WACC) The RTE Corporation expects to pay a dividend next year of $2.22. It expects its cash dividends to grow 5% per year forever. RTE has a debt ratio of $L = 35\%$. Its borrowing rate is $r_d = 9\%$. RTE pays corporate taxes at the rate of 30%. If $r_f = 6\%$, $r_M = 12\%$, and RTE's common stock is currently selling for $20 per share:

a. What is the current (leveraged) required return, r_e, on RTE's common stock?

b. What is RTE's WACC?

c. What is RTE's unleveraged required return, r?

d. What unleveraged beta is implied by r?

PROBLEM SET C

C1. (Capital structure arbitrage) Companies A and B are identical except for their capital structures. A has a debt ratio of 25%. B has a debt ratio of 33.33%. Suppose that the interest rate on both companies' debt is 10% and that investors can also borrow at a 10% interest rate.

a. An investor owns 5% of the common stock of company A, half of which is financed through borrowings. What investment-loan package involving B will produce identical returns?

b. An investor owns 10% of the common stock of B, none of which is financed through borrowings. What investment-loan combination involving A will produce identical returns?

C2. (WACC and net-benefit-to-leverage) Both the common stock and long-term bonds of Crib-Tick, Inc., makers of baby furniture, are traded publicly on the NYSE. Currently, the market value of Crib-Tick common stock is $14 per share, and there are 4 million shares outstanding. Crib-Tick's latest earnings were $2.09 per share, and next year's dividend is expected to be $1.02 per share. Five years ago, Crib-Tick paid a dividend of $0.72 per share. Crib-Tick has long-term bonds with a total market value of $30 million. The bonds mature in 2006 and have an 8% coupon. They are currently selling for $880. (Assume the bonds have 22 more coupon payments until maturity.) In addition to long-term bonds, Crib-Tick has $5 million in notes payable and $10 million in other current liabilities. Current market conditions are $r_f = 6\%$ and $r_M = 13.75\%$. Crib-Tick has a beta of 1.1, and it pays corporate taxes at a rate of 30%. It has estimated $T^* = 0.18$. What would you estimate is Crib-Tick's WACC?

C3. (Time-value-of-money puzzle) Ida Rather's Knot Corporation, a modest rope manufacturing company in the northeast corner of the Yukon, has been contacted by Wile E. Coyote and offered an investment opportunity that will pay her $2500 per month for 60 months. Ida must invest $10,000 now and borrow $90,000 from Wile E. at 16% APR, for a total initial investment of $100,000. The entire loan must be paid back at the end of the 60 months (principal and interest will total $199,242.62). There are no taxes. Assume that this investment is riskless, as Wile E. Coyote has claimed. Under what conditions would you recommend that Ida undertake this investment?

APPENDIX: MANAGING CAPITAL STRUCTURE

This appendix reviews additional practical considerations that managers weigh when managing their company's capital structure. The appendix reviews industry effects and the role of debt ratings in choosing a capital structure. Coverage ratios and comparative credit analysis are also widely used by managers.

INDUSTRY EFFECTS

We have a pretty good understanding of the main factors that affect a company's choice of capital structure. But financial theory doesn't tell us *precisely* how they determine a company's *optimal* capital structure. In practice, companies usually apply the Behavioral Principle to select an *appropriate* capital structure. They look to the capital structure choices of comparable companies for guidance about their choice of capital structure.

Studies show systematic differences in capital structures across industries. These are due mostly to differences in

1. the degree of operating risk
2. availability of tax shelter provided by things other than debt, such as accelerated depreciation, investment tax credits, and operating tax loss carryforwards
3. the ability of assets to support borrowing

Debt Ratings

Differences among average industry capital structures, however, are only part of the story. A company can't simply adopt the industry average debt ratio, because differences exist among companies in any particular industry with respect to tax position, size, competitive position, operating risk, business prospects, and other factors. Companies also differ in their willingness to bear financial risk and in their desire to maintain access to the capital markets.

In practice, a company's bond rating has important implications concerning the choice of capital structure. Table 12.2 shows the debt rating definitions of two major rating

TABLE 12.2
Bond Rating Definitions

MOODY'S INVESTORS SERVICE[a]	STANDARD & POOR'S[b]
Investment Grade Ratings	
Aaa	**AAA**
Bonds rated Aaa are judged to be of the best quality. They carry the smallest degree of investment risk and are generally referred to as "gilt edged." Interest payments are protected by a large or by an exceptionally stable margin, and principal is secure. Although the various protective elements are likely to change, such changes as can be visualized are most unlikely to impair the fundamentally strong position of such issues.	Debt rated AAA has the highest rating assigned by Standard & Poor's. Capacity to pay interest and repay principal is extremely strong.
Aa	**AA**
Bonds rated Aa are judged to be of high quality by all standards. Together with the Aaa group, they comprise what are generally known as high-grade bonds. They are rated lower than the best bonds because margins of protection may not be as large as in Aaa securities, fluctuation of protective elements may be of greater amplitude, or there may be other elements present that make the long-term risk appear somewhat larger than the Aaa securities.	Debt rated AA has a very strong capacity to pay interest and repay principal and differs from the higher-rated issues only in small degree.
A	**A**
Bonds rated A possess many favorable investment attributes and are to be considered as upper-medium-grade obligations. Factors giving security to principal and interest are considered adequate, but elements may be present that suggest a susceptibility to impairment some time in the future.	Debt rated A has a strong capacity to pay interest and repay principal, although it is somewhat more susceptible to the adverse effects of changes in circumstances and economic conditions than debt in higher-rated categories.
Baa	**BBB**
Bonds rated Baa are considered medium-grade obligations (they are neither highly protected nor poorly secured). Interest payments and principal security appear adequate for the present, but certain protective elements may be lacking or may be characteristically unreliable over any great length of time. Such bonds lack outstanding investment characteristics and in fact have speculative characteristics as well.	Debt rated BBB is regarded as having an adequate capacity to pay interest and repay principal. Whereas it normally exhibits adequate protection parameters, adverse economic conditions or changing circumstances are more likely to lead to a weakened capacity to pay interest and repay principal for debt in this category than in higher-rated categories.

(continued on following page)

(Table 12.2 Bond Rating Definitions *continued from previous page*)

Speculative Grade Ratings

Ba

Bonds rated Ba are judged to have speculative elements; their future cannot be considered as well assured. Often the protection of interest and principal payments may be very moderate, and thereby not well safeguarded during both good and bad times over the future. Uncertainty of position characterizes bonds in this class.

B

Bonds rated B generally lack characteristics of the desirable investment. Assurance of interest and principal payments or of maintenance of other terms of the contract over any long period of time may be small.

Caa

Bonds rated Caa are of poor standing. Such issues may be in default, or elements of danger with respect to principal or interest may be present.

Ca

Bonds rated Ca represent obligations that are speculative in a high degree. Such issues are often in default or have other marked shortcomings.

C

Bonds rated C are the lowest-rated class of bonds, and issues so rated can be regarded as having extremely poor prospects of ever attaining any real investment standing.

BB

Debt rated BB has less near-term vulnerability to default than other speculative issues. However, it faces major ongoing uncertainties or exposure to adverse business, financial, or economic conditions that could lead to inadequate capacity to meet timely interest and principal payments. The BB rating category is also used for debt subordinated to senior debts that is assigned an actual or implied BBB– rating.

B

Debt rated B has a greater vulnerability to default but currently has the capacity to meet interest payments and principal repayments. Adverse business, financial, or economic conditions are likely to impair capacity or willingness to pay interest and repay principal. The B rating category is also used for debt subordinated to senior debt that is assigned an actual or implied BB or BB– rating.

CCC

Debt rated CCC has a currently identifiable vulnerability to default and is dependent on favorable business, financial, and economic conditions to meet timely payment of interest and repayment of principal. In the event of adverse business, financial or economic conditions, it is not likely to have the capacity to pay interest and repay principal. The CCC rating category is also used for debt subordinated or senior debt that is assigned an actual or implied B or B– rating.

CC

The rating CC is typically applied to debt subordinated to senior debt that is assigned an actual or implied CCC rating.

C

The rating C is typically assigned to debt subordinated to senior debt that is assigned an actual or implied CCC– debt rating. The C rating may be used to cover a situation where a bankruptcy petition has been filed but debt-service payments are continued.

CI

The rating CI is reserved for income bonds on which no interest is being paid.

D

Debt rated D is in payment default. The D rating category is used when interest payments or principal payments are not made on the date due even if the applicable grace period has not expired, unless S&P believes that such payments will be made during such grace period. The D rating also will be used upon the filing of a bankruptcy petition if debt-service payments are jeopardized.

[a]Moody's applies numerical modifiers 1, 2, and 3 in each generic rating classification from Aa through B in the corporate bond rating system. The modifier 1 indicates that the security ranks in the higher end of its generic rating category; the modifier 2 indicates a mid-range ranking; and the modifier 3 indicates that the issue ranks in the lower end of its generic rating category.
[b]The ratings from "AA" to "CCC" may be modified by the addition of a plus or minus sign to show relative standing within the major rating categories. *Sources: Moody's Bond Record* (New York: Moody's Investors Service, April 1996), p. 3, and *Standard & Poor's Bond Guide* (New York: Standard & Poor's, April 1996), p. 12.

agencies, Moody's Investors Service, Inc., and Standard & Poor's Corporation. The highest four rating categories are known as **investment grade ratings.** For Moody's, the investment grade ratings are Aaa, Aa, A, and Baa. For Standard & Poor's, investment grade ratings are AAA, AA, A, and BBB. Ratings lower than investment grade are called **speculative grade ratings.**

Each agency distinguishes different levels of credit quality within each rating category below triple-A. Moody's attaches the numbers 1 (high), 2 (medium), and 3 (low). Standard & Poor's attaches a plus sign for the highest and a minus sign for the lowest. For example, a medium-grade single-A credit would be rated A2 by Moody's and A by Standard & Poor's, and would be of somewhat higher quality than one rated A3 by Moody's or A- by Standard & Poor's.

As you can see by reading table 12.2, the ratings are indicators of the likelihood of financial distress, as judged by the rating agencies. Bonds in the top three investment grade categories are judged from "favorable" to "gilt edged." They have a capacity to pay interest that ranges from "strong" to "extremely strong." Bonds rated in the lowest category (Baa or BBB) offer investors less protection than higher-rated bonds. The risk of financial distress is greater for lower-rated bonds.

The distinction between investment grade and speculative grade ratings is important because of institutional investment restrictions. To qualify as *legal investments* for commercial banks, bonds must usually be investment grade. In addition, various state laws impose minimum rating standards and other restrictions for bonds to qualify as legal investments for savings banks, trust companies, public pension funds, and insurance companies. Bonds rated speculative grade fail to qualify as legal investments for many financial institutions. A company's bond rating is very important, then, to maintaining access to the capital markets on acceptable terms.

The National Association of Insurance Commissioners (NAIC) has established six bond rating categories. The amount of reserves an insurance company must maintain for each bond investment depends on the bond's rating. Bonds rated NAIC-3 or below are speculative grade. They require significantly more capital.[7] With the introduction of this new rating system and capital-maintenance standards, speculative grade bonds have become much less attractive to insurance companies. The yields a company requires from speculative grade bonds are significantly higher, to compensate for the greater amount of capital they must maintain.

> **INVESTMENT GRADE RATING** A debt rating in one of the four highest rating categories.
>
> **SPECULATIVE GRADE RATING** A debt rating below the four highest rating categories.

Choosing a Bond Rating Objective

A company can choose a bond rating objective. Such a choice involves a decision about (1) the chance of future financial distress and (2) the desire to maintain access to the capital markets. When it looks as if a company would gain value from raising its proportion of debt financing, but the company chooses not to (by having a higher rating objective), the value that is missed can be viewed as a "margin of safety." The desired margin of safety is determined by how much risk of future financial distress, or restricted market access, the company is willing to bear. A single-A rating would seem to be a reasonable rating target, but some companies are more or less risk averse than this standard implies.

Bond Ratings and Financial Ratios

Once a company has chosen its rating target, what financial steps should the company take to hit the target? The rating agencies use many criteria to rate a bond. For example, in the case of industrial companies, Standard & Poor's evaluates (1) operating risk, (2) market position, (3) margins and other measures of profitability, (4) management quality, (5) conservatism of

---

[7]NAIC-2 corresponds to Moody's Baa (and to Standard & Poor's BBB). NAIC-3 corresponds to Moody's Ba (and to Standard & Poor's BB). Life insurance companies' reserve requirements for NAIC-3 bonds are five times as high as for NAIC-2 bonds. Property and casualty insurance companies can account for bonds rated NAIC-2 or higher (investment grade) based on their historical cost but must account for bonds rated NAIC-3 or lower (speculative grade) based on their current market value.

TABLE 12.3
Senior Debt Ratings as Indicators of Credit Quality

	KEY FINANCIAL RATIOS[a]					
Senior Debt Rating[b]	AAA	AA	A	BBB	BB	B
Interest coverage ratio	21.39x	10.02x	5.67x	2.90x	2.25x	0.74x
Fixed-charge coverage ratio[c]	6.96	5.31	3.42	2.22	1.62	0.85
EBITDA/Interest[d]	31.68	14.78	8.25	5.02	3.46	1.56
Funds from operations/Total debt	109.8%	75.4%	49.1%	30.3%	20.2%	9.8%
Free operating cash flow/Total debt	53.8	27.9	19.5	3.9	0.7	(1.7)
Pretax return on permanent capital	25.1	19.1	16.0	11.8	10.2	6.2
Operating income/Sales	21.2	17.1	14.6	12.3	11.9	8.7
Long-term debt/Capitalization	9.7	18.9	28.8	40.7	50.2	62.2
Total debt/Adjusted capitalization (including short-term debt)	22.6	28.3	36.7	45.3	55.6	71.4
Total debt/Adjusted capitalization (including short-term debt and 8x rents)	36.1	40.1	46.8	56.1	65.5	76.5

[a]Median of the 3-year simple arithmetic averages for the period 1992–1994 for firms whose senior debt had the indicated rating.
[b]As assigned by Standard & Poor's.
[c]Based on full rental charges, rather than the one-third of rental charges used in the SEC fixed-charge-coverage calculation.
[d]EBITDA = earnings before interest, taxes, depreciation, and amortization.
Source: Global Sector Review (New York: Standard & Poor's, October 1995), p. 10.

accounting policies, (6) fixed-charge coverage, (7) leverage (including off-balance-sheet debt) compared to liquidation value of assets, (8) adequacy of cash flow to meet future debt-service obligations, and (9) future financial flexibility in light of future debt-service obligations and planned capital expenditure requirements.

Each factor bears on the risk of future financial distress. The rating agencies weigh their assessments of relevant factors and reach a decision. There is no all-purpose formula. In fact, several factors are difficult to quantify. Nevertheless, certain key credit statistics for comparable companies whose debt carries the target rating offer useful guidance.

Table 12.3 shows how the values of ten key credit statistics vary across the six highest rating categories assigned by Standard & Poor's. Note how all the ratios are progressively better, the higher the company's senior debt rating. Taken together, they go a long way toward distinguishing a stronger credit rating from a weaker one.

Having selected a rating target, a company can use the values of the key credit statistics of comparable companies with that target rating as a rough guide to the ratio targets it should set for itself. We'll show you how to do this in the last section of this chapter.

IMPORTANT FACTORS AFFECTING A COMPANY'S CHOICE OF CAPITAL STRUCTURE

There are five basic considerations involved in a company's choice of capital structure: **1.** ability to service debt, **2.** ability to use interest tax shields fully, **3.** protection against illiquidity afforded by assets, **4.** desired degree of access to capital markets, **5.** dynamic factors and debt management over time. Let's look at each of these factors in turn.

Ability to Service Debt

A careful financial manager will not recommend that a company take on more debt unless she is confident the company will be able to service the debt, that is, be able to make the contractually required payments on time, even under adverse conditions. Many companies appear to maintain a margin of safety, or unused debt capacity, to control the risk of financial distress and maintain access to the capital markets.

There are various measures of debt servicing capacity. One is the **interest coverage ratio:**

$$\text{Interest coverage ratio} = \frac{\text{EBIT}}{\text{Interest expense}} \qquad (12.10)$$

where EBIT denotes earnings before interest and income taxes. Rental (including lease) payments include an interest component. Fixed charges, which include interest expense and one-third of rental expense, represents a better indicator of true interest expense. To take these factors into account, we can calculate a **fixed-charge coverage ratio:**[8]

$$\text{Fixed-charge coverage ratio} = \frac{\text{EBIT} + 1/3 \text{ Rentals}}{\text{Interest expense} + 1/3 \text{ Rentals}} \qquad (12.11)$$

The 1/3 rentals is an attempt to approximate the interest component of rental expense.

To avoid default, a company must meet its principal repayment obligations as well as its interest obligations on schedule. A more comprehensive measure of a company's ability to service its debt obligations is its **debt-service coverage ratio:**

$$\text{Debt-service coverage ratio} = \frac{\text{EBIT} + 1/3 \text{ Rentals}}{\text{Interest expense} + 1/3 \text{ Rentals} + \dfrac{\text{Principal repayments}}{1 - \text{Tax rate}}} \qquad (12.12)$$

The amount of principal repayments is divided by 1 minus the tax rate because principal repayments are not tax deductible. They are paid with after-tax dollars, whereas interest expense and rental expense are tax deductible.

The coverage ratios can be used in pro forma analysis to gauge the impact of a new issue.

INTEREST COVERAGE RATIO Earnings before interest and income taxes divided by interest expense. Equation (12.10).

FIXED-CHARGE COVERAGE RATIO Earnings before interest and income taxes plus one-third rental charges, divided by interest expense plus one-third rental charges. Equation (12.11).

DEBT-SERVICE COVERAGE RATIO Earnings before interest and income taxes plus one-third rental charges, divided by interest expense plus one-third rental charges plus the quantity principal repayments divided by one minus the tax rate. Equation (12.12).

Pro Forma Credit Analysis

EXAMPLE

A company has EBIT of $25 million and interest expense of $10 million. It is considering issuing $50 million of 10% debt. Calculate its pro forma interest coverage ratio, assuming the entire proceeds are invested in plant under construction. Recalculate it assuming the investment produces additional EBIT of $10 million per year.

In the first case,

$$\text{Interest coverage ratio} = \frac{25}{10 + (50)(0.1)} = 1.67x$$

In the second case,

$$\text{Interest coverage ratio} = \frac{25 + 10}{10 + 5} = 2.33x$$

A company can evaluate the impact of alternative capital structures using *sensitivity analysis*. The company calculates the interest coverage ratio, fixed-charge coverage ratio, and debt-service coverage ratio for each capital structure under a variety of projected business scenarios. Then the calculated values are compared with benchmarks that reflect the company's desired credit rating.

---

[8]The fixed-charge coverage ratio in equation (12.11) is the one specified by the Securities and Exchange Commission. However, some analysts prefer to use total rentals rather than one-third this amount. For example, table 12.3 shows the definition Standard & Poor's uses.

Ability to Use Interest Tax Shields Fully

Companies using debt financing must generate sufficient income from operations to claim the deductions. A company that does not pay income taxes and does not expect to become a tax-payer has less incentive to incur additional debt. The tax shields would go unused. That would raise the after-tax cost of the debt, and the additional debt would also increase the risk of in-curring the costs of financial distress. A company can carry tax losses forward. But the added debt will be beneficial only if the expected present value of these tax shields exceeds the ex-pected present value of the costs of financial distress plus the expected value of the increase in agency costs.

A company's capital structure should probably contain no more debt than its future tax position will let it use. For example, companies in industries with other substantial tax shelter opportunities, such as oil and gas companies (with their depletion allowances) and steel mak-ers (with their depreciation and loss carryforwards), should have lower leverage ratios than companies in other industries.

As we've said before, there are frequent changes to the tax code. Such changes compli-cate this analysis and can cause the company's target capital structure to change over time.

Ability of Assets to Support Debt

A company should not incur additional debt if doing so would involve a significant chance of insolvency. The risk of insolvency depends not only on the projected debt-service coverage but also on the company's ability to generate cash through additional borrowing, the sale of equity securities, or the sale of assets.

Assets vary in their ability to support debt. Lower-risk assets with more stable market values provide better collateral for debt. This allows a company to borrow a larger proportion of such assets' market value. For example, a real estate company, or a credit company, can generally support a relatively large amount of leverage.

EXAMPLE | *Leverage and Discovering Oil*

Imagine you bought 200 acres of land on which to create a catfish ranch. You paid $100,000 for the land and have an $80,000 mortgage on it. You plan to use an additional $60,000 of your own money to develop the ranch. You figure the project has an NPV of $40,000, so the total value of the project is $200,000 (= 100 + 60 + 40) at a cost of $160,000. Therefore, your ranch project has a 40% leverage ratio (its proportion of debt financing is $L = 80/200$).

In the process of digging a pond for the catfish, you discover oil on your land. An analy-sis of the discovery puts the new value of your land at $15.25 million. Now your project is only about $L = 0.5\%$ debt financed! But not to worry. You can, of course, increase your lever-age by borrowing against the increased market value of your land. ■

Desired Degree of Access to Capital Markets

A company planning a substantial capital expenditure program will want to maintain access to the capital markets on acceptable terms. This requires adequate credit strength. Histori-cally, a company large enough to sell debt publicly could be reasonably confident of main-taining such access by maintaining a senior debt rating of single-A or better. In 1983, the "junk bond" market expanded rapidly and appeared to lessen the need to have such a high credit standing for maintaining market access. In 1990, however, the junk bond market all but collapsed, emphasizing the risk inherent in increasing leverage to such an extent that a com-pany's debt rating falls below investment grade.

Corporate Debt Management Over Time

The four factors just discussed all affect a company's capital structure target. The capital market imperfections view of capital structure also plays a role. A company might appear to deviate from the normal financing preference order. This could be, for example, because one large issue has proportionally lower transaction costs than two or more smaller issues. Similarly, a company that needs only a relatively small amount of external funds would tend to use bank lines of credit rather than issue securities, even if issuing securities would appear to be better.

The dynamic process can even make it appear that a company has *no* target capital structure. For example, if a company takes advantage of an attractive but temporary financing opportunity (say, the opportunity to issue tax-exempt securities prior to the date the authority to issue such securities expires), its capital structure may move away from its "target." Such apparent deviations in a company's capital structure policy can simply reflect the dynamic nature of an optimal capital structure.

CHOOSING AN APPROPRIATE CAPITAL STRUCTURE

In this section we'll tie together the considerations just discussed into a single framework for determining an appropriate capital structure. To do this we'll use comparative credit analysis and pro forma capital structure analysis. A *comparative credit analysis* suggests a range of target capital structures that might be appropriate. A *pro forma capital structure analysis* shows the impact of the alternatives within the target range on the company's credit statistics and reported financial results, and indicates whether the company will be able to fully use tax shield benefits. This enables the company to select a specific target capital structure.

Comparative Credit Analysis

In practice, a comparative credit analysis is the most widely used technique for selecting an appropriate capital structure. This approach is an application of the Behavioral Principle. It involves the following steps:

1. Select the desired rating objective.
2. Identify a set of comparable companies that also have the target senior debt rating.
3. Perform a comparative credit analysis of these companies to define the capital structure (or range of capital structures) most consistent with this rating objective.

We have discussed five considerations that enter into the capital structure decision. Choosing a target debt rating actually encompasses three of the five. The only two not covered are the ability to the use tax benefits and debt management considerations, such as issuance expenses, which affect the immediate preference order of the various sources of funds. We must evaluate these two factors separately.

As we said earlier, a single-A rating provides a compromise between maintaining capital market access and getting more tax savings from additional leverage. However, more conservative companies and companies with very heavy future financing programs might strive for a higher rating. Other companies that are willing to bear greater financial risk might set a lower rating target.

Comparative Credit Analysis

Table 12.4 on page 458 illustrates a comparative credit analysis of specialty chemicals companies that are comparable to the company being analyzed, Washington Chemical Corporation. There are six specialty chemicals companies with rated debt. The senior debt ratings (Moody's/Standard & Poor's) range from a low of Ba1/BB+ to a high of A2/A.

(continued on following page)

(Comparative Credit Analysis *continued from previous page*)

Washington Chemical has decided on a target senior debt rating "comfortably within" the single-A range. Three of the companies in table 12.4 have at least one senior debt rating in the single-A category, and Johnson Chemical and Wilson Chemical are rated in the middle of the single-A category by both agencies.

Washington Chemical is significantly more profitable than one of the A2/A issuers and only slightly less profitable than the other. Washington Chemical's debt-to-capitalization,

TABLE 12.4

A Comparative Credit Analysis of Specialty Chemicals Companies

	WASHINGTON CHEMICAL CORPORATION	MYERS CHEMICALS CORP.	NORTHWEST CHEMICALS INC.	DELAWARE CHEMICALS CORP.	WESTERN INDUSTRIES	JOHNSON CHEMICAL INC.	WILSON CHEMICAL CORP.
Senior debt rating (Moody's/Standard & Poor's)	—	A3/BBB+	Ba1/BBB–	Baa2/BBB	Ba1/BB+	A2/A	A2/A
Profitability							
Operating profit margin	7.4%	5.9%	1.9%	4.5%	8.9%	4.1%	9.2%
Net profit margin	3.9	2.6	1.0	2.3	2.2	2.3	4.1
Return on assets	4.8	3.2	2.2	4.9	2.8	4.3	4.9
Return on common equity	10.3	9.2	5.0	13.9	8.8	10.8	10.0
Capitalization							
Short-term debt	$ 16	$ 60	$ 10	$ 10	$ 10	$ 8	$ 36
Senior long-term debt	$158	$144	$ 49	$163	$110	$140	$245
Capitalized lease obligations	—	22	10	20	—	—	1
Subordinated long-term debt	—	—	—	13	80	8	—
Total long-term debt	158	166	59	196	190	148	246
Minority interest	—	—	3	2	—	—	—
Preferred equity	—	2	35	5	—	—	—
Common equity	321	253	165	334	162	278	659
Total capitalization	$479	$421	$262	$537	$352	$426	$905
Long-term debt ratio	33%	39%	23%	36%	54%	35%	27%
Total-debt-to-adjusted-capitalization ratio	35	47	25	38	56	36	30
Funds-from-operations-to-long-term-debt ratio	60	42	45	35	27	51	63
Funds-from-operations-to-total-debt ratio	55	31	39	33	25	49	55
Liquidity							
Current ratio	2.4x	1.9x	2.7x	2.1x	1.9x	2.2x	2.6x
Fixed-Charge Coverage Ratio							
Last 12 months	3.5x	2.3x	2.4x	3.3x	2.0x	3.3x	3.7x
Latest fiscal year	4.3	4.0	3.8	2.9	2.3	4.4	4.2
One year prior	5.6	3.0	3.2	2.7	2.8	5.4	5.7
Two years prior	6.3	4.0	2.8	2.2	3.8	7.9	4.9

cash-flow-to-debt, and fixed-charge coverage ratios fall between the higher and lower of the two values for each ratio exhibited by the two A2/A specialty chemicals companies. Washington Chemical's ratios are substantially better than those of Myers Chemicals, which is a borderline triple-B–single-A. Washington Chemical concluded from this analysis that its financial condition is of medium-grade single-A quality. ■

We need to clarify one point regarding this example. We have emphasized the importance of basing financial decisions on market values, but the financial ratios in table 12.4 contain some book value items. This is because it is simply not practical to include current market values in every case. The rating agencies consider the market value of a company's assets in assessing its leverage. But they view these assets on a liquidity basis rather than on a going-concern basis. The most significant, practical, and common adjustment is to use the market value (based on the common stock price) in place of the book value of equity.

The actual debt-to-capitalization ratio should value the common equity component on the basis of the liquidation value of the assets rather than on the basis of even the company's prevailing share price (which reflects the value of the company on a going-concern basis). Assets such as proven oil and gas reserves, which are relatively liquid, will support a higher degree of leverage than less liquid assets. New plant and equipment will tend to support greater leverage than an equal book value amount of old plant and equipment. But determining these liquidating values is necessarily subjective, because there aren't typically liquid markets for fixed assets, and appraisals generally aren't available. Still, the quality of assets will tend to vary systematically from one industry to another. Thus, for a particular rating category, the debt-to-capitalization ratios for companies in one industry, when compared with the debt-to-capitalization ratios for companies in another industry whose debt bears the same rating, will reflect interindustry differences in liquidating asset value.

An analysis like the one in table 12.4 is necessarily imperfect. But if comparable companies are chosen carefully, and if differences between the comparable companies and the company being analyzed are carefully weighed, the comparative credit analysis can produce useful guidelines.

Comparative Credit Analysis (continued)

E X A M P L E

As we said, in the final analysis the choice of capital structure requires judgment. Before reaching a decision, Washington Chemical evaluated its expected profitability. Washington Chemical believed that its profitability would exceed that of its single-A competitors. Based on its careful consideration of all these factors, Washington Chemical decided to try to stay within the following ranges:

Annual fixed-charge coverage ratio: $3.50x$ to $4.00x$

Annual funds-from-operations-to-total-debt ratio: 50% to 60%

Long-term debt ratio: 30% to 35%

Before deciding where to aim within each of these ranges, Washington Chemical decided to

- Confirm its ability to fully use the estimated tax shield benefits, particularly under somewhat adverse conditions
- Assess the impact of these obligations on its future financing requirements

Table 12.5 on pages 460 and 461 contains a pro forma capital structure analysis.

In its evaluation, Washington Chemical realized the importance of considering a reasonably pessimistic case as well as its expected case. Consequently, there are four cases considered in table 12.5. They correspond to two degrees of leverage (long-term debt ratio of 30% and 35%) and two operating scenarios (10% growth and 5% growth).

(continued on following page)

(Comparative Credit Analysis *continued from previous page*)

It is evident from cases 1 and 2 that Washington Chemical could justify a 35% long-term debt ratio in the expected case. Both the fixed-charge coverage and the funds-from-operations-to-total-debt ratios increase steadily and remain comfortably within their target ranges. Moreover, Washington Chemical could fully use the tax benefits of ownership and fully claim all interest deductions.

Under a more pessimistic scenario, cases 3 and 4 show that Washington Chemical's fixed-charge coverage and funds-from-operations-to-total-debt ratios would eventually fall below their target ranges. The deterioration is less severe in case 4, because the long-term debt ratio is only 30%. However, the external equity financing requirement is greater. Washington Chemical decided to finance itself with a leverage ratio of 1/3. ■

TABLE 12.5

A Pro Forma Capital Structure Analysis

		PROJECTED AHEAD				
	Initial	**1 Year**	**2 Years**	**3 Years**	**4 Years**	**5 Years**
Case 1: Leverage at upper end of range/expected case operating results						
Pre-interest taxable income[a]	$ 61	$ 67	$ 74	$ 81	$ 89	$ 98
Interest	18	20	22	24	26	28
Surplus (Deficit)[b]	$ 43	$ 47	$ 52	$ 57	$ 63	$ 70
Earnings before fixed charges and income taxes[c]	$ 70	$ 77	$ 85	$ 93	$ 102	$ 113
Fixed charges[d]	20	22	24	26	28	30
Fixed-charge coverage	3.5x	3.5x	3.5x	3.6x	3.6x	3.8x
Net income	$ 30	$ 33	$ 36	$ 42	$ 45	$ 51
Noncash expenses	65	72	79	84	94	102
Funds from operations[c]	95	105	115	126	139	153
Dividends	(10)	(11)	(12)	(14)	(15)	(17)
Internal cash generation	85	94	103	112	124	136
Capital expenditures	(125)	(125)	(125)	(135)	(150)	(160)
Cash required	$ 40	$ 31	$ 22	$ 23	$ 26	$ 24
External debt requirement	$ 20	$ 17	$ 14	$ 15	$ 17	$ 17
External equity requirement[e]	$ 20	$ 14	$ 8	$ 8	$ 9	$ 7
Funds from operations to total debt[f]	55%	55%	56%	57%	59%	60%
Case 2: Leverage at lower end of range/expected case operating results						
Pre-interest taxable income[a]	$ 61	$ 67	$ 74	$ 81	$ 89	$ 98
Interest	18	19	21	23	25	26
Surplus (Deficit)[b]	$ 43	$ 48	$ 53	$ 58	$ 64	$ 72
Earnings before fixed charges and income taxes[c]	$ 70	$ 77	$ 85	$ 93	$ 102	$ 113
Fixed charges[d]	20	21	23	25	27	28
Fixed-charge coverage	3.5x	3.7x	3.7x	3.7x	3.8x	4.0x
Net income	$ 30	$ 33	$ 36	$ 42	$ 45	$ 51
Noncash expenses	65	72	79	84	94	102
Funds from operations[c]	95	105	115	126	139	153
Dividends	(10)	(11)	(12)	(14)	(15)	(17)
Internal cash generation	85	94	103	112	124	136
Capital expenditures	(125)	(125)	(125)	(135)	(150)	(160)
Cash required	$ 40	$ 31	$ 22	$ 23	$ 26	$ 24
External debt requirement[g]	$ 17	$ 15	$ 12	$ 13	$ 15	$ 15
External equity requirement[g]	$ 23	$ 16	$ 10	$ 10	$ 11	$ 9
Funds from operations to total debt[f]	55%	56%	57%	59%	61%	63%

(continued)

TABLE 12.5

A Pro Forma Capital Structure Analysis *(continued)*

	Initial	1 Year	2 Years	3 Years	4 Years	5 Years
			PROJECTED AHEAD			
Case 3: Leverage at upper end of range/pessimistic case operating results						
Pre-interest taxable income[a]	$ 61	$ 64	$ 67	$ 71	$ 74	$ 78
Interest	18	20	22	24	27	30
Surplus (Deficit)[b]	$ 43	$ 44	$ 45	$ 47	$ 47	$ 48
Earnings before fixed charges and income taxes[c]	$ 70	$ 74	$ 78	$ 82	$ 86	$ 90
Fixed charges[d]	20	22	24	26	29	32
Fixed-charge coverage	3.5x	3.4x	3.3x	3.2x	3.0x	2.8x
Net income	$ 30	$ 30	$ 33	$ 33	$ 33	$ 33
Noncash expenses	65	70	72	77	82	88
Funds from operations[c]	95	100	105	110	115	121
Dividends	(10)	(10)	(11)	(11)	(11)	(11)
Internal cash generation	85	90	94	99	104	110
Capital expenditures	(125)	(125)	(125)	(135)	(150)	(160)
Cash required	$ 40	$ 35	$ 31	$ 36	$ 46	$ 50
External debt requirement	$ 20	$ 18	$ 17	$ 19	$ 23	$ 25
External equity requirement[e]	$ 20	$ 17	$ 14	$ 17	$ 23	$ 25
Funds from operations to total debt[f]	55%	52%	50%	48%	46%	44%
Case 4: Leverage at lower end of range/pessimistic case operating results						
Pre-interest taxable income[a]	$ 61	$ 64	$ 67	$ 71	$ 74	$ 78
Interest	18	19	21	23	26	28
Surplus (Deficit)[b]	$ 43	$ 45	$ 46	$ 48	$ 48	$ 50
Earnings before fixed charges and income taxes[c]	$ 70	$ 74	$ 78	$ 82	$ 86	$ 90
Fixed charges[d]	20	21	23	25	28	30
Fixed-charge coverage	3.5x	3.5x	3.4x	3.3x	3.1x	3.0x
Net income	$ 30	$ 30	$ 33	$ 33	$ 33	$ 33
Noncash expenses	65	70	72	77	82	88
Funds from operations[c]	95	100	105	110	115	121
Dividends	(10)	(10)	(11)	(11)	(11)	(11)
Internal cash generation	85	90	94	99	104	110
Capital expenditures	(125)	(125)	(125)	(135)	(150)	(160)
Cash required	$ 40	$ 35	$ 31	$ 36	$ 46	$ 50
External debt requirement[g]	$ 17	$ 16	$ 15	$ 17	$ 20	$ 28
External equity requirement[g]	$ 23	$ 19	$ 16	$ 19	$ 26	$ 28
Funds from operations to total debt[f]	55%	53%	51%	50%	48%	46%

[a]As computed for federal income tax purposes. Estimated to grow at 10% per annum in the "expected case" and 5% per annum in the "pessimistic case."

[b]Calculated as pre-interest taxable income minus interest.

[c]Estimated to grow at 10% per annum in the "expected case" and 5% per annum in the "pessimistic case."

[d]Assumes rental expense of $6 million per year. Under the SEC method, one-third of this amount is included in fixed charges.

[e]Calculated to preserve a ratio of 35% long-term debt financing to 65% additional common equity.

[f]The amount of total debt at the end of the initial year is $174 (= 16 + 158 from table 12.4). The debt level for any single year projected ahead is the initial amount plus the sum of the annual external debt requirements up to the year in question. The debt level projected ahead 2 years is $205 (= $174 + 17 + 14) so that funds from operations to total debt equals 56% (= 115/205) in Case 1.

[g]Calculated to preserve a ratio of 30% long-term debt financing to 70% additional common equity.

APPENDIX SUMMARY

This appendix described and illustrated a practical procedure a company can use to select and manage an appropriate capital structure. The procedure involves two important steps.

- First, the company conducts a *comparative credit analysis* of comparable companies. The values of key financial ratios for each company are then calculated to determine the relationship between senior debt rating and capital structure. A bond rating provides estimates for both the relative risk of financial distress and the relative access to capital markets. The rating choice (such as a single-A rating) and the results of the comparative credit analysis allow a company to specify reasonable ranges for its key financial ratios.
- The second step in the procedure involves conducting a *pro forma capital structure analysis*. This tests, among other things, the company's ability to fully use the tax shields from its target capital structure. The result of this two-step process is a target capital structure that balances the advantages against the costs of a change in financial leverage.

APPENDIX REVIEW ACTIVITIES

APPENDIX QUESTIONS

1. Why is a pro forma analysis an important prerequisite to choosing a capital structure?
2. What is the major reason that subordinated debt is typically rated lower than senior debt?
3. Explain why selecting a target senior debt rating is a reasonable approach to choosing a capital structure. Explain why a target senior debt rating of single-A is a prudent objective when there is only a very limited new issue market for non-investment-grade debt, and when investor willingness to purchase triple-B-rated debt is likely to be highly sensitive to the state of the economy.
4. A company's capital structure consists solely of debt and common equity. What form would an exchange offer take if the company believes it is
   a. Overleveraged?   b. Underleveraged?
5. Why is it so important to note that the required return is not a historical cost of funds? Cite two factors that can render the use of a company's historical cost of funds (to evaluate a new investment) potentially damaging to the company.

CHALLENGING QUESTIONS

6. Why would lenders be willing to lend a larger proportion of the market value of tangible assets such as plant and equipment than of the market value of intangible assets such as "special" formulas and goodwill?
7. Suppose that a company wishes to maintain a capital structure that is consistent with an A senior debt rating. Under what circumstances would the company maintain a lower degree of leverage than a cross section of single-A-rated companies?
8. The development of the new-issue junk bond market had important implications for capital structure choice. The existence of a viable junk bond market means that companies can comfortably maintain higher degrees of leverage than they could prior to the development of this market. Do you agree or disagree? Justify your answer.

APPENDIX PROBLEMS

A1. (Coverage ratio) A company's latest 12 months' EBIT is $30 million, and its interest expense for the same period is $10 million. Calculate the interest coverage ratio.

A2. (Coverage ratio) The company in the preceding problem also had $15 million of rental expense during the latest 12 months. Calculate the company's fixed-charge coverage ratio.

A3. (Coverage ratio) The company in the two preceding problems also had $6 million of principal repayments during the latest 12 months. Its marginal tax rate is 40%. Calculate the debt-service coverage ratio.

B1. (Comparative credit analysis) Bixton Company's new chief financial officer is evaluating Bixton's capital structure. She is concerned that the company might be underleveraged, even though the company has larger-than-average research and development and foreign tax credits when compared to other companies in its industry. Her staff prepared the industry comparison shown below.

Rating Category	Fixed-Charge Coverage	Cash Flow/ Total Debt	Long-Term Debt/ Capitalization
Aa	4.00–5.25x	60–80%	17–23%
A	3.00–4.30	45–65	22–32
Baa	1.95–3.40	35–55	30–41

a. If Bixton's objective is to achieve a credit standing that falls, in the words of the chief financial officer, "comfortably within the 'A' range," what target range would you recommend for each of the three credit measures?

b. Before settling on these target ranges, what other factors should Bixton's chief financial officer consider?

c. Before deciding whether the target ranges are really appropriate for Bixton in its current financial situation, what key issues specific to Bixton must the chief financial officer resolve?

B2. (Comparative credit analysis) Sanderson Manufacturing Company would like to achieve a capital structure consistent with a Baa2/BBB senior debt rating. Sanderson has identified six comparable companies and calculated the credit statistics shown below.

Company:	A	B	C	D	E	F
Senior debt rating	Baa2/BBB	Baa3/BBB–	Baa2/BBB	Baa1/A–	Baa1/BBB–	Baa2/BBB+
Return on assets	5.2%	5.0%	5.4%	5.7%	5.2%	5.3%
Long-term debt/cap	38%	41%	45%	40%	25%	43%
Total cap ($MM)	425	575	525	650	210	375
Cash flow/LT debt	39%	43%	28%	46%	57%	43%
Fixed-charge cov	2.57	2.83	2.75	2.38	3.59	2.15

a. Sanderson's return on assets is 5.3%, and it has a total capitalization of $600 million. What are reasonable targets for long-term debt/capitalization, cash flow/long-term debt, and fixed-charge coverage?

b. Are there any companies among the six that are particularly good or bad comparables? Explain.

c. Suppose Sanderson's current ratio of long-term debt to total capitalization is 60% but its fixed-charge coverage is 3.00. What would you recommend?

B3. (Pro forma coverage ratios) A company has $100 million of earnings before interest and taxes and $40 million of interest expense.

a. Calculate this company's interest coverage ratio.

b. Calculate the pro forma interest coverage ratio, assuming the issuance of $100 million of 10% debt with the issue proceeds to be invested fully in a plant under construction.

c. Calculate the pro forma interest coverage ratio, assuming the issuance of $100 million of 10% debt with the proceeds to be invested temporarily in commercial paper that yields 8%.

BIBLIOGRAPHY

Agrawal, Anup, and Nandu J. Nagarajan. "Corporate Capital Structure, Agency Costs, and Ownership Control: The Case of All-Equity Firms," *Journal of Finance,* 1990, 45(4):1325–1331.

Arzac, Enrique R. "On the Capital Structure of Leveraged Buyouts," *Financial Management,* 1992, 21(1):16–26.

Ashton, D., and D. Atkins. "Interactions in Corporate Financing and Investment Decisions—Implications for Capital Budgeting: A Further Comment," *Journal of Finance,* 1978, 33(5):1447–1453.

Barton, Sidney L., Ned C. Hill, and Srinivasan Sundaram. "An Empirical Test of Stakeholder Theory Predictions of Capital Structure," *Financial Management,* 1989, 18(1):36–44.

Bar-Yosef, Sasson. "Interactions of Corporate Financing and Investment Decisions—Implications for Capital Budgeting: Comment," *Journal of Finance,* 1977, 32(1):211–217.

Baskin, Jonathan. "An Empirical Investigation of the Pecking Order Hypothesis," *Financial Management,* 1989, 18(1):26–35.

Ben-Horim, Moshe, Shalom Hochman, and Oded Palmon. "The Impact of the 1986 Tax Reform Act on Corporate Financial Policy," *Financial Management,* 1987, 16(3):29–35.

Bergman, Yaacov Z., and Jeffrey L. Callen. "Opportunistic Underinvestment in Debt Renegotiation and Capital Structure," *Journal of Financial Economics,* 1991, 29(1):137–172.

Bradley, Michael, Gregg A. Jarrell, and E. Han Kim. "On the Existence of an Optimal Capital Structure: Theory and Evidence," *Journal of Finance,* 1984, 39(3):857–878.

Bruner, Robert F., and E. Richard Brownlee II. "Leveraged ESOPs, Wealth Transfers, and 'Shareholder Neutrality:' The Case of Polaroid," *Financial Management,* 1990, 19(1):59–74.

Castanias, Richard P. "Bankruptcy Risk and Optimal Capital Structure," *Journal of Finance,* 1983, 38(5):1617–1635.

Chang, Chun. "Capital Structure as an Optimal Contract Between Employees and Investors," *Journal of Finance,* 1992, 47(3):1141–1158.

Chang, Rosita P., and S. Ghon Rhee. "The Impact of Personal Taxes on Corporate Dividend Policy and Capital Structure Decisions," *Financial Management,* 1990, 19(2):21–31.

Chaplinsky, Susan, and Greg Niehaus. "The Tax and Distributional Effects of Leveraged ESOPs," *Financial Management,* 1990, 19(1):29–38.

Chatrath, Arjun, Mukesh Chaudhry, Sanjay Ramchander, and Jandhyala L. Sharma. "Gains from Leverage," *Financial Management,* 1993, 22(4):21–22.

Collins, J. Markham, and William S. Sekely. "The Relationship of Headquarters Country and Industry Classification to Financial Structure," *Financial Management,* 1983, 12(3):45–51.

Cordes, Joseph J., and Steven M. Sheffrin. "Estimating the Tax Advantage of Corporate Debt," *Journal of Finance,* 1983, 38(1):95–105.

Dann, Larry Y., and Wayne H. Mikkelson. "Convertible Debt Issuance, Capital Structure Change and Financing-Related Information: Some New Evidence," *Journal of Financial Economics,* 1984, 13(2):157–186.

Davis, Alfred H. R. "Effective Tax Rates as Determinants of Canadian Capital Structure," *Financial Management,* 1987, 16(3):22–28.

DeAngelo, Harry, and Ronald W. Masulis. "Optimal Capital Structure Under Corporate and Personal Taxation," *Journal of Financial Economics,* 1980, 8(1):3–30.

Denis, David J. "Organizational Form and the Consequences of Highly Leveraged Transactions: Kroger's Recapitalization and Safeway's LBO," *Journal of Financial Economics,* 1994, 36(2):193–224.

Easterwood, John C., and Palani-Rajan Kadapakkam. "The Role of Private and Public Debt in Corporate Capital Structures," *Financial Management,* 1991, 20(3):49–57.

Emery, Douglas R., and Adam K. Gehr, Jr. "Tax Options, Capital Structure, and Miller Equilibrium: A Numerical Illustration," *Financial Management,* 1988, 17(2):30–40.

Ezzell, John R., and William A. Kelly, Jr. "An APV Analysis of Capital Budgeting Under Inflation," *Financial Management,* 1984, 13(3):49–54.

Ezzell, John R., and James A. Miles. "Capital Project Analysis and the Debt Transaction Plan," *Journal of Financial Research,* 1983, 6(1):25–31.

Fischer, Edwin O., Robert Heinkel, and Josef Zechner. "Dynamic Capital Structure Choice: Theory and Tests," *Journal of Finance,* 1989, 44(1):19–40.

Friend, Irwin, and Larry H. P. Lang. "An Empirical Test of the Impact of Managerial Self-Interest on Corporate Capital Structure," *Journal of Finance,* 1988, 43(2):271–281.

Froot, Kenneth A., David S. Scharfstein, and Jeremy C. Stein. "Risk Management: Coordinating Corporate Investment and Financing Policies," *Journal of Finance,* 1993, 48(5):1629–1658.

Harris, John M., Jr., Rodney L. Roenfeldt, and Philip L. Cooley. "Evidence of Financial Leverage Clienteles," *Journal of Finance,* 1983, 38(4):1125–1132.

Harris, Milton, and Artur Raviv. "Capital Structure and the Informational Role of Debt," *Journal of Finance,* 1990, 45(2):321–350.

Harris, Milton, and Artur Raviv. "The Theory of Capital Structure," *Journal of Finance,* 1991, 46(1):297–356.

Haugen, Robert A., and Lemma W. Senbet. "Bankruptcy and Agency Costs: Their Significance to the Theory of Optimal Capital Structure," *Journal of Financial and Quantitative Analysis,* 1988, 23(1):27–38.

Hodder, James E., and Lemma W. Senbet. "International Capital Structure Equilibrium," *Journal of Finance,* 1990, 45(5):1495–1516.

Hull, Robert M., and Richard Moellenberndt. "Bank Debt Reduction Announcements and Negative Signaling," *Financial Management,* 1994, 23(2):21–30.

Janjigian, Vahan. "The Leverage Changing Consequences of Convertible Debt Financing," *Financial Management,* 1987, 16(3):15–21.

Jensen, Gerald R., Donald P. Solberg, and Thomas S. Zorn. "Simultaneous Determination of Insider Ownership, Debt, and Dividend Policies," *Journal of Financial and Quantitative Analysis,* 1992, 27(2):247–264.

John, Kose. "Risk-Shifting Incentives and Signalling Through Corporate Capital Structure," *Journal of Finance,* 1987, 42(3):632–641.

John, Kose, Lemma W. Senbet, and Anant K. Sundaram. "Cross-Border Liability of Multinational Enterprises, Border Taxes, and Capital Structure," *Financial Management,* 1991, 20(4):54–67.

John, Teresa A., and Kose John. "Top-Management Compensation and Capital Structure," *Journal of Finance,* 1993, 48(3):949–974.

Kale, Jayant R., Thomas H. Noe, and Gabriel G. Ramirez. "The Effect of Business Risk on Corporate Capital Structure: Theory and Evidence," *Journal of Finance,* 1991, 46(5):1693–1716.

Kang, Joseph C., and Ira Horowitz. "Insider Equity Ownership and Financial Leverage," *Financial Management,* 1993, 22(4):20–21.

Kester, W. Carl. "Capital and Ownership Structure: A Comparison of United States and Japanese Manufacturing Corporations," *Financial Management,* 1986, 15(1):5–16.

Leland, Hayne E. "Corporate Debt Value, Bond Covenants, and Optimal Capital Structure," *Journal of Finance,* 1994, 49(4):1213–1252.

Lewellen, Wilbur G., and Douglas R. Emery. "Corporate Debt Management and the Value of the Firm," *Journal of Financial and Quantitative Analysis,* 1986, 21(5):415–426.

Long, Michael S., and Ileen Malitz. "The Investment-Financing Nexus: Some Empirical Evidence." In Joel M. Stern and Donald H. Chew, Jr., eds., *The Revolution in Corporate Finance.* New York: Basil Blackwell, 1986:112–118.

Long, Michael S., and Ileen Malitz. "Investment Patterns and Financial Leverage." In Benjamin Friedman, ed., *Corporate Capital Structure in the United States.* Chicago, Ill.: University of Chicago Press, 1985:325–348.

MacKie-Mason, Jeffrey K. "Do Taxes Affect Corporate Financing Decisions?" *Journal of Finance,* 1990, 45(5):1471–1494.

Masulis, Ronald W. "The Effects of Capital Structure Change on Security Prices: A Study of Exchange Offers," *Journal of Financial Economics,* 1980, 8(2):139–178.

Masulis, Ronald W. "The Impact of Capital Structure Change on Firm Value, Some Estimates," *Journal of Finance,* 1983, 38(1):107–126.

Mauer, David C., and Wilbur G. Lewellen. "Debt Management Under Corporate and Personal Taxation," *Journal of Finance,* 1987, 42(5):1275–1291.

Mauer, David C., and Alexander J. Triantis. "Interactions of Corporate Financing and Investment Decisions: A Dynamic Framework," *Journal of Finance,* 1994, 49(4):1253–1277.

Mehran, Hamid. "Executive Incentive Plans, Corporate Control, and Capital Structure," *Journal of Financial and Quantitative Analysis,* 1992, 27(4):539–560.

Miles, James A., and John R. Ezzell. "Reformulating Tax Shield Valuation: A Note," *Journal of Finance,* 1985, 40(5):1484–1492.

Miles, James A., and John R. Ezzell. "The Weighted Average Cost of Capital, Perfect Capital Markets, and Project Life: A Clarification," *Journal of Financial and Quantitative Analysis,* 1980, 15(3):719–730.

Miller, Merton H. "Debt and Taxes," *Journal of Finance,* 1977, 32(2):261–275.

Miller, Merton H. "Leverage," *Journal of Finance,* 1991, 46(2):479–488.

Modigliani, Franco, and Merton H. Miller. "Corporate Income Taxes and the Cost of Capital: A Correction," *American Economic Review,* 1963, 53(June):433–443.

Modigliani, Franco, and Merton H. Miller. "The Cost of Capital, Corporation Finance and the Theory of Investment," *American Economic Review,* 1958, 48(June):261–297.

Myers, Stewart C. "Interactions in Corporate Financing and Investment Decisions—Implications for Capital Budgeting," *Journal of Finance,* 1974, 29(1):1–25.

Myers, Stewart C. "Presidential Address: The Capital Structure Puzzle," *Journal of Finance,* 1984, 39(3):575–592.

Myers, Stewart C. "The Search for Optimal Capital Structure." In Joel M. Stern and Donald H. Chew, Jr., eds., *The Revolution in Corporate Finance.* New York: Basil Blackwell, 1986: 91–99.

Myers, Stewart C., and Nicholas S. Majluf. "Corporate Financing and Investment Decisions When Firms Have Information That Investors Do Not Have," *Journal of Financial Economics,* 1984, 13(2):187–221.

Opler, Tim C., and Sheridan Titman. "Financial Distress and Corporate Performance," *Journal of Finance,* 1994, 49(3):1015–1040.

Patterson, Cleveland S. "The Effects of Leverage on Revenue Requirements of Public Utilities," *Financial Management,* 1983, 12(3):29–39.

Pilotte, Eugene. "The Economic Recovery Tax Act of 1981 and Corporate Capital Structure," *Financial Management,* 1990, 19(4):98–107.

Ravid, S. Abraham. "On Interactions of Production and Financial Decisions," *Financial Management,* 1988, 17(3):87–99.

Rogers, Ronald C., and James E. Owers. "Equity for Debt Exchanges and Stockholder Wealth," *Financial Management,* 1985, 14(3):18–26.

Ross, Stephen A. "The Determination of Financial Structure: The Incentive Signalling Approach," *Bell Journal of Economics,* 1977, 8(Spring):23–40.

Scott, David F., Jr., and John D. Martin. "Industry Influence on Financial Structure," *Financial Management,* 1975, 4(1):67–73.

Shleifer, Andrei, and Robert W. Vishny. "Liquidation Values and Debt Capacity: A Market Equilibrium Approach," *Journal of Finance,* 1992, 47(4):1343–1366.

Shrieves, Ronald E., and Mary M. Pashley. "Evidence on the Association Between Mergers and Capital Structure," *Financial Management,* 1984, 13(3):39–48.

Taggart, Robert A., Jr. "Consistent Valuation and Cost of Capital Expressions with Corporate and Personal Taxes," *Financial Management,* 1991, 20(3):8–20.

Taggart, Robert A., Jr. "A Model of Corporate Financing Decisions," *Journal of Finance,* 1977, 32(5):1467–1484.

Titman, Sheridan, and Roberto Wessels. "The Determinants of Capital Structure Choice," *Journal of Finance,* 1988, 43(1):1–19.

Viswanath, P. V. "Strategic Considerations, the Pecking Order Hypothesis, and Market Reactions to Equity Financing," *Journal of Financial and Quantitative Analysis,* 1993, 28(2):213–234.

Williams, Joseph. "Perquisites, Risk, and Capital Structure," *Journal of Finance,* 1987, 42(1):29–48.

DIVIDEND POLICY

1. Explain the timing of the dividend declaration date, ex-dividend date, record date, and payment date.

2. Explain why dividend policy does not matter in a perfect capital market environment.

3. Explain why capital market imperfections (asymmetric taxes, asymmetric information, and transaction costs) create an environment in which a company's dividend policy can affect its total value.

4. Apply the three-step approach to the dividend decision outlined in the chapter to determine an appropriate dividend action for a company.

5. Distinguish special and extra dividends from regular cash dividends.

6. Explain the financial significance of stock dividends and stock splits and why a stock dividend is not a perfect substitute for a cash dividend.

7. Explain the possible advantages of share repurchases over cash dividend payments.

DIVIDEND POLICY A company's decision to pay out a portion of its earnings to its shareholders in cash.

Acompany's **dividend policy** is an established guide for the company to determine the amount of money it will pay out as dividends. Don't you think it's reasonable that a company should give its owners part of the profit? Why not share the wealth? But suppose the company has positive-NPV projects it can invest the money in. Might the shareholders be better off if the company retains and reinvests the money? If so, another alternative is for the company to pay the dividends, and then change its capital structure by issuing new debt or equity to get the money to invest in the positive-NPV projects.

A dividend policy, then, involves a trade-off among cash dividends, capital budgeting, and capital structure. We're interested in whether this dividend policy trade-off affects the value of the company. Just like capital structure, dividend policy doesn't matter in a perfect capital market environment. However, the same three groups of persistent capital market imperfections that cause capital structure to affect a company's value also cause dividend policy to affect its value, but to a lesser extent.

As with capital structure, there are conflicting viewpoints about dividend policy. But also like capital structure, dividend policy is relevant in practice, because companies certainly behave as though it matters. The empirical evidence shows consistent patterns of dividend policy, and it shows significant average stock price reactions to dividend changes. These suggest there are definite reasons for following certain policies, that some policies are superior to others. You might think companies are all following the Behavioral Principle and just copying each other. We think this is too simplistic. We'll explain why in this chapter.

DIVIDEND POLICY AND THE PRINCIPLES OF FINANCE

◆ *Capital Market Efficiency:* Recognize that the potential to increase company value through dividend policy is smaller than the potential to increase company value through the introduction of *valuable new ideas* and wise use of the company's *comparative advantages.* The potential value differential is also smaller for dividend policy than it is for capital structure policy.

◆ *Risk-Return Trade-Off:* Recognize that the difference between receiving the dividend now and getting it later is risk and the time value of money. It is a risk-return trade-off that does not affect the value of the company.

◆ *Signaling:* Consider any possible change in dividend policy carefully, because dividend changes convey information to outsiders and can be misunderstood.

◆ *Behavioral:* Use the information contained in the dividend decisions of other companies.

◆ *Two-Sided Transactions:* Repurchasing shares from a takeover raider at a premium to their fair market value transfers wealth away from the other stockholders.

◆ *Valuable Ideas:* Look for opportunities to create value by supplying a dividend policy that is in short supply, perhaps resulting from changes in tax law.

◆ *Time Value of Money:* Include any time-value-of-money tax benefits from dividend choices.

467

DIVIDEND POLICY IN PRACTICE

PAYOUT RATIO The ratio of cash dividends paid to earnings.

Thus far, for simplicity, we've characterized a dividend policy simply as a **payout ratio** (the ratio of dividends paid to earnings; see chapter 6). However, it's more complex than this. A company's payout ratio typically varies over time. For example, a small and rapidly growing company may retain all its earnings for many years to help finance its growth. As a company matures, typically it begins to pay dividends at some point and then, over time, increases the proportion of its earnings that are paid out in dividends. About 50% of the earnings of all U.S. corporations over the past half-century have been paid out as dividends. The actual dividend policies of companies provide a useful backdrop for our discussion of dividend policy.

Characteristics of Corporate Dividend Policies

In practice, publicly traded companies prefer to (1) pay at least some minimum level of dividends on a regular basis, (2) maintain a stable payout ratio and dividend rate, (3) make orderly changes in the dividend rate, and (4) avoid cutting an established dividend rate.

Sharing the Profits   Smaller and younger companies generally do not pay cash dividends. At some point in its life cycle, a company decides that it is sufficiently "mature" to share the profits. This may be due to a desire to demonstrate the company's stability, a decline in profitable investment opportunities, investor desires for at least some minimal level of cash distributions, a desire to broaden the market for the company's stock to include investors who are prohibited from buying non-dividend-paying stocks, or other factors. Among New York Stock Exchange–listed companies, for example, in any given year between 75% and 90% of the common stocks pay cash dividends.

Dividends Are More Stable than Earnings   Figure 13.1 illustrates the pattern of corporate earnings and dividends from World War II to the present. Dividends are more stable than earnings. This is also true for most individual companies, as illustrated in figure 13.2. See how dividends track cash flow per share much more closely than earnings per share.

FIGURE 13.1
Corporate dividends and earnings from World War II to the present.

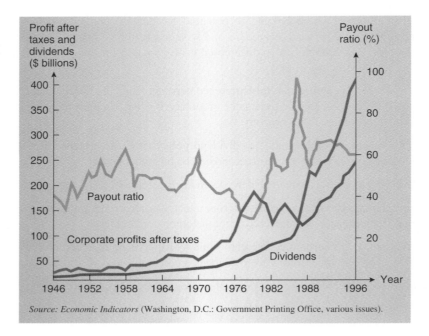

Source: Economic Indicators (Washington, D.C.: Government Printing Office, various issues).

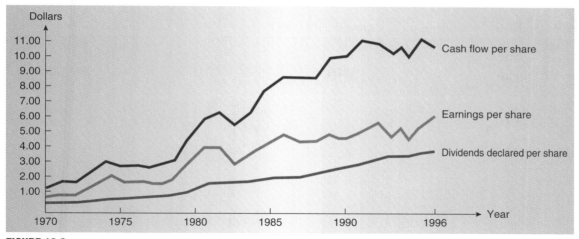

FIGURE 13.2
Earnings, cash flow, and dividends per share for Exxon Corporation, 1970–1996.

Regular Payment and Regular Changes

Dividend-paying companies usually make quarterly payments. Once they begin paying dividends, companies strive to continue making regular payments. In fact, companies frequently highlight the length of their uninterrupted dividend records when declaring a dividend. Furthermore, most companies review their dividend policies at least once annually, often during the same quarter each year. Many companies increase the quarterly dividend each year.

Reluctance to Cut the Dividend

Companies exhibit a strong aversion to cutting an established *dividend rate* (that is, a total dollar amount per period). This is probably because a dividend cut serves as a negative signal.

Table 13.1 on page 470 summarizes the dividend changes U.S. companies announced during the period 1972–1996. Fewer than 3% of the dividend actions taken during the period involved either dividend decreases or *dividend omissions* (reducing the dividend rate to zero). Dividend increases and *dividend resumptions* (paying dividends once again after having previously cut the dividend rate to zero) outnumbered decreases and omissions by more than 8 to 1. Lack of changes in the dividend rate outnumbered decreases and omissions by more than 30 to 1.

You can see that the numbers of dividend decreases and omissions increased sharply—and the numbers of dividend increases and resumptions decreased sharply—during the recession periods 1974–1975, 1980–1982, and 1990–1991. Investors generally interpret dividend reductions as a signal that the company's earnings prospects have worsened. This can adversely affect a company's share price and, in some cases, the share prices of other companies in the same industry.

Extra and Special Dividends

Table 13.1 also indicates that a minority of companies declared *extra dividends* or *special dividends* during the period 1972–1996. **Extra dividends** are paid, in addition to a "regular" quarterly dividend, to distribute unusual—and unsustainable—earnings. They tend to be considerably more variable in amount than regular dividend payments. Extra dividends usually occur near the end of the fiscal year (October–December quarter for most companies), as in the next example. How would you interpret this? Companies appear to pay extra dividends when the year-end review reveals unusually high earnings, and they wish to pay out their target percentage of earnings but do not wish to falsely signal a higher sustainable level of earnings. Many companies in cyclical businesses declare extra dividends when earnings are at a cyclical peak. They increase the regular dividend rate only when they believe they have reached a higher level of sustainable earnings.

EXTRA DIVIDEND A dividend in addition to regular dividends, paid when earnings are unusually high.

TABLE 13.1
Dividend Changes Announced by Publicly Owned U.S. Companies, 1972–1996

YEAR	NUMBER OF FIRMS TAKING DIVIDEND ACTION	DIVIDEND INCREASED	DIVIDEND RESUMED	DIVIDEND DECREASED	DIVIDEND OMITTED	EXTRA OR SPECIAL DIVIDEND DECLARED
1972	About 9,800	1,563	107	73	103	980
1973	About 9,800	2,197	116	37	114	1,105
1974	About 9,800	2,120	139	86	228	1,097
1975	About 9,800	1,648	129	186	266	1,013
1976	About 9,800	2,624	137	74	117	1,047
1977	Over 10,000	2,984	120	68	138	968
1978	Over 10,000	3,211	105	46	105	997
1979	Over 10,000	2,968	71	46	131	829
1980	Over 10,000	2,445	51	88	160	719
1981	Over 10,000	2,160	45	103	198	640
1982	Over 10,000	1,590	46	258	315	515
1983	Over 10,000	1,833	66	106	126	480
1984	Over 10,000	1,774	58	65	116	435
1985	Over 10,000	1,560	35	68	139	428
1986	Over 10,000	1,513	46	96	189	359
1987	Over 10,000	1,590	54	74	104	403
1988	Over 10,000	1,705	38	62	117	501
1989	Over 10,000	1,658	41	85	160	524
1990	Over 10,000	1,263	39	143	266	385
1991	Over 10,000	1,086	50	187	250	322
1992	Over 10,000	1,333	53	131	146	317
1993	Over 10,000	1,635	75	87	106	368
1994	Over 10,000	1,826	52	59	77	384
1995	Over 10,000	1,882	51	49	73	358
1996	Over 10,000	2,165	37	50	81	457
Total	Over 249,000	48,333	1761	2327	3825	15,631

Source: Standard & Poor's, *Annual Dividend Record,* 1974–1997.

SPECIAL DIVIDEND A dividend to distribute cash the company receives in a special situation, such as the sale of a subsidiary.

Special dividends are often declared when a company finds itself with substantial excess cash it wishes to distribute to its shareholders. For special dividends, this excess cash usually comes from sources beyond normal operating results, such as the sale of a subsidiary or a decision to liquidate the company. Both extra and special dividends are less effective devices for signaling a change in a company's earnings prospects than changes in the regular dividend.

EXAMPLE

Alcoa's Extra Dividends

Aluminum Company of America (Alcoa), the world's largest aluminum producer, declared regular quarterly cash dividends of $0.20 each in 1989 and 1990. Alcoa earned $5.34 per share in 1989 and declared an extra dividend of $0.70 per share on January 19, 1990. In view of the proximity to Alcoa's December 31 year-end, it seems appropriate to add the extra dividend to 1989's regular cash dividends in calculating the payout ratio for 1989:

$$\text{Payout ratio} = \frac{4(0.20) + 0.70}{5.34} = 28\%$$

Similarly, in 1990 Alcoa earned $3.30 per share. It declared an extra dividend of $.09 per share on January 18, 1991. The implied payout ratio for 1990 is:

$$\text{Payout ratio} = \frac{4(0.20) + 0.09}{3.30} = 27\%$$

Between 1991 and 1994, Alcoa's earnings per share varied between $0.40 and $1.64, and Alcoa did not declare any extra dividends subsequent to those year-ends. However, it continued to pay $0.20 per quarter in regular cash dividends. ∎

Industry Differences

Payout ratios vary systematically across industries. What might explain this? We suspect it's due, at least in part, to the similar investment opportunities that companies within a particular industry face. These differences may be industry-related.

Table 13.2 summarizes differences in average industry payout ratios. The electric utility industry has had the highest payout ratios. The building materials, drugs and health care, and life insurance industries generally have had the lowest payout ratios. The oil industry's five-year average payout ratio varied more than the others.

Declaration of Dividends

A dividend must be declared by the company's board of directors.[1] When the board declares a dividend, it specifies a **record date** and a **payment date.** The time line presented in figure 13.3 on page 472 shows the relative timing of the key dividend-related dates. Each *shareholder of record* (owner of shares according to the company's stock ownership record) as of the close of business on the record date will receive a check dated on the payment date for the dividends declared on the shares owned. Effective July 3, 1995, stock transactions must be settled by the third business day following the transaction. Consequently, the major stock exchanges and

RECORD DATE The date when stock owners are identified to receive the next dividend payment.

PAYMENT DATE The date the dividend is paid.

TABLE 13.2
Industry Differences in Payout Ratio

Industry	FIVE-YEAR INDUSTRY AVERAGE			Overall 1980–1994
	1980–1984	1985–1989	1990–1994	
Building materials	29.9%	13.3%	19.1%	20.8%
Drugs and health care	16.4	23.4	25.6	21.8
Life insurance	30.6	25.8	21.6	26.0
Textiles	28.4	39.7	15.5	27.9
Foods	28.0	26.4	31.3	28.6
Metals and mining	20.0	21.1	45.5	28.9
Paper and paper products	26.7	30.3	40.3	32.4
Business equipment	32.0	31.4	34.8	32.7
Steel	24.1	30.7	49.9	34.9
Aerospace and aircraft	33.5	59.8	18.5	37.3
Oil	14.3	75.8	29.1	39.7
Chemicals	33.0	72.2	50.1	51.8
Electric utilities	72.7	84.8	81.9	79.8
Average	29.9%	41.1%	35.6%	35.5%

Source: Compustat.

[1]Legal restrictions on dividend payments are discussed below.

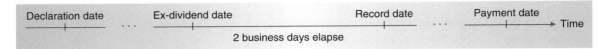

FIGURE 13.3
A time line for dividend-related events.

EX-DIVIDEND DATE The date shares begin trading without dividend rights.

securities dealers (in the over-the-counter market) establish an **ex-dividend date** two business days prior to the record date. On that date the shares begin trading *ex-dividend,* that is, without dividend rights. Consequently, a stock normally opens for trading on the ex-dividend date at approximately the preceding day's closing price less the amount of the dividend per share.

EXAMPLE

Dividend-Related Events for General Electric Company in 1994

General Electric Company established the following declaration, ex-dividend, record, and payment dates for the dividends it declared during 1994 (when stock transactions had to be settled by the fifth business day following the transaction):

Quarter	Declaration Date	Ex-Dividend Date	Record Date	Payment Date	Dividend Per Share
1	2/11/94	3/2/94	3/8/94	4/25/94	$0.36
2	6/24/94	6/28/94	7/5/94	7/25/94	0.36
3	9/16/94	9/26/94	9/30/94	10/25/94	0.36
4	12/16/94	12/23/94	12/30/94	1/25/95	0.41

Note the regularity in the pattern of dates and payments. ■

Legal Limitations on Dividend Payments

Two forms of legal restrictions on dividend payments are important. To start with, most bond indentures, loan agreements, and preferred stock agreements usually contain restrictions on the amount of common dividends a company can pay. These limitations are designed to minimize the company's agency costs.

State laws also impose restrictions. They are designed to prevent excessive cash distributions. Most states prohibit a company from paying dividends if doing so would render it insolvent. Many also prohibit companies from making dividend payments out of accounts that fall outside a legally defined "surplus." In some cases, this surplus includes only retained earnings; in others it also includes paid-in capital. In some states, a company can distribute current earnings, even though prior losses had eliminated its surplus.

These limitations are seldom troublesome to a healthy company. They help prevent unhealthy companies from expropriating wealth from lenders and other creditors.

Self-Check
1. List four characteristics of corporate dividend policies.
2. Which are more stable, dividends or earnings?
3. Why are companies reluctant to cut their dividend?
4. What are extra dividends, and when do companies pay them?
5. What happens on the ex-dividend date?
6. Why do payout ratios vary systematically across industries?
7. How can we make use of this systematic variation when selecting an appropriate payout ratio?

DOES DIVIDEND POLICY MATTER?

As we've said, a company's choice of dividend policy does not affect its value in a perfect capital market environment. The perfect capital market environment is the place to start the analysis of financial policy. But actual capital markets are not *perfect,* and capital market imperfections affect our conclusions about dividend policy. However, because the capital markets are so efficient, a company's value is less affected by its dividend policy than by its capital budgeting decisions and capital structure policy. Despite this, a company should use its dividend policy to whatever extent possible to maximize shareholder wealth.

After demonstrating dividend irrelevance in a perfect capital market environment, we'll relax our assumptions and see how that affects dividend policy.

What Is Dividend Policy?

Although we have characterized dividend policy as simply a payout ratio, it is more than that. Dividend payments are generally made in cash. Because a company has alternative uses for cash, confusion can occur among the dividend, capital budgeting, and capital structure policies. For example, if making a capital expenditure will reduce the company's cash dividends by the amount of the expenditure, then the dividend decision would simply be the result of the investment decision. We could not distinguish the valuation effect of a dividend change from that of a change in capital budget. The two policies would simply mirror each other. Similarly, if the capital budget is held constant, and the company issues new debt to finance the dividend, dividend policy would simply be a result of the capital structure policy.

If we maintain constant capital budgeting and capital structure policies, we may have too little or too much cash for dividends. In a strict sense, then, a pure dividend policy decision involves only a trade-off between retaining earnings on the one hand and selling new shares to obtain the cash to pay dividends on the other. Although some companies (mostly utilities) have maintained a high payout ratio of regular quarterly cash dividends and *simultaneously* sold new issues of common stock, they are not typical.

To understand the role of dividends, then, we must isolate the effect of a change in cash dividends from the company's choices of investments and capital structure. Otherwise, we would not be analyzing dividend policy exclusively.

Another complication is the method of payment. There are different ways to distribute cash to shareholders. A company can make regular payments (say, quarterly) or it can make larger irregular payments of "special" dividends. Instead of paying any dividends, it can use the cash to repurchase shares, which may have tax advantages.

Dividends in a Perfect Capital Market Environment

The crux of the dividend irrelevance argument is that fair market transactions are neutral and don't transfer wealth. Let's look at the transactions involved with a dividend and examine how it is financed.

When a company pays a dividend, money is simply transferred from one form to another. Before payment of the dividend, the money is in the form of a shareholder claim on the company's assets. After payment of the dividend, the shareholder has cash. But as long as the transfer is a fair market transaction in a perfect capital market environment, the value is the same.

Another transaction we need to consider is selling new shares. Again, this is simply a transfer of money from one form to another. Before the transaction, the new investors have cash. After exchanging the cash for new shares, the new investors have an equal-value claim on the company's assets. As long as the transfer is a fair market transaction in a perfect capital market environment, the value is the same.

Now let's consider a dividend under three different cases. In the first case, the company has the necessary cash and simply reduces its cash account to pay the dividend. The "offsetting" amount in the double-entry system is an equal reduction in the shareholder equity account. This is the transfer of money from one form, a claim on the company, to another form, cash in the shareholder's "hand."

In the second case, the company does not have the cash to pay the dividend, so it issues new shares in exchange for cash, which temporarily increases the total value of the company. Then the company makes the dividend payment, which reduces total company value back to its pre-new-share value. Because both transactions are simply fair market transactions that transfer money from one form to another, each party's value is the same, and after both transactions, company value is unchanged.

Figure 13.4 illustrates the second case. The company pays out 20% of its value as a cash dividend. It then raises an equal amount of cash by selling new shares. The new shareholders own 20% of the company.

Think about what happened in this second case. In effect, existing shareholders—through the company's transactions—sold part of their claim on the company to the new investors.

In our third case, a shareholder wants a cash dividend and thus wants the company to make the transactions in figure 13.4. But the company has decided not to pay the dividend because it does not want to go to the trouble of making the two transactions. The existing shareholder can go out and find a new investor and sell some shares directly to that new investor in exchange for cash. The net effect of this direct sale is the same as the company's two transactions in the second case. Part of the existing shareholder's claim would go to the new investor in exchange for cash. As long as it is a fair market transaction in a perfect market environment, neither party gains nor loses value. This direct transaction—a shareholder selling some shares to get cash—is called a **homemade dividend.**

HOMEMADE DIVIDEND
The sale of some shares of stock to get cash that would be similar to getting a cash dividend.

Figure 13.5 illustrates a homemade dividend. Let's compare alternatives. When the company pays a cash dividend and sells additional shares to pay for it, total value is unchanged. But the number of shares outstanding increases, and the value per share (the stock price) declines. The original shareholders are just as well off, because even though their shares are worth less and they have the same number of shares, they have cash that is equal to their decline in share value. With a homemade dividend, the original stockholders sell some of their shares, and the number of outstanding shares does not change, so the stock price does

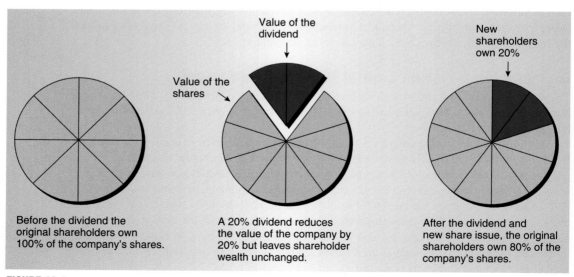

FIGURE 13.4
The transfer of value when a company pays a cash dividend and finances it with a new share issue.

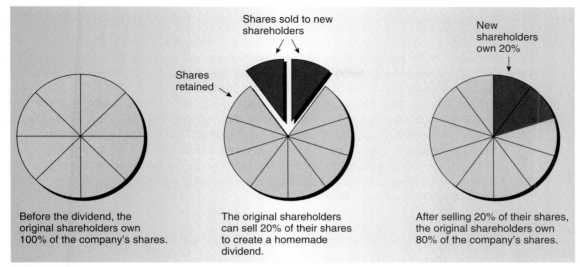

Shares sold to new shareholders

New shareholders own 20%

Shares retained

Before the dividend, the original shareholders own 100% of the company's shares.

The original shareholders can sell 20% of their shares to create a homemade dividend.

After selling 20% of their shares, the original shareholders own 80% of the company's shares.

FIGURE 13.5
The transfer of value when the original shareholders sell some of their shares to create a homemade dividend.

not change. The original stockholders are just as well off, because even though they have fewer shares worth the same per share, they have cash that is equal to their decline in share value.[2]

Therefore, despite the differences in the number of shares outstanding and the difference in stock (per-share) price, value is maintained. The two alternatives leave the original shareholders equally well off. Thus dividend policy is irrelevant—in a perfect capital market environment.

Illustration of Dividend Irrelevance to Company Value and Stockholder Wealth

EXAMPLE

Consider a company that's decided to make, but has not yet announced, a major new capital investment in a project that will cost $10 million. The project has a positive NPV of $20 million. The company has $10 million in cash available to finance the capital investment project if it so chooses. The company has 10 million shares of stock currently outstanding, selling for $24 each, and no debt. So the company's total value is $240 million (= [24]10 million) before the project announcement and $260 million (= 240 + 20) after.

To determine whether paying dividends affects shareholder wealth, let's look at two alternatives facing the company. The alternatives are (1) pay no cash dividend and finance the project with cash, or (2) pay a cash dividend of $1 per share and obtain $10 million in new external financing for the project. To make a fair comparison of alternatives, the company must sell $10 million in new shares with the dividend alternative. Otherwise, any difference could be due to factors other than the difference in dividend policy. The sale of new stock finances the project by replacing the $10 million in equity that the company pays out as dividends.

With no dividend, the company simply uses the cash to finance the project. In that case, each share would be worth $26 (= 260/10). If all the shareholders want the $10 million dividend, they can sell 384,615 (= 10,000,000/26) of their shares to get it.

(continued on following page)

---

[2]The original shareholders sell 20% of their holdings (which corresponds to two of the ten slices in the pie chart). Problem B1 at the end of the chapter provides a numerical example consistent with the pie charts in figures 13.4 and 13.5.

(Illustration of Dividend Irrelevance to Company Value and Stockholder Wealth continued from previous page)

With a dividend, the company pays out $10 million cash and sells $10 million worth of new shares. After payment of the dividend, each share will be worth the predividend share price ($26) minus the dividend ($1), or $25. Note that paying the dividend does not affect shareholder wealth; it's $26 before and 25 + 1 = $26 after.

To get the $10 million to finance the project, the company must sell 400,000 (= 10,000,000/25) fair-priced new shares. Then the company will have 10.4 million shares outstanding, worth $25 each, for a total company value of $260 million (= [25]10.4 million). That $260 million is exactly what the company's total value was before the dividend–new-share transactions. Therefore, the dividend does not change the company's total value or the wealth of its shareholders. In effect, it simply allows original shareholders to "cash in" part of their equity in the company. ■

But Aren't Capital Gains Riskier than Dividends?

Dividends represent cash in hand. Reinvesting that cash in the hope of realizing greater dividends and/or additional capital gains sometime in the future represents a risky prospect. So aren't shareholders better off getting a dividend?

At this point, we hope you recognize an opportunity to apply the Principle of Risk-Return Trade-Off and answer, "No, not necessarily." The difference between the dividend now and later is risk and the time value of money. Therefore, if we want the dividend now, we must accept a lower return on the investment in those shares. The issue is whether the existing shareholders or some "new" shareholders are going to invest the $10 million in the new project.

Shareholders who decide that future dividends and capital gains are *excessively* risky (as opposed to being in accordance with the risk-return trade-off) can sell some of their shares. This involves transaction costs, but it does enable shareholders to satisfy individual risk-return objectives. Moreover, holding fixed the company's capital investment program and capital structure, paying a dividend does not alter its risk profile or that of its shareholders. Therefore, the uncertainty of future dividends and capital gains does not invalidate the dividend irrelevance argument.

Shareholder Preference for Current Income

Suppose shareholders want a regular flow of income. Wouldn't they prefer the company to pay dividends rather than reinvest the cash? Not in a perfect market. As we have already explained, they can sell shares on a regular basis to generate income. In a perfect market, a preference for current income does not alter the conclusion that dividend policy is irrelevant. Dividend policy would not affect company value or stockholder wealth, regardless of individual stockholders' preferences regarding liquidity or risk. Why, then, do rational market participants act as if it *did* matter?

Capital Market Imperfections

The perfect market view leaves out taxes, transaction costs, and information asymmetries. If capital gains are taxed at a lower rate than dividends, shareholders paying taxes on both types of income should prefer getting the income as capital gains rather than as dividends.

There are also psychological theories that provide a rationale for why some individuals prefer cash dividends over capital gains. These theories argue that for psychological reasons, dividends and capital gains are not perfect substitutes for one another. For example, a lack of self-control provides a reason for an investor to prefer regular cash dividends. If the investor had to sell stock to get income, he might sell more and spend too much, thereby using up his capital too quickly for his own good. These psychological reasons are additional capital market imperfections that can make dividend policy relevant.

Finally, it may be that dividend policy can be used, less expensively than other methods, to convey information to the public.

All of these concerns are valid. Capital market imperfections, including asymmetric information considerations, contribute to the relevance of dividend policy.

Self-Check

1. What does the term *dividend policy* mean?

2. What is a homemade dividend?

3. Why are homemade dividends and cash dividends perfect substitutes in a perfect capital market?

THE ROLE OF INCOME TAXES

Tax laws change with some regularity. As in the case of capital budgeting projects, you must know the relevant tax laws before making decisions on dividend policy. Currently, personal taxes are higher on dividends than on capital gains. The maximum tax rate on capital gains is 28% versus 36% in the top bracket for ordinary income.[3] In addition, there is the valuable capital gains tax-timing option—postpone the tax on a gain, and claim the tax reduction on a loss.[4] The capital gains tax-timing option further lowers the *effective* tax rate on capital gains. Previous versions of the Internal Revenue Code have also included such a tax differential.

From a tax viewpoint, then, shareholders prefer capital gains over dividends, and hence low payout ratios, because capital gains are effectively taxed at a lower rate than dividends. Therefore, shareholders who are paying taxes on both types of income may prefer capital gains rather than dividends. But transaction costs to create a homemade dividend offset the tax gain. Thus other shareholders who want liquidity and face large enough transaction costs can still be better off with the dividend. Even if transaction costs to create a homemade dividend are not very high, tax-exempt shareholders who want liquidity will prefer dividends as long as transactions are not costless. This is because they can save the transaction costs, but they cannot save taxes because they do not pay taxes.

Corporate shareholders actually have a "reversed" tax preference. Currently, large corporate shareholders pay income tax at a 35% marginal rate and are not taxed on 70% of the dividends received from unrelated corporations (see chapter 2). A corporate shareholder would therefore pay tax on dividend income at the rate of 10.5% (= [1 − 0.70]0.35), because only 30% of the dividends it receives are taxable. In contrast, corporate shareholders pay tax on long-term capital gains at rates up to 35%. Thus corporate investors may prefer dividends over capital gains from the tax perspective.

The Effect of Personal Taxes on Company Value

EXAMPLE

Suppose dividends are taxed at a 36% rate and capital gains are not taxed. We can show that a dividend-paying company will have a lower value than an otherwise identical non-dividend-paying company.

(continued on following page)

---

[3]In addition, as of 1997, there is a surcharge for incomes in excess of $256,500, which raises the marginal tax rate on ordinary income to 39.6%.
[4]Recall that capital gains are taxed at the time of the sale of the asset, not as they accrue. So the tax liability for a capital gain is reinvested and earns the time value of money until the tax payment is actually made.

(The Effect of Personal Taxes on Company Value *continued from previous page*)

Company A has a $50 share price. It pays no dividend. Investors expect its share price to be $57.50 after 1 year. Shareholders thus expect a capital gain of $7.50 per share. The expected return is 15% (= 7.50/50) both before and after tax.

Company B is identical except that it will pay a $5 dividend per share at the end of the year. The ex-dividend price will be $52.50 (= 57.50 − 5.00). Its shares and those of company A are equally risky. So company B's shares must also provide a 15% after-tax return.

What is company B's share price? The tax on the dividend is $1.80 (= [0.36]5.00). The after-tax dividend is $3.20 (= 5.00 − 1.80). An investor will have $55.70 (= 52.50 + 3.20) per company B share. To provide a 15% return, each share of company B must be worth, today, the present value of its expected future value. That is,

$$\text{Share price} = \frac{55.70}{1.15} = \$48.43$$

What's the pretax return on company B's shares? It is

$$\text{Pretax return} = \frac{57.50 - 48.42}{48.43} = 18.73\%$$

Therefore, Company B's shares must provide a higher expected pretax return (18.73% versus 15%). This higher return is to compensate for the tax liability. ■

Considering two companies of equal risk, the one that offers a lower dollar return after taxes will have the lower stock price. After all, investors will require *identical after-tax returns* from both companies.

Tax Clienteles

The *clientele effect* (discussed in chapter 12) is also important in the study of dividend relevance. The clientele effect refers to investors "sorting" themselves into groups, each of which prefers the companies it invests in to follow a particular type of policy. When applied to dividend policy, the clientele effect refers to those investors who prefer one dividend policy over another for a particular reason.

The clientele effect lessens, and may even eliminate, the rationale for the tax differential view of dividend policy. As you might guess from our forgoing discussion, there are natural clienteles for high-cash-dividend stocks and low-cash-dividend stocks. There is extensive empirical evidence that identifies investor clienteles. On the basis of their tax positions, investors choose stocks with high or low cash dividends. A company's dividend policy simply appeals to different tax clienteles. Each tax clientele can invest in the shares of companies whose dividend policies best suit that clientele's tax posture. As long as there is a sufficient supply of investment opportunities for each group, no premium is needed to buy a preferred investment instrument. With no premium, dividend policy would again be irrelevant—in spite of the apparent tax asymmetry.

Where does this leave us concerning taxes? Income taxes can affect the sort of dividend policy shareholders want. But the clientele effect reduces the importance of taxes. Changes in the tax system are probably more important than the level of taxes at any particular time. They can create profitable opportunities for a company to offer a dividend policy that becomes attractive because of a tax law change but is in short supply. However, such opportunities are limited. Further, while an optimal dividend policy can contribute to the profitability of a company, the possibility of extraordinary success rests primarily on the company's real investment decisions.

Self-Check

1. On the basis of taxes only, would a U.S. tax-paying stockholder prefer that the company favor dividends or capital gains?

2. How does the existence of tax clienteles affect our conclusion that the differential taxation of dividends and capital gains can affect dividend policy?

TRANSACTION COSTS

Transaction costs can also cause dividend policy to matter. There are two types: flotation costs and commission charges, and legal and policy restrictions.

Flotation Costs and Brokerage Commissions

Flotation costs and brokerage commissions vary inversely with the size of the transaction. This makes it cheaper for a company to sell a large block of shares than for individual shareholders to make small purchases to reinvest their dividends. Likewise, it's cheaper for a company to pay a cash dividend than it is for individual shareholders to make small sales to create a homemade dividend. Therefore, the effect of such transaction costs depends on shareholder preferences and reinforces the clientele effect.

In recent years the growth of the discount brokerage industry has reduced commissions. However, the greatest commission reductions have occurred in connection with larger share transactions, so these frictions still tend to favor a clientele effect.

Dividend Reinvestment Plans

Dividend reinvestment plans offer shareholders the option to reinvest their dividends with little or no brokerage commission. This reduces the penalty a high-dividend-payout policy would otherwise impose on shareholders who wish their dividends to be reinvested. These plans also have permitted companies to reduce issuance costs substantially, perhaps to as little as 2% (versus 4% to 5% for normal-size public offerings). However, they do not eliminate the tax bias in favor of capital gains because shareholders must recognize the reinvested dividends as income. Nevertheless, by reducing flotation costs, dividend reinvestment plans may have led to increased payout ratios for those companies, such as electric utility companies, whose investor clienteles desire a relatively high level of dividend income.

DIVIDEND REINVESTMENT PLAN A program that gives shareholders the option to reinvest their dividends in a company's common stock with little or no brokerage commission.

Legal and Policy Restrictions

Certain institutions are prohibited, by law or policy, from investing in the common stocks of companies that do not have an established history of regular dividend payments. Others, such as many trust and endowment funds, can use only dividend income as a matter of policy. These investors prefer at least some minimum level of regular dividend income to maintain institutional decision-making flexibility. Legal and policy restrictions create indirect transaction costs.

Net Effect of Transaction Costs

We believe the tax bias favoring capital gains exerts a stronger influence than transaction costs on what a company's dividend policy ought to be. We think the majority of our colleagues in the finance profession would agree. Consequently, the combined effect of taxes and transaction costs favors retentions over dividends to some degree.

Self-Check

1. How do brokerage commissions affect the choice between homemade dividends and true dividends?

2. What sort of legal and policy restrictions give companies an incentive to pay at least a small dividend?

3. What's the net effect of taxes and transaction costs on dividend policy?

SIGNALING AND THE DIVIDEND ADJUSTMENT MODEL

Dividend changes can affect a stock's market value if investors believe such changes convey useful information. For example, suppose a company has rarely changed its dividend rate, and each time the rate was changed, the company's earnings also subsequently changed in the same direction. Investors would then interpret future changes in the dividend rate as a signal that management believes the company's earnings prospects have changed. A dividend increase would be a positive signal of greater future earnings. A dividend decrease would be a negative signal of lower future earnings.

Because of the informational content of dividend changes, simply paying out residual cash flow on a year-by-year basis may not be in the shareholders' best interest. Such a policy would lead to a dividend level and a payout ratio that could fluctuate wildly, depending on year-to-year changes in the availability of attractive investment projects. In fact, most companies seek slow changes in dividends. Look back at figure 13.1 and notice that yearly payout ratios varied inversely with earnings to produce a fairly smooth curve of growing dividends. This is no coincidence.

TARGET PAYOUT RATIO
The long-term average payout ratio a company tries to achieve.

Research based on interviews with corporate executives shows that managers think a company should aim toward a long-term **target payout ratio** to give shareholders a "fair share" of the company's earnings. The following model was created to explain dividend changes:

$$\text{DPS}_1 - \text{DPS}_0 = \text{ADJ} \, [\text{POR}(\text{EPS}_1) - \text{DPS}_0] \tag{13.1}$$

Currently the company's dividends are DPS_0 per share. It has a target payout ratio of POR. It will adjust (ADJ) its dividend rate, but less than fully, as its earnings per share (EPS) change. If the company always paid out its target ratio, then its dividends per share in the coming period would be $\text{DPS} = \text{POR}(\text{EPS}_1)$. But companies "manage" their dividend payments so as to produce a smooth progression in dividends, so ADJ < 1. Dividends progress toward the target level over several periods rather than all at once. This reduces the likelihood that a dividend increase will have to be "rolled back" in the future. Because of this "stickiness," dividend changes serve as a signaling device. A company will not increase its dividend rate unless it believes the increase is sustainable because of a higher sustainable level of earnings.

EXAMPLE   *Adjusting Dividends for EPS Changes at Snapple*

Snapple Corporation has historically paid out 40% of its earnings as dividends. Snapple's treasurer believes it is appropriate to adjust the dividend rate in a gradual manner. She applies the dividend adjustment model (13.1) with ADJ = 2/3. Snapple earned $5.00 per share last year and paid dividends of $0.50 per quarter, or $2.00 per year. She believes earnings will reach $6.00 per share this year and stay at that level into the foreseeable future. According to the model (13.1), how would the dividend rate change this year and the next four?

Using (13.1), the first year dividend is

$$DPS_1 - DPS_0 = ADJ[POR(EPS_1) - DPS_0]$$
$$DPS_1 - 2.00 = (2/3)[0.4(6.00) - 2.00]$$
$$DPS_1 = 2.266667 \cong 2.27$$

The next year, the dividend becomes

$$DPS_1 - 2.266667 = (2/3)[0.4(6.00) - 2.266667]$$
$$DPS_1 = 2.355556 \cong 2.36$$

Figure 13.6 shows the pattern of dividend changes. The dividend rate moves to the steady-state dividend rate $2.40 per year [= 0.4(6.00)], each year closing two-thirds of the remaining gap. ■

Self-Check

1. How do investors usually interpret a dividend increase? A dividend decrease?

2. How do stock prices usually react to a dividend increase? A dividend decrease? Why?

3. Explain the dividend adjustment model in your own words.

DIVIDEND POLICY GUIDELINES

Establishing a company's dividend policy involves a variety of conflicting and sometimes confusing considerations. Almost any dividend decision of a company with a diversified shareholder mix will disappoint at least some of its shareholders.

Determining an appropriate dividend policy for a company involves a three-step approach. The company must (1) estimate its future residual funds, (2) determine an appropriate target payout ratio, and (3) decide on the quarterly dividend.

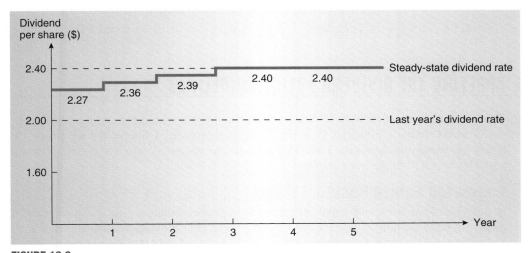

FIGURE 13.6
The adjustment of the dividend rate to a change in earnings per share.

Step 1: Estimate Future Residual Funds

Start with the company's earnings and cash flow projections over a reasonable time horizon. Five years is typical. At a minimum, a company should pay out cash that it cannot invest in positive-NPV projects. After considering investor-related factors, it might decide to pay out more than this minimum. However, because of flotation costs, it's usually unwise for a company to pay out so much more than the minimum as to trigger the need for new equity.

Many factors complicate this analysis. Capital budgeting projects often come in large units, and they are subject to substantial variation from their projected timing and cost. As economic and business conditions change, so will the desired portfolio of capital expenditure projects. Similarly, future operating cash flow is not entirely predictable. Thus, analyzing even the most carefully prepared cash flow projections will suggest a range of distributable amounts, a range of funds needs, and hence a range of *feasible target payout ratios.*

Step 2: Determine an Appropriate Target Payout Ratio

Applying the Behavioral Principle provides a good starting point for establishing a target payout ratio. The payout ratios of comparable companies—essentially those in the same industry, of nearly the same size, and with similar product mix and other operating characteristics—will suggest a range of *customary payout ratios* for that industry or industry segment. A company should consider the range of feasible target payout ratios together with the range of customary payout ratios and any special shareholder mix considerations in setting its long-term target payout ratio.

Step 3: Set the Quarterly Dividend Rate

Given its target payout ratio and its earnings and cash flow projections, a company should establish its quarterly dividend rate at the highest *comfortably sustainable* level. That is, the dividend rate should be sustainable at least over the planning horizon. Prudence dictates setting the actual rate somewhat below the expected maximum to compensate for the uncertainty of the earnings and cash flow forecasts. Most corporations find it advantageous to review dividend policy in a particular quarter each year, thus creating a predictable pattern. If a company wants to increase its dividend, it may be better to make one significant increase per year than several tiny ones each quarter.

Self-Check

1. What are the three steps in the recommended approach to dividend decisions?

2. How can you use comparable companies to determine an appropriate payout ratio?

APPLYING THE DIVIDEND POLICY GUIDELINES

The board of directors of Major Pharmaceutical Company is considering whether to change the dividend. Major's Financial Planning Group has prepared a five-year plan, which the board has tentatively approved. Table 13.3 provides the projected values of certain financial variables drawn from the five-year plan.

Estimated Future Residual Funds

Major's board has tentatively approved a five-year capital expenditure plan. It calls for expenditures of $335 million on positive-NPV projects. The plan provides for capital investment amounting to $45.0 million in year 1, $54.0 million in year 2, $74.0 million in year 3, $72.0 million in year 4, and $90.0 million in year 5. Over the five-year period, Major projects aggregate residual funds of $115.0 million.

TABLE 13.3

Projecting Dividends for Major Pharmaceutical Company

	Initial	Year 1	Year 2	Year 3	Year 4	Year 5	Totals
			PROJECTIONS				
Earnings per common share	$4.32	$ 5.00	$ 6.00	$ 7.20	$ 8.50	$ 10.00	
Number of common shares (millions)		× 10	× 10	× 10	× 10	× 10	
Earnings available for common		$50.0	$60.0	$72.0	$ 85.0	$100.0	$367.0
Depreciation and other noncash charges		12.0	14.0	16.0	19.0	22.0	83.0
Funds from operations available for reinvestment or dividends		62.0	74.0	88.0	104.0	122.0	450.0
Capital investment requirement		45.0	54.0	74.0	72.0	90.0	335.0
Residual funds		$17.0	$20.0	$14.0	$ 32.0	$ 32.0	$115.0
Assuming No Change in the Dividend							
Dividend per share	$1.44	$ 1.44	$ 1.44	$ 1.44	$ 1.44	$ 1.44	
Payout ratio	33%	29%	24%	20%	17%	14%	
Residual funds		$17.0	$20.0	$14.0	$ 32.0	$ 32.0	$115.0
Dividend requirements		14.4	14.4	14.4	14.4	14.4	72.0
Surplus (deficit)		$ 2.6	$ 5.6	$(0.4)	$ 17.6	$ 17.6	$ 43.0
One Possible Set of Dividends (Alternative A)							
Dividend per share	$1.44	$ 1.70	$ 1.70	$ 1.70	$ 2.70	$ 3.70	
Payout ratio	33%	34%	28%	24%	32%	37%	
Residual funds		$17.0	$20.0	$14.0	$ 32.0	$ 32.0	$115.0
Dividend requirements		17.0	17.0	17.0	27.0	37.0	115.0
Surplus (deficit)		—	$ 3.0	$(3.0)	$ 5.0	$ (5.0)	$ 0.0
Another Possible Set of Dividends (Alternative B)							
Dividend per share	$1.44	$ 1.68	$ 1.88	$ 2.00	$ 2.64	$ 3.30	
Payout ratio	33%	34%	31%	28%	31%	33%	
Residual funds		$17.0	$20.0	$14.0	$ 32.0	$ 32.0	$115.0
Dividend requirements		16.8	18.8	20.0	26.4	33.0	115.0
Surplus (deficit)		$ 0.2	$ 1.2	$(6.0)	$ 5.6	$ (1.0)	$ 0.0

Target Payout Ratio

The projected residual funds of $115.0 million represent 31% of projected earnings available for common. These amount to $367.0 million for the five-year period. A detailed analysis of Major's shareholder group would be expensive and time consuming. However, Major's treasurer realizes that as long as their dividend policies are clearly articulated and stable, particular industries and particular companies tend to attract certain shareholder clienteles.

Major's payout ratio has averaged 33.5% over the past ten years and 32.2% over the past five. Major's financial staff has also analyzed the payout policies of Major's closest ten competitors in the *ethical drug segment* of the pharmaceutical industry. Major derives more than 90% of its sales revenue and operating income from this industry segment. The average payout ratio for these companies for the preceding year was 36.6%. The range of payout ratios was 18.6% to 53.7%. Major's treasurer concluded that a payout ratio in the range from 30% to 40% would be appropriate. Major projects heavy capital expenditure requirements beginning in year 3. She therefore feels that Major's payout ratio will remain below the industry average.

Analyzing the Impact of Alternative Dividend Policies

Table 13.3 also illustrates how to evaluate alternative dividend policies. A company would normally examine several such alternatives before deciding on a particular dividend action.

The current indicated annual dividend rate is $1.44 per share. Suppose Major maintains this dividend rate through year 5. Its payout ratio trends steadily downward. Major would retain substantial residual funds.

Two alternative policies are considered. Under both alternatives, Major would pay out all the estimated residual funds to shareholders. Alternative B provides for increases each year. It avoids the very large increases in years 4 and 5 that alternative A calls for. Also, the payout ratio is less variable and closer to the long-run target under alternative B.

Major reassesses its dividend policy each year. Major is therefore more concerned about year 1 than the later years. It appears that Major can sustain a $0.24 increase in its dividend rate to $1.68 per share per year. Such an increase seems appropriate in light of Major's improved earnings prospects. Other considerations might indicate that a dividend rate different from $1.68 is more appropriate. But the analysis of Major's estimated residual funds position is the best starting place for such an analysis.

What about years 4 and 5? Alternative B suggests very large dividend increases. They will necessarily be reconsidered in the future. Major would implement them only if it continues to find them sustainable.

Special Considerations for the Privately Held Company

The preceding example applies only to *publicly traded companies*. In most cases, *privately held* companies don't have informational effects to worry about. However, tax considerations and the owners' liquidity needs are of great importance.

Because of taxes, the owners of a privately held company can normally benefit more from capital gains than from dividends. Double taxation is avoided. If the company is sold, the reinvested earnings will have benefited from tax deferral. They will be taxed at capital gains rates, which might be lower than ordinary income tax rates. For this reason, Internal Revenue Service regulations prohibit excessive earnings retention. But the definition of "excessive" is not clear. Privately held companies are usually smaller than publicly traded companies. They consequently have less financial flexibility and somewhat more variable liquidity requirements. Greater retentions are therefore warranted to compensate for the higher liquidity risks they face. Minimizing dividend payouts—especially until a surplus has been built up—may therefore be financially prudent as well as beneficial from a tax standpoint.

Self-Check

1. Why is it useful to consider more than one dividend policy alternative?

2. What special dividend policy considerations apply to privately held companies?

SHARE REPURCHASES

SHARE REPURCHASE
A company's use of cash to buy back shares of its own common stock.

Companies that want to distribute cash to their shareholders usually do so by declaring cash dividends. A **share repurchase** is an alternative to a cash dividend. The company spends the cash on repurchasing shares of its common stock. For example, IBM once offered to buy up to 4 million shares of its common stock. At the time, IBM had more than $6 billion in cash and marketable securities on its balance sheet. IBM actually bought 2,546,000 shares at a cost of $280 per share, for a total cost of about $713 million.

Share Repurchase versus Dividends

We showed that if a company is expanding, shareholders are indifferent between (1) dividend payout with the issuance of new shares and (2) retention of earnings—in a perfect capital market environment. Similarly, in a perfect capital market environment, if a company is contracting (the mirror image of expanding), shareholders are indifferent between dividend payout and using earnings to repurchase outstanding shares. Our next example illustrates this point.

Illustration of Equivalence of Dividends and Share Repurchases

Suppose International Paper (IP) has decided to distribute $50 million cash. IP has 10 million shares outstanding. It expects to earn $2.50 per share, and the current market value per share is $25. IP could pay a cash dividend of $5 per share, implying an ex-dividend value of $20 per share. Alternatively, it could use the $50 million to repurchase 2,000,000 (= 50,000,000/25) shares. After the share repurchase, each share would be worth

$$\frac{10{,}000{,}000(25) - 50{,}000{,}000}{10{,}000{,}000 - 2{,}000{,}000} = \$25$$

Therefore, as long as IP repurchases shares at the current market price of $25, a shareholder who doesn't sell will have the same wealth per share as a shareholder who does sell, namely $25 per share. The only difference is that one person has the wealth in the form of cash and the other has it in the form of stock. Similarly, if IP paid the $5 dividend, each shareholder would have an identical $25 per share value in the form of $5 in cash plus a share of stock worth $20. ■

Note that to the extent IP pays a repurchase price in excess of the market price, there is a *transfer of wealth* to the shareholders who sell from those who do not.

Greenmail: Wealth Transfer Through Share Repurchases

Let's continue our IP example. Suppose IP decides to spend $50 million to buy shares for $30 each from one of its shareholders. IP can purchase 1,666,667 (= 50,000,000/30) shares. Following the share repurchase, each share will be worth

$$\frac{10{,}000{,}000(25) - 50{,}000{,}000}{10{,}000{,}000 - 1{,}666{,}667} = \$24$$

There is a transfer of wealth *to* the selling shareholders amounting to $8,333,333 (= [30 − 25] 1,666,667), and there is a transfer of wealth *from* the remaining shareholders amounting to the same $8,333,333 (= [25 − 24]8,333,333). In the past, many companies have paid premiums to buy back shares from a takeover raider. When they do, the takeover raider effectively expropriates a portion of the other shareholders' collective wealth. This expropriation of wealth has come to be known by the colorful name **greenmail.** ■

GREENMAIL Repurchasing shares at a premium price from a takeover raider.

EPS Impact

Less sophisticated market participants often misunderstand how a share repurchase affects shareholder wealth. They judge its impact in terms of earnings per share (EPS). In the first example, before the cash distribution, IP had a price-earnings ratio (P/E) of 10 (= 25/2.50). After the cash distribution, IP should have a P/E of 8 (= 20/2.50). But this is true regardless of whether the cash is distributed as a dividend or through share repurchase. Neither IP's capital structure nor its capital budgeting policies are affected by the method of cash distribution. The share repurchase alternative would result in a projected EPS of

$$\frac{2.50(10{,}000{,}000)}{8{,}000{,}000} = \$3.125$$

However, although the EPS is higher with the share repurchase, each share would still be worth

$$3.125(8) = \$25$$

The increase in projected EPS is just offset by the decline in the P/E (from 10 to 8).

The confusion over the impact of share repurchases results from the mistaken belief that share repurchase will not alter the P/E. But if the P/E remained unchanged, the risk-return relationship would differ between the alternatives. This would be inconsistent with the Principles of Capital Market Efficiency and Risk-Return Trade-Off.

Advantages of Repurchasing Shares

In the first IP example, the share repurchase program did not affect shareholder wealth. But this conclusion depends on our assumption of a perfect capital market. Asymmetric taxes can change this conclusion. Because of lower effective taxes on capital gains, taxable individual shareholders would generally prefer that the company repurchase shares instead of paying a dividend.

Suppose dividends are taxed at a 50% rate and capital gains at a 20% rate. Shareholders would have to pay $25,000,000 (= [0.5]50,000,000) in total taxes on the dividend distribution, but no more than $10,000,000 (= [0.2]50,000,000) in total taxes on the share repurchase (depending on the tax basis of the shares).

On the other hand, dividends paid to other corporations are taxed at a lower rate than capital gains because of the 70% dividends-received deduction. Consequently, corporate shareholders usually prefer dividends over capital gains. The overall net tax advantage (or disadvantage) of share repurchase versus dividends thus depends on the shareholder mix.

Self-Check

1. What is a share repurchase?

2. Why is a share repurchase a substitute for a dividend?

3. How does a share repurchase affect projected EPS? Doesn't that mean the share price should rise?

STOCK DIVIDENDS AND STOCK SPLITS

Companies do not always pay dividends in cash. Frequently companies pay **stock dividends.** For example, suppose a company declares a 5% stock dividend. Then a shareholder will receive 5 new shares for each 100 shares owned.

STOCK DIVIDEND A dividend that is paid in the form of additional shares of common stock.

STOCK SPLIT Splitting each share into a greater number of shares.

A company can achieve much the same financial effect through a **stock split.** Although there is a technical difference between the two, stock dividends and stock splits represent alternative ways to rearrange a company's capital accounts on its balance sheet. Neither affects the net worth of the company, or the proportionate ownership interest of any of its shareholders. Stock dividends and stock splits, however, may send a signal to the market.

Accounting for Stock Dividends and Stock Splits

A stock dividend proportionally increases the number of shares each shareholder owns. The accounting treatment of "small" and "large" stock dividends is different. A "small" stock dividend is one that is less than 20% to 25% of the previously outstanding shares. The two accounting treatments are:

> **For a small stock dividend:** The *fair market value* of the shares distributed in the stock dividend is transferred from the retained earnings account to the *paid-in capital* and *capital contributed in excess of par value* accounts on the company's balance sheet.

> **For a large stock dividend:** The *par value* of the shares distributed in the stock dividend is transferred from the retained earnings account to the *paid-in capital* account on the company's balance sheet.

Stock dividends are a transaction that reallocates part of the company's retained earnings into either the paid-in capital or the capital contributed in excess of par value accounts. For a small stock dividend, the accounting treatment is like a cash dividend (which reduces retained earnings) and sale of new shares at their fair market value (which increases the paid-in capital and capital contributed in excess of par value accounts by the amount that retained earnings were reduced). Because of certain problems,[5] large stock dividends were treated differently. For this case, only the par value of the new shares was moved from retained earnings to paid-in capital.

The accounting treatment for a stock split is simpler:

For a stock split: No change is made in the dollar amounts of the paid-in capital, capital contributed in excess of par value, or retained earnings accounts. The number of shares and par value per share are adjusted for the new shares that are distributed.

For a 2-for-1 stock split, the number of shares is doubled and the par value per share is cut in half. If the company is implementing a 3-for-2 split, the number of shares is increased by 50% and the par value per share is reduced by one-third. The following example illustrates the mechanics of the accounting for a small stock dividend, a large stock dividend, and a stock split.

A 10% Stock Dividend, a 100% Stock Dividend, and a 2-for-1 Stock Split

EXAMPLE

Table 13.4 on page 488 illustrates the balance sheet impact of a *10% stock dividend,* a *100% stock dividend,* and a *2-for-1 stock split* for a company whose shares are selling at $30.

For the 10% stock dividend, 100,000 new shares are distributed. This is treated as a small stock dividend. The $3 million *fair market value* of these shares is taken out of retained earnings, with $1 million added to paid-in capital at par value (because the par value is $10 per share) and the balance, $2 million, is added to the capital contributed in excess of par value account.

For a 100% stock dividend, 1,000,000 new shares are distributed. This is treated as a large stock dividend because the distribution exceeds 20% to 25% of the previously outstanding shares. For a large stock dividend, only the par value of the new shares is taken from retained earnings and put into the paid-in capital account. As you can see in table 13.4, $10 million (=[10]1,000,000) is moved from retained earnings to paid-in capital.

For the 2-for-1 stock split, 1,000,000 new shares are distributed. The only change in the balance sheet accounts is the notation that outstanding shares are now 2,000,000 and the par value is reduced from $10 per share to $5.

In all cases, the company's net worth remains $100 million. ■

General Electric Company's 1994 Stock Split

EXAMPLE

General Electric Company announced a 2-for-1 stock split on March 17, 1994. Holders of record on April 28, 1994, received one additional share on May 13, 1994, for each share held on the record date. (Sounds a lot like a stock dividend, doesn't it?) Prior to the stock split, GE had approximately 926,564,000 shares outstanding. Following the split, it had approximately 1,853,128,000 shares outstanding. GE did not alter the dividend rate. Thus, the stock split effectively doubled the dividend from $0.36 to $0.72 per quarter. ■

---

[5]For example, the fair market value of the new shares distributed could exceed the total value of retained earnings.

TABLE 13.4

Comparison of the Balance Sheet Impact of a 10% Stock Dividend, a 100% Stock Dividend, and a Two-for-One Stock Split

COMMON STOCKHOLDERS' EQUITY INITIALLY	
Paid-in capital ($10 par value; 1,000,000 shares)	$ 10,000,000
Capital contributed in excess of par value	20,000,000
Retained earnings	70,000,000
Common stockholders' equity	$100,000,000
COMMON STOCKHOLDERS' EQUITY FOLLOWING 10% STOCK DIVIDEND	
Paid-in capital ($10 par value; 1,100,000 shares)	$ 11,000,000
Capital contributed in excess of par value	22,000,000
Retained earnings	67,000,000
Common stockholders' equity	$100,000,000
COMMON STOCKHOLDERS' EQUITY FOLLOWING 100% STOCK DIVIDEND	
Paid-in capital ($10 par value; 2,000,000 shares)	$ 20,000,000
Capital contributed in excess of par value	20,000,000
Retained earnings	60,000,000
Common stockholders' equity	$100,000,000
COMMON STOCKHOLDERS' EQUITY FOLLOWING 2-FOR-1 STOCK SPLIT	
Paid-in capital ($5 par value; 2,000,000 shares)	$ 10,000,000
Capital contributed in excess of par value	20,000,000
Retained earnings	70,000,000
Common stockholders' equity	$100,000,000

Stock Dividends versus Stock Splits

Companies generally use stock dividends when they are making relatively small stock distributions and use stock splits for larger ones. For example, the rules of the New York Stock Exchange prescribe that companies should make share distributions of less than 25% through stock dividends rather than stock splits.

Another difference between stock splits and stock dividends is based on state laws where a corporation is chartered. Some states allow dividends to be paid from retained earnings (or from retained earnings and capital contributed in excess of par value). By reducing retained earnings, a stock dividend can reduce the ability of a corporation to pay cash dividends. A stock split would have no such effect. In practice, this possible effect on the ability to pay cash dividends is rarely ever significant.

Financial Impact of Stock Dividends and Stock Splits

Both the 100% stock dividend and 2-for-1 stock split each doubled the number of shares outstanding. But they did not affect the company's liquidity position, capital budget, leverage, or any operating variable. Consequently, barring any informational effects, a stock dividend or a stock split should leave the stock market value of a company unchanged. Hence, a proportional reduction in the company's share price should occur:

$$\text{Price}_{After} = \frac{\text{Price}_{Before}}{1 + \% \text{ stock dividend}} = \frac{\text{Price}_{Before}}{\text{Stock split factor}}$$

For example, if the price per share is $60 before a 100% stock dividend or a 2-for-1 split, it should be $30 afterwards.

So what is the value of a stock dividend or of a stock split?

According to the Signaling Principle, actions convey information. The principal benefit of a stock dividend or stock split is probably the information it conveys. About half the shares listed on the New York Stock Exchange, for example, tend to trade in the range between $10 and $30 per share in any particular year, as illustrated in table 13.5.

Stock dividends and stock splits are usually associated with companies that have (or at least believe they have) excellent growth prospects. A stock split, in particular, may signal management's expectation that the company's share price would, in the absence of the split, move out of, or further above the top end of, this customary trading range. If so, investors ought to react favorably to the news of an impending stock split.

In connection with a stock split, companies frequently announce their desire to reduce the price of a share to a more popular trading range. More important, there is evidence that investors react positively to this signal. A stock split, normally involving a greater reduction in share price than a stock dividend, is likely to have the greater informational content of the two.

Following a stock dividend, companies often maintain the cash dividend per share. Following a stock split, companies typically either reduce the per-share cash dividend less than proportionally, or else maintain it, as GE did. These actions increase the cash dividend payout. Such increases are generally interpreted as positive signals.

By reducing the share price to a more popular trading range, a stock split—and to a lesser degree, a stock dividend—may increase trading activity in a stock and thus improve its liquidity. By increasing the number of shares outstanding (and increasing the volume of trading activity), a stock split—and to a lesser degree, a stock dividend—may broaden the ownership of a company's shares. However, the evidence on both points is not conclusive.

Stock Dividend versus Cash Dividend

Companies sometimes declare a stock dividend in lieu of a cash dividend to conserve cash and yet convey information. Do you think investors miss the significance of the switch? When a company substitutes a stock dividend for a cash dividend because of financial difficulty, investors will probably view this as negative rather than positive information.

Self-Check

1. What is a stock dividend, and what is a stock split? How do they differ?
2. How does a stock dividend work?
3. What is the value to shareholders of a stock dividend or a stock split?

TABLE 13.5

Distribution of Prices of New York Stock Exchange-Listed Common Stocks, 1967–1996

Price Group	AS OF JANUARY 6, 1967		AS OF JANUARY 7, 1972		AS OF FEBRUARY 3, 1978		AS OF DECEMBER 31, 1984		AS OF DECEMBER 31, 1990		AS OF DECEMBER 31, 1996	
	Number of Firms	Percentage of Total	Number of Firms	Percentage of Total	Number of Firms	Percentage of Total	Number of Firms	Percentage of Total	Number of Firms	Percentage of Total	Number of Firms	Percentage of Total
Under $10	77	6.1%	105	7.4%	283	18.0%	219	14.5%	604	35.6%	440	15.8%
$10–$19⅞	282	22.3	350	24.8	561	35.7	448	29.6	589	34.7	802	28.9
$20–$29⅞	327	25.8	355	25.2	457	29.0	384	25.3	283	16.7	643	23.1
$30–$39⅞	251	19.9	241	17.0	163	10.4	238	15.7	111	6.6	390	14.0
$40–$49⅞	139	10.9	173	12.3	64	4.1	112	7.4	56	3.3	220	7.9
$50–59⅞	73	5.8	71	5.1	22	1.4	56	3.7	26	1.5	112	4.0
$60–99⅞	102	8.0	91	6.5	18	1.1	50	3.3	21	1.2	145	5.2
$100 and over	14	1.2	25	1.7	4	0.3	8	0.5	7	0.4	31	1.1
Total	1265	100.0%	1411	100.0%	1572	100.0%	1515	100.0%	1697	100.0%	2783	100.0%
Closing value of Dow Jones Industrial Average	808.74		910.37		770.96		1211.57		2633.66		6448.27	

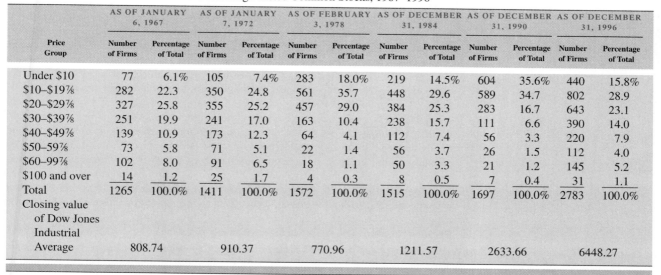

SUMMARY

This chapter examined dividend policy. We examined the historical record and discussed why a company's choice and implementation of its dividend policy might affect a company's value.

- Publicly traded companies have historically paid dividends on a regular basis, maintained both a stable payout ratio and dividend rate, made orderly changes in the dividend rate, and avoided whenever possible cutting a past dividend rate. There are systematic industry differences in payout policies.
- Dividend policy is irrelevant in a perfect capital market environment.
- Asymmetric information, asymmetric taxes, and transaction costs are persistent capital market imperfections that can cause dividend policy to affect a company's value.
- A company should use its dividend policy to whatever extent possible to maximize shareholder wealth. Its payout policy should be determined chiefly in keeping with its investment opportunities and internal funds needs.
- But also important are
  - market reactions to the company's changes, *or* lack of changes, in its dividend policy;
  - changes in laws that create a demand for innovative dividend policies that might be profitable;
  - shareholder preferences for capital gains and dividends;
  - shareholder preferences for liquidity;
  - the relative transaction costs of selling shares for the company versus the shareholders selling them; and
  - any legal or policy restrictions on the company and its shareholders concerning dividend policy.
- The individual tax system imposes a bias in favor of capital gains and against dividends. The system of corporate taxation does just the opposite for corporate investors. Depending upon the circumstances, tax-exempt pension funds may have preferences in either direction. As a result, high-income individual investors appear to gravitate toward low-payout companies, and corporate investors prefer high-payout companies.
- Transaction costs for the company impose a bias in favor of retained earnings over new share issues. However, transaction costs for investors impose at least some bias in favor of dividends over retained earnings for investors who want some minimum level of dividend income.
- The clientele effect, which involves investors investing in companies that have adopted dividend policies that are best for them, reduces or even eliminates tax and transaction cost considerations.
- Dividend policy may act as a signaling device. Simply paying out residual earnings year by year is unwise because it could cause the dividend rate to fluctuate wildly. This would reduce the information value of dividends.
- The chapter outlined and illustrated the application of a three-step set of dividend policy guidelines.
  - The appropriate dividend action depends on the company's future earnings and cash flow prospects and anticipated funds requirements. A company should determine what percentage of its earnings it expects to have available for distribution over its planning horizon (typically five years). This percentage depends on its earnings and cash flow prospects, the availability of attractive investment opportunities, and the company's chosen capital structure policy.
  - The second step involves deciding on an appropriate target payout ratio. A company should determine whether a higher or a lower payout ratio is warranted in view of the company's particular shareholder mix but should avoid setting the target payout ratio at a level that would trigger the need for an additional equity issue. The payout ratios of comparable companies provide a useful guide in this regard. Generally, a shareholder mix dominated by upper-income individual shareholders would argue for a payout ratio somewhat below that justified solely on the basis of residual earnings considerations, whereas a shareholder mix dominated by corporate shareholders, retired individuals, and tax-exempt institutions would argue for the opposite.
  - Decide on quarterly dividends that are comfortably sustainable.
- Companies can repurchase shares in lieu of distributing cash dividends. Share repurchases are usually more beneficial from a tax standpoint to individual shareholders. Nontaxable institu-

tional shareholders may prefer, and corporate shareholders usually will prefer, a dividend distribution. A company's shareholder mix helps determine whether a share repurchase program is preferable to a dividend distribution—or whether the company should use some combination of the two.

- Although there are some accounting differences between stock dividends and stock splits, their financial significance depends on signals accompanying the action, such as the positive signal of an increase in cash dividends.

EQUATION SUMMARY

(13.1) $$DPS_1 - DPS_0 = ADJ [POR(EPS_1) - DPS_0]$$

CHAPTER REVIEW ACTIVITIES

SELF-TEST PROBLEMS

1. (Dividend adjustment model) Last year's dividend for Woolridge Outfitters was $1.00. This year's earnings per share are $4.00, and Woolridge's target payout ratio is 40%. Using the dividend adjustment model, equation (13.1), what would be this year's dividend with each of the following adjustment factors?
   a. 70%   c. 100%
   b. 0%

2. (Accounting for a stock dividend and a stock split) Ligon Diagnostics has the capital accounts shown on its balance sheet below.

Common Stockholders' Equity	
Paid-in capital ($1 par value, 5,000,000 shares)	$ 5,000,000
Capital contributed in excess of par value	45,000,000
Retained earnings	100,000,000
Total	$150,000,000

The common shares are selling for $35 each.
   a. Show the capital accounts for a 10% stock dividend.
   b. Show the capital accounts for a 3-for-2 stock split.

SOLUTIONS TO SELF-TEST PROBLEMS

1. We use the dividend adjustment equation:

$$DIV_1 - DIV_0 = ADJ[POR(EPS) - DIV_0]$$

where $DIV_0 = \$1.00$, $EPS = \$4.00$, and the adjustment factor ADJ assumes different values.
   a. With 70% adjustment, $DIV_1 - 1.00 = 0.70[0.40(4.00) - 1.00]$

$$DIV_1 = \$1.42$$

   b. With 0% adjustment, $DIV_1 - 1.00 = 0.00[0.40(4.00) - 1.00]$

$$DIV_1 = \$1.00$$

   c. With 100% adjustment, $DIV_1 - 1.00 = 1.00[0.40(4.00) - 1.00]$

$$DIV_1 = \$1.60$$

Notice in part **b** that the dividend stays fixed, while in part **c** the dividend equals the payout ratio (40%) times earnings. In part **a,** the partial adjustment of 70% is a compromise between the 0% and 100% adjustment policies.

2. a. For a 10% stock dividend, 500,000 new shares are issued. The market value of these shares, $17,500,000 (= (35)500,000), is moved from retained earnings into the paid-in capital and contributed capital accounts. The par value is unchanged, so $500,000 is put into the paid-in capital account and the balance is put into capital contributed in excess of par:

Common Stockholders' Equity	
Paid-in capital ($1 par value, 5,500,000 shares)	$ 5,500,000
Capital contributed in excess of par value	62,000,000
Retained earnings	82,500,000
Total	$150,000,000

b. For a 3-for-2 stock split, 2,500,000 new shares are issued. The dollar amounts in each capital account are unchanged. The par value is adjusted to reflect the increased number of shares: par value = 5,000,000/7,500,000 = $0.66⅔.

Common Stockholders' Equity	
Paid-in capital ($0.66⅔ par value, 7,500,000 shares)	$ 5,000,000
Capital contributed in excess of par value	45,000,000
Retained earnings	100,000,000
Total	$150,000,000

QUESTIONS

1. Consider the following four dates: April 10, April 24, April 27, and May 5. Match them with the following:
   a. Ex-dividend date
   b. Record date
   c. Payment date
   d. Declaration date

2. Among the following alternatives, which is the most common pattern of dividend policy?
   a. A stable payout ratio where dividend payments vary with earnings.
   b. A stable payment rate per share where dividend payments are more stable than earnings.
   c. Dividend payments that vary each year according to the company's capital investment opportunities.
   d. A stable payment rate per share with a once-a-year "extra payment" based on the company's earnings so that dividend payments are more stable than earnings.

3. Briefly explain why dividend policy is irrelevant in a perfect capital market environment.

4. Briefly explain why the signal of paying a dividend can cause dividend policy to affect a company's value.

5. Explain what we mean by the term *dividend clientele*. How does the existence of dividend clienteles lessen or even eliminate the tax differential view of dividend policy in a perfect market?

6. True or False?
   a. Evidence shows that, on average, a dividend decrease affects the company's stock price negatively but a dividend increase has no effect on the company's stock price.
   b. A large majority of companies follow a dividend policy that specifies a fixed payout ratio, so that the dollar amount each quarter fluctuates according to the company's earnings.
   c. Typically, a company has a target payout ratio that it aims for over time, but the payout ratio for any particular quarter can be substantially different from this target.
   d. To pay a cash dividend, it is only necessary for the company to have sufficient retained earnings to afford the dividend payment. (If false, cite two factors that could preclude a company from paying a dividend.)
   e. Dividends are normally paid quarterly, whereas bond interest payments are normally made semiannually.

7. Cite two examples of how transaction costs might affect a company's choice of dividend policy.

8. Briefly describe our three-step approach to the dividend decision.

9. What is the difference between a stock dividend and a stock split, and what conditions make one more likely to be used than the other?

10. In what sense are share repurchases and dividend payments substitutes for one another? Under what circumstances, if any, are they perfect substitutes?

11. What are the major advantages of a share repurchase over a cash dividend?

12. Explain why a company's share price falls on the dividend ex-date. By how much would you expect it to fall? Does it matter whether the dividend is paid in cash or additional stock?

13. Can it *ever* happen that a person owns shares of stock but does not receive the same cash dividend per share paid to other shareholders, or that a person no longer owns shares of stock but does receive a cash dividend?

14. Illustrate how a company's repurchasing its own shares will increase the company's leverage. Ignore taxes and assume a perfect capital market environment.

15. How might the cost of issuing new stock affect a company's choice of dividend policy?

CHALLENGING QUESTIONS

16. Describe conditions under which a company might find it advantageous to substitute a stock dividend for an increase in its cash dividend.

17. What is the basis for the view that a company's total market value is invariant to its choice of dividend policy? Cite three broad types of capital market imperfections that might cause the dividend policy of a company to have an effect on the value of that company. Give three examples (one for each type) where such an imperfection would cause a company's dividend policy to have an effect on the value of that company. Explain *how* each of the three examples you gave would cause a company's dividend policy to have an effect on the value of that company.

18. A few years ago, Allegis Corporation (now UAL Corp.) announced that it expected to declare a special dividend of not less than $50 per share to be paid out of the after-tax proceeds from the sale of its Hilton International and Westin Hotels & Resorts hotel subsidiaries and Hertz Corp. car rental subsidiary. Its quarterly common dividend rate at the time was $0.25 per share.

    a. What does the special dividend announcement tell you about Allegis Corporation's ability to reinvest profitably the after-tax proceeds from the sale of its subsidiaries?

    b. Why do you suppose Allegis Corporation planned to pay a special dividend, rather than increase the regular dividend?

    c. Allegis Corporation eventually used the after-tax proceeds to repurchase approximately $3 billion worth of its common stock. It acted at the behest of at least one large shareholder. What does the large shareholder's preference for a share repurchase rather than a special dividend seem to indicate about that shareholder's tax position?

19. Mega Electric Company has been denied its request for an electricity rate increase. Mega has continued to pay $2 per share per year in cash dividends in anticipation of receiving permission to increase electric rates. As a result of the denial, Mega's payout ratio will go over 100% within 12 months unless something is done quickly.

    a. Mega Electric's chairman asks you, as the utility's chief financial officer, to study the advisability of paying a $1 cash dividend and a $1 common stock dividend in order to "preserve the dividend and not send a negative signal to the market." How would you respond to the chairman?

    b. Mega Electric's president comes to you with a "better idea." She suggests paying a $1 cash dividend and distributing the "rest" of the dividend as $1 face amount of a new 12% debenture. (Assume the 12% interest rate would make the debenture worth its par value.) How would you respond to the president?

20. If the price of a share of common stock can be expressed as the present value of the future dividend stream, how could it be that dividend policy is irrelevant?

21. Suppose a company is facing the possibility of a necessary dividend rate cut because of poor economic conditions. Suppose further that you are a member of the company's board of directors. How would you respond to the argument of another board member that the company should publicly deny the possibility of such a cut until the board has decided that the cut is an unavoidable necessity? The other member's argument is that unless the company denies the possibility of a dividend cut, its stock price will drop. If the cut can be avoided, the drop will have been unnecessary, and the company's stockholders will have suffered needlessly.

22. Our discussion in this chapter leads to a less than completely satisfying conclusion. Specifically, we do not provide a prescription that specifies *exactly* how to maximize shareholder wealth through dividend policy. If you will recall, our prescription concerning capital structure was somewhat similar. Now the question: Suppose the good fairy can tell you exactly how to optimize both your company's capital structure policy and your company's dividend policy. Although the good fairy wants to be good to you, he does not want to be too good to you and has offered to provide you with the optimal prescription for your company's capital structure policy *or* your company's dividend policy, but not both. Based on what you now know of the potential gains to be had from each policy, which one would you choose to optimize? Explain your reasoning.

23. It has been argued by a journalist that electric companies should not be allowed to pay cash dividends because such a prohibition would (a) reduce their need to raise external capital, thus (b) reducing their transaction costs, so that (c) they would have a lower cost of capital, and consequently (d) lower utility rates, and (e) make customers better off. Utility stockholders would receive capital gains instead of dividends, which (because of lower tax rates or tax deferral) would lower their taxes. Do you think a legal restriction preventing utilities from ever paying a cash dividend would result in this chain of events? If not, where does the logic break down?

PROBLEM SET A

A1. (Extra dividend) Escarraz Soy Products has the following quarterly earnings per share and has paid a regular quarterly dividend of $0.30.

Quarter	1	2	3	4	Total
Earnings per share	$0.60	$1.10	$1.20	$0.90	$3.80
Dividends per share	0.30	0.30	0.30	0.30	1.20

Escarraz wants the annual payout to be 40% of earnings. What extra dividend in the fourth quarter would give the company its planned payout?

A2. (Extra dividend) Sensor Technologies pays a regular dividend of $.10 per quarter plus an extra dividend in the fourth quarter equal to 40% of the amount that annual earnings per share exceeds $2.00.

a. If annual earnings per share are $2.80, what is the fourth-quarter extra dividend?

b. If annual earnings per share are $1.75, what is the fourth-quarter extra dividend?

A3. (Taxes on cash dividends versus repurchased shares) The board of directors of General Motors is debating the payment of an extra $500 million in cash dividends on common stock versus repurchasing $500 million of common shares.

a. Assume that GM pays a cash dividend of $500 million and that the marginal tax rate of its investors is 40%. What is the tax liability?

b. Assume that GM repurchases $500 million of common shares. The tax basis of these shares for the selling shareholders is $300 million. Assuming a 40% tax rate, what is the tax liability on the capital gain?

A4. (Accounting for a stock dividend) Deryl Martin Interests has the common stock accounts shown below. The stock has a $22 per share market value. If Deryl Martin pays a 5% stock dividend, show the revised common stock accounts.

Paid-in capital ($0.42 par value, 1,000,000 shares)	$ 420,000
Capital contributed in excess of par value	4,720,000
Retained earnings	8,200,000
Common stockholders' equity	$13,340,000

A5. (Accounting for a stock split) Bendeck Brake has the common stock accounts shown below. Bendeck stock is selling for $21.00 per share. If Bendeck has a 2-for-1 stock split, what will be the revised common stock accounts for the company?

Paid-in capital ($0.42 par value, 1,000,000 shares)	$ 420,000
Capital contributed in excess of par value	4,720,000
Retained earnings	8,200,000
Total common stockholders' equity	$13,340,000

A6. (Market prices following a stock split or stock dividend) Assume that IBM is selling for $180 per share. IBM implements one of the following stock dividends or stock splits, and no other change in the value of the company occurs. What is the value of one share for each of the following?

a. An 8% stock dividend.

b. A 50% stock dividend.

c. A 3-for-2 stock split.

d. A 2-for-1 stock split.

A7. (Market prices following a stock split) General Electric is selling for $90 per share. The board of directors declares a 3-for-2 stock split.

a. What is the market price per share after the split if there is no further information to cause investors to revalue the company?

b. Suppose that the board of directors increases cash dividends substantially and investors increase the value of General Electric by 10%. What should be the market price per share reflecting the split and the new information?

A8. (Accounting for stock dividends and stock splits) Shore Electronics Corporation's common stock is selling for $44 per share and its common stockholders' equity is shown below.

Paid-in capital ($4 par value, 5,000,000 shares)	$ 20,000,000
Capital contributed in excess of par value	30,000,000
Retained earnings	50,000,000
Common stockholders' equity	$100,000,000

a. Show the impact of a 50% stock dividend. (*Hint:* This is a large stock dividend, not a small one.)

b. Show the impact of a 3-for-2 stock split.

c. Describe how the stock market would react to each event. How would you explain the difference in reaction?

PROBLEM SET B

B1. (Cash versus homemade dividends) Refer to figures 13.4 and 13.5. A company currently has 8,000 shares outstanding that are worth $100 each. The company's shareholders desire a dividend of $20 per share. Assume a perfect capital market.

a. Suppose the company pays a dividend of $20 per share and sells new shares to raise $160,000 to replace the cash it paid out. Show that these steps do not alter the wealth of the original shareholders. What percentage of the company do they end up owning?

b. Suppose instead the shareholders raise $160,000 by selling some of their own shares. How many shares must they sell? Show that the two dividend alternatives leave them equally well off.

B2. (Dividend adjustment model) Regional Software has made a bundle selling spreadsheet software and has begun paying cash dividends. The company's chief financial officer would like the company to distribute 25% of its annual earnings (POR = 0.25) and adjust the dividend rate to changes in earnings per share at the rate ADJ = 0.75. Regional paid $1.00 per share in dividends last year. It will earn at least $8.00 per share this year and each year in the foreseeable future. Use the dividend adjustment model, equation (13.1), to calculate projected dividends per share for this year and the next four.

B3. (Dividend policy) A company has 20 million common shares outstanding. It currently pays out $1.50 per share per year in cash dividends on its common stock. Historically, its payout ratio has ranged from 30% to 35%. Over the next 5 years it expects the earnings and discretionary cash flow shown below.

	1	2	3	4	5	Thereafter
Earnings	100	125	150	120	140	150+ per year
Discretionary cash flow	50	70	60	20	15	50+ per year

a. Over the 5-year period, what is the maximum overall payout ratio the company could achieve without additional financing?

b. Recommend a reasonable dividend policy for paying out discretionary cash flow in years 1 through 5.

B4. (Cash dividend versus share repurchase) Consider a company that has decided to make, but has not yet announced, a large "bonus" cash dividend amounting in the aggregate to $5 million. The company has 1 million shares outstanding that sell for $20 each. The company has no debt; there are no taxes; and all transactions take place in a perfect capital market. Using calculations like those in the illustration of dividend irrelevance in a perfect capital market, show that shareholders will be indifferent between whether the company pays out the "bonus" as a dividend or uses the money to buy back $5 million of its shares.

B5. (Dividend change after a stock split) In July 1995 International Paper Co. announced a 2-for-1 stock split. At the same time, it announced that the quarterly dividend rate, which had been 42 cents per pre-split share, would become 25 cents a share after the stock split.
   a. Did International Paper increase its dividend rate? Explain.
   b. How would you expect the market to react to this dual announcement?

B6. (Share repurchase) A company's common stock is trading at a P/E ratio of 12. Its projected earnings per share are $2.00, and its share price is $24. All its shareholders are tax exempt. An open market purchase would result in projected earnings per share of $2.30. How would you expect the announcement of the share repurchase program to affect the company's share price?

B7. (Extra dividends) Aluminum Co. of America (Alcoa) recently announced a new dividend policy. The company said it would pay a base cash dividend of 40 cents per common share each quarter. In addition, the company said it would pay 30% of any excess in annual earnings per share above $6.00 as an extra year-end dividend.
   a. If Alcoa earns $7.50 per share in 1997, what percentage of its 1997 earnings would it pay out as cash dividends under the new policy?
   b. For what types of companies would Alcoa's new dividend policy be appropriate? Explain.

B8. (Dividend policy) Gotham Manufacturing Corporation (GMC) pays quarterly cash dividends on its common stock. Suppose GMC projects earnings per share of $3.00 this year and $2.70, $3.30, $3.90, and $3.60 over the next succeeding 4 years, respectively, and believes it can maintain a long-term payout ratio of 1/3. GMC revises its dividends once per year, and the quarterly dividend is one-fourth of the annual dividend. Which of the following annual cash dividend (in $) patterns would you recommend:
   1. 1.00, 1.00, 1.00, 1.30, 1.20?
   2. 1.00, 0.90, 1.10, 1.30, 1.20?
   3. 1.00, 1.00, 1.10, 1.20, 1.20?
   4. 1.00, 0.90, 1.20, 1.20, 1.20?

B9. (Greenmail) When a company repurchases shares of its common stock from a takeover raider, the payment for the shares is referred to as greenmail. The common stock of Trans-World-Dilemma (TWD) has a current price of $30 per share. If TWD has 10 million shares outstanding and it buys back 1 million shares from Karl I. Can, paying Karl $35 per share for the block of shares:
   a. What should be the company's share price immediately following the buy-back?
   b. How has the payment of greenmail affected the holders of the other 9 million shares?

B10. (Greenmail) Easy Mark, Inc. has a contentious minority shareholder who owns 10% of the company's 50 million outstanding shares. Easy Mark's share price is $12 per share, but the minority shareholder wants the company to repurchase her shares for $15 each. Assume all transactions take place in a perfect capital market (including no taxes).
   a. How would such a repurchase affect the minority shareholder's wealth?
   b. How would such a repurchase affect Easy Mark's share price?
   c. How would such a repurchase affect the wealth of Easy Mark's other shareholders?
   d. What do you conclude regarding the impact of greenmail on shareholder wealth?

PROBLEM SET C

C1. (Dividends, share repurchases, and taxes) Cardinal Computer Corporation has developed a phenomenally successful software package that makes it very easy to combine spreadsheet modeling and basic financial calculations. As a result, Cardinal has $20 million of excess cash that is available for distribution to its shareholders. All of Cardinal's shareholders invested at the company's inception and consequently have a negligible tax (cost) basis in their Cardinal shares. Cardinal has 10 million shares outstanding.

a. Assuming dividend income is taxed at a 40% rate and capital gains income is taxed at a 20% rate, calculate the impact on shareholder wealth of a $20 million cash dividend distribution and a $20 million share repurchase.

b. Under what circumstances, if any, would Cardinal's shareholders be better off having Cardinal retain and reinvest the cash in short-term financial instruments rather than pay it out to shareholders?

BIBLIOGRAPHY

Ambarish, Ramasastry, Kose John, and Joseph Williams. "Efficient Signalling with Dividends and Investments," *Journal of Finance,* 1987, 42(2):321–343.

Ang, James S. *Do Dividends Matter? A Review of Corporate Dividend Theories and Evidence.* Monograph 1987-2, Graduate School of Business Administration, New York University, New York, 1987.

Ang, James S., David W. Blackwell, and William L. Megginson. "The Effect of Taxes on the Relative Valuation of Dividends and Capital Gains: Evidence from Dual-Class British Investment Trusts," *Journal of Finance,* 1991, 46(1):383–399.

Bajaj, Mukesh, and Anand M. Vijh. "Dividend Clienteles and the Information Content of Dividend Changes," *Journal of Financial Economics,* 1990, 26(2):193–220.

Baker, H. Kent, Gail E. Farrelly, and Richard B. Edelman. "A Survey of Management Views on Dividend Policy," *Financial Management,* 1985, 14(3):78–84.

Bhagat, Sanjai, James A. Brickley, and Uri Loewenstein. "The Pricing Effects of Interfirm Cash Tender Offers," *Journal of Finance,* 1987, 42(4):965–986.

Black, Fischer. "The Dividend Puzzle," *Journal of Portfolio Management,* 1976, 2(Winter):5–8.

Born, Jeffrey A. "Insider Ownership and Signals—Evidence from Dividend Initiation Announcement Effects," *Financial Management,* 1988, 17(1):38–45.

Bortz, Gary A., and John P. Rust. "Why Do Companies Pay Dividends?: Comment," *American Economic Review,* 1984, 74(December):1135–1136.

Brennan, M. J., and T. E. Copeland. "Beta Changes Around Stock Splits: A Note," *Journal of Finance,* 1988, 43(4):1009–1014.

Brennan, Michael J., and Anjan V. Thakor. "Shareholder Preferences and Dividend Policy," *Journal of Finance,* 1990, 45(4):993–1019.

Brown, Keith C., and Scott L. Lummer. "The Cash Management Implications of a Hedged Dividend Capture Strategy," *Financial Management,* 1984, 13(4):7–17.

Chang, Rosita P., and S. Ghon Rhee. "The Impact of Personal Taxes on Corporate Dividend Policy and Capital Structure Decisions," *Financial Management,* 1990, 19(2):21–31.

Conroy, Robert M., Robert S. Harris, and Bruce A. Benet. "The Effects of Stock Splits on Bid-Ask Spreads," *Journal of Finance,* 1990, 45(4):1285–1295.

Cotter, James F., and Marc Zenner. "How Managerial Wealth Affects the Tender Offer Process," *Journal of Financial Economics,* 1994, 35(1):63–97.

Dann, Larry Y. "Common Stock Repurchases: An Analysis of Returns to Bondholders and Stockholders," *Journal of Financial Economics,* 1981, 9(2):113–138.

DeAngelo, Harry, and Linda DeAngelo. "Dividend Policy and Financial Distress: An Empirical Investigation of Troubled NYSE Firms," *Journal of Finance,* 1990, 45(5):1415–1432.

Denis, David J. "Defensive Changes in Corporate Payout Policy: Share Repurchases and Special Dividends," *Journal of Finance,* 1990, 45(5):1433–1456.

Denis, David J., Diane K. Denis, and Atulya Sarin. "The Information Content of Dividend Changes: Cash Flow Signaling, Overinvestment, and Dividend Clienteles," *Journal of Financial and Quantitative Analysis,* 1994, 29(4):567–587.

Eades, Kenneth M. "Empirical Evidence on Dividends as a Signal of Firm Value," *Journal of Financial and Quantitative Analysis,* 1982, 17(4):471–500.

Feldstein, Martin, and Jerry Green. "Why Do Companies Pay Dividends?" *American Economic Review,* 1983, 73(March):17–30.

Finnerty, John D. "The Behavior of Electric Utility Common Stock Prices Near the Ex-Dividend Date," *Financial Management*, 1981, 10(4):59–69.

Gay, Gerald D., Jayant R. Kale, and Thomas H. Noe. "Share Repurchases Mechanisms: A Comparative Analysis of Efficacy, Shareholder Wealth, and Corporate Control Effects," *Financial Management*, 1991, 20(1):44–59.

Gordon, Myron J. "Dividends, Earnings, and Stock Prices," *Review of Economics and Statistics*, 1959, 41(May):99–105.

Grinblatt, Mark S., Ronald W. Masulis, and Sheridan Titman. "The Valuation Effects of Stock Splits and Stock Dividends," *Journal of Financial Economics*, 1984, 13(4):461–490.

Hansen, Robert S., Raman Kumar, and Dilip K. Shome. "Dividend Policy and Corporate Monitoring: Evidence from the Regulated Electric Utility Industry," *Financial Management*, 1994, 23(1):16–22.

Jensen, Gerald R., Donald P. Solberg, and Thomas S. Zorn. "Simultaneous Determination of Insider Ownership, Debt, and Dividend Policies," *Journal of Financial and Quantitative Analysis*, 1992, 27(2):247–264.

John, Kose, and Larry H. P. Lang. "Insider Trading Dividend Announcements: Theory and Evidence," *Journal of Finance*, 1991, 46(4):1361–1390.

Kalay, Avner. "Signaling, Information Content, and the Reluctance to Cut Dividends," *Journal of Financial and Quantitative Analysis*, 1980, 15(4):855–869.

Kale, Jayant R., Thomas H. Noe, and Gerald D. Gay. "Share Repurchase through Transferable Put Rights," *Journal of Financial Economics*, 1989, 25(1):141–160.

Lamoureux, Christopher G., and Percy Poon. "The Market Reaction to Stock Splits," *Journal of Finance*, 1987, 42(5):1347–1370.

Lewellen, Wilbur G., Kenneth L. Stanley, Ronald C. Lease, and Gary G. Schlarbaum. "Some Direct Evidence on the Dividend Clientele Phenomenon," *Journal of Finance*, 1978, 33(5):1385–1399.

Lintner, John. "Distribution of Incomes of Corporations Among Dividends, Retained Earnings, and Taxes," *American Economic Review*, 1956, 46(May):97–113.

Litzenberger, Robert H., and K. Ramaswamy. "The Effect of Personal Taxes and Dividends on Capital Asset Prices: Theory and Empirical Evidence," *Journal of Financial Economics*, 1979, 7(2):163–195.

Litzenberger, Robert H., and K. Ramaswamy. "The Effects of Dividends on Common Stock Prices: Tax Effects or Information Effects," *Journal of Finance*, 1982, 37(2):429–443.

Loderer, Claudio, and David C. Mauer. "Corporate Dividends and Seasoned Equity Issues: An Empirical Investigation," *Journal of Finance*, 1992, 47(1):201–226.

Maloney, Michael T., and J. Harold Mulherin. "The Effects of Splitting on the Ex: A Microstructure Reconciliation," *Financial Management*, 1992, 21(4):44–59.

McNichols, Maureen, and Ajay David. "Stock Dividends, Stock Splits and Signaling," *Journal of Finance*, 1990, 45(3):857–880.

Millar, James A., and Bruce D. Fielitz. "Stock-Split and Stock Dividend Decisions," *Financial Management*, 1973, 2(4):35–45.

Miller, Merton H., and Franco Modigliani. "Dividend Policy, Growth, and the Valuation of Shares," *Journal of Business*, 1961, 34(October):411–433.

Miller, Merton H., and Myron S. Scholes. "Dividends and Taxes," *Journal of Financial Economics*, 1978, 6(4):333–364.

Miller, Merton H., and Myron S. Scholes. "Dividends and Taxes: Some Empirical Evidence," *Journal of Political Economy*, 1982, 90(6):1118–1141.

Mohanty, Sunil K. "Returns from Hedged Dividend Capture Programs and Dutch Auction Rate Preferred Stock," *Financial Management*, 1994, 23(1):11–13.

Ofer, Aharon R., and Daniel R. Siegel. "Corporate Financial Policy, Information, and Market Expectations: An Empirical Investigation of Dividends," *Journal of Finance*, 1987, 42(4):889–911.

Ofer, Aharon R., and Anjan V. Thakor. "A Theory of Stock Price Responses to Alternative Corporate Cash Disbursement Methods: Stock Repurchases and Dividends," *Journal of Finance*, 1987, 42(2):365–394.

Papaioannou, George J., and Craig M. Savarese. "Corporate Dividend Policy Response to the Tax Reform Act of 1986," *Financial Management*, 1994, 23(1):56–63.

Robin, Ashok J. "The Impact of the 1986 Tax Reform Act on Ex-Dividend Day Returns," *Financial Management*, 1991, 20(1):60–70.

Shefrin, Hersh M., and Meir Statman. "Explaining Investor Preference for Cash Dividends," *Journal of Financial Economics*, 1984, 13(2):253–282.

Spudeck, Raymond E., and R. Charles Moyer. "Reverse Splits and Shareholder Wealth: The Impact of Commissions," *Financial Management*, 1985, 14(4):52–56.

Sterk, William Edward. "Option Pricing: Dividends and the In- and Out-of-the-Money Bias," *Financial Management*, 1983, 12(4):47–53.

Talmor, Eli, and Sheridan Titman. "Taxes and Dividend Policy," *Financial Management*, 1990, 19(2):32–35.

Venkatesh, P. C. "Trading Costs and Ex-Day Behavior: An Examination of Primes and Stocks," *Financial Management*, 1991, 20(3):84–95.

Vermaelen, Theo. "Common Stock Repurchases and Market Signalling: An Empirical Study," *Journal of Financial Economics*, 1981, 9(2):139–183.

Wansley, James W., William R. Lane, and Salil Sarkar. "Managements' View on Share Repurchase and Tender Offer Premiums," *Financial Management*, 1989, 18(3):97–110.

Woolridge, J. Randall, and Donald R. Chambers. "Reverse Splits and Shareholder Wealth," *Financial Management,* 1983, 12(3):5–15.

Zivney, Terry L., and Michael J. Alderson. "Hedged Dividend Capture with Stock Index Options," *Financial Management,* 1986, 15(2):5–12.

LONG-TERM FINANCING ALTERNATIVES

OBJECTIVES

1. Cite and briefly describe the four main classes of long-term corporate debt.

2. Describe the maturity, interest rate, sinking fund, call option, and covenant features of long-term corporate debt.

3. Summarize the main characteristics of a Eurobond.

4. Explain the advantages and disadvantages of lease financing.

5. Calculate the net advantage to leasing and the lease's IRR.

6. Describe the main features of common and preferred stock.

Chapters 8 through 10 examined capital budgeting. In this chapter, we look at external ways of financing capital assets. When a company's capital requirements exceed its ability to generate cash internally, the company must raise funds externally. Businesses usually finance long-term assets with long-term capital.

No doubt you've borrowed money before. If you have a credit card, you borrow money each time you use it. The card issuer pays the merchant, and you must repay the card issuer. If you always pay when you're billed, the loans are *interest-free.* You simply repay the amount you borrowed; no interest is charged. If you don't pay right away, however, you begin to owe interest.

Credit card loans are easy to arrange. (Maybe that's why there is so much credit card debt in the United States![1]) You don't have to sign a new loan agreement each time you use the card. But you did enter into a form of loan agreement when your application was approved. The agreement has a lot of fine print, which spells out the loan terms. (Have you ever read it?) For example, it tells you the interest rate and how interest is calculated.

You may have also entered into more formal, longer-term loan arrangements. Have you gotten student loans to pay part of the cost of your education? Have you borrowed to buy a car? It won't be too long before you are taking out a mortgage loan to buy a house. Borrowing money is something individuals normally do. So do companies.

When a company decides to issue securities, it must decide several things. Does its capital structure policy call for equity or debt? Should the debt have a fixed or a variable interest rate? When should it mature?

---

[1] About $400 billion at the end of 1995, according to the Federal Reserve Board.

Should it include a sinking fund, which will retire it in installments? Should the company retain a call option so that it can call in the debt and refund it if interest rates drop? Would international debt financing be better than domestic debt? Would leasing be better than borrowing and buying? These are just a few of the points we'll discuss in this chapter.

LONG-TERM FINANCING AND THE PRINCIPLES OF FINANCE

◆ *Self-Interested Behavior:* Look for the most advantageous ways to finance the company, such as the lowest-cost debt alternative.

◆ *Two-Sided Transactions:* Set a price and other terms that investors will find acceptable when issuing securities.

◆ *Signaling:* Recognize that announcing the company's decision to issue securities conveys information about the company.

◆ *Risk-Return Trade-Off:* Recognize that riskier securities must offer investors a higher expected return.

◆ *Capital Market Efficiency:* Use the market value of a company's securities as the best measure of their value.

(continued on following page)

(Long-Term Financing and the Principles of Finance *continued from previous page*)

◆ *Options:* Recognize the value of a bond's call option. It's valuable because it enables the issuing company to redeem the debt and replace it at a lower cost if interest rates drop.

◆ *Valuable Ideas:* Look for ways to reduce financing costs by creating innovative securities that reduce issuing costs and/or raise investors' risk-adjusted after-tax returns.

◆ *Comparative Advantage:* Contract with underwriters to bear the risk in issuing securities if they can bear that risk more cheaply.

◆ *Incremental Benefits:* Calculate the net advantage of leasing versus borrowing and buying, as well as the net advantage to refunding a bond on the basis of the incremental after-tax benefits the transaction will produce.

◆ *Time Value of Money:* Use discounted cash flow analysis to compare the costs and benefits of financing decisions, such as alternative securities to sell, lease versus borrow and buy, and bond refunding.

THE LONG-TERM FINANCING MENU

Every time a company raises funds externally, it must decide which type or types of securities to issue. Transaction costs play a role, because they are proportionately smaller for larger issues. The fixed cost is spread out over a larger issue. The variable costs are greater for relatively smaller issues.

Debt, common stock, and preferred stock are the main sources of external long-term corporate financing. Table 14.1 shows the relative proportions of funds U.S. companies raised by issuing common stock, preferred stock, and long-term debt between 1972 and 1996. Over that 25-year period, common stock, preferred stock, and long-term debt accounted for 13.8%, 5.6%, and 80.6%, respectively, of the funds raised.

The total amount of common stock issued at any time is sensitive to stock market conditions. Companies try to take advantage of rising markets when the demand for common stock is relatively strong. New-issue activity tends to increase during periods of rising share prices. Correspondingly, companies are usually reluctant to sell new issues of common stock when the share price is low by historical standards.

Similarly, the volume of fixed-income security issues (preferred stock and debt) tends to vary with the level of long-term interest rates. During periods of rising long-term interest rates, companies tend to favor short-term borrowing. Then, if and when long-term interest rates fall, many companies start replacing the short-term debt with long-term fixed-income securities.

Self-Check

1. Among debt, common stock, and preferred stock, which provides the largest proportion of external financing by companies? Which accounts for the smallest?

2. Why are the volumes of common stock and debt financing sensitive to market conditions?

TABLE 14.1
The Main Sources of Domestic External Long-Term Financing by U.S. Companies, 1972-1996 (dollar amounts in millions)

YEAR	AGGREGATE DOMESTIC EXTERNAL FINANCING[a]	PERCENTAGE REPRESENTED BY			PERCENT CHANGE IN S&P 500 INDEX DURING YEAR	MOODY'S AVERAGE OF YIELDS ON Aa-RATED CORPORATE BONDS
		Common Stock	Preferred Stock[b]	Debt[c]		
1972	$ 41,957	23.1%	8.0%	68.9%	15.63%	7.48%
1973	33,390	23.2	10.1	66.7	−17.37	7.66
1974	38,313	10.4	5.9	83.7	−29.72	8.84
1975	53,619	13.8	6.4	79.8	31.55	9.17
1976	53,356	15.6	5.2	79.2	19.15	8.75
1977	53,792	14.6	7.3	78.1	−11.50	8.24
1978	47,230	15.9	6.0	78.1	1.06	8.92
1979	51,102	15.2	7.1	77.7	12.31	9.94
1980	73,694	22.9	4.9	72.2	25.77	12.50
1981	70,441	33.4	2.6	64.0	−9.73	14.75
1982	84,198	30.2	6.1	63.7	14.76	14.41
1983	119,949	37.0	6.0	57.0	17.27	12.42
1984	132,531	14.0	3.1	82.9	1.40	13.31
1985	201,269	14.4	3.2	82.4	26.33	11.82
1986	381,936	13.2	4.7	82.1	14.62	9.47
1987	367,863	11.8	6.3	81.9	2.03	9.68
1988	385,625	9.3	5.7	85.0	12.40	9.94
1989	325,034	8.0	4.1	87.9	27.25	9.46
1990	340,049	5.7	6.1	88.2	−6.56	9.56
1991	465,243	10.3	5.9	83.8	26.31	9.05
1992	559,827	10.2	5.6	84.2	4.46	8.46
1993	754,969	10.9	4.1	85.0	7.06	7.04
1994	582,569	8.2	6.4	85.4	−1.54	8.15
1995	641,979	8.9	6.7	84.4	37.57	7.72
1996	660,692	12.5	5.0	82.5	22.95	7.55
Total	$6,520,627	11.8%	5.4%	82.8%		

[a]Aggregate amount raised through the issuance of common stock, nonconvertible preferred stock, nonconvertible debt, and convertible securities.
[b]Includes convertible preferred and preference stock.
[c]Includes convertible debt.
Sources: Federal Reserve Bulletin, Board of Governors of the Federal Reserve System, Washington, D.C., various issues; *Daily Stock Price Record: New York Stock Exchange,* Standard & Poor's Corporation, New York, various issues; and *Moody's Bond Record,* Moody's Investors Service, Inc., New York, various issues.

TYPES OF LONG-TERM DEBT

There are four main classes of long-term corporate debt: secured, unsecured, tax-exempt, and convertible. We'll cover the first three here. The fourth class, convertible debt, is discussed in enhancement topic E, Derivatives and Hedging.

Secured Debt

Secured debt is backed by specific assets. This backing reduces the lenders' risk and, therefore, the bonds' required return. Mortgage bonds, collateral trust bonds, equipment trust certificates, and conditional sales contracts are the most common types of secured debt.

MORTGAGE BOND A bond secured by a lien on specific assets.

Mortgage Bonds
Mortgage bonds are secured by a lien on specific assets of the issuer. The assets are described in detail in the legal document, called a *mortgage,* that grants the lien. If the issuer defaults—fails to make a required payment—or fails to perform some other provision of the loan contract, lenders can seize the assets that secure the mortgage bonds and sell them to pay off the debt obligation. The extra protection the mortgage provides lowers the risk. In turn, that lowers the required return. But the issuer sacrifices flexibility in selling assets. The assets can be sold only with the mortgage bondholders' permission or with suitable replacement collateral.

Collateral Trust Bonds
Collateral trust bonds are similar to mortgage bonds except that the lien is against securities, such as common shares of one of the issuer's subsidiaries, rather than against real property such as plant and equipment.

Equipment Trust Certificates and Conditional Sales Contracts
Equipment trust certificates and conditional sales contracts are frequently issued to finance the purchase of aircraft or railroad rolling stock. The two financing mechanisms are similar. The borrower obtains title to the assets only after it fully repays the debt.

Unsecured Debt

NOTES Unsecured debt with an original maturity of ten years or less.

DEBENTURES Unsecured debt with an original maturity greater than ten years.

Unsecured long-term debt consists of notes and debentures. By securities industry convention, **notes** are unsecured debt with an original maturity of ten years or less. **Debentures** are unsecured debt with an original maturity greater than ten years. Notes and debentures are issued on the strength of the issuer's general credit. A financial contract (the bond indenture) specifies their terms. They are not secured by specific property. If the issuer goes bankrupt, noteholders and debentureholders are classified as general creditors.

Debentures may have different levels of seniority. *Subordinated debentures* rank behind more *senior debentures* in payment of interest and principal, and in claims on the company's assets in the event of bankruptcy. This subordinated position exposes lenders to greater risk. Subordinated debentures therefore have a higher required return than senior debt of the same company.

Tax-Exempt Corporate Debt

Under the Internal Revenue Code, companies can issue tax-exempt bonds for specified purposes. Congress grants tax-exempt bonding authority from time to time to encourage investment in specified types of projects that are in the public interest. The Tax Reform Act of 1986 sharply reduced the list of activities that qualify for tax-exempt financing. Activities that still qualified following that act include solid waste disposal and hazardous waste disposal facilities.

When a project qualifies for tax-exempt financing, holders of the tax-exempt bonds do not have to pay federal income tax on the interest payments they receive. Consequently, they are willing to accept a lower interest rate than on taxable debt. This creates a tax asymmetry. As a general rule, if a company plans to construct facilities that qualify for tax-exempt financing, it should use such financing to the maximum extent.

Self-Check

1. What are the four main classes of long-term corporate debt?

2. What's the difference between secured and unsecured debt?

3. Why is issuing tax-exempt debt beneficial to a company (when a project qualifies for it)?

MAIN FEATURES OF LONG-TERM DEBT

Long-term debt issues (initial maturity of one year or greater) have several common features:

- *Stated maturity.* This is the date the borrower must repay the money it borrowed.
- *Stated principal amount.* This is the amount the borrower must repay.
- *Stated coupon rate of interest.* The interest rate is usually a fixed rate, but it can be a variable rate that's adjusted according to a specified formula.
- *Mandatory redemption (or sinking fund) schedule.* Some bonds contain a sinking fund, whereas others are repaid in a single sum at maturity. A sinking fund involves a sequence of principal repayments prior to the maturity date. Bonds are redeemed in cash at their face amount or else through capital market purchases.[2] The purpose of a sinking fund is to spread out the redemption of the bond over time to decrease the likelihood of default.
- *Optional redemption provision.* The issuer has the right to call the issue (or some portion of it) for early redemption. A schedule of optional redemption prices is specified at the time of issue. Callable bonds usually provide for a grace period immediately following issuance. Bonds are *noncallable* during this period. Many long-term issues contain a weaker provision. The bonds are only *nonrefundable*. The issuer can call the bonds and redeem them for cash or the proceeds from an equity issue (or in some cases, out of the proceeds of a junior debt issue). During the nonrefundable period, the issuer cannot use the proceeds from a new debt issue that ranks senior to, or on a par with, the outstanding debt to refund it.

Protective Covenants

Debt issues contain **covenants** that impose restrictions on the long-term bond issuer. They are contained in a financial contract that is designed to protect the bondholders. For public debt issues, this contract is called a *bond indenture*. A trustee acts as agent for the bondholders and monitors the issuer's compliance with the provisions of the indenture. For a private issue, the contract is called a *bond agreement* or *note agreement*. These contracts specify the maturity, interest rate, and other terms mentioned earlier. In many cases they include a number of restrictive covenants. The covenants often spell out financial tests that must be met before the borrower can (1) incur additional indebtedness (*debt limitation*), (2) use cash to pay dividends or make share repurchases (*dividend limitation*), (3) mortgage assets (*limitation on liens* and/or a *negative pledge clause*), (4) borrow through one of its subsidiaries (*limitation on subsidiary borrowing*), (5) sell major assets (*limitation on asset dispositions*), (6) merge with another company or sell substantially all its assets to another company (*limitation on merger, consolidation,* or *sale*), or (7) sell assets and lease them back (*limitation on sale-and-leaseback*).

COVENANTS Restrictions on the debt issuer imposed by an indenture or a bond (or note) agreement.

Debt Covenants

EXAMPLE

A debt limitation covenant prohibits a borrower from issuing additional long-term debt if it would cause the issuer's interest coverage ratio (EBIT to total interest) to fall below 3.00 times (an *interest coverage test*), or if it would cause its ratio of tangible assets to long-term debt to fall below 1.50 times (an *asset coverage test*). A dividend covenant restricts cash dividends

(*continued on following page*)

---

[2]If the bonds are selling at or above par value, the company will call individual bonds that have been chosen randomly and pay the owner the par value. If the bonds are selling below par value, the indenture usually permits the company to repurchase bonds in the open market to satisfy the sinking fund requirement.

(Debt Covenants *continued from previous page*)

or share repurchases to $10,000,000 plus 50% of cumulative earnings (less the cumulative amount already used for this purpose) since the date of issuance of the bonds.[3]

Any covenant can restrict the company's flexibility. For example, the interest coverage test can restrict its ability to issue new debt. Suppose the company's earnings before interest and taxes (EBIT) are $39 million, and interest is $10 million. How much additional 6% debt can the company incur without reducing the interest coverage ratio below 3.00?

If interest expense rises to $13 million, interest coverage will be 3.00 times (= 39/13). The extra $3 million (= 13 − 10) of interest will allow the company to issue $50 million (= 3/0.06) of debt. ■

Events of Default

EVENTS OF DEFAULT
Events that permit the lenders to demand immediate repayment of the debt.

Bond indentures and bond agreements also specify **events of default.** If the issuer fails to pay interest or repay principal promptly, defaults on another debt issue, or fails to adhere to one of the covenants, the lenders can demand immediate repayment of the debt. Often, however, bondholders will try to negotiate before pursuing default proceedings, because they usually do not want to take ownership of the company.

Self-Check

1. What are the main features of long-term debt instruments?
2. What is a sinking fund schedule? What is its main purpose?
3. What is an optional redemption schedule? Why is it valuable to a company?
4. What are bond covenants? What is their main purpose?

DESIGNING A LONG-TERM DEBT ISSUE

Companies that wish to borrow must offer attractive debt opportunities to potential lenders. Borrowers design the terms of their long-term debt. The Principle of Two-Sided Transactions applies here. The issuer's choices are guided by how much compensation investors will require for the package of features selected.

Choice of Debt Maturity

Ideally, a company would choose a debt maturity that causes its outflow obligations to be in line with its expected inflows. This would bring the total debt service stream into line with its projected total operating cash flow stream. A debt repayment schedule that bunches the company's debt repayment obligations within a few brief periods involves greater insolvency risk than a schedule that spreads these obligations over a longer period. But the matching does not have to be exact. For example, if the company is growing rapidly or changing in significant ways (such as improving profitability), issuing shorter-maturity debt will allow it to renegotiate its debt contract in the future, after its financial condition has improved.

Significance of Including a Sinking Fund   A sinking fund requires the company to repay the debt in installments, rather than in a lump sum. It has two important consequences. First, the need to make principal repayments creates a monitoring device. Second, a sinking

---

[3]See enrichment topic C, Financial Contracting, for a discussion of the use of bond covenants in the financial contracting process.

fund shortens the bond issue's effective maturity from its stated maturity. The company isn't borrowing all the money for the entire life of the issue.

For example, suppose a debt issue that matures in ten years requires equal sinking fund payments at the end of years 6 through 10. Therefore, only one-fifth of the issue is actually borrowed for the entire ten years. One-fifth each is borrowed for only six years, seven years, and so on. This issue has what might be thought of as an effective maturity of eight years. On a time-weighted basis, the debt will be repaid in an average of 8 years. This effective maturity is called **average life.**

AVERAGE LIFE Repayment-weighted average maturity of a debt issue.

Maximum Maturity   Maturities can vary widely and have gotten longer within the past few years. Some companies have issued debt with 40- or 50-year maturities. The Coca-Cola Company even issued 100-year debentures.

Setting the Coupon Rate

Most debt issuers select a coupon rate that will make the bonds worth par. However, at times tax or other factors can make it advantageous either to set the coupon rate below the prevailing market rate or to let the interest rate float according to some specified formula.

Deep-Discount Bonds   In 1981 and 1982, interest rates were very high by historical standards. Many companies issued *deep-discount bonds*. They carried very low interest rates and were sold at prices well below their principal amounts. For example, Du Pont sold $600 million principal amount of 6% debentures due 2001 at a price of 46.852% ($468.52 per $1,000 bond) on November 19, 1981. Recall that in chapter 6 we defined *zero-coupon bonds,* which would be the deepest-discount bonds possible, because they make only a single payment at maturity. Among many others, Beatrice Foods sold $250 million principal amount of zero-coupon notes due February 9, 1992, at a price of 25.50% on February 2, 1982.

Some investors, particularly pension funds, found the deep-discount bonds and zero-coupon bonds attractive. The bonds generally have a call price equal to their par value. Unless the bonds have a call price schedule well below their par value, it is unlikely that a company would ever exercise its call option. Although a reduced risk of a call benefits the bondholders, it is at the expense of the issuer's refunding flexibility.

The discount also reduces the lender's reinvestment risk. In the case of a zero-coupon bond, the investor's "income" each period is effectively reinvested at the issue's yield to maturity, regardless of what interest rates are at the time. This protects the investor's total return from interest rate movements between the dates of issuance and maturity. The absence of reinvestment risk also enables investors such as pension funds to match their investment income against future liabilities more closely than they could with alternative investments. This feature is more valuable at higher levels of interest rates.

Issuers also found the deep-discount bonds and zero-coupon bonds attractive because of a tax asymmetry. At one time, issuers were permitted to deduct an equal portion of the discount (the difference between par value and the issue price) each period. Thus, interest could be deducted at a faster rate than it accrued. This feature is more valuable at higher bond yields. It substantially reduced the effective after-tax cost of the debt. Because most purchasers of zero-coupon bonds were tax-exempt, the manner of amortizing the discount did not affect them.

Fixing the Coupon Rate or Letting It Float   Banks and finance companies earn returns on assets that fluctuate with interest rate movements. They often find it best to issue floating-rate long-term debt.

Most other companies choose to fix the interest rate on long-term debt issues. They adjust the mix of fixed- and floating-rate debt by altering the mix of short-term bank debt and commercial paper on the one hand, and fixed-rate longer-term debt on the other. Before deciding whether to issue floating-rate intermediate- or long-term debt, a company should at least compare the prospective terms for such an issue against the following alternatives:

- Issuing a sequence of shorter-term issues, whose successive maturities match the successive interest-rate adjustment dates
- Issuing fixed-rate debt that matures the day the floating-rate issue does

In the first case, the sequence of shorter-term issues will involve roughly the same degree of interest-rate risk as the longer-term floating-rate issue. The sequence of shorter-term issues will involve greater issuance expenses than the longer-term floating-rate issue. In the second case, the floating-rate issue exposes the issuer to the risk that interest rates will change. Therefore, it is not surprising that industrial companies generally borrow long term on a fixed-rate basis to fund investments in fixed assets. By contrast, when the issuer's revenues are sensitive to movements in interest rates, borrowing on a floating-rate basis may actually reduce the company's financial risk by aligning the fluctuations in revenues and interest expense.

Setting the Optional Redemption Provisions

BOND REFUNDING Replacing an outstanding bond before its maturity with a new bond.

The optional redemption provision is a call option that gives the issuer the right to buy back the issue. Setting the optional redemption provisions involves two questions: Should the issue include a call option? If so, what form should it take? In a perfect capital market environment, an issuer would not derive any net benefit from including a call provision, because lenders would require a yield premium sufficient to compensate them fully for the risk of a call. However, market imperfections might make a call provision advantageous in some situations. The appendix to this chapter discusses when a call provision is advantageous and explains how to evaluate a bond refunding. **Bond refunding** is replacing an outstanding bond before its maturity with a new bond. When current interest rates are below the fixed interest rate on the outstanding bond, refunding may be profitable.

Design of Call Provisions   The call provision included in corporate debt issues has become highly standardized. The first year's call price is normally equal to the public offering price plus the coupon rate. Thereafter, the annual call prices decrease by equal amounts to par, at which price the bonds are callable over the remaining years to maturity. Usually the call provision also imposes limits on the issuer's ability to exercise the option. In the public market, long-term manufacturing company debt issues are nonrefundable for ten years but can be called and paid for out of excess cash or out of the proceeds of an equity issue. Long-term electric utility debt issues are nonrefundable for five years. Long-term telephone utility debt issues are noncallable (for any reason) for five years.

EXAMPLE   *An Optional Redemption Price Schedule for a Long-Term Bond*

Table 14.2 contains an optional redemption price schedule for a long-term bond. The bond has a 25-year maturity. It bears a 10% coupon. Its issue price is 95 (95% of par, or $950 per $1000 principal amount). The initial year's redemption price equals the offering price plus the coupon, 95 + 10 = 105. The bond is callable at par during the last 5 years. The call price steps down annually by equal amounts. There are 20 steps. What is the size of each step?

Each step is $0.25 (= [105 − 100]/20).

Bond Put Options   Interestingly, within the past few years, some corporate issuers have begun to include *put* options in their debt issues. The put option represents a mechanism for reducing agency costs. It limits the possibility of *claim dilution,* such as the loss in value that would result if a company effected a leveraged buyout. The put option limits this loss by permitting holders to force early redemption.

TABLE 14.2
Optional Redemption Price Schedule

YEAR	CALL PRICE	YEAR	CALL PRICE	YEAR	CALL PRICE
1	105.00[a]	8	103.25	15	101.50
2	104.75[a]	9	103.00	16	101.25
3	104.50[a]	10	102.75	17	101.00
4	104.25[a]	11	102.50	18	100.75
5	104.00[a]	12	102.25	19	100.50
6	103.75	13	102.00	20	100.25
7	103.50	14	101.75	21–25	100.00

[a]Bond is not refundable out of the proceeds of a debt issue that ranks senior to, or on a par with, this bond.

Frequency and Timing of Debt Issues

Economies of scale make larger issues relatively more attractive. Larger issues also help pro-mote a relatively liquid secondary market for the bonds. Consequently, companies issue long-term debt in large discrete amounts and plan their debt issues carefully. Because of capital market efficiency, it is unlikely that any single company will be able to gain by speculating on interest rate movements.

When a company plans to issue debt, it may be possible to obtain a modest reduction in the total cost of the transaction with short-term debt management. A company should not issue debt when conditions look volatile or temporarily bad. For example, the supply of funds for non-investment-grade bonds tends to shrink during periods of tight money or particularly volatile interest rates. Also, a large U.S. Treasury financing can temporarily depress the debt market. Therefore, issuers should remain flexible with respect to timing in order to prevent temporary factors from adversely affecting their cost of borrowing.

Self-Check

1. What does the average life of a debt issue measure?

2. What is a deep-discount bond? What is a zero-coupon bond?

3. What types of companies prefer fixed-interest-rate bonds? What types prefer floating-rate debt?

4. What does the optional redemption price schedule for a long-term bond usually look like?

RECENT INNOVATIONS IN THE BOND MARKET

Debt contracts are designed to meet the needs of both borrowers and lenders. Most debt inno-vations involve some form of risk reallocation as compared to conventional debt instruments. Risk reallocation adds value by transferring risks away from issuers or investors to others bet-ter able to bear them. Risk reallocation may also be beneficial if a company can design a se-curity that better suits the risk-return preferences of a particular class of investors. Investors with a comparative advantage in bearing some types of risks will pay more for innovative se-curities that allow them to specialize in bearing such risks. This section describes five recent debt innovations: commodity-linked bonds, collateralized mortgage obligations, floating-rate notes, credit-sensitive notes, and extendible notes.

Commodity-Linked Bonds

Commodity-linked bonds were developed in response to rising and increasingly volatile prices. The principal repayment, and in some cases the coupon payments, are tied to the price of a particular commodity, such as oil or silver, or a specified commodity price index. Such bonds are often structured to enable the producer of a commodity to hedge its exposure to a sharp decline in commodity prices and thus in its revenues. Such securities effectively increase a company's debt capacity by shifting the debt service burden from times when the commodity producer is least able to pay to periods when it is most able to do so. Commodity-linked bonds are analogous to variable-rate loans indexed to some measure of current interest rates.

EXAMPLE

An Oil-Indexed Debt Issue

An oil producer could design an "oil-indexed" debt issue with interest payments that rise and fall with the level of oil prices. Investors might be willing to accept significantly lower yields for two reasons. First, the company's after-interest cash flows would be more stable than in the case of a straight, fixed-rate debt issue. This reduces default risk. Second, some investors may be seeking a "play" on oil prices not otherwise available in the commodity futures or options market. In this latter sense, many securities innovations that reallocate risk also add value by "completing the market." ∎

Collateralized Mortgage Obligations

Collateralized mortgage obligations (CMOs) address a somewhat different kind of "reinvestment risk"—one that investors in mortgage pass-through certificates found troublesome.[4] Most mortgages are prepayable at par at the option of the mortgagor after some brief period. The fact that many mortgages will be paid off if interest rates decline creates a significant "prepayment" risk for investors. If their principal is returned prematurely, they will have to reinvest at lower rates.

To address this prepayment risk, CMOs repackage the mortgage payment stream from a portfolio of mortgages into several series of debt instruments. They are prioritized in terms of their right to receive principal payments. In the simplest form, each series must be repaid in full before any principal payments can be made to the holders of the next series. In this way, a CMO effectively shifts most of the mortgage prepayment risk to the lower-priority class(es). The higher-priority class(es) benefit from a significant reduction in the uncertainty as to when the debt obligation will be fully repaid.

Floating-Rate Notes

Floating-rate notes are one of the innovative securities developed in response to rising and increasingly volatile interest rates. They adjust interest payments to correspond to changes in market interest rates. Floating-rate notes thus reduce the lender's principal risk by transferring interest-rate risk to the borrower. This transfer naturally exposes the *issuer* to floating interest-rate risk. But such a reallocation of interest-rate risk can be of mutual benefit to issuers with assets whose values are directly correlated with interest-rate changes. For this reason, banks and finance companies are prominent among issuers of these securities.

Credit-Sensitive Notes

A new security can increase shareholder value by reducing agency costs. These costs arise out of the inherent conflicts of interest among professional corporate managers, stockholders, and bondholders. For example, managers can increase shareholder value at the expense of bond-

---

[4]Mortgage pass-through certificates consist of ownership interests in a portfolio of mortgages. Principal and interest payments are passed through pro rata to certificate holders.

holders (through claim dilution discussed in enrichment topic C) by leveraging up the company. *Credit-sensitive notes* bear a coupon rate that varies inversely with the issuer's credit standing. The coupon increases if the issuer's credit standing falls.

These securities, however, have a potentially serious risk to the issuer: The interest-rate adjustment mechanism will tend to increase the issuer's debt service burden just when it can least afford it. For instance, if operating cash flows diminish because of a recession, the company's credit rating could fall. The credit-sensitive notes would reduce operating cash flows even further.

Extendible Notes

Extendible notes increase stockholder value by reducing the underwriting commissions and other transaction costs associated with raising capital. They give the issuer or investor the option to extend the security's maturity. For example, extendible notes generally provide for an interest-rate adjustment every two or three years. They thus represent an alternative to rolling over two- or three-year note issues without incurring additional issuance expenses.

Self-Check

1. What is a commodity-linked bond, and what types of companies might find it attractive to issue such bonds?

2. What are collateralized mortgage obligations (CMOs)? How do they reallocate mortgage prepayment risk?

3. Why do banks often issue floating-rate notes?

4. What are credit-sensitive notes?

5. What are extendible notes?

INTERNATIONAL DEBT FINANCING

A company can sell U.S.-dollar-denominated bonds to U.S. investors in the domestic bond market, or to foreign investors in the Eurobond market. Alternatively, a company can sell bonds denominated in a foreign currency. However, issuing bonds denominated in a foreign currency involves a foreign exchange risk. The issuer must either realize foreign currency from its operations or purchase foreign currency to meet its future debt service obligations on this debt. We consider this possibility in chapter 15.

Dollar-Denominated Borrowing in the Eurobond Market

A **Eurobond** is a bond issued outside the country in whose currency it is denominated. Companies headquartered in the United States issue dollar-denominated Eurobonds to investors in Europe (hence the prefix *Euro*) and other areas outside the United States. Eurobonds denominated in other currencies are also issued, but U.S.-dollar-denominated bonds often represent more than half the new bonds issued in the Eurobond market.

The Eurobond market developed during the 1960s when the U.S. government levied an interest equalization tax on the purchase of foreign securities by U.S. investors and imposed restrictions on capital exports by American companies. Large U.S. balance-of-payments deficits continued the outflow of dollar funds. The U.S.-imposed withholding tax on interest payments by domestic companies to foreign investors discouraged foreign investment of these funds in domestic bond issues for many years. Instead, foreign investors avoided this withholding tax by purchasing Eurobonds issued by special-purpose subsidiaries of U.S. companies established in the Netherlands Antilles, which enjoyed a special status as a result of its tax treaty with the United States. The 30% withholding tax was eliminated in 1984,

EUROBOND A bond issued outside the country in whose currency it is denominated.

permitting U.S. companies to sell debt directly to foreign investors free of this tax. Nevertheless, the Eurobond market continues to thrive.

Characteristics of Eurobonds

Dollar-denominated Eurobond issues are as varied as domestic bond issues. Most are straight debt issues, but convertible Eurobonds and Eurobonds with warrants are not uncommon. Nevertheless, there are important differences between the domestic bond market and the Eurobond market:

- The Eurobond market is essentially unregulated. It is a truly international market. Hence, Eurobond yields are somewhat less susceptible to government influence than domestic bond yields. Nevertheless, arbitrage activity ensures that Eurobond yields normally track domestic bond yields fairly closely.

- Eurobond investors usually own assets denominated in several currencies. The relative attractiveness of dollar-denominated Eurobonds, and hence the relationship between bond yields in the domestic bond market and the dollar-denominated Eurobond market, depend on U.S. dollar exchange rates. When the U.S. dollar is appreciating relative to the other major currencies, Eurobond investors tend to increase their purchasing of dollar-denominated Eurobonds (as well as other dollar-denominated assets). This activity can drive Eurobond yields below domestic bond yields and create an attractive borrowing opportunity for U.S. companies. This gives rise to a so-called *Eurobond market window.*

- Because of investors' exchange rate sensitivity, Eurobond maturities are usually shorter, and issue sizes generally smaller, than in the domestic market.

- Eurobonds are generally *bearer bonds.* Issuing bonds in bearer form makes it more difficult to refund them prior to maturity, because most buyers can be contacted directly only when they come to the paying agent to claim their interest payments.

- Eurobonds pay interest *annually.* Because domestic bonds generally pay interest semi-annually, domestic and Eurobonds must be compared based on their annual percentage yields.

EXAMPLE   *Comparing Domestic and Eurobond Borrowing Costs*

A company can issue a 10-year public debt issue at par bearing a 12% coupon in the domestic market. It can also issue 12 1/8% Eurobonds. The total issuance expenses are identical for both issues. We can use the coupon rates to compare the borrowing costs. From equation (5.9), the annual percentage yield for the domestic bond is $(1.06)^2 - 1 = 12.36\%$. For the Eurobond issue it is 12.125%. Therefore, the Eurobond issue is slightly cheaper in spite of its higher coupon rate. ■

The Eurobond market is an alternative to borrowing domestically. Table 14.3 presents the mix of domestic and international bond financing by U.S. companies from 1984 to 1996. The volume of Eurobond financing picked up sharply in 1985 and 1993, when the strength of the U.S. dollar and other factors led to a sharp increase in foreign demand for dollar-denominated bonds.

Self-Check

1. What is a Eurobond? How did the Eurobond market develop?

2. How do dollar-denominated Eurobonds differ from U.S. domestic bonds?

3. What adjustment do you usually have to make in order to compare the cost of issuing Eurobonds with the cost of issuing domestic bonds?

TABLE 14.3

Volume of Domestic and International Bond Financing by U.S. Companies, 1984–1996 (dollar amounts in millions)

YEAR	DOMESTIC[a]	INTERNATIONAL[a]	TOTAL[a]	PERCENT DOMESTIC	TRADE-WEIGHTED DOLLAR EXCHANGE RATE[b]
1984	$ 81,153	$ 17,986	$ 99,139	81.9%	138.19
1985	84,047	40,889	124,936	67.3	143.01
1986	155,737	42,858	198,595	78.4	112.22
1987	125,185	19,565	144,750	86.5	96.94
1988	117,844	17,958	135,802	86.8	92.72
1989	140,455	18,221	158,676	88.5	98.60
1990	103,523	15,517	119,040	87.0	89.09
1991	197,713	23,141	220,854	89.5	89.84
1992	297,647	26,721	324,368	91.8	86.61
1993	406,146	41,000	447,146	90.8	93.18
1994	343,508	49,914	393,422	87.3	91.32
1995	419,691	66,375	486,066	86.3	84.25
1996	490,222	87,314	577,536	84.9	87.34
Total	$2,962,871	$467,459	$3,430,330	86.4	

[a]Includes convertible debt.
[b]Index for which March 1973 = 100.
Sources: Securities Data Company, Inc., and *Federal Reserve Bulletin,* Board of Governors of the Federal Reserve System, Washington, D.C., various issues.

LEASING

You may have rented a bike, a car, or other item. Maybe you rented a trailer to take all your stuff to school. Such rentals are usually for short periods, maybe just a day. But companies often rent equipment and real estate—and sometimes entire plants—for much longer periods.

Leasing is at least 3000 years old. Records show that the Phoenicians chartered ships. Since that time, chartering, a form of ship leasing, has played a major role in the financing of maritime activities.

Lease financing has also expanded to cover just about any type of capital equipment, and its use has grown very rapidly in recent decades. This is partly because capital equipment has become increasingly complex and costly—and quickly obsolete. More importantly, companies in capital intensive industries, such as railroads, airlines, and utilities, have been unable to make full use of the tax deductions that result from asset ownership. Lease financing provides a way to effectively transfer tax deductions from those who can't use them to those who can.

What Is a Lease?

A **lease** is a rental agreement that goes on for a year or longer. Under a lease agreement the owner of an asset (the *lessor*) grants another party (the *lessee*) the exclusive right to use the asset during the specified term of the lease in return for a specified series of payments.

LEASE A rental agreement that extends for one year or longer.

Payments are typically made monthly, quarterly, or semiannually. The first lease payment is usually due the date the lease agreement is signed. Payments are normally constant, like a mortgage or car payment. However, this time pattern can be altered, for example, to provide for lower payments during the early years before the asset reaches its full potential to generate cash flow.

Often lease agreements also give the lessee the option to renew the lease or purchase the asset. Sometimes the purchase option specifies a fixed price, but usually it's the asset's fair market value at the date the lessee exercises the option. If the purchase option isn't exercised, the leased asset continues to belong to the lessor.

Types of Leases

With a *full-service lease,* the lessor (owner) is responsible for maintaining and insuring the assets and for paying any property taxes due on them. With a *net lease,* the lessee is responsible for these costs. *Operating leases* are short term and are generally cancelable at the lessee's option before the end of the lease term. *Financial leases* (or capital leases) are long term. They generally extend over most of the estimated useful economic life of the asset. Usually they cannot be canceled by the lessee before the end of the lease period. Those financial leases that *can* be canceled generally require the lessee to reimburse the lessor for any losses the cancellation causes.

Financial Leases

Financial leases represent an important source of long-term financing. Entering into a financial lease is like entering into a loan agreement. There is an immediate cash inflow equal to the value of the asset. The company realizes this value, because it gets the exclusive use of the asset without having to purchase it. The company realizes the same stream of economic benefits (other than tax deductions) that it would if it had purchased the asset.

On the other hand, the lease agreement calls for specified periodic payments, just like a loan agreement. Moreover, if the lessee fails to make timely lease payments, the lessee runs the risk of bankruptcy, just as it would if it missed an interest payment or principal repayment on a loan.

So the cash flow stream associated with a financial lease is similar in financial effect to the cash flow stream of a loan. This suggests an appropriate starting point for analyzing a financial lease: Compare it to the alternative of (1) borrowing to finance the purchase price of the asset and (2) repaying this loan over the lease term.

EXAMPLE   *Western Mining Corporation's Financial Lease*

Western Mining Corporation has a coal mine project under consideration. The project would cost $100 million. Among the required equipment, Western Mining needs three electric shovels. Each costs $10 million. Western Mining would use each electric shovel for 10 years before selling it. Western expects each electric shovel to be worth $500,000 after 10 years. The company can depreciate each electric shovel on a straight-line basis to its expected salvage value over 10 years for tax purposes. A finance company has offered to lease each electric shovel to Western. The lease would require annual payments of $1.745 million (payable at the end of each year) for 10 years for each shovel. Leasing would require Western to forgo the tax deductions associated with asset ownership.

Table 14.4 illustrates the direct cash flow consequences to the company of lease financing an electric shovel. The company does not have to spend $10 million to purchase the shovel. The effect is equivalent to a cash inflow of $10 million. However, Western must make periodic lease payments. It must also forgo the depreciation tax deductions and residual value of ownership. Partially offsetting the impact of these cash outflows, the lease payments are tax deductible. There is an effective initial net cash inflow of $10.0 million, which is followed by effective net cash outflows of $1.427 million in each of years 1 through 9 and $1.927 million in year 10.

In table 14.4, we assume that Western expects to pay taxes at a 40% marginal rate over the next 10 years. If the company does not expect to pay taxes during that period, the value of the depreciation tax deductions forgone would be zero, and the net cash flow column would change accordingly. ■

Table 14.4 provides only the direct cash flow consequences of the financial lease. As already noted, a financial lease has many of the attributes of a secured loan. In particular, a financial lease displaces a portion of the lessee's debt capacity. In the next section, we'll show how to take into account these debt capacity side effects when valuing a financial lease.

TABLE 14.4

Direct Cash Flow Consequences to Western Mining of Lease Financing an Electric Shovel (dollar amounts in thousands)

YEAR	0	1	2	3	4	5	6	7	8	9	10
Benefits of Leasing:											
Initial outlay (avoided)	+10,000										
Costs of Leasing:											
Lease payments[a]		−1745	−1745	−1745	−1745	−1745	−1745	−1745	−1745	−1745	−1745
Lease payment tax credit[b]		+698	+698	+698	+698	+698	+698	+698	+698	+698	+698
Depreciation tax credits forgone[c]		−380	−380	−380	−380	−380	−380	−380	−380	−380	−380
Salvage value forgone											−500
Net cash flow to lessee	+10,000	−1427	−1427	−1427	−1427	−1427	−1427	−1427	−1427	−1427	−1927

[a]Lease payments made annually in arrears.
[b]Assumes the lessee's marginal income tax rate is 40%.
[c]Assumes straight-line depreciation to a $500,000 terminal book value for tax purposes.

Leasing versus Borrowing and Buying

Lease financing is a substitute for debt. This is because a company must make its lease payments to continue to use the leased asset. Otherwise, the lessor can reclaim the asset (which it legally owns) and sue the lessee for the missed payment.

The consequences of failing to make a lease payment are the same as the consequences of failing to pay interest or repay principal on outstanding debt. The lessor becomes a creditor who can force the lessee into bankruptcy. Consequently, for purposes of financial analysis, a company's lease payment obligations belong in the same risk category as the company's interest and principal repayment obligations.

Advantages of Leasing

Leasing offers a number of possible advantages.

- *More efficient use of tax deductions and tax credits of ownership.* The main reason to choose lease financing is the lessor's ability to use the tax deductions and tax credits associated with asset ownership more efficiently than the lessee can.

- *Reduced risk.* Most leases are short-term operating leases. They provide a convenient way to use an asset for a relatively short period of time. Cancelable operating leases, such as computer leases, relieve the lessee of the risk of product obsolescence. This risk shifting is efficient. The lessor, such as the equipment manufacturer, is usually in a better position to assume the risk. This motivation for leasing reflects the Options Principle: The cancellation option is valuable.

- *Reduced cost of borrowing.* Lessors of assets that can be sold readily, such as vehicles, usually do not have to perform credit analyses quite as detailed as those conducted by general lenders. They are also more likely to be able to use "standardized" lease documentation. Both factors reduce transaction costs and so can result in a lower cost of borrowing for the lessee, particularly a smaller company that may face restricted access to conventional sources of funds.

- *Bankruptcy considerations.* In the case of aircraft and vessels, special provisions of the bankruptcy law give a lessor greater flexibility than a secured lender has to seize the asset in the event of bankruptcy, because the lessor owns the asset. Suppliers of capital to smaller or less creditworthy companies, for which the risk of financial distress is greater, often prefer to advance funds through a lease rather than a loan. Because the lessor retains ownership of the asset, it can seize it if the lessee defaults.

- *An alternative source of financing.* Leasing provides yet another alternative financing method. It may or may not be a better source. Leasing has even enabled transactions that debt covenants did not allow using other methods.[5] However, investors have learned about such loopholes, and more recent debt contracts include leasing restrictions.

Disadvantages of Leasing

There are two principal disadvantages to leasing. First, the lessee gives up the depreciation tax deductions associated with asset ownership. Second, the lessee generally doesn't get the residual value. As a prospective lessee, you should evaluate carefully the cost of losing these benefits. Only then can you decide if leasing is really cheaper than borrowing and buying.

Tax Treatment of Financial Leases

The Internal Revenue Service has established guidelines to distinguish true leases from installment sales agreements and secured loans. If the terms of the leasing arrangement satisfy the guidelines, the lessee can deduct for tax purposes the full amount of each lease payment, and the lessor is entitled to the tax deductions and tax credits of asset ownership.

Valuing a Financial Lease

The leasing and borrowing-and-buying alternatives must be evaluated as though the company's total after-tax obligation (either lease payments or debt service payments) will be exactly the same under either alternative. Otherwise you'd be comparing apples to oranges. By keeping the after-tax obligations the same, what we're really doing is determining which alternative provides the greater amount of financing *given the particular after-tax payment stream.*

The Net Advantage to Leasing

The *net advantage to leasing* equals the purchase price *minus* the present value of the incremental after-tax cash flows, the CFATs, associated with the lease. The net advantage to leasing (NAL) can be expressed in equation form as:

$$NAL = P - PV(CFATs) \tag{14.1}$$

where P is the purchase price and PV(CFATs) is the present value of the CFATs. The purchase price P is the amount of financing the lease provides. The present value PV(CFATs) is the amount of conventional debt financing the CFATs could support.

The net advantage to leasing can be written as

$$NAL = P - \sum_{t=1}^{N} \frac{(1-T)CF_t + TD_t}{[1+(1-T)r']^t} - \frac{SAL}{[1+r]^N} \tag{14.2}$$

where

D_t = the depreciation deduction (for tax purposes, *not* financial reporting purposes) in year t

CF_t = lease payments in year t

N = the number of periods in the life of the lease

NAL = the net advantage to leasing

P = the purchase price of the asset

r = after-tax weighted average cost of capital for the asset

r' = the before-tax cost of debt, assuming 100% debt financing for the asset

---

[5]In a leasing agreement that was later highly publicized, the U.S. Navy leased a fleet of oil tankers instead of getting congressional approval to finance them.

SAL = expected residual value of the asset at the end of the lease

T = the lessee's (asset user's) marginal ordinary income tax rate

The required return for computing the present value of the lease payments and the depreciation tax deductions is the lessee's after-tax cost of identically secured debt. This is because the lease payments belong to the same risk class as the company's debt payments. The lease obligation is secured because the lessor retains ownership of the asset. However, the debt is essentially 100% of the purchase price. So the financial lease obligation is not *overcollateralized*, as is usually the case with conventional secured debt financing. Therefore, the required return for the lease payments must also reflect the higher risk of not having the extra collateral protection.

The expected residual value of the asset—the salvage value—is discounted at a higher required return to reflect its greater riskiness. Residual value is more closely related to overall project economic risk than to financing risk. Therefore, the project's WACC (weighted average cost of capital) is used to compute the present value of the expected residual value.[6]

Equation (14.2) assumes the lease payments are made at the end of each period, rather than in advance, at the beginning of each period. Contracts often require lease payments in advance. In such cases, equation (14.2) is adjusted to reflect the exact payment timing.

Western Mining Corporation's Net Advantage to Leasing

EXAMPLE

Western Mining's cost of debt, assuming 100% debt financing with no overcollateralization, is 12.0% before taxes. The project's WACC is 15%. Western's marginal income tax rate is 40%. The forgone depreciation tax deductions are $950,000 per year (=[10,000,000 − 500,000]/10). The related tax savings forgone are $380,000 per year (= [0.4]950,000). Using equation (14.2), the net advantage to leasing for Western Mining is:

$$\text{NAL} = 10,000,000 - \sum_{t=1}^{10} \frac{(1-0.4)1,745,000 + 380,000}{[1+(1-0.4)0.12]^t} - \frac{500,000}{[1.15]^{10}}$$

$$= 10,000,000 - 9,930,644 - 123,592 = -\$54,236$$

The net advantage to leasing is negative. Western's ability to fully use the tax deductions associated with asset ownership is largely responsible for this negative value. The company should borrow and buy rather than lease the shovel. ∎

Internal-Rate-of-Return Approach

The IRR (internal-rate-of-return) approach bears the same relation to the net-present-value approach in leasing that it does in capital budgeting. The IRR is the discount rate that makes the net advantage to leasing in equation (14.2) equal zero:

$$\text{NAL} = P - \sum_{t=1}^{N} \frac{(1-T)\text{CF}_t + TD_t}{[1+\text{IRR}]^t} - \frac{\text{SAL}}{[1+\text{IRR}]^N} = 0 \qquad (14.3)$$

The IRR represents the *cost of lease financing*. It is an after-tax cost. If the lessee is taxable, the cost of lease financing includes the interest tax deductions lost on displaced debt. It also includes the tax deductions and tax credits and the residual value forgone as a result of lease financing rather than borrowing and buying the asset. If the IRR is less than the company's after-tax cost of identically secured debt, it should lease. Otherwise it should borrow and buy.

---

[6]The asset's residual value at the end of the lease term is also important for tax reasons. If the asset's residual value is expected to be insignificant, the Internal Revenue Service may take the position that the lease is not a true lease. It would then deny the tax deductibility of the portion of the lessee's lease payments that effectively represents principal repayments.

EXAMPLE   *The IRR of Western Mining's Proposed Lease Financing*

Let's apply the IRR approach to Western's proposed lease financing. The IRR solves the equation

$$0 = \$10{,}000{,}000 - \sum_{t=1}^{10} \frac{1{,}427{,}000}{(1 + \text{IRR})^t} - \frac{500{,}000}{(1 + \text{IRR})^{10}}$$

Solving this equation for IRR gives an IRR = 0.0758, or 7.58%.

| $N = 10$ | $r = 7.58$ | $PV = 10{,}000{,}000$ | $PMT = 1{,}427{,}000$ | $FV = 500{,}000$ |

The cost of lease financing is greater than Western's 7.20% after-tax cost of identically secured debt. Western should therefore borrow and buy the asset. ∎

Self-Check

1. What is a lease?
2. How is a financial lease different from an operating lease?
3. What are the main advantages of leasing as compared to conventional debt financing?
4. What are the main disadvantages of leasing?
5. What is the net advantage of leasing? What is the IRR of leasing?

COMMON STOCK

Large companies usually get most of their new common equity internally, that is, from retained earnings. But smaller, or rapidly growing, companies usually also issue new common stock. Even large companies sometimes issue new common equity. In addition, many companies have instituted dividend reinvestment or employee stock purchase plans that also generate common equity.

Main Features of Common Stock

Common stock is a perpetual security that is not redeemable by the issuer. All the issuer can do is offer to repurchase shares. Common stockholders are entitled to get any dividends the company's board of directors declares, but it is not contractually obligated to declare any.

A company's corporate charter specifies the features of its common stock. Many of these features are determined by the corporate laws of the state in which the company is incorporated.

Rights and Privileges of Common Stock

The rights and privileges fall into four categories, voting rights, dividend rights, liquidation rights, and preemptive rights. These are the same rights of ownership we discussed in chapter 1. Let's take a quick look at each.

Voting Rights   Voting may be either cumulative or noncumulative. *Cumulative voting* allows a shareholder to target her votes to a subset of the directors up for reelection. For example, a holder of 100 shares could cast all 100 votes for a single director. State law usually requires an annual election of directors, but many permit staggered elections. A popular structure is to have directors serve three-year terms, with one-third standing for reelection each year.

Shareholders can vote in person or can transfer that vote to a second party who can vote it by proxy. A *proxy* conveys the right to vote your shares to someone else. Management solicits shareholder proxies and usually secures sufficient proxies to assure the election of its nominated slate. However, dissident shareholders can also solicit proxies to mount a **proxy contest** for control. Although the odds of succeeding are long, dissidents have won some battles.

PROXY CONTEST A competition between shareholder groups to acquire a controlling number of voting rights (proxies) as part of a battle for corporate control.

Dividend Rights
State laws usually require that all shares belonging to a single class of common stock must share pro rata in any distributions of dividends to that class of shares. Some companies have two or more classes of common stock with different dividend rights, although this is very unusual in the United States.

Liquidation Rights
Common stockholders are entitled to share pro rata in any distributions of assets by a company when it winds up its affairs and liquidates.

Preemptive Rights
When common stockholders have *preemptive rights,* the company must offer any new issue of common stock—or a new issue of any securities that are convertible into common stock—to existing shareholders before it can offer them to any other prospective investors.

Classification of Shares

A company's corporate charter limits the number of *authorized shares* of common stock. A company can't issue shares unless it has authorized shares available. Increasing the number of authorized shares is usually noncontroversial, but it does require a shareholder vote.

Shares become *issued shares* when a company sells them to investors. Issued shares consist of *outstanding shares* and *treasury shares.* Outstanding shares are held by investors. Treasury shares are those that the company has repurchased from investors. Earnings per share and book value per share calculations are based on the number of outstanding shares.

Table 14.5 shows the shareholders' equity section of the 1996 balance sheet and the 1996 EPS (earnings per share) for E. I. du Pont de Nemours and Company. This company had 900 million shares of common stock authorized at year-end 1996. There were 579,042,725

TABLE 14.5

Shareholders' Equity and EPS of E. I. du Pont de Nemours and Company for 1996 (dollar amounts in millions except for per share amounts)

	AT 12/31/96
Preferred stock, without par value:	
$4.50 Series—1,672,594 shares	$ 167
$3.50 Series— 700,000 shares	70
	237
Common stock, $0.60 per value:	
900,000,000 shares authorized;	
579,042,725 shares issued	347
Additional paid-in capital	6,676
Reinvested earnings	4,908
Common stock held in trust	(1,459)
Common stockholders' equity	10,472
Total stockholders' equity	$ 10,709
Net income	$ 3,636
Preferred dividends	10
Available for common	$ 3,626
Average common shares outstanding	560,675,296
Earnings per common share	$ 6.47

Source: E. I. du Pont de Nemours and Company, *1996 Annual Report to Shareholders,* pp. 29, 30, 31, and 36.

issued shares and 15,495,795 shares with a book value of $1459 million held in trust for unearned employee compensation and benefits (you can think of these as treasury shares). Du Pont had an average of 560,675,296 common shares outstanding during 1996, and earned $6.47 per average outstanding share.

Shares of common stock are issued with or without par value. Because some states do not permit companies to sell shares at a price below par value, par values are generally very small. Par value therefore has little real significance.

Book Value per Common Share

Book value per common share is the ratio of (1) common stockholders' equity, adjusted for any liquidation premium on any preferred or preference stock the company may have outstanding, to (2) the number of common shares outstanding on that date:

$$\text{Book value per common share} = \frac{\text{Common stockholders' equity}}{\text{Number of common shares outstanding}} \qquad (14.4)$$

For example, Du Pont's book value per common share at year-end 1996 was $18.57 (= 10,472/(579 − 15)).[7]

Book value per common share is the value per share if the company's assets are sold and liabilities are paid off at the amounts shown on the balance sheet, including preferred stock paid off at its involuntary liquidation value. Book values generally bear no direct relation to the true liquidation values of a company's assets because, as we explain in chapter 3, book value is based on historical cost and accounting measures of depreciation.

Self-Check

1. What are the rights of common stockholders?

2. What is cumulative voting?

3. What is the difference between authorized shares, outstanding shares, and treasury shares?

4. What is the book value per share of common stock? How is it related to the market price per share?

PREFERRED STOCK

Preferred stock and *preference stock* are hybrid securities. They combine features of common stock and features of debt. They rank senior to common stock, and junior to debt, in claims on the company's operating income and on the company's assets in the event of liquidation. The only significant difference between preferred stock and preference stock is that preferred stock is senior. Dividends must be paid in full on the preferred stock before the company can pay dividends on its preference stock. Companies normally issue preference stock only when charter limitations prevent them from issuing additional preferred stock. Because of the basic similarity between the two, the balance of this section will refer simply to preferred stock.

---

[7]The 15 million shares held in trust are not included in shares outstanding. Du Pont's preferred stock does not carry any *liquidation premium*. But to illustrate how a liquidation premium affects the book value per common share calculation, suppose that the liquidation premium is 5%. Thus, the liquidation value of the preferred stock would be $249 million, or $12 million greater than its face amount. Reducing common stockholders' equity by this amount leads to

$$\text{Book value per common share adjusted for preferred stock liquidation premium} = \frac{10,460}{564} = \$18.55$$

Main Features of Preferred Stock

Preferred stock has the following key features:

- A *par value* or *stated value,* generally $25, $50, or $100 per share. Issues that are to be sold mainly to institutional investors are usually given a $100 par value. Issues targeted to individual investors are usually given a $25 par value, so that a round lot (100 shares) would cost only $2500.

- A stated *dividend rate.* Preferred stock pays dividends quarterly, like common stock, but at a stated rate, like debt. The dividends are not deductible for tax purposes. Also, preferred stock issues usually have a *cumulative dividend feature.* That is, missed dividends are accumulated. This cumulative amount must be paid in full before any cash dividends can be paid on common stock.

- An *optional redemption provision.* Preferred stock usually has optional redemption provisions similar to those found in debt issues.

- *Redeemability.* Preferred stock may be redeemable or nonredeemable. *Redeemable preferred stock* contains sinking fund provisions similar to those found in sinking fund debentures. *Nonredeemable preferred stock* is perpetual, like common stock. In general, the shorter the average life of the preferred stock issue, the more debt-like it is.

Financing with Preferred Stock

Why do companies issue preferred stock? Sinking fund preferred stock is like debt except that the dividend payments are not tax deductible. However, missing a scheduled dividend payment will not force the issuer into default.

Preferred stock dividends qualify for the 70% dividends-received deduction when the preferred stockholder is a corporation. Therefore, preferred stock yields are usually lower than the yields of comparable debt instruments. If a corporation does not have taxable income, because it is carrying forward tax losses from prior years or because of substantial other expenses, it could cost the company less than issuing tax-deductible debt. Thrift and commercial banks have been the heaviest issuers of floating-rate preferred stock.

There is another rationale for issuing preferred stock. Utility companies have been the heaviest issuers of fixed-dividend-rate preferred stock. Preferred stock generally represents between 10% and 15% of an electric utility company's capitalization. Regulated utilities can pass preferred dividends through to their customers, which gives them an incentive to issue preferred stock instead of common stock.

Self-Check

1. What is preferred stock? What are the main features of preferred stock?
2. What is the tax treatment of preferred dividends to (a) the issuing corporation, (b) dividend-receiving corporations, and (c) dividend-receiving individuals?

SUMMARY

Chapter 14 covers long-term financing alternatives, including debt, leases, common stock, and preferred stock.

- Many different types of financial securities make up the long-term financing menu. For example, securities may be equity, debt, or some combination. Securities may also be domestic or international.

- There are four main classes of long-term corporate debt: secured, unsecured, tax-exempt, and convertible debt.
- Mortgage bonds, collateral trust bonds, and equipment trust certificates are common forms of secured debt. Notes and debentures are unsecured debt.
- Debt instruments have a stated maturity, stated principal amount, stated coupon rate of interest (or interest-rate formula in the case of floating-rate debt), mandatory redemption schedule, optional redemption provision, and covenant restrictions designed to protect bondholders.
- The terms of a debt issue will affect the interest rate investors require. Provisions such as the covenants contained in an indenture should be carefully examined. Contractual agreements may be able to reduce agency costs, but such provisions are not costless. For example, restrictive covenants may reduce a company's interest cost, but only at the expense of operating flexibility.
- Recent innovations in the bond market include commodity-linked bonds, collateralized mortgage obligations, floating-rate notes, credit-sensitive notes, and extendible notes.
- Lease financing involves an extended rental agreement. The lessor grants the lessee the exclusive right to use the asset for a specified period. In return the lessee agrees to make a series of fixed lease payments. The lessor owns the asset. It can claim the tax benefits that accompany asset ownership and the asset's residual value at the end of the lease term. The sale of the tax deductions and tax credits of asset ownership is principally responsible for the widespread use of lease financing.
- The exact repayment schedule can affect a company's cost of financing. Compounding affects the cost, because of the time value of money. A sinking fund reduces the maturity of the issue. Therefore, a sinking fund may affect the cost of an issue because of differences in the term structure of interest rates.
- Flotation expenses are normally amortized for tax purposes on a straight-line basis over the life of the issue. This treatment is similar to depreciation on capital equipment.
- Lease financing is essentially equivalent to borrowing and buying the asset. The decision whether to lease must therefore be evaluated relative to borrowing and buying. The net advantage to leasing equals the purchase price of the asset minus the present value of the after-tax lease payment and depreciation tax savings (discounted at the after-tax cost of debt) and minus the present value of the salvage value (discounted at the WACC).
- The main source of new equity capital is retained earnings.
- The rights of stockholders include voting rights, dividend rights, liquidation rights, and the preemptive right.
- Preferred stock has a *par value* or *stated value* and stated *dividend rate,* paying dividends quarterly. If a preferred stock issue has a *cumulative dividend feature,* any missed dividends are accumulated and must be paid in full before any cash dividends can be paid on common stock. Preferred stock usually has optional redemption provisions similar to those found in debt issues. Preferred stock may be redeemable or nonredeemable. *Redeemable preferred stock* contains sinking fund provisions similar to those found in sinking fund debentures. *Nonredeemable preferred stock* is perpetual, like common stock.
- Preferred stock is a hybrid financial instrument. Adjustable-rate preferred stock, which has undergone a number of refinements, gives rise to a tax arbitrage when the issuer is nontaxpaying and the investors are corporations that can use the 70% dividends-received deduction.
- The chapter appendix covers bond refunding in detail. A company should refund outstanding bonds only if it will increase shareholder wealth. Discount the change in after-tax debt service payments at the after-tax cost of money for the new issue, and then subtract the after-tax costs and expenses associated with the refunding. A high-coupon debt issue should be called for optional redemption when its market value reaches its redemption value (or call price).

EQUATION SUMMARY

(14.1)
$$NAL = P - PV(CFATs)$$

(14.2)
$$NAL = P - \sum_{t=1}^{N} \frac{(1-T)CF_t + TD_t}{[1+(1-T)r']^t} - \frac{SAL}{[1+r]^N}$$

$$(14.3) \qquad \text{NAL} = P - \sum_{t=1}^{N} \frac{(1-T)CF_t + TD_t}{[1+\text{IRR}]^t} - \frac{\text{SAL}}{[1+\text{IRR}]^N} = 0$$

$$(14.4) \qquad \text{Book value per common share} = \frac{\text{Common stockholders' equity}}{\text{Number of common shares outstanding}}$$

CHAPTER REVIEW ACTIVITIES

SELF-TEST PROBLEMS

1. (Bond covenants) Dallas Instruments has a large bond issue whose covenants require: (1) that DI's interest coverage ratio exceed 4.0; (2) that DI's ratio of tangible assets to long-term debt exceed 1.50; and (3) that cumulative dividends and share repurchases not exceed 60% of cumulative earnings since the date of the issuance of the bonds. DI has earnings before interest and taxes of $70 million and interest expense of $14 million. Tangibles assets are $400 million and long-term debt is $175 million. Since the bonds were issued, DI has earned $200 million, paid dividends of $40 million, and repurchased $40 million of common stock. Is DI in compliance with its bond covenants?

2. (Comparing borrowing costs) Stephens Security has two financing alternatives: (1) A publicly placed $50 million bond issue. Issuance costs are $1 million, the bond has a 9% coupon paid semiannually, and the bond has a 20-year life. (2) A $50 million private placement with a large pension fund. Issuance costs are $500,000, the bond has a 9.25% annual coupon, and the bond has a 20-year life. Which alternative has the lower cost (annual percentage yield)?

3. (Net advantage to leasing) Arkansas Instruments can purchase a sonic cleaner for $1,000,000. The machine has a 5-year life and would be depreciated straight-line to a $100,000 salvage value. Hibernia Leasing will lease the same machine to AI for five annual $300,000 lease payments paid in arrears (at the end of each year). AI is in the 40% tax bracket. The before-tax cost of borrowing is 10% and the after-tax cost of capital for the project would be 12%.

a. What cash flows does AI realize if it leases the machine instead of buying it?

b. What is the net advantage to leasing (NAL)?

c. What is the IRR of leasing?

SOLUTIONS TO SELF-TEST PROBLEMS

1. For the interest coverage test:

$$\text{Interest coverage} = \$70 \text{ million}/\$14 \text{ million} = 5.0x$$

For the asset coverage test:

$$\text{Asset coverage} = \$400 \text{ million}/\$175 \text{ million} = 2.29x$$

For the dividend test:

$$\text{Payouts} = (\$40 \text{ million} + \$40 \text{ million})/\$200 \text{ million} = 40\%$$

DI is in compliance with these three bond covenants.

2. For either bond, we must find the discount rate that equates the future cash flows with the net proceeds that Stephens receives. We must account for the fact that one pays interest semiannually while the other pays interest annually.

For the public placement, the net proceeds are $49 million, and there are 40 semiannual periods over the life of the bond. The discount rate (per 6-month period) makes the present value of the future payments equal the net proceeds:

$$49,000,000 = \sum_{t=1}^{40} \frac{2,250,000}{(1+i)^t} + \frac{50,000,000}{(1+i)^{40}}$$

Solving this for i gives an interest rate of 4.6104% per 6 months. Compounding twice per year gives us the annual percentage yield: APY $= (1 + 0.046214)^2 - 1 = 0.09433 = 9.433\%$

For the private placement, we find the discount rate (annual in this case) that makes the present value of the future payments equal the net proceeds:

$$49,500,000 = \sum_{t=1}^{20} \frac{4,625,000}{(1+i)^t} + \frac{50,000,000}{(1+i)^{20}}$$

The APY for the private placement is 9.362%.

Even though the private placement has a higher nominal coupon rate, it has the advantage of lower issuance costs and an annual coupon (which causes some of the coupon payments to occur 6 months later than they would with semiannual coupons). The net effect is that the private placement is slightly cheaper.

3. a. At time 0, AI has a $1,000,000 cash inflow because it doesn't make this outlay. At times 1–5, the after-tax cost of the lease payment is $(1 - 0.40)300,000 = \$180,000$. At times 1–5, AI loses the depreciation charge of $180,000 $[= (1,000,000 - 100,000)/5]$. This costs AI an annual tax savings of $0.40(180,000) = \$72,000$. The annual cash outflow for years 1–5 is $\$180,000 + \$72,000 = \$252,000$.

At time 5, AI loses the salvage value of $100,000. If the salvage equals the book value, there is no tax consequence.

b. The annual cash flows are discounted at $(1 - 0.40)10\% = 6\%$. The salvage value is discounted at 12%. Using equation (14.2), the net advantage to leasing is:

$$\text{NAL} = P - \sum_{t=1}^{N} \frac{(1-T)\text{CF}_t + TD_t}{[1 + (1-T)r']^t} - \frac{\text{SAL}}{[1+r]^N}$$

$$= 1,000,000 - \sum_{t=1}^{5} \frac{(1-0.4)300,000 + 0.4(180,000)}{[1.06]^t} - \frac{100,000}{[1.12]^5}$$

$$= 1,000,000 - 1,061,515.67 - 56,742.69 = -\$118,258.36$$

Since the NAL is negative, AI is better off avoiding the lease and purchasing the equipment.

c. Using equation (14.3), the IRR of leasing is 10.65%:

$$\text{NAL} = P - \sum_{t=1}^{N} \frac{(1-T)\text{CF}_t + TD_t}{[1 + \text{IRR}]^t} - \frac{\text{SAL}}{[1 + \text{IRR}]^N} = 0$$

$$1,000,000 - \sum_{t=1}^{5} \frac{252,000}{[1 + \text{IRR}]^t} - \frac{100,000}{[1 + \text{IRR}]^t} = 0$$

| $N = 5$ | $r = 10.65$ | PV = 1,000,000 | PMT = 252,000 | FV = 100,000 |

QUESTIONS

1. Describe the difference between secured and unsecured debt.
2. What is a Eurobond?
3. Explain how the presence of a sinking fund affects the effective maturity of a debt issue.
4. Explain the reasons for including a call option in a corporate bond issue.
5. Explain the role of debt covenants.
6. Define the terms *lease, lessor,* and *lessee.* What is the relationship between a lessor and a lessee?
7. What are the principal advantages and disadvantages of lease financing?
8. What is by far the largest source of new external financing?
9. What is by far the largest source of new equity financing?
10. Why does the par value of common stock have little real significance?
11. Why is preferred stock viewed as a "hybrid" security?
12. Explain each of the following:
    a. Dividend rights
    b. Liquidation rights
    c. Preemptive rights
    d. Voting rights

CHALLENGING QUESTION

13. In what sense is preferred stock:
   a. "Expensive" debt?
   b. "Cheap" equity?

PROBLEM SET A

A1. (Bond covenants) Montgomery Business Products has a large bond issue whose covenants require: (1) that Montgomery's interest coverage ratio exceed 5.0; (2) that its ratio of tangible assets to long-term debt exceed 2.0; and (3) that cumulative dividends and share repurchases not exceed 50% of cumulative earnings since the date of the issuance of the bonds. Montgomery has earnings before interest and taxes of $90 million and interest expense of $20 million. Tangible assets are $500 million and long-term debt is $210 million. Since the bonds were issued, Montgomery has earned $150 million, paid dividends of $60 million, and repurchased $2 million of common stock. Is Montgomery Business Products in compliance with its bond covenants?

A2. (Comparing borrowing costs) Mitchell Automotive is considering two financing alternatives: (1) A publicly placed $75 million bond issue. Issuance costs are $1 million, the bond has an 8% coupon paid semiannually, and the bond has a 20-year life. (2) A $75 million private placement with Pearce Investment Partners, a large money management company. Issuance costs are $500,000, the bond has an 8.125% annual coupon, and the bond has a 20-year life. Which alternative has the lower cost (annual percentage yield)?

A3. (Net advantage to leasing) Hyland Music Company is planning to purchase a new computer system costing $90,000. The computer has a 5-year life and would be depreciated straight-line to a $10,000 salvage value. Stolz Leasing will lease the computer to Hyland for five annual $30,000 lease payments paid in arrears (at the end of each year). Hyland is in the 40% tax bracket. The before-tax cost of borrowing is 10% and the after-tax cost of capital for the project would be 14%.
   a. What cash flows does Hyland realize if it leases the machine instead of buying it?
   b. What is the net advantage to leasing (NAL)?
   c. What is the IRR of leasing?

A4. (Book value per share) Portland Trust has a book value of common stockholders' equity of $55,000,000. The company's financial statements show 2,000,000 authorized shares, 1,000,000 outstanding shares, and 200,000 treasury shares. What is the book value per share?

A5. (Average life of a bond) A debt issue repays principal in three equal installments at the end of years 18 through 20. What is its average life?

A6. (Floating-rate bond) Maberly Marina has a $1 million floating-rate mortgage bond outstanding. The interest rate will float with the 1-year Treasury rate plus 3%. The principal of the loan will remain unchanged for the next 5 years.
   a. What will Maberly's interest expense be if the Treasury rate is 5%, 6%, 9%, 7%, and 7% for the next 5 years?
   b. Suppose that Maberly has a floating-rate bond that charges the 1-year Treasury rate plus 3.25%, but that the rate is capped at 9%. This means that if the formula requires a rate above 9%, Maberly pays only 9%. What would Maberly's interest expense be for the next 5 years if interest rates are 5%, 6%, 9%, 7%, and 7%?

PROBLEM SET B

B1. (Cost of a bond with a sinking fund) A debt issue bears a 10% coupon and has a sinking fund that makes equal payments at the end of years 4 and 5. Interest is paid semiannually at the end of each period.
   a. What are the bond's cash flows for interest payments and repayment of principal?
   b. If the issuing company nets a price equal to 95% of the face amount of the debt, what is the annual pretax cost of the debt (annual percentage yield)?

B2. (Taxes and the cost of borrowing) A new debt issue bearing a 12% coupon and maturing in one lump sum at the end of 10 years involves issuance expenses equal to 2% of the gross proceeds.

a. Assume the issuing company pays tax at a 50% marginal rate. What is the after-tax cost of debt?

b. Suppose instead the company is not a taxpayer and expects never to be. What is the after-tax cost of debt?

c. Explain how your answer to part **b** would change if the company expected to pay taxes at a 50% rate after 5 years.

B3. (Cost of floating-rate debt) A new floating-rate debt issue pays interest annually based on the 1-year Treasury bill rate. Assume zero issuance cost. The issue matures in 5 years. The current 1-year Treasury bill rate is 9%, and the forecast 1-year rates over the next 4 years are 9.25%, 9.5%, 9.75%, and 10%. The coupon equals the beginning-of-period Treasury rate plus 1%. There is no sinking fund.

a. Project the debt service payment stream.

b. Calculate the pretax cost of debt.

c. Calculate the after-tax cost of debt, assuming a 34% tax rate.

B4. (Average life) A long-term debt issue in the amount of $100 million calls for mandatory redemption payments of $20 million each at the end of years 7, 8, and 9, and repayment of the remaining balance (called the *balloon*) at the end of year 10. Calculate the issue's average life.

B5. (Cost of borrowing alternatives) General Aviation Corporation has decided to issue $100 million of 10-year debt. It has three alternatives: (1) A U.S. public offering would require a 9% coupon with interest payable semiannually and $1 million of flotation expense. (2) A U.S. private placement would require a 9⅛% coupon with interest payable semiannually and $750,000 of flotation expense. (3) A Eurobond offering would require a 9⅛% coupon with interest payable annually and $1,250,000 of flotation expense. Assume a tax rate of 34%.

a. Calculate the APY cost of borrowing for each alternative.

b. Which alternative has the lowest cost of borrowing?

c. What other factors should General Aviation consider before it decides how to raise $100 million?

B6. (Cost of borrowing alternatives) Exxon Corporation has a 34% tax rate and has decided to issue $100 million of 7-year debt. It has three alternatives: (1) A U.S. public offering would require an 8% coupon with interest payable semiannually and $900,000 of flotation expense. (2) A U.S. private placement would require an 8⅜% coupon with interest payable semiannually and $500,000 of flotation expense. (3) A Eurobond offering would require an 8⅛% coupon with interest payable annually and $1,100,000 of flotation expense.

a. Calculate the after-tax cost of borrowing for each alternative.

b. Which alternative has the lowest cost of borrowing?

B7. (Bond covenant) A debt issue contains a dividend limitation. Cumulative dividends cannot exceed the sum of $25 million plus 60% of cumulative net income since the debt was issued 3 years ago. The company earned $50 million net income in each of those years. It paid total dividends of $15 million and $20 million the past 2 years and $25 million so far this year. How large a dividend could the company pay at the end of the third year without violating the dividend limitation?

B8. (Bond covenant) A debt issue contains a coverage test that prohibits a company from issuing additional debt if doing so would reduce its interest coverage below 2.50 times. Its earnings before interest and taxes are currently $100 million. Its interest expense is currently $25 million. How much additional 10% debt could the company incur under this test?

B9. (Bond covenant) An asset coverage test prohibits a company from issuing additional long-term debt if doing so would reduce the ratio of tangible assets to long-term debt below 1.50 times. A company currently has $1 billion of tangible assets and $400 million of long-term debt. How much additional long-term debt could it issue if it invests the entire proceeds in tangible assets?

B10. (Stockholder voting) A company has a large group of dissident shareholders who control 20% of the company's stock.

a. Suppose there are 15 board members all up for reelection and that voting is cumulative. How many directors could the dissident shareholders elect?

b. Suppose voting is noncumulative. How many directors could the dissidents elect?

c. Suppose there is cumulative voting but that only 5 directors are up for reelection because the directors' terms are staggered. How long would it take for the dissidents to get in the same position they would be in immediately after the election in part **a?**

d. Explain why the company's top management would prefer to have noncumulative voting for directors.

B11. (Net advantage to leasing) Look back at the Western Mining Corporation example (table 14.4). Suppose the lease rate is $1.7 million payable annually in arrears, and the cost of secured debt is 11%. The required return for the project is 14% assuming Western Mining's tax rate is 40% and 17% assuming its tax rate is zero. The depreciation schedule and residual value are unchanged.

a. Calculate the net advantage to leasing assuming Western Mining's tax rate is 40%. Should Western lease, or borrow and buy?

b. Calculate the net advantage to leasing assuming Western will never be able to use

the tax deductions associated with asset ownership. Should the company lease, or borrow and buy?

B12. (NAL and IRR of leasing) Allied Metals Inc. is considering leasing $1 million worth of manufacturing equipment under a lease that would require annual lease payments in arrears for 5 years. The net cash flow to lessee over the term of the lease (with zero residual value) is given below. Allied's cost of secured debt is 12%, and its cost of capital is 16%. Allied pays taxes at a 34% marginal rate.

Year	0	1	2	3	4	5
Net cash flow (thousands)	1000	−300	−275	−250	−225	−200

a. Calculate the net advantage to leasing.
b. Calculate the IRR for the lease.

c. Should Allied lease, or borrow and buy?

B13. (Net advantage to leasing) Lake Trolley Company is considering whether to lease or buy a new trolley that costs $25,000. The trolley can be depreciated straight-line over an 8-year period to an estimated residual value of $5000. Lake Trolley's cost of 8-year secured debt is 12%. The project's required return is 16% after tax and 20% before tax. National Trolley Leasing Corporation has offered to lease the trolley to Lake Trolley in return for annual payments of $5000 payable at the end of each year.

a. Specify the incremental cash flow stream associated with the lease, assuming Lake Trolley's marginal income tax rate is 40%.

b. Calculate the net advantage to leasing, assuming Lake Trolley's tax rate is 40%. Should Lake Trolley lease, or borrow and buy?

c. Calculate the net advantage to leasing, assuming Lake Trolley's tax rate is zero. Should Lake Trolley lease, or borrow and buy?

d. How would your answers to part **b** and **c** change if the residual value at the end of 8 years is $500?

B14. (NAL and IRR of leasing) Neighborhood Savings Bank is considering leasing $100,000 worth of computer equipment. A 4-year lease would require payments in advance of $22,000 per year. The bank does not currently pay income taxes and does not expect to have to pay income taxes in the foreseeable future. If the bank purchased the computer equipment, it would depreciate the equipment on a straight-line basis down to an estimated salvage value of $20,000 at the end of the fourth year. The bank's cost of secured debt is 14%, and its cost of capital is 20%.

a. Calculate the net advantage to leasing.

b. Calculate the IRR for the lease.

PROBLEM SET C

C1. (Cost of borrowing) A company issues a 10-year debt obligation that bears a 12% coupon rate and gives the investor the right to put the bond back to the issuer at the end of the fifth year at 103% of its face amount. The issue has no sinking fund. Interest is paid semiannually. The issuer's tax rate is 34%.

a. Calculate the after-tax cost of debt, assuming the debt remains outstanding until maturity.

b. Calculate the after-tax cost of debt, assuming investors put the bond back to the

company at the end of the fifth year. (*Note:* Any unamortized issuance expenses and any redemption premium can be deducted for tax purposes in the year of redemption.)

C2. (NAL and IRR of leasing) Show how to modify equations (14.2) and (14.3) to reflect the timing of lease payments when the lease calls for payments *at the beginning* of each year.

APPENDIX 14A: FINANCIAL DISTRESS AND BANKRUPTCY

BANKRUPTCY A legal process of settling a company's debt obligations under bankruptcy court supervision in which the claims on the company's assets are reorganized, or where its assets are liquidated or transferred to its creditors.

When a company borrows money, it enters into a contract to pay interest and repay principal in a timely manner. When the company doesn't generate enough cash to pay its debts, lenders take steps to make the borrower meet its obligations. If the company finds it cannot correct the situation, it will try to renegotiate the terms of the loan. If that proves impossible, the company may have no choice but to file for bankruptcy. **Bankruptcy** is a legal process for liquidating, reorganizing the claims on, or transferring to its creditors a company's assets to settle its debt obligations under bankruptcy court supervision.

The term *bankruptcy* has its origin in medieval Italy. When a merchant did not pay his debts, then lenders would destroy his trading bench. The word *bankruptcy* comes from the Italian term for broken bench, *banca rotta.*

REORGANIZATION The restructuring of a debtor's business and its debts under a court-approved plan designed to restore it to financial health.

Until modern times, the legal system generally favored creditors and treated a financially distressed debtor quite harshly. The first official laws covering bankruptcy were adopted in England in 1542 under King Henry VIII. The law treated a bankrupt individual as a criminal. Punishments ranged from imprisonment in debtors' prison to the death penalty in more serious cases!

LIQUIDATION The process of closing a debtor's business, in which its assets are sold and the proceeds are used to repay its debts.

Today, bankruptcy law offers two ways to resolve financial distress: (1) reorganization and (2) liquidation. **Reorganization** (under Chapter 11 of the bankruptcy code) creates a plan to restructure the debtor's business and restore its financial health. **Liquidation** (under Chapter 7 of the bankruptcy code) is a more extreme solution. Under liquidation, the debtor stops operating the business, its assets are sold, usually piecemeal, and the cash proceeds are paid to the company's creditors according to strict rules of priority. We will discuss both forms of bankruptcy, but we will emphasize reorganization, because U.S. bankruptcy law favors reorganization. However, the bankruptcy laws of most other countries favor liquidation.

FIGURE 14.1
Number of business failures and aggregate liabilities of companies entering bankruptcy, 1971–1995.
Source: Business Failure Record (New York: Dun & Bradstreet, 1996).

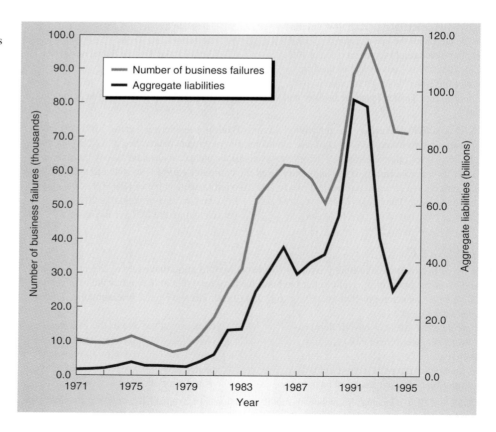

Corporate Financial Distress in the 1990s

The number of business failures accelerated in 1990–1992 (figure 14.1). Business failures rose by 21% in 1990, by 45% in 1991, and by 10% in 1992. The aggregate liabilities of companies entering bankruptcy increased by 33% in 1990 to $56 billion and by 73% in 1991 to $96.8 billion. Both the number and the aggregate liabilities of companies entering bankruptcy have fallen since 1992, although the number of companies entering remains high. As the number and size of bankruptcies grew, bankruptcy came to be regarded as a more acceptable strategy for dealing with financial distress.

Not only has the number of bankruptcies increased sharply, but unprecedented numbers of very large companies have failed. Table 14.6 lists the 25 largest U.S. bankruptcies involving nonbank companies through the end of December 1994. All but one (Penn Central) occurred since 1982, and 17 took place since the beginning of 1990. Several of these bankruptcies, including those of Federated Department Stores, R. H. Macy, Allied Stores, and Southland, followed on the heels of a leveraged buyout.

This experience wasn't limited to the United States. Olympia & York (fourth-largest bankruptcy in table 14.6) is headquartered in Toronto, and Maxwell Communication (sixth largest) is based in London. Both had extensive operations in the United States and filed for bankruptcy court protection in the United States.

TABLE 14.6

The 25 Largest U.S. Bankruptcies of Nonbank Companies[a]

RANK	COMPANY	BANKRUPTCY DATE	ASSETS ($ MILLIONS)
1	Texaco, Inc.	04/12/87	35,892
2	Federated Dept. Stores	01/15/90	7,913
3	Continental Airlines Hldgs.	12/03/90	7,656
4	Olympia & York Devel. Ltd.	05/14/92	7,023
5	Penn Central	06/21/70	6,851
6	Maxwell Communication Corp.	12/16/91	6,352
7	LTV Corp.	07/17/86	6,307
8	Columbia Gas System, Inc.	07/31/91	6,196
9	Macy (R.H.) & Co., Inc.	01/27/92	4,812
10	Eastern Air Lines, Inc.	03/09/89	4,037
11	Allied Stores Corp.	01/15/90	3,502
12	Walter Industries, Inc.	12/27/89	3,462
13	Southland Corp.	10/24/90	3,439
14	Trans World Airlines, Inc.	01/31/92	3,277
15	Public Service Co. of New Hampshire	01/28/88	2,639
16	Pan Am Corp.	01/08/91	2,441
17	Farley, Inc.	09/24/91	2,408
18	Manville Corp.	08/26/82	2,298
19	JWP, Inc.	12/21/93	2,281
20	E-II Holdings, Inc.	07/15/92	2,141
21	Ames Department Stores	04/25/90	2,130
22	Carter Hawley Hale Stores	02/11/91	2,045
23	Circle K Corp., The	05/15/90	2,045
24	Continental Info. Systems	01/13/89	1,926
25	NVR L.P.	04/06/92	1,901

[a]Excluding firms whose primary businesses are banking, insurance, brokerage, or similar financial products.
Source: The 1995 Bankruptcy Yearbook and Almanac (Boston, Mass.: New Generation Research, 1995), p. 62.

Four Aspects of Financial Distress

FINANCIAL DISTRESS
The condition in which a company is unable to pay its debts as they come due.

A company is in **financial distress** when it is having significant trouble paying its debts as they come due. A variety of terms are used to describe a financially distressed company. Four of the more widely used terms are *bankrupt, in default, failed,* and *insolvent.* They have different shades of meaning.

A company is *bankrupt* when it has filed a petition for relief from its creditors under the bankruptcy code, or when it has consented to a filing by its creditors. A company is *in default* when it violates one of the terms of a loan agreement or bond indenture. A company is said to have *failed* if it meets one of several criteria created by Dun & Bradstreet, a leading provider of information about distressed companies. A company is *insolvent* when it is unable to pay its debts. It's useful to distinguish between technical insolvency and bankruptcy insolvency. *Technical insolvency* occurs because of a lack of cash. *Bankruptcy insolvency* occurs when the company's total liabilities exceed the fair market value of its total assets. Technical insolvency may be just a temporary condition. Bankruptcy insolvency usually indicates a more serious distressed condition.

Reorganization Outside Bankruptcy

Bankruptcy is time consuming and expensive. For these reasons, financially distressed companies usually try to reorganize outside bankruptcy before filing for bankruptcy.

Reorganization Techniques   A company can restructure its liabilities outside bankruptcy in one of three ways: (1) exchange new securities for existing securities, (2) solicit securityholders' consent to modify the terms of existing securities, and (3) repurchase existing securities for cash. Each technique requires the company to persuade its securityholders to alter the terms of their investment in the company.

Exchange Offers   If a company finds itself unable to service its debt, it can offer to exchange new securities for some of the outstanding debt. These new securities might consist of common stock, preferred stock, or new debt securities with a lower interest rate or a longer amortization schedule. These transactions reduce the company's leverage ratio and its debt obligations.

Amending the Terms of Outstanding Securities   A company may try to amend its indenture if it can no longer satisfy some of the terms. For example, a company might no longer satisfy a covenant to maintain a specified minimum net worth. The company can solicit the written consent of the debtholders to relax or, perhaps, eliminate the restrictive covenant. To obtain their consent, the company might have to pay cash or increase the interest rate on the debt.

Repurchasing Securities for Cash   Repurchases for cash by a financially troubled company are unusual. Such a company usually does not have enough cash on hand and would probably have trouble arranging credit. Yet, some voluntary debt reductions have taken the form of cash repurchases of outstanding debt. This can get rid of a particularly troublesome debt issue.

Self-Check

1. Cite three ways that a company can restructure its liabilities outside bankruptcy.

2. Why does amending restrictive covenants involve making a payment to debtholders?

Chapter 11 of the Bankruptcy Code—Reorganization

The guiding principle of Chapter 11 reorganizations is that a debtor should be given the opportunity to negotiate with its creditors and achieve a consensual plan of reorganization *provided that the going-concern value of the reorganized debtor exceeds its liquidation value.* Even though a company may not be able to meet its current financial obligations, it may still be able to operate profitably after its debts are restructured. Chapter 11 gives the debtor the opportunity to determine whether restructuring is feasible and in the best interest of its creditors.

Reorganization Value versus Liquidation Value

E X A M P L E

Consider a steel manufacturer with just a single steel mill. The scrap value of the mill is well below its book value. The company owes $100 million, the economy is in a recession, and the company cannot cover its interest payment obligations. The scrap value of the mill plus the value of the land it occupies would provide a total liquidation value of $30 million. The company expects that once the economy recovers from the recession, it will be able to earn a competitive return on its steel-making assets. The present value of the expected cash flows is $60 million. The steel manufacturer cannot service $100 million of debt, and the amount of its liabilities exceeds the value of its assets. But liquidation would be wasteful. The going-concern value is more than the liquidation value, so a higher value can be realized through reorganization. ■

Reorganization in Bankruptcy

Chapter 11 offers a debtor the opportunity to freeze its debts while it attempts to negotiate a reorganization plan with creditors. Reorganization is an administrative procedure. It allows a distressed, but otherwise economically viable, company to survive as a going concern. The objective of this process is to preserve the going-concern value of the debtor.

Debtor in Possession   Table 14.7 on page 532 describes the Chapter 11 process. The company commences this process by filing a *petition for relief.* The company then becomes a **debtor in possession.** It is in possession of the same assets and business it had before the bankruptcy filing. It can continue to operate its business with the same officers and the same board of directors it had before.

DEBTOR IN POSSESSION A company that continues to operate its business under Chapter 11 bankruptcy protection.

Automatic Stay   The bankruptcy code imposes an *automatic stay* of any further efforts by creditors to collect their debts or by secured creditors to seize the collateral securing their loans. This is one of the fundamental protections provided debtors by the bankruptcy code. The automatic stay stops all collection efforts, all foreclosure actions, and all harassment against the debtor. It enables the debtor to hold on to its assets while it strives to put together a plan of reorganization.

Plan of Reorganization   The main objective of the Chapter 11 process is to come up with a **plan of reorganization.** It is crucial to the company's survival as a going concern. The plan of reorganization contains a business plan for the company, establishes a new capital structure, shows how the old debts will be paid off, and provides for the distribution of cash, new securities, and other consideration among the company's creditors and shareholders. The plan must satisfy requirements specified in the bankruptcy code in order for a bankruptcy court to confirm it.

PLAN OF REORGANIZATION A document that contains a blueprint for reorganizing the debtor and its business.

TABLE 14.7
How Chapter 11 Works in a Successful Reorganization

HOW CHAPTER 11 WORKS

Firm Files for Chapter 11 Protection

A firm files for Chapter 11 protection from its creditors either when it is no longer able to pay its debts as they come due or when it anticipates future liabilities that it will not be able to meet. It has usually attempted an out-of-court restructuring but failed to achieve one.

The Chapter 11 Bankruptcy Process

The bankruptcy judge issues an automatic stay.
The firm becomes a *debtor in possession*. The firm operates its business as before the bankruptcy filing except that the bankruptcy court must approve all significant decisions. All debts are frozen. Creditors are precluded from seizing the debtor's property or trying to enforce collection. Lawsuits are suspended.

Different creditor classes form committees.
Generally, the largest seven creditors within each class of creditors are appointed to the committee. Equityholders may also form a single committee or one committee for preferred stockholders and one for common stockholders, if the firm has preferred stock outstanding. The creditors' committee(s) can ask the bankruptcy court to appoint an examiner to investigate possible fraud or mismanagement. They can also petition the bankruptcy court to appoint a trustee to run the firm.

The committee and the debtor negotiate a plan of reorganization.
For the first 120 days after filing for bankruptcy, the firm has the exclusive right to propose a plan of reorganization. Thereafter, unless the bankruptcy court extends the period of exclusivity, any interested party can submit a plan.

Creditors approve the proposed plan of reorganization.
Generally, each class of creditors must approve the plan.[a] A majority of the creditors holding at least two-thirds of the bonds in the class who vote must approve the plan in order for the class to accept it.

The bankruptcy court confirms the plan of reorganization.
The reorganization plan must satisfy the requirements of the bankruptcy code before the bankruptcy court can confirm it.

Reorganized Firm Emerges from Bankruptcy

The reorganized debtor must execute the plan of reorganization. The debtor emerges from Chapter 11 when it has satisfied the conditions in the plan.

[a]The *cramdown* exception is described in the text.

Priority   The liabilities, called *claims,* and equity interests are classified in order of decreasing priority, as follows.

1. Administrative expenses, such as legal, accounting, and trustee fees.
2. Priority claims, which are unsecured claims created in the ordinary course of business and certain "small" claims (for example, wages up to $2000 per person earned within 90 days of the filing).
3. Secured debt.
4. Unsecured senior debt.
5. Subordinated debt.
6. Preferred stock.
7. Common stock.

TABLE 14.8
Summary of the Requirements for Confirming a Plan of Reorganization

SUMMARY OF THE REQUIREMENTS FOR CONFIRMING A PLAN OF REORGANIZATION
1. The plan must be feasible.
• The reorganized debtor must have positive net worth.
• It is unlikely that the reorganized debtor will wind up back in bankruptcy in the foreseeable future.
2. The plan cannot discriminate unfairly among creditors of equal classes.
3. At least one class of creditors must accept the plan, but the cramdown procedure can allow confirmation over the objections of one or more classes of creditors.
• Need at least two-thirds approval in amount of allowed claims that vote *and*
• Need more than one-half approval in number of allowed claims that vote.
4. The plan must satisfy the fair-and-equitable test.
• If an *impaired* class votes against the plan and would receive less than the full amount of its claims under the plan, all junior classes must get nothing under the plan.[a]
• If an *unimpaired* class votes against the plan, it is treated as having approved the plan.
5. The plan must satisfy the best-interests-of-creditors test.
• If the holder of a claim or interest votes against the plan, the claim holder must receive at least as much under the plan as the holder would receive if the debtor were liquidated.

[a]A class is impaired when it will receive cash and securities that are worth less than the amount of its claims.

Absolute Priority   The **absolute priority doctrine** holds that the assets of the debtor should be distributed among creditors and shareholders according to the hierarchy just listed. A more senior claim must be paid in full before a junior claim is permitted to receive *any* distribution. However, senior creditors often find it expedient, in practice, to allow a reorganization plan to deviate from absolute priority. Making a small distribution to a dissenting class can benefit senior creditors when that achieves their support and speeds up the reorganization process.

ABSOLUTE PRIORITY DOCTRINE The legal doctrine that the assets of the debtor should be distributed according to a strict hierarchy.

Requirements for Confirmation   A plan of reorganization must be *feasible* and it must satisfy four basic standards of *fairness*. Table 14.8 summarizes these requirements.

Cramdown   The **cramdown** procedure permits the bankruptcy court to confirm a proposed plan over the objections of one or more classes of creditors. The plan must pass the following test. If a class rejects the plan, (1) it must provide the holders with property whose value is at least equal to the allowed amount of their claims or else (2) no junior class receives anything.[1]

CRAMDOWN The ability of the bankruptcy court to confirm a *plan of reorganization* over the objections of some classes of creditors.

Cramdown

EXAMPLE

Olympic Computer Company is preparing a plan of reorganization. Table 14.9 on page 534 provides Olympic Computer's latest balance sheet. The company has 1000 shares of preferred stock with a par value of $100 per share and a liquidation value of $110 per share. It has 1000 shares of common stock with no par value. It also has $3 million of bank debt (secured by accounts receivable), $2 million of mortgage debt (secured by machinery, equipment, and real estate), and $3 million of subordinated debt (expressly subordinated to the bank debt).

(*continued on following page*)

---

[1]A cramdown plan satisfies the absolute priority doctrine.

(Cramdown *continued from previous page*)

Suppose that an appraisal of Olympic Computer's assets reveals a liquidation value of $1 million for the machinery, equipment, and real estate, $2 million for the receivables, and $1 million for the inventory. The mortgage holder would be paid $1 million, leaving a $1 million deficiency. The banks would be paid $2 million, also leaving a $1 million deficiency. Suppose that administrative claims and tax claims total $1 million. Table 14.10 shows how the available assets would compare to the unsecured claims in a Chapter 7 liquidation.

There is $1 million of cash but $9 million of unsecured claims. Unsecured claimants would be entitled to a cash distribution equal to 1/9 of their claims. Because of the subordination provision, the bank debt is entitled to the share that would otherwise be paid to subordinated debt. Therefore, the banks would be entitled to 4/9 of the cash distribution, and the subordinated debtholders would get nothing.

A careful analysis of Olympic Computer reveals that it has a value of $6 million on a going-concern basis. Suppose also that the $1 million of cash is not needed to run the business. Then Olympic Computer's *reorganization value*—its value as a going concern plus the value of any excess assets—is $7 million.

Table 14.11 illustrates the distributions that would occur in a cramdown. Subtracting $1 million of administrative and tax claims and $3 million for the secured claims from the $7 million of reorganization value leaves $3 million available for distribution to the unsecured claims. These claims total $9 million. Unsecured claims can thus realize $0.33 on the dollar. Note that because Olympic Computer is insolvent, the preferred stockholders and common stockholders will not receive anything in a cramdown.

Trade creditors receive $1.333 million. Because of the subordination provision, subordinated debtholders must pay over to the banks the lesser of (1) their entire share or (2) enough to repay the banks in full. That is, a class of creditors cannot receive an amount that exceeds their claims. The subordination provision makes an additional $1.333 million available for the banks. However, $1 million brings their total distributions to $3 million, the amount of their original claims. The $0.333 million excess remains with the subordinated debtholders. The mortgage bondholders receive 3/9 of their $1 million deficiency, or $0.334 million. ■

TABLE 14.9

Balance Sheet of Olympic Computer Company

OLYMPIC COMPUTER COMPANY			
Balance Sheet before Reorganization **($ millions)**			
Assets		**Liabilities and Stockholders' Equity**	
Cash	$1.0	Accounts payable	$4.0
Accounts receivable[a]	3.0	Bank debt	3.0
Inventory	2.0	Subordinated debt[c]	3.0
Fixed assets[b]	1.0	Mortgage bonds	2.0
Real estate[b]	1.0	Preferred stock	0.1
		Common stock	(4.1)
		Total liabilities and	
Total assets	$8.0	stockholders' equity	$8.0

[a]Pledged to secure the bank debt.
[b]Pledged to secure the mortgage bonds.
[c]Subordinated to the bank debt.

TABLE 14.10
Distributions to Olympic Computer Creditors in Liquidation

DISTRIBUTIONS TO OLYMPIC COMPUTER CREDITORS IN LIQUIDATION

($ millions)

Available Cash		Unsecured Claims	
Cash on balance sheet	$1.0	Accounts payable	$4.0
Liquidation of assets	4.0	Banks' deficiency	1.0
Administrative & tax claims	(1.0)	Subordinated debt	3.0
Secured interests	(3.0)	Mortgagee's deficiency	1.0
Total cash available	$1.0	Total unsecured claims	$9.0

CASH DISTRIBUTIONS

	Secured Claim	Unsecured Claim	Total Distribution
Trade creditors	—	$0.444	$0.444
Banks	$2.0	0.444	2.444
Subordinated debtholders	—	—	—
Mortgage bondholders	1.0	0.112	1.112
Total	$3.0	$1.0	$4.0

TABLE 14.11
Distributions to Olympic Computer Creditors in a Cramdown

DISTRIBUTION TO OLYMPIC COMPUTER CREDITORS UNDER REORGANIZATION

($ millions)

Available Consideration		Unsecured Claims	
Going-concern value	$6.0	Accounts payable	$4.0
Cash on balance sheet	1.0	Banks' deficiency	1.0
Administrative & tax claims	(1.0)	Subordinated debt	3.0
Secured interests	(3.0)	Mortgagee's deficiency	1.0
Total available consideration	$3.0	Total unsecured claims	$9.0

DISTRIBUTIONS

	Secured Claim	Unsecured Claim	Total Distribution
Trade creditors	—	$1.333	$1.333
Banks	$2.0	1.0	3.0
Subordinated debtholders	—	0.333	0.333
Mortgage bondholders	1.0	0.334	1.334
Preferred stockholders	—	—	—
Common stockholders	—	—	—
Total	$3.0	$3.0	$6.0

Advantages and Disadvantages of Reorganizing Under Chapter 11

A reorganization under Chapter 11 has advantages and disadvantages compared to an out-of-court restructuring. They are summarized in table 14.12.

TABLE 14.12

Advantages and Disadvantages of Reorganizing Under Chapter 11

ADVANTAGES	DISADVANTAGES
1. Filing the bankruptcy petition automatically stays all creditor collection efforts.	1. The debtor's business is disrupted for some period of time, in part because the debtor cannot pay pre-petition creditors. Some of its former vendors, suppliers, and customers may decline to do business with a bankrupt company.
2. The bankruptcy process provides the debtor with a single forum—bankruptcy court—for conducting negotiations and resolving disputes.	2. A debtor in possession must meet stringent reporting requirements.
3. The bankruptcy court can authorize debtor-in-possession financing for working capital purposes.	3. The bankruptcy court must approve all transactions outside the ordinary course of business.
4. The bankruptcy court can authorize the debtor in possession to reject unfavorable leases and other contracts.	4. A bankruptcy filing may trigger the filing of claims that would not have been asserted in an out-of-court restructuring (for example, a claim concerning a potential environmental cleanup liability).
5. All claims (including contingent claims) can be dealt with at one time and a plan developed for discharging them.	5. The need for official committees to represent creditors and stockholders, as well as legal and financial advisors for these committees (paid for by the debtor), can make bankruptcy much more expensive than an out-of-court restructuring.
6. Interest stops accruing on unsecured claims.	6. The debtor's management might lose control of the company through either the appointment of a trustee or the adoption of a creditors' reorganization plan.
7. Claims resulting from the rejection of leases or contracts are capped.	
8. If a proposed plan has been accepted by at least two-thirds in dollar amount of claims, and by more than one-half in number of claims, actually voting in each class of creditors, the bankruptcy court can confirm it over the objection of dissenting creditors.	
9. Even if a class of creditors rejects the plan, the court can still confirm it under the cramdown rules.	
10. Once the plan is confirmed, all of the debtor's creditors and stockholders are bound by its terms.	
11. Restructuring through bankruptcy may enable the debtor to avoid having to pay taxes on the income that results when debt is retired at less than its face amount.	

On balance, a private out-of-court restructuring can save significant direct and indirect costs. It does so mainly by avoiding the delays inherent in a bankruptcy restructuring. The private alternative is more likely to work when the debtor's liabilities are concentrated in the hands of a fairly small number of banks or other large, sophisticated financial institutions.

Prepackaged Plans of Reorganization

In a **prepackaged bankruptcy,** the debtor and creditors negotiate a plan of reorganization and then file it along with the bankruptcy petition. A prepackaged bankruptcy attempts to combine the advantages—and avoid the disadvantages—of the bankruptcy process and out-of-court restructurings. The requirements for confirming a prepackaged plan are the same as in a traditional reorganization.

PREPACKAGED BANK-RUPTCY A plan of reorganization negotiated between the debtor and creditors and then filed along with the bankruptcy petition.

The prepackaged bankruptcy process has some advantages relative to alternative methods of reorganization. (1) Approval is easier to obtain. Exchange offers usually require 90% or 95% of the debtholders to accept the exchange offer. The bankruptcy code sets lower acceptance levels. (2) The confirmed plan is binding on all debtholders, whether they vote to accept the plan or not. (3) Filing for bankruptcy often permits the debtor to realize tax advantages that are not available in an out-of-court restructuring. (4) Filing for bankruptcy allows the debtor to reject burdensome leases and other contracts.

Crystal Oil Company's Prepackaged Bankruptcy

EXAMPLE

The first significant prepackaged bankruptcy was of Crystal Oil Company, an independent oil and gas producer headquartered in Louisiana, in 1986. It emerged from bankruptcy less than 3 months later with its capital structure completely reorganized. Total indebtedness was reduced from $277 million to $129 million. Debtholders received common stock, convertible notes, convertible preferred stock, and warrants to purchase common stock in exchange for the old debt.

Crystal Oil's reorganization plan had been presented to creditors 3 months prior to the bankruptcy filing. All seven classes of public debtholders accepted the plan. However, Crystal Oil's two most senior creditors, Bankers Trust and Halliburton Company, did not initially accept the plan. Both had liens on Crystal Oil's oil and gas properties. Bankers Trust eventually accepted a revised plan. Halliburton never did. The bankruptcy court approved the plan over Halliburton's objection. ■

Chapter 7 of the Bankruptcy Code—Liquidation

When the prospects for reorganizing a debtor are so poor that it would be unreasonable to invest further time, effort, and financial resources in the effort, the only alternative is liquidation. The company or its creditors file a petition under Chapter 7 (bankruptcy with intent to liquidate the company). In some cases, the parties to a Chapter 11 cannot agree upon a plan of reorganization and decide to convert to a Chapter 7. Pan Am Corporation and Eastern Airlines are examples.

Liquidation is preferable to reorganization when selling the debtor's assets in liquidation would produce value that exceeds the debtor's reorganization value. Usually, the key variables are time and risk. For instance, the financial advisors of the debtor may believe that the realizable economic value of the debtor will eventually exceed the liquidation value. But suppose the value to be realized and the time it would take are highly uncertain. In that case, the expected present value of the debtor's assets as a going concern might be less than their currently realizable liquidation value. Then liquidation is in the best interest of creditors.

Self-Check
1. What is a prepackaged bankruptcy? How does it work?
2. What are the advantages of a prepackaged bankruptcy?
3. When is it better to liquidate a debtor than to attempt a reorganization?

APPENDIX 14A SUMMARY

- A company seeks protection from its creditors under Chapter 11 when it's no longer able to pay its debts as they come due, or when it anticipates future liabilities that it will not be able to meet. Chapter 11 has a guiding principle. A debtor should be given the opportunity to negotiate with its creditors and achieve a plan of reorganization, provided that the value of the reorganized debtor exceeds its liquidation value.
- An out-of-court restructuring is normally less expensive and less time consuming than a Chapter 11 reorganization.
- When a distressed company's liquidation value exceeds its reorganization value, it should file for liquidation under Chapter 7.
- A prepackaged bankruptcy has several advantages over an out-of-court restructuring. It is an effective way to deal with the holdout problem.
- Absolute priority is not always observed in bankruptcy. In many cases, making a small distribution to a dissenting class will be advantageous to senior creditors. Buying dissenters' support is likely to speed up the reorganization process and reduce expenses.

APPENDIX 14A REVIEW ACTIVITIES

QUESTIONS

1. What is the purpose of the bankruptcy code? When should a company file for bankruptcy?
2. How do a Chapter 7 liquidation and a Chapter 11 reorganization differ?
3. What is the basic premise of Chapter 11?
4. Under what circumstances will:
   a. reorganization be preferred over liquidation?
   b. liquidation be preferred over reorganization?
5. Explain what is meant by the absolute priority doctrine. What are the arguments for and against enforcing absolute priority in reorganization?
6. How would the following classes of claims and interests be ordered for bankruptcy purposes?
   a. Accounts payable
   b. Legal fees due to the bankruptcy process
   c. First mortgage bonds
   d. Common stock
   e. Unsecured bank debt
   f. Second mortgage bonds
   g. Bank debt secured by current assets
   h. Preferred stock
   i. Debentures subordinated to all bank debt
   j. Tax claims

PROBLEMS

B1. (Value of debt received in a reorganization) A reorganization plan provides that creditors will receive new debt. It will pay a 10% coupon annually and mature in a lump sum at the end of 10 years. The debtor's financial advisors estimate that the required return for the new debt is 16%. What is the new debt worth as a percentage of its face amount?

B2. (Distributions in bankruptcy) In the cramdown example presented in this appendix, suppose that Olympic Computer's subordinated debt is subordinated not only to the bank debt but also to the accounts payable and the mortgage bonds. How would the distributions in a cramdown change?

B3. (Distributions in bankruptcy) A company had assets worth $700 million. It borrowed $100 million, which was secured by a mortgage on its newest factory. The company also borrowed $200 million on an unsecured basis. The company subsequently goes bankrupt, and its assets are then worth just $150 million. Its newest factory can be sold for only $50 million. Who gets what?

B4. (Liquidation) Boris Baking is in bankruptcy. Since it is worth less as a going concern than in liquidation, the company will be liquidated. The company's balance sheet prior to bankruptcy is:

ASSETS		LIABILITIES AND STOCKHOLDERS' EQUITY	
Cash	$ 500	Accounts payable	$1500
Accounts receivable	2000	Bank loan	1500
Inventory	2000	Mortgage bond	4000
Fixed assets	5000	Subordinated debenture	2500
		Preferred stock	500
		Common stock	(500)
Total assets	$9500	Total liabilities & equity	$9500

The bank loan is secured by accounts receivable and the mortgage bond is secured by fixed assets. The subordinated debenture is subordinated to the mortgage bond.

The liquidation values for the assets are $500 for cash, $1600 for accounts receivable, $1000 for inventory, and $2500 for fixed assets. How will the $5600 total liquidation value be allocated among the company's claimants? Assume that there are $500 of administrative expenses (for legal and accounting fees) and that absolute priority is followed.

APPENDIX 14B: BOND REFUNDING

A bond's optional redemption provision is a valuable call option. It gives the issuer the right to redeem the bond prior to maturity. If interest rates rise throughout the life of the issue, the call option will expire worthless. But if interest rates fall sufficiently, the issuer can call the bond and replace it with lower-cost debt.

Replacing an outstanding bond with a new bond before its scheduled maturity is referred to as *refunding*. A well-managed company will look for opportunities to refund its debt at a profit. We'll show you how a company can evaluate a bond refunding opportunity to decide whether it's in the shareholders' interest to refund.

A call provision isn't free. Consider the other side of the transaction, the bondholders' viewpoint. If interest rates fall and the issuer calls the bond, the bondholders will have to reinvest their funds at a lower interest rate. A higher required return is needed to compensate them. Therefore the company must decide whether including a call feature is worth the price.

What Gives Rise to Profitable Bond Refunding Opportunities?

Volatile interest rates create profitable bond refunding opportunities. Figure 14.2 on page 540 illustrates that between 1985 and 1987, and again between 1993 and 1994, interest rates on corporate bonds decreased sharply. These decreases gave rise to profitable refunding opportunities.

Debt Service Parity

When a company refunds debt, its capital structure may change. It's important to calculate the net benefit to shareholders of a refunding exclusive of these side effects. One method of neutralizing them is called the *debt service parity (DSP) approach*. The basic idea is simple.

Construct a replacement debt obligation that has the same after-tax payments, period-by-period, as the outstanding debt obligation. If this stream of after-tax debt service payments will support sufficient new debt to cover the cost of retiring the outstanding issue *and* cover all transaction costs, then refinancing will provide a net benefit to the company's shareholders. The DSP approach values the incremental after-tax cash flows by computing their present value at the after-tax cost of the new debt issue.

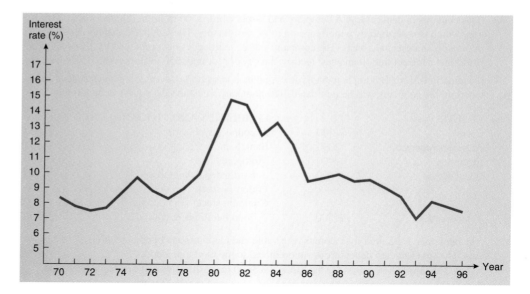

FIGURE 14.2
Average yield on AA-rated long-term corporate bonds, 1970–1996. *Sources: Moody's Bond Record,* Moody's Investors Service, Inc., New York, various issues.

The DSP principle extends beyond cash flows. Parity implies that all rights and obligations of the old issue must also be maintained in the new. Therefore, the sinking fund schedule and maturity of the hypothetical new issue must be identical to those remaining on the old issue.

For example, a debt issue with a remaining life of six years would be evaluated against a hypothetical refunding issue with a six-year life. Note that if the refunding were undertaken, the actual new issue might have a maturity other than six years. The maturity of the actual new issue is a separate decision. The company should choose the features of the new debt only after it has determined that refunding is advantageous.

Self-Check

1. What does it mean to refund a bond issue?

2. What gives rise to profitable bond refunding opportunities?

3. Briefly describe the debt service parity (DSP) approach to bond refunding.

Tax Considerations

As with other financial decisions, the refunding decision must reflect the related tax consequences. This involves adjusting the cash flows and the discount rate appropriately. As we've said, tax laws change, so the current tax treatment must be used.

All of the expenses connected with a refunding are tax deductible, some during the year of the refunding and the others over the life of the new issue. The basic rule is (1) expenses connected with retiring the old issue may be deducted in the year of the refunding, and (2) expenses connected with the new issue (including any discount or premium) must be amortized over its life.

Those expenses that are deductible in the year the refunding occurs include:

- The call premium—the difference between the call price and par value.
- The unamortized balance of issuance expenses on the old debt.

The Net Advantage of Refunding

A company should undertake a refunding only if it will increase shareholder wealth. The *net advantage of refunding* (NA) equals the present value savings (PVS) minus the total cost (Cost) of the refunding:

$$NA = PVS - Cost \qquad (14.5)$$

Both PVS and Cost are computed on a present value after-tax basis. If the present value savings exceed the total cost, NA is positive and the refunding is attractive.

Transaction costs can affect the refunding decision. We will include their effect on the decision but will not explain the details of calculating the after-tax transaction cost of refunding. Problem C1 at the end of appendix B explores this aspect.

Under the debt service parity approach, PVS equals the present value of the after-tax interest savings. The discount rate is the after-tax cost of the new debt issue.

The net advantage of refunding high-coupon debt can be expressed as

$$NA = \sum_{n=1}^{N} \frac{(1-T)(r-r')D}{[1+(1-T)r']^n} - (1-T)(P-D) - Trans \qquad (14.6)$$

where the variables are defined as

D = par value of the old debt

N = number of periods until the old debt is scheduled to mature

P = call (strike) price of the old debt (excluding accrued interest)

r = coupon rate on the old debt

r' = coupon rate on a new debt issue sold at par

T = issuer's marginal ordinary income tax rate

Trans = after-tax transaction costs of refunding

The first term in equation (14.6) represents the present value of the after-tax savings from replacing the old debt at the new interest rate. The second and third terms represent the after-tax cost of buying back the old debt (the call premium) and issuing the new debt.

Analyzing a High-Coupon Bond Refunding Opportunity

EXAMPLE

Palo Alto Refinancing (PAR) specializes in helping consumers refinance their personal debt. PAR's managers have decided that charity begins at home. The company has a $100 million bond issue outstanding, which is scheduled to mature in a single lump sum 15 years from today. This issue has a 12% coupon rate (6% semiannual). PAR can call them at a strike price of $1050 each. PAR can issue new 15-year noncallable debt at par value if they carry a 10.40% coupon rate (5.20% semiannual). The other terms of the new bonds are identical to those of the old bonds. PAR's marginal income tax rate is 34%. After-tax transaction costs are $2 million. Table 14.13 on page 542 shows the calculation of the net advantage of refunding the 12% issue.

The after-tax interest savings per period amount to

$$(1-T)(r-r')D = (1-0.34)(0.06-0.052)100,000,000 = \$528,000$$

The discount rate is the after-tax cost of the new debt, 3.432% (= [1 − 0.34]5.20). The present value of the stream of savings is

$$\sum_{n=1}^{30} \frac{528,000}{(1.03432)^n} = \$9,794,266$$

(*continued on following page*)

(Analyzing a High-Coupon Bond Refunding Opportunity *continued from previous page*)

The call price exceeds the par value by $50 per bond. There are 100,000 bonds (= 100,000,000/1000) outstanding. PAR will incur an after-tax redemption cost of $5,300,000 (= [1 − 0.34][50]100,000 + 2 million). The net advantage of refunding is

$$NA = 9,794,266 − 5,300,000 = \$4,494,266$$

Why Companies Issue Callable Bonds

In a perfect capital market environment, including a call provision would be a zero-sum game. Any gain to the party on one side of the transaction would be exactly offset by a loss to the party on the other side of the transaction. (Recall the Principle of Two-Sided Transactions.) We've identified three capital market imperfections. These imperfections might explain why companies often include call provisions in bonds they issue.

Asymmetric Information and the Possibility of Wealth Expropriation   When a company borrows, debtholders may require a higher rate of interest because of the possibility of asset substitution. Later on, when a company has not engaged in asset substitution, the debt can increase in value. The company may be able to recoup this increase in value from the debtholders by exercising its call option. In this way the call option offers a bonus for companies that forgo their asset-substitution option.

Taxes   A company can benefit from including a call option when it is taxed at a higher marginal rate than bondholders. When this is so, the call option is worth more to the issuer than the after-tax cost of the interest rate premium it must pay bondholders to obtain this privilege. This is another example of how a tax asymmetry can create a non-zero-sum game.

TABLE 14.13
The Net Advantage of Refunding PAR's Outstanding 12% Bonds

		Old Issue	New Issue
I.	Conditions		
	Principal amount	$100,000,000	$100,000,000
	Coupon	12%	10.40%
	Maturity	15 years	15 years
		Before Taxes	**After Taxes**
II.	Interest Savings		
	Interest on old bonds per period	$ 6,000,000	$ 3,960,000
	Interest on new bonds per period	5,200,000	3,432,000
	Interest savings per period	800,000	528,000
	Present value savings[a]		$ 9,794,266
III.	Total Cost		
	Redemption premium	$ 5,000,000	$ 3,300,000
	After-tax transaction costs		2,000,000
			$ 5,300,000
IV.	Net Advantage		
	Present value savings		$ 9,794,266
	Total cost		5,300,000
	Net advantage of refunding		$ 4,494,266

[a]The discount rate is 3.432% per semiannual period (= [1 − 0.34]5.2).

Transaction Costs Calling bonds involves lower transaction costs than repurchasing them in the open market. A company might expect its credit standing to improve prior to the debt's maturity. It would then refund the debt. Lower transaction costs provide an incentive to include a call provision.

Timing Considerations

Suppose a company determines that refunding a debt issue would be profitable. It should also consider that it might be more profitable to postpone the refunding. If the call price exceeds the market price of the bonds, then calling the bonds immediately involves a transfer of wealth from the shareholders to the bondholders. It equals the difference between the aggregate redemption price for the bonds and their aggregate market value immediately prior to the announcement of the call.

If capital markets were perfect, this transfer of wealth could be avoided by following a simple decision rule: Call a (nonconvertible) bond issue only when the market price of the bonds (including accrued interest) reaches the *effective call price,* that is, the stated call price plus accrued interest. However, because transaction costs are not zero, the timing issue is not so simply resolved.

In practice, companies often call their high-coupon bond issues for redemption before their market value reaches the call price. Issuers thus face a call-or-wait decision. Even if immediate refunding is (apparently) profitable, a greater value might be possible if the company postpones the refunding. Making the refund-or-wait decision requires assessing the relative likelihood of favorable changes in future interest rates.

Self-Check

1. What does it mean to say that the net advantage of refunding a bond issue is positive?

2. True or false? Discounting the change in the after-tax debt service payment at the after-tax cost of the new issue is consistent with the debt service parity (DSP) approach.

3. Why might refunding high-coupon debt involve an opportunity cost?

4. Why do companies issue callable bonds?

APPENDIX 14B REVIEW ACTIVITIES

QUESTIONS

1. What is a high-coupon bond refunding?
2. Explain briefly the debt service parity approach to evaluating the net advantage of a proposed bond refunding.
3. Explain why a company should not necessarily refund an outstanding debt issue the instant the net advantage of refunding first becomes positive.
4. Why might a company find it advantageous to include an optional redemption feature in its debt issue?

PROBLEMS

B1. (Net advantage of refunding) A company has outstanding a $50 million debt issue that bears a 15% coupon (7.5% semiannual). It matures in a lump sum at the end of 10 years. The call price is $1100 per bond. A new 10-year debt issue would require a 12.5% coupon (6.25% semiannual). The company's marginal income tax rate is 40%.

a. Calculate the semiannual after-tax savings that would result if the company issued $50 million of 12.5% debt.

b. Calculate the net advantage of refunding the 15% debt issue.

B2. (Net advantage of refunding) Tara Corporation has $70 million of 12% bonds outstanding. It can call the bonds at a price of $1100 per bond. The bonds have a remaining life of 10 years. Tara is considering refunding the issue with a new $70 million issue of 11% bonds. Tara's tax rate is 40%. What is Tara's net advantage of refunding the outstanding bonds?

B3. (Net advantage of refunding) The Kaplan Corporation sold $50 million of 25-year, 10% bonds during a period of very high interest rates 10 years ago. Kaplan can now refund that bond issue with 15-year, 8% bonds, which would sell at par value. There is a 5% call premium. Kaplan's tax rate is 40%. What is Kaplan's NA of refunding the outstanding bonds?

C1. (Including detailed transaction costs in the net advantage of refunding) The net advantage of refunding high-coupon debt can be expressed as

$$NA = \sum_{n=1}^{N} \frac{(1-T)(r-r')D + T[(E-U)/N]}{[1+(1-T)r']^n}$$
$$-(1-T)(P-D) - [E - (1-T)F - TU] - (P-B)$$

where D, N, P, r, r', and T are defined as in equation (14.6) and
B = the market price of the old debt issue (excluding accrued interest);
E = the underwriting commissions and other expenses associated with the new debt issue;
F = the tax-deductible, out-of-pocket expenses associated with the refunding; and
U = the unamortized balance of issuance expenses on the old debt.

a. Issuance expenses are tax-deductible over the life of the debt issue on a straight-line basis. Interpret the term $T[(E-U)/N]$.

b. The unamortized balance of issuance expenses on the old debt can be written off for tax purposes in the year of refunding. Interpret the term TU.

c. Suppose bonds are redeemed at a price that exceeds their market value. Bondholders benefit at the expense of shareholders. Interpret the term $P-B$. Why is it subtracted?

d. Explain how the tax treatment of issuance expenses in bond refunding is like the tax treatment of equipment cost in capital budgeting.

C2. (Net advantage of refunding with detailed transaction costs) Northern Gas Company has outstanding $100 million principal amount of 12% debentures (6% payable semiannually) that mature in a lump sum at the end of 20 years. The unamortized balance of issuance expenses is $500,000. A par-value $100 million noncallable refunding issue would require a 10% coupon (5% semiannual) and $750,000 of issuance expenses. The 12% issue is callable at a price of $1020 per bond (pretax), and miscellaneous debt retirement costs amount to $3.00 per bond. Northern Gas's marginal income tax rate is 40%.

a. Calculate the net advantage of refunding, assuming the bonds have a market value of $1020 each.

b. How would your answer to part **a** change if the 12% debentures were selling at a market price of $1017 per bond.

BIBLIOGRAPHY

Alderson, Michael J., and Brian L. Betker. "Liquidation Costs and Capital Structure," *Journal of Financial Economics,* 1995, 39(1):45–70.

Allen, David S., Robert E. Lamy, and G. Rodney Thompson. "Agency Costs and Alternative Call Provisions: An Empirical Investigation," *Financial Management,* 1987, 16(4):37–44.

Asquith, Paul, and David W. Mullins, Jr. "Convertible Debt: Corporate Call Policy and Voluntary Conversion," *Journal of Finance,* 1991, 46(4):1273–1290.

Aziz, Abdul, and Gerald H. Lawson. "Cash Flow Reporting and Financial Distress Models: Testing of Hypotheses," *Financial Management,* 1989, 18(1):55–63.

Barber, Brad M. "Exchangeable Debt," *Financial Management,* 1993, 22(2):48–60.

Barrow, Janice M., and Paul M. Horvitz. "Response of Distressed Firms to Incentives: Thrift Institution Performance Under the FSLIC Management Consignment Program," *Financial Management,* 1993, 22(3):176–184.

Bayless, Mark E., and J. David Diltz. "An Empirical Study of the Debt Displacement Effects of Leasing," *Financial Management,* 1986, 15(4):53–60.

Beranek, William, and Steven L. Jones. "The Emerging Market for Trade Claims of Bankrupt Firms," *Financial Management,* 1994, 23(2):76–81.

Betker, Brian L. "An Empirical Examination of Prepackaged Bankruptcy," *Financial Management,* 1995, 24(1):3–18.

Bhagat, Sanjai, James A. Brickley, and Jeffrey L. Coles. "The Costs of Inefficient Bargaining and Financial Distress: Evidence from Corporate Lawsuits," *Journal of Financial Economics,* 1994, 35(2):21–247.

Bi, Keqian, and Haim Levy. "Market Reaction to Bond Downgradings Followed by Chapter 11 Filings," *Financial Management,* 1993, 22(3):156–162.

Billingsley, Randall S., Robert E. Lamy, M. Wayne Marr, and G. Rodney Thompson. "Split Ratings and Bond Reoffering Yields," *Financial Management,* 1985, 14(2):59–65.

Bowlin, Oswald D. "The Refunding Decision: Another Special Case in Capital Budgeting," *Journal of Finance,* 1966, 21(1):55–68.

Brick, Ivan E., William Fung, and Marti Subrahmanyam. "Leasing and Financial Intermediation: Comparative Tax Advantages," *Financial Management,* 1987, 16(1):55–59.

Brick, Ivan E., and Oded Palmon. "The Tax Advantages of Refunding Debt by Calling, Repurchasing, and Putting," *Financial Management,* 1993, 22(4):96–105.

Brick, Ivan E., and S. Abraham Ravid. "Interest Rate Uncertainty and the Optimal Debt Maturity Structure," *Journal of Financial and Quantitative Analysis,* 1991, 26(1):63–82.

Brick, Ivan E., and Buckner A. Wallingford. "The Relative Tax Benefits of Alternative Call Features in Corporate Debt," *Journal of Financial and Quantitative Analysis,* 1985, 20(1):95–105.

Brown, David T., Christopher M. James, and Robert M. Mooradian. "The Information Content of Distressed Restructurings Involving Public and Private Debt Claims," *Journal of Financial Economics,* 1993, 33(1):93–118.

Campbell, Cynthia J., Louis H. Ederington, and Prashant Vankrudre. "Tax Shields, Sample-Selection Bias, and the Information Content of Conversion-Forcing Bond Calls," *Journal of Finance,* 1991, 46(4):1291–1324.

Cason, Roger L. "Leasing, Asset Lives and Uncertainty: A Practitioner's Comments," *Financial Management,* 1987, 16(2):13–16.

Chance, Don M. "Default Risk and the Duration of Zero Coupon Bonds," *Journal of Finance,* 1990, 45(1):265–274.

Chatfield, Robert E., and R. Charles Moyer. "'Putting' Away Bond Risk: An Empirical Examination of the Value of the Put Option on Bonds," *Financial Management,* 1986, 15(2):26–33.

Chatterjee, Sris, Upinder S. Dhillon, and Gabriel G. Ramirez. "Coercive Tender and Exchange Offers in Distressed High-Yield Debt Restructurings: An Empirical Analysis," *Journal of Financial Economics,* 1995, 38(3):333–360.

Chatterjee, Sris, Upinder S. Dhillon, and Gabriel G. Ramirez. "Resolution of Financial Distress: Debt Restructurings via Chapter 11, Prepackaged Bankrupcies, and Workouts," *Financial Management,* 1996, 25(1):5–18.

Christensen, Donald G., and Hugo J. Faria. "A Note on the Shareholder Wealth Effects of High-Yield Bonds," *Financial Management,* 1994, 23(1):10.

Coats, Pamela K., and L. Franklin Fant. "Recognizing Financial Distress Patterns Using a Neural Network Tool," *Financial Management,* 1993, 22(3):142–155.

Collins, J. Markham, and Roger P. Bey. "The Master Limited Partnership: An Alternative to the Corporation," *Financial Management,* 1986, 15(4):5–14.

Cowan, Arnold R., Nandkumar Nayar, and Ajai K. Singh. "Calls and Out-of-the-Money Convertible Bonds," *Financial Management,* 1993, 22(4):106–116.

Cowan, Arnold R., Nandkumar Nayar, and Ajai K. Singh. "Underwriting Calls of Convertible Securities: A Note," *Journal of Financial Economics,* 1992, 31(2):269–278.

Crabbe, Leland E., and Jean Helwege. "Alternative Tests of Agency Theories of Callable Corporate Bonds," *Financial Management,* 1994, 23(4):3–20.

De, Sankar, and Jayant R. Kale. "Contingent Payments and Debt Contracts," *Financial Management,* 1993, 22(2):106–122.

DeGennaro, Ramon P., Larry H. P. Lang, and James B. Thomson. "Troubled Savings and Loan Institutions: Turnaround Strategies Under Insolvency," *Financial Management,* 1993, 22(3):163–175.

Diamond, Douglas W. "Seniority and Maturity of Debt Contracts," *Journal of Financial Economics,* 1993, 33(3):341–368.

Dyl, Edward A., and Stanley A. Martin, Jr. "Setting Terms for Leveraged Leasing," *Financial Management,* 1977, 6(4):20–27.

Eberhart, Allan C., William T. Moore, and Rodney L. Roenfeldt. "Security Pricing and Deviations from the Absolute Priority Rule in Bankruptcy Proceedings," *Journal of Finance,"* 1990, 45(5):1457–1470.

Eberhart, Allan C., and Lemma W. Senbet. "Absolute Priority Rule Violations and Risk Incentives for Financially Distressed Firms," *Financial Management,* 1993, 22(3):101–116.

Elgers, Pieter T., and John J. Clark. *The Lease/Buy Decision.* New York: The Free Press, 1980.

Emery, Douglas R., J. Ronald Hoffmeister, and Ronald W. Spahr. "The Case for Indexing a Bond's Call Price," *Financial Management,* 1987, 16(3):57–64.

Emery, Douglas R., and Wilbur G. Lewellen. "Refunding Noncallable Debt," *Journal of Financial and Quantitative Analysis,* 1984, 19(1):73–82.

Emery, Douglas R., and Wilbur G. Lewellen. "Shareholder Gains from Callable-Bond Refundings," *Managerial and Decision Economics,* 1990, 11:57–63.

Fabozzi, Frank J., and Uzi Yaari. "Valuation of Safe Harbor Tax Benefit Transfer Leases," *Journal of Finance,* 1983, 38(2):595–606.

Fields, L. Paige, and Eric L. Mais. "The Valuation Effects of Private Placements of Convertible Debt," *Journal of Finance,* 1991, 46(5):1925–1932.

Finnerty, John D. "Evaluating the Economics of Refunding High-Coupon Sinking-Fund Debt," *Financial Management,* 1983, 12(1):5–10.

Finnerty, John D. *An Illustrated Guide to Bond Refunding Analysis.* Charlottesville, Va.: The Financial Analysts Research Foundation, 1984.

Finnerty, John D. "Indexed Sinking Fund Debentures: Valuation and Analysis," *Financial Management,* 1993, 22(2):76–93.

Finnerty, John D. *Project Financing: Asset-Based Financial Engineering.* New York: Wiley, 1996.

Finnerty, John D. "Refunding Discounted Debt: A Clarifying Analysis," *Journal of Financial and Quantitative Analysis,* 1986, 21(1):95–106.

Finnerty, John D., Andrew J. Kalotay, and Francis X. Farrell, Jr. *The Financial Manager's Guide to Evaluating Bond Refunding Opportunities.* Cambridge, Mass.: Ballinger Publishing Company, 1988.

Gilson, Stuart C., Kose John, and Larry H. P. Lang. "Troubled Debt Restructurings: An Empirical Study of Private Reorganization of Firms in Default," *Journal of Financial Economics,* 1990, 27(2):315–354.

Gombola, Michael J., Mark E. Haskins, J. Edward Ketz, and David D. Williams. "Cash Flow in Bankruptcy Prediction," *Financial Management,* 1987, 16(4):55–65.

Gosnell, Thomas, Arthur J. Keown, and John M. Pinkerton. "Bankruptcy and Insider Trading: Differences between Exchange-Listed and OTC Firms," *Journal of Finance,* 1992, 47(1):349–362.

Hochman, Shalom, and Ramon Rabinovitch. "Financial Leasing Under Inflation," *Financial Management,* 1984, 13(1):17–26.

Hodges, Stewart D. "The Valuation of Variable Rate Leases," *Financial Management,* 1985, 14(1):68–74.

Hotchkiss, Edith Shwalb. "Postbankruptcy Performance and Management Turnover," *Journal of Finance,* 1995, 50(1):3–21.

Houston, Joel F., and S. Venkataraman. "Optimal Maturity Structure with Multiple Debt Claims," *Journal of Financial and Quantitative Analysis,* 1994, 29(2):179–197.

Hsueh, L. Paul, and David S. Kidwell. "Bond Ratings: Are Two Better Than One?" *Financial Management,* 1988, 17(1):46–53.

Hull, Robert M., and Richard Moellenberndt. "Bank Debt Reduction Announcements and Negative Signaling," *Financial Management,* 1994, 23(2):21–30.

Jalilvand, Abolhassan, and Tae H. Park. "Default Risk, Firm Characteristics, and the Valuation of Variable-Rate Debt Instruments," *Financial Management,* 1994, 23(2):58–68.

Jensen, Marlin R. H., and William N. Pugh. "Valuation Effects of Cancelled Debt Offerings," *Journal of Financial and Quantitative Analysis,* 1991, 26(3):425–432.

Jog, Vijay M., Igor Kotlyar, and Donald G. Tate. "Stakeholder Losses in Corporate Restructuring: Evidence from Four Cases in the North American Steel Industry," *Financial Management,* 1993, 22(3):185–201.

John, Kose. "Managing Financial Distress and Valuing Distressed Securities: A Survey and a Research Agenda," *Financial Management,* 1993, 22(3):60–78.

John, Kose, Larry H. P. Lang, and Jeffry Netter. "The Voluntary Restructuring of Large Firms in Response to Performance Decline," *Journal of Finance,* 1992, 47(3):891–918.

John, Teresa A. "Accounting Measures of Corporate Liquidity, Leverage, and Costs of Financial Distress," *Financial Management,* 1993, 22(3):91–100.

Johnson, James M., Robert A. Pari, and Leonard Rosenthal. "The Impact of In-Substance Defeasance on Bondholder and Shareholder Wealth," *Journal of Finance,* 1989, 44(4):1049–1058.

Kalotay, Andrew, and Bruce Tuckman. "Sinking Fund Prepurchases and the Designation Option," *Financial Management,* 1992, 21(4):110–118.

Kaplan, Steven N., and Jeremy C. Stein. "How Risky Is the Debt of Highly Leveraged Transactions?" *Journal of Financial Economics,* 1990, 27(1):215–246.

Kim, In Joon, Krishna Ramaswamy, and Suresh Sundaresan. "Does Default Risk in Coupons Affect the Valuation of Corporate Bonds? A Contingent Claims Model," *Financial Management,* 1993, 22(3):117–131.

Krishnan, V. Sivarama, and R. Charles Moyer. "Bankruptcy Costs and the Financial Leasing Decision," *Financial Management,* 1994, 23(2):31–42.

Laber, Gene. "Bond Covenants and Forgone Opportunities: The Case of Burlington Northern Railroad Company," *Financial Management,* 1992, 21(2):71–77.

Lease, Ronald C., John J. McConnell, and James S. Schallheim. "Realized Returns and the Default and Prepayment Experience of Financial Leasing Contracts," *Financial Management,* 1990, 19(2):11–20.

Lewellen, Wilbur G., and Douglas R. Emery. "On the Matter of Parity Among Financial Obligations," *Journal of Finance,* 1981, 36(1):97–111.

Lewis, Craig M., and James S. Schallheim. "Are Debt and Leases Substitutes?" *Journal of Financial and Quantitative Analysis,* 1992, 27(4):497–512.

Livingston, Miles. "Measuring the Benefit of a Bond Refunding: The Problem of Nonmarketable Call Options," *Financial Management,* 1987, 16(1):38–40.

Loderer, Claudio P., and Dennis P. Sheehan. "Corporate Bankruptcy and Managers' Self-Serving Behavior," *Journal of Finance,* 1989, 44(4):1059–1076.

Long, Michael S., and Stephan E. Sefcik. "Participation Financing: A Comparison of the Characteristics of Convertible Debt and Straight Bonds Issued in Conjunction with Warrants," *Financial Management,* 1990, 19(3):23–34.

Lovata, Linda M., William D. Nichols, and Kirk L. Philipich. "Defeasing Discounted Debt: An Economic Analysis," *Financial Management,* 1987, 16(1):41–45.

Mauer, David C., Amir Barnea, and Chang-Soo Kim. "Valuation of Callable Bonds Under Progressive Personal Taxes and Interest Rate Uncertainty," *Financial Management,* 1991, 20(2):50–59.

Mitchell, Karlyn. "The Call, Sinking Fund, and Term-to-Maturity Features of Corporate Bonds: An Empirical Investigation," *Journal of Financial and Quantitative Analysis,* 1991, 26(2):201–222.

Mooradian, Robert M., "The Effect of Bankruptcy Protection on Investment: Chapter 11 as a Screening Device," *Journal of Finance,* 1994, 49(4):1403–1430.

Mukherjee, Tarun K. "A Survey of Corporate Leasing Analysis," *Financial Management,* 1991, 20(3):96–107.

Nayar, Nandkumar, and Michael S. Rozeff. "Ratings, Commercial Paper, and Equity Returns," *Journal of Finance,* 1994, 49(4):1431–1449.

The 1995 Bankruptcy Yearbook and Almanac. Boston, Mass.: New Generation Research, 1995.

Ogden, Joseph P. "Determinants of the Relative Interest Rate Sensitivities of Corporate Bonds," *Financial Management,* 1987, 16(1):22–30.

Opler, Tim C. "Controlling Financial Distress Costs in Leveraged Buyouts with Financial Innovations," *Financial Management,* 1993, 22(3):79–90.

Opler, Tim C., and Sheridan Titman. "Financial Distress and Corporate Performance," *Journal of Finance,"* 1994, 49(3):1015–1040.

Petersen, Mitchell A., and Raghuram G. Rajan. "The Benefits of Lending Relationships: Evidence from Small Business Data," *Journal of Finance,* 1994, 49(1):3–37.

Peterson, Pamela, David Peterson, and James Ang. "The Extinguishment of Debt Through In-Substance Defeasance," *Financial Management,* 1985, 14(1):59–67.

Rajan, Raghuram G. "Insiders and Outsiders: The Choice Between Informed and Arm's-Length Debt," *Journal of Finance,* 1992, 47(4):1367–1400.

Roberts, Gordon S., and Jerry A. Viscione. "The Impact of Seniority and Security Covenants on Bond Yields: A Note," *Journal of Finance,* 1984, 39(5):1597–1602.

Schall, Lawrence D. "Analytic Issues in Lease vs. Purchase Decisions," *Financial Management,* 1987, 16(2):17–20.

Schallheim, James S. *Lease or Buy?* Boston, Mass.: Harvard Business School Press, 1994.

Schallheim, James S., Ramon E. Johnson, Ronald C. Lease, and John J. McConnell. "The Determinants of Yields on Financial Leasing Contracts," *Journal of Financial Economics,* 1987, 19(1):45–68.

Scholes, Myron S., and Mark A. Wolfson. "Employee Stock Ownership Plans and Corporate Restructuring: Myths and Realities," *Financial Management,* 1990, 19(1):12–28.

Schultz, Paul. "Calls of Warrants: Timing and Market Reaction," *Journal of Finance,* 1993, 48(2):681–696.

Shulman, Joel, Mark Bayless, and Kelly Price. "Marketability and Default Influences on the Yield Premia of Speculative-Grade Debt," *Financial Management,* 1993, 22(3):132–141.

Singh, Ajai K., Arnold R. Cowan, and Nandkumar Nayar. "Underwritten Calls of Convertible Bonds," *Journal of Financial Economics,* 1991, 29(1):173–196.

Slovin, Myron B., Marie E. Sushka, and John A. Polonchek. "Corporate Sale-and-Leasebacks and Shareholder Wealth," *Journal of Finance,* 1990, 45(1):289–300.

Smith, Clifford W., Jr., and Lee M. Wakeman. "Determinants of Corporate Leasing Policy," *Journal of Finance,* 1985, 40(3):896–908.

Thatcher, Janet S. "The Choice of Call Provision Terms: Evidence of the Existence of Agency Costs of Debt," *Journal of Finance,* 1985, 40(2):549–561.

Usmen, Nilufer. "Currency Swaps, Financial Arbitrage, and Default Risk," *Financial Management,* 1994, 23(2):43–57.

Vu, Joseph D. "An Empirical Investigation of Calls of Non-Convertible Bonds," *Journal of Financial Economics,* 1986, 16(2):235–265.

Waheed, Amjad, and Ike Mathur. "The Effects of Announcements of Bank Lending Agreements on the Market Values of U.S. Banks," *Financial Management,* 1993, 22(1):119–127.

Wingler, Tony R., and G. Donald Jud. "Premium Debt Tenders: Analysis and Evidence," *Financial Management,* 1990, 19(4):58–67.

INTERNATIONAL CORPORATE FINANCE

1. Describe the five basic types of foreign exchange transactions: spot transactions, forward transactions, currency futures, currency swaps, and currency options.

2. Describe each of the four key international market relationships: interest rate parity, purchasing power parity, unbiased forward exchange rates, and the international Fisher effect.

3. Explain how a company can use forward market transactions and foreign currency option transactions to hedge its foreign currency risk exposure.

4. Evaluate the net present value of a foreign capital budgeting project.

5. Calculate the cost of borrowing in terms of the domestic currency when issuing debt denominated in a foreign currency.

6. Explain the pitfall in borrowing in whichever currency affords the lowest interest rate.

MULTINATIONAL CORPORATION A company that operates in more than one country.

Successful companies today have a global perspective and operate in many countries. As a result, the distinction between U.S. companies and foreign companies has become blurred as the leading companies have evolved into truly **multinational corporations.**

The Coca-Cola Company sells its familiar soft drink virtually everywhere and derives two-thirds of its sales and three-quarters of its operating profits outside the United States. Exxon Corporation produces oil and gas in the North Sea, off Norway and the United Kingdom, and in Australia, Indonesia, and Malaysia. The Walt Disney Company has huge theme parks located near Paris and Tokyo. Australia's News Corporation owns the Fox Broadcasting Network, Twentieth Century Fox film studio, HarperCollins Publishers, and TV Guide. Japan's Toyota Motor Corporation manufactures automobiles in California and Kentucky.

The principles of finance don't stop at the border. They apply no matter where the company has its base and where it operates. The fundamental goal of an international company also remains unchanged: maximize shareholder wealth. The main complication concerns foreign currencies, but multinational corporations must also contend with changing interest rates and inflation rates among countries. They must manage the complex risks they face.

We'll help you understand how the foreign exchange markets operate and the methods they afford for handling foreign exchange risk. We'll also show how to take foreign exchange risk into account when evaluating proposed capital budgeting projects and analyzing foreign-currency-denominated financing alternatives.

INTERNATIONAL CORPORATE FINANCE AND THE PRINCIPLES OF FINANCE

◆ *Self-Interested Behavior:* Seek out investments that offer the greatest expected risk-adjusted real return.

◆ *Two-Sided Transactions:* You can use derivatives to transfer foreign exchange risk to others. Derivatives do not eliminate risk; they only transfer it.

◆ *Valuable Ideas:* Look for opportunities to develop derivatives or design arrangements that enable companies to cope better with the risks they face in their foreign operations. Also, look for opportunities to develop new positive-NPV financing mechanisms.

◆ *Comparative Advantage:* Transfer foreign exchange risk to other parties if they are willing to bear these risks more cheaply.

◆ *Options:* Recognize the value of hidden options in a situation, such as the foreign exchange options in some derivative instruments.

◆ *Incremental Benefits:* Calculate the net advantage of a foreign project on the basis of the incremental after-tax cash flows the project will provide.

◆ *Risk-Return Trade-Off:* To transfer risk to another party, you must offer a return that fully compensates for the amount of risk transferred.

(continued on following page)

(*International Corporate Finance and the Principles of Finance continued from previous page*)

◆ *Diversification:* Diversifying internationally is valuable when the returns from a foreign investment are not perfectly correlated with the returns on any subset of the U.S. market portfolio.

◆ *Capital Market Efficiency:* You cannot forecast foreign exchange rate movements precisely. You should use forward rates as quoted in the foreign exchange market rather than internal exchange rate forecasts.

◆ *Time Value of Money:* Use discounted cash flow analysis to measure the net present value of a foreign investment project.

THE FOREIGN EXCHANGE MARKET

FOREIGN EXCHANGE MARKET The market that trades one country's currency for another country's currency.

A large American department store chain has signed an agreement to import fine English china. The contract calls for the American company to pay the British exporting company in British pounds. To do so, the American company must purchase British pounds in the foreign exchange market. The **foreign exchange market** is the market that trades one country's currency for another country's currency. In our example, the American company would exchange U.S. dollars for British pounds in the foreign exchange market and pay the exporter's invoice. Alternatively, if the contract had specified payment in U.S. dollars, the exporter would have received dollars and then sold the dollars for British pounds in the foreign exchange market.

The foreign exchange market is the world's largest financial market. It is a worldwide market, but London, New York, and Tokyo are the major centers of activity. The larger commercial banks and the central banks are the principal market participants, and corporations generally buy and sell currencies through a commercial bank. Most of the trading takes place in six currencies: U.S. dollar ($), German mark (or simply, mark; DM), French franc (FF), Swiss franc (SF), Japanese yen (¥), and British pound (£). Table 15.1 lists 20 currencies and their symbols.

The foreign exchange market is an over-the-counter market. The large commercial banks and investment banks are the major participants. Some other participants include importers, who need foreign currency to pay for the goods they import; money managers, who buy and sell foreign stocks and bonds; and multinational companies, who invest in facilities and sell goods in foreign markets.

TABLE 15.1
Twenty Currencies and Their Symbols

Country	Currency	Symbol	Country	Currency	Symbol
Australia	Dollar	A$	Italy	Lira	₤
Belgium	Franc	BF	Japan	Yen	¥
Botswana	Pula	P	Kuwait	Dinar	KD
Canada	Dollar	Can$	Mexico	Peso	Ps
Chile	Peso	$	Saudi Arabia	Riyal	SR
Denmark	Krone	DKr	South Africa	Rand	R
France	Franc	FF	South Korea	Won	₩
Germany	Deutsche mark	DM	Switzerland	Franc	SF
India	Rupee	Rs	United Kingdom	Pound	£
Israel	Shekel	NIS	United States	Dollar	$

Exchange Rates

An **exchange rate** is the price of one country's currency expressed in terms of another country's currency. For example, a rate of $1.70 per £1 means that 1 pound costs $1.70 (£1 = $1.70). Put somewhat differently, 1 U.S. dollar costs 0.5882 pounds, because 1/1.70 = 0.5882 ($1 = £0.5882). The exchange rate can be expressed equivalently in terms of either dollars per pound or pounds per dollar.

An exchange rate is used to convert an amount expressed in one currency into another.

EXCHANGE RATE The price of one country's currency expressed in terms of another country's currency.

Using an Exchange Rate to Convert from One Currency to Another   E X A M P L E

Your sorority can buy a used two-decker London bus for £15,000. (You'll use it to drive everyone to home football games and other important events.) The exchange rate is $1.70 per £1. How many dollars will you need to buy it?

Purchasing the bus will cost $25,500 (= [15,000]1.70).

The U.S. dollar–pound exchange rate can be expressed equivalently in terms of either dollars per pound or pounds per dollar. The exchange rates could also be expressed indirectly in terms of a third currency—say, the Swiss franc: SF1.50/$ and SF2.55/£. Figure 15.1 illustrates these currency relationships. Given any two, it's easy to find the third.

The direct and indirect methods of expressing an exchange rate are equivalent. In our example, the dollar–pound exchange rate implicit in the exchange rates SF1.50/$ and SF2.55/£ is £0.5882/$ (or equivalently, $1.70/£) because

$$\frac{\dfrac{SF1.50}{\$}}{\dfrac{SF2.55}{£}} = \frac{£0.5882}{\$}$$

If the equivalence didn't hold, there would be a riskless arbitrage opportunity.

A Riskless Currency Arbitrage Opportunity   E X A M P L E

Suppose British pounds were trading at a price of SF2.60/£ in Switzerland and $1.70/£ in New York while Swiss francs were trading for SF1.50/$ in New York. In that case, the pound would be overvalued in Switzerland relative to the other two currencies. A foreign exchange trader who purchased $100 worth of pounds in New York would obtain £58.82 (= [100]0.5882). Selling the pounds in Switzerland would yield SF152.93 (= [58.82]2.60). The Swiss francs could be sold in New York for $101.96 (= [152.93]0.6667), yielding a riskless arbitrage profit of $1.96 per $100 invested. ■

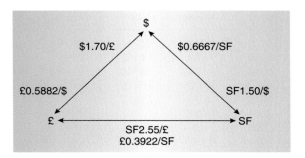

FIGURE 15.1
The relationship among the values of three currencies.

In practice in foreign exchange trading, all exchange rates are expressed in terms of the U.S. dollar. For example, SF1 = $0.66, DM1 = $0.60, £1 = $1.70, and so on. Traders find it convenient to quote exchange rates indirectly in terms of a single currency, the U.S. dollar.

Types of Foreign Exchange Transactions

There are five types of foreign exchange transactions: spot transactions, forward transactions, currency futures, currency swaps, and currency options. Let's take a look at each.

SPOT TRADE The purchase or sale of a currency for "immediate" delivery, which actually occurs two business days after the trade takes place.

Immediate Transactions   **Spot trades** involve the purchase and sale of a currency for "immediate" delivery, which actually occurs two business days after the trade takes place. Figure 15.2 illustrates what a typical table of foreign exchange rates published in a financial newspaper looks like. Suppose the exchange rates shown in the table applied on February 12, 1997. The table furnishes the *spot foreign exchange rates* quoted by Bankers Trust Co. for trading amounts of $1 million or greater as of 3 P.M. the preceding two trading days. For example, the British pound is quoted in the table at £1 = $1.6950 for February 11 and £1 = $1.6865 for February 12, indicating a slight decrease in the value of the pound (relative to the dollar) between February 11 and February 12.

The table also reports currency *cross rates* for actively traded currencies. They show the value of any currency in terms of any other currency. For example, considering the Canadian dollar (Can$)–U.S. dollar ($) exchange rate, Can$1.2035 = $1 (in the upper left-hand corner) is equivalent to $0.83091 = Can$1 (in the lower right-hand corner).

FORWARD CONTRACT A contract for the purchase and sale of an item, such as a currency, for future delivery based on a price that is agreed upon today.

Forward and Futures Contracts   A **forward contract** covers the purchase and sale of an item, such as a currency, for *future* delivery based on a price (the exchange rate) that is agreed to *today*. When the forward contract involves a currency, it is referred to as a *currency forward*. Figure 15.2 shows *forward exchange rates* in addition to spot exchange rates for British pounds, Canadian dollars, French francs, Japanese yen, Swiss francs, and German marks. In each case the rates are shown for 30, 90, and 180-day forward contracts. Forward contracts typically have a term between 1 and 52 weeks. For example, a company could purchase pounds for immediate delivery at an exchange rate of £1 = $1.6865 on Wednesday, February 12, 1997. On that same day, a company could also contract for 30-day delivery at an exchange rate of £1 = $1.6779, called the forward exchange rate, and for 180-day delivery at a forward rate of £1 = $1.6341. A company entering into a 30-day forward contract on February 12 to purchase British pounds would agree to exchange $1.6779 per pound on March 14 when the contract settles.

FIGURE 15.2
Foreign exchange rate tables.

| | | | | KEY CURRENCY CROSS RATES | | | | | |
| | | | | Late New York Trading Feb. 12, 1997 | | | | | |
	Dollar	Pound	SFranc	Guilder	Yen	Lira	D-Mark	FFranc	CdnDlr
Canada	1.2035	2.0283	.79834	.63027	.00831	.00096	.71024	.20896	—
France	5.7595	9.706	3.8206	3.0162	.03976	.00458	3.3989	—	4.7856
Germany	1.6945	2.8557	1.1240	.88741	.01170	.00135	—	.29421	1.4080
Italy	1258.7	2121.3	834.96	659.18	8.689	—	742.81	218.54	1045.9
Japan	144.86	244.13	96.093	75.863	—	.11509	85.488	25.151	120.37
Netherlands	1.9095	3.2181	1.2667	—	.01318	.00152	1.1269	.33154	1.5866
Switzerland	1.5075	2.5406	—	.78947	.01041	.00120	.88964	.26174	1.2526
U.K.	.59337	—	.39361	.31074	.00410	.00047	.35017	.10302	.49303
U.S.	—	1.6853	.66335	.52370	.00690	.00079	.59014	.17363	.83091

EXCHANGE RATES
Wednesday, February 12, 1997

The New York foreign exchange selling rates below apply to trading among banks in amounts of $1 million and more as quoted at 3 P.M. Eastern time by Bankers Trust Co. Retail transactions provide fewer units of foreign currency per dollar.

Country	U.S. $ equiv. Wed.	U.S. $ equiv. Tue.	Currency per U.S. $ Wed.	Currency per U.S. $ Tue.	Country	U.S. $ equiv. Wed.	U.S. $ equiv. Tue.	Currency per U.S. $ Wed.	Currency per U.S. $ Tue.
Argentina (Peso)	1.0004	1.0004	.9996	.9996	90-Day Forward	.17252	.17437	5.7965	5.7350
Australia (Dollar)	.7503	.7450	1.3328	1.3423	180-Day Forward	.17132	.17313	5.8370	5.7760
Austria (Schilling)	.08397	.08478	11.91	11.80	Germany (Mark)	.5908	.5970	1.6925	1.6750
Bahrain (Dinar)	2.6522	2.6522	.3771	.3771	30-Day Forward	.5909	.5970	1.6924	1.6750
Belgium (Franc)	.02828	.02856	35.36	35.01	90-Day Forward	.5904	.5966	1.6937	1.6763
Brazil (Real)	.04129	.04264	24.22	23.45	180-Day Forward	.5892	.5953	1.6971	1.6797
Britain (Pound)	1.6865	1.6950	.5929	.5900	Greece (Drachma)	.006266	.006333	159.60	157.90
30-Day Forward	1.6779	1.6865	.5960	.5929	Hong Kong (Dollar)	.12802	.12806	7.8110	7.8090
90-Day Forward	1.6595	1.6683	.6026	.5994	India (Rupee)	.05907	.05907	16.93	16.93
180-Day Forward	1.6341	1.6427	.6120	.6088	Indonesia (Rupiah)	.0005568	.0005568	1796.01	1796.01
Canada (Dollar)	.8299	.8288	1.2050	1.2065	Ireland (Punt)	1.5785	1.5830	.6335	.6317
30-Day Forward	.8269	.8261	1.2093	1.2105	Israel (Shekel)	.5378	.5378	1.8594	1.8594
90-Day Forward	.8207	.8201	1.2185	1.2193	Italy (Lira)	.0007955	.0008034	1257.01	1244.76
180-Day Forward	.8125	.8123	1.2307	1.2310	Japan (Yen)	.006911	.006930	144.70	144.30
Chile (Peso)	.003448	.003448	290.03	290.03	30-Day Forward	.006919	.006938	144.53	144.13
China (Renminbi)	.211757	.211757	4.7224	4.7224	90-Day Forward	.006929	.006948	144.33	143.93
Colombia (Peso)	.002208	.002208	453.00	453.00	180-Day Forward	.006943	.006965	144.04	143.57
Denmark (Krone)	.1532	.1547	6.5295	6.4625	Jordan (Dinar)	1.5328	1.5328	.6524	.6524
Ecuador (Sucre) Floating rate	.001445	.001445	692.00	692.00	Kuwait (Dinar)	3.4596	3.4596	.2891	.2891
Finland (Markka)	.25310	.25336	3.9510	3.9470	Lebanon (Pound)	.001825	.001825	548.00	548.00
France (Franc)	.17375	.17558	5.7555	5.6955	Malaysia (Ringgit)	.3704	.3698	2.6995	2.7045
30-Day Forward	.17342	.17525	5.7664	5.7060	Malta (Lira)	3.0534	3.0534	.3275	.3275
					Mexico (Peso) Floating rate	.0003670	.0003670	2725.02	2725.02
					Netherlands (Guilder)	.5244	.5299	1.9070	1.8870
					New Zealand (Dollar)	.5850	.5825	1.7094	1.7167
					Norway (Krone)	.1544	.1548	6.4775	6.4605

(continued on following page)

(Foreign exchange rate tables *continued from previous page*)

Country	U.S. $ equiv.		Currency per U.S. $		Country	U.S. $ equiv.		Currency per U.S. $	
	Wed.	*Tue.*	*Wed.*	*Tue.*		*Wed.*	*Tue.*	*Wed.*	*Tue.*
Pakistan (Rupee)	.0471	.0471	21.25	21.25	30-Day Forward	.6642	.6688	1.5055	1.4952
Peru (new Sol)	.4237	.4237	2.3600	2.3600	90-Day Forward	.6624	.6673	1.5097	1.4986
Philippines (Peso)	.04533	.04533	22.06	22.06	180-Day Forward	.6607	.6649	1.5135	1.5040
Portugal (Escudo)	.006769	.006769	147.73	147.73	Taiwan (Dollar)	.038387	.038461	26.05	26.00
Saudi Arabia (Riyal)	.26681	.26681	3.7480	3.7480	Thailand (Baht)	.03911	.03911	25.57	25.57
Singapore (Dollar)	.5365	.5366	1.8640	1.8635	Turkey (Lira)	.0004264	.0004264	2345.05	2345.05
South Africa (Rand)	.3927	.3931	2.5465	2.5439	United Arab (Dirham)	.2723	.2723	3.6725	3.6725
South Korea (Won)	.0014584	.0014584	685.70	685.70	Uruguay (New Peso)				
Spain (Peseta)	.009153	.009234	109.25	108.30	Financial	.001247	.001247	801.75	801.75
Sweden (Krona)	.1637	.1632	6.1100	6.1275	Venezuela (Bolivar)				
Switzerland (Franc)	.6647	.6693	1.5045	1.4940	Brady rate	.02137	.02137	46.80	46.80
					SDR	1.32768	1.32790	.75319	.75307
					ECU	1.21633	1.21899		

Special Drawing Rights (SDR) are based on exchange rates for the U.S., German, British, French, and Japanese currencies. Source: International Monetary Fund.

European Currency Unit (ECU) is based on a basket of community currencies. Source: European Community Commission.

Note that the forward rates for pounds are lower than the spot rate. In the next section we'll see why. If a company purchased pounds for 30-day delivery, it would get more pounds for its dollar than it would in a spot purchase (£0.5960/$ versus £0.5929/$). The pound is therefore said to trade at a *forward discount* relative to the dollar, because forward pounds are "cheaper" than spot pounds. This forward discount can be expressed on a nominal annualized basis as

$$\text{Forward discount} = 12 \left(\frac{\text{30-day Forward rate} - \text{Spot rate}}{\text{Spot rate}} \right) = 12 \left(\frac{0.5960 - 0.5929}{0.5929} \right) = 6.27\%$$

Note that the Japanese yen is trading at a *forward premium* relative to the dollar, because forward yen are more expensive than spot yen.

EXAMPLE

A Forward Contract

Your sorority does not have $25,500. You can raise the money from parents and friends, but it will take 180 days. The owner of the bus agrees to deliver the bus in 180 days in return for £15,500. How many dollars will it cost if you buy £15,500 180 days forward and the forward exchange rate is £1 = $1.6341?

Purchasing the pounds forward will cost $25,328.55 (= [15,500]1.6341). You will pay this amount in 180 days to take delivery of the £15,500. ∎

Forward contracts can be customized to suit a corporation's particular requirements as to amount, currency, settlement date, and other matters. Voiding a forward contract, however, is difficult and is subject to negotiation with the other party to the contract.

Currency Futures

Currency futures markets also exist. Currency futures are like currency forwards except that a **futures contract** is standardized and exchange traded. A **currency future** is a futures contract that is denominated in a particular foreign currency. Because of this standardization, currency futures generally are less costly and enjoy more liquid markets than (non-exchange-traded) forward contracts. With a futures contract, a company can close out its position at any time simply by selling the contract (or repurchasing the contract if it had previously sold it). The choice between a forward contract and a futures contract thus involves a trade-off. Forward contracts can be customized, but futures contracts have greater liquidity and lower transaction costs.

Currency futures, like currency forwards, have premiums or discounts that reflect market expectations of exchange rates at future dates.

Currency Swaps

In the third type of foreign exchange transaction, the **currency swap,** two parties swap equivalent amounts of two currencies and agree to exchange a series of specified payment obligations denominated in one currency for payment obligations denominated in another. When payments are due, one party generally pays the other the difference in value caused by changes in the exchange rate. Currency swaps can be arranged directly between two companies seeking to borrow in each other's home currency. More commonly, companies swap currency with commercial banks, which are in a better position to effect such transactions.

FUTURES CONTRACT A standardized, exchange-traded contract for the purchase and sale of an item, such as a currency, for future delivery based on a price that is agreed upon today.

CURRENCY FUTURE A futures contract that is denominated in a particular foreign currency.

CURRENCY SWAP An agreement to swap equivalent amounts of currency and exchange payment obligations expressed in two different currencies.

A Currency Swap

EXAMPLE

Imperial Chemicals Industries PLC (ICI), a British company, would like to make an investment in the United States. Texaco Inc. (Texaco) is an American company that would like to make an investment in the United Kingdom. They can both borrow in their respective national currencies and enter into a currency swap. Suppose a 10-year British pound loan to ICI requires a 12% APR, whereas a 10-year U.S. dollar loan to Texaco requires a 9% APR. Texaco and ICI agree to exchange interest and principal payment obligations.

Suppose each company needs the equivalent of $100 million. Each company borrows this sum in its home currency, and the two companies enter into a currency swap. Texaco's debt service stream (assuming the debt matures in a lump sum and pays annual interest) under a currency swap arrangement with ICI is given in table 15.2 on page 556.

In this example, Texaco borrows $100 million and exchanges the $100 million with ICI for £62.5 million. In each of the subsequent 10 years, Texaco agrees to pay ICI £7.5 million (= [0.12]62.5), and ICI agrees to pay Texaco $9 million (= [0.09]100). Texaco then makes an interest payment of $9 million on its loan. At the time of the last interest payment, Texaco agrees to pay ICI £62.5 million, and ICI agrees to pay Texaco $100 million. Texaco then pays $100 million to repay its loan. The payment obligations of ICI and Texaco are netted: On the basis of prevailing exchange rates, one party will have to write the other party a check for the net amount owed when each payment is due.

The currency swap effectively converts Texaco's $100 million 9% U.S. dollar loan into a £62.5 million 12% British pound loan. ∎

Why does a currency swap offer a cost advantage over simply borrowing the needed foreign currency directly in the foreign capital market? Briefly, the answer is market imperfections. Tax asymmetries and national regulations can restrict international capital flows and restrict the free flow of capital across national boundaries. These frictions lead to differences

TABLE 15.2
Texaco's Debt Service Stream (currency amounts in millions)

	YEAR 0		YEARS 1–10		YEAR 10	
	$	£	$	£	$	£
Borrow $	+100					
Swap $ for £	−100	+62.5				
Interest on $ loan			−9			
Swap payments			+9	−7.5	+100	−62.5
Repay $ loan					−100	
Net cash flow	0	+62.5	0	−7.5	0	−62.5

in relative borrowing costs that give a comparative advantage to two companies, or (as is more often the case recently) to a company and one of its commercial banks, to engage in a currency swap.

Currency Options

CURRENCY OPTION The right to buy (a call option) or sell (a put option) a specified amount of a particular foreign currency at a stated price within a specified time period.

Currency Options A forward contract or a futures contract obligates the parties to make the foreign currency exchange specified in the contract. In contrast, a **currency option** conveys the *right* to buy (in the case of a call option), or sell (for a put option), a specified amount of a particular foreign currency at a stated price within a specified time period. Commercial banks sell customized currency options, and standardized currency options are traded on option exchanges.

The option holder's gain will depend on the change in the exchange rate. The maximum loss, however, is limited to the cost of the option, because the option holder does not have to actually make the exchange.[1]

Self-Check

1. What is the foreign exchange market?

2. What is an exchange rate? If the dollar–pound rate is $1.75/£, what is it when expressed in pounds per dollar?

3. What is a spot exchange rate? What is a forward exchange rate?

4. What is a currency future? How is it different from a currency forward?

5. What is a currency swap? How can a company use a currency swap to convert a dollar loan into, say, a French franc loan?

▌HEDGING AGAINST FOREIGN CURRENCY RISKS

FOREIGN EXCHANGE RISK The risk that a payment denominated in a foreign currency will change in value due to a change in a foreign exchange rate.

When some of the cash flows a company expects to receive, or anticipates having to pay, are denominated in a foreign currency, the company faces foreign currency risk. **Foreign exchange risk** (or foreign currency risk) is the risk that the value of a cash flow will change as a result of a change in the exchange rate. For example, suppose that Boeing has a contract to sell two aircraft to British Airways. The contract calls for delivery of both in one year against payment in British pounds. The value of the contract is £200 million. Suppose the spot dollar–pound exchange rate expected one year hence is £1 = $1.60. Then the aircraft contract has an expected value of $320 million. But suppose the dollar–pound exchange rate is £1 = $1.50

---

[1]For more on options, see enrichment topic B, Options and Contingent Outcomes, and enrichment topic E, Derivatives and Hedging.

when British Airways makes payment. In that case, British Airways will still pay £200 million, but Boeing will receive only $300 million when it converts the pounds into dollars.

Exchange Rate Volatility

The exchange rates between the major currencies are not fixed by government policy. Rather, they can float up or down in response to supply and demand. The central bank of each major country does intervene in the foreign exchange market from time to time. It buys or sells its currency in order to smooth exchange rate fluctuations. It tries to keep its exchange rate at a level it deems appropriate. For example, it may wish to reduce its exchange rate in order to boost exports. However, intervention can affect the situation only temporarily when exchange rates are floating. Attempts to force a different exchange rate are soon swamped by market forces.

Figure 15.3 shows how the values of the Australian dollar, British pound, German mark, and Japanese yen moved in relation to the U.S. dollar between 1980 and 1996. All four currencies exhibit considerable volatility.

Hedging Techniques

Boeing can eliminate its foreign currency risk exposure by hedging. **Hedging** means establishing a financial position whose change in value will offset a recognized risk. To create a foreign exchange hedge, Boeing should enter into a foreign currency transaction that would generate an offsetting gain in case the pound's value depreciated relative to the expected future spot rate before receipt of payment (a $20 million gain if the pound were to depreciate to $1.50/£).[2] We will explain two basic foreign currency hedging techniques: (1) forward market transactions and (2) currency option transactions.

HEDGING Establishing a financial position whose change in value will offset the change in value of a risky financial instrument.

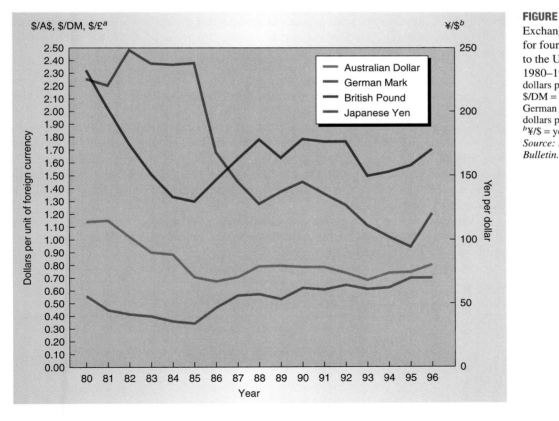

FIGURE 15.3
Exchange rate fluctuations for four currencies relative to the U.S. dollar, 1980–1996.   [a]$/A$ = U.S dollars per Australian dollar, $/DM = U.S. dollars per German mark, and $/£ = U.S. dollars per pound.
[b]¥/$ = yen per U.S. dollar.
Source: Federal Reserve Bulletin.

---

[2]You can read more about hedging in enrichment topic E, Derivatives and Hedging.

Before describing them, we should mention one other strategy for Boeing that you may have thought of. Boeing could negotiate payment in U.S. dollars. But the Principle of Two-Sided Transactions should indicate why invoicing in dollars does not eliminate foreign currency risk. It eliminates *Boeing's* foreign currency risk exposure—but transfers it to British Airways, which must now pay in dollars. The Principle of Risk-Return Trade-Off implies that the risk transfer will require compensation to British Airways in the form of a reduced transaction price.

Let's see how forward market transactions can be used to hedge foreign currency risk.

EXAMPLE

Hedging Foreign Currency Risk in the Forward Market

Boeing could hedge its foreign currency risk exposure by selling a £200 million forward contract for delivery in 1 year. That strategy converts the £200 million receivable into a known dollar amount. Suppose the 1-year forward rate is £1 = $1.60. Then the forward sale will net Boeing $320 million 1 year hence. Table 15.3 shows the consequences to Boeing of hedging in this manner in three different future exchange rate scenarios.

Suppose the British pound depreciates to £1 = $1.50. Boeing receives £200 million from British Airways, which is worth $300 million. But Boeing delivers the £200 million under the forward contract for $320 million. There is a $20 million profit (320 − 300) on the forward contract that restores the value of the aircraft contract to the originally expected $320 million value. Suppose instead the British pound appreciates to £1 = $1.70. The £200 million Boeing receives is worth $340 million. But it must deliver pounds at an exchange rate of £1 = $1.60 to settle the forward contract. The $20 million loss on the forward contract leads to a net (of gain or loss on hedging) realized value of $320 million on the aircraft contract. Indeed, regardless of what happens to the spot rate 1 year hence, Boeing will realize $320 million because of the forward contract. Losses are avoided—but so are gains—under a forward contract hedge. ■

Forward market transactions are useful for hedging foreign currency risk exposures that are certain as to amount and timing. But life is not always quite so simple.

Suppose that Boeing and Airbus are competing for the order and that British Airways will not make a decision for several weeks (while it studies the bids). If Boeing sells pounds forward but does not win the contract, it will lose money if the British pound appreciates. Boeing can avoid this outcome and still hedge its foreign currency risk by purchasing an option to sell £200 million at a stated exchange rate in one year. The most Boeing can lose in that case is the cost of the option.

Currency options represent a useful hedging tool when the quantity of foreign currency to be received or paid is uncertain. The following rules indicate how to choose between forward contracts and currency options.

TABLE 15.3
Possible Outcomes of Boeing's Forward Market Hedge

SPOT EXCHANGE RATE, 1 YEAR HENCE	VALUE OF ORIGINAL CONTRACT (MILLIONS)	GAIN (LOSS) ON FORWARD CONTRACT (MILLIONS)	NET REALIZED DOLLAR VALUE (MILLIONS)
£1 = $1.50	£200 = $300	$20	$320
£1 = $1.60	£200 = $320	—	320
£1 = $1.70	£200 = $340	(20)	320

- When the quantity of foreign currency to be received (paid) is known, sell (buy) the currency forward.

- When the quantity is unknown, buy an option to sell (buy) enough of the foreign currency to cover the maximum amount of foreign currency that might be received (paid).

Self-Check

1. What is foreign exchange risk? What is hedging?

2. Explain how a company can use a forward market transaction to hedge foreign currency risk.

3. How could a company use a foreign currency money market transaction (borrowing in the foreign currency) to hedge foreign currency risk?

4. Explain how a company can use currency options to hedge foreign currency risk.

INTERNATIONAL INTEREST RATES AND EXCHANGE RATES

As we have seen in our discussion of currency swaps, interest rates are not the same in every market. One factor affecting interest rates is the exchange rate between currencies. Even in a perfect capital market, interest rates and exchange rates would be closely linked. This relationship is referred to as interest-rate parity. **Interest-rate parity** is the relationship between the spot and forward exchange rates and the interest rates for two countries. The next example illustrates this interaction.

INTEREST-RATE PARITY
The relationship between the spot and forward exchange rates and the interest rates for two countries.

Relationship Between International Interest Rates and Exchange Rates

E X A M P L E

Suppose you have the following two investment alternatives. You can buy a 1-year U.S.-dollar-denominated note that pays 10% interest at maturity, or a 1-year British-pound-denominated note that pays 12% interest at maturity. Which would you select?

You can't answer the question until you take into account how many pounds you get for your dollars today, and how many dollars you would get for your pounds 1 year from today. The forward exchange market provides the needed information.

Suppose the dollar-pound spot rate is $1.70/£ and the 1-year forward rate is $1.60/£. The pound is trading at a forward discount. This example will demonstrate why. If you invest $1000 in the U.S.-dollar-denominated note, you will receive $1100 at maturity. If you instead convert the $1000 into British pounds at the spot rate, you will receive £588.24 (= 1000/1.70). If you purchase the British-pound-denominated note, then you will receive £658.83 (= [588.24]1.12) at maturity. By selling the pounds forward, you would ensure that the £658.83 would purchase $1054.13 (=[658.83]1.60). The dollar-denominated note is the more profitable investment.

Moreover, you can earn a riskless arbitrage profit by borrowing British pounds, selling them in the spot market for U.S. dollars, investing the dollars at 10%, and selling the dollars you will receive at maturity forward against the pound.

If you borrowed £588.24 and bought $1000 (= [588.24]1.70), the investment of those dollars would yield $1100, which would produce £687.50 (= 1100/1.60) under the forward contract. After paying £70.59 (= [588.24]0.12) of interest and repaying the British pound borrowing, you have a £28.67 (= 687.50 − 588.24 − 70.59) arbitrage profit. Arbitrage will continue until the interest-rate differential is equivalent to the differential between the spot and

(continued on following page)

(Relationship Between International Interest Rates and Exchange Rates *continued from previous page*)

forward rates. The interest-rate differential between U.S. dollars and British pounds for investments of identical risk can be expressed in ratio form as[3]

$$\frac{1 + r_£}{1 + r_\$}$$

where $r_£$ and $r_\$$ are the pound and dollar interest rates, respectively. The differential between the spot exchange rate (s_0) and the forward exchange rate (f_t) can be expressed as

$$\frac{s_0}{f_t}$$

Interest-rate parity holds that

$$\frac{1 + r_£}{1 + r_\$} = \frac{s_0}{f_t} \qquad\qquad (15.1)$$

In this example, interest-rate parity would hold if arbitrage activity raises the 1-year forward rate to \$1.67/£, for then

$$\frac{1 + r_£}{1 + r_\$} = \frac{1.12}{1.10} = 1.02 = \frac{\$1.70/£}{\$1.67/£} = \frac{s_0}{f_1}$$

Interest-rate parity requires the difference between the forward and spot exchange rates to offset the difference between the interest rates in the two countries. *It ensures that a forward currency discount exactly offsets the higher interest rate on comparable investments in that currency.* If U.S.-dollar-denominated investments provided a higher interest rate, then the British pound would trade at a forward premium. In that case, the larger number of dollars to be received upon future sale of pounds would fully compensate for the lower British interest rate. Evidence indicates that interest-rate parity normally holds, at least to a close approximation, in the Eurocurrency markets.

Self-Check

1. What is interest-rate parity?

2. The spot exchange rate is \$0.7432 = 1 Canadian dollar, and the 180-day forward rate is \$0.7518 = 1 Canadian dollar. Which country has the higher interest rate, the United States or Canada?

3. The spot exchange rate is \$0.6085 = 1 German mark and the 180-day forward rate is \$0.6159 = 1 German mark. Is the interest rate higher in Germany or the United States?

INTERNATIONAL INFLATION RATES AND EXCHANGE RATES

Inflation rates also affect exchange rates and interest rates. Suppose a loaf of bread costs \$1 in the United States. What should it cost in Britain? According to the law of one price, \$1 should also buy a loaf of bread in Britain and in every other market. This will happen only if the foreign exchange rate between two currencies adjusts by the difference in the rates of inflation in the countries that issued the two currencies. If the inflation rate is 3% in the United States and

---

[3]The interest rates $r_£$ and $r_\$$ both apply to the same period of time; for example, both might be one-year interest rates.

5% in Britain, then the British pound would have to fall by (1.05/1.03) − 1, or about 2% per year, for the (equivalent) dollar price of bread to remain the same in both countries.

The condition just described is referred to as purchasing power parity.[4] It is formally stated in terms of expected inflation rates. **Purchasing power parity** requires that the expected difference in inflation rates equals the difference between the spot exchange rate now and the spot exchange rate expected in the future. The difference in expected inflation rates is expressed in ratio form as

$$\frac{1 + E[i_£]}{1 + E[i_\$]}$$

where E is the expected value of the quantity in brackets, and $i_£$ and $i_\$$ are the British and U.S. inflation rates, respectively. This ratio must equal the difference between the spot exchange rate (s_0), expressed in dollars per pound, and the expected future spot exchange rate $(E[s_t])$, which is[5]

$$\frac{s_0}{E[s_t]}$$

Purchasing power parity holds that

$$\frac{1 + E[i_£]}{1 + E[i_\$]} = \frac{s_0}{E[s_t]} \qquad\qquad (15.2)$$

PURCHASING POWER PARITY The hypothesis that the expected difference in inflation rates in two countries equals the difference between the spot exchange rate now and the spot exchange rate expected in the future.

Relationship Between International Inflation Rates and Exchange Rates   E X A M P L E

Let's continue the previous example. Suppose the expected inflation rate is 8% in the United States and 10% in Britain. If the current spot rate is $1.70 = £1, purchasing power parity will hold if the expected spot rate 1 year forward is $1.67 = £1. Equation (15.2) can be used to solve for the expected spot rate:

$$\frac{1 + E[i_£]}{1 + E[i_\$]} = \frac{s_0}{E[s_1]}$$

$$\frac{1.10}{1.08} = \frac{\$1.70/£}{E[s_1]}$$

$$E[s_1] = \$1.67/£$$

Purchasing power parity ensures that the expected change in the spot exchange rate offsets the difference between the expected inflation rates in the two countries. *The higher inflation rate is fully offset by the expected rate of depreciation of that country's currency.*

Self-Check

1. Explain what purchasing power parity means.

2. The spot exchange rate is $0.9553 = 1 Brazilian real. If the expected inflation rate is lower in the United States than in Brazil, should the expected future spot rate be higher or lower than the current spot rate? (Assume the rates are quoted in dollars per real.)

3. The spot rate is $0.7026 = 1 Swiss franc. If the Swiss inflation rate is expected to be lower than that in the United States, what is expected to happen to the future spot rate?

---

[4]Purchasing power parity differs from the law of one price in that the law of one price refers to individual goods whereas purchasing power parity refers to the general price level for all goods, for example, as measured by the consumer price index.
[5]The inflation rates $i_£$ and $i_\$$ both apply to the same period of time, for example, both might be one-year inflation rates. The exchange rate $E(s_t)$ is the one expected to hold at the end of this period.

UNBIASED FORWARD RATES AND THE INTERNATIONAL FISHER EFFECT

There are two other conditions that will hold in a well-behaved market. One links forward and spot exchange rates. The other explains how real interest rates relate.

Unbiased Forward Exchange Rates

Suppose foreign exchange market participants do not care about risk—that is, they are risk neutral. Then the forward rate would depend solely on what market participants expect the future spot rate to be. For example, suppose the expected spot rate for British pounds is £1 = $1.50. What would be the forward rate? It would have to be £1 = $1.50. If it were higher than this rate, everyone would want to sell pounds, but no one would be willing to sell dollars forward. If it were lower than this rate, everyone would want to sell dollars, but no one would be willing to sell pounds forward. Therefore, the *unbiased forward exchange rate* condition states that the expected spot exchange rate equals the forward rate:

$$E[s_t] = f_t \qquad (15.3)$$

This condition does not require the actual future spot rate to equal the historical forward rate. Foreign exchange market participants are not assumed to be perfect forecasters. All that is required is that, on average, the forward rate equals the future spot rate. Evidence shows that it does. However, the evidence also indicates that when the forward rate predicts a sharp change (either up or down) in the spot rate, the forecast change tends to overstate the actual change. Thus, the forward rate is not *always* an unbiased predictor of the future spot rate.

International Fisher Effect

Chapter 9 showed that the required return in nominal terms (r_n) results from simply compounding the required real return (r_r) and the expected inflation rate (i):

$$(1 + r_n) = (1 + r_r)(1 + i)$$

so that

$$1 + r_r = \frac{1 + r_n}{1 + i}$$

Many years ago, Irving Fisher argued that the nominal interest rate observed in the financial markets fully reflects investors' collective expectation regarding the inflation rate. It does so in order to compensate them for inflation's effects on the real value of their investments. This phenomenon is now called the *Fisher effect*. If follows from the Principle of Self-Interested Behavior: Investors seek out investments that offer the greatest expected risk-adjusted real return. Arbitrage ensures that in a perfect capital market, two debt instruments denominated in different currencies but of equivalent risk will offer the same expected real return.

If the Fisher effect holds, then the difference in nominal interest rates must equal the difference in expected inflation rates:

$$\frac{1 + r_£}{1 + r_\$} = \frac{1 + E[i_£]}{1 + E[i_\$]} \qquad (15.4)$$

INTERNATIONAL FISHER EFFECT The difference in nominal interest rates must equal the difference in expected inflation rates.

We refer to equation (15.4) as the **international Fisher effect** because it follows from the (domestic) Fisher effect.

Equation (15.4) follows from equations (15.1), (15.2), and (15.3). The four relationships are mutually consistent. If any three of them hold, then they all must hold.

International Fisher Effect

Let's continue the investments example. We know that $r_£ = 0.12$, $r_\$ = 0.10$, $i_£ = 0.10$, and $i_\$ = 0.08$. We can verify that equation (15.4) holds:

$$\frac{1.12}{1.10} \approx 1.02 \approx \frac{1.10}{1.08}$$

Interpretation of the International Fisher Effect

Let's rewrite equation (15.4) as

$$\frac{1 + r_£}{1 + E[i_£]} = \frac{1 + r_\$}{1 + E[i_\$]} = 1 + r_r$$

The international Fisher effect says that the real interest rate is the same in every country.

There isn't much empirical evidence concerning the international Fisher effect. As a general rule, the countries with the highest inflation rates also tend to have the highest interest rates. Thus, real interest rates vary less than nominal interest rates. As we have noted, there are various impediments to the free international flow of capital. As a result, arbitrage activity cannot achieve a single real interest rate that applies in all market segments.

Self-Check

1. What is the unbiased forward exchange rate condition?

2. The one-year forward rate is 121 Japanese yen per U.S. dollar. According to the unbiased forward exchange rate condition, what is an unbiased estimate of the spot rate in one year?

3. What is the international Fisher effect?

4. The interest rate is higher in Italy than in Germany. How does the international Fisher effect explain this?

INTERNATIONAL CAPITAL BUDGETING DECISIONS

Companies should evaluate foreign investment opportunities using the same principles they apply to domestic projects. A foreign project, however, involves several complications. The incremental after-tax cash flows are denominated in foreign currencies. These foreign currencies may not be freely convertible into U.S. dollars. Foreign investment projects may also entail a risk of expropriation by the host country's government. In addition, foreign taxes must be considered, the cost of capital for a foreign project may differ from that for a domestic project, and there may be a cost advantage to raising funds in the foreign country or in the international capital market.

After cash flows are adjusted for these factors, a company has two alternative methods of applying the NPV criterion to foreign projects. The first is to calculate the incremental cash flows in the local currency, convert them into dollars at appropriate projected foreign exchange rates, and discount at the dollar-denominated required return. The second method is to do the entire NPV calculation in the local currency and then convert the foreign-currency-denominated NPV into dollars at the current exchange rate. The two procedures, applied correctly, will produce the same NPV.

Estimating the Incremental Cash Flows

So long as a company can hedge its foreign currency risk exposure, it should not use internal foreign exchange forecasts to make investment decisions. It should use the forward rates quoted in the foreign exchange market. If forward rates are not available far enough into the future, then the company should use the key relationships between interest rates, exchange rates, and inflation rates to estimate expected future spot exchange rates.

EXAMPLE

The Incremental After-Tax Cash Flows for AlliedSignal's German Project

AlliedSignal Inc. is considering building a plant in Germany to manufacture automotive parts for the Central European market. The plant is expected to cost DM50 million. AlliedSignal's project staff has projected the following incremental after-tax cash flows in German marks:

Year	1	2	3	4	5
Cash flow (DM millions)	15	17	20	20	17

The current dollar–mark exchange rate is DM1 = $0.60. This implies a $30 million (= [0.60]50) project cost. AlliedSignal can project future exchange rates by applying the key relationships between interest rates, exchange rates, inflation rates, and expected future spot exchange rates.

Suppose the 1-year riskless return is 8% in the United States (the equivalent annual 1-year Treasury note rate) and 6% in Germany, and that the expected inflation rate in the United States is 5% per annum for each of the next 5 years. Under interest rate parity, equation (15.1), and unbiased forward exchange rates, equation (15.3), the expected spot rate 1 year hence satisfies

$$\frac{1.06}{1.08} = \frac{\$0.60}{E[s_1]}$$

$$E[s_1] = \$0.6113$$

Under purchasing power parity, equation (15.2),

$$\frac{1 + E[i_{DM}]}{1.05} = \frac{0.60}{0.6113}$$

$$1 + E[i_{DM}] = 1.03059$$

The expected inflation rate in Germany for the next year is 3.059%. Suppose the real interest rate is expected to remain constant over the next 5 years in each country. Then the projected German inflation rate is 3.059% per year for each of the next 5 years. AlliedSignal should check to make sure that its cash flow forecast is consistent with a 3.059% German inflation rate.

Under purchasing power parity, equation (15.2), the expected spot exchange rate t years hence (1 ≤ t ≤ 5) satisfies

$$E[s_t] = \$0.60\left(\frac{1.05}{1.03059}\right)^t$$

The projected German mark cash flows can be converted into U.S. dollars:

Year	1	2	3	4	5
Cash flow (DM millions)	15	17	20	20	17
Exchange rate ($/DM)	0.6113	0.6228	0.6345	0.6465	0.6586
Cash flow ($ millions)	9.17	10.59	12.69	12.93	11.20

Lack of Convertibility   Unlike Germany, many foreign countries place restrictions on a company's ability to convert local currency into dollars or other "hard" currencies. This is often the case in Third World countries that have very limited hard currency reserves. If the free cash flow is not freely convertible into U.S. dollars—that is, if the U.S. parent is not free to convert the foreign currency into U.S. dollars and transfer the dollars outside the foreign country—then the annual cash flows may overstate the true benefits that the project sponsor can expect to realize. Recall from chapter 8 that the NPV calculation implicitly assumes that interim cash flows can be reinvested at the project's cost of capital. When the local currency is not freely convertible into U.S. dollars, the incremental cash flow stream should reflect the actual expected U.S. dollar cash remittances (including interest on reinvested balances that can be remitted in U.S. dollars) at the time the project sponsor expects to realize these U.S. dollar flows.

Expropriation and Other Political Risks   Investing in a foreign country entails political risk. An incoming foreign government might not honor a previous government's agreement to permit convertibility, or the foreign government might impose discriminatory taxes. Worst of all, it might expropriate the company's property for its own use (euphemistically called "nationalization").

Political risks should be incorporated in discounted cash flow analysis by adjusting the incremental cash flows, rather than by adjusting the discount rate.

Adjusting for Political Risk

EXAMPLE

Suppose that the expected cash flows for a project are

Year	1	2	3	4
Cash flow ($ millions)	20	30	30	40

Let's say the project sponsor fears that there is a 50% probability that the project will be expropriated at the end of 2 years when a new government may come to power. The expected cash flow stream to be discounted is

Year	1	2	3	4
Cash flow ($ millions)	20	30	15	20

Calculating the probability of expropriation is highly subjective. But that does not mean the risk should be ignored. If expropriation risk is significant, it is important to gauge the sensitivity of NPV to the probability of expropriation. Break-even analysis—determining the probability of expropriation during any particular year that would reduce the NPV to zero—is often used.

Domestic Currency Approach

Returning to the AlliedSignal example, we would like to demonstrate calculating the project's NPV with both the domestic currency approach and the foreign currency approach. To use the domestic currency approach, the cash flows are converted into U.S. dollars and an appropriate risk-adjusted discount rate is estimated. Then the NPV can be calculated.

Calculating the NPV for AlliedSignal's German Investment

EXAMPLE

AlliedSignal's marginal income tax rate for the project is 23.8%. The pretax cost of debt for the project is 10% based on a project debt ratio (L) of 25%, or $r_d = 0.10$. The debt ratio is consistent with AlliedSignal's capital structure objective. Next we'll use the CAPM to calculate AlliedSignal's required return on equity.

(continued on following page)

(Calculating the NPV for AlliedSignal's German Investment *continued from previous page*)

AlliedSignal calculates a (leveraged) project beta of 1.10. The riskless return is 8%, and the expected return on the market portfolio is 16.6%. The (leveraged) required return on equity for the project is

$$r_e = 8 + 1.10(16.6 - 8) = 17.46\%$$

The required return for the dollar-denominated incremental cash flow stream is then the weighted average cost of capital:

$$\text{WACC} = 0.25(0.762)(0.1) + 0.75(0.1746) = 15.00\%$$

The project NPV is

$$\text{NPV} = -30.0 + \frac{9.17}{1.15} + \frac{10.59}{(1.15)^2} + \frac{12.69}{(1.15)^3} + \frac{12.93}{(1.15)^4} + \frac{11.20}{(1.15)^5} = \$7.29 \text{ million}$$

Foreign Currency Approach

Let's verify that calculating the project NPV in German marks does not alter the dollar NPV. First, we calculate the approximate German mark required return. Then we'll discount the cash flows in German marks, and finally convert the present value to dollars.

Based on the international Fisher effect, the required return in German marks must satisfy the relationship

$$\frac{1 + r_{DM}}{1 + r_{\$}} = \frac{1 + r_{DM}^*}{1 + r_{\$}^*}$$

where r_{DM} and $r_{\$}$ are the 1-year riskless returns, and r_{DM}^* and $r_{\$}^*$ are the required returns in DM and $, respectively. Then

$$\frac{1.06}{1.08} = \frac{1 + r_{DM}^*}{1.15} \quad or \ r_{DM}^* = 12.87\%$$

The NPV of the project in German marks is

$$\text{NPV} = -50.0 + \frac{15.00}{1.1287} + \frac{17.00}{(1.1287)^2} + \frac{20.00}{(1.1287)^3} + \frac{20.00}{(1.1287)^4} + \frac{17.00}{(1.1287)^5} = \text{DM}12.15 \text{ million}$$

Converting this amount to U.S. dollars gives

$$\text{DM}12.15 \text{ million}(\$0.60/\text{DM}) = \$7.29 \text{ million}$$

Properly calculated, the domestic and foreign currency approaches produce the same result.

Self-Check

1. Describe the two alternative methods of applying the NPV criterion to foreign capital budgeting projects. Should they both lead to the same NPV?

2. How can you allow for expropriation risk in the NPV analysis of a capital project?

FINANCING FOREIGN INVESTMENTS

Today, bond issues are regularly launched in New York, London, or Tokyo and traded almost immediately in every time zone. Increasingly, domestic debt and equity issues are sold overseas as well as in the United States, and foreign debt and equity issues are also sold in the

United States. The capital markets have become global, and for this reason it is important for financial managers to maintain a global perspective when raising funds.

A company that wants to borrow funds to finance a foreign capital budgeting project can (1) borrow U.S. dollars in the United States and export the funds to the foreign country, (2) borrow U.S. dollars in the Euromarket, (3) borrow in the foreign country, or (4) borrow in whichever currency and in whichever market affords the lowest interest cost. The fourth strategy is particularly tempting but also very risky, as many *former* corporate treasurers will attest!

Financing in the Euromarket

In addition to the separate domestic capital markets, there is a large supranational Euromarket. A *Eurobond* is a bond that a company or some other type of issuer sells outside the country in whose currency it is denominated. In financial circles, the prefix *Euro* means "outside of." For example, Eurodollar bonds are denominated in U.S. dollars and issued, held, and traded outside the United States. Eurobonds exist in U.S. dollars, Canadian dollars, German marks, French francs, Japanese yen, British pounds, and many other currencies.

Long-Term Loans   Eurobonds have become a major source of capital. The Euromarket is a large unregulated market; it is basically free of the restrictions that apply to domestic offerings. The Euromarket offers a viable alternative to the domestic capital market for a company that wants to raise short-term or long-term funds. From time to time, U.S. companies have found it advantageous to sell entire bond issues in the Eurobond market, rather than domestically, and to borrow in different currencies. A few years ago, the World Bank introduced *global bonds,* which are designed to qualify for immediate trading in any domestic capital market and in the Euromarket, and hence to reach the broadest group of investors. In all these cases, the issuer enters the Euromarket hoping to exploit an opportunity to raise funds at a lower cost than domestically.

Short-Term Loans   In addition to issuing Eurobonds to raise long-term funds, companies can also borrow short-term funds in the Euromarket. The interest rate on such loans is usually tied to LIBOR. The *London Interbank Offered Rate,* or LIBOR, is the interest rate at which large international banks lend each other funds in the London money market. Most loans consist of Eurodollars, which are U.S. dollar deposits in banks outside the United States. But loans are also granted in other currencies. Most Eurodollar loans are overnight. The overnight rate is referred to as *overnight LIBOR.* But banks also lend each other Eurodollars for longer periods, such as for one week at *7-day LIBOR,* for one month at *1-month LIBOR,* and so on. There are similar interest rates for other Eurocurrencies, such as sterling (British pound) LIBOR, French franc LIBOR, and so on.

Dollar LIBOR is important in the commercial loan market. Many short-term loans, including those in the United States, bear interest at a rate tied to LIBOR. For example, the interest rate on a loan might be stated as 3-month LIBOR plus 1%. The interest rate adjusts quarterly. If 3-month LIBOR increases to 6% from 5%, the interest rate increases to 7% from 6%. Similarly, floating-rate Eurobonds usually have an interest rate that is tied to LIBOR.

Foreign Bonds   A *foreign bond* is issued by a foreign company or government in the country in whose currency it is denominated. For example, *Yankee bonds* are denominated in U.S. dollars and issued in the United States by foreign companies or governments. They are different from Eurobonds. A U.S. company sells Eurobonds outside the United States; a foreign company sells Yankee bonds in the United States. Other examples of foreign bonds are Bulldog bonds (issued in Britain), Matador bonds (Spain), Rembrandt bonds (Netherlands), and Samurai bonds (Japan). Foreign bonds often face tougher restrictions and disclosure standards than bonds sold by domestic issuers. As a result, the Eurobond market has grown more rapidly than the markets for foreign bonds.

Choice of Currency

AlliedSignal could borrow $30 million and purchase DM50 million, or it could borrow DM50 million. Borrowing dollars to fund a German mark investment entails foreign exchange risk. If AlliedSignal borrows dollars and the German mark depreciates relative to the dollar, the company's German automotive plant will be worth fewer dollars. Also, in that case, AlliedSignal will have to dedicate a larger proportion of its mark-denominated project cash flow to service its U.S.-dollar-denominated debt. The opposite would occur if the mark appreciated relative to the dollar. AlliedSignal can hedge against this foreign exchange risk by borrowing in marks.

Interest rate parity implies that when credit risk is held constant, any difference in nominal *pretax* yields between two different currencies is exactly offset by the expected change in the spot exchange rate during the term of the loan. The currency of borrowing does not matter. Income taxes or international capital market frictions can cause the choice of currency to make a difference, however. For example, government-imposed capital controls can create opportunities to reduce a borrower's after-tax cost of debt by choosing one currency over another.

EXAMPLE   *Calculating AlliedSignal's Cost of Borrowing in a Foreign Currency*

Suppose that AlliedSignal can borrow 5-year funds in U.S. dollars for its new plant at an interest rate of 10% APR or 5-year funds in German marks at an interest rate of 8% APR. The mark-denominated loan calls for sinking fund payments of DM10 at the end of years 2 and 3 and DM15 at the end of years 4 and 5. First we verify that the pretax dollar cost of debt (before transaction costs) is 10%. Table 15.4 presents AlliedSignal's debt service in U.S. dollars. The cost of debt is the return c that solves the equation

$$0 = -30.0 + \frac{2.4452}{1+c} + \frac{8.7192}{(1+c)^2} + \frac{8.3754}{(1+c)^3} + \frac{11.2491}{(1+c)^4} + \frac{10.6693}{(1+c)^5}$$

so that $c = 10.0\%$.

AlliedSignal's marginal ordinary income tax rate is 50% on both its U.S. income and its German income. Its after-tax cost of debt on the U.S. dollar loan (before transaction costs) is $0.10(1 - 0.5) = 5.00\%$.

Suppose instead that AlliedSignal borrows and repays the German marks through its German subsidiary. Its after-tax cost of debt, expressed in terms of dollars, is given in table 15.5. In this case, the cost of debt is the return c that solves the equation

$$0 = -30.0 + \frac{1.2226}{1+c} + \frac{7.4736}{(1+c)^2} + \frac{7.3602}{(1+c)^3} + \frac{10.4733}{(1+c)^4} + \frac{10.2742}{(1+c)^5}$$

so that $c = 5.96\%$.

The after-tax cost of the loan in German marks exceeds the after-tax cost of the U.S. dollar loan. Note that the mark is appreciating relative to the dollar, but only the actual interest expense, not the cost to AlliedSignal of repaying the more expensive marks, is tax deductible.

As a rule, borrowing in the weaker currency usually minimizes the expected after-tax cost of debt. That is, interest rate parity applies to pretax yields, not after-tax yields. Also, it is normally cheaper to borrow in high-tax-rate countries. However, neither statement is *always* true. We recommend that when evaluating alternative currency borrowing options, you calculate the after-tax cost of each before deciding which to select. ■

TABLE 15.4
AlliedSignal's Debt Service in U.S. Dollars

	YEAR				
	1	**2**	**3**	**4**	**5**
Principal amount (DM millions)	50	50	40	30	15
Interest at 8% (DM millions)	4	4	3.2	2.4	1.2
Principal payment (DM millions)	—	10	10	15	15
Total debt service (DM millions)	4	14	13.2	17.4	16.2
Exchange rate ($/DM)	×0.6113	×0.6228	×0.6345	×0.6465	×0.6586
Debt service ($ millions)	2.4452	8.7192	8.3754	11.2491	10.6693

TABLE 15.5
After-Tax Debt Service for AlliedSignal's German Mark Loan

	YEAR				
	1	**2**	**3**	**4**	**5**
Debt service (DM millions):					
Principal payment	—	10	10	15	15
Interest payment	4	4	3.2	2.4	1.2
Tax saving (at 50%)	(2)	(2)	(1.6)	(1.2)	(0.6)
Total	2	12	11.6	16.2	15.6
Exchange rate	×0.6113	×0.6228	×0.6345	×0.6465	×0.6586
Debt service ($ millions)	1.2226	7.4736	7.3602	10.4733	10.2742

American Depository Receipts

As with debt, a company can raise equity in its domestic capital market, in one of the foreign national capital markets, or in the Euromarket. Likewise, foreign companies can raise equity in the United States.

A foreign company can raise funds in the United States by issuing *American depository receipts,* or ADRs. An ADR is a security that represents ownership of shares of a foreign common stock. The foreign shares are held in trust, which issues the ADRs in the United States. ADRs are publicly traded, and their price is expressed in U.S. dollars. An agent bank converts each dividend into U.S. dollars before paying it to U.S. shareholders. Foreign companies like ADRs because the securities laws are less demanding for ADRs than for shares issued directly to U.S. investors. There are about 700 separate issues of ADRs.

Self-Check

1. What is the Eurodollar bond market? Are there Euromarkets for bonds denominated in other currencies besides U.S. dollars? Name a few.

2. Why might it be advantageous to borrow in one currency rather than another?

3. Taking tax factors into account, is it usually better to borrow in a weaker currency or in a stronger currency? In a high-tax-rate country or a low-tax-rate country?

4. What are ADRs? Where are they issued and traded? If you look up the price of an ADR, in what currency will it be quoted?

SUMMARY

A multinational company's objective is the same as that of a purely domestic company: to maximize shareholder wealth. International dimensions are increasingly relevant to financial decisions.

- An international financial manager needs additional analytical tools to cope with complications in the form of cash flows denominated in foreign currencies, foreign political risk, foreign government regulations and capital constraints, and foreign tax systems. Managers need these tools to take advantage of opportunities that are available in the foreign exchange market and in foreign capital markets to reduce foreign exchange risk. Information from those markets enables a financial manager to ensure that financial decisions are not biased, perhaps unknowingly, by foreign exchange rate factors.

- A critical first step toward developing these tools involves understanding the four key international financial market relationships: interest-rate parity, purchasing power parity, unbiased forward exchange rates, and the international Fisher effect.
  - Interest-rate parity requires the difference between the forward and spot exchange rates to offset the difference between the interest rates in the two countries.
  - Purchasing power parity states that the difference between the expected inflation rates in two countries equals the expected change in the spot exchange rate.
  - The unbiased forward exchange rate condition states that the forward exchange rate equals the expected future spot exchange rate.
  - The international Fisher effect holds that real rates of interest must be the same in all the world's capital markets.
  These four relationships do not hold exactly because of government regulations and other market imperfections. But they are a useful approximation to reality and represent a good starting point for analysis.

- The foreign exchange market offers a low-cost means of hedging foreign exchange risk. International financial managers would be wise to utilize this relatively cheap insurance and not to speculate on exchange rate movements. We explained how to use forward and futures contracts and currency options to reduce or eliminate exposure to foreign exchange risk.

- International capital budgeting projects involve foreign exchange considerations. But because of the four key international market relationships, it makes no difference which currency is used in the calculations.
  - The foreign currency approach involves estimating cash flows in the foreign currency, calculating an NPV in the foreign currency at the foreign currency required return, and then converting the foreign currency NPV to the domestic currency.
  - The domestic currency approach involves converting the foreign cash flows into the domestic currency, and then calculating a domestic currency NPV at the domestic currency required return.
  The incremental cash flow stream and the discount rate should be calculated with respect to the same currency; which currency does not matter so long as the key international market relationships all hold. In particular, ensure that the inflation rate implicit in the forecast cash flow stream is consistent with purchasing power parity.

- A foreign project can be financed in the sponsoring company's domestic capital market, in the Euromarket, in the host country's capital market, or in some other country's capital market. The cost of funds for each alternative should be calculated after tax on a consistent basis. It should be expressed in terms of the same currency, the same frequency of compounding, and so forth. The company should select the lowest-cost alternative, taking into consideration any particular benefit from hedging foreign exchange, political, or other risks.

- A company should not always borrow in the currency that has the lowest stated interest rate. That currency is likely to appreciate, which can offset the apparent saving.

- Trading on U.S. exchanges has become very significant in American Depository Receipts (ADRs), representing shares of foreign companies.

EQUATION SUMMARY

(15.1)

$$\frac{1 + r_\pounds}{1 + r_\$} = \frac{s_0}{f_t}$$

(15.2)
$$\frac{1+E[i_£]}{1+E[i_$]} = \frac{s_0}{E[s_t]}$$

(15.3)
$$E[s_t] = f_t$$

(15.4)
$$\frac{1+r_£}{1+r_$} = \frac{1+E[i_£]}{1+E[i_$]}$$

CHAPTER REVIEW ACTIVITIES

SELF-TEST PROBLEMS

1. (Currency cross rates) Consider the following exchange rates: $0.08640 = 1 Austrian schilling; $0.02787 = 1 Indian rupee; $0.7432 = 1 Canadian dollar.

a. How many schillings, rupees, and Canadian dollars are equivalent to $1.00?

b. How many schillings equal one rupee?

c. How many rupees equal one Canadian dollar?

d. How many Canadian dollars equal one schilling?

2. (Interest-rate parity) The spot rate is $1.6403 = £1 and the 180-day forward rate is $1.6344 = £1. If the interest rate in the United States is 5.00% APR, what should be the interest rate in the United Kingdom?

3. (Purchasing power parity) The spot rate is $0.600 per German DM. If the inflation rates are 3% in the United States and 5% in Germany, what is the expected spot rate in one year?

SOLUTIONS TO SELF-TEST PROBLEMS

1. a. 1/0.08640 = 11.574 Austrian shillings = $1.00
   1/0.02787 = 35.881 Indian rupees = $1.00
   1/0.7432 = 1.3455 Canadian dollars = $1.00

   b. $$\frac{\$0.02787}{\text{rupee}} \div \frac{\$0.08640}{\text{schilling}} = 0.3226 \text{ schillings per rupee}$$

   c. $$\frac{\$0.7432}{\text{Canadian dollar}} \div \frac{\$0.02787}{\text{rupee}} = 26.6667 \text{ rupees per Canadian dollar}$$

   d. $$\frac{\$0.08640}{\text{schilling}} \div \frac{\$0.7432}{\text{Canadian dollar}} = 0.1163 \text{ Canadian dollars per schilling}$$

2. Since the forward rate is one-half year forward, the one-half year interest rate in the United States is 5%/2 = 2.5%. Use this rate in equation (15.1), the interest-rate parity formula:

$$\frac{1+r_£}{1+r_$} = \frac{s_0}{f_t}$$

$$\frac{1+r_£}{1+0.025} = \frac{1.6403}{1.6344}$$

$$r_£ = 0.0287$$

The U.K. 6-month interest rate is 2.87%, which is 5.74% (= [2]2.87%) APR. Because the British pound is expected to depreciate in value over the next 6 months, the U.K. interest rate must be higher than the U.S. rate or else arbitrage profits would be possible.

3. Find the expected spot rate in 1 year with equation (15.2):

$$\frac{1+E[i_{DM}]}{1+E[i_$]} = \frac{s_0}{E[s_t]}$$

$$\frac{1+0.05}{1+0.03} = \frac{0.600}{E[s_t]}$$

$$E[s_t] = \$0.5886 \text{ per DM}$$

QUESTIONS

1. Explain the important differences between a forward contract for a particular foreign currency and a futures contract for the same currency. What are the relative advantages of each?

2. Explain each of the following relationships:
   a. interest-rate parity
   b. purchasing power parity
   c. unbiased forward exchange rates
   d. international Fisher effect

3. What happens if the conditions required for unbiased forward exchange rates to hold are satisfied in the market for U.S. dollars and British pounds but:
   a. the forward rate (expressed as $ per £) is greater than the expected future spot rate (expressed as $ per £)?
   b. the forward rate (expressed as $ per £) is less than the expected future spot rate (expressed as $ per £)?

4. Explain which of the following represents the stronger requirement: (a) the forward rate always equals the expected future spot rate, or (b) the forward rate always equals the future spot rate.

5. Explain why a corporate treasurer would be unwise to follow a policy of always borrowing in whichever currency affords the lowest stated interest rate.

6. Suppose the Japanese yen–German mark spot exchange rate is ¥1 = DM0.012 and the expected spot rate 1 year hence is ¥ = DM0.015. What is the relationship between the expected inflation rates in Japan and Germany for the coming year?

CHALLENGING QUESTIONS

7. Show that if interest-rate parity, purchasing power parity, and unbiased forward exchange rates all hold, then so does the international Fisher effect. What happens when any one of the first three parity relationships fails to hold?

8. Suppose the expected average annual inflation rates in Canada and Great Britain over the next 5 years are 7% and 10%, respectively. Interest-rate parity and purchasing power parity hold, and forward exchange rates are unbiased. What is the relationship between the 5-year interest rates in Canada and Great Britain?

9. Show that if any one of the four parity relationships fails to hold, at least one other must also fail to hold.

PROBLEM SET A

A1. (Currency cross rates) Consider the following exchange rates: $0.005872 = 1 Hungarian forint; $0.03797 = 1 Philippino peso; $0.5406 = 1 Dutch guilder.
   a. How many forints, pesos, and guilders are equivalent to $1.00?
   b. How many forints equal one peso? How many pesos equal one guilder? How many guilders equal one forint?

A2. (Interest-rate parity) The spot rate is $0.7432 = 1 Canadian dollar and the 180-day forward rate is $0.7518 = 1 Canadian dollar. If the interest rate in the United States is 5.00% APR, what should be the interest rate in Canada?

A3. (Purchasing power parity) The spot rate is $0.7500 per Swiss franc. If the inflation rates are 3.5% in the U.S. and 1.5% in Switzerland, what is the expected spot rate in one year?

A4. (Currency cross rates) Using the foreign currency cross rates in figure 15.2:
   a. Find the price of a Canadian dollar in Swiss francs.
   b. Find the price of a Swiss franc in Canadian dollars.
   c. Show that the currency cross rates in **a** and **b** are equivalent.

A5. (Forward discounts or premia) Using the foreign exchange rates for Tuesday in figure 15.2:
   a. Is the German mark trading at a forward discount or at a forward premium to the U.S. dollar? Calculate the 30-day, 90-day, and 180-day forward premium or discount.
   b. Is the Japanese yen trading at a forward discount or at a forward premium to the U.S. dollar? Calculate the 30-day, 90-day, and 180-day forward premium or discount.

A6. (Currency cross rates) The Swiss franc–Japanese yen exchange rate is SF1 = ¥96.18. The Swiss franc-German mark exchange rate is SF1 = DM1.125. What is the Japanese yen–German mark exchange rate?

A7. (Purchasing power parity) The dollar–pound exchange rate is £1 = $2.00. The expected rates of inflation in the United States and Great Britain are 4% and 8% APR, respectively. Calculate the one-year forward exchange rate required under purchasing power parity.

A8. (Purchasing power parity) Suppose the interest rates in the United States and Switzerland are 8% and 4% APR, respectively, and the projected inflation rates are 5% and 1% APR, respectively. Verify that equation (15.4) holds. What is the real interest rate?

A9. (Hedging) Using the Boeing example, show that if the future spot rate is £1 = $1.25, the forward contract hedge will produce a net realized dollar value of $320 million. Show that the same result occurs if the future spot rate is £1 = $2.00.

A10. (NPV versus IRR criterion) Calculate the U.S. dollar and German mark internal rates of return for AlliedSignal's automotive plant and apply the IRR criterion. Which criterion is superior, IRR or NPV?

PROBLEM SET B

B1. (Currency cross rates) The table of currency cross rates is partially filled in. Please fill in the missing exchange rates. The values in the table are the units of the foreign currency of the country in a particular row equivalent to the currency in the column. For example, in the Germany row and Dollar column, 1.6434 DM = $1.00. In the U.S. row and the D-Mark column, $0.60849 = 1 DM, which is the reciprocal of 1.6434.

Key Currency Cross Rates

	Dollar	Pound	Peso	Yen	D-Mark	CanD
Canada	1.3455	_____	_____	_____	_____	......
Germany	1.6434	_____	_____	_____	......	_____
Japan	123.32	_____	_____	......	_____	_____
Mexico	7.8210	_____	......	_____	_____	_____
U.K.	.60964	......	_____	_____	_____	_____
U.S.	......	1.6403	.12786	.00811	.60849	.74322

B2. (International borrowing costs) A company faces two borrowing alternatives. It can issue 6-year debt domestically that bears a 10% APR coupon and that matures in a lump sum at the end of 6 years. Issuance expenses are 1% of the principal amount. Alternatively it can issue a 10¼% Eurobond that matures in a lump sum at the end of 6 years. Issuance expenses are 1.25% of the principal amount. The issuer's tax rate is 50%.

a. Calculate the after-tax cost of the domestic issue.

b. Calculate the after-tax cost of the Eurobond issue, and express this cost on an

equivalent semiannually compounded basis.

c. Which issue is cheaper? Explain.

B3. (International borrowing costs) Look back at AlliedSignal's cost of borrowing in German marks on page 568. Suppose AlliedSignal's marginal ordinary income tax rate is 34%. Ignore issuance expenses.

a. Calculate the after-tax cost of the U.S.-dollar-denominated issue.

b. Calculate the after-tax cost of the German-

mark-denominated issue expressed in U.S. dollars.

B4. (Interest-rate parity) The 3-month riskless interest rate in U.S. dollars is 8% APR. The 3-month riskless interest rate in Swiss francs is 3% APR. The dollar–franc exchange rate is SF1 = $0.66.

a. Calculate the 3-month forward rate required under interest rate parity.

b. Suppose the 3-month forward rate is SF1 = $0.68. Describe how a riskless arbitrage profit could be earned.

c. Quantify the profit in both dollars and Swiss francs.

B5. (Interest-rate parity) The spot rate for U.S. dollars and German marks is $1 = DM1.50. The 1-year forward rate is $1 = DM1.40.

a. Under interest-rate parity, what is the 1-year U.S. dollar interest rate if the 1-year German mark interest rate is 5%?

b. Under interest-rate parity, what is the 1-year German mark interest rate if the 1-year U.S. dollar interest rate is 10%?

c. What mathematical relationship must hold between the U.S. dollar and German mark 1-year interest rates if interest-rate parity prevails?

B6. (Arbitrage opportunity) Gold is selling for $450/oz. in New York and £300/oz. in London.

a. Suppose it were costless to transport gold between New York and London. What would the dollar–pound exchange rate have to be if the law of one price is to hold?

b. Suppose the dollar–pound exchange rate is £1 = $1.70. Describe how arbitrageurs could realize a riskless arbitrage profit.

c. Quantify the profit in both dollars and British pounds.

B7. (Unbiased forward exchange rates) The Swiss franc–German mark spot exchange rate is SF1 = DM1.20. The 1-year forward rate is SF1 = DM1.30.

a. What is your best estimate of the spot rate expected 1 year from now?

b. If the expected spot rate were SF1 = DM1.40, would anyone want to sell Swiss francs forward? to sell German marks forward?

c. If the expected spot rate were SF1 = DM1, would anyone want to sell Swiss francs forward? to sell German marks forward?

B8. (Hedging transactions) TransAtlantic Airlines (TAA) expects to receive DM5 million from a German tour operator in 30 days. Because TAA's expenses are in U.S. dollars, the company wishes to hedge its foreign currency risk. The current spot exchange rate is DM1 = $0.60, and the 30-day forward exchange rate is DM1 = $0.58.

a. How many U.S. dollars should TAA expect to receive if it does not hedge?

b. Suppose the spot exchange rate at the time the tour operator pays is DM1 = $0.56. How much would hedging have saved TAA?

c. If 30-day interest rates are 10% APR in the United States and Germany, would TAA be better off (1) borrowing German marks for 30 days, investing them, and using the DM5 million it receives to repay the loan or (2) selling DM5 million forward to hedge its risk?

d. If the 30-day interest rates in the United States and Germany are 10% and 14% APR, respectively, would TAA be better off borrowing marks for 30 days and using the DM5 million to repay the loan, or selling DM5 million forward?

B9. (Interest-rate parity) In problem B8, suppose the 30-day interest rate in the United States is 12% APR. What would the 30-day interest rate have to be in Germany in order for TAA to be indifferent between (1) entering into a 30-day forward contract and (2) creating a 30-day foreign currency money market hedge by borrowing in the foreign currency?

B10. (Purchasing power parity) Consider again AlliedSignal's proposed automotive plant on page 564. What are the expected real rates of interest in Germany and in the United States? Why must these rates of interest be equal when interest-rate parity and purchasing power parity hold and forward exchange rates are unbiased?

B11. (International capital budgeting) With AlliedSignal's proposed automotive plant, suppose that the projected riskless interest rates (APR) in the United States and Germany are given below.

Maturity (years)	1	2	3	4	5
United States	8%	9%	9%	10%	10%
Germany	6%	7%	8%	9%	10%

a. Calculate the spot exchange rates expected 1, 2, 3, 4, and 5 years hence.

b. Calculate the projected incremental cash flow stream in dollars on the basis of the projected spot exchange rates in part **a**.

c. Calculate the NPV of the project based on the cash flow stream in part **b**.

B12. (International capital budgeting analysis) Northern Chemical Company is considering building a petrochemical plant in Scotland. The plant would cost $100 million. The projected incremental cash flow stream is given below. The current spot exchange rate is £1 = $1.50. The 1-year riskless return is 8% in the United States and 12% in the United Kingdom. The expected inflation rate in the United States is 5% per year for the next 7 years. The expected inflation rate in the United Kingdom is constant over this time period, too.

Year	1	2	3	4	5	6	7
Cash flow (£ millions)	30	40	40	50	50	50	50

a. What is the expected inflation rate in the United Kingdom for the next 7 years?
b. Calculate the expected spot exchange rates for each of the next 7 years.
c. Calculate the projected incremental cash flow stream in dollars.
d. If the dollar required return is 14%, what is the NPV in dollars?

e. Calculate the British pound required return.
f. Calculate the NPV in British pounds.
g. Are the project NPVs in parts **d** and **f** equal? Explain.

B13. (International borrowing costs) Verify that if AlliedSignal can deduct for tax purposes the appreciation in the cost of marks that must be repaid, its after-tax cost of the mark-denominated loan, expressed in U.S. dollars, closely approximates the after-tax cost of the U.S.-dollar-denominated loan, 5.00%.

PROBLEM SET C

C1. (Forward interest rates) The 2-year interest rate is 10% per year semiannually compounded. The 1-year interest rate is 8% per year semiannually compounded. If there is no opportunity for riskless arbitrage, what is the 1-year forward interest rate?

C2. (Hedging transactions) Generalize the Boeing example to demonstrate that:
a. The net realized dollar value will be $320 million regardless of the future spot exchange rate when the British pounds are sold forward.
b. The net realized dollar value will be $320 million regardless of the future spot ex-
change rate when the British pounds are sold spot and the dollar proceeds invested at an interest rate that satisfies interest-rate parity.

C3. (Law of one price) *The Economist* (April 15, 1995) reported the following prices for a Big Mac hamburger in different countries, along with the exchange rates given below.

Country	Price of Big Mac	Exchange Rate
Australia	A$2.45	A$1.35/US$
Britain	£1.74	£0.62/US$
Canada	C$2.77	C$1.39/US$
France	FFr18.5	FFr4.80/US$
Germany	DM4.80	DM1.38/US$
Japan	¥391	¥84/US$
United States	$2.32	—

a. Calculate the exchange rates implied by the law of one price.
b. Are the prices consistent with the law of one price?

c. How would you interpret your answers to parts **a** and **b?** Are exchange rates out of equilibrium? Is the law of one price invalid? Is there some other explanation?

BIBLIOGRAPHY

Aggarwal, Reena, Ricardo Leal, and Leonardo Hernandez. "The Aftermarket Performance of Initial Public Offerings in Latin America," *Financial Management,* 1993, 22(1):42–53.

Alexander, Gordon, Cheol S. Eun, and S. Janakiramanan. "Asset Pricing and Dual Listing on Foreign Capital Markets: A Note," *Journal of Finance,* 1987, 42(1):151–158.

Anvari, M. "Efficient Scheduling of Cross-Border Cash Transfers," *Financial Management*, 1986, 15(2):40–49.

Baldwin, Carliss Y. "Competing for Capital in a Global Environment," *Midland Corporate Finance Journal*, 1987, 5(Spring): 43–64.

Cebenoyan, A. Sinan, George J. Papaioannou, and Nickolaos G. Travlos. "Foreign Takeover Activity in the U.S. and Wealth Effects for Target Firm Shareholders," *Financial Management*, 1992, 21(3):58–68.

Chang, Jack S. K., and Soushan Wu. "On Hedging Jump Risks in the Foreign Exchange and Stock Markets," *Financial Management*, 1994, 23(1):15.

Chen, Haiyang, Michael Y. Hu, and Joseph C. P. Shieh. "The Wealth Effect of International Joint Ventures: The Case of U.S. Investment in China," *Financial Management*, 1991, 20(4):31–41.

Collins, J. Markham, and William S. Sekely. "The Relationship of Headquarters Country and Industry Classification to Financial Structure," *Financial Management*, 1983, 12(3):45–51.

Constand, Richard L., Lewis P. Freitas, and Michael J. Sullivan. "Factors Affecting Price Earnings Ratios and Market Values of Japanese Firms," *Financial Management*, 1991, 20(4):68–79.

Cooper, Ian A., and Evi Kaplanis. "Cost to Crossborder Investment and International Equity Market Equilibrium," eds. J. Edwards, Julian Franks, C. Mayer, and Stephen Schaefer. In: *Recent Developments in Corporate Finance*, Cambridge, England: Cambridge University Press, 1986.

Cornell, Bradford. "Spot Rates, Forward Rates and Exchange Market Efficiency," *Journal of Financial Economics*, 1977, 5(1): 55–65.

Cornell, Bradford, and Alan C. Shapiro. "Managing Foreign Exchange Risks," *Midland Corporate Finance Journal*, 1983, 1(Fall):16–31.

Crutchley, Claire, Enyang Guo, and Robert S. Hansen. "Stockholder Benefits from Japanese–U.S. Joint Ventures," *Financial Management*, 1991, 20(4):22–30.

Doukas, John, and Nickolaos G. Travlos. "The Effect of Corporate Multinationalism on Shareholders' Wealth: Evidence from International Acquisitions," *Journal of Finance*, 1988, 43(5):1161–1175.

Dufey, Gunter, and S. L. Srinivasulu. "The Case for Corporate Management of Foreign Exchange Risk," *Financial Management*, 1983, 12(4):54–62.

Eun, Cheol S., and Bruce G. Resnick. "Exchange Rate Uncertainty, Forward Contracts, and International Portfolio Selection," *Journal of Finance*, 1988, 43(1):197–215.

Fatemi, Ali M. "Shareholder Benefits from Corporate International Diversification," *Journal of Finance*, 1984, 39(5):1325–1344.

Fisher, Irving. *The Theory of Interest.* New York: Augustus M. Kelley, 1965.

Frankel, Jeffrey A. "The Japanese Cost of Finance: A Survey," *Financial Management*, 1991, 20(1):95–127.

Gultekin, Mustafa N., N. Bulent Gultekin, and Alessandro Penati. "Capital Controls and International Capital Market Segmentation: The Evidence from the Japanese and American Stock Markets," *Journal of Finance*, 1989, 44(4):849–870.

Hodder, James E. "Evaluation of Manufacturing Investments: A Comparison of U.S. and Japanese Practices," *Financial Management*, 1986, 15(1):17–24.

Howe, John S., and Kathryn Kelm. "The Stock Price Impacts of Overseas Listings," *Financial Management*, 1987, 16(3):51–56.

Hunter, William C., and Stephen G. Timme. "A Stochastic Dominance Approach to Evaluating Foreign Exchange Hedging Strategies," *Financial Management*, 1992, 21(3):104–112.

John, Kose, Lemma W. Senbet, and Anant K. Sundaram. "Cross-Border Liability of Multinational Enterprises, Border Taxes, and Capital Structure," *Financial Management*, 1991, 20(4):54–67.

Kaplan, Steven N., and Bernadette A. Minton. "Appointments of Outsiders to Japanese Boards: Determinants and Implications for Managers," *Journal of Financial Economics*, 1994, 36(2):225–258.

Kaufold, Howard, and Michael Smirlock. "Managing Corporate Exchange and Interest Rate Exposure," *Financial Management*, 1986, 15(3):64–72.

Levis, Mario. "The Long-Run Performance of Initial Public Offerings: The UK Experience 1980–1988," *Financial Management*, 1993, 22(1):28–41.

Manzon, Gil B., Jr., David J. Sharp, and Nickolaos G. Travlos. "An Empirical Study of the Consequences of U.S. Tax Rules for International Acquisitions by U.S. Firms," *Journal of Finance*, 1994, 49(5):1893–1904.

Marr, M. Wayne, John L. Trimble, and Raj Varma. "On the Integration of International Capital Markets: Evidence from Euroequity Offerings," *Financial Management*, 1991, 20(4):11–21.

Medewitz, Jeanette N., and Keith A. Olson. "An Investigation into the Market Valuation Process of Closed-End Country Funds," *Financial Management*, 1994, 23(1):13–14.

Megginson, William L., Robert C. Nash, and Matthias Van Randenborgh. "The Financial and Operating Performance of Newly Privatized Firms: An International Empirical Analysis," *Journal of Finance*, 1994, 49(2):403–452.

Merton, Robert C. "Presidential Address: A Simple Model of Capital Market Equilibrium with Incomplete Information," *Journal of Finance*, 1987, 42(3):483–510.

Pettway, Richard H., Neil W. Sicherman, and D. Katherine Spiess. "Japanese Foreign Direct Investment: Wealth Effects from Purchases and Sales of U.S. Assets," *Financial Management*, 1993, 22(4):82–95.

Prowse, Stephen D. "The Structure of Corporate Ownership in Japan," *Journal of Finance*, 1992, 47(3):1121–1140.

Rhee, S. Ghon, and Rosita P. Chang. "Intra-Day Arbitrage Opportunities in Foreign Exchange and Eurocurrency Markets," *Journal of Finance*, 1992, 47(1):363–380.

Rogalski, Richard J., and James K. Seward. "Corporate Issues of Foreign Currency Exchange Warrants: A Case Study of Financial Innovation and Risk Management," *Journal of Financial Economics,* 1991, 30(2):347–366.

Shapiro, Alan C. *International Corporate Finance,* 2nd ed. Cambridge, Mass.: Ballinger, 1988.

Shapiro, Alan C. *Multinational Financial Management,* 3rd ed. Boston: Allyn and Bacon, 1989.

Smith, Clifford W., Jr., Charles W. Smithson, and L. Macdonald Wakeman. "The Evolving Market for Swaps," *Midland Corporate Finance Journal,* 1986, 3(Winter):20–32.

Thomadakis, Stavros, and Nilufer Usmen. "Foreign Project Financing in Segmented Capital Markets: Equity versus Debt," *Financial Management,* 1991, 20(4):42–53.

Usmen, Nilufer. "Currency Swaps, Financial Arbitrage, and Default Risk," *Financial Management,* 1994, 23(2):43–57.

Part V

WORKING CAPITAL MANAGEMENT

Many of a company's day-to-day operating decisions involve its working capital, its *current* assets and liabilities. In part V, we'll apply the principles of finance to the problems of working capital management. Making good day-to-day management decisions is critical to maximizing stockholder wealth.

Chapter 16 deals with cash and working capital management. These are assets and liabilities the company expects to receive and pay, respectively, in cash within a year. Managing them properly is important because it affects the company's ability to meet its obligations as they come due.

Chapter 17 examines economic decisions about accounts receivable and inventories. A company invests in both along with its investments in fixed assets. We'll show you how a company can make sure that its investments in receivables and inventories are profitable.

Finally, chapter 18 deals with financial planning, the problems of coordinating the company's various financial activities. Careful planning can be critical; a company must be prepared to deal with problems as it meets them. A company that doesn't plan for its future might find that it doesn't have one!

CASH AND WORKING CAPITAL MANAGEMENT

OBJECTIVES

1. Explain the composition of a company's working capital accounts and calculate the cash conversion cycle.

2. Cite the motives for holding cash and marketable securities.

3. Describe and apply some of the popular cash management models.

4. Identify float and the methods that companies use to reduce float costs.

5. Describe the mechanics of short-term borrowing through accounts payable, short-term bank loans, and commercial paper.

6. Estimate the costs of the primary sources of short-term funds.

7. Describe the growing applications of electronic data interchange (EDI).

A checking account is a place to "collect" money between inflows and outflows. The account acts like a pool. It's useful because you can add money in any amount, say $87.35, and conveniently take it out in completely different amounts, say $11.52 and $34.27. The catch is that you cannot take out more than what is in the pool, so you have to manage the pool to make sure there is enough for the outflows. But you can arrange to have money added automatically, whenever you run short, by using "check-bouncing protection." Whenever money is added to your account to cover a check, you effectively take out a loan.

Many people also use a credit card. They can charge things and then get one bill for all their recent charges. They can pay the bill off entirely, or they may be able to pay only part of it, thereby effectively taking out a loan.

Checking accounts, check-bouncing protection, and credit cards are just a few of the many tools available for managing your money.[1] Companies use similar tools to manage their money. For example, companies create check-bouncing protection by establishing a credit line.

Suppose you have a choice. Which loan is cheaper, check-bouncing protection or credit card debt? The answer is to take the one with the lowest after-tax APY. In this chapter, we will tell you how a company can answer such questions.

Companies make short-term financial decisions just about every day. Where should we borrow? Where should we invest our cash? How much liquidity should we have? The options come rapidly. Investment bankers want you to sell commercial paper, a bank wants to lend you money, and a supplier is willing to offer you trade credit. Which one is offering the best deal? Another bank wants you to purchase its lockbox services. Should

---

[1]If you're like us, even with all these tools, it's a constant challenge to balance your checkbook.

you do it? After much complaining, your largest customer is threatening to stop doing business with you unless you immediately convert your ordering and invoicing systems over to EDI (electronic data interchange). How would that affect your costs and cash flow?

Working capital decisions are fast paced because they reflect a company's day-to-day operations. The principles of finance, along with hard work and imagination, provide guidance for sound, value-maximizing decisions.

CASH, WORKING CAPITAL MANAGEMENT, AND THE PRINCIPLES OF FINANCE

Finance theory and real-world considerations are in constant contact in working capital management. Hence, the principles of finance are constantly in use.

◆ *Time Value of Money:* Compare the benefits and costs of alternative uses and sources of money using after-tax APYs.

◆ *Incremental Benefits:* Calculate the incremental after-tax cash flows connected with working capital decisions.

◆ *Risk-Return Trade-Off:* Recognize that risk-return trade-off decisions are part of a company's choice of financing working capital.

(continued on following page)

(Cash, Working Capital Management, and the Principles of Finance *continued from previous page*)

◆ *Options:* Look for hidden options and recognize their value, such as the option to refinance long-term debt.

◆ *Capital Market Efficiency:* Periodically evaluate routine capital market alternatives to make sure they continue to be competitive. Also, be careful to distinguish between routine transactions made in an efficient capital market, and unique transactions that are not subjected to such intense competition. For example, decisions to grant credit or to use a particular supplier are essentially private, and so the prices and risks should be checked against those in a competitive marketplace.

◆ *Behavioral:* Use common industry practices as a starting place for operating efficiently.

◆ *Comparative Advantage:* Consider subcontracting business activities to outside vendors if the vendors can provide the services more cheaply and competently.

◆ *Two-Sided Transactions:* Don't act unethically to gain short-term profit at the expense of a supplier or a customer, because such behavior can damage or even destroy a profitable long-term relationship.

OVERVIEW OF WORKING CAPITAL MANAGEMENT

WORKING CAPITAL MANAGEMENT The management of current assets and current liabilities.

Much of a financial manager's time is devoted to **working capital management.** Recall that a company's net working capital consists of its current assets minus its current liabilities. *Current assets,* principally cash and short-term securities, accounts receivable, and inventories, are assets that can normally be converted into cash within one year. *Current liabilities,* principally short-term borrowings, accounts payable, and taxes payable, are obligations that are expected to come due within one year. Working capital management involves all aspects of the administration of current assets and current liabilities.

The goal of working capital management is shareholder wealth maximization, avoiding negative and seeking positive-NPV decisions. Some methods that managers use in practice to make working capital decisions do not use the principles of finance. Rather, they use imprecise rules of thumb or poorly constructed models. You should avoid such methods. Working capital decisions can and should be made to maximize shareholder wealth.

Working capital management involves making the appropriate investments in cash, marketable securities, receivables, and inventories, as well as the level and mix of types of short-term financing. Working capital management includes several basic business relationships.

- *Sales impacts.* The company must determine appropriate levels of receivables and inventories. Granting easy credit to customers and keeping high inventories may help boost sales and fulfill orders quickly, but they raise costs.

- *Liquidity.* The company must choose levels of cash and marketable securities, taking into account liquidity needs and any required compensating balances.

- *Relations with stakeholders.* Suppliers and customers are intimately affected by the management of working capital. Customers are concerned with quality, cost, availability, and the service reputation of the company. Likewise, the company has similar concerns about its suppliers. The company's reputation depends in large measure on how it manages its short-term assets and obligations.

- *Short-term financing mix.* The company must choose the mix of short-term financing, as well as the proportions of short- and long-term financing, taking into account its profitability and risk objectives.

Table 16.1 shows the composition of the current assets and current liabilities for all U.S. manufacturing corporations in recent years. Notice the sheer size of the investment in short-term assets. The investment shown in the table is only for manufacturing companies; additional working capital is owned by wholesaling and retailing companies, service companies, and others. Also, notice that the percentage of total assets invested in short-term assets has declined substantially in recent years. Most of this decline in short-term assets has been accomplished by the reduction in the relative amount of inventories required to operate these companies. Finally, notice that short-term debt of various types accounts for roughly 24% of the total financing of the company.

Philosophies About Financing Working Capital

In its day-to-day operations, the company must maintain *liquidity*.[2] At the same time, it wants to operate as efficiently and profitably as possible. There is a tension between risk and return that manifests itself in managerial philosophies about how working capital should be financed. We can characterize a company's philosophy about how it finances working capital as the maturity-matching approach, the conservative approach, and the aggressive approach.

Maturity-Matching Approach to Financing Working Capital In the maturity-matching approach, the company hedges its risk by matching the maturities of its assets and liabilities (panel A of figure 16.1 on page 584). The company finances seasonal variations in current assets with current liabilities of the same maturity. It finances long-term assets by issuing long-term debt and equity securities. In addition, in most cases there is a permanent component of current assets. Inventories and receivables will remain above some minimum level. This permanent component of current assets is also financed with long-term capital. As panel A of figure 16.1 illustrates, short-term borrowing (including temporary increases in payables as well as bank borrowings, commercial paper, and so on) mirrors the seasonal swings in current assets. Short-term borrowing under this sort of policy would fall to zero at seasonal low spots.

Conservative Approach to Financing Working Capital Under the maturity-matching approach, a company depends on short-term financing for its temporary current

TABLE 16.1
Current Assets and Liabilities of All Manufacturing Corporations

	PERCENTAGE OF TOTAL ASSETS					DOLLARS INVESTED IN 1996
	1960	1970	1980	1990	1996	
Current Assets						
Cash	6.0%	4.3%	2.8%	2.4%	2.8%	$ 102.4 billion
Marketable securities	4.8	0.7	2.5	2.0	2.9	104.8
Accounts receivable	15.6	17.3	17.0	13.9	12.8	454.4
Inventory	23.6	23.0	19.8	14.3	11.9	424.0
Other current assets	2.3	3.5	2.8	3.4	4.1	147.5
Total current assets	52.3%	48.8%	44.9%	36.0%	34.5%	$1233.1 billion
Current Liabilities						
Notes payable	3.9%	6.3%	5.0%	6.2%	3.7%	$ 131.1 billion
Accounts payable	7.9	8.5	9.9	7.9	8.0	286.7
Accruals and other current liabilities	9.0	9.9	12.0	11.6	12.3	439.7
Total current liabilities	20.8%	24.7%	26.9%	25.7%	24.0%	$ 857.5 billion

Source: Quarterly Financial Report for Manufacturing, Mining, and Trade Corporations, U.S. Department of Commerce, various dates.

[2]Recall that liquidity refers to how quickly and easily assets can be bought or sold without loss of value. Cash is the most liquid asset.

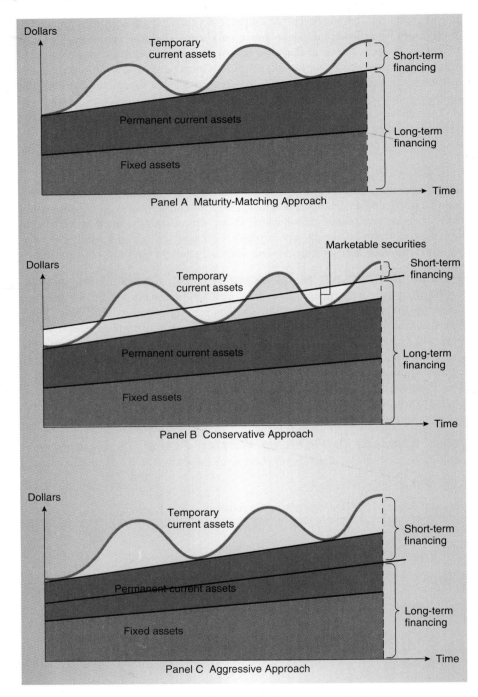

FIGURE 16.1

Three philosophies of financing working capital.

assets. The company assumes that funds will always be available. It also gambles that their cost will not rise dramatically. If general economic conditions worsen or if the company's own circumstances deteriorate, the company might have trouble getting the money it needs. Another possibility is that funds are available, but only at a much higher cost. To guard against the risks of a credit shutoff or a cost increase, the conservative approach uses more long-term and less short-term financing than the maturity-matching approach.

The conservative approach is shown in panel B of figure 16.1. Long-term financing is used to finance all of the company's long-term assets, all of its permanent current assets, and some of its temporary current assets. As you can see in panel B, only when asset needs are high will the company use short-term financing. At other times, when asset needs are low, the company actually has more long-term financing than it has total assets. At these times, the company invests the excess funds in marketable securities. By financing a portion of its seasonal needs for funds on a long-term basis, the company builds in a margin of safety.

Aggressive Approach to Financing Working Capital

One problem with the maturity-matching and conservative approaches is that long-term funds generally cost more than short-term funds. The term structure is usually upward sloping. Because of this, many managers prefer an aggressive approach to financing working capital (figure 16.1, panel C). The aggressive approach uses less long-term and more short-term financing. The goal is to raise profitability. We know from the Principle of Risk-Return Trade-Off that without some sort of market imperfection, higher expected profitability comes only at the expense of greater risk.

Costs of the Three Approaches to Financing Working Capital

We can think of the maturity-matching approach as the base-case scenario. If interest rates rise unexpectedly, a company using the aggressive approach loses relative to less aggressive (maturity-matching and conservative) companies. This is because companies with more long-term financing locked in at the lower rate will have lower financing costs. But if interest rates fall, the situation is reversed and the aggressive company is a winner. This is because companies with more long-term financing may be stuck with either higher interest costs or the cost of refinancing.

Therefore, because of the possibility that funds might become more expensive or even unavailable, a company without ready access to capital markets should be more conservative. The availability of financing at a fixed cost can be ensured by locking in long-term financing. In contrast, a company with ready capital market access can be more aggressive.

Some managers gamble on the direction of interest rates. A manager who expects a decline in interest rates will use the aggressive approach. The aggressive manager shortens the average maturity of the company's debt by financing more with short-term and less with long-term debt. A manager who expects interest rate increases will use the conservative approach. This manager lengthens the average maturity of the company's debt by financing more with long-term and less with short-term debt.

If interest rates in fact move in the direction that the manager forecasts, the company will realize additional profits. However, if interest rates move in the "wrong" direction, the interest rate gamble will backfire and the company will be less profitable. On the basis of the Principle of Capital Market Efficiency, we caution against such gambling. Our recommendation is that the company apply the Principle of Comparative Advantage instead. For example, a shoe company might work on manufacturing higher-quality shoes at lower cost instead of guessing the direction of interest-rate movement.

Self-Check

1. What is working capital management? What are examples of major financial decisions that are made in working capital management?

2. Compare and contrast the maturity-matching, conservative, and aggressive approaches to financing working capital.

3. If a company is afraid that its access to borrowing in the future might be restricted by its banks and other lenders, which of the three approaches should it follow?

4. Which approach benefits the company if interest rates rise? Which one benefits the company if interest rates fall?

CASH CONVERSION CYCLE

CASH CONVERSION CYCLE The length of time between the payment of a company's accounts payable and the receipt of cash from its accounts receivable.

The **cash conversion cycle** is the length of time between the payment of accounts payable and the receipt of cash from accounts receivable.

Without credit, a company's cash is tied up from the moment it purchases inventory until it collects its accounts receivable. Suppose a company holds its inventory 50 days and collects its accounts receivable in 30 days. Then it would take 80 days for the original investment to be converted back into cash.

However, with supplier credit, the company's money is not invested for the entire 80 days. Figure 16.2 illustrates this cycle with 20-day supplier credit. On day 0, goods are delivered from the supplier, go into inventory, and result in an account payable. In 50 days, the goods are sold for credit, and the accounts receivable are collected 30 days later, on day 80. However, the company does not have to put up its own money until it pays its accounts payable on day 20. With 20-day supplier credit, the company's cash is invested for 60 days, day 20 to day 80. Thus in this instance, the cash conversion cycle is 60 days.

The cash conversion cycle is equal to the inventory conversion period, plus the receivables collection period, minus the payables deferral period:

$$\begin{array}{c} \text{Cash} \\ \text{conversion} \\ \text{cycle} \end{array} = \begin{array}{c} \text{Inventory} \\ \text{conversion} \\ \text{period} \end{array} + \begin{array}{c} \text{Receivables} \\ \text{collection} \\ \text{period} \end{array} - \begin{array}{c} \text{Payables} \\ \text{deferral} \\ \text{period} \end{array} \qquad (16.1)$$

The inventory conversion period is the average time between buying inventory and selling the goods:

$$\begin{array}{c} \text{Inventory} \\ \text{conversion} \\ \text{period} \end{array} = \frac{\text{Inventory}}{\text{Cost of sales}/365} = \frac{365}{\text{Inventory turnover}} \qquad (16.2)$$

The receivables collection period, or days' sales outstanding (DSO), is the average number of days it takes to collect on accounts receivable:

$$\begin{array}{c} \text{Receivables} \\ \text{collection} \\ \text{period} \end{array} = \frac{\text{Receivables}}{\text{Sales}/365} = \frac{365}{\text{Receivables turnover}} \qquad (16.3)$$

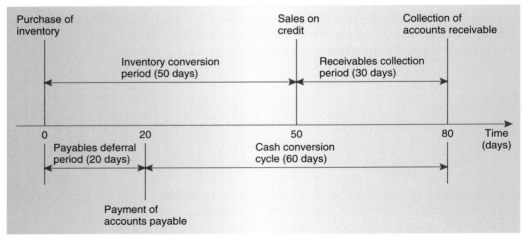

FIGURE 16.2
Cash conversion cycle.

The payables deferral period is the average length of time between the purchase of the materials and labor that go into inventory and the payment of cash for these materials and labor:

$$\frac{\text{Payables}}{\text{deferral}} = \frac{\text{Accounts payable} + \text{Wages, benefits, and payroll taxes payable}}{(\text{Cost of sales} + \text{Selling, general, and administrative expenses})/365} \quad (16.4)$$

EXAMPLE

Cash Conversion Cycle for Clark Pharmaceuticals

Suppose Clark Pharmaceuticals has the financial information given below. What is Clark's cash conversion cycle?

Inventory	Accounts receivable	Accounts payable	Wages, benefits, and payroll taxes payable	Sales	Cost of sales	Selling, general, and administrative expenses
$1.40 million	$1.70 million	$0.40 million	$0.10 million	$20.0 million	$10.0 million	$1.00 million

Using equation (16.2), the inventory conversion period is 51.1 days:

$$\frac{\text{Inventory}}{\text{conversion}} = \frac{1,400,000}{(10,000,000/365)} = 51.1 \text{ days}$$

Using equation (16.3), the receivables collection period is 31.0 days:

$$\frac{\text{Receivables}}{\text{collection}} = \frac{1,700,000}{20,000,000/365} = 31.0 \text{ days}$$

Using equation (16.4), the payables deferral period is 16.6 days:

$$\frac{\text{Payables}}{\text{deferral}} = \frac{(400,000 + 100,000)}{(10,000,000 + 1,000,000)/365} = 16.6 \text{ days}$$

Using equation (16.1), the cash conversion cycle is 65.5 days:

$$\text{Cash conversion cycle} = 51.1 + 31.0 - 16.6 = 65.5 \text{ days.}$$

Self-Check
1. What is the cash conversion cycle?
2. What happens to the cash conversion cycle when: (a) the inventory turnover increases? (b) the receivables turnover decreases? (c) a company pays its accounts payable more quickly because credit terms have become less attractive?

CASH MANAGEMENT

Corporations use increasingly sophisticated cash management systems to monitor their cash and marketable securities and maintain their needed liquidity at minimum cost. Cash and marketable securities are managed together, because marketable securities are so liquid and funds can be moved from one to the other quickly and cheaply. In fact, corporations usually report only the total of the two on the balance sheet.

A company's cash management decision can be broken into two parts. First, how much liquidity (cash plus marketable securities) should the company have? Second, what should be the relative proportions of cash and marketable securities in maintaining that liquidity?

Demands for Money

There are three basic motives for holding cash: (1) the transactions demand, (2) the precautionary demand, and (3) the speculative demand.

The **transactions demand** is simply the need for cash to make everyday payments for such things as wages, raw materials, taxes, and interest. The transactions demand for cash exists because of imbalances between cash inflows and outflows. The need for transactions balances depends on the size of the company. The larger the company, the more transactions it makes. The transactions demand also depends on the relative timing of cash inflows and outflows. The more closely they match, the less cash is needed to carry the company until more inflow arrives.

The **precautionary demand** is essentially the margin of safety required to meet unexpected needs. The more uncertain the cash inflows and outflows, the larger the precautionary balance should be.

Finally, the **speculative demand** is based on the desire to take advantage of unexpected profitable opportunities that require cash. This motive accounts for a smaller percentage of corporate cash holdings than of individual cash holdings. For the most part, companies hold cash for transactions and precautionary reasons. Readily available bank borrowing can generally be used to meet the speculative demand for cash.

In addition to the three basic demands for cash, many companies hold cash in compensating balances. A **compensating balance** is an account balance that the company agrees to maintain. It provides indirect payment to the bank for its loans or other services. Commercial banks may accept or require compensating balances in lieu of direct fees.

If a bank wants $1000 of compensation for a service, the bank can simply charge a fee of $1000. Alternatively, if the interest rate is 5%, a compensating balance of $20,000 left at the bank in a non-interest-bearing account for one year would provide the bank with the same $1000 (= [0.05]20,000) (indirect) compensation. Although direct fees are much more popular than they were in the past, a substantial number of corporations still keep compensating balances.

Short-Term Investment Alternatives

The following is a list of several types of marketable securities. They are shown in order of increasing level of risk and return.

- *U.S. Treasury securities. Treasury bills* (T-bills) have an original maturity of one year or less when they are issued. *Treasury notes* and *bonds* have an original maturity of one year or more. These securities have the lowest risk and greatest liquidity, but because of the risk-return trade-off, they also offer the lowest yield. Companies can buy and sell these securities directly. Companies can also invest in these securities for very short periods by using repurchase agreements, or *repos,* with securities dealers.

- *U.S. federal agency securities.* These securities are backed to varying degrees by the U.S. government. Many are nearly as liquid as U.S. Treasury securities but have a slightly higher risk and return.

- *Negotiable certificates of deposit.* Negotiable CDs are time deposits issued by domestic or foreign commercial banks that can be sold to a third party.[3] *Eurodollar certificates of deposit* generally have higher risk and return than domestic CDs.

- *Short-term tax-exempt municipals. Munis* are short-term securities, issued by state and local governments, and are exempt from federal taxation. Several of these are short-term securities issued in anticipation of cash receipts. They are Tax Anticipation Notes (TANs), Revenue Anticipation Notes (RANs), and BANs (Bond Anticipation Notes).

- *Bankers' acceptances.* Bankers' acceptances are drafts that a commercial bank has "accepted." Their value is based on the accepting bank's credit standing.

---

[3]Consumer CDs are usually non-negotiable. They can only be sold back to the issuing bank.

- *Commercial paper.* These securities are unsecured promissory notes that corporations issue. Commercial paper seldom has an original maturity of more than 270 days.[4] Most commercial paper has an original maturity between 30 and 180 days and is issued only by very creditworthy corporations.

- *Preferred stock and money-market preferred stock.* Preferred stock pays dividends that qualify for the 70% dividends-received deduction. Most preferred stock is a long-term security subject to market value fluctuations. Money-market preferred stock differs from other preferred stock. It is a short-term security that has a floating dividend rate that is reset frequently to reflect current interest rates. Therefore, it has lower risk and return, being much less subject to market value fluctuation, just like other short-term securities.

Transactions Demand Models

How much cash does a company need to conduct its transactions? A simple and useful approach to answering this question treats cash management as an inventory management problem. In this approach, the company manages its inventory of cash on the basis of the cost of holding cash (rather than marketable securities) and the cost of converting marketable securities to cash. The best policy minimizes the sum of these costs.

Baumol Model The Baumol cash management model assumes the company can predict its future cash requirements with certainty, cash disbursements are spread uniformly over the period, the interest rate (the opportunity cost of holding cash) is fixed, and the company pays a fixed transaction cost each time it converts securities to cash.

The Baumol model has a sawtooth pattern of cash balances, which is shown in figure 16.3. The company sells C dollars worth of marketable securities and deposits the funds in its checking account. The cash balance decreases steadily to zero as the cash is spent. Then the company sells C dollars of marketable securities and deposits the funds in the checking account, and the pattern repeats itself. Over time, the average (mean) cash balance will be $C/2$. The time value (opportunity cost) of funds is the interest rate, i, times the average balance, $iC/2$. Likewise, if each deposit is for C dollars and the company needs to deposit a total of T dollars in its account during the year, the total number of deposits (and the number of saw

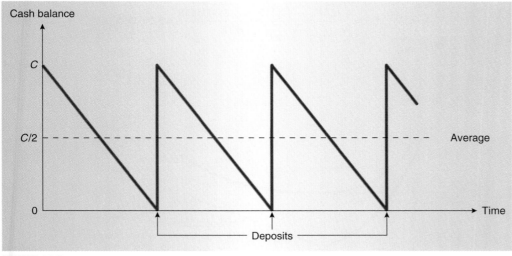

FIGURE 16.3
Cash balances with the Baumol model.

[4]So long as its maturity does not exceed 270 days, it does not have to be registered with the Securities and Exchange Commission (SEC).

teeth per year in figure 16.3) is equal to T/C. The annual transaction cost will be cost per deposit times the number of deposits, which is bT/C.

The annual cost of meeting the transactions demand is the transaction cost plus the opportunity (time value) cost:

$$\text{Cost} = b\left(\frac{T}{C}\right) + i\left(\frac{C}{2}\right) \tag{16.5}$$

where

T = annual transactions volume in dollars (uniform through time)

b = fixed cost per transaction, i = annual interest rate, C = size of each deposit

The decision variable is C, the deposit size. Increasing C increases the average cash balance and the opportunity cost as well. However, increasing C reduces the number of deposits, thereby lowering the annual transaction cost. Figure 16.4 shows this trade-off between the two costs. The best or optimal deposit size, C^*, provides the minimum total cost, $Cost^*$.

The optimal deposit size is

$$C^* = \sqrt{\frac{2bT}{i}} \tag{16.6}$$

The optimal deposit size is a function of the transaction cost b, the annual transactions volume T, and the annual interest rate i. C^* is positively related to b and T and negatively related to i. Note that the optimal deposit size is not linearly related to these variables. For example, if T doubles, then the optimal deposit size will also increase—but it won't double.

EXAMPLE

Using the Baumol Model at Fox

Let's say Fox, Inc. needs $12 million in cash next year. It believes it can earn 12% per year on funds invested in marketable securities, and converting marketable securities to cash costs $312.50 per transaction. What does this imply for Fox?

Using equation (16.6), Fox's optimal deposit size is

$$C^* = \sqrt{\frac{2bT}{i}} = \sqrt{\frac{2(312.50)(12,000,000)}{0.12}} = \$250,000$$

FIGURE 16.4
Annual costs for the Baumol model.

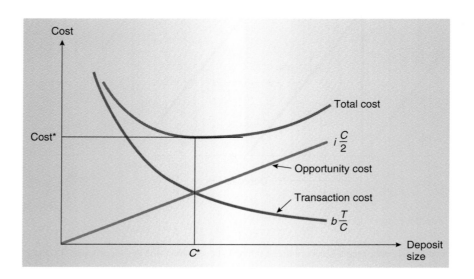

Using equation (16.5), the annual cost is $30,000.

$$\text{Cost} = 312.50 \left(\frac{12,000,000}{250,000} \right) + 0.12 \left(\frac{250,000}{2} \right) = 15,000 + 15,000 = \$30,000$$

The subparts of the solution are: $T/C = 48$ = deposits per year; $b(T/C) = 312.50(48) = \$15,000$ = transaction costs per year; $C/2 = \$125,000$ = average cash balance; $i(C/2) = 0.12(125,000) = \$15,000$ = annual opportunity cost of funds. Fox would make about one deposit per week of $250,000. The average cash balance is $125,000, transaction costs are $15,000, opportunity costs are $15,000, and the total annual cost is $30,000. ∎

Miller-Orr Cash Management Model

The Miller-Orr cash management model is more realistic than the Baumol model. It allows the daily cash flows to vary according to a probability function. For example, suppose we can assume that the expected net cash flow (combined inflows and outflows) follows a normal distribution with a mean of zero and has a standard deviation of $50,000 per day. This incorporates the realistic uncertainty about future cash flows. Figure 16.5 illustrates the Miller-Orr model.

The Miller-Orr model uses two control limits and a return point. The lower control limit, LCL in the figure, is determined outside the model. The upper control limit, UCL, is $3Z$ above the lower control limit. The model uses a return point that is Z above LCL. The return point is the target level the company returns to whenever the cash balance hits a control limit.

When the cash balance hits LCL, the company sells Z of marketable securities and puts the money in the checking account. This brings the cash balance back up to the return point. Whenever the balance hits the upper limit, $2Z$ of marketable securities are purchased with money from the checking account, putting the balance back to the return point. This procedure produces an average cash balance of LCL + (4/3)Z.

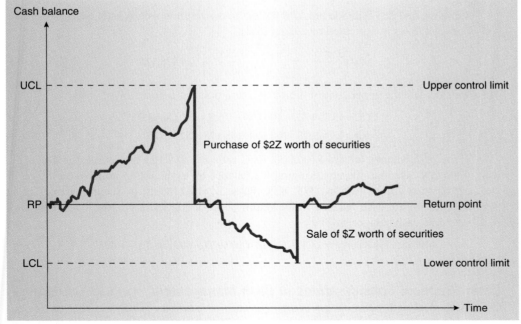

FIGURE 16.5
Cash balances with the Miller-Orr model.

Although LCL is set outside the model, UCL and the return point depend on the LCL and on Z. The return point is simply LCL + Z, and the UCL equals LCL + 3Z. The variable Z depends on the cost per transaction, *b*, the interest rate per period, *i*, and the standard deviation of the net cash flows, σ. The interest rate and the standard deviation of cash flows must be defined for the same unit of time, which is most often per day. Z is then

$$Z = \left(\frac{3b\sigma^2}{4i}\right)^{1/3} \tag{16.7}$$

As we noted above, the return point, RP, upper control limit, UCL, and average cash balance are:

$$RP = LCL + Z$$
$$UCL = LCL + 3Z$$
$$\text{Average cash balance} = LCL + (4/3)Z$$

A higher cost per transaction or greater variation in the cash flow results in a larger Z and a larger difference between LCL and UCL. Likewise, a higher interest rate results in a smaller Z and a smaller range.

The Miller-Orr model is a good example of *management by exception*. Managers allow the cash balance to fluctuate within specified limits. Only when these limits are violated do managers take action, and that action is planned ahead of time. The model is useful for managing transactions cash balances.

EXAMPLE

Using the Miller-Orr Model at KFC

Suppose KFC has estimated the standard deviation of its daily cash flows (outflows minus inflows for the day) to be σ = $50,000 per day. In addition, the cost of buying or selling marketable securities is $100. The APR is 10%. Because of its liquidity requirements and compensating balance agreements, KFC has a lower control limit of $100,000 on its cash balances. What would be KFC's upper control limit and return point, using the Miller-Orr model?

First, we find Z. We divide the APR by 365 to convert it to a daily rate, because the variability of cash flows is expressed on a daily basis.

$$Z = \left(\frac{3b\sigma^2}{4i}\right)^{1/3} = \left[\frac{3(100)(50,000)^2}{4(.10/365)}\right]^{1/3} = \$88,125$$

Then we calculate the upper control limit and return point.

$$UCL = LCL + 3Z = 100,000 + 3(88,125) = \$364,375$$
$$RP = LCL + Z = 100,000 + 88,125 = \$188,125$$

If the cash balance falls to $100,000, KFC sells Z = $88,125 of securities and puts the cash in the cash account, thereby bringing the balance up to the return point of $188,125. If the cash balance climbs to $364,375, KFC buys 2Z = $176,250 of securities from cash, thereby reducing the cash balance to the return point of $188,125 (= 364,375 − 176,250). KFC's average cash balance will be

$$\text{Average cash balance} = LCL + (4/3)Z = 100,000 + (4/3)(88,125) = \$217,500$$

Other Practical Considerations in Cash Management The Baumol and Miller-Orr models deal with optimizing a company's cash transactions balances. Other factors not included in these models also affect cash balances. For example, a company may have a compensating balance requirement. In such a case, the company's average cash balance is the greater of its balance needed for transactions and its compensating balance requirement. The compensating balance is costly, then, only if it raises the balance the company would maintain anyway. Frequently, it is costly.

The optimal amount of marketable securities is the total liquidity desired minus cash balances. The company invests in a variety of marketable securities, taking into account its possible future cash needs as well as the transaction costs, maturities, riskiness, and investment yields.

Some companies maintain unusually large portfolios of marketable securities. Although some of the portfolios may be maintained for liquidity purposes, responding to special tax situations may also be the motive. Sometimes companies have foreign operations in countries with different tax laws, and they can benefit by investing the cash abroad rather than returning it to the United States and paying U.S. income taxes on it.

Float

When you write a check, there's a delay before the funds are taken out of your checking account. This delay occurs because of the time your check is in the mail, the time needed to process the check, and the time it takes the banking system to remove the funds from your account. During this delay, you are benefiting from float. **Float** is the difference between the available or collected balance at the bank and the company's book or ledger balance.

$$\text{Float} = \text{Available balance} - \text{Book balance} \qquad (16.8)$$

Float arises from timing differences that occur when you are paying your bills or collecting from customers. Float, then, is between the company and outsiders such as customers or suppliers. There are two kinds of float, disbursement float and collection float.

FLOAT The difference between the company's available or collected balance at its bank and the company's book or ledger balance.

DISBURSEMENT FLOAT The positive float that is created between the time when a check is written and when it is finally cleared out of the checking account.

COLLECTION FLOAT The negative float that is created between the time that you deposit a check in your account and when funds are made available.

Disbursement Float   When you write a check, your book or ledger balance is reduced by the amount of the check, but your available or collected balance at the bank is not reduced until the check finally clears. This difference is **disbursement float.**

Disbursement Float at Huskie Oil
EXAMPLE

Suppose the Huskie Oil Corporation has $50,000 for both its book balance and its bank balance. If Huskie writes a $1000 check that takes 4 days to clear, during this period, $1000 of disbursement float has been created. Huskie's book balance declines by the amount of the check, from $50,000 to $49,000, but the bank balance is unchanged until the check clears. What is Huskie's float on this check?

Using equation (16.8), the float is

$$\text{Float} = 50,000 - 49,000 = \$1000$$

After the check clears, the book and bank balances will both be $49,000 and there is no more disbursement float. ■

Collection Float   Float can be either positive or negative. Suppose you receive a check and deposit it in your bank. Until the funds are credited to your account, your book balance will be higher than your actual balance. In this case, you are experiencing **collection float.**

Collection Float at Huskie Oil
EXAMPLE

Let's say Huskie has a $50,000 cash balance on both its ledger balance and its available bank balance. If Huskie receives a $5000 check and deposits it in its checking account, funds are not made available on this particular check for 2 days. Its book balance increases by $5000, but its bank balance is unchanged until the funds are finally available. What is the float?

(continued on following page)

(Collection Float at Huskie Oil *continued from previous page*)

Using equation (16.8), the float is

$$\text{Float} = 50,000 - 55,000 = -\$5000$$

This negative float of $5000 is Huskie's collection float. ∎

Float Management Techniques   Companies use several devices and procedures to manage float.

- *Wire transfers* Large payments can be made with wire transfers instead of with paper checks. Sending a wire transfer is more expensive than writing and mailing a paper check, but a wire transfer reduces the cost of float because it's immediate.

- *Zero balance accounts (ZBAs)* These are special disbursement accounts that maintain a zero balance. Funds are automatically transferred in when a check is presented on a ZBA.

- *Controlled disbursing* This technique may use disbursing accounts at several banks in addition to the master account at the company's lead bank. As with ZBAs, funds are put into the accounts on an as-needed basis. The banks notify the company about what funds are needed. The company then wires the needed funds to the banks. Conversely, the bank notifies the company about excess funds and wires them out.

- *Centralized processing of payables* By centralizing payables, a cash manager knows when all bills must be paid and can make sure that funds are available and bills are paid on time. Prompt bill paying causes better relations with vendors. In addition, the company avoids late penalties while reducing its cash balances.

- *Lockboxes* Lockboxes are post office boxes to which a company directs its incoming checks. A bank is engaged to open the lockbox several times per day, process the checks, and collect them. Cash managers face two problems: the choice of lockbox locations and the assignment of customers to particular lockboxes. By strategically locating the lockboxes around the country and by using efficient banks, companies can reduce their float substantially. Float is reduced by shortening mail times (from customers to the lockbox), processing times (by using efficient banks), and availability times (the amount of time it takes for funds to be made available on checks after they are presented to banks).

EXAMPLE   *Cost of a Wire Transfer*

You need to transfer $100,000 from Houston to Chicago. If you mail a check, it will cost $1.00 for postage and clearing the check, and it will take a total of 5 days for the funds to be transferred. During the money's 5-day travel, you are suffering an opportunity cost, because the $100,000 is not earning 3% APY interest. Alternatively, you could avoid the opportunity cost by wiring the money at a cost of $12.00, which would instantaneously transfer the funds with no float. Which is cheaper?

$$\text{Cost} = \text{Fixed costs} + \text{Float costs}$$
$$\text{Cost of check} = 1.00 + 100,000(0.03)(5/365) = 1.00 + 41.10 = \$42.10$$
$$\text{Cost of wire transfer} = 12.00 + 0 = \$12.00$$

The wire transfer is substantially cheaper. ∎

Profitability of a Lockbox System at The Gap

Let's say The Gap currently collects all of its customer payments in Nashville. By going to a new lockbox system with boxes in Atlanta and St. Louis, The Gap expects to reduce the time from when customers mail their checks to when the funds are collected. It expects the time to fall from an average of 8 days to an average of 5 days, a 3-day savings. The Gap collects $100,000 per day. The extra costs associated with the lockbox are $12,000 per year. The Gap's opportunity cost of funds is 10% per year. What is the expected annual profit from using the new system?

Reduction in float = (100,000/day)(3 days)	= $300,000
Value of float reduction = 300,000 (0.10)	= 30,000
Less: Annual operating cost	= 12,000
Net before-tax profit from lockbox system	= $ 18,000

The reduction in float of $300,000 permanently frees up this amount of cash. Invested at 10%, this is worth $30,000 per year. Subtracting the $12,000 yearly cost of operating the system gives an expected before-tax profit of $18,000 per year. ∎

Self-Check

1. What are the three basic motives for holding cash?

2. Describe three short-term investment alternatives.

3. Explain graphically and with equations (1) the Baumol cash management model and (2) the Miller-Orr cash management model.

4. What is float? What causes float? What are the two kinds of float? Explain how each of the following can help a corporation manage its float: (a) wire transfers, (b) zero balance accounts, (c) controlled disbursing, (d) centralized processing of payables, (e) lockboxes.

SHORT-TERM FINANCING

The phrases *short-term funds* and *intermediate-term funds* refer to the original maturity of the debt obligation. Short-term funds are debt obligations that were originally scheduled for repayment within 1 year. Intermediate-term funds are debt obligations that were originally scheduled to mature between 1 and perhaps as many as 10 years from the date of issue. These time periods vary in practice.

Another useful distinction concerns the source of funds from which the loan is to be repaid. Companies typically arrange short-term loans to finance seasonal or temporary needs. Intermediate-term loans are to be repaid over a period of years. If the loan is short term (due in a year or less), lenders are mainly concerned with the company's working capital position and its ability to liquidate current assets—collecting on receivables and reducing inventories according to seasonal patterns—to generate cash to meet the company's current debt service obligations. For an intermediate-term loan, lenders are more concerned with the longer-term profitability of the company's operations.

There are three main sources of short-term funds: *trade credit* (borrowing from suppliers), *bank loans* (borrowing from banks), and *commercial paper* (selling short-term debt securities in the open market). This section discusses each of these sources of short-term funds, describes how to estimate the cost of funds from each source, and provides a framework for comparing these costs on a consistent basis.

Trade Credit

TRADE CREDIT Credit extended by one business to another to facilitate the sale of its goods and services.

Trade credit is credit extended by one company to another. Businesses routinely grant trade credit on the sales of their goods and services. Purchasers of raw materials, manufactured products, and services are generally permitted to wait until after the goods or services are delivered to pay for them. Trade credit is the largest single source of short-term funds for businesses, representing approximately one-third of the current liabilities of nonfinancial corporations. Because suppliers are often more liberal in extending credit than financial institutions, trade credit is a particularly important source of funds for small companies.

CASH DISCOUNT An incentive offered to purchasers of a company's product to make payment within a specified time period, such as 10 days.

When extending trade credit, the seller specifies the period of time allowed for payment and often offers a **cash discount** if payment is made more quickly. For example, the terms "2/10, net 30" are frequently encountered; they mean the buyer can take a 2% cash discount if payment is made within 10 days (the *discount period*). Otherwise, the full amount is due within 30 days (the *net period*).

Trade credit can be a significant source of funds. For example, suppose a company purchases $50,000 worth of supplies each day on terms of 2/10, net 30. The company always pays in exactly 10 days. In this case, the company will owe its suppliers 10 times $50,000, or $500,000, less the 2% discount. Its suppliers are providing almost $500,000 of funds the company can use in its business. If the company pays at the end of 30 days, the total amount of trade credit would be 30 days of purchases, which is $50,000 times 30, or $1,500,000. The extra $1 million dollars in financing comes at a cost of the 2 percent discount.

Cost of Trade Credit If no discount is offered, or if payment is made soon enough that the discount can be taken, there is no cost to the company for the use of the supplier's credit. When cash discounts are offered but not taken, however, trade credit involves a cost. It should be obvious that when a company offers a discount for early payment, the discounted price is the "real" price of the goods. That is, if the invoice is for $100 and a 2% discount is offered for early payment, the "real" price is $98. If the company does not pay its bill within 10 days, it is effectively borrowing $98 and paying $2 interest for the loan by forgoing the discount.

Equation (5.8) is the formula for computing the APR. Similarly, the APR for trade credit is

$$\text{APR} = \left(\frac{\text{discount\%}}{100\% - \text{discount\%}}\right)\left(\frac{365}{\text{total period} - \text{discount period}}\right) \tag{16.9}$$

The APR formula is widely used, but it understates the true annual interest rate because it ignores the effect of interest compounding. The true interest cost is the APY (equation 5.9), which for trade credit is

$$\text{APY} = \left(1 + \frac{\text{discount\%}}{100\% - \text{discount\%}}\right)^{\left(\frac{365}{\text{total period} - \text{discount period}}\right)} - 1 \tag{16.10}$$

EXAMPLE | *Cost of Trade Credit for Radio Shack*

What's the cost to Radio Shack if it skips the discount and pays at the end of the total credit period if credit terms are 2/10, net 30? Using equation (16.9), the APR is

$$\text{APR} = \left(\frac{2\%}{100\% - 2\%}\right)\left(\frac{365}{30 - 10}\right) = 37.24\%$$

This example can be visualized with the help of figure 16.6. Radio Shack would pay $2 of interest on a $98 loan. The loan is for only 20 days, so the loan is rolled over $365/(30-10) = 365/20 = 18.25$ times per year.

For such a high interest rate, the difference between the APR and the APY can be substantial. Using equation (16.10), the APY is 44.59%.

$$N = 0.05479\ (= 20/365)\quad \mathbf{r = 44.59}\quad PV = 98\quad PMT = 0\quad FV = 100$$

$$APY = \left(1 + \frac{2\%}{100\% - 2\%}\right)^{\left(\frac{365}{30-10}\right)} - 1 = 44.59\%$$

As the Radio Shack example illustrates, trade credit can be very expensive when a cash discount is offered but not taken. So it's important to evaluate the implicit cost of not taking the discount. Other sources of credit may be quite a bit cheaper.

Effective Use of Trade Credit   Trade credit offers certain advantages as a source of short-term funds. It's readily available, at least to companies that regularly pay their suppliers on schedule. Also, it's informal. If the company is now paying its bills within the discount period, it can get additional credit simply by delaying the payment until the end of the net period or perhaps later (but at the cost of forgoing the discount).

Trade credit is also more flexible than other means of short-term financing. The company does not have to negotiate a loan agreement, pledge collateral, or adhere to a rigid repayment schedule. In particular, the consequences of delaying a payment beyond the net period are much less onerous than those resulting from failure to repay a bank loan on schedule. For these and other reasons, trade credit is particularly valuable to smaller companies, which often have difficulty obtaining credit elsewhere.

Stretching Accounts Payable   Companies may also "stretch" accounts payable by postponing payment beyond the end of the net period. Such stretching lowers the financing cost computed in equations (16.9) and (16.10) because the loan period is extended without any increase in cost.

For example, with credit terms of 2/10, net 30, paying in 40 rather than 30 days lowers the APR from 37.24% to 24.83%. It lowers the APY from 44.59% to 27.86%. Suppliers sometimes tolerate such delinquencies during periods when the buyer has large seasonal funds requirements. To minimize any adverse consequences, however, the buyer should keep the supplier fully informed of its situation. It should also try to keep current on its repayment obligations with the supplier over the rest of the year.

Stretching the payments on accounts payable is a good example of the Principle of Two-Sided Transactions. Paying late may be a zero-sum game, and what you save for yourself is a cost imposed on your supplier. The buyer must be careful to avoid excessive stretching of accounts payable. Excessive stretching may cause the company to incur other implicit costs, such as a deterioration in its credit ratings, strained relations with suppliers, or both.

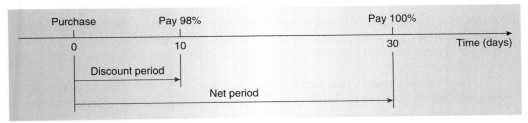

FIGURE 16.6
Cost of trade credit.

These results can lead to less attractive repayment terms in the future and perhaps to higher prices as suppliers attempt to pass through to the buyer the cost of the buyer's delinquent payments. These implicit costs of trade credit, although difficult to estimate, should be carefully evaluated. In particular, smaller companies that may at times rely heavily on trade credit for short-term financing should assess the implicit as well as explicit costs of the trade credit.

Statement Billing versus Invoice Billing   In many business relationships, particularly where the number of purchases is small, the supplier sends a separate bill for each purchase. This is called *invoice billing*. Obviously, this can result in a lot of paperwork.

In *statement billing,* several invoices are collected together into a single statement and the customer is asked to pay after the statement is presented. A common arrangement is monthly statements. The supplier's "month" might run from the 25th of one month until the 25th of the next month. On the 25th day of the month, the supplier collects all of the invoices over the last month and sends the statement with credit terms such as "2/10, net EOM." If the statement was prepared on, say, April 25, this allows the customer to take a 2% discount if the bill is paid by the 10th of the next month, which is May 10. If the discount is not taken, the net amount is due on EOM, the end of the month, which is May 31.

Self-Check

1. What are the three main sources of short-term funds? What are the main differences among them? Which is the largest source?

2. What is trade credit? What are its advantages compared to other sources of short-term funds?

3. What does "3/10, net 20" mean?

4. What is the cost of trade credit when the borrower pays within the discount period?

5. Why does trade credit create an implicit cost when a company doesn't pay within the discount period?

Secured and Unsecured Bank Loans

Commercial bank lending is second in importance to trade credit as a source of short-term financing. Commercial banks also provide intermediate-term financing (maturity between 1 and 10 years). Banks provide loans in a wide variety of forms that are tailored to the specific needs of the borrower. Banks generally lend to their most creditworthy customers on an unsecured basis. But when a borrower represents a significant credit risk, the bank may ask it to provide some form of security, such as a lien on receivables or inventory. Finance companies also lend on a secured basis.

TRANSACTION LOAN A loan extended by a bank for a specific purpose. In contrast, lines of credit and revolving credit agreements involve loans that can be used for various purposes.

LINE OF CREDIT An *informal* arrangement between a bank and a customer establishing a maximum loan balance that the bank will permit the borrower.

Short-Term Unsecured Loans   Short-term unsecured bank loans take one of three basic forms: a specific *transaction loan,* a *line of credit,* or a *revolving credit.* Such loans are generally regarded as "self-liquidating": The lender expects that the assets the company purchases with the loan proceeds will generate sufficient cash to repay the loan within a year. Short-term unsecured loans are evidenced by a promissory note that specifies the amount of the loan, interest rate, and repayment terms. Short-term unsecured loans typically bear interest at a floating rate.

Banks make a **transaction loan** for a specific purpose. For example, a bank may lend a home builder funds to pay for building houses. The loan agreement requires the company to repay the bank when the houses are sold.

A **line of credit** is an arrangement between a bank and a customer concerning the maximum loan balance the bank will permit the borrower at any one time. Banks normally extend credit lines for a one-year period, with one-year renewals granted as long as the bank continues to find the borrower's credit acceptable.

Banks generally don't like borrowers to use credit lines to cover their long-term funds requirements, so banks require borrowers to be out of bank debt periodically for some specified amount of time (for example, 30 consecutive days each year). Inability to meet such a requirement gives the bank an early warning of potential trouble. If the company is unable to meet this requirement, the bank will insist that the company get additional long-term financing to be able to meet it. Most credit lines are informal arrangements. If the prospective borrower's credit deteriorates, the bank is not legally obligated to advance funds.

A **revolving credit agreement** represents a legal commitment to lend up to a specified maximum amount any time during a specified period. In return for this legal commitment, the borrower must pay a *commitment fee,* typically between 0.25% and 0.5%, on the difference between the permitted maximum and the amount actually borrowed. This fee increases the company's cost of borrowing and compensates the bank for committing itself to making extra funds available to the company. Revolving credits are evidenced by short-term notes that usually mature in 90 days. The borrower can roll these over automatically as long as the notes mature no later than the date the revolving credit agreement expires. Revolving credits often extend beyond one year, and the borrower often has the option to convert the revolving credit to a term loan when the revolving credit expires.

REVOLVING CREDIT AGREEMENT A *legal* commitment where a bank promises to lend a customer up to a specified maximum amount during a specified period.

Term Loan

Bank term loans represent intermediate-term debt, but the similarity between their pricing and that of short-term bank loans makes it appropriate to discuss them in this chapter. A bank **term loan** is a loan for a specified amount that requires the borrower to repay it according to a specified schedule. A term loan generally matures in one to ten years, but banks permit longer maturities under special circumstances. Repayment is normally at regular intervals in equal installments.

In some cases the loan may provide for a larger final payment, called a *balloon payment,* or simply repayment at maturity in one lump sum, called a *bullet maturity.* A loan with a bullet maturity is like a typical corporate bond. The interest is paid periodically over the life of the loan, but the principal is repaid in one lump sum at the end. Banks often extend revolving credits that the borrower can convert into a term loan. A three-year revolving credit convertible into a five-year term loan at the end of the third year is not uncommon. Term loans usually carry a floating interest rate.

TERM LOAN An intermediate term loan (1–10 years) for a specified amount. Term loans are usually repaid according to a specified schedule.

Cost of Bank Financing

Except for a rather small percentage of loans that bear interest at a fixed rate, commercial banks charge interest at a rate that floats. Generally, the interest rate floats with the bank's **prime rate,** which is a benchmark rate that banks may use to price loans.[5] Banks often use other benchmark rates besides prime. These are usually based on the bank's cost of funding the loan. For example, commercial banks often offer their larger, more creditworthy customers the option of selecting interest rates based on (1) one of the London Interbank Offered Rates (LIBOR), the rates at which prime banks offer one another deposits in the London market, or (2) the interest rate the bank pays on large certificates of deposit. Nevertheless, the prime rate serves as the base lending rate in most cases.

PRIME RATE The benchmark interest rate that banks charge large, creditworthy corporations.

A bank adjusts its prime rate to reflect changes in its cost of funds. In addition, commercial banks frequently offer loans at "money market rates" that are below prime to compete with the commercial paper market, which we will discuss in a moment. Banks charge less creditworthy customers a higher rate, usually expressed as a percentage over prime, depending on the customer's credit standing. For example, if a bank's prime rate is 12%, then it might lend to a local manufacturing company at prime plus 0.5%, or 12.5%, and to a local

---

[5]It used to be the interest rate banks charged their largest, most creditworthy customers. Currently, however, banks often lend to their best customers at below prime rate.

merchant at prime plus 2%, or 14%. The interest rates on these loans would vary with changes in the bank's prime rate. If the bank raises its prime rate to 12.5%, the interest rate on the manufacturing company's loan would automatically become 13%, and the interest rate on the merchant's loan would automatically become 14.5%.

A compensating balance requirement, generally between 10% and 20% of the size of the loan, is in addition to interest charges. This requirement may be a minimum, but more commonly it is a required *average* deposit balance during a particular interest period. Such an average gives the borrower greater flexibility, because a high balance one day can offset a low balance on another day. Compensating balance requirements are more common when credit is tight in the entire economy. In any case, a compensating balance adds to the cost of a loan in those instances where a company has to maintain a higher cash balance than it otherwise would.

Despite the many differences in bank loan contracts, calculating the cost of a loan is not difficult. As with trade credit, we can calculate the APR. It is

$$\text{APR} = \left(\frac{\text{Net cost of loan}}{\text{Cash advance}}\right)\left(\frac{1}{f}\right) \tag{16.11}$$

where f is the fraction of a year that the loan is outstanding. For example, for a three-month loan, $f = 0.25$.

The APY is:

$$\text{APY} = \left(1 + \frac{\text{Net cost of loan}}{\text{Cash advance}}\right)^{1/f} - 1 = \left(\frac{\text{Net repayment}}{\text{Cash advance}}\right)^{1/f} - 1 \tag{16.12}$$

In the analysis that follows, we'll give only the APR formulas based on equation (16.11). In each case, the comparable APY formula would be based on equation (16.12).

True Interest Cost with Compensating Balances
When interest is paid in arrears (that is, at the end of an interest period) and compensating balances are required, the true interest cost of the loan is higher than the rate quoted on the principal amount of the loan. The compensating balance reduces the effective loan proceeds, raising the cost of the usable funds. The higher interest cost with a compensating balance is

$$\text{APR} = \left(\frac{\text{Net cost of loan}}{\text{Cash advance}}\right)\left(\frac{1}{f}\right) = \left(\frac{\text{Interest charges}}{\text{Loan amount} - \text{Compensating balance}}\right)\left(\frac{1}{f}\right) = \left(\frac{rPf}{P - B}\right)\left(\frac{1}{f}\right) \tag{16.13}$$

where

> P = amount of the loan
>
> f = loan term
>
> r = interest rate on loan amount
>
> B = increase in the company's average cash balances due to the compensating balance requirement
>
> rPf = interest charges

The financing costs for the loan above consist of interest expense, and the net loan proceeds are the loan amount reduced by the amount of the compensating balance requirement.

Equation (16.13) assumes the compensating balances don't earn interest, which is generally the case. But if the compensating balances earn some yield, y, the interest so earned, yBf, reduces the cost of the loan. In that case, the cost of the loan is

$$\text{APR} = \left(\frac{\text{Interest charges} - \text{Interest received}}{\text{Loan amount} - \text{Compensating balance}}\right)\left(\frac{1}{f}\right) = \left(\frac{rPf - yBf}{P - B}\right)\left(\frac{1}{f}\right) \tag{16.14}$$

Loans with Compensating Balance Requirements

Suppose a Wendy's franchisee borrows $100,000 for 1 year. The bank charges interest at prime rate plus 0.50%. It also requires a 10% compensating balance, which the franchisee would not otherwise have kept. If the prime rate averages 11.50%, what is the APR?

Using equation (16.13), the APR is

$$\text{APR} = \left(\frac{rPf}{P-B}\right)\left(\frac{1}{f}\right) = \left[\frac{0.12(100,000)(1)}{100,000-10,000}\right]\left(\frac{1}{1}\right) = \frac{12,000}{90,000} = 13.33\%$$

In the absence of any compensating balance requirements, the true interest cost would have been simply 12%. We can look at this problem another way.

The franchisee borrows $100,000 at the first of the year and repays the $112,000 at the end of the year. However, because $10,000 stays in the bank the whole year, the franchisee takes out only $90,000 at the first of the year and must pay $102,000 at the end. This produces a 1-year interest rate of 13.33%.

$N=1$	$r=\mathbf{13.33}$	$PV=90,000$	$PMT=0$	$FV=102,000$

Suppose the franchisee could deposit the compensating balance in a time deposit account earning 5% interest. Then the financing costs would be reduced by the amount of interest earned, which would be 5% of 10,000, or $500. The APR is now 12.78%

$N=1$	$r=\mathbf{12.78}$	$PV=90,000$	$PMT=0$	$FV=101,500\ (=102,000-500)$

$$\text{APR} = \left(\frac{rPf-yBf}{P-B}\right)\left(\frac{1}{f}\right) = \left[\frac{0.12(100,000)(1)-0.05(10,000)(1)}{100,000-10,000}\right]\left(\frac{1}{1}\right) = \frac{11,500}{90,000} = 12.78\%$$

True Interest Cost of Discount Loans   Many loans are **discount loans,** which require the borrower to pay the interest in advance. The loan proceeds are reduced by the interest cost. The stated loan amount is P, but the borrower gets only $P-rPf$, where f is the borrowing period expressed as a fraction of a year. Often, f is computed using a 360-day year. With an interest expense of rPf, with a "true" loan amount of $P-rPf$, and adjusting for a loan period of f, the APR is

DISCOUNT LOAN A loan that requires the borrower to pay the interest in advance.

$$\text{APR} = \left(\frac{rPf}{P-rPf}\right)\left(\frac{1}{f}\right) = \frac{r}{1-rf} \tag{16.15}$$

As you would expect because of the time value of money, the true interest cost is higher when interest is paid in advance than when it is paid in arrears. If a compensating balance were also required, other adjustments would be needed as well.

Famous Amos's Cost for a Discount Loan

Let's say Famous Amos is paying interest on a discount basis at the rate of 12% per year for a $100,000, 3-month loan. There is no compensating balance requirement. What is Famous Amos's true cost of this loan?

Using equation (16.15), the APR is

$$\text{APR} = \frac{r}{1-rf} = \frac{0.12}{1-0.12(0.25)} = \frac{0.12}{0.97} = 12.37\%$$

(continued on following page)

(Famous Amos's Cost for a Discount Loan *continued from previous page*)

The APY is 12.96%.

  N = 0.25   **r = 12.96**   PV = 97,000   PMT = 0   FV = 100,000

Summary of Cost of Single-Payment Loans

Figure 16.7 summarizes costs of four types of single-payment $100, 3-month loans at 12% APR. The types are based on whether interest is paid in arrears (at the end of the year, cases 1 and 2) or in advance (a discount loan, cases 3 and 4) and on whether a compensating balance is required (cases 2 and 4) or not (cases 1 and 3). Figure 16.7 shows how the loan's APY is increased by compensating balances, by paying interest on a discount basis, and by more frequent compounding.

The APY for a Discount Installment Loan

Instead of a single-payment loan, the bank may require the borrower to repay the loan on an installment basis. The APY of an installment loan can be found by solving for the periodic interest rate and then annualizing it.

EXAMPLE

Famous Amos's Cost for a Discount Installment Loan

Suppose Famous Amos is borrowing another $100,000 at what the bank calls a 12% interest rate. In this case, the note is discounted at 12% for 3 months (total discount of 3%). Amos will repay the loan in three installments of $25,000 each at the end of the first 2 months and $50,000 at the end of 3 months. So Amos gets $97,000 (= $100,000 − [0.12][0.25]100,000), and its true interest cost is the r that solves

$$97,000 = \frac{25,000}{(1+r)} + \frac{25,000}{(1+r)^2} + \frac{50,000}{(1+r)^3}$$

Solving for r gives $r = 1.3658\%$ per month. The APR is 16.39% (= [12]1.3658), and the APY is 17.68% (= [1.013658]^{12} − 1).

FIGURE 16.7
Costs of four types of single-payment loans.

Loan amount = $100, Interest rate = 12%, Loan term = 3 months

(1) Interest in arrears
    No compensating balance

100   −103
————————————————→ Time
0   0.25

APR = (3/100)4 = 12.00%

APY = (103/100)⁴ − 1 = 12.55%

(2) Interest in arrears
    10% compensating balance

90   −93
————————————————→ Time
0   0.25

APR = (3/90)4 = 13.33%

APY = (93/90)⁴ − 1 = 14.01%

(3) Discount loan (interest in advance)
    No compensating balance

97   −100
————————————————→ Time
0   0.25

APR = (3/97)4 = 12.37%

APY = (100/97)⁴ − 1 = 12.96%

(4) Discount loan (interest in advance)
    10% compensating balance

87   −90
————————————————→ Time
0   0.25

APR = (3/87)4 = 13.79%

APY = (90/87)⁴ − 1 = 14.52%

Famous Amos's "12%" discount installment loan illustrates vividly, once again, why it's so critical to understand and account for the exact terms of a loan agreement. Two loans with the same quoted interest rate may have substantially different APYs because of differences in how interest is calculated or differences in the timing of repayments.

Security   Commercial banks often ask lenders to provide security for their loans. When the bank is lending on a short-term basis, it may ask the borrower to pledge liquid assets such as receivables, inventories, or marketable securities. The pledge of collateral may take the form of a "floating lien" against one or more classes of short-term assets without specifying them in detail. More commonly, banks will ask the borrower to specify in detail the collateral for the loan (such as a list of the receivables it is pledging). Depending on the quality of the receivables, a company can usually borrow between 70% and 90% of the face value of the receivables it pledges. With inventories that are easily sold, a company can probably borrow between 50% and 75% of the inventory's retail value.

For loans secured by receivables, commercial banks normally charge the prime rate plus a premium of up to five percentage points. The bank's cost of processing the receivables affects the rate it charges. The higher the processing cost, the higher the interest rate. However, there are normally no compensating balances on such loans. Interest rates on loans secured by inventory have a similar range. The premium is generally lower the higher the quality of the receivables or inventory pledged. Finance companies also make secured loans, but they usually do so at higher rates than commercial banks charge.

The main benefit from pledging is that a company can borrow more than it could on an unsecured basis. In return, the company incurs extra administrative and bookkeeping costs and sacrifices some degree of control over its receivables and inventories. In some cases, the borrower's customers pay what they owe directly to the bank. Pledged inventories are sometimes physically separated out and given special handling.

Commercial Paper

The largest, most creditworthy companies are able to borrow on a short-term basis by selling **commercial paper.** More than 4000 companies issue this form of security. Commercial paper consists of unsecured promissory notes that have a maturity of up to 270 days. It is possible for commercial paper to have a maturity longer than 270 days, but such an issue would have to be placed privately or else registered with the Securities and Exchange Commission.

COMMERCIAL PAPER
Short-term, unsecured promissory notes, sold by large businesses, that have a maturity of up to 270 days.

Market for Commercial Paper   Commercial paper is sold either directly or through dealers. Large industrial companies, utilities, and medium-size finance companies generally sell their paper through dealers, who typically charge a commission of ⅛ of 1% on an annualized basis. Such dealer-placed paper typically has a maturity of between 30 and 180 days. Principal buyers include other business companies, insurance companies, pension funds, and banks.

Roughly 40% of all commercial paper is sold directly to investors. Large finance companies, such as General Motors Acceptance Corporation or General Electric Capital, typically sell their paper directly. They tailor the maturities and the amounts of the notes to fit the needs of investors, who consist principally of corporations investing excess cash on a short-term basis. Maturities range from 1 to 270 days. In contrast to most industrial companies, the large finance companies use the commercial paper market as a permanent source of funds because of the finance companies' assets and the lower cost of commercial paper relative to bank financing.

Computing the True Cost of Commercial Paper   Interest on commercial paper is paid on a discount basis. For example, if 120-day prime commercial paper carries a 12% interest rate, then the APR (based on a 360-day year), using equation (16.15) is

$$\text{APR} = \frac{r}{1 - rf} = \frac{0.12}{1 - 0.12(120/360)} = 12.5\%$$

Because of the many different ways to state interest rates, we remind you yet again to compute carefully the APY of each alternative.[6] The one with the lowest APY is the lowest-cost alternative.

Issuers of commercial paper generally maintain a backup line of credit to provide insurance against any problems selling commercial paper. If a company cannot pay off its commercial paper at maturity, the backup line of credit is used. Banks generally charge an annualized fee of ¼ to ½ of 1% for such backup lines, which increases the cost.

EXAMPLE

GMAC's Cost of Commercial Paper

Let's say General Motors Acceptance Corporation (GMAC) issues $50 million of 90-day commercial paper at 10%. The paper is discounted, so GMAC receives $48.75 million (= 50 − [0.10][0.25]50). Using equation (16.11), the APR is

$$APR = \left(\frac{1,250,000}{48,750,000}\right)\left(\frac{1}{0.25}\right) = \left(\frac{1,250,000}{48,750,000}\right)(4) = 10.26\%$$

GMAC "rolls over" its paper four times per year, selling new commercial paper to replace each issue as it matures.

Assuming a backup line of credit costing 0.25% of the funds received and legal and other out-of-pocket costs amounting to another 0.50% per year, GMAC's total APR cost is

$$Cost = 10.26\% + 0.25\% + 0.50\% = 11.01\%$$

Rating Considerations   The credit quality of commercial paper is rated by agencies such as Moody's Investors Service and Standard & Poor's Corporation. The agencies apply similar rating criteria. Moody's has two basic commercial paper rating categories: "Prime" and "Not Prime." The Prime category is subdivided into P-1 (highest quality), P-2, and P-3. Standard & Poor's has four basic commercial paper rating categories: A, B, C, and D. The A category corresponds to Moody's Prime category and is subdivided into A-1+ (highest), A-1, A-2, and A-3.

Paper with the highest rating, P-1/A-1+, carries the lowest cost of borrowing and the smallest chance of interrupted market access. At times the yield differential between paper rated P-1/A-1+ and P-3/A-3 has been more than two full percentage points. Furthermore, in market crises, the market for paper rated lower than P-1/A-1 can dry up. Even in the best of times, there is normally no market for commercial paper rated lower than P-3/A-3, and the market for commercial paper rated P-3/A-3 is very limited.

Companies with paper rated P-3/A-3, and some companies with paper rated P-2/A-2, may be able to lower their borrowing cost with an irrevocable letter of credit. The letter of credit is a form of insurance that raises the rating and lowers the interest rate. If the present value of the interest savings exceeds the cost, this is a positive-NPV decision.

Contracting Costs, Agency Costs, and Short-Term Debt

A variety of factors affect a company's choice of amount and mix of short-term debt as well as the overall maturity structure of the company's debt. These factors include (1) the cost of each source of funds, (2) the desired level of current assets, (3) the seasonal component of current assets, and (4) the extent to which a company uses the maturity-matching approach to hedge its debt structure.

---

[6]In this case, the APY is 13.03%. This comes from a 12.5% APR with compounding 3 times per year (every 120 days in a 360-day year) (= [1 + 0.125/3]³ − 1).

Beyond the basic factors just cited, several contracting costs and agency costs also affect the company's use of short-term debt.

- *Flotation costs.* The costs of issuing long-term securities like bonds and common stock are generally much higher than the costs of arranging short-term borrowings. Consequently, the company issues these long-term securities only infrequently. In the interim, companies borrow short-term from banks or issue commercial paper. As these short-term borrowings build up, they are eventually replaced with long-term securities.

- *Restricted access to sources of long-term capital.* Legal restrictions limit the types of loans that institutional investors can make. It may not be attractive for smaller companies, or larger companies whose debt would be rated below investment grade, to sell long-term debt securities. They may have to rely on trade credit, bank financing, or finance company borrowing.

- *Less restrictive terms.* Public and private debt normally carry penalties for early repayment. Such a penalty is simply the cost of the "hidden" option to refinance. Because of this cost, the more likely a company is to want to repay early, the more attractive bank financing becomes, because bank financing generally does not have such a penalty.

- *Bankruptcy costs.* Bankruptcy costs create a bias in favor of longer maturities, because every time short-term financing comes due, there is the "hidden" option to default. Shareholders must decide whether it is worth it to "repurchase" the assets from the debtholders or to "walk away."[7]

- *The company's choice of risk level.* The company's attitude toward risk will help determine its philosophy about financing its working capital and, more generally, its choice of short- versus long-term financing. Because of possible increases in interest rates, companies whose shareholders are not well diversified, as is often the case with owner-managed businesses, frequently choose the conservative approach.

Self-Check

1. Why do banks often require a borrower to pledge receivables or inventory as security for a loan?

2. Does a compensating balance requirement always increase the cost of a bank loan? If not, when do they and when don't they?

3. Why is the true interest cost of a discount loan always greater than the stated discount rate?

4. Describe the following four basic forms of bank loans: (a) line of credit, (b) revolving credit, (c) transaction loan, (d) term loan.

5. What is commercial paper? Who are the main issuers and who are the main investors? What is responsible for the rapid growth of the commercial paper market?

ELECTRONIC DATA INTERCHANGE (EDI)

More and more, an increasing volume of business transactions is being made using **electronic data interchange (EDI).** EDI is the exchange of information electronically, directly from one computer to another, in a structured format. By moving the information in this way, companies save time, personnel costs, materials costs, and costs due to errors.

ELECTRONIC DATA INTERCHANGE (EDI) The exchange of information electronically, directly from one business's computer to another's, in a structured format.

---

[7]For more on this, see enrichment topics B and C, Options and Contingent Outcomes, and Financial Contracting.

Let's follow a simple business transaction to see the potential value of EDI. First, assume you want to buy something using traditional paper documents and mail delivery. You contact a supplier about availability and price. You then place an order. The supplier acknowledges the purchase order. When the goods are shipped, the supplier also sends shipping documents and an invoice. When it is time to pay, you send a check along with remittance information through the mail. After getting the check, the supplier credits your account and deposits the check in its bank. Finally, the money is transferred from your bank account to the supplier's.

Now consider the same transaction using EDI. In North America, the American National Standards Institute (ANSI) sets EDI standards for such things as invoices, shipping information, purchase orders, customer account information, requests for quotations, and many others.

Each step in the traditional paper-based process causes time delays and labor costs. In addition, the paper-based system is prone to errors. There are also uncertainties in paper-based systems because participants do not know the status of the transaction. By simplifying the process and sending information almost instantaneously, EDI reduces labor costs, substantially reduces errors, and makes possible a much higher degree of control over the company's resources.

Using EDI, some companies have been able to operate with much lower investments in inventories, to provide their customers with better service, and to be more price competitive. In fact, the economic advantages of EDI are so compelling that some companies either require that all transactions be done with EDI or charge a fee, such as $50, for paper documents.

By increasing the availability and lowering the cost of high-quality information, EDI is changing the way companies manage their working capital assets. There are also some special kinds of EDI that can be considered a subset of the overall EDI architecture. Electronic funds transfer (EFT) is the transfer of money electronically from one bank to another bank. Financial EDI (FEDI) is the exchange of information between a bank and its customers (such as information about checks paid, account balances, lockbox information, and other things).

Self-Check

1. What does EDI stand for? What is it and what are its advantages?

2. Which of the following will increase or will decrease in an EDI system compared to a paper-based system? (a) The time between the sending and receipt of a purchase order, (b) the number of times that information must be keypunched into the computer, (c) the number of errors that employees make in handling a customer's orders, (d) the amount of managerial control over resources such as inventory levels.

SUMMARY

Chapter 16 covers the nature of working capital management, cash management practices, short-term financing sources, and electronic data interchange.

- Working capital management is the management of the company's short-term assets and liabilities.
- The cash conversion cycle is the length of time between when a company pays its accounts payable and collects on its accounts receivable. The cash conversion cycle is equal to the inventory conversion period plus the receivables collection period minus the payables deferral period.
- Businesses need stores of cash for three reasons: to conduct ordinary transactions when cash flows are uneven (the transactions demand), to avert default on obligations (the precautionary demand), and to take advantage of investment opportunities (the speculative demand). Bank requirements for compensating balances also contribute to the demand for cash balances.
- The Baumol model and the Miller-Orr model are two well-known models that minimize the cost of accommodating the transactions demand for cash.

- Float is the difference between the checking account balance at the bank and the balance on the company's ledgers; the available balance minus the book balance. Companies use zero balance accounts, wire transfers, controlled disbursing, centralized processing of payables, and lockboxes to manage float.
- Trade credit, bank loans, and commercial paper are the main sources of short-term financing. The APY of each source depends on the specific terms in its contract.
- Electronic data interchange is the direct exchange of information between the computers of two businesses. A wide variety of documents can be electronically exchanged with the structured formats in EDI.

EQUATION SUMMARY

(16.1)
$$\text{Cash conversion cycle} = \text{Inventory conversion period} + \text{Receivables collection period} - \text{Payables deferral period}$$

(16.2)
$$\text{Inventory conversion period} = \frac{\text{Inventory}}{\text{Cost of sales}/365} = \frac{365}{\text{Inventory turnover}}$$

(16.3)
$$\text{Receivables collection period} = \frac{\text{Receivables}}{\text{Sales}/365} = \frac{365}{\text{Receivables turnover}}$$

(16.4)
$$\text{Payables deferral period} = \frac{\text{Accounts payable} + \text{Wages, benefits, and payroll taxes payable}}{(\text{Cost of sales} + \text{Selling, general, and administrative expenses})/365}$$

(16.5)
$$\text{Cost} = b\left(\frac{T}{C}\right) + i\left(\frac{C}{2}\right)$$

(16.6)
$$C^* = \sqrt{\frac{2bT}{i}}$$

(16.7)
$$Z = \left(\frac{3b\sigma^2}{4i}\right)^{1/3}$$

(16.8)
$$\text{Float} = \text{Available balance} - \text{Book balance}$$

(16.9)
$$\text{APR} = \left(\frac{\text{discount\%}}{100\% - \text{discount\%}}\right)\left(\frac{365}{\text{total period} - \text{discount period}}\right)$$

(16.10)
$$\text{APY} = \left(1 + \frac{\text{discount\%}}{100\% - \text{discount\%}}\right)^{\frac{365}{\text{total period} - \text{discount period}}} - 1$$

(16.11)
$$\text{APR} = \left(\frac{\text{Net cost of loan}}{\text{Cash advance}}\right)\left(\frac{1}{f}\right)$$

(16.12)
$$\text{APY} = \left(1 + \frac{\text{Net cost of loan}}{\text{Cash advance}}\right)^{1/f} - 1 = \left(\frac{\text{Net repayment}}{\text{Cash advance}}\right)^{1/f} - 1$$

(16.13)
$$\text{APR} = \left(\frac{\text{Net cost of loan}}{\text{Cash advance}}\right)\left(\frac{1}{f}\right) = \left(\frac{\text{Interest charges}}{\text{Loan amount} - \text{Compensating balance}}\right)\left(\frac{1}{f}\right)$$
$$= \left(\frac{rPf}{P - B}\right)\left(\frac{1}{f}\right)$$

(16.14)
$$\text{APR} = \left(\frac{\text{Interest charges} - \text{Interest received}}{\text{Loan amount} - \text{Compensating balance}}\right)\left(\frac{1}{f}\right) = \left(\frac{rPf - yBf}{P - B}\right)\left(\frac{1}{f}\right)$$

(16.15)
$$\text{APR} = \left(\frac{rPf}{P - rPf}\right)\left(\frac{1}{f}\right) = \frac{r}{1 - rf}$$

CHAPTER REVIEW ACTIVITIES

SELF-TEST PROBLEMS

1. (Cash conversion cycle) Dennis Lasser has collected some information about a food wholesaler in order to estimate its cash conversion cycle. The accumulated information is given below. What will Dennis find the cash conversion cycle to be?

Inventory turnover = 10x	Inventory conversion period = 365/10 = 36.5 days
Receivables turnover = 20x	Receivables collection period = 365/20 = 18.25 days
Payables turnover = 25x	Payables deferral period = 365/25 = 14.6 days

2. (Cost of short-term funds) D. M. Ferguson and Associates is considering three alternative sources of short-term funds. What is the cost of each source?

   a. Skipping the discount on accounts payable—the terms are 1/10, net 30.
   b. Borrowing from the bank at 10%, interest in arrears, with a 20% compensating balance requirement.
   c. Selling 90-day commercial paper, with a discount rate of 13%.

3. (Baumol cash management model) A corporation projects a need for $10,000 of cash next year. It believes it can earn 12.5% per year on funds that are invested in marketable securities and that converting marketable securities to cash involves a cost of $1.00 per transaction.

   a. What is the optimal deposit size using the Baumol model?
   b. What is the average cash balance and the number of deposits per year?
   c. What is the annual total cost, opportunity cost of funds, and transactions cost?

SOLUTIONS TO SELF-TEST PROBLEMS

1. Using equation (16.1), the cash conversion cycle is 40.15 days.

$$
\begin{array}{ccccc}
\text{Cash} & & \text{Inventory} & \text{Receivables} & \text{Payables} \\
\text{conversion} & = & \text{conversion} + & \text{collection} & - \text{deferral} = 36.5 + 18.25 - 14.6 = 40.15 \text{ days} \\
\text{cycle} & & \text{period} & \text{period} & \text{period}
\end{array}
$$

2. a. Using equation (16.9), the cost of skipping the discount is 18.43%.

$$
\text{APR} = \left(\frac{1}{99}\right)\left(\frac{365}{30 - 10}\right) = 18.43\%
$$

   b. Using equation (16.13), the cost of the bank loan is 12.5%.

$$
\text{APR} = \left(\frac{rPf}{P - B}\right)\left(\frac{1}{f}\right) = \left(\frac{0.10}{1 - 0.20}\right)\left(\frac{1}{1}\right) = \frac{0.10}{0.80} = 12.5\%
$$

   c. Using equation (16.15), the cost of the commercial paper is 13.44%.

$$
\text{APR} = \frac{r}{1 - rf} = \frac{0.13}{1 - 0.13(90/360)} = \frac{0.13}{0.9675} = 13.44\%
$$

   The bank loan is the cheapest source of funds.

3. a. Using equation (16.6), the optimal deposit size is $400.

$$
C^* = \sqrt{\frac{2bT}{i}} = \sqrt{\frac{2(1.00)(10,000)}{0.125}} = \sqrt{160,000} = \$400
$$

   b. The average cash balance is C/2 = 400/2 = $200. The number of deposits per year is T/C = 10,000/400 = 25 times per year.
   c. Using equation (16.5), the annual cost is $50.

$$
\text{Cost} = b\left(\frac{T}{C}\right) + i\left(\frac{C}{2}\right) = (1.00)\frac{10,000}{400} + (0.125)\frac{400}{2} = 25 + 25 = \$50
$$

The annual opportunity cost is $i(C/2) = 0.125(200) = \$25$. The annual transaction cost is $b(T/C) = 1.00(25) = \$25$.

QUESTIONS

1. Cite and describe three alternative philosophies about how a company finances its working capital.
2. Describe the cash conversion cycle and discuss its importance to working capital management.
3. Cite and describe three basic motives for holding cash.
4. Explain the concept of float.
5. List and describe five marketable securities that are available to a corporation that has funds to invest short term. Order them from the lowest risk (and return) to the highest.
6. Cite and describe three alternative types of short-term bank loans.
7. What is Electronic Data Interchange (EDI)? What are the principal economic advantages of EDI over the traditional paper-based system?

CHALLENGING QUESTIONS

8. What are the assumptions of the Baumol cash management model? What are the Miller-Orr model's assumptions?
9. Briefly explain how each of the following can be used to reduce a company's float costs:
   a. Wire transfers
   b. Zero balance accounts (ZBAs)
   c. Controlled disbursing
   d. Centralized processing of payables
   e. Lockboxes
10. Why are interest rates on short-term loans not necessarily comparable to each other? Give three possible reasons.

PROBLEM SET A

A1. (Cash conversion cycle) Auburn Hair Products has an inventory turnover of 6 times per year, a receivables turnover of 10 times, and a payables turnover of 12 times. What is Auburn Hair's inventory conversion period, the receivables collection period, and the payables deferral period? What is the cash conversion cycle?

A2. (Cash conversion cycle) Baklava Baking Corporation is interested in its cash conversion cycle. A Baklava manager has assembled the data given below (in $millions) for your use. Estimate each of the following:
   a. Inventory conversion period
   b. Receivables collection period
   c. Payables deferral period
   d. Cash conversion cycle

Inventory	Accounts receivable	Accounts payable	Wages, benefits, and payroll taxes payable	Sales	Cost of sales	Selling, general, and administrative expenses
$1.00	$0.80	$0.40	$0.15	$25.0	$10.0	$1.50

A3. (Baumol cash management model) A company projects a need for $2 million cash per month. Its projected 30-day investment yield is 9% APR. The cost of converting securities into cash is $300 per transaction.
   a. How much cash would it raise each time it sells securities?
   b. How often should the company plan to sell securities?
   c. What will be the average cash balance?
   d. What is the annual opportunity cost of funds, transactions costs, and total costs?

A4. (Miller-Orr cash management model) Suppose that the cash flows of a company are uncertain and have an estimated standard deviation of $100,000 per day. The interest rate is 9% per year and the cost of converting securities into cash or vice versa is $300 per transaction. The lower control limit is zero. (*Hint:* Don't forget to convert the annual interest rate into a daily rate.)
   a. Calculate the return point and upper control limit.
   b. When and in what amounts should the company buy and sell securities?
   c. What is the average cash balance?

A5. (Float) Suppose a Footlocker franchisee has $20,000 in both its book balance and its bank balance. If the franchisee writes a $2000 check that takes 4 days to clear, what is its disbursement float?

A6. (Float) Gerry Johnson writes a $100 check on Monday, a $200 check on Tuesday, and a $300 check on Wednesday. It takes exactly 2 days for the checks to be presented and funds taken from Gerry's account. What is Gerry's disbursement float on Monday, Tuesday, Wednesday, Thursday, and Friday?

A7. (Cost of trade credit) Calculate the cost of skipping the discount and paying at the end of the net period for each of the following credit terms. Calculate the cost of each in two ways, one way for APR (that ignores the effect of intrayear compounding) and another way for the APY (that does account for intrayear compounding).

    a. 1/10, net 30   c. 2/15, net 45
    b. 6/10, net 70

A8. (Cost of trade credit) Trade credit terms are 2/10, net 40.

    a. What is the true interest cost of skipping the discount and paying on day 40? Estimate both the APR and the APY.

    b. If payment is stretched to day 55 (15 days late), calculate the true interest cost of skipping the discount if the supplier accepts the payment without penalty at that time. Again, estimate both the APR and the APY.

A9. (Cost of trade credit) Suppose you are offered trade credit terms of 1.5/15, net 50. What is the APR cost of this trade credit if you skip the discount and pay at the end of the net period? What would be the APR cost if you "stretched" the payable and paid after 75 days?

A10. (Cost of bank loan) A bank loan agreement calls for an interest rate equal to prime rate plus 1%. If prime rate averages 9% and non-interest-earning compensating balances equal to 10% of the loan must be maintained, what are the APR and the APY of the loan?

A11. (Cost of commercial paper) The discount rate for a 54-day issue of commercial paper is 8.50%. What are the APR and the APY? Assume a 360-day year.

A12. (Cost of commercial paper) Specific Motors Acceptance Corporation sells medium-term commercial paper with a 180-day maturity. If SMAC sells the commercial paper at an annualized discount rate of 11%, calculate the APR and the APY. Assume a 360-day year.

A13. (Cost of wire transfer versus paper check) Say you need to transfer $250,000 from Houston to Chicago. If you mail a check, it will cost $1.00 for postage and clearing the check, and it will take a total of 5 days for the funds to be transferred. During the money's 5-day travel, you will suffer an opportunity cost because the $250,000 is not earning 3% APY interest. Alternatively, you can avoid the opportunity cost by sending a wire transfer costing $12.00, which instantaneously transfers the funds with no float. Calculate the cost of each alternative. Which is cheaper?

PROBLEM SET B

B1. (Baumol cash management model) A company uses the Baumol model and projects a need for $2 million cash per month. Its projected 30-day investment yield is 9% APY. The cost of converting securities into cash is $300 per transaction.

    a. How much cash would the company raise each time it sells securities?

    b. How often should the company plan to sell securities?

    c. What will be the average cash balance?

    d. What are the annual opportunity cost of funds, the annual transaction costs, and the annual total cost?

B2. (Baumol cash management model) Sturbens Electrical Systems pays its $4,000,000 annual payroll expenses out of a Wyoming bank. The disbursements are roughly uniform throughout the year. Sturbens makes deposits into the account from its master account in a Chicago bank. Each deposit involves a fixed cost of $200. The opportunity cost of funds is 4%, because the funds are earning 4% in Chicago and the corporate account in Wyoming receives no interest.

    a. What is the optimal deposit size? What are the annual opportunity cost of funds, annual transaction cost, and annual total cost?

    b. Assume that interest rates have risen substantially, and that Sturbens now has an opportunity cost of funds of 8%. If Sturbens continues to use the same deposit size that you determined in part **a,** what would be its annual opportunity cost of funds, annual transactions cost, and annual total cost?

    c. Recompute the optimal deposit size, assuming the new 8% opportunity cost. What are the opportunity cost, transaction cost, and total cost using the recomputed deposit size?

B3. (Float) The book and available balances for a company's checking account for the last 7 days are given below. What is the daily float? For the 7 days, what is the average book balance, average available balance, and average float?

Day:	Monday	Tuesday	Wednesday	Thursday	Friday	Saturday	Sunday
Book balance:	$100,000	50,000	70,000	100,000	110,000	110,000	110,000
Available balance:	$120,000	100,000	60,000	80,000	130,000	130,000	130,000

B4. (Float) Patin Risk Management Company writes the checks and makes the deposits indicated in the table below. Assume that when Patin writes a check, it takes 3 days for the check to clear and funds to be removed from Patin's available balance at the bank. When Patin makes a deposit, it takes 1 day for the funds to be made available at the bank. Indicate each day the amount of Patin's available balance at the bank, disbursement float, availability float, and total float.

Day	Checks written	Deposits	Book balance	Available balance	Disbursement float	Availability float	Total float
1	0	0	10,000	10,000	0	0	0
2	500	1000	10,500				
3	800	0	9,700				
4	800	0	8,900				
5	0	0	8,900				
6	0	2000	10,900				
7	900	0	10,000				
8	0	0	10,000				
9	0	0	10,000				
10	0	0	10,000				

B5. (Cost of wire transfer versus paper check) If you send money to company headquarters with a wire transfer, it costs a fixed $10 and there is no float. On the other hand, if you write a check and mail it, the fixed cost is only $1.50 and the transfer of funds will occur in 5 days (due to mail times, processing times, and clearing times). The opportunity cost of funds is 8% per year. Assume a 365-day year.

a. What is the cost of a wire transfer and the cost of a paper check if the amount being forwarded to headquarters is $5000?

b. What is the cost of a wire transfer and the

cost of a paper check if the amount being forwarded to headquarters is $25,000?

c. What is the break-even point between a wire transfer and a paper check?

B6. (Lockbox) The Denver Bakery Products Company currently collects all of its customer payments in Denver. By going to a new lockbox system with boxes in Denver, Boston, and Atlanta, Denver Bakery Products can reduce the total time it takes to convert customer payments into available funds by an average of 2.50 days. The company collects an average of $120,000 per day. The extra costs associated with the lockbox system are $7500 per year. The opportunity cost of funds is 6% per year. What is the expected annual profit of using the new system?

B7. (Lockbox) A Columbus bank has made a proposal to operate a lockbox for you. Checks cleared through the lockbox amount to $20,000 per day, and the lockbox will make these funds available to you 2.5 days faster.

a. If the Columbus bank will provide the lockbox services in exchange for a $30,000 compensating balance, is its proposal attractive?

b. Instead of a compensating balance, the bank proposes to provide lockbox services on a fee basis, charging an annual fee of $1000 plus $0.10 per check. You

expect 40,000 checks per year to be processed through the lockbox. If the opportunity cost of funds is 6% APR, what is the annual profit associated with accepting the fee-based proposal?

c. Which is more profitable to you, the compensating balance proposal in part **a** or the fee-based proposal in part **b**?

B8. (Fees versus compensating balance) The bank services you receive cost $500 per month. You have a $100,000 average balance at the bank, on which the bank gives you earnings credits of 0.4% per month.

a. Is your compensating balance sufficient to cover your service charges? If not, what additional amount do you owe the bank?

b. What minimum compensating balance would cover your $500 service charge?

B9. (Cost of bank loan) For a *1-year* loan of $100 with a nominal annual interest rate of 15%, determine the cash flows and the annual percentage yield (APY) for each of the following loans:
   a. interest in arrears
   b. discount loan
   c. interest in arrears with a 10% compensating balance
   d. discount loan with a 10% compensating balance

B10. (Cost of bank loan) For a *3-month* loan of $100 with a nominal annual interest rate of 15%, determine the cash flows and the annual percentage yield (APY) for each of the following loans:
   a. interest in arrears
   b. discount loan
   c. interest in arrears with a 10% compensating balance
   d. discount loan with a 10% compensating balance

B11. (Cost of bank loans) Jim Booth has discussed a $250,000 1-year loan with several different banks. What are the APR and the APY of each alternative? Which loan is the cheapest?
   a. A 15% annual rate on a simple interest loan (interest in arrears), with no compensating balance and interest due at the end of the year.
   b. An 11% annual rate on a simple interest loan (interest in arrears), with a 20% compensating balance requirement and interest due at the end of the year.
   c. A 14% annual rate on a discount loan with no compensating balance. Interest is due at the beginning of the year.

B12. (Cost of installment loan) The Bank of Corpus Christi will give you an installment loan for $50,000 that will be repaid in 12 equal monthly installments. The loan is a 12% add-on loan, which means you must pay 12% on the original loan advance (not just the remaining balance). Your total payments will be $56,000 (the principal of $50,000 plus $6000 of interest), so your monthly payment is $4666.67. What annual percentage yield (APY) are you paying on the loan?

PROBLEM SET C

C1. (Float) Gravel Shirt Company has daily deposits of $40,000 that take 1 day to clear, $80,000 that take 2 days to clear, and $30,000 that take 3 days to clear.
   a. What is the average daily collection float?
   b. What is the weighted average collection delay? (Weight the delays by the dollar volume of the deposits.)
   c. If Gravel added a part-time evening clerk costing $15,000 per year, it could reduce the average collection delay by 0.30 days. If the opportunity cost of funds is 10% per year, what is the annual profitability of adding this clerk?

C2. (Fees versus compensating balances) First Bank of New Orleans has the schedule of service charges given below. Your monthly usage of the services is also given.

Service:	Deposits	Checks cleared	Wire transfers	Account maintenance	ACH transactions	Consulting
Per item:	$0.50	$0.15	$15.00	$25.00	$0.05	$200.00
Number:	400	3000	10	6	1000	0.5

   a. What is your total service charge for the month?
   b. The bank gives you earnings credits equal to the earnings credit rate times your available balance. If the earnings credit rate is 3.6% (0.3% per month) and your available balance is $300,000, how much in earnings credits did you accumulate during the month?
   c. The bank will invoice you for the difference between service charges and earnings credits if the earnings credits are insufficient to cover the service charges. Excess earnings credits are lost. How much do you owe the bank?
   d. What available balance is necessary to exactly cover your service charges for the month?

BIBLIOGRAPHY

Anvari, M. "Efficient Scheduling of Cross-Border Cash Transfers," *Financial Management,* 1986, 15(2):40–49.

Aziz, Abdul, and Gerald H. Lawson. "Cash Flow Reporting and Financial Distress Models: Testing of Hypotheses," *Financial Management,* 1989, 18(1):55–63.

Baumol, William J. "The Transactions Demand for Cash: An Inventory Theoretic Approach," *Quarterly Journal of Economics,* 1952, 66(November):545–556.

Brown, Keith C., and Scott L. Lummer. "The Cash Management Implications of a Hedged Dividend Capture Strategy," *Financial Management,* 1984, 13(4):7–17.

Brown, Keith C., and Scott L. Lummer. "A Reexamination of the Covered Call Option Strategy for Corporate Cash Management," *Financial Management,* 1986, 15(2):13–17.

Gentry, James A. "State of the Art of Short-Run Financial Management," *Financial Management,* 1988, 17(2):41–57.

Gentry, James A., R. Vaidyanathan, and Hei Wai Lee. "A Weighted Cash Conversion Cycle," *Financial Management,* 1990, 19(1):90–99.

Gilmer, R. H., Jr. "The Optimal Level of Liquid Assets: An Empirical Test," *Financial Management,* 1985, 14(4):39–43.

Hill, Ned C., and William L. Sartoris. *Short-Term Financial Management: Text and Cases.* Englewood Cliffs, N.J.: Prentice Hall, 1995.

Kallberg, Jarl G., and Kenneth K. Parkinson. *Current Asset Management.* New York: John Wiley, 1984.

Kamath, Ravindra R., Shahriar Khaksari, Heidi Hylton Meier, and John Winklepleck. "Management of Excess Cash: Practices and Developments," *Financial Management,* 1985, 14(3):70–77.

Miller, Merton H., and Daniel Orr. "A Model of the Demand for Money by Firms," *Quarterly Journal of Economics,* 1966, 80(August):413–435.

Pohlman, Randolph A., Emmanuel S. Santiago, and F. Lynn Markel. "Cash Flow Estimation Practices of Large Firms," *Financial Management,* 1988, 17(2):71–79.

Richards, Verlyn D., and Eugene J. Laughlin. "A Cash Conversion Cycle Approach to Liquidity Analysis," *Financial Management,* 1980, 9(Spring): 32–38.

Sartoris, William L., and Ned C. Hill. "A Generalized Cash Flow Approach to Short-Term Financial Decisions," *Journal of Finance,* 1983, 38(2):349–360.

Stone, Bernell K., and Tom W. Miller. "Daily Cash Forecasting with Multiplicative Models of Cash Flow Patterns," *Financial Management,* 1987, 16(4):45–54.

Winger, Bernard J., Carl R. Chen, John D. Martin, William J. Petty, and Steven C. Hayden. "Adjustable Rate Preferred Stock," *Financial Management,* 1986, 15(1):48–57.

ACCOUNTS RECEIVABLE AND INVENTORY MANAGEMENT

In this chapter we'll discuss receivables and inventories, which are integral parts of working capital management. Receivables and inventories are important for several reasons. First, they make up a large investment in assets. Second, they represent a tremendous volume of transactions and decisions. Third, they involve a large proportion of jobs. Finally, receivables and inventories are important because if they are managed poorly, an otherwise healthy company can actually be pushed into financial distress.

In practice, managing receivables and inventories often falls to new employees, including those who have just received their business degrees. From this vantage point, new managers apply the principles of finance to day-to-day decisions at the core of the business. Competent use of these resources is essential to the company's short-term operation and long-term health. Therefore, inventory and receivables managers often work under close supervision. Employees who do well can earn promotion, and those who do poorly can find themselves out of work.

RECEIVABLES, INVENTORY, AND THE PRINCIPLES OF FINANCE

◆ *Incremental Benefits:* Calculate the incremental cash flows for receivables and inventory decisions.

◆ *Time Value of Money:* Compare the NPV of alternative receivables and inventory decisions.

◆ *Two-Sided Transactions:* Look for situations that are non-zero-sum games; these may be profitable for you *and* your supplier or customer. Receivables and inventory decisions can be used to reduce financial contracting costs and routine transaction costs.

- ◆ *Self-Interested Behavior:* Carefully evaluate and monitor the creditworthiness of your credit customers as well as the quality of goods and services from your suppliers.

- ◆ *Comparative Advantage:* Consider subcontracting business activities to outside vendors if they can provide the services more cheaply and competently.

- ◆ *Behavioral:* Use common industry practices that provide a starting place for operating efficiently.

ACCOUNTS RECEIVABLE MANAGEMENT

Credit sales create accounts receivable. There are two types of credit: trade credit and consumer credit. As chapter 16 discusses, *trade credit* occurs when one company buys goods or services from another without simultaneous payment. Such sales create an account receivable for the supplier (seller) and an account payable for the buying company. **Consumer credit,** or retail credit, is created when a company sells goods or services to a consumer without simultaneous payment.

Most business transactions use trade credit. At the retail level, payment mechanisms include cash, checks, credit extended by the retailer, and credit extended by a third party (such as MasterCard, Visa, or American Express). The use of trade credit and consumer credit is so commonplace that we tend to take them for granted. If you ask why companies grant credit, managers often say they must because competitors do. Although true, this response is simplistic and does not address the fundamental reasons for the extensive use of credit.

CONSUMER CREDIT OR RETAIL CREDIT Credit granted by a business to consumers for the purchase of goods or services.

Why Is Credit So Pervasive?

Trade credit is effectively a loan from one company to another. But it is a loan that is tied to a purchase, like the special-financing offers we explored in chapter 5. The product and loan (credit) are bundled together. Why does this bundling occur?

One answer is that bundling controls financial contracting costs that are created by market imperfections. By using trade credit, both sides of the transaction must be able to lower the cost or risk of doing business. Some specific market considerations follow.

1. *Financial intermediation.* Generally, the interest rate of a trade credit loan benefits both partners. It is lower than the customer's alternative borrowing rates but higher than short-term investment rates available to the supplier. A successful transaction makes the supplier a convenient and economical "bank" for the customer and makes the customer a reliable short-term investment for the supplier.

2. *Collateral.* Suppliers know how to handle the goods as collateral better than other lenders such as banks. When collateral is repossessed after a default on payment, the collateral is more valuable in the hands of a supplier, who has expertise in producing, maintaining, and marketing this collateral.

3. *Information costs.* A supplier may already possess the information needed to evaluate customer creditworthiness. A company accumulates important information about its customers in its normal business relations. This same information may be a sufficient basis on which to make credit-granting decisions. If a bank wants to lend to this same customer, making the credit-granting decision entails costs. Such costs give a supplier a cost advantage over a bank.

4. *Product quality information.* A supplier generally has better information than the customer about the quality of its products. If a supplier is willing to grant credit to customers who buy its products, this is a positive signal about product quality. Credit can provide a cheaply enforced product quality guarantee. If the product is of acceptable quality, the customer pays the trade credit on time. If the product is of low quality, the customer ships it back and refuses to pay. Of course, a supplier can offer a product quality guarantee, but this can be expensive and time consuming for a customer to enforce if payment has already been made. (For a highly reputable supplier who readily honors all guarantees, the extension of credit adds little as a product quality signal.)

5. *Employee opportunism.* Companies try to protect themselves from employee theft in a variety of ways. One is to separate the employees who authorize transactions, who physically handle products, and who handle the payments. This segregation of duties makes it much more difficult for dishonest employees to steal merchandise or money without being caught. Trade credit helps separate the various functions.

6. *Steps in the distribution process.* If a supplier sells to a customer, but the goods must pass through the hands of shippers (such as rail, truck, sea, or air transporters), then it is simply impractical to have payments exchanged at each step in the distribution process. By granting credit to the ultimate buyer, the payments mechanism bypasses all of the agents in the distribution process, requiring only one payment from the ultimate buyer to the original seller.

7. *Convenience, safety, and buyer psychology.* Sometimes it is inconvenient to pay at the time of purchase. Carrying a lot of cash increases the likelihood of being robbed as well as the possibility of losing or misplacing cash. Convenience and safety are important for both business and retail customers, but psychology is also important, especially at the retail level. Most retailers know that their customers would probably buy less if they had to pay with cash or check instead of with credit. "Plastic money" just does not seem like real money. Credit can be an important part of marketing.

The Basic Credit-Granting Decision

The basic analysis for credit-granting decisions is the same as for other financial decisions. Credit should be granted whenever granting credit is a positive-NPV decision.

$$\text{NPV} = \text{PV of future net cash inflows} - \text{outlay}$$

For a simple credit-granting decision, the NPV is

$$\text{NPV} = \frac{pR}{(1+k)^t} - C \qquad (17.1)$$

At time zero, we invest C in a credit sale. The investment might be the cost of goods sold and sales commissions. The sale amount is R, the probability of payment is p, and the expected payment is pR. The customer's probability of payment is estimated subjectively or with the help of statistical models. The payment is expected at time t. The required return is k. If the NPV is negative, then credit should not be granted. We would like a positive NPV.

We can also calculate an indifference (zero-NPV) payment probability, p^*. If a credit customer has a payment probability exceeding p^*, then granting credit has a positive NPV. This indifference payment probability is found by setting the NPV in equation (17.1) equal to zero and solving for p:

$$p^* = \frac{C(1+k)^t}{R} \qquad (17.2)$$

Simple Credit-Granting Decision

E X A M P L E

Boy Scouts of America (BSA) has a customer who wants to purchase $1000 of goods on credit. BSA estimates that the customer has a 95% probability of paying the $1000 in 3 months and a 5% probability of a complete default (paying no cash at all). Assume an investment of 80% of the amount, made at the time of the sale, and a required return of 20% APY. What is the NPV of granting credit, and what is the indifference payment probability?

Using equation (17.1), the NPV is $107.67.

$$\text{NPV} = \frac{pR}{(1+k)^t} - C = \frac{0.95(1000)}{(1+0.20)^{0.25}} - 800 = 907.67 - 800 = \$107.67$$

Therefore, granting credit is profitable, and it should be granted.

Using equation (17.2), the indifference payment probability is 83.7%.

$$p^* = \frac{C(1+k)^t}{R} = \frac{800(1+0.20)^{0.25}}{1000} = \frac{837.31}{1000} = 83.7\%$$

This result is consistent with the NPV calculation. BSA's estimate of a 95% payment probability exceeds the indifference value of 83.7% and indicates that BSA should grant credit. ∎

The NPV rule is the best method for evaluating credit-granting decisions. However, calculations can be quite complicated. The investment in the sale may not be made at time zero. In addition, the expected payments may occur at various times rather than at a single point in time. For example, with payment due in 30 days, the customer might have a 60% probability of paying in 30 days, a 30% probability of paying in 60 days, a 5% probability of paying in 90 days, and a 5% probability of never paying. No matter how complicated the situation, however, the NPV rule should be used.

Credit-Policy Decisions

CREDIT PERIOD The length of time that the customer is granted credit.

DISCOUNT PERIOD The period during which a customer can "take" the *discount.*

DISCOUNT A percentage a customer can deduct from the net amount of the bill if payment is made before the end of the *discount period.*

INVOICE The written statement from a supplier about goods that were shipped along with the amount due and the payment dates.

INVOICE DATE Usually the date when goods are shipped. Payment dates are set relative to the invoice date.

INVOICE BILLING Billing customers with each individual shipment or service.

STATEMENT BILLING Billing customers for all the charges for a billing period.

Credit-policy decisions affect a company's revenues and costs. For example, consider a policy of granting credit more easily. A more liberal credit policy should increase the cost of goods sold, gross profit, bad debt expenses, the cost of carrying additional receivables, and administrative costs. However, the more liberal policy might or might not increase net profit. A policy's profitability depends on the incremental benefits and incremental costs. These are the additional gross profits generated by the liberal policy minus the increase in costs, such as bad debt costs, carrying costs on increased receivables, and administrative costs.

Depending on the industry, credit policy can vary from being crucial to being irrelevant. A retail store may need a competitive policy to survive, whereas an electric utility must simply grant credit according to government regulation. Credit-policy decisions involve all aspects of receivables management. They include (1) the choice of credit terms, (2) setting evaluation methods and credit standards, (3) monitoring receivables and taking actions for slow payment, and (4) controlling and administering the company's credit functions.

Credit Terms

Credit terms are the contract between the supplier and credit customer specifying how the credit will be repaid. In our discussion of accounts payable in chapter 16, we used the term "2/10, net 30." As the seller, you are now *offering* such credit terms instead of *receiving* them. For the 2/10, net 30 credit terms, you are offering a total **credit period** of 30 days from the date of the invoice, a **discount period** of 10 days, and a 2% **discount** if paid on or before the end of the discount period.

The **invoice** is a written statement about goods that were ordered, along with their prices and the payment dates. In other words, the invoice is simply the bill for purchases. The **invoice date** is usually the date the goods are shipped. When a company is using **invoice billing,** the invoice that accompanies shipment is a separate bill to be paid. When invoices are numerous, a company may use statement billing instead of invoice billing. With **statement billing,** all of the sales for a period such as a month (for which a customer receives invoices, too) are collected into a single statement and sent to the customer as one bill.

Although any alternative set of credit terms is possible, only a few sets of terms tend to be used in a particular industry. These credit terms reflect the industry's specific circumstances, as well as general economic conditions. The accompanying box describes several basic types of commonly used credit terms.

TRADE CREDIT TERMS

CIA (cash in advance) and **CBD (cash before delivery)** Payment must be received before the order is shipped.

COD (cash on delivery) The shipper collects the payment (on behalf of the seller) upon delivery.

Cash Payment is due when the goods are delivered. Unlike COD, cash terms allow the customer to mail the payment. Effectively, cash terms allow the customer up to about 10 days to pay.

Standard terms: "net 30" or "net 60" Payment is due in full 30 or 60 days from the date of the invoice.

Discount terms: "2/10, net 30" Discount terms include a discount percentage, discount payment date, and net date. The buyer can take a 2% discount if the payment is made by the 10th day following the invoice date. Otherwise, the full amount is due 30 days following the invoice date.

Prox terms: "10th prox," "25th prox," "2/10, prox net 30" Prox or proximate refers to the next month. All invoices dated prior to a defined cutoff are to be paid by a date in the next month. Invoices with "10th prox" must be paid by the 10th of the next month and invoices with "25th prox" by the 25th of the next month. Similarly, "2/10, prox net 30" means that invoices paid by the 10th of the next month receive a 2% discount. If payment is not made by the 10th, then the full amount is due by the 30th.

Seasonal dating: "2/10, net 30, dating 120," or "2/10, net 30, 60 extra" For seasonal items such as sporting goods, some clothing, or Christmas items, payment is sometimes scheduled to be due near the buyer's selling season. The "dating 120" or the "60 extra" mean that the clock does not start until 120 or 60 days after the invoice date. Although seasonal dating does give buyers a longer time to pay, sellers benefit by encouraging buyers to make earlier purchase decisions. This lowers the seller's inventory costs by reducing the amount of time the goods spend in inventory.

Consignment The seller ships the goods to the buyer, but the buyer is not required to pay until the goods have been sold or used.

Letter of credit A letter of credit is an agreement by which a financial institution (a bank or other financially strong party) substitutes its creditworthiness for that of the customer. The supplier can require a letter of credit when the payment risk is high. When terms specified in the letter of credit are met, such as delivery of the goods, the bank will make payment on behalf of the customer. Letters of credit frequently are used in international trade.

Electronic credit terms The seller is paid directly from the buyer's bank account by an automated clearing house (ACH) transaction. Transfer usually occurs right after delivery. Electronic credit terms reduce administrative costs and uncertainties about payment dates. They also reduce supplier accounts receivable and buyer accounts payable.

Credit terms also specify the evidence of indebtedness. Most credit sales are made on an **open account** basis, which means that customers simply purchase what they want. The invoice they sign when receiving the shipment provides evidence that they received the goods and have accepted an obligation to pay. Suppliers usually establish a credit limit for each customer. It is the maximum total amount of outstanding invoices that the customer is permitted. If the cumulative bills reach the credit limit, further credit is denied until the customer makes some payment or gets the credit limit raised. Credit limits are an effective way to limit the amount that can be lost to default.

For large purchases or nonregular customers, a customer may be required to sign a promissory note. Because of time and expense and the low risk of default, promissory notes are not used for routine sales.

OPEN ACCOUNT A credit account where the customer makes purchases and the signed invoices are evidence of indebtedness.

Self-Check

1. What is trade credit? How is it different from consumer credit? Explain how both arise in the normal course of business transactions.

2. Why is credit so pervasive?

3. What should be the basis for credit-granting decisions?

4. What are the four main aspects of credit-policy decisions?

CREDIT STANDARDS AND CREDIT EVALUATION

Credit standards are the criteria used to grant credit. They depend on the variables that determine the NPV of the sale: investment in the sale, probability of payment, required return, and payment period. A higher probability of default, delayed payments, and the necessity of expensive collection efforts all reduce the NPV.

Table 17.1 gives three pairs of numerical examples of how each of these variables can cause a sale to be profitable or unprofitable. The first pair shows the effect of a lower probability of payment. A lower probability results in a negative NPV. The second pair shows the effect of delayed payment. The time value of money on a two-month payment delay more than eliminates the profit. The final pair emphasizes the role of collection costs. The present value of the collection costs is an added cost of the sale. Higher collection costs reduce the NPV and can even cause it to be negative. Collection costs have a fixed component, costs that are independent of the amount of the credit sale. These fixed administrative or collection costs often make small credit sales unprofitable.

Unfortunately, these individual factors that reduce the profitability of a credit sale often reinforce one another. For example, a customer who is likely to make late payments is also more likely to default and to require extra collection efforts. The management of credit policy, then, must include establishing credit standards and then evaluating individual customers against these standards. To do this, managers must know how to analyze creditworthiness.

Sources of Credit Information

There are several valuable internal and external sources of information. The primary *internal sources* are:

1. A credit application, including references.
2. The applicant's previous payment history, if credit has previously been extended.
3. Information from sales representatives and other employees.

Several important *external sources* of credit information include:

1. Financial statements for recent years. These financial statements can be analyzed to get insights into the customer's profitability, debt obligations, and liquidity.
2. Reports from credit-rating agencies such as Dun & Bradstreet Business Credit Services (D&B). These agencies supply credit appraisals of thousands of companies and estimates of their overall strength. D&B appraises the credit of a company relative to that

TABLE 17.1
Effects of Default Risk, Delayed Payments, and Collection Costs

SALE	INVESTMENT	PROBABILITY OF PAYMENT	COLLECTION PERIOD	PV OF COLLECTION COSTS	COST OF FUNDS	NPV
Effect of Default Risk						
$1000	$ 850	.99	1 month	0	20%	$125.07
1000	850	.85	1 month	0	20%	−12.82
Effect of Delayed Payment						
$2000	$1925	.99	1 month	0	20%	$25.14
2000	1925	.99	3 months	0	20%	−33.22
Effect of Collection Costs						
$ 100	$ 80	.95	1 month	$ 5	20%	$8.57
100	80	.95	1 month	20	20%	−6.43

of other companies of comparable financial strength and assigns composite credit appraisal ratings between 1 ("high") and 4 ("limited").

3. **Credit bureau reports.** These reports provide factual information about whether a company's financial obligations are overdue. Credit bureau reports also give information about any legal judgments against the company.

4. **Industry association credit files.** Industry associations sometimes maintain credit files. Industry associations and your direct competitors are frequently willing to share credit information about customers.

Two basic approaches to evaluating a credit application are the *judgmental* approach and the *objective* approach. The judgmental approach uses a variety of credit information, as well as specific knowledge and experience, to reach a decision. The objective approach uses numerical cutoffs or scores that must be reached for credit to be granted. The "five Cs of credit" are used with the judgmental approach. Credit scoring is an example of an objective approach.

Five Cs of Credit

The **five Cs of credit** are five general factors that credit analysts often consider when making a credit-granting decision.

> **FIVE CS OF CREDIT** Five characteristics that are used to form a judgment about a customer's creditworthiness. The five Cs of credit are character, capacity, capital, collateral, and conditions.

1. *Character.* The commitment to meet credit obligations. Character is best measured by a credit applicant's prior payment history.

2. *Capacity.* The ability to meet credit obligations with current income. Capacity is evaluated by looking at the income or cash flows on the applicant's income statement or statement of cash flows.

3. *Capital.* The ability to meet credit obligations from existing assets if necessary. Capital is evaluated by looking at the applicant's net worth.

4. *Collateral.* The collateral that can be repossessed in the case of nonpayment. Collateral value depends on the cost of repossessing and on the possible resale value.

5. *Conditions.* General or industry economic conditions. Conditions external to the customer's business affect the credit-granting decision. For example, improving or deteriorating general economic conditions can change interest rates or the risk of granting credit. Likewise, conditions in a particular industry can affect the profitability of granting credit to a company in that industry.

Credit-Scoring Models

Assessing a company's ability to pay its debts is a complex judgment, because many factors affect creditworthiness. One tool many companies use is credit scoring. **Credit scoring** combines several financial variables into a single score, or index, that measures creditworthiness. The score is often a linear combination of several specific variables. A score based on four financial variables could be

> **CREDIT SCORING** A statistical technique where several financial characteristics are combined to form a single score to represent a customer's creditworthiness.

$$S = w_1X_1 + w_2X_2 + w_3X_3 + w_4X_4 = 2X_1 - 0.3X_2 + 0.1X_3 + 0.6X_4$$

where

X_1 = net working capital/sales (expressed as %) X_2 = debt/assets (%)

X_3 = assets/sales (%) X_4 = net profit margin (%)

The *w*s are the coefficients (or weights) that are multiplied by the *X*s (financial characteristics) to create the overall credit score. The positive coefficients for X_1, X_3, and X_4 mean that a higher value results in a higher credit score. The negative coefficient for X_2 means that a higher debt/assets ratio reduces the credit score.

EXAMPLE

Calculating Credit Scores for a Business Customer

What are the credit scores for the two customers with the following characteristics?

	Customer 1	Customer 2
X_1 = net working capital/sales (%)	15%	8%
X_2 = debt/assets (%)	40%	55%
X_3 = assets/sales (%)	105%	110%
X_4 = net profit margin (%)	12%	9%

Customer 1's credit score is 35.7.

$$S = 2.0(15) - 0.3(40) + 0.1(105) + 0.6(12) = 30 - 12 + 10.5 + 7.2 = 35.7$$

Customer 2's credit score is 15.9.

$$S = 2.0(8) - 0.3(55) + 0.1(110) + 0.6(9) = 16 - 16.5 + 11 + 5.4 = 15.9$$

If the company expects a zero NPV for customers with a score of 25, customer 1 should get credit, and customer 2 should be denied credit. ■

Credit-scoring models are constructed by using sophisticated statistical methods to analyze the payment records of many past customers. Such models offer several advantages.

1. They enable the creditor to accept the clearly good customers and reject the clearly bad customers very quickly. The creditor then can devote costly evaluation talent to analyzing the "close calls."

2. They allow different loan processors to apply consistent standards across all credit applicants. They also make changing the standards easy. The company could change the cutoff from 25 to, say, 28. This change would then apply equally to all loan applicants.

3. They are "objective" and can help the company avoid bias or discrimination.

There are important disadvantages of credit-scoring models, too.

1. The models are only as good as the payment records used to construct the models. Many samples do not have a rich enough set of bad loans to build an effective scoring model. In addition, the models have to be updated occasionally. When the model is updated with a new sample, there is some "inbreeding" whereby the new model is built on data that eliminated many bad customers.

2. Credit-scoring models work best when applied to large populations of loan applicants. Consumer loan databases often include many thousands of loans, and credit-scoring models can be built readily. Unfortunately, the number of business loans in a database is often too small to be statistically reliable. Consequently, credit-scoring models are more often used for evaluating consumer loans than for evaluating business loans, which more often relies on judgmental methods.

Credit scoring is frequently used on consumer credit card applications and for personal loans and car loans. For a credit card application, the following scoring sheet (sometimes called a weighted application blank) is often used.

Telephone	Yes = 4 points, No = 0 points
Income	Above $40,000 = 3 points
	$20,000–$40,000 = 2 points
	below $20,000 = 0 points

Employment	more than 3 years with current employer = 3 points
	1–3 years with current employer = 2 points
	less than 1 year with current employer = 1 point
	Self-employed = 1 point
	Unemployed = 0 points
Residence	Own = 3 points
	Rent = 1 point
	more than 3 years at current address = 2 points
	1–3 years at current address = 1 point
	0–1 years at current address = 0 points
Credit report	Good = 10 points
	Fair = 4 points
	Bad = −5 points
	None = 0 points

Consumer Credit-Scoring Model

EXAMPLE

Suppose Marcelle Welch is applying for a credit card. After graduating with her business degree, Marcelle has a new job earning $45,000 per year. She has just moved to her new job and has rented an apartment. Her telephone is connected, and she has a good credit report. What is her credit score?

Telephone	4 points
Income	3
Employment	1
Residence	1
Credit report	10
Total score	19 points

If the cutoff is 15, Marcelle qualifies for the credit card. ■

Self-Check

1. What are the main sources of credit information? Which are internal and which are external sources?

2. What are the five Cs of credit? Explain how credit analysts use them to decide whether or not to grant credit.

3. Explain how a company can use a credit-scoring model to decide whether or not to grant credit. How is such a model constructed?

4. What are the main advantages and disadvantages of using credit-scoring models to evaluate customer creditworthiness?

MONITORING ACCOUNTS RECEIVABLE

Monitoring accounts receivable is critical because of the size of the investment. If the quality is surprisingly high or low, several relevant questions arise: Are the company's credit standards too low or too high? Has a change in general economic conditions affected customer creditworthiness? Is something fundamentally wrong with the evaluation system?

In any case, a reliable, early warning about deterioration of receivables can make it possible to take action to prevent a worsening. Conversely, a reliable, early indication of improvement in the quality of receivables might inspire the company to be more aggressive in its receivables policies.

Widely used techniques to monitor the quality of receivables include aging schedules, the average age of receivables, collection fractions, and receivables balance fractions. Let's take a look at each in turn.

Aging Schedules

AGING SCHEDULE A table showing the dollar amounts and the percentages of total accounts receivable that fall into several age categories.

An **aging schedule** is a table showing the total dollar amounts and the percentages of total accounts receivable that fall into several age classifications. It provides a picture of the quality of outstanding accounts receivable. Such schedules usually show those receivables that are 0 to 30 days old, 30 to 60 days old, 60 to 90 days old, and over 90 days old.

The next example shows how an aging schedule is prepared. All of the company's outstanding invoices are collected and sorted according to their ages. These are then summarized on the aging schedule.

E X A M P L E   *Building an Aging Schedule for the Provo Palace*

On September 30, the Provo Palace prepares a list of all of its outstanding invoices from its database system and sorts them by their original dates. The invoices for each month up to the current date are collected together and totaled, as shown in table 17.2. As you can see, the September invoices, which are 0–30 days old, are substantially more than for the previous months because most of the older invoices have already been collected.

Amounts are usually shown in both dollars and percentages. The percentage breakdown can be readily compared with previous aging schedule breakdowns to see if the current situation is different from past experience. ■

The aging schedule depends on the credit terms offered, customer payment habits, and trends in recent sales. For example, if a company changes its credit terms, such as giving customers a longer credit period, the aging schedule will reflect this change. If customers are paying more quickly, the percentage in the youngest categories will increase and the percentage in the older categories will decrease. Likewise, a change in the company's sales can affect the aging schedule. If sales increase during the current month, the percentage of 0-to-30-day receivables will increase. Conversely, a sales decrease tends to reduce the percentage of 0-to-30-day receivables.

Average Age of Accounts Receivable

AVERAGE AGE OF ACCOUNTS RECEIVABLE The weighted average age of all of the company's outstanding invoices.

In addition to an aging schedule, managers commonly compute an **average age of accounts receivable,** the average age of all of the company's outstanding invoices. There are two common ways to make the computation. The first is to calculate the weighted average age of all individual outstanding invoices. The weights used are the percentages that the individual invoices represent out of the total amount of accounts receivable.

A simplified way to calculate the average age of accounts receivable is to use the aging schedule. Here, all receivables that are 0 to 30 days old are assumed to be 15 days old (the midpoint of 0 and 30), all receivables that are 30 to 60 days old are assumed to be 45 days old, and all receivables that are 60 to 90 days old are assumed to be 75 days old. Then the average age is computed by taking a weighted average of 15, 30, and 45. The weights are the percentages of receivables that are 0 to 30, 30 to 60, and 60 to 90 days old, respectively.

TABLE 17.2

Aging Schedule for Provo Palace

OUTSTANDING INVOICES SEPTEMBER 30

Invoice Number	Invoice Date	Invoice Amount		
1041	7/7	$ 1,200		
1049	7/13	1,000	$ 3,400	Total for July
1060	7/27	800		
1061	7/27	400		
1063	8/5	1,500		
1066	8/12	1,000		
1067	8/12	500		
1072	8/15	800	$ 8,300	Total for August
1073	8/16	1,200		
1080	8/23	1,200		
1083	8/25	1,500		
1084	8/26	600		
1087	9/2	1,000		
1089	9/5	1,400		
1090	9/5	500		
1092	9/7	1,000		
1093	9/10	1,200		
1094	9/14	700		
1095	9/15	400	$11,800	Total for September
1096	9/18	900		
1097	9/20	1,000		
1098	9/22	800		
1099	9/25	1,000		
1100	9/25	500		
1101	9/28	1,400		
Total		$23,500	$23,500	

AGING SCHEDULE, SEPTEMBER 30

Age	Amount	Percent
0–30 days	$11,800	50.2%
30–60 days	8,300	35.3
60–90 days	3,400	14.5
over 90 days	0	0
Total	$23,500	100.0%

Average Age of Accounts Receivable for Provo Palace   ▪ EXAMPLE

What is the average age of accounts receivable for Provo Palace?

Using the aging schedule in table 17.2, and the midpoint for each category (for example, 15 for the 0–30-day category), we estimate that the weighted average is 34.29.

Average age $= 0.502(15) + 0.353(45) + 0.145(75) = 7.53 + 15.885 + 10.875 = 34.29$ days

The same phenomena that affect an aging schedule will affect an average age. Changes in credit terms, payment habits, or sales levels can increase or decrease the average age.

Collection Fractions and Receivables Balance Fractions

Two other measures used to monitor the quality of receivables are collection fractions and receivables balance fractions. **Collection fractions** are the percentages of sales collected during various months. For example, the collection fractions show the percentage of June's sales that are collected in June, as well as the percentage collected in each month thereafter (July, August, and September). After a month's billings have all been collected, the collection fractions sum to 100%. The pattern of the collection fractions is compared with an expected or budgeted collection pattern to see whether collections are faster or slower than expected.

     Receivables balance fractions are the percentages of a month's sales that remain uncollected (and part of accounts receivable) at the end of the month of sale and at the end of succeeding months. For example, receivables balance fractions would include the percentage

TABLE 17.3
Collection Fractions and Receivables Balance Fractions

MONTH: SALES:	AUG 1000	SEPT 1000	OCT 1000	NOV 1000	DEC 1200	JAN 1500	FEB 1800	MAR 2000
Panel A								
Collections from:					↓			
Current month	100	100	100	100	110	135	160	175
Previous month		500	500	500	480	550	680	800
Two months previous			350	350	340	350	420	525
Three months previous				50	50	60	70	120
Total collections				1000	980	1095	1330	1620

Collections of December sales

Panel B								
Collection fractions from:								
Current month	0.100	0.100	0.100	0.100	0.092	0.090	0.089	0.088
Previous month		0.500	0.500	0.500	0.480	+ 0.458	0.453	0.444
Two months previous			0.350	0.350	0.340	0.350	+ 0.350	0.350
Three months previous				0.050	0.050	0.060	0.070	+ 0.100 = 1.00

↑ Collection fractions for the month   ↑ Fractions of December sales collected

Panel C								
Accounts receivable from:								
Current month	900	900	900	900	1090	1365	1640	1825
Previous month		400	400	400	420	540	685	840
Two months previous			50	50	60	70	120	160
Three months previous				0	0	0	0	0
Total accounts receivable				1350	1570	1975	2445	2825

Panel D								
Receivables balance fractions from:								
Current month	0.900	0.900	0.900	0.900	0.908	0.910	0.911	0.913
Previous month		0.400	0.400	0.400	0.420	0.450	0.457	0.467
Two months previous			0.050	0.050	0.060	0.070	0.100	0.107
Three months previous				0.000	0.000	0.000	0.000	0.000

↑ Receivables balance fractions for the month

of June's sales that remain outstanding at the end of June and in the months of July, August, and September. The key point to notice about collection fractions and receivables balance fractions (compared to aging schedules) is that collections and receivables outstanding are always expressed as a *percentage of original sales.*

If sales go up or down after the given month, collections and receivables are always compared with their original month of sale instead of with later sales figures. Data from each month's sales are always treated separately. June's collection fractions and balance fractions are never mixed in with those of another month. Hence collection fractions and receivables balance fractions are more reliable measures of quality than aging schedules, particularly when sales are increasing or decreasing. The following example illustrates how to use collection fractions and balance fractions to monitor the quality of receivables.

Connecticut Micro Systems's Collection Fractions and Receivables Balance Fractions

E X A M P L E

Connecticut Micro Systems, Inc. expects its collection fractions and receivables balance fractions to be:

	Collection Fraction	Balance Fraction
Original month	0.10	0.90
month t+1	0.50	0.40
month t+2	0.35	0.05
month t+3	0.05	0.00

These expected fractions are based on the company's credit terms and on its best estimate of what the payment habits of its customers should be. Note that the expected collection fractions sum to 1.00, but the balance fractions do not. The balance fraction declines from its previous value by the amount collected during the month.

Table 17.3 on p. 626 is a schedule showing monthly sales and the pattern of collections over several months tied back to the original month's sales. What are the collection fractions, receivables balance fractions, and dollar amounts of receivables outstanding that go with these data? How would you assess the behavior of collections and receivables compared to the expected fractions?

Panel A of table 17.3 shows how each month's sales are subsequently collected. For example, December's $1200 of sales were collected as follows: $110 in December, $550 in January, $420 in February, and $120 in March. Panel B shows the collection fractions that correspond to panel A. For example, December's sales collection fraction for December is $110/1200 = 0.092$. For January it is $550/1200 = 0.458$, for February $420/1200 = 0.350$, and for March $120/1200 = 0.100$.

Panel C shows this information in terms of receivables yet to be paid, the total and by age. For example, December's total accounts receivable of $1570 are made up of remaining receivables of $1090 from December sales, $420 from November sales, and $60 from October sales. The progression through panel C follows the diagonal, by subtracting the collections (panel A) according to the formula

$$\frac{\text{Receivables from one month previous}}{\text{Receivables from two months previous}} - \frac{\text{Collections from two months previous}}{}$$

For example, receivables in December from the previous month (420, in panel C) minus collections in January from two months previous (350, in panel A) equals receivables in January from two months previous ($420 - 350 = 70$, in panel C).

(continued on following page)

(Connecticut Micro Systems's Collection Fractions and Receivables Balance Fractions *continued from previous page*)

Panel D presents this information in terms of receivables balance fractions. The receivables balance fraction is the value in panel C divided by the original month's sales. For example, the receivables balance fractions in January are for the current month, one month previous, and two months previous: 0.910 (= 1365/1500), 0.450 (= 540/1200), and 0.070 (= 70/1000).

The collection fractions and receivables balance fractions are evaluated by comparing them to their expected sizes. In November, the collection fractions in panel B are exactly equal to the expected levels. Likewise, in November, the receivables balance fractions in panel D are equal to their expected levels. However, the quality of receivables then deteriorates. You can see that by the end of March, the collection fractions for the current month and the previous month are below expectations, and the collection fractions for late collections (from sales three months previous) are higher. It is taking longer to collect.

This collection slowdown also shows up in the receivables balance fractions for March in panel D. Because of delayed collections, the receivables balance fractions are higher than expected. Connecticut Micro Systems may have a receivables problem. If its credit terms were not changed, it could be that the company is granting credit to less creditworthy customers or is managing collections poorly. ■

Pursuing Delinquent Credit Customers

Your best credit customers pay their bills promptly and are very easy to deal with. A few credit customers will prove to be complete deadbeats, and it will be difficult to recover anything from them no matter how hard you try. Other customers fall in between these two extremes, and dealing successfully with these marginal credit customers can be a key to profitability.

Businesses follow a number of specific steps in the collection process, depending on how long overdue the account is, the size of the debt, and other factors. A typical collection process can include these steps.

1. *Letters.* When an account is overdue by a few days, a "friendly reminder" may be sent. If payment is not received, one or two more letters might be sent, with the tone of the letters becoming more severe and demanding.

2. *Telephone calls.* After the first couple of letters, the customer is phoned. If the customer is having financial troubles, a compromise might be worked out. A partial payment is better than no payment.

3. *Personal visits.* The salesperson who made the sale can visit the customer to request payment. Other special collectors besides the salesperson can be used.

4. *Collection agencies.* The account is turned over to a collection agency that specializes in collecting past due accounts. Collection agencies usually collect a fee, such as one-half of whatever is recovered, and they recover only a fraction of the accounts they go after. So a company's loss can be a very large portion of the accounts turned over.

5. *Legal proceedings.* If the bill is large enough, legal action may be used to obtain a judgment against the debtor.

The collection process can be viewed as a capital budgeting process wherein the company wants to use the collection procedures that generate the highest NPV. When collection is viewed this way, there are a few important principles to follow. The sequence of collection efforts begins with the least expensive and proceeds to increasingly more expensive techniques only after earlier methods have failed. Letters may cost the company only $0.50, whereas telephone calls may average, say, $5.00, and personal visits can cost $20 to $100. Controlling the size of the investment in the collection effort can improve the NPV.

The early collection contacts are more upbeat and friendly, and the later contacts are not the least bit friendly. This is because many marginal customers will pay if asked and because future sales to these customers might be profitable. Once it becomes clear that there is limited potential for future profitable sales, collection efforts become much more aggressive.

Collection decisions follow capital budgeting principles. Sunk costs, which can be the uncollected investments made in goods sold, are eventually ignored. The collection sequence should be the one that results in the maximum NPV. Once the expected cash flow from continuing the collection effort is less than the additional cost of continuing, the correct decision is to stop pursuing the customer.

Changing Credit Policy

Credit policy can be changed by altering terms, standards, or collection practices. A change in credit policy can affect sales. It can also affect the cost of goods sold, bad debt expenses, carrying costs on accounts receivable, and other administrative costs. We can calculate the NPV of a credit policy change.

The NPV of Changing Credit Policy

EXAMPLE

A company currently uses credit terms of net 30. It is considering a switch to 2/10, net 30. The expected effects of this more liberal policy are:

	Current Policy	Proposed Policy
Credit terms	net 30	2/10, net 30
Sales	$1,000,000	$1,050,000
Cost of sales (at time 0)	$600,000	$630,000
Bad debt losses	1.5% of sales	1.0% of sales
	0.015(1,000,000) = 15,000	0.01(1,050,000) = 10,500
Collection pattern	1.5 months (98.5% pay here on average) (1.5% never pay)	0.5 months (70%) 1.5 months (29%) (1% never pay)
Required return	1% per month	1% per month
Sales less bad debt	$985,000	$1,039,500
Discounts taken	$0	0.02(0.70)(1,050,000) = $14,700
Sales less bad debt and discounts	$985,000	$1,024,800

The expected cash flows for the current policy are:

$$\begin{array}{lll} -600{,}000 & 985{,}000 & \\ \hline 0 & 1.5 \text{ months} & \text{time} \end{array}$$

The current policy requires $600,000 at time zero and has an expected inflow of $985,000 (the sales of $1,000,000 less 1.5% bad debt) in 1.5 months. At a required return of 1% per month, the NPV of one year's sales under the current policy is

$$\text{NPV (current policy)} = \frac{0.985(1{,}000{,}000)}{(1+0.01)^{1.5}} - 600{,}000 = 970{,}408 - 600{,}000 = \$370{,}408$$

The expected cash flows for the proposed policy are:

$$\begin{array}{llll} -630{,}000 & 720{,}300 & 304{,}500 & \\ \hline 0 & 0.5 \text{ months} & 1.5 \text{ months} & \text{time} \end{array}$$

The proposed policy results in a 5% increase in sales and cost of goods sold, an outlay of $630,000 at time 0. Note that 70% of our customers pay early and take the 2% discount,

(continued on following page)

(The NPV of Changing Credit Policy *continued from previous page*)

resulting in a cash flow of 0.70(0.98)(1,050,000) = $720,300 at time 0.5 months. The balance of the customers who pay, 29% of sales, pay in 1.5 months. These customers pay 0.29(1,050,000) = $304,500. So the NPV of one year's sales for the proposed policy is:

$$\text{NPV (proposed policy)} = \frac{0.70(0.98)(1,050,000)}{(1.01)^{0.5}} + \frac{0.29(1,050,000)}{(1.01)^{1.5}} - 630,000$$

$$= 716,725 + 299,989 - 630,000 = \$386,714$$

Because the proposed policy has the greater NPV ($386,714 versus $370,408), the company would be better off with the proposed change in credit policy. The tricky part of this kind of decision is determining whether there is a third credit policy that would be even better than the proposed one we have just analyzed. This is essentially the same question we faced in capital budgeting. Our answer is still just as unsatisfying: You just have to do the best you can. ■

Most companies in an industry use similar credit policies. Competitive pressures, as well as similar contracting cost structures, tend to cause credit policies to be strikingly similar. Therefore, the Behavioral Principle can be useful. When you are considering your own credit policy, a good starting point is the credit policies of other companies in the industry. Then, on the basis of your own strategic directions or changing economic conditions, you should consider credit policies that might be better for your company.

Self-Check

1. How do companies monitor the quality of their receivables?

2. What does an aging schedule show? How is one prepared?

3. Explain how a company can use collection fractions and receivables balance fractions to monitor its accounts receivable. Are they more useful as measures of quality than aging schedules?

4. Describe the five steps that are usually part of the collection process.

5. How can information about your main competitors' current credit policies be useful to your company in setting its credit policy?

INVENTORY MANAGEMENT

Inventories play a crucial role in a company's purchasing-production-marketing process. Some inventories are a physical necessity for the company. For example, partly built cars must be on the assembly line. Oil in transit must fill up oil pipelines. Other inventories are buffer stocks that are necessary at several points in the purchasing-production-marketing process. If the food is not in the grocery store when customers want it, the store cannot sell it. Likewise, if needed parts are delayed or out of stock, an assembly line can be shut down. Some goods, such as grain or coal, are shipped in such large quantities that it can take a year or more to use up one shipment.

Manufacturing companies generally carry three types of inventories: raw materials, work-in-process, and finished goods. The size of a company's raw materials inventories depends on factors such as the anticipated level of production, production seasonality, and supply reliability. The size of the company's work-in-process inventories depends mainly on the overall length of each production cycle and the number of distinct stages in the cycle. Finally, the size of the company's finished goods inventories depends primarily on the rate of sales (units of product per unit of time), cost of carrying the inventory, cost of ordering replacement stocks, and cost of running out of an item (maybe losing the sale or even the customer). In general, larger inventories give the company greater sales and operating flexibility, but they also cost more.

The Economic Order Quantity (EOQ) Model

A simple and useful inventory management model is the economic order quantity (EOQ) model. This model is derived in the following manner. Suppose that units are removed from inventory at a constant rate S (the rate at which goods are sold, in the case of finished goods inventories). Assume that there is a fixed reordering cost, F, per order regardless of the number of units reordered and that it costs C to carry a unit in inventory for an entire period. Note that the EOQ model assumes *constant* inventory usage or sales and *instantaneous* inventory replenishment.

Under these assumptions, the inventory level behaves as shown in figure 17.1.[1] The inventory begins at Q units and is reduced at a constant rate until it reaches zero. At that point, the inventory is instantaneously replenished with another Q units, and the process starts over. Over the year, the inventory fluctuates between Q and zero, and the number of saw teeth in the figure is the number of orders per year.

The total annual cost is made up of two components, ordering costs and carrying costs. The ordering cost is the cost per order, F, times the number of orders per year. The number of orders per year is the annual usage (in units) divided by the order size, S/Q, so the annual ordering cost is $F(S/Q)$.

The annual carrying cost is the carrying cost per unit, C, times the average inventory, which is $Q/2$. Thus the annual carrying cost is $C(Q/2)$.

The total annual cost is the sum of these two components:

$$\text{Total cost} = \text{Ordering cost} + \text{Carrying cost} = F\frac{S}{Q} + C\frac{Q}{2} \tag{17.3}$$

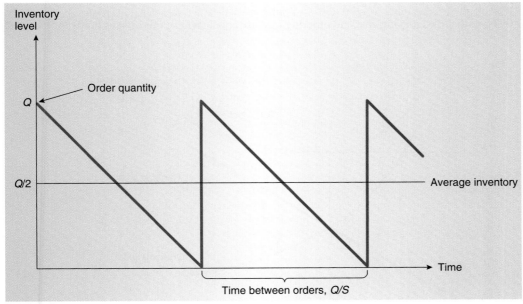

FIGURE 17.1
Inventory levels for the EOQ model.

---

[1]If figure 17.1 looks suspiciously familiar, that's probably because it's essentially identical to figure 16.3, the Baumol cash management model. The two models have equivalent structures.

ECONOMIC ORDER QUANTITY (EOQ) The order quantity that minimizes total inventory costs.

Figure 17.2 shows ordering costs and carrying costs as a function of Q, the order size, which is the decision variable. Note that an increase in Q increases the carrying cost but decreases the ordering cost. Total cost can be minimized by finding the order quantity that balances the two component costs. That order quantity is the **economic order quantity (EOQ)**, as shown in figure 17.2.[2] The formula for EOQ is

$$EOQ = \sqrt{\frac{2FS}{C}} \tag{17.4}$$

EXAMPLE

OfficeMax's EOQ

Suppose OfficeMax sells personal copying machines at the rate of 1800 units per year. The cost of placing one order is $400, and it costs $100 per year to carry a copier in inventory. What is OfficeMax's EOQ? Using the EOQ, find the average inventory, number of orders per year, time interval between orders, annual ordering cost, annual carrying cost, and annual total cost.

Using equation (17.4), the EOQ is 120 copiers.

$$EOQ = \sqrt{\frac{2FS}{C}} = \sqrt{\frac{2(400)(1800)}{100}} = \sqrt{14,400} = 120 \text{ copiers}$$

Average inventory = EOQ/2 = 120/2 = 60 copiers
Number of orders per year = S/EOQ = 1800/120 = 15 times per year
Time interval between orders = EOQ/S = 120/1800
$$= 0.0667 \text{ years } ([0.0667]365 = 24.3 \text{ days})$$
Annual ordering cost = F(S/EOQ) = 400(1800/120) = 400(15) = $6000
Annual carrying cost = C(EOQ/2) = 100(120/2) = 100(60) = $6000
Using equation (17.3), OfficeMax's total annual cost is $12,000.

$$\text{Total cost} = 400\frac{1800}{120} + 100\frac{120}{2} = 6000 + 6000 = \$12,000$$

Note that the carrying cost and ordering cost are equal (6000); this always holds for EOQ. ■

FIGURE 17.2
Annual costs for the EOQ model.

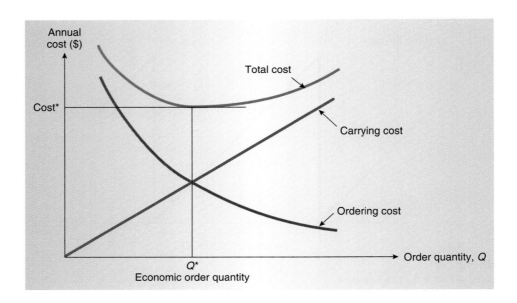

---

[2]The form of the EOQ model is identical to the one for C^*, the optimal deposit size in the Baumol cash management model. So we'll make your day and skip the mathematical derivation.

Quantity Discounts

Many suppliers offer a quantity discount to encourage larger orders. For example, a supplier might offer a price discount for ordering 10,000 or more units. If your EOQ is currently more than the discount quantity, you get the discount without doing anything.

If your EOQ is less than the discount quantity, you have to increase your order size to get the discount. The trade-off is between higher inventory costs and a lower price for purchases. If the discounts exceed the cost of the extra inventory, then you should increase the order size to get the discounts. To analyze this decision, we can adjust the total cost function by adding in the price discounts:

$$\text{Total cost} = \text{Ordering cost} + \text{Carrying cost} - \text{Price discounts}$$

$$= F\frac{S}{Q} + C\frac{Q}{2} - dS \tag{17.5}$$

where d is the price discount per unit.

The best order size is the one that provides the lowest total cost: either the result of using equation (17.4) to find the EOQ without price discounts or the result of using equation (17.5), which reveals the cost outcome of ordering the larger quantity and getting the price discounts.

The EOQ and Quantity Discounts at OfficeMax

EXAMPLE

Continuing our OfficeMax example, where the EOQ was 120, let's say the dealer offered a quantity discount of $3 per unit for orders of 200 or more. Should OfficeMax order 200 each time to get the discount?

OfficeMax must compare the total cost of ordering the larger quantity to get the discount with the total cost of ordering the EOQ. We calculated the total cost using the EOQ to be $12,000. Using equation (17.5), the total cost of ordering 200 units each time is $8200.

$$\text{Total cost} = 400\frac{1800}{200} + 100\frac{200}{2} - 3.00(1800) = 3600 + 10,000 - 5400 = \$8200$$

The order size of 200 increases the inventory costs from $12,000 per year (with the EOQ) to $13,600 (= 3600 + 10,000). The company receives discounts of $3.00 per unit on *the entire year's purchases* (1800 units). The total discounts received (5400) are more than the $1600 increase in ordering and carrying costs. The total costs decline by $3800 when the quantity discount is taken. Thus raising the order size to 200 is worth it. ■

Inventory Management with Uncertainty

The EOQ model makes simplifying assumptions: Future demand is known with certainty, inventory is used at a constant rate, and delivery is instantaneous (or equivalently, the lead time is known with certainty). Each factor, of course, actually has some uncertainty. A company can protect itself from this uncertainty by maintaining **safety stocks**—that is, a buffer inventory.

Figure 17.3 on page 634 shows the company's inventory level over time, with a safety stock and other more realistic assumptions. In the figure, the company uses inventory down to the reorder point. At the reorder point, the company orders its EOQ, but there is a lead time until the order arrives. During this lead time, the company might have a *stockout* if demand is large. A stockout occurs when the company cannot immediately make a sale because of a lack of inventory. Stockouts can create customer bad will and/or cause lost sales. To guard against a stockout, the reorder point includes the expected lead-time demand plus a safety stock.

SAFETY STOCKS Inventory buffer stocks that a company holds to hedge uncertainties in delivery times, usage, or sales.

$$\text{Reorder point} = \text{Expected lead-time demand} + \text{Safety stock} \tag{17.6}$$

With uncertainties, annual inventory cost has three components:

$$\text{Annual cost} = \text{Ordering cost} + \text{Carrying cost} + \text{Stockout costs} \tag{17.7}$$

FIGURE 17.3

Inventory levels with uncertain demand and a safety stock.

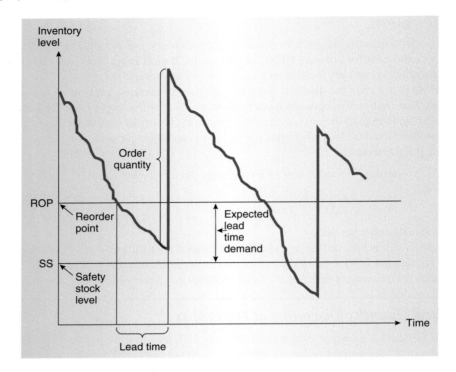

The expected stockout cost is the probability of a stockout times the cost of a stockout. A larger safety stock reduces the expected stockout cost but raises the reorder point. Thus a larger safety stock increases the inventory carrying cost, because the average inventory level is equal to EOQ/2 *plus* the safety stock. Again, there is a trade-off between costs. But again, the optimal inventory policy provides the lowest total cost.

E X A M P L E

Order Quantity and Reorder Point at Oxford Arms

Oxford Arms sells bullet-proof vests through mail orders. Oxford sells 5000 vests per year, with a fixed cost of $60 per order and a carrying cost of $15 per unit average inventory. Oxford's EOQ is therefore 200 vests.

$$EOQ = \sqrt{\frac{2FS}{C}} = \sqrt{\frac{2(60)(5000)}{15}} = \sqrt{40,000} = 200 \text{ vests}$$

This order quantity implies 25 orders per year (= 5000/200) and an ordering cost of $1500 per year (= [25]60). What are Oxford's optimal safety stock and reorder point?

The average lead-time demand is 20 vests, so the reorder point will be the safety stock plus 20. The average inventory will be the safety stock plus EOQ/2 = 100. Oxford is considering several safety stock levels ranging from none to 30. Estimates of the expected stockout cost for various sizes of safety stock are given in table 17.4.

Note in table 17.4 that the expected stockout cost starts high and declines at a rapid but diminishing rate. Adding the first 5 units to the safety stock reduces the expected stockout cost by $500, from $1200 to $700. The annual carrying cost of the 5 units of safety stock is only $75 (= [5]15), so the total cost declines by $425 (= 500 − 75). As long as the expected stockout cost declines faster than the carrying cost increases, increasing the safety stock is beneficial. A safety stock of 20 and a reorder point of 40 provide the lowest total cost. This is the optimal safety stock and reorder point, because it balances the component costs off against each other. ∎

TABLE 17.4

Finding the Reorder Point and Safety Stock

REORDER POINT[a]	SAFETY STOCK	AVERAGE INVENTORY[b]	STOCKOUT COST[c]	CARRYING COST[d]	ORDERING COST[e]	TOTAL COST[f]
20	0	100	$1200	$1500	$1500	$4200
25	5	105	700	1575	1500	3775
30	10	110	450	1650	1500	3600
35	15	115	250	1725	1500	3475
40[g]	20[g]	120	150	1800	1500	3450[g]
45	25	125	90	1875	1500	3465
50	30	130	50	1950	1500	3500
55	35	135	30	2025	1500	3555
60	40	140	25	2100	1500	3625

[a]Reorder point = Lead time demand + Safety stock = 20 + Safety stock.
[b]Average inventory = $Q/2$ + Safety stock = 100 + Safety stock.
[c]Stockout costs are management's estimates for each safety stock level.
[d]Carrying cost = Average inventory times $15.
[e]Ordering cost = $F(S/Q)$ = $60(25) = $1500.
[f]Total cost = Stockout cost + Carrying cost + Ordering cost.
[g]Indicates the cost-minimizing reorder point and safety stock.

ABC System of Inventory Control

The **ABC system of inventory control** categorizes inventory into one of three groups—A, B, or C—on the basis of critical need. The most important items are A items, and the least important are C items. For example, suppose 10% of inventory items make up 80% of the total inventory value. These might be the A items. The B items might compose 30% of the total *number* of items but only 15% of the total inventory value. The C items would be 60% of the number of items but would make up only 5% of total inventory value. Figure 17.4 shows the

ABC SYSTEM OF INVENTORY CONTROL A system of inventory control that categorizes inventory items as very important (A items), which are managed very carefully, fairly unimportant (C items), which are managed very casually, and items that fall between these two extremes (B items).

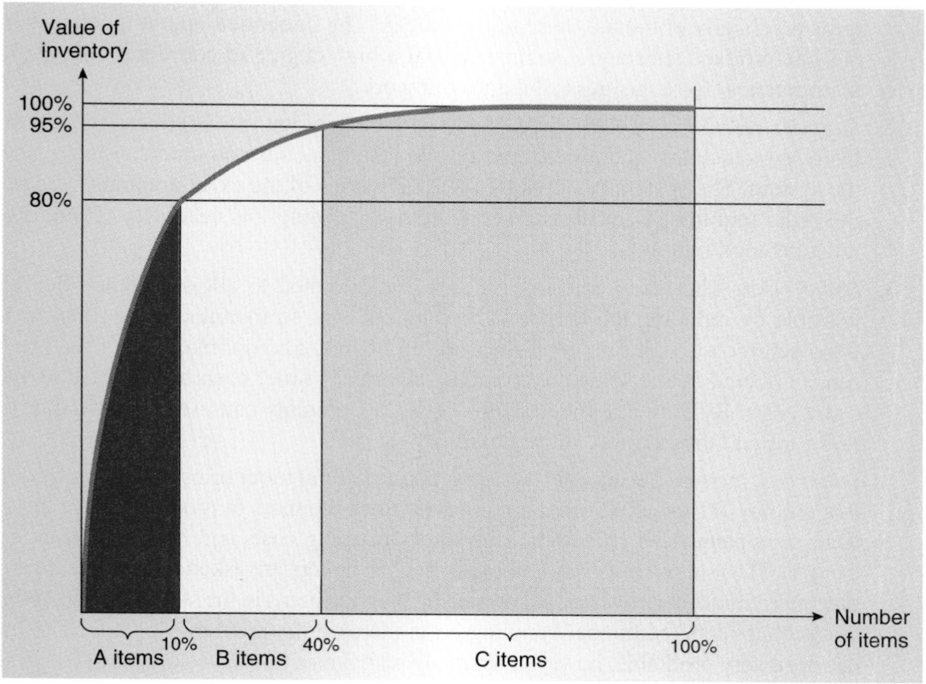

FIGURE 17.4
The ABC system of inventory control.

relationship between the number of items and their cumulative investment for the ABC inventory system.

Because they are the most critical, the A items are managed very carefully. The B items are managed with less care, and the C items are managed the least carefully. For example, for a car company, engines, transmissions, and in fact all of the components of the cars under production are A items and are managed very carefully. On the other hand, office supplies such as paper clips, pencils, and paper are ordered when needed without much supervision.

Materials Requirement Planning (MRP) Systems

MATERIALS REQUIRE-MENT PLANNING (MRP) SYSTEMS Computer-based systems that plan backward from the production schedule to make purchases and manage inventory levels.

Companies often produce or supply more than one product, and each product may have a large number of components. Typically, this means the company has multiple suppliers. Coordinating and scheduling can become complex, so companies rely on **materials requirement planning (MRP) systems.** MRP systems are computer-based systems that plan backward from the production schedule to make purchases and manage inventory. These large software systems combine information about the production process and the supply process to determine when the company should place purchase orders. Done properly, MRP assures that production proceeds smoothly without interruptions due to inventory stockouts.

Just-in-Time (JIT) Inventory Systems

JUST-IN-TIME (JIT) INVENTORY SYSTEMS Systems that schedule materials to arrive exactly as they are needed in the production process.

Just-in-time (JIT) inventory systems greatly reduce inventories. The philosophy of a JIT system is that materials should arrive exactly as they are needed in the production process. The system requires careful planning and scheduling, and extensive cooperation between suppliers and manufacturers is needed throughout the production process. All of this is facilitated by electronic data interchange (EDI), which we discussed in chapter 16. A JIT system can reduce raw materials inventories, work-in-process inventories, and finished product inventories.

The success of a JIT system depends on several factors.

1. *Planning requirements.* JIT requires a coordinated, integrated plan for the entire company. Recall that one of the basic functions of inventories is to serve as a buffer stock at various stages of the production process. By careful planning and scheduling, JIT systems practically eliminate these buffer stocks. The integrated operating environment of JIT can produce substantial savings. But if a high degree of coordination and planning is impractical for a business, JIT does not work.

2. *Supplier relations.* The company must work closely with its suppliers for JIT to work. Delivery schedules, quantities, quality, and instantaneous communication are all part of the system. The system requires frequent deliveries of the exact amounts needed and in the order required. Careful marking—often bar coding—is necessary. Therefore, there must be good relations.

3. *Setup costs.* The manufacturing process is redesigned to allow as much flexibility as possible by reducing the length of production runs. In manufacturing, there is often a fixed setup cost each time a production run begins. The optimal size of the production run is affected by the setup cost (much as inventory order costs are affected by the fixed order cost). By reducing these setup costs, the company can use much smaller production runs and thus achieve more flexibility.

4. *Other cost factors.* Because JIT systems require careful monitoring and control, companies that employ JIT usually limit the number of their suppliers in order to reduce these costs. Many companies can reduce their inventory carrying costs and inventory setup costs by using a JIT system. However, nothing is free. Suppliers are asked to improve quality, provide more frequent deliveries, sequence and barcode items in the shipments, and other such things. Suppliers' additional handling costs increase the price they charge. The trade-off has been very profitable, however, for many companies that have adopted JIT.

5. *Impact on credit terms.* JIT systems would be impossible without electronic data interchange (EDI). Because many aspects of the purchasing-production-marketing process are now handled electronically, trade credit is also becoming automated. When electronic credit terms are used, payment is not made, say, 30 days after an invoice date. Rather, payment can be made shortly—such as only a day—after delivery and use of materials. This essentially eliminates accounts payable for a company, which was a major source of short-term financing. On the other hand, collecting electronically eliminates the supplier's accounts receivable. EDI also eliminates the costs and risks associated with paper-based payables and receivables systems.

Self-Check

1. What is the EOQ (economic order quantity)? What cost does it minimize?

2. Explain how the EOQ is related to the rate at which items are removed from inventory, the fixed reordering cost, and the carrying cost.

3. What is safety stock, and what is its purpose?

4. Explain how a just-in-time (JIT) inventory system works. What factors determine how well it works? What is the purpose of such a system?

SUMMARY

Accounts receivable and inventories are large investments in assets that support the company's process of buying materials, transforming them into final products, and selling them. These investments, like capital budgeting projects, are measured in terms of their NPV. As with capital budgeting, a company should avoid negative-NPV decisions and seek out positive NPVs.

- Trade credit is used as a device to reduce financial contracting costs created by market imperfections.
- The NPV of granting credit is the present value of all of the expected cash flows that occur if credit is extended.
- An indifference payment probability can be derived where customers with a payment probability above this critical value are designated profitable (positive-NPV) customers.
- Credit policy includes the choice of (1) credit terms, (2) evaluation methods, and (3) credit standards, as well as the process of monitoring the quality of outstanding receivables, pursuing delinquent customers, and administering the credit functions.
- A variety of credit terms have been designed to allow suppliers and customers to carry on mutually profitable associations. See the "Trade Credit Terms" box for several examples.
- The five Cs of credit are character, capacity, capital, collateral, and conditions. Subjective credit evaluation methods use the five Cs.
- Credit-scoring models create a single credit score for a customer. This score is supposed to be an objective measure of creditworthiness.
- Aging schedules, collection fractions, and receivables balance fractions are used to monitor the quality of outstanding accounts receivable.
- Pursuing delinquent credit customers is a balancing act between the cost of pursuit, the likelihood of maintaining a profitable relationship with a marginal customer, and the amount of cash that can be collected.
- Changing credit policies can be evaluated with the same NPV framework that is used for making basic credit-granting decisions. The optimal policy generates the largest NPV.
- The EOQ (economic order quantity) is the order size that minimizes the total inventory cost.

- When uncertainties in deliveries or demand exist, companies maintain safety stocks. The reorder point is the safety stock level plus the expected lead-time demand that provides the minimum total cost.

- The ABC system of inventory control categorizes inventory into three groups—A, B, and C—on the basis of critical need. The most important items (A items) are managed the most carefully. The relatively less important items (C items) are the least closely managed.

- Computer-based materials requirement planning (MRP) systems plan backward from production schedules to make purchases and plan inventories.

- Just-in-time (JIT) inventory systems schedule arrivals of materials exactly when they are needed. JIT systems can greatly reduce inventories. When electronic data interchange (EDI) is used with JIT, companies often reduce both their payables and receivables.

EQUATION SUMMARY

(17.1)
$$\text{NPV} = \frac{pR}{(1+k)^t} - C$$

(17.2)
$$p^* = \frac{C(1+k)^t}{R}$$

(17.3)
$$\text{Total cost} = \text{Ordering cost} + \text{Carrying cost} = F\frac{S}{Q} + C\frac{Q}{2}$$

(17.4)
$$\text{EOQ} = \sqrt{\frac{2FS}{C}}$$

$$\text{Total cost} = \text{Ordering cost} + \text{Carrying cost} - \text{Price discounts}$$

(17.5)
$$= F\frac{S}{Q} + C\frac{Q}{2} - dS$$

(17.6)   Reorder point = Expected lead-time demand + Safety stock

(17.7)   Annual cost = Ordering cost + Carrying cost + Stockout costs

CHAPTER REVIEW ACTIVITIES

SELF-TEST PROBLEMS

1. (Credit-granting decision) Murfreesboro Air Handling Systems wants to buy 10 compressors from you at a price of $800 each. Your cost of supplying each compressor is $650, and you estimate that Murfreesboro has a 95% probability of paying you in 2 months. There is also a 5% probability that they will pay you nothing. Your opportunity cost of funds is 1.2% per month. Find the following:

   a. the expected payment from Murfreesboro,   c. the net present value of extending credit.
   b. the present value of the expected payment, and

2. (Changing credit policies) Conn Music Company is considering a new credit policy that has much more lenient credit standards. Sharon Conn estimates that the new policy will affect the several key variables shown below. Assume that the cost of goods sold is a cash outlay at time 0, and that the expected sales (net of bad debt) are collected at the end of the collection period. Which policy is better?

	Current Policy	Proposed Policy
Annual sales	$4.8 million	$6.0 million
Cost of goods sold/Sales	60%	60%
Bad debt/Sales	1%	3%
Collection period	3 months (.25 years)	4 months (1/3 year)
Required return	10%	10%

3. (Economic order quantity) Lake Charles Office Supply sells 10,000 boxes of photocopy paper per year. The ordering cost is $24 per order and the carrying cost is $3 per unit average inventory per year. Demand for the boxes is uniform through time and replenishment of inventory is instantaneous.

a. What is the economic order quantity?

b. What is the average inventory, number of orders per year, and the time interval between orders?

c. What is the annual carrying cost, ordering cost, and total cost?

SOLUTIONS TO SELF-TEST PROBLEMS

1. a. The expected payment is $10(800)(0.95) = 8000(0.95) = \$7600$

b. The present value of $7600 received in 2 months discounted at 1.2% per month is

$$PV = 7600 / (1.012)^2 = \$7420.83$$

c. Your investment in the sale is $10(650) = \$6500$

$$NPV = \$7420.83 - \$6500 = \$920.83$$

The sale is profitable because it has a positive net present value.

2. The net present value of the current policy is

$$NPV \text{ (current policy)} = -0.6(4.8 \text{ million}) + \frac{0.99(4.8 \text{ million})}{(1 + 0.10)^{0.25}}$$

$$= -2.88 \text{ million} + 4.640 \text{ million} = \$1.760 \text{ million}$$

The net present value of the proposed policy is

$$NPV \text{ (proposed policy)} = -0.6(6.0 \text{ million}) + \frac{0.97(6.0 \text{ million})}{(1 + 0.10)^{0.3333}}$$

$$= -3.6 \text{ million} + 5.638 \text{ million} = \$2.038 \text{ million}$$

The proposed policy is better. It increases one year's NPV by $0.278 million (= 2.038 − 1.760).

3. a. The economic order quantity is

$$EOQ = \sqrt{\frac{2FS}{C}} = \sqrt{\frac{2(24)(10,000)}{3}} = \sqrt{160,000} = 400 \text{ boxes}$$

b. The average inventory is EOQ/2 = 400/2 = $200.

The number of orders per year is $S/EOQ = 10,000/400 = 25$ times per year.

The time interval between orders is $EOQ/S = 400/10,000 = 0.04$ years.

c. The annual ordering cost is $F(S/EOQ) = 24(10,000/400) = 24(25) = \$600$.

The annual carrying cost is $C(EOQ/2) = 3(400/2) = 3(200) = \$600$.

Using equation (17.3), the annual total cost is

$$\text{Total cost} = F\left(\frac{S}{Q}\right) + C\left(\frac{Q}{2}\right) = 24\frac{10,000}{400} + 3\frac{400}{2} = 600 + 600 = \$1200$$

QUESTIONS

1. What is meant by the phrase 1/10, net 40?

2. Trade credit presumably exists because it allows two trading partners to reduce the costs and risks of doing business. Explain how each of the following examples can make trade credit mutually beneficial for a supplier and customer.

a. Suppliers know how to handle collateral better than other lenders such as banks.

b. Suppliers already possess the information needed to evaluate creditworthiness.

c. The extension of credit is a positive signal about product quality.

d. Trade credit reduces employee opportunism.

3. Cite and discuss five reasons for the extensive use of trade credit.

4. Optical Supply Company offers credit terms of 2/10, net 60. If Optical Supply is considering a change in its credit terms to one of those indicated below, explain whether the change should increase or decrease sales.

a. 2/10, net 30   c. 3/15, net 60
b. net 60   d. 2/10, net 30, 30 extra

5. What are the five Cs of credit? Explain why each is relevant.
6. What is a credit-scoring model? What are possible advantages and disadvantages of using credit-scoring models?
7. Describe the steps involved in a typical collection process.
8. The basic economic order quantity (EOQ) model deals with which two of the following three costs? (1) Ordering costs, (2) Carrying costs, and (3) Stockout costs.
9. Explain the logic of an ABC system of inventory control.
10. What is meant by the term *safety stocks?* Why would a company normally find it beneficial to maintain safety stocks in its inventory?
11. What are the factors on which the success of a JIT system depends?

CHALLENGING QUESTIONS

12. Explain how financial contracting costs, created by market imperfections, can lead to the use of trade credit.
13. Why are credit-scoring models used more for consumer loans than for business loans?
14. Explain how a company's inventory and accounts receivable management problems are like a capital budgeting problem.

PROBLEM SET A

A1. (NPV of granting credit) A credit sale of $15,000 has a 95% probability of being repaid in two months and a 5% probability of a complete default. If the investment in the sale is $12,000 and the required return is 15% per year, what is the NPV of granting credit?

 A2. (NPV of granting credit) For each of the following items sold on credit, estimate the net present value of granting credit.

Item	Sale Price	Investment in Sale	Collection Period	Required Return	Probability of Payment
Refrigerator	$1200	$1000	3 months	12%	0.80
Jewelry	300	150	12 months	14%	0.95
Stereo	800	550	6 months	13%	0.90

A3. (Break-even payment probability) For each of the following items sold on credit, estimate the probability of payment that is required for the seller to break even (have a zero net present value from granting credit).

Item	Sale Price	Investment in Sale	Collection Period	Required Return
Refrigerator	$1200	$1000	3 months	12%
Jewelry	300	150	12 months	14%
Stereo	800	550	6 months	13%

 A4. (Economic order quantity model) Assume that annual usage is 12,000 units, that the fixed order cost is $60 per order, and that the carrying cost is $4 per unit average inventory. Find the average inventory, number of orders per year, carrying cost, ordering cost, and total cost for the order sizes indicated below.

Order size (units)	200	400	600	800	1000
Average inventory	___	___	___	___	___
Orders per year	___	___	___	___	___
Annual carrying cost	___	___	___	___	___
Annual ordering cost	___	___	___	___	___
Total annual cost	___	___	___	___	___

A5. (Economic order quantity) Knoxville Accountants LLP consumes 100,000 packets of plain copier paper annually. The usage is roughly constant throughout the year. The carrying cost of this inventory is $2.00 per unit average inventory per year. The ordering and delivery cost is a fixed $100 per order.

a. What is the economic order quantity?

b. How many orders will be placed per year using the EOQ?

c. What is the average inventory level?

d. What is the total annual inventory cost?

A6. (Value of JIT) Meridian Ceramics is studying the economics of converting its manufacturing over to a just-in-time system. There are several benefits and costs that must be weighed. Total inventories are expected to decline by $4 million, saving an estimated $600,000 per year. Labor savings in tracking inventories are expected to save another $100,000 per year. The additional demands placed on Meridian's suppliers are expected to increase the cost of purchases by about 2% of annual purchases, about $250,000 per year. Equipment needed to operate the JIT system should cost about $150,000 per year. The system will facilitate a savings of $20,000 per year in administering the company's billing and payables systems. Finally, the JIT system will allow Meridian to gain new customers that should add $300,000 annually to gross profits. If these estimates are correct, what would be the impact of a JIT system on Meridian's annual before-tax profits?

PROBLEM SET B

B1. (NPV of extending credit) The Salt Lake Ski Company wants to make a $200,000 credit purchase from your company. Your investment in the credit sale is 70% of the amount of the sale. You estimate that Salt Lake has a 95% probability of paying you on time, which is in 3 months, and a 5% probability of paying nothing. If the opportunity cost of funds is 18% per year, what is the net present value of granting credit?

B2. (NPV of extending credit) Squires Sports Equipment Company is selling $4000 of rubber mats to the Springfield Fitness Center. Squires will invest $3400 in the sale. Squires has credit terms of 2/10, net 30, and estimates that Springfield has a 50% probability of taking the discount and paying on day 10, a 40% probability of paying the net amount on day 30, and a 10% chance of defaulting. If Springfield Fitness defaults, Squires estimates that it will recover nothing. If the opportunity cost of funds is 12% compounded annually, what is the net present value of granting credit? Assume a 365-day year.

B3. (Changing credit policies) Vulcan Games is considering a new credit policy that has much more stringent credit standards. Vulcan's analysts estimate that the new policy will affect several key variables shown below. Assume that the cost of goods sold is a cash outlay at time zero, and that the expected sales (net of bad debt) are collected at the end of the collection period. Which policy is better?

	Current Policy	Proposed Policy
Annual sales	$15 million	$14 million
Cost of goods sold/Sales	72%	72%
Bad debt/Sales	4%	2%
Collection period	2 months (0.1667 years)	1 month (0.08333 years)
Required return	15%	15%

B4. (Aging schedule) The accounts receivable for the Boulder Skimobile Company include the following 12 invoices:

Invoice	Invoice date	Amount
522	March 3	$1200
530	March 12	1800
533	April 2	600
540	April 4	2400
544	April 12	1800
548	April 25	1200
550	May 5	1200
551	May 8	2400
552	May 12	1200
553	May 15	1800
554	May 16	2400
555	May 27	1200

Prepare an aging schedule as of May 31 for Boulder Skimobile in the following format:

Age	Accounts Receivable	Percent
0–30 days	$xx,xxx	xx.x%
30–60 days	xx,xxx	xx.x
60–90 days	xx,xxx	xx.x
Total	$xx,xxx	100.0%

B5. (Average age of accounts receivable) Wilson Licensing has the aging schedule shown below. Assume that the receivables in each age category have an age equivalent to the midpoint of the range. Calculate an average age of accounts receivable for Wilson Licensing.

Age	Accounts Receivable	Percent
0–30 days	$400,000	53.33%
30–60 days	250,000	33.33
60–90 days	100,000	13.33
Total	$750,000	100.0%

B6. (Changing credit policies) The Deep River Company is considering the liberalization of its credit terms and credit standards in order to increase sales and, hopefully, profits. The ad hoc management team charged with evaluating this credit liberalization has gathered the information shown below. Assume that the cost of goods sold is equivalent to an investment at time zero and that the expected sales (net of bad debt) are received at the end of the predicted collection period. Which policy is more profitable for the Deep River Company?

	Current policy	Proposed policy
Annual sales	$10 million	$11 million
Collection period	0.10 years	0.20 years
Bad debt/Sales	1%	2%
Cost of goods sold/Sales	85%	85%
Annual required return	15%	15%

B7. (Economic order quantity) Sartoris Steel Products uses 200,000 tons of coal per year. The carrying cost per unit average inventory is $10, and the fixed cost per order is $1000.

a. What is the economic order quantity? What is the annual cost of using the EOQ?

b. The coal supplier will not ship partial carloads of coal, so Sartoris can order coal only in multiples of 1000 tons. What should Sartoris use as the order quantity? What is the annual cost?

B8. (Economic order quantity) Waters Printing Company orders 6 rolls of paper every week. The ordering and setup cost is $500 and the annual carrying cost is $1000 per unit average inventory. Assume a 52-week year.

a. What is the annual cost of ordering 6 rolls at a time?

b. What is the economic order quantity and the annual cost of using the EOQ?

c. Assume that Waters cannot order fractional rolls. If your EOQ in part **b** above was not an integer value, what is the annual cost of using the next integer-valued order size above the EOQ? What is the annual cost of using the closest integer-valued order size below the EOQ? What order size do you recommend?

B9. (Economic order quantity) Your annual usage is 50,000 units, the carrying cost per unit is $1, and the ordering cost is $250 per order.

a. What is the EOQ and the total annual cost?

b. Your warehouse will allow a maximum inventory level of 3000 units. If the order size is constrained by this, what is the total annual cost?

c. What is the maximum annual rent you would pay for additional warehouse space that would relieve your warehouse space constraint?

B10. (Economic order quantity with quantity discounts) The annual usage of toggle switches is 10,000 units per year, at a uniform rate through the year. The ordering cost is $50 per order, and carrying costs are $4.00 per unit average inventory per year.
a. What is the economic order quantity? What is the annual cost using the EOQ?
b. If the supplier offers a quantity discount of $0.10 per unit if you order in quantities of 250 or more, what should you do? What is the annual cost of following your recommendation?
c. If the supplier offers a quantity discount of $.10 per unit if you order in quantities of 1000 or more, what should you do? What is the annual cost of following your recommendation?

B11. (Reorder point) Alabama Central Hospital has established an economic order quantity for its obstetrics kits of 60 units. The lead time before orders arrive and are ready for use is 4 days. The average usage is 4 kits per day, and Alabama Central has determined that it would like to have a safety stock of 10 kits.
a. What is the expected lead-time demand?
b. What should Alabama Central use as its reorder point?

B12. (Safety stock) General Enzyme Company uses an average of 5 tons of beta medium per day. Because the lead time between a reorder and delivery is 4 days, expected lead-time demand is 20 tons. The economic order quantity is 80 tons. Because their usage is somewhat random, GE carries a safety stock to reduce the probability of a stockout. Based on the annual costs estimated below, which reorder point and safety stock would minimize total annual costs?

Safety Stock	Reorder Point	Ordering Cost	Carrying Cost	Stockout Cost
0	20	$10,000	$10,000	$12,000
5	25	10,000	12,500	7,000
10	30	10,000	15,000	4,000
15	35	10,000	17,500	2,000
20	40	10,000	20,000	1,000

PROBLEM SET C

C1. (Collection fractions and receivables balance fractions) Texas Chili Products collects 20% of its sales in the month of the sale, 50% in the month following the sale, 25% in the second month following sale, and 5% in the third month following sale.

Month	October	November	December	January	February	March
Sales	$500	$500	$500	$500	$700	$900

a. For a given month's sales, what percentage of that month's sales should be outstanding at the end of the sale month, in the first month after the sale, the second month after sale, and the third month after sale?
b. Assume that collections proceed as predicted. Calculate the level of accounts receivable for January, February, and March from the sales information above.
c. Provide an aging schedule for accounts receivable outstanding at the end of March.

C2. (Credit scoring) The Flint Area Credit Union (FACU) uses a credit-scoring system to screen its car loan applications. It uses the following scoring system:

Telephone:	Yes +5	No 0		
Home:	Own (no mortgage) +6	Own (mortgage) +3	Rent +2	
Years at present address:	<6 months 0	6 months– 2 years +1	>2 years +2	
Monthly income:	<1000 +1	1000–2000 +2	2000–3500 +3	>3500 +4
Years at present job:	<6 months 0	6 months– 2 years +1	>2 years +2	

Family size (including applicant): 1 +2	2 +5	3–5 +3	>5 +1
Previous loan experience:	none 0	loan pmts on time +5	loan pmts late −5	

Account with FACU:	yes +2	no 0		
Number of bank accounts:	0 0	1 +2	2 +3	>2 +4
Loan/Value ratio:	<50% +4	50–75% +2	75–90% +1	>90% −3
Credit report:	good +5	limited +2	poor −5	

FACU's disposition of a credit application is as follows:

0–20 points	deny credit
21–24 points	investigate further and base decision on further analysis
25 or more points	grant credit

Apply the credit scoring system to the following two loan applicants and decide the disposition of each loan request.

a. Jorge is buying a $20,000 car, putting $6000 down and borrowing the remaining $14,000. Jorge has a telephone, is renting an apartment (where he has lived for 3 months), and is making $3000 per month. He has been with his present employer for 3 years. He is single. He has a savings account with FACU and has two additional bank accounts. He has not previously borrowed from FACU. His credit report is good.

b. Flavia is buying a $24,000 car and is asking for a $23,000 loan to help her make the purchase. Flavia has a telephone, is renting an apartment (where she has lived for 3 years), and is making $2400 per month. She has been with her present employer for 10 months. She is single. She has no accounts with FACU and has two bank accounts. Flavia has not previously borrowed from FACU. Her credit report is bad.

C3. (EOQ and safety stocks) Brown Pontiac maintains an inventory of tires. The dealer uses tires at a constant rate of 1000 per month. The dealer's cost of placing a new order is $500 per order. The cost of carrying a tire in inventory for a year is $12.

Safety stock	100	125	150	175	200
Stockouts per year	75	50	35	30	30

a. Calculate the economic order quantity.

b. Brown Pontiac has found that if it is out of stock when a customer arrives, it will make the eventual sale only 20% of the time. For each lost sale, Brown Pontiac loses the net margin of $30 per tire. Lost sales as well as back orders involve record-keeping costs of $10 per stockout. Brown Pontiac has estimated the benefit of maintaining safety stocks given above. What level of safety stock should Brown Pontiac maintain?

BIBLIOGRAPHY

Adams, Paul D., Steve B. Wyatt, and Yong H. Kim. "A Contingent Claims Analysis of Trade Credit," *Financial Management,* 1992, 21(3):95–103.

Ben-Horim, Moshe, and Haim Levy. "Management of Accounts Receivable Under Inflation," *Financial Management,* 1983, 12(1):42–48.

Brick, Ivan E., and William K. H. Fung. "The Effect of Taxes on the Trade Credit Decision," *Financial Management,* 1984, 13(2):24–30.

Brick, Ivan E., and William K. H. Fung. "Taxes and the Theory of Trade Debt," *Journal of Finance,* 1984, 39(4):1169–1176.

Carpenter, Michael D., and Jack E. Miller. "A Reliable Framework for Monitoring Accounts Receivable," *Financial Management,* 1979, 8(4):37–40.

Emery, Gary W. "A Pure Financial Explanation for Trade Credit," *Journal of Financial and Quantitative Analysis,* 1984, 19(4): 271–285.

Gallinger, George W., and A. James Ifflander. "Monitoring Accounts Receivable Using Variance Analysis," *Financial Management,* 1986, 15(4):69–76.

Gentry, James A., and Jesus M. De La Garza. "A Generalized Model for Monitoring Accounts Receivable," *Financial Management,* 1985, 14(4):28–38.

Kim, Yong H., and Joseph C. Atkins. "Evaluating Investments in Accounts Receivable: A Wealth Maximizing Framework," *Journal of Finance,* 1978, 33(2):403–412.

Lee, Yul W., and John D. Stowe. "Product Risk, Asymmetric Information, and Trade Credit," *Journal of Financial and Quantitative Analysis,* 1993, 28(2):285–300.

Lewellen, Wilber G., and Robert O. Edmister. "A General Model for Accounts-Receivable Analysis and Control," *Journal of Financial and Quantitative Analysis,* 1973, 8(2):195–206.

Long, Michael S., Ileen B. Malitz, and S. Abraham Ravid. "Trade Credit, Quality Guarantees, and Product Marketability," *Financial Management,* 1993, 22(4):117–127.

Mian, Shehzad L., and Clifford W. Smith, Jr. "Accounts-Receivable Management Policy: Theory and Evidence," *Journal of Finance,* 1992, 47(1):169–200.

Scherr, Frederick C. "Optimal Trade Credit Limits," *Financial Management,* 1996, 25(1):71–85.

Smith, Janet Kilholm. "Trade Credit and Informational Asymmetry," *Journal of Finance,* 1987, 42(4):863–872.

Stone, Bernell K. "The Payments-Pattern Approach to the Forecasting and Control of Accounts Receivable," *Financial Management,* 1976, 5(3):65–82.

Stowe, John D. "An Integer Programming Solution for the Optimal Credit Investigation/Credit Granting Sequence," *Financial Management,* 1985, 14(2):66–76.

FINANCIAL PLANNING

Financial planning creates a "blueprint" for the company's future. Planning is necessary to (1) establish the company's goals, (2) choose operating and financial strategies, (3) forecast operating results against which to monitor and evaluate performance, and (4) create contingent plans for dealing with unforeseen circumstances. Good financial planning involves all parts of the company and its policies and decisions about such things as liquidity, working capital, inventories, capital budgeting, capital structure, and dividends. Therefore, financial planning is a critical part of financial management.

In practice, companies make, and periodically update, financial plans. Major corporations, such as Toys R Us, Wal-Mart, Citicorp, and McDonald's, are almost constantly reassessing their environment and measuring the condition and future viability of their financial plan against that environment.

Successful companies don't simply react to events as they unfold. They are prepared to deal swiftly and effectively with both favorable and unfavorable developments. Competitive forces in the capital markets—and in other markets—make it difficult to find positive-NPV decisions. However, mistakes and poor planning make negative-NPV outcomes an ever-present possibility!

In this chapter, we develop a framework for financial planning. We'll look at both short- and long-term planning models, because the typical short-term plan is simply a more detailed part of a company's long-term plan.

FINANCIAL PLANNING AND THE PRINCIPLES OF FINANCE

◆ *Valuable Ideas:* Use both bottom-up and top-down processes to increase the chance of uncovering valuable ideas.

◆ *Behavioral:* Use common industry practices as a good starting place for the planning process.

◆ *Self-Interested Behavior:* Carefully evaluate and monitor the financial plan's impact on the company and its stakeholders.

◆ *Incremental Benefits:* Forecast the company's cash flows and analyze the incremental cash flows of alternative decisions.

◆ *Time Value of Money:* Compare the NPVs of alternative financial plans.

◆ *Two-sided Transactions:* Look for situations that are not zero-sum games and thus may be profitable to you *and* your supplier or customer, perhaps by reducing financial contracting costs and routine transaction costs.

◆ *Comparative Advantage:* Consider subcontracting business activities to outside vendors if they can provide the services more cheaply and competently.

THE FINANCIAL PLANNING PROCESS

A company is a dynamic system. Decisions and policies about liquidity, working capital, inventories, capital budgeting, capital structure, and dividends (among other things) interact continually. Figure 18.1 illustrates this interaction in a flow-of-funds framework.

The main net source of funds is the company's operations. The company uses its fixed assets, together with labor, raw materials, and other inputs, to produce products and services to sell. Sales revenue minus cost of goods sold and operating expenses (such as selling, general, and administrative expenses) equals the company's operating income. An important question in connection with financial planning is how operating income responds to increases in output. The answer depends on the company's operating leverage. Recall from chapter 11 that the higher the fixed-cost component of total costs, the greater is operating leverage.

Net income is left after interest expense and taxes are paid. Net income can be paid out as dividends, or it can be retained and reinvested. The company's dividend policy determines the split between dividends and retained earnings. Dividend policy interacts with the company's capital budget. A higher payout ratio increases the amount of external financing needed to meet the capital budget. Both of these policies in turn interact with the company's capital structure policy. The combination of the company's financing needs, its dividend policy, and its capital structure policy determines the mix of debt and equity in any required new external financing.

The company's financing needs are determined mainly by its capital budget and internal cash generation. The capital budget is in turn affected by projected sales. Increased sales will eventually require expenditures for planned expansions and new equipment. In addition, higher production rates cause machines to wear out faster, so the need for replacement investment also increases. Higher sales levels will also require additional investment in working capital.

The company's planned investment in current assets (net of increases in payables), along with its liquidity policy, determines the net increase or decrease in short-term borrowing. The rest of the company's borrowing needs, the residual, should be on a long-term basis. The company might issue some preferred stock in addition to (or in place of) long-term debt, depending on its tax position and capital structure objectives. The company's tax position is essentially the amount of tax deductions and credits from depreciation, depletion allowance, and interest expense.

The total long-term borrowing requirement includes the residual just noted plus any required debt repayments and planned early refunding. Finally, the terms of the debt (and/or preferred stock) issues must be determined in light of the company's financing policy. Any resulting debt issuance changes the company's interest expense. This will affect net income—and the planning "circle" is complete.

The process illustrated in figure 18.1 is a continuing one. Remember, the company's total sources of funds must equal its total uses of funds in any finite planning period. For relatively short periods of time, this equality might require either unintended changes in cash balances or unplanned short-term borrowing. But the company should strive to avoid these inefficiencies through good financial planning. All six of the basic financial policies must be determined simultaneously. This requires certain trade-offs. These trade-offs can be analyzed within a financial planning model.

FINANCIAL PLANNING
The process of evaluating the investing and financing alternatives available to the company. It includes attempting to make optimal decisions, projecting the consequences of these decisions for the company in the form of a financial plan, and then comparing future performance against that plan.

The Financial Plan

Figure 18.1 provides a starting point for financial planning. **Financial planning** is a process of evaluating the impact of alternative investing and financing decisions. Decisions, such as the company's capital budget or a debt restructuring, are then projected as part of a financial plan. Subsequently, outcomes are measured against the plan.

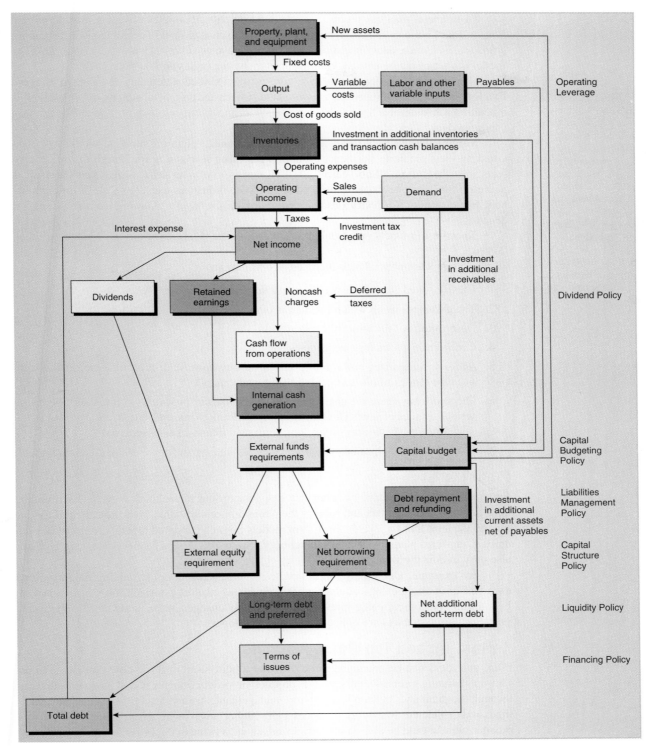

FIGURE 18.1
Interaction of financial decisions in a flow-of-funds framework.

A financial plan has inputs, a model, and outputs. Examples of inputs include projections of sales, collections, costs, interest rates, and exchange rates. The company's current position (cash balance, debt obligations, and so on) and alternative decisions are also inputs. The model is a set of mathematical relationships among the inputs and outputs.

The outputs of a financial plan are pro forma financial statements and a set of budgets. **Pro forma financial statements** are projected (forecasted) financial statements. A **budget** is a detailed schedule of a financial activity, such as an advertising budget, a sales budget, or a capital budget.

Companies use both short- and long-term financial planning models. Models are classified by their planning horizon. A model's **planning horizon** is the length of time it projects into the future. "Short-term" usually means a year or less. A five-year horizon is common for a long-term planning model, but some industries use a ten-year or longer horizon. For example, a forestry products company might have a planning horizon of several decades.

Short-term models are detailed and very specific. Long-term models tend to be much less so.

A complete financial plan includes, at a minimum,

1. Clearly stated strategic, operating, and financial *objectives*
2. The *assumptions* on which the plan is based
3. Descriptions of the underlying *strategies*
4. *Contingency plans* for emergencies
5. *Budgets,* categorized and summarized in various ways, such as by time period, division, and type (for example, cash, advertising, and capital)
6. The *financing program,* categorized and summarized in various ways, such as by time period, sources of funds (for example, bonds, bank loans, and stock), and types of funds (for example, short-term versus long-term, and internal versus external)
7. A set of period-by-period *pro forma financial statements* for the entire planning horizon

Planning Cycles

Financial plans are updated on a regular basis, according to a planning cycle. Each update adds the latest information and renews the planning horizon—that is, it projects into the future by the length of the cycle. Short-term models might be updated monthly, weekly, or even daily. Long-term plans might be updated once, twice, or perhaps four times a year. Updates also vary in how thorough they are.

For example, a company might update its short-term model by adding the latest data each week but might extend another month (renew the planning horizon) only once a month. In addition, the company might review and make any changes in the model itself only once a year. Similar procedures are typical for long-term models.

Bottom-Up and Top-Down Planning

Plans and ideas can be generated through either a bottom-up or a top-down process. A bottom-up planning process starts at the product or production level and proceeds upward through the plant and division levels to top management. At each level, ideas are added, modified, and/or deleted. Managers at successively higher levels, who are in a position to take a broader view, should be able to see things that are not visible to the lower levels. Higher management levels can also propose efficient combinations or eliminations that are unlikely to be suggested by the affected employees.

The top-down planning process starts with the company's top management and its strategic plans and goals and proceeds downward through the organization's levels. Top management makes strategic decisions. These decisions often create, increase, shrink, or eliminate such things as the company's products, divisions, and international marketing efforts. Managers describe how strategic decisions will be implemented. At each successively lower managerial level, the required actions become more specific.

Critics of the bottom-up process say it often fails to produce a coherent strategy for the company as a whole and can cause the company to appear chaotic and poorly managed. Critics of the top-down process say it tends to exaggerate the role of top managers and often results in bad investments and missed opportunities because top management may not be in touch with what is going on "in the field." But the bottom-up and top-down processes actually complement one another. Good planning requires both. Ideally, valuable new ideas are supported no matter where or how they originate.

Phases of the Financial Planning Process

Financial planning has three phases: *formulating* the plan, *implementing* the plan, and *evaluating* performance. Involvement in the three phases depends on the manager's specific role. For example, salespersons may have special insights into marketing forecasts, and engineers may have special expertise in developing cost estimates. A financial plan should be formulated by using the kinds of bottom-up and top-down processes we just described.

In the implementation phase, budgets with specific objectives, resource allocations, and operating policies are used to clarify each manager's responsibilities for contributing to the company's goals. During implementation, circumstances change and opportunities evolve. A company should alter its plans to adapt to, and take advantage of, changing circumstances. Consequently, a good budgeting system should be *flexible*. A budget is simply part of a financial plan, and plans need to be adapted to new opportunities and circumstances.

In the evaluation phase, the company compares its overall performance to the financial plan. Managers and their units are evaluated in terms of how well their performance compares to the objectives. In this process the conditions that actually prevailed, which can be very different from those expected and forecasted, are taken into account.

Benefits of Financial Planning

The goal of the planning process is to help maximize the value of the company. Toward this end, there are several benefits a company hopes to realize from the planning process:

1. *Standardized assumptions.* The planning process can expose inconsistencies in decision-making methods. For example, when managers differ in their forecasts of future conditions, the more optimistic manager's plan will look better—even if there is no other difference between the plans. A similar problem occurs when managers use different required returns to evaluate the same project. Such differences bias the planning process in favor of one manager's proposals. Planning requires explicit assumptions that can themselves be evaluated and then must be agreed upon. Standardized assumptions make it possible to compare the alternatives.

2. *Future orientation.* The planning process forces you to think about the future. Doing so generates new ideas and can eliminate bad ideas.

3. *Objectivity.* Because assumptions and models are made explicit, planning can expose decisions that are based on politics or emotions. Planning therefore increases the objective pursuit of organizational goals.

4. *Employee development.* The planning process includes input from many people. The ability to provide such input increases an employee's perceived stake in the company. People who are empowered through the budgeting process may be better motivated to carry out the company's plans. The planning process also educates participants about the company. This fosters coordination and cooperation. It also helps prepare an employee for career advancement in the company.

5. *Lender requirements.* Financial plans, sometimes very detailed, are necessary for borrowing—especially for the first time. Such plans indicate the use of the borrowed money and show the company's expected future inflows and outflows, including the loan's interest and principal repayments.

6. *Better performance evaluation.* It's possible for a manager to make good decisions but to have bad performance because of an unexpected downturn in the economy. Similarly, bad decisions can have favorable outcomes as a result of just plain good luck. For example, when net income is higher than expected because interest rates and borrowing costs were lower than expected, the high performance is not due to superior managerial decision making. A financial plan provides a benchmark against which to identify reasons for the differences between outcomes and forecasts. Then the company can avoid punishing good decisions because of bad outcomes or rewarding bad decisions because of good outcomes.

7. *Preparing for contingencies.* A good financial plan includes contingency plans for unlikely outcomes. The planning process can identify potential, if unlikely, conditions that would cause significant problems. This enables the company to plan appropriate reactions should such an unlikely contingency occur. For example, the planning process might reveal a possible shortage of funds. The company that has prearranged contingency financing will be able to continue to operate efficiently—regardless of its cash flow.

In the next section, we will discuss cash budgeting, which usually has a short-term planning horizon and focuses on the cash flows of the company.

Self-Check

1. What is financial planning? What benefits can a company derive from it? Why is sound financial planning critical to a company's success?

2. What are pro forma financial statements? How are they created?

3. What is a budget? How is it related to the company's financial plan? What does each include?

4. Contrast top-down and bottom-up planning.

5. What are the major benefits from the financial planning process?

CASH BUDGETING

CASH BUDGETING The process of summarizing a company's expected cash inflows and cash outflows as well as the expected cash and loan balances.

Cash budgeting is the process of projecting (forecasting) and summarizing a company's cash inflows and outflows expected during the planning horizon. The cash budget also shows the monthly cash balances and any short-term borrowing used to cover cash shortfalls. Monthly cash budgets typically have a 6- to 12-month planning horizon. A positive net cash flow for a month can increase cash, reduce outstanding loans, or be used elsewhere in the business. Similarly, negative net cash flows can reduce cash or be offset with additional borrowing.

For the most part, cash budgets are used in short-term plans, so they include substantial detail. However, the amount of detail also depends on the size of the company and on the present stage of projects in the planning horizon. Projections farther out in the planning horizon are less detailed. Small companies are less complex, and their cash budgets are less detailed. Because of the complexity of larger companies, more detail is required to take into account all of the factors that affect their cash flows.

Most cash budgets are based on sales forecasts, because so many cash flows are tied to sales. Inflows from sales depend on the amount of sales and also on the proportion that are cash versus credit sales. The time delays involved in collecting on credit sales depend on credit terms and payment patterns.

Several cash outflows also depend on sales. The cost of goods sold reflects raw materials purchases, wages, and production costs for inventories based on anticipated sales. Selling costs, including commissions, are often directly linked to sales.

Other cash expenditures do not fluctuate with current sales. These include capital expenditures; rent, lease, and debt payments; and some types of salaries and tax payments. Such fixed cash outflows are also included in the cash budget. Our next example shows how to create a cash budget.

Cash Budgeting at the Monet Paint Company

EXAMPLE

The cash managers of Monet Paint are preparing a cash budget for the 6 months from April through September. Their cash management model is based on the following assumptions:

1. The recent and forecasted (April on) sales (in thousands) are:

Feb.	Mar.	Apr.	May	Jun.	Jul.	Aug.	Sep.	Oct.
400	500	600	700	800	800	700	600	500

2. Twenty percent of sales is collected in the month of sale, 50% is collected in the month following the sale, and 30% is collected in the second month following the sale.

3. Purchases are 60% of sales, and purchases are paid for 1 month prior to the sale.

4. Wages and salaries are 12% of sales and are paid in the same month as the sale.

5. Rent of $10,000 is paid each month. Additional cash operating expenses of $30,000 per month will be incurred for April through July, decreasing to $25,000 for August and September.

6. Tax payments of $20,000 and $30,000 are expected in April and July, respectively. A capital expenditure of $150,000 will occur in June, and the company has a mortgage payment of $60,000 in May.

7. The cash balance at the end of March is $150,000, and managers want to maintain a minimum balance of $100,000 at all times. The company will borrow the amounts necessary to assure that the minimum balance is achieved. Any cash above the minimum will be used to pay off any loan balance until it's eliminated.

The cash budget in table 18.1 on page 654 is based on these assumptions. The top part of the table presents the cash receipts, which reflect the sales predicted in assumption 1 and the collection pattern in assumption 2. The cash disbursements for each month reflect the checks that must be written to satisfy assumptions 3 through 6. April's beginning cash balance is the end-of-March cash balance in assumption 7. Monthly net cash flows are total receipts minus total disbursements for the month.

The lower portion of table 18.1 projects the beginning and ending cash balances for each month, amounts borrowed or repaid on short-term loans, and the cumulative short-term loan balance. It is important to follow the logic in this section of the cash budget.

The monthly net cash flow plus the beginning balance for the month gives an available balance. The available balance is compared to the desired minimum $100,000 balance. If the available balance is too low, the company borrows enough to bring the balance up to $100,000. Any amount above the minimum can be used to repay any outstanding short-term loans. The ending cash balance is the available balance plus the month's borrowing and minus

(continued on following page)

(Cash Budgeting at the Monet Paint Company *continued from previous page*)

the month's loan repayments. Finally, the cumulative loan balance is the previous month's loan balance plus any additional borrowing and minus any loan repayments this month. Note that Monet projects negative net cash flows for April, May, and June, which will require the company to borrow each month and build up its loan balance. Beginning in July, the projected positive net cash flows will enable Monet to pay off its outstanding loan balance and to accumulate a substantial ending cash balance by the end of September. ■

The purpose of a cash budget is to ensure a company's smooth financial operation over the planning horizon. The cash budget identifies the amounts and timing of any surplus or needed funds and is the basis for planning the company's uses and sources of funds. For example, there is often a benefit to maturity matching short-term investments to particular cash needs that are identified in the cash budgeting process. Once these needs have been quantified, the company can select from among the short-term investment alternatives discussed in chapter 16.

Monet's cash budget is a monthly budget. It could be further divided into weekly or daily flows. There are cash flow patterns within the month, which can be incorporated into the daily or weekly budgets. For example, wage and salary cash flows will occur on predictable days. Similarly, payments for rent, loans, and even trade credit are often known in advance. These more detailed daily and weekly cash budgets enable a company to monitor its short-term finances very closely.

TABLE 18.1

Cash Budget for the Monet Paint Company

	CASH BUDGET, APRIL–SEPTEMBER					
Sales	**April** $600,000	**May** $700,000	**June** $800,000	**July** $800,000	**August** $700,000	**September** $600,000
Cash Receipts:						
Collections (current) 20%	$120,000	$140,000	$160,000	$160,000	$140,000	$120,000
(previous month) 50%	250,000	300,000	350,000	400,000	400,000	350,000
(2nd month previous) 30%	120,000	150,000	180,000	210,000	240,000	240,000
Total cash receipts	490,000	590,000	690,000	770,000	780,000	710,000
Cash Disbursements:						
Purchases	420,000	480,000	480,000	420,000	360,000	300,000
Wages and salaries	72,000	84,000	96,000	96,000	84,000	72,000
Rent	10,000	10,000	10,000	10,000	10,000	10,000
Cash operating expenses	30,000	30,000	30,000	30,000	25,000	25,000
Tax installments	20,000			30,000		
Capital expenditure			150,000			
Mortgage payment		60,000				
Total cash disbursements	552,000	664,000	766,000	586,000	479,000	407,000
Ending Cash Balance:						
Net cash flow	−62,000	−74,000	−76,000	184,000	301,000	303,000
Beginning cash balance	150,000	100,000	100,000	100,000	122,000	423,000
Available balance	88,000	26,000	24,000	284,000	423,000	726,000
Monthly borrowing	12,000	74,000	76,000			
Monthly repayment				162,000		
Ending cash balance	$100,000	$100,000	$100,000	$122,000	$423,000	$726,000
Cumulative loan balance	$ 12,000	$ 86,000	$162,000	$ 0	$ 0	$ 0

Self-Check
1. What is a cash budget? How is it created?
2. What is the typical planning horizon for a cash budget?
3. Why do companies prepare cash budgets?

PRO FORMA FINANCIAL STATEMENTS

Companies continually make decisions. For example, they choose the schedules, amounts, processes, innovations, and pricing connected with such things as their products, marketing, production, labor, and inventories. Before making such decisions—and to help them make the best ones—they want to know the effects of alternative choices. Although it is not possible to predict the future perfectly, the effects of many decisions can be predicted with reasonable accuracy.

Pro forma financial statements show the effects of the company's decisions on its future financial statements. Companies use pro forma financial statements throughout the planning process to assess the effects of alternative decisions on various items of interest, such as sales and net income. In addition to helping in the decision-making process, pro forma statements also help the company create contingent plans for responding to unexpected situations.

A complete financial plan includes a set of pro forma financial statements, which show the company's planned financial position at regular points over the planning horizon. These statements are based on the actual decisions made as a result of the planning process, and on the agreed upon sales and other forecasts. Our next example illustrates the use of pro forma financial statements.

Pro Forma Financial Statements for Bluestem Crafts Stores

EXAMPLE

Bluestem Crafts operates several stores in medium-size towns in the Southwest. It has decided to expand into the Southeast. Pro forma financial statements for next year are shown in table 18.2 on page 656, along with the latest income statement and current balance sheet.

Bluestem forecasts increased sales and profits next year for existing stores. However, new stores are not expected to break even in their first year because of startup and extra promotional costs.

Cost of goods sold and selling, general, and administrative expenses are expected to rise somewhat faster than sales. The result will be a small increase in earnings before interest and taxes and a correspondingly modest increase in net income. Because of a recent decline in interest rates, Bluestem expects interest expense to be unchanged, even though total debt will increase. Bluestem is not planning any cash dividends during the next year.

Bluestem's balance sheet shows a $5.8 million increase in assets as receivables, inventories, and fixed assets all increase. This increase in assets is financed with $3.7 million from retained earnings, a $600,000 increase in accounts payable, and a $1.5 million increase in bank loans.

Income statements beyond next year are expected to show increased profitability as the new stores get over their "shakedown period" and become profitable. Of course, Bluestem may continue to expand, and future growth decisions will depend on the success of this year's new stores. ■

TABLE 18.2
Pro Forma Financial Statements for Bluestem Crafts Stores

	INCOME STATEMENT		
	Current	Projected	Change
Sales	$74,000,000	$95,000,000	$21,000,000
Less cost of goods sold	45,500,000	59,000,000	13,500,000
Less depreciation	500,000	600,000	100,000
Gross profit	28,000,000	35,400,000	7,400,000
Less selling & administrative expenses	21,000,000	28,000,000	7,000,000
Earnings before interest and taxes	7,000,000	7,400,000	400,000
Less interest	500,000	500,000	—
Earnings before taxes	6,500,000	6,900,000	400,000
Less taxes	3,000,000	3,200,000	200,000
Net income	3,500,000	3,700,000	200,000
Less cash dividends	—	—	
Addition to retained earnings	$ 3,500,000	$ 3,700,000	$ 200,000

	BALANCE SHEET		
Assets:			
Cash and marketable securities	$ 3,000,000	$ 3,000,000	—
Accounts receivable	4,600,000	6,000,000	$ 1,400,000
Inventory	9,500,000	12,400,000	2,900,000
Total current assets	17,100,000	21,400,000	4,300,000
Net plant and equipment	6,500,000	8,000,000	1,500,000
Total assets	$23,600,000	$29,400,000	$ 5,800,000
Liabilities and Equity:			
Accounts payable	$ 3,400,000	$ 4,000,000	$ 600,000
Bank loans	1,700,000	3,200,000	1,500,000
Other short-term debt	3,000,000	3,000,000	—
Total current liabilities	8,100,000	10,200,000	2,100,000
Long-term debt	3,500,000	3,500,000	—
Stockholders' equity	12,000,000	15,700,000	3,700,000
Total liabilities and equity	$23,600,000	$29,400,000	$ 5,800,000

In addition to pro forma financial statements, companies create many specialized budgets that show in greater detail each unit's resources and responsibilities. Table 18.3 lists statements and budgets that are often created in the planning process. For example, a sales budget provides sales forecasts in units and total revenues, shown in various ways such as by product, division, geographical region, and store. The production budget shows the planned quantities of various items to be produced. Planned production equals forecasted sales plus the desired ending inventory minus the beginning inventory. The purchasing budget specifies the quantities and costs of the necessary production input items. These and other budgets must be carefully coordinated.

Which budgets and statements managers are concerned with depend on their role in the company. For example, top management and the board of directors often focus on the combined pro forma financial statements for the entire company. These officials coordinate the company's investing, financing, production, and liquidity; they must understand the entire company's operations.

Middle managers need other kinds of information to do their specific jobs. Specialized budgets are provided for each managerial responsibility. For example, personnel managers are given training budgets for training current personnel and recruiting budgets for recruiting

TABLE 18.3

Statements and Budgets Produced in the Financial Planning Process

FINANCIAL STATEMENTS	
Income statement	Projected revenues, expenses, net income, and additions to retained earnings
Balance sheet	Projected assets, liabilities, and equity
Statement of cash flows	Projected cash flows for operations, investing, and financing
SPECIALIZED BUDGETS	
Cash budget	Cash inflows, cash outflows, and cash balances
Sales budget	Planned sales in units and in dollar volume. Various sales budgets may be produced for different divisions, product lines, regions, and even individual stores and individuals
Production budget	Scheduled production (quantities and costs)
Purchasing budget	Planned purchases of the raw materials the firm uses in production, goods for resale, and supplies used in operating the firm
Advertising budget	Planned advertising campaigns and their cost
Capital budget	Purchase of long-term assets
R&D budget	Research-and-development plans for the period
Personnel training and recruiting budget	Planned expenses for training employees and recruiting new employees
Administrative budgets	Administrative expenses for each plant, store, department, or managerial unit in the organization

new employees. The recruiting budget has funds for advertising job opportunities, visiting college campuses, and hosting job candidates on visits to the company.

Pro forma financial statements omit many details in order to provide a "big picture" of the company. This big picture is important and is especially useful to the board of directors, CEO, CFO, and other top managers. But the many specialized budgets provide important detailed guidance to other employees. For example, a salesperson probably does not need to know the company's leverage policy, liquidity objective, dividend policy, and the like. The salesperson, however, does need to know about the availability and prices of new and existing products and must be familiar with the resources available to help in selling them. Each of the company's units and managers should have the budgets and parts of the financial plan that are relevant to their responsibilities.

Percent of Sales Forecasting Method

Although pro forma statements and budgets are very useful, they can be complex and time consuming to produce. Consequently, managers often use a shortcut method to create them: the percent of sales forecasting method. This method is a crude but easy way to estimate the funds required to finance growth.

Sales growth requires additional investments in receivables, inventories, and fixed assets, so the company must have financing to grow. Some short-term financing comes spontaneously from the additional sales, because accounts payable and accruals such as wages and taxes payable naturally increase with an increase in sales. Other financing can come from retained earnings. Any remaining necessary financing must come from other sources, such as additional borrowing.

The Percent of Sales Forecasting Formula The percent of sales forecasting formula is based on the following equation:

$$\begin{matrix} \text{Additional} \\ \text{financing} \\ \text{needed} \end{matrix} = \begin{matrix} \text{Required} \\ \text{increase} \\ \text{in assets} \end{matrix} - \begin{matrix} \text{Increase} \\ \text{in liabilities} \end{matrix} - \begin{matrix} \text{Increase in} \\ \text{retained} \\ \text{earnings} \end{matrix}$$

$$AFN = (A/S)gS_0 - (L/S)gS_0 - [M(1+g)S_0 - D] \qquad \text{(18.1)}$$

where

AFN = additional financing needed

A/S = the increase in assets required per dollar increase in sales

L/S = the increase in liabilities provided per dollar increase in sales

S_0 = sales for the current year

g = growth in sales

M = net profit margin on sales

D = cash dividends planned for common stock.

EXAMPLE

Forecasting Financing Needs at Cohen Energy Management Systems

Cohen Energy Management Systems is a small company with excellent growth opportunities. Cohen's sales last year were $2 million. They are expected to grow 25% in the coming year to $2.5 million. Cohen believes that it has access to $250,000 of external capital and wants to know whether this is sufficient to finance its planned growth.

Cohen requires additional assets (receivables, inventories, and fixed assets) equal to 60% of the increase in sales. Short-term liabilities (accounts payable and other accruals) will increase by 10% of the sales increase. The net profit margin is 8%, and Cohen plans to pay a $50,000 cash dividend next year.

Using equation (18.1), the additional financing required is $100,000.

$$AFN = (0.60)500,000 - (0.10)500,000 - [(0.08)2,500,000 - 50,000]$$
$$= 300,000 - 50,000 - 150,000 = \$100,000$$

From this, we can see that Cohen requires an additional $300,000 of assets to support its sales growth. Spontaneous financing from short-term liabilities that increase with sales provides $50,000 of the needed funds. After payment of the $50,000 dividend from the expected net income of $200,000, this year's retained earnings will provide $150,000 of funds. This leaves a need for only $100,000 more to finance the expected sales growth. Cohen will be fine, then, because it has access to up to $250,000 of additional financing. ■

Cash Flow Break-Even Point

CASH FLOW BREAK-EVEN POINT The point below which the company will need either to obtain additional financing or liquidate some of its assets to meet its fixed costs.

Over the planning horizon, the **cash flow break-even point** is the point below which the company will need either to obtain additional financing or liquidate some of its assets to meet its fixed costs (for example, salaries and administrative costs, interest and principal payments, and planned cash dividends). The existence of the cash flow break-even point is pivotal in that it "forces" the company to address contingency plans for possible, but perhaps unlikely, bad outcomes.

Please understand that we're not suggesting that forecasting outcomes above this break-even point is all that is necessary to continue in business. Still, a temporary downturn in economic conditions may force a company below the cash flow break-even point. Costly financial distress and eventual bankruptcy might result, even if the company's portfolio of projects has a positive NPV.

The probability of falling below cash flow breakeven during a planning horizon provides a measure of the company's total risk. This probability depends both on the variability of sales and on how close the company is to its cash flow break-even point when adversity begins to set in.

It's important to keep the possible effects of financial leverage and operating leverage in mind when preparing the financial plan for a company. Both are sources of risk. Therefore, to control the risk that it will be unable to meet, for example, its contractual debt payment obligations, a company can, to whatever extent possible, (1) change its financial leverage, (2) change its operating leverage and, consequently, its break-even point, or (3) change some combination of the two. To the extent that a company cannot control its operating leverage, the company should use the planning process to control risk by creating contingency plans for dealing with bad outcomes.

Alternatives When Funds Are Inadequate

Many rapidly growing companies find themselves short of cash—even though they are profitable. In such cases, the company has several options to consider.

1. *Reduce the growth rate.* The company can choose to reduce its funds requirement to a manageable level by not fully meeting the demand for its product. One thing that might reduce demand is to raise the selling price. If implemented successfully, this approach has the added benefit of increasing the company's income, which provides additional funds that can be reinvested to finance growth. (See our discussion of the price-setting option in chapter 10.)

2. *Sell assets.* If there are any assets that are not required to run the company, it can sell those assets and reinvest the proceeds. Such an alternative would need to be analyzed as a capital budgeting project under capital rationing. (See chapter 10.)

3. *Obtain new external financing.* Among other things, a company can issue new securities, arrange loans, lease or rent assets, or use venture capital financing. Because these choices can affect capital structure, they must be made in conjunction with the company's capital structure policy. (See chapter 12.)

4. *Reduce or stop paying dividends.* Cash dividends use funds that could otherwise be reinvested. However, there are many factors to consider before making this decision. (See our discussion of dividend policy in chapter 13.)

Managers must weigh the benefits and costs of each alternative carefully before deciding on a course of action. Most important, the problem will not cure itself. Consider this simple rule: An unprofitable company that does not have substantial unused production capacity cannot grow into profitability.[1]

Growth does not usually increase the company's return on its existing assets. Growth in the form of a simple expansion of existing operations would normally have a lower *rate* of return than the return on existing assets. Growth is attractive—in spite of this lower return—only when the growth has a positive NPV, that is, when the expected return exceeds the required return. Growth can lead to disaster when it has a negative NPV. An unprofitable company should consider the abandonment option if it's unable to move itself into profitability without growth.

It's also important to remember that rapid expansion is risky. Expansion often means sales in new markets or even sales of new products—both of which are likely to be riskier than the company's current operations. Consequently, companies often limit their growth through capital rationing to control the company's risk. (See our discussion of the potential benefits of capital rationing in chapter 10.)

Long-Term Planning Models

Thus far we have focused on short-term planning models. Companies also use long-term planning models, where the planning horizon depends on the nature of the industry. Most companies use a five- or ten-year planning horizon. Some industries, such as electric utilities, have even longer horizons. Long-term planning models incorporate the company's strategic commitments of resources. They are built around periodic pro forma financial statements over the planning horizon.

---

[1]A company with substantial unused capacity might become profitable if it can grow. If it can expand sales, for example through better marketing, and earn a positive contribution margin on the increased sales, its *return ratios* will improve. (See chapter 4.)

EXAMPLE

Whittaker Industries' Long-Term Planning Model

Whittaker Industries has a 7-year planning model that includes detailed financial statements for the next 7 years. Some of the data from Whittaker's pro forma income statements, statements of cash flows, and balance sheets are summarized and presented in table 18.4. This table provides a good overview of several of the company's strategic decisions.

The company intends to expand from 1999 to 2001. You can see this in the large investing cash flow (the negative cash flow is an investment) for the first 3 years. Net fixed assets also increase substantially on the balance sheet in the early years of the plan. In the fourth year, 2002, some of the short-term debt expected to be accumulated to finance construction will be refinanced with long-term mortgages. Sales growth is expected to be slow for the first 3 years but much faster in years 4 through 6 of the plan. In year 7, sales growth is expected to taper off. The sales growth in years 4 through 6 is accompanied by planned increases in working capital. The company plans to hold dividends constant for 4 years, until after the construction is completed and net income has begun increasing in response to the sales expansion. In years 5 and 6, if all goes well, the company will be able to substantially increase the dividend on its common shares.

In the first 3 years of the plan, Whittaker's total asset turnover and current ratio fall slightly. Thereafter, these ratios improve. Late in the 7-year plan, the company's overall financial health is expected to have improved to the point where other strategic decisions might be considered, such as additional growth, paying off debt, or repurchasing some common shares. ■

Self-Check

1. How do companies use pro forma financial statements?

2. What role do business unit budgets play in the operation of the company?

3. What is the relationship among the additional financing needed, the required increases in assets, the increase in liabilities, and the increase in retained earnings?

4. If a profitable but rapidly growing company finds itself short of cash, what steps can it take to deal with the problem?

AUTOMATING FINANCIAL FORECASTING

Computer technology has greatly benefited cash budgeting and the entire planning process. Spreadsheet software lends itself to cash budgeting and pro forma financial statement analysis. You probably already know how to use a computer spreadsheet package. The main benefit of a spreadsheet is its flexibility. It can be updated very easily, which reduces the clerical burden. A spreadsheet is ideally suited to answer "what-if" questions. For example, changing the February sales projection would cause other changes that ripple through the entire annual cash budget. You can make such changes in seconds when you are using a spreadsheet.

An Example of an Automated Forecast

When Justin Case started his new job as treasurer of the You 'N' Me Toy Company (YNMTC), he found the company did not have a formal cash budgeting system. The owner said, "Don't worry, we have plenty of money in the bank." However, Mr. Case wanted to create a cash management model for the company's activities just the same. (Somewhat surprisingly, the owner agreed, saying, "We need this model, Justin Case.")

YNMTC is a small manufacturer with a stable customer base and stable supplier relationships. Accurate cash inflow and cash outflow data are available. Table 18.5 on page 662

TABLE 18.4

Whittaker Industries' Seven-Year Plan, 1999–2005

	1999	2000	2001	2002	2003	2004	2005
Selected Income Statement Items							
Sales	60.00	62.00	65.00	80.00	95.00	105.00	110.00
Net income	3.00	3.10	3.25	4.00	4.75	5.25	5.50
Dividends	0.60	0.60	0.60	0.60	0.90	1.20	1.25
Statement of Cash Flow Summary							
Operating cash flow	6.50	6.25	6.50	7.50	6.50	7.50	8.00
Investing cash flow	−8.00	−9.00	−8.00	−2.00	−2.00	−4.00	−3.00
Financing cash flow	1.00	2.50	1.50	−4.00	−2.00	−2.00	−2.00
Total cash flow	−0.50	−0.25	0.00	1.50	2.50	1.50	3.00
Balance Sheet Summary							
Cash	4.00	3.75	3.75	5.25	7.75	9.25	12.25
Receivables	9.00	9.30	9.75	12.00	14.25	15.75	16.50
Inventory	7.20	7.45	7.70	9.60	11.40	12.60	13.20
Total current assets	20.20	20.50	21.20	26.85	33.40	37.60	41.95
Net fixed assets	35.00	42.00	48.00	50.00	52.00	54.00	56.00
Total assets	55.20	62.50	69.20	76.85	85.40	91.60	97.95
Payables and accruals	3.60	3.72	3.90	4.80	5.70	6.30	6.60
Other short-term debt	10.00	12.00	13.00	6.00	6.85	7.50	7.75
Total current liabilities	13.60	15.72	16.90	10.80	12.55	13.80	14.35
Mortgages	12.00	12.00	12.00	19.00	19.00	19.00	19.00
Other long-term debt	14.40	17.08	19.95	23.30	26.25	27.15	28.70
Stockholders' equity	15.20	17.70	20.35	23.75	27.60	31.65	35.90
Total liabilities and equity	55.20	62.50	69.20	76.85	85.40	91.60	97.95
Selected Financial Ratios							
Sales/total assets	1.09	0.99	0.94	1.04	1.11	1.15	1.12
Current assets/current liabilities	1.49	1.30	1.25	2.49	2.66	2.72	2.92
Divdends/net income	20.0%	19.4%	18.5%	15.0%	18.9%	22.9%	22.7%
Net income/stockholders' equity	19.7	17.5	16.0	16.8	17.2	16.6	15.3
Total debt/total assets	72.5	71.7	70.6	69.1	67.7	65.4	63.3

shows the information Justin Case gathered. Justin then had to decide on the form of the model, what period(s) it would cover, and how frequently it would be updated.

In his accounting classes, Justin learned that accountants go to great lengths to avoid having an account with a negative balance. For example, they create what are called contra accounts for dealing with negative amounts. We in financial management don't feel so constrained. We recognize that an account with a negative balance can be equivalently viewed as being a positive amount on the other side of the balance sheet. The two sides are mirror images: A negative asset is a liability, and a negative liability is an asset. We can recognize the Principle of Two-Sided Transactions in this relationship. For example, "negative debt" is money someone else owes you—so it is an asset. Similarly, a "negative marketable security" is simply money you owe someone else—so it is a liability.

Justin used this fact to simplify his short-term financial planning model of YNMTC. He created a short-term investment (borrowing) account to use as a "plug" for balancing the balance sheet. The account consists of marketable securities when it is positive, but it becomes a short-term bank loan whenever it must be negative to make the balance sheet balance. A negative balance in this account indicates that the company needs to arrange for more short-term financing.

Justin's short-term investment (borrowing) account simplifies the model-building process. Letting the account be positive *or* negative avoids the problem of automating "conditional" accounts. Conditional accounts require a more complex set of equations. For example,

TABLE 18.5

Information About the You 'N' Me Toy Company, Compiled by Justin Case

1. The payment pattern for revenues is estimated to be as follows: 40% of sales are for cash, 10% are paid for 1 month after the sale, 50% are paid for 2 months after the sale, and bad debt is negligible.
2. The treasury department believes that the cash account should be set to start each month in the amount of $10,000 plus 60% of next month's salaries and wages plus 70% of this month's accounts payable. It also believes YNMTC can earn 0.6% per month on its short-term investments. The model will adjust the cash account with the short-term investment (borrowing) account.
3. YNMTC appears to purchase raw materials each month in the amount of 30% of the predicted sales for the month after next plus 20% of next month's predicted sales plus 10% of this month's sales. Purchases are paid for in the month following their purchase, and there are no discounts available to YNMTC from its suppliers. The cost of raw materials averages 60% of sales.
4. YNMTC pays salaries and wages of $7000 plus 18% of this month's sales.
5. YNMTC is depreciating its net fixed assets at the rate of 1% of *net* fixed assets per month.
6. YNMTC pays a cash dividend of $2000 every month.
7. The long-term debt on the YNMTC balance sheet carries a 12% APR, and payments are made quarterly in December, March, June, and September.
8. Taxes for YNMTC are at the rate of 35% of taxable income (including rebates for negative taxes). Taxes are paid monthly.
9. Sales in October and November of this year were $40,000 and $60,000, respectively. Sales forecasts for the next 11 months ($ thousands) are

Dec	Jan	Feb	Mar	Apr	May	Jun	Jul	Aug	Sep	Oct
100.00	170.00	150.00	125.00	100.00	70.00	65.00	90.00	175.00	50.00	70.00

BALANCE SHEET AS OF NOVEMBER 30

Cash	$ 76.00	Accounts payable	$ 77.00
Short-term investment (borrowing)	70.00	Accrued interest	6.00
Accounts receivable	56.00	Long-term debt	300.00
Inventory	122.00	Common stock	70.00
Net fixed assets	391.00	Retained earnings	262.00
Total assets	$715.00	Liabilities + stockholders' equity	$715.00

with the short-term investment (borrowing) account, if YNMTC is investing money (the account is positive), then the amount invested is shown as a current asset. But if YNMTC is borrowing money (that is, if the account is negative), then the amount is normally shown in an entirely different account as a current liability with a positive balance.

Table 18.6 presents output from Justin Case's automated financial planning model, based on the information in table 18.5. The short-term investment (borrowing) account is projected to be negative in January and February. Thus it seems that during January and February, YNMTC will have to either (1) obtain additional financing in the amounts indicated (the absolute value of the negative balance), to maintain its target level for the cash account, or (2) allow the cash account to fall below the target.

Table 18.7 on page 664 presents the spreadsheet equations (or data) in Justin's model for the first month of the planning period, December, which is shown in column F. In principle, the general form of such equations is simple:

$$\text{Ending balance} = \text{Starting balance} + \text{Increases} - \text{Decreases} \qquad (18.2)$$

The trick to building the model is to identify correctly all the potential increases and decreases for a given account. For example, the inventory account increases with the purchase of raw materials and decreases with the sale of finished goods. A purchase of raw materials also increases accounts payable or decreases cash. A sale of finished goods increases accounts receivable or increases cash.

TABLE 18.6

Cash Budget and Pro Forma Income Statements and Balance Sheets for the You 'N' Me Toy Company, Based on the Information in Table 18.5

CASH BUDGET FOR DECEMBER THROUGH AUGUST													
	Oct	Nov	Dec	Jan	Feb	Mar	Apr	May	Jun	Jul	Aug	Sep	Oct
SALES	40.00	60.00	100.00	170.00	150.00	125.00	100.00	70.00	65.00	90.00	175.00	50.00[a]	70.00[a]
A/R COLLECTIONS			66.00	108.00	127.00	150.00	127.50	100.50	83.00	77.50	111.50		
INTEREST INCOME			0.42	0.01	−0.13	−0.06	0.24	0.56	0.76	0.66	0.52		
CASH INFLOW			66.42	108.01	126.87	149.94	127.74	101.06	83.76	78.16	112.02		
PAYABLES PAID			77.00	89.00	84.50	70.00	53.50	43.50	47.00	77.00	59.00		
SALARIES & WAGES PAID			25.00	37.60	34.00	29.50	25.00	19.60	18.70	23.20	38.50	16.00[a]	
TAXES PAID			2.98	8.24	6.66	4.78	2.97	0.79	0.48	2.39	8.90		
INTEREST PAID			9.00	0.00	0.00	9.00	0.00	0.00	9.00	0.00	0.00		
DIVIDENDS PAID			2.00	2.00	2.00	2.00	2.00	2.00	2.00	2.00	2.00		
STARTING CASH			76.00	94.86	89.55	76.70	62.45	52.21	54.12	77.82	74.40		
ENDING CASH			94.86	89.55	76.70	62.45	52.21	54.12	77.82	74.40	53.55		
S-T INVESTMENT CHANGE (cash budget)			−68.42	−23.52	12.56	48.92	54.51	33.27	−17.12	−23.00	24.48		
S-T INVESTMENT CHANGE (balance sheet)			−68.42	−23.52	12.56	48.92	54.51	33.27	−17.12	−23.00	24.48		

MONTHLY PRO FORMA INCOME STATEMENTS											
	Oct	Nov	Dec	Jan	Feb	Mar	Apr	May	Jun	Jul	Aug
SALES	40.00	60.00	100.00	170.00	150.00	125.00	100.00	70.00	65.00	90.00	175.00
COST OF RAW MATERIALS			60.00	102.00	90.00	75.00	60.00	42.00	39.00	54.00	105.00
SALARIES & WAGES			25.00	37.60	34.00	29.50	25.00	19.60	18.70	23.20	38.50
DEPRECIATION			3.91	3.87	3.83	3.79	3.76	3.72	3.68	3.64	3.61
INTEREST EXPENSE			3.00	3.00	3.00	3.00	3.00	3.00	3.00	3.00	3.00
INTEREST INCOME			0.42	0.01	−0.13	−0.06	0.24	0.56	0.76	0.66	0.52
TAXABLE INCOME			8.51	23.54	19.04	13.65	8.48	2.25	1.38	6.82	25.42
TAXES			2.98	8.24	6.66	4.78	2.97	0.79	0.48	2.39	8.90
NET INCOME			5.53	15.30	12.37	8.87	5.51	1.46	0.90	4.43	16.52
DIVIDENDS			2.00	2.00	2.00	2.00	2.00	2.00	2.00	2.00	2.00
CHANGE IN RETAINED EARNINGS			3.53	13.30	10.37	6.87	3.51	−0.54	−1.10	2.43	14.52

CURRENT BALANCE SHEET AND MONTHLY PRO FORMA BALANCE SHEETS											
	Oct	Nov	Dec	Jan	Feb	Mar	Apr	May	Jun	Jul	Aug
CASH		76.00	94.86	89.55	76.70	62.45	52.21	54.12	77.82	74.40	53.55
S-T INVESTMENT (BORROWING)		70.00	1.58	−21.94	−9.38	39.53	94.04	127.31	110.19	87.19	111.66
ACCOUNTS RECEIVABLE		56.00	90.00	152.00	175.00	150.00	122.50	92.00	74.00	86.50	150.00
INVENTORY		122.00	151.00	133.50	113.50	92.00	75.50	80.50	118.50	123.50	67.00
NET FIXED ASSETS		391.00	387.09	383.22	379.39	375.59	371.84	368.12	364.44	360.79	357.19
TOTAL ASSETS		715.00	724.53	736.33	735.21	719.58	716.09	722.05	744.95	732.38	739.40
ACCOUNTS PAYABLE		77.00	89.00	84.50	70.00	53.50	43.50	47.00	77.00	59.00	48.50
ACCRUED INTEREST		6.00	0.00	3.00	6.00	0.00	3.00	6.00	0.00	3.00	6.00
LONG-TERM DEBT		300.00	300.00	300.00	300.00	300.00	300.00	300.00	300.00	300.00	300.00
COMMON STOCK		70.00	70.00	70.00	70.00	70.00	70.00	70.00	70.00	70.00	70.00
RETAINED EARNINGS		262.00	265.53	278.83	289.21	296.08	299.59	299.05	297.95	300.38	314.90
LIABILITIES + STOCKHOLDERS' EQUITY		715.00	724.53	736.33	735.21	719.58	716.09	722.05	744.95	732.38	739.40

[a]Required for other computations.

TABLE 18.7
Spreadsheet Equations for the Output Shown in Table 18.6 (The months of October through October are in columns D through P)

LINE	COLUMN A	COLUMN F
4		DEC
5	SALES	100.00
6	A/R COLLECTIONS	0.4*F5 + 0.1*E5 + 0.5*D5
7	INTEREST INCOME	0.006*E42
8	CASH INFLOW	+F6 + F7
9		
10	PAYABLES PAID	+E48
11	SALARIES & WAGES PAID	7.0 + 0.18*F5
12	TAXES PAID	+F32
13	INTEREST PAID	+E49 + F28[a]
14	DIVIDENDS PAID	2.00
15	STARTING CASH	+E41
16	ENDING CASH	+F41
17	S-T INVESTMENT CHANGE (cash budget)	+F15 − F16 + F8-F10-F11-F12-F13-F14
18	S-T INVESTMENT CHANGE (balance sheet)	+F42-E42
19		
20		
21		
22	MONTHLY PRO FORMA INCOME STATEMENTS	
23		DEC
24	SALES	+F5
25	COST OF RAW MATERIALS	0.6*F24
26	SALARIES & WAGES	+F11
27	DEPRECIATION	0.01*E45
28	INTEREST EXPENSE	0.01*E50
29	INTEREST INCOME	+F7
30	TAXABLE INCOME	+F24-F25-F26-F27-F28 + F29
31		
32	TAXES	0.35*F30
33	NET INCOME	+F30-F32
34		
35	DIVIDENDS	+F14
36	CHANGE IN RETAINED EARNINGS	+F33-F35
37		
38		
39	CURRENT BALANCE SHEET AND MONTHLY PRO FORMA BALANCE SHEETS	
40		DEC
41	CASH	10.0 + 0.6*G11 + 0.7*F48
42	SHORT-TERM INVESTMENT (BORROWING)	+F53-F41-F43-F44-F45
43	ACCOUNTS RECEIVABLE	0.06*F5 + 0.5*E5
44	INVENTORY	E44 + F48-F25
45	NET FIXED ASSETS	+E45-F27
46	TOTAL ASSETS	+F41 + F42 + F43 + F44 + F45
47		
48	ACCOUNTS PAYABLE	0.1*F5 + 0.2*G5 + 0.3*H5
49	ACCRUED INTEREST	+E49 + F28-F13
50	LONG-TERM DEBT	+E50
51	COMMON STOCK	+E51
52	RETAINED EARNINGS	+E52 + F36
53	LIABILITIES + STOCKHOLDERS' EQUITY	+F48 + F49 + F50 + F51 + F52

[a]This equation repeats every 3 months, with zero for the intervening months.

Account changes in double-entry accounting always maintain the "balance" of the balance sheet. When the offsetting accounts are on the same side of the balance sheet, an increase in one account causes a decrease in the other, and vice versa. For example, a cash purchase of raw materials causes an increase in inventory and a decrease in cash. When the offsetting accounts are on opposite sides of the balance sheet, the changes are in the same direction. An increase in one account causes an increase in the other, and a decrease in one causes a decrease in the other. For example, a credit purchase of raw materials causes an increase in inventory and an increase in accounts payable.

Once he had entered the equations into the December column, Justin *block-copied* them into subsequent columns for January through August. Then he put in "corrections" for two of the model's rows: (1) Each sales forecast was entered separately, and (2) he put in zeros in line 13 for the months in which YNMTC does not make a cash interest payment.[2]

In the cash budget, Justin put in two different equations for the short-term investment change as a check on the model. The first equation (cash budget) tracks the actual cash flows. This change is the sum of the increases and decreases in short-term investment (borrowing). The second equation (balance sheet) is the change in short-term investment (borrowing) that results from forcing the balance sheet to balance. This second change is the short-term investment (borrowing) ending balance minus its starting balance. If these two equations do not produce the same answer, then there is an error—the model is not internally consistent.

Before you build your own model, three warnings are in order. First, do not be alarmed if the values in the cells are incorrect or show ERR as you are entering the equations for a model. (Become alarmed only if such things remain when you *think* you are finished.) Second, even very simple errors can cause *many* of the spreadsheet cells to show nonsensical amounts or ERR or can cause the CIRC indicator to identify circular reasoning. (Circular reasoning is a situation where two or more cells are functions of one another, simultaneously.) This sometimes alarming result occurs because the model is a set of interwoven relationships. A single error can have an enormous ripple effect. Finally, remember that numbers can look okay but in fact be totally *wrong!* We do not mean to discourage you, but an impressively printed spreadsheet can be deceiving: There can be serious errors even though the numbers look fine. You should always check your model and its output very carefully to limit the possibility of errors.

"What-If" Questions: The Power of a Spreadsheet Package

After he had built the financial planning model shown in tables 18.6 and 18.7, it occurred to Mr. Case that actual sales virtually never turn out to be what was expected. Therefore, he decided to consider the possibilities of higher- or lower-than-expected sales. Tables 18.8 on page 666 and 18.9 on page 667 present output from his model, assuming that sales are 80% and 120% of forecast levels, respectively.

Table 18.8 can be produced from Justin's model by following these steps:

1. Insert a blank row between lines 3 and 4 [the Lotus spreadsheet command is /, W, I, A4 . . A4].
2. Copy line 6 (old line 5) to new line 4 [the Lotus spreadsheet command is /, C, A6 . . P6, A4].
3. Enter 0.8 *F4 in cell F6 (old cell F5).
4. Copy cell F6 to G6 . . P6 [the Lotus spreadsheet command is /, C, F6 . . F6, G6 . . P6].

Table 18.9 can then be produced from the model in table 18.8 by following these steps:

1. Enter 1.2 *F4 in cell F6.
2. Copy cell F6 to G6 . . P6 [the Lotus spreadsheet command is /, C, F6 . . F6, G6 . . P6].

[2]Note that unless you specify differently, the copy command maintains the relationship among the cells rather than maintaining specific cell identities. For example, if cell G6 has the equation [E5 + F4] in it, and you copy G6 to L12, the equation becomes [J11 + K10].

TABLE 18.8

Cash Budget and Pro Forma Income Statements and Balance Sheets for the You 'N' Me Toy Company, with 80% of Forecast Sales

CASH BUDGET FOR DECEMBER THROUGH AUGUST

	Oct	Nov	Dec	Jan	Feb	Mar	Apr	May	Jun	Jul	Aug	Sep	Oct
SALES	40.00	60.00	80.00	136.00	120.00	100.00	80.00	56.00	52.00	72.00	140.00	40.00[a]	56.00[a]
A/R COLLECTIONS			58.00	92.40	101.60	120.00	102.00	80.40	66.40	62.00	89.20		
INTEREST INCOME			0.42	0.09	0.01	0.06	0.28	0.54	0.69	0.60	0.48		
CASH INFLOW			58.42	92.49	101.61	120.06	102.28	80.94	67.09	62.60	89.68		
PAYABLES PAID			77.00	71.20	67.60	56.00	42.80	34.80	37.60	61.60	47.20		
SALARIES & WAGES PAID			21.40	31.48	28.60	25.00	21.40	17.08	16.36	19.96	32.20	14.20[a]	
TAXES PAID			1.44	5.65	4.40	2.89	1.44	−0.30	−0.54	0.98	6.19		
INTEREST PAID			9.00	0.00	0.00	9.00	0.00	0.00	9.00	0.00	0.00		
DIVIDENDS PAID			2.00	2.00	2.00	2.00	2.00	2.00	2.00	2.00	2.00		
STARTING CASH			76.00	78.73	74.48	64.20	52.80	44.61	46.14	65.10	62.36		
ENDING CASH			78.73	74.48	64.20	52.80	44.61	46.14	65.10	62.36	45.68		
S-T INVESTMENT CHANGE (cash budget)			−55.15	−13.59	9.29	36.57	42.83	25.83	−16.28	−19.20	18.78		
S-T INVESTMENT CHANGE (balance sheet)			−55.15	−13.59	9.29	36.57	42.83	25.83	−16.28	−19.20	18.78		

MONTHLY PRO FORMA INCOME STATEMENTS

	Oct	Nov	Dec	Jan	Feb	Mar	Apr	May	Jun	Jul	Aug
SALES	40.00	60.00	80.00	136.00	120.00	100.00	80.00	56.00	52.00	72.00	140.00
COST OF RAW MATERIALS			48.00	81.60	72.00	60.00	48.00	33.60	31.20	43.20	84.00
SALARIES & WAGES			21.40	31.48	28.60	25.00	21.40	17.08	16.36	19.96	32.20
DEPRECIATION			3.91	3.87	3.83	3.79	3.76	3.72	3.68	3.64	3.61
INTEREST EXPENSE			3.00	3.00	3.00	3.00	3.00	3.00	3.00	3.00	3.00
INTEREST INCOME			0.42	0.09	0.01	0.06	0.28	0.54	0.69	0.60	0.48
TAXABLE INCOME			4.11	16.14	12.58	8.27	4.13	−0.86	−1.55	2.79	17.67
TAXES			1.44	5.65	4.40	2.89	1.44	−0.30	−0.54	0.98	6.19
NET INCOME			2.67	10.49	8.17	5.38	2.68	−0.56	−1.01	1.82	11.49
DIVIDENDS			2.00	2.00	2.00	2.00	2.00	2.00	2.00	2.00	2.00
CHANGE IN RETAINED EARNINGS			0.67	8.49	6.17	3.38	0.68	−2.56	−3.01	−0.18	9.49

CURRENT BALANCE SHEET AND MONTHLY PRO FORMA BALANCE SHEETS

	Oct	Nov	Dec	Jan	Feb	Mar	Apr	May	Jun	Jul	Aug
CASH		76.00	78.73	74.48	64.20	52.80	44.61	46.14	65.10	62.36	45.68
S-T INVESTMENT (BORROWING)		70.00	14.85	1.26	10.55	47.12	89.95	115.78	99.50	80.29	99.07
ACCOUNTS RECEIVABLE		56.00	78.00	121.60	140.00	120.00	98.00	73.60	59.20	69.20	120.00
INVENTORY		122.00	145.20	131.20	115.20	98.00	84.80	88.80	119.20	123.20	78.00
NET FIXED ASSETS		391.00	387.09	383.22	379.39	375.59	371.84	368.12	364.44	360.79	357.19
TOTAL ASSETS		715.00	703.87	711.76	709.34	693.51	689.19	692.43	707.43	695.84	699.93
ACCOUNTS PAYABLE		77.00	71.20	67.60	56.00	42.80	34.80	37.60	61.60	47.20	38.80
ACCRUED INTEREST		6.00	0.00	3.00	6.00	0.00	3.00	6.00	0.00	3.00	6.00
LONG-TERM DEBT		300.00	300.00	300.00	300.00	300.00	300.00	300.00	300.00	300.00	300.00
COMMON STOCK		70.00	70.00	70.00	70.00	70.00	70.00	70.00	70.00	70.00	70.00
RETAINED EARNINGS		262.00	262.67	271.16	277.34	280.71	281.39	278.83	275.83	275.64	285.13
LIABILITIES + STOCKHOLDERS' EQUITY		715.00	703.87	711.76	709.34	693.51	689.19	692.43	707.43	695.84	699.93

[a]Required for other computations.

TABLE 18.9

Cash Budget and Pro Forma Income Statements and Balance Sheets for the You 'N' Me Toy Company, with 120% of Forecast Sales

		CASH BUDGET FOR DECEMBER THROUGH AUGUST											
	Oct	Nov	Dec	Jan	Feb	Mar	Apr	May	Jun	Jul	Aug	Sep	Oct
SALES	40.00	60.00	120.00	204.00	180.00	150.00	120.00	84.00	78.00	108.00	210.00	60.00[a]	84.00[a]
A/R COLLECTIONS			74.00	123.60	152.40	180.00	153.00	120.60	99.60	93.00	133.80		
INTEREST INCOME			0.42	−0.07	−0.27	−0.18	0.19	0.59	0.83	0.73	0.56		
CASH INFLOW			74.42	123.53	152.13	179.82	153.19	121.19	100.43	93.73	134.36		
PAYABLES PAID			77.00	106.80	101.40	84.00	64.20	52.20	56.40	92.40	70.80		
SALARIES & WAGES PAID			28.60	43.72	39.40	34.00	28.60	22.12	21.04	26.44	44.80	17.80[a]	
TAXES PAID			4.52	10.83	8.92	6.66	4.49	1.87	1.51	3.79	11.60		
INTEREST PAID			9.00	0.00	0.00	9.00	0.00	0.00	9.00	0.00	0.00		
DIVIDENDS PAID			2.00	2.00	2.00	2.00	2.00	2.00	2.00	2.00	2.00		
STARTING CASH			76.00	110.99	104.62	89.20	72.10	59.81	62.10	90.54	86.44		
ENDING CASH			110.99	104.62	89.20	72.10	59.81	62.10	90.54	86.44	61.42		
S-T INVESTMENT CHANGE (cash budget)			−81.69	−33.45	15.83	61.26	66.19	40.70	−17.96	−26.81	30.18		
S-T INVESTMENT CHANGE (balance sheet)			−81.69	−33.45	15.83	61.26	66.19	40.70	−17.96	−26.81	30.18		

		MONTHLY PRO FORMA INCOME STATEMENTS									
	Oct	Nov	Dec	Jan	Feb	Mar	Apr	May	Jun	Jul	Aug
SALES	40.00	60.00	120.00	204.00	180.00	150.00	120.00	84.00	78.00	108.00	210.00
COST OF RAW MATERIALS			72.00	122.40	108.00	90.00	72.00	50.40	46.80	64.80	126.00
SALARIES & WAGES			28.60	43.72	39.40	34.00	28.60	22.12	21.04	26.44	44.80
DEPRECIATION			3.91	3.87	3.83	3.79	3.76	3.72	3.68	3.64	3.61
INTEREST EXPENSE			3.00	3.00	3.00	3.00	3.00	3.00	3.00	3.00	3.00
INTEREST INCOME			0.42	−0.07	−0.27	−0.18	0.19	0.59	0.83	0.73	0.56
TAXABLE INCOME			12.91	30.94	25.50	19.03	12.84	5.35	4.31	10.84	33.16
TAXES			4.52	10.83	8.92	6.66	4.49	1.87	1.51	3.79	11.60
NET INCOME			8.39	20.11	16.57	12.37	8.34	3.48	2.80	7.05	21.55
DIVIDENDS			2.00	2.00	2.00	2.00	2.00	2.00	2.00	2.00	2.00
CHANGE IN RETAINED EARNINGS			6.39	18.11	14.57	10.37	6.34	1.48	0.80	5.05	19.55

		CURRENT BALANCE SHEET AND MONTHLY PRO FORMA BALANCE SHEETS									
	Oct	Nov	Dec	Jan	Feb	Mar	Apr	May	Jun	Jul	Aug
CASH		76.00	110.99	104.62	89.20	72.10	59.81	62.10	90.54	86.44	61.42
S-T INVESTMENT (BORROWING)		70.00	−11.69	−45.14	−29.31	31.95	98.14	138.84	120.89	94.08	124.26
ACCOUNTS RECEIVABLE		56.00	102.00	182.40	210.00	180.00	147.00	110.40	88.80	103.80	180.00
INVENTORY		122.00	156.80	135.80	111.80	86.00	66.20	72.20	117.80	123.80	56.00
NET FIXED ASSETS		391.00	387.09	383.22	379.39	375.59	371.84	368.12	364.44	360.79	357.19
TOTAL ASSETS		715.00	745.19	760.90	761.07	745.64	742.99	751.67	782.47	768.91	778.87
ACCOUNTS PAYABLE		77.00	106.80	101.40	84.00	64.20	52.20	56.40	92.40	70.80	58.20
ACCRUED INTEREST		6.00	0.00	3.00	6.00	0.00	3.00	6.00	0.00	3.00	6.00
LONG-TERM DEBT		300.00	300.00	300.00	300.00	300.00	300.00	300.00	300.00	300.00	300.00
COMMON STOCK		70.00	70.00	70.00	70.00	70.00	70.00	70.00	70.00	70.00	70.00
RETAINED EARNINGS		262.00	268.39	286.50	301.07	311.44	317.79	319.27	320.07	325.11	344.67
LIABILITIES + STOCKHOLDERS' EQUITY		715.00	745.19	760.90	761.07	745.64	742.99	751.67	782.47	768.91	778.87

[a]Required for other computations.

Looking at table 18.8, we see a case of "good news and bad news." The good news is that with lower-than-expected sales, YNMTC will not need to obtain additional financing to maintain its target level of cash; in none of the months is the short-term investment (borrowing) balance negative. The bad news is that total projected net income over the planning horizon declines from $70,890 to $41,130.

Similarly, table 18.9 reveals that higher-than-expected sales will require an even greater amount of additional financing but that total projected net income increases from $70,890 to $100,660. Although growth can have its problems, You 'N' Me would be happy to have higher-than-expected sales, but, true to his name, Justin Case also considered lower-than-expected sales to help create contingency plans.

Self-Check

1. Why is spreadsheet software so useful in preparing financial plans?

2. In building a financial planning spreadsheet model, why is it convenient to use a single item to represent both short-term investments (when the amount is positive) and short-term borrowing (when the amount is negative)?

SUMMARY

Financial planning is an organized process of gathering information, analyzing alternative decisions, developing goals and plans, implementing the plans, and evaluating performance against those plans. The financial plan is a "blueprint" for the future. The purpose of planning and budgeting is to draw out the best of the company's units and individuals to achieve the company's overall goals.

- A company should prepare a financial plan on a regular basis, preferably at least annually. Any company that doesn't plan for its future may not have one.
- A financial plan has three phases: (1) the formulation phase where the plan is designed, (2) the implementation phase where the plan is put into action, and (3) the evaluation phase where future performance is measured against the plan.
- Top-down financial planning relies on top managers to dominate the strategic decisions, while a bottom-up planning style tends to make decisions based on ideas that percolate up from lower levels in the company.
- Good financial planning uses both bottom-up and top-down processes in an effort to get the most from the company's units and individuals.
- Pro forma financial statements are used to summarize the overall impact on the company of the production, marketing, and financing decisions that have been made.
- A company's financial plan should consist of (1) a *long-term financial plan* that covers a period of at least three to five years, (2) a *short-term financial plan* that covers the coming year and agrees with the first year of the long-term plan, and (3) a detailed *cash budget* for the coming year.
- A complete financial plan includes, at a minimum:
    Clearly stated strategic, operating, and financial *objectives*
    The *assumptions* on which the plan is based
    Descriptions of the underlying *strategies*
    Contingency plans for emergencies
    Budgets, categorized and summarized in various ways, such as by time period, division, and type (for example, cash, advertising, purchasing, and capital)
    The *financing program,* categorized and summarized in various ways, such as by time period, sources of funds (for example, bonds, bank loans, stock), and types of funds (for example, short- versus long-term, internal versus external)
    A set of period-by-period *pro forma financial statements* for the entire planning horizon.

- A company's business units should be intimately involved in the planning process, each unit preparing its own financial plan. The corporate staff must provide overall guidance by ensuring that all business units base their plans on a consistent set of assumptions (supplied by the corporate staff), checking the business unit plans for reasonableness, and consolidating the business unit plans into the overall financial plan for the company.

- A cash budget summarizes the company's expected cash inflows and outflows as well as its expected cash and loan balances.

- A company should regularly (at least monthly) monitor its performance against the short-term plan and the cash budget.

- The *cash flow break-even point* over a planning horizon is a pivotal point for addressing contingency plans for possible, even if unlikely, bad outcomes.

- The probability of falling below cash flow break-even during a planning horizon provides a measure of the company's total risk.

- Computer technology has greatly benefited cash budgeting and the entire planning process. Because of its flexibility, spreadsheet software lends itself to cash budgeting and the analysis of pro forma financial statements. Changes can be made easily and "what if" questions can be easily investigated.

EQUATION SUMMARY

$$\begin{array}{c} \text{Additional} \\ \text{financing} \\ \text{needed} \end{array} = \begin{array}{c} \text{Required} \\ \text{increase} \\ \text{in assets} \end{array} - \begin{array}{c} \text{Increase} \\ \text{in liabilities} \end{array} - \begin{array}{c} \text{Increase in} \\ \text{retained} \\ \text{earnings} \end{array}$$

(18.1) $$\text{AFN} = (A/S)gS_0 - (L/S)gS_0 - [M(1 + g)S_0 - D]$$

(18.2) $$\text{Ending balance} = \text{Starting balance} + \text{Increases} - \text{Decreases}$$

CHAPTER REVIEW ACTIVITIES

SELF-TEST PROBLEMS

1. (Cash budgeting) At the beginning of January, the South Carolina Sportsplex has $150,000 of cash on hand. The company forecasts the cash flows for the first six months of the year given below. The S.C. Sportsplex wants to maintain a cash balance of at least $100,000 at all times. If the balance falls below that level, the company will borrow to bring its balance up to $100,000. If more than $100,000 of cash is available, it will use the excess to reduce its short-term borrowing.

     Show the monthly net cash flow, borrowing (if any), loan repayments, cash balance, and cumulative borrowing balance.

Cash flows (thousands)

	Jan	Feb	Mar	Apr	May	June
Cash inflows	100	120	150	320	350	240
Cash outflows	150	180	200	290	240	180

2. (Pro forma financial statements) Columbus Distributors has the following balance sheet:

Balance Sheet, today

Cash	$ 500,000	Accounts payable	$ 1,000,000
Accounts receivable	3,500,000	Bank loan	1,500,000
Inventory	3,000,000	Long-term bond	2,000,000
Fixed assets	3,000,000	Stockholders' equity	5,500,000
Total assets	$10,000,000	Total liabilities & equity	$10,000,000

Next year, Columbus Distributors is planning for a major sales increase of 40%. Sales are currently $15,000,000, and they should increase to $21,000,000 next year. Cash, receivables, and inventory will increase proportionally to sales. Fixed assets will increase by $500,000. Payables will also increase proportionally to sales. The bank loan will increase to $2,000,000. Sinking fund payments will decrease the bond balance by $200,000. Columbus has a 6.0% net profit margin and is expecting to pay a nominal dividend of $100,000 to its common stockholders.

Prepare a pro forma balance sheet for next year. Does the balance sheet show that extra external funds are needed, or that excess funds are available for investment?

3. (Percent of sales forecasting method) Lafayette Oil Company has current sales of $50 million. Lafayette estimates that an additional dollar of sales requires an investment of $1.25 and generates spontaneous short-term financing of $0.10. Lafayette has an 8% net profit margin and expects to pay out dividends equal to 25% of its net profit.

How much additional financing is needed if Lafayette plans to expand sales by 10% next year?

SOLUTIONS TO SELF-TEST PROBLEMS

1.

	Cash flows (thousands)					
	Jan	**Feb**	**Mar**	**Apr**	**May**	**June**
Cash inflows	100	120	150	320	350	240
Cash outflows	150	180	200	290	240	180
Net cash flow	−50	−60	−50	30	110	60
Beginning cash balance	150	100	100	100	100	130
Cash available	100	40	50	130	210	190
Monthly borrowing	0	60	50	0	0	0
Monthly repayment	0	0	0	30	80	0
Ending cash balance	100	100	100	100	130	190
Cumulative borrowing	0	60	110	80	0	0

2. For Columbus, next year's net income is predicted to be:

$$\text{Net income} = (\text{Net profit margin})(\text{Sales}) = 0.06(21,000,000) = \$1,260,000$$

The addition to retained earnings is net income minus dividends:

$$\text{Addition to retained earnings} = 1,260,000 - 100,000 = \$1,160,000$$

Cash, receivables, inventory, and payables should all increase by 40%. Fixed assets, the bank loan, and the mortgage all change by the amounts specified.

Balance Sheet, next year

Cash	$ 700,000	Accounts payable	$ 1,400,000
Accounts receivable	4,900,000	Bank loan	2,000,000
Inventory	4,200,000	Long-term bond	1,800,000
Fixed assets	3,500,000	Stockholders' equity	6,660,000
Total assets	$13,300,000	Subtotal	$11,860,000
		Additional financing	1,440,000
		Total liabilities & equity	$13,300,000

The company must commit $13,300,000 to its assets, but the company's financing and retained profits provide only $11,860,000 of financing. Consequently, Columbus must raise an additional $1,440,000 in order to accommodate its plans.

3. Sales increase = $g(S_0) = 0.10(50 \text{ million}) = \$5 \text{ million}$

Next year's total sales = $(50 + 5) \text{ million} = \$55 \text{ million}$

Next year's net profit = $M(55 \text{ million}) = (0.08)55 \text{ million} = \$4.4 \text{ million}$

Next year's cash dividend = 25% of next year's profit = $(0.25)4.4 \text{ million} = \$1.1 \text{ million}$

Therefore:

Required increase in assets = $(A/S)g(S_0) = 1.25(5 \text{ million})$	$6.25
−Increase in liabilities = $(L/S)g(S_0) = 0.10(5 \text{ million})$	−0.50
−Increase in retained earnings = $M(1 + g)(S_0) - D = 4.4 - 1.1 =$	−3.30
Additional financing needed	$2.45 million

QUESTIONS

1. What would a complete financial plan include, at a minimum?
2. What is the difference between bottom-up and top-down planning?
3. Assume you are working for a business and one of your colleagues is whining that the business is wasting too many resources on its financial planning. Because this person is your friend, outline for him some of the major benefits of the financial planning process that, hopefully, justify its cost.
4. Indicate whether each of the following would typically increase or decrease a company's need for additional external financing.

a. An increase in cash dividends
b. An increase in the net profit margin
c. A decrease in the credit period offered by the company's suppliers
d. A decrease in the credit period offered to the company's customers
e. An increase in corporate income tax rates

5. A rapidly growing company does not have access to sufficient external financing to accommodate its planned growth. What alternatives does it have to avoid running out of cash?
6. True or false?

a. The three phases of the financial planning process are formulating the plan, implementing the plan, and evaluating performance.
b. Top-down financial planning relies on top managers to dominate the strategic decisions, while a bottom-up planning style tends to make decisions based on ideas that percolate up from lower levels in the company.
c. A major advantage of financial planning is that various managers are given an in-crease in flexibility and a reduction in ac-countability.
d. Most U.S. companies have a very short-term planning horizon, seldom exceeding 1 year.
e. In the implementation phase, every man-ager receives a copy of all of the pro forma financial statements and budgets.
f. The use of computer technology and spreadsheet software in financial plan-ning has greatly diminished in recent years.

7. What are the advantages in using a computer spreadsheet package for your financial planning (in-stead of doing it by hand, using a pencil and calculator)?

PROBLEM SET A

A1. (Cash budgeting) Steve Ferris has $6000 in the bank and has a part-time job earning $500 per month. Estimates for his monthly college expenses for his senior year are given below. Steve has a loan agreement where his bank will lend him money when he runs out, such that he will even-tually have a zero cash balance and will be accumulating a debt obligation. What is Steve's fore-casted cash balance and loan balance for the 9 months? How much will he owe when he graduates in May?

Sept.	Oct.	Nov.	Dec.	Jan.	Feb.	Mar.	Apr.	May
4000	1000	1000	1500	4000	1000	1500	1000	1500

A2. (Cash budgeting) Tulsa Well Supply Company has a cash balance at the end of June of $1,200,000 and predicts the net cash flows (in thousands) given below for the next 6 months. If Tulsa must keep a cash balance of at least $1,000,000 at all times, when and how much will it need to borrow to maintain this minimum cash balance?

July	Aug.	Sept.	Oct.	Nov.	Dec.
220	205	−325	−625	100	360

A3. (Additional financing needed) Rodeo Supply Company is planning to increase its sales by 20% next year. The sales increase will require a total additional investment in receivables, inventory, and fixed assets of $750,000. Increases in liabilities such as accounts payable and other accruals will supply $175,000 of financing. Rodeo also expects total profits of $225,000 next year and will not pay any cash dividends. How much external financing is required to finance the sales in-crease?

A4. (Additional financing needed) Chris Hughen is studying his company's financing requirements for next year. Chris estimates that the company must invest an additional $100 in assets and that short-term liabilities will increase spontaneously by $10. He also estimates that the company will earn profits of $70 and that it has access to additional external financing of $50. What is the largest dividend that the company can pay and still have adequate funds to finance its additional assets?

PROBLEM SET B

B1. (Percent of sales forecasting) In 1998, the sales for Amalgamated Meat Loaf Company were $12,000,000. Several balance sheet items varied directly with sales as follows:

Cash	Accounts receivable	Inventory	Net fixed assets	Accounts payable	Other accruals
3%	20%	15%	25%	10%	5%

The net profit margin for Amalgamated Meat Loaf is 6%, and the company pays out an annual dividend equal to 25% of net income. The balance sheet for December 31, 1998, is:

Amalgamated Meat Loaf
Balance Sheet, December 31, 1998

Cash	$ 360,000	Accounts payable	$1,200,000
Accounts receivable	2,400,000	Other accruals	600,000
Inventory	1,800,000	Short-term loan	800,000
Total current assets	4,560,000	Total current liabilities	2,600,000
Net fixed assets	3,000,000	Long-term debt	1,000,000
Total assets	$7,560,000	Stockholders' equity	3,960,000
		Total liabilities and equity	$7,560,000

a. If sales increase by 25% to $15,000,000 in 1999, what additional financing is needed?
b. Assume that the additional financing needed is acquired by increasing the short-term loan. Create a balance sheet for December 31, 1999, showing the financial position of Amalgamated Meat Loaf at that time.

B2. (Cash budgeting) Merrimack Resorts has projected the cash flows for the 6 months of April through September given below. Prepare a schedule showing the monthly cash flow, borrowing, loan repayments, cash balance, and cumulative loan balance. Merrimack has a beginning cash balance of $150 and wishes to maintain a minimum cash balance of at least $100. If the company has cash balances in excess of the minimum, the excess will be used to reduce any outstanding loan balances.

	Apr	May	Jun	Jul	Aug	Sep
Cash inflows	100	100	175	250	300	250
Cash outflows	200	200	250	250	175	125

B3. (Cash budgeting) The management team of Dark Adventures has asked you to prepare a monthly cash budget for the 6 months from October through March. Because the sales of Dark Adventures are seasonal, peaking around the turn of the year, cash budgeting is critical to the company. To facilitate your preparation of the cash budget, they have supplied you with the following information:

1. The recent and forecasted (starting in Oct.) sales (in thousands) are:

Aug.	Sep.	Oct.	Nov.	Dec.	Jan.	Feb.	Mar.	Apr.
400	500	600	700	800	800	700	600	500

2. Twenty-five percent of sales are collected during the month of sale, 50% is collected in the month following the sale, and 25% is collected in the second month following the sale.
3. Purchases are 50% of sales and are paid for 1 month prior to sale.
4. Wages and salaries are 24% of sales and are paid in the same month as the sale.
5. Rent of $4000 is paid each month. Additional cash operating expenses of $8000 per month will be incurred for October and November, $20,000 for December and January, and $8000 for February and March.
6. Tax installments of $10,000 are planned for October and January. A capital expenditure of $100,000 will occur in October, and the company has a mortgage payment of $5000 due every month.

7. The cash balance at the end of September is $125,000, and the managers want to maintain a minimum balance of $60,000 at all times. The company will borrow the amounts necessary to assure that the minimum balance is achieved. If the cash balance is above the minimum and there is still a loan balance from previous months, excess funds will be applied to the loan balance until it is eliminated.

B4. (Pro forma financial statements) Kennesaw Leisure Products has the following balance sheet:

Balance Sheet, current date (thousands)

Cash	$ 50	Accounts payable	$ 70
Accounts receivable	220	Bank loan	180
Inventory	300	Long-term mortgage	200
Fixed assets	210	Stockholders' equity	330
Total assets	$780	Total liabilities & equity	$780

In the year just completed, Kennesaw had sales of $600,000, with net income of $60,000 and a net profit margin of 10%. The company expects the same profit margin on next year's sales. Kennesaw paid no dividend this year and does not plan to pay one next year. Next year, Kennesaw is planning on a substantial sales increase. Assume that cash, accounts receivable, inventory, and accounts payable will increase proportionally to the sales increase. Furthermore, the existing level of fixed assets is sufficient to accommodate the planned sales increase, the mortgage loan will be amortized by $10,000, and the bank loan cannot be increased.

a. Assume that sales increase by 10%. Prepare a pro forma balance sheet showing the company's financial position at the end of next year. If the balance sheet does not otherwise balance, indicate on the balance sheet the amount of additional external funds that are needed or the excess funds that are available for investment.

b. Assume that sales increase by 20%. Prepare a pro forma balance sheet showing the company's financial position at the end of next year. If the balance sheet does not otherwise balance, indicate on the balance sheet the amount of extra external funds that are needed or the excess funds that are available for investment.

B5. (Percent of sales forecasting) Current sales of $1,000,000 are expected to increase by 20% next year. The investment in additional assets to finance this growth should be 150% of the sales increase. Short-term liabilities (such as accounts payable and other accruals) will provide financing equivalent to 15% of the sales increase. The company's net income is predicted to be 20% of total sales, and the company plans to pay a cash dividend equal to one-third of net income. How much additional financing is needed to finance the company's growth?

PROBLEM SET C

C1. (Pro forma financial statements) The table below shows the income statement and balance sheet for the current year for Dellva Machine Products Company. The table also gives assumptions about what Dellva expects during the next year. Based on this information, complete the projected balance sheet and income statement for Dellva Machine Products.

Income Statement

	Current	Projected	Assumptions for next year
Sales	$54,000,000	$	20% increase
Less cost of goods sold	25,000,000		20% increase
Less depreciation	1,500,000	_____	$500,000 increase
Gross profit	$27,500,000	$	
Less selling & administrative expenses	16,000,000	_____	$1,500,000 increase
Earnings before interest and taxes	$11,500,000	$	
Less interest	1,500,000	_____	$1,000,000 increase
Earnings before taxes	$10,000,000	$	
Less taxes	4,500,000	_____	45% of earnings before taxes
Net income	$ 5,500,000	$	
Less cash dividends	1,000,000	_____	Unchanged
Addition to retained earnings	$ 4,500,000	$	

Balance Sheet

Assets:			
Cash and marketable securities	$ 2,000,000	$	See note below
Accounts receivable	4,500,000		$1,000,000 increase
Inventory	5,500,000	_____	$1,000,000 increase
Total current assets	$12,000,000	$	
Net plant and equipment	8,000,000	_____	$1,000,000 increase
Total assets	$20,000,000	$	
Liabilities and Equity:			
Accounts payable	$ 2,500,000	$	$500,000 increase
Bank loans	2,000,000		See note below
Other short-term debt	1,500,000	_____	Unchanged
Total current liabilities	$ 6,000,000	$	
Long-term debt	5,000,000		Unchanged
Stockholders' equity	9,000,000	_____	Add new retained earnings
Total liabilities and equity	$20,000,000	$	

NOTE: Dellva wants cash and marketable securities to be at least $2,000,000. If the company has more funds (from total liabilities and equity) than it needs for its planned assets, the excess funds will be added to cash and marketable securities. On the other hand, if the company's asset requirements (total assets) exceed its total financing (total liabilities and equity not including bank loans), Dellva will use short-term bank loans to raise the needed funds. (In other words, the cash and marketable securities or bank loans accounts are the plug accounts that will cause the balance sheet to balance. Extra funds are invested in cash and marketable securities, or a funds shortage is covered by bank borrowing.)

C2. (Automated forecasts) Mathew T. Box, III, grandson of the founder and currently CEO of the M. T. Box Company, has been concerned about the company's short-term financial management. The treasurer of M. T. Box, Mary Hoover, has gathered the following information and is asking you to create a cash budget, monthly pro forma income statements, and monthly pro forma balance sheets for the next 6 months for M. T. Box.

1. The payment pattern for revenues is estimated to be as follows: 20% of sales are for cash, 15% are paid for 1 month after the sale, 55% are paid for 2 months after the sale, 9% are paid for in 3 months, and 1% are uncollectible.
2. The cash account should be set to start each month in the amount of $15,000 plus 65% of next month's salaries and wages plus 75% of this month's accounts payable. The cash account will be adjusted with the short-term investment (borrowing) account, and Mary Hoover believes M. T. Box can earn 9% APR on its short-term investments.
3. Purchases of raw materials each month are in the amount of 35% of the predicted sales for the month after next plus 25% of next month's predicted sales plus 8% of this month's sales. Purchases are paid for in the following month, and there are no discounts available from suppliers. The cost of raw materials averages 68% of sales.

4. The company pays salaries and wages of $15,000 plus 14% of this month's sales.
5. Fixed assets are being depreciated at the rate of 1% of net fixed assets per month.
6. The company pays a cash dividend of $2000 every month.
7. The long-term debt on the balance sheet carries a 15% APR, and payments are made quarterly in December, March, June, and September.
8. Taxes are at the rate of 35% of taxable income (including rebates for negative taxes). Taxes are paid monthly.
9. Mary Hoover is expecting the company to make a purchase of $150,000 in fixed assets at the end of April.
10. Sales for October, November, and December of this year were $60,000, $90,000, and $150,000, respectively. Sales forecasted for the next 8 months are (in thousands):

Jan.	Feb.	Mar.	Apr.	May	Jun.	Jul.	Aug.
250	235	190	160	110	90	135	260

Balance Sheet as of December 31

Cash	$ 170	Accounts payable	$ 160
Short-term investments (borrowing)	90	Accrued interest	0
Accounts receivable	195	Long-term debt	600
Inventory	157	Common stock	120
Net fixed assets	615	Retained earnings	347
Total assets	$1227	Liabilities + stockholders' equity	$1227

C3. (Automated forecasts) The following information has been gathered for Dunn Manufacturing, Inc. Ulysses R. Dunn, the founder, manager, and majority shareholder, is trying to get a "handle" on financial planning. Use the following information to create a cash budget, monthly pro forma income statements, and monthly pro forma balance sheets for the next 9 months for Dunn Manufacturing and U. R. Dunn.

1. The payment pattern for revenues is estimated to be as follows: 20% of sales are for cash, 10% are paid for 1 month after the sale, 50% are paid for 2 months after the sale, 18% are paid for 3 months after the sale, and 2% are uncollectible.

2. The cash account is targeted to start each month in the amount of $20,000 plus 70% of next month's salaries and wages plus 75% of this month's accounts payable. The cash account will be adjusted with the notes payable account, which currently costs 1.1% per month on the balance.

3. Dunn purchases raw materials each month in the amount of 40% of the predicted sales for the month after next plus 10% of next month's predicted sales plus 15% of this month's sales. Purchases are paid for in the following month, and there are no discounts available to Dunn from its suppliers. The cost of raw materials averages 65% of sales.

4. Dunn pays salaries and wages of $27,000 plus 10% of this month's sales.

5. Dunn is depreciating its net fixed assets at the rate of 0.9% of net fixed assets per month.

6. Dunn pays a cash dividend of $5000 every month.

7. The long-term debt on the Dunn balance sheet carries a 12% APR, and payments are made quarterly in December, March, June, and September.

8. Taxes for Dunn Manufacturing are at the rate of 34% of taxable income (including rebates for negative taxes). Taxes are paid quarterly (end of December, March, June, and September) on the basis of what the tax liability is *expected to be over the next quarter.* The model you build must be used in conjunction with trial and error to determine the correct tax payments to avoid encountering the problem of circular reasoning (CIRC). (*Hint*: Initially, just let the taxes "use up" what is currently in the prepaid tax account and go negative.)

9. Dunn expects to purchase $275,000 worth of fixed assets at the end of July.

10. Sales for January, February, and March of this year were $320,000, $345,000, and $365,000, respectively. Sales forecasted for the next 11 months are (in thousands):

Apr.	May	Jun.	Jul.	Aug.	Sep.	Oct.	Nov.	Dec.	Jan.	Feb.
410	430	350	325	300	220	265	290	375	350	370

Balance Sheet as of March 31

Cash	$210	Accounts payable	$177
Accounts receivable	256	Notes payable	219
Inventory	437	Accrued interest	0
Prepaid taxes	43	Long-term debt	650
Other assets	15	Common stock	150
Net fixed assets	674	Retained earnings	439
Total assets	$1635	Liabilities + stockholders' equity	$1635

BIBLIOGRAPHY

Carpenter, Michael D., and Jack E. Miller. "A Reliable Framework for Monitoring Accounts Receivable," *Financial Management,* 1979, 8(4):37–40.

Elmer, Peter J., and David M. Borowski. "An Expert System Approach to Financial Analysis: The Case of S&L Bankruptcy," *Financial Management,* 1988, 17(3):66–76.

Emery, Gary W. "Some Empirical Evidence on the Properties of Daily Cash Flow," *Financial Management,* 1981, 10(1):21–28.

Fabozzi, Frank J., and Leslie N. Masonson, eds. *Corporate Cash Management: Techniques and Analysis.* Homewood, Ill.: Dow Jones- Irwin, 1985.

Ferguson, D. M., and Ned C. Hill. "Cash Flow Timeline Management: The Next Frontier of Cash Management," *Journal of Cash Management,* 1985 (May/June):12–22.

Finnerty, John D. *Corporate Financial Analysis.* New York: McGraw-Hill, 1986.

Francis, Jack Clark, and Dexter R. Rowell. "A Simultaneous Equation Model of the Firm for Financial Analysis and Planning," *Financial Management,* 1978, 7(1):29–44.

Maier, Steven F., and James H. Vander Weide. "A Practical Approach to Short-Run Financial Planning," *Financial Management,* 1978, 7(4):10–16.

TOPICS IN FINANCIAL MANAGEMENT

TOPIC D: Issuing Securities and the Role of Investment Banking
TOPIC E: Derivatives and Hedging
TOPIC F: Mergers and Acquisitions

This section provides additional background material designed to enrich your understanding and broaden your knowledge of financial management.

Topic D examines how companies go about issuing securities. Companies need capital to grow and acquire additional assets. They usually finance the purchase of long-term assets with long-term capital. Retained earnings are one source of long-term capital. But when capital requirements exceed the company's ability to generate cash internally, it must raise funds externally. Issuing new securities is an important source of additional external capital.

Some securities derive their value from other assets. Such securities are called *derivatives*. For example, an option gets its value from the underlying asset. Topic E examines derivatives and how these securities are used in financial management to manage a company's risk, through what is called *hedging*.

Topic F covers mergers and acquisitions. Such transactions are mega-capital budgeting decisions that often involve investment–financing interactions and special legal, tax, and accounting considerations. Despite any special considerations, however, the fundamental principles still apply—a merger or acquisition should be undertaken only when it creates value.

T O P I C   D

Issuing Securities and the Role of Investment Banking

A healthy company needs capital to maintain its assets, as well as to grow and acquire additional assets. Companies usually finance the purchase of long-term assets with long-term capital. Retained earnings are the major source of internal long-term capital. But when capital requirements exceed the company's ability to generate cash internally, it must raise funds externally.

In this topic, we further examine external sources of long-term capital. In chapter 14, we focused on the various alternative sources of capital. Our focus here is on how companies go about obtaining the financing they have decided to use. In particular, we look at how companies issue securities (as opposed to borrowing money from banks) and the markets in which they issue them. We explore the investment banking process and consider how investment bankers can help companies obtain additional external financing, and at what cost.

Sometimes companies issue securities directly to private investors. Private placement can eliminate certain requirements but, at the same time, reduce the liquidity of the securities.

Finally, we consider the benefits and costs of changing from a private company to a company with publicly traded securities.

ISSUING SECURITIES, INVESTMENT BANKING, AND THE PRINCIPLES OF FINANCE

◆ *Two-Sided Transactions:* When issuing securities, set a price and other terms that investors will find acceptable.

◆ *Signaling:* Recognize that announcing a public offering of common stock usually leads to a negative stock market reaction because it suggests that the company's managers think the company's stock is overvalued.

◆ *Valuable Ideas:* Look for opportunities to develop new securities that reduce issuers' funding costs and raise investors' risk-adjusted after-tax return.

◆ *Options:* Value the rights distributed to shareholders just as you would any other call option.

◆ *Comparative Advantage:* Contract with underwriters to bear the risk in issuing securities—if they can bear that risk more cheaply.

◆ *Risk-Return Trade-Off:* Look for innovative securities that reduce the investors' risk, which will enable you to pay a lower interest rate than an otherwise identical conventional security would require.

◆ *Capital Market Efficiency:* Use the market price at which a company's common shares are actively trading as the best measure of their value.

ISSUING SECURITIES

Just as there are various financing alternatives, which we described in chapter 14, there is a choice of issue methods. Larger companies usually make a **general cash offer,** also referred to as a *registered public offering.* The procedure is much the same for debt and equity. The issuer must satisfy the securities laws, which are enforced by the Securities and Exchange Commission (SEC). In particular, securities sold in a public offering must be registered with the SEC. The company can then offer the securities to investors at large, usually with the help of **underwriters.** Underwriters are middlemen who buy securities from the issuing companies and sell them to others. In most cases, they also guarantee the price the issuer will receive.

A company can also offer new common stock directly to existing holders. This procedure is called a **rights issue** (or *rights offering*). It's different from a general cash offer in several ways, including lower issuance costs. Interestingly, rights issues are rare in the United States but common elsewhere, for reasons we will explain.

Many companies, particularly smaller ones, issue debt securities directly to investors through a **private placement.** Any type of security can be privately placed, but most private placements involve debt. Privately placed securities are not registered for sale to the public. Private placements must satisfy the requirements for exemption from registration under the Securities Act of 1933. These requirements limit the investors to whom unregistered securities may be offered for sale. There are also significant restrictions on resale to other investors, which make such securities less liquid. As a result, a private placement tends to be more expensive than a general cash offer because investors demand a premium for the lack of liquidity.

There are foreign markets for securities, too. The **Eurodollar bond market** is the market outside the United States for U.S.-dollar-denominated bonds. At times, the Eurodollar bond market provides more attractive new issue terms than the U.S. market. It therefore pays a prospective bond issuer to keep an eye on the Eurodollar bond market.

General Cash Offers

When a company issues securities in a general cash offer, it must register them with the SEC.[1] A general cash offer involves the following steps.

What to Issue? Managers must first decide how much they need to raise and what type of security to issue. The company's target capital structure will affect the decision. But other considerations, such as the specific terms available and management's view of how its common stock is priced, also play a role.

Management must obtain board approval to issue new securities. Shareholder approval is required if the company needs to increase the number of authorized shares of common or preferred stock.

Registration Statement The prospective issuer must prepare and file a **registration statement** with the SEC.[2] The registration statement contains a *preliminary* **prospectus.** A preliminary prospectus is also called a *red herring* because of a warning legend that must be printed on its cover in bold red letters. A prospectus gives the information about the issuer and the proposed issue that investors need to make their decision to invest.

The SEC reviews the registration statement and makes comments. Once this review process is complete, the issuer and the underwriters can agree on the pricing terms for the new issue.

Pricing The issuer and underwriters negotiate the terms of the offering and the underwriters' compensation. The issuer then files the final amendment to the registration statement, which contains the *final prospectus.* Figures D.1 on page 680 and D.2 on page 681 show the cover and summary pages from a typical prospectus. After registration, the securities can be traded freely by investors.

Closing The offering *closes* three business days later. Corporate securities transactions customarily settle, or close, in the United States on the third business day following the transaction date. At the closing, the issuer delivers the securities. The underwriters simultaneously deliver payment, net of their fees. The underwriters then deliver the securities to investors in return for payment.

---

[1]The Securities Act of 1933 (the 1933 Act) and its related rules regulate interstate issues of securities. All the states have their own laws to regulate intrastate securities issues. An offering limited to one state only is registered with the state securities department, rather than the SEC. In addition, each state's "blue sky" laws regulate the sale of any securities (including SEC-registered) within that state.

[2]There are some exemptions from this requirement. Footnote 1 mentioned the intrastate exemption. There is a commercial paper exemption for notes that will mature within 270 days of issue. There is also a small-issue exemption. Regulation A under the 1933 Act provides for an abbreviated offering statement when the issue will raise no more than $1.5 million.

2,795,000 Shares

MICROSOFT®

Microsoft Corporation

Common Stock

Of the 2,795,000 shares of Common Stock offered hereby, 2,000,000 shares are being sold by the Company and 795,000 shares are being sold by the Selling Stockholders. See "Principal and Selling Stockholders." The Company will not receive any of the proceeds from the sale of shares by the Selling Stockholders.

Prior to this offering, there has been no public market for the Common Stock of the Company. For the factors which were considered in determining the initial public offering price, see "Underwriting."

See "Certain Factors" for a discussion of certain factors which should be considered by prospective purchasers of the Common Stock offered hereby.

THESE SECURITIES HAVE NOT BEEN APPROVED OR DISAPPROVED BY THE SECURITIES AND EXCHANGE COMMISSION NOR HAS THE COMMISSION PASSED UPON THE ACCURACY OR ADEQUACY OF THIS PROSPECTUS. ANY REPRESENTATION TO THE CONTRARY IS A CRIMINAL OFFENSE.

	Initial Public Offering Price	Underwriting Discount(1)	Proceeds to Company(2)	Proceeds to Selling Stockholders(2)
Per Share	$21.00	$1.31	$19.69	$19.69
Total(3)	$58,695,000	$3,661,450	$39,380,000	$15,653,550

(1) The Company and the Selling Stockholders have agreed to indemnify the Underwriters against certain liabilities, including liabilities under the Securities Act of 1933.

(2) Before deducting expenses of the offering estimated at $541,000, of which $452,000 will be paid by the Company and $89,000 by the Selling Stockholders.

(3) The Company has granted to the Underwriters an option to purchase up to an additional 300,000 shares at the initial public offering price, less the underwriting discount, solely to cover overallotments. If such option is exercised in full, the total Initial Public Offering Price, Underwriting Discount and Proceeds to Company will be $64,995,000, $4,054,450 and $45,287,000, respectively.

The shares are offered severally by the Underwriters, as specified herein, subject to receipt and acceptance by them and subject to their right to reject any order in whole or in part. It is expected that the certificates for the shares will be ready for delivery at the offices of Goldman, Sachs & Co., New York, New York on or about March 20, 1986.

Goldman, Sachs & Co.

Alex. Brown & Sons
Incorporated

The date of this Prospectus is March 13, 1986.

FIGURE D.1

Prospectus cover page.

PROSPECTUS SUMMARY

The following summary is qualified in its entirety by the more detailed information and Consolidated Financial Statements appearing elsewhere in this Prospectus. All information relating to the Company's Common Stock contained in this Prospectus, except as presented in the Consolidated Financial Statements, reflects the conversion of all outstanding shares of Preferred Stock into Common Stock on the date of this Prospectus.

The Company

Microsoft designs, develops, markets, and supports a product line of systems and applications microcomputer software for business and professional use. The Microsoft Software Product Line chart inside the front cover of this Prospectus illustrates the evolution and diversity of the Company's product line. Microsoft's systems software products include Microsoft® MS-DOS®, a 16-bit microcomputer operating system used on IBM PC and IBM compatible computers, and computer language products in six computer languages. The Company offers business applications software products in the following categories: word processing, spreadsheet, file management, graphics, communications, and project management. The Company's products are available for 8-bit, 16-bit, and 32-bit microcomputers, including IBM, Tandy, Apple, COMPAQ, Olivetti, AT&T, Zenith, Wang, Hewlett-Packard, DEC, Siemens, Philips, Mitsubishi, and NEC. Microsoft develops most of its software products internally using proprietary development tools and methodology. The Company markets and distributes its products domestically and internationally through the original equipment manufacturer ("OEM") channel and through the retail channel primarily by means of independent distributors and dealers and by direct marketing to corporate, governmental, and educational customers.

The Offering

Common Stock offered by the Company	2,000,000 shares(1)
Common Stock offered by the Selling Stockholders	795,000 shares
Common Stock to be outstanding after the offering	24,715,113 shares(1)
Proposed NASDAQ symbol	MSFT
Use of Proceeds	For general corporate purposes, principally working capital, product development, and capital expenditures.

Selected Consolidated Financial Information
(In thousands, except per share data)

	Year Ended June 30,				Six Months Ended December 31,	
	1982	1983	1984	1985	1984	1985
					(Unaudited)	
Income Statement Data:						
Net revenues	$24,486	$50,065	$97,479	$140,417	$62,837	$85,050
Income before income taxes	5,595	11,064	28,030	42,843	18,219	29,048
Net income	3,507	6,487	15,880	24,101	9,996	17,118
Net income per share	$ .17	$ .29	$ .69	$ 1.04	$ .43	$ .72
Shares used in computing net income per share	21,240	22,681	22,947	23,260	23,253	23,936

	December 31, 1985	
	Actual	As Adjusted(1)(2)
		(Unaudited)
Balance Sheet Data:		
Working capital	$57,574	$96,502
Total assets	94,438	133,366
Total long-term debt	—	—
Stockholders' equity	71,845	110,773

(1) Assumes the Underwriters' over-allotment option is not exercised. See "Underwriting."

(2) Gives effect to the sale of shares offered by the Company hereby. The net proceeds have been added to working capital pending their use. See "Use of Proceeds."

FIGURE D.2
Prospectus summary page.

EXAMPLE   *GM's General Cash Offer of Common Stock*

General Motors Corporation reported net losses of $2.0 and $4.5 billion in 1990 and 1991, respectively. It forecast another operating loss in 1992. In addition, effective January 1, 1992, GM adopted Financial Accounting Standards Board Statement No. 106, *Employers' Accounting for Postretirement Benefits Other Than Pensions* (primarily postretirement medical, dental, vision, and life insurance benefits). This accounting change reduced GM's stockholders' equity by $20.6 billion.

GM decided to sell a new issue of common stock as one step in rebuilding its stockholders' equity. GM chose the general cash offer method. It filed a registration statement with the SEC on April 24, 1992. After receiving the SEC's comments, GM prepared the amendment. On May 20, 1992, GM filed the amended registration statement with the SEC, sold 57 million shares of its $1⅔ par value common stock at $39 per share, and realized net proceeds of $2.2 billion. ■

Primary versus Secondary Offerings   The GM common stock offering was a **primary offering.** In a primary offering a company sells newly issued securities to investors. Sometimes insiders or large institutional shareholders sell securities they hold in a registered public offering. Such an offering is known as a secondary offering. Shareholders sell previously issued securities that they purchased from the company or other investors.

EXAMPLE   *GM Pension Funds' Secondary Offering*

Companies sometimes find it advantageous to issue common shares to their pension funds in lieu of making cash contributions. The share issue augments the stockholders' equity but the stockholders don't have to pay the flotation costs they would incur in a public offering. At some point the pension funds might decide to sell some or all of these shares for diversification purposes. On March 13, 1995, General Motors Corporation contributed 173,163,187 shares of GM Class E Common Stock to its pension plans.

The GM pension plans subsequently decided to sell 42,550,000 of these shares in a registered secondary offering. On June 8, 1995, the pension plans sold the shares in a global offering for $42.375 each, realizing net proceeds of $1.75 billion. ■

With a public offering, underwriters usually publish advertisements like the one in figure D.3 to advertise their role. These are called *tombstone advertisements* because of their appearance.

The ad in figure D.3 lists three groups, called **syndicates,** of underwriters. The first is a group of U.S. Underwriters (31.05 million shares). The second is a group of International Underwriters (8.05 million shares). The third is a group of Asian Underwriters (3.45 million shares). Merrill Lynch & Co. and Goldman, Sachs & Co. acted as joint global coordinators, coordinating the selling activity of the three syndicates and redistributing shares from one to another according to the demand for the offering.

Self-Check

1. What's the difference between a general cash offer and a rights issue?

2. What are the steps involved in a general cash offer?

3. What is an underwriter? A private placement?

4. What is the difference between a primary offering and a secondary offering?

This announcement is under no circumstances to be construed as an offer to sell or as a solicitation of an offer to buy any of these securities.
The offering is made only by the Prospectus.

June 8, 1995

42,550,000 Shares

General Motors Corporation

Class E Common Stock

Dividends are paid by General Motors Corporation on Class E Common Stock
based on the earnings of its wholly-owned subsidiary

Electronic Data Systems Corporation

Price $42.375 Per Share

Joint Global Coordinators

Merrill Lynch & Co.   **Goldman, Sachs & Co.**

Of the 42,550,000 shares sold, 40,550,000 shares were sold by the General Motors Special Hourly Employees
Pension Trust under the General Motors Hourly-Rate Employees Pension Plan and 2,000,000 shares were sold
by a trust under the General Motors Retirement Plan for Salaried Employees. United States Trust Company of
New York is the trustee for the General Motors Special Hourly Employees Pension Trust and Bankers Trust
Company is the trustee for a trust under the General Motors Retirement Plan for Salaried Employees

Advisor to United States Trust Company of New York

Wasserstein Perella & Co.

Copies of the Prospectus may be obtained in any State or jurisdiction in which this announcement is circulated from only
such of the undersigned or other dealers or brokers as may lawfully offer these securities in such State or jurisdiction

31,050,000 Shares
The above shares were underwritten by the following group of US Underwriters.

Merrill Lynch & Co.   **Goldman, Sachs & Co.**   **Lehman Brothers**

CS First Boston   **Morgan Stanley & Co.**   **Salomon Brothers Inc**

Bear, Stearns & Co. Inc.   Alex. Brown & Sons   Commerzbank Capital Markets Corporation
Dean Witter Reynolds Inc.   Dillon, Read & Co. Inc.   A.G. Edwards & Sons, Inc.   Furman Selz
Hambrecht & Quist LLC   Invemed Associates, Inc.   Kemper Securities, Inc.
Lazard Freres & Co. LLC   Montgomery Securities   J.P. Morgan Securities Inc.   Oppenheimer & Co., Inc.
PaineWebber Incorporated   Prudential Securities Incorporated   Robertson, Stephens & Company
Smith Barney Inc.   UBS Securities Inc.   Wertheim Schroder & Co.
Advest, Inc.   Sanford C. Bernstein & Co., Inc.   Cowen & Company   Dain Bosworth   Duff & Phelps Securities
First of Michigan Corporation   Janney Montgomery Scott Inc.   Edward D. Jones & Co.
C. J. Lawrence/Deutsche Bank   Legg Mason Wood Walker   Morgan Keegan & Company, Inc.
Needham & Company, Inc.   Principal Financial Securities, Inc.   Rauscher Pierce Refsnes, Inc.
Raymond James & Associates, Inc.   SoundView Financial Group, Inc.   Stephens Inc.
Sutro & Co. Incorporated   Wheat First Butcher Singer   M.R. Beal & Company   Doft & Co., Inc.
Ferris, Baker Watts   First Manhattan Co.   Luther, Smith & Small Inc.   Roney & Co.   Scott & Stringfellow, Inc.
Muriel Siebert & Co., Inc.   Stifel, Nicolaus & Company   Utendahl Capital Partners, L.P.   William K. Woodruff & Company

8,050,000 Shares
The above shares were underwritten by the following group of International Underwriters.

Merrill Lynch International Limited   **Goldman Sachs International**   **Lehman Brothers**

CS First Boston   **Morgan Stanley & Co.**   **Salomon Brothers International Limited**

ABN AMRO Hoare Govett   Cazenove & Co.   Credit Lyonnais Securities   Deutsche Bank
Dresdner Bank   NatWest Securities Limited   UBS Limited   S.G. Warburg Securities

3,450,000 Shares
The above shares were underwritten by the following group of Asian Underwriters.

Merrill Lynch International Limited   **Goldman Sachs (Asia) L.L.C.**   **Lehman Brothers**

HSBC Corporate Finance Limited   The Nikko Securities Co. (Asia) Limited   Nomura International (Hong Kong) Limited
Robert Fleming & Co. Limited   LG Securities Co., Ltd   Peregrine Capital Limited   J.B. Were & Son

INVESTMENT BANKING AND THE COST OF ISSUING SECURITIES

A company can market its securities itself (as the U.S. government does), but most use investment bankers because of their expertise and experience. Table D.1 shows the ranking of the 15 leading securities underwriters in the United States and worldwide during 1996. Note that the five largest companies accounted for more than 55% of all underwritten securities offerings in the United States.

Investment Bankers

The **investment banker** serves as an intermediary between the issuer and the purchasers. Investment bankers usually provide advice regarding the type and terms of the security to issue and the market that provides the most attractive terms. They also help prepare the documentation (such as the prospectus) and underwrite and price the new issue.

Investment bankers also devote much time and energy to designing new securities. They try to develop new securities that will reduce issuers' funding costs and increase investors' after-tax risk-adjusted returns. In keeping with the Principle of Valuable Ideas, they do so to generate profitable securities marketing opportunities.

Underwriting

There are two types of underwriting: (1) purchase and sale and (2) best efforts. A true underwriting agreement involves a *purchase and sale,* in which an investment bank purchases the securities from the issuer at a fixed price and agrees to reoffer them to investors at a specified price less a specified commission. The securities company bears the risk that the entire issue may not be saleable at the initial offering price. If it is not, the securities company will sell the securities at the market clearing price and bear the loss. A purchase-and-sale underwriting thus involves a form of insurance.

In a *syndicated public offering,* an underwriting group, or syndicate, is formed to purchase the securities from the issuer and reoffer them to investors. The lead managing underwriter assembles a syndicate consisting of those securities companies it believes can best market the issue successfully.

Nonunderwritten Offerings

Securities issues sold through investment bankers are not always underwritten. In a *best-efforts* agreement, an investment bank commits to use its best efforts to market the securities to investors. There is no commitment to pur-

chase, and therefore there is little financial risk to the investment banker. Informally, the securities company may be called a *best-efforts underwriter,* even though it never owns the security. Public offerings of the securities of smaller, lesser-known companies are often handled on a best-efforts basis. This may be due to the risk involved: The issuer is unable to find a securities company willing to enter into a purchase-and-sale commitment (at least at an acceptable price).

In connection with private placements, securities companies customarily serve as *agent* for the issuer. The issuer sells the securities directly to investors. Securities companies help negotiate the terms of sale but don't underwrite the issue. Such offerings are sold on a best-efforts basis.

Some companies, including finance companies, may bypass the investment banks altogether and issue securities directly to investors. This reduces issuance expenses. The strategy can be cost effective when the issuer has a natural market it can exploit, such as current security holders.

In most cases, however, the investment banker has superior access to market information and to the channels of distribution. These advantages result from the investment banker's day-to-day interaction with prospective investors. Normally it is more economical for an issuer to sell securities through an investment banker.

Underwriters' Compensation

For their services in an underwritten public offering, underwriters charge a **gross underwriting spread.** It is calculated as a percentage of the public offering price of the issue. This spread has three components. The *management fee,* usually 15 to 20% of the total, compensates the managing underwriters for their assistance in designing the issue, preparing the documentation, forming the syndicate, and directing the offering process. The *underwriting fee,* usually 15% to 20% of the total, compensates for the underwriting risk. The *selling concession,* generally 60% to 70% of the total, compensates for the selling effort.

Underwriters' compensation represents a significant portion of the flotation expense. Table D.2 on page 686 provides a flotation expense breakdown for public offerings of various types and sizes during the period 1975–1996. It is generally most expensive to float a common stock issue and least expensive to float an issue of (nonconvertible) bonds. This reflects differences in underwriting risks. It is also due to the higher selling commissions required to distribute common stock issues, large portions of which are usually marketed very broadly to individual investors. Note the significant economies of scale in issuing securities.

TABLE D.1

Leading Managing Underwriters of Public Securities Offerings in 1996

	ALL DOMESTIC ISSUES[a] (FULL CREDIT TO LEAD MANAGER) JANUARY 1, 1996–DECEMBER 31, 1996			
Rank	Manager	Amount ($ millions)	%	Issues
1	Merrill Lynch	155,921.8	16.3	1,113
2	Lehman Brothers	100,713.7	10.6	782
3	Goldman Sachs	98,621.3	10.3	799
4	Salomon Brothers	96,364.2	10.1	632
5	Morgan Stanley	83,726.4	8.8	531
6	J.P. Morgan	68,730.4	7.2	469
7	Credit Suisse First Boston	60,108.4	6.3	453
8	Bear Stearns	42,364.0	4.4	373
9	Donaldson Lufkin & Jenrette	34,780.9	3.6	243
10	Smith Barney	29,880.4	3.1	375
11	NationsBank	19,417.4	2.0	278
12	Chase Manhattan	17,529.4	1.8	130
13	PaineWebber	16,081.0	1.7	131
14	Prudential Securities	14,177.2	1.5	137
15	UBS	10,668.0	1.1	129
	Industry Totals	954,246.1	100.0	8,937

[a]Full credit is given to the lead managing underwriter.
Source: Investment Dealers' Digest, January 6, 1997, p. 32.

	WORLDWIDE OFFERINGS[a] (ALL DEBT AND EQUITY) JANUARY 1, 1996–DECEMBER 31, 1996			
Rank	Manager	Amount ($ millions)	%	Issues
1	Merrill Lynch	187,702.6	13.0	1,329
2	Goldman Sachs	124,661.6	8.6	938
3	Lehman Brothers	112,239.7	7.8	875
4	Salomon Brothers	110,293.6	7.6	715
5	Morgan Stanley	105,484.0	7.3	675
6	J.P. Morgan	87,178.9	6.0	601
7	Credit Suisse First Boston	83,534.5	5.8	602
8	Bear Stearns	45,891.9	3.2	399
9	Donaldson Lufkin & Jenrette	35,615.1	2.5	264
10	Deutsche Morgan Grenfell	33,517.1	2.3	222
11	SBC Warburg	32,479.1	2.3	169
12	UBS	30,706.5	2.1	263
13	Smith Barney	30,397.2	2.1	386
14	ABN AMRO Hoare Govett	22,336.1	1.5	158
15	Chase Manhattan	21,248.0	1.5	159
	Industry Totals	1,442,778.0	100.0	11,891

[a]Full credit is given to the lead managing underwriter.
Source: Investment Dealers' Digest, January 6, 1997, p. 47.

TABLE D.2

Gross Underwriting Spread and Out-of-Pocket Expenses as Percentage of Offering Price for Registered Public Offerings, 1975–1996

ISSUE SIZE ($ MILLIONS)	COMMON STOCK			PREFERRED STOCK			CONVERTIBLE PREFERRED AND CONVERTIBLE DEBT			BONDS		
	Gross Underwriting Spread (%)	Out-of-Pocket Expense[a] (%)	Total (%)	Gross Underwriting Spread (%)	Out-of-Pocket Expense[a] (%)	Total (%)	Gross Underwriting Spread (%)	Out-of-Pocket Expense[a] (%)	Total (%)	Gross Underwriting Spread (%)	Out-of-Pocket Expense[a] (%)	Total (%)
Under 10.0	8.72	7.41	16.13	6.27	4.22	10.49	8.36	7.01	15.37	3.08	2.47	5.55
10.0 to 24.9	6.46	2.85	9.31	2.51	1.07	3.58	4.67	2.04	6.71	1.02	1.10	2.12
25.0 to 49.9	5.80	1.61	7.41	2.08	0.55	2.63	3.27	1.05	4.32	0.88	0.59	1.47
50.0 to 99.9	5.18	0.97	6.15	2.00	0.35	2.35	2.71	0.59	3.30	0.78	0.39	1.17
100.0 to 199.9	4.77	0.68	5.45	2.81	0.31	3.12	2.34	0.40	2.74	0.81	0.29	1.10
200 to 500	4.57	0.50	5.07	2.99	0.21	3.20	1.98	0.19	2.17	0.76	0.14	0.90
Over 500	4.61	0.29	4.90	2.87	0.13	3.00	1.27	0.09	1.36	0.73	0.10	0.83

[a]Includes legal fees, accounting fees, SEC filing fee, blue sky expenses, and printing, mailing, and miscellaneous out-of-pocket expenses.
Source: Securities Data Company

Negotiated versus Competitive Offerings

A company can offer securities publicly using either competitive bidding or a negotiated offering. Under **competitive bidding,** the issuer specifies the type of securities it wishes to sell and invites securities companies to bid for the issue. It puts the securities up for bid, and the bidding process determines which investment bankers will market the issue and at what price.

In a **negotiated offering,** the issuer selects one or more securities companies to manage the offering and works closely with them to design the terms of the issue and determine the appropriate time to issue the securities. Currently, registered public utility holding companies are required to offer securities competitively, but other companies are free to choose the offering technique. Other electric utilities tend to offer debt and preferred stock by competitive bid (except during periods of heightened market volatility) but generally sell common stock on a negotiated basis. Railroads frequently sell equipment trust certificates through competitive bidding.

Are Competitive Offerings Cheaper?

Which offering method costs less? The question has been hotly debated, and the evidence is inconclusive. However, recent studies suggest that the competitive process usually does not lead to significant cost savings, except perhaps during stable market periods when strong competition among bidding groups results in lower costs. Competitive bidding generally results in lower underwriting spreads, but competitive underwritings may involve greater underwriting spreads than negotiated underwritings during periods of great market uncertainty.

Moreover, the negotiated offering process offers greater flexibility in the design of the securities and the timing of the issue. The issuer has not committed in advance to a specific set of terms (for example, maturity and redemption terms) or to a particular offering date (in competitive bidding, the date bids are to be received).

A negotiated offering also gives securities companies the opportunity to form the most effective selling group for the issue. Rather than splitting them into competing bidding groups, the negotiation process provides a stronger incentive for securities companies to assess the demand for, and stimulate interest in, the issue prior to pricing. Because they know that they will have the securities to sell, they will not hesitate to begin marketing activities. Competitive bidders, in contrast, would lose their marketing investment if they were not selected.

Shelf Registration

The Securities and Exchange Commission's Rule 415 is commonly known as **shelf registration.** Rule 415 allows a company to register an inventory of securities of a particular type sufficient to cover its financing requirements for up to two years and sell the securities whenever it chooses. The securities remain "on the shelf" until the issuer finds market conditions sufficiently attractive to sell them.

Shelf registration has improved companies' financing flexibility. A company does not have to file a new registration statement each time it offers securities, which reduces flotation costs. Securities can be sold within minutes. Also, a single shelf registration statement can cover many types of debt securities. This permits issuers to design the security at the time they sell it to exploit any special investor preferences and minimize their cost of funds.

Rule 415 has effectively extended competitive bidding to issues of securities by the roughly 2000 large companies that qualify to use shelf registration. Securities companies and institutional investors can bid for securities that a company has on the shelf. But the evidence is mixed on whether Rule 415 has had any impact on transaction costs.

Other Costs of Issuing Securities

In addition to the gross underwriting spread, there are out-of-pocket expenses, such as lawyers' and accountants' fees, and engraving, printing, and mailing costs. Out-of-pocket expenses tend to be fixed expenses and are therefore a significant cost factor only in connection with small offerings.

Any market price decline associated with the announcement of the offering and subsequent marketing activity is also a cost. This last cost is most significant in connection with public stock offerings.

Market Impact of a Stock Issue
A company's share price often declines upon the announcement of a public offering. This may seem puzzling. If the corporation intends to invest the issue proceeds in positive-NPV projects, the share price should increase. But evidence indicates that the Signaling Principle is at work.

The share price falls because the offering apparently sends a negative signal to investors. This reaction has been explained in terms of asymmetric information. If management acts in its shareholders' best interest, it will refrain from issuing shares when it believes the company's stock is relatively undervalued in the market and will choose to sell new shares when it believes the company's shares are relatively overvalued. Accordingly, the announcement of the new issue may signal overvaluation and lead to a negative market reaction. Taking this line of reasoning a step further, the larger the size of the offering, the more the share price should decrease.

Self-Check

1. Explain the difference between a negotiated and a competitive offer.

2. Distinguish between an underwritten and a best-efforts agreement.

3. What is the role of the underwriters in a general cash offer? What are the three components of the gross underwriting spread?

4. What is a shelf registration?

5. Why might a company's stock price decline when the company announces a public offering of new common shares?

PRIVATE PLACEMENTS

Instead of selling securities to the general investing public, companies can sell securities directly to institutional investors through a private placement.

Features of Privately Placed Securities

Privately placed securities are not registered and therefore are not freely tradable. For this reason, securities regulations require companies to offer securities privately only to investors sophisticated enough to make an independent determination of their investment merits. Such investors include life insurance companies, property and casualty insurance companies, credit companies, pension funds, and wealthy individuals. Table D.3 on page 688 shows the principal sources of private placement funds. Table D.4 on page 688 lists the 25 largest private placement buyers. The dominant role of life insurance companies is evident in both.

Advantages of a Private Placement

A private placement offers the following advantages in comparison with a public offering:

◆ *Lower issuance costs* for smaller issues. A private placement avoids the costs of registering the securities, printing prospectuses, and obtaining credit ratings. Also, the private placement agent's fee is generally a lot less than the underwriting expenses for a comparable public offering and can be avoided altogether if the issuer negotiates directly with investors.

◆ *Issues can be placed more quickly* for companies that do not qualify for shelf registration. Registering securities requires time to prepare the registration statement and have the SEC review it.

◆ *Greater flexibility of issue size.* The private market is more receptive to smaller issues. Issues of only a few million dollars each are not uncommon. Public debt

TABLE D.3
Lender Shares in the Traditional Market for Private Placements, 1990–1992

TYPE OF LENDER	SHARE OF DOLLAR VOLUME
Life insurance companies	82.6%
Foreign banks	3.6
U.S. commercial banks	3.3
Pension, endowment, and trust funds	1.7
Finance companies	1.4
Property and casualty insurance companies	1.4
Mutual funds	0.7
Thrifts	0.7
Others	4.6
Total	100.0%

Source: Carey et al. (1993), p. 27.

TABLE D.4
Twenty-five Largest Buyers of Private Placements in the United States, 1993 (in $ millions)

RANK	COMPANY	AMOUNT
1	Prudential Life Insurance	$5000.00
2	Metropolitan Life Insurance	4104.10
3	Teachers Insurance and Annuity	4050.00
4	John Hancock Mutual Life	3932.00
5	Principle Financial Group	3462.30
6	CIGNA	3200.00
7	New York Life	1800.00
8	Travelers Insurance	1455.00
9	Mass Mutual	1300.00
10	Pacific Mutual Life	1039.00
11	Northwestern Mutual Life	954.70
12	American General	850.00
13	Lincoln National Life	714.80
14	Great-West Life & Annuity	651.50
15	Hartford Insurance	650.00
16	Mutual of Omaha	625.00
17	Nationwide Life	625.00
18	Mimlic Asset Management	532.50
19	New England Mutual Life	437.30
20	Aegon USA	400.00
21	State of Wisconsin Investment Board	400.00
22	Provident Life & Accident	387.50
23	Lutheran Brotherhood	337.90
24	America United Life	242.70
25	Canada Life Assurance	241.90

Source: Private Placement Letter (September 19, 1994), p. 6.

and preferred stock issues of less than $50 million principal amount are usually more costly, because their small size decreases their liquidity and thus lessens their attractiveness to investors.

◆ *Greater flexibility of security arrangements* and other terms. Private investors are capable of analyzing complex security arrangements, and it is easier to tailor the terms of an issue to suit both sides of the transaction. It is also easier to obtain lenders' consents to a change in terms should the company's circumstances change, both because the debtholders are sophisticated and also because there are fewer of them.

◆ *Lower cost of resolving financial distress.* Private debt tends to be easier than public debt to restructure, because it will generally involve fewer and more sophisticated investors. Empirical research has found that financial distress is more likely to be resolved outside bankruptcy when more of the company's debt is owed to banks, but is less likely to be resolved outside bankruptcy when the company has more than one public debt issue outstanding.

◆ *More favorable share price reaction than a public offering.* Studies have found that the stock market generally reacts positively to the announcement of private placements of debt, convertible debt, and equity. The larger private placements of debt have tended to elicit the most positive market response, and the positive impact tends to be especially large for companies that have never issued debt publicly. These results are consistent with the notion that private placement leads to reduced information asymmetries, increased monitoring, and certification.

In connection with a public offering, the investment banks investigate the affairs of the issuer on behalf of the investing public (the process is referred to as *due diligence*). In a private placement, the institutional investors conduct their own investigation. Private placement may therefore allow investors access to information about a company that isn't available to the general investing public. With respect to monitoring, privately placed debt issues usually have more restrictive covenants than comparable public debt issues. The tighter covenants improve monitoring efficiency. Finally, the purchasers—because they tend to be large, sophisticated institutional investors—are making a comment about the company's quality in their very willingness to purchase and hold the company's securities.

A larger private placement, because of the accompanying increased commitment of funds, may intensify all of these considerations, thereby communicating greater confidence in the company's quality.

Disadvantages of a Private Placement

A private placement has the following disadvantages relative to a public offering:

◆ *Higher yield.* To compensate for the lack of liquidity, purchasers of privately placed securities require a yield premium relative to publicly traded securities. Purchasers of privately placed common stock require a substantial discount to the price at which the shares would trade in a liquid secondary market.

◆ *More stringent covenants and more restrictive terms.* Private issuers are often not public companies and thus not subject to the SEC's reporting requirements. Private purchasers insist on tighter covenant restrictions to compensate for the greater agency costs. The covenants alert investors when something has "gone wrong," such as a sharp reduction in net worth. Private lenders have also insisted on tighter protection against *event risk,* the risk that stockholders might initiate events such as a leveraged buyout that could expropriate bondholder wealth. These covenants can limit a company's operating flexibility, possibly forcing it to pass up profitable investment opportunities.

Rule 144A Private Placements

SEC Rule 144A has broadened the market for private-placement financing in the United States, especially for foreign issuers. In a **Rule 144A private placement,** the issuer sells its unregistered securities to one or more investment banks, which then resell the securities to "qualified institutional buyers" (QIBs).[3] This process is much like an underwritten public offering.

Self-Check

1. Who are the main purchasers of privately placed securities?

2. What are the advantages and disadvantages of a private placement as compared to a general cash offer?

3. What is a Rule 144A private placement?

---

[3]A QIB generally is defined as a financial institution that invests on a discretionary basis at least $100 million in securities of unaffiliated companies or Treasury securities. QIBs can trade freely with each other in securities that have not been registered with the SEC.

RIGHTS ISSUES

Instead of offering common stock directly to the general public, a company may offer new stock to its current shareholders on a privileged-subscription basis. This is called a rights offering, because the company distributes to its shareholders *rights* to subscribe for additional shares at a specified price.

From World War II to the 1960s, roughly two-thirds of all common stock issues were rights issues. But beginning in the late 1960s, virtually all large U.S. companies, which tend to have widely dispersed shareholdings, obtained shareholder approval to eliminate preemptive rights. However, companies outside the United States tend to rely heavily on rights offerings to raise additional equity capital. For example, the London Stock Exchange changed its rules in 1975 to allow general cash offers. Nevertheless, rights issues continue to be the predominant method of external equity financing there. In some countries, companies are required by law to sell new share issues through rights offerings.

EXAMPLE   *Eurotunnel's Two Rights Issues*

The Eurotunnel project, begun in 1984 and completed in 1994, involved the construction of twin-bore rail tunnels beneath the English Channel to link the rail systems of France and the United Kingdom. When cost overruns made it necessary to raise additional common equity, Eurotunnel conducted an underwritten rights issue in November 1990 that raised £532 million (net of expenses).

Further cost overruns necessitated another equity offering. This time Eurotunnel raised £816 million (net of expenses) through an underwritten rights offering in May and June 1994. ■

How a Rights Offering Works

In a rights offering, the company distributes to each shareholder one right for each share the holder owns as of the specified *record date* for the offering. Rights are call options on newly issued shares. The company will indicate the number of rights required to purchase one new share of stock. For instance, stockholders may be given rights to buy one new share for every three shares already owned. As with other market-traded options, a right has a time until expiration and a strike price. The time until expiration is called the *subscription period*. The strike price for a specified number of rights is called the *subscription price*.

Shareholders can either (1) exercise the rights and subscribe for shares or (2) sell the rights if they are transferable (they usually are). If the shareholders do neither, the rights expire, worthless, at the close of business on the expiration date. If shareholders wish to purchase extra shares, they can purchase additional rights from other shareholders who choose to sell their rights. If the company gives shareholders an *oversubscription privilege* to purchase the shares for which other shareholders fail to subscribe, they can buy them from the issuer to the extent that they are available.

Value of Rights

The Options Principle states that options are valuable. Because a right is a call option, then, it will always have a positive value prior to its expiration. Enrichment topic B shows that the value of an option, and therefore of a right, is a function of (1) the strike price, (2) the value of the underlying stock, (3) the time until expiration, (4) the variance of the underlying stock's return, and (5) the riskless return. In addition, the value of a right depends on its dilutive effect, which is caused by its creation of new equity. Loosely speaking, the dilutive effect is the difference between the strike price (the new equity) and the market value (existing equity). Recall that when the value of the underlying stock is more than the strike price, a call option is in-the-money. The smaller the strike price relative to the share price, the more valuable the call option.

To encourage subscription, rights are issued in-the-money. That is, the issuer sets the subscription price at less than the market price of its stock on the record date. Because of the short time to expiration, the exercise value—which is based on the difference between the strike price and share price—is the main thing that determines the value of a right. That is, with a very short life, the time premium of the in-the-money option is negligible. For simplicity, then, we ignore the time premium on the right.

The initial value of each right just after the offering is announced, and when the stock is trading *rights-on* (that is, the rights are still attached to the stock), is approximately

$$R = \frac{P_R - S}{N + 1} \tag{D.1}$$

where R is the value of the right, P_R is the market value of a share trading rights-on, S is the strike price, and N is the number of rights to purchase one new share.

The Long Island Lighting Company Rights Offering

A number of years ago the Long Island Lighting Company offered 6,402,515 additional shares of its common stock to its current shareholders on the basis of one new share for seven rights (that is, each seven shares already owned), plus a subscription price of $17.15 per new share during the 18-day subscription period. At the time, shares were trading at $18.375. What was the approximate value of each right?

Using equation (D.1), the initial value of each right was

$$R = \frac{18.375 - 17.15}{7 + 1} = \$0.1531$$

After the ex-date, the stock is said to trade *ex-rights* because the purchaser of the shares is not entitled to receive the rights. On the ex-date, then, the share price decreases by the value of the right, which is no longer attached to it. Therefore, the share price ex-rights, P_E, is

$$P_E = P_R - R \qquad \text{(D.2)}$$

In the case of the Long Island Lighting rights offering,

$$P_E = \$18.375 - \$0.1531 = \$18.2219$$

Immediately after the ex-date, the market value of each right will vary with the price of the company's common stock:

$$R = \frac{P_E - S}{N} \qquad \text{(D.3)}$$

In this equation we divide by N, rather than $N + 1$, because the rights have separated from the shares.

Underwritten Rights Offering

Companies would generally prefer to have an investment banker stand ready to purchase unsubscribed shares on an underwritten basis rather than have to reduce the subscription price to ensure a successful offering, as with the Eurotunnel rights offerings. The underwriters are paid a standby fee for each share offered for subscription, plus a take-up fee payable on shares acquired by the underwriters through the exercise of rights during the subscription period and on shares remaining unsubscribed at the end of the period.

Advantages and Disadvantages of a Rights Offering

The fundamental idea underlying a rights offering is to provide shareholders with the option to retain their proportionate ownership in a company when it sells additional common shares. However, because of the separation of ownership and control, this probably benefits only shareholders with large holdings.

It's often argued that a rights offering is beneficial to shareholders because they can buy shares at a bargain price or because they perceive the rights as a kind of dividend. But a stockholder receives no benefits from the rights other than the option of retaining proportionate ownership. The company's share price falls on the ex-date, and the decrease in price offsets the value of a right, as in the case of a stock dividend. The shareholder is just as well off after the rights offering as before it, provided that he either sells the rights or exercises them.

The main benefit of a rights offering is that it protects existing shareholders from a potential loss of wealth that can result from a public offering. To induce sales, shares are offered at a price below the current market value. In a public offering, this inducement transfers wealth from existing shareholders to the purchasers of the newly created shares. The rights offering avoids this wealth transfer. It gives the inducement to existing shareholders, so long as they sell or exercise their rights.

A rights offering may also be more beneficial than a public offering to a company that does not have broad market appeal or a company that has concentrated stock ownership, because it enables the selling effort to be focused on investors who already own shares and are therefore familiar with the company. In addition, common stock issued in a rights offering can be purchased on margin, whereas common stock issued in a public offering cannot.

On the other hand, there are two principal disadvantages to a rights offering: It generally takes longer to complete, and it eliminates the possible transaction cost savings of selling large blocks of shares to institutions that don't currently own the stock.

Dividend Reinvestment Plans

Many companies sponsor dividend reinvestment plans. A **dividend reinvestment plan (DRP)** allows each common stockholder to use her dividends to purchase shares of the company's common stock. In a *new-issue DRP*, the company sells newly issued shares to its shareholders. The price is often slightly (up to 5%) below the stock's market price. New-issue DRPs resemble rights offerings; in effect, the company offers new shares pro rata to existing shareholders. An *open-market DRP* is different. In such a plan, the company uses the reinvested dividends to repurchase shares on behalf of shareholders. A new-issue DRP is a source of new capital; an open-market DRP is not.

Self-Check

1. Is a right a call option or a put option? What are the primary determinants of the value of a right?

2. What is the difference between a share trading rights-on and a share trading ex-rights?

3. What are the advantages and disadvantages of a rights offering as compared to a general cash offer?

4. What is a dividend reinvestment plan (DRP)?

DILUTION

Practitioners often worry about possible dilution when a company sells additional common shares. **Dilution** refers to a decrease in equity value per common share. The term has at least three different meanings:

1. Dilution in percentage ownership
2. Dilution in price (a market value change)
3. Dilution in book value or earnings per share (a book value change)

Can you see why the three are not identical? The three meanings create confusion. Worse, it also leads to misconceptions about the impact of accounting dilution. The real issue is whether there is a loss of shareholder wealth. As we have said many times, it's market value that matters!

Dilution in Percentage Ownership

Dilution in percentage ownership occurs whenever a company sells additional shares and a shareholder's percentage voting interest falls. The following example illustrates that no change in shareholder wealth need occur.

EXAMPLE *Dilution in Percentage Ownership*

Let's say you own 10,000 shares of Reliable Fabrics Corporation, a company your father founded. (He gave you the shares as a graduation gift!) There are 200,000 shares outstanding, so you own 5% (= 10,000/200,000) of the company. You get 5% of the dividends and cast 5% of the votes.

Suppose Reliable needs to sell 50,000 shares to finance expansion. It sells the shares in a general cash offer. You don't buy any. Your percentage ownership falls to 4% (= 10,000/250,000). Your ownership has been diluted. But has your wealth been affected? Not necessarily. Suppose your shares were worth $12 each before the offering and Reliable issued the new shares for $12 each. Prior to the new issue, Reliable was worth $2.4 million (= [12]200,000). You owned 5%, worth $120,000 (= [0.05]2.4 million). After the new issue, you own 4%, also worth $120,000 (= [0.04]3.0 million). So the decrease in percentage ownership has not changed your wealth. ∎

A rights issue would let you maintain your percentage ownership. If this is important to you and your fellow shareholders, a rights offering may be the way to go.

Dilution in Value

Let's tackle the next two forms of dilution at the same time. The following example illustrates how dilution in book value can occur without any dilution in market value.

Dilution in Value: Market Value versus Book Value

International Nickel Corporation plans to build a new nickel smelter, which will cost $36 million. Table D.5 on page 694 shows that the company currently has 10 million shares outstanding but no debt. Its share price is $10, giving International Nickel equity with a market value of $100 million. The company's equity has a book value of $14 per share.

Let's consider two possibilities. First, suppose the project NPV is $20 million. Announcing the project causes the share price to rise by $2 (= 20/10) to $12. (The prospectus for the offering contains enough information for investors to gauge the project's NPV.) International Nickel will have to sell 3 million (= 36 million/12) new shares to raise the $36 million project cost. Its aggregate market value rises to $156 million (= [12]13 million). Its aggregate book value rises to $176 million (= 140 + 36) while its book value per share falls to $13.54 (= 176/13). The NPV is positive, and International Nickel should undertake the project, despite the dilution in book value per share.

Suppose instead the project's NPV is −$10 million. Announcing the project would cause the share price to fall by $1 (= 10/10) to $9. International Nickel would have to sell 4 million (= 36 million/9) new shares. Its aggregate market value would be $126 million (= [9]14 million). Its aggregate book value would again be $176 million while its book value per share would fall to $12.57 (= 176/14). Once again book value per share falls, but by more than in the case of a positive-NPV project.

Book value per share falls in both cases. This *always* happens when the market-to-book ratio is less than 1. But market value, not book value, is what matters. The company should undertake the project if its NPV is positive—even though book value per share suffers dilution. Market value per share sends the right signal. The negative-NPV project dilutes market value per share (to $9 from $10). The positive-NPV project has the opposite effect. ■

Some practitioners worry instead about dilution in earnings per share. But it can be just as misleading as dilution in book value. For example, EPS might be higher or lower if the project NPV is positive or negative. In table D.5, financing the project with equity dilutes EPS but more so in the negative-NPV case.[4]

Self-Check

1. What are the three types of dilution? Which one should be of paramount concern to stockholders?

2. True or False?

a. If new shares are sold for more than the current book value per share, the book value per share will increase.

b. If new shares are sold for more than the current book value per share, the market value per share will increase.

c. The company announces a positive-NPV project that will be financed by issuing new shares. Assume no issuing costs or signaling. The market price per share should increase.

---

[4]Problem B9 asks you to verify the EPS calculations.

TABLE D.5
The Impact of International Nickel's Equity Offering

	PRIOR TO THE OFFERING	NEW PROJECT HAS POSITIVE NPV	NEW PROJECT HAS NEGATIVE NPV
Number of common shares	10,000,000	13,000,000	14,000,000
Share price	$10.00	$12.00	$9.00
Aggregate market value	$100 million	$156 million	$126 million
Aggregate book value	140 million	176 million	176 million
Book value per share	$14.00	$13.54	$12.57
Market/Book	0.71	0.89	0.72
Return on book equity	12%	12%	12%
Return on new equity		13	12
Earnings	$16,800,000	$21,480,000	$21,120,000
Earnings per share	$1.68	$1.65	$1.51
Project NPV		$20 million	−$10 million

GOING PUBLIC AND GOING PRIVATE

When a company's common stock is not registered for listing on an exchange or for trading in the over-the-counter market, it's said to be privately held. Privately held companies normally do not have to file regular quarterly financial reports with the SEC. Therefore they are also private in the sense that much of the information concerning them isn't public.

When a company first sells its common stock to the investing public in an **initial public offering (IPO)**, it becomes publicly held. It also becomes subject to the regular reporting requirements of the securities laws. On the other hand, when a small group of investors (usually including the company's managers) buys up all the common stock, the company is said to *go private* because it becomes privately held.

Going Public

Companies go public through an IPO. It is a watershed event in the life of a company. The decision to go public depends on a number of factors. The key stockholders must conclude that the advantages outweigh the disadvantages.

To make a successful IPO, a company must (1) find capable underwriters to sponsor and assist it and (2) complete its offering at an acceptable price. Its ability to achieve these goals will depend largely on its profitability and future prospects. A company that wishes to go public normally tries to do so when it believes the stock market is most receptive.

Table D.6 shows how the volume of IPOs varied during the 22-year period from 1975 to 1996. The receptivity of investors depends to a great extent on the overall prospect for capital gains, which depends on the tone of

the stock market and on how investors expect these capital gains to be taxed. The new-issues booms of 1980 to 1983 and 1991 to 1996 (and still continuing in 1997) both coincided with major stock market rallies. The first rally also began soon after the 1978 reduction in the capital gains tax rate and was enhanced by another reduction in 1981.

Preparing the Company to Go Public Before going public, companies may have to modify some of their practices and put dealings with insiders on an arm's-length basis. Individuals from outside the company usually have to be added to the board of directors to monitor the company's performance on behalf of public investors. The company will have to change its accounting procedures to conform to generally accepted accounting principles, including regular audits, if they do not conform already.

Pricing the Offering Underwriters generally try to price an IPO 10% to 15% below the expected trading price. In some cases it is substantially more than 15% "underpriced." Underwriters apparently underprice IPOs to increase their attractiveness and the likelihood that the shares will perform well in the aftermarket. However, research shows that IPOs generally underperform the market for up to three years after the initial price surge following their issuance.

Advantages of Going Public

There are several advantages to going public.

New Capital Going public enables a company to raise additional capital. Also, shares generally bring a higher price in the public market than in the venture capital or private placement markets.

TABLE D.6
Volume of Initial Public Offerings, 1975–1996

| | INITIAL PUBLIC OFFERINGS | | | S&P 500 INDEX | |
YEAR	Number	Aggregate Value	Average Size	Beginning of Year	Change During Year
1975	5	$ 176	$35.2	68.6	31.5%
1976	40	337	8.4	90.2	19.2
1977	31	221	7.1	107.5	−11.5
1978	38	225	5.9	95.1	1.1
1979	62	398	6.4	96.1	12.3
1980	149	1,387	9.3	107.9	25.9
1981	347	3,055	8.8	135.8	−9.7
1982	122	1,339	10.9	122.6	14.7
1983	683	12,438	18.2	140.6	17.3
1984	355	3,808	10.7	164.9	1.4
1985	353	8,348	23.6	167.2	26.4
1986	702	18,088	25.8	211.3	14.6
1987	522	17,109	32.8	242.2	2.0
1988	228	5,940	26.1	247.1	12.4
1989	209	6,082	29.1	277.7	27.3
1990	172	4,519	26.3	353.4	−6.6
1991	367	16,411	44.7	330.2	26.3
1992	517	24,138	46.7	417.1	4.5
1993	709	41,721	58.8	435.7	7.1
1994	607	28,341	46.7	466.5	−1.5
1995	584	30,241	51.8	459.3	34.1
1996	874	50,013	57.2	615.9	20.3

Sources: Securities Data Company and Bloomberg, L.P.

Liquidity and Diversification for Current Shareholders   Existing shareholders usually sell portions of their shares as part of the IPO. This gives them a cash return on their investment and allows them to diversify their investment portfolios.

Creation of a Negotiable Instrument   Going public makes the common stock negotiable and creates a visible market value. After going public, the company usually finds it easier to acquire other companies in exchange for shares of its stock. If all else is equal, marketable securities are worth more because of their greater liquidity.

Increased Equity Financing Flexibility   A publicly traded company is able to raise additional equity more quickly and more cheaply than it could were it not public.

Enhanced Company Image   Because of the standards investment bankers apply before agreeing to take a company public, going public represents a milestone in a company's development.

Disadvantages of Going Public

Going public is not without disadvantages, however.

Expense of Going Public   Going public involves significant expenses—generally from 6 to 13% of the amount of the offering, and even more for very small offerings. Going public can also take a substantial amount of valuable management time.

Higher Estate Valuation   Negotiability increases a stock's value because of liquidity. Estate tax obligations are consequently greater when a stock is publicly traded. On the other hand, a public market provides a way of selling shares to get cash to pay the tax.

Dilution of Ownership Interest   Existing shareholders lose a portion of their ownership interest to public shareholders. This can be a significant change, and existing shareholders can even lose voting control.

Disclosure Requirements   A public company is subject to regulations governing regular reporting to shareholders, proxy solicitation and insider trading, and other matters. A public company must publicly report on a regular basis information regarding its operating results, financial condition, significant business developments, and other sensitive matters such as officers' compensation and transactions between the company and its management.

Accountability to Public Shareholders and Market Pressure to Perform in the Short Term

As a result of information asymmetries, the managers of a publicly held company might make decisions that look good in the short run but are significantly inferior in the long run. "Managing" quarter-to-quarter earnings can also hamper a company's operating flexibility.

Pressure to Pay Dividends

Public shareholders expect the company to begin paying dividends eventually. This may not be best if the company is able to reinvest the funds in positive-NPV projects.

Decision to List the Shares on an Exchange

When a company goes public, it must decide where its shares will trade. Each of the exchanges and NASDAQ have established minimum listing requirements (net income, shares held by other than insiders, and so forth) and reporting requirements. The NYSE's minimum requirements for listing are the most demanding. In order to have its stock listed on an exchange or quoted in the NASDAQ, a company that meets the listing/quotation criteria files an application, pays a modest fee, and agrees to abide by the disclosure requirements and other rules.

Are there benefits to listing the stock on the NYSE or some other exchange rather than having it quoted on NASDAQ? An exchange appoints a single market maker for each stock it lists. The market maker commits its capital to maintain an orderly market and must adhere to the rules of the exchange. In contrast, there is no central market and no single market maker committed to an over-the-counter (OTC) stock. Many companies feel that prestige is associated with their stock being exchange listed. Research shows that exchange markets have lower transaction costs. However, they are not necessarily more liquid than the NASDAQ market. Also, many prestigious companies, including Apple Computer, Intel, and Microsoft, have remained with NASDAQ even though they could qualify for exchange listing.

Going Private

Going private is the reverse of going public. When a small group of investors (usually in conjunction with members of senior management) purchases the entire common equity of a publicly traded company, the company becomes privately held. It is no longer subject to the financial reporting requirements of a public company. If the disadvantages of being publicly owned outweigh the advantages, it's possible to revert to private ownership. Because going public and going private each involve substantial transaction costs, we don't observe companies frequently switching back and forth.

Self-Check

1. What are the advantages of going public?

2. What are the disadvantages of going public?

SUMMARY

There are many alternative ways to issue securities, including through investment bankers. In a given situation, a company must weigh the costs and benefits and choose its best alternative.

- A company that needs to raise long-term funds externally can sell securities in the public market or in the private market. It can sell them directly to investors or engage a securities company to assist it.
- The bulk of the securities issued by U.S. companies are sold in the domestic market in negotiated underwritten offerings.
- The initial decision involves what type of security to sell. Most important, the company must decide in light of its capital structure objectives and its current financial condition whether to sell debt or equity securities. Economies of scale involved in issuing securities make it impractical for a company to sell debt and equity securities each time it needs funds

in the exact debt and equity proportions embodied in the company's target capital structure.

- After deciding what type of security to sell, the company must determine which market offers the most attractive terms. The private market offers some advantages but also suffers some disadvantages relative to the public market. The private market is generally more attractive than the public market for small debt issues or for debt issues backed by complex security arrangements. The Eurobond market is another alternative.
- There are a number of sources of additional common equity capital: retained earnings, public offerings of new shares, rights offerings of new shares to current shareholders, private placement of new shares, sale of new shares through a dividend reinvestment or employee stock plan, or a contribution of shares in lieu of cash to the company's pension plan. Public offerings account for most of the new common equity capital companies raise from external sources.

- New securities can be marketed in a variety of ways. For example, they may be underwritten by one or more investment banking companies, sold on a best-efforts basis by one or more investment banking companies, sold directly to the public by the company, or, in the case of common stock, sold through either a rights offering or a dividend reinvestment plan to current shareholders.

- Issuance costs are proportionately lower for larger issues.

- Bonds have lower explicit issuance costs than common stock for comparable dollar amounts.

- Common stock is most often issued through a general cash offer on a negotiated basis. Rights offerings are rare in the United States but are the typical method of offering additional common stock in many other countries.

- Dilution is a reduction in the market value per equity share that accompanies the issue of new shares. The term *dilution* is also applied to a reduction in the percentage of shares owned or a reduction in earnings per share.

- Going public is a watershed event in a company's life. It enables a company to raise capital and creates a negotiable instrument for use in acquisitions or for other purposes but obligates a company to make regular financial disclosures and to deal with a new constituency, its public shareholders. A company should go public only if it has determined that the advantages outweigh the disadvantages of being publicly held.

EQUATION SUMMARY

(D.1)
$$R = \frac{P_R - S}{N + 1}$$

(D.2)
$$P_E = P_R - R$$

(D.3)
$$R = \frac{P_E - S}{N}$$

TOPIC REVIEW ACTIVITIES

SELF-TEST PROBLEM

1. (Value of a right) Rollins Company common stock is selling for $33.50 per share. Rollins has announced an offer of additional shares of its common stock to current shareholders on the basis of one new share for four rights plus a subscription price of $27.50 per new share.
   a. What is the value of one right?
   b. What should happen to the stock price when it goes ex-rights?

SOLUTION TO SELF-TEST PROBLEM

1. a. The value of a right is:

$$R = \frac{P_R - S}{N + 1} = \frac{33.50 - 27.50}{4 + 1} = \frac{6.00}{5} = \$1.20$$

   b. When the stock goes ex-rights, the stock should drop by $1.20, the value of a right.

QUESTIONS

1. How do public and private financing differ?
2. Cite three advantages and the major disadvantage of private financing.
3. What are the three meanings of the term *dilution?* Why are they different? Which ones are important to shareholders?
4. Why would you expect debt securities sold in a Rule 144A private placement to offer a lower yield than the same securities sold in a traditional private placement?
5. Name the three explicit transaction cost components of the gross underwriting spread in an underwritten public offering.

6. Explain why the real transaction cost of an issue consists of the market impact as well as the gross spread.
7. What is a rights offering?
8. Explain the difference between a negotiated and a competitive offering.
9. Explain why the announcement of a public offering of common stock generally has a negative impact on the company's share price.
10. Describe the major advantages and disadvantages of going public.
11. How is stockholders' wealth affected when a company sells new shares of common stock for a price:
    a. Greater than its book value?
    b. Less than its book value?

CHALLENGING QUESTIONS

12. Explain why a company making a new securities issue, especially one that includes some component of equity, must be concerned with more than simply the explicit transaction costs such as underwriter fees.
13. Explain why the shelf registration process might lead to a more efficient capital market.

PROBLEM SET A

A1. (Underwriting costs) Green Shoe Company needs to raise $20 million for a new project.
    a. It can sell new stock for an estimated price of $24. If the underwriting spread and out-of-pocket expenses will total 9% of the offering price, what will be the net proceeds per share to Green Shoe? How many shares will Green Shoe have to sell to raise its needed funds?

b. It can sell new bonds for an estimated price of $1010. If the underwriting spread and out-of-pocket expenses will total 3.5% of the offering price, what will be the net proceeds per bond to Green Shoe? How many bonds will Green Shoe have to sell to raise its needed funds?

A2. (Underwriting costs) Eurosport Spas is issuing 1,200,000 shares at an offering price of $20 per share. The management fee is $0.25 per share, the underwriting fee is $0.25 per share, and the selling concession is $0.75 per share.

a. What is the gross underwriting spread per share? What is the total dollar amount of the underwriting costs?

b. What are the gross underwriting costs as a percentage of the offering price?

A3. (Rights issue) Upton Signal Company has 600,000 outstanding shares with a market value of $40 per share. Upton has announced a rights offering of 200,000 new shares with a subscription price of $30 each.

a. What is the total market value of the company before the rights offering? What should be the total market value of the company after the rights issue?

b. How many rights will be needed to purchase a new share?

c. What is the value of one right?

d. What should be the ex-rights price of Upton Signal stock?

A4. (Value of a right) When Mammalcloners Company goes ex-rights, the market price per share is expected to drop from $44.50 to $43.25. What is the value of one right?

A5. (Cost of private placement versus public offering) Base Metal Company is considering the two debt financing alternatives shown below. What is the cost of funds from each source? (Calculate the yield to maturity assuming semiannual compounding.)
Private placement: 20-year maturity, 8.20% coupon paid semiannually, offering price = 100% of face value, and issuing costs = 1.5% of the offering price.
Public offering: 20-year maturity, 8.00% coupon paid semiannually, offering price = 100% of face value, and issuing costs = 4.0% of the offering price.

PROBLEM SET B

B1. (Flotation costs and cost of preferred stock) A company is considering issuing preferred stock that bears an 8% APR dividend rate (payable quarterly). The issue is perpetual. Issuance expenses are 1%.

a. What is the cost of this preferred stock?

b. How does your answer to part **a** change if the preferred stock matures in one lump sum after 10 years?

c. How does your answer to part **b** change if the issue has a sinking fund calling for equal payments in years 9 and 10?

B2. (Public offering versus rights issue) Consider a company about to make a new equity issue. The company feels it can make either a public offering or a rights issue to all existing shareholders. The company wants to raise $14.4 million, net new equity capital. The current share price is $30, with 3 million shares outstanding. Under Plan I, a

public offering would be made as follows: 600,000 new shares would be underwritten at a market price of $26 per share and a net price to the company of $25 per share. Theoretically, after the issue is completed, the market price per share will be $29.17. Under Plan II, a rights offering (one right per share issued to each current shareholder) would be made with the following features: 1 million new shares would be sold at $15 each, and 3 rights would be necessary to buy each share. Total flotation costs would be $600,000 for Plan II. Theoretically, after the issue is completed, the market price per share should be $26.25. Assuming that the company's actual goal is to maximize shareholder wealth, which of these plans would be better, and why?

B3. (Rights issue) The A.B. Sea Company wishes to raise $100 million through a rights offering. It has 70 million shares outstanding, trading at $25 per share. It wishes each right to be worth at least $0.20 initially.

a. Find the subscription price and subscription ratio.

b. After the offering commences, the shares trade at a price of $23 per share. What is the value of one right?

c. In what situations is a rights offering more appropriate than a general public offering?

d. What is the principal drawback to a rights offering?

B4. (Review, capital-asset-pricing model) The riskless return is 6%. The expected return on the market portfolio is 14%. A stock's beta is 1.35. Calculate the cost of equity capital.

B5. (Review, dividend growth model) A stock's current market price is $25. The expected annual cash dividend is $1 per share. In addition, investors expect the company to pay a 4% dividend in common stock. The expected growth rate of the cash dividend is 10% per year.

a. Calculate the cost of retained earnings.

b. If a new share issue would require 5% flotation costs, what is the cost of the new issue?

B6. (Dilution) Consider again the dilution in percentage ownership example, the Reliable Fabrics example in the section on Dilution. Suppose Reliable needs to raise $650,000 to finance a project with an NPV of $200,000.

a. How will the announcement of the project affect Reliable's share price?

b. How many shares will Reliable have to sell to raise $650,000?

c. What has happened to your wealth?

d. Is there a direct connection between the change in percentage ownership and the change in shareholder wealth?

B7. (Dilution) Consider again the dilution in percentage ownership example, the Reliable Fabrics example in the section on Dilution. Suppose Reliable will invest the new issue proceeds in a project with a zero NPV. But in order to sell the shares, Reliable will have to offer them at $10 each.

a. How will the announcement of the new issue affect Reliable's share price?

b. How will the new issue affect your wealth?

c. What conclusion can you draw about the effect on share-holder wealth of selling shares for less than their market value? Is this conclusion related to the change in percentage ownership?

B8. (Cost of preferred stock) A perpetual preferred stock issue can be sold for $25 per share. It would require a quarterly dividend rate of $0.50 per share. The underwriting fees and out-of-pocket expenses amount to 1.75% of the public offering price. What is the cost of preferred stock?

B9. (Dilution) Look back at table D.5. International Nickel currently earns a 12% return on book equity.

a. Calculate the company's earnings and EPS.

b. Suppose the project has a positive NPV, and the company earns a 13% return on the equity it invests in the project. Calculate earnings and EPS.

c. Suppose the project has a negative NPV, and the company earns a 12% return on the project equity. Calculate earnings and EPS.

d. Redo part **b** assuming the company earns a 15% return on project equity.

B10. (Dilution) Public Service Company of New York has 20,000,000 common shares outstanding. Its share price is $30. Book value per share is $50. Public Service plans to raise an additional $100 million by selling shares. It will invest the proceeds in a new electric generating plant. Its regulators allow Public Service to earn a 10% return on equity.

a. Suppose the project has a $10 million NPV. Investors are aware of this at the time of the offering. What happens to market value per share, book value per share, and EPS?

b. Redo part **a** assuming project NPV is −$20 million.

c. Public Service currently has 10,000 shareholders who own equal numbers of shares. All the additional shares will be sold to new investors. Calculate the dilution in percentage ownership in parts **a** and **b.**

d. Which measure of dilution, if any, indicates a change in shareholder wealth?

BIBLIOGRAPHY

Affleck-Graves, John, Shantaram P. Hegde, Robert E. Miller, and Frank K. Reilly. "The Effect of the Trading System on the Underpricing of Initial Public Offerings," *Financial Management,* 1993, 22(1):99–108.

Aggarwal, Reena, and Pietra Rivoli. "Fads in the Initial Public Offering Market?" *Financial Management,* 1990, 19(4):45–57.

Alderson, Michael J., and Donald R. Fraser. "Financial Innovations and Excesses Revisited: The Case of Auction Rate Preferred Stock," *Financial Management,* 1993, 22(2):61–77.

Allen, David S., Robert E. Lamy, and G. Rodney Thompson. "The Shelf Registration of Debt and Self Selection Bias," *Journal of Finance,* 1990, 45(1):275–288.

Arshadi, Nasser, and Thomas H. Eyssell. "Regulatory Deterrence and Registered Insider Trading: The Case of Tender Offers," *Financial Management,* 1991, 20(2):30–39.

Asquith, P., and D. W. Mullins. "Equity Issues and Offering Dilution," *Journal of Financial Economics,* 1986, 15(1/2):61–89.

Bae, Sung C., and Haim Levy. "The Valuation of Firm Commitment Underwriting Contracts for Seasoned New Equity Issues: Theory And Evidence," *Financial Management,* 1990,19(2):48–59.

Barry, Christopher B. "New Directions in Research on Venture Capital Finance," *Financial Management,* 1994, 23(3):3–15.

Barry, Christopher B., and Robert H. Jennings. "The Opening Price Performance of Initial Public Offerings of Common Stock," *Financial Management,* 1993, 22(1):54–63.

Barry, Christopher B., Chris J. Muscarella, and Michael R. Vetsuypens. "Underwriter Warrants, Underwriter Compensation, and the Costs of Going Public," *Journal of Financial Economics,* 1991, 29(1):113–136.

Benveniste, Lawrence M., and William J. Wilhelm. "A Comparative Analysis of IPO Proceeds Under Alternative Regulatory Environments," *Journal of Financial Economics,* 1990, 28(1/2):173–208.

Bhagat, Sanjai. "The Effect of Management's Choice Between Negotiated and Competitive Equity Offerings on Shareholder Wealth," *Journal of Financial and Quantitative Analysis,* 1986, 21(2):181–196.

Bhagat, Sanjai, James A. Brickley, and Ronald C. Lease. "The Authorization of Additional Common Stock: An Empirical Investigation," *Financial Management,* 1986, 15(3):45–53.

Bhagat, Sanjai, M. Wayne Marr, and G. Rodney Thompson. "The Rule 415 Experiment: Equity Markets," *Journal of Finance,* 1985, 40(5):1385–1401.

Bowers, Helen M., and Robert E. Miller. "Choice of Investment Banker and Shareholders' Wealth of Firms Involved in Acquisitions," *Financial Management,* 1990, 19(4):34–44.

Brickley, James A., and Kathleen T. Hevert. "Direct Employees Stock Ownership: An Empirical Investigation," *Financial Management,* 1991, 20(2):70–84.

Carey, Mark, Stephen Prowse, John Rea, and Gregory Udell. *The Economics of the Private Placement Market.* Washington, D.C.: Board of Governors of the Federal Reserve System, December 1993.

Carter, Richard B., and Frederick H. Dark. "The Use of the Over-Allotment Option in Initial Public Offerings of Equity: Risks and Underwriter Prestige," *Financial Management,* 1990, 19(3):55–64.

Carter, Richard, and Steven Manaster. "Initial Public Offerings and Underwriter Reputation," *Journal of Finance,* 1990, 45(4):1045–1067.

Chang, Saeyoung. "Employee Stock Ownership Plans and Shareholder Wealth: An Empirical Investigation," *Financial Management,* 1990, 19(1):48–58.

Dawson, Steven M. "Initial Public Offer Underpricing: The Issuer's View—A Note," *Journal of Finance,* 1987, 42(1):159–162.

Drake, Philip D., and Michael R. Vetsuypens. "IPO Underpricing and Insurance Against Legal Liability," *Financial Management,* 1993, 22(1):64–73.

Eckbo, B. Espen, and Ronald W. Masulis. "Adverse Selection and the Rights Offer Paradox," *Journal of Financial Economics,* 1992, 32(3):293–332.

Ferreira, Eurico J., Michael F. Spivey, and Charles E. Edwards. "Pricing New Issues and Seasoned Preferred Stocks: A Comparison of Valuation Models," *Financial Management,* 1992, 21(2):52–62.

Fields, L. Paige, and Eric L. Mais. "Managerial Voting Rights and Seasoned Public Equity Issues," *Journal of Financial and Quantitative Analysis,* 1994, 29(3):445–457.

Garfinkel, Jon A. "IPO Underpricing, Insider Selling and Subsequent Equity Offerings: Is Underpricing a Signal of Quality?" *Financial Management,* 1993, 22(1):74–83.

Greene, Jason T., and Susan G. Watts. "Price Discovery on the NYSE and the NASDAQ: The Case of Overnight and Daytime News Releases," *Financial Management,* 1996, 25(1):19–42.

Grinblatt, Mark, and Chuan Yang Hwang. "Signalling and the Pricing of New Issues," *Journal of Finance,* 1989, 44(2):393–420.

Gupta, Atul, and Leonard Rosenthal. "Ownership Structure, Leverage, and Firm Value: The Case of Leveraged Recapitalizations," *Financial Management,* 1991, 20(3):69–83.

Handa, Puneet, and A. R. Radhakrishnan. "An Empirical Investigation of Leveraged Recapitalizations with Cash Payout as Takeover Defense," *Financial Management,* 1991, 20(3):58–68.

Hanley, Kathleen Weiss. "The Underpricing of Initial Public Offerings and the Partial Adjustment Phenomenon," *Journal of Financial Economics,* 1993, 34(2):231–250.

Hanley, Kathleen Weiss, A. Arun Kumar, and Paul J. Seguin. "Price Stabilization in the Market for New Issues," *Journal of Financial Economics,* 1993, 34(2):177–198.

Hansen, Robert S., and Paul Torregrosa. "Underwriter Compensation and Corporate Monitoring," *Journal of Finance,* 1992, 47(4):1537–1556.

Jain, Bharat A., and Omesh Kini. "The Post-Issue Operating Performance of IPO Firms," *Journal of Finance,* 1994, 49(5):1699–1726.

James, Christopher, and Peggy Wier. "Borrowing Relationships, Intermediation, and the Cost of Issuing Public Securities," *Journal of Financial Economics,* 1990, 28(1/2):149–172.

Jegadeesh, Narasimhan, Mark Weinstein, and Ivo Welch. "An Empirical Investigation of IPO Returns and Subsequent Equity Offerings," *Journal of Financial Economics,* 1993, 34(2):153–175.

Johnson, James M., and Robert E. Miller. "Investment Banker Prestige and the Underpricing of Initial Public Offerings," *Financial Management,* 1988, 17(2):19–29.

Kadapakkam, Palani-Rajan, and Sarabjeet Seth. "Trading Profits in Dutch Auction Self-Tender Offers," *Journal of Finance,* 1994, 49(1):291–306.

Karpoff, Jonathan M., and Daniel Lee. "Insider Trading Before New Issue Announcements," *Financial Management,* 1991, 20(1):18–26.

Kidwell, David S., M. Wayne Marr, and G. Rodney Thompson. "Eurodollar Bonds, Alternative Financing for U.S. Companies: A Correction," *Financial Management,* 1986, 15(1):78–79.

Levis, Mario. "The Long-Run Performance of Initial Public Offerings: The UK Experience 1980–1988," *Financial Management,* 1993, 22(1):28–41.

Loderer, Claudio, and David C. Mauer. "Corporate Dividends and Seasoned Equity Issues: An Empirical Investigation," *Journal of Finance,* 1992, 47(1):201–226.

Loderer, Claudio, Dennis P. Sheehan, and Gregory B. Kadlec. "The Pricing of Equity Offerings," *Journal of Financial Economics,* 1991, 29(1):35–58.

Logue, Dennis E., James K. Seward, and James P. Walsh. "Rearranging Residual Claims: A Case for Targeted Stock," *Financial Management,* 1996, 25(1):43–61.

Masulis, Ronald W., and A. N. Korwar. "Seasoned Equity Offerings: An Empirical Investigation," *Journal of Financial Economics,* 1986, 15(1/2):91–118.

Megginson, William L., Robert C. Nash, and Matthias Van Randenborgh. "The Financial and Operating Performance of Newly Privatized Firms: An International Empirical Analysis," *Journal of Finance,* 1994, 49(2):403–452.

Megginson, William L., and Kathleen A. Weiss. "Venture Capitalist Certification in Initial Public Offerings," *Journal of Finance,* 1991, 46(3):879–904.

Miller, Merton H. "Financial Innovation: The Last Twenty Years and the Next," *Journal of Financial and Quantitative Analysis,* 1986, 21(5):459–471.

Miller, Robert E., and Frank K. Reilly. "An Examination of Mispricing, Returns, and Uncertainty for Initial Public Offerings," *Financial Management,* 1987, 16(2):33–38.

Moore, Norman H., David R. Peterson, and Pamela P. Peterson. "Shelf Registrations and Shareholder Wealth: A Comparison of Shelf and Traditional Equity Offerings," *Journal of Finance,* 1986, 41(2):451–464.

Myers, Stewart C., and Nicholas S. Majluf. "Corporate Financing and Investment Decisions When Firms Have Information That Investors Do Not Have," *Journal of Financial Economics,* 1984, 13(2):187–222.

Persons, John C. "Signaling and Takeover Deterrence with Stock Repurchases: Dutch Auctions versus Fixed Price Tender Offers," *Journal of Finance,* 1994, 49(4):1373–1402.

Pinegar, J. Michael, and Ronald C. Lease. "The Impact of Preferred-for-Common Exchange Offers on Firm Value," *Journal of Finance,* 1986, 41(4):795–814.

Rogowski, Robert J., and Eric H. Sorensen. "Deregulation in Investment Banking: Shelf Registrations, Structure, and Performance," *Financial Management,* 1985, 14(1):5–15.

Schultz, Paul H., and Mir A. Zaman. "Aftermarket Support and Underpricing of Initial Public Offerings," *Journal of Financial Economics,* 1994, 35(2):199–219.

Slovin, Myron B., Marie E. Sushka, and Yvette M. Bendeck. "The Intra-Industry Effects of Going Private Transactions," *Journal of Finance,* 1991, 46(4):1537–1550.

Stein, Jeremy C. "Convertible Bonds as Backdoor Equity Financing," *Journal of Financial Economics,* 1992, 32(1):3–22.

Viswanath, P. V. "Strategic Considerations, the Pecking Order Hypothesis, and Market Reactions to Equity Financing," *Journal of Financial and Quantitative Analysis,* 1993, 28(2):213–234.

TOPIC E

Derivatives and Hedging

Modern financial engineering emerged in the 1970s in response to a very real problem: Financial markets had become more volatile, compared to the previous 20 years. Because this volatility could affect company value, managers sought to avoid it. Initially, many companies tried to build better forecasting models. If they could predict price changes, they could avoid the risk. Not surprisingly, these forecasting efforts were generally unsuccessful because of the Principle of Capital Market Efficiency. Putting into practice the Principle of Valuable Ideas, financial engineers developed a variety of derivative instruments that companies can use to manage financial risk.

Recall that a *derivative* is a financial instrument whose value depends on the price of some other asset. There are four basic types of derivatives. We call them the *basic building blocks* because they are used to build more complex derivatives and other securities. The basic building blocks can be used to analyze or "build" more complex securities. For example, recall that a convertible bond is a *hybrid security* composed of a "straight" bond and a call option on the issuer's common stock.

Organized options markets and financial futures markets were two of the most significant financial developments of the 1970s. The development of the swaps markets was one of the most significant developments of the 1980s. These new financial instruments increased the ability of investors to change their return distributions. Insurance protects against a potential but unlikely loss. You pay the insurance company to bear the risk. Similarly, these new financial markets made it possible to pay others to bear financial risk.

Here, we'll describe the basic types of derivatives and show how companies use them to manage their financial risks. We'll build on our discussion of futures, options, and hedging foreign exchange risk in chapter 15 to show you how companies use derivatives to hedge other kinds of risk.

DERIVATIVES AND HEDGING AND THE PRINCIPLES OF FINANCE

◆ *Valuable Ideas:* Look for opportunities to develop derivatives that enable companies to cope better with the financial risks they face.

◆ *Options:* Recognize the value of options contained in derivatives.

◆ *Two-Sided Transactions:* Use derivatives to pay others to take risks. Derivatives do not eliminate financial risk; they only transfer it.

◆ *Risk-Return Trade-Off:* To transfer risk to another party, you must offer a return that fully compensates for the amount of risk transferred.

◆ *Capital Market Efficiency:* You cannot forecast movements in interest rates, commodity prices, and foreign exchange rates precisely because these financial prices have a significant random component in an efficient market. Use the financial markets' consensus forecasts.

◆ *Comparative Advantage:* Paying others to bear financial risk may be valuable if they can bear the risk more cheaply.

OPTIONS

The first basic building block we'll examine is the option. Recall that a **derivative** is a financial instrument whose value depends on the price of some other asset. An option fits this definition. As you know, the value of a stock option depends on the price of the underlying shares.

Recall that an *option* conveys a right without an obligation. According to the Options Principle, that's why options are valuable. With a *call option* on a stock, you have the right to buy a specified amount of stock (usually 100 shares in the case of a standardized market-traded stock option) at a specified price within some stated time period. A *put option* provides the right to sell. The specified price is the *strike price*. These instruments are traded in the options markets.

Options Markets

Options are traded on organized exchanges and in the over-the-counter (OTC) market. The Chicago Board Options Exchange (CBOE) began operations in 1973. It initially traded only call options on about two dozen stocks. Trading volume grew rapidly, and so did the number of option contracts available. By January 1997 the CBOE listed puts and calls on 881 common stocks. Today it is the largest options exchange in the world in aggregate dollar value of contracts traded. Among U.S. securities exchanges, only the New York Stock Exchange (NYSE) is bigger. Stock options are also traded on four other exchanges: the American Stock Exchange, Philadelphia Stock Exchange, NYSE, and Pacific Stock Exchange. There is also an OTC market. It deals primarily in nonstandardized options.

Figure E.1 shows a typical price quotation for options listed on an exchange. It comes from the *Wall Street Journal* of January 24, 1997, and shows the previous day's trading in put and call options on General Motors (GM) common stock. Newspapers usually provide quotations only for actively traded options. GM's stock closed at $61⅞. The options have a strike price of $55, $60, or $65. They expire in February 1997, March 1997, or June 1997. The Vol. (volume) column gives the number of contracts to buy or sell 100 shares traded that day. The column headed Last gives the last trading price. For example, the March 60 call last traded at $3.75 per underlying share, or $375 per contract. A total of 436 contracts to buy 43,600 shares traded that day.

On each options exchange, the members meet during trading hours on the floor of the exchange to buy and sell options. Floor brokers execute buy orders and sell orders

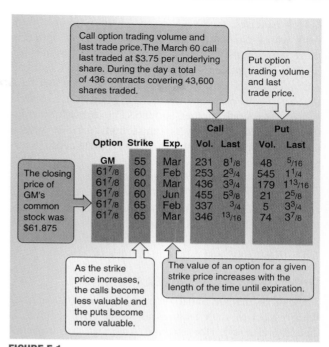

FIGURE E.1

A typical price quotation for listed options.
Source: *Wall Street Journal*, January 24, 1997, p. C19.

for their customers. Each exchange employs clerks who observe the trading and transmit the latest trading information to other options exchanges and news services around the world.

The five options exchanges jointly own the Options Clearing Corporation (OCC) and clear all their option trades through the OCC. Figure E.2 shows how the OCC interposes itself between every option buyer and seller. The option buyer and seller agree on the price and strike a deal. At this point, the OCC steps in. It places itself between the two traders, effectively becoming both the buyer of the option from the writer and the writer of the option to the buyer. The OCC substitutes its promise to deliver for the option seller's promise to deliver. When an option

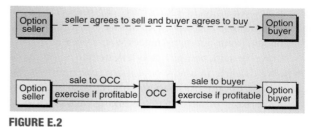

FIGURE E.2

The role of the OCC.

holder exercises, the OCC arranges with a member company whose clients have written that particular option to make good on the option obligation. The OCC stands behind this obligation. The OCC effectively makes all call option contracts written on a particular security that have the same strike price and the same expiration date perfect substitutes for one another, and the same is true for put option contracts. This lowers transaction costs because it saves the cost of having to conduct a separate credit investigation for each seller.

In recent years, the number of traded options has greatly increased. There are options on common stocks, of course. There are also traded options on foreign currencies, on debt instruments such as U.S. Treasury securities, on stock market indexes such as the Standard & Poor's 500 Index (S&P 500), and on futures contracts.

Over-the-Counter Options

The options that are traded on exchanges are standardized with respect to such features as strike price, expiration date, exercise style (for example, American or European), and settlement arrangements. This enhances their liquidity. But there is a drawback. If an investor or a company wants a nonstandard option, it can't obtain such an option on an exchange. The investor can try to obtain what she wants in the OTC market. Like the OTC market for stocks, the OTC market for options consists of securities dealers who craft customized options to meet investor demand. A potential option buyer calls an OTC dealer to negotiate an option contract's exercise price, expiration date, underlying stock, and so on and a mutually acceptable price for the option.

To compete with the OTC market, the CBOE recently introduced FLEX options. These allow some flexibility in designing options on the S&P 500, S&P 100, and Russell 2000 indexes. The OTC market still offers greater flexibility in option design.

Options and Financial Management

Options have a wide range of uses in financial management. We first introduced you to options in our discussion of the Options Principle in chapter 2. Enrichment topic B, Options and Contingent Outcomes, explores options in broad generalities. There, we explain the basis for valuing an option and point out many places where options exist.

As we've said, companies often include an option to redeem bonds early in a new debt issue. The option to redeem is a call option. Enrichment topic D, Issuing Securities and the Role of Investment Banking, describes how some companies, especially in other countries, sell new common stock to their shareholders through rights offerings. Rights are call options.

Finally, recall that options exist in many situations, even though they are sometimes hard to spot. But keep in mind how important it is to look for options, because they affect value—in some cases dramatically.

An Option Pricing Model

Now let's take a look at how to value options. To keep matters simple, we'll value only stock options. We'll value calls first and then puts.

Fischer Black and Myron Scholes derived a very useful model for valuing options. The Black-Scholes option pricing model (OPM) is

$$\text{CALL} = P_0 N(d_1) - SN(d_2)e^{-\Delta tk} \qquad \text{(E.1)}$$

where

$$d_1 = \frac{\ln(P_0/S) + \Delta tk}{\sigma\Delta t^{1/2}} + \frac{\sigma\Delta t^{1/2}}{2} \qquad \text{(E.2)}$$

$$d_2 = d_1 - \sigma\Delta t^{1/2} \qquad \text{(E.3)}$$

and

$N(d)$ = the cumulative distribution function (cdf) for a standardized (mean = 0, $\sigma = 1$) normal random variable. This is the probability that an outcome is less than or equal to d. $N(d)$ is given in the table in appendix B to this book for values of d from $d = -3.09$ to $d = 3.09$, in increments of 0.01.

σ = the standard deviation of the (continuously compounded) return on the underlying asset

Δt = the time (in years) until the option expires

k = the riskless APR with continuous compounding

S = the strike price of the option

P_0 = the current value of the underlying asset

$\ln$ = the natural (base e) logarithm function

Let's take a closer look at equation (E.1). P_0 is the current share price; $Se^{-\Delta tk}$ is the present value of the strike price, which you would pay in the future if you exercise the call option; and $N(d_1)$ and $N(d_2)$ are probabilities. We know that for any given strike price, a call option is more valuable the higher the market price of the underlying asset. We also know that for any given asset price, a call option is less valuable the higher the strike price. Thus, it seems reasonable that CALL, the value of a call option, should increase with P_0 and decrease with S. The probabilities $N(d_1)$ and $N(d_2)$ take into account the uncertainty concerning the future share price and, consequently, whether the option will ever be exercised, and if it is, what value will be realized. So while we can't show you the complex mathematics that led Black and Scholes to their remarkable discovery, at least we hope you can see that the formula appears reasonable.

Using the Black-Scholes OPM is very practical for two reasons. First, except for σ, the parameter inputs needed are specified in the option contract or are readily observable in currently operating markets. Second, the model usually provides a very good approximation of the true value of an option, even though some of its assumptions may not be perfectly satisfied.

Valuing Call Options As you might expect by now, violations of the perfect market assumption do not harm the model's usefulness. However, it may surprise you to find out that the distinction between an American and a European type of option is not important unless there are cash flows associated with the underlying asset before the option expires. Recall that you can exercise an American option any time during its life. Also, you are generally better off selling, rather than exercising, one prior to its expiration. Thus, with a few adjustments, you can usually use the Black-Scholes OPM to value American as well as European call options.

Applying the Black-Scholes OPM to Value a Call Option   EXAMPLE

Suppose a non-dividend-paying stock is selling for $28 per share. The standard deviation of the return from owning a share of this stock is estimated from the returns on the stock during a recent representative historical period and is found to be 0.30. The APR for the riskless return with continuous compounding is 6%. The option has a strike price of $30, and there are 9 months until expiration. What is a call option on this stock worth?

First list the parameter values: $P_0 = 28$, $\sigma = 0.30$, $k = 0.06$, $S = 30$, and $\Delta t = 0.75$. Then $\sigma \Delta t^{1/2} = 0.259808$. From equation (E.2), d_1 is

$$d_1 = \frac{\ln(P_0/S)}{\sigma \Delta t^{1/2}} + \frac{\Delta t k}{\sigma \Delta t^{1/2}} + \frac{\sigma \Delta t^{1/2}}{2} = \frac{\ln(28/30)}{0.259808} + \frac{0.75(0.06)}{0.259808} + \frac{0.259808}{2}$$

$$d_1 = -0.265553 + 0.173205 + 0.129904 = 0.037556 \approx 0.04$$

From equation (E.3):

$$d_2 = d_1 - \sigma \Delta t^{1/2} = 0.037556 - 0.259808 = -0.222252 \approx -0.22$$

From appendix B, we have

$$N(d_1) = N(0.04) = 0.5160$$
$$N(d_2) = N(-0.22) = 0.4129$$

Finally, from equation (E.1):

$$\text{CALL} = P_0 N(d_1) - S N(d_2) e^{-\Delta t k} = 28(0.5160) - 30(0.4129) e^{-0.045} = \$2.61$$

An option like this one should sell in the market for a price of about $2½ to $2¾. ■

What Happens When the Share Price Falls?   EXAMPLE

Suppose the non-dividend-paying stock in the previous example was instead selling for $26 per share. With everything else the same, we would have $P_0 = 26$, $\sigma = 0.30$, $k = 0.06$, $S = 30$, and $\Delta t = 0.75$. As before, $\sigma \Delta t^{1/2} = 0.259808$. From equation (E.2), d_1 is

$$d_1 = \frac{\ln(P_0/S)}{\sigma \Delta t^{1/2}} + \frac{\Delta t k}{\sigma \Delta t^{1/2}} + \frac{\sigma \Delta t^{1/2}}{2} = \frac{\ln(26/30)}{0.259808} + \frac{0.75(0.06)}{0.259808} + \frac{0.259808}{2}$$

$$d_1 = -0.550795 + 0.173205 + 0.129904 = -0.247686 \approx -0.25$$

(continued on following page)

(What Happens When the Share Price Falls? *continued from previous page*)

Equation (E.3) yields

$$d_2 = d_1 - \sigma \Delta t^{1/2} = -0.247686 - 0.259808 = -0.507494 \approx -0.51$$

From appendix B, we have

$$N(d_1) = N(-0.25) = 0.4013$$
$$N(d_2) = N(-0.51) = 0.3050$$

Finally, from equation (E.1),

$$CALL = P_0 N(d_1) - SN(d_2)e^{-\Delta tk} = 26(0.4013) - 30(0.3050)e^{-0.045} = \$1.69$$

Although the option is \$2 further out-of-the-money, its value decreases by less than \$2. ■

Exercise Value and Time Premium of a Call Option

Option value can be broken into two parts; the exercise value and the time premium. If a call option is in-the-money ($P_0 > S$), the exercise value is $P_0 - S$. If the call option is out-of-the-money ($P_0 < S$), you won't exercise it and the exercise value is zero. Thus, the exercise value is the greater of $P_0 - S$ and zero.

Exercise value of a call option = Maximum of ($P_0 - S$, 0)

Prior to expiration, the market value of a call option generally exceeds its exercise value. We say that an option "is worth more alive than dead." The excess of the market value above the exercise value is called the time premium.

Time premium of an option = Market value − Exercise value

In the two call option examples above, the option was out-of-the-money because the stock price (\$28 for the first ex-ample and \$26 for the second) was below the strike price (\$30). The exercise value of these options is zero. The time premium of these options is the excess of the market value of these call options over the exercise value, which is \$2.61 for the first example and \$1.69 for the second.

Valuing Put Options

The value of a put option can be expressed in terms of the value of a similar call option:[1]

$$PUT = CALL + Se^{-\Delta tk} - P_0 \tag{E.4}$$

You can value a put option by substituting equation (E.1) into equation (E.4).

---

[1]This relationship reflects the concept of *put-call parity*, which is discussed in enrichment topic B, Options and Contingent Outcomes. According to this concept, we can express the value of either option in terms of the value of the other (and the present value of the strike price and the current value of the asset).

EXAMPLE

Valuing a Put Option

What is the value of a 9-month put option, with $S = \$30$, on a non-dividend-paying stock that is selling for \$28 per share if $\sigma = 0.30$ and $k = 6\%$? We computed the value of a call option under the same conditions in our first example. It was \$2.61. Therefore, from equation (E.4):

$$PUT = CALL + Se^{-\Delta tk} - P_0 = 2.61 + (30)e^{-0.045} - 28 = \$3.29$$

Note that the option's time premium equals \$1.29, which is its market value minus its exercise value.

Next let's extend our second example. The value of the put option if the stock has a current value of \$26 is

$$PUT = CALL + Se^{-\Delta tk} - P_0 = 1.69 + (30)e^{-0.045} - 26 = \$4.37$$

The put option is \$2 further in-the-money. But the option's value doesn't increase by \$2. ■

Exercise Value and Time Premium of a Put Option

A put option has a positive exercise value only when it is in-the-money, that is, the stock price is below the strike price ($P_0 < S$). If a put option is out-of-the-money, the exercise value of the put option is zero. Thus, the exercise value of a put option is:

Exercise value of a put option = Maximum of ($S - P_0$, 0)

A put option's time premium is the market value minus the exercise value. For the put option examples above, when the stock price is $28, the strike price is $30, and the put value is $3.29, the exercise value is $2 (= 30 − 28) and time premium is $1.29. When the stock price drops to $26 and the strike price and put value are $30 and $4.37, the exercise value is $4 (= 30 − 26) and the time premium is $0.37.

Self-Check

1. How does an increase in the strike price affect the value of a call option? A put option?

2. What is put-call parity?

3. What are the five variables that you use in the Black-Scholes option pricing model to value an option?

4. What is the exercise value and the time premium of a call option? Of a put option?

WARRANTS

A **warrant** is a long-term call option that is issued by a company. It entitles the holder to buy shares of the company's common stock at a stated price for cash. Companies, particularly smaller ones, often find it more attractive to issue convertible bonds, or bonds with warrants, than to issue straight debt. In addition, smaller companies often include warrants as a "sweetener" to a new issue of common stock or a privately placed debt issue.

A convertible bond (or convertible preferred share) entitles the holder to exchange the bond (or preferred share) for a stated number of shares of the issuing company's common stock. Convertible securities thus incorporate a call option that lets the owner profit if the company's share price goes up.

Recall that standardized call options traded in the options market are written by investors against outstanding shares of a company's stock. By contrast, warrants are issued by the company, often as part of a package that includes the issuer's common stock, preferred stock, or bonds. Warrants are like rights because the underlying security is newly issued equity. But warrants usually do not expire for several years, and some companies, such as Allegheny Corporation, have even issued perpetual warrants.

Main Features of Warrants

The provisions of a warrant are essentially the same as those of a conventional call option. A warrant specifies the underlying common stock, the number of shares, a strike price, an expiration date, and the option type (American or European). Sometimes a warrant contains an early redemption feature, which enables the issuer to trigger its exercise prior to the expiration date.

An Issue of Warrants

EXAMPLE

A large and actively traded issue of warrants was sold by American Express Company in two *tranches* (parts). American Express distributed 932,000 common share purchase warrants to its common stockholders and then sold an additional 900,000 such warrants to the public at a price of $12.625 per warrant. Each American Express warrant entitled the holder to purchase, at any time within 5 years of the issue date, one share of American Express common stock at a strike price of $55 per share. The strike price was 17.0% over the previous closing price of American Express common stock. The terms of the warrant permitted American Express to accelerate the expiration date if the price of American Express's common stock traded at or above a price of $95 per share for a period of 10 consecutive trading days.

The American Express warrants were also redeemable at the company's option beginning 2 years from the issue date at a price of $40 per warrant. This redemption feature, like the redemption feature on a convertible bond, permits the issuer to force exercise of the call

(continued on following page)

(An Issue of Warrants *continued from previous page*)

option. Some warrants provide for a "step-up" or increase in the strike price. Warrants like those issued by American Express provide for adjustment of the strike price if the issuer pays a common stock dividend, splits its common stock, distributes some of its assets (other than cash dividends), or issues stockholders rights to purchase shares at a discount from the prevailing market price, and in some other circumstances.[2] However, as is generally the case, American Express warrant holders are not entitled to vote or to receive dividends, and the strike price is not adjusted for cash dividend payments to common stockholders. ■

Financing with Warrants

Companies can sell warrants separately, as American Express did, or in combination with other securities. Because of the efficiency of the capital markets, when a company issues warrants at their fair market price, the cash it receives is fair compensation for the potential equity interest it gives up. Nevertheless, issuing warrants may add value by reducing agency costs.[3] Including warrants along with an issue of debt allows lenders to share in the upside if the project financed with the debt issue is very profitable. As a result, lenders will accept a lower interest rate on the debt issue.

Valuing Warrants

Figure E.3 illustrates the relationship between the value of a warrant and the price of the underlying shares.[4] Warrants are long-term call options. We can value them like any other call option. But there is one important adjustment. Issuing warrants is dilutive because new shares are created. We must take this dilution into account. To do so, divide the call option value by a dilution factor:

$$W = \frac{C}{1 + P} \tag{E.5}$$

where W is the value of the warrant, C is the value of a call option to purchase one common share, and P is the propor-

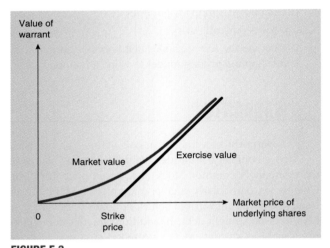

FIGURE E.3
Relationship between the value of a warrant and the price of the underlying shares.

tionate increase in the number of common shares that would result from exercising the warrants.

We use equation (E.5) to value warrants before they are issued. How about after the issue? In an efficient market, their dilutive impact is already fully reflected in the issuer's common stock price, so $W = C$ after issuance.

Self-Check

1. What are the major differences between a warrant and a conventional call option?

2. Why are warrants considered to be dilutive?

---

[2]The strike price is usually adjusted only if the dilutive factors would require an adjustment of at least 5%. In addition, the $40 redemption price and the $95 acceleration price of the American Express warrants would be adjusted along with the strike price.
[3]See enrichment topic C, Financial Contracting, for a discussion of optimal financial contracts.
[4]This is the same relationship described for other call options in enrichment topic B, Options and Contingent Outcomes.

CONVERTIBLE SECURITIES

The conversion features of convertible bonds and convertible preferred stock are very similar. In our discussion we will concentrate on convertible bonds, but our comments will also apply to most convertible preferred stock.

Main Features of Convertible Debt

A **convertible bond** is a bond that is convertible, at the option of the bondholder, into shares of the issuer's common stock. You can think of it simply as a straight bond with call options attached. Convertible debt has the same coupon rate, maturity, and optional redemption features that typify a straight bond. It also has the following conversion features:

◆ Each bond is convertible at any time prior to maturity into common stock at a stated *conversion price*. This (strike) price usually exceeds the issuer's share price at the time of issue. In other words, the conversion option is normally issued out-of-the-money. The conversion premium is generally between 10% and 20%. Dividing the face amount of the convertible bond by the conversion price gives the *conversion ratio*. It is the number of shares of common stock into which each bond can be converted. The conversion terms are normally fixed for the life of the issue, although some convertible securities provide for one or more step-ups in the conversion price over time.

◆ The conversion price is usually adjusted for stock splits, stock dividends, or rights offerings with a discounted offering price. It is also adjusted when the company distributes assets (other than cash dividends) or indebtedness to its shareholders.

◆ Bondholders who convert do not receive accrued interest. Therefore, bondholders rarely convert voluntarily just before an interest payment date.

◆ If the bonds are called, the conversion option will expire just before (usually between three and ten days before) the redemption date.

Valuing Convertible Bonds

A convertible bond can be modeled as a straight bond plus a nondetachable warrant. From the Options Principle, you know that the value of a warrant can never be negative. Therefore, in a perfect capital market environment, the value of a convertible bond can never fall below its value as a straight bond. Similarly, the value of a convertible bond also can never fall below its conversion value. Figure E.4 illustrates the relationship among the bond value, con-

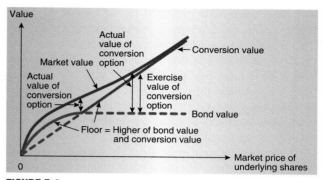

FIGURE E.4
Bond value, conversion value, and actual market value of a convertible bond.

version value, and actual market value of a convertible bond.

The market value of a convertible bond equals the sum of the bond value and the actual value of the conversion option. Note in figure E.4 that the market value of the convertible bond always exceeds both the bond value and the conversion value. When the underlying share price rises above the conversion price, the conversion option becomes in the money. In that share price range, the actual market value of the convertible bond equals the bond value plus the exercise value of the conversion option plus the conversion option's time premium. When the underlying share price is very low, the convertible bond's market value approximates the bond value. When the share price is very high, the convertible bond's market value approximates the conversion value.

We can value a convertible bond by valuing the bond and warrant components separately. The value of a convertible bond exactly equals the sum of the two component values in a perfect capital market.

Convertible Preferred Stock

The main buyers of convertible securities are either entirely tax-exempt investors or those who cannot benefit directly from the corporate 70% dividends-received deduction. Consequently, under most market conditions, issuers of convertible securities have been able to obtain essentially the same terms (chiefly nominal annual interest or dividend rate and conversion premium) whether they issued the convertible security as debt or as preferred stock.

Convertible preferred stock is similar to convertible debt; it is preferred stock that is convertible at the holder's option into shares of the issuer's common stock. Issuers who are in a tax-paying position and expect to remain so for a number of years find it cheaper to issue convertible debt than convertible preferred stock. Interest payments are tax deductible, whereas dividend payments are not. The tax deductions reduce the cost of capital. Interest deductions are much less valuable to issuers who do not expect to be in a tax-paying position for a number of years. They are worthless if the issuer will *never* be able to claim them for tax purposes. Thus, in either case, non-tax-paying companies that wish to issue convertible securities issue convertible preferred stock.

Convertible preferred stock is usually perpetual, whereas convertible debt has a stated maturity and usually has a sinking fund. The rating agencies view perpetual convertible preferred stock as "true" equity for credit rating purposes.

Convertible Exchangeable Preferred Stock

A company that is only temporarily not in an income-tax-paying position can issue *convertible exchangeable preferred stock.* Such securities are convertible preferred stock that is exchangeable at the option of the company into convertible *debt* of the company. The company would exercise this option as soon as it became tax paying. The nominal annual interest rate on the convertible debt equals the nominal annual dividend yield on the convertible preferred stock issue, and the issues have equivalent conversion terms. A non-tax-paying company can reap the advantages of issuing convertible preferred stock while preserving the flexibility to reissue it in the form of debt should it become a taxpayer before the issue is converted.

Exchangeable Debentures

Companies have also issued bonds that are exchangeable for the common stock of another company. The debentures are in effect "convertible" into the common stock of the other company. But in all other respects, exchangeable debentures are like conventional convertible bonds. Exchangeable debentures may be attractive to a company that owns a block of another company's common stock when it would like to raise cash and intends eventually to sell the block. The company may want to defer the sale, because it believes the shares will increase in value or because it wants to defer the capital gains tax liability.

Forced Conversions

Convertible bonds are normally callable subject to a schedule of fixed redemption (strike) prices that decline over the life of the issue. This call provision allows the issuer to force holders to convert the debt into common stock whenever the conversion value exceeds the call price. Most convertible bond indentures require the issuer to notify

bondholders of the call prior to the redemption date, generally 30 days in advance. Securityholders can convert at any time during this notice period.

How Forced Conversion Works As we have noted, the market value of a convertible bond always exceeds its conversion value unless the conversion option is about to expire. The difference between the market and conversion values reflects the conversion option's time premium. If the underlying common stock is non-dividend-paying, convertible bondholders never voluntarily convert, no matter how high the conversion value becomes. They can always realize greater value by selling the bond. Even when the underlying common stock is paying cash dividends, convertible bondholders do not voluntarily convert if the dividends they would receive after conversion are less than the interest they receive now.

Suppose the market value of the underlying common stock exceeds the call price. Calling the convertible issue motivates holders to convert, because converting is more profitable than tendering the bonds for cash redemption. A company should follow the forced conversion strategy that maximizes shareholder wealth. If the company calls convertible bonds when their conversion value is less than the effective call price, the bonds will not be converted, and wealth will be transferred from shareholders to bondholders. If the company calls convertible bonds when the conversion value exceeds the call price, bondholders will simply convert. The forced conversion strategy that maximizes shareholder wealth is the one that minimizes bondholder value: In a perfect capital market, a company should call convertible bonds when their conversion value reaches the *effective call price* (optional redemption price plus accrued interest).

Judged by the standards of the perfect capital market, most companies appear to wait "too long" to call their convertible bonds. They usually wait until the conversion value exceeds the call price by a seemingly wide margin— at least 20% is the practitioner's rule. Why do they behave this way? As we well know by now, actual markets are not perfect. In addition, if the market price of the issuer's common stock falls—and remains—below the conversion price during the 30-day notice period, the redemption value will exceed the conversion value, and bondholders will surrender their bonds for cash rather than convert. In that case, the company may have to raise enough cash to cover the cash redemption value on short notice. That could involve significant transaction costs. This explains why companies normally wait to call their convertible bonds until the conversion value exceeds the effective call price by a comfortable margin.

There is also an agency cost involved with trying to force conversion. A failed attempt is very embarrassing for the company's executives and could even lead to someone being fired. This tends to bias the executives toward waiting for an even larger margin.

Time Incorporated's Forced Conversion

Time Incorporated called its Series C $4.50 cumulative convertible preferred stock for redemption at a price of $54.9375, including accrued dividends. The issue was convertible into 1.5152 shares of Time common stock at a conversion price of $33 per share. The market price of the common stock was $46⅜, representing a 40.5% premium over the conversion price. Time was paying dividends on its common stock at the rate of $1.00 per share per year. A holder who converted at that time would suffer a decrease in annual dividend income amounting to $2.98 (= 4.50 − [1.5152]1.00) per preferred share. Consequently, few holders had converted voluntarily.

The market value of the common stock provided a *redemption cushion* over the redemption price amounting to:

$$\text{Redemption cushion} = \frac{\left(\genfrac{}{}{0pt}{}{\text{Conversion}}{\text{ratio}}\right)\left(\genfrac{}{}{0pt}{}{\text{Market price of}}{\text{common stock}}\right) - \left(\genfrac{}{}{0pt}{}{\text{Redemption}}{\text{price}}\right)}{\text{Redemption price}} \qquad \text{(E.6)}$$

$$\text{Redemption cushion} = \frac{(1.5152)(46.375) - 54.9375}{54.9375} = 27.9\%$$

This cushion gave holders a strong incentive to convert when Time called the issue. With the assistance of investment bankers, the entire issue was converted. ■

Self-Check

1. What is a convertible bond? What is convertible preferred stock? What are the main differences between them?

2. What are the main features of convertible debt?

3. What is convertible exchangeable preferred stock? Why do companies issue it?

4. What is forced conversion? Why do companies want to force conversions? What is the optimal time to force a conversion?

INTEREST-RATE SWAPS

Often, a company wishes to replace fixed-rate debt with floating-rate debt, or vice versa. Such a substitution involves transaction costs. The company can avoid these by entering into an interest-rate swap. The swap enables the company to recharacterize an existing debt obligation rather than having to pay the cost of replacing it in its entirety.

A **swap** contract obligates two parties to exchange specified cash flows at specified intervals. In an **interest-rate swap,** the cash flows are determined by two different interest rates.

Swaps were introduced in 1981, and their use has grown rapidly. Table E.1 on page 712 shows the growth in the interest-rate swap market since 1987. The number of contracts grew 10-fold and the total notional principal amount involved in these transactions grew 19-fold. The market is still growing.

How an Interest-Rate Swap Works

The two parties to an interest-rate swap exchange interest payment obligations. One might be at a specified fixed rate, say 8%, and the other at a floating rate, say 6-month LIBOR (London Interbank Offered Rate, at which banks in the London money market lend each other funds). They

TABLE E.1
Interest-Rate Swaps Outstanding, 1987–1995

	1987	1988	1989	1990	1991	1992	1993	1994	1995
Number of contracts	34,127	49,560	75,223	102,349	127,690	151,545	236,126	248,798	347,966
Notional principal amount in billions of U.S. dollars	$682	$1010	$1539	$2311	$3065	$3850	$6178	$8816	$12,811

Source: Smithson (1995), p. 53, and Smithson (1997), p. 59. Reprinted by permission.

might be different floating rates. Coupon payments *but not the principal* are swapped. The payments are based on a *notional principal amount;* it's only *notional* because the two parties don't exchange principal, they simply use the principal amounts to calculate the amounts of interest they owe each other. The interest payment obligations are conditional. If one party defaults, the other is released from its obligation.

Figure E.5 illustrates an interest-rate swap. In its simplest form, called a *fixed-rate–floating-rate swap,* one interest rate is fixed and the other is floating. One party pays out a series of cash flows determined by the fixed interest rate R_1. It receives a series of cash flows determined by the floating interest rate R_2. The cash flows for the other party are the mirror image of those shown in figure E.5.

A swap has lower default risk than a loan. Two features account for this. No principal changes hands, and the

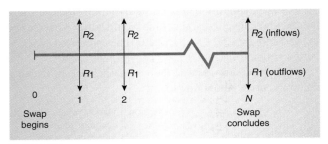

FIGURE E.5
An interest-rate swap.

payments are netted. Each party calculates what it owes the other. The party owing the greater amount writes a check to the other for the difference.

EXAMPLE   *McDonald's Interest-Rate Swap*

Let's say that McDonald's Corporation enters into the following fixed-rate–floating-rate swap. It agrees to pay 6-month LIBOR and to receive 8%, based on $100 million notional. Net payments will be made semiannually. The amount of the first payment is determined on the swap date. LIBOR is 6%. Six months later McDonald's receives a check for $1,000,000 (= 100,000,000[0.08 − 0.06]/2). By then LIBOR has risen to 7%. Six months later McDonald's receives a check for $500,000 (= 100,000,000[0.08 − 0.07]/2). LIBOR has risen further to 9%. At the end of the third period, McDonald's writes a check for $500,000 (= 100,000,000[0.09 − 0.08]/2). ■

Interest-rate swaps are used to change fixed-rate loans into floating-rate loans, and vice versa, or to change the index on a floating-rate loan.

EXAMPLE   *How Interest-Rate Swaps Are Used*

Suppose McDonald's issued $100 million of 10-year fixed-rate bonds 3 years ago. The interest rate is 7.50%. The issue has 7 years remaining. McDonald's now enters into a 7-year fixed-rate–floating-rate swap like the one in the previous example. Every 6 months McDonald's pays interest at a 7.50% rate on the bonds. It receives interest at an 8% rate and pays 6-month LIBOR in the swap. Its net interest cost is

Pay bondholders	7.50%
Receive from swap counterparty	8.00
Pay swap counterparty	6-month LIBOR
Net interest cost	6-month LIBOR − 0.50%

In effect, McDonald's has converted its fixed-rate bonds to floating-rate bonds paying 6-month LIBOR minus 0.50%. ∎

The Changing Market for Swaps

Swaps are not traded on exchanges. In the early days of the swap market, financial institutions arranged swaps by finding two counterparties who wanted to swap. The intermediary took no risk; it simply acted as agent. Swaps have evolved into a standardized product, and the intermediary's role has changed. It became important for intermediaries to put the transactions on their books. This exposed the intermediaries to default risk. The Principle of Comparative Advantage came into play. Commercial banks, with their greater capitalizations and comparative advantages in handling high-volume, standardized transactions and in extending credit, replaced investment banks as the main intermediaries.

Table E.2 shows the ten largest swap dealers in 1993. Nine were commercial banks. Three of these (Compagnie Financière de Paribas, Crèdit Lyonnais, and Banque Indosuez) were French.

Value Added by Interest-Rate Swaps

In the 1980s, many market participants and academic researchers argued that comparative advantage was responsible for the rapid growth of the interest-rate swap market.

The Comparative Advantage Argument

The argument went like this. Suppose a BBB-rated company can borrow on a floating-rate basis at LIBOR plus 0.50% and on a fixed-rate basis at 12%. An AAA-rated bank can borrow at LIBOR or at 10.50%. The BBB-rated company must pay a rate premium of 1.50% in the fixed-rate market but only 0.50% in the floating-rate market. The BBB-rated company has a comparative advantage in the floating-rate market. The AAA-rated bank has a comparative advantage in the fixed-rate market. Suppose the bank borrows fixed-rate, the company borrows floating-rate, and they swap. The company agrees to pay the bank 11%, and the bank agrees to pay LIBOR. Figure E.6 on page 714 illustrates the swap and the net interest cost to each party.

The company pays a net interest cost of 11.50%. It saves 0.50%. The bank pays LIBOR − 0.50% and also saves 0.50%. Sound too good to be true? It is! The argument is appealing. Unfortunately, it ignores arbitrage. With no barriers to capital flows, arbitrage would eventually eliminate any comparative advantage. Over time, the swap market would shrink, not grow!

TABLE E.2

Ten Largest Swap Dealers, 1993

RANK	FIRM	NOTIONAL PRINCIPAL AMOUNT OUTSTANDING ($ MILLIONS)
1	J. P. Morgan	453,080
2	Compagnie Financière de Paribas	431,728
3	Chemical Banking	411,782
4	Bankers Trust New York	315,879
5	Merrill Lynch	308,000
6	Crèdit Lyonnais	302,885
7	Citicorp	254,596
8	Chase Manhattan	237,773
9	BankAmerica	214,817
10	Banque Indosuez	184,924

Interest-rate swaps and currency swaps.
Source: Smithson, Smith, and Wilford (1995), p. 248.

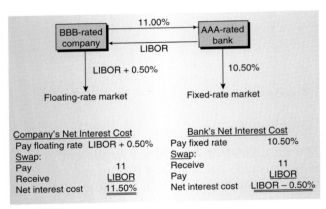

FIGURE E.6
Fixed-rate–floating-rate swap and the comparative advantage argument.

A simple comparison of interest rates can be misleading. A swap is mutually beneficial only if it is superior *for each party* to a straight borrowing that is *identical in design and risk*. In a competitive market, there is no reason why the difference in floating rates for two companies should be the same as the difference in fixed rates. Consequently, there is also no reason why the fixed-rate–floating-rate differential should be the same for every company. This differential depends on the company's cash flow characteristics. If two companies differ, so will their fixed-rate–floating-rate differentials.

A Better Explanation   We think there is a better explanation for the growth of the interest-rate swap market. Market imperfections, such as transaction costs, can explain much of the growth. Suppose a company has information, which is not available to the market, that leads it to believe that its credit quality will improve. It is generally cheaper and easier to refund short-term debt than long-term debt. Issuing short-term floating-rate debt and swapping into fixed-rate will enable the company to exploit its information advantage. In our example, suppose the BBB-rated company's credit improves so that it can borrow at LIBOR + 0.25%. It replaces its bank loan facility with a new one, leaving the swap in place. Its cost of funds drops to 11.25% (= LIBOR + 0.25% + 11.00% − LIBOR).

We'll explain later on how companies can use interest-rate swaps to manage their interest-rate risk exposure. Companies can enter into a swap with any number of large financial institutions. The success of swaps should therefore come as no surprise. Recall that the creation of a market for a security increases its liquidity, thus increasing its value by lowering transaction costs. The markets for swaps and other interest-rate derivatives have grown with the increase in hedging by companies.

Self-Check

1. What is an interest-rate swap? How does one work?

2. Why do companies enter into interest-rate swaps?

3. How do interest-rate swaps add value? Is comparative advantage responsible for the growth in the interest-rate swap market?

4. How are interest-rate swaps useful in hedging interest-rate risk?

5. Explain why an interest-rate swap involves less default risk than simply exchanging two debt obligations.

FORWARDS AND FUTURES

You may think derivatives are new. Some are, but others aren't. Futures contracts on commodities have been traded on organized exchanges since the 1860s. Forward contracts are even older. The Chicago Board of Trade (CBOT) opened in 1842. It initially traded forwards. It introduced commodity futures in 1865. Financial futures are newer. The International Monetary Market of the Chicago Mercantile Exchange (CME) introduced foreign currency futures in 1972 and interest-rate futures in 1975.

Forward Contracts

As we said in chapter 2, a **forward contract** obligates the holder to buy a specified amount of a particular asset at a stated price on a particular date in the future. All these terms are fixed at the time the forward contract is entered into. The specified future price is the *exercise price*. Most forward contracts are for commodities or currencies. (We discussed foreign exchange forwards in chapter 15.)

At contract origination, the net present value of a forward contract is zero because the exercise price is set equal to the expected future price. Neither buyer nor seller will realize a profit unless the actual market price of the asset differs from the exercise price at maturity. If the actual price exceeds the exercise price, the contract holder profits. If the actual price is lower than the exercise price, the holder suffers a loss. Under the Principle of Two-Sided Transactions, the holder's gain (loss) is the contract seller's loss (gain).

National Refining's Forward Contract

National Refining Corporation enters into a forward contract to purchase 10,000 barrels of oil at $17 per barrel in 90 days from Lone Star Oil & Gas. The purchase obligation is $170,000 (= [17]10,000). Suppose the price of oil is $20 when the contract matures. National Refining realizes a profit of $3 per barrel, or $30,000. ■

A forward contract has two-sided default risk. Lone Star might fail to deliver the oil, and National Refining might fail to pay for it.[5] This credit risk is important in determining who is able to transact in the forward market. Access is usually limited to large corporations, governments, and other creditworthy parties.

Two other features of forward contracts are noteworthy. First, there are no intermediate cash flows. Value is conveyed only at maturity. Second, most forward contracts require *physical delivery* of the asset in exchange for the cash purchase price. However, some can be *cash-settled*, which requires the party with the loss to pay that sum to the other party.

Futures Contracts

As noted in chapter 15, the basic form of a futures contract is identical to that of a forward contract. A **futures contract** obligates the holder to buy a specified quantity of a particular asset at a specified exercise price at a specified date in the future. A futures contract differs from a forward contract with respect to realizing gains or losses. With a forward contract, gains or losses are realized only on the settlement date. With a futures contract, they are realized daily. Also, futures contracts are traded on organized exchanges, whereas forwards are traded over the counter. Futures contracts are actively traded on more than 60 exchanges in more than two dozen countries. There are futures contracts for agricultural commodities, precious metals, industrial commodities, currencies, stock market indexes, and interest-bearing securities. These securities include Treasury bills, Treasury notes, Treasury bonds, and Eurodollar deposits.

Some futures contracts (notably agricultural futures) require physical delivery. Others (notably stock index futures and Eurodollar futures) are cash-settled. In practice, few futures contracts are held to maturity and exercised. Most are closed out by doing a reverse trade on the futures exchange. For example, a person who bought a futures contract can close out her position by selling an identical contract.

Market for Futures   Futures are traded on exchanges through open outcry. Trading takes place in a trading ring on the exchange floor. Exchange members who want to trade enter the ring and announce their intention to trade. When a buyer and seller agree on terms, the updated price is posted on a board near the trading ring.

Unlike the stock exchanges and the options markets, there are no central market makers on the futures exchanges. As a result, futures prices can exhibit considerable volatility. To limit this volatility, the futures exchanges have established price limits. Futures prices cannot change by more than the indicated limit on any particular day.

Low Default Risk   A futures contract has less default risk than a forward contract. Three features of futures markets are responsible. (1) Futures contracts are *marked to market* and *settled* at the end of every business day. When a futures contract loses value during the day, the holder pays the seller at the end of the day a sum equal to the day's loss. (2) There are *margin requirements*. Each buyer and seller must post a performance bond, which is adjusted daily. (3) There is a *clearinghouse*. Each party to a futures transaction really enters into a transaction with the clearinghouse. If either party defaults on a payment, the clearinghouse will make the payment. It first applies any funds in the defaulting party's margin account. If that is not enough, then the clearinghouse covers the difference.

Greater Liquidity   Futures contracts are more liquid than forward contracts for two reasons. Futures are standardized contracts, and they are traded on organized exchanges.

How an Interest-Rate Futures Contract Works

We'll use the Treasury bond futures contract to illustrate how an interest-rate futures contract works. The underlying instrument is a hypothetical bond with a $100,000 par value, a 20-year maturity, and an 8% coupon. The contract price is quoted with respect to this bond. However, the contract seller can choose from among several actual Treasury bonds that are acceptable to deliver. Settlement is made by physical delivery.

---

[5]The CBOT developed futures contracts after many forward contracts defaulted.

| EXAMPLE | *A Treasury Bond Futures Contract* |

Suppose you buy one contract, which specifies delivery in 6 months at a price of 96 (that is, 96% of the face amount, or $96,000 in total). You are said to be *long* the contract, and the seller is said to be *short* the contract. Each day your position and the seller's position will be marked to market as the value of the futures contract changes. As interest rates go up, the value of the futures contract (the value of the 8% bond) goes down. As interest rates go down, the value of the futures contract goes up. Under the Principle of Two-Sided Transactions, as the value of your long position goes down, the value of the seller's short position goes up by the same amount. As the value of your long position goes up, the value of the seller's short position goes down by the same amount.

At the end of 6 months you will take delivery of Treasury bonds in exchange for the $96,000 agreed-on price. Your gain (or loss) will depend on whether you can sell the bonds for more (or less) than the $96,000 you paid for them. If you don't want to take delivery, you can close out your position by selling one Treasury bond contract. The clearinghouse will net your long and short positions. If the 8% bond increased in value while you owned the futures contract, you'll have a profit; in the opposite case, you'll have a loss. ∎

Growth of the Futures Market

Figure E.7 illustrates the growth of the Treasury bond and Eurodollar CD futures markets between 1981 and 1992. The number of Treasury bond contracts traded grew fivefold to 70 million per year. The number of Eurodollar CD contracts traded grew many times faster to 59 million per year. Each Eurodollar CD contract is for $1 million

whereas each Treasury bond contract is for $100,000. Thus the underlying principal amount is actually greater in the Eurodollar futures market than in the Treasury bond futures market.

As we observed in the swap market, the interest-rate futures markets have expanded because of the increase in hedging activity.

Self-Check

1. Describe the main differences between a forward contract and a futures contract. What do they have in common?

2. Explain why a futures contract involves less default risk than a forward contract.

3. How does an interest-rate futures contract work?

4. What factors account for the growth of the futures markets?

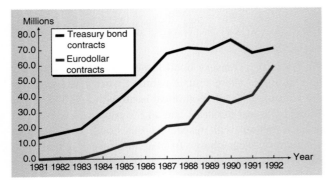

FIGURE E.7
Yearly volume of financial futures contracts, 1981–1992.

HEDGING

We've mentioned several times that derivatives are used in hedging and that an increase in hedging helps to explain the growth in the options, swaps, and futures markets. Chapter 15 showed how a company can use currency futures and options to hedge foreign exchange risk. Now we'll see how companies use the instruments we've described to hedge other types of risk.

How a Hedge Works

You may recall from chapter 15 that a company engages in hedging in order to reduce its sensitivity to changes in the price of a commodity, a foreign exchange rate, or an interest rate. Figure E.8 illustrates the rationale for hedging. **Hedging** involves taking an offsetting position by buying or selling a financial instrument whose value changes in the opposite direction from the value of the asset being hedged. Suppose an increase in interest rates would decrease the value of the company. In panel (a), the company's value decreases as interest rates increase. This may be a result of interest rates increasing on floating-rate debt that the company has outstanding. It might reflect a rise in long-term interest rates just as the company is about to issue new bonds. You could also think of r as the price of jet fuel to an airline, or the cost of British pounds to a U.S. importer of British goods.

If the company can take a position in a derivative whose value will increase as interest rates increase, it can neutralize the impact of the interest-rate increase. In panel (b), the value of the hedge position follows the dashed line. The hedge position is carefully selected so that changes in its value offset changes in the value of the asset being hedged. Panel (b) illustrates a *perfect hedge*. The value changes offset each other precisely, so the value of the company is unaffected. Perfect hedges are difficult to construct. Nevertheless, proper hedging should substantially reduce the company's exposure to price risks.

Hedging with Options

Options provide an opportunity to hedge against a bad outcome while preserving the opportunity to benefit from a good outcome. Imagine that General Holding Company has purchased 1 million shares of Family Entertainment's

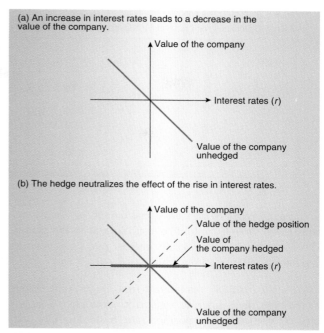

FIGURE E.8
The rationale for hedging.

common stock. General Holding would like to sell the stock. However, it is near year-end. Deferring the sale would defer tax on the gain General Holding has realized. But General Holding is concerned that the shares might decline in value before year-end. Let's see how General Holding can hedge this risk.

Using Options to Hedge at General Holding

EXAMPLE

General Holding can purchase put options. Family Entertainment's current share price is $28. If General Holding buys put options on 1 million shares at $28 per share, it will be fully hedged against risk of loss. Table E.3 on page 718 illustrates the possible outcomes. Suppose Family Entertainment's share price falls to $20. General Holding's 1 million shares lose $8 each. But the put is worth $8 per share. The gain just offsets the loss. On the other hand, if Family Entertainment's share price rises, General Holding has a gain. It has hedged against the risk of a loss without affecting its opportunity to benefit from a rise in Family Entertainment's share price.

Hedging is not costless, however. General Holding must pay the option seller. Why? The Principle of Two-Sided Transactions provides the answer. General Holding transfers the risk of loss to the option seller, who must be compensated in order to be willing to accept this risk. General Holding will purchase the put only if it believes that the price of the option is at least as great as the value it realizes by transferring the risk. ∎

TABLE E.3
Possible Outcomes for General Holding's Option Hedge

SHARE PRICE AT TIME OF SALE	GAIN OR (LOSS) ON SHARES		GAIN OR (LOSS) ON HEDGE		NET GAIN OR (LOSS)
	Per Share	Total	Per Share	Total	
$20	$(8)	$(8,000,000)	$8	$8,000,000	—
25	(3)	(3,000,000)	3	3,000,000	—
30	2	2,000,000	—	—	$2,000,000
35	7	7,000,000	—	—	7,000,000

Many types of derivative instruments are really options (even though "option" doesn't appear in the name). Three we should mention are interest rate caps, interest rate floors, and interest rate collars.

Caps and Floors An *interest-rate cap* pays the holder if the specified interest rate (for example, 3-month LIBOR) rises above a specified rate. A floating-rate borrower who buys a 7% cap will never have to pay more than 7%. Any period in which 3-month LIBOR exceeds 7%, the seller of the cap contract pays the difference between the actual rate and 7% multiplied by the notional amount and the fraction of the year (in this case 0.25). The cap contract is like a call option on 3-month LIBOR with a strike price of 7%. It hedges the contract holder against a rise in rates.

An *interest-rate floor* places a lower limit on the interest rate. For example, an investor in floating-rate notes that pay 3-month LIBOR + 1% who purchases a 4% floor contract can never receive less than 5% interest any period. The floor contract is like a put option on 3-month LIBOR with a strike price of 4%. It hedges against a drop in rates.

Collars Finally, an *interest-rate collar* is just a package consisting of a cap and a floor. For example, a 4%/7% collar consists of a 4% floor and a 7% cap. It hedges against rates falling outside a particular range.

Hedging with Interest-Rate Swaps

A floating-rate borrower can hedge against a change in interest rates by entering into a swap to pay fixed and receive floating. The BBB-rated company in the comparative advantage example entered into such a swap. The swap converted its interest cost from LIBOR + 0.50% floating to 11.50% fixed.

Hedging with Forwards and Futures

Because forwards and futures are basically identical in structure, we'll present only a futures example. The critical factor in futures hedging is determining the hedge ratio. The *hedge ratio* is defined by

$$\text{Hedge ratio} = \frac{\text{Volatility of bond to be hedged}}{\text{Volatility of hedging instrument}} \quad \text{(E.7)}$$

Consider two other hedging situations. Suppose Delta Airlines is concerned about a possible rise in the cost of jet fuel. It could hedge by buying oil futures. Suppose Nike is about to receive payment in French francs for a large shipment of running shoes just like the ones you wear. It could sell French franc futures to hedge against the risk of a decline in the value of the franc.

Hedging with Futures at PepsiCo

PepsiCo Inc. plans to issue $50 million of bonds. It needs 1 month to prepare the documentation, and it is concerned that interest rates might rise by a full percentage point before it can sell the issue. It could sell Treasury bond futures to hedge this risk.

If it were prepared to issue debt immediately, it could sell 10% notes that mature in a lump sum at the end of 30 years. If its new-issue rate increases to 11%, the 10% issue will fall in value to $91.2751 per $100 par value.

$$PV = \sum_{t=1}^{60} \frac{5}{(1.055)^t} + \frac{100}{(1.055)^{60}} = 91.2751$$

$$N = 60 \quad r = 5.5 \quad PV = 91.2751 \quad PMT = 5 \quad FV = 100$$

The change in value is 8.7249 (= 100 − 91.2751).

PepsiCo estimates that the yield on an 8% 20-year Treasury bond would also increase by 1%, from 9% currently to 10%. At a 9% yield, the 8% Treasury bond is worth $90.7992 per $100 par value.

$$PV = \sum_{t=1}^{40} \frac{4}{(1.045)^t} + \frac{100}{(1.045)^{40}} = 90.7992$$

$$N = 40 \quad r = 4.5 \quad PV = 90.7992 \quad PMT = 4 \quad FV = 100$$

At a 10% yield, it is worth $82.8409 per $100 par value.

$$PV = \sum_{t=1}^{40} \frac{4}{(1.05)^t} + \frac{100}{(1.05)^{40}} = 82.8409$$

$$N = 40 \quad r = 5.0 \quad PV = 82.8409 \quad PMT = 4 \quad FV = 100$$

The change in value is 7.9583 (= 90.7992 − 82.8409).

From equation (E.7), the hedge ratio is

$$\text{Hedge ratio} = \frac{8.7249}{7.9583} = 1.0963$$

PepsiCo needs to sell short 1.0963 8% Treasury bonds for each bond to be hedged. PepsiCo needs to sell short

$$\text{Number of contracts} = (\text{Hedge ratio}) \left(\frac{\text{Principal amount to be hedged}}{\text{Par value of hedging instrument}} \right) \qquad \text{(E.8)}$$

Each futures contract covers $100,000 principal amount of bonds, so

$$\text{Number of contracts} = (1.0963) \left(\frac{50,000,000}{100,000} \right) = 548 \text{ Treasury bond contracts}$$

To verify, suppose interest rates rise by 1%. The missed issuance opportunity will cost PepsiCo

$$0.087249(50,000,000) = \$4,362,450$$

But it will earn a profit on the futures contracts equal to

$$548(0.079583)100,000 = \$4,361,148$$

This profit offsets 99.97% of the opportunity cost. ∎

Self-Check

1. Explain a company's rationale for hedging. How does a hedge work?

2. A company might win a contract to sell goods to a British company in exchange for pounds sterling. How could it go about hedging its sterling/dollar foreign exchange risk?

3. A company is considering borrowing on a floating-rate basis. How could it hedge its interest-rate risk?

4. What are interest-rate caps and floors? How are they like options?

5. How could a company use interest-rate futures to hedge an upcoming issue of long-term debt?

SUMMARY

Financial markets have become more volatile in recent years, and companies actively seek ways to hedge their risk exposure. Financial engineers have responded by developing new hedging instruments. These don't eliminate risk. Rather, they transfer it to other parties who are willing to bear it at lower cost.

There are four basic derivatives: options, swaps, forwards, and futures. They can be used to build more complex securities. Once you understand these basic building blocks, you will be able to analyze complex securities more easily.

- An option conveys a right without an obligation. A call option gives the right to buy, a put option the right to sell. Companies can issue call options, known as warrants, to raise equity. They can package them with debt to create convertible bonds or exchangeable bonds. Valuing options can be difficult. Various option valuation models have been developed. The Black-Scholes OPM is one that is widely used.

- The Black-Scholes OPM can be used to value options on stocks. It is also useful for valuing warrants and the option component of convertible bonds. Remember to adjust for the dilution factor when valuing warrants that have not yet been issued.

- Financing with convertible debt represents a form of what practitioners call deferred equity financing. The issue is debt until it is converted. A convertible bond derives its value from two sources: its value as a straight bond and the value of the underlying common stock into which it can be converted.

- Companies, particularly smaller ones, often find it advantageous to issue convertible bonds or bonds with warrants. These securities generally have lower agency costs than straight debt. If the company pursues riskier projects, the option feature lets securityholders share in the payoff from really good outcomes.

- A company that is not tax paying, and does not expect to be in the foreseeable future, should issue convertible preferred stock rather than convertible debt. If it expects to become tax paying soon, it should consider issuing convertible exchangeable preferred stock. It can exchange convertible debt for the convertible preferred when it begins paying income taxes.

- In a perfect capital market, a convertible debt issue should be called for redemption, in order to force its conversion into common stock, when its conversion value reaches its effective call price (the optional redemption price plus accrued interest). With costly transactions, including the chance of a "failed conversion," companies usually call only when the conversion value exceeds the effective call price by at least 20%.

- Interest-rate swaps entered the marketplace in 1981. Their use has grown rapidly. The two parties to a swap exchange interest but not principal. Payments are based on a notional principal amount. Swaps can be used to transform fixed-rate debt into floating-rate debt, and vice versa. Interest-rate swaps are useful in hedging interest-rate risk. The swap market has grown in response to the increase in hedging by companies.

- A company that wants to transform some fixed-rate debt into floating-rate debt should compare the cost of refunding the fixed-rate debt and the cost of entering into a fixed-rate–floating-rate swap. It should select the lower-cost alternative.

- Forwards and futures are contracts that obligate the holder to buy a specified amount of a particular asset at a stated price on a particular date in the future. Futures are standardized, forwards are not. Futures are exchange-traded. Forwards are traded over the counter. Forwards allow greater flexibility in design, whereas futures are more liquid and have less default risk. Both are useful for hedging commodity price risk, foreign exchange risk, and interest-rate risk.

- A company can use derivatives to reduce its exposure to commodity price, foreign exchange, or interest-rate risk. It should decide how much risk it wants to transfer. It should make sure that any transaction it considers will work properly. If it considers more than one alternative, it should select the one with the lowest cost.

EQUATION SUMMARY

(E.1) $\quad$ CALL $= P_0 N(d_1) - SN(d_2)e^{-\Delta tk}$

(E.2) $\quad d_1 = \dfrac{\ln(P_0/S) + \Delta tk}{\sigma \Delta t^{1/2}} + \dfrac{\sigma \Delta t^{1/2}}{2}$

(E.3) $\quad d_2 = d_1 - \sigma \Delta t^{1/2}$

(E.4) $\quad$ PUT $=$ CALL $+ Se^{-\Delta tk} - P_0$

(E.5) $\quad W = \dfrac{C}{1+P}$

(E.6) $\quad$ Redemption cushion $=$

$$\dfrac{\left(\begin{matrix}\text{Conversion} \\ \text{ratio}\end{matrix}\right)\left(\begin{matrix}\text{Market price of} \\ \text{common stock}\end{matrix}\right) - \left(\begin{matrix}\text{Redemption} \\ \text{price}\end{matrix}\right)}{\text{Redemption price}}$$

(E.7) $\quad$ Hedge ratio $= \dfrac{\text{Volatility of bond to be hedged}}{\text{Volatility of hedging instrument}}$

(E.8) $\quad$ Number of contracts $=$

$$(\text{Hedge ratio})\left(\dfrac{\text{Principal amount to be hedged}}{\text{Par value of hedging instrument}}\right)$$

TOPIC REVIEW ACTIVITIES

SELF-TEST PROBLEMS

1. (Exercise value and time premium of a call option) Philip Morris stock is currently selling for $119⅞ per share. What is the exercise value and the time premium of these two Philip Morris options?
   a. A call option with a strike price of $115 and a market value of $6⅝.
   b. A call option with a strike price of $125 and a market value of $1.

2. (Put-call parity) A BankAmerica call option with a $115 strike price has a value of $5⅞. The market price of the stock is $113¼ and the present value of the strike price is $113.00. What should be the value of a put option on BankAmerica with the same maturity and strike price?

3. (Value of a convertible bond) Xygot Company has a convertible bond outstanding that is convertible into 20 common shares. Xygot common shares are selling for $35 per share. A similar nonconvertible bond would be expected to sell for about $900.
   a. The convertible bond is selling for a premium of $75 above the greater of its conversion value and its straight-bond value. What is the market price of the convertible bond?
   b. What is the value of the conversion option of the convertible bond?
   c. Xygot can call the bond and force conversion at a redemption price of $1050. Should Xygot call the bond today?

4. (Interest-rate swap payments) Suppose that Intel enters into a swap agreement where it agrees to pay LIBOR plus 0.5% and it receives a fixed 8.0%. The notional amount is $100 million and the net payments are made semiannually.
   a. What is Intel's cash flow if LIBOR is 6.00%?
   b. What is Intel's cash flow if LIBOR is 8.50%?

SOLUTIONS TO SELF-TEST PROBLEMS

1. a. This option is in-the-money and its exercise value is $P_0 - S = 119⅞ - 115 = \$4⅞$. The time premium is the market value minus the exercise value, which is $6⅝ - 4⅞ = \$1¾$.
   b. This option is out-of-the-money, so its exercise value is $0. The time premium is the market value minus the exercise value, which is $1 - 0 = \$1$.

2. Using the put-call parity relationship, we can write the value of a put as:

   PUT $=$ CALL $+ Se^{-\Delta tk} - P_0$

   PUT $= 5⅞ + 113.00 - 113¼$
   $$= 5.875 + 113.00 - 113.25 = 5.625 = \$5⅝$$

3. a. The conversion value $=$ (Conversion ratio)(Stock price) $= 20(35) = \$700$. Since the straight-bond value is $900, the convertible is worth $75 more than the greater of $700 or $900, which is $975.
   b. The value of the conversion option of the convertible bond is the value of the convertible bond minus the straight-bond value $= 975 - 900 = \$75$.
   c. Xygot should not call the bond and pay $1050 for it when its market value is only $975. The optimal time to call the bond is when the conversion value reaches the effective call price, which is the redemption value plus accrued interest. Ignoring the accrued interest, in a perfect capital market, Xygot should wait to call the bond until the stock price reaches $1050/20 = \$52.50$.

4. a. For this 6-month period, Intel receives 8.0% and pays 6.5%, so Intel receives $100,000,000(0.08 - 0.065)/2 = \$750,000$. Intel receives this sum from its swap counterparty.
   b. In this period, Intel receives 8.0% and pays 9.0%, so Intel's cash flow is $100,000,000(0.08 - 0.09)/2 = -\$500,000$. Intel must pay the swap counterparty.

QUESTIONS

1. What is a derivative?
2. What are the variables that affect the value of a call option?
3. What is the relationship between the values of a call option and a put option?
4. What is a warrant?
5. What is a convertible security?
6. Explain why a convertible bond can be viewed as a package consisting of a straight bond and warrants.
7. What is an interest-rate swap?
8. Warrants are often referred to as "sweeteners" to a bond issue, as though the company can "throw them into the deal" at no cost. Explain why it is, or is not, costless for the company to include warrants with a bond issue.
9. Explain why futures contracts are similar to forward contracts. How are they different?
10. What is the basic rationale for hedging?
11. Explain how each of the following instruments is used to hedge interest-rate risk:
   a. interest-rate swap
   b. option to buy a bond
   c. interest-rate future

CHALLENGING QUESTIONS

12. Consider the following statement: "A call option is a great way to make money. If the asset goes up in value, you get the increase, but if the asset goes down in value, you do not exercise the option and do not lose any money. Therefore, everyone should invest in call options." Is this statement true, false, or part true and part false? Explain why.
13. We pointed out that common stock in a company that has some debt can be viewed as a call option. Explain why.
14. Explain why a convertible bond can be viewed as a combination of (1) the underlying common stock that it is convertible into and (2) a put option exercisable at the conversion price.
15. Why does the time premium of an option increase (decrease) as the value of the underlying asset moves toward (away from) the strike price?
16. Explain why it is possible to view an interest-rate swap as a portfolio of forward contracts.
17. Explain why a futures contract can be viewed as a sequence of forward contracts. Each day the old forward contract is settled and a new one is written.

PROBLEM SET A

A1. (Exercise value and time premium of call or put options) What are the exercise values and the time premiums of the following options?
   a. An Exxon call with a strike price of $100 and a market value of $4¼. Exxon stock is selling for $102⅞.
   b. An Exxon put with a strike price of $100 and a market value of $1½. Exxon stock is selling for $102⅞.
   c. A Lucent call with a strike price of $55 and a market value of $4¼. Lucent stock is selling for $53⅞.

   d. A Lucent put with a strike price of $55 and a market value of $4⅜. Lucent stock is selling for $53⅞.

A2. (Put-call parity)
   a. General Electric stock is selling for $103. A call option with a strike price of $105 is selling for $3¼ and the present value of the strike price is $104. What should a put with the same strike price and maturity be worth?
   b. An IBM option is close to expiration. The strike price is $140, the stock price is $148¾, and the put price is $½. The present value of the strike price is $139.90. What should the $140 call with the same expiration be worth?

A3. (Value of a convertible bond) OEM Corporation has a convertible bond outstanding that is convertible into 25 common shares. OEM common shares are selling for $40 per share. A similar nonconvertible bond would be expected to sell for about $950.
   a. The convertible bond is selling for a premium of $50 above the greater of its conversion value and its straight-bond value. What is the market price of the convertible bond?
   b. What is the value of the conversion option of the convertible bond?
   c. OEM can call the bond and force conversion at a redemption price of $1080. Should OEM call the bond today?

A4. (Interest-rate swap payments) Coke enters into a swap agreement where it agrees to pay a fixed 8.5% and receive LIBOR plus 0.5%. The notional amount is $300 million and the net payments are made semiannually.
   a. What is Coke's cash payment or receipt if LIBOR is 6.00%?
   b. What is Intel's cash payment or receipt if LIBOR is 10.00%?

A5. (Caps, floors, and collars) What will the holder of the following contracts pay or receive?
   a. You buy a 9% interest-rate cap to hedge against interest-rate increases on a large bond. What do you pay or receive if the interest rate is 7%? 9.5%?
   b. You buy a 5% floor. What do you pay or receive if the interest rate is 6%? 4.5%?
   c. You buy a 5%/9% collar. What do you pay or receive if the interest rate is 4.5%, 6%, or 9.5%?

A6. (Valuing a call option) Redo the Black-Scholes OPM example, assuming $P_0 = 28$, $S = 30$, $\Delta t = 0.75$, $k = 0.6$ and $\sigma = 0.40$. (This is identical to the example in the text except that the standard deviation is larger.) Why has the value of the call option increased?

A7. (Valuing a call option) Redo problem A6 assuming $\Delta t = 2.00$. Why has the value of the call option increased?

PROBLEM SET B

B1. (Call and put valuation) Suppose a stock is selling for $48.50 per share, the standard deviation of the return from owning a share of this stock is 24% per year, and the riskless return with continuous compounding is 5% APR. According to the Black-Scholes OPM:

a. What is a call option on this stock worth if the option has a strike price of $50 and 8 months until expiration?

b. What is a put option on this stock worth if the option has a strike price of $50 and 8 months until expiration?

c. What is a call option on this stock worth if the option has a strike price of $50 and 4 months until expiration?

d. What is a put option on this stock worth if the option has a strike price of $50 and 4 months until expiration?

B2. (Put valuation) According to the Black-Scholes OPM, what is the value of a 6-month put option with a strike price of $40 on stock selling for $37.75 if the standard deviation of the return to the stock is 28% per year and the riskless return with continuous compounding is 7% APR?

B3. (Call valuation, and time premium and exercise value) Suppose the standard deviation of a stock's return is 25% per year and the riskless return with continuous compounding is 6% APR. According to the Black-Scholes OPM:

a. What is a 6-month call option on this stock worth if the strike price is $30 and the stock is currently selling for $28? What are the time premium and exercise value of this option?

b. What is a 6-month call option on this stock worth if the strike price is $30 and the stock is currently selling for $32? What are the time premium and exercise value of this option?

c. What is a 6-month call option on this stock worth if the strike price is $30 and the stock is currently selling for $34? What are the time premium and exercise value of this option?

B4. (Call valuation for differing volatilities) Consider a 9-month call option with a strike price of $25 on a stock that currently sells for $25. According to the Black-Scholes OPM, if the riskless return with continuous compounding is 6% APR:

a. What is the value of this option if σ is 35%?

b. What is the value of this option if σ is 30%?

c. What is the value of this option if σ is 25%?

B5. (Call value for a deep out-of-the-money option) According to the Black-Scholes OPM, what is the value of a call option with a strike price of $110 and 3 months until expiration on an asset that has a current market value of $90 and a σ of 30% per year if k is 10%?

B6. (Call valuation for differing interest rates) Consider a 6-month call option with a strike price of $20 on a stock that currently sells for $21. According to the Black-Scholes OPM, if σ is 30%:

a. What is the value of this option if k is 4%?

b. What is the value of this option if k is 7%?

c. What is the value of this option if k is 10%?

B7. (Call value, exercise value, and time premium) What is the current value of a European call option with an exercise price of $20 and an expiration date 9 months from now if the stock is non-dividend-paying and is now selling for $24.38, the variance of the return on the stock is

0.48, and the riskless return is 6% APR? What is the current exercise value of this call option? What is the current time premium?

B8. (Interest-rate swaps and comparative advantage) Tokai Bank can borrow at a fixed rate of 9% or at LIBOR. A manufacturing company can borrow at a fixed rate of 12% or at LIBOR + 1%.

a. Is there a mutually advantageous opportunity to engage in an interest-rate swap? Explain.

b. Suppose the bank offers to pay the manufacturing company LIBOR in return for payments at 11½%. How should the manufacturing company respond?

c. The manufacturing company proposes to pay 10½% in return for LIBOR. Is such a swap advantageous for the bank?

d. What fraction of the net cost benefit does each party realize under the swap terms in part **c?**

B9. (Interest-rate swaps and comparative advantage) Triple-A-rated Exxon Corporation can borrow at a fixed rate of 8.5% or at LIBOR + 0.10%. Single-B-rated Cajun Drilling Company can borrow fixed-rate at 12% or floating-rate at LIBOR + 2%.

a. Is there a mutually advantageous opportunity to engage in an interest-rate swap? Explain.

b. Suppose Exxon proposes that Cajun pay 11% in return for LIBOR. Should Cajun accept the offer?

c. Suppose Exxon proposes that Cajun pay 9.5% in return for LIBOR. Should Cajun accept the offer?

B10. (Hedging with a put option) Petrie Stores holds 200,000 shares of Toys 'R' Us common stock. It plans to sell the shares but would like to delay the sale for 3 months for tax reasons. Toys 'R' Us is trading at $40. The standard deviation of the return on the stock is 28% per year. The riskless return with continuous compounding is 6% APR. The stock is not expected to pay dividends for the next 3 months.

a. How could Petrie Stores hedge the risk of a decline in the Toys 'R' Us share price?

b. How much would an at-the-money put option on 200,000 shares cost?

c. How much would the put option cost with a strike price of $35?

d. Compare the advantages and disadvantages of the two option alternatives.

B11. (Interest-rate cap) Dayton, Duvalier, and Dice (Three D) plans to acquire Neptune Candy Company through a leveraged buyout. It will borrow $1 billion of the purchase price from its banks. The interest rate is 3-month LIBOR + 1%. Three D would like to protect against its interest cost rising above 10%.

a. How can Three D hedge this risk?

b. Suppose Three D buys a 9% interest-rate cap contract. LIBOR varies over the next 8 quarters as shown in the table below. How much interest does Three D pay each quarter?

Quarter	1	2	3	4	5	6	7	8
3-month LIBOR (%)	7.50	6.75	8.50	10.25	11.50	12.25	9.75	7.50

   c. How much does the party who sold the cap contract have to pay Three D each quarter?

B12. (Interest-rate collar) An interest-rate collar provides for an 8% floor and 10% cap. The notional amount is $100 million. The periodic interest rates are shown in the table in problem B11. Calculate the amount of the payment the seller of the collar contract will make or receive each quarter.

B13. (Hedging a new bond issue) Kmart plans to issue $100 million of bonds. It needs 1 month to prepare the documentation. It is concerned that interest rates might rise before it can sell the issue. Its current new-issue rate is 9% for 30-year bonds.

   a. How could Kmart use futures contracts to hedge this risk?

   b. The yield on 8% 20-year Treasury bonds is 7.50%. Kmart's treasurer estimates that the yield on these bonds will rise to 8.50% if Kmart's borrowing cost rises to 10%. Calculate the hedge ratio.

   c. Calculate the number of Treasury bond futures contracts Kmart should sell to hedge its risk.

   d. Calculate Kmart's missed issuance opportunity cost and profit on the futures contracts if interest rates rise by 1%.

   e. Recalculate the hedge ratio, number of contracts, missed issuance opportunity cost, and profit on the futures con- tracts if the yield on 20-year Treasury bonds rises by 0.5% when Kmart's borrowing cost rises by 1%.

PROBLEM SET C

C1. (Implied standard deviation) What standard deviation of the return to a stock is implied by the Black-Scholes OPM for the following situation? A 5-month call option with a strike price of $35 sells for $2.03, k is 6%, and the stock is currently selling for $32.75. (Do not solve this problem. Indicate *how* you might solve it.)

C2. (Put-call parity) Use put-call parity to show that the combination of buying an asset, buying a put with a strike price of S, and selling a call with a strike price of S is equivalent to simply buying a riskless bond that has a maturity value of S.

C3. (Puzzle: Using options as alternative securities) Suppose you live in a state that has a usury law prohibiting interest charges above 9% APR, but current market rates are 18% effective annual for a project for which you have the opportunity to provide 6-year debt financing. Show how you can use option contracts on an asset that is connected with the project to provide the project with a 6-year "loan" of $250,000, from which you will earn the market rate of 18% per year with interest payments of $45,000 per year and a principal repayment of $250,000 at the end of 6 years.

BIBLIOGRAPHY

Arak, Marcelle, Arturo Estrella, Laurie Goodman, and Andrew Silver. "Interest Rate Swaps: An Alternative Explanation," *Financial Management,* 1988, 17(2):12–18.

Bell, David E., and William S. Krasker. "Estimating Hedge Ratios," *Financial Management,* 1986, 15(2):34–39.

Black, Fischer. "Fact and Fantasy in the Use of Options and Corporate Liabilities," *Financial Analysts Journal,* 1975, 31(July-August):36–41, 61–72.

Black, Fischer, and Myron Scholes. "The Pricing of Options and Corporate Liabilities," *Journal of Political Economy,* 1973, 81(May/June):637–654.

Brown, Keith C., and Donald J. Smith. "Default Risk and Innovations in the Design of Interest Rate Swaps," *Financial Management,* 1993, 22(2):94–105.

Chang, Jack S. K., and Soushan Wu. "On Hedging Jump Risks in the Foreign Exchange and Stock Markets," *Financial Management,* 1994, 23(1):15.

Emery, Douglas R., and John D. Finnerty, "Using a PERCS-for-Common Exchange Offer to Reduce the Costs of a Dividend Cut," *Journal of Applied Corporate Finance,* 1995, 7(4):77–89.

Grant, Dwight. "Rolling the Hedge Forward: An Extension," *Financial Management,* 1984, 13(4):26–28.

Howe, John S., and Peihwang Wei. "The Valuation Effects of Warrant Extensions," *Journal of Finance,* 1993, 48(1):305–314.

Hunter, William C., and Stephen G. Timme. "A Stochastic Dominance Approach to Evaluating Foreign Exchange Hedging Strategies," *Financial Management,* 1992, 21(3):104–112.

Koppenhaver, G. D. "Bank Funding Risks, Risk Aversion, and the Choice of Futures Hedging Instrument," *Journal of Finance,* 1985, 40(1):241–255.

Kumar, Raman, Atulya Sarin, and Kuldeep Shastri. "The Behavior of Option Price Around Large Block Transactions in the Underlying Security," *Journal of Finance,* 1992, 47(3):879–890.

Lauterbach, Beni, and Paul Schultz. "Pricing Warrants: An Empirical Study of the Black-Scholes Model and Its Alternatives," *Journal of Finance,* 1990, 45(4):1181–1209.

Maldonado, Rita, and Anthony Saunders. "Foreign Exchange Futures and the Law of One Price," *Financial Management,* 1983, 12(1):19–23.

McCabe, George M., and Charles T. Franckle. "The Effectiveness of Rolling the Hedge Forward in the Treasury Bill Futures Market," *Financial Management,* 1983, 12(2):21–29.

Merton, Robert C. "Theory of Rational Option Pricing," *Bell Journal of Economics and Management Science,* 1973, 4(Spring):141–183.

Nance, Deana R., Clifford W. Smith, Jr., and Charles W. Smithson. "On the Determinants of Corporate Hedging," *Journal of Finance,* 1993, 48(1):267–284.

Rendleman, Richard J., Jr., and Brit J. Bartter. "Two-State Option Pricing," *Journal of Finance,* 1979, 34(5):1093–1110.

Smithson, Charles W. *Managing Financial Risk: 1995 Yearbook.* New York: CIBC Wood Gundy, 1995.

Smithson, Charles W. *Managing Financial Risk: 1997 Yearbook.* New York: CIBC Wood Gundy, 1997.

Smithson, Charles W., Clifford W. Smith, Jr., and D. Sykes Wilford. *Managing Financial Risk: A Guide to Derivative Products, Financial Engineering, and Value Maximization.* Burr Ridge, Ill: Irwin, 1995.

Sprenkle, Case. "Warrant Prices as Indications of Expectations," *Yale Economic Essays,* 1961, 1:179–232.

Titman, Sheridan. "Interest Rate Swaps and Corporate Financing Choices," *Journal of Finance,* 1992, 47(4):1503–1516.

TOPIC F

Mergers and Acquisitions

Acquisitions attract headlines because of the drama of the battle for control. Not long ago, the front page of the *Wall Street Journal* carried an article headlined "Bidding War: Offers for RJR Pit KKR and Shearson in a Battle for Turf," which announced the bid of Kohlberg Kravis Roberts & Company (KKR) for control of RJR Nabisco. Five days earlier, a management-led group had announced its intention to develop a proposal, in conjunction with Shearson Lehman Hutton, to acquire RJR Nabisco in a leveraged buyout valued at $75 per common share. A leveraged buyout is an acquisition that is financed mainly, sometimes more than 90%, by borrowing. The KKR bid amounted to $90 per share. The battle for control unfolded over the ensuing six-week period. It involved three bidding groups, no fewer than ten of the leading investment banks, and a veritable army of lawyers, information agents, accountants, and commercial banks. KKR finally prevailed when it offered to pay $109 per common share, 45% more than the management-led group's original proposal and a staggering aggregate bid of $25 billion.

In this topic, we'll show you how to analyze corporate acquisitions. An acquisition is like a "mega" capital budgeting project. As such, a company should acquire another company only if it will increase shareholder wealth. However, a corporate acquisition involves special legal, tax, and accounting issues. We'll explain how to tailor capital budgeting techniques to evaluate a corporate acquisition. We'll also describe other valuation techniques—especially comparative analysis—that are widely used in practice.

Agency problems are important in corporate acquisitions. How will the target respond? Under the Principle of Self-Interested Behavior, we would expect that managers would not sit by passively when facing a possible acquisition of "their" company. In fact, corporate managers go to great lengths to erect barriers to forestall unwanted suitors from acquiring their companies (and perhaps eliminating their jobs in the process). We'll describe these measures and their potential impact on shareholder wealth.

MERGERS AND ACQUISITIONS AND THE PRINCIPLES OF FINANCE

◆ *Self-Interested Behavior:* Look for opportunities to make profitable acquisitions. Acquire another company only if doing so increases shareholder wealth for your company.

◆ *Two-Sided Transactions:* Acquiring another company usually requires paying a premium over the prevailing market price large enough to get the acquiree's shareholders to sell their shares.

◆ *Comparative Advantage:* Recognize that a merger of companies that have different comparative advantages might have a positive NPV.

◆ *Behavioral Principle:* Look to comparable acquisitions for guidance regarding a reasonable price to pay for an acquisition.

◆ *Valuable Ideas:* Look for opportunities to redesign securities or the structure of an acquisition transaction to enhance value.

◆ *Incremental Benefits:* Calculate the net advantage of an acquisition on the basis of the incremental after-tax cash flows the acquisition will provide.

◆ *Risk-Return Trade-Off:* Merging two companies through an exchange of shares benefits the bondholders of both, because their expected return increases while their risk decreases.

◆ *Diversification:* Diversifying through a conglomerate merger will benefit shareholders only if they could not achieve such diversification on their own.

◆ *Capital Market Efficiency:* The method of accounting for an acquisition does not affect the benefits shareholders derive from it.

◆ *Time Value of Money:* Use discounted-cash-flow analysis to measure the net advantage of an acquisition.

WHAT'S SPECIAL ABOUT A MERGER?

A corporate acquisition is usually a substantial capital investment for the acquiring company. Table F.1 on page 728 lists the ten largest merger and acquisition transactions that have taken place in the United States through year-end 1996. Note that five of these occurred in 1996! Because of its size, an acquisition can have a greater impact on shareholder wealth than other forms of capital investment. The analytical tools and basic decision rules of capital budgeting still apply. However, particular care must be taken in applying these tools because of the enormous size and complexity of the investment.

A corporate acquisition can take the form of either a merger or a consolidation. A **merger** involves a combination of two companies, the acquiror and the acquiree. The *acquiror* absorbs all the assets and liabilities of the acquiree and assumes the acquiree's business. The *acquiree* loses its independent existence, often becoming a subsidiary of the acquiror.

In a **consolidation,** two or more companies combine to form an entirely new entity. The distinction between acquiror and acquiree becomes blurred, because shares of each of the consolidating companies are exchanged for shares of the new company. Both of the consolidating companies lose their independent existence, often becoming subsidiaries of the new company or, in combination, becoming the new company.

Lockheed's and Martin Marietta's "Merger of Equals"   EXAMPLE

Between 1985 and 1995, the federal defense budget for research and development, test and evaluation, and procurement had shrunk by almost two-thirds in real terms (dollars of constant purchasing power). This reduction placed pressure on aerospace/defense companies to consolidate in order to achieve production economies and remain competitive.

In August 1994, Lockheed Corporation and Martin Marietta Corporation, two of the nation's leading aerospace companies, announced a consolidation, which they proclaimed a "merger of equals." They would form a new corporation, Lockheed Martin Corporation, which would have two special-purpose subsidiaries. One would be merged with and into Lockheed, and the other would be merged with and into Martin Marietta. As a result, Lockheed and Martin Marietta would become wholly owned subsidiaries of Lockheed Martin. ■

When two companies of roughly equal size combine, they often choose to consolidate. When they are of unequal size, one company acquires the other through merger. Usually the larger company acquires the smaller, although this is not always the case. The distinction between a merger and a consolidation is important in a legal sense, but the same analytical techniques apply to both.

Accordingly, we will assume that one party to a corporate combination can be identified, or at least treated for analytical purposes, as the acquiror, and we'll use the terms *corporate acquisition* and *merger* interchangeably to refer to corporate combinations in general.

A merger involves the acquisition of an entire company. Buying a company, with its own portfolio of assets and

TABLE F.1

The Ten Largest Merger and Acquisition Transactions in the United States Through Year-End 1996 (dollar amounts in billions)

ACQUIRING FIRM	ACQUIRED FIRM	APPROXIMATE PRICE PAID[a]	YEAR ANNOUNCED
Kohlberg Kravis Roberts & Co.	RJR Nabisco, Inc.	$24.6	1988
British Telecommunications PLC-U.K.	MCI Communications Corp.[b]	21.6	1996
Bell Atlantic Corp.	NYNEX Corp.	19.5	1996
Disney (Walt) Co.	Capital Cities/ABC Inc.	19.0	1995
SBC Communications	Pacific Telesis Group	16.7	1996
Beecham Group PLC-U.K.	Smithkline Beckman Corp.	16.1	1989
WorldCom Inc.	MFS Communications Co.	14.1	1996
Boeing Co.	McDonnell Douglas Corp.	13.3	1996
Chevron Corp.	Gulf Corp.	13.2	1984
Philip Morris Companies Inc.	Kraft Inc.	13.1	1988

[a]Based on the number of shares of common stock acquired.
[b]Remaining 80% interest.
Source: Houlihan Lokey Howard & Zukin, *Mergerstat Review 1997,* p. 166.

its own liabilities, is more complicated than buying a new machine or building a new plant. In addition, complex tax issues must often be resolved. For these reasons, estimating the incremental cash flows is inherently more difficult than the measurement problems encountered in capital budgeting projects of the types discussed in chapters 8 through 10.

Also, how a company finances an acquisition takes on added importance. The economics of the investment and how the company finances it tend to interact, because the acquisition can alter the acquiror's financial structure. Thus, estimating the required return is also inherently more difficult in the case of corporate acquisitions than in other forms of capital investment. Yet accuracy is often crucial because of the amount of corporate funds that the acquiror must commit to the transaction.

Self-Check

1. What is a merger? What is a consolidation? How do they differ?

2. A corporate acquisition can be viewed as a special type of capital budgeting project. In what respects is it more complicated than a typical capital budgeting project?

WHY COMPANIES MERGE

A company may have a number of possible motives for seeking to merge with a particular company. Each should be judged against the objective of maximizing shareholder wealth.

When Do Mergers Create Value?

The shareholders of an acquiring company can benefit from a merger only if the two companies are worth more in combination than separately. To provide a framework for discussion, suppose that acquiror and acquiree are worth V_A and V_B in total market value (that is, the total market value of their assets), respectively. They would be worth V_{AB} in total market value in combination. The acquiror must normally offer the acquiree's shareholders some pre-mium, P_B, above V_B to induce them to sell their shares. The acquiror also incurs various costs and expenses, *Expenses*. The **net advantage to merging (NAM)** to the acquiror's shareholders equals the difference between (1) the total market value of the company post-merger net of the cost of completing the transaction and (2) the total market value of the companies before the merger:

$$\text{NAM} = V_{AB} - (V_B + P_B) - \text{Expenses} - V_A$$
$$= [V_{AB} - (V_A + V_B)] - P_B - \text{Expenses} \quad \text{(F.1)}$$

If the net advantage to merging is positive, the merger would increase the wealth of the acquiror's shareholders. The term in brackets in equation (F.1) represents what is commonly referred to as the *synergistic effect* of a merger. The whole is worth more than the sum of the parts when this expression is positive. Under the Principle of

Two-Sided Transactions, the premium P_B represents both a gain to the acquiree's shareholders and a cost to the acquiror's shareholders. Even if the synergistic effect is positive, the acquiror's shareholders will benefit only if the premium P_B and the *Expenses* are less than the synergistic

benefits. One of the more interesting issues in the area of mergers and acquisitions is the size of P_B in relation to $V_{AB} - (V_A + V_B)$. If P_B is large enough, NAM can be negative. In that case, the acquiror will have "overpaid" for the acquisition.

Calculating the Net Advantage to Merging

EXAMPLE

Company A, with a total market value of $50 million, is planning to acquire company B, which has a total market value of $15 million. Company A estimates that the merged company will be worth $75 million as a result of operating and other efficiencies. Company A's investment bankers have advised that company A will have to pay a $6 million premium in price to acquire company B. Merger-related costs and expenses will amount to $1 million. Applying equation (F.1), we find that the net advantage to merging is

$$NAM = [75 - (50 + 15)] - 6 - 1 = \$3 \text{ million}$$

Synergy creates $10 million of value (= $75 - [15 + 50]$). Of this amount, $6 million is paid to company B's shareholders, and $1 million covers transaction-related expenses. Company A's shareholders wind up with a net increase in their wealth of $3 million. Thus the merger would benefit both companies' shareholders. ■

Evidence suggests that mergers do tend to produce synergy, at least when the two companies are in the same industry, and that the stockholders of acquired companies tend to benefit handsomely. Target stockholders generally receive takeover premiums averaging between 30% and 50% for their shares. In contrast, the shareholders of acquiring companies tend to realize only very modest gains. This sharing of benefits is probably due to capital market efficiency, reflecting the impact (actual or potential) of competing acquirors.

Valid Motives for Merging

A merger can be economically beneficial only if the sum of the parts exceeds the whole. There are at least four situations in which this can happen.

Achieve Operating Efficiencies and Economies of Scale

Two companies may decide to merge in order to achieve *operating efficiencies* or to take advantage of *economies of scale*. The merged companies can eliminate duplicate facilities, operations, or departments.[1] Consider two airlines with overlapping routes. By merging their operations, they can better coordinate scheduling and eliminate excess capacity.

Achieving operating efficiencies is more likely to result from a horizontal or vertical merger than from a conglomerate merger. A **horizontal merger** combines two

companies in the same line of business. A **vertical merger** involves integrating forward toward the consumer, or backward toward the source of supply, in a particular line of business. A **conglomerate merger** joins companies in unrelated businesses. The merger of two airlines is a horizontal merger. When a company purchases one of its parts suppliers, that is a vertical merger. Most mergers in the United States since World War II have been of the conglomerate type.

One means of achieving operating efficiencies involves combining two companies that have complementary resources. For example, a small computer company might have a skilled product engineering staff and one or more unique products but might lack management expertise and a strong sales staff. A second computer company, perhaps older and larger, might have strong management and an established sales network but lack state-of-the-art products. A merger could be mutually beneficial, because each company has something the other needs. Such a case is an application of the Principle of Comparative Advantage. But a merger will be beneficial to both only if it enables each company to obtain what it needs more cheaply than it could have if it had remained on its own.

Two companies in the same line of business might also merge in order to achieve economies of scale in production, distribution, or some other phase of their operation. Economies of scale occur when the average unit cost of goods sold decreases as output expands. For example, a higher volume of production might permit a company to build larger, more efficient plants than the smaller ones it must build now. Achieving economies of scale in production is a key motive underlying most horizontal mergers.

---

[1]Something to consider if you are thinking of pursuing a career in financial management: The financial staff of the acquiree is usually one of the first redundancies to be eliminated!

EXAMPLE	*Lockheed's and Martin Marietta's Horizontal Merger*

The Lockheed–Martin Marietta combination would create a leading U.S. aerospace company, which would have the critical mass and economies of scale necessary to compete effectively in the global business environment. The boards of directors of the two companies expected the merger to enhance the combined companies' position in commercial markets, give rise to an estimated $200 million per year of pretax operating cost savings, and create a broader product platform from which the combined business could grow. ■

Operating efficiencies and economies of scale are the main sources of any synergy. A conglomerate merger has the least potential for generating them. In any case, one must be careful in assessing potential operating efficiencies and potential economies of scale. They may never be realized. For example, merging an insurance broker and a securities broker to achieve economies of distribution may fail to yield the anticipated benefits if the brokers cannot (or simply will not) sell each other's products.

EXAMPLE	*Potential Economies Are Not Always Realized*

After Sears, Roebuck & Co. acquired Dean Witter Reynolds Inc., it placed Dean Witter stockbrokers in more than 300 of its approximately 850 retail stores nationwide. Dean Witter brokers complained about the "socks and stocks" marketing strategy, saying it was difficult to drum up business from people shopping for clothing, vacuum cleaners, and lawn mowers. Within a few years, Sears had reduced the number of Dean Witter outlets by more than two-thirds. ■

Realize Tax Benefits Suppose a company has tax loss carryforwards it cannot fully use. Merging with a profitable company that pays income taxes might prove mutually beneficial. Under some circumstances, the company with a loss can use its tax loss carryforwards to shelter some—or perhaps all—of the profitable company's income from taxation. For example, when the Penn Central Corporation emerged from bankruptcy, in effect it was able to use its substantial tax loss carryforwards by acquiring tax-paying companies.[2]

Here is another possible tax benefit. Consider a company in a mature industry that is generating a large amount of free cash flow. If the company distributes the cash to its shareholders, they will have to pay tax (unless shares are repurchased at a price that is less than the shareholders' tax basis in the shares). But they won't have to pay tax if the company instead invests the cash in the shares of other companies. Whether the acquiror's shareholders truly gain depends on whether the acquisition has a positive net present value when compared to the other possible alternative uses of the cash.

Capture Surplus Cash Mergers may be motivated by the acquiror's desire to use the acquiree's cash. Companies with substantial cash and a shortage of capital investment opportunities may therefore look like sitting ducks for acquisition unless they can invest the cash or distribute it to their shareholders.

Grow More Quickly or More Cheaply A company may find that it can grow more quickly or more cheaply by acquiring other companies than through internal development. It's generally quicker to obtain new products, new facilities, or a national distribution network by acquiring a company that has already developed them. A company may be able to acquire assets, such as oil and gas reserves, more cheaply by purchasing another company than by developing— or in this case exploring for—its own. Acquiring a local company may be the most cost-effective means of establishing a secure market position in a foreign market. The desire to secure a position in the U.S. market probably is largely responsible for the sharp increase in the number of foreign acquisitions of U.S. companies in recent years.

---

[2]Under current tax law, the merger must have a valid business purpose, apart from taxes, in order for the Internal Revenue Service to permit the profitable company to use the other company's tax net operating loss carryforwards (NOLs). The Tax Reform Act of 1986 tightened restrictions on one company's ability to use another company's NOLs to shelter part of its operating income from taxation following an acquisition. It is no longer possible for an acquiring company to use its NOLs to shelter gain on the sale of the acquiree's assets (for example, assets in a subsidiary with a very low tax basis) following the corporate acquisition, which was one of the strategies Penn Central adopted.

Sandoz A.G.'s Acquisition of Genetic Therapy Inc.

In August 1995, Sandoz A.G., one of the world's largest pharmaceutical companies, acquired Genetic Therapy Inc., which is developing human gene therapy delivery systems. Sandoz paid $295 million for Genetic Therapy, whose annual sales revenues were just $17.2 million. Why would Sandoz pay such a high price for a relatively small company? Genetic Therapy's research and development efforts were yielding promising opportunities—new product options—and options have value! ■

Questionable Motives for Merging

Companies also cite other motives for mergers. Three of the more questionable motives involve diversification, reducing the cost of debt, and enhancing earnings per share.

Diversification   Diversification is generally one of the main motives behind a conglomerate merger. At first glance, this motive seems reasonable because of the Principle of Diversification. But diversification will benefit the acquiror's shareholders *only if they could not achieve such diversification more cheaply on their own.*

A Conglomerate Merger Might Not Increase Shareholder Wealth

Two companies plan to merge through an exchange of shares. The companies are in unrelated businesses, so there is no synergistic effect. Company A has 1 million shares worth $40 each, and company B has 3 million shares worth $20 each. Each company is debt free. Company B will issue 2 new shares of its stock (worth $20 each, for a total of $40) for each share of company A (worth $40). (There is no merger premium in this case.) Table F.2 on page 732 shows the impact of the merger. The total market value of each company is the weighted average of its value in the three possible states of the economy. For example, the value of company A is

$$\text{Value of Company A} = 0.4(50) + 0.5(36) + 0.1(20) = \$40 \text{ million}$$

The value of company B is calculated the same way. Combining companies A and B combines their respective values. The value of the combined company is $100 million (= 40 + 60). Because there are 5 million shares, each share is worth $20 (= 100/5).

Suppose a shareholder owned 1000 shares of company A and 500 shares of company B prior to the merger. Her shares were worth

$$\$50,000 = (40)(1000) + (20)(500)$$

Following the merger, she owns 2500 shares of company B (the original 500 shares plus 2000 more received in exchange for her 1000 shares of company A), which are worth the same $50,000 (= [20]2500).

Shareholder wealth has not changed.[3] ■

The homemade diversification argument is like the homemade dividends argument given in chapter 13 and the individual borrowing (leverage) argument given in chapter 12. They rest on the assumption that there are no market imperfections. Because there are, corporate diversification may create value. As already noted, diversifying at the company level may be more tax efficient than paying out the excess cash to shareholders.

---

[3]Note that the merger might actually make her *worse off* if there are no close substitutes for each company, because the merger in that case would reduce her investment opportunities. Before the merger, she owned the shares of the two companies in the ratio 4:1 by market value ($40,000 of company A and $10,000 of company B). They combine in the ratio 2:3 ($40 million of company A and $60 million of company B). After the merger, she effectively owns them in this new ratio.

TABLE F.2

Diversification Through Merging May Not Increase Shareholder Wealth (dollar amounts in millions except share prices)

	NUMBER OF SHARES	TOTAL VALUE IN STATE			TOTAL MARKET VALUE	SHARE PRICE
		Boom	Stable Growth	Recession		
Probability		0.4	0.5	0.1		
Company A	1 million[b]	$ 50	$36	$20	$ 40	$40
Company B	3 million	75	54	30	60	20
Combined[a]	5 million[b]	125	90	50	100	20

[a]Company A and company B combine through an exchange of shares. Company B issues 2 million new shares in exchange for company A's 1 million outstanding shares.
[b]Company A's 1 million shares are eliminated in exchange for 2 million shares of company B.

Reduced Cost of Debt   A larger (merged) company may achieve economies of scale in issuing securities. If the merged company makes larger issues than the two companies would separately, the merger may result in lower transaction costs. However, lower issuance expenses aren't likely to contribute much to the value of a merger.

But suppose the two companies combine by exchanging shares. Such a merger can lower the combined company's cost of borrowing but it can also benefit bondholders at the expense of shareholders. The problem here is the reverse of the problem of *claim dilution* with respect to capital structure. Stockholders can expropriate wealth from bondholders by diluting the bondholders' claim on the assets.[4]

This same phenomenon can work in reverse, against the stockholders. Diversification via merger can reduce the probability of bankruptcy and, consequently, the bondholders' required returns. The expected return to each class of the companies' debtholders increases, and their risk de-

creases. It follows from the Principle of Risk-Return Trade-Off that the debtholders of each company are unambiguously better off. But if the merger does not alter the two companies' combined returns, the stockholders must be worse off. The bondholders gain at the expense of stockholders, because each company effectively guarantees the debt of the other. Notwithstanding the lower borrowing cost, each company's shareholders are worse off as a result of the merger.

Enhanced Earnings per Share   A company can increase its earnings per share by exchanging its shares for those of another company whose shares have a lower price-earnings ratio. Some managers believe this is beneficial because they think it will increase the company's share price. However, such share-for-share exchanges increase earnings per share *even if no real gain results from the merger.* (We'll return to this point later on.) Shareholders will benefit only if the net advantage to merging is positive.

Self-Check

1. What is the net advantage to merging (NAM)? How is it calculated?

2. List four valid motives that companies may have for merging. Explain each one.

3. What is the difference between a horizontal merger and a vertical merger? How are they different from a conglomerate merger?

4. Two unrelated companies plan to merge. Their joint announcement says that the shareholders of both will

benefit from diversification. Do you agree? Why or why not?

5. Company A with high leverage acquires company B with a debt-free capital structure. The companies exchange shares on the basis of their respective fair market values. Why might the shareholders of company B object to this merger?

---

[4]Claim dilution is explained more fully in enrichment topic C, Financial Contracting.

TECHNICAL ISSUES

When one company acquires another, three sets of technical issues arise: the legal form of the transaction, its tax status, and its accounting treatment. These three sets of issues are interrelated. Figure F.1 summarizes the alternatives.

LEGAL FORM	TAX STATUS	ACCOUNTING TREATMENT
Merger or consolidation Purchase of stock Purchase of assets	Tax-free Taxable	Pooling of interests Purchase accounting

FIGURE F.1
Legal, tax, and accounting issues involved in mergers.

Form of Transaction

There are three basic ways of effecting a corporate acquisition: (1) merger or consolidation, (2) purchase of stock, and (3) purchase of assets.

Merger or Consolidation   In a merger, the acquiror absorbs the acquiree. The acquiror automatically obtains all the assets and assumes all the liabilities of the acquiree, which loses its corporate existence. But suppose the acquiror wishes the acquiree to survive as a separate entity. Then the acquiror can merge the acquiree with a special-purpose subsidiary. The acquiree becomes a wholly owned subsidiary of the acquiror.

A merger or consolidation must comply with each corporation's charter. Many corporate charters require a simple majority of the company's shareholders to approve a merger or consolidation. Some require a two-thirds majority.

A merger or consolidation offers the most flexible means of structuring a tax-free acquisition. It is also generally easier and less costly to complete than either of the other two forms of acquisition.

Purchase of Stock   An acquiror can purchase the acquiree's stock. It still obtains the acquiree's assets and liabilities, but no shareholders' meetings are involved. A prospective acquiror can also bypass management and make a **tender offer** directly to the company's shareholders. It is only an *offer* to purchase; any shareholders who do not like the price offered can refuse to sell their shares. But if the price is high enough, the shareholders will sell their shares. This can create problems for the acquiror, however. If the acquiror purchases fewer than 80% of the acquiree's voting securities, it will not be able to consolidate the acquiree for tax purposes. Also, if any of the acquiree's shares remain outstanding, there is a minority interest in the subsidiary, which creates potential agency problems.[5]

Purchase of Assets   An acquiror may purchase only the selling company's assets. The liabilities of the seller, other than those specifically assumed by the buyer, remain the responsibility of the seller. There is thus substantially less likelihood that hidden liabilities will be discovered after the transaction to the detriment of the buyer. There is also no problem with minority shareholders. In addition, the buyer's shareholders usually do not have to approve the transaction, and most corporate charters require only 50% approval by the seller's shareholders. The three main drawbacks to this structure are that (1) it's more difficult to achieve a tax-free transaction, (2) transferring the title of ownership to individual assets is costly and time consuming, and (3) distributing the cash proceeds to shareholders usually triggers an income tax liability to the shareholders in addition to any tax the company may owe.

Texaco's Acquisition of Getty Oil   EXAMPLE

The federal government challenged the merger of Texaco and Getty Oil Company, at the time the third and twelfth largest oil companies in the United States, because of the two companies' overlapping gasoline marketing operations in the northeastern United States.

The actual percentage of potential mergers contested on antitrust grounds is small. Those involving very large companies, and horizontal acquisitions, appear to be the most likely to be challenged. Many of those that are questioned can survive the challenge by having the acquiror agree to sell assets in the affected market(s) to restore competition, as Texaco agreed to do. ■

---

[5]Consequently, an acquiror that purchases shares from less than all of the acquiree's shareholders—for instance, through a tender offer—generally follows this purchase with a formal merger in order to eliminate the minority interest.

Antitrust Considerations

A merger transaction must comply with federal antitrust law, state anti-takeover statutes, the corporate charter of each company, and federal and state securities laws. There are three main federal antitrust statutes. The Clayton Act has become the chief weapon the government uses to contest mergers that it feels may lessen competition. It forbids a company to purchase the assets or the stock of another company if the purchase might substantially lessen competition, or tend to create a monopoly, in any line of commerce or in any section of the country.

Other Legal Considerations

Several other legal issues must be addressed in merger situations. For example, there are special rules relating to tender offers. Also, the acquiror should examine the indenture covenants for the acquiree's outstanding debt to determine whether any of its debt issues will have to be repaid at par upon a change in control.

Tax Considerations

The tax issues that arise in connection with mergers are very complex. All we can do is summarize some of the key aspects. The Internal Revenue Service assumes that an acquisition is taxable unless stringent conditions are met. In a **tax-free acquisition,** the selling shareholders are treated as having *exchanged* their old shares for substantially similar new shares. The acquiror's tax basis in each asset whose ownership is transferred in the transaction is the same as the acquiree's. Each selling shareholder who receives only stock does not have to pay any tax on the gain realized as a result of the acquisition until the shares are sold.

In a **taxable acquisition,** the selling shareholders are treated as having *sold* their shares. The acquiror can, if it wants, increase the tax basis in the assets it acquires to the fair market value of the consideration it pays to acquire them (including the fair market value of the acquiree's liabilities assumed by the acquiror).

From the seller's perspective, the main benefit of a tax-free transaction is deferral of tax on any gain realized on the sale of the business. The seller who receives stock in the acquiror also has a continuing equity interest in the en-terprise and can share in any post-merger benefits. From the buyer's perspective, the main benefit of a tax-free transaction derives from the acquiror's ability to take advantage of the existing tax attributes of the acquiree, such as net operating loss carryforwards.

Requirements for Tax-Free Treatment

The Internal Revenue Code imposes a variety of conditions that must be met for a transaction to be tax free. If these conditions are not met, the transaction is taxable.

To Be or Not To Be Tax Free

A tax-free transaction benefits a shareholder who has a gain because it permits deferral of tax on the gain. A taxable transaction benefits a shareholder who has a loss and has sufficient taxable income to offset it because it creates a tax deduction. A taxable transaction also gives the acquiror greater flexibility in financing the acquisition. Under the Principle of Two-Sided Transactions, the interests of the acquiror and those of the selling shareholders often conflict. The "high" market value of the assets that can make writing up their tax basis advantageous is likely to be reflected in a "high" share price for the acquiree, which creates the capital gain.

As a general rule, structuring an acquisition as a taxable transaction in order to be able to write up the tax basis of the acquiree's assets is not a tax-effective strategy under current U.S. tax law. The seller must pay tax on the difference between the purchase price received and its tax basis in the assets. In an efficient market, this tax liability will be reflected in the purchase price the buyer pays. Because this difference is then depreciated over several years, the net present value of the asset write-up must be negative.

Accounting Considerations

Acquisitions often involve difficult accounting issues. One of the more important issues, in practice, is whether to structure the acquisition as a pooling of interests or as a purchase. In an efficient capital market, the choice of accounting technique should not affect market value, because it does not affect cash flows. Nevertheless, professional managers often take great pains to structure transactions so as to achieve a particular accounting treatment.

EXAMPLE   *Lockheed–Martin Marietta Tax-Free Combination*

The Lockheed–Martin Marietta combination was structured so as to qualify as a tax-free exchange of shares. Each of Lockheed's 66,179,422 outstanding common shares was exchanged for 1.63 Lockheed Martin shares. Each of Martin Marietta's 100,680,090 outstanding common shares was exchanged for one Lockheed Martin share. ■

Pooling of Interests   In a **pooling of interests,** the assets, liabilities, and operating results of the companies involved in the merger are added together without any adjustment to their recorded values. The financial statements of the companies are combined as though the companies had always been commonly owned.

Pooling-of-Interests Accounting

Company B acquires company A, by giving company A's shareholders $60 million of its common stock. Table F.3 shows the accounting impact. The balance sheets of the two companies are added line by line. The *book values* of equity are combined. The $60 million market value of equity that company B pays company A's shareholders does *not* enter into this calculation. The combined book equity is $115 million. The new company is owned jointly by the former shareholders of both companies. The old shareholders of company A now own shares of company B. ■

Purchase Method   Under the **purchase method** of accounting, one of the companies is identified as the acquiror. It is treated as having purchased the assets of the other company. The purchase price, after adding the fair market value of the liabilities the acquiror assumes, is allocated to the acquired assets. Any excess of the purchase price over the fair market value of the net assets acquired is recorded as *goodwill,* which the acquiror must amortize over a period not exceeding 40 years.[6] This represents a noncash charge against the acquiror's net income.

Purchase Accounting

Company B acquires company A, using cash from issuing $60 million of new common stock. Table F.4 on page 736 shows the accounting impact. Company A's fixed assets have a book value of $30 million, but a fair market value of $42 million. Its debt has a book value of $10 million but is worth only $7 million. Company A's assets are written up by $12 million. Its debt is written down by $3 million. The acquisition eliminates company A's book equity of $40 million because company A's shares are purchased and retired but the purchase price for company A increases the merged company's equity by $60 million.

Table F.4 also shows the calculation of goodwill. The fair market value of company A's assets exceeds that of its liabilities by $55 million. But company B paid $60 million. The $5 million excess represents goodwill. You might think of goodwill as a company's "franchise" value: the reputational capital it has built up for itself and its products through years of successful operation. ■

TABLE F.3

Accounting for an Acquisition: Pooling-of-Interests Method (dollar amounts in millions)

	COMPANY A	COMPANY B	COMBINED
Assets			
Working capital	$20	$ 35	$ 55
Fixed assets	30	65	95
Total	$50	$100	$150
Liabilities and Equity			
Debt	$10	$ 25	$ 35
Equity	40	75	115
Total	$50	$100	$150

---

[6]If there is a deficiency, it reduces the carrying value of long-term assets.

TABLE F.4
Accounting for an Acquisition: Purchase Method (dollar amounts in millions)

	COMPANY A	COMPANY B	ADJUSTMENTS	COMBINED
Assets				
Working capital	$20	$ 35		$ 55
Fixed assets	30	65	+12[a]	107
Goodwill	—	—	+5[b]	5
Total	$50	$100		$167
Liabilities and Equity				
Debt	$10	$ 25	−3[c]	$ 32
Equity	40	75	−40[d]	
			+60[e]	135
Total	$50	$100		$167

[a]To record the write-up of company A's assets to fair market value.
[b]Calculation of goodwill:

Purchase price paid for company A's equity		$60
Fair market value of company A's assets	$62	
Fair market value of company A's liabilities	7	
Fair market value of company A's net assets		55
Goodwill		$ 5

[c]To revalue company A's debt to fair market value.
[d]The acquisition eliminates company A's equity.
[e]To record the equity company B issues to raise the cash to pay for company A.

Acquisitions that qualify for pooling-of-interests accounting usually also qualify as tax free, and taxable acquisitions are usually accounted for as purchases.

Self-Check

1. What are the three basic ways of effecting a corporate acquisition? What are the distinguishing features of each approach?

2. What are the main differences between a tax-free acquisition and a taxable acquisition? Why would a seller with a low tax basis in her stock prefer a tax-free acquisition, other things being equal?

3. What are the main differences between the pooling-of-interests and purchase methods of accounting for an acquisition? Does the choice of accounting method affect shareholders wealth?

4. Why do antitrust concerns sometimes arise in connection with mergers? Which type of merger is most likely to raise them?

COMPARATIVE ANALYSIS OF MERGERS

There are two main ways to value corporate acquisitions: by comparative analysis and by discounted-cash-flow analysis. The two approaches differ in one fundamental respect. Comparative analysis is used to determine a "reasonable" price to pay: We infer the value from the prices that were paid for companies in comparable transactions. The discounted-cash-flow approach is used to calculate the impact of an acquisition on shareholder wealth, given a particular acquisition cost. It can also be used to estimate the maximum price an acquiror could pay without reduc-

ing the wealth of its shareholders. These two approaches are therefore complementary. When used properly together, they yield more useful information than either approach could separately.

The Merger Premium

The acquiror usually must pay a premium over the price at which the acquiree's shares are trading in the market (or would trade if the target company were publicly held). The premium reflects the value of obtaining control of the acquiree. Comparative analysis can be used to determine a "reasonable" premium.

Investment bankers look at comparable acquisitions to gauge a reasonable premium to offer for the target com-

TABLE F.5
Premiums Paid in Acquisitions of Publicly Traded Companies, 1977–1996

| YEAR | NUMBER OF ACQUISITIONS | PERCENT PREMIUM PAID OVER MARKET PRICE | | | | | | AVERAGE | MEDIAN | DOW JONES INDUSTRIAL AVERAGE DURING YEAR | |
| | | 0.1–40.0 | | 40.0–80.0 | | OVER 80.0 | | | | | |
		Amount	%	Amount	%	Amount	%			High	Low
1977	218	120	55	70	32	28	13	41	36	999.75	800.85
1978	240	116	48	90	38	34	14	46	42	907.74	742.12
1979	229	95	41	91	40	43	19	50	48	897.61	796.67
1980	169	75	44	61	36	33	20	50	45	1000.17	795.13
1981	166	80	48	54	33	32	19	48	42	1024.05	824.01
1982	176	80	45	66	37	30	18	47	44	1070.55	776.92
1983	168	101	60	53	32	14	8	38	34	1287.20	1027.04
1984	199	118	59	68	34	13	7	38	34	1286.64	1086.57
1985	331	231	70	71	21	29	9	37	28	1553.10	1184.96
1986	333	222	67	82	24	29	9	38	30	1955.60	1502.30
1987	237	155	65	66	28	16	7	38	31	2722.42	1738.74
1988	410	255	62	113	28	42	10	42	31	2183.50	1879.14
1989	303	187	62	88	29	28	9	41	29	2791.41	2144.64
1990	175	105	60	48	27	22	13	42	32	2999.75	2365.10
1991	137	92	67	35	26	10	7	35	29	3168.83	2470.30
1992	142	84	59	40	28	18	13	41	35	3413.21	3136.58
1993	173	110	64	48	28	15	9	39	33	3794.33	3241.95
1994	260	155	60	80	31	25	10	42	35	3978.36	3593.35
1995	324	214	66	77	24	33	10	45	29	5235.62	3817.28
1996	381	253	66	104	27	24	7	37	27	6560.91	5032.94
Total	4771	2848	60	1405	29	518	11				

Sources: W. T. Grimm & Co., *Mergerstat Review 1988,* pp. 94–95, and Houlihan Lokey Howard & Zukin, *Mergerstat Review 1997,* pp. 23–24.

pany's shares. This reflects the Behavioral Principle: Look to comparable acquisitions for guidance regarding a reasonable price to pay. The *premium paid* is defined as

$$\text{Premium paid} = \frac{\text{Purchase price per share} - \text{Target's share price pre-merger}}{\text{Target's share price pre-merger}} \quad \text{(F.2)}$$

The target's share price pre-merger is usually measured 30 days before the initial announcement date of the acquisition in order to prevent preannouncement effects from biasing the analysis. The required premium tends to vary from one industry to another, depending on the industry's prospects. It also varies from one company to another within an industry, depending on that company's financial and business characteristics and relative prospects. The required premium may also depend on the state of the stock market.

Premiums Paid in Past Deals

Table F.5 shows the distribution of premiums paid in acquisitions for the period 1977–1996. The annual average premium has varied between a low of 35% in 1991 and a high of 50% in 1979 and again in 1980. The annual median premium has varied between a low of 27% in 1996 and a high of 48% in 1979. A recent study found that acquisition premiums during the 1974–1985 period were approximately double those of the 1963–1973 period, which was a period of generally rising share prices. That study also found that the acquisition premium behaves counter-cyclically, varying inversely with the Standard & Poor's 500 Index.[7]

---

[7]Nathan and O'Keefe (1989). The reasons for this behavior are not entirely clear. One possibility is that takeovers occur when the target company is undervalued. Undervaluation may be more severe during recessions (when share prices are depressed).

EXAMPLE	*Analysis of Premiums Paid*

An acquisition target currently has 10,000,000 shares outstanding. They are trading at $27. This gives the target a current market value of $270 million. The acquiror's financial staff analyzes ten recent acquisitions of companies in the same industry. It finds that the merger premiums fall between 50% and 66%. It also considers whether there has been any merger speculation or other factors that might have inflated the target's share price. It concludes there were none.

The premiums paid suggest that a reasonable acquisition value is between $405 million (= [270]1.5) and $448 million (= [270]1.66). A reasonable offering price would fall between $40.50 (= 405/10) and $44.80 (= 448/10) per share. Discounted-cash-flow analysis, discussed next, and tactical considerations will determine what price the acquiror should initially offer.[8] ∎

Self-Check

1. What is a merger premium and how is it calculated?
2. Why is it wise to calculate the merger premium using the share price 30 days before the initial announcement of the acquisition?

DISCOUNTED-CASH-FLOW ANALYSIS

We have pointed out that an acquisition is a special type of capital budgeting problem. A company acquires another company, instead of just one project. Even though acquisitions are more complex, discounted-cash-flow (DCF) analysis is still useful. We must be careful not to overlook any of the complexities that might affect shareholder value. But when applied correctly, DCF analysis is helpful to an acquiror in deciding whether an acquisition would benefit its shareholders if it can buy the target for the price it is considering paying. DCF analysis is also useful in determining the maximum price the acquiror can afford to pay. We illustrate both uses of the technique in this section.

Empire State Pharmaceutical is a proprietary drug manufacturer with annual sales of $1.2 billion. Empire State is considering acquiring another publicly traded proprietary drug manufacturer, Garden State Drugs. Garden State has annual sales of $600 million. The acquisition would increase Empire State's sales by 50%. It would also lead to significant economies in marketing, and it could expand Empire State's product line more quickly than Empire State would be able to by developing similar drugs on its own. The net benefit of the potential acquisition depends, of course, on how much Empire State would have to pay to acquire Garden State.

Table F.6 illustrates how you could use DCF analysis to evaluate Empire State's possible acquisition of Garden

State. We assume that Empire State has already decided that it would not be advantageous to step up the tax basis of Garden State's assets. Empire State elected to use a ten-year time horizon for its analysis. Projected amounts are rounded to the nearest million.

Determining the Net Acquisition Cost

The first step is to determine what it would cost Empire State to acquire Garden State. The **net acquisition cost (NAC)** is the investment the acquiror makes when it purchases the acquiree:

$$
\begin{array}{ll}
& \text{Cost of purchasing target's equity} \\
+ & \text{Transaction costs} \\
- & \underline{\text{Target's excess assets}} & \text{(F.3)} \\
& \text{Net investment in target's equity} \\
+ & \underline{\text{Cost of assuming target's debt}} \\
& \text{Net acquisition cost (NAC)}
\end{array}
$$

Let's take a closer look at each item in equation (F.3).

Cost of Purchasing Target's Equity Garden State has 10,000,000 shares outstanding. Its share price is $32. Empire State plans to purchase all of Garden State's outstanding stock for cash through a tender offer at a price of $48 per share (16 times earnings), which represents a 50% premium. Purchasing Garden State's shares, then, will cost $480 million.

Cost of Assuming Target's Debt Garden State currently has $100 million of debt outstanding, which bears in-

---

[8]Discounted-cash-flow analysis will indicate the maximum price the acquiror can afford to pay. The acquiror must then determine an appropriate bidding strategy. But don't offer the maximum initially—give yourself room to raise the bid later.

TABLE F.6

Discounted-Cash-Flow (DCF) Analysis of the Acquisition of Garden State Drugs (dollar amounts in millions)

	YEAR										
	0	**1**	**2**	**3**	**4**	**5**	**6**	**7**	**8**	**9**	**10**
Purchase of equity[a]	$ 480.0	—	—	—	—	—	—	—	—	—	—
Cost of debt assumed	92.6	—	—	—	—	—	—	—	—	—	—
Transaction costs	5.0	—	—	—	—	—	—	—	—	—	—
Acquiree's excess cash	(35.0)	—	—	—	—	—	—	—	—	—	—
Net acquisition cost	$ 542.6	—	—	—	—	—	—	—	—	—	—
Incremental Free Cash Flow:											
Revenue	—	$672	$753	$843	$944	$1057	$1184	$1326	$1486	$1664	$1864
Cost of goods sold[b]	—	336	376	421	472	529	592	663	743	832	932
SG&A	—	251	276	304	334	367	404	444	489	538	591
Depreciation (tax)	—	13	15	15	18	19	22	25	28	30	35
Pretax operating profit	—	72	86	103	120	142	166	194	226	264	306
Income taxes[c]	—	36	43	52	60	71	83	97	113	132	153
Net operating profit	—	36	43	51	60	71	83	97	113	132	153
Depreciation (tax)	—	13	15	15	18	19	22	25	28	30	35
Net operating cash flow	—	49	58	66	78	90	105	122	141	162	188
Net investment in working capital[d]	—	$(15)	$(18)	$(20)	$(25)	$(28)	$(32)	$(36)	$(40)	$(43)	$(50)
Investment in fixed assets	—	(22)	(25)	(30)	(35)	(40)	(45)	(50)	(50)	(50)	(50)
Operating economies net of taxes[e]	—	10	11	12	13	15	15	15	15	15	15
Incremental free cash flow	—	22	26	28	31	37	43	51	66	84	103
Terminal Value of Net Assets:											
Nondisposition basis[f]	—	—	—	—	—	—	—	—	—	—	2472
Disposition basis[g]	—	—	—	—	—	—	—	—	—	—	1842
Incremental Net Cash Flow:											
Nondisposition basis	$(542.6)	$ 22	$ 26	$ 28	$ 31	$ 37	$ 43	$ 51	$ 66	$ 84	$2575
Disposition basis	$(542.6)	$ 22	$ 26	$ 28	$ 31	$ 37	$ 43	$ 51	$ 66	$ 84	$1945

Required return = WACC = $(1 - L)\, r_e + L\,(1 - T)\, r_d = (2/3)(0.2032) + (1/3)(0.5)(0.12) = 15.55\%$

IRR (Nondisposition basis) = 20.40%
IRR (Disposition basis)   = 17.59%
NPV (Nondisposition basis) = $236.5 million
NPV (Disposition basis)   = $ 88.0 million

[a]Estimated as 16 times prior year's earnings (a purchase price of $48.00 per share).
[b]Excluding depreciation.
[c]Assumes a 50% marginal income tax rate.
[d]Increase in inventories and receivables net of increase in payables.
[e]Estimated after-tax savings resulting from eliminating redundant overhead and redundant production facilities and marketing some of Garden State's products through Empire State's distribution network.
[f]Calculated as 16 times terminal year's earnings ($142.7 million) plus the amount of debt outstanding at the investment horizon ($188.3 million). This calculation assumes that Empire State does not sell the shares of Garden State; it continues to hold them (nondisposition case).
[g]Calculated as 16 times terminal year's earnings ($142.7 million) plus the amount of debt outstanding at the investment horizon ($188.3 million) and net of capital gains tax at a 34% rate (with a tax basis of $450 million) and net also of transaction costs ($10 million). This calculation assumes that Empire State sells the shares of Garden State at the end of the 10th year and pays any resulting tax liability if there is a gain (or receives a tax benefit if there is a loss on disposition).

terest at a 10% rate, payable annually in arrears. The debt matures in one lump sum at the end of ten years and is callable at par. Empire State will be able to assume this debt.

Assuming the obligation for servicing Garden State's debt reduces the amount of new debt that Empire State can issue to finance (part of) the cost of the acquisition. Cash that Empire State uses to service the debt it assumes is not available to service new debt. In other words, assuming the 10% debt involves an opportunity cost. This opportunity cost equals the maximum amount of new debt that Empire State could issue, subject to the constraint that the after-tax period-by-period debt service payments of the hypothetical new issue are the same as those of Garden State's debt that Empire State would assume.[9]

If Empire State is permitted to assume the debt, *and* if the opportunity cost of assuming the debt is less than the cost of retiring it immediately, Empire State should assume the debt rather than retire it. Empire State should include the opportunity cost as part of the net acquisition cost. It must also be subtracted from the amount of new debt Empire State could otherwise issue to finance the acquisition. If instead the opportunity cost of assuming Garden State's debt is greater than the cost of retiring it immediately, the debt should be retired. The cost of retiring it must then be included in the net acquisition cost.

Empire State's pretax cost of a new debt issue (before issuance expenses) is 12%. Its marginal ordinary income tax rate is 50%. Assuming the 10% debt would require after-tax interest payments of $5 million per year. Newly issued debt would have an after-tax interest cost of 6% per year. *The opportunity cost of assuming Garden State's outstanding debt equals the present value of the after-tax debt service with Empire's after-tax cost of debt serving as the discount rate:*

$$PV(\text{debt assumed}) = \sum_{t=1}^{10} \frac{5}{(1.06)^t} + \frac{100}{(1.06)^{10}} = \$92.6 \text{ million}$$

 | $N = 10$ $r = 6$ **PV = 92.6** $PMT = 5$ $FV = 100$ |

Because the cost of assuming the 10% debt is less than the $100 million cost of retiring it, Empire State is better off assuming the debt. The net advantage is $7.4 million (= 100.0 − 92.6).

How Much New Debt Can Empire State Issue?

Empire State's financial staff has studied the capital structure policies of large pharmaceutical companies in the manner described in chapter 12. On the basis of that analysis, Empire State believes that it could finance the acquisition on a long-term basis with a debt-to-total-value ratio of 1/3 without any adverse impact on its senior debt rating or on how it might choose to finance other projects. The amount of new long-term debt that Empire State can issue is the amount it can have outstanding after the acquisition less the amount of debt displaced by the debt it assumes in the acquisition:

$$\text{Added debt} = (L)\text{NAC} - \text{PV(debt assumed)} \qquad \textbf{(F.4)}$$
$$= (1/3)542.6 - 92.6 = \$88.3 \text{ million}$$

where L is the acquiror's target debt-to-total-value ratio. This calculation uses NAC = $542.6 million, which is calculated in Table F.6.

Target's Excess Assets and Transaction Costs

The gross cost of Empire State's acquisition before transaction costs is $572.6 million (= 480.0 + 92.6). However, after analyzing Garden State's financial statements, Empire State believes that Garden State has approximately $35 million of excess cash and marketable securities that it will be able to apply toward the purchase price. Empire State has estimated that investment bankers' fees and other expenses net of taxes will total $5 million.

Note that excess assets represent a potential pitfall. Companies like to pay as much of the acquisition cost as they can with the acquiree's cash. But what appears as excess cash may in fact be tied up as compensating balances, or it may be overseas and repatriating it could trigger a significant tax liability.

Net Acquisition Cost   Empire State's net acquisition cost of acquiring Garden State's net assets is $542.6 million. The calculation is shown in table F.6.

Cost of purchasing target's equity	$480.0
+ Transaction costs	5.0
− Target's excess assets	(35.0)
Net investment in target's equity	450.0
+ Cost of assuming target's debt	92.6
Net acquisition cost (NAC)	$542.6

If the target's debt became payable immediately as a result of the acquisition, the cost of retiring target's debt would be the face amount, $100 million. In that case, the net acquisition cost would be $550 million (= 450 + 100). Whenever you evaluate the possible acquisition of a company that has debt outstanding, check whether the acquisition will trigger immediate repayment. If it will, but if assuming the debt would be cheaper than retiring it, you will probably want to find an alternative legal structure that will avoid acceleration.

Incremental Free Cash Flow

Empire State believes that Garden State's revenue will grow at the rate of 12% per year, the historical growth rate. Empire State also believes that the cost of goods sold will grow at the same rate, whereas selling, general, and administrative expense (SG&A) will grow at 10% per year. Annual depreciation expense for tax purposes is estimated from Garden State's published financial reports and from Empire State's estimate of Garden State's required capital

---

[9]This method of analysis, the *debt service parity (DSP)* approach, is described more fully in appendix 14B.

expenditure program. The forecasted operating economies represent Empire State's estimate of the benefits it will realize by eliminating redundant production facilities and from marketing some of Empire State's products through Garden State's distribution network.

There are some important potential pitfalls. It is easy to be too optimistic about the acquiree's growth prospects. It is also easy to be overly optimistic about the synergistic benefits from the merger. The more dissimilar the acquiree's and the acquiror's businesses, the more difficult it will be to find true synergies. It is also easy to underestimate the amount of investment that will be required. The older the acquiree's plant and equipment, the higher the required post-merger capital expenditures.

The projected incremental free cash flow stream is shown in table F.6. In year 1, net operating cash flow is expected to be $49 million. Empire State estimates that $15 million of this amount will have to be invested in additional inventories and receivables, and $22 million will have to be invested in fixed assets. It also believes that operating economies will provide $10 million of after-tax savings, leaving $22 million of incremental free cash flow. Empire State estimates that annual incremental free cash flow from Garden State's operations should grow to $103 million in year 10.

Terminal Value of Net Assets

An acquiree's terminal value is the estimated value of its net assets (total assets net of current liabilities, which equals the sum of shareholders' equity and long-term debt) at the end of the time period used in the acquisition analysis. We estimate terminal value by comparing the results of owning the acquiree with the results of selling it. For our example, the first case (nondisposition) assumes that Empire State continues to own Garden State for an indefinite period beyond the investment horizon. The second case (disposition) assumes that Empire State sells all the common stock of Garden State at the investment horizon. If Empire State were to sell Garden State after the investment horizon, the present value of any resulting tax liabilities would have to be taken into account. The value of Garden State in that case would lie between the two values estimated in the following paragraphs.

In the first case, Garden State's terminal value is estimated by applying an appropriate multiple to Garden State's pro forma earnings in year 10 estimated as though Garden State were on a stand-alone basis. Empire State would pay $480 million to purchase Garden State's equity. Garden State's net income is $30 million per year according to its latest income statement. The purchase price represents a multiple of 16 times earnings:

Multiple of earnings paid

$$= \frac{\text{Cost of purchasing target's equity}}{\text{Target's net income before extraordinary items}} \quad \text{(F.5)}$$

$$= \frac{480}{30} = 16$$

In year 10, Garden State would have $100 million principal amount of 10% debt plus $88.3 million of 12% debt, giving rise to $10.3 million of after-tax interest expense. Subtracting this from Garden State's estimated year-10 net operating profit of $153 million leaves $142.7 million of earnings. Multiplying by 16.0 gives a terminal value of $2283.2 million for Garden State's equity. Adding the terminal value of Garden State's debt, $188.3 million, gives the terminal value of Garden State's net assets:

$$\text{TV(NA)} = \text{TV(equity)} + \text{TV(debt)} - \text{Taxes} - \text{Expenses} \quad \text{(F.6)}$$

$$= 2283.2 + 188.3 - 0 - 0 = \$2471.5 \text{ million}$$

where TV(NA) is the terminal value of net assets, TV(equity) is the terminal value of shareholders' equity, TV(debt) is the terminal value of long-term debt (and capitalized lease and preferred stock) obligations, *Taxes* represents any taxes incurred in realizing the terminal value, and *Expenses* represents any other expenses incurred in realizing the terminal value. TV(NA) rounded to the nearest million is $2472 million, which appears in table F.6 as the terminal value of net assets on a nondisposition basis.

In the second case, tax liabilities and transaction costs must be taken into account. Empire State estimates that if it sold Garden State, it would incur $10 million of transaction costs. Its net proceeds are $2273.2 million (= 2283.2 − 10). Its tax basis equals what it pays to purchase Garden State's shares (that is, the net investment in target's shares after taking into account excess assets and transaction costs), $450 million. Empire State would realize a long-term capital gain equal to the difference between the net proceeds from the sale of the equity and the net investment in the target's shares, $1823.2 million (= 2273.2 − 450).[10] Empire State's financial staff estimates a future capital gains tax rate of 34%. Empire State would incur capital gains tax of $620.0 million (= [0.34]1823.2). Substituting into equation (F.6), this leaves

$$\text{TV(NA)} = \$2283.2 + 188.3 - 620.0 - 10 = \$1841.5 \text{ million}$$

TV(NA) rounded to the nearest million is $1842 million, which appears in table F.6 as the terminal value of net assets on a disposition basis.

---

[10]Its original tax basis in the shares of Garden State equals the cost of purchasing the shares ($480 million) plus transaction costs ($5 million) minus the portion of the purchase price paid for with the target's excess cash ($35 million). The net amount is $450 million. The net sales proceeds realized upon the sale of the shares equal the sale price ($2283 million) net of transaction costs ($10 million).

The calculation of terminal value is often critical. By assuming a high enough future multiple, an acquiror can justify any purchase price. But it seems more prudent to assume that the future acquisition multiple will be no greater than the current acquisition multiple, as we did in the illustration.

DCF Analysis

We have calculated the incremental net cash flow stream in table F.6. Next we must estimate the required return. As we have noted, an acquisition is a form of capital investment. Therefore we must estimate the weighted average cost of capital (WACC) for the acquisition. We can use the procedure outlined in chapter 11.

The debt ratio is $L = 1/3$. Empire State's financial staff has analyzed pharmaceutical companies comparable to Garden State. It estimated a required return to equity of

$r_e = 0.2032$. The cost of debt is $r_d = 0.12$. Substituting these values into equation (11.1), the weighted average cost of capital formula, gives

$$\text{WACC} = (2/3)(0.2032) + (1/3)(0.5)(0.12) = 0.1555, \text{ or } 15.55\%$$

Note that as in capital budgeting, the debt ratio is the acquiror's long-run target proportion of debt financing.

The incremental net cash flow stream is discounted at the required return WACC = 0.1555 to obtain the net present value of the acquisition, NPV(acquisition):

$$\text{NPV(acquisition)} = -\text{NAC} + \sum_{t=1}^{N} \frac{\text{CFAT}_t}{(1 + \text{WACC})^t} \qquad \text{(F.7)}$$

where CFAT_t is the (unleveraged) incremental net cash flow during period t, and N is the investment horizon. CFAT_N includes the terminal value of the acquisition (at the investment horizon) estimated from equation (F.6).

EXAMPLE   *Calculating the NPV of a Potential Acquisition*

Applying equation (F.7) to Empire State's proposed acquisition of Garden State indicates NPV(acquisition) = $236.5 million on a nondisposition basis and NPV(acquisition) = $88.0 million on a disposition basis. Both values are given at the bottom of table F.6. The WACC approach indicates that the acquisition of Garden State at a price representing 16 times Garden State's earnings would be profitable. ∎

Calculating terminal value on both bases reveals the sensitivity of the acquisition decision to this value and, in this case, to the multiple applied to the terminal year's earnings. Note that the present value of the incremental net cash flow stream, exclusive of terminal value, is −$346.1 million. The terminal value must be at least $1468.6 million (= $[346.1]1.1555^{10}$) for the NPV to be positive. The NPV of a proposed acquisition is usually very sensitive to the estimated terminal value. Therefore, it is important to consider carefully the assumptions made in arriving at the estimate. It is also wise to calculate the break-even terminal value, which makes NPV(acquisition) equal to zero.

Maximum Price the Acquiror Can Afford to Pay

There is one additional use for DCF analysis. We can calculate the maximum price the acquiror could afford to pay for the target. Given the incremental net cash flow stream and discount rate, the maximum price is the one that makes NPV(acquisition) equal to zero. Valuing Garden State on a disposition basis, Empire State could afford to pay approximately $568.0 million (the original $480 mil-

lion price plus the $88.0 million net present value), or $56.80 (= 568/10) per share. At that price, Garden State's shareholders would experience a 110% gain (56.80 versus the current 27), whereas Empire State's shareholders would expect only to break even at best.[11]

---

[11]Empire State could actually afford to pay an even higher price before NPV becomes zero. A higher price increases Empire State's tax basis in Garden State's shares and reduces the future capital gains tax liability. For a purchase price of $568.0 million, the tax liability would be $590.0 million (= 0.34[2273.2 − 538.0]); it would be $620.0 million if the price paid for the stock were $480 million.

THE MEDIUM OF PAYMENT

Acquirors usually pay for acquisitions in cash, stock, or some combination of the two. Achieving tax-free treatment requires that the acquiror pay at least 50% of the purchase price in its stock, although in many cases the acquiror has the flexibility to issue preferred stock instead of common stock.

Choice of Medium of Payment

Figure F.2 breaks down merger transactions during the period 1975–1996 according to the medium of payment. Overall, 41% of the acquisitions were cash only, 41% were stock only, 1% were debt only, and the other 17% were paid for in a combination of stock, cash, and debt. The proportion of cash-only transactions fell sharply between 1988 and 1992. The proportion involving a combination of stock, cash, and debt generally increased through the 20-year period. Combinations of stock and debt arise in two-tiered tender offers, wherein shareholders of the target usually get debentures in the second tier of the transaction. Combinations of cash and debt are common in acquisitions of privately held companies wherein the sellers often take a note from the buyers as part of the purchase price.

Common Stock and Net Acquisition Cost

Common stock tends to become a more popular medium of payment among acquirors during periods of rising stock prices. Acquirors are reluctant to pay in stock when they feel their shares are depressed in price. However, the shareholders of publicly traded acquirees, particularly the *risk arbitrageurs* who generally replace a significant portion of the public shareholders by buying their shares as soon as an acquisition is announced, prefer cash as the medium of payment. When an acquisition occurs, they want to take their profits and move on. Receiving cash saves them the trouble and cost of having to sell securities in the open market.

Acquirors often decide to pay in common stock when they think their share price is attractive. That is, they think it is "cheaper" to pay in common stock than in cash. But whether it really is cheaper depends on (1) how the transaction is structured and (2) what happens to the share price after the transaction is announced.

Suppose Empire State wished to buy Garden State in an exchange of common stock. If managers of the two companies agreed on a fixed price of $480 million payable in Empire State common stock, the net acquisition cost would remain $542.6 million regardless of what happened to Empire State's share price. But in stock-for-stock acquisitions it is customary to negotiate an *exchange ratio*—that is, so many shares of Empire State for each share of Garden State. If the acquiror's share price then increases, so does the net acquisition cost. Of course, if the acquiror's share price falls, the net acquisition cost falls also.

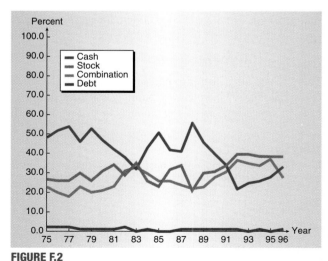

FIGURE F.2
Trend in medium of payment, 1975–1996.
Source: Houlihan Lokey Howard & Zukin, *Mergerstat Review 1997,* pp. 13–14.

EXAMPLE   *Impact on the Net Acquisition Cost in a Stock-for-Stock Acquisition*

Assume that Empire State has 50 million shares outstanding that are trading at a price of $32 each. Garden State has 10 million shares outstanding. Suppose Empire State offers to pay $48 for each Garden State share. It would have to exchange 1.5 (= 48/32) of its shares for each Garden State share. Empire State would have to issue 15 million (= [1.5]10) new shares. As a result, Garden State's former shareholders would own 23% (= 15/[15 + 50]) of Empire State after the acquisition. Suppose the exchange ratio is fixed. Suppose also that stock market investors believe the market value of Empire State's equity should be $2168 million after the acquisition. This value is the sum of Empire State's current market value ($1600 million) plus the value of the shares issued in exchange for Garden State's shares ($480 million) plus the NPV in the disposition case ($88.0 million). In that case, Empire State's share price would rise to $33.35 per share (= 2168/65) and its cost of purchasing Garden State's shares would increase to $500.25 million (= 33.35[1.5]10) from $480 million. The fixed exchange ratio effectively appropriates 23% of the NPV (= [500.25 − 480]/88) for Garden State's former shareholders.

Let's assume instead that investors believe the market value of Empire State's equity after the merger should be only $1950 million. Then Empire State's share price would fall to $30 (= 1950/65), and its cost of purchasing Garden State's shares would fall to $450 million (= 30[1.5]10). Its net acquisition cost would fall from the $542.6 million in table F.6 to $512.6 million. In this way, Garden State's former shareholders would share the burden of the decline in value of Empire State's shares. Thus an acquiror's shareholders are better off in a stock-for-stock transaction than in a cash-for-stock transaction if the acquiror overpays. ■

Acquirees realize that they will share the burden of a decline in the acquiror's share price if the exchange ratio is fixed. As a result, acquirees often try to negotiate a *flexible exchange ratio* designed to assure them a fixed dollar price for their shares. For example, suppose Empire State's share price falls to $30 upon announcement of the acquisition, but the exchange ratio adjusts to 1.60 Empire State shares per Garden State share. Garden State's shareholders would still realize $48 (= [1.60]30) per share.

Dilution in Earnings Per Share

There is one other factor to consider when common stock is the medium of payment. A publicly traded acquiror is usually concerned about the impact an acquisition will have on its future reported earnings per share. As we noted earlier, an acquisition can increase earnings per share under pooling-of-interests accounting when the acquiror's price-earnings multiple exceeds the target's. However, when the acquiree's price-earnings multiple exceeds the acquiror's, the accounting impact is just the opposite.

Table F.7 illustrates the dilutive case. In the absence of any operating economies or other synergistic benefits, the market value of the combined entity is just the sum of the market values of the acquiror and the acquiree. Because the acquiror has the lower price-earnings multiple, its earnings per share are diluted from $5.00 to $4.29 per share. However, its price-earnings multiple increases from $10.0x$ to $11.7x$.

TABLE F.7

Illustration of the Dilutive Impact of an Acquisition on Reported Earnings per Share

	ACQUIROR	ACQUIREE	COMBINED
Total earnings	$50,000,000	$10,000,000	$60,000,000
Number of shares	10,000,000	5,000,000	14,000,000[a]
Earnings per share	$ 5.00	$ 2.00	$ 4.29
Share price	$50.00	$40.00	$50.00
Price-earnings ratio	10.0x	20.0x	11.7x

[a]Acquiror exchanges 0.8 common share for each of the acquiree's common shares, issuing a total of 4 million new shares.

You should appreciate that as long as transactions take place in an efficient capital market, dilution in earnings per share will have only an accounting impact. Dilution is *not* an indicator of a proposed acquisition's impact on shareholder wealth. It should not affect which medium of payment the acquiror chooses.

Self-Check

1. Over the last 20 years, what has been the most frequent medium of payment in corporate acquisitions? Are there any noticeable trends in use of the various methods of payment?

2. Why does paying for an acquisition with stock raise the cost of a positive-NPV acquisition and reduce the cost of a negative-NPV acquisition?

MERGER TACTICS

Many merger and acquisition transactions take place on a "friendly" basis. The two parties agree to merge. Then they negotiate the legal form of the transaction, price, method of payment, and other terms. But many transactions are unfriendly. Management of the target may resist the potential acquiror's overtures. If they refuse to negotiate, the potential acquiror can take its offer directly to the target's shareholders along either of two avenues: a tender offer or a proxy contest. Managers and boards of directors have shown remarkable creativity in designing takeover defenses to thwart such threats to their security. You've probably heard the term *shark repellents,* which is used to describe them in the media.

Tender Offers

Few events in business pack as much drama—or engender as much bitterness—as a hostile tender offer by one company for the shares of another. Recall that a tender offer is an offer to purchase shares of stock at a stated price from shareholders who are willing to sell shares at that price. The buyer decides on a tender price and on the other terms of the offer, files the tender offer documents with the Securities and Exchange Commission, and when the SEC clears these documents for distribution to securityholders, the buyer publicly announces its offer to purchase their shares.

Tender offers may be either friendly or hostile to the target's management. In a hostile tender offer, the management of the target company takes steps, often including litigation, to contest the offer. *Hostile raids* became an established acquisition strategy more than 20 years ago when one of the leading securities companies assisted International Nickel of Canada in a successful hostile tender offer for ESB.

Tender offers are frequently employed when incumbent management refuses to negotiate with the prospective acquiror. An example is the battle for control over RJR Nabisco, which is discussed in the next section. In other cases, management may be indifferent to a proposed acquisition. A tender offer lets the shareholders decide for themselves whether they like the acquiror's offer. The tender price usually represents a substantial premium over the target's prevailing share price, and tender offers are almost always made exclusively in cash.

Advantages of Tender Offers   Cash tender offers present an acquiror with several potential advantages. First, a cash tender offer represents the quickest means of obtaining control of another company. There are no terms to be negotiated and no securities to be registered. Tender offers also have a shorter minimum waiting period for government antitrust review. However, tender offers are regulated, and Securities and Exchange Commission rules do not permit an all-out blitzkrieg. The securities laws require disclosure (within 10 days) when an acquiror buys 5% or more of any class of a company's equity securities, as well as disclosure of tender offers or exchange offers to acquire a class of equity securities of a publicly traded company.

A second advantage is that a tender offer provides greater flexibility than other acquisition strategies. A company can tender for just enough shares to give it effective control. In the case of a publicly traded company whose shares are widely held, this may require tendering for only 20% to 40% of the outstanding shares. The acquiror can set conditions of the offer so that, for example, it does not have to buy any shares unless the required minimum number is tendered. Once the acquiror has purchased these shares, resistance on the part of the acquiree's management normally lessens. The acquiror can then effect a merger structured as a tax-free reorganization to achieve 100% ownership.

Third, a cash tender offer represents the simplest way for a foreign company to buy a U.S. company. U.S. investors would generally be reluctant to swap shares of a U.S. company for securities of a foreign company for legal and other reasons. A cash tender offer gets around this problem.

Fourth, open-market purchases of the target company's stock followed by a cash tender offer give the potential acquiror an opportunity for profit. The cash tender price effectively puts a floor under the target's share price and alerts the financial community that the target company is "in play." If a higher bidder emerges, the original bidder can take some consolation from the profits it realizes on the shares it owns.

Contested Tender Offers Tender offers are often contested by the target's management, which may mount an aggressive public relations campaign, file lawsuits, bid for the other company's shares, and take other steps.

Unexpected tender offers are a source of concern to management. There is a 20-day minimum period that the tender offer must remain open, which seems painfully short to a company that gets caught by surprise. In addi-tion, current tender offer regulations require the target company to disclose its response within 10 business days of the commencement of the offer.

Proxy Contests

Tender offers are expensive because the bidder must pur-chase enough shares to secure control. Alternatively, one or more individuals who oppose incumbent management can initiate a **proxy contest.** A *proxy* conveys the right to vote the shares of the person who grants the proxy. The dissidents solicit shareholders' proxies to vote their shares in favor of their own slate of directors at the next annual meeting of stockholders. However, a proxy fight is expen-sive and time consuming, and few succeed.

E X A M P L E	*Brooke Group's Proxy Battle with RJR Nabisco Management*

In December 1995, Brooke Group took the first step in its proxy battle with RJR Nabisco's management. Brooke Group, controlled by investor Bennett LeBow, and investor Carl Icahn had tried unsuccessfully to convince the board of directors of RJR Nabisco to spin off the Nabisco food division in order to separate it from the company's tobacco business. Nabisco's board expressed a willingness to consider the spinoff but said that it would need time to figure out how best to separate the two businesses.

Brooke Group then solicited RJR Nabisco's shareholders on the issue. More than 50% of the company's shareholders voted in favor of a resolution supporting an immediate spinoff and another resolution giving shareholders the right to call a special shareholders' meeting. However, these resolutions were not binding on the board, which still refused to agree to an immediate spinoff. Thus in February 1996, Brooke Group announced that it would propose its own slate of dissident directors with a stated goal of spinning off the food business.

They launched a proxy contest in April 1996 but lost, leaving RJR Nabisco manage-ment in place to pursue its own strategy. ■

Shareholders seem to prefer cash in hand—espe-cially when it represents a large premium over the prevail-ing share price—to the mere promise that the company's financial prospects will improve in the future under new management. This observation is consistent with the Prin-ciple of Risk-Return Trade-Off. It is not surprising, then, that the vast majority of contests for control take the form of cash tender offers rather than proxy fights.

Defensive Tactics

Corporate managers often react negatively to unsolicited takeover bids. One would hope that their motive in doing so is to achieve the highest possible value for the com-pany's shares rather than merely exhibit the Principle of Self-Interested Behavior to protect their jobs. The courts have generally held that the directors of a company have a responsibility to obtain maximum value for shareholders. Corporate managers have devised a host of defensive tac-tics. Table F.8 lists some of the more popular ones. These tactics include anticipatory steps that management and the board take to reduce the risk of getting blindsided. But they can also entrench management. The poison pill has become controversial. In at least two cases, the Delaware Chancery Court ordered the board of directors to redeem poison pills in order to let shareholders choose between a restructuring plan supported by the board and an outside bidder's cash tender offer. The responsive tactics are more extreme, and many involve the sale of assets or securities.

Implications for Shareholder Wealth The use of defensive tactics raises serious questions about how they affect shareholder wealth. If they entrench inefficient man-agement, shareholder wealth must suffer. Studies have concluded that corporate charter amendments that autho-rize a staggered election of directors or supermajority vot-ing do not adversely affect stock prices but that targeted share repurchases (greenmail) cause shareholders who do not receive favored treatment to suffer a loss of wealth.

TABLE F.8
Frequently Used Takeover Defensive Tactics

DEFENSIVE TACTIC	DESCRIPTION
Anticipatory Tactics	
Dual class recapitalization	Company distributes a second class of common stock that possesses superior voting rights (for example, 10 votes per share). New shares cannot be sold. Shareholders who wish to sell must exchange new shares for regular shares with only 1 vote per share. Over time, management's voting power increases as other shareholders sell their shares.
Employee stock ownership plan (ESOP)	Company sells a large block of common stock (or voting preferred stock) to a company-sponsored ESOP and repurchases an equivalent number of common shares in the open market. Company votes the ESOP's shares until they are distributed to employees, which typically takes place over several years.
Poison pill	Company issues rights to its shareholders (typically, one nondetachable right per common share) that entitle the shareholders to purchase at one-half the market price (1) shares of the company's common stock if a potential acquiror buys more than a specified percentage of the company's shares (flip-in poison pill) or (2) shares of the acquiror's common stock following an acquisition of the company (flip-over poison pill). The acquiree's board of directors can redeem the rights for a nominal sum (typically, $0.05 per right) if it approves of the acquisition.
Staggered election of directors	Company's board of directors is divided into three equal classes. Only one class stands for reelection each year. A hostile raider cannot obtain control through a single proxy contest.
Supermajority voting/fair-price provision	Company's charter is amended to require a supermajority (for example, 80%) of the company's common shares to be voted in favor of a merger that has not been approved by the company's board of directors. (If it is board approved, a simple majority usually applies.) A fair-price provision allows the board of directors to waive the supermajority voting provision if the acquiror agrees to pay all shareholders the same price. The fair-price provision is designed to prevent a two-tier bid, in which shareholders who sell their shares in the initial tender often receive one price and the remaining shareholders who are "merged out" in the second stage receive a lower price.
Responsive Tactics	
Asset purchases or sales	Company purchases assets that the bidder does not want or that would block the bidder by creating an antitrust problem. Company sells the "crown jewel" assets that the bidder wants.
Leveraged recapitalization	Company borrows a large sum of money and distributes the loan proceeds along with any other excess cash to its shareholders as a dividend. A recapitalization is designed to make it more difficult for a takeover raider to make the acquisition with borrowed funds.
Litigation	Company files suit against the bidder alleging violation of state takeover statute(s), antitrust laws, securities laws, or other laws or regulations.
Pac-Man defense (or counter tender offer)	Company makes a counterbid for the common stock of the potential acquiror.
Share repurchases or sales	Company uses excess cash or borrows cash with which to finance a large share repurchase program. Alternatively, the company might instead repurchase shares only from the takeover raider, any premium over fair market value representing "greenmail." As a third alternative, the company can sell shares to a "friendly" third party.
Standstill agreement	Prospective acquiror agrees during the term of the agreement (1) not to increase its shareholdings above a specified percentage and, in many cases, (2) to vote its shares with management.

The Agency Problem in the Bid Response The managers' role in determining the company's response to an unsolicited takeover bid reflects a potentially serious agency problem. Many companies have established golden parachutes in order to reduce this agency problem. A *golden parachute* provides generous payments to managers who lose their jobs as a result of a takeover. In some cases these payments have been substantial. For example,

the RJR Nabisco leveraged buyout discussed in the next section resulted in payments to employees totaling $166 million. Golden parachutes are designed to align the objectives of shareholders and managers. However, if they are too generous, then under the Principle of Self-Interested Behavior, they could give management an incentive to sell the company on terms that may not be the most advantageous ones for shareholders.

Self-Check

1. What is a tender offer? How are tender offers used in battles for corporate control?

2. What are the main advantages of a tender offer as compared with alternative acquisition methods?

3. What is a proxy contest, and how does one work?

4. What are some of the defensive tactics that companies use in their efforts to ward off unwanted suitors?

5. What is a golden parachute? What agency problem is it designed to avoid? How might it create an agency problem of its own?

LEVERAGED BUYOUTS

A **leveraged buyout (LBO)** is an acquisition that is financed principally, sometimes more than 90%, by borrowing on a secured basis. Lenders look to the collateral value of the company's assets as security for their loans. They look to the operating cash flow from these assets to service this debt. LBOs are often used to take a company private.[12]

The RJR Nabisco Leveraged Buyout

Kohlberg Kravis Roberts & Co. (KKR) acquired RJR Nabisco, Inc. in 1988. It is a landmark transaction because it is the largest merger transaction ever accomplished.

On October 20, 1988, RJR Nabisco announced that a management group contemplated paying about $75 per share in cash to acquire the company, for an aggregate value of $17.6 billion. Four days later KKR announced that it was offering to acquire the company for $90 per share in cash and securities (plus $108 for each outstanding share of preferred stock). Several rounds of bidding ensued. KKR finally prevailed when it raised its bid to $109 per share ($81 of it in cash). The leveraged buyout cost $26 billion (including over $1 billion of transaction costs). KKR's common equity investment was a mere $1.5 billion, just 5.8% of the cost of the acquisition.

The transaction was so large that it caused a small blip in the U.S. money supply. Senior bank borrowings provided 49% of the funds. Subordinated lenders provided 19% of the funds. The new common stockholders provided 8% of the funds. They invested $500 million in pay-in-kind extendible debt securities and $1.5 billion in common stock. The pay-in-kind securities permitted RJR Nabisco to pay interest on them in the form of additional notes rather than cash. The securities issued in a second merger step provided the remaining 24% of the funds.

Agency Problems and the RJR Nabisco LBO

The RJR Nabisco LBO illustrates two significant agency problems. First, the management-led group announced that it was contemplating bidding $75 per share—far below the $109 acquisition price. The relatively low initial bid undoubtedly reflects the Principle of Two-Sided Transactions: The better the deal for the managers, the worse the deal would be for the shareholders. If shareholders had sold their shares to the management-led group, that group would have reaped a windfall of $34 per share, or more than $7.5 billion in the aggregate. Fortunately, the board of directors immediately formed a special outside committee and took steps to enable the company's shareholders to realize "full value" for their shares.

Second, the LBO caused RJR Nabisco's bonds to fall in price by approximately 20% to 30%. The fall in bond value reflected a transfer of wealth to the shareholders from the bondholders. This illustrates the problem of claim dilution with respect to capital structure, which we referred to earlier. The huge amount of additional borrowing reduced the credit standing of the bonds because RJR Nabisco's assets and operating cash flow didn't change. Soon after the LBO announcement, Moody's Investors Service downgraded the bonds from A-1 to Ba-2. Worse, the transaction sent shock waves through the corporate bond market as bond investors became concerned that other corporate bonds might be subject to similar *event risk.* Investors began to demand new protective bond covenants, called *super poison puts,* that would force issuers to redeem bonds at par in the event that a change in control occurred. Event risk is, of course, another form of agency cost. The demand for super poison puts represents the bondholders' attempt to reduce this cost.

---

[12]The advantages of being public or private are discussed in enrichment topic D, Issuing Securities and the Role of Investment Banking.

What Makes an Attractive LBO Candidate?

The ideal LBO candidate has relatively low operating risk. This permits the company to take on an unusually high degree of financial risk. In addition, an issue of subordinated debt provides comfort to senior lenders, much like true equity. The actual financing structure for a leveraged buyout will depend crucially on the perceived riskiness of the company's business, its cash flow characteristics, and the quality of its assets. These factors determine how much debt the company's operations can support. Investment bankers (or leveraged buyout companies) try to determine the maximum amount of debt the company's operations can support. The comparative approach, together with the DCF approach, will suggest a reasonable purchase price. This price, together with the company's borrowing capacity, will indicate the maximum degree of leverage for the buyout.

Self-Check

1. What is a leveraged buyout? What distinguishes it from other acquisitions?

2. Describe two agency problems that can arise in a leveraged buyout.

3. What is event risk? How do bond investors deal with it?

SUMMARY

A merger represents a special form of capital budgeting decision. One company acquires the entire portfolio of assets, and usually the liabilities as well, of another company. Such a transaction has special legal, tax, and accounting consequences. A merger is larger, more complex, and thus more difficult to analyze than undertaking a single project.

- Companies have a variety of motives for merging, but a merger can benefit both the acquiror's shareholders and the acquiree's shareholders only if (1) the two companies are worth more together than they are apart and (2) the increase in value is large enough to offset the transaction costs involved. Merging benefits the acquiror's shareholders only if they can realize some of this net gain.

- Valid motives for merging include operating efficiencies and economies of scale, tax benefits, surplus cash, and more rapid growth or cheap assets.

- Questionable motives for merging include diversification, reducing the cost of debt financing, and increasing earnings per share.

- The acquiror must choose what legal form the acquisition should take: merger or consolidation, purchase of stock, or purchase of assets.

- A proposed merger must comply with federal antitrust and securities laws and with each company's charter. An acquiror can merge or consolidate with the acquiree, purchase the acquiree's stock, or purchase only (some portion of) the acquiree's assets.

- The acquiror must evaluate its tax position, the target's tax position, and the tax position of the target's shareholders and decide whether it prefers a tax-free transaction or a taxable transaction.

- Generally, the acquiror is also concerned about the accounting impact of an acquisition, even though the available evidence indicates that the choice of accounting method does not affect valuation. It can choose between pooling-of-interests and purchase accounting treatments. Acquirors also often place a constraint on how much dilution in earnings per share they are willing to accept.

- The acquiror can use comparative analysis to determine a range of merger premiums—and a reasonable price range.

- The acquiror can use discounted-cash-flow (DCF) analysis to evaluate the net present value of the acquisition. DCF analysis can (and should!) also be used to determine the maximum price the acquiror can afford to pay (which is likely to depend on the legal form and tax status of the acquisition).

- The acquiror must decide how it wishes to pay for the acquisition: cash, common stock, other securities, or some combination. Its choice is restricted by the legal form of transaction, tax status, and accounting treatment it chooses. Common stock has a potential advantage in that the target's shareholders bear part of the risk that the acquiror has overpaid.

- Considering all its prior decisions and the probable response(s) of the target, the acquiror must decide how to proceed with the transaction, such as with a cash tender offer or a friendly proposal to merge. The defensive barriers the target has already erected affect this decision. Prior to proceeding with the transaction, the acquiror must comply with all applicable legal and regulatory requirements.

- A leveraged buyout (LBO) is an acquisition that is financed principally by borrowing on a secured basis.

- As the transaction proceeds—or as the battle for control unfolds—the acquiror may have to alter some of its earlier decisions if it finds that its objectives conflict with those of the target. But throughout this process, the acquiror must not lose sight of the fact that its ultimate objective is to maximize the wealth of its stockholders.

EQUATION SUMMARY

(F.1) $NAM = V_{AB} - (V_B + P_B) - Expenses - V_A$

$= [V_{AB} - (V_A + V_B)] - P_B - Expenses$

(F.2) $Premium\ paid = \dfrac{Purchase\ price\ per\ share - Target's\ share\ price\ pre\text{-}merger}{Target's\ share\ price\ pre\text{-}merger}$

(F.3)
$$\dfrac{\begin{array}{l}Cost\ of\ purchasing\ target's\ equity \\ + Transaction\ costs \\ - Target's\ excess\ assets\end{array}}{\begin{array}{l}Net\ investment\ in\ target's\ equity \\ + Cost\ of\ assuming\ target's\ debt\end{array}}$$
$$Net\ acquisition\ cost\ (NAC)$$

(F.4) $Added\ debt = (L)NAC - PV(debt\ assumed)$

(F.5) $\dfrac{Multiple\ of}{earnings\ paid} = \dfrac{Cost\ of\ purchasing\ target's\ equity}{\begin{array}{l}Target's\ net\ income \\ before\ extraordinary\ items\end{array}}$

(F.6) $TV(NA) = TV(equity) + TV(debt) - Taxes - Expenses$

(F.7) $NPV(acquisition) = -NAC + \displaystyle\sum_{t=1}^{N} \dfrac{CFAT_t}{(1 + WACC)^t}$

TOPIC REVIEW ACTIVITIES

SELF-TEST PROBLEMS

1. (Net advantage to merging) Agrawal Services is acquiring Mandelker Manufacturing. Prior to the merger, Agrawal's equity had a total value of $170 million and that of Mandelker was worth $60 million. After the merger, Agrawal is expected to have a market value of $260 million. Agrawal gave Mandelker shareholders a $20 million premium for their shares. In addition, Agrawal incurred $3 million of acquisition costs.
   a. What is the net advantage to merging for Agrawal?
   b. What is the total synergistic effect in this merger? By how much did the synergy exceed the premium and other acquisition costs?
2. (Earnings per share) Youhaul has 4,000,000 shares outstanding that are trading at $25 each. Z-Rocks has 2,000,000 shares outstanding that are trading at $20 each. Youhaul earns $2.00 per share, and Z-Rocks earns $2.50 per share. If the companies merge, their total combined earnings will be the same as before the merger.
   a. Calculate each company's price-earnings ratio.
   b. Suppose Youhaul acquires Z-Rocks in a stock-for-stock swap based on current market values. What is the exchange ratio? What happens to Youhaul's earnings per share?
   c. Suppose that Youhaul's managers (stupidly) believe that Youhaul is profiting as long as its earnings per share do not decline as a result of the merger. What is the maximum number of shares offered to Z-Rocks stockholders that they can issue and achieve this? What is the exchange ratio?
3. (Comparative analysis) Fleming Corporation is planning to acquire Southwest Purveyors, a food wholesale distributor. Fleming's financial staff has gathered the data shown below regarding acquisitions involving companies in the food service industry. Price is the price paid in the acquisition. Southwest's latest 12 months' earnings are $35 million, its latest 12 months' cash flow is $48 million, and its

current aggregate book value is $175 million. Calculate a reasonable range of acquisition values for Southwest.

Acquiree	Business	Price/ Earnings	Price/ Cash Flow	Price/ Book Value
Ferri Foods	wholesale	8x	5.0x	1.5x
Chowderhead	fast food	12	6.2	2.2
Conrad's	wholesale	8	4.5	1.6
Puri Curry	fast food	11	7.0	2.1
Burtin's Bar	fast food	10	7.5	2.4
Foodmasters	wholesale	7	4.8	1.3

SOLUTIONS TO SELF-TEST PROBLEMS

1. a. Using equation (F.1), the net advantage to merging is:

   $$NAM = 260 - (60 + 20) - 3 - 170 = \$7\ million$$

   Agrawal's stockholders gain a net $7 million.
   b. The total synergy is $V_{AB} - (V_A + V_B) = 260 - (170 + 60)$ = $30 million. Since premium and acquisition costs are $P_B + E = 20 + 3 = \$23$ million, the net advantage to merging is $30 - 23 = \$7$ million.
2. a. Price-Earnings ratio (Youhaul) = $25/2.00 = 12.50x$
   Price-Earnings ratio (Z-Rocks) = $20/2.50 = 8.00x$
   b. In order to receive their current value ($20 per share), Z-Rocks shareholders would have to receive 0.80 shares of Youhaul stock per share of Z-Rocks stock. Youhaul would issue $0.8(2,000,000) = 1,600,000$ new shares to Z-Rocks stockholders. The EPS are summarized in this table:

Company	Shares outstanding	Total earnings	Earnings per share
Youhaul (before)	4,000,000	$ 8,000,000	$2.00
Z-Rocks (before)	2,000,000	5,000,000	2.50
Youhaul (after)	5,600,000	13,000,000	2.32

   c. EPS will be at their current level ($2.00) as long as no more than $13,000,000/\$2.00 = 6,500,000$ total shares are outstanding. This means that Youhaul can issue an additional 2,500,000 shares above its pre-merger shares outstanding. If it did this, the EPS picture before and after the merger is:

Company	Shares outstanding	Total earnings	Earnings per share
Youhaul (before)	4,000,000	$ 8,000,000	$2.00
Z-Rocks (before)	2,000,000	5,000,000	2.50
Youhaul (after)	6,500,000	13,000,000	2.00

3. Because Southwest is a food wholesaler, the financial data for the wholesale acquisitions are more relevant than those for the fast food acquisitions. A reasonable approach is to take the average of the multiples for the comparable companies and then apply them to Southwest.

$$\text{Average Price/Earnings} = (8 + 8 + 7)/3 = 7.67x$$

$$\text{Price for Southwest} = 7.67(\text{Earnings}) = 7.67(35 \text{ million})$$
$$= \$268.45 \text{ million}$$

$$\text{Average Price/Cash Flow} = (5 + 4.5 + 4.8)/3 = 4.77x$$

$$\text{Price for Southwest} = 4.77(\text{Cash flow})$$
$$= 4.77(48 \text{ million}) = \$228.96 \text{ million}$$

$$\text{Average Price/Book Value} = (1.5 + 1.6 + 1.3)/3 = 1.47x$$

$$\text{Price for Southwest} = 1.47(\text{Book value})$$
$$= 1.47(175 \text{ million}) = \$257.25 \text{ million}$$

These estimates suggest a price in the $225 million to $270 million range.

QUESTIONS

1. Define the following terms: *merger, consolidation, horizontal merger, vertical merger,* and *conglomerate merger.*
2. Explain the valid motives that two companies may have for merging.
3. The Diversification Principle states that diversification is beneficial. Diversification is one of the main justifications managers give when undertaking conglomerate mergers. Explain why the justification is usually invalid notwithstanding the Diversification Principle.
4. How can a merger create financial synergy? How can it create business synergy? What is the difference between these two types of synergy?
5. How is the net advantage to merging usually divided between shareholders of acquirors and shareholders of acquirees?
6. Describe the three basic ways of effecting a corporate acquisition, and explain the distinguishing features of each.
7. Describe the main differences between a tax-free acquisition and a taxable acquisition. Which of these does a seller generally prefer and which does a buyer generally prefer?
8. Describe the main differences between the pooling-of-interests method and the purchase method of accounting for acquisitions. Should the choice of accounting technique affect market value in an efficient market?
9. Define the term *tender offer,* and explain how a company can acquire another company through a tender offer. What are the main advantages of a tender offer relative to other acquisition methods?
10. Define the term *proxy contest,* and explain how an investor group can gain control of a company through a proxy contest. What are the main disadvantages of a proxy contest relative to a cash tender offer?
11. Describe the main defensive tactics that companies have used in an effort to fight off unwanted suitors. How would you expect the use of such tactics to affect shareholder wealth? Describe the agency problem that arises in connection with defensive tactics to thwart unwanted bids.
12. What distinguishes a leveraged buyout from other types of acquisitions?

CHALLENGING QUESTION

13. At the time the Delaware Chancery Court ruled in favor of Time Inc. and let it proceed with its purchase of Warner Communications, Time's shares were trading at around $144 per share. Paramount Communications had bid $200 per share for Time's common stock. Time's board of directors refused to let the shareholders vote on the proposed Warner Communications transaction and argued that their long-term strategy had greater value for the Time shareholders. After the court decision, Paramount withdrew its bid.
   a. What do Time's actions reveal about the existence of agency costs?
   b. How could you reconcile the board's argument that its long-term strategy has a present value in excess of $200 per share with the fact that the stock was trading at just $144 per share?

PROBLEM SET A

A1. (Merger premium) Carbondale Scientific was worth $40 per share. What is the merger premium offered in the following two cases?
   a. Edwardsville Biotechnics offers $55 cash per share.
   b. Edwardsville Biotechnics offers 1.40 Edwardsville shares per Carbondale share. Edwardsville shares are worth $48 each following the takeover announcement.

A2. (Merger premium) Company A has 4 million outstanding shares and a market price of $30 per share. Company B has 1 million shares outstanding and a market price of $45 per share.
   a. Company A offers 2.0 shares of its stock per share of company B. If the price of company A stays at $30 per share, what is the merger premium offered?
   b. Company A offers 2.0 shares of its stock per share of company B. If the price of company A drops by $2 per share, what is the merger premium offered?

A3. (Net advantage to merging) LSU Company is acquiring TT Company. Prior to the merger, LSU's equity had a total value of $340 million and that of TT was worth $120 million. After the merger, LSU is expected to have a market value of $500 million. LSU is giving TT shareholders a $40 million premium for their shares. In addition, LSU incurred $6 million of acquisition costs.
   a. What is the net advantage to merging for LSU?
   b. What is the total synergistic effect in this merger? By how much did the synergy exceed the premium and other acquisition costs?

A4. (Net advantage to merging) Ace Homebuilding and Brace Homebuilding will merge. Ace has a total market value of $50 million, and Brace has a total market value of $75 million. Their merger will lead to operating efficiencies and will produce a present value savings of $10 million.
  a. What is the total market value of the merged companies?
  b. If the merger would entail expenses amounting to $5 million, is there a net advantage to merging?
  c. If Ace buys Brace's outstanding shares, paying Brace's common stockholders a $3 million premium, will the acquisition be advantageous to Ace's shareholders? How is the net advantage to merging divided between the two companies' shareholders?

A5. (Earnings per share) Two companies plan to merge. Prior to the merger, the acquiror has earnings per share of $5 and a price-earnings ratio of 20. The acquiree has earnings per share of $2 and a price-earnings ratio of 10. The acquiror has 10 million shares of stock, and the acquiree has 5 million shares.
  a. How many shares must the acquiror exchange for each of the acquiree's shares if the shares are exchanged at their respective market values (that is, no premium)?
  b. Calculate the acquiror's earnings per share after the merger.
  c. Calculate the acquiror's price-earnings ratio after the merger.
  d. What conclusion can be drawn from parts **b** and **c?**

A6. (Earnings per share) Lux Company has 1000 shares outstanding that are trading at $50 each. MCD has 200 shares outstanding that are trading at $40 each. Lux earns $4.00 per share, and MCD earns $2.00 per share. If the companies merge, their total combined earnings will be the same as before the merger.
  a. Calculate each company's price-earnings ratio.
  b. Suppose Lux acquires MCD in a stock-for-stock swap based on current market values. What is the exchange ratio? What happens to MCD's earnings per share?
  c. What is the maximum number of shares that can be offered to MCD stockholders that would not cause Lux's earnings per share to drop?

PROBLEM SET B

B1. (NPV of an acquisition) Company A intends to acquire company B. The acquisition will cost company A $100 million. Company A plans to install new management, "fix" the company, and sell it at the end of 5 years. The projected incremental free cash flow stream company A expects to realize from the acquisition, which reflects the anticipated operating improvements, is given below. In addition, the projected after-tax sales proceeds amount to $200 million.

Year	1	2	3	4	5
Cash flow ($ millions)	10	20	30	40	50

  a. Calculate the NPV of the acquisition, assuming a 20% cost of capital.

  b. Calculate the internal rate of return for the acquisition.
  c. Calculate the payback period for the acquisition.
  d. Should company A proceed with the acquisition?

B2. (Effect of a merger on bondholders) Two companies in unrelated businesses plan to merge. There are three possible states of the economy. The table below shows the returns to the shareholders of each company and the debtholders of company B in each state of the economy. Company B has $50 million principal amount of debt, and company A has no debt.

	Boom	Stable Growth	Recession
Probability	0.3	0.5	0.2
Company A	$200 million	$100 million	$25 million
Company B			
Debt	50	50	25
Equity	100	50	—

  a. What is each company worth?
  b. A merger would not produce any operating efficiencies or economies of scale. What is the merged company worth? What is the debt of the merged company worth? What is the equity of the merged company worth?
  c. Should the companies merge?

B3. (Effect of a merger on bondholders) Suppose the two companies in Problem B2 are in the same industry and a merger will produce $30 million of synergistic benefits (in all three states of the economy) but require $2 million of expenses.
  a. How will a merger affect the bondholders?
  b. How will a merger affect the shareholders of each company?
  c. Should the companies merge?

B4. (Purchase accounting) The purchase price in an acquisition is $275 million. Consultants estimate that the fair market value of the assets acquired is $180 million. Investment bankers estimate that the fair market value of the liabilities assumed in the acquisition is $30 million. Calculate the amount of goodwill.

B5. (Takeover premium paid) National Permanent Credit Corporation just acquired Specific Capital Corporation. National paid $50 per Specific share. Specific's closing share price 30 days prior to the merger announcement was $35. Calculate the premium paid.

B6. (Valuing a takeover target) International Oil Company has oil and gas reserves consisting of 25 million barrels of oil and 60 billion cubic feet of natural gas. Judging by the prices at which oil and gas reserves have recently sold, 1 barrel of oil is equivalent to 6000 cubic feet of natural gas.
  a. Calculate the number of barrels of oil equivalent in International's reserves.
  b. Regal Oil Corporation is contemplating a bid for International based on the value of International's assets. Petroleum reserves have recently sold for $8.50 per barrel of oil equivalent, and Regal estimates that International's other assets are worth $52.5 million. Calculate the estimated value of International's assets.

B7. (NPV of an acquisition) Razorback Computer Corporation is preparing to make a bid for the common shares of Windy City Software. Razorback would acquire the shares for cash but not write up Windy City's assets. Windy City has 5 million shares outstanding, which are trading at a price of $30 per share and a price-earnings multiple of 10. Windy City has $50 million principal amount of 8% debt, which pays interest annually in arrears and matures in a lump sum at the end of 6 years. Razorback's marginal income tax rate is 40%. Razorback estimates that it will have to pay a 50% premium to acquire Windy City and also pay $3 million of after-tax transaction costs. Windy City has no excess cash. Razorback's target debt-to-equity ratio is 1/3, its pretax cost of new debt is 10%, its cost of capital for the acquisition is 16.5%, and the incremental free cash flow stream for the next 6 years is given below.

Year	1	2	3	4	5	6
Cash flow ($ millions)	25	30	35	40	45	50

a. Calculate the NPV and IRR of the acquisition on a nondisposition basis, assuming the estimated year-6 net operating profit is $75 million.
b. Calculate the NPV and IRR of the acquisition on a disposition basis, assuming a 6-year investment horizon.
c. Should Razorback make the acquisition if it has to pay $45 per share?
d. What is the maximum price Razorback can afford to pay on a disposition basis with a 6-year investment horizon?

B8. (NPV of an acquisition) Razorback Computer Corporation in Problem B7 has a leveraged beta of 1.25. The riskless return is 8%, and the risk premium on the market portfolio is 8%.
a. Calculate the cost of capital for Razorback's acquisition.
b. Calculate the NPV of the acquisition on a nondisposition basis, assuming the debt issued to finance the acquisition matures in a lump sum at the end of 6 years.
c. Calculate the NPV of the acquisition on a disposition basis, assuming the debt issued to finance the acquisition matures in a lump sum at the end of 6 years.

B9. (Pooling of interests and purchase accounting) Eastern Shore Chemicals plans to acquire Ocean State Chemicals for $50 million. The two companies' balance sheets are shown below. The fair market value of Ocean State's working capital is $12 million, of its fixed assets is $32 million, and of its debt is $4 million.

	Ocean State	Eastern Shore
Assets ($ millions)		
Working capital	$ 10	$ 25
Fixed assets	25	125
Total	$ 35	$ 150
Liabilities and Equity ($ millions)		
Debt	$ 5	$ 50
Equity	30	100
Total	$ 35	$ 150

a. Suppose Eastern Shore exchanges shares of its common stock for the outstanding shares of Ocean State's common stock. How would the balance sheet of the combined company look? Which method of accounting did you apply?
b. Suppose Eastern Shore issues new common stock for cash and uses the cash to purchase Ocean State's shares. How would the balance sheet of the combined company look? Which method of accounting did you apply?
c. Which method of accounting should Eastern Shore apply?

B10. (Earnings per share) Company A has 1,000,000 shares outstanding that are trading at $25 each. Company B has 2,000,000 shares outstanding that are trading at $50 each. Company A earns $2.50 per share, and company B earns $4.00 per share.
a. Calculate each company's price-earnings ratio.
b. Suppose company B acquires company A in a stock-for-stock swap based on current market values. What happens to company B's earnings per share? Does that mean that company B's shareholders are better off as a result of the merger? Explain.

B11. (Effect of a merger on bondholders) With regard to Empire State's acquisition of Garden State, suppose Garden State's new-issue rate is 13%.
a. What is the market value of the $100 million of outstanding bonds?
b. Would the acquisition help or hurt Garden State's bondholders?
c. What is the cause of this transfer of wealth?

B12. (NPV of an acquisition) Big Sky Airlines would like to acquire Far West Commuter Air and integrate Far West's route structure into its system. Big Sky would acquire Far West's shares for cash but not write up Far West's assets. Far West has 2 million shares outstanding. Its share price is $24, its earnings per share are $4, and it has no debt and no excess cash. Big Sky's debt-to-equity ratio is 2-to-1. Its pretax cost of debt is 14% (annual interest), its cost of equity is 20%, and its marginal income tax rate is 40%. If Big Sky acquires Far West, it projects a year-8 net operating profit of $45 million and the incremental free cash flows given below.

Year	1	2	3	4	5	6	7	8
Cash flow ($ millions)	6	10	12	14	18	22	25	30

a. Calculate the NPV and IRR of the acquisition on a nondisposition basis, assuming Big Sky pays a 1/3 premium for Far West's shares and $500,000 of after-tax acquisition expenses.
b. Calculate the NPV and IRR of the acquisition on a disposition basis under the same assumptions as in part a and assuming an 8-year investment horizon.
c. Should Big Sky make the acquisition if it has to pay a 1/3 premium for Far West's shares?

B13. (Calculating exchange ratios) Ajax Air Products and Central Combustion have agreed to an exchange of common stock under which Ajax would acquire Central. Ajax's common stock is trading at $40 per share, and Central's common stock is trading at $20 per share. Each company has 10 million shares outstanding.

a. Calculate the exchange ratio, assuming Ajax does not pay a premium.
b. Calculate the exchange ratio, assuming Ajax pays a 25% premium to acquire Central.
c. If the exchange ratio determined in part **b** is fixed and the announcement of the merger causes Ajax's share price to fall 10%, by how much would you expect Central's share price to change?

PROBLEM SET C

C1. (NPV of an acquisition) Excelsior Paper Products Company is considering acquiring the Spring Lake Greeting Card Company. Excelsior would have to pay $100 million for Spring Lake, 90% of which it would borrow at a 10% annual interest rate. The $100 million purchase price represents a multiple of 8 times this year's incremental free cash flow. Excelsior's marginal income tax rate is 40%. Its long-term debt ratio is 50%. Spring Lake's incremental free cash flow is expected to grow at the rate of 10% per year into the foreseeable future. All available free cash flow will be used first to pay interest, next to repay principal (until the acquisition loan is fully repaid), and then to

pay dividends. The unleveraged cost of equity capital for similar acquisitions is 14%. The riskless return is 6%, and the excess return on the market portfolio is 8%. Calculate the NPV of the acquisition, assuming a 6-year investment horizon.

C2. (Acquisition price range) American Car Rental has agreed to acquire Big Apple Car Rental. American's financial staff has gathered the data shown below regarding acquisitions involving companies in the automobile industry. Price is the price paid in the acquisition. Big Apple's latest 12 months' earnings are $25 million, its latest 12 months' cash flow is $40 million, and its current aggregate book value is $175 million. Calculate a reasonable range of acquisition values for Big Apple.

Acquiree	Business	Price/ Earnings	Price/ Cash Flow	Price/ Book Value
Central	rental	$10x$	$5.8x$	$1.5x$
Eastern	manufacturing	7	4.3	1.2
Western	manufacturing	6	4.0	1.1
South Central	rental	11	6.7	1.6
Southwestern	rental	12	7.8	1.4
Panhandle	manufacturing	8	4.9	1.3

BIBLIOGRAPHY

Agrawal, Anup, Jeffrey F. Jaffe, and Gershon N. Mandelker. "The Post-Merger Performance of Acquiring Firms: A Re-Examination of an Anomaly," *Journal of Finance,* 1992, 47(4):1605–1622.

Agrawal, Anup, and Gershon N. Mandelker. "Large Shareholders and the Monitoring of Managers: The Case of Antitakeover Charter Amendments," *Journal of Financial and Quantitative Analysis,* 1990, 25(2):143–162.

Agrawal, Anup, and Ralph A. Walkling. "Executive Careers and Compensation Surrounding Takeover Bids," *Journal of Finance,* 1994, 49(3):985–1014.

Ambrose, Brent W., and William L. Megginson. "The Role of Asset Structure, Ownership Structure, and Takeover Defenses in Determining Acquisition Likelihood," *Journal of Financial and Quantitative Analysis,* 1992, 27(4):575–590.

Ambrose, Brent W., and Drew B. Winters. "Does an Industry Effect Exist for Leveraged Buyouts?" *Financial Management,* 1992, 21(1):89–101.

Amihud, Yakov, Baruch Lev, and Nickolaos G. Travlos. "Corporate Control and the Choice of Investment Financing: The Case of Corporate Acquisitions," *Journal of Finance,* 1990, 45(2):603–616.

Arzac, Enrique R. "On the Capital Structure of Leveraged Buyouts," *Financial Management,* 1992, 21(1):16–26.

Baldwin, Carliss Y., and Sugato Bhattacharyya. "Choosing the Method of Sale: A Clinical Study of Conrail," *Journal of Financial Economics,* 1991, 30(1):69–98.

Banerjee, Ajeyo, and James E. Owers. "Wealth Production in White Knight Bids," *Financial Management,* 1992, 21(3):48–57.

Benjamin, Harvey E., and Michael B. Goldberg. *Leveraged Acquisitions: Private and Public.* New York: Practising Law Institute, 1984.

Berkovitch, Elazar, and Naveen Khanna. "How Target Shareholders Benefit from Value-Reducing Defensive Strategies in Takeovers," *Journal of Finance,* 1990, 45(1):137–156.

Bertin, William J., Farrokh Ghazanfari, and Khalil M. Torabzadeh. "Failed Bank Acquisitions and Successful Bidders' Returns," *Financial Management,* 1989, 18(2):93–100.

Bhagat, Sanjai, and Richard Jefferis. "Voting Power in the Proxy Process: The Case of Antitakeover Charter Amendments," *Journal of Financial Economics,* 1991, 30(1):193–225.

Boot, Arnoud W. A. "Why Hang On to Losers? Divestitures and Takeovers," *Journal of Finance,* 1992, 47(4):1401–1424.

Bradley, Michael, Anand Desai, and E. Han Kim. "Synergistic Gains from Corporate Acquisitions and Their Division Between the Stockholders of Target and Acquiring Firms," *Journal of Financial Economics,* 1988, 21(1):3–40.

Brickley, James A., Jeffrey L. Coles, and Rory L. Terry. "Outside Directors and the Adoption of Poison Pills," *Journal of Financial Economics,* 1994, 35(3):371–390.

Brous, Peter A., and Omesh Kini. "A Reexamination of Analysts' Earnings Forecasts for Takeover Targets," *Journal of Financial Economics,* 1993, 33(2):201–226.

Brown, David T., and Michael D. Ryngaert. "The Model of Acquisition in Takeovers: Taxes and Asymmetric Information," *Journal of Finance,* 1991, 46(2):653–670.

Brown, Keith C., and Michael V. Raymond. "Risk Arbitrage and the Prediction of Successful Corporate Takeovers," *Financial Management,* 1986, 15(3):54–63.

Bruner, Robert F. "Leveraged ESOPs and Corporate Restructuring," *Continental Bank Journal of Applied Corporate Finance,* 1988, 1(Spring):54–66.

Bruner, Robert F., and Kenneth M. Eades. "The Crash of the Revco Leveraged Buyout: The Hypothesis of Inadequate Capital," *Financial Management,* 1992, 21(1):35–49.

Cebenoyan, A. Sinan, George J. Papaioannou, and Nickolaos G. Travlos. "Foreign Takeover Activity in the U.S. and Wealth Effects for Target Firm Shareholders," *Financial Management,* 1992, 21(3):58–68.

Chaplinsky, Susan, and Greg Niehaus. "The Role of ESOPs in Takeover Contests," *Journal of Finance,* 1994, 49(4):1451–1470.

Chowdhry, Bhagwan, and Vikram Nanda. "The Strategic Role of Debt in Takeover Contests," *Journal of Finance,* 1993, 48(2):731–745.

Conrad, Jennifer, and Cathy M. Niden. "Order Flow, Trading Costs and Corporate Acquisition Announcements," *Financial Management,* 1992, 21(4):22–31.

Davidson, Wallace N., III, Dipa Dutia, and Louis Cheng. "A Re-Examination of the Market Reaction to Failed Mergers," *Journal of Finance,* 1989, 44(4):1077–1084.

DeAngelo, Harry, and Linda DeAngelo. "Proxy Contests and the Governance of Publicly Held Corporations," *Journal of Financial Economics,* 1989, 23(1):29–59.

Fabozzi, Frank J., Michael G. Ferri, T. Dessa Fabozzi, and Julia Tucker. "A Note on Unsuccessful Tender Offers and Stockholder Returns," *Journal of Finance,* 1988, 43(5):1275–1283.

Franks, Julian, Robert Harris, and Sheridan Titman. "The Post-merger Share-Price Performance of Acquiring Firms," *Journal of Financial Economics,* 1991, 29(1):81–96.

Gosnell, Thomas F., Sylvia C. Hudgins, and John A. MacDonald. "The Acquisition of Failing Thrifts: Returns to Acquirers," *Financial Management,* 1993, 22(4):58–68.

Hayn, Carla. "Tax Attributes as Determinants of Shareholder Gains in Corporate Acquisitions," *Journal of Financial Economics,* 1989, 23(1):121–153.

Healy, Paul M., Krishna G. Palepu, and Richard S. Ruback. "Does Corporate Performance Improve After Mergers?" *Journal of Financial Economics,* 1992, 31(2):135–176.

Hirschey, Mark, and Janis K. Zaima. "Insider Trading, Ownership Structure, and the Market Assessment of Corporate Sell-Offs," *Journal of Finance,* 1989, 44(4):971–980.

Hite, Gailen L., and Michael R. Vetsuypens. "Management Buyouts of Divisions and Shareholder Wealth," *Journal of Finance,* 1989, 44(4):953–970.

Jarrell, Gregg A., and Annette B. Poulsen. "The Returns to Acquiring Firms in Tender Offers: Evidence from Three Decades," *Financial Management,* 1989, 18(3):12–19.

Jensen, Michael C. "Agency Costs of Free Cash Flow, Corporate Finance, and Takeovers," *American Economic Review,* 1986a, 76(May):323–329.

Jensen, Michael C. "Eclipse of the Public Corporation," *Harvard Business Review,* 1989 (September–October):61–74.

Jensen, Michael C. "The Takeover Controversy: Analysis and Evidence," *Midland Corporate Finance Journal,* 1986b, 4(Summer):6–32.

Kaplan, Steven. "Management Buyouts: Evidence on Taxes as a Source of Value," *Journal of Finance,* 1989, 44(3):611–632.

Kaplan, Steven N. "The Staying Power of Leveraged Buyouts," *Journal of Financial Economics,* 1991, 29(2):287–314.

Kaplan, Steven, and Michael S. Weisbach. "The Success of Acquisitions: Evidence from Divestitures," *Journal of Finance,* 1992, 47(1):107–138.

Lam, Chun H., and Kenneth J. Boudreaux. "Conglomerate Merger, Wealth Redistribution and Debt: A Note," *Journal of Finance,* 1984, 39(1):275–281.

Lee, Chun I., Stuart Rosenstein, Nanda Rangan, and Wallace N. Davidson, III. "Board Composition and Shareholder Wealth: The Case of Management Buyouts," *Financial Management,* 1992, 21(1):58–72.

Lee, D. Scott. "Management Buyout Proposals and Inside Information," *Journal of Finance,* 1992, 47(3):1061–1080.

Lehn, Kenneth, Jeffrey Netter, and Annette Poulsen. "Consolidating Corporate Control: Dual-Class Recapitalizations versus Leveraged Buyouts," *Journal of Financial Economics,* 1990, 27(2):557–580.

Lehn, Kenneth, and Annette Poulsen. "Free Cash Flow and Stockholder Gains in Going Private Transactions," *Journal of Finance,* 1989, 44(3):771–788.

Lewellen, Wilbur G., and Michael G. Ferri. "Strategies for the Merger Game: Management and the Market," *Financial Management,* 1983, 12(4):25–35.

Loderer, Claudio, and Kenneth Martin. "Corporate Acquisitions by Listed Firms: The Experience of a Comprehensive Sample," *Financial Management,* 1990, 19(4):17–33.

Loderer, Claudio, and Kenneth Martin. "Postacquisition Performance of Acquiring Firms," *Financial Management,* 1992, 21(3):69–79.

Martin, Kenneth J., and John J. McConnell. "Corporate Performance, Corporate Takeovers, and Management Turnover," *Journal of Finance,* 1991, 46(2):671–688.

McWilliams, Victoria B. "Managerial Share Ownership and the Stock Price Effects of Antitakeover Amendment Proposals," *Journal of Finance,* 1990, 45(5):1627–1640.

McWilliams, Victoria B. "Tobin's *q* and the Stock Price Reaction to Antitakeover Amendments," *Financial Management,* 1993, 22(4):16–17.

Mian, Shehzad, and James Rosenfeld. "Takeover Activity and the Long-Run Performance of Reverse Leveraged Buyouts," *Financial Management,* 1993, 22(4):46–57.

Michel, Allen, Israel Shaked, and You-Tay Lee. "An Evaluation of Investment Banker Acquisition Advice: The Shareholders' Perspective," *Financial Management,* 1991, 20(2):40–49.

Mitchell, Mark L., and J. Harold Mulherin. "The Stock Price Response to Pension Terminations and the Relation of Terminations with Corporate Takeovers," *Financial Management,* 1989, 18(3):41–56.

Morck, Randall, Andrei Shleifer, and Robert W. Vishny. "Do Managerial Objectives Drive Bad Acquisitions?" *Journal of Finance,* 1990, 45(1):31–48.

Muscarella, Chris J., and Michael R. Vetsuypens. "Efficiency and Organizational Structure: A Study of Reverse LBOs," *Journal of Finance,* 1990, 45(5):1389–1414.

Nathan, Kevin S., and Terrence B. O'Keefe. "The Rise in Takeover Premiums: An Exploratory Study," *Journal of Financial Economics,* 1989, 23(1):101–119.

Neely, Walter P. "Banking Acquisitions: Acquirer and Target Shareholder Returns," *Financial Management,* 1987, 16(4):66–73.

Newbould, Gerald D., Robert E. Chatfield, and Ronald F. Anderson. "Leveraged Buyouts and Tax Incentives," *Financial Management,* 1992, 21(1):50–57.

Niden, Cathy M. "An Empirical Examination of White Knight Corporate Takeovers: Synergy and Overbidding," *Financial Management,* 1993, 22(4):28–45.

Opler, Tim C. "Controlling Financial Distress Costs in Leveraged Buyouts with Financial Innovations," *Financial Management,* 1993, 22(3):79–90.

Opler, Tim C. "Operating Performance in Leveraged Buyouts: Evidence from 1985–1989," *Financial Management,* 1992, 21(1):27–34.

Opler, Tim, and Sheridan Titman. "The Determinants of Leveraged Buyout Activity: Free Cash Flow Versus Financial Distress Costs," *Journal of Finance,* 1993, 48(5):1985–1999.

Palepu, Krishna G. "Predicting Takeover Targets: A Methodological and Empirical Analysis," *Journal of Accounting and Economics,* 1986, 8(March):3–36.

Servaes, Henri. "Tobin's *Q* and the Gains from Takeovers," *Journal of Finance,* 1991, 46(1):409–420.

Shrieves, Ronald E., and Mary M. Pashley. "Evidence on the Association Between Mergers and Capital Structure," *Financial Management,* 1984, 13(3):39–48.

Slovin, Myron B., Marie E. Sushka, and Carl D. Hudson. "Deregulation, Contestability, and Airline Acquisitions," *Journal of Financial Economics,* 1991, 30(2): 231–252.

Smith, Brian F., and Ben Amoako-Adu. "Minority Buyouts and Ownership Characteristics: Evidence from the Toronto Stock Exchange," *Financial Management,* 1992, 21(2):41–51.

Song, Moon H., and Ralph A. Walkling. "The Impact of Managerial Ownership on Acquisition Attempts and Target Shareholder Wealth," *Journal of Financial and Quantitative Analysis,* 1993, 28(4):439–457.

Stulz, Rene M., Ralph A. Walkling, and Moon H. Song. "The Distribution of Target Ownership and the Division of Gains in Successful Takeovers," *Journal of Finance,* 1990, 45(3):817–834.

Sullivan, Michael J., Marlin R. H. Jensen, and Carl D. Hudson. "The Role of Medium of Exchange in Merger Offers: Examination of Terminated Merger Proposals," *Financial Management,* 1994, 23(3):51–62.

Thomas, Hugh. "Seller Selection of M&A Advisors," *Financial Management,* 1993, 22(4):17–18.

Vijh, Anand M. "The Spinoff and Merger Ex-Date Effects," *Journal of Finance,* 1994, 49(2):581–609.

Wansley, James W., William R. Lane, and Ho C. Yang. "Abnormal Returns to Acquired Firms by Type of Acquisition and Method of Payment," *Financial Management,* 1983, 12(3):16–22.

Weaver, Samuel C., Robert S. Harris, Daniel W. Bielinski, and Kenneth F. MacKenzie. "Panel Discussion: Merger and Acquisition Valuation," *Financial Management,* 1991, 20(2):85–96.

Using a Business Calculator

A business calculator is an absolute must in today's business environment whether you are doing finance, accounting, marketing, production, strategy, or human resource management. You can easily learn to make the time-value-of-money calculations we illustrate here. However, with just a little more effort, you can also learn to do so much more with your calculator, such as calculating averages, standard deviations, depreciation, linear regression coefficients, and breakeven amounts. The list is almost endless.

There are many different business calculators on the market today. The one you choose depends on your own personal preferences. We have chosen the Texas Instruments BAII PLUS to illustrate the use of a business calculator.

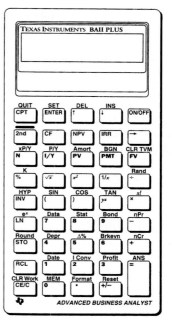

Key strokes are illustrated by boxes. An unshaded box indicates the function shown on the face of the key. For example, the four-key-stroke sequence 3 $+$ 2 $=$ adds the numbers 3 and 2 using the red keys with + and = on them. A shaded box preceded by a $2nd$ indicates the function shown in grey above the key. For example, 4 $2nd$ $x!$ computes 4 factorial (4 times 3 times 2 times 1) using the secondary function shown above the times key, which is the red key with × on it.

Assumed Payments per Period *(very important)*

Your calculator can assume any number of payments per period. For simplicity, our calculations here, and throughout the book, *always* assume the mode is set to 1.00. For example, if there are 12 monthly payments per year over 5 years, we make the conversion and use N = 60.

To set your calculator for use with our calculations:

$2nd$ P/Y 1 $ENTER$ CE/C CE/C

This setting continues indefinitely (even though the calculator is turned off and on), until it is changed.

Decimal Place Display

Your calculator always calculates with 9-digit accuracy. However, the numbers it displays depend on the number of decimal places to which you have it set. Our calculations generally display 2, 3, or 4 decimal places.

To set the number of decimal places displayed to three:

$2nd$ $Format$ 3 $ENTER$ [the display will show: DEC = ☐ 3.000] CE/C CE/C

This setting also continues indefinitely (even though the calculator is turned off and on), until it is changed.

End-of-Period Annuity Cash Flows

Your calculator can assume that annuity cash flows occur either at the end of the period or at the beginning of the period. For simplicity, our calculations *always* assume the mode is set to end-of-period annuity cash flows. If a small BGN appears above the number display, the mode is set to beginning-of-period annuity cash flows. Otherwise, the mode is already set to end-of-period annuity cash flows.

To set the mode to end-of-period annuity cash flows:

⟦2nd⟧ ⟦BGN⟧ [the display should show BGN; if it shows END, hit ⟦CE/C⟧] ⟦2nd⟧ ⟦SET⟧ ⟦CE/C⟧ ⟦CE/C⟧

This setting also continues indefinitely (even though the calculator is turned off and on), until it is changed.

EXAMPLES

Present Value of a Single Future Cash Flow

The present value of $5000 to be received in 4 years at 12% APY is $3177.59:

⟦4⟧ ⟦N⟧ ⟦1⟧ ⟦2⟧ ⟦I/Y⟧ ⟦0⟧ ⟦PMT⟧ ⟦5⟧ ⟦0⟧ ⟦0⟧ ⟦0⟧ ⟦FV⟧ ⟦CPT⟧ ⟦PV⟧ = −3177.59

Future Value of a Current Amount

The future value of $2000 to be received in 7 years at 9% APY is $3656.08:

⟦7⟧ ⟦N⟧ ⟦9⟧ ⟦I/Y⟧ ⟦2⟧ ⟦0⟧ ⟦0⟧ ⟦0⟧ ⟦PV⟧ ⟦0⟧ ⟦PMT⟧ ⟦CPT⟧ ⟦FV⟧ = −3656.08

Present Value of an Annuity

The present value of $200 per month for 5 years (60 months) at 9% APR (0.75% per month) is $9634.67:

⟦6⟧ ⟦0⟧ ⟦N⟧ ⟦.⟧ ⟦7⟧ ⟦5⟧ ⟦I/Y⟧ ⟦2⟧ ⟦0⟧ ⟦0⟧ ⟦PMT⟧ ⟦0⟧ ⟦FV⟧ ⟦CPT⟧ ⟦PV⟧ = −9634.67

Future Value of an Annuity

The future value of $50 per week for 3 years (156 weeks) at 6% APR (0.5% per week) is $11,772.37:

⟦1⟧ ⟦5⟧ ⟦6⟧ ⟦N⟧ ⟦.⟧ ⟦5⟧ ⟦I/Y⟧ ⟦0⟧ ⟦PV⟧ ⟦5⟧ ⟦0⟧ ⟦PMT⟧ ⟦CPT⟧ ⟦FV⟧ = −11,772.37

Annuity Cash Flows for a Present Value

The monthly payments for a $100,000 20-year (240 months) mortgage at 8.16% APR (0.68% per month) are $846.43:

⟦2⟧ ⟦4⟧ ⟦0⟧ ⟦N⟧ ⟦.⟧ ⟦6⟧ ⟦8⟧ ⟦I/Y⟧ ⟦1⟧ ⟦0⟧ ⟦0⟧ ⟦0⟧ ⟦0⟧ ⟦0⟧ ⟦PV⟧ ⟦0⟧ ⟦FV⟧ ⟦CPT⟧ ⟦PMT⟧ = −846.43

Annuity Cash Flows for a Future Value

Suppose you are going to save some money from the paycheck you get every 2 weeks, and you will earn 4.42% APR (0.17% per 2-week period) on your savings. To save up $10,000 over 2.5 years (65 pay periods), you will need to put aside $145.63 from each paycheck:

⟦6⟧ ⟦5⟧ ⟦N⟧ ⟦.⟧ ⟦1⟧ ⟦7⟧ ⟦I/Y⟧ ⟦0⟧ ⟦PV⟧ ⟦1⟧ ⟦0⟧ ⟦0⟧ ⟦0⟧ ⟦0⟧ ⟦FV⟧ ⟦CPT⟧ ⟦PMT⟧ = −145.63

Interest Rate for a Present Value

A $15,000 10-year (120-month) loan requiring monthly payments of $206.96 has an APR of 11.04%:

⟦1⟧ ⟦2⟧ ⟦0⟧ ⟦N⟧ ⟦1⟧ ⟦5⟧ ⟦0⟧ ⟦0⟧ ⟦0⟧ ⟦PV⟧ ⟦2⟧ ⟦0⟧ ⟦6⟧ ⟦.⟧ ⟦9⟧ ⟦6⟧ ⟦+/−⟧ ⟦PMT⟧ ⟦0⟧ ⟦FV⟧ ⟦CPT⟧ ⟦I/Y⟧ = 0.92 ⟦×⟧ ⟦1⟧ ⟦2⟧ ⟦=⟧ 11.04

Interest Rate for a Future Value

To save $1,000,000 by investing $155.50 per month for 35 years (420 months), your investments must earn an APR of 12.00%:

$\boxed{4}\,\boxed{2}\,\boxed{0}\,\boxed{N}\,\boxed{0}\,\boxed{PV}\,\boxed{1}\,\boxed{5}\,\boxed{5}\,\boxed{6}\,\boxed{5}\,\boxed{0}\,\boxed{+/-}\,\boxed{PMT}\,\boxed{1}\,\boxed{0}\,\boxed{0}\,\boxed{0}\,\boxed{0}\,\boxed{0}\,\boxed{0}\,\boxed{FV}\,\boxed{CPT}\,\boxed{I/Y} = 1.00\,\boxed{\times}\,\boxed{1}\,\boxed{2}\,\boxed{=}\,12.00$

Present Value of Annuity Cash Flows and a Future Value

The present value of a 10%-coupon ($50 semiannually) corporate bond that pays $1000 at maturity in 8 years (16 semiannual periods) and has a yield to maturity of 12% (6% semiannually) is $898.94:

$\boxed{1}\,\boxed{6}\,\boxed{N}\,\boxed{6}\,\boxed{I/Y}\,\boxed{5}\,\boxed{0}\,\boxed{PMT}\,\boxed{1}\,\boxed{0}\,\boxed{0}\,\boxed{0}\,\boxed{FV}\,\boxed{CPT}\,\boxed{PV} = -898.94$

Interest Rate for Annuity Cash Flows and a Future Value

The yield to maturity of a 6%-coupon ($30 semiannually) corporate bond that pays $1000 at maturity in 5.5 years (11 semiannual periods) and currently sells for $833.87 is 10%:

$\boxed{1}\,\boxed{1}\,\boxed{N}\,\boxed{8}\,\boxed{3}\,\boxed{3}\,\boxed{.}\,\boxed{8}\,\boxed{7}\,\boxed{+/-}\,\boxed{PV}\,\boxed{3}\,\boxed{0}\,\boxed{PMT}\,\boxed{1}\,\boxed{0}\,\boxed{0}\,\boxed{0}\,\boxed{FV}\,\boxed{CPT}\,\boxed{I/Y} = 5.00\,\boxed{\times}\,\boxed{2}\,\boxed{=}\,10.00$

NPV and IRR for Uneven Cash Flows

CF0	CF1	CF2	CF3	CF4	CF5
−110,000	45,000	45,000	45,000	10,000	60,000

The NPV at a cost of capital of 12% and the IRR for the above cash flows from a capital budgeting project are $38,483.20 and 25.73%, respectively:

$\boxed{CE/C}\,\boxed{CE/C}\,\boxed{CF}\,\boxed{2nd}\,\boxed{CLR\ Work}\,\boxed{1}\,\boxed{1}\,\boxed{0}\,\boxed{0}\,\boxed{0}\,\boxed{0}\,\boxed{+/-}\,\boxed{ENTER}\,\boxed{\downarrow}\,\boxed{4}\,\boxed{5}\,\boxed{0}\,\boxed{0}$

$\boxed{0}\,\boxed{ENTER}\,\boxed{\downarrow}\,\boxed{3}$ [3 is the number of times the cash flow repeats] $\boxed{ENTER}\,\boxed{\downarrow}\,\boxed{1}\,\boxed{0}\,\boxed{0}$

$\boxed{0}\,\boxed{0}\,\boxed{ENTER}\,\boxed{\downarrow}\,\boxed{ENTER}\,\boxed{\downarrow}\,\boxed{6}\,\boxed{0}\,\boxed{0}\,\boxed{0}\,\boxed{0}\,\boxed{ENTER}\,\boxed{\downarrow}\,\boxed{ENTER}\,\boxed{2nd}\,\boxed{QUIT}$ [all the cash flows have been entered]

$\boxed{NPV}\,\boxed{1}\,\boxed{2}$ [12 is the cost of capital (required return)] $\boxed{ENTER}\,\boxed{\downarrow}\,\boxed{CPT} = 38,483.20$

IRR $\boxed{CPT} = 25.73$

at a 20% cost of capital, the NPV is $13,726.85:

$\boxed{NPV}\,\boxed{2}\,\boxed{0}\,\boxed{ENTER}\,\boxed{\downarrow}\,\boxed{CPT} = 13,726.85$

Cumulative Distribution Function for the Standard Normal Random Variable

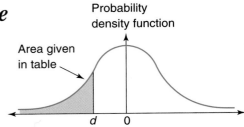

For example, N[−1.15] = .1251 and N[1.57] = .9418

d	0.00	0.01	0.02	0.03	0.04	0.05	0.06	0.07	0.08	0.09
−3.0	.0013	.0013	.0013	.0012	.0012	.0011	.0011	.0011	0010	.0010
−2.9	.0019	.0018	.0018	.0017	.0016	.0016	.0015	.0015	.0014	.0014
−2.8	.0026	.0025	.0024	.0023	.0023	.0022	.0021	.0021	.0020	.0019
−2.7	.0035	.0034	.0033	.0032	.0031	.0030	.0029	.0028	.0027	.0026
−2.6	.0047	.0045	.0044	.0043	.0041	.0040	.0039	.0038	.0037	.0036
−2.5	.0062	.0060	.0059	.0057	.0055	.0054	.0052	.0051	.0049	.0048
−2.4	.0082	.0080	.0078	.0075	.0073	.0071	.0069	.0068	.0066	.0064
−2.3	.0107	.0104	.0102	.0099	.0096	.0094	.0091	.0089	.0087	.0084
−2.2	.0139	.0136	.0132	.0129	.0125	.0122	.0119	.0116	.0113	.0110
−2.1	.0179	.0174	.0170	.0166	.0162	.0158	.0154	.0150	.0146	.0143
−2.0	.0227	.0222	.0217	.0212	.0207	.0202	.0197	.0192	.0188	.0183
−1.9	.0287	.0281	.0274	.0268	.0262	.0256	.0250	.0244	.0239	.0233
−1.8	.0359	.0351	.0344	.0336	.0329	.0322	.0314	.0307	.0301	.0294
−1.7	.0446	.0436	.0427	.0418	.0409	.0401	.0392	.0384	.0375	.0367
−1.6	.0548	.0537	.0526	.0516	.0505	.0495	.0485	.0475	.0465	.0455
−1.5	.0668	.0655	.0643	.0630	.0618	.0606	.0594	.0582	.0571	.0559
−1.4	.0808	.0793	.0778	.0764	.0749	0735	.0721	.0708	.0694	.0681
−1.3	.0968	.0951	.0934	.0918	.0901	.0885	.0869	.0853	.0838	.0823
−1.2	.1151	.1131	.1112	.1093	.1075	.1056	.1038	.1020	.1003	.0985
−1.1	.1357	.1335	.1314	.1292	.1271	.1251	.1230	.1210	.1190	.1170
−1.0	.1587	.1563	.1539	.1515	.1492	.1469	.1446	.1423	.1401	.1379
−0.9	.1841	.1814	.1788	.1762	.1736	.1711	.1685	.1660	.1635	.1611
−0.8	.2119	.2090	.2061	.2033	.2005	.1977	.1949	.1922	.1894	.1867
−0.7	.2420	.2389	.2358	.2327	.2296	.2266	.2236	.2206	.2177	.2148
−0.6	.2743	.2709	.2676	.2643	.2611	.2578	.2546	.2514	.2483	.2451
−0.5	.3085	.3050	.3015	.2981	.2946	.2912	.2877	.2843	.2810	.2776
−0.4	.3446	.3409	.3372	.3336	.3300	.3264	.3228	.3192	.3156	.3121
−0.3	.3821	.3783	.3745	.3707	.3669	.3632	.3594	.3557	.3520	.3483
−0.2	.4207	.4168	.4129	.4090	.4052	.4013	.3974	.3936	.3897	.3859
−0.1	.4602	.4562	.4522	.4483	.4443	.4404	.4364	.4325	.4286	.4247
−0.0	.5000	.4960	.4920	.4880	.4840	.4801	.4761	.4721	.4681	.4641

d	0.00	0.01	0.02	0.03	0.04	0.05	0.06	0.07	0.08	0.09
0.0	.5000	.5040	.5080	.5120	.5160	.5199	.5239	.5279	.5319	.5359
0.1	.5398	.5438	.5478	.5517	.5557	.5596	.5636	.5675	.5714	.5753
0.2	.5793	.5832	.5871	.5910	.5948	.5987	.6026	.6064	.6103	.6141
0.3	.6179	.6217	.6255	.6293	.6331	.6368	.6406	.6443	.6480	.6517
0.4	.6554	.6591	.6628	.6664	.6700	.6736	.6772	.6808	.6844	.6879
0.5	.6915	.6950	.6985	.7019	.7054	.7088	.7123	.7157	.7190	.7224
0.6	.7257	.7291	.7324	.7357	.7389	.7422	.7454	.7486	.7517	.7549
0.7	.7580	.7611	.7642	.7673	.7704	.7734	.7764	.7794	.7823	.7852
0.8	.7881	.7910	.7939	.7967	.7995	.8023	.8051	.8078	.8106	.8133
0.9	.8159	.8186	.8212	.8238	.8264	.8289	.8315	.8340	.8365	.8389
1.0	.8413	.8439	.8461	.8485	.8508	.8531	.8554	.8577	.8599	.8621
1.1	.8643	.8665	.8686	.8708	.8729	.8749	.8770	.8790	.8810	.8830
1.2	.8849	.8869	.8888	.8907	.8925	.8944	.8962	.8980	.8997	.9015
1.3	.9032	.9049	.9066	.9082	.9099	.9115	.9131	.9147	.9162	.9177
1.4	.9192	.9207	.9222	.9236	.9251	.9265	.9279	.9292	.9306	.9319
1.5	.9332	.9345	.9357	.9370	.9382	.9394	.9406	.9418	.9429	.9441
1.6	.9452	.9463	.9474	.9484	.9495	.9505	.9515	.9525	.9535	.9545
1.7	.9554	.9564	.9573	.9582	.9591	.9599	.9608	.9616	.9625	.9633
1.8	.9641	.9649	.9656	.9664	.9671	.9678	.9686	.9693	.9699	.9706
1.9	.9713	.9719	.9726	.9732	.9738	.9744	.9750	.9756	.9761	.9767
2.0	.9773	.9778	.9783	.9788	.9793	.9798	.9803	.9808	.9812	.9817
2.1	.9821	.9826	.9830	.9834	.9838	.9842	.9846	.9850	.9854	.9857
2.2	.9861	.9864	.9868	.9871	.9875	.9878	.9881	.9884	.9887	.9890
2.3	.9893	.9896	.9898	.9901	.9904	.9906	.9909	.9911	.9913	.9916
2.4	.9918	.9920	.9922	.9925	.9927	.9929	.9931	.9932	.9934	.9936
2.5	.9938	.9940	.9941	.9943	.9945	.9946	.9948	.9949	.9951	.9952
2.6	.9953	.9955	.9956	.9957	.9959	.9960	.9961	.9962	.9963	.9964
2.7	.9965	.9966	.9967	.9968	.9969	.9970	.9971	.9972	.9973	.9974
2.8	.9974	.9975	.9976	.9977	.9977	.9978	.9979	.9979	.9980	.9981
2.9	.9981	.9982	.9982	.9983	.9984	.9984	.9985	.9985	.9986	.9986
3.0	.9987	.9987	.9987	.9988	.9988	.9989	.9989	.9989	.9990	.9990

Answers to Selected Problems

Chapter 2

B1. a. 26.67%; 9.6%   b. Rivas   c. 17.78%; 28.00%

B3. $4523.49

B5. a. $11,000; $10,000   b. $12,000; $10,909.09
c. $11,000; $9166.67

B7. Sell now; above $240,000

C1. a. 20%; 100%; −100%

Chapter 3

B1. (amounts in millions)   a. $170; $300   b. $200; $300
c. $170   d. $160   e. $70; $100   f. $330; $160; $170

B3. (amounts in millions)   a. $400; $475   b. $975;
$1175   c. $275

B5. a. $3964.50; 28%; 15.86%   b. $15,418.00; 31%;
23.72%   c. $34,370.50; 36%; 27.50%

C1. $750,000

Chapter 4

B3. a. Yes   b. $1.5 million   c. $750,000   d. $750,000
e. $833,333

B4. a. 6%; 1.67x; 10%; 33.33%   b. $12,500; $15,000
c. 6%; 1.83x; 11.01%; 40.82%

Chapter 5

B1. 12%

B3. $10,345.11

B5. a. 0.666%   b. 8%   c. 8.3%

B7. 16.18%

B9. $2444.33

B11. $123,364.92

B13. $5758.11

B15. $6035.23

B17. a. 17.67 periods   b. 8 periods   c. 4.96 periods

B19. $13,022.81

B21. a. 0.9%   b. 10.8%   c. 11.35%

B23. Borrow from Bob's bank.

B25. $16,790.88

C1. a. $4628.21   b. $3441.79

C3. a. $61,857.65   b. $32.65

C5. $47,908.26

C7. $430.38

C9. $3930.82

C11. 5.946%

Chapter 6

B1. 8.106%

B3. October 9, 2012

B5. a. $1208.29   b. 9.34%   c. 9.44%

B7. 3.33%

B9. a. $1012.97; 1072.62; 1118.88   b. $1022.56;
1129.68; 1218.41   c. $1003.51; 1019.17; 1030.54

B11. a. $12.64   b. $7.70

B13. $5.13

B15. $873.79

C1. a. 13.42%; 13.87%   b. 13.40%; 13.85%
c. 13.41%; 13.86%

C3. Minus 11 cents per share

Chapter 7

B1. 8%; 16%

B3. 3.92

B5. 25.92

B7. 12%

B9. a. 4.8%; 3.3%   b. 57.76; 37.41   c. 0.16
d. 0.00344

C3. a. −0.09%; 3.76%   b. 8.6; 47.88   c. 11.65   d. 0.57

C5. a. −0.21%; −0.09%   b. 23.52; 9.39   c. 10.16
d. 0.68

Topic A

B1. a. No   b. Less than $2.25

B3. a. Profitable   b. Not profitable   c. Not profitable

Topic B

B1. a. $1080   b. $230   c. $50; yes

B4. $742,925

B5. $9143

C1. a. $1.88   b. $1.93   c. $1.93

Topic C

B1. $750,000

B3.   a. $500,000   b. As little as $350,000, but no more than $500,000

B5.   Zero

C1.   a. $20 million   b. $20 million; $12.5 million

Chapter 8

B1.   a. 0%   b. $9.09   c. Yes

B3. $2.57 million

B5.   a. 60%; 56%   b. 7.72%; 22.47%   c. Microwave blower

B7.   a. $2679.46; $1339.73   b. 21.86%; 21.86% c. 1.268; 1.268   d. 2.5 years; 2.5 years   e. Project A; it creates more value

B9.   a. 3 years   b. 3.67 years   c. 77.14%   d. $32,110 e. 1.18   f. 17.09%

B11. a. $85,369; $82,096   b. 44.83%; 48.40%

B13. a. $87.75; yes   b. −31.12%; not according to this criteria   c. 1.7 years   d. 3.2%

C1.   a. $0.31; $2.51; 15.13%; 16.97%   b. Both   c. Both d. Project B

Chapter 9

B1.   a. $6065   b. $8000   c. Expense

B3. $24,008

B5. $682

B7.   −$0.67 million

B9.   a. $240,000; $474,696   b. $300,000; $843,370 c. 68.63%

B11. a. $500,000; $70,000; $500,000   b. $122,892 c. $4,622,892

B13. $1,030,800

B15. Machine A; it has the better EAA

C1.   Yes, NPV = $18,975

Chapter 10

B1. $200,000

B3.   Sell, NPV = $352,455

B5. $4.16 million

B7.   a. No   b. $10 million   c. $5.703 million

B9.   a. $157,006   b. $157,006

B10. $146,194

C2. $34,496

Chapter 11

B1.   15%

B3.   20%

B5.   Invest in B and C

B6.   13.73%

B8.   15.2%

B11. 14.25%

C1.   c. 14.2%

C3.   1.46

Chapter 12

B1.   18.17%

B3.   a. $40,625   b. $7109

B5.   Use the 15% debt capital structure; there's a slight disadvantage to debt financing

C2.   11.17%

Chapter 13

B1.   a. 80%   b. 1600 shares

B3.   a. 33.86%

B5.   a. Yes

B7.   a. 27.3%

B9.   a. $29.44 per share   b. Collectively, they lost $5 million

Chapter 14

B1.   b. 11.78%

B3.   b. 10.45%   c. 6.91%

B5.   a. 6.13%; 6.19%; 6.15%

B7. $55 million

B9. $800 million

B11. a. $13,907; lease   b. $131,260; lease

B13. b. −$226.30; borrow and buy   c. −$1001.04; borrow and buy   d. They become $597.24 and $45.52, and leasing would be better in both cases

C1.   a. 8.2% APY   b. 8.61% APY

Chapter 15

B2.   a. 5.19% APY   b. 5.27% APY

B3.   a. 6.60%   b. 7.26%

B5.   a. 12.5%   b. 2.67%   c. Equation (15.1)

B7.   a. SF1 = DM1.30   b. Yes; no   c. No; yes

B9.   15.862%

B11. a. 0.6113$/DM, 0.6226, 0.6168, 0.6223, 0.6000

b. $9.1695 million, 10.5842, 12.336, 12.446, 10.200

c. $6,275,018

C1. 12.38%

Chapter 16

B1. a. $400,000   b. 5 times per month   c. $200,000
d. $18,000; 18,000; 36,000

B3. (In $000s) 20, 50, −10, −20, 20, 20, 20, 92.857,
107.143, 14.286

B5. a. $6.98; 10.00   b. $29.28; 10.00   c. $7756.25

B7. a. Yes; expected annual profit = $20,000   b. −$2000
c. Compensating balance proposal

B9. a. 15.00%   b. 17.65%   c. 16.67%   d. 20.00%

B11. a. 15.00%   b. 13.75%   c. 16.28%; alternative b is
cheapest

C1. a. $290,000   b. 1.93   c. −$6300

Chapter 17

B1. $42,298

B2. $137.87

B5. 33.00 days

B7. a. 6324.55; $63,245.55   b. 6000; $63,333.33

B9. a. 5000; $5000   b. $5666.67   c. $66.67

B11. a. 16 kits   b. 26 kits

C1. a. 80%, 30%, 5%, 0%   b. $400, 550, 575, 575, 735,
955

C3. a. 1000   b. 150

Chapter 18

B1. a. $765,000

B5. $110,000

Topic D

B1. a. 8.329% APY   b. 8.399% APY   c. 8.405% APY

B3. a. $21.43; 15 shares   b. $0.1047

B5. a. 14.16%   b. 14.38%

B7. a. Decrease to $11.60 per share   b. Decrease $4000

B8. 8.39%

Topic E

B1. a. $3.74   b. $3.60   c. $2.40   d. $3.07

B3. a. $1.54; $0   b. $1.83; $2   c. $1.50; $4

B5. $0.88

B7. $6.75; $4.38; $2.37

B9. a. Yes   b. No   c. Yes

B11. a. Buy an interest rate cap or sell (short) futures on
short-term debt   b. $18.75 million, 16.88, 21.25,
22.50, 22.50, 22.50, 22.50, 18.75   c. $0.00 million,
0.00, 0.00, 3.13, 6.25, 8.13, 1.99, 0.00

C1. 32%

Topic F

B1. a. $59.3 million   b. 34.45%   c. 4 years   d. Yes

B2. a. $115 million; 100   b. $215 million; 50; 165   c. No

B5. 43%

B7. a. $167.19 million; 27.75%   b. $175.16 million;
28.16%   c. Yes   d. $80.03

B9. a. Pooling of interests   b. Purchase

B11. a. $83.72 million   b. Helps them, value increases to
$88.70 million   c. Risk reduction, Empire would be
guaranteeing the bonds

B13. a. 0.5   b. 0.625   c. Increase to $22.50

C1. $49.08 million

AUTHOR INDEX

N after a page number refers to footnote reference

N after a page number refers to footnote reference
Entries in bold type are key terms/marginal glossary items in text

PHOTO CREDITS

TABLE III
Future Value Factors for an Annuity, FVAF, Compounded at r Percent for n Periods: $FVAF_{r,n} = \sum_{t=1}^{n}(1+r)^{n-t} = \dfrac{(1+r)^n - 1}{r}$ (for non-zero r)

Discount Rate, r

Number of Annuity Pmts, n	0%	1%	2%	3%	4%	5%	6%	7%	8%	9%	10%	12%	14%	16%	18%	20%	25%	30%	35%	40%	45%	50%
1	1.0000	1.0000	1.0000	1.0000	1.0000	1.0000	1.0000	1.0000	1.0000	1.0000	1.0000	1.0000	1.0000	1.0000	1.0000	1.0000	1.0000	1.0000	1.0000	1.0000	1.0000	1.0000
2	2.0000	2.0100	2.0200	2.0300	2.0400	2.0500	2.0600	2.0700	2.0800	2.0900	2.1000	2.1200	2.1400	2.1600	2.1800	2.2000	2.2500	2.3000	2.3500	2.4000	2.4500	2.5000
3	3.0000	3.0301	3.0604	3.0909	3.1216	3.1525	3.1836	3.2149	3.2464	3.2781	3.3100	3.3744	3.4396	3.5056	3.5724	3.6400	3.8125	3.9900	4.1725	4.3600	4.5525	4.7500
4	4.0000	4.0604	4.1216	4.1836	4.2465	4.3101	4.3746	4.4399	4.5061	4.5731	4.6410	4.7793	4.9211	5.0665	5.2154	5.3680	5.7656	6.1870	6.6329	7.1040	7.6011	8.1250
5	5.0000	5.1010	5.2040	5.3091	5.4163	5.5256	5.6371	5.7507	5.8666	5.9847	6.1051	6.3528	6.6101	6.8771	7.1542	7.4416	8.2070	9.0431	9.9544	10.9456	12.0216	13.1875
6	6.0000	6.1520	6.3081	6.4684	6.6330	6.8019	6.9753	7.1533	7.3359	7.5233	7.7156	8.1152	8.5355	8.9775	9.4420	9.9299	11.2588	12.7560	14.4384	16.3238	18.4314	20.7813
7	7.0000	7.2135	7.4343	7.6625	7.8983	8.1420	8.3938	8.6540	8.9228	9.2004	9.4872	10.0890	10.7305	11.4139	12.1415	12.9159	15.0735	17.5828	20.4919	23.8534	27.7255	32.1719
8	8.0000	8.2857	8.5830	8.8923	9.2142	9.5491	9.8975	10.2598	10.6366	11.0285	11.4359	12.2997	13.2328	14.2401	15.3270	16.4991	19.8419	23.8577	28.6640	34.3947	41.2019	49.2578
9	9.0000	9.3685	9.7546	10.1591	10.5828	11.0266	11.4913	11.9780	12.4876	13.0210	13.5795	14.7757	16.0853	17.5185	19.0859	20.7989	25.8023	32.0150	39.6964	49.1526	60.7428	74.8867
10	10.0000	10.4622	10.9497	11.4639	12.0061	12.5779	13.1808	13.8164	14.4866	15.1929	15.9374	17.5487	19.3373	21.3215	23.5213	25.9587	33.2529	42.6195	54.5902	69.8137	89.0771	113.330
11	11.0000	11.5668	12.1687	12.8078	13.4864	14.2068	14.9716	15.7836	16.6455	17.5603	18.5312	20.6546	23.0445	25.7329	28.7551	32.1504	42.5661	56.4053	74.6967	98.7391	130.162	170.995
12	12.0000	12.6825	13.4121	14.1920	15.0258	15.9171	16.8699	17.8885	18.9771	20.1407	21.3843	24.1331	27.2707	30.8502	34.9311	39.5805	54.2077	74.3270	101.841	139.235	189.735	257.493
13	13.0000	13.8093	14.6803	15.6178	16.6268	17.7130	18.8821	20.1406	21.4953	22.9534	24.5227	28.0291	32.0887	36.7862	42.2187	48.4966	68.7596	97.6250	138.485	195.929	276.115	387.239
14	14.0000	14.9474	15.9739	17.0863	18.2919	19.5986	21.0151	22.5505	24.2149	26.0192	27.9750	32.3926	37.5811	43.6720	50.8180	59.1959	86.9495	127.913	187.954	275.300	401.367	581.859
15	15.0000	16.0969	17.2934	18.5989	20.0236	21.5786	23.2760	25.1290	27.1521	29.3609	31.7725	37.2797	43.8424	51.6595	60.9653	72.0351	109.687	167.286	254.738	386.420	582.982	873.788
16	16.0000	17.2579	18.6393	20.1569	21.8245	23.6575	25.6725	27.8881	30.3243	33.0034	35.9497	42.7533	50.9804	60.9250	72.9390	87.4421	138.109	218.472	344.897	541.988	846.324	1311.68
17	17.0000	18.4304	20.0121	21.7616	23.6975	25.8404	28.2129	30.8402	33.7502	36.9737	40.5447	48.8837	59.1176	71.6730	87.0680	105.931	173.636	285.014	466.611	759.784	1228.17	1968.52
18	18.0000	19.6147	21.4123	23.4144	25.6454	28.1324	30.9057	33.9990	37.4502	41.3013	45.5992	55.7497	68.3941	84.1407	103.740	128.117	218.045	371.518	630.925	1064.70	1781.85	2953.78
19	19.0000	20.8109	22.8406	25.1169	27.6712	30.5390	33.7600	37.3790	41.4463	46.0185	51.1591	63.4397	78.9692	98.6032	123.414	154.740	273.556	483.973	852.748	1491.58	2584.68	4431.68
20	20.0000	22.0190	24.2974	26.8704	29.7781	33.0660	36.7856	40.9955	45.7620	51.1601	57.2750	72.0524	91.0249	115.380	146.628	186.688	342.945	630.165	1152.21	2089.21	3748.78	6648.51
25	25.0000	28.2432	32.0303	36.4593	41.6459	47.7271	54.8645	63.2490	73.1059	84.7009	98.3471	133.334	181.871	249.214	342.603	471.981	1054.79	2348.80	5176.50	11247.1990	24040.7	50500.3
30	30.0000	34.7849	40.5681	47.5754	56.0849	66.4388	79.0582	94.4608	113.283	136.308	164.494	241.333	356.787	530.312	790.948	1181.88	3227.17	8729.99	23221.6	60501.1	154107	383500
35	35.0000	41.6603	49.9945	60.4621	73.6522	90.3203	111.435	138.237	172.317	215.711	271.024	431.663	693.573	1120.71	1816.65	2948.34	9856.76	32422.9	104136	325400	987794	2912217
40	40.0000	48.8864	60.4020	75.4013	95.0255	120.800	154.762	199.635	259.057	337.882	442.593	767.091	1342.03	2360.76	4163.21	7343.86	30088.7	120393	466960	1750092	6331512	22114663
45	45.0000	56.4811	71.8927	92.7199	121.029	159.700	212.744	285.749	386.506	525.859	718.905	1358.23	2590.56	4965.27	9531.58	18281.3	91831.5	447019	2093876	9412424	40583319	167933233
50	50.0000	64.4632	84.5794	112.797	152.667	209.348	290.336	406.529	573.770	815.084	1163.91	2400.02	4994.52	10435.6	21813.1	45497.2	280256	1659761	9389020	50622288	260128295	1275242998